Saints & Sinners

ANTTI P. BALK

An Account of
Western Civilization

THELEMA PUBLICATIONS
Helsinki · Washington D.C. · London

Thelema Publications LLC

UK: BCM Agape, London WC1N 3XX

US: PO Box 10102, Washington, DC 20018-0102

First published 2008
First paperback edition 2010

© Antti Pekka Balk, 2008

The author asserts the moral right to be
identified as the author of this work in accordance
with the UK Copyright, Designs and Patents Act 1988.

All Rights Reserved. No part of this publication, in part or in whole, may be reproduced, transmitted or utilized, in any form or by any means, electronic or mechanical, or other means, now known or hereafter invented, including photocopying, recording, or by any information storage and retrieval system, without permission in writing from the copyright holder, except as permitted by the UK Copyright, Designs and Patents Act 1988 or under the terms of a licence issued by the Copyright Licensing Agency Ltd, Saffron House, 6-10 Kirby Street, London, England EC1N 8TS. Applications for the copyright holder's written permission to reproduce any part of this publication should be addressed to the publisher.

Every effort has been made to provide proper acknowledgement of original sources. The publisher apologizes for any errors or omissions that may have occurred and would be grateful if notified of any corrections that should be incorporated in subsequent reprints or editions of the work.

British Library Cataloguing in Publication Data

Balk, Antti P.
Saints & sinners: an account of Western civilization
1. Civilization, Western
I. Title
909'.09821

Library of Congress Catalog Card Number: 2008-901785

ISBN: 978 952 5700 00 8 (hardback)
ISBN: 978 952 5700 53 4 (paperback)

"Explore the rivers of the soul, whence and in what order thou has come."

— Zarathushtra Spitama (628-551 BCE)

EGYPT - A PROLOGUE

After having endured incredible hardships, having wandered up from Africa over the last million years, having battled through the ice ages, man, finding the earth suddenly flowering and animals surrounding him, moved from gathering food, from hunting and fishing to producing food, to farming and breeding cattle. Proper organized agriculture was established a couple of millennia later, circa 8000 BCE.

The turning-point seems to have been the occurrence of two forms of wheat that had a large, full head of seeds. Before the 8th millennium BCE, wheat was not the exuberant plant it is today—it was merely one of many wild grasses that spread throughout the Middle East. By a genetic accident, the wild wheat crossed with one variety of goat-grass, forming a fertile hybrid. Because its seeds were attached to the husk in such a way that they scatter in the wind, this hybrid, which we now call emmer, was able to propagate naturally.

There was a second accident, which perhaps came about because emmer was already cultivated. It crossed with another variety of goat-grass and produced an even larger hybrid: the bread wheat. Now there existed a beautiful ear of corn, but because it was too tight to break up, it would never scatter in the wind. And if it did break up, the chaff would fly off and every grain would fall exactly where it grew. All of a sudden man and the cereal had come together: man needed to harvest the ears and scatter the seeds in order for the vegetable to spread and multiply; the life of each, man and the plant, now depended on the other.

In all likelihood, it was Egypt where agriculture really took off. Every year, the River Nile overflows, and when it subsides again, a thin layer of fertilizing mud is poured over the land. Drillings made forty-five feet into the strata of the world's longest river prove most revealing; the layers are more shallow where the ridges have become covered, and deeper where the hollows have filled up. Since the average thickness is five inches to a hundred years, the age of the plains of the Nile adds up to roughly 10,000 years, and since agriculture, or any other civilization that is based on permanent settlement, can only have become possible after the Nile had begun to yield its fertile mud, the time frame for the actual settling of Egypt can thus be determined.

As the valley floor was formed, or carpeted with soil, by the annually overflowing river, Egypt became a very desirable place in which to live. Khem, the native name of Egypt, means "black" and refers precisely to the fertile, black soil of the Nile Valley. Khem was also the name of the Egyptian father-god. He represented the power of generation, and was regarded in the ancient times as the god of harvest and protector of crops. Linguistically and ethnologically, Khem is equivalent to "Ham" mentioned in the Book of Genesis, the youngest son of Noah, and the progenitor of the Egyptians, Nubians, and Canaanites.

According to legend, the god Osiris was once a good and beloved king, who reclaimed the predynastic Egyptians from savagery and brought them civilization. Isis, the sister and wife of Osiris, discovered wheat and barley growing wild, and Osiris introduced the cultivation of these grains amongst his people, who presently abandoned cannibalism and adopted a corn diet. The Agricultural Revolution in the cultivation of plants and the domestication of animals brought on the crucial realization that man dominates his environment in its most important aspect, not physically but at the level of living things—plants and animals. This was accompanied by an equally powerful social revolution.

It now not only became possible but necessary for man to settle. This creature that had roamed the Earth for a million years had to make the fateful decision: whether he would cease to be a nomad and become a villager—civilization rests on that decision.[1] Osiris taught his still half-savage subjects how to fashion agricultural implements, and was the first to gather fruit from trees, to train the vine to poles, and to tread the grapes. Though the Egyptians were beer people, we also know a great deal about their wines, by way of written records, paintings, and archæological finds. By the 5th Dynasty, if not before, Egypt was producing both red and white wine, which were called the right and left eye of Horus, respectively.

Ancient as wine is, beer is even older, as attested by brewers' slops found on Neolithic middens. The Egyptians had words for more than eighty different

---

[1] The word "civilization" itself derives from the Latin *civitas*, "city."

varieties of beer, differentiated by the various plants and herbs mixed into the wort. Isis is addressed as not only "Our Lady of Bread," but also "Our Lady of Beer." Most of these beers were medicinal, used as they were as carriers for other medicinal herbs, and like bread, formed a part of the salary. In fact, it has been said that man was a brewer even before he was a baker—some even believe that brewing was the very impetus behind the domestication of grains.

Every ceremony and ritual in Egypt involved bread, in one form or another, throughout the life of her civilization. For centuries, she was the bread basket of the Western world, supplier of grain for all the ovens of the Mediterranean. The metaphor of baked bread as divine substance arose in the earliest days of mankind; the hieroglyph for the verb "to give offering" is a loaf of bread on a woven reed tray. Fire, a novel metaphor for the cosmic forces that surround us, is, despite all its magic, entirely of the natural realm. Spontaneous and self-creating, it rains down from heavens or bursts out from the earth. It is a metaphor of divine force only nominally under man's control—a good servant, but a bad master. Bread, on the other hand, is entirely a human invention.

Grass, nourishing as it does only animals, is, like fire, wholly of the Natural Kingdom, but the seeds of grass can feed humans as well. Flour, made from these seeds, is itself a new substance, a substance unlike the grass or its seeds. It is more like the substance of the Earth itself, but edible, and a product of the hand and vigour of man and man alone; for most of the world, the appetite for bread is an essential part of being human. It is no accident that every civilization throughout history has been based on grain: bread is not only the central food of daily life, but the symbol of sociability—"to break bread" remains our term for establishing and sustaining social relationships.

Water, mixed with flour, becomes remarkably like flesh, not only in its colour, but also in yielding like flesh, being warm to the touch; also like flesh, it is better to eat when cooked. Bread can be moulded into any shape or form, and once baked, holds that mould. Too much or too little heat can spoil it, but once baked, it is "of one flesh." Here arises a suspicion of a miracle. Baked bread is not like green grass, not like yellow grain, nor brown flour—not anything like its parts. It is neither gaseous like fire, nor wet like water, or dry like flour, yet all these elements join together to form bread. Should the means to make it become diminished, men feel more in need than without any other foods. The Hamito-Semitic word for bread is *aysh*, which literally translates as "life."

According to legend, it was Osiris who instituted the cult of the gods and built the first temples, where worship was practised according to the rules he laid down. The ancient Egyptian word *Netjer* has such implications as "god," "holy," "divine," and "sacred." All of them are likely correct to some extent, but it has so far been impossible to render an exact translation. In a society where every man is thought to be endowed more or less with powers which we would today call supernatural, the distinction between gods and men is fairly blurred, or rather has barely emerged. The notion of gods as superhuman beings equipped with powers surpassing in degree and kind everything man possesses, has only slowly evolved in the course of history. Primitive man regarded the supernatural beings not greatly, if at all, superior to himself.

The great gods of ancient Egypt were certainly not exempt from the common lot. Like men, they grew old and died; like men, they were composed of body and soul; and thus, like men, were subject to all the passions and frailties of the flesh. When their time came, they passed away from the cheerful land of the living to reign as dead gods over dead men in the realm of the dead.[2]

The mythology of Egypt is not a hollow tale of wars or battles with giants. Men do not fight their gods, struggle with, or oppose them. There is no *Armageddon* or *Götterdämmerung*; just betrayal by a trusted friend, and a murder committed in jealousy. There are no avenging armies of heavenly hosts; only the judgements of a family about the actions of one of their own against another—the archetype of the human family. The heart and soul of their "greatest story ever told" lay in the deep and abiding loyalty of a woman for her man, and her grief at his death.

The versions of the stories of Isis and Osiris which have come down to us as a single piece, woven together into a simplified, theatrically-styled plot, are

---

[2] At first sight, life in ancient Egypt may seem as one long preoccupation with death and the afterlife. This is largely because the homes of the Egyptians, built by the Nile, are buried under twenty feet of river mud, under new towns, under new corn fields. Their tombs, on the other hand, lying at the edge of the desert, are naturally on raised land, and all the archæologists need to do is to break them open.

Greek interpretations of older Egyptian originals: Eager to make his beneficent discoveries known to all mankind, Osiris left the regency of Egypt to Isis, and visiting all the inhabited Earth, diffused the blessing of agriculture wherever he went. Loaded with the wealth that had been showered upon him by the grateful nations, he returned to Egypt, and on account of the blessings he had bestowed upon mankind was unanimously hailed as *Onnophiris*, "the Good One," and henceforward worshipped as a deity. His brother, Set, however, plotted against him.

At a banquet of the gods, Set fooled Osiris into trying out a coffin, which he then slammed shut and cast into the Nile. The coffin was carried by the river to the delta town of Byblos, where it became caught in a tamarisk tree. Isis discovered the coffin and brought it back—the story to this point is attested only by the Greek Plutarch, though Set was identified as the murderer as early as the Pyramid Era of the Old Kingdom.

Taking advantage of Isis' temporary absence, Set cut the body to fourteen pieces, and cast them into the Nile—in the Egyptian texts this alone accounts for the murder of Osiris. Isis searched the land for the severed members of her husband, and was eventually able to piece together his body, whole save for the penis, which had been swallowed by a crocodile, according to Plutarch, or by a fish, according to the original Egyptian sources. She replaced the penis with a reasonable facsimile, and she is often portrayed in the form of a kite being impregnated by the ithyphallic corpse of Osiris.

To rule, each new Pharaoh had to marry the queen or the daughter of the former ruler. She may have been his mother or his sister, yet she alone had the power to enroyal him and to grant him the right to sit on the throne. The throne was the hieroglyph of Isis, who got her name from the Greek translation of the Coptic *Esi*. In the earliest representations, she is depicted as crowned with the empty throne of her murdered husband—the horned disk of Hathor was merged with the Isian headgear only in later dynasties. In a way, it is the throne that makes the king: he receives his authority by assuming his place on the throne.

The custom throughout the known world at the time was that a king must be whole and virile. Anything less and the land and her people will suffer. This goes back to the linking of the land's fertility with the king's. A deposed ruler, such as Osiris, and any sons he might have, were castrated to make certain that no one would make a claim to the throne. This was the reason behind the flight of Isis and Anubis from the vengeance of Set. As the son of his father, Anubis had to be preserved from the same fate.

In some Egyptian texts, the scattering of the body parts is likened to the scattering of grain in the fields, a reference to Osiris' role as a vegetation god, who dies with the autumn harvest and is reborn again when the grain sprouts in springtime. It is the periodicity of plants and vegetation in general which depends on moisture that is most striking. Plants die down in the heat of summer, trees shed their leaves in autumn, all nature sleeps or dies in winter, and awakens in spring. The most enlightened priests, says Plutarch, specify that Osiris is the "principle of moisture," the power and cause of all generation, the substance of every seed, the definitive symbol of all death and rebirth.

According to Plutarch, the Egyptians saw the Nile as an outflow of Osiris and the earth as the body of Isis—in becoming intermixed with the soil, the Nile-Osiris therefore fertilizes the Earth-Isis. "Osiris gardens," wood-framed barley hotbeds in the shape of the god, were frequently placed in tombs, and the plants which sprouted from these beds were held to symbolize the resurrection of life after death. Nevertheless, it is the dying down that attracts most attention; the rites of Osiris are, though he rises again, essentially rites of lamentation. Committing the seed to the ground with hope of their appearing again or coming to fruition, the ancients did many things like attendants at a funeral in mourning for the dead.

According to the native Egyptian account, when Isis had reassembled the corpse of her husband, she and her sister, Nephthys, sat down beside it and wailed a dirge which became the model of all ancient Egyptian lamentations for the dead. Touched by their sorrow, the sun-god Ra sent down from heaven Anubis, who with the aid of Isis and Nephthys, of Thoth and Horus the Elder, pieced together the broken body of Osiris and swathed it in linen bandages. Isis spoke the magic words, as instructed by Thoth, over the murdered god, who not only resurrected, but sired a son, Horus the Younger, who avenged his father's death by killing Set and ascending the throne. Isis is thus seen to be the mother of the king, and appears as such throughout the iconography of ancient Egypt.

Mummification was not practised in predynastic times. On the contrary, it was the done thing to cut up the bodies of the dead and remove the flesh as the impure part before a subsequent ritual reassembly—a custom which is echoed in the stories of Isis and Osiris. Many features of these rituals have been handed down to historic times, when they were affixed to the collection of spells now known as the "Book of the Dead."[3] In the second and even in the first prehistoric age, this custom was still a common one, but it began to die out in dynastic times, vanishing completely during the 6th Dynasty.

No culture at any stage of human history has been able to subsist without a religion of some sort and the faith it brings of the existence of man's most essential part, the soul. The idea of the immortality of the soul justifies the need for a religion, which even the most atheistic of states have been unable to suppress. The Pyramid Texts provide the earliest evidence of man's quest for salvation. The ancient Egyptians saw in the resurrection of Osiris a pledge of everlasting life for themselves beyond the grave. They believed that every man would live forever in the Other World, providing that his surviving family did for his body what the gods had done for the body of Osiris.

Being the first living thing to die, Osiris became the ruler of the dead. In the minds of the Egyptians, he was the one who decides who is worthy of admittance into the realm of eternal light, rest, and peace. Having once been a man and subject to the human passions and weaknesses, Osiris knew that the other gods could not appreciate human fallibility. Prayers and chants were addressed to him throughout Egyptian history, in hopes of securing his blessing and entrance to the afterlife which he ruled.

At first, Osiris was only associated with the funerary rituals of the Egyptian monarch, the Pharaoh, who was believed to become Osiris after his death. Over time, this soteriology was developed in both concept and ritual practice, and became popularized. The original royal privilege was gradually extended to every class of society, until about 1400 BCE, it had become an elaborate mortuary cult through which anyone with the means could hope to partake of the salvation it offered. From the Middle Kingdom onwards, it was the regular practice to address every dead Egyptian as "Osiris So-and-So." A passage in the later Book of the Dead (c. 1200 BCE) has the deceased, once ritually identified with Osiris, declaring that he comprehends the whole range of time in himself, thereby asserting his superiority to it.

---

[3] More properly the "Book of Coming Forth by Day," but also known as the "Book of Thoth"; in its complete form, a collection of 42 books dealing with cosmology, theology, and priestly discipline—the only extant part pertains to the long and arduous journey of the soul after death.

Osiris had several cult centres, but two cities above all others were associated with his myth. One of them was Busiris in the Nile Delta, which boasted the possession of his backbone. The other was Abydos in Upper Egypt, which professed to the possess his head. Abydos, once an obscure place, became from the end of the Old Kingdom the most sacred spot in Egypt. His tomb there was to the Egyptians what the Holy Sepulchre would much later be to the Christians. The one wish of every pious man was that his corpse should rest in hallowed ground close to the grave of the glorified Osiris.

The great annual mystery-play, in which the passion, death, and resurrection of Osiris were re-enacted, drew thousands of people to Abydos from every part of Egypt. In it was set forth, first, what the Greeks called his *agôn*, his contest with his evil brother, Set; then his *pathos*, his suffering, or downfall and defeat, his wounding, his death, and his burial; and finally, his *anagnorisis*, his resurrection either as himself or as his posthumous son, Horus.

Of all Egyptian, and probably of all ancient deities, none has lived so long or had so deep and wide an influence as Osiris. The immeasurable vogue which he enjoyed made his devout worshippers pile upon him the attributes and powers of many other gods. Local tradition had the Sun end its daily course at Abydos, and enter into the realm of the dead in the mysterious region below the western horizon, and thus Osiris, the lord of the dead, became identified with the setting Sun. His popularity endured until the final phases of Egyptian history—reliefs still exist of Roman Emperors, conquerors of Egypt, making offerings to him in his temples. He stands as the prototype of the great class of "Dying-Gods," who die that they may live again.

In art, Osiris is always depicted in human form swathed in mummy wrappings, because he was that which survives death and decay. He is often also depicted with green skin, alluding to his role as a god of vegetation. He wears a crown known as the *atef*, composed of the tall, conical white crown of Upper Egypt with red plumes on either side. His hands protruding, he holds a crook against his left shoulder with his left hand and a flail against his right shoulder with his right hand. His sacred colour is black, signifying the fertile black land (*Khem-et*) of the Nile—the sacred colour of Set, his brother and enemy, is red, connoting the barren red land (*Deshr-et*, the desert) and its hot, scorching wind.

Ancient Egypt fashioned the world's first civilized society out of river mud and the inhospitable desert with little more than ink and papyrus. Thoth, the ibis-headed deity, was the scribe of the gods and the god of scribes. His hieroglyph was the ibis-bird because the gesture of the ibis searching for food in the river mud is similar to that of the wrist and hand of the scribe writing and drawing.

Thoth was shown as attendant in almost every major scene involving the gods. He was credited with having caused a deluge to punish mankind for its wickedness. In this episode, related in the Book of the Dead, he had acted jointly with Osiris. Both of these deities had also ruled on Earth after the human race had begun to flourish again. Thoth was considered the inventor of hieroglyphics, and as such, he was associated with all the arts and sciences that depend on writing, including astronomy, mathematics, geometry and land surveying, medicine, botany, and chemistry.

The Egyptian writing started out as a form of pictography, each word having its own symbol, but early on, transferred meaning was developed, where each symbol would account for a specific sound so that these symbols could be used in different meanings and in different combinations. Gradually each regular syllable acquired its own specific symbol, and in the end, each letter had a different symbol, at which point approximately 29 letter and 80 word symbols were used altogether, shortening the writing considerably, as do the abbreviations (i.e. ABC, d.t.d., lbs, mph, Ph.D., etc.) that we use today.

In the Old Kingdom, a special shorthand for everyday use, called hieratic, or "sacerdotal," was developed, where the different hieroglyphs gradually shortened in order to be easier to draw with a reed pen. Over time, this form of writing transformed so much that the original shapes disappeared. At this latter stage, the writing is called demotic, or "popular." Ultimately, the Phœnician, Hebrew, Arabic, and Sanskrit alphabets are all based on the ancient pictograms of Egypt.

By the Middle Kingdom, the Egyptian textbooks would satirize every trade except that of the scribe, making the profession that much more desirable, and two adventure stories, one of an exiled nobleman called Sinuhe, the other of a shipwrecked sailor, foretell the voyages of Ulysses, Æneas, and Sindbad. One scribe glorifies himself and his colleagues in the fashion that is common to poets in all ages: all is trivial, "but a book makes him remembered through the mouth of its reciter."[4]

---

[4] Papyrus Chester Beatty IV

A culture is a multiplier of ideas, where each new innovation quickens and enlarges the power of the rest. Science has for its initial purpose the making of tools for life. Man tries to discern the laws of nature, or how natural things behave, in order that he may conquer them, rule over them, shape them to his own ends. Every stage in the domestication of plants and animals requires inventions, which start out as technical devices and from which emanate scientific principles.

The earliest agricultural tools were very simple: the mightiest invention was, of course, the furrowing plough, a wedge used to divide the soil. Though the wedge itself is an important mechanical invention, the plough is something much more fundamental—as a lever which lifts the soil, it was among the first applications of the lever principle. Settled agriculture breeds a technology from which all science takes off, and the true men of science soon begin to seek knowledge for its own sake.

The ancient Egyptians worshipped Thoth as the author of every work on every branch of knowledge, both human and divine. While he wears many crowns, his primary one is the globe of a full moon framed by two crescents. This association of Thoth with the Moon dates all the way back to Neolithic times. As the "Measurer of the Moon" and her phases, Thoth stands as the first scientist of mankind, seeding the beginnings of astronomy, geometry, and mathematics. Astronomy was the first science to be developed, and became a model for all the others, because it could be turned into exact numbers; in contrast to the background of religion and magic, the fundamental tenets of astronomy are pure science.

The rudiments of astronomy exist in every culture, and played an important role in the concerns of early people all over the globe. The reason for this is obvious: astronomy is the knowledge that guides us through the cycle of seasons; for example, according to the apparent movement of the Sun. There can thus be fixed a time when man should sow, when he should reap, and when he should move his herds. All settled cultures make use of a calendar in guiding their plans.

The whole life of nature is ruled by the existence of periodic events: the rotation of the Earth gives rise to successive days; the path of the Earth round the Sun brings about the annual recurrence of the seasons; even our own bodily life, with its recurrent heartbeats and breaths, is essentially periodical. In fact, the presupposition of periodicity is fundamental to our conception of life itself, and without this periodicity, the very means of measuring time as a quantity would be gone.

For many thousands of years, men only knew what time of year it was by looking at the natural calendar of the sky, and dated the sowing of crops and their religious rites by the rising and setting of Sirius or of some other easily recognizable star or constellation. Calendrical computation have to be seen as the primary cause of the rise of scientific astronomy, whether the calendar was needed for religious or agricultural purposes—the two are hardly separable in early days.

The studies of the phases of the Moon date from the days of the cave and stone knife, charting the cycle on antlers and thighbones. The nomadic and semi-nomadic lifestyles of early man obscured the diurnal and annual fluctuations in the path of the Sun, because these changes are horizon-related. For a nomad, the horizon travels alongside with him, unfixed, unmeasurable, altered by every change in geography, a strangely personal possession of the beholder, yet the possessor of all. The impact of the Sun is marked by the seasons and changes of the Earth and stars, but not by the day sky. The phases of the Moon, on the other hand, are everywhere the same, and though artificial light has made these phases pass almost unnoticed today, in climates where the skies are clear, human life was largely influenced by moonlight. The regular observation of the changes of the Moon predates the first villages, but once people settled, they became aware of the cycles in the patterns of the Sun on the now fixed horizon.

It depends on man's social and geographic conditions whether he will notice periodicity most in plants or animals. A nomad will note the recurrent births of animals and human children, and will connect these with the lunar year. Ritual centred very early round the Moon, whose cycle is long, but not too long, though probably only after her supposed influence on vegetation was first surmised. In a way, the Moon works magic herself: she waxes and wanes, and all the vegetable kingdom seems to wax and wane with her, all except the lawless onion.

Since he was originally associated with the Moon, Thoth became the god of time and time-measurement, and so of astronomy. But as the "Reckoner of Times and Seasons," he was depicted with a symbol combining the Sun's disk and the Moon's crescent upon his head, and the Egyptian inscriptions said his knowledge and powers of calculating "measured out the heavens and planned the Earth." His hieroglyphic name, *Tahuti*, is usually construed to mean "he who balances."

The ancient Egyptians originally employed a calendar based on the Moon. This earlier calendar was, like that of all ancient peoples, a calendar of twelve lunar months; the length of each being 30 days, making the year 360 days long. The Egyptians annually inserted five supplementary or "epagomenal" days in the end of every year in order to establish a harmony between lunar and solar time. This "civil" or secular calendar, which was introduced after the start of dynastic rule in Egypt, supplanted or perhaps only supplemented at first, the "sacred" calendar of old. Still, the calendar year remained approximately six hours too short. The Egyptians did not count a leap year, wherefore they had all the names of the months travel backwards through the seasons, a month in 120 years, returning to their original positions only after a period of 1460 (365 x 4) years, which is called a Sothic Cycle.

The Egyptians began their year with the heliacal rising of the brightest night star, Sothis, which in dynastic times immediately preceded the flooding of the Nile, on which Egypt depended. The heliacal rising of a star or constellation occurs when the star is seen rising in the eastern horizon just before sunrise (its heliacal setting is when it sets in the west immediately after sunset). The rising of bright stars during the night were used to divide the time of darkness into hours; and since in summer, at the time of Sothis' heliacal rising, twelve are seen to rise before dawn, the night hours were twelve. In the rainless Egypt, the hours of the night could almost always be discerned from the stars, and because in the south the night and day are reasonably equal in length, it was natural enough to divide the day into twelve hours as well.

As the messenger of the gods, Thoth was equated by the Greeks with Hermes, and for this reason, his centre of worship is still known to us today as Hermopolis. At Hermopolis, it was said that from Thoth were brought forth eight children, the most notable of which was Amoun, "the Hidden One." The Greeks associated the latter with the highest of their gods, and held his Egyptian oracle in great respect. They referred to him as Jupiter-Ammon or the Zeus of Thebes.

Viewed as a primordial creation-deity by the priests of Hermopolis, Amoun was the patron god of Thebes from earliest times, worshipped by the Thebans as the Lord of the Universe. Each "nome," or district, had its own *Netjer*, usually in animal form, but this same divinity tended to be identified with the deity of another nome. Thoth, for example, was portrayed as the sacred ibis in one district and as a baboon in another. The idea thus arose that the various gods and goddesses might just be different manifestations of the same creative power.

Amoun is always depicted in human form, a man crowned with the various attributes of his power. He is the first truly human man, because it is the ability of the soul to civilize itself that makes man different from animals. His primary crown and emblem is a pair of stone tablets, for the written word is the primary vehicle of civilization. This is the source of the image of the tablets holding the Ten Commandments, for Amoun represents the original social contract between eternity and the soul. The usage of the word "Amen" by the Hebrews is presumed to have originated in the Egyptian custom of taking oaths in the name of Amoun. In Isaiah 65:16, the "God of Truth" is in Hebrew *Elohi-Amen*.

Amoun is the archetype of the contract itself, of the civilized honour of agreements between souls maintained here on Earth. He is the invisible, hidden force of civilization, the magic power of organized effort among human beings, the whole that is greater than the sum of its parts. The earliest demonstration of his immense power lay in the network of irrigated fields that fed the growing nation of Egypt. The natural disadvantage of the Nile's flooding was thereby turned into the agricultural bounty of an empire.

The development of agriculture is a central prerequisite to the formation of a state. The most important functions of the state are the defence of the domain and the regulation of the water resources. The evolution of Egyptian agriculture was almost entirely dependent on the Nile, flowing mightily from the south to the north through the fertile flood lands of the Nile Valley. Still, this river can be viewed as the passage between equatorial Africa and the countries of the Mediterranean, at the mouth of which three continents meet. From there the caravan routes would head to various directions. Egypt was self-sufficient in her agriculture and her trade was modest, comprising mainly of luxury items. To the Egyptians, the Nile Valley was a "Beloved Land," where drought and bloom were in regular flux.

Qanats are a late construction of an urban civilization, and imply the existence of laws to govern water rights and land tenure, as well as other social relations. In an agrarian community, the rule of law is of a different nature from the nomad law that governs the theft of a sheep or a goat. The social structure is bound up with the regulation of matters that affect the community as a whole: access to the land, the maintenance and control of water rights, the precious structure on which the seasonal harvest depends.

A large system of irrigation extending over an empire requires a strong central authority. All the cities in Egypt rested on an invisible base of communication through which authority was able to be present and heard everywhere, directing orders from and information towards the centre. The network of authority was sustained by three advanced inventions: the roads, the bridges, and the messages. These are the typical first targets in revolutions, for if they are severed then authority is cut off and breaks down.

The seclusion of the Nile Valley acted as a safeguard to the development of political unity. About 5,000 years ago, all of Egypt became a thoroughly firm political entity, where a strict division of labour prevailed. The production took place in large, temple-led units. While cattle-breeding—symbolized by the crook—was initially important, farming—represented by the flail—soon became the central means of livelihood. Unlike her neighbours in Africa and Asia, Egypt was not dependent on the rains to ensure its food supply: the Nile rose with predictable certainty, inundating the land and allowing for continuous cultivation of crops. The success of the harvest depended, in addition to the level of the floodwater, on the condition of a complex series of canals dug to facilitate irrigation, which needed to be maintained and controlled by a strong central authority, personified by the Pharaoh. Not until the arrival of the Greeks in the 4th century BCE did the Egyptians rid themselves from the fluctuations of the Nile.

The structure of society and its relation to the royal court remained unchanged, a product of the secure, cyclical nature of the Egyptian environment. This is also why ancient Egypt is often accused of having had a stagnant culture, regardless of the dynamic changes that are dramatically evidenced throughout her history in the lives and art of her people. The Egyptian religion is an elegant philosophy of dance and joy, nurtured by a secure, relaxed world view that reflects the relatively comfortable conditions of the Nile Valley, and by the sense of boredom grown out of such leisure time.

It is no accident that all the first great strides towards civilization were made under despotic and theocratic governments, like those of Egypt, Babylon, and Peru, where the monarch claimed and received the humble allegiance of his subjects in the dual character of a king and a god. Nor is it an exaggeration to say that, at this early period, despotism was the best friend of humanity, and paradoxical as it may seem, of liberty. After all, there was more liberty in the best sense, liberty to think one's own thoughts and to build one's own destiny, under the most crushing tyranny, than under the apparent freedom of savagery, where the lot of the individual is carved in stone from the cradle to the grave.

The idea of early kingdoms as the kind of despotisms where the people existed solely for their sovereign, is wholly inapplicable to the ones discussed here. On the contrary, the sovereign existed only for his subjects, his life was only valuable so long as he performed the duties of his office by ordering the course of nature for the benefit of his people. The minute he failed to do so, the care and the devotion which had hitherto been heaped upon him ceased and shifted into hatred and scorn; he was dishonourably dismissed, and thankful to escape with his life. Deified one day, he was executed as a traitor the next. If the ruler of the people is also their god, he is, or should be, their preserver as well—if he will not preserve them, he must make room for another who will. A monarch like that is steeped in an elaborate ceremonious etiquette, a cobweb of prohibitions and observances, whose purpose is not to add to his dignity, much less to his comfort, but to restrain him from actions which, by disturbing the balance of nature, might involve himself, his people, and the universe in one collective cataclysm.

Primitive art in Egypt, Assyria, and Greece, represented either magical ceremonies, processions, sacrifices, embodied prayers, or else the images of the deities related to those rites. The monumental building of pyramids, begun as early as the Old Kingdom, had a profound effect on both the society and economy of Egypt. Cult and later also temple establishments became an important element in the life of the nation, and their financial dependency on the central authority was gradually lessened. The gradual shift in landownership from the central authority to the religious establishments began to undermine the very foundation on which the state stood. While these changes did not affect agricultural production, they were slowly preparing conditions for a return to the situation before the creation of one state by weakening the royal authority.

Initially, the chief beneficiaries of the king's favours were the religious centres near the capital, and only in the 5th Dynasty did provincial temples begin to receive land donations, which would turn them into economically independent institutions. From then on, the royal temple establishments began to represent a major economic force in the realm, and started to act as the principal clearing-houses for the distribution of national produce.

The official doctrine concerning the relationship of the Pharaoh with the *Netjer* was redefined and systematized sometime before the 5th Dynasty in order to fit him in a new system with the sun-god Ra of Heliopolis at its head. While perhaps the best known of Egyptian deities today, Ra was evidently unknown by name in both ancient Greece and Rome, and is consequently also a comparatively recent introduction in the Western world. In any case, the rise in importance of the sun-god led to his recognition as the state-god of the Old Kingdom, and the appearance of his name in royal names and titles reflect this fact. Whilst still being dubbed Horus, the king became also a "son of the god Ra."

Amoun's cult rose in prominence as Thebes rose to a pre-eminent political position within Egypt. Up until the Middle Kingdom, Amoun was merely a local god of Thebes, but during the 11th Dynasty, he became identified with the great sun-god as Amon-Ra, the father of the gods, the fashioner of men, the creator of cattle, the lord of all beings.

By the New Kingdom, Amon-Ra was made the supreme god of the entire realm and the "king of the gods." The Pharaohs, previously considered the sons of Ra, came now to be regarded as incarnations of Amon-Ra. Amoun assumed the role of a primæval deity in the cosmology of the New Kingdom, creating Earth and Sky out of his thought. The Egyptian architecture also experienced its heyday during the New Kingdom—the most massive temple ever built was constructed for Amon-Ra at Karnak.

The Karnak catalogues show that the temple owned 700,000 hectares of land, over 400,000 heads of livestock, and had its own navy. The worthiest form of worship was building for the god: originally, in the 3rd millennia BCE, Karnak had nothing but a shrine; during the golden age of Egypt, everything changed. Success in war, and the new trade routes that followed, made the Pharaohs more and more generous—the god was clearly on their side.

Karnak became the greatest dynastic cult centre of the Pharaohs, the power plant of the entire kingdom, and apparently also the greatest economic force in the realm. Every Pharaoh wanted to leave a memento of himself at Karnak, to contribute to the creative process. The obelisks of one ruler were left behind the walls erected by his jealous successors. The pylons disappeared behind more and more magnificent structures.

It is the Pharaoh who is always depicted as adoring the gods, though in reality, instead of performing rituals every day, he delegated these duties to the priests. But once every year, the Pharaoh had to affirm his divine rights: this necessitated a rite that was his alone, at the culmination of which even the high priest was not allowed be present. Each year, during the flood season, the Pharaoh left Memphis, from his palace, which stood in the Nile Delta, and journeyed up towards Karnak. The statue of Amoun was brought forth from the shrine of the god, wrapped up in linen cloth, and delivered to the royal barge. The common folk gathered on the river banks to watch the Pharaoh conducting his shrouded god to Karnak's smaller sister temple in Luxor.

The Pharaoh alone knew the rite, although everyone knew that at the end of it he would surely be a god. In Luxor, whose temple was connected with the rejuvenating powers of Amoun, the Pharaoh shut himself, his wife, and the effigy up in a small dark room at the furthest end of the temple, where the king's conception and divine birth was ritually re-enacted. This divine procreation is carved and painted in great detail on the walls of the two of the oldest temples in Egypt, those of Deir el-Bahri and Luxor—the inscriptions attached to the paintings leave no doubt as to the meaning of the scenes. As a result of the ritual, the regent was regenerated, recreated, if you will; his right to rule, his royal power, was reaffirmed. Amoun had once again accepted him and revealed him unto the world as his legitimate heir and representative on Earth.

But the power the high priest of Amoun rivalled that of the Pharaoh, causing political problems similar to modern Church-State rivalry. The priests of Amoun acted as the book-keepers, and operated at the kernel of power. They had become very influential by the New Kingdom, even posing a threat to some of the weaker Pharaohs, and needed to be appeased through donations. Their landholding increased to encompass almost one-third of Egypt's land. Through these enormous donations, the priests became powerful in both economic and political sense.

The papyri tell of great expeditions financed by the priests of Karnak: Amoun was not only the lord of creation, but also the lord of the eastern desert, and in that capacity, the owner of the rich mineral deposits, gold and the other precious metals. Expeditions penetrated also the deep south, the other side of Nubia. From there the god obtained exotic animals for his amusement. Between the years 1500 and 1000 BCE, Karnak was delivered over 30 metric tons of gold; invaluable lapis lazuli, or biblical "sapphire," was shipped from hundreds of kilometres off the coast. By 1100 BCE, Karnak was a centre of international trade unequalled in all the history of Egypt.

As the power of Karnak increased so did the power of its priests. By 1000 BCE, there were 80,000 people working in the service of the temple. A huge amount of dwellings were constructed for the needs of the priesthood—storage depots took up the whole western extremity of the district. All the property belonged to Amoun, but who was entitled to make use of it in this world, the priests or the Pharaoh?

The demise of kingship in the late period was largely a result of the fact that the Pharaohs attempted to take the gold from the temples, which, of course, the priests vigorously objected to, creating a schism that ended in the downfall of Egypt. The foreigners, who had for so long been the vassals of Egypt, decided to exploit the opportunity, and in the mid-8th century BCE, Egypt fell to conquerors. Rather than pushing aside the ancient deities, the foreign-born rulers of Egypt—the Persians, the Greeks, and the Romans—adopted the local customs and rituals; some of them were even embalmed.

The recorded history of ancient Egypt extends over a period of three thousands years. This vast time span opens with the legendary Menes, the king who unified the upper and lower kingdoms circa 3100 BCE, and closes with the conquest of Egypt by the Greeks in 332 BCE. The selection of these dates is, of course, arbitrary: Westerners looking at the ancient Middle East feel compelled to set definable limits, to describe dynasties and historical periods, even if the Egyptians themselves felt no such compulsion.

When Herodotus visited Egypt in 450 BCE, he was told by the priests of Memphis that they were in possession of a papyrus roll listing 330 royal predecessors to Menes and that this list covered the last 11,340 years of Egyptian history. His Greek readers, themselves heirs to ancient tradition, were first taken aback by these claims, but eventually came to accept them as proof of the antiquity of Egypt. The Egyptian civilization was the single most stable culture humanity has ever produced; the "Children of the Sun" succumbed not to stagnation, but to Alexander the Great.

CHAPTER 1

When we look for the first traces of civilization in the Nile Valley, we have to go back in time thousands of years and still we will find early traces of some primitive culture in the strata and the graves, proving that man has lived in these parts at least ten thousand years. This is not the case in Greece, not so far as it has been populated by the Greeks, who as late as the time of Homer, were held in disdain by the Egyptian priests, and considered nothing but an infant race. Even then it was a well-known fact that the land had been previously inhabited by older tribes, usually referred to collectively as the Pelasgians.

It is clear that the Greek-speaking peoples were immigrants, northern tribes from the lowlands of Danube or from farther north still, and linguistically related to the Germans, Celts, and Slavs. In several waves, the Hellenes, as they called themselves, arrived in the domain of the then prevailing culture of the land, now called Cretan or Minoan. Having adopted the oldest culture produced by inland Europe, they penetrated the south, where they met a much superior civilization, one the Ægean people had attained with the aid and stimulus of Egypt and Phœnicia.

The proximity of the coast of Greece to the nearby islands had led to the development of a homogeneous, maritime civilization. The first advanced civilization in Europe sprang, not from a well-watered river plain like in Egypt, Babylon, India, and China, but from the rugged landscape of the Ægean. Islands such as Crete became part of an enormous centre of commerce, an interaction sphere based on ideal standards of life. The farmers, herders, and craftsmen, who lived there some 4,000 years ago in scattered inland villages, created one of the most remarkable cultures of all time.

The Cretans used a certain kind of pictography acquired from the Egyptians, but the numerous documents discovered are so hard to decipher that it cannot be decided for certain when the Greek tongue was adopted there. No written history of the earliest phases of the Greeks have been preserved, but these phases are clearly reflected in legends and myth and in the archæological finds, which confirm the existence of human habitation on the island from the 8th millennium BCE onwards. Far ahead of its time with paved roads and running water, the Cretan culture thrived in reality and later in the lore of Plato as Atlantis.

Sir Arthur Evans, who excavated the famous palace of Knossos, named the culture "Minoan" after Minos, the legendary king of Crete. Ancient authors speak of him as a wise lawgiver and a fair judge, while Homer[5] even calls him a "companion of mighty Zeus." Thucydides says that Minos was the first man to hold sway over the Ægean with his fleet, and Plato mentions that the Attic Peninsula paid a heavy tribute to the Cretan King. At the height of their power, the Minoans achieved political and economic dominance over whole the eastern Mediterranean. Theirs was a sophisticated and generally peaceful culture that enjoyed the profits of a healthy market economy.

The island of Crete itself, a crossroads linking the three continents of Europe, Asia, and Africa, was repeatedly invaded and periodically conquered because of its strategic position in the sea. Trade in goods and ideas allowed for the growth and development of their advanced civilization. Trading ties existed with North Africa and Asia Minor, as witnessed in the writings on Egyptian temples and by archæological finds. Having unique charm and variety, the Minoan arts and crafts were without comparison against many of their contemporaries. Since all the countries in the region were not even aware of the existence of one another, strange and exaggerated tales began to circulate about the size, scope, and wonders of the Minoan civilization. The legends of Dædalus, of Theseus and the Minotaur, all concern the Minoans. The civilization that built the great palaces, rose and fell within a period of twelve hundred years, from circa 2200 BCE to 1000 BCE, with the last two centuries in a period of great decline.

The Minoans probably originated in coastal Asia Minor, where they became a seafaring people, who eventually settled on what are now islands of modern Greece. Archæological evidence comes mainly from the Minoan cultural centre on Crete, where several palaces have revealed a wealth of exquisitely detailed and colourful frescoes, vases, and other artefacts. However, in the late 1960s, archæologists began to uncover a vast underground city on the volcanic island of Thera, 70 miles north of Crete, and it is estimated that

---

[5] *Odyssey*, xix. 179

teams of archæologists will need several hundred years to reveal and study the immense quantity of finds. A great volcanic eruption in the 17th century BCE buried the Theran town of Akrotiri under layers of ash, pumice, and rock, preserving its Minoan heritage.

The Minoan art differed from all the other art of the Bronze Age in its themes and style: instead of stylizing, the Minoan artists depicted their surroundings realistically, and at the same time, delicately. From what we can tell, they led a peaceful and idealistic life; their motifs were not of warriors, subdued foes, and maimed slaves like those of their contemporaries. The Minoans paintings depicted humans, animals, and flowers—the most common theme being the woman.

In its time, Thera was a flourishing stronghold of the Minoan Empire, employing its gigantic fleet to control all sea trade on the Mediterranean. Although the Minoan capital was located at Knossos on Crete, Thera provided much of the military and political power that the Minoans used to defend themselves against the Greeks. The Minoans were not aggressive; they did not sail to conquer—they had everything they could possibly need. The fact that they did not fall a prey to their bloodthirsty neighbours was due to the primitiveness of the ships and seamanship of the latter.

The cataclysmic eruption of 1628 BCE created an explosive crater over six miles wide, stretching half a mile below sea level. It sent a tidal-wave nearly half the height of the Empire State Building onto the coast along the Mediterranean. The eruption displaced more than five times the volume of Krakatoa, covering the Minoan Empire with a heavy layer of ash. Stones from the explosion were hurled at least as far as the Black Sea. A roaring cloud of gas and dust filled the sky, causing periods of unusual darkness throughout Egypt and China.

The blast and tidal waves destroyed the Minoan coastal fortifications and damaged the great shipping industry. The ash fallout had a major impact on Crete, and though it did not have enough effect to destroy the Minoan way of life, it did cause an agricultural crisis, economic depression, and an influx of refugees. "The Great Island" nevertheless continued to enjoy comparative prosperity for a time, while the influence of her civilization kept on spreading in the Greek mainland.

However, about a generation after the great eruption of Thera, most of the important sites in central and southern Crete were destroyed by fire; great waves resulting from the eruption damaged settlements along the northern coast of Crete, while Knossos was shattered by a series of earthquakes that either preceded or accompanied it. Magnificent new palaces were erected on the ruins of the old ones and the cities around them expanded, starting the Second Palace Period. Destruction was not confined to cities and palaces, however, but extended to country houses, farms, and rural shrines, and many settlements were never again inhabited. Nobles at rural villas controlled areas in much the same way as feudal lords did in the Middle Ages. Their ships carried the products of Minoan and other cultures throughout the Ægean and eastern Mediterranean.

The great palace of Knossos was destroyed again at the end of the 15th century BCE, bringing in the Third Palace Period, and yet again in the mid-14th, beginning the Post-Palatial Period. This time, none of the Minoan palaces were rebuilt, and the Greek-speaking Mycenæans from mainland Greece filled the power vacuum. The tribes and cultures of the Mycenæans and the Minoans began to mix, the Mycenæans being the dominant group, and the lever of culture declined, as is common when less sophisticated people subjugate a more sophisticated one. The Hellenes represented the fusion of these two cultures, a brilliant product in the history of mankind.

At the beginning of the 12th century BCE, the scribe of Pharaoh Ramesses III wrote that "the northern countries, which are in their isles, are restless in their limbs." All the world of the Ægean was inflamed with migration. There was nothing new in the process of migration itself, but until about 1200 BCE, the southward migration of the Greek tribes had been fragmentary, and incapable of overturning the development of civilization. But in this last stage, known as the Dorian migration, the torrent of arrivals was so rapid and concentrated, that the civilization, which could no longer absorb it, began to decline.

The immigrants brought with them their language, which proved more precious an asset than many other treasures. The Greek language manifests a rare, even unique, musicality in its liveliness and finesse, its richness in nuances and colour, its melodiousness, its strength, and its elasticity. It had all the prerequisites of the most perfect language ever spoken or written, and thus also of a medium to the noblest literature that the ancient world has ever produced.

Instead of adopting the Cretan pictography, the Greeks borrowed their writing from the Phœnicians. The letters (consonants and the vowels A and E, numbering 28 in all) of the West-Semitic Hebreo-Phœnician writing were transmitted to Greece around the 10th century BCE. The Phœnicians, who on their trade trips wandered about the countries of the Mediterranean, simplified the alphabet they had developed and settled for 21 or 22 letters. The Greeks, in their turn, added a couple of new ones. The Phœnician language, like Hebrew, was written from right to left, so when Greek came to be written from left to right, the shape of the letters changed.

Comparative study has shown that each time epic literature has been born out of natural impulse, and not from artificial stimulation or from a wish to imitate, it has required very special conditions. What is at once noticeable in the heroic poems is that hardly anyone is safely and quietly at home. The heroes are fighting in far-off lands or voyaging by sea—we hear little of tribal or even of familial bonds. The real centre is never the hearth, but the leader's ship or tent. In short, the heroic spirit, as portrayed in heroic poetry, was the product of a society cut loose from its roots, of an age of migrations, of the shifting of populations.

The songs of heroes heard by Homer retain scarcely any memory of the great and peaceful civilization of Crete. The age they depict is the Age of Heroes, c. 1200 BCE, when the Mycenæan culture had died out and piracy and cattle-lifting ran rampant. In settled, social conditions, "most of the heroes"—as Jane Harrison has well remarked—"would sooner or later have found themselves in prison." The Trojan War, described by Homer in the *Iliad*, took place, according to the Greeks, in 1184 BCE and was presumably one of a series of wars waged during the 13th and 12th centuries BCE. It was probably also connected with the last and most important of the invasions from the north, which brought the Iron Age to Greece.

Horses were the pride and joy of some Homeric kings; the noble creatures were only used in war, in cart races, and mule breeding—not to ride as yet. The idea must have been as startling in its day as the invention of a flying machine. For one thing, riding required a bigger, stronger horse; the horse was originally quite a small animal that could not carry a man for long. Riding as a serious use began in the nomad tribes that bred horses. The riders were men out of Central Asia, Persia, Afghanistan, and beyond; the Greeks called them Scythians, a collective name for the new and frightening creature.

The rider is visibly more than man, head-high above others, moving with bewildering force so that he bestrides the living world. Mounting the horse was a more than human gesture, it was a symbolic act of dominance over all the creation. We know this for sure from the awe and dread that the horse inspired—horsemen were a terror that swept over the lands that did not know the technique of riding. Excluding Thessaly, the land of studfarms, horses remained unusually rare and expensive everywhere in Greece. When the other Greeks beheld the Thessalian horsemen, they believed the steed and rider to be one—which is how the legend of the Centaur came about.

The conditions that gave birth to Homer were presented by the extinguishment of a pre-existent culture. Adventurers from north came upon a land rich in spoils, where the chieftain might sack a city and dower himself and his band of reckless followers with sudden wealth. Such a contact of old and new, of settled splendour besieged by rampant adventure, went to the making of a heroic age, its vices and virtues, its apparent beauty and hidden ugliness. The warlike heroes of Homer "toil not, neither do they spin." They do nothing creative or constructive, they just live and laugh, rape and ravage, wasting the resources of the civilization which they are in process of destroying.

Evidently, the heroes of the Trojan War enjoyed great popularity—their adventures and deeds were praised and preserved by tradition, until time was ripe to affix them onto the pages of world literature. The *Iliad* and *Odyssey* have received more lasting and more universal admiration than any other pieces of poetry. Homer, a blind minstrel, whom the Greeks considered the author of these two books, lived sometime before the 7th century BCE. That is all we know of him, and the theories of skeptical philologists have been free to romp about. Homer is not much more than a name, and there is no reason to deprive the author of it. Apparently, he lived in Asia Minor of the 8th century, not at any rate much earlier, judging from the cultural patterns his works reflect.

A heroic age is the age of the individual, and luckily for society, cannot last. If a society is to endure, it must strike its roots deep in the soil, be it native or foreign. The band of adventurers must either disband and go home, or else settle anew on the land which they have conquered. Their wanton, reckless leader must become a sober, domesticated, law-making and law-abiding king, whose followers have to "beat their swords into plowshares, and their spears into pruninghooks."

Like Herodotus says, it was Homer and Hesiod who created the Greek theology and named the characteristic duties of the principal gods, thus reconciling the local cults and discouraging the remnants of the older religions. The Homeric poems were considered veritable sources of knowledge and quoted as zealously as the later generations have quoted the Bible. The modern mind, limited by the canonical Olympus, the Olympus which is "all for the Father," has forgotten the Great Mother. Yet it is clear that the rites of the Olympians had been superimposed on a different order of worship. The contrast between the two classes of rites is so marked and distinct, that an unbroken development from one to the other seems almost impossible.

In historical times, descent was traced in Greece mostly through the father. But the primitive Greek goddesses reflect another state of affairs, a relationship traced through the mother, the state of society known as matriarchal. The modern patriarchal society focuses its religious anthropomorphism on the relationship of the father and the son, but at Athens, male kinship was preceded by female kinship. Crete was to the end "of the Mother"—her art completely lacked the most popular image of the Bronze Age, the male sovereign, warrior, conqueror of people; even in her language, she refused to recognize the empty patriarchalism of "fatherland."

In the ancient days, the only relationships that could be proved, and that therefore were worth troubling about, were through the mother. Women were worshipped as deities for their ability to give birth, nurture, and otherwise care for their young. The tribes were ruled by queens, and the women were viewed as the Strong Ones. At Athens, a city once subject to Crete, we find evidence of succession to the throne by marriage with a royal princess: two of the most ancient kings of Athens, namely Cecrops, an Egyptian, and Amphictyon, are said to have married the daughters of their predecessors.

In a state of society where noble rank is reckoned only through women, where descent through the mother is everything, and the descent through the father is nothing, no objection exists to uniting girls of the highest rank to men of humble origin, even to foreigners or slaves, provided that in themselves the men seem like suitable mates. If they, like their consorts, be of royal and divine descent, so much the better—but it is nowise imperative that they be so. The king was not king by inheritance, but by right of conquest, and in the most stable dynasties, the new king was always a stranger, a foreigner.

The Greek myths contain mythological elements from different cultures and from different stages of history. In the Ægean region, before the arrival of the proto-Greeks around 2000 BCE, most deities were Chthonian, or earthly, in character. The Great Mother Goddess was almost necessarily envisaged as the Earth—Ga was also Ma. And Mother Earth bore not only fruits, but also the human race. In the words of the poet Asius, "Divine Pelasgos on the wood-clad hills, Black Earth brought forth, that mortal man might be."

Pelasgos claimed no father, yet he—the first father—had a mother. A local mother must inevitably have preceded Gaia, the abstract and universal, for primitive man tends not to deal in abstractions: each local hero claimed descent from a local earth-nymph or mother; and each local mother, the real parent, is eventually merged in the great all-mother Gê.

To the early tribes, the need for fertility was essential, both in their women, to combat the high mortality rate, and in the herds of wild creatures that provided most of their food. The woman who was exceptionally fertile was regarded with great awe, seen as someone with special powers, highly favoured by the supernatural being that caused her to give birth so often. A fertile woman with her large breasts and wide hips, spread by continuous childbearing, would become an ideal, a copy of the Earth Mother, seen by the tribe as her earthly counterpart. The Earth Mother and each and every local nymph was mother not only of man, but of all living creatures; she was *Potnia Theron*, the "Lady of the Wild Things."

We can give the goddess no proper name; we rightly call her the Great Mother and the "Lady of the Wild Things," but this is as far as we can go. She has been called Isis and Cybelê, but for neither name is there a shred of evidence; primitive man will shirk from addressing his gods by a personal name, delicately shrouding them in class epithets. Given these adjectival names, it is clear that the deities are as many as the moods of the worshipper: should he be kind, they are Kindly Ones; should he feel vengeful, they become Vengeful Ones.

The word *heros* itself is adjectival—by "hero" was meant "mighty," "exalted," and "venerable." In Homer, the hero was the strong man alive, mighty in battle; in cult, the hero was the strong man after death, fortified with a greater, because a ghostly, strength. The avoidance of the actual given name of a dead man is an instructive propriety that lives on today. The newly dead becomes "he" or "she," as the actual name feels, at least for a time, too intimate. The tendency in all primitive minds is to remove the little whatever that is too close, calling one's friend "the tall one," or "the young one," or "the fair one," and never pronounce his silent name. Before long, this delicate instinct crystallizes into a definite ritual prescription, gathering about it the cautious Solonic utilitarianism of *De mortuis nil nisi bene*.

To ancient humanity, anyone who fitted the concept of an ideal man or woman was considered more than human and gradually elevated to the earthly image of a god. The hero, like all primitive divinities, had for his sphere of beneficence the whole circle of human activities, for a primitive community cannot afford to departmentalize its deities. The local hero had to help his kinsmen to fight, to secure fertility for themselves and their crops, to act as oracle when the community was disconcerted, and in general be ready for any emergency that might arise.

The general principle in mythology is that the reputed death-place of a hero is far more significant than his place of birth. This is due to the fact that, among a people who practise hero-worship, the death-place and the tomb are where the cult is set up. For the Olympian gods were erected temples, images, and altars, for the Chthonian gods and heroes were dug hearths, trenches, and *megara*[6]. The Great Mother was mother of the dead as well as the living, keeping ward in the metropolis of the dead.

At Philius, Hebe, a local heroine, had a sacred grove, "most holy from ancient days." Her sanctuary was an asylum, and it was considered her greatest honour that "slaves who took refuge there were safe and prisoners released hung their fetters on the trees in her grove." It was common in ancient days for sanctuaries to also be asylums, for whenever an immigrant conqueror reduces a whole land to subjection, he tends, perhaps from superstitious awe, to let the conquered retain their local sanctuary, the one place safe from his tyranny. Hebe Ganymeda, the female correlative of Ganymede, was later promoted to the Homeric Olympus, but significantly only as cupbearer and wife of Herakles.

Into every village in Greece descended the lowest steps of the stairway that reached sometimes—though not always or even often—up to the summit of Olympus itself. Whenever a local hero or heroine became famous beyond his own parish, the Olympian religion did its best to meet him or her half-way.

---

[6] s. *megaron*, a natural chasm or cleft later helped out by art

Herakles was of the primitive Pelasgian stock, his name signifying merely the "young dear hero." No pains were spared to affiliate him: he was allowed the Olympian burnt sacrifice, made a son of god through Zeus' intrigue with a mortal maiden, Alkmene; he died, but "ascended as a spirit to his father Zeus in Olympus," where he was wedded to Hebe, herself only just translated.

The view of Herakles changed considerable over time, focusing first on how badly he managed despite his obvious gifts. As time passed, the focus shifted to his virtues: he was considered a saint by the Stoics for his example of ultimately obtaining deitification through enduring the ordeals of the world; the Romans valued him highly as he best fit their idea of a hero. Herakles may have emerged as a Panhellenic god, dubbed *Soter*, a saviour, and *Neulos Emelos*, a good shepherd, but far more often the fate of a hero was to remain the object of a local cult. This, of course, nowise barred the local identification of the heroes and heroines with the mighty Olympians.

It was natural enough in day when man was mainly concerned with hunting and fighting, that agriculture and the ritual attendant on it should fall to the woman. To this social necessity was added, and still is among many primitive communities, a deep-seated superstition. Primitive man refuses to interfere with agriculture, assuming it to be magically dependent for success on woman, and connected with childbearing. Common to all primitive tribes are ceremonies of sympathetic magic, the gist of which is the mimicking of nature's processes. The women of the ancient Attica fasted seated on the ground because the earth was desolate; they rose and revelled, they stirred the *megara* to mimic the impulse of spring—when they no longer knew why they did these things they made a goddess their prototype.

So long as and wherever man lives mostly by hunting, the figure of the "Lady of the Wild Things" will satisfy his imagination. As soon as he becomes an agriculturist, however, the Great Mother must necessarily, in addition to being the mother of all living creatures, be also the mother of corn. She is still the Earth Mother, *Gê Mêtêr*, but in a limited sense, as *Dêmêtêr* or the "barley mother"; to Greece she probably came from Crete, bringing her name with her (*deai*, Cretan for "barley"). She first visited Attica, where she revealed to Triptolemus the mysteries of the grain called by her name. The goddess then sent the boy out into the world to teach the starving humanity to plow, sow, harvest the crop, bake the bread, and grow the fruit—all crafts which had thus far been unknown to Greeks.

Agriculture began to bind men together with the ties of civilized life. The connection between primitive law and agriculture is very close, even as the name of the earliest law recorded, the "Ploughman's Curses," testifies. Similar precepts have come down to us under the name of the thrice-plougher, Triptolemus, who also happened to be the first lawgiver of the Athenians. He told men: "Honour your parents; Sacrifice to the Gods from the fruits of the earth; Injure not animals."

It was mainly in connection with agriculture that the Earth Goddess developed her double form as Mother and Maid. The ancient "Lady of the Wild Things" was both in one, but at Eleusis, the two figures were clearly outlined: Demeter and Kore[7] are two persons, but one goddess. When both appear together in art, they are often so alike as to be indistinguishable.

The Eleusinian Mysteries, held annually in honour of Demeter and Kore, were the most sacred and revered of all the ritual celebrations of ancient Greece. Standing as the foundation of the unity of all Hellenic peoples, they were instituted in the city of Eleusis, some fourteen miles west of Athens, possibly as far back as the early Mycenæan period, and went on for almost two thousand years—more than the span of the Classical Greek and Roman civilizations put together.

So strongly did these mysteries underlie Greek culture that each September, a peace was declared throughout the Greek-speaking world for the fifty-five days of their celebration on the Eleusinian plain. At this "Place of Happy Advent," tradition held, the goddess Demeter was reunited with her daughter, Kore, who had been abducted into the underworld by its lord and ruler, Pluto. The legend goes, that after the Eleusinians had built their temple to Demeter, she had remained with them, longing for her daughter and refusing to rejoin the other gods and goddesses on Mount Olympus. What is more, she had also refused to make the seeds sprout in the dark earth, causing all the world to suffer famine.

Even the gods suffered from the lack of burnt sacrifice, so Zeus sent his minions to intercede with her, but she yielded not. Finally, the king of the gods sent Hermes down to Hades, to bid the lord of the underworld for the return of Kore to her mother. Pluto reluctantly agreed, and only after having

---

[7] a/k/a Persephone

succeeded in making Kore eat a single pomegranate seed—just enough to ensure, by some sort of divine symmetry, that she would always spend one third of the year with him. And so Kore was able to leave the underworld and reunite again with her mother on Earth.

By no means was Eleusis the only place in Greece where annual festivals in honour of a goddess of grain and the yearly renewal of life were featured; similar rituals were typical to many centres of the ancient eastern Mediterranean civilization, including islands as far north as Samothrace, as far east as Cyprus, and as far south as Crete. Besides the twofold Mother and Maid, Greek religion had a number of female trinities: we find not only three Gorgons, but three Furies, three Fates, three Graces, three Seasons, and, as a multiple of three, nine Muses.

In the Chthonian ritual, three was a sacred number: the dead were thrice invoked, sacrifice was offered to them on the third day, mourning lasted for three days; the court of the Areopagus, which was watched over by the deities of the underworld, sat on three days; at the three ways was the threefold Hekate of the underworld worshipped. Threefold divinities naturally arose to keep ward over such a ritual, and when the powers of the underworld came to preside over agriculture, the transition from two to three seasons naturally tended in the same direction. For two seasons a duality was enough: the Mother for the fertile summer, the Maid for the infertile winter. As soon as the seasons became three, a trinity was required.

While all female trinities rose out of dualities, not every duality became a trinity. Where personification had become complete, as was the case with Demeter and Kore, no third figure could be added. Where the divine pair was still called by nothing but adjectival titles that had not yet crystallized into proper names, a person more or a person less mattered little. Thus there is a trinity of Furies, Fates, Graces, and Seasons, but the *Thesmophoroi* (from *thesmoi*, "laws," and *phoria*, "carrying," in reference to Demeter and Kore as "law-bearers") always remain, because of the clear outlines of goddesses, a duality.

It is well worth noting that the trinity-form was confined only to the female deities. In Zeus and Apollo, the Greek religion had the figures of the Father and the Son, but no trace is found of any male trinity. What is more, Zeus and Apollo, incomers from the north, stand alone in this relationship. The fatherhood of Poseidon is not emphasized, nor is the sonship of Hermes.

There is no universal development of the Father and the Son as there was of the Mother and the Maid—dualities and trinities both are characteristic of the primæval goddess.

According to Pythagoras[8], "women who were married to men had the names of the Gods, being successively called virgins (*kôre*), then brides (*nymphê*), and subsequently mothers (*mêtêr*)." All you need to do is to invert his statement, and you have the gist of matriarchal theology.

Nymphs are of course everywhere, but to a primitive society, the two principal stages of womanhood are obviously Mother and Maid. When these conditions crystallized into divinities in the form of Demeter and Kore, they appear as mother and daughter, but primarily the stages expressed are Mother and Maid, woman mature and woman before maturity. Of these two, the form of the Mother was in early days the more prominent, while Kore as daughter rather than maiden is the product of mythology, as the Mother Goddess has for her attribute of motherhood a son rather than a daughter.

The relation of these early matriarchal, unwedded goddesses, be they Mother or Maid, to the accompanying male figures is altogether maternal and feminine, in the middle between a mother and a lover. Detached from achievement themselves, they choose a champion to inspire and protect; they ask him, not to love or adore, but to do great deeds. Demeter has her Triptolemus, Hera her Iason, Athena her Perseus, her Herakles, and her Theseus. Their glory is in the deeds of the hero, their grace is his protection. The arrival of patriarchal conditions puts an end to this noble companionship, shutting the goddesses off into a servile domesticity.

According to some scholars, the Greek creation myth bears witness to the arrival into the Ægean region of Indo-European populations, who brought with them new gods and a new cosmogony. The Titans are the children of Earth, primitive giants rebellious against the new Olympian order.

Gaia, the Earth, daughter of Chaos (the void), gave virgin birth to Ouranos (the heaven), Ourea (the mountains), and Pontos (the sea). In relation with Ouranos, she bore the twelve Titans and a variety of monsters, who were imprisoned in the depths of the earth. The youngest of the Titans, Kronos (the time), became the supreme ruler by castrating his father, and to prevent the same from ever happening to him, swallowed each of his own

---

[8] as quoted by Diogenes Laërtius

children—Hestia, Hera, Demeter, Poseidon, and Pluto—immediately following their birth. His sister and partner, Rhea, soon grew tired of this, wrapping a stone in swaddling cloth for the birth of the next child. Kronos thus swallowed a rock instead of Zeus, the last born, who upon reaching maturity, forced his father to egest all the children he had swallowed.

In the great battle that ensued, most of the Titans sided with Kronos, afraid of losing their position to the younger gods. Zeus, with the help of the Cyclops and Hecatoncheires, whom the Titans had imprisoned in Hades, defeated his father and took possession of the world as king of the gods, residing on Mount Olympus. Mad that her children had all been scourged or killed by the next generation of gods, Gaia had her new-born son, Typhon, challenge the Olympians. So horrid was he, with his thundering voice, his serpentine body, and his hundred heads, that the gods fled from Olympus to Egypt, where they concealed themselves in various animal forms. However, they soon recovered from their initial fright, returning to Olympus and expelling the Giants; after Zeus had, using his thunderbolts, crushed Typhon under Mount Etna, which still heaves with his convulsions. Others of the old order also received special punishments; Atlas, for example, was transformed into the mountain range which still bears his name.

According to this same myth—related by Hesiod in his *Theogony*—Zeus created the first woman, Pandora, out of the clay of the earth. But to the primitive matriarchal Greece, Pandora had been a real goddess, in form and name, and men did sacrifice to her.[9] Pandora, the all-gifted, is in ritual and matriarchal theology the earth as Kore, yet in the patriarchal mythology of Hesiod, her great figure is strangely changed and diminished. She is no longer earth-born, but created, the handiwork of Olympian Zeus.

Zeus the Father will admit no great Earth Goddess, Mother and Maid in one, into his patriarchal Olympus. Her figure is primæval, so he needs to remake it: woman, once the inspirer, is henceforth the temptress—she who created all things divine and mortal, has become their toy, endowed only with physical beauty and the tricks and flattery of a slave. To Zeus, the birth of the first woman is nothing but a great Olympian jest: "So said the father of men

---

[9] E.g. the Oracle-Monger instructing Peisthetærus in *The Birds* of Aristophanes recites from his sacred scroll: "They must first sacrifice a white-fleeced goat to Pandora."

and gods, and laughed aloud."[10]

These myths are a necessary outcome of the shift from matriarchy to patriarchy, and this shift in itself is a necessary stage in the evolution of man. Matriarchy bestowed upon women a false, since a superstitious, prestige. Patriarchy came with the inevitable facing of an actual fact: man realized that he had something to do with conception, namely, insemination. When man outgrew his belief in the magical potency of woman, he proceeded by an excusable practical logic to treat women as second-rate citizens, weaker, and not as intelligent as men. He was to no longer live in harmony with nature, he was to have dominion over her.

In the Homeric Olympus, there is mirrored a family group of the basic patriarchal type, a type that is so familiar to us that it hardly attracts any attention. Zeus, "the Father of Men and Gods," reigns supreme; Hera, while ever in significant revolt, nevertheless occupies the subordinate place of a wife; Hestia and Demeter, Poseidon and Pluto, are their younger siblings, and the rest of the divinities are grouped around them as sons and daughters.

Yet if we burrow into local cults we discover that, should these mirror the civilization of the worshippers, this civilization is something other than patriarchal. At Eleusis, Demeter and Kore reign supreme—neither Pluto nor Triptolemus ever challenges their supremacy. At Argos, Hera, subject in Olympus, reigns alone; at Athens, Athena is no god's wife—affiliated as she in a loose way is to Poseidon, that relation is not one of subordination, but of rivalry and ultimately of conquest. Apollo may have held the oracle at Delphi in historical times, but even he was preceded by a succession of goddesses: "First, in this prayer of mine, I give the place of highest honour among the gods to the first prophet, Earth; and after her to Themis, for she was the second to take this oracular seat of her mother, as legend tells. And in the third allotment, with Themis' consent and not by force, another Titan, child of Earth, Phœbe, took her seat here. She gave it as a birthday gift to Phœbus, who has his name from Phœbe."

St. Augustine[11], in relating the tale about the rivalry between Athena and Poseidon, writes that the victor was determined by the vote of the citizens, both men and women, since it was customary those days for women to

---

[10] *Works and Days*, ll.59

[11] *De Civitate Dei*, xviii. 9

participate in public affairs. The men voted for the god, the women for the goddess, and since the former exceeded the latter by one, Athena prevailed. However, to appease Poseidon's wrath, the menfolk inflicted a threefold punishment on the womenfolk—"they would no longer have any vote, none of their children would be named after their mothers; and no one was to call them Athenians," after their goddess.

The myth is ætiological, mirroring a shift in the social structure of Athens. The citizens were summoned by Cecrops, whose name tradition associates with the introduction of the patriarchal form of marriage. "In Athens Cecrops was the first to join one woman to one man," says Athenæus, quoting Aristotle's far-travelled student and colleague, Clearchus of Soli, "before his time unions had been loose and promiscuity was general. . . .earlier men did not know who was their own father, there were so many [possible ones]." According to tradition, Cecrops was the first to call Zeus the Highest, and with the worship of the Father were introduced the social conditions of patriarchy.

Hera appears outwardly all wife, queen in Olympus by virtue of her marriage to Zeus; yet a mere glance at the local myth and cult show that their Sacred Marriage, the prototype of all human wedlock, was not from the beginning. In the ancient Argonautic legend, it is not Zeus, but Hera, the Queen of Thessaly and the patron of Iason, who is dominant. At Olympia, where Zeus in historical times ruled if anywhere supreme, the ancient Heraion long predates the Temple of Zeus. In the remote Arcadia, Hera had three sanctuaries and three epithets: in the spring, she was called *Parthenos*, "Child," in the summer, she was celebrated as *Teleia*, "Full-Grown," and in the winter, she became *Chera*, "Widow." Long before she had any connection with Zeus, she already reflected the three stages of a woman's life, of which the middle one did not yet imply a patriarchal wedlock.

Even Homer is still haunted by the memory of days when Hera was a mistress in her own right; or what else could her ceaseless rebellion and the unending strife with the king of the gods signify? What means her persistent tyranny over Herakles, whom Zeus loves, but cannot protect? Forcibly married, she is never really a wife: Zeus and Hera merely become *omobômioi*, "sharers of one altar," against which liaison the older female divinities are only too often powerless.

Oddly enough, when the Great Mother re-emerges, she does it as

Aphrodite. This goddess is more Nymphê the Bride, but she is the bride of the old order, never the wife, for she never tolerates perpetual patriarchal wedlock—her will is clearly for love, not for marriage. Once she is admitted to the patriarchal Olympus, there is a futile attempt to attach her to one husband, Hephaistos the Craftsman. He does not achieve happiness with her; on that all the legends agree. Aphrodite is in very principle unfaithful to him, and has children with all men possible, save her husband.[12] It is made evident in Homer that she is a newcomer to Olympus, hardly tolerated and always thankful to get away. Her Homeric epithets, *Kypris* and *Kythereia*, prove that she is originally a local goddess of the island in the south, never truly at home in the cold and gloomy north.

Another voucher of her late arrival into mainland Greece is that in Homer she is a departmental goddess, having for her sphere a single human passion. The earlier forms of divinities are invariably deities of larger import, gods of all work. It is the gradual dispersion of the tribes, together with their consequent isolation from one another, that favours differentiation in the ways of conceiving and worshipping the deities whom they have brought with them from their original home, and thus discrepancies of myth and ritual will emerge, and in time, convert a nominal distinction between the divinities into a real one. The eventual fusion of tribes and the influence of literature then brings together a number of local divinities, which, if they are to stay together, divide their functions and attributes. They have thus become so distinct that their original identity cannot be discerned, but they can now take their place side by side as departmental divinities in the national pantheon.

Poseidon, locally *Phytalmios*, the god of growth, has been reduced to a deity of one element. Hermes, having at home dominion over flocks and herds, over all life and growth, is here a mere herald. The Roman Cicero, who wrote a book *On the Nature of the Gods*, says that there were five different gods who had that same name, and it is obvious that all the things we are told of this messenger of Olympus, could not easily from the beginning have referred to

---

[12] Sexuality was perceived as a divine, regenerative force to be channelled through women until ascetic patriarchy relegated such notions to the realm of heresy and witchcraft. Aphrodite was not only the goddess of love, but the goddess of eroticism; her power to remain a virgin no matter how many lovers she had terrified men more than all the lightning bolts of Zeus ever could.

the one and the same god. The popularity, which Homer and his Olympus won, led to the local cults being discarded or adapted to the worship of Zeus, Apollo, and the others. These Panhellenic gods were honoured with public celebrations, games, and poetry contests, which gradually became a strong bond uniting all the geographically scattered Greeks.

By the 8th century BCE, the Greeks were already both traders and warriors, artists and perhaps even thinkers, and they had organized into the best known of Greek institutions, independent and autonomous, economic and political units that were city-states. This organization inaugurated a period of stability, wealth, further expansion of population, plus social and economic experimentation, which turned Greece into a Mediterranean power to be reckoned with.

The great political event that dominates the whole Attic history, and in fact, makes the history of Athens possible, is the merging of numerous independent districts with Athens under one king and one government. According to legend, this change was brought about by Theseus, who, quite consistently, is also told to have liberated his country from the domination of Crete, to have repulsed the alien aggressions, and to have banished the foreign denizens, such as the Amazons, the battle against whom played such a prominent part in the decorative art of Greece. The merging that came about with Theseus was not complete, however; Eleusis, standing on her own plain, retained her independence for a long time.

The Spartans, on the other hand, had decided to meet the challenge of land-hunger, not by trade and colonization like the Athenians, but by expansion at the expense of their neighbours. After conquering Messenia, they subjugated the Messenians, and bound them to the land as helots, serfs of the Spartan state. However, in order to maintain their control over the helots, the Spartan citizens had to submit to political and military discipline of the harshest kind. In return for the lands that they had appropriated, the Spartans had to relinquish their own individual liberties: male citizens were trained for war from the age of seven, living their lives as wardens of an armed fortress in the midst of a hostile and potentially rebellious alien population. Directing all of their resources into the maintenance of their state did afford the Spartans exceptional stability; but it was the stability of the barracks, and as much creative.

CHAPTER 2

Greek traders and colonists had wandered about the whole Mediterranean basin by the late 7th century BCE, and were spreading northward to the Black Sea; southward to North Africa in the areas left unclaimed by the Phœnicians; eastward to Asia Minor; and westward to southern Italy, Sicily, France, and Spain. Trade with the colonies enabled many of the poleis in Hellas to turn themselves into manufacturing centres or to focus on developing specialized crops such as the olive and the grape, produce that could be traded for grain, minerals, and fur.

Wealth and seafaring had generated broad-mindedness and sophistication that often formed a potent contrast to the blood orgies of legends and myth. The early geographer, Hecatæus of Miletus, made a discovery on his extensive travels that shook the foundations of the belief in the pre-eminence of the Greek aristocracy. The Greek aristocrats traced their pedigree six or seven generations back to a god or perhaps rather to the promiscuity of a god. But when Hecatæus journeyed through Egypt, the priests took him to see the graves of the kings, showing him the mummies of Egyptian families dating back 20 or 30 generations. That was when he saw the truth, that is to say the falsity of the claims that the Greek aristocrats descended from the gods, and as soon as he returned, he would spread the word of his discovery to everyone he met.

Around 600 BCE, just when the Gods of Olympus were losing touch with reality, fading and succumbing to their own sumptuous perfection, there came a fresh religious impulse into Greece: the Thracian Bacchos, arrived as *theos xenikos*, a "foreign deity," among the Greeks, who were to call him Dionysos.

Long before his arrival, the Greeks had nature-gods: Demeter was the goddess of the corn; Poseidon, the god of the growth of plants; and Charites were the givers of all increase. But each of these and many other nature-gods had now passed into a state of complete anthropomorphism, representing human rather than merely physical relations, hopelessly cut off from their plant and animal ancestry. Demeter was now much more mother than corn;

Hermes, in spite of his herm-shape and phallic worship, was all but forgotten as a spirit of generation in flocks and plants, being now perceived as a young man in all his human grace. In art, Hermes and Dionysos still appeared as they were worshipped—as herms. The symbol of both as fertility-gods was, of course, the phallos. It was impossible to distinguish the young Dionysos from Hermes.

Pan was a solitary god, who wandered among the heaths and woods, and dwelt on mountains and in caves. To a people of goat-herds, like the Arcadians, the goat was the personification of life and generation—to a people of cowherds, the ox was a more suitable vehicle. Dionysos the bull-god was god of all growing things, of every tree and plant and product of nature—only later exclusively of the vine.

Plutarch, discussing the identity of Dionysos and Osiris, says that the Greeks regarded the former as not only the lord and originator of wine, but of the whole *hugra phusis*, the "moist principle"—representing not only the liquid fire of the grapes, but also the sap rushing in young trees, the blood throbbing in the veins of young animals, all the mysterious and unchecked tides that ebb and flow in the Natural Kingdom. Both appeared in ritual as slain and dismembered, and in both cases, there was clearly some form of resurrection of the god, or a new birth as a little child.

Honouring Dionysos was the appropriate task of the women of every Greek city. Every spring, they who ordinarily could not leave the house, abandoned their babies and met together on the barren mountain tops, where they sang and danced to awaken the infant Dionysos from his sleep. They not only nursed and mothered the young god, but young plants and animals as well. As mothers, they had the power to make the earth bloom and the wild animals come to them.

The affiliation of the worship of the wine-god to that of the corn-goddess is eminently important. The winnowing-fan, a simple agricultural instrument figured in the mystic rites of Dionysos, is intrinsically and inevitably an instrument of Demeter. According to tradition and affirmed by art, Dionysos was placed at birth in a winnowing-fan as in a cradle, and from this, he derived the epithet of *Liknites*, "He of the Winnowing-Fan."

The wind is, of course, the natural winnower, but man can assist the wind by throwing the cob up against the wind, which blows away the chaff, while the heavier grain falls to the ground. Two tools—dissimilar in shape and made of different materials—were used in ancient times for winnowing: the *ptuon*, the "chaff-consumer" of Homer, was an oar-like pole with a long handle, made of wood and later of iron, broadened at the end to work as a shovel; the *liknon*, a *vannus* in Vergil, was made of wicker-work and shaped like an old-fashioned scuttle.

The latter was not as convenient as the former, since the labourer had to squat to scoop up the grain and then stand up again to toss it against the wind. It could hold more grain, however, and double as a basket—to hold grain or fruit or sacred relics—and as a cradle for a child. The worship of Dionysos, and later the Orphic mysteries, would adopt the *liknon*, the winnowing-curb, and leave the *ptuon*, the winnowing-shovel, to Demeter.

The shift from winnowing-fan to fruit-basket represents the transition from agriculture to viticulture, from Demeter to Dionysos. The vine-growers have turned their winnowing-fans into fruit-baskets, taken over from the winnowing-fan its proper symbolism and applied it to the fruit-basket. Both the *liknon* and the *vannus* begin as winnowing-fans and end as baskets for fruit or corn. The child rises out of the *cornucopia*, a symbol of fertility; he is the fruits of the earth. The beautiful archaic symbolism that refuses to discriminate between the human and the natural sees in earth the mother, in marriage the plough, in man the sower, and in the fruits of the earth the new-born child.

The worship by women of Liknites, the child in the cradle, reflects the primitive, matriarchal stage of society, an age when the principal conceived function of a woman was motherhood, while the more advanced, patriarchal function of wedded wife was hardly speculated. The closest relationship of parent and child mirrored in mythology is surely not that of the mother and the daughter, but that of the mother and the son. That he is the son of his mother is both the main point and chief note in the mythology of Dionysos. The relationship of the father and the son, Zeus and Apollo, Yahweh and Yeshua, reflects yet a further advance in civilization.

The cult of Dionysos, based on the worship of Mother and Son, gave women a freedom and a rank possible only among the primitive peoples of the north. In a matriarchal civilization, the Son is still naturally only the attribute of motherhood. As long as the worship is primarily in the hands of women, they tend to keep the male divinity in the one shape they can keep him—as a babe. But were their cult to advance with civilization, were their god to have male worshippers, he must grow to a man.

At Athens, Dionysos is a bridegroom, not a new-born child. His development from child to man was probably precipitated by his appropriation of the vine, for a god of intoxication will be worshipped by males at least as much as by females. Dionysos is then a primitive nature-god possessed by an intoxicating spirit, the male correlative as it were of Kore, transfigured by this new element of intoxication and revel.

Though the primary note of the religion of Dionysos was always the cult of an intoxicant, wine is not the only intoxicant, and certainly not the most primitive. Man has never been without the rudimentary means of intoxication: long before he had advanced to agriculture, he had a drink made of naturally fermented honey, a drink now known as mead; he offered to the Chthonian divinities libations of honey—this was the ancient Nectar of the Gods.

Greece acquired beer from its neighbours, notably from the northern barbarians. War and drink, Ares and Dionysos, have always been the preferred divinities in the north.[13] The drinks that the Thracians made of fermented grain, their various beers and crude malt spirits, gave to Bacchos the names of Bromios, Braites, and Sabazios. What the countless number of primitive beers have in common is that they are all alcoholic beverages made of fermented grain, appear with the introduction of agriculture, supersede mead, and are in turn superseded by wine. When "He of the Cereal-Intoxicant" became "He of the Grape-Wine," the implement that had been a winnowing-fan was transformed into a grape-basket.

The Thracians never conquered Greece, so there was no historical reason for their god to impose himself. He no doubt owed his supremacy to the introduction and rapid spread of vine; his characteristic gift, by which he won hearts and minds of men, was wine—wine made not out of barley, but out of the juice of the grape. A newly-imported plant will attach itself to the local divinity, whoever he or she be. The olive attached itself to Athena, who was there before its arrival, and increased the prestige of the goddess. In all the southern European countries, olive oil took the place of butter, which was hard to keep fresh in a warm climate. Still, the supersession of butter by oil was a quiet and inconspicuous advance, not a triumphant step forward like the advent of the vine.

---

[13] Herodotus asserts that the thirst of the northerners was often their undoing: lured to a rival's camp, their chieftains drank themselves senseless and were easily slain.

Not that the Greeks were a nation of drunkards; on the contrary, their way of life was modest, almost ascetic. A couple of elegant clay pots and finely cut wooden rinks satisfied their need for luxury; few fishes and salt cakes, figs and olives, formed their regular meals; mixing two thirds of wine with one third of water was considered excessive. When they came in contact with northern peoples like the Thracians, who drank in earnest, they were both amazed and disgusted. There is no question that with respect to wine and food as to everything else, the Greeks were true to their motto: *mêden agan*, "nothing to excess."

In all of this predominated the same, not moral, but æsthetic economy, which also manifested itself in the Greek architectural forms and in the subjects, concepts, and imagery of their poetry. This strange sobriety is perhaps the central phenomena of Greek culture and such that has never been encountered since. The Greek simplicity, misconstrued in the 18th century as austerity, dignity, and purity of the soul, was in reality nothing but the lesser refinement of life and the surer limitation of scope that produced the firm, clear, unbending contours of the Greek way of life. Their much praised temperance, self-discipline, and love of moderation is confined to the fact that in everything they were characterized by the comfortable medium size, a reasonable and "due proportion."

Large drinking cups were characteristic to the northern barbarians. Originally made of the huge horns of the large breed of cattle common to the north, these were later set in silver and gold, and sometimes actually made of precious metals. When the savage tastes an intoxicant for the first time, a great delight overwhelms him; he is sure that he is possessed by a spirit, not figuratively, but literally; he is mad, but with a divine madness. Not only did the Greeks dilute their wine with several parts of water, tempering the madness of the god, but they saw in Dionysos the god of spiritual as well as physical intoxication. The wine-drinker tends to treat the beer-drinker as an inferior person. Wine in itself is finer, rarer beverage, and Sabazios, god of the cheap cereal drink, brings sleep rather than inspiration.

According to the legend as related by Euripides, Dionysos, as a thank-you for being greeted as god everywhere he went, taught men the cultivation of vine. After establishing his cult across the known world, he returned to Greece, bringing his Thracian rites with him, and demanding to be worshipped as a god. Pentheus, King of Thebes, had him arrested, tried, scourged, and thrown into prison. For this, Dionysos drove all the women of Thebes mad, including Agaue, mother of Pentheus. They became Mænads, going out into the mountains to conduct the Dionysian orgies—the word *orgia* (from *erga*, "works") originally connoted a divine service. Pentheus imprudently followed Agaue and her companions, who fell upon him, inflamed by wine and religious ecstasy, tearing him to pieces. Thus was the length and breadth of Hellas converted to the religion of Dionysos, and he moved on.

A Mænad means simply a "mad woman," and the Mænads are the female worshippers of Dionysos of whatever stock, maddened, or as the ancients would say, inspired by his spirit. The Mænad is, however, only one, if the most common, of the many names applied to the worshipping women. In Thrace, they were called Bacchæ, in Athens, Lenai, in Delphi, Thyiades, in Lydia, Bassarids, in Macedon, Clodones and Mimallones, etc. The terms *Mænad* and *Bacchæ* were themselves adjectival, and thus could be applied not only to the female worshippers of Dionysos, but to those of any orgiastic deity.

Homeric theology was wholly untouched by Orphism: the human divinities of Olympus, being as they are distinctive and departmental, share no kinship with the partless and passionless *Protogonos*. The Olympians claim neither omnipotence nor omniscience; in no sense are they creators, sources of life. Homer has no cosmogony, only a marvellous, ready-made human society. His gods are immortal simply because death would shade and spoil their splendour, not because they should be the perennial sources of life or its ultimate purpose. Concerning themselves as little with the before as with the hereafter, the Olympians are, in the strictest sense, human.

Anthropomorphism may provide lovely motifs for art, but the spirit which makes Eros a boy rolling a hoop, Apollo a youth aiming a stone at a lizard, and Nike a woman fastening her sandal, is hardly religious. And while the art of painting was as important as sculpture in ancient Greece, no examples of it other than vase-paintings have been preserved.[14] The visual arts were not at the centre of Hellenic life; music was.

---

[14] The Greek vase-painters were considered artisans, not artists, and at Athens, they lived and worked in the same district as the city's prostitutes.

What we usually define as music is actually a quite limited concept. In normal usage, it means for us the Western music that has developed in Europe during the last two and a half millennia. This definition excludes a large number of older and extra-European phenomena, such as the playing and singing practised in ancient high cultures. The history of Western music is usually begun with Greece, though the Greeks themselves gave a much broader significance to the word *mousikê*, the Art of the Muses, than the derived word "music" has today; in fact, they associated all artistic presentations with it, including the literary ones. The singer was thought to be directly inspired by god, even as every prayer was a song. There can be no doubt that music, the most intimate and moving of arts, has done much to create as well as to express the religious feelings, thus modifying more or less deeply the fabric of belief for which alone it at first sight seems to cater.

The importance of the ancient Greek music to posterity is evident from the fact that many modern musical terms are Greek loans; including the words "melody," "rhythm," and "harmony," "orchestra" and "chorus," "lyre," "zither," and "guitar," and many, many another. Music had such an effect on the Greek soul that it could be used to heal the sick. Even the military rested on music, considered as it was the most efficient means to tactical cohesion: the flutist was as the most important man in both infantry and galley. The announcements of the herms, who made the way known to the traveller, were all written in hexameter, and all the poets were primarily composers. The new lyricist was, above all, the inventor of a new melody, the word taken out of its literal meaning. Tyrtæus and Pindar, Alcæus and Sappho had been singers, while the epics themselves were originally sung, and later at the very least melodramatically recited.

The step from the *epos*, the narrative, to the *drama*, the enactment, is a monumental one, not taken in Greece until after centuries of epic achievement, and then taken suddenly, almost inadvertently, and quite irrevocably. Most primitive religions do have ritual or *dromena*, "things done," but in the religion of Dionysos was fathered the *drama*, a "thing acted" in the stage sense. Clear as the analogy between the two seems today, no other Greek divinities have drama, only *dromena*. The transition came about in the cult of Dionysos and in his alone; his nurses are not only Mænads, but also Muses; from him alone comes the beauty and enchantment of their song, "Hail, thou child of beautiful Semele, none that is mindless of thee can fashion sweet minstrelsy."

In the early Athenian form of drama, the *chorus*, the band of dancing and singing men, was always dressed up as Satyrs, and Aristotle claimed that tragedy had developed from these Satyr-plays; according to him, the word *tragodia* itself means a "goat-song" (*tragos* = goat). Yet the real impulse to the drama lay in no sacrificial goat-song, but in the principal, and in its essence, dramatic conviction of the Dionysian religion, that the worshipper can not only worship but become his god. Neither Zeus nor Athena have drama, because no worshipper of theirs, even for one passionate moment, ever believed he could become, or be, his god.

Only in the orgiastic religions can the rapturous moments of energized enthusiasm come about, and only in orgiastic religion did the Greek drama arise. Early worshippers of Dionysos apparently re-enacted the gruesome fate of Pentheus by whipping themselves into a frenzy and tearing a live bull to pieces with their teeth. These terrifying rites, accompanied by loud music and the clashing of cymbals, were intended to thrust the revellers into a state of ecstasy. They hoped thereby to transcend their earthly bonds, to allow the soul to temporary free itself from the body—the Greek word *ekstasis* means literally "to be placed outside." Only by standing outside itself, by giving up its individual identity, could the soul achieve a condition of *enthousiasmos*, the state of being "inside the god," believed by the worshippers to be a taste of what they would one day enjoy in eternity.

Tragedy was a kind of a composite work of art, formed by the scene, text, mime, song, and dance, and held together by music. The instrumentations were, according our own standards, simple, almost deficient. The Greek music knew no hair instruments, used horns only in signalling purposes, and was, by and large, merely vocal, employing instruments almost exclusively in accompaniment and only rarely and very scantily in solo performances—the whole tragedy orchestra was formed by a guitarist and one or two flutists. Above all, it rejected polyphony: Greek vocal music was sung either solo or in chorus, but always monophonously. The primary accompanying instruments were the *aulos*, a reed instrument, and the *kithara*, a stringed one.[15] The performance of the principal vocalist shifted between rhapsodies, duets, and monologous arias.

---

[15] associated with Dionysos and Apollo, respectively

To be called "lyric," a poem had to be sung with a lyre accompanying. These types of performances were evidently ancient, though this form of poetry was perfected before all on the island of Lesbos, where in the late 7th century BCE, there lived perhaps the greatest Greek lyric poet, Sappho. She was renowned for her charming and graceful yet passionate love poetry, addressed, as it happens, to women—hence our modern term "lesbian." She was a well-respected noblewoman, the idol of the daughters of the aristocracy, whom she seems to have given expert tutoring in music and etiquette. When they subsequently married, she wrote the wedding songs that were instrumental in her rise to renown. Sappho, like most ancient literary giants, became the subject of fables; in fact, the Greeks held her in so great a respect that they referred to her as the "Tenth Muse."

The musician has played as great a part as the prophet and the thinker in the founding of religion. Every faith has its appropriate music, the differences between the creeds being expressed to a significant degree in their respective musical notations.[16] Orpheus, the quintessential bard, whose masterful singing and music upon the lyre could tame wild beasts and even move rocks and trees, came, of course, from the home of music, the north. As Conon the Mythographer attests, "the stock of the Thracians and Macedonians is music-loving."

Orpheus, whom Diodorus places two generations later than Dionysos, apparently won the hearts of the men of Thrace and Macedon by his music, but refused to reveal his mysteries to women, whom he since the loss of his wife had hated indiscriminately. The men were wont to assemble on certain fixed days in Libethra, at a large building suitable for the celebration of their orgiastic rites, and before going in, they always laid down their arms in front of the entrance. Realizing their opportunity, the women seized the arms, slew the men, and tore Orpheus to pieces, throwing his limbs to the monsters of the sea to devour.[17]

The above details, supplied by Conon in his *Narrations*, are no doubt

---

[16] Æschylus asserts that Orpheus preferred the calm and soothing sound of the Greek lyre over the harsh Phrygian flutes and cymbals used in Bacchos' frenzied rites.

[17] According to legend, Orpheus' singing head and playing lyre drifted down the River Hebrus, out to sea, and onto the shores of Lesbos, where the Muses buried it, making the Lesbians adept at music.

ætiological. Still, we can discern behind them a basis of historical fact, an outrage of the Thracian women against a real immigrant prophet, whose reforms they perceived as blasphemy of their own rites. Instead of revering Dionysos, he accounted Apollo the greatest of the gods: each morning, he climbed Mount Pangæus to watch Apollo bring up the Sun and to greet him. The Mænads tore Orpheus to pieces, not because he was an incarnation of their god, but because he despised them and they hated him. There is always about him a touch of the reformers' smugness, and it is impossible not to feel sympathy for the determined women who went to put a stop to all this sun-watching and lyre-playing.

The modern reader thinks of Orpheus as two things: as a magical musician, which he was; and as a passionate lover, which he originally was not. The myth of Eurydice is very interesting indeed, but not as a love story. It is a piece of theology taken over from Dionysos that had initially nothing to do with Orpheus. A priest of Dionysos, Orpheus took on his resurrection as well as his death; this is the germ from which sprang the sentimental love story. *Semelê*, the green earth, comes up from below, year by year, and with her comes her son Dionysos, who was thought to have gone to fetch her. *Eurydice*, finally, is the "Wide-Ruless," one of those universal, adjectival names appropriate to any and every goddess.

Orpheus was a Thracian, and yet it is primarily through his influence at Athens that we know him: there he took a primitive superstition, rooted deeply in the savage rite of Dionysos, and gave it new spiritual significance. In the Dionysian orgies, live animals were not only torn to pieces, but devoured raw—it was believed that the god entered the worshippers and possessed them through this eucharist of living flesh. But Orpheus sought to obtain that godhead by wholly different means: he replaced the old Dionysian *omophagia*, the ritual devouring of the raw flesh of a sacrificial animal, with the offering and consumption of cakes of meal and honey in commemoration of the slain Son of God.

Though Dionysos as Bromios, Braites, Sabazios, as god of intoxication, was much, Dionysos as Zagreus, Nyktelios, Isodaites, he who is "a meal shared by all" was infinitely more. In the breaking of bread, and even more in the drinking of wine, both physical and spiritual life is renewed, equanimity and magnanimity are restored, reason and morality rule again. We will not share a meal with a man we hate—it is regarded as a sacrilege that leaves the body and soul sick. The first breaking of bread and drinking of wine together is the seal of a new friendship; the last eaten in silence at parting speaks louder than any words. The sacrament of bread and wine is spread for the newly married, as it is for the newly dead.[18]

The Orphics turned the most barbarous element of their own religion not just into a vague monotheism, but into a sacrament of spiritual purification, the ritual consumption of the body of god. To the Orphics, man was a child of Earth and starry Heaven; his body of the earth, but his soul "rooted in the celestial element." The Orphic way of atonement is to stop the repetition of behaviour that reduces human life to a circle of repetitiousness in parody of the cyclic rhythms of nature, binding us eternally to a wheel of false catharsis prepared by our distant forebears, the earth-born Titans.

Entirely Orphic, rather than Dionysian, are also the regulations as to the peace and order to be observed: "Within the place of sacrifice no one is to make a noise, or clap his hands, or sing, but each man is to say his part and do it in all quietness and order as the priest and the Archibacchos direct."[19] Still more striking is the rule that if any member should act riotously, an officer appointed by the priest shall set against him the *thyrsus* of the god; the phallic staff, in a truly Orphic fashion, has transformed from the symbol of revel and license, into the sign of an orderly conducted worship.

The coming of Dionysos brought to the Greek religion a new spiritual impulse, central to which was the ascetic notion that the body is the tomb of the soul, that this world is but preparation to a higher life, and that man, by mystically uniting with the divinity, can be redeemed. In the Eleusinian Mysteries, generally regarded as the high point of Greek religion, all that was not a part of primitive harvest festival was borrowed from the cult of Dionysos.

Unlike the Egyptians, the Greeks had not developed a doctrine of immortality out of the symbolism of the corn, but when that doctrine came to them from without, the symbolism of the seed was ready at hand. The worship of Dionysos in its Orphic form, arriving at Eleusis, modified the

---

[18] The making of wine involved symbolism reminiscent of the tending of the dead and the hope for resurrection: the blood of the grape was fermented in subterranean, tomb-like containers, which, when opened, released the god, who returned from the grave to celebrate his new birth.

[19] from the inscription on a temple column at the Baccheion of Athens

simple rites of the Mother and the Maid: at Eleusis, the god was know by the title of Iacchos, and worshipped amidst not only the goddesses Demeter and Kore, but also the gods Pluto and Zeus, the god of the underworld and the god of the sky respectively—in this conjunction linked to the vegetative power of the earth, and the fertilizing showers of the sky.

In a far-off time, Eleusis was an independent city-state, before the stately procession of the mysteries had defiled over the low chain of barren hills, which divides the flat Eleusinian corn plain from the more spacious olive field of the Athenian plain. Though Athens ultimately emerged to political supremacy, it was Eleusis to which the Thracian migrant, Eumolpus, first brought his rites, and she maintained her religious hegemony to the end. Athens did what she could: she built herself an Eleusinion and instituted Lesser Mysteries; the *hiera* or "sacred objects" were brought from Eleusis, and Iacchos, who had his sanctuary at Athens, made a return visit—but the final initiation still took place at Eleusis and the *hierophant* is always and forever a Thracian Eumolpid, a member of the hereditary priesthood.

The festival of the mysteries was held on two separate occasions during the Athenian year (each city-state had its own calendar), and each and every candidate was twice initiated. The Lesser Mysteries were celebrated in the spring, at Athens, to welcome the return of vegetation; the Greater at harvest time, in Eleusis. Iacchos was a god made by the Athenians in their own image: as they were guests at Eleusis, so was their god. Large crowds of worshippers from all over Greece—later from all over the Roman Empire—would gather to make the sacred pilgrimage between the two cities and participate in the secret rites. Each new initiate, known as a *mystes*, would receive preliminary guidance from an experienced sponsor, a *mystagogos*, who would usually be from one of the leading families of Eleusis. A *mystes* who returned a second time to Eleusis was referred to as an *epoptes*.

The Lesser Mysteries were a sort of a preliminary purification for the Greater, being founded, according to tradition, in order that Herakles, tainted though he was with the blood of the Centaurs, might be initiated. In the Greater Mysteries, those of Demeter, Dionysos was to the end only a visitor; in the Lesser, a later foundation, he shared the honours with her daughter Kore. Iacchos at Eleusis is not the beer-god, nor the wine-god, but the son-god, the "Child of Semele"—the same as Liknites, "He of the Cradle," whom the Thyiades year by year wakened to new life on Mount Parnassus. Pursuant to the sacred dogma, "A virgin shall conceive and bear a son," this mystic child was born of a maiden.

The union of the sky-god Zeus with the virgin-goddess Kore was ritually represented by the union of the *hierophant* with the priestess, who acted the parts of the god and goddess. The torches having been extinguished, the couple descended into a murky place, while the *mystai* awaited in anxious suspense the result of the *hieros gamos*, on which they believed their salvation to depend. After a while, the *hierophant* reappeared, and in a blaze of light, exhibited to the congregation the supreme revelation of a "green ear of corn reaped," declaring the birth of a sacred child: "Unto us a Child is born, unto us a Son is given."

In the wake of political and economic strength came a blossoming of Hellenic culture, particularly in Ionia, where a tradition of Greek philosophy began with the speculations of Thales, Anaximander, and Anaximenes. Uniting all of ancient Greece was the Homeric religion; the sanctuary of Delphi, with its famous oracle, became the greatest national shrine; the Eleusinian rites became a state religion, politically and socially sacred. The Orphics were dissenters, living in small communities, and following an ascetic lifestyle—intended to symbolize the renunciation of the Titanic side of human nature, and to ultimately liberate the spirit from the "tomb of the body" and the "sorrowful wheel of generation."

The earliest Greek we can link to Orphism is the 6th-century BCE thinker, Pherecydes. Through Heraclitus and Empedocles to Plato and Plotinus, the Orphic wisdom followed the Greek thought like a dark shadow. Orphism influenced the works of the tragics Æschylus and Sophocles, those of the most favoured of Greek poets, Pindar, and of the greatest poet of Rome, Vergil; Pythagoras was an Orphic initiate.

A pupil of Pherecydes, Pythagoras was forced to flee his birthplace on the island of Sámos because of Polycrates, the tyrant of Syracuse. He settled at Croton, in southern Italy, where he established the famous Pythagorean school of philosophy, mathematics, and natural science. People from all classes of society came to his school to hear his lectures, among them women, even though the law in those days forbade the participation of women in public meetings. Indeed, these Orphic Pythagoreans tended to revive religious ideas that were matriarchal rather than patriarchal, the house of Pythagoras being even known to the people of Metapontum as "the temple of Demeter."

Pythagoras became the first famous exponent of Orphism and was the individual most responsible for disseminating it throughout ancient Greece. He gathered together his more talented disciples, male and female, founding around 530 BCE an order that preached modesty, rigorous self-discipline, patience, and self-control. Discipline has always been a part of religious practice, mental and otherwise. Long ago, all intellectual acts, anything that did not involve working with the hands, was prayer, or something much like it. To read a book, to study a mental discipline, was to pray—a categorization still common in the East. Pythagoras believed that all relations could be reduced to number relations, a generalization that stemmed from his observations in mathematics, astronomy, and music.

Some mathematicians still relate their art to their religion as an attempt to behold the perfection of the created universe. From the deductive regularity of the propositions of geometry, we may discern a model for the laws which govern the universe, both physical and moral. "The first and noblest of Sciences," geometry may have been man's first exercise in abstraction outside of language. The word means to "measure the earth," and this was no doubt its first application. In time, it became sacred as well as practical, for the ancients reckoned all its figures to be of religious significance.

Being the first to observe that natural phenomena, especially that of the astronomical world, may be expressed in mathematical formulas, Pythagoras maintained that numbers were not only the symbols of reality, but the very substance of things. Through numbers a divine order was imposed on the world, invisible to the eye, but discernible by the mind. The Heavens, Pythagoras taught, are the realm of pure number, where objects move in perfect circles, a realm that is best perceived through pure reason; the Earth, realm of sense and appearances, is where human souls are condemned.

It was not any of these particular doctrines of the school so much as the prevalent notion among the Pythagoreans concerning the scope and aim of philosophy, that influenced the subsequent course of speculation among the Greeks. The "philosophers" of the day called themselves by the noun *sophos*, a "wise man" or a "sage"—Pythagoras was the first to use instead the title *philosophos*, a "lover of wisdom." His school was devoted to the cultivation of not only philosophy in the modern sense, but also of mathematics, music, and even gymnastics, the aim of the organization being primarily ethical; the oath ascribed to Hippocrates may have originally been drawn up for a Pythagorean sect.

The most important scientific discovery of the Pythagorean school was the fact that the diagonal of a square is not a rational multiple of its side, a result which revealed the existence of irrational numbers. This upset not only Greek mathematics, but also the Pythagoreans' own belief that integers and their ratios could alone account for geometrical properties. They never ceased to study this subject, adopting as their emblem the pentagram, a five-pointed star that has for its centre a regular pentagon; this figure contains within itself an unusual amount of irrational variables, and became, in time, a magical symbol for Faust and the other mediæval wizards.

Besides the above-mentioned geometric theorem, the Pythagoreans, who had to make do without either algebra or the Arabic numerals, are also credited with the discovery of the numerical ratios that determine the concordant scale. They noticed that vibrating strings produce harmonious tones when the ratios of the lengths of the strings are whole numbers, and that these ratios can be extended to other instruments—it is from this discovery that all Western music derive.

All in all, the Pythagorean school made an outstanding contribution to science: its members invented the Multiplication Table, knew that the Earth is round and that it rotates on its axis, and raised important scientific problems which would not be solved until a millennium and a half later. In a sense, they invented the whole Western science: by associating measurements of length with musical tones, they made the first known reduction of a quality (sound) into a quantity (length and ratio).

The time-honoured tradition that Pythagoras forbade his disciples to eat beans, for which various reasons, more or less fabulous, were invented by ancient and mediæval writers, has been refuted by modern scholars, who understand the phrase, *Kyamon apechete*, "Abstain from beans," to refer not so much to an obscure dietary prescription, as to a principle of practical prudence. Beans, black and white, were the means of voting in Magna Græcia, and abstaining from beans would, therefore, refer only to avoiding politics—a warning well warranted by the troubles which the school was involved in due to the active part it took during the lifetime of its founder in the struggles of the popular with the aristocratic party in southern Italy.

You see, the early Pythagorean order was a notable political factor, gaining ground in many southern Italian communities. Croton enjoyed for some time a great prosperity under the Pythagorean rule, but eventually a revolt broke out, led by a Crotonian called Kylon. The rebels took the Pythagoreans by surprise at a symposium, killed many, and banished the rest. Most of the brethren died during the uprising, presumably also Pythagoras. Those who lived settled at Thebes and Phlius, where they revived the order. Withing its ranks rose two divergent groups, dedicated to religion and science respectively—it was the latter group which would come under the leadership of Archytas of Tarentum.

The theoretical doctrines first taught by Pythagoras were strictly adhered to, so much so that the Pythagoreans were known for their constant citation of the *ipse dixit* of their founder. As soon as the legends began to grow around his name, he was ascribed many tenets which were only introduced by later Pythagoreans, such as Archytas, Philolaus, and Aristoxenus.

Before the year 300 BCE, the Pythagorean school vanished from view once again, only to be revived by the neo-Pythagoreans at Rome and Alexandria in the 1st century BCE. Unlike the Ionians, who related philosophy to knowledge only[20], the Pythagoreans, being religiously and ethically inclined, aspired to bring philosophy into relation with life as well as with knowledge. Aristotelianism, which reduced philosophy to knowledge, never could challenge Christianity, as neo-Pythagoreanism did, by claiming that the teachings of its founder offered a way of life preferable to its Christian counterpart.

---

[20] The most important achievement of the early Ionian thinkers was the development of "logic," the view that it is necessary to give reasons for one's conclusions and to persuade others by arguments based on evidence.

CHAPTER 3

The existing culture could still be perceived and ruled in its entirety; the artistic and scientific traditions were neither old nor broad. The scope of experience consisted of barely a dozen generations; of homogeneous flora and fauna; of two opposite coasts and the sea between them, which, rife as it was with islands and blocked up by Crete in the south, had almost the character of an inland body of water—while the isthmuses and robust mountain ranges of the familiar peninsula had given birth to even smaller centres.

On the whole, the tardiness, inconvenience, and hazardousness of travel, along with the distrustful seclusion of the ancients, made their view narrow right from the start. Everything was concrete in the literal meaning of the word: coalescent, concentrated on the tiniest area, condensed to the smallest scale possible. The Greek conception of state was not the vague philosophical idea which it was dimly outlined as in the perception of the 18th century; nor was it anything like the pan-nationalism and imperialism of our day, occupying itself with gigantic nations and entire continents; it was not generally the object of judicial reasoning as which the whole Modern Era, the Middle Ages, and even the Roman Imperial Period readily treated it; it signified quite simply each *polis*, the tangible, easy to manage, corporeal entity, that is, a small town; a clearly defined human habitat, with a religious, political, military, and economic centre: a shrine, a square, a fort, and a harbour.

By today's standards, Athens was a reasonably significant trading town, Sparta a mountain-village, Thebes a fairly large market-town, and Olympia a tiny parish. These places were large enough to create all the social and intellectual discrepancies, and small enough to cause the most intimate friction and interaction between all their inhabitants. The peninsula, to the extent it was Greek, had the land area of the state of South Carolina, and the population of the city of Los Angeles. The distance from the northernmost point of the country, Mount Olympus, to its southern extremity, Cape Tænarum, was roughly equivalent to the distance from Chicago to Detroit by air, and can be covered today in less than an hour.

Greek expansion was facilitated in the 6th century by the fact that the great powers of the eastern Mediterranean were temporarily distracted by the contest between Persia and Assyria for control over the Fertile Crescent, a contest that had aversely affected the Phœnician shipping industry and thus led to the temporary decline of Carthage. After Babylon was finally (539 BCE) conquered by Cyrus the Great, founder of Persepolis and the Persian Empire, Greek expansion eastward came to a halt. At the same time, an alliance between Carthage in North Africa and the Etruscans in central Italy cut off the western Greeks from their homeland.

Though the past period of intense economic activity and expansion had caused radical changes in Greek life on the mainland, the model of government was still the traditional oligarchy of some sort, a government run by the aristocracy, a small élite of warriors and landowners. The population of Greece kept on growing, causing sudden prosperity for the manufacturer and trader, but also land-hunger, inflation, and decline of the peasantry and the part of the aristocracy that depended on landed holdings. The feelings of resentment generated by this situation between the agricultural and commercial sectors of the population manifesting themselves widely in the form of bloody internal riots.

Sparta was not affected by these crises, but the responses of Athens set the course of her history for the next two centuries. At this juncture, a man called Draco entered the stage, making his name immortal by codifying the laws, that is, by knitting them together in that rigid spirit which we still call Draconian today. Indolence was punishable by death in exactly the same fashion as murder and robbery, and though Draco himself was a bit worried about the fact that the punishment was the same for every transgression, he apparently could not see the least breach of law deserving nothing but the maximum punishment.

With time, the laws of Draco were found too harsh, and when his party lost its prestige, the laws were revoked, and in 594 BCE, the leader of the opposite party, the equally famous Solon, replaced them with a new code of laws. His first political measures were to cancel all mortgages and free all those who had been sold into slavery because of their debts. He then restructured society by dividing the population into four classes based on income; while only citizens of the top two classes could take office, all the four groups were allowed to vote on legislation and to elect their governing officials. The laws of Solon are considered insurmountably upright—the punishments they impose were carefully crafted to fit each specific offence.

However, the pressures of class struggle would cause a temporary abrogation of the Solonic reforms. For a time, full power was exercised by popular leaders from the impoverished aristocracy supported by the disgruntled peasantry. Solon had to witness the system of government which he had brought into force evaporate, when Pisistratus proclaimed himself tyrant of Athens. Pisistratus never formally annulled the Solonic laws, however, nor was his dictatorship continuous, for he was banished from the city a couple of times.

He clearly used his autocracy wisely and sensibly, for his reign (561-527 BCE) marked an economic and cultural rise of Athens. Exports increased and yielded returns, which were used, among other things, to build an aqueduct. Pisistratus' great cultural accomplishment was appointing a committee to compile the songs of the *Iliad* and *Odyssey*, and it is believed that the wording of the poems as we know them derives from this editorial work. The songs were arranged not for what we would nowadays call a publication, but for public recitation at the great festival of *Panathenaia*, or "All Athens." Homer was, of course, already known at Athens, but in a scrappy way, and not until now was he publicly, officially promulgated.

Just outside the gates of the city was celebrated a festival of Dionysos called the Rural Dionysia. He had always been the god of the people, the god of the "working classes"—the upper classes worshipped not the Spirit of Spring, but their own ancestors. It was Pisistratus who realized that Dionysos had to be transplanted from the fields of Attica to the city of Athens itself. The old sanctuary of the god was left to its fate, a new and finer precinct consecrated to the god, a new temple built (534 BCE) at the south side of the Acropolis where the present Theatre of Dionysos stands. The ever conservative countryside is the natural stronghold of a landed aristocracy, having fixed traditions—the city, with its closer contacts and more rapid changes, its acquired, not inherited, wealth, leans towards democracy.

Using his popularity with the masses, Pisistratus effected political reforms that ultimately completed the work begun by Solon. Under his leadership, Athens was transformed into a limited democracy, and his successor, Cleisthenes (fl. 510 BCE), would turn the chaos of conflicting factions into an integrated political unit. To discourage the division of the populace along class lines, Attica was divided into ten wards, composed of aristocrats, craftsmen, traders, and peasants alike. Although Cleisthenes was from the aristocracy himself, he reduced its power by establishing at the Eleusinion the Council of the Five Hundred, made up of fifty members from each ward. As the chief organ of government, it prepared the business of the *Ekklesia*, in which every citizen had a voice and a vote. The popular assembly gathered on the Pnyx, known today as the "Hill of Democracy," located to the west of the Acropolis.

The Athenian army, now composed of free citizens rather than of slaves or mercenaries, was placed under the direction of ten democratically-elected generals, again one from each ward. By the time of Cleishenes' death, the Athenian government was ready to resume its expansionist policies and even to do battle with the mighty Persian Empire if necessary.

During the period from 560 to 546 BCE, most of the Greek colonies in Asia Minor had been subjugated and made vassals to Lydia by its rich king, Crœsus. They had nevertheless retained most of their independence, and their trade had even increased, since coins—a Lydian novelty—were introduced into their society. Thus, when Cyrus the Great had exhorted them to abdicate Lydia at the beginning of his campaign, they had lent no ear to his persuasions. When he had then crushed the Lydian kingdom in 546, the Greek cities had asked to stay under his rule on the same terms that had been in force under Crœsus. Cyrus had replied by relating a subtle educational anecdote about the flutist who tried to allure fishes ashore; when the creatures paid no attention to his lures, he captured them in his net, where they danced and wriggled, and he needed not to play for them.

Fearful of becoming slaves to the Persians, the people of the Greek colonies prepared for resistance, but quickly humbled themselves before the superior Persian army that was sent to meet them. One after the other, all the Greek cities in Asia and the coastal islands, all except for Sámos, surrendered and became part of the Persian Empire. The people were not enslaved, but they did have to pay taxes, supply men for the Persian army, and install tyrants meeting the prior approval of the Persian king. A coastal town called Phocæa, northwest of Smyrna, alone refused to submit: the Phocæans gathered their women and children, their servants and chattels, in ships and sailed west; after various adventures, they finally settled and founded the city of Massilia—modern Marseilles.

Still, judging from the stories related by Herodotus, the Greek colonies that had fallen into Persian hands were in no great peril. During the internal conflicts that shook the Persian Empire following the death of Cambyses, the Greek cities remained calm, and after King Darius had consolidated his power and could resume foreign policy, the Greeks followed him obediently. On his orders, they erected a raft bridge over the strait of Bosporus, so the King and his army could march to Europe in 513 BCE, and begin an expedition against the Scythians in what is now Bulgaria and Romania.

Having migrated from Asia in the 7th century BCE, the Scythians were masters of a great stretch of the European steppes for some four hundred years. Frightened by the screams of Persian asses, a sound they had never heard before, the Scythians retreated but were never defeated by Darius' army. After a few insignificant conquests, the Persians were forced to withdraw over the bridge the Greeks had faithfully guarded for the whole duration of the campaign. The Persian army would have been besieged and slaughtered if the Greek colonies of Asia Minor had not remained loyal to the King. Both parties drew wrong conclusions from this incident: Darius thought that he could rely on the Greek colonies, and the Greek colonies thought the Persian army was not undefeatable and that it was the perfect time to revolt.

The Persian Wars began in 499 BCE, with the revolt of the Ionian city of Miletus, a Greek polis that had been under Persian rule since 546, when Crœsus' army was defeated by Cyrus the Great. The Milesian Tyrant, Histiæus, and his deputy, Aristagoras, believed they could worm themselves in a position of authority. The main reason of the revolt was not a hatred against the Persians, but more the fact that the Greek colonies could not develop into mature poleis if they were governed by pro-Persian tyrants. The Persians were known for their tolerance towards other cultures and it seems evident that the Greeks revolted not against the Great King of Persia, but against the Greek tyrants installed by him.

The Greeks felt that the poleis provided a superior way of life to that of the barbarians, that is, all non-Greeks who lived under autocratic rule. The narratives which Greek literature provides of tyrants, domestic and foreign, originate, almost exclusively, from sources that are strongly prejudicial against them. As the *Politics* of Aristotle makes clear, the anti-despotic bias of the Greeks is based on the fact that the power of the despot is unlimited, and as such, unconstitutional.

The Persian conquest of Asia Minor threatened the trade of Athens with the

Greek colonies on the Black Sea, so when Miletus began her revolt against the Persian rule, the Athenian Assembly voted to send military aid to Ionia. But the Milesians failed in their revolt, and by 494 BCE, Ionia had been crushed entirely and its population deported. Since the system of Persian-installed tyrants had proven a failure, Persia decided to establish a species of democracy in her Greek colonies; yet the trade and culture of the Asian Greeks continued to decrease even as their unrest grew, and many immigrated to Hellas or to the colonies in the west—the age of great economic and cultural prosperity had come to an end.

In 490 BCE, the Persian fleet crossed the Ægean, conquering several small Greek islands. It then moved against the Greeks on the mainland, relying not only on its superior force, but also on the divisions among the Greek cities. Athenian tradition sees this expedition as a retaliation against Athens for aiding the rebellious Miletus after having sworn allegiance to the Persian King. But from Darius' point of view, it seems more likely that his new campaign was only a sequel to the one in 492—an attempt to gain control over the Ægean via strongholds in Thrace, on several Greek islands, and in Athens itself. This theory is also supported by the fact that the tyrant Hippias, exiled from Athens back in 510, travelled along with the Persian fleet. The Athenians evidently feared the Persian goal was to annex Athens indirectly to their empire by installing a pro-Persian tyrant.

Greek resistance was organized with lukewarm success at first. The Athenians chose as their general a nobleman called Miltiades, who, besides being a victim of the Persians, was also a personal enemy of Hippias. He managed to persuade the majority of the hesitant citizens to fight an open battle with the Persian army. His carefully planned strategy enabled the outnumbered Athenians to force the Persians into hand-to-hand combat, something in which the hoplites were superior. The Persians retreated, leaving 6,000 dead on the plain of Marathon.

An Athenian messenger ran the twenty-six miles from Marathon to Athens in order to announce the victory and warn against a naval attack by the Persian fleet. He died on the spot, but his run is still commemorated every four years in the Olympic games. Warfare, like athletics, was considered by the Greeks a ritual activity: in ancient times, the lighting of the Olympic fire took place, not before the first athletic event, but after and because of it—the athlete who won the prototypal foot-race had the honour of lighting the sacrificial fires at the Altar of Zeus.

The Battle of Marathon was a high-water mark in the history of Athens: the unexpected result, a Greek victory, contributed to both the Athenian self-confidence and exchequer; it was a badge of honour for the men who fought there; and perhaps most important of all, it reaffirmed Athens' commitment to democracy over despotism. Following his triumph at Marathon, Miltiades was given the command over the Greek fleet. Unfortunately, he wanted to gain personal power over the Thracian Chersonese (the Gallipoli Peninsula) and used the fleet shamelessly to further these ends. He was sued and died in prison the following year.

Persia was the greatest empire in the world at that time, the most powerful heir to the great civilizations of the Fertile Crescent, which had dominated the area for over a thousand years; her defeat at Marathon was an insult that could not be forgotten. However, Darius died before he could mount a full-scale invasion, and a ten-year period of restive peace followed, owing to the need of his son and successor, Xerxes, to put down the revolts against Persian rule in Babylon and Egypt.

In the meantime, the Athenians had discovered rich silver deposits in Attica, and with their newfound wealth and commercial resources, were able to purchase both ships and allies for their second great encounter with the Persians. When the new Persian attack was finally mounted in 480 BCE, most of the Greek cities united in the defence of Hellas, save for Sparta, which sent only a small force, and Thebes, which defected to the Persian side—an omen of things to come.

Xerxes led an enormous Persian army across the Hellespont, now the Dardanelles, the strait separating Asia from Europe. After marching around the coast of the Ægean to Greece, his forces quickly conquered all of Attica. The Athenians, however, had evacuated most of the population of their city to the nearby island of Salamis, and as long as the Greek fleet with some 300 warships at its disposal remained afloat, there was no possibility of total Persian domination over Greece. Not keen to risk battle at open sea, the Athenians managed to lure their Persian opponents in the small Strait of Salamis with a fake message. The narrow channel prevented the Persians from using all their fleet at once and minimized the advantage given by the greater manoeuvrability of their ships. The larger Greek triremes used their underwater rams to sink the smaller Persian ships, resulting in a major Greek victory, which did much more than just save the Athenians from destruction.

Xerxes' fleet had suffered heavy losses—according to Herodotus over 200 ships—and was forced to withdraw to Phaleron, from whence it eventually returned to the Hellespont. Faced with the impossible task of provisioning and supporting his huge army with a depleted fleet, Xerxes had no option but to withdraw the majority of his forces from Greece. At the same time, the western Greeks in Sicily, under the leadership of Syracuse, crushed the Carthaginian army sent by the Persians.

Superior weapons, armour, and tactics may explain the Greek victories from a military standpoint, but the decision to fight at all against a vastly greater force is truly remarkable. Independence was a powerful motivation for the Greeks: even if they had surrendered and become Persian subjects, they could probably have kept their religion, basic government, and traditions; instead, the aristocrats and the poorer men who rowed the warships chose to defend the freedom of their poleis despite the overwhelming odds against them. The victory of the Greek at the Battle of Salamis strengthened both their spirit and their will, and dealt a fatal blow to the morale and reputation of the Persian army.

Xerxes' defeat to the Greeks encouraged a widespread revolt within the Persian Empire and he was forced to return home. A part of his army was left in Thessaly, Thrace, and Macedon, so Persia still remained a threat to Greek independence. The Athenians, who wanted their city back, advocated an offensive war, but Sparta felt safer behind her isthmus wall. Finally, in 479 BCE, the Persian army, which had wintered in northern Greece, attacked once more.

The battle took place at Platæa, situated at the southern border of Bœotia. It was more characteristic than Salamis for battles of the day, that is, it was chaotic. This time, the Athenians were joined by Sparta, and it was primarily the Spartans who forced their way through the enemy, winning the battle for the Greeks. At the same time, the Athenian fleet crossed the Ægean, destroying the remains of the Persian fleet and the Persian army at the naval base of Mycale in Asia Minor. The Ionian Greeks, who had been forced to serve in the Persian army, took the side of Athens and Sparta, aiding them during these final battles—an Ionic revolt thus begun and ended the Persian Wars.

After the victory at Mycale, all the Greek cities throughout the Ionian coast rose in rebellion and expelled the Persian tyrants and garrisons. With the

Syracusans having defeated the Carthaginians at the Battle of Himera the year before, the way was opened for westward expansion once more. By destroying the Persian sea power, the Greeks had secured protection against further invasions from the east, and were now masters of the Ægean Sea.

Nothing seemed to stand in the way of the unification of the entire Mediterranean under Greek rule. Unfortunately, the Persian Wars were one of the rare occasions when most Greek cities forgot their internal struggles and formed an alliance. The unity that had been maintained, with the greatest of difficulty, during the Persian invasions could not withstand the pressures of peace and prosperity. The Greeks may not have lost territory again, but they did lose their internal unity.

To the Persians, the fiasco suffered in Greece was, of course, no great catastrophe. To them, the Wars had only meant the same kinds of border-disputes as the Scythian campaigns of Cyrus and Darius. The Persian Empire continued to be the greatest and mightiest nation in the world for a few more generations, but to Western civilization her subsequent history is of little impact.

The immense wealth which the Greek cities now enjoyed, combined with the sense of unlimited potential for expansion that now seized them, resulted in a renewed period of growth and experimentation. Many Greeks reckoned that the ideals and institutions that they had fashioned in the 6th century had withstood the severest test of all, contest with the mighty Persian Empire. After the conquest of Mycale, the Athenian fleet conquered the Thracian Chersonese. This and other expeditions, against Byzantium for example, were led by the Spartan Pausianus. Sparta rather focussed on controlling the Peloponesse, however, and though she tried to built a big fleet herself and to prevent Athens from rebuilding her city walls, both enterprises failed and everyone had to accept Athens as the foremost city in Hellas.

Pericles of Athens (c. 495-429 BCE) faced the future with the confident belief that man, now liberated from the fetters of tradition, convention, and superstition, could overcome any challenge presented to him. Under his rule, Athens prospered, with most of her citizens and residents living better lives than anywhere else at the time, expressing their newfound self-confidence in the literary, artistic, and intellectual activity that made the 5th century BCE one of the most glorious periods in Western civilization.

A truly unique time in all of history, this period of Athenian domination under the rule of Pericles has become known as the "Golden Age of Athens." Never before or since have so many revolutionary ideas been created in one place. Much of what was then brought about still remain a cornerstone of Western culture, for in the ancient Greek civilization, it was precisely the thoughts conceived during the 5th century—the political system, architecture, sculpture, drama, historical writing, medicine, philosophy, rhetoric, and science—that have most affected our own.

The Athenian-led victory over the "tyrannical" East was one of the decisive events of Western history: without it, the practice of representative self-government might well have disappeared. Inspired by Athens' example, many Greek cities expelled their tyrants and established democracies of the Athenian type. Unfortunately, Greek culture remained wedded to the philosophy of political particularism: the egocentrism of the city-state ultimately triumphed over the potential of creating a world empire that their economic and intellectual inventiveness certainly offered. The great enthusiasm that followed the hard-fought victory soon disintegrated into petty quarrels between the victors: the "Golden Age" was also a period of almost ceaseless internal warfare; one bloody conflict after another raged between and among Sparta and Athens and their allies, weakening all the cities of Hellas.

The fear of a possible Persian reprisal led many of the poleis in the eastern Mediterranean to unite in a defensive alliance, known as the Delian League (478-454 BCE), though a transliteration of its Greek title, "the Athenians and their allies," reveals who predominated—the other members merely contributed ships to a fleet and money to a treasury to be disposed at will by Athens.

In the early 440s, the Athenian Assembly accepted Pericles' proposal to initiate a public reconstruction programme of temples and other structures in public sanctuaries on a scale never before seen in a Greek city-state. The new buildings seemed spectacular not only because they were lavishly expensive, but also because their massive scale, copious decoration, and surrounding open spaces formed a glaring contrast to the private architecture of 5th-century Athens.

Pericles apparently proposed that the immense cost of his Acropolis rebuilding programme be paid for with money collected by the Delian League, though whether it actually was or was not remains unknown. However the great civic improvements were paid for, it was Pericles who persuaded the city of Athens to undertake them. The work began in 447 BCE, and continued until completion a decade later.

The Acropolis—the high place of Athens—had been the site of temples dedicated to Athena Polias and other patron deities for centuries before it was laid waste by the Persians. The purpose of the Parthenon was to house a new, nearly forty feet high image of the goddess, portrayed in battle armour, holding in her outstretched hand a six-foot likeness of Nike, the goddess of victory. The placing of this huge and expensive statue in the new Parthenon appears to have been more a political than a religious act, for the women of Athens continued to take their annual *peplos* tribute to the old cult statue.

While the Orphic movement manifested many elements towards genuine piety, the Olympian religion was nothing but superficial storytelling, empty ceremonial, and childish fear of demons and spirits. In tempestuous weather or high seas, before battle or after immoral behaviour, Greeks grew fearful of their gods. After surviving any of these troubles, they thankfully left gifts, or paid for sacrifices[21], at the appropriate shrine. A temple was the house of a god or goddess, that is, of his or her cult statue. The earliest edifices survive only in clay models which convey perfectly their intimate, homelike nature. The actual temples were constructed of wood and adobe, had a single rectangular room—a *naos*—with thatched roof, and a small front porch—a *pronaos*—supported by wooden columns.

While the emergence of rationalistic thinking among a small set of philosophers produced explanations of the cosmos that required no deities, the majority of Greeks—farmers and craftsmen—remained quite traditional in fulfilling their religious obligations. The men honoured the patron gods of their cities, their families, or their professions; the women invoked their favourite gods and goddesses at annual feasts. The Olympians were highly political, favouring those who gave them gifts. Wealthy Greeks spent a great deal of money on festivals, and sacrificed valuable animals in the sacred precincts. The new Parthenon was, above all, a patriotic shrine that, by honouring Athena, glorified the proud polis of Athens herself.[22]

---

[21] The superstitious Greek hailed not Orpheus or Dionysos, but Prometheus the Fire-giver as the greatest benefactor of humanity.

[22] Personal religious experiences, being individual and asocial, can never be national; in order to unite a nation, a religion has to consist of practices.

The climax of over four centuries of Greek temple architecture, what remains of the Parthenon still crowns the Athenian Acropolis. To reflect the Panhellenic claims of Pericles, the building was uniquely designed as a Doric temple with several Ionic features: instead of the usual six Doric columns, there were eight across each end, and counting the corner columns both times, each side had twice-plus-one the number of columns at each end; the dimensions of the temple platform, 230 by 102 feet, followed the same proportion. Instead of clay, the roof tiles were marble. The *pronaos* had six Doric columns; the *naos* itself was extremely high, to hold the colossal gold and ivory statue by Phidias (c. 490-425 BCE). The inside walls were surrounded by a two-storey Doric colonnade, creating an interior aisle that ran around the goddess; complementing the Doric *naos* was an *epinaos*, a rear portico with four Ionic columns. Light was provided by the high entrance doorways and probably also by lamps that burned olive oil, sacred to Athena.

Artistic developments in free-standing sculpture provide the most striking demonstration of the innovation and variety in the depiction of the human form characteristic to the 5th-century Greek art. Phidias' dazzling creation won him fame and the friendship of leaders such as Pericles, as well as invitations from other Greek poleis to sculpt statues for their temples. He went on to create the famous statue of Zeus seated on a throne for the main temple in the sanctuary at Olympia, counted among the Seven Wonders of the World.

Buildings, open spaces, fields, and villages in ancient Athens and its vicinity continue to live in words that are still used in all the cultural languages. To the southwest of the Acropolis stood once a place called the Kerameikos, which housed, among other things, an industrial area; this is how the pottery, or "ceramics," that were produced not only there but also at other locations, got its name. In this same area was located the Agorâ, a square toward which unfolded two covered porticoes, the more famous of which was called the Stoa Poikile, the painted colonnade—the great Periclean painter Polygnotus decorated it with mythological figures. A little further to the south stands to this day a hill called the Areopagus, where ruled the court of law by the same name, dispensing justice in accord with the laws of Solon.

In the east, outside the city walls, stood the *Stadion* or Stadium: properly speaking, the name stands for a linear measure, being the equal to 600 Greek feet—this was the length of the running track and how the Stadium got its name. Outside the city were also many an athletic field known as a *gymnasion* or gymnasium. These were used not only in the physical education of the youth, but in military drills, and to some extent, also in the training of the mind. A gymnasium was usually an open place enfolded by a colonnade, with a number of indoor facilities for bathing, wrestling, and other such activities.

Finally, to the south of the Acropolis stood the two institutions that have given posterity not only words in language, but also all the things for which these words stood. Using spars from the Persian ships taken as booty in the Wars, Pericles erected here the *Odeion* or Odeon, which was the first indoor theatre and served as a prototype for modern auditoriums; instead of providing the optimal experience for the audience, the building was designed to emphasize the grandeur of the music hall itself, and was used, above all, in the song contest held during the Panathenaia. This annual festival took place every July, being a magnificent patriotic event that ended in a parade. It featured games such as horse racing, chariot racing, and a regatta, but also literary and musical programme; the latter were performed at the Odeon.

Near the Odeon lay the Theatre of Dionysos, where the Western form of dramatic art first saw the light of day. The Greek theatre was originally made up simply of an altar surrounded by the *orchestra* or the "circular dancing-place" of the chorus, but nearly all the theatres were later altered into semi-circles. When the Victorians found their ruins, they were without colour because it had faded over the years, and many people still think the Greek theatre consisted of white buildings with white scenes and white costumes—when it in actual fact consisted of much dancing, loud music, and bright colours. In ancient times, the theatrical performances were always tied to specific religious festivals; our modern custom is, of course, in direct contrast—we tend to close rather than open our theatres on our holy days.

The feast of Dionysos was celebrated with theatrical performances twice during the Athenian year, the biggest celebration being held in March. The theatre opened at sunrise, and the entire day was consecrated to august and passionate religious attention. For the five or six days of the Great Dionysia, all of Athens would be in a state of exceptional sanctity, as under a taboo: it was unlawful to even distain a debtor, and any personal assault, however minor, was considered sacrilege.

Passing through the entrance gate to the theatre, the Athenian citizen would find himself at once on holy ground. He was within a *temenos*, or sacred precinct, a place separated from the common land and dedicated to a divinity. As he entered the actual theatre, he would pay nothing[23] for his seat—his attendance was an act of worship, and from the social point of view, obligatory.

Though the theatre (from *theâtron*, a "seeing place") was open to all Athenian citizens, and indeed, to resident non-citizens, the ordinary man would not dare to even think of seating himself in the front row. In this row, and in this row only, the seats had backs, and the central seat had even arm rests. The entire row was permanently reserved, not for rich men who could afford to hire "booths," but for certain state officials, all of whom were priests.

The *dithyramb*, or the Dionysian song which possessed the infectious quality that led his votaries to adopt it as a ritual chant, became the subject for competition at the Dionysian festivals, and with its formalization, lost all the spontaneity it had originally possessed. After the public was discovered to be an incompetent critic, deciding on the result of the contest was turned over to special judges; the poet who prevailed was awarded with a laurel crown, the symbol of spring.

Three tragedians got to compete with three tragedies and one satire each, and three comedy-wrights would compete each with their own comedy (from *komos*, "drunken revel"). The works of four of these 5th-century Athenian price-winners are still performed in the theatres of all the civilized countries. Their names are Æschylus, Sophocles, Euripides, and Aristophanes.

Æschylus was some 30 years older than Sophocles, and 45 years Euripides' senior. All three were exceptionally prolific: Æschylus wrote at least eighty-two dramas, Sophocles hundred-and-twenty-three, Euripides over ninety. Still extant are seven, seven, and eighteen respectively, along with a host of fragments. Many other tragic playwrights are known by name (e.g. Frynichus, who had performed even before the Persian Wars), but it is Æschylus who we are accustomed to regard as true founder of Greek drama. It was he who brought a second actor to drama, thus making dialogue possible; before him, there had been but one drama actor, instituted by the semi-legendary Thespis—hence our "thespian." It is clear who this actor was, the one actor with the double part: Death to be carried out and Summer to be carried in. He was the bough-bearer, the only possible actor in the one-part play of the

---

[23] In fact, while the Athenian empire survived, the tribute sent by the subject poleis was carried through the orchestra and presented to the audience.

renewal of life and the return of the year.

Since drama arose out of a ritual dance, the chorus, a band of dancers, remained its centre and kernel. Sophocles increased the number of the chorists from twelve to fifteen, but more importantly, he added one more actor, moving drama yet further away from its original Dionysian spirit. The three were called the *protagonist*, the *deuteragonist*, and the *tritagonist*, meaning respectively something like the first, the second, and the third contender; the first of these was still trusted with the biggest and most important roles.

Euripides was, from our point of view, the last Attic tragic playwright simply because hardly any of the dramas that were written after him are preserved. He was more interested in the thrill of the action than in the lyric side of drama, and thus used the chorus more sparingly and in a more operatic manner than his predecessors. The orthodox Hellenes would eventually complain that the plays enacted before them had "nothing to do with Dionysos."[24] Greek drama had developed over a single generation in Athens from the *dithyramb* as rapturous spring-song into an insipid heroic spectacle, from an oratory-like choral performance into a proper play.

Euripides has had a great significance to modern theatre as well, and it is particularly notable that, in the end, all that we call comedy derives from the dramatical observations and instructions contained in his plays. Of the Attic comedy, only eleven plays of Aristophanes are extant; he wrote likely fifty in all. Most of his comedies were political revues with singing and dancing, coupled with a conservative tendency and an impetuous attack against the important figures of his day; these were fundamentally a regional form of comedy that appealed only to the Athenians, and after Athens lost her superpower status, the age of Aristophanes came to an abrupt end. But the effect of the development of drama on the whole of Greek life and religion, on the whole of subsequent literature and thinking, was immeasurable.

Every aspect of Greek life rested on the base of religion; government, justice, warfare, trade, even eroticism and social life, sports and theatre: all was under the protection of the gods, and in a way, had the nature of a permanent liturgy. The rich Greek pantheon consisted of some local deities and many more borrowed from other cultures, but most, sooner or later, mingled in the mystery melting-pot, each becoming "multiform,"

---

[24] *ouden pros ton Dionuson*

"omnipresent," "first-born," "saviour," and such. In short, the several divinities by the end of the 5th century BCE were in practice all really one, and this one god was mystically conceived as *daimôn*, a potency, rather than *theos*, a personal divinity.

Monotheism was, by that time, the common property of all educated minds—people no longer believed in the self-made caricatures of gods, that had been Offenbachian from the start. The famous statement of Herodotus was that Homer and Hesiod had only "yesterday or the day before" made a theogony for the Hellenes and given "the titles to the gods and distributed to them honours and arts, and set forth their forms." The Pythagoreans taught that Homer must suffer a punishment in Hades for the frivolous tales which he had been spreading. Homeric mythology had presented poets with the material for the innumerable crushing diatribes aimed at the anthropomorphic religion, so eagerly recycled by the Church Fathers in their time. Heraclitus says of his countrymen that "they pray to these images, as if one were to talk with a man's house." Plato thought that Homer and his fellow-poets lied too much to be tolerated in a well-ordered society. "A man of sense ought not to say, nor will I be very confident, that the description which I have given of the soul and her mansions is exactly true," states the *Phædo*, after Socrates has finished describing the judgement that befalls the dead.

Herodotus (c. 480-425 BCE) became known as the father of history because he was the first person to write down facts about events that really happened, as they really happened. He is also thought to have invented the principle used in modern journalism: to record facts accurately, even when they are not what the government wants written down. The emergence of fresh ideas in Greek medicine during this period is associated with the name of Hippocrates of Cos (c. 460-377), a younger contemporary of Herodotus the Historian. He made giant strides in putting medical diagnosis and treatment on a scientific basis—earlier medical practices were largely dependent on magic and ritual. Hippocrates taught that physicians should base their knowledge on careful observation of patients and their response to remedies; he insisted that empirically-grounded clinical experience was the only path to treatments that would not do the sick more harm than good. The oath bearing his name that most medical doctors still take at the beginning of their professional careers continues to remind us of his contribution to medicine.

CHAPTER 4

Athens and Sparta vied with each other for the dominance of the Greek mainland with varying success. Their respective political systems had become dissimilar due to different historical circumstances, but also because of their sharply divergent politico-philosophical standpoints. Athens was a naval power, and as such, assimilated many outside influences, while Sparta clung stubbornly to her own culture-bound ways. From the 6th century BCE on, democracy was the predominant form of government in Athens, while Sparta was ruled oligarchically. The Athenians stood by their principle of political equality, whereas the Spartans were unwilling to renounce their aristocratic faith, according to which all political wisdom, experience, and skill belonged to the ruling layer of society.

Aristotle's basic observation about Greek society, that "the human being is an organism of the polis," is often mistranslated as "man is naturally a political animal." The Athenian democracy was, in fact, very different from its modern counterpart. Citizenship was possible only to free male adult Athenian property-owners, who were required to serve in the polis army from when they were 18 until they turned 60. Only free men were allowed to participate in decision-making, whereas women and slaves were left outside of it—slaves did not always even have civil rights. It is estimated that of the 400,000 Athenians, 40,000 could participate in the functions of the Popular Assembly. Actual attendance may have been still a lot lower, for many decisions required a quorum of only 6,000.

There prevailed no equality in the Delian League, which was the foundation of Athens' supremacy: the Athenian fiscal authorities collected the taxes from the Allies; the imperial Athenian democracy alone dictated how these taxes were to be used, and because Athens granted citizenship only very sparingly, the Allies were in reality tributary vassals just waiting for an opportunity to reclaim their freedom.

Greek political life was chaotic and often extremely dangerous; it was a time of continuous unrest and endless party-political mass murders in the poleis that were dependent on Athens. Malcontent political factions were always plotting a new coup—sometimes with the aid of hostile poleis. The democratized legal system made Athens the first litigious society, public figures often facing lawsuits filed by their political enemies. However, as there were no lawyers or judges yet, citizens had to defend themselves before juries of several hundred laymen: generals who lost battles could face execution; people could be "ostracised," i.e. forced into exile by a vote of the Assembly, simply because a majority deemed them a danger, even if no law had been broken. These exiles then sometimes aided the enemies of their own cities.

After witnessing the growth of Athens' military and naval power during the Persian Wars, Sparta saw Athens as a threat to its dominance of the peninsula; Athens, too, was fearful and suspicious of the Spartan army, the most formidable infantry force in all Greece, perceiving it as a threat to her Panhellenic ambitions and own security. The allies of Athens and Sparta further added to the friction by presenting to their respective leaders real and imaginary grievances against the other side. Of the eighty years that followed the victory over the Persians, peace prevailed only on ten; the Athenians sustained immense losses of life even during their days of prosperity.

As the Persian threat abated, many of the founding poleis of the Delian League sought to pull out from it. Athens naturally opposed these attempts, as the Athenian leaders knew that the weakening of the League would inevitably weaken the Athenian power both in the Ægean and the Black Sea. At the same time, the resentment against Athens grew, especially in those poleis whose main interest lay in trade with Magna Græcia, where the Persian threat was practically non-existent; Ionia, prohibited by Athens from trading with Persia, was now suffering from her protectors more than she ever had from her persecutors. Many of the members began to look to Sparta—the only independent major power on the mainland—for aid and protection.

The Athenian campaigns against Cyprus and Egypt, led by Pericles and financed by funds drawn from the treasury of the Delian League, ended in utter disaster: 850 ships were destroyed with their crew still on them. With the expansion eastward thus halted, Athens turned her envious eyes toward the rich plantations of her sister poleis in Sicily. Between Athens and Sicily, however, stand not only Sparta, but a number of other Greek cities that either desired to retain their independence or were bound by close ties to Athens' commercial rivals, especially Corinth.

The last quarter of the 5th century was thus to be filled with that great struggle of life and death known as the Peloponnesian War, during which reciprocal cruelty was indescribable, and the wholesale slaughter of captives and thinkers became an everyday phenomenon. When it ended after twenty-eight years in 404 BCE, Sparta had defeated Athens with Persian financial aid, in return to which Persia regained control over the Greek cities in Asia Minor for another half a century. The Delian treasury was empty, and the peerless selection of artists that had first flocked to Periclean Athens departed for richer shores. Deprived of its colonies, Athens erupted in a social conflict where rich landowners fought peasants and craftsmen.

The Peloponnesian War ultimately ended in the overthrow of the world's first democracy: the treaty dictated by the occupiers nowise altered the constitution of Athens, but the fierce internal struggles were tearing the city apart; to protect themselves from the growing demands for the annulment of debts and land distribution, the Athenian landowners sought to combat political democracy and to erect a hierarchical society; they finally appealed to the Spartan general Lysander, who promptly followed the invitation to come and rearrange the internal conditions of Athens favourable to Sparta. With his support, an aristocratic government consisting of thirty members was installed, the leading figure of these so-called "Thirty Tyrants" being Critias, an eloquent and learned man, student of Socrates no less.

Among the close relatives of Critias was Plato (c. 428-348 BCE), himself no supporter of democracy, and an admirer of the much better organized Spartan form of government. After the death of Plato's father, his mother had married an associate of Pericles, so he was politically connected to both oligarchy and democracy, though his experience of politics was not of Pericles, but of the demagogues like Cleon and Hyperbolus. Born to one of the most prominent aristocratic families of Athens, he supposedly descended from Codrus, the last legendary king of Athens, through his father, Ariston, and was related to Solon through his mother, Perictione. Several of his relatives were involved in anti-democratic politics, not least his uncle Critias, who tried to persuade him to join the oligarchical rules of the city.

For eight months, Critias set up a fearful tyranny and had scores of people slain and banished. The number of Athenian emigrants grew fast, and from their number rose the democratic leader Thrasybulus. At the head of a small posse, he marched towards Athens, the clash taking place roughly half-way between Cape Sunion and Athens, on the south side of the city. Critias fell and the reign of the Thirty Tyrants came to an end; but the financial and military strength of Athens were forever shattered.

Instead of embarking on the political career for which his family had prepared him, Plato had fortunately joined his two older brothers in becoming a student of Socrates. We know not for sure whether he had other teachers during his youth, who they were, or what he learned from them; the earlier extant biographies of Plato have been written centuries after his death and bear little resemblance to what we nowadays expect from a proper biography. To make matters worse, Plato scarcely ever talks about himself in his dialogues; in fact, he does so only twice, once in the *Apology* and once in the *Phædo*, both times in connection with the trial and forced suicide of Socrates. Most of what we read on Plato's life is plain guess, hypotheses built on top of hypotheses by generations upon generations of scholars.

Under Socrates' influence and disillusioned by what he witnessed in the Athenian politics of his youth, culminating in the condemnation and death (399 BCE) of his beloved mentor at the hands of democracy[25], Plato came to the conclusion that the fate of mankind was bereft of hope unless there was a profound change in men's education, and especially in the education of those keen on becoming statesmen. As he tells us in his *Seventh Letter*, he felt that the only salvation of politics would require that "either those who are pursuing a right and true philosophy receive sovereign power in the States, or those in power in the States by some dispensation of providence become true philosophers." He was to become the theoretician of this new society, rationalized in the *Republic*, and justified by the cosmology of *Timæus*.

Unlike his mentor Socrates, who wrote nothing, Plato was exceptionally prolific; his fame rests on his more than two dozen dialogues that cover nearly every topic and are apparently all still extant. He is, in fact, the earliest Greek philosopher whose work is preserved down to our times; of the works of the philosophers who lived before him we have only fragments, and most of them

---

[25] Although there was considerable freedom of speech at Athens, Socrates was tried for expressing ideas that were in conflict with traditional religious beliefs; in fact, the whole Socratic revolution has been described by Nietzsche as the outright destruction of Hellenic culture and the beginning of the prolonged cultural decline of the West, where the good life became unworldly in a way it had never been in ancient Greece.

quotations by later students. However, Plato's thought can hardly be called revolutionary, for it was built on the work of his predecessors, that of Parmenides and Pythagoras, of the "pre-Socratics" and the Sophists, perhaps more than we can ascertain—but the form in which he presented it left all the earlier philosophers hopelessly in the shadow.

Plato's greatest creation is the philosophical dialogue: philosophical ideas are advanced, discussed, and criticized in the context of a conversation or debate involving two or more people. As a voice he employed Socrates, whose unique personality had made such a profound impression on the young Plato. Such as Plato depicts him, he probably was not in reality, but the fact that he is more a fictional than historical character does not diminish his value; a person who stirred the imagination of the people around him that strongly, becoming the ideal man for so many, must have been a person of quite exceptional proportions.

Reason to Plato, like to the Greek tradition in general, is most distinctly manifest in the Logos, the word; language, the medium through which reason articulates being, is a central topic throughout Plato's dialogues. Seeing bad poetry and bad rhetoric alike as pathological forms of the inescapable dissociation of word and world, he constantly addresses the question of how to purge language of its potential deceptiveness; the central vehicle he envisioned for this purpose was dialectic, the dialogue that refines and articulates the true shape and tendency of speech and understanding. This dialectic was presented mimetically in the dialogues themselves, which were thus representations not merely of philosophical views, but of philosophy at work, of human beings engaged in the distinctly human and civilized activity of intelligent debate.

Plato's dialogues made him the reformer and perfecter of language, the master of character description and staging, of logic and irony, of prosaic and festive, comic and pathetic depiction. Yet we cannot ascertain exactly when Plato wrote each one of these works, or even whether all or only a part of them were "published," that is, made available outside his school, during his lifetime. The earliest collection of Plato's works consists of some 35 dramatic dialogues and 13 letter on philosophical and related subjects. The authenticity of some of the dialogues and most of the letters has been disputed, and their precise chronological ordering remains unclear, though stylistic and thematic considerations give credence to the traditional division into three periods.

The earliest writings, begun sometime after 399 BCE, are seen by many as memorials to the life and teaching of Socrates; they include a series of short dialogues that take the same form, ending with no clear and definitive solution to the problems raised. Upon encountering someone who claims to know much, Socrates pleads ignorance and seeks assistance from this sage; however, as Socrates begins to raise questions, it becomes clear that his interlocutor knows not what he claims to know, and Socrates is proved to be the wiser one, for he knows at least that he knows not; such knowledge is seen as the beginning of wisdom. This group of dialogues includes "A Discussion of Justice," the first book of the *Republic*, widely regarded as Plato's greatest philosophical achievement.

Sometime after Plato's first excursion to Sicily, where he most likely met with Pythagoreans and befriended Archytas of Tarentum, he decided—rather than to risk his life in active politics—to open a school where he would educate future leaders of poleis. The school was called the Academy because it stood in the middle of beautiful parkland near a grove sacred to an old hero called Academus. There he remained, apart from two more trips to Sicily, until his death, discussing philosophy and teaching students both male and female.

The dialogues of the middle period were begun after the founding of the Academy, and defend the doctrines commonly thought of as Platonism; they are not in dialogue form, nor do they exhibit the Socratic method, though Socrates continues to be the main character in many of them. At the heart of Plato's philosophy is his doctrine of Ideas—probably an attempt to reconcile the dire conflict between Heraclitus' doctrine of change and Parmenides' doctrine of immutability, an attempt to tie together the One and the Many, the Being and the Becoming. Ultimately, his view of knowledge, his concept of the state, his notion of justice, and his theory of ethics must all be understood in terms of this one doctrine. Even those who find its metaphysical content awkward, use in their everyday language words like "idea," "ideal," "idealist," thus unconsciously paying homage to Plato's doctrine of Ideas.

The foundational myth of Platonism, "the Allegory of the Cave," is illustrated in the *Republic*: it describes individuals chained deep within the recesses of a cave. Bound so that vision is restricted, they cannot see one another; the only thing visible is the wall of the cave upon which shadows are cast by statues of animals and objects that pass before a brightly burning fire. Breaking free, one of the individuals escapes from the cave into the light of day; with the aid of the Sun, that person sees for the first time the real world, and returns to the cave with the tidings that the things they have hitherto seen are but shadows and that the real world awaits them if they are only willing to struggle free of their shackles.

For Plato, the shadowy environment of the cave symbolized the physical world of Becoming, the escape into the sunlit setting outside the transition to the ideal realm of Being, which he considered the proper object of knowledge. Utilizing the image of the Divided Line, Plato emphasized the ethical implication of this distinction: the ideal forms are the source of all good, while base, earthly matter is the source of the world's evils. The imperfect, transitory, changeable world of everyday life cannot be used to understand the perfect, eternal, and unchangeable Heavens.

One unfortunate consequence of this view was Plato's rejection of empiricism, the notion that knowledge is derived from sense experience. The Ionian science assumed that the world was knowable by observation, thought and labour joining together; it was the world view of the peasant and craftsman. Platonic dualism describes the cosmos as knowable only to the pure reason of the few, who consequently had the right to rule over the many, as the Heavens rule the Earth, as the mind rules the body, as the master rules the slave; it was the world view of the rich landowner.

In Plato's ideal political community, a particular person's class is determined by an educational process that begins at birth and proceeds until that individual has reached the maximum level of education compatible with personal interest and ability. By completing the entire educational process, one becomes a philosopher-king: one whose mind is so developed that he can grasp the Ideas, and thus make the wisest decisions.

Justice, for Plato, was the principle of each thing performing the function most appropriate to its nature, a principle of the proper adjudication of Being and Becoming. In political terms, this principle is embodied in a society where citizens perform the tasks for which they are best suited. Reason is to rule, but justice is ideally allied with the traditional Greek virtues: temperance is the virtue peculiar to the artisan class, courage is the unique virtue of the military class, and wisdom characterizes the rulers. The just state is one in which each class duly performs its own function without encroaching upon the duties of the other classes. Thus the rule of reason is seen not as a tyranny, but as a harmonious rule of the happily unified individual and society.

Plato's ethical theory rests entirely on the presumption that virtue is knowledge and can be taught—this has to again be understood in terms of his doctrine of Ideas. He conceived them as arranged hierarchically, the ultimate Idea being that of the Good, which, like the Sun in the cave allegory, illuminates all the other Ideas. For Plato, knowledge involves judgement concerning the being of things, not a mere acquaintance with them in perception, and knowledge of the Idea of the Good is the source of guidance in moral decision-making; he argued that to know the good is to do the good—anyone who behaves immorally does so out of ignorance.

Plato did not believe in freedom in any conventional meaning of the word; even the philosopher-kings are subject to discipline of the strictest kind. He divides the human soul into three parts: the reason, the will, and the desire. The just person is the one in whom the rational part, supported by the will, controls the desires. By an obvious analogy, in the threefold class structure of his ideal state, the enlightened philosopher-kings, supported by the military, govern the rest of society. His kings and soldiers do not acquire the virtues demanded by their office either by personal experimentation or by being exposed to the varying impressions of this world. The authority of their seniors thoroughly prevent them from straying to any alternative course. They are kept strictly orthodox and can only think very exalted thoughts; many would consider this not thinking at all.

What is more, Plato seems to have been quite blind to the defects of the city-state. He evidently believed that the Greeks could forever live in the poleis created by their own culture, or in some communities that improved upon them. His Utopian world, like its real life contemporary, was not one of universal peace. The Greeks fought wars to gain wealth, power, and prestige, to strike awe into the hearts of the conquered, to secure trade monopolies and perhaps also livelihood and living space for a growing population that was eating away the standard of living.

Plato's Academy became very famous, and most of his life was dedicated to teaching and running his school; except, that is, for the two more sojourns in Sicily, at the court of Dionysius the Younger, the eldest son of the Dionysius he had met during his first trip there. In 367 BCE, the elder Dionysius died, and his brother-in-law, Dion, who had previously befriended Plato, invited him to come and school the young Dionysius for his future kingship. Seeing this as a way to fulfill his goal for a philosopher-king, Plato accepted the invitation and assumed control over the boy's studies. The new tyrant of Syracuse was tutored in mathematics and philosophy alike, but although he let Plato influence himself to the extent of reducing the number of courses on his dinner table, he showed no willingness to rearrange his domain after the doctrines of his teacher. He later fell out with Dion, whom Plato soon followed to Athens, where he had been exiled. Plato continued correspondence with Dionysius, trying to reconcile him with Dion.

In 361 BCE, Dionysius lured Plato into a trap by convincing him that he wanted to become a philosopher. Plato made one last trip to Sicily, but yet again his excursion into Syracusan politics proved a complete and utter failure. He was trapped in Syracuse until 360 BCE, when Dion seized power and exiled Dionysius. Plutarch says that when the former tyrant was later asked why he had been unable to retain even what his father had created, he answered: "My father embarked on his venture at a time when democracy was hated, but I at a time when despotism was odious." Dion was in turn soon murdered by his close Athenian associate, Calippus, another of Plato's students. After extensive riots, the tyranny of Syracuse was crushed by Timoleon, a fervent democrat, who had murdered his own brother after the latter had tried to establish autocracy in Corinth.

The concluding years of Plato's life were spent writing and lecturing at the Academy; the works of this later period include the *Timæus*, a semi-mythical description of the origin and nature of the universe, and the *Laws*, his last and—though unfinished—longest work. In it, he returns to the character of the ideal republic in a more realistic and pessimistic manner, with civic piety and religion taking much of the burden of education away from philosophy. The figure of Socrates no longer shares any part in these final works.

Plato died around 348 BCE, at about the age of eighty. He was succeeded as head of the Academy, not by Aristotle, who had for twenty years been a student and then a teacher at the Academy, but by his nephew, Speusippus (c. 407-339 BCE). The influence of Plato's thought is seen in the enduring vitality of the Platonic tradition through subsequent centuries; the Academy kept functioning, under one guise or another, for more than a thousand years after the death of its founder. It produced a ballast of scientific and mathematical innovations, linking 5th-century BCE Pythagorean mathematics with Egyptian geometry and arithmetic done in Alexandria; the major philosophers of late Hellenism, most notably Plotinus and Proclus, were self-professed Platonists.

After the closing of the Academy in 529 CE by the Christian Emperor Justinian, who objected to its pagan teachings, Neoplatonism continued to flourish in the Byzantine and Islamic world, and was a strong intellectual factor throughout the Latin Middle Ages.

Aristotle (384-322 BCE) was not a citizen of Athens, but had come from the town of Stagira in Thrace. After Plato died, he left Athens, but as the Macedonians had just then conquered and destroyed Stagira, he travelled as a lecturer and teacher to the city of Assos in Asia Minor, and thence to Mytilene in Lesbos. From there he was summoned by Philip of Macedon to his court at Pella to tutor his son, Alexander. After staying there for seven years, Aristotle finally returned to Athens, where he founded a school at a gymnasium which was located near a sacred grove called the Lykeion; it is better know in its Latin form as the Lyceum. The school was called Peripatetic, because the students would study and converse with Aristotle as they strolled along the walkway (Gr. *peripatos*).

Many of Aristotle's works are still extant, but his writing is so unpolished that many scholars contend that instead of his own work, it is only the notes of his pupils that are preserved. At any rate, these texts were of the utmost importance to the Western culture, be it scientific or artistic, secular or ecclesiastical. Aristotle was the first to divide the sciences into groups according to their field of research, yet wrote himself essays on nearly every branch: on logic, physics, psychology, biology, ethics, politics, and æsthetics. Such was his pre-eminence that throughout the Middle Ages, his every pronouncement was accepted without question; not before the founders of modern science led the 16th- and 17th-century rebellion against his authority was the deductive logic he used discovered as fruitless, for it left no room for experimentation and induction.

While the several hundred city-states of Greece were wasting their strength keeping an eye on and squabbling with one another, in the north of Hellas a political might was emerging whose power and determination were of entirely different order. Macedon, all through the age of the Greek city-states, was an anomaly: it was a Greek kingdom. Although poets and scholars from Athens and other poleis were frequent quests at the court of Pella—Euripides, for example, ended his days there—the Macedonians were never counted among the Hellenes. The few existing Panhellenic institutions, such as the religious council of the Amphictyonic League in Delphi, had no seat for the Macedonians; they were looked on as no better than barbarians, because they had never developed or adopted the polis.

Located northeast of the Greek mainland and northwest of Asia Minor, Macedon was firmly entrenched on the European continent. The Macedonians were thus the Greeks who had to compete with all the European tribes, many of which were warlike. In a way, their kingdom served as a buffer for all the other Greeks, as it stood between the tribal Europeans and the Greek city-states. The kings of Macedon, always busy enough keeping their Illyrian vassals in check and defending their western and northern borders, generally stayed out of the Greek politics. The first Macedonian king who purposely turned to this direction was Philip II, the father of Alexander the Great.

The kings claimed the throne by right of inheritance, but they had to be approved by the army. Beneath the monarch stood an aristocracy with limited power, and like in all monarchies that shared power with a nobility, the balance of power constantly shifted from the king to the aristocrats and back again. Into this situation, at the height of the political turmoil enveloping the Greek world, stepped King Philip, who unified the kingdom of Macedon. He swiftly pacified all the European tribes to the north, seized gold and silver mines through his conquest of Amphipolis to the south, and began building new cities and large standing armies.

At Athens, which had of old considerable amount of interests to attend in the coast of Thrace, Philip's conquests created ill-will and riots. The early democratic leaders of the city were men of the aristocratic class with the wealth and public-speaking skills to sway the masses: a tireless opponent of Philip, the fierce and impetuous Demosthenes (384-322 BCE) is known and admired as the greatest rhetorician of ancient Greece. Those of his speeches that were aimed directly at Philip are called the *Philippics*, a word that is still used today, if in a broader meaning. The rhetoric of Demosthenes would have a great bearing on posterity, for it was in due course imitated by the foremost Roman rhetorician, Cicero; however, filled as they are with day-to-day political questions of the 4th century BCE, Demosthenes' extant speeches are scarcely of interest to anyone other than the historian.

Contemporaneously to Demosthenes, there also lived in Athens an orator and political writer by the name of Isocrates (436-338 BCE). He was slightly younger than Plato, and is described in the *Phædrus* as someone "who will marvelously improve as he grows older." He, too, was born to a wealthy Athenian family, living and writing in the same cultural situation as Plato; he, too, had studied with Socrates, as well as with a variety of Sophists; and he, too, ran a school of higher learning at Athens. His writings, like Plato's, are essential to understanding 4th-century BCE politics and scholarship.

Isocrates' teaching methods dominated the rhetorical techniques of ancient Greece and influenced mediæval European liberal education. Rhetoric, as an art and a curriculum subject, is a Greek invention; a fact that can still be discerned from its name and from all its terminology. Yet it is primarily its Latin form that has affected Western humanistic culture: Cicero related Isocrates' style of teaching oratory through his writings, and it remained the standard of excellence for rhetoric education in Europe until the Renaissance.

Isocrates wanted to be a leading figure in the Athenian politics, but was born with a weak voice that could not be heard by crowds, and suffered from an acute case of stage fright. In his forties, he finally decided that if he could not be a civic leader, he would train the future leaders of the city. Public speaking, the central subject in Isocrates' school, was one of the most important processes for a person in Athens to master, because almost all the important business of the polis was conducted in the open forum where persuasion skills are essential. The majority of Isocrates' speeches were written to be published, rather than spoken, and he is credited with making a literary form of oratory.

The fact that a substantial part of the ancient Greek literature that is still extant consists of speeches and of essays on rhetoric, is not as strange as it may seem to us today. In the ancient times, there were neither newspapers nor printing-presses, and oral presentation played a crucial role in every kind of literary success—even the politicians often had to plead before a public that was used to hearing poets and literary narrators and whose ear was trained to appreciate the resonance and verbosity of language. That the Greeks in general thought of language as a musical phenomenon is made apparent by the incredible sensitivity with which they discerned errors in pronunciation, accentuation, and word order, related in numerous anecdotes and parallelled only by the fine ear of the Italians in regard to singing.

Even though Greek was the first language to reflect on the higher scientific and philosophical questions, it had almost no foreign loans, while at the same time, it had an uncanny ability to express even the most abstract things in a plastic fashion, the ability in the fullest Platonic sense to move about in the world of Ideas. It is not a least bit surprising in these circumstances that rhetoric would develop into an art and even a science, which on top of everything would be deemed quite useful and necessary, for eloquence was something that could be learned and taught.

Isocrates' school attracted young men from all over the Greek-speaking world, many of whom went on to become eminent leaders of their day. His twenty-one extant speeches all concern the politics of ancient Greece. Isocrates was not concerned with the development of rhetorical theory, but with the development of efficient leaders for Greece: the rhetorician's community has a claim on him that he cannot refuse—the rhetorician must always endeavour to be a good citizen and to make good citizens of others.

In *Against the Sophists*, Isocrates voices his opposition to not only the oversimplified rhetorical techniques advanced by the Sophists, but also the philosophy of rhetoric taught by a rival school, namely Plato's Academy. In contradistinction to all the rival rhetoricians, Isocrates did not believe that any general rules could be applied to rhetoric. In his opinion, all general principles must fail, because they sieve out the particulars of any given situation, which have to be taken into account in every truly good moral and rhetorical decision; Isocrates thus rejected the belief of those who sought absolute truth: Plato and the other philosophers.

Where rhetoric seeks to have certain opinions prevail over other, competing opinions, philosophy—which originally included the individual sciences—seeks impersonal truths. Isocrates argued that the tedious, abstract arguments of Plato on metaphysics, epistemology, axiology, and human nature were plain and simple nonsense: he was a practical, down-to-earth person who wanted to solve the problems at hand. He asserted that public business is of the paramount importance; the urgency of civic affairs will not wait for a philosopher to resolve his questions of absolute truth. The philosophers' higher obligation was "to educate men for their current affairs, to help them learn to make wise decisions in the face of limited knowledge." Metaphysical speculation is a waste of both time and energy.

Knowledge is tentative; we cannot know anything for sure. What we can have is good opinions, ones that help explain life in a way that promotes getting along in this world. Isocrates agreed with Plato in championing traditional Greek values, but he did so for reasons different from Plato's.

Isocrates believed those values to be useful, but not necessarily the true or only values. Plato wanted to instill in the people a passion for those values because they were real, eternal, and unchanging; they could thus lend a unity of purpose and meaning to Athenian life, a reason to live and participate.

Isocrates fully realized that his relativistic value system lacked the power to draw people together under a common bond of unity and fraternity that would stabilize society. He therefore promoted a political ideal which he thought could bring that unity, namely Panhellenism—an ideal he thought could be achieved only through education. Like so many academics today, Isocrates saw education as the deliverer. He remained for nearly half a century the most famous, influential, and successful teacher of aspiring young politicians. His most famous oration, called the *Panegyrikos*, composed for the Olympic festival of 380 BCE, and laboured over for ten years, strongly urges the Greeks to unite under the joint leadership of Athens and Sparta against the common Persian foe.

One autumn afternoon in 338 BCE, Athens and her allies met Philip of Macedon in a decisive battle near the Bœotian town of Chæronea. The great military feat that carried the day for the Macedonians was a cavalry charge by Philip's 18-year-old son, Alexander. The Greeks suffered a crushing defeat that brought to a definitive end the petty state politics of Hellas. The independent city-state, the polis, had ceased to exist.

All this was very painful to the old Isocrates, who had not taken into account that the success of his ideas could spell a catastrophe for his native Athens, and he saw no other solution to his inner conflict than taking his own life at the very moment his dreams of a united Hellas would become a reality. Philip immediately began to work at consolidating his power in Greece, and still the same year, created the Hellenic League. Ostensibly an alliance of free poleis, Philip was its head, and for all intents and purposes, king of Greece.

The Macedonian troops occupied Corinth, Thebes, and Chalcis, while their opponents were either executed or exiled. Toward Athens, however, whose fleet was still in fair condition, Philip was inclined to show more generosity. The city had to break up its naval alliance and hand over its colonies in the Thracian Chersonese, but the prisoners of war were released without ransom. The results of this clemency were such as Philip had intended: he was suddenly a popular person in Athens, which now erected for him a statue in the town square, and made him and his son honorary citizens.

But the King was not done yet; the Persian Wars still festered in the Greek memory, and as the Spartan invasion of Persia in 379 BCE had showed, it was entirely possible to defeat the mightiest empire known to man. Thus, in 337 BCE, Philip announced that the League would attack Persia in retaliation for the Wars, and the next year, he stood poised to carry out his audacious invasion of the Persian Empire, only to have an assassin's sword finish off his great campaign.

Alexander, upon ascending the Macedonian throne in the summer of 336 BCE, found himself surrounded by conspirators at home and threatened by insurrection abroad. After quickly disposing of all domestic enemies by ordering their execution, he descended on Thessaly, where the partisans of independence had gained the upper hand, and restored Macedonian rule. Before anyone knew it, Alexander was in Corinth, and the Hellenic League acknowledged him the commander-in-chief of all the armed forces of Greece; he was twenty-one.

In the spring of 334 BCE, Alexander started east at the head of an allied Greek army, on what was to be the greatest conquest of ancient times. He began his war against Persia by crossing the Hellespont into Asia. To conquer Persia would be to conquer the world, for the Persian Empire ruled most of the known civilization: Asia Minor, Syria, Phœnicia, Palestine, Egypt, and Babylonia. Alexander had little to go on: he had no funds, he had no navy, and his army of Macedonian and Greek troops numbered only 30,000 infantry and just 5,000 cavalry.

Alexander's strategy was beautifully simple: by moving quickly and starting with a few sure victories, he could acquire money and supplies; through his focus on the coastal cities, he would soon control all the ports, rendering it impossible for the Persian navy to make landfall. He would then take the battle right to the centre of the enemy forces, and throw himself into the heart of the battle; his enemies were stupefied, while his own troops grew fiercely loyal to the commander who took both them and himself into harm's way.

At the River Granicus, near the ancient city of Troy, Alexander charged an army of Persians and Greek mercenaries totalling 40,000 men; his forces not only decimated the enemy, but according to tradition, lost only 110 men. After this battle, he quickly overran all of Asia Minor, and after seizing every last coastal city, he turned inland towards Syria in 333 BCE. There he met the main Persian army, commanded by King Darius III, near a city called Issus. Just as in Chæronea, Alexander again led an astonishing cavalry charge against a vastly superior opponent, forcing the Persians to break ranks. The exact size of Darius's army is unknown, but the ancient tradition that it numbered 500,000 men can be safely dismissed as a fantastic exaggeration.

Cut off from his base, Darius fled, leaving his mother, wife, and children to the mercy of Alexander, who treated them with the respect due for royalty. The Persian King ran northward towards Babylonia with much of his army, leaving Alexander free to proceed south. He quickly seized all the coastal towns along the Phœnician and Palestinian coasts; the strongly-fortified Tyre, absolutely central to Persian naval operations, offered stubborn resistance, but in 332 BCE, after a siege of seven months, Alexander took it by storm. Next, he captured Gaza, and when he entered Jerusalem, he was hailed as a deliverer.

Alexander's conquest of Egypt was bloodless and peaceful. He was welcomed by the Egyptians as a pleasant alternative to tyrannical Persian rule. Even though he spent only a year in Egypt, Alexander had a tremendous effect on the country; he was a merciful ruler who allowed the Egyptians to continue their native customs. He showed great respect towards their gods and especially towards the Apis-bull, whom the Persians had so grievously offended during the reign of Artaxerxes Ochus. At the country's ancient capital, Memphis, Alexander gave offerings to the sacred bull-god and was crowned Pharaoh.

His plans entailed a longer journey to Persia, Central Asia, and India; but first, Alexander wanted to visit the oasis of Siwa and consult the oracle of Amoun. During the Persian occupation, the people of Egypt had rediscovered their illustrious past; a sort of romanticism, which included chivalric romances and archæological excesses, had taken rise. The old religion was revived, often in the form of reactionary priestly rule, worship of animals and of ancient Pharaohs, magic and mysteries. The last mentioned came to mean a great deal to the Greek conquerors, and subsequently to the Roman counterparts, who eagerly introduced them, thus preserving a substantial part of the Egyptian heritage down to our days, in whatever form it may be known.

When Alexander reached Siwa, he was greeted by the priests and worshippers at the temple as "Amoun," the living incarnation of the god. In the Greek mind, Amoun was the same divinity as their own Zeus, and the merger of these two cults brought new blood to the old religion; Alexander would go as far as issue coins that portrayed himself wearing the ram-horned cap of the "Zeus of Thebes."

Egypt was also the first country where Alexander would found a city to bear his name. On his way to the oracle, Alexander had admired the stretch of land between the Mediterranean and Lake Mareotis, and the nearby island. The location was ideal for a regional capital, being as it was intermediate between Greece and the rest of Egypt. An excellent seaport could be formed by joining the island of Pharos to the bay shore: the light on the island[26] eventually lent its name to all such lighthouses. On the south side, Alexandria would have a river port on Lake Mareotis; the lake was connected by a canal with an eastern branch of the Nile, giving the city great access to the inland. The river communicated with the Red Sea by another canal, so Alexandria could further serve as a gateway to the Indian Ocean. The city plan was designed by Dinocrates of Rhodes, the outline of the city walls being marked by Alexander himself.

Egypt's new capital was born on the 7th of April, 331 BCE. She may have been named after Alexander, but he never saw a single building rise there. Leaving behind a small contingent, Alexander reorganized his forces at Tyre, and started for Mesopotamia with an army of 40,000 infantry and 7,000 cavalry. Having crossed the Euphrates and the Tigris, he met Darius near the ancient Assyrian capital of Nineveh, laid waste by the Chaldæans three centuries earlier. According to the doubtlessly exaggerated accounts of antiquity, the Persian army numbered a million men; it was utterly defeated in the Battle of Gaugamela, on the 1st of October, 331 BCE.

Feeling that their king could no longer lead them effectively, the Persian nobility, under the leadership of his brother Bessus, killed Darius, and left his body for the Greek army to discover. Alexander, however, pushed on, killing Bessus and as many nobles as he could find. The Persian Empire had now officially come to an end.

The Persians had amassed immense wealth from the tribute paid by the various states under their control. The great and rich Babylon surrendered to Alexander in January of 330 BCE, and the city of Susa, with its vast treasures, was soon conquered. Finally, in midwinter, he forced his way into Persepolis,

---

[26] one of the Seven Wonders of the World

the Persian capital; having started with no money at all, Alexander now controlled the fattest treasury that had ever existed. After plundering the royal exchequer, he burned the city down in a drunken stupor, thereby completing the destruction of the Persian Empire.

Alexander's kingdom now stretched along and beyond the southern shores of the Caspian Sea, including modern Afghanistan and Pakistan, and northward into present-day Uzbekistan and Tajikistan. It took Alexander only three years, from the spring of 330 BCE to the spring of 327 BCE, to conquer this vast stretch of land; now the master of what was then the whole known world, he had pushed his army to the very limits of civilization as he knew it.

But he still craved for more; seeing that the world extended further, Alexander pushed east, partly out of curiosity and partly out of a desire to conquer all the land within the boundaries of the River Oceanus. In order to complete his conquest of the ancient Persian Empire, which had once included part of western India, Alexander led his army across the Indus in 326 BCE, and invaded the Punjab as far as the Beas River. There, his men refused to go further.

Marching his men back through the Iranian desert, Alexander reached Babylon in 324 BCE. He was then, quite literally, king of the world, and began implementing the strategies for the consolidation of his empire; he spent about a year organizing his domains, and made a survey of the Persian Gulf in preparation for new campaigns. In June of 323 BCE, he contracted a fever and died at the age of 33. His body was carried back to Egypt for burial, but the exact location of his tomb remains a mystery.

CHAPTER 5

It is uncommon in history for human events to become focussed on a single individual; even more rarely is that focus justified. Alexander the Great, however, is one notable exception: the Age of Alexander was an age created by Alexander, for it was he who permanently branded world culture with a Greek character. His conquest of the East led to a unification of the Eastern and the Western cultures into a common "Hellenistic" culture.

As Alexander led his triumphal march across the known world, Greece quickly spread its influence over an area twenty times larger than its own. The expanding activities of the West made it necessary to have a suitable venue outside the winding and shallow passages of the Nile. Alexandria was born out of necessity, and her rapid ascend to dominance showed just how important she was. The Hellenistic era is also frequently called the Alexandrian era. The former appellation refers to the fact that Greek civilization was no longer tied to small autonomous states, the latter to the fact that Alexandria had begun to supersede Athens as the focal point of Greek culture.[27]

The society and culture of the pre-Alexander "Hellenic" world was pretty much reserved for those who were Hellenes by birth; its political, ethical, and even epistemological ideas were bound up with particular social conditions. The gradual opening of Hellenic culture was made possible, above all, by the philosophical reflections of various thinkers who appeared on the Greek soil prior to Alexander, such as Socrates, Plato, and Aristotle. The last mentioned was for seven years the tutor of Alexander.

The main elements contributed by these philosophers were the concepts of rationality and logic, with which came greater awareness of the reality that the laws and customs of society are mere conventions. This led to varied reactions: some, like the Cynics, suggested that man should move away from these conventions; others, like Socrates, suggested that conventions should be

---

[27] The Athenians were proud of their democratic system and held its universal advancement important; but direct democracy was no longer suitable for the empire of Alexander.

maintained in the interest of law and order. Whatever the various different opinions on this matter may have been, Greek culture was unavoidably moving away from particularism towards a more universal awareness.

To further this development, the Stoics subsequently advanced the notion that freedom is purely an inner quality, and as such, independent of external circumstances. This suggested that any man or, indeed, any woman, could be free if only they were wise, thus opening up Greek culture to every rational being. As a citizen of a polis, the private individual had only felt as a part, a member, or an organ in his cramped, specific community, which was all to him; now, in the spirit of Stoicism, he was told that the real commonwealth is the cosmos—hence the term "cosmopolitan"—and the responsibilities of the townsman and the father come to be viewed through the eyes of a Cynic philosopher.

The first cosmopolitan civilization known to man was ultimately made possible because previous upheavals had already overturned the original units of regional culture. Adequately uprooted and dispersed, the East had been rendered rather indifferent by its many conquerors and was easily lulled into passive acceptance of what the West had to offer. For the Macedonians did more than just control territory—they actively exported Hellenistic culture: not only art, literature, and philosophy, but also religion, politics, and law. This exportation of culture was an entirely new idea, an idea that would, more than anything else, influence all the civilizations and cultures that would later spring from this soil: the Roman Empire, the Jewish Diaspora, Christianity, and Islam.

As the Greek way of life was disseminated throughout the civilized regions of antiquity, their lively form of public debate also became common. With the Greeks spread their language, which, while losing some of its Attic elegance, developed into a Panhellenic standard-language, the *Koinê*, Greek for "common"—the old dialects died out. It was during this period that Greek culture became a world culture, developing that flexible and shrewd, liberal and pluralistic spirit which we are accustomed to consider especially Hellenic.

The Battle of Issus (333 BCE) not only made Alexander the master of East and of Palestine, but opened a new period of history for the Jews.[28] Whatever may be thought of the historical value of Flavius Josephus' account on

---

[28] Alexander and Alexandra are still popular Jewish names.

Alexander's personal visit to Jerusalem, the Palestinian Jews were now brought into direct contact with Greek civilization. Prior to this, there had been scarcely any intercourse between the Hebrews and the Greeks. According to the Jewish historian, his countrymen would join Alexander's troops "on this condition, that they should continue under the laws of their forefathers, and live according to them."

In any case, Alexander allowed the Jews a free enjoyment of their religious and civil liberties, further rewarding those of them who went to war with him by granting them equal rights with the Macedonians. And when the Samaritans rebelled against him in 331 BCE, he added a part of Samaria to Judæa. The founding of Alexandria proved likewise of a great significance to the Jews. They would enjoy many privileges here, and for the next few centuries, this town in the delta would form a centre through which Judaism spread to the Greek-speaking world, and where evolved Hellenistic Judaism, culminating in Philo.

For all appearances, the Hellenistic world was a Greek secular culture: the official language was Greek, and all writings were penned in Greek, using Greek literary devices and styles; different ideas were tolerated and even encouraged, but each of them was presented within a Greek framework. At a glance, it would seem that the Eastern influence had been circumvented by Western culture; this was not the case, however.

The influence of the East was there, though cloaked in the guise of Greek language and thought: i.e. Babylonian astrological fatalism could easily be disguised in the garments of Stoic cosmology, and Persian theological dualism in those of Platonism. The currents of Oriental thought would work and evolve underground, utilizing the analytical techniques of the Greek philosophers to reshape their myths and symbols into logical and rational systems of theology, until they could present themselves to the world three centuries later at the beginning of the Common Era.

When Alexander died in 323 BCE, there was no specific successor to claim his kingdom. We will never know whether he would, or could, have unified this huge empire, and it might have crumbled into nothing within a few years. In any case, his death guaranteed that the empire which he had built would never last. He had left it, in his own words, "to the strongest"—an ambiguous testament, which resulted in bloody conflicts for the next half a century.

Egypt was more fortunate than any other land in Alexander's kingdom in that she gained as her new ruler the most cunning and skillful of his generals, namely Ptolemy. He was also called Lagos, for that was the name of his formal father, but he was believed to be the son of Philip of Macedon, giving him a particularly influential position amongst Alexander's generals. While holding the reins of the most fertile and easily defended province, in the name of Alexander or whoever else was formally in charge, he took exceptional care of the land, enriching and developing its resources by peaceful means, until he proclaimed himself king of Egypt nineteen years later.

Several of Ptolemy's colleagues also became satraps with similar aspirations, but the boundaries of their provinces were not as natural. Some of these men have defied oblivion, including Antigonus in Phrygia, Lysimachus in Thrace, and Eumenes in Cappadocia and Paphlagonia. Macedon and Greece remained under the rule of Antipater, but Perdiccas, who ruled in Babylonia, demanded authority over all the others. The lot is usually referred to by the collective term of *Diadochi*, meaning simply "successors."

The political realm had adopted imperialism and its complement, cosmopolitism. The most popular form of government was absolutism, but the enlightened kind: Antigonus Gonatas would dub kingship *endoxos douleia*, "noble servitude," and the Diadochi were wont to give themselves either the epithet of *Euergetes*, "benefactor," or that of *Soter*, "saviour." The outer form of rule consisted of the typical apparatus of a great dynastic régime: of a cabinet, a court etiquette, the audiences, the orders, the proclamations, a standing army, the sanctity of the sovereign, and the taking of an oath in the name of the *Tuchê* of the king. There rose the new concepts of "subject" and "private person," who, as is almost always the case, enjoy more personal liberty and safety under an absolute monarchy than under an incalculable democracy.

In the war that erupted between the Diadochi, the majority of them allied against Perdiccas. He then marched on Egypt, but a number of his troops drowned while attempting to cross the Nile. This aroused such a great indignation that his own officers murdered him in his tent still that same night. Now Antipater in his turn claimed rightful heirship to the entire empire that Alexander had built. In Asia Minor, Antigonus fought against Eumenes, who was eventually imprisoned and executed after several years of artful politicizing. The former became very powerful and a new coalition was therefore formed against him. He, too, fell in due time, and Persia, Babylonia, and Syria were subjugated in his place by a certain fortunate soldier called

Seleucus Nicator.

The march of Seleucus to Babylon took place on the 1st of October in 312 BCE, marking the beginning of an era known as the Seleucid period. The Seleucid calendar spread far and wide in the East over several centuries, and Arab astronomers presumably utilized it from time to time right down to our own day. The reign of the Seleucids lasted over two centuries (until 64 BCE) and most of the rulers were named either Seleucus or Antiochus. The regions beyond the Euphrates were soon lost and the centre of gravity in the kingdom shifted early on from Babylonia to Syria.

Situated between Egypt and Syria, Palestine would become the bone of contention between their respective rulers, the continuous wars between the Ptolemies and the Seleucids causing a great deal of disturbance in the internal matters of Judæa. However, after the Battle of Ipsus (301 BCE), Palestine remained annexed to Egypt practically a whole century (until 202 BCE). When Seleucus founded Antioch around 300 BCE, he attracted Jews to his new capital by granting them equal rights with his Greek subjects, rights that were gradually extended into all the principal cities of Asia Minor. Antioch soon came to be regarded as the third city of the world, being surpassed only by Alexandria and Rome.

The rule of the first three Ptolemies proved even more popular with the Jews than that of the Seleucids. During its first century, the Ptolemaic government was the most enlightened in the world, and Egypt was the only country where peace remained unbroken, and commerce and science could evolve without restraint. Alexandria grew into one of the largest, if not the largest metropolis in the world, having at its height about half a million inhabitants, of all sorts. It was from its foundation an international city, whose busy trade brought strange peoples and cargoes from as far away as India and China. It was not only a port, but a manufacturing centre, of glass and metal work, of papyrus and silk, of scents and incense, and of weaving, especially of carpets. It had a reputation for culture and learning, but also for extravagance and splendour, similar to that of 15th-century Florence.

The Library of Alexandria, actually two or more libraries in the Egyptian capital, has achieved almost a mythical stature within the study of Classics from the time of the Renaissance. The idea of a formal institution for scholars of different fields, complete with a library, was new, and the Museum was modelled after the Lyceum of Aristotle. Its immediate precursors were the shrines of the Muses, which were no longer just cult centres, but also a focus for literary competitions and festivals. The word *Musæum* itself is merely the Latin form of the Greek for "temple of the Muses," and as the Muses were the goddesses of the arts, so was the Museum the temple of the arts and sciences. As a shrine built for the glorification of the Muses, the Museum contained, from the beginning, lecture halls, observatories, laboratories, porticoes for peripatetic discussions, living quarters, a dining hall, a garden, a zoo, the shrine itself, and, presumably, the library.

The administrator of the Museum was a priest appointed by the king, while its collection was the responsibility of a separate librarian. Though its exact location is unknown, it is supposed to have been within the walls of the royal palace, which stood in the Brucheion, the Greek quarter of the city. Here one hundred scholars lived, maintained by the state, and while lacking the technical aids that are employed by modern academics, developed quite modern methods of working. They collected, catalogued, analyzed, critiqued, annotated, edited, and abridged the works of their predecessors, literary giants such as Homer, Hesiod, Plato, and Aristotle—this first systematic study of Greek literature resulted in the invention of the concepts of accent and grammar. The scholars at Alexandria also gathered translations of Egyptian, Assyrian, Persian, Indian, Jewish, and other cultures' literature, having nearly 1,000,000 works in their possession by the late Ptolemaic period.

Above all, the Hellenistic Greeks distinguished themselves in mathematics (especially geometry), astronomy, and physics, the last three centuries BCE being the golden age of Greek science. In medicine and biology, all the promises of Hippocrates and Aristotle were not met, and chemistry was hardly even recognized as a branch of science. But, as a whole, the study of natural sciences made considerable progress. Prior to the late 17th century CE, scientific study in its modern form advanced the furthest precisely at the Museum of Alexandria during the era of the first Ptolemies.

Unlike his father, Ptolemy II Philadelphus (r. 283-244 BCE) turned his back on military campaigns and focussed on building his capital. More "Egyptian" than his Macedonian-born father, he married his sister Arsinoë, a custom widely accepted among ancient Egyptians, but despicable to the Greeks. The gods of Egypt were not neglected either; the vast endowments were not taken away from the temple establishments, but used for the extensive rebuilding projects which resulted in the most magnificent temples that we know. A second or "daughter" library, the Serapeion, was established in the temple of Serapis, a popular god created by the Ptolemies through the synthesis of Zeus, Pluto, Osiris, and Apis. This library, located in the Rhakotis, or Egyptian quarter, was open to all, not just to government-sponsored scholars, and held copies of many of the scrolls of the Museum.

The first mention of the Great Library itself is found in a 2nd-century BCE Jewish document, the so-called *Letter of Aristeas*, a propagandistic account of the first translation of the *Pentateuch* by the seventy-two elders of Israel, six from each tribe. This Greek translation was apparently commissioned by the Museum's founder, Demetrius, under the patronage of Ptolemy I Soter, and completed during the reign of the second Ptolemy. The designation *Septuagint* was later extended to cover the rest of the Old Testament and the non-canonical books that were rendered into Greek during the two following centuries.

There was a remarkable difference between the theological opinion of the Babylonian and the Alexandrian Jew. In and around Antioch, the Jews read and studied the *Tanakh* in the original Hebrew, which was comparatively easy to them since the Chaldæan tongue was related to the language of Canaan. The Jews in Egypt and throughout Europe, commonly known as Hellenistic Jews, soon forgot Hebrew. The *Septuagint* rendered the Old Testament books into Greek terms and concepts that often were inaccurate, misleading, or plain mistranslated from the original texts. As a consequence, the Hellenistic Jews were less punctilious in their observance of the Law. And, like the Samaritans, they displayed schismatic tendencies by erecting a rival temple to that in Jerusalem.

The Hebrews of Palestine, on the other hand, retained a marked hostility to the ideas and practices that had evolved among other peoples. Their resistance to the introduction of Gentile rituals and customs into Jerusalem formed the backdrop for many famous scenes in their rebellion. The annual tribute demanded by the early Ptolemies was light, and as long as it was paid regularly, the Palestinian Jews were free to manage their own affairs under their high priests, at whose side stood the Sanhedrin of Jerusalem as a council of state.

The reason for, and at the same time, the result of cosmopolitism was the rapacious propagation of global economy, the like of which the world had never seen before. Alexander had set up a common system of currency for his entire domain, and the coinage began to standardize by denomination as well as by design—his rapid ascendancy and lasting importance are well documented in the coins of the ancient world. His conquests had opened up the Eastern trade: from Persia, India, and China were brought, in abundant numbers, hitherto unknown luxury items. People began to risk venturing on the open seas, whereas they had previously remained timid ashore.

The Persian example was followed in building the roads of the empire, which would relay the traffic of immense caravan trains. The hotel system, unknown to the earlier antiquity, began to flourish. Numerous banks were founded, at the head of which stood the almighty central bank of Alexandria, as well as vast cartels of major traders, ship-owners, and shipping-agents; even world exhibitions already existed. A refined system of taxation—to which Egypt lent its millennial experience—spun its web over the astonished humanity; there were stamps and taxes for everything.

For Greece proper, the world conquest meant poverty, decrease of population, and decline. Following the release by Alexander of the immense amounts of money that had until then laid idle at the treasure vaults of the great kings of Persia, a depreciation in the value of currency and a rise in prices took place. The long-term financial crisis led to civic unrest and blood-soaked riots. Wholly novel to the age was the dawning of a new kind of humane sentiment: the art of war was beginning to recognize some elementary human rights, an almost romantic chivalry being often demonstrated; the lot of slavery and even its justification were pondered upon, the counterpart to which was the rise of a mass proletariat of working people.

Transplanted on alien soil, Greek culture became the province of a privileged aristocracy that ruled over a foreign populace. It was a turbulent, pessimistic time: Cynics, Sophists, Platonists, Peripatetics, and others offered new philosophical and moral ways of coping with life and the unpredictable world. The so-called Hellenistic poets, the Greek poets of 3rd- and 2nd-century BCE Alexandria, are noted for an extremely sophisticated, intellectual, and frequently artificial type of poetry. Living as they did in a largely rootless society, their art turned in on itself, with emphasis placed on art for art's sake; their elegant poems were carefully crafted for a cultivated, well-read audience, trained to look for witty turns of phrase, clever plays on tradition, and obscure allusions to earlier literature and mythology.

New religions were in demand during the international phase which followed Alexander's conquest, as the glory days of the Olympian gods were long over. There was also a unique market for the worldly wisdom and explanations of the universe offered by the philosophers. From Aristotle on, a great many of them wrote short "evangelical" tracts, proclaiming the glad tidings of the importance of philosophical contemplation in a troubled world, exhorting men to its practice. The multitude of names leads us to the conclusion that the world was absolutely swarmed with philosophers of a more or less broad following and influence. Around 300 BCE were born the two most important schools, in terms of subsequent influence on men's thoughts about themselves and the world. Both taught a philosophy that was essentially pragmatic and non-metaphysical. Both sought a mental equilibrium, and not the comprehension of the whole universe through reason, the goal of the earlier philosophers.

The first, Epicurean school, does not enjoy the same noble reputation today as the second one does, but about Epicurus himself even his contemporary adversaries have nothing but good things to say. Epicurean philosophy, being materialistic and atheistic, with the avowed intention of freeing men from superstition of all kinds and thus allowing him to attain peace of mind, free from vain fears, was Athenian in both its origin and character. The Greeks lived almost wholly in this world; to them, the hereafter was a hazy and a fundamentally unreal realm of shadows, and the Orphic sermons on the redemption of the flesh and the transmigration of the souls seemed entirely foreign to their disposition; they thus indulged, to fullest extent, in the reality at hand. Their playful light-heartedness and sensuous worldliness was manifest to the level of their greeting: *Khaire*, "Rejoice!"

In the Greek mind, religion was specially connected rather with the notion of a feast than of a fast. Thucydides of Athens was certainly not by nature a reveller, yet religion was to him mainly a "rest from toil." To the Old Oligarch, thoroughly orthodox and even pious, the gist of religion appears to have been decorous social enjoyment; in a laid-back aristocratic fashion, he rejoices that there are religious ceremonials to provide the less well-to-do citizens with appropriate amusements that they would otherwise lack—as a part of the splendour of Athens, he notes that "she celebrates twice as many religious holidays as any other city." The Greeks were artistic people wholly devoid of gravity, which is why their true-to-life realism possessed none of the coarse roughness, tedious concretism, or empty banality that would later characterize its Roman counterpart.

Within the doctrine of Epicurus, in itself simple and scientific, lay a potential for misinterpretation. According to Epicurus, the object of life was the search for delight (Gr. *hêdonê*, whence the term "hedonism") and the avoidance of suffering, for death is the end of life. Inasmuch as pleasures, if indulged in without discipline and balance, will soon grow boring and even bring suffering, Epicurus wanted to equilibrate them and to choose only the ones that endure the longest without causing any pain afterwards. This is how he arrived at the importance of moderation, good company, mental tranquillity, and meditation; gaiety and levity only lead to greater agony. He based his materialistic world view on the atomic theory of Democritus, who only now, through Epicurus, gained note in wider circles. In the privileged upper classes, those inclined to Epicureanism were the ones who had devoted themselves to arts, poetry, and other peaceful pursuits. The other new school, Stoicism, was in many ways un-Greek, which, perhaps, is precisely why it had the future on its side, among both the Romans and their heirs.

The Stoics based their doctrine on the suitable tenets of all the earlier philosophers, but their aim was not as much the ordering of their thoughts as of their lives. They had arrived at an aristocratic cosmopolitism that emphasized the similarities between people rather than their obvious differences: Nature tricks the fool into thinking that She is volatile, intricate, and diversified; in reality Nature is—to him who can penetrate Her mysteries—fixed, coherent, and uniform. The Stoics therefore urged people to live life "one flock on a common pasture feeding together under a common law." They insisted that all the offices of public authority should have a legal foundation, and that all the people, women and slaves included, are entitled to equal protection of the law. According to the Stoics, all things were held together by the same all-pervading force, the Logos, or reason; humans are rational beings, who as such, understand this rational, natural order.

The ever-firmer trend towards monotheism is partly linked to the influence of the East; Zeno, who is usually considered as the founder of the Stoic school, was, in actuality, a Phœnician from the island of Cyprus. Central concerns to all the schools of the day were establishing personal ethics and understanding the ultimate deity. The Stoic believed in one god, even though He could be worshipped under different names. He was a benevolent and omnipotent divinity, who took care of His children and wanted them to live in virtue. Itinerant philosophers became a sort of popular clergy, frequenting the marketplaces and private homes. The problem of the existence of evil, however, became as severe a stumbling-block to the Stoics as it has done to all the other advocates of theism. The average Stoic accepted Sin as something that had to be fought against, and considered Duty to be the struggle against Sin.

The proclamations made at the Stoa of Zeno and at the Garden of Epicurus were the last notable contribution of Athens to the history of antiquity. Far away from the focus of world events, the once mighty republic had been turned into a quiet university town. Its subsequent accomplishments have only rarely been of any interest to posterity.

By the close of the 2nd century BCE, the series of great international wars that had started with Alexander's conquests ended in one of the contending superpowers—the republic of Rome—gaining victory. Rome herself had initially been just a regular city-state; but she had, in a certain sense, solved the problem that Athens, Sparta, Thebes, and the other Greek poleis had been unable to solve: she had managed to rise beyond the borders of a city-state.

The upper classes in general, and above all, those men who gradually ascended to the leadership of the united world of the Roman Empire, were adherents of Stoicism. Whereas the Epicureans urged the wise man to withdraw from the distractions and dangers of political life, the Stoics emphasized his Duty to the State, his commitment to politics. To the Stoic philosopher, *Jus Gentium*, the common international law of all nations, was more natural than the conflicting laws and juridical systems of different poleis, tribes, and nations. Roman law differed from Athenian and Jewish law in that it was intended for all the people and was not merely the property of one tribe. It applied to Roman citizens (*Jus Civile*) as well as to the Roman subjects that were not citizens, and forms the basis of the Western legal system. By the 1st century BCE, Roman Italy had developed, if not into a perfectly modern nation-state, at least into an extensive territorial whole, with common citizenship and common legislation. Gradually, law and order became established as the cohesive forces of political communities; the world of warring tribes and city-states had become the united world of the later Græco-Roman culture.

The rationalistic notion of human equality as preached by the Stoics was an integral part of the cosmopolitan citizenship of the Roman Empire. Stoicism, however, never evolved into a religious denomination, a parochial organization, nor did it develop any actual, formal articles of faith. Common to Stoic humanism, the parodies at cost of the old divinities, and the paradisal dream of archaic children of nature—the characteristic traits of the day—was gazing towards the past. The novelties came from the East.

The Romans had adopted an extremely tolerant attitude towards most religions. Everyone was allowed to believe in whatever he wanted to as long as he did not disturb others or injure the State. The Olympian waxworks did not satisfy the genuine religious needs of the people. The gods of Olympus, as well as the great number of Greek and Italian local deities more or less loosely affiliated with them, paled quickly and early in the Roman era. The Stoics had given their deontological ethics a strict religious significance, for the concern of which the blissful gods of Epicurus, cut loose from the affairs of men and even the ordered ways of nature, were completely inadequate. All of these would have to give way for the monumental importation of Oriental deities, which ceased only after the triumph of Christianity, and lent the Classical world a group of foreign divinities and myths.

The Roman conquests in Asia and Africa brought the nation under the influence of diverse mystery cults, each of which had its own saviour god or goddess, such as Mithras, Attis, or Isis. Each of these saviour deities had in some way overcome death, or performed some feat whose effects guaranteed a happy afterlife for the initiates, the "true philosophers" of Socrates. Some of the divinities had also instituted sacraments: after slaying the bull as a salvific blood sacrifice, Mithras had dined with the sun-god, and this supper had become the Mithraic cultic meal, the *Myazd*.

The concept of the saviour, the Greek *Soter*, the deity incarnate on Earth, matured above all within the Hellenistic culture, which bestowed the epithet, among others, upon Herakles, Osiris, and Mithras; it was also readily given to many of the heads of the philosophical schools, like Epicurus for example; later it became an epithet of the Roman Emperors.

Mithras was the Græco-Roman name for the Indo-Iranian god Mitra or Mithra. The origin of Mithraism dates from the time when the Indians and Persians still formed one people, for the god figures in the religion and the scriptures of both peoples, namely the Vedas and the Avesta respectively. Mitra is a part of the Hindu pantheon, while Mithra is one of several minor deities under Ahura-Mazda in the Zoroastrian hierarchy of divinities. In the northwest of the Iranian highlands, Mithra retained his place as principal deity even after the Zoroastrian reform. Following the conquest of Babylon, this Persian cult came in contact with Chaldæan astrology and the national worship of Marduk. During the period when the two priesthoods of Mithra and Marduk co-existed in the capital, much was borrowed by the Magi from the Chaldæi. Travelling farther to the northwest, this altered form of Mithraism became the state religion of Armenia, whose rulers adopted Mithradates as their royal name—as did five kings of Georgia. When Mithraism entered Asia Minor, it came across the Phrygian cult of Attis and Cybelê, from which it adopted yet more ideas and practices.

After Alexander's conquest, Mithraism had come in touch with the Western world, but Hellenism—and especially Greece itself—remained singularly free from its influence. The success of Mithraism in the West was not secured until the Romans had taken possession of Pergamon, occupied Asia Minor, and stationed two legions on the Euphrates. The same features that shocked and repulsed the Greeks may have actually attracted the less sophisticated Romans and barbarians of the West. The theory of both the new birth and the remission of sins through the shedding of blood have their origin in savagery, and naturally appeal to peoples in whom the savage instincts are still strong.

Since Mithraism passed as a Phrygian cult, it would also share in the official recognition which Phrygian religion had long enjoyed in Rome, spreading rapidly from Persia to Tunisia, the Rhine, even London. It gained currency first in the frontier stations of the Roman army, because the legionaries were its chief apostles; at the same time, however, Eastern slaves and foreign traders carried out its mission work in the cities. More than one Emperor must have partaken in the holy sacrament known as the *taurobolium*, where the new initiates were baptized with the blood of an ox, to wash away their sins; this part of the ceremonial was closely parallelled in the cult of Cybelê, the Great Mother of Asia Minor, which had been brought to Rome a century earlier.

The cult of Mithras satisfied many of the same needs that would later attract people to Christianity. It was a fraternity where rank and reciprocal duty were predicated not upon accepted social norms, but on the secret bonds of a closed circle, an underground network of close allegiances operating within the larger social framework of the Roman Empire. A Mithraic community was not just a religious congregation, but a social and legal body with its own *magistri*, *curatores*, *defensores*, and *advocati*. While women were not allowed as members, they could console themselves by forming associations devoted to Cybelê, at whose worship only women were permitted to be present.[29]

For future generations, the importation of Greek ideas and customs into Rome was more important than the arrival of Oriental gods. She came in superficial contact with Hellenic culture even as she conquered the Greek cities in southern Italy and Sicily, from which she stole many treasures for the benefit and edification of her own citizens. During the First Punic War, for example, the municipal sun-dial of Catania was confiscated, dragged all the way to Rome, and placed at a public location, where it told the time wide off the mark for about a century, due to the much more northern latitude.[30]

For all that, the Roman understanding of Greek life and of its institutions grew with time, and as it deepened, Roman literature finally saw the light. Livius Andronicus, the first Latin author whose name has reached posterity, was himself born a Greek; he was taken prisoner by the Romans during their conquest of Tarentum, but was soon released, and stayed with his captors as a teacher. He needed a reading book for his students, and the only thing he could come up with was to translate the *Odyssey*, the basic textbook for all children in the Hellenic world.

Latin got its name from the great plain of Latium that circles Rome, after the Romans had risen, lifted by the advantageous position of their city and their own political prowess, to the leadership of the Latin tribes. The evolution of Latin from a language of farmers—poor in expression though capable even early on of producing a substantial legal terminology with all the abstract concepts that go with it—into a more and more nuanced cultural and literary language, was largely due to Greek. All of Roman poetry was, strictly speaking, merely translated literature. The first two truly significant Roman poets, Catullus and Lucretius, both of whom died around 55 BCE, were

---

[29] Sociologically speaking, it cannot be denied that, in certain tasks, those of the same gender work together more harmoniously than when both sexes try to work in unison.

[30] It was from Carthage that Rome acquired Sicily, Sardinia, Corsica, Spain, Numidia (Algeria), and Tunisia.

immensely dependent on Greek prototypes.

About the life of the latter we know hardly anything, wherefore it is highly unlikely that he belonged to Cæsar's circle of acquaintances. Epicureanism, which from the days of its founder had been one of the most maligned schools of philosophy, provided a motif for the most peculiar didactic poem of world literature: a compelling plea for atheism, *De Rerum Natura*, "On the Nature of Things," is a six-volume work written entirely in dactylic hexameter, whose main purpose was to discredit the existence of the gods and fate by explaining various phenomena through physics, based on the atomic theory of Democritus. In it, Titus Lucretius Carus very perceptively, and at the same time, very poetically, outlines the transitory nature of the soul, the deceptiveness of religion, the birth and evolution of life, and the beginning of culture. It is apparent, however, that the later generations were never avid readers of Lucretius, for although his works are positively filled with witty and thought-provoking hexameters, hardly any famous Latin quotations come from them.

Like most of Rome's distinguished poets, Gaius Valerius Catullus was a provincial, an outsider, born into a family of Celtic descent in the town of Verona in Cisalpine Gaul, the region between the Alps and the Apennines. The Celts were one of the great founding civilizations of Europe, the first European people north of the Alps to emerge into recorded history. The word *Keltoi* was first used in the 5th century BCE, by which time the Celtic peoples had established themselves in France and Spain, as far south as Cádiz, and in the Po Valley of upper Italy. Theirs was an adventurous and inventive culture with a highly-developed religion unifying all their tribes from Galatia to Ireland. Forbidden as they were by religious prohibition to write in their own languages, the Celts of Cisalpine Gaul and Spain wrote in Latin. Not only Catullus, but also Publius Valerius Cato, Marcus Terentius Varro, Cæcilius Statius, Lucius Pomponius, Trogus Pompeius, and even Vergil, were Celts. Just like their descendants in the Modern Era, the Celts of the Roman world contributed to the language of their conquerors rather than to their own.

Despite Catullus' frequent jokes about his poverty, we know that he came from a wealthy aristocratic family. His father was prominent and rich enough to be friends with Julius Cæsar, and sent his young son to learn the ways of the city in Rome. There he was noticed by an anything-but-virtuous woman, whom he calls Lesbia, and who is generally considered to have been Clodia Metelli, sister of Cicero's infamous antagonist, Publius Clodius Pulcher, and the wife of the former consul Metellus Celari. They embarked on a torrid affair that provided the material for most of Catullus' intensive but graceful poetry. That the name Lesbia is a pseudonym is clear: the Roman love poets would routinely employ such false names, cleverly selecting them so that the object of their affection could put her real name in place of the fictitious one.

In addition to providing a suitable metric equivalent for Clodia's real name, the name Lesbia, "a woman from the island of Lesbos," directly recalls the most famous Lesbian, the passionate Greek poetess, Sappho—the Ægean island itself was associated both with beautiful women and cultured refinement. By addressing Clodia as Lesbia, Catullus therefore suggests a woman not only of beauty, grace, and culture, but also of strong passions. His poems, some of them written in Sapphic stanzas, chronicle their affair from flirtation through passion to bitter betrayal. His most famous poem is a translation of Sappho, reckoned as the first poem that he addressed to Clodia, to highlight his choice for her pseudonym. From Sappho, he also got the themes for his famous wedding songs, composed for his friends.

His poem of the innumerable kisses—*Vivamus, mea Lesbia, atque amemus*; let us live, my Lesbia, and let us love—has not only literary, but also philological interest. The word *basium*, or romantic kiss, which appears in the most frequently quoted verse—*Da mi basia mille, deinde centum*; Give me a thousand kisses, then a hundred—was imported to the Latin tongue precisely by Catullus. Kiss, in Latin, is normally *osculum*, and *basium* was originally probably a Celtic word. Through Catullus' little love poem, the word was appropriated into Latin, which then lent it to the modern Romance languages, being *baiser* in French and *bacio* in Italian.

The elegant, sincere, and passionate eroticism of Catullus would form the model for the mediæval tradition of courtly love. However, his first poem was dedicated to a fellow-Celt and friend, Cornelius Nepos, whom Catullus named as the first person brave enough to write a universal history in three volumes; in fact, he was the first person ever to write a universal history. Born around 100 BCE in the Po country, Nepos would later suffer the bitter fate of turning into the dread and nuisance of all little schoolboys; his sole extant work, *De Viris Illustribus*, a collection of gritty, moralizing biographies of illustrious men has, throughout the centuries, been used as the elementary Latin textbook in every Western school.

With his friends Cinna and Licinius Calvus, Catullus belonged to a set of

Roman poets who consciously turned for their inspiration, not to the traditional, "respectable" genres such as the epic, but to the Hellenistic poets, and in the case of Catullus and his friends, incorporated this untraditional form of poetry into the carefree lifestyle of the young socialite. These revolutionary poets came to be known as Neoteric—the term derives from a Greek comparative adjective, signifying "newer" or "rather new."

Being founded on an essentially utilitarian ideal, early Roman poetry was largely didactic in nature; its celebration of nationalistic themes presented useful models of behaviour while focusing on the glory of the fatherland and its leaders. Catullus, in contrast, celebrates the most un-Roman values, such as love affairs and orgies; in general, private enjoyment rather than the public good. His short and passionate life gave him so much inspiration that his early Greek and Alexandrian models were unable to stifle his personality. It appears so prominently, especially in his shorter poets, as to be exceedingly rare in the history of poetry, and it has made him the most eminent Roman poet of all.

Modern readers tend to overlook Catullus for precisely the same reason he seems ever so familiar: we expect poets to explore themes of intimately personal nature and to write heavily in the first person—which was not the case in antiquity, and least of all in Rome. Time and again, his poems seem to consciously celebrate a life of frivolity and excess, purposely mocking the opinion of moralists such as Sallust or Cato; yet for all his witty playfulness and erudition, the most impressive thing about Catullus is his uncanny ability to portray vividly both the rapture of someone caught up in a fresh affair and the torment of romance gone sour—his poems to Lesbia transcend in this respect both his Hellenistic models and the Roman traditions.

Despite all his ribaldry and ridicule of authority, Catullus is very much an aristocrat in his outlook, deeply conservative in his opinions, and has a constant concern for the bottom line. He thus represents not only a literary, but a social phenomenon, providing a rare glimpse into the life of a rich and gifted member of the Roman aristocracy amidst the tumult of the late Republic; his poetry presents a welcome corrective to the dreary picture painted by the chaotic and violent politics of the period—he makes it evident that life mostly went on as usual despite the uncertainties of the times.

Catullus is noted for numerous satirical epigrams on the folly and crudity of his contemporaries. His words of abuse on Cæsar are, remarkably enough, preserved, and characteristically to the poet, Catullus does not delve any deeper into the political acts of the Emperor, but merely calls him a scoundrel and accuses him of sexual perversion and of a close relationship to his financial supporter, the banker Mamurra. Though Catullus had deeply offended Cæsar with his verses, as recorded by the great Roman biographer, Gaius Suetonius Tranquillus, in his *Lives of the Cæsars*, when the poet apologized, the Emperor invited him to dinner that very same day, and resumed his usual friendly relations with the poet's father.

CHAPTER 6

Gaius Julius Cæsar was born in Rome on the 13th day of the month of Quintilis, in the year 100 BCE. His father, Gaius Cæsar, died in Pisa when Cæsar was 16 years old, so it was his mother Aurelia, who proved most influential in his life. Because of their close relationship, young Julius was heavily influenced by the political views of his maternal family, in particular his uncle, Gaius Aurelius Cotta. Although not particularly rich or influential, they were still patricians, members of Rome's original aristocracy, even if this status no longer provided much political advantage.

At the time of Julius' birth, Roman political life was dominated by one man, Gaius Marius (157-86 BCE), a plebeian general married to Cæsar's Aunt Julia. Marius' greatest claim to fame was defeating the Teutones and the Cimbri, and successfully ending the Jugurthine War. As a *Popularis*, Marius advocated the direct ratification of legislation through the Assembly of the People. In this, he was opposed by the Optimates, those patricians who believed everything should be ratified by the Senate and who saw the Populares as revolutionaries.

The Social War witnessed the emergence of a new Optimate champion, Lucius Cornelius Sulla, a former lieutenant of Marius'. In 88 BCE, many of the cities of Greece supported King Mithradates VI of Pontus in his attack on Roman-controlled territories in the east, for he had promised to help the Greeks regain their independence. When Marius attempted to assume Sulla's command against Pontus, Sulla marched into Rome, setting off the First Civil War. Defeated by patrician forces, Marius fled to Africa, while Sulla marched on Asia, where he beat the King of Pontus in the First Mithradatic War (88-84 BCE). Not only was the punishment of all the rebellious Hellenic cities severe, but the campaigns fought on Greek soil left much of Greece in ruins.

Marius had all his personal enemies killed when he returned to Rome in 86 BCE. Before dying from a stroke just a few days after being elected to the consulship for an unprecedented seventh time, he had his nephew by marriage appointed to the lifelong position of *flamen Dialis*, priest of Jupiter. The spiritual guidance of the day was monopolized by the philosophers, not by the weak and archaic priesthood, so the appointment only served to identify Cæsar with extremist politics. In 84, he committed himself further to the radical side by breaking his engagement with Cossutia, daughter of his uncle Cotta, and marrying Cornelia, daughter of Lucius Cornelius Cinna, an associate of Marius'.

History might have been very different if Sulla had not returned to crush the Populares in 82 BCE. He appointed himself Dictator, giving him emergency powers. He used his army to strengthen the rights of the patricians, thereby curtailing those of the Popular Assembly. Before retiring from politics in 79 BCE, Sulla was to massacre his enemies by the thousands, and try to wash away the memory of Marius by scattering his ashes in the Tiber and tearing down his statues.

A priest of Jupiter was forbidden to ride a horse, touch a sword, or even look at an enemy of Rome; upon Cinna's death, however, Sulla demanded that Cæsar divorce Cornelia. When Cæsar refused, he came close to losing both his life and property, but his friends and family, including Cotta, begged Sulla to spare him. According to Suetonius, Sulla exclaimed: "Have your way and take him; only bear in mind that the man you are so eager to save will one day deal the death blow to the cause of the aristocracy, which you have joined with me in upholding; for in this Cæsar there is more than one Marius."

Despite his pardon, Cæsar thought it wise to leave Rome for a while, entering military service first in Asia and then in Cilicia. Upon learning of Sulla's death in 78 BCE, he returned and began his political career as a public prosecutor. After building a reputation as an orator, Cæsar went on to study rhetoric in Rhodes, and did not return until 73 BCE. He was captured by pirates on his way to Rome, and was kept captive for 38 days. He persuaded them to raise his ransom from twenty talents to fifty, thereby increasing his prestige. After raising a naval force, he defeated his captors and had them crucified. Again, when the King of Pontus began the Third Mithradatic War (74-63 BCE), Cæsar gathered an army of provincial troops in Asia and triumphed over Mithradates' generals. Since Cæsar was a private citizen without any *imperium*, both acts were against Roman law and highly unconstitutional, but no charges were ever filed against him.

When Cæsar re-entered the political stage in 69 BCE, he clearly expressed his Populist tendencies by praising his uncles Cinna and Marius in the funeral oration for his late aunt Julia. After his first wife died later that year, he married Pompeia, a distant relative of Gnæus Pompeius Magnus—commonly known as Pompey—a former lieutenant of Sulla's. Upon being elected Quæstor, the first rung on the Roman *cursus honorum*, Cæsar left for Hispania Ulterior. He ruled his Spanish province well, making humane laws, while at the same time, taking care of improving his personal finances; he returned to Rome a rich man, was elected Ædile in 65 BCE, Pontifex Maximus in 63 BCE, and a Prætor in 62 BCE—Pompeia he divorced after a scandal.

Pompey, who owed his distinction to two lightning campaigns against the remaining Marian faction in Sicily and Africa, was called "the Butcher" by his enemies; Pompey himself assumed the name Magnus, "the Great." His demand for a triumph had been met by Sulla despite the fact that Pompey was neither a Prætor much less a Consul, the usual prerequisite for this honour. However, after crushing the attempted coup of Lepidus in 78 BCE, he had forced the Senate to confer proconsular power to enable him to deal with the Marian general in Spain. Thought Pompey was defeated by the illustrious Quintus Sertorius, the Spanish general was soon assassinated by one of his own officers. On returning to Rome with his army, Pompey coerced the Senate into electing him to the shared consulship with Marcus Licinius Crassus for 70 BCE—notwithstanding the fact that he was six years too young to legally hold that important office and had never actually been a Senator.

A bitter struggle broke out in Judæa following the death of Queen Salome (76-67 BCE) between her two sons, Hyrcanus and Aristobulus, and in 64 BCE, Pompey was invited to act as an mediator in the contest for the royal throne. He ruled in favour of Hyrcanus the high priest, whose supporters opened the gates of Jerusalem to the Romans, but met fierce resistance from Aristobulus' supporters on the Temple Mount. After a three-month siege, during which thousands of the defenders were slain, the Temple fortress was taken. Pompey caused great dismay among the Jews by entering the Temple itself and the Holy of the Holies within, but unlike the later Roman conquerors, he did not plunder it of its treasures. Nevertheless, his demise is called for in the apocryphal "Psalms of Solomon," written shortly after the event.

The fall of Jerusalem in 63 BCE marked the beginning of Israel's vassalage to Rome—the whole of Judæa was absorbed into the political framework of the Roman Republic. At home, the return of Pompey was anticipated with a mixture of hope and fear: he had conquered greater and richer lands than any general before him; he had arranged the conditions in these far-away lands without consulting the Roman authorities; and he had under his command a great and thoroughly loyal army. There was no reason to believe that he would not seize the power also in Italy.

Pompey was, however, to surprise both his friends and his enemies. Having barely landed in Brundisium, he disbanded his forces and proceeded to Rome without a military escort. His great triumphal procession, complete with elephants, was unlike any celebrated before. After pointing out that he held no state office and was therefore not entitled to any triumph at all, the Senate humiliated Pompey further by refusing to ratify his arrangements in the East or to allocate land for his veterans.

Although Cæsar came from an aristocratic family that held a seat in the Senate, he did not have enough money to bride his way into the consulship. He promised to champion Pompey's cause and aligned himself with land speculator Crassus, who, like Pompey, had been one of Sulla's lieutenants during the First Civil War, and had become Rome's richest man by exploiting the bloody Sullan proscriptions. Thus was born the first so-called Triumvirate, a coalition of three men, having at its disposal the fame and popularity of Pompey, the political genius of Cæsar, and the immense wealth of Crassus, its aim being to attain control over the government machinery and use it for their own gain. This "three-headed monster," the name given to it by Varro, the most erudite man in all Rome, soon held the whole republic in its sway.

In the eyes of the public, the foremost of the Triumvirs was definitely Pompey, the least prominent of them being Cæsar, a man then in his forties who had done nothing remarkable other than winning the elections. But Crassus was widely hated by the Romans for his part in the Sullan proscriptions, and Pompey's skills, considerable as they were, did not extend beyond the battlefield. Cæsar, on the other hand, was a born orator. If he needed Crassus' wealth and Pompey's influence, they needed Cæsar just as much for his consummate ability to manipulate the plebeians. To cement the coalition, his daughter Julia divorced her coæval husband and was given in marriage to Pompey, seven years older than her father.

With a Populist Consul, Rome had in 59 BCE for the first time in the history of the Republic something resembling a majority government. All the measures Pompey had taken in the lands that he had conquered were given official approval, while Cæsar personally introduced, contrary to the prevailing custom, a bill for the allotment of land. During the previous centuries, duties like this had been tied to the office of the Tribunes. The public land of Compania, plus the extra land that would be bought with the income resulting from Pompey's conquests, were to be divided amongst 20,000 settlers, part of them veterans, part of them poor of the capital. Among the less controversial, but sorely-needed initiatives executed by Cæsar were the tightening of the laws to punish the misconduct of provincial governors and the arrangements that made the business of the Senate more public.

Cæsar also resolved the great controversy that had prevailed between the Senate and the tax collectors, the Publicans. The capitalists and aristocrats, who had last made contracts to collect income from the Eastern Provinces, insisted that the amount which they had committed to pay was too high, and demanded that it be lowered significantly. Cæsar gave the Publicans everything they had asked for, although a great part of the spoils flowed into the Triumvir chests. For reasons of convenience, the Triumvirs took care that the most prominent men of the Optimate party, the ultra-conservative moralist Marcus Porcius Cato and the eloquent rhetorician Marcus Tullius Cicero, would be banished from Rome.

Pompey and Crassus having gotten what they wanted, it was finally Cæsar's turn: with the help of Pompey, Cæsar was assigned three legions[31] and given a five-year command of Cisalpine Gaul and Illyricum, starting from the 1st of March, 59 BCE—the Romans originally began their year in March, or Martius, dedicated to Mars, the patron god of the Roman State. When the governor-designate of Transalpine Gaul suddenly died, the Senate bowed to necessity and assigned also this province, along with a fourth legion, to Cæsar.

The Romans had an uncanny ability to deceive themselves; they would conquer the whole then known world from Britain to Egypt, from Euphrates to Gibraltar, pretending the entire time that everything was happening under duress. This time the excuse was the alleged crossing of the Celtic Helvetii into Roman sphere of influence and the invasion of Gaul by the Germanic tribe of the Suebi. The truth was that, in order for Cæsar to secure another consulship on his return to Rome, he needed to build up an army and a

---

[31] The nominal strength of a legion was 5,000 men.

reputation to match those of Pompey.

The battles that followed are related in a classic work, *Commentarii de Bello Gallico*, the notes of Ceasar regarding the Gallic Wars, written at the close of each year, and sent to the Senate in Rome, apparently as a supplement to a future application for a triumph. As a work of propaganda, its purpose was rather to boost the political reputation of the author than to tell the truth about the Wars, but its value as an historical source lay in the fact that it contains virtually all we know on this important subject—no other information simply exists. To make things worse, the use of Cæsar in the teaching of Latin has only increased its popularity.

Cæsar's account consists of more or less colourful stories concerning the life and ways of the tribes with which he came in contact, an information faithfully repeated in every English, French, and German textbook on ancient history. He tells, for example, of Gallic priests, the Druids, whose power was formidable since they pronounced judgement on every dispute and could ban people from the community.

According to Cæsar, the Druids also carried out human sacrifices—stuck live people into gigantic wicker men, which they then set on fire. This charge has been repeated many times since, but as has often been pointed out, the only writers besides Cæsar to make this accusation are those who have read Cæsar[32]; upon reading his work closely, one discovers that he never claimed to have actually witnessed such a sacrifice—in fact, there is not a single eye-witness account of a human sacrifice performed by a Druid in all of written history; nor is there any piece of native tradition or a shred of archæological evidence to support the charge. Insular tradition actually points in the opposite direction: the Druids' reverence for life was so strong that they refused to raise a sword to defend themselves when the Roman soldiers massacred them on the Isle of Mona (now Anglesey).

Due to his splendid victories in Gaul, Cæsar rose swiftly in popularity, while Pompey, still a far greater man in the eyes of the Romans, was held responsible for all the mischief that the Triumvirate had caused. When the Senate tried to annul the Agrarian Laws that had been formed during Cæsar's consulship, Pompey and Cæsar came closer to each other. In May of 56 BCE,

---

[32] Although Pontifex Maximus, Cæsar never mentions making sacrifices to thank the gods for his victories, and in fact, discusses religion only when dealing with the Gauls and the Germans.

a famous meeting of public authorities was held at Lucca, just inside the borders of Cisalpine Gaul. Among the attendants were almost two-hundred Senators, including governors from Spain and Sardinia—it was as if the Senate had moved to the provinces.

The negotiation between Cæsar, Pompey, and Crassus breathed new life into their pact: Cæsar's command was extended by another five years, until the 1st of March, 49 BCE; Pompey would be made Consul for 55 BCE and given the command in Spain for the next five years; Crassus was to be his fellow-Consul and receive a similar five-year tenure in Syria, Rome's newest and richest province. It was further agreed that Cæsar would be granted a second consulship upon the termination of his command in Gaul.

In 56 BCE, the Gallic tribe of the Veneti rose to revolt, supported by the Morini and Menapii from the Lower Rhine region. They also asked and received the aid of their British kinsmen, and to nominally punish the Britons for their help, Cæsar decided to conquer the British Isles. In the summer of 55 BCE, Cæsar landed on the coast of Kent, but accomplished little at this time. His expedition to Germany had also been brief, and Gaul remained far from pacified. He must have realized that it would take more than terrorist-like lightning stikes to subdue the Celts. Nevertheless, he would launch a second expedition on Britain the very next year.

This time, Cæsar embarked from Portus Itius (modern Boulogne) with 800 ships, five legions, and 2,000 cavalry—a record which would stand until the D-Day landings of 1944. His forces managed to penetrate Britain all the way to Middlesex, but as Plutarch laconically relates: ". . .in several battles which he fought did more hurt to the enemy than service to himself, for the islanders were so miserably poor that they had nothing worth being plundered of. When he found himself unable to put such an end to the war as he wished, he was content to take hostages from the king, and to impose a tribute, and then quitted the island."

Possibly due to their belief in the immortality of the soul, the Celts were uncommonly bold warriors. In battle, they used their two-horsed chariots to circle the enemy while throwing spears, thus causing the enemy alignment to fall into confusion. They then drove to a distance, climbed down from their chariots, and began fighting on foot. If they were losing, they simply climbed back on their chariots, and retreated in safety. "In action, therefore," says Julius Cæsar, "they combine the mobility of cavalry with the staying power of foot soldiers."

All this notwithstanding, of the Celtic lands, only Ireland and the Isle of Man were never conquered by Rome. But though the northern part of Britain was invaded, it never settled under Roman administration. As a major European nation, the Celtic civilization was devastated first by the Romans and later by the expansion of the Germanic tribes.

Cæsar's blood-soaked return to Gaul marked a turning-point in his life, a period of personal crisis: in 54 BCE, while the Wars were still raging, he received word of the deaths of two of the most important people in his life—his daughter Julia, and his mother Aurelia. Julia, who was married to Pompey and the object of deep affection to both her husband and father, had been the sole tie between these two men, and the death of Crassus effectively dissolved the First Triumvirate the next year.

You see, Crassus thirsted for battle-glory to match that of the other two Triumvirs, and had chosen Syria as his province in order to start a war against the Parthians of Persia and to conquer for Rome the most essential parts of Alexander the Great's empire. The Parthians, however, had not given the Romans the slightest justification for breaking the peace, so the preparations of Crassus aroused great indignation in Rome. His campaign turned into a disaster unequalled in the history of the Roman Republic, when he fell with nearly all his army in the Battle of Carrhæ (53 BCE) near the biblical Haran.[33] Nevertheless, the Parthians, for some reason, did not try to profit from their victory or make a solid attempt to invade the Eastern Provinces, whose heavily overtaxed inhabitants would probably have welcomed them as deliverers.

On the 18th of January, 52 BCE, Clodius was murdered by gladiators and other armed rogues led by the Optimate Tribune, Titius Annius Milo, a long-time rival of his. In the riots that followed, a mob torched the body of Clodius on the Forum of Rome, whereupon the Senate building caught fire and burned down. Pompey finally intervened and forced the Senators to choose between himself and Milo, promising that he would no longer support Cæsar. He was elected sole Consul, with the responsibility to re-establish law and order; his status was unmatched in the history of the Republic in this and some other

---

[33] Upon being brought the severed head of the rich Crassus, the Parthian victor had it sneeringly filled up with molten gold.

regards—never had so much power been fixed in the hands of one man. After marrying the daughter of the Optimate Metellus Scipio, whose father was among the bigwigs of the aristocratic party, Pompey made his father-in-law his fellow-Consul. It was now clear to everyone that his friendship with Cæsar had come to an end.

In his *Commentarii de Bello Civili*, "Commentaries on the Civil War," Cæsar voices his discontent with Pompey and the Senate. As a propagandistic work, it—like *The Gallic Wars* before it—is exemplary: dry but literarily effective matter-of-factness instils in the reader a feeling of security, a feeling that one is not being deliberately manipulated. Cæsar particularly emphasizes the fact that Pompey ruled Spain with great force of arms through his subordinates; never before had anyone been a Consul in Rome, and at the same time, a Proconsul in charge of a province and a great standing army—this was surely a symptom of an imperial régime.

The Senate began to make motions to suspend Cæsar's command and to incapacitate him in the event of a future confrontation, but they were vetoed by his Tribune friends, who were quickly expelled from the governing council. Cæsar was legally entitled to keep his army until his term in Gaul expired, and had further been given the privilege of consular candidacy for 48 BCE without being present in the capital.[34] While his enemies were trying hard to annul this dispensation, Cæsar dazzled the world with his many victories.

The last great battle, where the heroic Arvernian Vercingetorix united almost all of Gaul against Rome, ended with the siege and capture of Alesia. After that, the Gauls would submit without resistance to the domination of Rome. The great Gallic revolt had occurred at a most auspicious time for Cæsar, so auspicious in fact that one might almost claim Vercingetorix to have been a Cæsarean agent; the suppression of the rebellions in 52 BCE was so efficient that the Gallic provinces remained pacified even through the decades of civil war that were to follow.

On the 11th of January, 49 BCE, Cæsar, accompanied by half a legion, finally stood beside the Rubicon, a small stream separating Cisalpine Gaul from ancient Italy. An apparition of the great god Pan reportedly appeared on

---

[34] Though Cæsar, like all the other Populists before him, had used the people on his way to power, he never trusted them, sending his soldiers home to vote in the time of the elections.

the river, and was taken by the troops as a sign that the gods favoured a crossing, even though it meant war. With the words *Alea jacta est*, "the die is cast," Cæsar crossed into Italy. Pompey was appointed commander-in-chief of the Roman armed forces—those Tribunes who tried to use their constitutional right of veto were banished, and joined Cæsar's army. He marched through Italy almost without any resistance, for town after town welcomed him, and many of Pompey's troops deserted to his side, but he did not catch up with their leader, who fled from Brundisium to Greece on the 17th of March. The Senate having fled to Capua, even the state treasury was left for Cæsar to loot.

After securing his position in Rome, Cæsar headed with nine legions towards Spain to render harmless the seven legions that formed the Spanish army of Pompey. The bloodlust which Cæsar had displayed in dealing with the Gauls and Germans did not extend to Roman citizens. Cæsar used his cavalry to cut the supply lines of the Pompeian legions, and in forty days, had succeeded in subduing a more experienced army without a battle. The troops who were willing he enrolled in the ranks of his own army, the rest he allowed to go free and even to join Pompey in Macedon if they so wished. On his way back, he captured the major Greek town of Marseilles, severely punishing her for having taken the losing side.

Cæsar then had himself appointed Dictator for 11 days, long enough to conduct the consular elections for 48 BCE, which he predictably won with Publius Servilius Isauricus, son of the Isauricus under whom he had earlier served. He also took the time to decree an extension of Roman citizenship to his loyal friends, the people of Cisalpine Gaul, to regulate the finances, and to assign new provincial governors. After resigning his dictatorship, he set out for Greece to confront Pompey.

Pompey's army was composed of varied people, recruited partly from Greece, partly from the East, whereas Cæsar had the advantage of a homogenous army composed mainly of Roman enlistees. After much vacillation, Cicero had decided to join Pompey, but was shocked with what he saw; staying only long enough to make some sarcastic remarks, the orator withdrew his support before the final defeat of Pompey at Pharsalus on the 9th of August, 48 BCE.

After the epochal Battle of Pharsalus, Cæsar pursued Pompey to Egypt, landing there on the 29th of September with just 4,000 men, only to find to his great dismay that Pompey had been stabbed in the back the previous day by an officer of King Ptolemy.[35] Cæsar then marched boldly through Alexandria with his lictors in all the glory of a Roman Consul—a spectacle that naturally caused great consternation in independent Egypt. He demanded the Egyptian state treasury to pay him ten million drachmas, an amount which he claimed the late Ptolemy XI Auletes owed him, and began rearranging the government of the country.

Back in 52 BCE, the Romans had appointed as the interim queen of Egypt the 16-year-old Cleopatra, who was supposed to marry her 10-year-old brother; according to the ancient Egyptian code of succession, the king's son must marry the king's daughter—the law had been such for thousands of years. Four year later, Ptolemy XII Neos Dionysus was duly proclaimed king, but Cleopatra was banished from the country by his advisors in order to acquire all the power. She assembled an army in Syria, came back, and made an unsuccessful attempt to dethrone her little brother. She then fled to Alexandria, where she demanded the aid and protection of Cæsar, who knew that to control Egypt's grain supply was to control of the city of Rome.

Cæsar was keen to support the now 19-year-old Cleopatra against her young brother-husband, whose army and fleet then besieged him in the Greek quarter where the Museum was located. The apocryphal "burning of the Library" during Cæsar's occupation of Alexandria in 48 BCE has been described as the greatest calamity to befall the ancient world, one that erased the most complete collection of Hellenistic and Middle Eastern literature in one great fire. The legend evidently rose from Livy's account of the Alexandrian Wars, now lost, but quoted by all subsequent writers on the topic, starting with Seneca. Livy apparently claimed that after Cæsar set fire to the docks to block Ptolemy's fleet, the flames consumed the nearby warehouses storing both grain and 400,000 rolls of papyrus. Scholars have disputed fiercely over this conflagration since Roman times, debating whether the actual library was burned or if these scrolls had anything at all to do with the Museum.

Be it as it may, Cæsar was at any rate relieved by reinforcements sent from Judæa by Antipater, the arrival of which induced the local Jews to throw their

---

[35] The assassination of Pompey was a severe blow for Cæsar, both personally and politically. He had, without doubt, a deep respect for the man whom fate had made his opponent, and upon receiving his corpse erected a huge sepulchral monument in his honour.

support behind Cæsar, enabling him to move from desperate defence to powerful offence; by the end of March, 47 BCE, Cæsar had crushed and killed Ptolemy in the Battle of the Delta, effectively conquering his kingdom. Judæa, which had been Pompey's private fiefdom until his defeat at Pharsalus, was now officially annexed to Rome by Cæsar. The Idumæan Antipater was rewarded with the rights of Roman citizenship and the office of procurator over all the Jewish territories in the Roman province of Syria. He then appointed two of his sons, Phasael and Herod, governors of Jerusalem and Galilee respectively, and began rebuilding the walls of the Holy City.

Cleopatra VII Philopator, and through her Egypt, became a client of Cæsar personally rather than of Rome. She was married to her still younger brother, and when her younger sister escaped from the hands of her custodians and attempted an armed coup, she was captured and graced Cæsar's triumph in Rome. Cleopatra herself also followed Cæsar to Rome, where the two lived together, and where she soon bore him a son, who was named Ptolemy Cæsarion.

The mistress of Egypt, the heiress of the Macedonian kings who had ruled the land for three-hundred years, the greatest woman of her time, Cleopatra was learned, intelligent, luminous, and enchanting. Of all the ancient authors, Plutarch is the only one whose superlatives concerning her physical appearance stay within reasonable bounds: he tells us that Cleopatra's "actual beauty was not in itself so remarkable; it was the charm of her presence that was irresistible." She was especially well versed in languages, being able to converse with Egyptians, Syrians, Arabs, Medians, Parthians, and Hebrews without having to consult an interpreter. In the *Talmud*, the collection of ancient Judaic lore, there is an indignant entry relating how Cleopatra once enquired the learned Pharisees how they thought the resurrection would take place and should it be assumed to happen with one's clothes on or in the nude.

The pro-Cæsarean Consuls for 47 BCE appointed Cæsar Dictator once more, this time for an unprecedented period of ten years, thus securing his legal position in an otherwise precarious situation. Later that year, he left for Africa to crush his opponents, and in 46 BCE, he was in Spain putting down resistance there. After Scipio was crushed at Thapsus[36], Cato chose a "Roman

---

[36] Scipio escaped but, foreseeing capture, took his own life. The Roman knights' preferred method of suicide, like that of the Japanese samurai, was disembowelment (Jap. *harakiri*).

death" to preserve dignity after defeat. Cicero could not pass the opportunity to write a panegyric about Cato, which Cæsar was forced to counter with his *Anti-Cato*. Not until 45 BCE was the entire Roman world conquered. In March of that year, Cæsar gained a decisive victory over his enemies near Munda, after having overcome the greatest perils he had ever faced. His report to the Senate was brief: *Veni, Vidi, Vici*, "I came, I saw, I conquered."

Alone among his compatriots, Cæsar appears to have realized that Rome as a city-state could survive no longer. By his time, the Roman citizens had degenerated into a proletariat that subsisted largely on electoral bribery, triumphs, feasts, and above all, on the state grain dole. It would have been detrimental to confine the citizenship to the people of Rome; on the contrary, all nationalities should, sooner or later, be bound to the Roman empire. With this goal in mind, Cæsar enlarged the Senate from 600 to 900, including among its members many new citizens from the provinces. Since most of the new Senators were his supporters, and therefore automatically his clients, he was ensured to always have a majority, strengthening his control over the governing council.

In the past, people like Clodius and Milo had formed armed bands, organized in *collegia*, to disturb elections and to intimidate the masses; the upshot was, of course, violence, unrest, and social disorder. Radical reforms were initiated by Cæsar to deal with this problem, starting with the banning of all the organizations suspected of having political aims. The Jews were exempt from this, however, possibly as a reward for their invaluable assistance during the Alexandrian Wars. A special legal status was created for them, and survived in its broad outlines into later times: the Hebrew *ethnos* was a corporation with administrative, judicial, and financial powers; governed by an *ethnarch*, its members were dispensed not only from military service, but from paying the billeting of the Roman troops in their territories. Cæsar's decrees not only advantaged Jewish people in Rome and abroad, but helped to promote the status and appeal of Judaism itself.

To fulfill his goal of improving the social condition in Rome and of spreading citizenship throughout the empire, Cæsar instituted a massive colonization programme. Around 80,000 families were offered new lives in more than twenty newly-founded Roman colonies, among them the rebuilt cities of Corinth and Carthage. Veterans of the Civil Wars were allocated farms and given a cash bonus, while the rights of Roman citizenship were extended over all of Gaul north of the Po River and to many present-day Spanish and French cities. The teachers of philosophy and of Liberal Arts were conferred privileges to ensure that Rome would become a centre of culture. In addition, citizenship was automatically granted to every physician and scholar regardless of nationality.

To consolidate his substantial work, Cæsar drew up the legislation regulating how the new towns were to be governed. Recognizing that discrepant laws led to rebellions in the provinces, Cæsar made provincial governors accountable to Rome, and all Italian cities subject to the same laws and taxes. This code, *Lex Julia Municipalis*, was to form the cornerstone and foundation of both municipal and provincial administration and would endure until the fall of the Roman Empire.

One historic outcome of annexing most of Western Europe to Rome was that the French, for one, still speak a Romance language. Latin, originally a minor Italic dialect used by farmers and herders in the villages underlying the Palatine Hill, spread alongside the Roman domination to the rest of Italy, and by the 1st century CE, superseded nearly every other language there—except for Greek, which continued to be spoken throughout the Magna Græcia of southern Italy. Vulgar Latin, spread by the soldiers and colonists of Rome over the different quarters of the Empire, began from the 7th century CE on to diverge into separate dialects, from which evolved the Romance languages of today: Italian, Rhætian, Provençal, French, Catalan, Spanish, Portuguese, Romanian, and Sardinian.

From the Greek point of view, the victories of Rome had led to the absurd situation where there existed two sets of world language and of world literature. After Greece was annexed by the Romans, they became more and more thoroughly bilingual. From then on, Greek literature was as much a part of the canon of the Empire as was its Latin cousin. This applied especially to everything produced at the daybreak of Common Era and thereafter, at which time no one any longer entertained the idea of an independent Greece.

Whilst the Roman culture was disseminated throughout the West, the Greek was allowed to prevail in the East. Some Roman colonies were, indeed, established there, but these too became Hellenized and finally Rome herself succumbed to the division into East and West, something which has left deep marks in all the subsequent history. In the eastern half of the Empire, knowledge of Latin was akin to a thin veneer, evaporating the minute the political supremacy of Rome vanished. As soon as the Hellenic East would obtain its own political centre in Constantinople, she was to announce the deep resentment she felt towards the barbaric Rome.

Unlike the Greek, the Roman was not hidebound to his own language and literature. Above and beyond these, he constantly sees before him the Greek masters and rivals, whose works he, after the manner of Horace, "pores over night and day,"[37] wishing he could produce "something greater than the Iliad"[38] (Propertius, of the *Æneid*). In return, the Greeks act like they were unaware of their competition; they teach themselves Latin only for practical, economic, and political, reasons, not in order to promote Roman literature. While the works of the Greek authors—starting, of course, with Homer—were incessantly translated into Latin, only few Roman authors ever received a Greek rendition. Whereas the cultured Roman was bilingual, the cultured Greek was, and would remain, unilingual.

Even though Greek historians might have referred to Rome as a "Hellenic polis," even though sympathetic—or well-compensated—Greek writers were known to praise the Hellenic forefathers of the Romans, even the most "Philhellenic" Romans stayed faithful to their maternal language even when most enthusiastically imitating the Greek models. Thus was born a literature that dared not only to imitate, but also to compete with the Greek letters. This challenge seemed even more bitter when the people cultivating this new literature had become the masters of the world.

Cæsar personally busied himself with the writing of more than just war journals, though nothing besides them is extant. In his youth, he had penned even some fiction, among other works, a panegyric to Herakles and a drama about Œdipus. He also wrote a discourse on astronomy called *De Astris*, "On the Stars"—in this field he was considered a professional, since, as Pontifex Maximus, he performed for the Roman Republic the duties which in our time belong to that scientific institution which publishes the almanac.

It was known in Rome long before Cæsar that the solar year was approximately 365 days and six hours in length. The early Roman calendar had twelve months, each of them having either 29 or 31 days—30-day months

---

[37] *nocturna versate manu, versate diurna*

[38] *Nescio quid maius nascitur Iliade*

were not used, because even numbers were considered unlucky, and because a middle day, called the *Idus* or Ides, was required in every month. The year began in March, but only had 355 days, wherefore an intercalary month was needed every other year. This was not simply added to the end of the year, but instead, the 29-day February was cut short at the end of its 23rd day, and the 25-day *mensis intercalaris* was observed thereafter. Thus the leap day is, even today, on the 24th of February and not at the end of the month.

However, the Roman calendar eventually drifted far away from the position of the seasons. The Pontifex Maximus was not always a skilful mathematician, and moreover, it often happened that he used his power for political purposes—by adding an extra leap month or by leaving a required one out, he could lengthen or shorten the term of his friends or foes as necessary. The Romans originally identified the years by the names of the reigning Consuls, but gradually people started to feel need for a fixed starting-point, from which numbering could commence; during Cæsar's pontificate, a chronology was instituted *ab urbe condita*, "from the founding of the city," something that was held to have taken place on the day which by current reckoning would be the 21st of April, 753 BCE.

During the last stormy decade of the Republic, the Roman year was counted 354 days without any kind of intercalaries, whereupon the almanac had arrived eighty days ahead of the actual date. It is easy to imagine the impact this had on the businessman, farmer, and the holidaymaker. In his office as Pontifex Maximus, Cæsar carried through his great calendar reform, the one that has his name and which, in its principal points, is still in use today. With the help of the Greek mathematician and astronomer Sosigenes, Cæsar put the Roman calendar in order. The Julian Calendar which, as we all know, prescribes 365 days to a year, and adjusts the deviation every four years, is identical to the 3rd-century BCE calendar of Aristarchus of Alexandria. It also moved the opening of the year from March to January, while retaining the old names of the months: e.g. October literally means the eighth month, even though it became the tenth after the reform.

The last six months of Cæsar's life seem to have been dedicated to colossal building projects and preparing a huge new campaign against the Parthians, to avenge their defeat of Crassus and to secure the border in that quarter. Cæsar may have realized that, after half a century of civil war, only a war against external enemies could unite the Roman people—in the words of Livy:

Externus timor, maximum concordiæ vinculum, "Fear of the foreigner [is] the chief bond of harmony." The legions assembled for this purpose garrisoned the vicinity of Rome, while others were stationed at Macedon.

Cæsar had made clear that he intended to rule the provinces through honest, supervised civil servants, not through a poor and greedy nobility. Republican tradition had enabled men of noble birth to compete for offices by climbing the political ladder, but Cæsar made this impossible. It was precisely from the ranks of the disgruntled patricians that his most bitter enemies emerged; more than sixty of Rome's most prominent men would form a conspiracy against his life.

No matter what Cæsar did, the Optimates would twist and bend it to appear tyrannical. After his timely calendar reform, on being told that Lyra would rise the next morning, Cicero said, "yes, in accordance with the edict," implying that even the movement of constellations depended on the pleasure of the great Cæsar. In him, they saw only the threat of a king—a word which was irrevocably linked with the word "tyrant" in Hellenistic history. On his return from the Latin Festival held at the Alban Mount, Cæsar rode into Rome on horseback; as he entered the Capitol, some of the plebeians actually hailed him as King. Although he rejected the title, his enemies were greatly offended by the episode.

The evening before his murder on the Ides of March, Cæsar attended an intimate supper with his friends, where he spoke prophetically about his death. The soul of the conspiracy appears to have been Gaius Cassius Longinus, a man who Cæsar respected and had pardoned after the Battle of Pharsalus. Cassius felt disregarded because, even though he was promised the governorship of Syria, he was not to receive a command in the upcoming campaign against Persia. It was he who persuaded Marcus Junius Brutus, his brother-in-law—whose greatest claim to fame lay in his descent from the Lucius Junius Brutus who had murdered the last king of Rome—to join the plot.

Like Cassius, Brutus had fought on the side of Pompey at Pharsalus, but had subsequently accepted the clemency of Cæsar. Having had an affair with Brutus' mother, Servilia, Cæsar acted as father to him, and had secured the election of both Brutus and Cassius to the high office of Prætors. Once Brutus had gotten the idea into his head, however, he became obsessed with the thought of demonstrating himself worthy of his ancestry.

Having just dismissed his bodyguard, Cæsar was detained outside Pompey's Theatre, and all others present who had sworn to protect him fled in fear of death. Cæsar himself silently took a stab after another, but when he saw Brutus holding a blade in the midst of the conspirators, he exclaimed in Greek: *Kai su, teknon*, "Even you, my child?" The Greek phrase was quoted as such even by its Latin recounter Suetonius, but thanks to Shakespeare, it has attained renown in its Latin rendition: *Et tu, Brute*, "Even you, Brutus?"

The Senators fled to different quarters of Rome, while panic and confusion spread over the city. The friends and relatives of Cæsar stayed out of sight as well as they could, and the most prominent of them, such as his first lieutenant, Marc Antony, and his most trusted general, Marcus Lepidus, dared not to remain at home. Under the cover of night, Lepidus joined his troops, who were waiting outside the city, and took a part of his army to the Martian Field. Simultaneously, Marc Antony took possession of the war-chest, which Cæsar had accumulated for the Parthian campaign. He then made contact with the Cæsar's assassins through the intermediation of Cicero, and arranged by proxies an extraordinary pre-dawn session of the Senate. Before the crowing of the cock, he had hammered out a compromise, allowing him to retain consulship while absolving the murderers from any culpability for their actions.

On the next day, Brutus addressed the people at the Forum Romanum, and they listened quietly without expressing any more disapproval than favour. From time immemorial, *regicide*, or the murder of a king, was considered justified and even honourable in both Greece and Rome, and had the approval of public opinion. The assassins imagined that the old Republican system would recover by magic, if only the tyrant was done away with; they did not in the least consider the vast army waiting by the gates of the city, against which they had not one cohort to command. They were completely blind to the reality that the rule of the Roman aristocracy was beyond recall—even the mighty Cæsar would have been incapable of overthrowing the system had its destruction not been long overdue; his assassination condemned Rome to another, much bloodier civil war, which also meant that she would never again have the manpower to conquer the fertile plains of Babylonia.

Without Cæsar, his assassins were an insignificant lot; their lives had only had meaning while Cæsar made use of them. Neither the fanatical Brutus nor the unpopular Cassius had the talent required to effect reforms or to build a new leadership. Many educated Romans mourned for Cæsar, who, despite his arrogance, had been a great general, a consummate orator, and an exceptionally erudite man, renowned for his magnanimity. The lower classes were equally fascinated by the lavish presents which were bequeathed in his last will to every Roman citizen. Yet Suetonius describes the Jews as the most assiduous mourners at Cæsar's funeral, returning for several nights in succession, lamenting "after the fashion of their country." In three months, Rome had become too hot a place for the conspirators; the houses of Brutus and Cassius were burned by a mob, and the murderers fled the city.

Cæsar's death seemed to have disturbed the order of nature itself, the unusual darkness of the sun being one of the most widely attested phenomena of this period of antiquity.[39] Some claimed to have witnessed his spirit rise from the funeral pyre in a form of an eagle ascending to heaven, but it was the appearance of a comet during the celebration in honour of Jupiter-Julius that was taken as a proof that his soul had been received into the number of the immortals. As a dead hero, Cæsar was officially deified by the Senate, an event which only a few short years earlier the Romans would have thought impossible. They had killed him because they thought he was setting himself up to be a king, and now he took his place in the court of the gods.

Gaius Octavius Thurinus, the 19-year-old son of Cæsar's niece Atia, then entered the stage. After Octavian had ascertained the contents of his great uncle's will and confirmed his adoption, he left for Brundisium, where Cæsar's veterans greeted him as the son and successor of their late commander. Octavian was now the one who gave the orders in the Senate, and occupying Rome with his legions, he had the Assembly of the People elect him Consul, against all statutes and customs, for he had not yet reached the age of twenty. As a partner in the highest office of the State, he secured his cousin, Quintus Pedius. But their position was still precarious, forcing Octavian to make peace with Antony and Lepidus. This new alliance, concluded between the three in March of 43 BCE for 5 years, beginning from the start of 42 BCE, was called the Second Triumvirate.

The three men agreed to jointly put the affairs of the empire in order, dividing its provinces and offices between themselves. Antony acquired the

---

[30] *Antiquities*, xiv. 309; *Georgics*, i. 466; *Julius Cæsar*, 69; *Natural History*, vii. 93.

Gallic provinces excluding Gallia Narbonensis, which, along with Spain, was given to Lepidus. Octavian took over Sicily, Sardinia, and Africa, and since Italy was left in the hands of the Consuls, they retained the control of her. The authority of this Triumvirate was officially affirmed by a legislative enactment of the Senate and just as tyrannical as that wielded by Cæsar.

It was dangerous to have the Republican leaders in Italy while the Triumvirs themselves were fighting in the Balkans, besides which their need for money was great. Citing the failure of Cæsar's clemency policy as justification, Octavian and Antony robbed and massacred 200 senators and 2,500 knights, "the chief factions surrendering their enemies to each other, and for this purpose not sparing either their friends or brothers, so much did animosity towards others overpower the love of the kindred." (Appian: *The Civil Wars*) Cicero, to whom Octavian was substantially indebted for his success, died valiantly. Quintus Pedius, an honourable and virtuous man, was so shocked when he saw the list that he died of shame.

Lepidus was promised a consulship for the next year. In return, he gave up one of his armies, so that Octavian and Antony could, with ten legions each, conquer back the Eastern Provinces, where the champions of liberty, Brutus and Cassius had, by robbing the towns of Asia Minor and Syria of money and men, put together a large army. Two battles were fought in the fall of 42 BCE at Philippi in Macedon where the Republicans were defeated. After the first, Cassius took his own life; after the second, Brutus followed the example. Porcia, daughter of Cato, also committed suicide, upon receiving word of her husband Brutus' death in Rome. Here ends the history of the Roman Republic.

CHAPTER 7

When the will of Cæsar was unsealed, Cleopatra, Queen of Egypt, had hoped their three-year-old son, Cæsarion, would have been proclaimed heir, and since this wish was not fulfilled, it is understandable that her feelings towards Octavian were not particularly warm. She was also accused of lending Cassius money for war, and Antony sent her strict instructions to appear in Cilicia to answer for her politics. Antony was immediately enchanted by Cleopatra, a fact that is not surprising if one believes the descriptions made about this woman by the ancient authors. At the time, Cleopatra was 28 years of age, and according to Plutarch, "in the time of life when women's beauty is most splendid, and their intellects are in full maturity." When she returned to Egypt, Antony followed her eagerly, spending few pleasurable months at the court of Alexandria amidst amusements and excesses, the nature of which Plutarch very eloquently relates.

In 41 BCE, Consul Lucius Antonius, brother of Marc Antony, joined Fulvia, the wife of Antony, in a plot to incite a revolt against Octavian in order to beguile Antony into Italy. Octavian's most trusted lieutenant, Marcus Vipsanius Agrippa, besieged their forces at the Etruscan town of Perugia, and before long, they were forced to capitulate. Octavian had a few hundred of their supporters executed, but sent the conspirators themselves unharmed to Antony. He met his banished relatives at Athens, whither they had been accompanied by a number of prominent Romans. One of these was General Ventidius Bassus, whom Antony sent to fend off the Parthians, who, under the command of another Roman exile, Quintus Labienus—son of the Titus Labienus who aided Cæsar in his conquest of Gaul—had began to conquer the Eastern Provinces.

Meanwhile, Antony allied with Sextus Pompeius, one of Pompey's sons, who had managed to subjugate southern Spain, Sardinia, and Sicily with an army and fleet composed mainly of slaves. He proceeded to besiege the coastal towns of southwestern Italy in 40 BCE, while Antony sailed for Brundisium with all of his troops. The soldiers were tired of fighting, however, and

Octavian's emissaries procured a very lucrative treaty with Antony, greatly mitigated by the rather opportune death of Fulvia in Greece. It was probably the threatening situation in the East that persuaded Antony to relinquish all his lands in the West. The treaty was sealed with the marriage of Antony and Octavia, half-sister of Octavian.

Sextus, whom the allies had abandoned, did nowise throw away his axe. During the following winter, he besieged Italy so effectively that there was a shortage of food in Rome, and the people threw stones at the Triumvirs in the Forum. They found it wisest to try and come to a settlement with Sextus, who was now asked to join the Triumvirate. In 39 BCE, the infamous meeting depicted by Shakespeare in his tragedy *Antony and Cleopatra* took place at Misenum between Antony, Octavian, and Sextus. The last mentioned was allowed to retain control of Sicily, Sardinia, Corsica, and even the Peloponnese, in return to which he would immediately withdraw his food blockade. The Triumvirate had suddenly expanded to a Quadrivirate, for Africa was still occupied by Lepidus.

But the peace stood on shallow ground: to appease Sextus, Octavian had married his sister-in-law, but the two divorced soon after the Treaty of Misenum was signed, and Octavian remarried with the famous Livia, who was kindly relinquished by her husband, Tiberius Claudius Nero. The next year, Sextus resumed hostilities, accusing Antony of deceit. In 37 BCE, Antony arrived at Tarentum with Octavia, who got her brother to conclude a fresh agreement with her husband: Antony would help Octavian at sea, where Sextus was too great a foe for him, and Octavian would in turn send a powerful army into the East to fight the Parthians. The Triumvirate was renewed for another five-year period, but Sextus was not crushed for good until the following year, when he fled with a few ships to Asia Minor, where he was captured and executed.

Most of Sextus' troops went over to the side of Lepidus, who had declared himself independent from the Triumvirate at the hour of its victory. This, however, he should not have done: accompanied by only a few men, Octavian proceeded straight to Sextus' camp and appealed to his troops, who immediately and down to the last man defected to his side—the forsaken Lepidus had to beg for mercy. He lost Africa and was confined to Italy, but got to keep his life and his high office as Pontifex Maximus, to which he had been elected after it was left vacant by the death of Cæsar.

Octavian had acquitted himself remarkably well of the dangers that came with ruling Italy, and his position grew more secure every passing minute. Antony, on the other hand, was detested in all the Eastern Provinces for his cruel taxation, which exceeded all previously practised by Roman procurators. In Judæa, Antipater and his sons had to take severe measures to exact the money, and in the ensuing riots, the King was killed. The Hasmonean pretender, Antigonus, who had been rejected by Cæsar, seized the opportunity to ally himself with Persia and to reclaim the throne of his fathers. The vast majority of the Jewish nation supported him, thus reviving the Maccabean dynasty. As a counter-measure, Antony proclaimed the son of Antipater, Herod, a half-Jewish, half-Arab Idumæan, as king.

Once Antony had routed the Parthians in Syria and was in a position to release sizeable forces for operations against Judæa, Antigonus' fate was sealed. Jerusalem fell to the legions after a five-month siege, and the last of the Maccabean kings was executed. All testimonials agree that Herod was a cruel tyrant, who managed to keep his throne by timely renouncing the man to whom he owed his position. Still, his long reign (37-4 BCE) forms, on the material level, perhaps the most glorious epoch in the history of the Jews. With his massive building projects, the establishment of a solid bureaucracy, and the development of economic resources, and the expansion of his territories, Herod the Great did much for his people.

The War against Persia had brought Antony both losses and dishonour, but he nevertheless held a triumph in Alexandria—a fact that must have greatly offended the Roman people, who missed this glorious spectacle. But it was the way he treated Octavia, a most refined Roman matron, by abandoning her for Cleopatra, that really aroused the anger of the Roman world. On one beautiful summer afternoon, the virtuous Octavia received a letter of divorce, and Octavian made sure that both the Romans and posterity would know how Antony, having forfeited his honour, lived in splendour and vice with the treacherous Queen of Egypt. The whole of Italy acknowledged Octavian as her champion against the man who had given up everything Roman and fallen into the lifestyle of a debauched Oriental despot.

The war propaganda reached its apex in early 32 BCE, when Octavian ordered the forcible retrieval of Antony's last will and testament, which was deposited with the Vestal Virgins, who naturally refused to hand it over without a struggle; it not only declared Cæsarion as Cæsar's lawful heir, but that Antony wanted to be buried in Alexandria even if he died in Rome. People began to think that if Antony were allowed to gain victory, the first city of the world would be Alexandria, instead of Rome.

Not only Italy, but all the Western Provinces were now eager supporters of Octavian's cause. On his orders, the Senate issued a declaration of war, which was officially aimed at the Queen of Egypt. Antony gathered a vast army for the imminent confrontation, and his navy was initially many times superior, but his officers soon began to flee to the enemy side in alarming numbers. As usual, Octavian had transferred the command over to Agrippa, and one of the decisive battles of world history took place on the 2nd of September, 31 BCE, when Agrippa gained a glorious naval victory at Actium on the coast of Epirus. On the 1st of August, 30 BCE, Octavian appeared in person at Alexandria.

Cleopatra, the false information of whose death had led to the suicide of her husband, Antony, attempted at first to put a spell on the victor, Octavian. He would not, however, let himself to be enthralled, and when Cleopatra realized that she would be taken to Rome as a prisoner of war and paraded in a triumph for all the Romans to see, she too took her own life[40], on the 29th of August, at the age of 39. The young Cæsarion, said to look remarkably like his father, was murdered[41] on the orders of Octavian, who had thus become the indisputable ruler of the old world. Egypt was thenceforward a province of Rome—her richest province to be sure.

Julius Cæsar had abolished the Roman Republic, which was not that hard since its foundations had been shaky for a long time. Cæsar had carried out economic reforms to solve the debt problems which had demoralized the Republic since its birth, for the interest rates tended to soar sky-high in times of war. He had the interests lowered and a quarter of all debts cancelled,

---

[40] The death she chose made a very strong statement. The venomous snake, asp, was the symbol of the power of the Egyptian Pharaohs; its bite was said to bestow eternal life on the victim. The teeth of the Egyptian cobra are as sharp as awls, and capable of envenoming up to ten people at a time. As opposed to a poison taken orally, asp's venom gets straight into the bloodstream, offering an easy, quick, and painless death. By exposing herself to the serpent's kiss, Cleopatra achieved immortality the Egyptian way, cheating not only the Romans, but almost death itself.

[41] Her remaining children were, however, spared, and her gold-plated statue stood in Rome for three hundred years.

while taking steps to bring more coins into circulation, thereby increasing liquidity. Though these precaution were taken to resolve an immediate socio-economic crisis, they laid the foundation for the amazing recovery that took place during the reign of his adopted son. Having rid himself of all rivals, Octavian continued the work begun by his beloved adoptive father, and was wise enough not to repeat the mistakes committed by Cæsar.

The world greeted him with cheers not so much because he was the victor, but because he had ended the war. Of the 56 years that had passed since the first confrontation between the Sullan and Marian parties, not many had been without war, and nearly all the quarters of the empire had had to suffer. Octavian imitated Cæsar's clemency by sparing most of his enemies, and the Senate gave him the title of *Augustus*, which in Greek—the second official language of the realm—was *Sebastôs*; it implies something akin to exalted, eminent, or majestic, and obscured the blood-stained name of Octavian in all the subsequent chronicles. The word also had religious connotations, and seemed to elevate him somewhat above the human level, giving new prestige to the man who already had the right to call himself *Cæsar Divi Filius*, the "Son of the Divine Cæsar."

Unlike Cæsar, Augustus managed to avoid any hint of an attempt to set himself up as a Hellenistic-style monarch. With Anthony defeated and the threat to Roman traditions gone, Rome could return to the noble ideals that had made her great in the days of the early Republic. Her citizens would see the return of the glorious age when they were world conquerors, subduing foreign adversaries, before corruption and greed had embroiled them in constant internal warfare. The Empire was ostensibly a continuation of the Republic, with the same constitutional offices, though Augustus actually occupied all the key positions. He was *Imperator*, the commander-in-chief, a title which referred, of course, to his military status, and was to be added to the full name of every subsequent ruler, before all the other components—the word "emperor" is derived precisely from this appellation.

To appease public opinion, Augustus adopted another title to be used in Rome, before the Senate and the people; this was *Princeps Senatus*, "the First of the Senate," an expression from which every European language derives the word "prince." At the same time, however, the right to declare war and to conclude peace was transferred from the Assembly of the People to the Emperor, along with the control of foreign policy, so that he had the power to determine the status of each and every dependent state, nation, and prince, whether they be in an imperial or a senatorial province. After Lepidus died, Augustus also assumed the office of Pontifex Maximus, highest overseer of religion—thus completing his control over all aspects of Roman public life.

Augustus took pride in his religious reforms, boasting that he had renovated all the temples in Rome, these having fallen into neglect and decay during the years of political turmoil. The most prominent new temple complex was that built in honour of Apollo on the Palatine Hill overlooking the city, recalling the Athenian Parthenon, and suggesting that Augustan Rome, like Periclean Athens, was to be a centre of art and learning. But, above all, Augustus wanted to appear as a prince of peace in a world that was weary of war. His elaborate rebuilding programme not only provided a vital boost to the Roman economy, but provided tangible signs of the return to peace and prosperity.

Everywhere the citizens were reminded of the source of their good fortune by the erection of effigies of the Emperor and arches covered with reliefs emblazoning his great deeds of valour. The Great Altar of Peace, *Ara Pacis*, erected by the Senate to celebrate the *Pax Augusta* in 13 BCE, is still partially preserved. In reality, there was no peace in all the reign of Augustus, nor did the Romans ever wage wars of conquests with more determination and sense of purpose. During the Augustan Age, the northern border of the Empire was advanced over those areas which would later form Romania, Bulgaria, Yugoslavia, Hungary, Austria, Switzerland, southern Germany, and the Netherlands.

As Imperator, Augustus had, according to an old Republican principle, the right to keep a bodyguard, albeit during the time of the Republic, the commander-in-chief had had to relinquish his guards when he arrived in Rome. Augustus developed this ancient statute further, founding the famous "Prætorian Guard," which was composed of 9,000 men quartered near the capital; its commanders, the Prefects, were among the highest government officials. After this permanent guard was further supplemented with a police force, the Emperor had within his reach a sufficient number of troops to keep the city in order.

The monthly dole of grain to the people of Rome continued just as it had in the last decades of the Republic, and in the time of Augustus, the number of recipients reached quarter of a million. The people once pleaded to the Emperor also when the prices of wine went up, but he replied by directing the thirsty to the splendid aqueducts which his associate, Agrippa, had just finished building.

As we all know, the people of Rome were not only kept in bread, but also provided with circuses. At least two theatres were built in Rome during the reign of Augustus; one is the Theatre of Marcellus, which with its renovated façade draws people even today. The other arenas have now disappeared, for example the artificial lake that Augustus constructed on the banks of the Tiber in order to arrange naval battles; the water there was drained through a pipeline built expressly for the purpose, and there once competed on the reservoir thirty great warships and a number of smaller vessels, manned by 3,000 gladiators in all. Trained more elaborately than the legionaries, successful gladiators of the Græco-Roman world made as pretty a penny as the professional football players of today's North America; news of their battles spread by word of mouth, boys idolized them, and women were known to have affairs with them.

Still, the claim to fame of the Augustan Age rests largely on its literature. Augustus realized how steady a buttress literature could be for the new form of government. The name of Mæcenas, a great statesman and, at a time, a trusted minister of Augustus, has become synonymous with a patron of arts. He was immensely rich, and kept his house on the Esquiline Hill open to gifted and learned men. Vergil, Horace, and Varius, among many others, profited from his generosity.

As a contrast to Cæsar, who had been internationally inclined and had little appreciation for the typically Roman, Augustus believed in the value and vitality of Roman traditions, thus inaugurating the "Classical period" of Latin literature. All the letters that were older than the late Republic acquired the reputation of being old-fashioned and clumsy. Hardly any of the earlier writers were born Roman, and although the Romans rather indiscriminately imitated Greek literature of all periods and were in their personal level of education closer to the Alexandrians, they nevertheless soon got accustomed to regarding the Periclean literature alone as exemplary.

These traditions dominated, slightly modified, the whole of the Imperial period. All the Roman poets, even Quintus Horatius Flaccus (65-8 BCE), who had fought against Augustus at Philippi, yearned for peace to wash away the bloodstains of the Civil Wars; all felt the necessity of moral and religious rebirth, and awaited a golden age with confidence. During his final years in particular, Horace did his part to promote the patriotic reconstruction, and this semi-official poetry is his most consummate. The *Secular Hymn*, which Horace was commissioned to compose for the famous centenary of 17 BCE, is perhaps the most successful poem of occasion ever written. The festival, attended by the highest officials of the Empire, was supposed to herald the coming of a new and a happier age and the conclusion of the old, gloomy and turbulent era. As Pontifex Maximus, Augustus was able to challenge the validity of the almanac, according to which that year was nowhere near the turn of the Roman century.

It is well known that Augustus also left some much deeper marks in the calendar. Even as he restored Cæsar's Julian Calendar, which during the war years had fallen slightly into disarray, he had the Senate take a day out of February and insert it into the month of Sextilis. The reason was fairly human: Julius Cæsar had lent his name to July, which had thirty-one days. The next month was supposed to be named after Augustus[42], but according to the original Julian Calendar, it had only thirty days—which simply would not do. Thus August got its thirty-first day, while February shrank to just twenty-eight days.

The foremost name among the Classics was that of Publius Vergilius Maro (70-19 BCE), a highly admired and respected man even during his own lifetime—it thus fell upon him to write the eulogy of the age. We could say that Vergil began that already in his *Georgics*, a pæan well fitting the new agricultural policy. He had earlier imitated the pastorals of Theocritus in his *Eclogues*, but the former work reveals his originality, even though the motif itself was derived from Hesiod. It was "factual poetry," full of details pertaining to everyday life, but had a radiance which only Vergil could give to everything he wrote. He was himself a provincial in the sense that he preferred to live in the farm that he had been allocated by Augustus as a compensation for the losses suffered in the great sequestration of landed property.

Gratitude does partly explain the adoration Vergil expressed towards Augustus as the Saviour of the Fatherland. Yet long before, in 40 BCE, he had foretold in his fourth eclogue the coming of such a deliver in words that in the Middle Ages were considered a prophecy about the birth of Christ. Vergil's

---

[42] Augustus was actually born in September; August was selected by him to celebrate his defeat of Cleopatra that month.

reputation as a seer was, however, born already in antiquity, and there were people only few decades after his death who believed the future could be foreseen by opening any of his works at random. In mediæval folklore, Vergil held the status of a mighty magician and his name—connected to the word *virga*, signifying a magic wand—was surrounded with extensive legends.

Nevertheless, Vergil did not honour his benefactor in a way a slave or an opportunist would have. Everything points to the fact that his own thoughts were perfectly compatible with those of Augustus: both men were convinced that the nation's salvation lay in rekindled patriotism and in a return to the old Roman simplicity and a strong government. If we bear in mind this like-mindedness, it is easier for us to understand how Vergil, unlike most government-sponsored authors, has managed to produce great poetry.

The writing of the *Georgics*, which comprised, as it were, the aspect of the question relating to domestic policy, was presumably encouraged by Mæcenas; according to tradition, Augustus himself commissioned Vergil to write the *Æneid*—its object was nothing less than defining the world political purpose of Rome. This was expressed in the famous words: "Yours be the care, O Rome, to subdue the whole world for your empire! These be the arts for you—the order of peace to establish, them that are vanquished to spare, and them that are haughty to humble!"

Still, heroism can hardly be deemed the strongest feature in this epic that recounts how Æneas, son of Venus, founded the Roman empire. The Julians traced their ancestry back to the goddess, so this was a rather unsubtle reminder of Augustus' divine lineage. The form of the poem is Homeric, but the spirit is Vergil's own—and he was more of a dreamer than a man of action. The turbulent scenes are cloaked in a veil of melancholy, subtlety, and delicacy, pointing forward to finer forms of the chivalric ideal.

The *Æneid* formed the basis for Vergil's immense reputation and has, in all ages except our own, been considered his greatest work. He wrote this epic for eleven years, yet it remained unfinished on his passing. On his death-bed, he ordered the manuscript to be burned, but Augustus decreed his order to be discarded, and chose three learned men to edit the work. They were not to change or add anything, but instead, they could leave out all that which they considered half-finished.

All through the Middle Ages, the poems of Vergil served as a nearly universal source of knowledge, and until the 18th century, he was seen as the greatest poet of the ancient times, greater even than Homer. He became above all a classic, and there are still those who regard him greater than all the rest. All his poems have been used diligently as textbooks throughout the centuries, and have thus left quite a few marks in modern languages. It is exceedingly difficult to find anything that would surpass his verses. He knew how to embrace the abundant linguistic and poetical potentialities that Latin had acquired over the years, when he portrayed, with refined alliterations and assonances, the most diverse sense impressions, from the distant roar of waves hitting the cliffs, through the hoofbeat of a galloping horse, to the silence of the night.

Publius Ovidius Naso (43 BCE-18 CE), the third great poet of the Augustan Era, was not a part of Mæcenas' circle. He was at least twenty years younger than the famous *mecenate*, and when he had achieved the peak of his reputation, both Vergil and Horace had already passed away. His most enduring and best deserved claim to fame was his *Metamorphoseon*, a compilation of exquisitely retold fables of antiquity. The "Metamorphoses" was of an immense importance to the literature and art of later generations, for it is primarily through this work that the legends and myths of antiquity were conveyed to the Christian West.

Ovid's credits include the theatrically and musically so workable tale of Orpheus and Eurydice, and he has lent material for Shakespeare's *Midsummer Night's Dream* and for numerous other less lasting dramas of mythological theme. The compilation of metamorphoses ends—not counting the brief epilogue in which the poet predicts that his work will live for ever—with a poem that relates how Julius Cæsar was transformed into a comet and how he and the other gods look approvingly at his son and successor, Augustus.

In his own lifetime, Ovid would quickly become a *persona non grata* in Rome. The reason for this depreciation seems to have been his promiscuous lifestyle, which so poorly fit the reconstruction programme. He was a celebrated figure in those aristocratic circles that gathered around Julia, the daughter of the Emperor. These circles did not hold the old Roman virtues in too much respect, and the poems with which Ovid gained their affection were undoubtedly quite frivolous. This incurred the wrath of Augustus, who had him exiled to Tomis, a remote outpost on the shores of the Black Sea, where he died a decade later.

Posterity has, on the contrary, regarded Ovid worthy of the greatest respect; the Middle Ages, in particular, were his heyday. Despite its rather cynical matter-of-factness, his *Ars Amatoria*, "Art of Love," which expertly and elegantly disentangles the science of seduction, became a guide for countless number of troubadours and minnesingers. Since this work artfully merges sexual immorality with literary finesse, it is deemed questionable even by most of its modern readers. In the Middle Ages, it was rendered four times into the French tongue, and in the catalogue of manuscripts, its author appeared above even Vergil himself.

There is no sign that Cæsar ever considered in earnest the great rebuilding dilemmas which Augustus was to solve so triumphantly. His extensive use of the famous white Carrara marble for public monuments was merely a part of the larger plan to make Imperial Rome an equal of 5th-century BCE Athens—he could justly boast that he received a city of brick and left a city of marble. The architects describe an abundance of the forums, market halls, baths, theatres, and mausoleums of his time, many of which are preserved to this day. Not that the imperial construction industry was confined to the capital: Augustus systematically organized the road network, which gave occasion to the still-enduring adage that all roads lead to Rome.

The Roman roads were built on a base of gravel which was cemented over and then covered with slabs of stone. The roads were 12 feet wide and enclosed by fences on either side. There were stables and guard houses at regular intervals to protect the travellers from marauders. Stations and roadhouses were established on the roadsides. The improved communications served primarily the interests of Rome, but during peace and under a decent government, the provinces also flourished like never before.

Romans needed straight and level roads on which to drive their chariots, allowing them to travel a hundred miles in a day. Caravans, on the other hand, had no wheels: goods were packed on the backs of camels, which walked along the roadside, utilizing the roads themselves only as landmarks. But the earlier private looting came to an end, and the administrators sent to the provinces were no longer autocrats by any means. The Roman legions were stationed at the imperial provinces, which were administered by imperial overseers, who held the simple title of either Prefect or Procurator. In each province, there was established an imperial treasury, or a *fiscus*, whence the modern terms *fiscal* and *confiscate*.

Egypt was a land that fell under the personal control of the Emperor. Augustus was the king of Egypt and the ruler of the Roman Empire, and his Egyptian title was far more valuable than emperorship, if not as impressive. He gave an edict that no high-ranking Roman could visit his kingdom without his express permission—seemingly to protect the nobles from Oriental corruption, but also to ensure that no one could covertly gain control of the Empire's grain supply and thus bring him to his knees. The revenues from Egypt were his personally, and managed by his agents. The grain tax was the Emperor's gift to his Roman clients, the plebeians.

Knowing Alexandria's reputation for unrest, Augustus founded a new city, Nicopolis, to the east, and stationed a large garrison there. At the same time, he installed a Prefect, abolished the city council, and stripped the Ptolemaic magistrates of all power, thereby forming a class of wealthy aristocrats living a life of leisure, relieved from any further duties. Besides the Greeks, the Jews—though not citizens—accounted for a significant part of the Alexandrian population, living in their own quarter, and originally exempt from many of the taxes; under Augustus, their ethnarch gave way to the re-established Sanhedrin, for which Herod the Great erected a new building in Jerusalem.

King Herod's crowning achievement, however, was a magnificent new port, which was called Cæsarea in honour of the Emperor; dedicated in 9 BCE, it was built to rival Alexandria in the trade with Arabia, from where spices, perfume, and incense were imported. A masterpiece of Roman engineering, its piers were made from hydraulic concrete, and protected by unique wave-breaking structures; it was not an Oriental town like Jerusalem, but laid out on a Greek grid plan, with a forum, an aqueduct, government offices, villas, baths, a circus, and pagan temples.

The death of Herod would be a signal for an insurrection which was finally put down by the Roman governor of Syria. In his last will and testament, Herod had divided his dominions between his three sons: the principal heir was Archelaus, who was appointed ruler of Judæa and Samaria. In 6 CE, after ten years of misrule, Augustus deposed him, and put a Procurator in his stead, thus transforming Judæa and Samaria into Roman provinces. Galilee and Peræa were allowed to remain royally-ruled vassal states, having for their king another of Herod's sons, Antipas.

In 14 CE, Augustus himself died at an old age and at the height of his reputation. Even though the relations between Augustus and his stepson, Tiberius[43], had never been warm, the latter was early on elected the former's successor, and already had a long experience as a general and a statesman when he took over the reins of the Empire. In fact, he was a 54-year-old man, who had seen all and done all, and scarcely thirsted any longer for either power or for great deeds. To the provincial governors who wanted to raise the taxes, Tiberius addressed the following words of wisdom: *Boni pastoris est tondere pecus, non deglubere,* "A good shepherd shears his flock, not skins it."

The Roman procurators of Judæa were subalterns of the Syrian governors, resided in Cæsarea, and went to Jerusalem only on special occasions. They commanded the military, maintained the peace, took care of the revenue, and generally refrained from meddling with the religious affairs—especially for fear of arousing the outrage of the Zealots, who regarded the payment of tribute to the Emperor as unlawful. The local government was left largely in the hands of the Sadducean priestly aristocracy, while the Sanhedrin in Jerusalem remained the supreme court of justice, with jurisdiction over Jews even in foreign cities.

In every region except Palestine, Jews were representatives of the principal intelligentsia, cut loose from the ties of agriculture. Alexandria, valuable as it was as the granary of the Empire, was also a thriving centre of trade between the East and the West. This cosmopolitan city drew Egyptians, Greeks, Romans, and Jews into a unique, if not entirely harmonious co-existence. The Alexandrian Library was an ideal place for scholars from these different cultures to meet and exchange ideas, being a repository for the literature and lore of the Alexandrian intelligentsia and of the Roman Empire in general. The Museum flourished not only during the Hellenistic era of the Ptolemies, but through the ceaseless turbulence of the Empire's most volatile and valuable city.

In Alexandria, Greek philosophy and Oriental mysticism were combined in a peculiar manner, and the Egyptian capital was a nursery for many of the Gnostic doctrines that spread to the Roman Empire. A remarkable dialogue developed between pagan, Judaic, and later, Christian thought, as religious thinking was refined and ideas were adapted not only from the other faiths common in Alexandria, but from the Zoroasterism of Persia, and even

---

[43] His full name was Tiberius Claudius Nero, like his father's.

Hinduism and Buddhism from India, which after the conquests of Alexander had come to a much livelier intercourse with the Mediterranean region. It was in Alexandria that the fusion of Greek philosophy and Jewish theology took place and found its greatest representative in Philo Judæus (30 BCE-45 CE), who through his allegorical interpretation of the Bible established a view of literature that knew no bounds.

Throughout the Empire, Jews endeavoured to treat the country of their residence as their homeland, by taking part in the pertinent pursuits and responsibilities. "So populous are the Jews," says Philo, "that no one country can hold them, and therefore they settle in very many of the most prosperous countries in Europe and Asia both in the islands and on the mainland, and while they hold the Holy City where stands the sacred Temple of the most high God to be their mother city, yet those which are their by inheritance from their fathers, grandfathers, and ancestors even farther back, are in each case accounted by them to be their fatherland in which they were born and reared." Philo was a Jew of the Dispersion, and observed the *mitzvot*, yet like many cosmopolitan Alexandrians of his time, worshipped the Greek divinities as well.

Yahweh had originally resembled the other deities common in ancient days. Never had he been particularly kindly a god. When we first encounter him, he is already, as the tribal god of the Hebrews, a mighty and sole god, and not merely a member of a group of gods competing with one another. Still, he is only the god of the Hebrews—the other tribes were presumed to have other divinities. Yahweh was a jealous god who did not want his people to adopt any of the other tribes' deities. Among the most unattractive sections of the Bible are those which relate his lengthy and triumphant struggle to defend himself and his people against the enticements of rival gods and goddesses.

Monotheism, as we have seen, was not the property of the Jews alone, but of much of Greek philosophy. Ancient thought had arrived at a single ultimate deity that had once created and now governed the universe. The Greeks, equipped with the powerful philosophy of Plato, and later of Aristotle, believed this Godhead to be inherently "unknowable." It was beyond human understanding, and any attempt to describe it could only end in failure. Since no form of contact with the material universe was considered appropriate, or indeed, possible, the idea arose that any relationship between the Ultimate Deity and the world would have to take place through some form of intermediary. The Greek solution was the Logos, an emanation of the Godhead, through whom it acted upon the world.

Yahweh, however, was totally different, being easily accessible and constantly busying himself with the particulars of everyday Jewish life. He could be experienced and explained in traditional human terms: hope, fear, jealously, and of course, vengeance. Whenever the Israelites needed a victory on the battlefield against their enemies, *Elohim Tzabaoth*, the "Lord of Hosts," was always there to assist his people and to plan the strategy with them. He was the very opposite of the philosophical construct of the Greek Unknowable; he walked the earth, conversed with Abraham, wrestled with Jacob, and appeared momentarily yet quite physically in all his glory before Moses on Mount Sinai. The god of the Hebrews was never far way, and could be reached just by calling out to him.

Believing the two worlds not to be irreconcilable, Philo introduced the concept of the Logos as an allegorical force of Yahweh. Philo's work bridged the chasm between Yahwism and the Greek idea of the Godhead. He postulated an *ousia*, a singular essence of God, which is the unknowable, and an *energeia* (Gr. energy), which could interact with and touch the lives of mortals. The Logos was the mediator who made it possible to realize the eternal energy of God, and therefore by extension, the essence of the Deity itself. Philo's doctrine became extremely popular among Jews and Gentiles alike, splitting the Godhead successfully into multiple personifications that pagan worshippers would later refine further from the trinitarian concept which is familiar to us today.

CHAPTER 8

Until the reign (37-41 CE) of Gaius Cæsar, otherwise known as Caligula, the Jews enjoyed, without any serious interruption, the universal tolerance which Rome extended to the religions of all her subject states. He began his career by throwing parties and organizing shows, which brought a great joy to all the people, for Tiberius had always been quite stingy in that respect. Caligula's favourite entertainment was the circus; he built a great racing track in the cove between the two hills of the Vatican, on the exact spot where St. Peter's Church now stands. In the centre of this arena he erected a gigantic stone obelisk, which he had with great trouble transported from Egypt, in a huge ship built expressly for this purpose. Caligula managed to quickly dispose of all the funds his predecessor had accumulated, and had to proceed with generating new income, which put an abrupt end to his popularity.

In the ancient chronicles, Caligula appears as a detestable monster, who committed every sort of mischief even when he had nothing to gain financially. His favourite phrase was allegedly borrowed from the tragedy-wright Accius: *Oderint, dum metuant*, "Let them hate me, so long as they fear me." Many modern scholars believe that he was an effective ruler, and probably not guilty of all the excesses attributed to him. However, his demands for the acknowledgement of his divinity were the most preposterous known in Roman history until the accession of Heliogabalus a couple of centuries later.

Everyone living within the borders of the Empire had the right to worship their own deities. The only form of religious service common to all was the cult of the Emperor's *Genius*, his guardian spirit. Caligula decreed that his effigy was to be erected, along with the emblems of Jupiter, to all places of worship, including synagogues. The Jews, of course, refused to erect or venerate any such images. The tensions and riots were recorded by Philo—along with his own participation as an envoy to Rome in 38 CE—in his *Delegation to Gaius* and *On Flaccus*, the latter referring to Caligula's replacement for the previous Alexandrian prefect.

Philo's eloquent plea before Caligula was in vain: Alexandria was once again embroiled in civil unrest; this time the extensive riots between the Greek and Jewish residents, an old Alexandrian problem, were precipitated by Caligula's appointment of Herod Agrippa—a debtor to many Alexandrian money-lenders—as King of Judæa. When the foreign minority at Jamnia set up an altar to the Emperor, the Jews of the city, unwilling to tolerate idolatry on the soil of Judæa, destroyed the shrine. Aghast, Caligula ordered Petronius, the Roman governor of Syria, to use violence, if necessary, to erect an enormous golden image in the Temple of Jerusalem itself. As rumours of the imperial edict spread, an open revolt seemed imminent. An appeal to the Emperor by Agrippa led to the toning down of the edict, but it was ultimately the assassination of Caligula that prevented the outbreak of a Jewish-Roman War.

With the accession of Claudius[44], Caligula's uncle and the last surviving member of the House of Cæsar, a brighter day dawned for the Romans and Jews alike. He owed his imperial dignity largely to the efforts of Agrippa, and out of gratitude, conferred upon him the whole kingdom of Herod the Great. The number of annual public holidays was increased to a staggering 159, in addition to which the Jews were allowed freely to observe their own festivals and the Sabbath. Claudius also sorted out the state finances by transforming the tax collection department into a fixed organization; the Imperial Treasury was upgraded into a state bank of sorts, which, among other things, lent money in return for interest.

At home and abroad, the Jews enjoyed valuable privileges. They had everywhere the right of residence and could not be expelled. (A notable exception was the expulsion of the Jews from Rome when they rioted on the instigation of Chrestus, but this was only for a short duration.) All Jewish communities had their synagogues or *proseuchai*, which also served as libraries and places of assembly, and numbered in the thousands—the most famous being that in Antioch. The Sanhedrin, now under the presidency of Gamliel the Elder, St. Paul's teacher, had greater authority than ever before. The Jews alone, in the sphere of the vast Empire, were exempt from bowing down to the image of the Emperor.

---

[44] Tiberius Claudius Nero Cæsar Drusus, born Tiberius Claudius Drusus Nero Germanicus

Another token of the freedom enjoyed by the Jews throughout the Roman Empire was their active proselytism. A plethora of Jewish miracle workers, healers, and magicians roamed the streets of Rome. Jewish wonder working was world-renowned—only the Egyptians were held in higher regard for their miracle and healing powers. Any itinerant rabbi worth his salt would have a full repertoire of miracles to perform among the crowds he encountered. In the Hellenistic world, just like in the Jewish one, miracles were not only possible, but everyday, and expected from prophets and holy men.

While the Sadducean and Pharisean religious parties competed for power in Judæa, the Messianic and apocalyptic ideas that gained expression in the Book of Daniel spread through the Jewish congregations to every corner of the Empire. Since the Babylonian Captivity, the Jews as a nation had looked for deliverance from a long succession of conquerors, from Cyrus the Great through Alexander to Julius Cæsar, until many had become convinced that only violent divine intervention could bring about their promised elevation "high above all nations of the earth." This view was entertained by a myriad of sectarian groups—each regarding itself as the elect—flourishing on the fringes of mainline Judaism. Christianity was one of these sects, driven by the conviction that the Kingdom of God was at hand. Within a few years of Jesus' supposed death, Christian communities were found all over the eastern Mediterranean, their founders unknown.

Palestine was the trunk-road between Asia and Africa, Babylonia and Egypt; the Mediterranean, the sea that washes its beaches, is fittingly so called, for it is the waterway that joins the West with the East. Due to the busy intercourse between the countries of the Mediterranean, it had long been impossible to maintain national peculiarities, the prerequisite of which is relative isolation. The language and literature of the Hellenes had spread over the entire region; Hellenistic Greek was also the common tongue of Jews outside Palestine at the time when it was used as an international language throughout the Empire. The only borders known to the Greek literature were the borders of the known world, *oikoumene*—it was world literature.

The leading authors of this world literature were often Greek only in name and in language, but this did not prevent them from adopting the self-important and patronizing attitude of the Greeks towards "barbarians." When St. Paul, a Jew of the Dispersion and a citizen of Rome, writes in Greek to the church of Corinth about the gift of tongues, he states as a self-evident fact:

"Therefore if I know not the meaning of the voice, I shall be unto him that speaketh a barbarian, and he that speaketh shall be a barbarian unto me." An immense paradox has thus become reality: the most exclusive world literature has become the most universal; the barbarians have become Hellenes, and are proud of their "Hellenism," considering it a matter of honour to imitate the old Greek masters more closely than their Greek contemporaries do.

Paul dedicated all his energy to expanding the early Church into a cosmopolitan body. In that day, the first step towards catholicism, that is to say, universalism, would naturally take place through Græcism. The Greek of Paul's letters is stylish, grammatical, and erudite, something which is made even more remarkable by the fact that Hebrew thought, Hebrew language forms, and Hebrew word-play can be discerned behind much of what they have to say. But Paul was also familiar with the religious and philosophical ideas of Greece, and soon after his conversion to Christianity, he planted himself against the Jewish wing of this new religion, his work as an organizer of the new sect winning him the title: "Apostle of the Gentiles."

Paul promoted the propagation of Christianity precisely by paving the road from Jewish sectarism to a universal religion. Prior to their contact with pagan philosophy, the Hebrews had been a tribe of bigots: no one who did not adhere to their narrow creed could live in their midst; no Gentile was considered worthy of Yahweh's interest. Paul saw the social inadequacy of their sectarian beliefs, and drew the logical conclusion from the fall of Zion and the flight of Israel—the Jews were not the sole concern of the Almighty. While Yahweh remained their god, He now became also the God of all mankind; thanks to Paul, it was now possible to become a Christian without having a circumcision.

As long as the Romans could not separate the Christians from the Jews, the Christians too were exempt from conscription and from paying tribute to the guardian spirit of the Emperor. However, as the number of Christians grew, it became painfully obvious that they were something entirely distinct from Jews. However, the Christians had inherited from their Judaic springhead that hard and fast spirit, which they managed to retain through their crucial years of growth, and which was of great advantage to them.

Public acts of worship were an integral part of the ancient political systems. The Christians were merely requested to give up their fundamental intolerance towards the gods and symbols of the State, and to demonstrate civic solidarity in its established forms. They were widely denounced as atheists, not in the least because of their lack of participation in public sacrifices and their abstinence from meat—at least such meat as was commonly sold in that day, namely meat from the temple abattoirs. Since they eschew sacrifice and tended to keep mostly to themselves, the Christians were also considered possible traitors to the State.

It is noteworthy that all the other religions were willing to compromise when it came to the adoration of the Emperor's *Genius*. The adherents of other faiths, who were not familiar with the Mosaic code, could do this freely, just as they honoured the sacred scriptures of one other. The Magi, coming from King Tiridates of Armenia, would worship in Emperor Nero[45] (r. 54-68) an emanation of Mithra, and at the same time as the Christians were persecuted, Mithraism was popular within the ranks of Rome's mighty army.

The Christians, a few private individuals, were not persecuted for believing in a different god; the position the Roman authorities adopted towards Christianity was a question entirely of internal policy, and not in the least a religious issue: Græco-Roman society was built on the subordination of the individual to the community, of the citizen to the State; it set the security of the commonwealth above that of the individual, be it in this world or the next.

The State kept a watchful eye on the antisocial and subversive Christians, who refused to bear arms for the common defence; who answered when asked to perform their military duty: "We cannot, for our Master has said: 'He who takes up the sword will perish by the sword.' We cannot fight for your earthly emperors." The martyr and the hermit, contemptuous of Earth and enraptured by contemplation of Heaven, was in the Christian opinion the highest ideal of humanity, displacing the old Roman ideal of the hero and patriot who, oblivious of self, lives and is prepared to die for the good of the country.

During the early years of his reign, Nero lowered the taxes, subsidized the poorer Senators, gave many entertainments of different kind, acted as a conscientious judge, promulgated a new fire safety act, began building a channel through the Isthmus of Corinth, and persecuted the "new and mischievous superstition" of the Christians—thus proclaims Suetonius in his

---

[45] Nero Claudius Cæsar Augustus Germanicus, born Lucius Domitius Ahenobarbus

summary of the good deeds of Nero as a contrast to all his crimes and malice.

The Christian movement was both widespread and diverse, uncoordinated and competitive, expressing a wide variety of doctrine within the broad religious inspiration of the age. To a certain extent, persecution is apt to consolidate the persecuted group in a purely mundane fashion; persecution binds the persecuted firmly together, creating an ever more efficient and disciplined whole. Paul set as a condition for salvation the membership in that church which he ruled over sovereignly. Whenever the pressure abated, various sectarian phenomena invariably sprang up.

Little is known about Simon Magus or the Simonians, and most of the information we do have is from their enemies, and as such, assuredly distorted. He is simultaneously described as a pagan, a Jew, a Christian, and a founder of a new religion of his own; a philosopher, a magician, a necromancer, and an arch-heretic; a false Apostle, a false Messiah, and a false incarnation of God—the "Father of All Heresies." He was born in the Samaritan village of Gitta, to parents named Antonius and Rachel. He was educated in Greek learning at Alexandria, later becoming a disciple of John the Baptist[46], whom he eventually succeeded.

While teaching at the great Phœnician city of Tyre, Simon beheld a prostitute on the roof of a brothel. Her name was Helena, but Simon recognized her immediately as the present incarnation of the primordial *Ennoia*, the "First Thought," the "Mother of All," the "Holy Spirit." She was the lost sheep, forced by her progeny, the angels, to wander through the centuries from vessel to vessel—including that of Helen of Troy. Simon purchased Helena from her master, and she became his constant companion during his travels and teachings. Their reunion was supposed to represent the dissolution of this world the angels had made and served as the model for the process of salvation to the Simonians.

Simon's miracle working and charisma enabled him and his disciples to establish a number of churches along the Palestinian-Syrian coast from Cæsarea to Antioch. Before long, however, Simon lost his churches to the more successful St. Peter, who followed in his footsteps. According to one rather dubious legend, Simon finally ended up in Rome and was defeated by the Apostle in magical combat. When Simon flew into the air to demonstrate

---

[46] some say Dositheus, a disciple of John the Baptist

his power to Emperor Nero, Peter cancelled his spell and sent him tumbling to the ground. A more plausible account has him dying peacefully among his flock in Antioch.

The Acts of the Apostles (8:9-24) portray Simon as attempting to purchase spiritual gifts from Sts. Peter and John—hence the term "simony." There is, however, strong evidence to suggest that this particular account was modified from a story about Paul, originally written by the early Petrine Christians. After the Petrines were finally reconciled with the Paulines, the references to Paul were changed to Simon, who no longer had the chance to defend himself.

In the tenth year of Nero's reign, half of Rome burned down; the fire raged for nine months, and many thousand were left homeless and destitute. The conflagration was apparently a misfortune, one of many that befell ancient Rome; but the people of the city were infuriated by the rumour that it was Nero himself who had started the fire in order to enjoy the spectacle. His younger contemporary, Publius Cornelius Tacitus, the historian, has written down a famous account of the things that followed: he says that to make that rumour disappear, Nero started persecuting the people who were infamous for their abominations and called Christians, accusing and executing them in various, calculated ways.

First, those were arrested who confessed, and then, on the strength of their testimony, a great multitude, who were accused of crimes against humanity, though not of burning the city. Even though these were wrong-doers who should be punished, Tacitus tells that people felt sorry for them, because "it was not, as it seemed, for the public good, but to glut one man's cruelty, that they were being destroyed." Unfortunately, he mentions nothing of Apostles Peter and Paul, who, according to Church tradition, fell victims to Nero's persecution.

Rome was rebuilt under a new building code which required greater fire-proofing. This necessitated the use of concrete, which was not only fire-resistant, but cheaper and much stronger than stone, especially when big open rooms had to be bridged. Because of the high quality mortar, Roman concrete construction allowed for ambitious building forms, regardless of the final facing hiding the underlying structure.[47] By adding vaults to the concrete

---

[47] Our words "cement" and "mortar" are derived from the Latin *cæmentum* and *mortarium*, respectively.

arches, the Romans could build high domes, which appeared for the first time in the Golden House of Nero, erected on a huge expropriated plot of fire-ravaged land near the Forum. Here the play of corvex and concave form, solids and voids, finally came into its own, to be rediscovered by Baroque architects in the 17th century.

The seven Roman procurators who ruled Judæa from 44 to 66 CE acted as though they were purposely trying to drive its population to revolt. Their objectives were to collect tribute, enrich themselves, and make sure that complaints about their inept administration did not reach the Emperor. The harsh taxation and the presence of a foreign army on Judæan soil were degrading enough, but what really aroused the ire of the Jews was the support given by the procurators to the Greek and Syrian population of the province. Rome usually governed the dependencies through her maintenance of the native aristocracy, but in Judæa, she found a ruling class based on the priesthood, not wealth. Consequently, the Romans chose instead as their partners in government the few wealthy landowners of the country, who were mostly foreign and detested the Jews.

The Pharisean party was content to ignore the Romans, but the Zealots, a splinter group of the Pharisees, wished to see them banished. They aimed to establish the Kingdom of Heaven on Earth—a kingdom ruled by God, not man. So, despite the precautionary efforts of King Agrippa II, the Zealots burst into an open rebellion in 66 CE, driving the Roman troops out from Jerusalem. In 67, Nero's best general, Vespasian[48], was put in charge of three legions in Judæa. He began suppressing the revolt by taking Galilee, the main Zealot centre, a task which took him an entire year to accomplish.

The Galileans had for their commander a moderate Pharisee named Josephus, who defended the mountain fortress of Jotapata with bravery and cunning, despite the fact that he had opposed the uprising. When the Romans took him a prisoner, he was immediately put in chains, but saved his life by playing the part of a prophet to Vespasian, predicting that the general would become Emperor. On the third year of the war, Vespasian finally made his approach to Jerusalem, where the remaining Jewish troops had sought shelter after most of their country was occupied. He was just about to mount a siege,

---

[48] Titus Flavius Vespasianus, later Cæsar Vespanianus Augustus

when news of Nero's suicide suddenly gave him something else to think about.

At the death of Nero, the highest leadership of the Empire fell into the hands of the military. According to Tacitus, it was a major discovery when the corps realized that emperors could be made elsewhere than at Rome. First, the governor of Hispania Terraconensis, Galba, was proclaimed Emperor by his soldiers. The army of the Rhine then chose Aulus Vitellius, the governor of Lower Germany, in his stead, but Otho, the governor of Lusitania, had already deposed Galba. The legions of Syria and Judæa now got involved in the dispute and proclaimed Vespasian as the true Emperor. The initiative, however, came from the Prefect of Egypt, Tiberius Julius Alexander, an Alexandrian Jew and a relative of Philo's. The prophesy of Josephus was thus fulfilled and Vespasian designated him his freedman, giving him an abundance of gifts, which Josephus acknowledged by adopting the Emperor's family name, Flavius.

Meanwhile, Jerusalem was devastated by a bloody civil war between three groups of Zealots, several Messianic claimants, and a multitude of Idumæans. The Roman siege of the Holy City was carried through by Vespasian's son, Titus[49], in 70 CE. Histories of the Jews written by Christians before the 20th century ended here. According to Josephus, the burning down of the Temple took place against Titus' will. Still, tens of thousands had been killed in battle, and tens of thousands more had been taken captive; male captives were, for the most part, killed, and the rest of the unhappy population was sold into slavery and scattered over all parts of the Empire.

The city was torn down to the ground, its soil ploughed over. Large areas of land were confiscated by the Roman State and used to settle newcomers, though many of the Jews remained as tenants on land that had previously owned. Taxation was heavy—particularly the tax for the temple of Jupiter Capitolinus, the principal god of the Empire. Despite all this, Judaism continued to attract converts—by the thousands. At the prayer of Yochanan ben Zacchai, Vespasian spared Jamnia, where the Rabbi was allowed to organize a new Sanhedrin, composed not of priests and politicians, but of the teachers of the Law.

Titus, the conqueror of Jerusalem, became almost a co-ruler with his father. The chief leaders of the revolt, a long train of chained captives, the

---

[49] also Titus Flavius Vespasianus

sacred vessels of the Temple, its seven-branched candelabrum, the golden shew-bread table, the purple curtains of the Inner Sanctum, and a roll of the Law, graced Titus' triumphal procession in the Imperial City. He brought with him a Jewish princess, whom he had fallen in love with and whom he intended to marry. She was Berenice, Agrippa I's daughter, whose fate inspired the famous tragedy by Racine. The Romans were vehemently opposed to the marriage, and Titus gradually realized that he had to send her back—*invitus invitam invisit*, as Suetonius puts it: to reluctantly dismiss the reluctant.

Coins were struck to commemorate the hard-earned victory, and the temple of Janus was closed as a sign of peace for the sixth time in the history of Rome. Yet three Jewish fortresses in Palestine still held out: Herodium, Machærus, and Masada. The first two fell in 71 CE, and the Roman procurator of Judæa, Flavius Silva, marched with the feared Tenth Legion (*Legio X Fretensis*) against the third the following year. Masada was, and is, an immense, mesa-shaped, over nine-hectare-wide hill of rocks in the Judæan Desert near the Dead Sea. Shortly before the beginning of the Common Era, the hill was converted into a fortress on the orders of Herod the Great.

The Romans finished a six-foot-thick siege wall in 73, built in order that no one remaining in the fortress could escape their vengeance. Masada was doomed; its fall was only a matter of time. The Sicarii, the most extreme of the Zealots, who had taken refuge in the fortress, made an shocking decision. They would rather commit a mass suicide than subject themselves to the slavery of Rome.

Orthodox Judaism upholds the idea of dying, or allowing oneself to be killed, for a just cause[50], but not suicide. The mass suicides at Masada, Gamala, and other strongholds rested on the uniquely Zealot concept of resurrection, a concept derived primarily from Prophets Daniel and Ezekiel: "Behold, O my people, I will . . . cause you to come up out of your graves, and bring you into the land of Israel. An ye shall know that I am the Lord, when I have opened your graves. . . And shall put my spirit in you, and ye shall live. . ." (Ezek. 37:12-14)

The death of these Jewish martyrs was related by Josephus. The Zealot leader, Eleazar ben Yair, delivered a speech to his troops, after which the married men killed their families. Those who remained alive, tossed a coin to

---

[50] cf. II Macc. 7

select the ten men who would slay the rest of the garrison. These ten chose by lot the one who would kill the nine others. He would then kill himself by falling on his sword. When the Romans stormed the walls, they found only corpses. Of the 976 Jews that had manned the fortress, only seven—two women and five children—were left to tell the tale. They had been hiding in a cistern, and the Romans were so moved when they found them that they spared their lives.

The story has long been doubted, since its only source is Josephus, who was nowhere near the scene of battle, but far away in Rome, where he wrote in Greek about the Jewish War and the antiquities of the Jews. In the archæological excavations that were made nearly two millennia later (1963-65), evidence was found, in the form of pot shards with the full name of Eleazar and the nicknames of others, supporting Josephus' account of the drawing of lots. However, while Josephus says 969 people perished at Masada, archæologists have located the skeletons of only twenty-five.

Vespasian and Titus exercised a suspicious vigilance over the Jews of the Empire. The regiments of auxiliary troops, composed of men from Samaria and Cæsarea, whose conduct had been largely responsible for the unrest, were removed from Judæa. The Tenth Legion occupied the ruins of Jerusalem in order to prevent its reconstruction by its former inhabitants, and to do away with all possible pretenders to the Jewish Throne or to the Messianic dignity. Masada became a symbol and an epic of national independence for the Jews, and is today a sacred spot in Israel. The recruits of the Israel Defense Forces swear in their oath of allegiance that: "Masada shall not fall again."

Vespasian greatly valued the booty acquired from the Judæan campaign, for he was known for his keen financial sense. He helped the Roman economy to its feet, and was instrumental in making trade and commerce flourish. He boosted employment in Rome by devising an extensive building programme, which crossed out all the expensive proposals and stopped the construction at the Golden House of Nero. In place of the palace garden, where an artificial salt-water lake was supposed to be dug, he erected the Amphitheatrum Flavium, commonly known as the Colosseum and counted among the Seven Wonders of the World.

On the 23rd of June, 79 CE, Vespasian died of natural causes at Reate, the ancient capital of the Sabines, where he was also born. Titus, the first Emperor to be the natural son of an Emperor, enjoys an immensely good reputation in the Roman annals. Suetonius dubs him *amor et deliciæ generis humani*, the "darling and delight of the human race," and says that he was handsome, dignified, graceful, and uncommonly strong. He was a skilled warrior, familiar with music and poetry, writing excellent verses himself and playing the zither exceptionally well. It is true that he also had a number of people assassinated, but Suetonius is careful to produce just causes and apologies for all these acts. Apparently, Titus' constant occupation was to do good deeds. One day at dinner, upon realizing he had not granted clemency to anyone or pleased the Romans with any beneficial act, he proclaimed: *Amici, diem perdidi*, "Friends, I have lost a day!"

Titus was succeeded by his younger brother, Domitian[51], after having reigned for only two years. Although Domitian took pride in being a patron of literature, especially of poetry, and even regarded himself as a poet, he had a bitter quarrel with the Stoics and other philosophers. Due to his constant shortage of funds, the tax of two drachmas established by his father for the temple of Jupiter Capitolinus was collected from the Jews with the utmost rigour. He persecuted those who tried to hide their ancestry and did not want to pay, which, according to Church tradition, cost the life of John the Evangelist far away in Ephesus. Yet, Domitian was in his own way a religious man, for contrary to his predecessors, he inflicted a severe punishment on those Vestals who had broken their vow of chastity.

Rightfully judged, the facts show that the reign of Domitian was beneficial to the Empire. He strengthened the defences at the Rhine and at the Danube, where Rome faced her most formidable enemies. Some ominous names of barbarian tribes now emerged at the forefront of history: the greatest threat was posed by the Marcomanni and the Daci, who occupied present-day Hungary and Romania, respectively, and were bribed to peace by Domitian.

Despite all their flaws, the Flavian Emperors were to be sorely missed by the people of the provinces. Culture and prosperity spread quickly in the border provinces during their reign, and their despotic cruelty, as rotten as it was, affected only a small portion of the population in the capital. Only by reading history backwards and putting too much emphasis on the critique of the day, can the Rome of the first Christian century be called a "sin-infested,

---

[51] Titus Flavius Domitianus

dying world." Rather, it had its best years ahead of it, years of stabilization, peace, and despite all the set-backs, increasing humaneness.

A provincial from Celtic Spain, Marcus Valerius Martialis (c. 40-104) came to the capital in his mid-twenties, befriending a wide variety of men and women, from emperors to slaves.[52] In his 1,500 satirical epigrams, Martial offers candid depictions of real life as he saw it, revealing the Rome of the Flavians in all its vice, bashfulness, hypocrisy, sensitivity, and absurdity. A singularly non-judgmental observer, he found even the ugly aspects of his surroundings filled with excitement and humour. The only things he deemed deserving of his scorn were sham and imposture: he was the first to use the term "plagiarism," calling those who perpetrated literary theft by the Latin word *plagiarius*, "plunderer."[53]

In 96, Domitian was assassinated by a conspiracy that included some of his closest servants and officers of the Prætorian Guard. As with the death of Tiberius, the Senate dreamed for a moment about the return of the Republic, but the rest of the world knew it to be a fantasy. The Senators consoled themselves by officially cursing the memory of the late Emperor, as a contrast to the deification of Augustus, Claudius, Vespasian, and Titus. They would choose an Emperor who was partial to the so-called "liberty," that is, wished to rule wisely by taking the Senate into fair consideration.

The new sovereign was one Marcus Cocceius Nerva, an aged and well-known Senator. Although his hands were tied by the lack of state funds left by Domitian, Nerva managed to carry out certain beneficial reforms. There was an acute need for cultivators of land in many parts of Italy, and Nerva laid out a plan to transfer peasants to these areas. To stimulate the birth-rate of the Italians, he instituted the important system of *alimenta*, which assigned funds to support the poorer parents, and was eventually extended to the provinces. Nerva, who was distrusted by the soldiers, many of whom suspected him of complicity in Domitian's murder, wisely adopted as his son and heir a tried and famous general, Marcus Ulpius Trajanus.

Trajan was the first Emperor whose immediate ancestry was not Italian, so

---

[52] It should be noted that, in many cases, Roman slaves were more refined and better educated than their masters, often serving as teachers or scribes. What is more, they could not only amass money (*peculium*) and property —including slaves of their own—but purchase their freedom.

[53] *Epigrammaton*, i. 52. 9

his election marked a significant departure from the old custom. He was a native of the Spanish Italica, and spent most of his time on the frontiers, maintaining and expanding the borders of the Empire. During his reign (98-117), Rome reached its greatest areal extent, stretching from the Persian Gulf to the southern borders of Scotland. Trajan restored and extended the ancient Appian Way, the first and foremost of the Roman consular roads, along with several other, lesser-known routes. In all, 50,000 miles of first-rate highway connected the diverse parts of the Empire, in addition to which municipal roads—250,000 miles in all—branched off to fortresses, legionary camps, small towns, villages, ports, and signal stations.

The main roads were used, apart from administrative and military purposes, to carry the mail, the delivery of which Augustus had organized, and for all the overland commercial and passenger traffic. The road network of Rome was so efficiently planned and the roads so well built, that it remained serviceable for almost 2,000 years—it was the most expedient method of land transport until the coming of the railway. In Britain, many Roman roads are still in use, as are the Roman-built roads and stone-bridges in central and southern Europe and Asia Minor.

During the reigns of the "Five Good Emperors," from 96 to 180 CE, peace prevailed on an wider area of land than ever before or since in all of Western history. Thanks to better storage techniques and a new harbour, Rome became less dependent on Egyptian grain, and Trajan even shipped Roman corn to Alexandria to relieve a famine. The civilian residents of Rome, who in the time of Trajan enjoyed peace and happiness, honoured him with the title of *Optimus*, "the Best." His reputation for goodness endured throughout the ages, for the subsequent emperors were officially called to become more fortunate than Augustus, and better than Trajan—*felicior Augusto, melior Trajano*.[54] In the Middle Ages, a legend circulated that God had brought Trajan back to life just so that he could convert to Christianity.

The Roman citizens who practised a different religion considered the Christians as anarchists and atheists, who showed no tolerance, but blasphemed that which was held sacred by the others. In is clear that the riots where martyrs were created were brought about not by the authorities, but by the pious followers of another religion. The early Christians made a habit of

---

[54] *Breviarium ab Urbe Condita*, viii. 5

adopting infants abandoned in public places, which seemed to support the common slander that they were sacrificing babies to their god, even if this act of charity was at worse intended to increase their number.[55] Before long, every disappearance of children left unattended in the marketplace was routinely attributed to Christians, and runaways were thought to be their victims. The odd madman who actually did kill a child was often called a Christian by the public, and some fallen pagans may even have emulated the common view of what the "wicked Christians do."

The standpoint of the Roman authorities is known through the famous letter that Trajan wrote to Pliny the Younger: Christians are not to be searched for, stated the Emperor, but should they be denounced, they are obligated to show civic responsibility by paying homage, like all good citizens, to the gods of the State, and only if they refuse to do this, are they to be punished. Anonymous information was disregarded and only the verifiably Christian received a punishment, which usually meant either penal servitude or banishment to a remote area. This law remained unmodified through many subsequent generations, while the Christians were building a global organization and becoming more and more audacious and great in number.

Only on exceptional occasions did catacombs serve for ordinary Christian worship even during the times of persecution. They were used solely for funeral services and for the feasts of martyrs. In the early days of Christianity, there were no buildings specially consecrated to divine service; the assemblies for worship were still held in private houses at the end of the 2nd Christian century and even later. *Ecclesia*, the Latin name for the Christian Church, was derived from the Greek term *Ekklesia*, signifying the political assembly of people at Athens. Early on, people like St. Ignatius of Antioch (c. 40-107) would try to organize and control these assemblies. He in particular invented the episcopal idea—bishops apart from laity. If we include St. Peter, Ignatius would have been the third Bishop of Antioch and the immediate successor of Evodius, receiving his episcopal consecration from the Apostles themselves.

In 114, a far-reaching conflict erupted with the Parthians, the age-old enemies of Rome, providing Trajan with glorious victories and turning

---

[55] Much later, Julian the Apostate (*Epistles*, xxii) would criticize the Christians for keeping their charity to themselves against the old Stoic tradition of philanthropy based on the brotherhood of man.

Armenia and Mesopotamia into Roman provinces. However, the great cities of Edessa and Nisibis, along with Seleucia, that noble outpost of Hellenism, revolted and were subdued only with great difficulty. After the failure of the assault which Trajan led personally against the mighty fortress of Hatra, news arrived of Jewish uprisings in lands far apart from one another. Even as the Roman legions were withdrawn to fight Persia, the Jews in the East took arms again against the Greeks of their cities. The agitation spread from Mesopotamia to Judæa, Cyprus, and Cyrene, bringing with it much bloodshed on the side of both the authorities and the rebels. In 116, Alexandria followed suit, starting yet another ethnic and religious clash fuelled by the grievances of the Judæan refugees.

Ill health forced Trajan to leave the Parthian campaign in the hands of others, and he expired on his long journey home. His ward and appointed successor, Publius Ælius Hadrianus (r. 117-138), had gone through similar career as a Roman Senator, serving with distinction as a legionary tribune, as a legionary commander, and finally as a provincial governor. Yet the two men were as different as night and day: Hadrian's first acts as Emperor were to abandon all the untenable conquests of Trajan beyond Euphrates and to conclude peace with the Parthians.

There is no major historian for his reign, but the anonymous author of the *Historia Augusta* informs us that Hadrian was a good soldier, who imposed strict discipline also upon himself; he could walk twenty Roman leagues (*mille passus*, 1.5 kilometres, from which derives the English "mile," 1,609 metres) in full gear. He also had an incredible memory: in no time at all, he would learn the names of all the new people who were constantly introduced to him, and after just a quick read, he knew every new book by rote. Every single detail of the state budget was known to him better than most of us know our personal finances. And even though Hadrian, like Trajan, was born in Spain, he had a better command of Greek than Latin, and was a prolific penman in both languages. He had a personal opinion on every possible question, and liked to debate with men of learning.

Science has never, not even during the "Golden Age of Rome," much fascinated the emperors or the Senate. Roman life was ruled by the practical wisdom that built roads, bridges, and amphitheatres, but did not concern itself with mathematics or the investigation of natural phenomena. Most of the thinkers of the Roman era were either of Greek or Egyptian extraction.

Elected archon while he was still a private citizen, Hadrian beautified Athens and restored many of the ancient poleis. During the Emperor's visit to Alexandria in 130, he restored the city, founded a new library in the temple of Augustus, and engaged in philosophical discussion at the Museum.[56]

As Hadrian considered himself especially familiar with astrology, he must have amused himself with the company of the great Alexandrian astronomer and geographer, Claudius Ptolemæus (c. 90-168). This man has lent his name to the Ptolemaic model of the universe, which was based on his own observations and on the earlier conclusions of the Greek Hipparchus, and can, with certain caveats, be regarded as one of the first truly scientific theories. Since the Greeks believed the perfect form of motion to be a circle, Ptolemy had the planets run on circles, or on circles running in turn on other circles. The Moon obviously revolves around the Earth, and it seemed just as obvious to Ptolemy that so did the Sun and the planets. It was a beautiful and workable theory, an article of faith for Muslims and Christians alike throughout the Middle Ages, but like so many other good theories, it was wrong.

Normally, an emperor would have made war and conquered new lands to make his mark and win the admiration back home, but most of Hadrian's reign elapsed in extensive tours of inspection, the purpose of which was to make the administration more efficient. In all quarters, mementoes were left of his broad-mindedness. He visited all the armies of the Empire to ensure that they were well-trained and disciplined, winning their favour by his interest in their welfare and in the correction of abuses. As a result of his 122 trip to Britain, a "Roman Wall," impressive remains of which remain standing to this day, was erected between Solway and Tyne, representing the northernmost expansion of the Empire.[57] In the British countryside, away from the towns, with their metalled, properly drained streets, their forums, baths, and amphitheatres, stood the great villas, many of which were occupied by native Britons who had acquired land and adopted Roman culture and customs. While little affected by Rome physically, the common people of this far-away island nevertheless

---

[56] Hadrian's visit was repeated seven decades later by Septimius Severus—known as a fierce enemy of the Christians—who rebuilt parts of the city, and at long last, re-established the Senate of Alexandria, abolished by Augustus.

[57] The frontiers of the empire had previously been formed mostly by natural boundaries such as a sea, a river, or a desert.

enjoyed the *Pax Romana*, with peace, communications, and markets like never before.

During the reign of Hadrian, peace prevailed on all the borders of the Empire; the only truly serious military operations he had to undertake were directed at the Palestinian Jews towards the end of his reign. After the revolts of 115-117, the Roman government was forced to take several anti-Jewish measures, including the prohibition of the circumcision of boys who had not yet reached the age to consent with the barbaric operation. At this conjuncture, it was announced that the Messiah had just appeared or, as the *Historia Augusta* puts it, "the Jews started a war because they were forbidden to mutilate their genitals."

Rabbi Aqiba, the most learned Sanhedrist of the day and the official religious leader of the Jews, acknowledged the claims of the new king. His name, Bar Kochba, "Son of the Star," appeared to fulfill the Mosaic prophecy that "there shall come a Star out of Jacob" (Num. 24:17). Roman coins of Titus and Vespasian, which celebrated their victory over Judæa, were overstruck with the palæo-Hebrew[58] legend "Eleazer the Priest," suggesting that a new high priest had been elected. Jewish warriors from all countries flocked around the "Prince of Israel," and for a duration of two years (132-134), Rome had no say in Jerusalem.

Hadrian's best general, Julius Severus, was recalled from his prestigious post as the governor of Britain, to command three Roman legions and seventeen auxiliary units. To starve the rebels and their sympathizers into submission, a policy of scorched earth was effected: fields were bared, trees uprooted, towns sacked, and houses burned down. The rebel strongholds fell one after another, and in the summer of 135, the fortress of Bethar, the last refuge of Bar Kochba, was captured and razed to the ground; its defenders never surrendered, but died of famine and thirst. The Romans, too, had suffered heavy casualties—so heavy, in fact, that in his report to the Senate, the Emperor omitted the traditional formula: "I and my army are well."

The 3rd-century Greek historian Dio Cassius tells of a land turned into a bleak wilderness, of jackals and wolves howling in the streets of the city. He records the destruction of fifty fortresses and 985 villages, and the slaying of

---

[58] a script from the 4th century BCE, which most Jews even then could not read

580,000 men. Many of the fugitives who escaped death fled to Arabia, which is how the country obtained its Jewish population—the rest were sold into slavery. To annihilate for ever any hope of the restoration of a Jewish kingdom, a pagan shrine was founded on the site of Jerusalem and settled by a colony of foreigners. The new city received the name of Ælia Capitolina in honour of Jupiter, and no Jew was allowed to even approach its environs.

Aqiba was seized and executed for violating this edict, as were at least nine other rabbis, but most fled to Persian Babylonia.[59] Judaism became decentralized and stopped seeking converts; the local synagogues became the new centres of Jewish life, as authority shifted from the centralized priesthood to local scholars and teachers, giving rise to Rabbinical Judaism. The Christians, on the other hand, were now fully distinguished from the Jews and permitted to establish themselves within the walls of Ælia, which became the seat of a flourishing bishopric.

The hands-on administration of Hadrian had so offended the Senators, that Antoninus[60] managed only with great difficulty to persuade them into deifying his adoptive father, earning him the name of Pius. The year 139 saw the dedication of the great mausoleum of Hadrian, where his ashes were deposited. This massive round structure on the right bank of the Tiber is the famous castle of Sant' Angelo, better known from mediæval history of Rome. The only Roman Emperor not to be vilified by enemies, Antoninus continued, in every respect, the traditions of his predecessors, and nothing of note took place during his reign.

---

[59] In fact, the Babylonian Diaspora retained its predominance for nearly two thousand years from the 6th century BCE to the 13th century CE.

[60] Titus Aurelius Fulvius Boionius Arrius Antoninus

CHAPTER 9

During the 2nd century, the Christian faith started to climb the social ladder: it rose from a religion of the slaves and the poor to a religion of the middle classes. Since Jesus had been thoroughly rejected by the Jews, virtually all the Christian Apologists were born pagan and became Christian after reading the Jewish scriptures. Based in cosmopolitan centres of the Empire, they were men who presented and justified the new faith to a largely hostile outside world. They gained much success by merging together Hellenistic Judaism and Platonic philosophy, which educated Romans neither could nor would forsake. There was none of the early Christians' focus on the Messiah or the end of the world; the Apologists' views of salvation were rooted in Greek mysticism, not in Jewish martyrology for sin.

In his search for truth, St. Justin Martyr (d. c. 167), the most prominent of the Apologists, studied all the popular philosophies of his day: Stoicism, Aristotelianism, and neo-Pythagoreanism. Finally, he was instructed in Middle Platonism, the most influential school of thinking which coloured everything else during that era, especially in its heavily religious concerns on the nature of the Deity and its relationship to humanity. Impressed by the devotion of Christian martyrs, Justin was eventually converted to their faith by an old Christian, who taught him about the Hebrew prophets. According to Justin, Christianity fulfilled the highest aspirations of Greek philosophy and was, therefore, the "true philosophy."[61]

Observing co-ownership, the early Christians dedicated some of their common meals—the *Agapes* or Love Feasts—to the memory of Christ. There are, however, no known Last Supper scenes in catacomb or sarcophagus art. In fact, the two-part sequence of eating and drinking, of breaking bread and then pouring a libation before drinking wine, summarizes the entire process of a Græco-Roman formal meal. In Paul's letter to the Corinthians, the Christian eucharist is still found in the midst of a real meal, but by the end of the 1st

---

[61] *sola philosophia tuta atque utilis*

century, the meal aspect was becoming less and less common.

The Christian authors of the 2nd century increasingly refer to the body and blood of Jesus Christ, the Greek for "Yeshua the Messiah"—Yeshua itself being a Hebrew name that means "saviour."[62] In the earliest instances, this reference appears to suggest kinship with Rabbi Yeshua, rather than a ritual consumption of symbolic flesh and blood under the guise of bread and wine. But fairly soon this ceremony was transformed into an actual sacrament, the continuously renewable, miraculous participation in the life of Christ—the same kind of participation we have already encountered in connection with the Greek mystery religions, which were much more widely spread, and often practised by Christian family members.

As one religion of salvation among many, Christianity had to fight fiercely for its position, and its tenets were decisively affected by what its rivals had to offer. Throughout every region where new Christian communities were flourishing, local church leaders caved in to public pressure, beginning to incorporate popular customs and festivals into ecclesiastical doctrine. The pagan elements attached to Christ were so close to the cult of Dionysos that Justin found himself apologizing for the similarities. The two were frequently confused with each other, and people often accused the Christians of *omophagia*, a practice commonly associated with the Dionysians. Justin would ask: "have you also believed concerning us, that we eat men; and that after the feast, having extinguished the lights, we engage in promiscuous concubinage?"

A wide variety of competing movements developed around Christianity, Judaism, and the Greek schools of philosophy, which were later declared heresies by the victors. The most significant of these various doctrines was Gnosticism, which evidently preceded the establishment of orthodox beliefs and churches in whole areas like Syria and Egypt. With Asia Minor, these formed a sort of a Hellenic America, where hundreds of flourishing Greek cities had sprung into existence, and where energies crippled in the impoverished homeland were given limitless opportunities to display themselves; not only had these colonies surpassed the mother country in material wealth, but they also cultivated intellectual interests. The Gnostics

---

[62] Consequently, the word "Saviour" (or *Soter*) was not adopted as an epithet of Jesus until Christianity had spread more widely through the Hellenistic world; the early Greek-speaking brethren called him *Kyrios*, "Master."

were, for the most part, representatives of the Græco-Roman intelligentsia; in fact, Gnostic Christianity claimed to be the only true Christianity, unfit for the profane, and set apart for the wise.

Although the educated had been thoroughly skeptical during the time of Julius Cæsar, they began to gradually move towards religiousness in the 2nd century. Even philosophy, Stoicism and Platonism, became more and more religious, while paganism exhibited a clear tendency towards monotheism. Serving first as co-Emperor with Antoninus Pius, the well-known philosopher Marcus Aurelius—whose diaristic thoughts were, typically enough, written down in Greek, and remain devotional texts of humanists to this day—became the sole Emperor upon the death of his adoptive father in 161. Six years later, he wrote the *Meditations*, the last work of Classical Stoicism, in which he expressed, in passing, his view of the Christians, which was not favourable. He says that he took objection to their lack of manners and to their theatrical behaviour at the face of death. In spite of his strong distaste for violence, the Emperor ordered the persecution of Christians in Vienna and Lyons for a brief period in 177; many Christians, including Justin, were killed during his reign.

Martyr's fate was sought after, incited, and encouraged. Never was there a shortage of those who would die in the name of their faith. Legends circulating in the form of letters and narratives added to the glory of the martyrs. The only branch of Christianity that cared not for martyrdom but actually ridiculed it, was Gnosticism. To the Gnostics, the testimony of blood was mere worship of the body, and as such, beneath their fully-realized spirit. Incidentally, the first anti-Gnostic writer was St. Justin Martyr, who wrote the treatise *Peri Anastaseos*, "On the Resurrection."

Before the 2nd century BCE, Judaism had developed a concept of the righteous dead rising to participate in the Kingdom of God to be established on Earth—bodily resurrection was therefore a prerequisite. But while Jews had always been this-world oriented and had little conception of a heavenly afterlife, the Hellenes were very different: they had absolutely no desire to be resurrected in the flesh, an idea which they found totally repugnant; for them, salvation after death was a question of freeing oneself from the bondage of matter and rejoining the divine as pure spirit.

The Roman philosopher Celsus, a vicious 2nd-century opponent of Christianity, said the doctrine of resurrection of the flesh to be "so repulsive that there is opposition to it even among Jews and Christians. . . the soul may have everlasting life, but corpses ought to be thrown away as worse than dung." The Gnostics of the early Christian period did not believe in last judgement and therefore neither in a "New Jerusalem" descending from the heavens. They taught that God's Kingdom is already within us and around us, if we just open our eyes and see.

The group of Christians which fought it way through countless heresies to become the Eastern Orthodox and Roman Catholic Churches, retained and secured its unity precisely because it had to struggle with these heresies and make compromises with them. It is without question that the Universal Church gained strength from the heresies she subdued. For example, the purpose of the Second Epistle of Peter was to dispute Gnostic libertinism, which taught the "freedom of the flesh" and mocked the orthodox hope of Christ's swift return. It was attributed to the Apostle, though it was written during the mid-2nd century at the earliest; Origen (185-254) was the first known Christian writer to mention it.[63]

The Gnostics possessed no central authority for either doctrine or discipline. Some of them functioned inside Jewish-Christian and mainline Christian groups, greatly influencing their beliefs from within, while others formed separate communities; but considered as a while, Gnosticism had not organization similar to that of the Universal Church. The Gnostic teachers were essentially individualists, who produced their own philosophical and speculative works without having to subscribe to any fixed set of beliefs. This naturally led to the formation of several different schools of Gnosticism, each with its own points of emphasis.

The obvious connection between all the schools of Gnosticism was the shared emphasis on the redemptive power of *Gnosis*, or knowledge. The Gnostics believed that evil forces have trapped our immortal souls in a mortal body, and that we keep reincarnating until we discover the hidden knowledge that will release us from the circle of rebirth. This knowledge is not acquired

---

[63] The First Petrine Epistle was in turn written in Rome—not in Babylon as claimed in verse 5:13—to the Christians in the Roman province of Asia Minor, i.e. to Paul's former mission. It contains exhortations to fortify the religious life and is aimed at catechumens. As its actual author is named Silvanus, a long-time associate of Paul. Promulgating it in the name of Peter was connected with the efforts of the Roman congregation at end of the 1st century to reinforce orthodoxy through epistles that represented the apostolic tradition.

from books or teachers, but through divine revelation. So even when they operated within a framework imposed by tradition and hierarchy, the Gnostics were seldom just the blind followers of some other prophet's revelation, but rather active seekers of their own prophetic visions.

The Syrian School represents the oldest phase of Gnosticism, since western Asia was the birthplace of the movement. Syria was also an important home to Christianity, its centre being Antioch, where Sts. Peter, Paul, and Barnabas established the first Christian community—the very word "Christian" was invented there. Born in Antioch, Basilides the Gnostic is said to have received a secret tradition from Glaucias, an interpreter of St. Peter. He may have studied philosophy in Alexandria with Valentinus, the other great thinker of the Hellenistic or Alexandrian School of Gnosticism, who himself had apparently been educated by Theodas, a pupil of St. Paul. Both moved to Rome during the reign of Pope Hyginus (c. 136-140), where the former preached a form of Christian Gnosticism that would have attained even greater popularity, had he not demonstrated that open disdain towards priesthood and authority which has been characteristic to Gnostics throughout the ages. When the latter was not elected pope after the end of St. Hyginus' reign, he abandoned the mainline Christian community of Rome, developing his own branch of Christian Gnosticism, which refined and elaborated the Basilidean system.

At Alexandria, the great Greek ecclesiastical writers, several of whom were born there, also pursued their studies with pagan rhetoricians. They set up their own schools, teaching Christian doctrine in the manner of pagan philosophers of the time. This development was facilitated by the allegorical interpretation of scripture, already employed for a long time by the Alexandrian Jews. The method was perfected by Clement of Alexandria (born Titus Flavius Clemens), the head of the Cathechetical School[64] from 199 to 202, and especially by Origen (or Origenes Adamantius), who succeeded him in 203, at the age of 18. The firm position that Platonism secured especially in Eastern Christendom was largely due to this versatile and broad-minded, though controversial ecclesiastic. Origen was the first systematic theologian, the most important extant statement of this being his *Peri Archon*, "On First Principles."

---

[64] Gr. *Didascaleion*

The "Christian philosophy" preached the monotheistic worship of the God of the Hebrew scriptures, a deity that was praised as superior to his pagan counterparts. It placed high value on a mode of life founded on Judaic ethics—something again praised as superior to the ethical philosophy of the pagans. At the same time, however, it used ideas from Greek philosophy to elucidate the Christian doctrine; it derived from Platonism the concept of the Logos, a force active in the world and serving as an intermediary between God and humanity. In theory, impersonal, immanent, and blindly evolving in the world, the Logos became—transfigured by both the pagan Soter cult and Alexandrian Judaism—so near to personification, that the Apologists could assert once and for all that the Word was made flesh in Jesus Christ.

Clement's three main works (*Protreptikos*, *Paidagogos*, and the unfinished *Stromateis*) were all directed at knowing and practising a moral, Christian life, in order that we might prepare for our ascent to God, the creator of all things. Clement only indirectly combatted Gnosticism by championing the "true" Christian Gnosis, which he esteemed above the belief of rank-and-file Christians.[65] He held the true Gnostics in higher regard because they had access to a sacred knowledge concerning the Word of God. Clement thus united knowledge with the act of faith, insisting that both are necessary for understanding how to live in accordance with God's will.

The Gnostic Basilides was succeeded by his son Isidorus, who founded on his teachings a church that never spread so widely as that of Valentinus, which proved a serious competitor to the Catholic Christianity in the 2nd and 3rd centuries CE. We learn from Clement that there were two main schools of Valentinianism: the Western school was represented by Ptolemæus and Heracleon, the Eastern by Theodotus and Marcus.

Ptolemæus is mostly noted for his letter to Flora[66], a noble lady who had written to him as Prom Presbyter to explain the meaning of the Hebrew Bible. Clement considers Heracleon the most eminent teacher of the Valentinian school, and while Origen devotes no work exclusively to the refutation of Gnosticism, a large part of his commentary on John is devoted to combatting Heracleon's commentary on the same Evangelist. In the East, the local worship left its mark more on the practice of the Gnostics than on their

---

[65] *Stromateis*, v. 11

[66] preserved verbatim by St. Epiphanius of Salamis (*Panarion*, xxxiii. 3-7)

theories; some modern scholars believe the liturgical system of the Catholic Church to be based on the Valentinian ritual systems developed by Theodotus and Marcus.

Theodotus is known only from the fragment of his writings preserved by Clement of Alexandria. Marcus the Conjuror's Egyptian system is outlined by his great orthodox contemporary, St. Irenæus of Lyons, in his five-volume anti-Gnostic work, *Elegchos kai Anatrope tes Psudonymou Gnoseus* (c.180-192), commonly known as "Against the Heresies," but this account was repudiated by the Marcosians. Besides his chief work, Bishop Irenæus wrote an open letter to a Roman presbyter named Florinus[67], who contemplated joining the Valentinians. When Florinus did apostatize, and became a Gnostic, Irenæus wrote an epistle to the Pope[68], imploring him to use his authority against the poor cleric.

However, the Gnostic Christians themselves had developed an astonishing literary activity, producing a quantity of texts far surpassing the contemporary output of orthodox literature. It is estimated that no less than three-fourths of the early Christians narratives about Jesus and his disciples emanated from Gnostic circles; Irenæus sneered that they were capable of producing a new gospel every day. Besides these, they penned both psalms and odes, and commentaries on other gospels, the bulk of which is unfortunately no longer extant; with the exception of a few Coptic translations and a number of Catholicized Syriac versions, only fragments remain of what must have once formed a large library.

When St. Paul and others mention the "Scriptures" they mean the Old Testament books, which the early Christians recited at their religious assemblies. Instead of regarding these as a prelude to Christianity, they believed that the Jewish scriptures spoke about Christ, not merely prophetically, but in types and allegories which the Holy Spirit revealed to the Christians. As for the New Testament, there was no notion of a canon yet; both oral and written form were considered authoritative, and were known to the early Christians as "tradition" or *paradosis*—the Greek word comes from the verb meaning "to deliver." Not only are there rabbinical parallels to the

---

[67] cited by St. Eusebius of Cæsarea (*Hist. Ecc.* v. 20)

[68] St. Victor I

early Christian preference for oral tradition, but Philo himself thought oral tradition to be superior to scripture; the oral accounts obviously change with the narrator, thereby averting the dogmatic assertion of a truth greater than the individual.

There were many different gospels in circulation, each based on the particular community's own oral tradition. These were copied by a scribe, line for line and word for word, in a very expensive and time-consuming process. During the first centuries of the Common Era, most Christians could not afford a copy of a gospel themselves, and those communities which could afford one used only a single gospel that they read aloud to one another on the Sabbath. By no means had any of these gospels met with universal acclaim; Irenæus was the first Church Father to quote the canonical Gospels, and used these quotes against the Gnostics.

By the end of the 2nd century there must have been close to forty gospels in existence, but early Church Fathers like Irenæus argued for the acceptance of just four. Many other bishops and elders disagreed, each preferring his own oral and written tradition.[69] It was still quite unclear which of the various forms of Christianity flourishing at the time had the best grounds to claim legitimacy, and the first fixed collection of New Testament books was in fact made by a heretic, Marcion of Sinope, around 150 CE. He had a gift for organizing unparalleled in the early Church. In Italy, Egypt, Syria, Palestine, Asia Minor, and even Persia, exquisitely organized Marcionite communities sprang up, complete with their own bishops and the rest of the ecclesiastical hierarchy, having similar worship and service as those of what later became the Universal Church.

Marcion wanted documents that had preserved the truth in a pure form, which ruled out the oral gospel since the sayings could not be confirmed and were therefore questionable. Besides, he was convinced that the disciples had completely misunderstood their master, and that Paul alone had understood Jesus. Yet only ten of the thirteen Epistles traditionally ascribed to Paul were included in Marcion's canon, and even parts of them were rejected as later interpolations by the conciliators of the Petro-Pauline controversy. The Gospel of Marcion itself was presumably a collection of sayings used among

---

[69] As late 451 CE, Theodoret of Cyrus said that there were at least 200 different gospels circulating in his own small diocese.

the Pauline churches of the day, though the later Patristic writers claim that Marcion merely mutilated the Gospel of Luke, the "follower of Paul." It is exceedingly difficult to believe that, if he indeed did do this, so keen a critic as Marcion would have retained certain verses which conflicted with his strong anti-Judaic views.[70] He felt that uniting the gospel of Christ with the Old Testament religion, was in direct contrast to, and a recession from the truth.

Marcion's criticism of the Old Testament was the same as that offered in modern times: how can one reconcile the conflict between the jealous, vengeful, and capricious God of the Hebrew scriptures with the God of love, forgiveness, and grace whom one meets in the New Testament, mainly in the Pauline Epistles? Most Christians today reject the horrible sayings and acts ascribed to God in many Old Testament documents, but Marcion actually demonstrated the contradictions between the Hebrew scriptures and the gospel in a massive work, the *Antitheses*. Orthodox Christian writers were from then on especially concerned to show the necessity of the Old Testament and explain the reasons for their God's apparent bloodthirst.

Marcion was no doubt aware of the criticism from the contemporary pagans like Celsus, who had demonstrated the gospels to be self-contradictory, and this may have influenced his decision to rely on one only. Another very popular heretic and a disciple of Justin Martyr, Tatian the Syrian, introduced the *Diatessaron*, a "harmony" that smoothed out the discrepancies in the four canonical Gospels and combined them into one in a chronological order using the Gospel of John as a framework. In his only extant work, *Address to the Greeks* (c. 160), Tatian says: "We do not act as fools, O Greeks, nor utter tales, when we announce that God was born in the form of man. I call on you who reproach us to compare your mythical accounts with our narrations." He then goes on to describe some of the countless Hellenic myths about gods who came to Earth, underwent suffering and ultimately death, for the benefaction of mankind—"But these things we have put forth only for argument's sake; for it is not allowable even to compare our notion of God with those who are wallowing in matter and mud."

Orthodoxy would not declare for any party in a while, and the Syrian Church used the *Diatessaron* as its sole gospel until the 5th century, but in the

---

[70] It should be noted that he only subtracted, and never added to the texts he accepted.

end, it was Irenæus' views that won. Around 180 CE, the Saint compiled from the wealth of gospels the first list of biblical texts that resembles today's New Testament. A now-famous passage in *Against the Heresies* declares his reasons for choosing precisely four gospels: "It is not possible that the gospels can be either more or fewer in number than they are . . . since there are four zones of the world in which we live, and four principal winds." He shrewdly defended the four gospels he had chosen by allowing the various heresies that accepted only one of the four to testify on behalf of the gospel to which they adhered; the Ebionites, Docetists, Marcionites, and Valentinians for the gospels of Matthew, Mark, Luke, and John respectively.

The fact that the names of the Apostles are attached to these four gospels in no way bear record to their actual authors. These are merely 2nd-century additions known as "pseudepigraphy"—authorship by an anonymous writer which is later attributed to a famous Scriptural character for authority. The general consensus today is that "Mark" wrote first and was revised by "Matthew" and "Luke," who added new material.

The original Mark, the work of an anonymous Gentile Christian, was considerably shorter than canonical Mark. It is commonly dated by the "Little Apocalypse" of Chapter 13, which prophecies great upheavals and the destruction of the Temple, and is thought to refer to the First Jewish War (66-70); hence Mark must have been written either in its midst or sometime thereafter. However, the author was not an historian; that is, he did not deal directly or critically with the evidence. He merely organized inherited stories into a sequence and shaped them into a coherent plot without seeking to portray Jesus' life story.

When Mark was later adopted by a dominant community, it was augmented with their own oral tradition, resulting in verses 6:45-8:26. This provided them not only with a complete codified form of their own values, but with the authority of a written gospel, all in one book. But Mark still lacks the Sermon on the Mount (Matt. 5-7), Luke's most famous parables (Luke 18-19), the infancy narratives, and the post-resurrection appearance stories—items that took on greater theological significance as Christianity matured. The early Christians conceived of Jesus as "put to death in the flesh" and quickened only "by the Spirit" (cf. Romans 8, I Peter 3:18); his corporeal appearance to the Apostles came with the Gospels. In fact, the whole Easter event, as portrayed by the Gospels, is missing from the 1st-century Epistles. Verses 16:9-20 were added to Mark sometime during the 2nd century in order to harmonize it with the other gospels—a quite common and perfectly acceptable practice in the ancient world.

As opposed to the old evangelical view that the four Gospels are independent and corroborative accounts, their strong similarities are now generally recognized as the result of copying; out of Mark's 661 verses, all except thirty-one are either repeated or parallelled in Matthew and Luke. There are also around four dozen instances were Matthew and Luke parallel each other very closely, word for word in some cases. In the 19th century, form critics finally ventured to suggest that both of the above must have had another common source, which the scholars designated "Q" (from the German *Quelle*).

The Q Gospel is a now-lost collection of codified oral traditions based on the set of stories that were circulating in the early Christian communities. It belongs to a genre that is called *logoi sophon* or "words of the wise" (after Prov. 22:17), and which is represented in the Hebrew scriptures by such books as Job, Proverbs, Ecclesiastes, Wisdom of Solomon, and Jesus Sirach[71]. Also, scholars have recently pointed out close similarities between its maxims and the Cynic school of philosophy, a Greek counter-culture movement spread by itinerant Cynic teachers.

Since the Q provided at most a simple "Jesus said" for the Master's sayings, Matthew and Luke had to come up with their own settings. The same kind of barebones frame is found in the Gnostic Gospel of Thomas (c. 50-60), which is thought to be based on an earlier stage of Q; a stage that exchanged stories about Jesus before any eschatological expectations were attributed to him, and before the Son of Man sayings found their way into the source gospel. The Q contains absolutely no notion of a suffering Christ, a divinity that has undergone death and resurrection as a act of redemption, and the Gospel of Thomas is equally devoid of any reference to the Master's death and resurrection.

The dating of Matthew and Luke is influenced by the picture they draw of the "parting of the ways" between Christianity and the wider Jewish establishment. The fact that Luke has also abandoned the expectation of an imminent end of the world places him even later. His gospel was modelled on

---

[71] Jesus was omitted when the name became sacred.

Greek historiography and the events therein are related in sequence, and for the first time, as a part of general history. Theophilus, to whom the Gospel is addressed, was born pagan and became a Christian after reading the Jewish scriptures, serving as the Bishop of Antioch from 169 to 177. Nor is there any reference to the Acts of the Apostles, written by the same author who drafted the final version of Luke, before the year 170—more than a century after the date frequently assigned to it.

Some see the Acts as a mid-2nd-century response by the Roman Church to Marcion's view of things, and there are certainly major discrepancies between the Acts and what Paul recounts in his Epistles. There is no way Paul could account for all the Christian congregations across the Empire, many of which were in existence before he even got there. Nor is one imparted any sense of vigorous missionary work on the part of the Jerusalem circle around Peter. Modern scholarship has been forced to admit that much of the Acts is nothing more than groundless fabrication. The book was crucial to the Roman Church because it honoured both Peter and Paul, but no other writer even mentions the *Pentecost*, that collective visitation of the Holy Spirit to the Apostles which the Acts claim started the whole missionary movement.

The later synoptics, Matthew and Luke, place the birth of Jesus at Bethlehem because the Prophet Micah had foretold that this would be the birthplace of the future "ruler in Israel" (5:2). The earliest references, on which Mark is based, insist that Jesus was born instead in Nazareth of Galilee. This conflict would be a minor one were it not for the fact that there was no town called Nazareth in Galilee at Jesus' birth. In a comic self-fulfilling prophecy, the Galilean town was established in the latter half of the 3rd century, after news of the Saviour's birthplace had spread. (It would appear that somewhere along the line, the Greek word, *Nazoraios*, deriving from *Nazirite*, Hebrew for a person "consecrated" to God[72], had become confused with the word *Nazarenos*, "native of Nazareth.")

Mark does not bother itself with the biography of Jesus prior to his baptism by John. To the early Christians, the Master's childhood, like his place and manner of birth, was irrelevant; God's Kingdom was at hand, and Jesus had

---

[72] "For behold, you shall conceive and bear a son. And no razor shall come upon his head, for the child shall be a Nazirite to God from the womb; and he shall begin to deliver Israel out of the hand of the Philistines." — Jud. 13:5

urged his followers to prepare for the new Heaven and Earth that would be created in their life-time. Considering his apocalyptic message and the instructions to repent and prepare for the Lord, a posterity-driven biography would have been absurd—there were not expected to be any future generations to read anything written in the present.

Working independently of each other, Matthew and Luke produced conflicting genealogies based on Old Testament numerology. According to the former, Jesus can be called the "seventh son thrice and one" of King David himself; an impressive paternal lineage that testifies to the powerful influence of numerology on the ancient world. While both Matthew (1:18-25) and Luke (1:26-35) tell us that Jesus was born of a virgin, Mark makes no such claim. Instead, the earliest of the synoptics describes Jesus as a decidedly Jewish Messiah, born quite naturally in the manner expected of a Davidic prince.

According to Mark (6:3), Jesus even had four brothers, who all must have been born after him, otherwise one of them would have been the heir apparent to the throne of David. Both the Eastern Orthodox and the Roman Catholic Church insist, however, that Mary was a "perpetual virgin" in the manner of Venus, which would make the brothers and sisters of Jesus the children of Joseph by a previous marriage. But if that were the case, Matthew's genealogy (1:1-16) would inevitably transfer the legal heirship to "the Lord's brother," James—according to Paul's earliest Epistle (Gal. 1:19, 2:9,12) merely an elder of the church in Jerusalem.

Celsus surmised the motive behind the virgin birth narrative, accusing the Christians of attributing a *parthenogenesis* to Jesus in order to imitate the pagan saviour-gods: ". . .a few years ago he began to teach this doctrine, being regarded by Christians as the Son of God. . . There is an authoritative account [of similar doctrines] from the very beginning, respecting which there is a constant agreement among all the most learned nations, and cities, and men. . . the Galactophagi of Homer, the Druids of the Gauls, and the Getæ. . . Linus, and Musæus, and Orpheus, and Pherecydes, and the Persian Zoroaster, discussed these topics. . . the fiction of [Jesus'] birth from virgin [is parallelled and preceded by] the Greek fables about Danæ, and Melanippe, and Auge, and Antiope. . ."

The Gentile converts could hardly be expected to leave behind Herakles and Mithra, who were virgin-born, in exchange for a Jewish Messiah who was not. These Hellenes could pick and choose among dozens of mystery cults and saviour-gods, each of which promised eternal bliss in a heavenly afterlife. Jesus, to all appearances, a mortal Palestinian rabbi, had little to offer the Hellenes, speaking as he did only to the sons of Abraham, exhorting them to "prepare the way of the Lord," who would build a New Jerusalem for His chosen people.

The Gospel of John differs considerably from the other canonical gospels, and of the four, took the longest to gain acceptance. It was written for the Gentile Christian of the early 2nd century—these new converts were wealthy, educated, and contemptuous of the Diaspora Jews who resided in their cities, enjoying the hospitality of Rome. John leaves out the offensive references to Jesus as a Messiah of the Jews, the awkwardness of Jewish patrilineage, and all the allusions to Davidic and Palestinian descent, which are characteristic to the earlier gospels.

John has Jesus state for the first time those things which the early Christians thought he was, but which he himself never claimed to be. Stripped from the synoptic and Judaic traditions, the Jesus of John is successfully placed in the role of the *Soter*, the saviour through whom every man must pass in order to achieve the higher realms. In the manner of the Orphic mysteries, he doth declare that "He that eateth my flesh, and drinketh my blood, dwelleth in me, and I in him." (6:56) This distinctly pagan element reaches into the very core of every mystery cult of the pagan world—Christianity had thus created the final, lasting reflection of the central religious concept of the Hellenistic era.[73]

---

[73] The terminology of the mysteries (e.g. *Soter, Logos, teles, epipsanes, baptismos*) was largely transported into Christian use (by Paul, Ignatius, Origen, Clement etc.); liturgy (especially of baptism and of eucharist) and organization (of the catechumenate) were affected by them. The Christian practices entitled "mystagogical" describe the process whereby initiates were to become "wedded to Christ" as Orphic initiates were to Dionysos, and led into a grand procession to the chapel for esoteric study and final initiation.

St. Cyril of Jerusalem describes an eventual eucharist ceremony where the initiate accepts communion as a substitute for the literal body of the Christ: "Thus we come to bear Christ in us, because His Body and Blood are distributed through our members; thus it is that, according to the blessed Peter, we become partakers of the divine nature." (*Mystagogical Catechesis*, iv. 3) According to even the modern Orthodox belief, a Christian's ultimate goal is *theosis*, Greek for "deification."

CHAPTER 10

The canon of the New Testament took near final form in many quarters by the end of the 2nd century CE, containing the four Gospels, the Acts, and the Pauline Epistles. Once the canonical Gospels began to be circulated together as a cohesive unit, scribes got used to seeing them together and passively harmonized them whenever discrepancies were found. The oral tradition eventually died out, being slowly displaced by the authority of the written word.

The Gospels were thoroughly sectarian writings, offering a bulwark against outside attack while legitimatizing parochial beliefs and practices. For instance, the burning issue of "table-fellowship," whether Jew could mix with Gentile, whether the ritually pure could break bread with the impure, was solved by having Jesus condemn the Pharisees for their obsession with purity, and having him consort even with outcasts. The question of whether Jewish Law still applied was similarly addressed by letting Jesus make rulings on it.

Meanwhile, the *Mishnah*[74], a collection of Jewish ethical and ritual laws, covering, for example, agriculture, Sabbath and feasts, marriage and divorce, civil and criminal matters, was completed in Palestine around 189 CE, and concurrently with the *Torah*, became the principal source of Rabbinical study, a sort of a constitution which even today holds together the dispersed communities of the Jews. Its editor was Rabbi Judah the Patriarch, and its compilation had been initiated some time earlier. Even though Syrian Aramaic had been established as the colloquial language of the Palestinian Jews several centuries BCE, the *Mishnah* was written in neo-Hebrew, used primarily for academic purposes.

Under Emperor Caracalla (r. 211-217), Jews, along with all the other free subjects of the Empire, received the rights of citizenship, the right to call themselves Roman, thus abolishing the distinction between the Roman colonists and the subjugated populations. By the 2nd century CE, the women

---

[74] Heb. "repetition"

of the Empire were not only highly educated, but involved in business and social life—concerts, theatres, festivals, travelling—with and without their spouses. They took part in a wide range of athletics, even bore arms and went to battle. Women of the Jewish communities, however, were excluded from active participation in public worship, social and political life, outside the family, and even from education. The most striking practical difference between the orthodox and the Gnostic Christians was in their respective positions towards women in congregation. It also gave occasion to the severest of quarrels and rebukes; for in the Gnostic congregations, women functioned as equals with the men.

The Gnostic scriptures, the Gospel of Mary and the Wisdom of Faith, portray Mary Magdalene as a teacher. After the crucifixion, the disciples asked Mary to tell them what Jesus had taught her in secret. And Mary taught them, until Peter angrily questioned her: "Did He really speak privately with a woman and not openly to us? Are we to turn about and all listen to her? Did He prefer her to us?" Shocked by the animosity of Peter, Mary answered: "My brother Peter, what do you think? Do you think that I have thought this up myself in my heart, or that I am lying about the Saviour?" At this point, Matthew took upon himself the role of an arbiter: "Peter you have always been hot tempered. Now I see you contending against the woman like the adversaries. But if the Saviour made her worthy, who are you indeed to reject her? Surely the Saviour knows her very well. That is why He loved her more than us."

As orthodox Christianity grew in strength and organization, the Gnostic sects came under increasing pressure and persecution. The greatest anti-Gnostic controversialist of the early Church was Tertullian (169-c.230), who devoted practically his whole life to combatting Gnosticism. One needs only to mention some titles of his works: *The Prescription against Heretics*, *Against Marcion*, *Against the Valentinians*, *On the Flesh of Christ*, and *On the Resurrection of the Flesh*. Known as the greatest theologian of the West until St. Augustine, he is described as utterly brilliant, highly sarcastic, and absolutely intolerant. The exasperated Church Father relates how the women in Gnostic congregations teach, debate, exorcise evil spirits, heal the sick, and dare even to baptize. The Gnostic Christians appointed women as ministers, even as bishops. These women prophesied, they assembled and administered their own groups.

Orthodox Christians answered the Gnostics by adding to the Pauline

Epistles the Letters of Pseudo-Paul to Timothy, to the Colossians, and to the Ephesians, wherein the woman is told to submit to the will of the man. By year 200 CE, the women of the orthodox congregations were silent (I Cor. 14:34-35). The ministerial and episcopal offices were strictly in the hands of men. In this regard, the Christian faith was exceptional, accompanied only by Judaism. In all other religions, women were priestesses, and even if some governing duties were reserved for men, the women could officiate at services and ceremonies.

The Christian Church, spreading as it was across the Roman Empire, was still a Greek church. The common language of most traders, craftsmen, and professionals was the Koinê. This was also the language of every Jew of the Dispersion, to whom the Gospel was originally preached. Every book of the New Testament was written in Greek. Latin was the official language of the western half of the Empire, stretching north and west from present-day Romania and Italy, and including North Africa west of Egypt. But even the western cities, such as Marseilles and Arles, that were centres of trade and commerce, had large Greek-speaking communities. The first Latin apologetic work expressly aimed at the educated Romans was the *Octavius* of Minucius Felix, written no earlier than the very end of the 2nd century.

Latin first occurs as a Christian language, not in Rome, but in Africa. Greek was initially the chosen language of the African clerics, but Latin was a more familiar tongue for the majority of the faithful—which is why it soon took the lead in the church and why Tertullian of Carthage, who penned some of his earlier works in Greek, ended up using Latin only. The legally-trained Tertullian's vigorous language formed the basis to the Latin of the Church Fathers, and incidentally, the unscriptural terms "Old and New Testament" were first employed by him.[75] Pope St. Victor I (r. 190-202), a fellow-African, was apparently the first Roman Bishop to use Latin, while St. Hippolytus (170-235), a 3rd-century theologian and martyr, was the last Christian Roman to employ the Greek tongue alone.

Bardesanes of Edessa (c. 154-223) is again referred to as "the last of the Gnostics," since he was probably the last major teacher to preach Gnosticism within the mainline Christian community. Born to wealthy Parthian parents, he obtained an excellent Græco-Persian education at the court of Edessa. This

---

[75] *Against Marcion*, iv. 6

independent Syrian city-state stood on the Silk Road, which begins on the Mediterranean coast at Antioch, passes across the Euphrates, and reaches the Armenian city of Nisibis through Edessa. Already familiar with the various ancient religions of western and southern Asia, Bardesanes converted to Christianity at the age of twenty-five, after hearing the preaching of Bishop Hystapes. Soon after, he in turn converted his close friend, King Abgar IX, who established Bardesanian Christianity as the Edessan state religion.[76] This Abgar, who ruled from 179 to 214, was also known as the Great, because under him Edessa, by then economically the most prominent city in northern Mesopotamia, achieved a status of the "Athens of the East."

When Edessa was conquered by Caracalla in 216, Bardesanes fled to Armenia, where he continued his preaching. As instrumental as he was in the introduction of Christianity into the region of Edessa, Bardesanes was considered heretical by the Christians who came after him. As with most early heretics, most of our information about his doctrines comes from the writings of his opponents, notably Ephræm Syrus of Edessa. Bardesanes was the first Syrian hymn-writer, and is thought to have composed, for example, the famous "Hymn of the Pearl" found in the apocryphal Acts of Thomas. Only a few words survive of the lyrics to his 150 hymns, but Saint Ephræm admitted stealing their meters for his own songs.

Until the discovery in 1945 of the twelve Gnostic codices near the Egyptian village of Nag Hammadi, the vast majority of our knowledge about Christian Gnostics was in the form of polemics by their orthodox adversaries. A great store of information on, rather than a refutation of Gnosticism, is the ten-volume series, written some time after 234, once called *Philosophoumena* and ascribed to Origen, but since the discovery of Books IV-X, known by the name of its real author, Hippolytus of Rome, and its true title, *Kata pason Aireseon Elegchos*, "Refutation of All Heresies." Its publication (1851) revolutionized the study of Gnosticism and rendered obsolete and nearly worthless all the previously published works on the subject.

Hippolytus wrote nearly half a century after St. Irenæus, whose disciple he had been, and thus describes a later development of Gnosticism than the Bishop of Lyons. What distinguishes Hippolytus from all the other early anti-Gnostic writers is his extensive quotation from the heretical writings in

---

[76] making Edessa the first officially Christian state in the world

framing his arguments against them. As he was in possession of a vast number of Gnostic writings, his information is priceless, for those writing were systematically sought out and burned by the Roman Church, a leader of which Hippolytus was from 199 to 217. He advocated strict ecclesiastical discipline and opposed "monarchianism"—which he names as one of the heresies in his book—against the stand of Calixtus, who was named pope over him in 217.

Pope St. Calixtus I came to power at a crucial time for the Church. Our knowledge about this pontiff is chiefly from two of his most bitter enemies, Hippolytus and Tertullian, both of whom challenged his orthodoxy. The early Church had been unforgiving on those who committed sins of murder, adultery, and fornication; mortal sin committed after baptism could not be pardoned. Through his famous edict, Calixtus allowed repentant sinners back into communion of the Church after they had performed public penance. What is more, Calixtus not only allowed the lower clergy to marry, but also excused the marriages of bishops that had been concluded before their conversion. Hippolytus and Tertullian perceived all this as a degradation of the Church, a resignation to lust and carnality that reflected not grace and holiness, but perversion and corruption.

Additional complaints included the facts that Calixtus did not ask converts from heresy to do penance for sins committed before baptism, and that he decreed mortal sins not to be a sufficient reason for defrocking a bishop. Calixtus' stand was that a bishop could pardon all sins. The congregation with its servants was fast becoming the Church with its deputies: the Pope in place of Christ, the head bishops in place of God's Word, priests and the rest of the hired army in place of the assembly with its representatives. Calixtus wanted to subdue the resistance by demanding, as the Bishop of Rome, power over the whole Church.

"From what source," objects Tertullian, "you usurp this right to 'the Church.' If, because the Lord has said to Peter, 'Upon this rock will I build My Church,' 'to thee have I given the keys of the heavenly kingdom;' or, 'Whatsoever thou shall have bound or loosed in earth, shall be bound or loosed in the heavens,' you therefore presume that the power of binding and loosing has derived to you, that is, to every Church akin to Peter, what sort of man are you, subverting and wholly changing the manifest intention of the Lord, conferring (as that intention did) this (gift) personally upon Peter?" The election of Calixtus so enraged Hippolytus that he left Rome and formed his own community outside the city, thus becoming the first Antipope in history. He and his group of followers remained in schism through the terms of two other regular Popes, St. Urban (223-230) and St. Pontian (230-235).

In 235, Emperor Alexander Severus was assassinated; his successor, Maximinus Thrax, was an ex-wrestler who had served solely in military, and was fit to rule the Empire only like a soldier. The capital he never visited, and is said to have confiscated the funds put aside for the Roman soup-kitchens and for the local entertainment, and even to have deprived the temples of their revenue. Since he hated his predecessor, who had favoured the Christians, Maximin ordered the leaders of the Church to be struck. Hippolytus and Pontian both found themselves exiled to the mines of Sardinia, where they achieved a reconciliation.

The Pope and the Antipope resigned their posts to make way for St. Anterus (235-236), whose successor, St. Fabian (236-250), would transport their bodies back to Rome for burial as martyrs. Before converting to Christianity, Prudentius had written a hymn about the ancient Hippolytus, son of Theseus, which gave rise to the legend that St. Hippolytus was torn to pieces by wild horses. Emperor Maximin was killed by his own men during the siege of Aquileia in 238. The quarrels of the many short-term emperors that took place between this incident and the accession of Diocletian (r. 284-305) have little fascinated posterity. Suffice it to say that they left the Christians pretty much alone.

The incessant exchange of ideas has had an undeniable effect on all the Western countries. One result of this intellectual exchange is the movement we now call Neoplatonism. And new it was, for the differences between it and the original Platonism were considerable. This last great philosophical structure of antiquity was erected at the Museum of Alexandria by Plotinus (c. 204-270), a disciple of Ammonius Saccas, who had also taught Origen the theologian. Neoplatonism stood for the decay of the original Greek thinking and the shift to mystical contemplations akin to Christianity. It portrayed this world as a flawed copy of its ideal, and therefore tried to concentrate rather on the perfection of the human soul, which would keep on reincarnating until it achieved a Buddha-like enlightenment.

After eleven years with Ammonius, Plotinus travelled with Emperor Gordian III to Persia, where he was exposed to Indian ideas. After the death of Gordian, Plotinus fled to Antioch and thence to Rome, where he established a school of philosophy which in many ways resembled a monastic order. Despite his association with many Christians, Plotinus never became a Christian himself. His writings are voluminous and bear witness to great erudition, yet they aim not at knowledge, but at redemption, which is achieved by uniting with "the One." In one essay, *Against the Gnostics*, he disputes Gnosticism while at the same time largely agreeing with most of its ideas.

Porphyry (c. 232-305) was a major contributor in the dissemination of Neoplatonism, particularly within the Roman Empire. After moving from Tyre to Rome in 263, he became a close friend and student of Plotinus. He is mostly known for assorting the works of Plotinus—all of which were in the form of shortish essays—into groups of nine, whence they became known as "The Enneads," *ennea* being the Greek for nine. Porphyry authored several philosophical works himself, including *Against the Christians*, a critical essay denouncing Christianity, and *Introduction to the Categories*, a commentary on Aristotle's take on Plato, which interestingly enough became the standard mediæval text on the subject.

The work of Plotinus was also carried on by Iamblichus (d. c. 330), who also came from present-day Lebanon, and whose numerological and magical speculations were synthesized in the 5th century into a great system of knowledge by the Greek Proclus. These masters, fanatically idolized by their disciples, bore more resemblance to theologians than philosophers. It was therefore natural that their opponents and, ultimately, conquerors, were men who represented not different thought, but different faith.

After the fall of Jerusalem, Babylonia began to gain increasing significance for the Jews, and in the period that followed, southern Mesopotamia became a new home to them. The Jewish communities flourished under their Exilarch, or "Prince of the Captivity," a powerful feudatory of the Parthian Empire. Always of the Davidic line, he was the supreme judge of his people, both in civil and in criminal matters, and exercised in many other ways a near absolute authority over them. Except for a short duration immediately following the conquest of the Arsacids by the neo-Persians, and during the brief rule of King Odenathus of Palmyra, the Jews of Babylonia enjoyed peace and independence.

It is also from southern Mesopotamia where Mani (216-276), the originator of Manichæism, came. His Persian name was Shariak, and he was born in the vicinity of Ctesiphon, the Sassanid capital. His parents are said to have been of noble Iranian descent, his mother even of Parthian royal lineage. His father was apparently a member of the Jewish-Christian baptizing sect of the Elkesaites, founded around 100 CE by a Syrian prophet known as Elkesai, the "hidden power of God." However, baptism as a Jewish practice predates John the Baptist, whose later followers, the Mandæans, rejected both Jesus and Judaism.

The only group of Gnostics to have survived into modern times, Mandæans live to this day in Iran and southern Iraq. Mandæism is named, not after its founder as are most sects, but after its name for the Godhead, *Manda D'Hayye*, "wisdom of life." And contrary to many other Gnostic schools, Mandæans believe that the reproduction of mankind through sexual behaviour and progeny is essential for man also as a spiritual being—which might partly explain the sect's endurance. The role of the First or Primal Man is a central aspect in the Mandæan creation myth, and was later meditated upon also by Mani. Indeed, Manichæism is sometimes classed as a form of Gnosticism, and styled Parsi Gnosis, as distinguished from Syrian and Egyptian Gnosis—ignoring the fact that the two systems, while they share the doctrine of the impurity of matter, start from entirely different principles, Manichæism from an absolute cosmic dualism between spirit and matter, Gnosticism from the notion of matter as gradual deterioration of the Godhead.

When Mani was twelve years old, he had his first vision, in which his heavenly "twin" appeared to him, and these visionary experiences eventually led to his expulsion from his father's sect. He confronted Shapur I (r. 241-272) on the day of his coronation, proclaiming a new religion, to which he was *Mani*, "the Vessel." He was invited to the court as tutor to the King's eldest son, but when the royal heir fell ill and died, Mani was imprisoned and condemned to death. He escaped first to the Arabian mountains, and thence to Caschar, where he encountered Bishop Archelaus, with whom he had the famous disputation on Christianity. After refusing to accept the orthodox dogma, Mani was banned by the Church, and again forced to flee, making converts everywhere he went.

Considering himself the last of the great prophets, Mani sought to reconcile the great religions of salvation into a new, syncretistic faith, which also incorporated elements from Greek philosophy, while refuting patriarchal

Judaism. He clearly intended his religion to be a world religion, the first-ever world religion in fact. He therefore adapted his doctrines to accommodate local beliefs and customs, and was regarded by his Christian followers as the Paraclete prophesied by Jesus in the Gospel of John, by his Buddhist disciples as the Lord Maitreya, and by his Parsi adherents as the Zoroastrian saviour Saoshyant.

After the death of King Shapur, Mani returned to Persia, where his following had vastly increased. He was allowed to preach freely by Shapur's successor, Hormizd I, who saw the advantage of having a single religion for the Iranian and non-Iranian parts of his empire. However, during the reign of Bahram I, son of Shapur and the successor of Hormizd, Mani was summoned before a council of Zoroastrian priests at Gondi Shapur. Upon refusing to recant his heresy, he was thrown to prison in chains, where he died after 26 days. His corpse was flayed, its skin was stuffed with straw, and crucified before the gates of the city.

The Manichæans—who by now had spread across Europe and Asia, and reached even China—would disappear as the result of centuries of persecution. In 287, Emperor Diocletian sentenced the leaders of the Roman Manichæans to the stake, condemning their followers partly to death by beheading and partly to forced labour in government mines. The Christians, on the other hand, had been allowed peace for half a century already, and the first thirteen years of Diocletian's reign were among the calmnest in the history of the early Church.

Christendom of the 4th century was no longer an insignificant sect formed by the meek or the subversive, whose members owned their few commodities between them and looked down upon power and wealth. A Christian could be wealthy, and he could be powerful. Christianity had, in fact, gained ground even at the imperial court; the Emperor's wife, Prisca, and his daughter, Valeria, were no strangers to its propaganda, and all four head eunuchs, Lucianus, Dorotheus, Gorgonius, and Andreas, had adopted the new faith and converted many of their subordinates.

Also in the Roman army did Christianity gain many adherents. One pagan holiday in 298, it came to pass in a certain North African town, that a centurion named Marcellus threw away his arms in front of all the celebrants, took off his military belt and legion insignia, and announced in a loud voice that he would follow no one besides the Christ Jesus. He was apprehended and duly executed as a deserter, but from the point of view of the authorities, the incident was a critical symptom of how the Christian faith undermined the oath of allegiance. Cæsar Galerius, who himself had previously dismissed a number of Christian officers from his army, spent the winter of 302 at Nicomedia with Emperor Diocletian, and we can safely assume that the rulers addressed the Christian question in their many, lengthy discussions.

In the end, Diocletian made a decision to dissolve all Christian associations and set bounds to the further progress of Christianity. On a February morning in 303, his officers marched with a small group of soldiers to the main ecclesiastical edifice in Nicomedia, had the church doors forced open, the holy scriptures brought out and burned, and then began dismantling the building with battering-rams. On the next day, a general edict was promulgated throughout the Empire, decreeing persecution of the Christians: they were forbidden to assemble, their churches were to be demolished, and the assets of their congregations confiscated. The authorities were ordered to refrain from producing fresh martyrs, but after a couple of puzzling attempts at arson in the Emperor's bedchamber, the orders were changed and the number of victims grew higher than Diocletian had probably intended, though not as high as Church tradition is wont to suggest.

The Empire of Diocletian used a tetrarchy, or rule of four. There was one Augustus and one Cæsar for the eastern and western parts of the Empire. The persecutions of the Christians raged worst in the East, where their number was highest and where Galerius succeeded Diocletian as Augustus in 305. Galerius appointed as his Cæsar Maximin Daia, who was not only his kinsman, but shared his views on Christianity. The rulers of Italy and Africa were also vicious enemies of the new religion, the wretched Severus and the despotic warriors Maximian and Maxentius alike.

In Gaul, the fate of the Christians was not as severe: Constantius Chlorus showed great tolerance towards them and Constantine acted from the start as their friend and protector. Constantine the Great was the illegitimate son of Emperor Constantius and Helena, a Bithynian barmaid, whom legend insists was a devout Christian; but it is highly probably that Constantine's position was dictated by political wisdom. In a contest which seems fairly even and uncertain, the support of any fanatical minority is useful. In the provinces ruled by his rivals, the number of Christians was high, and it depended largely on their fortune and misfortune whether Constantine would have success or not.

Only a few days before his death in 310, Galerius issued with Licinius and Constantine a peculiar edict which implied that the persecution had been wrongful and ineffectual, and by which Christians were given the right to freely practise their faith. Instead of having a new Augustus elected to succeed Galerius, Licinius and Maximin Daia divided his dominions between themselves, Licinius taking charge of the Balkan Peninsula and Maximin of Asia Minor. Since the relations between the rulers of the western half of the Empire were equally chilly, Constantine and Licinius soon found each other, whereupon Maxentius and Maximin formed a secret alliance of their own.

The war between Constantine and Maxentius broke out first, a battle being fought in Turin and another at Verona. Constantine, who had swiftly and without warning crossed the Alps at the pass of Mont Cenis, emerged as the victor in both battles. He then marched south and met Maxentius' army a little north of Rome at Saxa Rubra, where a third battle, made famous by ecclesiastical history, was fought in 312; a quarter of a century after the event, Bishop Eusebius revealed to the benighted world the well-kept secret that Constantine had been inspired to attack Maxentius by a vision that had appeared in the sky: a luminous cross and above it the Greek and the Latin writing *En touto nika* and *In hoc signo vinces*, both of which mean the same: "In this sign thou shalt conquer."

The miracle took place at high noon, making it that much more astonishing, and the Emperor, who till then had worshipped the Greek and Roman gods, was as surprised as the rest of them. According to the Christian apologist Lactantius, his consternation turned into faith when he saw a clarifying vision in a dream the following night: Christ himself appeared before him, showed him the celestial cross more closely, and advised him to prepare a war banner with the same design. However, a contemporary pagan panegyrist insists the Emperor's vision was of Apollo, and received at one of the sun-god's shrines back in Gaul.[77]

Be it as it may, Constantine gained a wonderful victory over the pagan Maxentius, whose army was routed and rushed in wild disorder onto the *Pons Mulvius*, one of the busiest bridges across the Tiber. The Milvian Bridge collapsed under the weight of the fleeing forces, and many soldiers fell into the river, among them also Maxentius, who in his heavy gear immediately

---

[77] *Panegyrici Latini*, vi. 21. 4-5

sank to the bottom and drowned.[78] The victor had his corpse fished out, its head chopped off, and taken with him to Rome, which he could now freely enter. Later, Constantine had the severed head sent to Africa along with a letter to Bishop Cæcilian of Carthage, in which he promised to pay a great sum of money to the church of that province.

Constantine's first act in Rome was to execute the sons of Maxentius, after which he disbanded for good the Prætorian Guard which Maxentius had reorganized, and had its fortified camp torn down, leaving the capital unprotected and incapable of defiance. The Senate hailed the Emperor as saviour of the world, erecting a triumphal arch to commemorate his victory. The largest triple arch in Rome, the Arch of Constantine was built with structures and decorations belonging to monuments from previous ages, and inscribed with quotations from Cicero.

After finishing his work in Rome, Constantine left for Milan and married off his sister Constantia to his ally Licinius, the Cæsar of the province of the Danube and the Balkans. Here the monarchs drew up their famous joint edict of religious tolerance: it declared that the two Emperors, upon deliberating as to what would be advantageous for the security and welfare of the Empire, had decided to concede equal rights to all religions.[79] They decreed the torn-down churches to be rebuilt and the confiscated assets to be returned to their rightful owners, hoping that "the Deity enthroned in Heaven" would grant favour and protection to the Emperors and their subjects.

While the Edict of Milan (313) granted the Christians freedom of worship, it endeavoured at the same time not to offend the pagans. The imprisoned Christians were released from the prisons and mines, the churches were filled again, and many who had fallen away sought forgiveness. During the times of persecution, Christians had been quite able to live according to their ideal; they were outside the society, recognizing neither its laws nor its official

---

[78] The defeat of Maxentius and the conquest of Rome is described by Eusebius in terms reminiscent of the biblical account of the destruction of the Pharaoh's army in the Red Sea; he apparently saw Constantine as a new Moses, come to lead the "true" chosen people into a New Jerusalem—just as his pagan contemporaries perceived in the "first Christian emperor" the ruler of the world prophesied in Virgil's fourth eclogue.

[79] The old, dismissed Emperor Diocletian was also summoned to Milan, but failed to show up, preferring to stay at his great palace in Salona (now Split, Croatia), leaving the world to run its course.

machinery—they could demand from one another the unconditional observance of their religious prescriptions. A Christian magistrate was not allowed to sentence anyone to death, and a Christian who had killed an enemy as a soldier risked exclusion from the community for a period of three years.

A decisive change in pursuing the ideal took place when Constantine embarked on turning the Christian Church into an instrument of temporal power. He invited the bishops to court and frequently to his table, calling them his brothers. The ecclesiastics were granted immunity and exempted from taxation and military service, as well as from obligatory state offices, such as the curial post, which was a great burden. The exemption from municipal offices was regarded as such a valuable privilege that the clergy now discovered an amazing number of vocations to their body. Crowds of people everywhere made for the churches, moved less by conviction than by the hope of reward. However, the disorder that soon followed in the administration of the provinces compelled the Emperor to modify the privilege.

While Constantine chose bishops as his counsellors, they again would often request his intervention. For the Church was not a single united body, the *corpus Christianorum* which he had assumed it to be, and as soon as the pressure from outside abated, fierce theological disputes broke out around questions that seemed unnecessarily casuistic to the Emperor. The first ecclesiastical schism to present itself was simple and understandable enough, pertaining as it did to the sort of a question that is quite familiar to the subsequent generations.

The newly-elected Bishop of Carthage, Cæcilian, was accused by his rival, Majorinus, of having participated in the surrender of holy scriptures to the authorities during the persecution of Diocletian. Cæcilian and his supporters answered with an accusation of exactly the same nature. Majorinus died shortly afterwards, however, and was succeeded as the party leader by the fiery Donatus, who managed to persuade seventy bishops into excommunicating his opponent. Cæcilian, of course, appealed to the Emperor, who organized a very thorough, and perhaps even objective inquiry.

Cæcilian was found by Constatine to be in the right, and his most prominent opponents were banished from the province. But the Donatists did not accept this verdict: in Africa, they outnumbered the orthodox Christians, each city having its rival Donatist and orthodox bishops, until the Arabs appeared there in the 7th century and converted both parties into Islam.

Branded as heretical and separated from communion with the Universal Church, they in turn denounced the Universal Church, invariably baptizing every new convert, since they did not recognize the baptisms of other communities.

While the wedding festivities were still under way in Milan, a couple of dispatches arrived there, which had the imperial brothers-in-law set off headlong in opposite directions: the Franks had attacked Gaul, forcing Constantine to leave for the Rhine, whereas Licinius was informed that Maximin Daia was marching across Syria towards Bosporus, despite the fact that it was the height of winter in Asia and there was a lot of snow. Maximin conquered Byzantium before Licinius could come to its assistance, but at Adrianople, he met an Illyrian cavalry of thirty thousand, which quickly routed his doubly superior army. Maximin fled to the East in order to assemble a new army, and from there promulgated an edict of toleration which surpassed that of Licinius in its goodwill towards Christianity. But three months later, he died a fugitive at Tarsus.

After the death of Galerius, the Emperor's widow Valeria, the daughter of Diocletian, had caught Maximin's eye. When she fended off his advances, he got angry, confiscated her property, and had many of her friends and servants slain.[80] Upon receiving word of his death, Valeria and her mother Prisca left their place of exile at Syria for the court of Licinius in Nicomedia. The two Christian ladies were kindly welcomed, but when the Emperor had young Candidianus, the son of Galerius and stepson of Valeria, detained and killed without any cause, she could stay at the court no longer. Dressed up as peasants, she and her mother fled westward, but made it no further than Thessalonica before they were uncovered, captured, sentenced to death, and executed. The children of Maximin, an eight-year-old boy and a seven-year-old girl, were also slain, and the same fate also befell the son of Emperor Severus. Licinius then took possession of Maximin's whole domain, and thus ruled all the eastern lands from Illyricum to Mesopotamia and Egypt.

The amity between Constantine and Licinius did not last long. In the fall of 314, about a year after Licinius had acquired the East, the two clashed at a

---

[80] Diocletian had tried many times to get his daughter to him in Salona, but Maximin took sadistic pleasure in being able to turn down the appeals of his former master.

village called Cibalis by the Sava River in Pannonia, where Constantine gained his first Pyrrhic victory. Licinius abandoned his camp at night and headed east, picking up his wife, his son, and his cash reserves from Sirmium on the way. He assembled a new army in Thrace, but after suffering another defeat at a place called Mardia near Adrianople, he withdrew to the mountains of Macedon. In the spring of 317, Licinius managed to negotiate peace with Constantine, albeit with heavy provisions.

Licinius was able to keep his throne, but the Illyrian general Valens, whom he had named Cæsar before the fateful battle, had to remove his purple after only a few days' reign, and was put to death on the orders of the victor. Licinius also had to cede his Danubian provinces and most of the Balkan Peninsula to Constantine, whose domains now stretched from Britain to the islands of the Ægean. The sons of Constantine, Crispus and Constantine, were made Cæsars in the West, whereas the younger Licinius was accorded the same dignity in the eastern half of the Empire.

The new treaty between the two Emperors remained in force for eight years, but when Licinius began to persecute the Christians, the outbreak of war became imminent. Licinius held great superiority at sea, but he was imprudent enough to wait for Constantine's army at Adrianople, suffering a crushing defeat on the 3rd of July, 324, in an uncharacteristically bloody battle for its time, the death toll rising to 30,000. He then retreated to the fortified port of Byzantium, which Constantine forthwith attempted to besiege. His son Crispus charged the Bosporus and Hellespont with his navy and gained a great naval victory, but before Byzantium was finally besieged, Licinius had already left for Chalcedon and managed to assemble one last army in Asia.

Constantia, residing nearby in Nicomedia, contacted her victorious brother, who promised that her husband would be allowed to live. Licinius surrendered, laid his diadem and his purple robe at the feet of Constantine, prostrating himself before the victor, who picked him up in an extremely condescending manner, and asked him to sit at his table. Licinius was then escorted to Thessalonica, where he was supposed to spend the rest of his days, but was arrested before long and shortly after executed for conspiring with the enemies of the State. All his statues were torn down and all his acts were declared null and void—something which evidently proved ill-considered, for Constantine brought many of the decrees back into force very soon. He was the sole master of the Empire, the reconstruction of which he could now begin.

CHAPTER 11

The existence of the Roman Empire was threatened by many serious perils, not the least of which were the lack of national unity and military weakness. Constantine strengthened the army, increasing the *limitanei*, the static frontier troops that guarded the borders, to 360,000 men; stationed inland was a new military body, the *Scholæ Palatinæ*, which numbered 194,500 men and took the place of the disbanded Prætorian Guard; the barbarian tribes living on the frontiers were also taken into the pay of the State as allies; several cities were fortified, and many new garrisons were established, further undermining the old Roman division between soldiers and civilians. With so many men under arms, as well as a struggling economy, the tax burden became hard to bear for the civilian population—the Byzantine historian Zosimus even claims that fathers were forced to hire out their daughters as prostitutes to pay their arrears.

The Christians, having previously acted according to their own rules as a state within a state, were now incorporated into the ruling machinery. They might aspire to amend society into complying with their ideals, but despite its decline, the Roman Empire was still so well regulated and organized, and its traditions so viable, that it was generally the Christian themselves who had to adapt to the surrounding society. The Church would allow its members to speak of the divinity of the Emperor, of the sacred palace and the sacred chamber, without fear of being denounced as an idolater. Blinded by the splendour of the imperial court, some bishops went so far as to glorify the Emperor as an "angel of the Lord" who, like the Son of God, would reign in Heaven.

It is obvious that Constantine's confession of Christianity was for a long period of time weak and ambiguous, and he would never risk falling into dispute with the adherent of other religions. He remained Pontifex Maximus all his life, and after his death, the pagans would elevate him, as was customary, to the rank of a divinity. He never stopped using Mithra's image or the words *Soli Invicto Comiti*, "To the Unconquerable Sun, my Companion," for Mithra had faithful worshippers above all in the army. In his coins, Constantine repeatedly declared the sun-god to be his guide and protector and the bestower of even the victory foreshadowed by the vision of a cross above the midday sun.

In the Julian Calendar, the 25th of December was reckoned as the Winter Solstice, and observed as the sun-god's birthday, the *natalis invicti*, the rebirth of the winter-sun, unconquered by the rigours of the season. In Egypt and Syria, the celebrations climaxed at midnight with a cry: "The virgin has brought forth! The light is waxing!" The Egyptians even represented the "newborn" Sun by the effigy of an infant which was brought forth and exhibited to his adorers.

Since the Gospels say nothing as to the day of Jesus' birth, the early Church did not celebrate it. During the 2nd century, among an obscure Gnostic sect at first, but soon generally among the Christians of the East, the 6th of January started to be regarded as the date of Nativity; the custom of commemorating the birth of Christ on that day gradually spread, until it was universally established in the East by the 4th century—the Western Church, however, never recognized this.

In Rome, which was still very much a stronghold of the old religion, the Catholic Fathers had noticed that the Christians were wont to take part in the pagan festivities connected with the 25th of December[81], and in 320 CE, decided to declare that day the Nativity of Christ.[82] In the East, the change was opposed, however: the Syrians did not introduce it until half a century later, whereas the independent Armenian Church still commemorates Jesus' birth on the 6th of January. Not that there was ever much pretence at the historical accuracy of the dates chosen, as shepherds simply do not abide "in the field, keeping watch over their flocks by night" in the dead of winter.

The Christian version of the holiday could not spread any faster than Christianity itself, wherefore "Christmas" was not celebrated in Ireland until the late 5th century; in England, Austria, and Switzerland until the 7th; in

---

[81] The minor Jewish holiday of Chanukah is also linked in timing to the Winter Solstice; the lighting of the nine-branched candelabrum (Heb. *Chanukiya*) commemorates a miracle of light conspicuously absent from the apocryphal story in the Maccabees.

[82] There had been a tradition in the West that Mary bore the Christ Child on the 25th day, but no one could seem to decide on the month.

Germany until the 8th; and in the Slavonic countries until the 9th and 10th centuries. Not that any of these lands lacked their own Yuletide celebrations. Paganism only disappeared by vanishing into Christianity, and many of the pagan midwinter customs, albeit in a watered-down form, entered the mainstream of Christmas celebration. This is why both Luther and Calvin abhorred the holiday and why the Puritans refused to even acknowledge it; to them, no day of the year could be more holy than the Sabbath—in Boston, Christmas was actually made illegal.

Emperor Constantine showed equal favour to both Christianity and Mithraism. As Pontifex Maximus, he oversaw the pagan worship and protected its rights. He may have placed Sunday under the protection of the State, but the believers in Mithra observed Sunday as well as Christmas. In fact, the Jewish Sabbath had always been observed on Saturday, the seventh day.[83] Constantine himself speaks not of the day of the Lord, but of the "venerable day of the Sun."[84] Temples and altars were still being built to the old gods with the consent and support of the Emperor, who concurrently subsidized the Christians in building the Lateran palace at Rome and the old St. Peter's Church.

It is estimated that during Constantine' reign, the Christians represented approximately five percent of the entire population of the Empire; in any case, they we decidedly in the minority. Yet Mithraism, since it allowed only male initiates, was at a serious disadvantage from the start. It was just one of several imported cults that enjoyed a large following at Rome and in other parts of the Empire. The chief competitor to Christianity was not Mithraism, but the great array of imported and official Roman cults falling under the rubric of "paganism."

Christians were still tied to their pagan roots and had yet to make a clear case as to why their god should be considered an equal to the older state-endorsed divinities. Early Church Fathers like Eusebius of Cæsarea, the author of Constantine's biography, compare and contrast Christ against his pagan counterparts, arguing that if He was false, then so were Herakles and Dionysos. From the very beginning, Constantine showered wealth and

---

[83] St. Ambrose allegedly kept Sabbath in Milan and Sunday in Rome, giving rise to the saying: "When in Rome, do as the Romans do."

[84] *Codex Justinianus*, iii. 12. 3

privileges upon the Christians, as new churches, each more flamboyant than the next, began to rise. At court and in the army, the quickest and surest path to promotion was yielding to this brilliant evidence of faith. Municipalities were raised to city status if all their inhabitants exchanged Jupiter for Jesus. Imperial gold did more in a decade than the miracles of all the apostles, the blood of all the martyrs, and the arguments of all the apologists in three centuries.

The Donatist schism had been a local one, and in the time of Constantine, the whole affair probably seemed nothing more than a personal power stuggle between two energetic clerics in an episcopal election. Of an entirely different magnitude was the feud over a word, or rather, a single letter, which ultimately divided the believers into Homoousians and Homoiousians. The same year that Constantine took over the Empire in its entirety, a dispute broke out in Egypt, where the learned and respected Presbyter Arius (c. 256-336) presented views on the second person of the Godhead, which his superior, Bishop Alexander of Alexandria, could not accept.

Found in each and every textbook on ecclesiastical history, Arius' doctrine concerned the nature of Christ, and was nowhere near as infantile and academic as it may seem today. Philo's Logos had for the Christians incarnated in the person of Jesus, but they now faced the question of whether he was to be worshipped as a god or if the worship was only to be directed at the invisible supernatural force that sent him to us. By no means did Arius deny the divinity of Christ, but he argued on philosophical grounds that the Son could not from all eternity co-exist with the Father, since then there would be two deities instead of one. The Son thus belongs to the creation of the Father, but is perfect in contradistinction to all other created beings, and can therefore be considered divine. But to Bishop Alexander, this simply did not go far enough and made Jesus appear less than God.

Alexander excommunicated Arius and condemned his doctrine, but he would not bend before his bishop, for in addition to being sure of his case, he had plenty of supporters in Egypt, including two bishops, seven presbyters, twelve deacons, and, we are told, 700 spiritual virgins. It soon became evident that most of the Eastern bishops, among them the often-mentioned Eusebius, agreed with him, and it was thus that the reading of the creed became customary, first in the Syrian Church—hence the name "Antiochene Creed."

The *Quicumque vult*[85], also known as the Athanasian Creed and always attributed to St. Athanasius (c. 297-373), the young deacon who supported Bishop Alexander, was unknown to the Eastern Churches until the 12th century, so he is unlikely its author. The earliest known copy of this creed was included in a prefix to a collection of homilities by Cæsarius of Arles (d. 542).

The rumours of a great doctrinal controversy soon reached the Emperor, who immediately sent both Arius and Alexander a letter asking them to avoid a public dispute that would cause division in the Church. Constantine recommended that they follow the example of Greek philosophers, who could peaceably debate an issue and finally come to an agreement on how things really were. "Constantine the Victor, Supreme Augustus, to Alexander and Arius. . . how deep a wound has not only my ears but my heart received from the report that divisions exist among yourselves. . . having enquired carefully into the origin and foundation of these differences, I find their cause to be of a truly insignificant nature, quite unworthy of such bitter contention. . . Restore my quiet days and untroubled nights to me, so that joy of undimmed light, delight in a tranquil life, may once again be mine."

When the Emperor realized that his letters had no effect at all, he made a brilliant move which had not previously occurred to anyone. He convoked the first-ever Ecumenical Council, requesting the bishops from three continents in very respectful letters to come promptly to the Asian town of Nicæa, present-day Iznik, near the Bosporus. The choice of location was favourable to the assembling of a large number of bishops, being easily accessible from nearly all the provinces, but especially from those of Asia, Syria, Palestine, Egypt, Greece, and Thrace; several bishops from outside the Roman Empire would also attend.

In order to expedite the assembling of the Council, the public conveyances and posts of the Empire were placed at the disposal of the bishops, and the Emperor provided generously for the maintenance of the participants. Among the most famous attendants were Eusebius of Cæsarea, Eustathius of Antioch, Macarius of Jerusalem, Eusebius of Nicomedia, and St. Nicholas of Myra. Alexander of Alexandria was accompanied by the young Athanasius as his secretary and deacon, while two Roman presbyters, Victor and Vincentius, represented the Pope.

---

[85] Lat. "whoever wishes" i.e. to be saved

The Council of Nicæa was opened by Constantine in the early summer of 325 with the greatest solemnity. His unbaptized majesty conducted the meeting of the bishops dressed up in fine silk embroidered with golden flowers, a purple robe hemmed with precious stones, a diadem of a new design, necklaces and bracelets glittering with gems, and wigs of different colours fashioned by the most eminent masters of the craft. He made an address expressing his intention to give legal validity to any conclusion the prelates, enlightened by the Holy Spirit, would reach, and listened patiently to their lively and long debates.

Finally, after two months and twelve days, the Council approved by vote the view that the Son was "of one substance with the Father," born not created[86]; the decision was made with 301 votes for and seventeen against. The Emperor announced that he was pleased to find the unanimity so great and that the light of truth had eclipsed the discord between Christians. He solemnly ratified the Council's verdict by proclaiming that anyone who was against its divinely inspired judgement would be banished—all but two of those present signed the revised statement of faith.

The Council was concluded with a glorious banquet that seemed a far cry from the commensality of the early Christian Agapes. In his *Vita Constantini*, Eusebius reports that: "Detachments of the bodyguard and other troops surrounded the entrance of the palace with drawn swords, and through the midst of them the men of God proceeded without fear into the innermost of the imperial apartments, in which some were the emperor's companions at table, while others reclined on couches arranged on either side. One might have thought that a picture of Christ's kingdom was thus shadowed forth, and a dream rather than reality."

Arius himself was banished to a far-away corner of Illyricum, while his writings and those of his sympathizers were ordered to be burnt, with those who henceforward were discovered to have them in their possession declared enemies of Christ. A reign of terror was proclaimed for all those who would not conform with the new, official Christian line: "Let none of you presume, from this time forward, to meet in congregations. To prevent this, we command that you be deprived of all the houses in which you have been

---

[86] This decision also formally and irreparably severed all official ties between Christianity and Judaism.

accustomed to meet. . . . and that these should be handed over immediately to the catholic church."

In the earliest Christian congregations, there was no difference between the laity and the clergy: "But be not ye called Rabbi: for one is your Master, even Christ; and all of ye are brethren. And call no man your father upon Earth; for one is your Father, which is in Heaven. Neither be ye called masters; for one is your Master, even Christ." (Matt. 23:8-10) Yet the clergy began to differentiate themselves from the laity early on, and by the 4th century, the ecclesiastics had turned into the mightiest of politicians, organized into a rank order resembling the army, a hierarchy reaching from altar boys and other lesser incumbents, through priests, bishops and archbishops, all the way to the primate.

The organization adopted by the Church derived its form from that of the civil administration of Rome. One of the most important units of the Christian organization, the *diocesis* or "bishopric," was christened after the Roman administrational unit of the same name. During the first three centuries CE, the local spiritual life centred around the episcopacy, an appellation that derives from the Greek word *episkopos*, "overseer." As a result of the spread of Christianity outside the main population centres, the bishops gradually delegated the administration of a portion of the diocesan territory to other ecclesiastics.

In imitation of the Mithraic priests, their Christian counterparts became "Fathers," despite Jesus' express proscription against the acceptance of such title (Matt. 23:9). It is irrelevant that he was not specifically repudiating the Mithraists, but the Jewish Sanhedrin, whose president was styled Father; the early Church had, following the example of Jesus, called God the Father. Mithra's chief priests wore a *mitra* as their badge of office, and the Christian bishops adopted also these "mitres." The Magi further carried a shepherd's staff, wore a ring and a robe that featured the sword of Mithra; identical garments are worn by Christian clergy to this day. The head of the Mithraic fathers always lived in Rome and was called *Pater Patrum* or *Pater Patratus*.

From the middle of the 3rd century on, wealthy Christians had been buying houses and outfitting them as churches, but as the Church grew in size and importance, these no longer met the needs of the community. The church began to emulate the *basilica* (lit. "royal hall") model of Roman public buildings, which were long, regular, and usually had a semicircular apse to the east, meaning they could be converted into liturgical spaces simply by replacing the throne with an altar. This change in the place of worship allowed for another change: the daily celebration of Mass. Initially said only on Sundays, the Mass could now be performed on any day of the week desired. This was not obligatory, however, and during the episcopacy of St. Augustine, for example, Hippo never had daily Mass.

Up until then, the bishop had been the normative presider at all Masses, but the growing size of the congregations and the increasing number of churches made it impossible for the bishop to conduct each and every Mass. This is how the priest began to preside over the Mass, a change that involved a substantial increase in the number of priests. The establishment of parishes from the 4th and 5th century on gradually relieved the bishops from many of their other original duties, though they naturally retained the right of supervision and supreme direction.

At the same time, the State began granting bishops other powers; they were exclusively empowered to take cognizance of the misdemeanours of the clergy, and every lawsuit filed against the latter had to be tried before a bishop—the development of canon law had begun. Even after a suit had begun before a civil magistrate, it was still permissible for either of the parties to transfer it to an episcopal court. A law of 333 ordered state officials to enforce the decisions of the bishops, whose testimonies alone were to be considered sufficient by all judges. Constantine's successors, however, prudently limited this jurisdiction to cases where both parties voluntary submitted to the bishop's court.

The organization of ecclesiastical provinces under metropolitans followed Diocletian's restructuring of the Empire. He had divided it into four great prefectures: those of Italy, Gaul, and Illyricum made up the bishopric of Rome; the fourth had five civil dioceses, Thrace, Asia, Pontus, the Orient, and Egypt. Since the most important cities in the East were Alexandria of Egypt and Antioch of Syria, the Bishop of Alexandria became the chief of all Egyptian bishops and metropolitans, while the Bishop of Antioch held the same power over Syria, Asia Minor, Greece, and the rest of the East. The supreme place of the bishops of these three cities was recognized as an "ancient custom" by the Council of Nicæa. The three other civil dioceses, Thrace, Asia, and Pontus, would undoubtedly have developed into separate patriarchates, were it not for the rise of Constantinople.

Well before the days of Constantine, the idea of "Rome" had become dissociated from the Eternal City on the Tiber. A Roman meant a Roman citizen wherever he lived, and since the 2nd century, the Roman population had been shifting to the eastern provinces, which had become the leading centres of economic activity. A low-lying city on a marshy plain, Rome had also been discarded as an administrative centre, the emperors preferring to live in Nicomedia and Milan, even in Trier[87] and York[88]. These places of residence were, however, only ever meant to be temporary ones, and Constantine seems early on to have set out plans to found a new, permanent capital, though he was uncertain for a long time as to where it should be situated.

For at least a moment, Constantine probably considered his own native town, the nowadays Serbian city of Niš, and then for a while Thessalonica, until one day it dawned upon him that the right location was Troy, not only the ancestral home according to Roman poetic tradition, but a strategically and commercially important spot at the southern mouth of the Hellespont. The Emperor actually began erecting gates and what not there, but the work was soon interrupted—by Christ himself, if we are to believe the legend. He appeared to Constantine and demanded that the city should be built on the Bosporus, not on the Dardanelles. The obliging Emperor headed there with his building materials and began to stake out a capital in Chalcedon, on the side of Asia, but Providence intervened once more.

Eagles, claims the legend, snatched all the poles and cables of the imperial architect in their talons, flew them over the narrow to the side of Europe, and dropped them down south of the deep-but-serene bay called the Golden Horn. Here lay Byzantium, a small Greek colony founded in the 7th century BCE; its unique location made it one of the great cities of history, and choosing it as the capital of the Roman Empire would have a profound impact on the destiny of both Europe and Asia.

For several years, Constantine was passionately absorbed in the construction of his city, and the work was done so fast that the walls, the

---

[87] i.e. Augusta Treverorum

[88] i.e. Eboracum

gates, and all the principal monuments were completed within a few years. The Senators whom he managed to persuade into leaving Rome and settling in the new city, were pleasantly surprised when they found perfect replicas of their Italian villas, built for them by the Emperor on the shores of the Thracian Bosporus. The city soon duplicated everything possessed by the old capital, transferring the actual identity of Rome to a new location.

The city was largely built of trees logged from the untouched forests in the shores of the Black Sea, but marble also was close at hand on the little island of Proconnessus in the Sea of Marmara; after all, this is where the sea got its name from. A host of existing monuments and statues were also shipped to the Bosporus from the ancient cities of Asia and Greece, in particular from Delphi, whose oracle had apparently lost all its authority.

The imperial palace was a massive and marvellous construct, wherefrom winding stairs led straight to the imperial gallery at the Hippodrome, a structure that could hold 80,000 spectators. A century and a half earlier, Emperor Septimius Severus had had this race track built at the old Byzantium, and it was now adorned with wonderful images, statues, and obelisks. On the Forum next to the Hippodrome was erected a statue that had once depicted the sun-god, but which had apparently had its head cut off and replaced with the Christian image of Emperor Constantine; on its pedestal was—or so they claim—embedded, in addition to a piece of the True Cross, the famous Palladium, which had been secretly transported from Rome, where it had rested for a thousand years without a single Roman ever having seen it.

We are further told that Constantinople was dedicated to the Virgin Mother of God, but long before the time of Constantine, Byzantium was considered dedicated to the Virgin Queen of Heaven. On the 11th of March in the year 330, the date that astrologers had selected for him, the Emperor inaugurated his new capital with ceremonies which were half pagan and half Christian, and went on for fourty days and fourty nights. He named the city "New Rome," but the name did not endure for long: the people called it *Konstantinoupolis*, the City of Constantine, and possibly just *Polis*, the City; nowadays it is called Istanbul, which is asserted to be a Turkish derivation of the neo-Greek saying *Eis tên polin*, "Into the city"—yet the culture and history associated with it has come to be known as Byzantine.

While Constantine was building his Constantinople, the bishops and other shepherds of the fold persistently carried on their theological debate. Arius had been long condemned and exiled, but it soon proved that his thoughts concerning the persons of the Godhead had more proponents than was initially believed, and instead of wearing thin, the subject was incessantly enriched with new views and terms. At Nicæa, the operative word had been *homoousion*, which was derived from the Greek words *homos*, "same," and *ousia*, "essence" or "substance"; it thus signified the sameness of substance or something to a similar effect, while the "Homoousians" were the majority that held the Son to be of the same substance as the Father, not created but born from eternity.

There now appeared divergent sects among the discredited Arians, one radical group even asserting that the Father and the Son were of a different substance altogether, but many others leaning towards the view that the Son was of similar though not entirely same substance as the Father. The last-mentioned group gathered under the banner of *homoiousion*, which meant "similar substance," and had been composed by combining the Greek word *homoios*, "similar," with the aforementioned *ousia*. The battle was now fought principally between the Homoousians and Homoiousians.

Instead of punishing the adherents of the heretical doctrine as Constantine had promised, the Emperor began protecting them from the zeal of the orthodox and from the particularly zealous Athanasius, who in 328 had succeeded Alexander as Bishop of Alexandria. St. Athanasius spent fifteen years and ten months of his 45-year reign in exile, most of it with other Egyptian monks or in Rome. While in exile, he wrote several works, many of which stress the importance of God's incarnation in the person of Jesus Christ; the Greek art of argumentation and discourse left an ineffaceable mark in the dogmatics, which he fashioned against the Arians, and he is now regarded by many as the most important theologian of the 4th century.

However, just three years after the Council of Nicæa, another synod was assembled in Jerusalem, where the Arians were a majority, and could thus condemn the doctrine that the Son was born of the Father from all eternity, and banish the bishops of Alexandria, Antioch, and Constantinople to the most remote corners of the Empire. The decision of Nicæa had thus ceased to be valid, and Arius could be summoned back from exile and called to the new capital only six years after its inauguration. He received a solemn reception when he appeared for the audience of the Emperor, but was suddenly and unexpectedly compelled by a call of nature to retire, immediately suffering a fatal seizure in a public washroom.

A year after the mysterious death of Arius, Emperor Constantine held with magnificent ceremonies, in his new capital, the 30th anniversary of his reign—none of his predecessors, excluding Augustus himself, had reigned that long. His 20th anniversary, which, too, was a significant event, Constantine had celebrated in the Old Rome, and its memory has been vividly preserved in history, for it was connected with a family tragedy rivalling the Greek legends. In the middle of the festivities, the Emperor had his son, Crispus, unexpectedly arrested, and after a private investigation, sent to prison and there soon executed. The young Licinius, who was also a Cæsar and an inheritor to the throne, met the same fate after his uncle rejected the pleads his sister offered for her only begotten son; incidentally, Constantia herself died soon after this incident. At approximately the same time, the Emperor's own wife, the intriguing little Empress Fausta, was put to death with hot steam in one of the palace baths.

The reasons behind all this are not entirely clear, and Constantine's obsequious biographer, Bishop Eusebius, skips over these events in expressive silence. Contemporary historians say that Crispus was accused of having an altogether too close a relationship with his young stepmother, and later ones claim that the whole incident was but a repetition of the ancient tragedy of Phædra: Fausta had tried to seduce Crispus, and when he had coldly rejected her, she had retaliated by making an accusation to her husband of his son's lecherous advances—thereby involving in the matter Licinius, who was a friend of Crispus' and knew the charges to be false. After Constantine had, in a moment of rash anger, had both of the youths executed, his mother, Helena, who grieved for her noble grandson, entered the stage and soon managed to convince the Emperor of Crispus' innocence and Fausta's guilt. After making Fausta pay for her treachery, the remorseful Constantine erected for Crispus a golden statue bearing the inscription: "To my son, wrongfully convicted."

The 30th anniversary of the Emperor was accompanied by events that were no less dramatic. The glorious festivities were celebrated in the shadow of an imminent Persian War. King Shapur II of Persia could also celebrate his thirtieth year of reign, although he was only twenty-nine and a half years of age; due to the untimely death of his father, he was crowned even before his birth, the regalia of the Persian monarchs having been ceremoniously placed on his mother's belly when she was pregnant with him.

The alarming state of foreign policy and the strenuous celebration of his jubilee thoroughly exhausted Constantine. Soon after the festivities, he left for Aquyrion, his palace, near Nicomedia, on the opposite shore of the Bosporus, in order to recover his strength and to enjoy the hot baths offered there. However, he fell seriously ill upon arrival, and when it became clear to him that his illness was fatal, he decided to have himself baptized, since he wished not to miss the joys of Heaven.

Dressed in clothes of purest white, he received the sacrament on his bed, which too was as white as driven snow, and from that moment onwards, he never wore any of the regular imperial garments again. When he passed away a few weeks later, the cries of grief and wails of sorrows echoed throughout the Roman Empire louder than ever before. The body of the Emperor was embalmed very carefully, then led in a magnificent procession to the Great Palace at Constantinople, where it was laid on a golden bed in one of the royal halls.

Whilst waiting for his sons and heirs, Constantine II, Constantius, and Constans, to return home from the distant provinces, the life in the palace followed its usual course: each day, at a specific time, the highest officials of the State, ministers and generals, were one at a time taken to a solemn audience with the late Emperor, who lay on his golden bed in his gem-embroidered purple robe with a glistering diadem on top of his wig. The high officials fell on their faces, then rose up reverentially to present their issues and make their reports, for it was written that no act of government could be carried out unless the Emperor was present.

Through the summer, through the autumn and the winter, the dead Emperor went on ruling in this manner, until his son Constantius arrived home the next year, allowing the clergy, the army, and the people to take their eminent deceased to the gold-plated mausoleum that was located in the Church of the Holy Apostles, where thirteen porphyry-sarcophagi, twelve for the apostles and the thirteenth in the centre of the circle for Emperor Constantine, lay waiting. Here the Bishop of Constantinople first uttered the words that, for a thousand years, were to follow the Byzantine Emperors: "Arise, O Lord of the World. The King of kings awaits thee for the Last Judgement."

The triumph of Christianity made the Bible world literature and thus elevated its writers beside the Greeks and Romans, or rather, above them. The prophets, psalmists, and evangelists usurped the places of honour at Parnassus; David ja Isaiah effaced Homer and Vergil. Rome had the oldest Hebrew community in Europe, and Jewish propaganda had not neglected to emphasize the æsthetic value of their scriptures. But by no means did the great masses of the Roman Empire adopt the new faith for æsthetic reasons, and it was indeed difficult for the cultured and educated to accept those barbaric writings which fought against every the recognized rule of language and taste. St. Augustine himself recounts how he had to change all his linguistic assumptions and his affection for the "stately prose of Cicero" in order to accommodate the rustic, childlike language of Scripture.

It meant a great deal to these people that the Old Testament forced out as the basis of tradition the whole mythical world of antiquity. This involved a decisive victory of the Orient over the Occident: the old Roman materialism had to gradually give way for all those spiritualistic ideas that emanated form the East and penetrated nearly every layer of society. Without this prerequisite, Christianity would never have spread as fast as it did. The rigorous opposition encountered by Christianity can be blamed partly on the at-times conscious reaction triggered by the repudiation of the heritage of the fathers; seeing the latter regain its former prestige was the chosen purpose of many.

Of Constantine's sons, the eldest, Constantine II, leaned towards paganism, but the middle one, Constantius II, was a zealous Christian who forbade pagan worship under pain of death, while the youngest, Constans I, attached the death penalty to marriages between Jews and Christians. In 340, Costantine II attempted to seize some of Constans' territory, and was killed in a battle near Aquileia; Constans was assassinated ten years later, and Constantius II became the sole Emperor once he had executed two of his paternal uncles, one maternal uncle, and eight cousins.

Of Contantine's family, only his two nephews, Gallus and Julian, now remained; the former was executed by Constantius' head chamberlain, Eusebius, in 354. Ammianus Marcellinus describes with warm sympathy the latter, who had for his epithet *Apostata*, "the Apostate." He had endured a harsh Christian upbringing, wherefore his disposition inclined him towards Greek philosophy. He studied rhetoric diligently at Athens under the renowned teachers Himerius and Proæresius, at the same time as the two men who would become the great Christian leaders of the time: St. Gregory of Nazianzus (c.325-389) and St. Basil the Great (329-379).[89]

When he finally became Emperor in 361, Julian famously attempted to stem the Christian tide and to organize the adherents of the old religion into a Church of their own, but his efforts were, like so many other similar reactions, doomed to failure. Property confiscated from pagan temples was restored, and public worship of all religions, Christian as well as pagan, was allowed once more. During this 4th-century "resurgence of paganism," many imported cults and even official Roman state religion experienced a brief surge in popularity, but their existence was increasingly threatened by the rapid spread of Christianity. Unlike Christians, pagans conducted no missionary work to seek converts and had never been exclusive in their worship. Julian sought to amend this by creating pagan religious houses and to establish a systematic pagan theology. His approach differed from traditional Hellenism in that it promoted religious fervour; his practice and frequency of sacrifice brought fanaticism to Hellenism.

The pagans of Alexandria lynched George, the Arian bishop sent to replace Athanasius during his third exile, when the good prelate proposed to erect a church over a ruined Mithræum near the city. In 363, Julian decreed the reconstruction of Yahweh's fallen Temple on Mount Moriah and the full restoration of Jewish worship, possibly with a view of securing the influence of the Mesopotamian Jews in his fateful campaign against the Persians. Sudden flames, however, burst forth from Temple Mount and rendered the rebuilding impossible, while Julian himself was fatally wounded by a Persian arrow after only two years of reign, and died surrounded by friends amid a constructive discussion concerning the immortality of the soul. Legend, not Ammianus, claims that his last words were: *Vicisti, Galilæe*, "Thou hast won, Galilean!"

When Christianity had then taken over the world, it had itself been conquered by world literature. Its adherents had attended the schools of the pagan writers, imitating them and gradually surpassing them. The great Christian writers, the "Church Fathers," would become the most prominent representatives of the Greek and Roman literature of their day. The Christian

---

[89] Julian later introduced a law that forbade Christians to teach Classical literature on the grounds that one should not teach what one does not believe.

Church was to nurse the cultural heritage of antiquity, and rescue it, along with the ancient literature, from the turbulences of the Great Migrations.

Julian was succeeded by the commander of his imperial guard, Jovian, who briefly reverted to Constans' policy by restoring the Christians their former rights and taking away those of the heathen, including the Jews. After less than a year, he was in turn succeeded by another Pannonian general, Valentinian, who took his younger brother, Valens, as his co-Emperor, and together were the last rulers to decree equal toleration to pagans and Christians. Their reign was, however, one of constant wars.

Roman legion war strategy did not work against barbarian cavalry, and since the 3rd century CE, the Roman army had more and more been recruited from among the barbarians themselves. By the time of Valentinian, it was entirely barbarian, officered by barbarians, armed and trained like the barbarians, and even beginning to be clad in the once-disdained barbarian dress—the words "soldier" and "barbarian" would be synonymous from then on. In addition to the barbarianized regular army, the Roman Empire also employed the troops of its allies, the *fœderati*. These tribes or "nations" of barbarians were admitted within the Empire and granted lands on which to live in return for military service. They were allowed to retain their own laws and their whole national organization, including their king. One such nation were the Goths, whom Valens had permitted to settle on the Danube in 376.

As a prelude, the westward migration of the nomadic Huns—a godless nation of horsemen, who, instead of cooking their meat, tenderized it on horseback under their bare buttocks—had crushed the Gothic power in the north of the Black Sea. Back in the 3rd century BCE, they had invaded China, where part of the Great Wall was built to exclude them. Leagued with the somewhat more humane Alani, who decorated their horses with the scalps of their enemies and worshipped a naked scimitar fixed in the ground, the Huns then crushed the great nation of the Ostrogoths and drove the Visigoths, along with their women, children, and cattle, over the wide Danube to the Roman side, where they were kept in camps for years, defrauded and assailed in every possible way, until they finally lost their patience and took up arms.

Emperor Valens died on a hot August day in 378, during the blood-soaked Battle of Adrianople, in which the Visigoths destroyed two-thirds of his army, leaving the eastern half of the Empire virtually defenceless. His brother,

Valentinian, had been succeeded three years earlier as the Emperor of the West by his son, Gratian, who had his hands full holding the field against the Germanic tribes that occupied the borders of the Rhine. In 379, he appointed his Spanish general, Theodosius, as co-Augustus, and sent him to the derelict East. Soon after, he fell seriously ill and received baptism from the orthodox Bishop of Thessalonica. Indeed, his reign is worth recollection above all from the perspective of church history: upon recovering, he became a zealous follower of Nicene Christianity at a time when Arianism was at its strongest, truly earning his posthumous title, St. Theodosius the Great.

CHAPTER 12

There has always been many forms of Christianity, lots of ways of being Christian. The learned and eloquent rhetorian Aurelius Symmachus, the Prefect of Rome and Proconsul of Africa during the reign of Theodosius, fought as long as he possibly could for religious freedom and tolerance, but had an overwhelmingly proficient, energetic, and pious opponent in the extraordinary Bishop of Milan, Aurelius Ambrosius, who in due course was declared a saint along with his monarch.[90]

In February of 380, Theodosius published with Gratian the notorious edict that all Roman subjects should profess the faith of the Bishops of Rome and Alexandria: "The rest, however, whom We adjudge demented and insane, shall sustain the infamy of heretical dogmas, their meeting places shall not receive the name of churches, and they shall be smitten first by divine vengeance and secondly by the retribution of Our own initiative, which We shall assume in accordance with the divine judgement."[91]

On 24th of November, Theodosius held at Constantinople his triumph celebrating the advantageous peace with the Goths. As soon as he arrived, he began expelling the Arians, who had been in possession of the seat of the Empire for over four decades, while the remnants of the Nicenes were without either church or pastor. After the Arian metropolitan Demophilus had fled the city, Theodosius determined that St. Gregory of Nazianzus should be bishop of the new orthodox see, and personally accompanied him to Hagia Sophia, where he was enthroned in presence of a huge crowd.

The Second Ecumenical Council was called by Theodosius in May, 381, to re-enact the Nicene Creed forty-five years after the Arians had been allowed to re-enter the Church, and to put an end to the new heresy of the Macedonians, the followers of Macedonius, who impugned the divinity of the

---

[90] the debate is reproduced in *Nicene and Post-Nicene Fathers*, Series II, Vol. X

[91] *Codex Theodosianus*, xvi. 1. 2

Holy Spirit. The Synod of Constantinople, as it is also called, was originally only an Eastern general council, but ranks as Ecumenical because its decrees were eventually received in the West also. It added to the Nicene confession of faith the clauses which declare that Holy Spirit should be "worshipped and glorified" equally with God and Jesus, leaving the creed very close to how it reads today.

The Council was originally attended by 186 bishops from the East, but thirty-six leaning towards heresy left after the opening sessions. It was initially presided over by St. Meletius of Antioch, but after his untimely death, St. Gregory succeeded him as president. Gregory's continued state of ill-health necessitated his resignation of not only the presidency of the Council, but of the See of Constantinople, which he had held for only a few months. He left both to St. Nectarius, and retired to his old home at Nazianzus, where he found the Church overrun with the heretical teaching of Apollinarius, who however perished shortly after Gregory himself.

At the close of the Council, Theodosius issued an imperial decree declaring that all the Eastern churches should be handed over to those bishops who held communion with Nectarius of Constantinople. The acts of the Council have disappeared, with the exception of the first canon, an important dogmatic condemnation of all shades of Arianism, Macedonianism, and Apollinarianism. In the summer of 382, another synod of the Eastern bishops was convoked in the Imperial City by Theodosius. Two of its canons are still extant, and were for long time falsely put among those of the Second Ecumenical Council.

In 383, Emperor Gratian was assassinated near Paris on behalf of an usurper named Magnus Maximus, who became the first Christian emperor to inflict death penalty on a heretic, Priscillian. The same year, Theodosius convoked yet another council, with the idle hope of uniting all factions and groups among the Christians. In fact, historians estimate that more Christian deaths resulted from this infighting between the various sects of Christianity than had been caused by pagan aggressions throughout all the preceding centuries.

In 385, Theodosius sent Cynegius, the Prefect of the East, around Egypt, Syria, and Asia Minor for the purpose of closing down the temples, breaking up the pagan associations, seizing or destroying the instruments of idolatry, and confiscating the consecrated property for the benefit of the Emperor, of the Church, or of the army. Theodosius could then turn against his rival, Maximus, who was defeated in battle and surrendered at Aquileia, where he and his guards were executed in 388.

A mob led by St. Theophilus, Bishop of Alexandria, set out to destroy all pagan temples in the city, including the Museum. When the Saint attempted to convert a temple of Dionysos into a church, a bloody riot ensued between pagans and Christians, the former taking refuge in the great Serapeion, home to the famous library. After a violent siege, the Christian first occupied, then demolished the fortified building. While the golden and silvery images were carefully melted, those of less valuable metals were scornfully smashed and cast into the streets. The colossal statue of Serapis itself was brought down and broken into pieces; the limbs were disgracefully dragged through the streets, and the carcass was burned in the Amphitheatre, amidst the cries of the people—the persecuted early Church of the 2nd century had by the end of the 4th become itself the persecutor.

Contemporary philosophers lamented the ruin of paganism as an astounding and dreadful legacy, which covered the earth with darkness and restored the ancient dominion of chaos and night. Such sentiments reached their peak during the eventful year of 391, when Theodosius refused to allow the Altar of Victory to be restored in the Roman Senate.[92] The perpetual flame at the temple of Vesta was put out, pagan sacrifices and the trickery of the augurs were to be punished as high treason against the State, one unforeseen consequence of which was that the language of the Etruscans fell forever into oblivion. The gladiator fights involved no paganism and were therefore allowed to continue, but the bloodless Olympic games were banned, not to be revived until fifteen centuries later. Ancient academies of learning were closed; education for anyone outside the Church came to an end. The Magi walled up their caves—Mithra had no martyrs to rival those who died for Christ.[93]

---

[92] Until then, the senators were still sworn on the altar of the goddess to observe the laws of the empire, and a solemn offering of wine and incense had preceded all their public deliberations.

[93] However, the lines that divided Mithraism from Christianity had been blurred due to the slow and steady absorption of the former by the latter during the centuries that the two existed side by side. Christians had no trouble incorporating Mithra's followers into their own ranks and many former Mithræums were converted into churches. Even today, many Christian edifices, most notably the Church of San Clemente in Rome, still contain well-preserved Mithræums in their vaulted crypts.

All Roman Emperors from Julius Cæsar to Gratian had born the dignity of Pontifex Maximus, high priest of the Roman gods. When Theodosius turned down the title as incompatible with his status as a Christian, the Christian bishops of Rome hungrily adopted it. Pope (*papa*), on the other hand, was the common title of all bishops, metropolitans, and abbots in the first few centuries and is still a common title in the East. In the West, it began in the 5th century to become the distinctive title of the Roman pontiff, but it was not until after the Great Schism of 1054, that Gregory VII—popularly known as Hildebrand—once and for all prescribed that the title should be confined to the bishops of Rome; the Pope became Pope only when there was no other Pope to oppose his claim.

More and more, the Christian liturgy became something that the congregation watched as the clergy appeared in magnificent vestments. The first mention of "sin" is found in the liturgy of St. Basil the Great, one of the Four Fathers of the Greek Church and the Bishop of Cæsarea from 370 to 379. People celebrating the Mass began to call themselves "thy humble, and sinful, and unworthy servants." This had an adverse effect on the number of Christians going to communion, which until then, had been practically each and every one of them. St. John Chrysostom, another Greek Father and the Bishop of Constantinople from 397 to 407, refers in his liturgy to the "terrible God" and the "terrible mysteries of Christ," yet he would later complain about how few parishioners came to communion.

The next development to follow was that the dividing line between the sanctuary and the people became more pronounced. There had been no separation at first, because in the earlier Masses, the whole congregation had sat around the holy table and eaten. But as the Mass became more formalized, the laity were restricted to the assembly area, while only the clergy were allowed in the sanctuary. This was soon segregated from the assembly by a communion rail, which later developed into the iconostasis.

A divergence of the liturgy between the East and the West begins in the 4th century. Though Greek had started to disappear as a liturgical language at Rome, parts of the liturgy were left in the original tongue, the creed often being recited in Greek down to Byzantine times. The evolution of the Latin liturgy was set in motion by the two psalm translations, *Magnificat* and *Gloria*; *Te Deum*, the foremost Christian hymn of praise, is supposed to have been written by Bishop Nicetas of Remesiana, who died in the year 400, about the same time as Prudentius and Ambrose.

Wanting an accurate, serviceable, and authorized Latin translation of the four Gospels for the liturgy, Pope St. Damasus (366-384) commissioned Sophronius Eusebius Hieronymus, a pupil of Gregory of Nazianzus acclaimed for his commentaries on Scripture, to revise the earlier versions, said to be as many as the manuscripts. Whether St. Jerome made his translations from the original Greek or adapted previous translations after bringing them more in line with the rapidly developing papal system, the official status of his revision diminished the authority of many popular versions. He must have enjoyed his assignment for he committed the next twenty years of his life to making an entirely new Latin translation of the Old Testament based on the ancient Hebrew texts. The first permanent wedge was thus to be driven between Western and Eastern Churches, for the latter used the Greek *Septuagint*, just as the early Christians had.

Since very few words have exact equivalents in another language, many of the early controversies centred around the Latin and Greek renditions of the various Hebrew terms and concepts. Besides employing, as occasion demanded, the words introduced by earlier writers, Jerome is personally responsible for at least 350 new words in the Latin vocabulary. Aside from the North African writers, no author had such influence on the development of Church Latin as Jerome did. But while his work was favoured in Rome from the 5th century on, the early Latin translations remained for hundreds of years dear to the Christians of Italy, Gaul, and Britain. Only after Latin ceased to be a living language did St. Jerome's critical and artificial translation become known as the common version, *Versio Vulgata*. It was not used everywhere even by the churches of the West until the Middle Ages.

It should also be noted that after the Councils had begun, it took yet half a century until the canon of the New Testament was established; the only New Testament books Jerome ever worked on were the Gospels, and the Vulgate as it has come down to us was created by assembling manuscripts from a variety of sources. While it can be said that the twenty-seven books of our present New Testament were determined by the 5th century, it took far longer to produce universal agreement.

The four Gospels and the Pauline Epistles were the first to be accepted by the whole Church. The Epistle to the Hebrews took some time to win general acceptance in the West, and there was similarly a general refusal to allow apocalyptic writings into the canon in the East. Consequently, St. Gregory of Nazianzus and St. Cyril of Jerusalem (c. 315-386) accepted all twenty-seven books except Revelation, while Pope St. Innocent I in 405 affirmed a twenty-six book canon that excluded Hebrews. St. John Chrysostom appears to have been the first to use the phrase "scriptures," *grammata*, to refer to both Old and New Testament. The same is signified by the Greek plural *biblia*, from which many modern languages derive the collective name for the accepted Judæo-Christian scriptures.

Papyrus, a quite perishable material, was used prior to the 4th century, and all writing had to be painstakingly copied on a regular basis in order to survive. No original autographs, manuscripts, or even fragments dating to the 1st and 2nd centuries are extant today. The earliest incomplete texts of the New Testament, the *Beatty Papyri* and the *Bodmer Papyri*, date from the 3rd century, and both exist only as small fragments of the various books. There are just over thirty papyrus manuscripts of New Testament books that can be dated before the 4th century—a tiny number in comparison with the scores of copies of Homer and other famous Greek authors of greater antiquity. Each copy further has its own oddities and errors—no two are completely identical, or the same as later manuscripts.

In the 4th century, the more durable vellum—commonly known as parchment—made from scraped sheepskin, began to supersede papyrus as the preferred writing medium. The *Codex Vaticanus*, so called because it is the most prized vellum manuscript in possession of the Vatican library, was torn at the end and does not reveal the whole list of books; the surviving part consists of twenty-one books of the present-day New Testament, including an incomplete Hebrews. The later 4th-century *Codex Sinaiticus*, discovered at Mount Sinai, has all the twenty-seven books of the present canon, but also includes Barnabas and Shepherd.

The Western Council of Hippo, in 393, was the first synod to specify the limits of the canon, and it accepted the current twenty-seven books, allowing only them to be read in church under the name of canonical writings. By prohibiting and burning all other texts, the Roman Church eventually convinced its members that this Bible represented the one original Christian view.

Many Christians did not, however, recognize the Church of Rome as their spiritual leader. Her ecclesiastical hierarchy set the laymen in a low position, as though outside the Church proper. And the farthest of all stood women, who had been deprived almost all functions in the orthodox Church by the end of the 2nd century. Some of the Christians fled to the Egyptian deserts to live alone (Gr. *monos*) with God, but only after the hermits had joined together in fixed monastic orders, did the ideals they represented begin to have an effect on Western culture. The rise of the monastic system was originally a protest against the formation of strict hierarchy—a lay movement that offered men and women equal opportunity to seek sanctification.

Just seven years after the Edict of Milan was promulgated, the Egyptian Pachomius (c. 290-346) introduced the first monastic rule, regulating cloistered life according to an austere model. Christianity had now discovered a system, within whose limits the faithful could live according to their religious ideal without disturbing society, the requirements of which were different. The immense popularity and quick spread of monasticism serves to show its necessity: by the end of the 4th century, there were hundreds of monasteries, and thousands of cells and caves scattered throughout the desert hills of Egypt; we hear of gigantic communities of as many as 3,000 monks and 1,800 nuns.

While Syrian and strictly Oriental monastic systems had no direct influence on those of continental Europe, all Christian monasticism ultimately stems from the Egyptian example. When St. Basil organized Greek monasticism after visiting Egypt in the 4th century, he set himself against the strictly eremitical life and insisted instead on common prayer, meals, and other functions. The monks and nuns would address one another as *fratres* and *sorores*, brothers and sisters, exactly as the early Christians had. Although women had lost their equality in congregations in less than two centuries, within the monastic system whey could lead comparatively independent lives for another thousand years.

Double monasteries, such as those of St. Basil and his sister, St. Macrina, were numerous throughout the East during the early centuries of monasticism. What is more, in most double monasteries, the supreme rule was in the hands of the abbess, and monks as well as nuns were subject to her authority. The justification for the position of a woman acting as the superior for a community of men is thought to have its origin in Jesus' words from the cross:

"Woman, behold thy son! Son, behold thy mother!"—it was also pointed out that maternity as a form of authority derives from nature, while paternal authority is merely legal.

In 394, after Gratian's younger brother and lawful successor, Valentinian II, had committed suicide, Theodosius became the last emperor to rule the entire Roman Empire. When he himself died a year later, the eastern half, having Constantinople for its capital, was inherited by his eldest son, Arcadius. The western half, including the city of Rome, fell to the younger brother, whose name was Honorius, and who was only ten years old at the time of his accession.

During the ensuing decades, Germanic tribes overran the entire western half of the Empire, and even those men who sought to maintain the power and authority of Rome and the Emperor, were often of Germanic extraction. One of these men was the Valdal Stilicho, guardian of Honorius, commander of the imperial army, and a husband to the Emperor's cousin; he was not, however, in good terms with the rulers of the eastern half, a fact that would lead to historic consequences.

Stilicho's main political adversary was the Visigoth Alaric, who had served as a general under Theodosius, but been bypassed by the sons of the Emperors in their distribution of government offices, thus deciding to act on his own political behalf. He gathered disgruntled *fœderati*, tribute payments for whom from Rome had been diminished, and had himself proclaimed Gothic king. He then marched his troops on Constantinople itself, but unable to take this well-defended city, he turned them towards Greece proper, where he plundered or raised a levy on all the even least bit prominent cities, including Eleusis[94].

The Athenians bought themselves off with money and organized a banquet in honour of Alaric, at which point they noted that he was a completely civilized person with excellent table manners. Alaric soon left Greece, however, for his negotiations with the court of Constantinople had led to the unexpected result that he was appointed commander-in-chief of Illyricum—the key province where the two halves of the Empire met—and sent to the West to lead his Goths in battle against Stilicho.

---

[94] whose ancient sanctuaries the Visigoths desecrated in 396, leaving the town desolate until the 18th century

Suffering defeats at Turin and Verona, Alaric had to vacate the soil of Italy, but to gain these victories, Stilicho had been forced to leave the Western Provinces without an army, allowing hordes of Germans to pour once more into Gaul and environs. The Alemanni, who took over the South German provinces, were known to their neighbours as Swabians[95]; the Burgundii, who hailed from the Isle of Bornholm, gave their name to Burgundy; and the lesser tribe of the Franks spread to the northern parts of future France.

Stilicho was executed on account of these disasters in the presence of the legions gathered at Pavia, leaving Rome without a general from that day on. Alaric with his Goths attacked Italy again, marched past the fortified Ravenna, where Emperor Honorius and his court had taken refuge, and headed for Rome, which was besieged and had to pay an enormous tribute in the form of gold, silver, silk, and the precious spice, pepper, to end the blockade.

Alaric then proceeded to negotiate once more with the Emperor, but when his demands were refused, he again attacked Rome, which capitulated after Ostia was taken and the supply of food to the city cut. While he had Attalus, the town prefect, appointed counter-Emperor, Alaric continued his negotiations with the court of Ravenna. After he realized that even this would not ensure the position of his tribe or even his own status, he marched on Rome for the third time in the year 410.

Thus of the matter Edward Gibbon, the most famous portrayer of the decline and fall of the Roman Empire: "Eleven hundred and sixty-three years after the foundation of Rome, the Imperial city, which had subdued and civilized so considerable a part of mankind, was delivered to the licentious fury of the tribes of Germany and Scythia." There were certainly barbarians in the ranks of the Roman troops and Romans on Alaric's side, so the situation was not quite as straightforward as Mr. Gibbon would have us believe.

The legends that tell of great devastation, plundering, and killing, are completely groundless; by the standards of the time, Rome can be said to have gotten off the Gothic invasion fairly cheaply. Alaric was a comparatively

---

[95] The practice of differentiating between the Alemanni and the Suebi first appeared in the 19th century, and has no historical foundation beyond the conflicting nationalistic views of Baden and Württemberg. Today, the French still call Germany *Allemagne*, while modern Germans refer to their home country as *Deutschland*, from the Latinized Celtic source *Teuton*, "people."

merciful invader, who did not occupy the city for more than three days, and many of the atrocities have later been attributed to the Roman slaves that had taken refuge in the Gothic army.

Thomas Hodgkin, in his authoritative history, *Italy and Her Invaders*, calls the Germans "an army of Puritans," and even Tacitus, in his most famous treatise, the *Germania*, reproached the Romans by holding up to them the superior morals of their invaders. More than half a century before the invasion, Bishop Ulfilas (c. 311-382) had given the barbarians a Gothic Bible, the so-called *Codex Argenteus*, named after its silver covers.[96] The property of the Church was scrupulously spared, and a festive procession carried sacred vessels from the caches of the pious, presumably marching straight through the rioting mob from the Field of Mars over the Tiber bridge to St. Peter's Basilica, accompanied by Alaric's personal guard.

The desecration of the city of Rome was so dramatic an event, that its actual importance is easily overestimated. It was, in itself, comparatively insignificant: Rome was no longer the capital of the Empire, not even an administrative centre to any prefecture or district; it was neither a great military centre like Trier, nor an important centre of commerce like Alexandria—it was nothing but a former metropolis, outsized by both Ravenna and Milan. Gibbon's *Decline and Fall of the Roman Empire* ends not with the fall of Rome, but with the fall of Constantinople.

More shocking to the contemporaries than the devastation itself was the traumatic realization that the Eternal City could be invaded in the first place, and that no city was ever completely safe from war. Alaric's army was the first enemy force to penetrate the soil of Rome since the days of the Celtic Brennus, and the spoils that the Goths acquired were therefore enormous. However, a large part of the city's diminished population was formed by a proletariat who lived at the expense of the State and whose support devoured funds that were desperately needed elsewhere.

Most importantly, the invasion caused the withdrawal of the Roman troops from Britain, and gave the final push to the Germanic conquests in the south. Emperor Honorius replied the British petition for assistance in 410 by

---

[96] Gothic disappeared as a spoken language between the 7th and 9th centuries, but Ulfilas' Bible translation remains the first major document of Germanic literature.

exclaiming that the Romans had their hands full defending their own land, and that the Britons would have to take care of their own defence from now on. Thenceforward, Britain ceased to be a province of Rome, and was exposed to the incursion of the Angles and Saxons, while the Vandals marched over the Pyrenees to Spain, where they settled in the province of Vandalusia, which still—having lost only one letter—carries their name.

After his epoch-making accomplishment, Alaric promptly continued his march towards Calabria, in order to conquer North Africa, the granary of the Empire, which was still loyal to Honorius. But his transport ships were lost in a storm, and shortly thereafter, he himself died of fever in Cosenza, at the age of only thirty-four. His troops diverted the Busento River temporarily from its course, dug a deep grave in the bed of the stream, and laid his body there alongside his trusty steed and his most splendid spoils. After the river was returned to its former course, the slaves who had done the work were killed so that no one could learn the secret of his final resting place and raid the tomb of the Visigothic king.

Alaric's brother-in-law, Ataulf, emerged as the next king of the Visigoths, and took them first to Gallic Aquitaine, between the Garonne and the Pyrenees, and thence to Spain, where the wandering tribe would finally find a permanent abode, though not quite yet in his time. While in Italy, he had captured Galla Placidia, sister of the Emperors, and taken her as his wife—on her, but by no means on her brothers' consent. Ataulf was murdered before long by one of his own officers, who imprisoned the princess and treated her badly, but she soon got an opportunity to take vengeance on her husband's murderer. His successor handed her over to her imperial brother at Ravenna for 600,000 measures of grain, which the Goths needed more urgently than they did her.

From the writings of Church Father Augustine, who at that time had been a bishop in the North African town of Hippo for fifteen years already, we may read of many even less uplifting incidents. He wrote his famous work on the City of God, *De Civitate Dei*, partly for the reason that he wanted to refute the accusation commonly advanced by pagans, that the weakness manifesting itself more and more clearly in the Roman Empire was caused by the Christian orientation towards the hereafter, if not actually by the wickedness of the Christians. Augustine could easily demonstrate that many cities and kingdoms had declined and fallen long before Christianity was even founded; according to him, decline was inherent in the cities of this world—the City of God alone was eternal.

Over fifteen years, Augustine's work of course developed into something much wider in scope and of much greater and more lasting importance. The basis of his thinking was the notion of man as the citizen of two worlds. The early secular communities, such as Babylon and the Roman Empire, were characterized by the negative qualities of man, such as lust for power, iniquity, and pride. Alongside the earthly powers had risen communities, where the Christian virtues, charity, humility, and obedience to God, prevailed. Augustine contended that the Christian Church was obliged to realize the City of God, that is, lead His chosen people through earthly vicissitudes to heavenly beatitude. As a representative of the City of God on Earth, the Church stood above secular power, which would be allowed to wield its might only by submitting to ecclesiastical supervision. He was naturally thinking of the spiritual authority of the Church, but those who came after him would think of its temporal power.

Aurelius Augustinus was of noble Roman African descent; his father was a pagan, his mother a Christian. He had, before converting to Christianity, tasted most of the carnal pleasures and studied many of the spiritual currents of the day, including Manichæism and Neoplatonism. It was with Plato's *Republic* as his model, that he had created his divine commonwealth. Neither were possible to implement, but thanks to Augustine, Plato's thought continued to subsist through all the long ages when his writings lay in oblivion. For no other author had a greater presence in mediæval libraries than Augustine, none were so widely read.

Determinism, perhaps the most significant theological doctrine of Augustine, got polished when it clashed with the opinion of Pelagius, an Irish monk who defended a heretical degree of free will.[97] In the course of this long and bitter conflict, Augustine developed his doctrines of Original Sin, Divine Grace, divine sovereignty, and predestination. It has never been easy for the

---

[97] Pelagius regarded the moral strength of man's Free Will (*liberum arbitrium*), when steeled by asceticism, as sufficient in itself to desire and attain the loftiest ideal of virtue. Man was created by God in His image and is, by nature, good, but can fall into sin through the misuse of his Free Will.

Christian Church to admit that people have the ability to make their own free decisions, if only on the account that this sort of freedom would appear to limit the omnipotence which Christianity accords its God. The power of decision, according to Augustine, lay with God, who in his infinite wisdom has made all the decisions for all the ages. However, if man has no free will, he cannot be morally accountable for his actions[98], which is why the Catholic Church never accepted Augustine's doctrine, and only out of respect for him, never publicly banned it.

Extreme determinism also carries another threat to orthodoxy, the idea of a great and irresistible force that sweeps away the commonplace, customary, and self-evident, and is known to attract people of strong character and rebellious nature. Augustine's faith, strengthened and inflamed through an immeasurable devotion, *credo quia absurdum*, finds its passionate expression in his *Confessions*. Besides being one of the most enduring books in all world literature, this work of prose, conceived around the year 400, also starts a whole new genre, the merciless, backward-looking and deep-probing self-analysis. Without it, we may never have been able to see the pride, egocentrism, and insincerity of the honest seeker of truth, who made his way from Manichæism and neo-Skepticism to Neoplatonism and Christianity.

The so-called Constantinian tradition obligated the Church to act reciprocally for the good of the State. The Church had to act as an intercessor for the whole society and especially for the Emperor. The people had to be raised as humble subjects, who observed the law and paid the taxes without a word of complaint. The adherents of other religions, the so-called "pagans," i.e. the people of the rural districts, by far the largest component of the population, had to be kept in check, and if at all possible, converted to Christianity. Religious unity was presumed to lead to the overall unity of the Empire.

At the end of the 4th and during the 5th century, Judaism, Manichæism, and Donatism were the heresies most in view. A law of 407, aimed at the Donatists, asserts for the first time that heretics should be placed on the same level as transgressors against the sacred majesty of the Emperor, a concept which was given a momentous role in later times. This was the first occasion

---

[98] which would, of course, also have clashed with the claimed authority of the Catholic Church to grant absolution

when a Catholic bishop advocated a decisive co-operation of the State in religious questions, and its right to inflict death on heretics.

Led by their king, Geiseric, the Arian Vandals crossed the strait of Gibraltar in 429 and marched triumphantly through North Africa, where they had come to free the multitude of Donatists, who were the target of a ruthless persecution by the orthodox. Only a few months after St. Augustine's death in 430, the Vandals invaded the bishopric of Hippo, which had, however, been evacuated before their arrival. The patristic writings had also been saved from falling into the hands of heretics; otherwise the history of the European peoples might have evolved quite differently than it did. Some years later, Geiseric invaded Carthage and founded there a pirate state that subsisted for a century.

It might be tempting to think that paganism simply declined and Christianity filled a vacancy—but it was really not quite like that. Christianity made little progress among rural people of the Empire, and despite laws against it, pagan faith remained persistently alive, being erased only slowly over centuries. There were, of course, peaceful Christians, gentle Christians, benevolent Christians, hermits interested only in their solitary salvation; but, almost inevitably, especially in cities, the Christian church and the pagan temple proved incompatible.

From the 5th century on, the title of Patriarch was bestowed upon the metropolitan bishops, who had begun to exercise more and more control over their provinces. In Alexandria, the conflict between secular and ecclesiastical authority was decided in 415, when the Roman prefect, Orestes—who was officially still in charge—objected to Patriarch Cyril's order that all Jews[99] be expelled from the city. Cyril's army of monks killed the prefect and, marauding through Alexandria, came across Hypatia, daughter of Theon, the last great mathematician of the Museum.

A Neoplatonic philosopher and astronomer in her own right, Hypatia was not only talented, but also extremely beautiful; her lectures were greatly admired, and an abundance of listeners, though not one theologian, gathered to hear them. Driving home without an attendant from one of her lectures, this independent woman scholar embodied the suspect nature of pagan science. She was dragged from her chariot, stripped naked, flayed alive, and

---

[99] who, until then, still outnumbered the Christian population

finally burned with the library of the Cæsareum for the greater glory of God, marking the end of paganism in Alexandria. St. Cyril made sure that the murder was never properly investigated, and that the guilty would not be punished.

There were, at the time, two main theological schools of thought within the eastern half of the Roman Empire: the "Alexandrian" and the "Antiochene" schools of Egypt and Syria respectively. The former school, to which St. Cyril belonged, had fought with the heresy of Arius, who had held the Son to be a part of the creation of the Father. Thus the orthodox Egyptians insisted especially on the divinity of the Son—had He not so completely united our humanity to Himself that He made it fully His own, we would not have been saved. The Syrian orthodoxy, on the other hand, had been threatened by Apollinarianism, which asserted that the Logos had assumed only human flesh, wherefore the Antiochene theologians were chiefly concerned to preserve the entire human nature of the Son. For them, it was the co-operation of the human with the divine which made possible our salvation—were Christ not fully human, we would not have been be saved.

In 428, a Syrian priest, Nestorius, was consecrated Patriarch of Constantinople. He immediately caused great controversy by arguing that the Virgin Mary, though the passive recipient of the Divine Logos, had given birth to the human Son only, and could therefore not be given the title of her pagan counterparts, *Theotókos*, or God-Bearer, for which St. Cyril had strongly lobbied. The monks of the capital, whom Nestorius had excommunicated on account of their opposition to his orthodox Antiochene teachings, appealed to the Emperor of the East, Theodosius II, son and successor of Arcadius, to call together a council.

In 431, the Third Ecumenical Council met at Ephesus, the metropolis of Roman Asia. Though Nestorius had camped nearby, he refused to appear before the Council, which was presided over by his mortal enemy, St. Cyril the Great. Thus the Council had no difficulty in affirming that Mary was indeed the *Theotókos*, or condemning the teachings of Nestorius, who was now dubbed the "Second Judas," a sneer at his Jewish descent.

Six days later, John, Patriarch of Antioch, arrived with his bishops, who had not been able to reach Ephesus in time for the Council, and met by themselves. They naturally sided with Nestorius, a graduate of the Antiochene school, against the bishops of the Council, deeming him innocent and issuing an accusation of heresy against Cyril. The second Theodosius, who had as little sense of humour as the first, ordered both Cyril and Nestorius to be confined, and the verdicts of both the Council of Ephesus and the Syrian bishops void. The envoys whom the Council was eventually allowed to send to the court finally persuaded the Emperor to accept its decrees.

The Syrian bishops made peace with Cyril in 433, while Nestorius himself requested permission to retire to his former monastery, where he stayed until his death in 451. The Christians in East Syria and Mesopotamia, however, remained in opposition to the Council and eventually produced a lasting schism of their own. Shut out from the Roman Empire, but protected by the Persian kings, this Nestorian Church flourished around Ctesiphon, Nisibis, and throughout Persia. Nestorians survive today in parts of Syria, Iraq, Iran, and India, though their creed contains no trace of the heresy after which they were named.

Things heated up again after the death of St. Cyril in 444. He was succeeded as the Patriarch of Alexandria by his nephew, Dioscurus, who became, with Archimandrite Eutyches of Constantinople, one of the most violent opponents of Nestorianism. Whereas Cyril had agreed with the Syrians in 433 that Christ had two natures, Eutyches insisted that Christ's humanity was absorbed in his divinity and that to accept two natures at all was Nestorian. When a Syrian bishop, Theodoret of Cyrus, condemned Eutychianism, Dioscurus retaliated by anathematizing him, and in 448, Theodosius II confined him to his diocese. Meanwhile, to top the confusion, Pope Leo I wrote a dogmatic epistle to Patriarch Flavian of Constantinople, condemning Eutyches, who was subsequently deposed in a local synod held at the capital.

Eutyches appealed to his friends, and in 449, the Eastern Emperor convoked the Second Council of Ephesus under the presidency of Dioscurus. This Council was dubbed by St. Leo as the *Latrocinium*, the "Robber Council," if not because it declared Eutyches orthodox and reinstated his offices, while excommunicating St. Flavian of Constantinople, along with Theodoret of Cyrus, Ibas of Edessa, Domnus II of Antioch, and a few other Syrian prelates, then because it completely ignored the papal epistle. To the Greeks, Rome was still a sort of colonial bishopric; after all, there were two million Christians in the East, and not two hundred thousand in the West.

One of the only two popes whom all later history has agreed to style "the

Great," Leo condemned everything the Council had done via letters and a Roman synod, absolved all whom it had condemned, and excommunicated everyone who had taken part in it. Theodosius II refused Leo's request to call a new general council to right the wrongs of Ephesus, but his sudden death less than a year later in 450—an event that raised more than a few eyebrows at this point—immediately altered the state of affairs. He was succeeded by his sister, St. Pulcheria, who soon after married and co-ruled with the elderly general Marcian, an intimate friend and follower of Nestorius.

The Council of Chalcedon, convoked by Emperor Marcian in 451, was impressive to say the least. The estimates of the number of bishops attending range from five to six hundred. No council before it had had such a great attendance, and few councils since then have surpassed its record until recent times. It was supervised by imperial commissioners, in accordance with the directions of Leo, whose legates presided. They accepted Theodoret and Ibas as members, declared as orthodox Theodore of Mopsuestia, the teacher of Nestorius and the originator of his heresy, and solemnly accepted the now-famous Tome of Leo as an expression of the orthodox faith concerning the person of Christ.

While the Council is commonly thought to have condemned Archimandrite Eutyches, it did not, in fact, deal with him at all, but with Dioscurus of Alexandria. As soon as the Council had assembled, the papal legates demanded that Dioscurus be deposed and banished because of Leo's orders. Without even examining the issue, they denounced the Second Council of Ephesus, placing the whole responsibility for its decrees on the Patriarch of Alexandria. He was thus deprived of office, not on account of erroneous beliefs, but on procedural grounds.

According to the Roman Catholic Church, the ecumenical episcopacy, or primacy, belongs to the Roman pontiff, which assertion was first made by Pope St. Stephen in the middle of 3rd century, and repeated by Leo the Great in the middle of the 5th, based on the leading position supposedly given to Peter in Matthew 16:18 and handed down to his successors. The problem was that St. Peter had provenly reigned at Antioch, not Rome, and founded the church of Alexandria through his disciple, St. Mark. Constantinople, on the other hand, had the presence of the all-powerful Emperor on its side. It was this controversy that reached its peak at Chalcedon.

The Council decided that the old Roman custom, by which the Emperor had the final say in ecclesiastical matters, was to continue. That may have been the end of the matter at Constantinople, but Pope Leo confirmed the decrees of Chalcedon only after eliminating the canon which elevated the Imperial City; Anti-Chalcedonian riots broke out in Egypt and in Syria, while the Armenians, who had been unable to attend the Council due to the Sassanian occupation, flatly rejected all its decisions.

As an expression of their national sentiment against the imperial garrisons, Roman officials, and the government-appointed patriarchs, the "Non-Chalcedonian" Christians of Egypt and Syria translated the Bible and liturgy into their own vernacular and formed what are known today as the Oriental Orthodox Churches. The heresy that was labelled the Monophysitic Error (from *mone physis*, one nature) appears to have been introduced later in a polemic fashion on behalf of the Chalcedonian Churches[100] and has certainly never reflected the real belief of the Non-Chalcedonians, whose persecution by the Byzantine Empire would not cease until the Arab invasion in the 7th century.

---

[100] In any case, the term was not used in the 5th, 6th, or even the 7th century.

CHAPTER 13

The other noteworthy episode of the mid-5th century was the dramatic final act in the saga of the Huns. At the beginning of the century, there was hardly a Hun State in the proper meaning of the word, though several autonomous Hun armies existed in the east. One of these armies rode through Asia Minor and acquired horses from the famed imperial stud farms in Cappadocia, where the finest steeds of antiquity were reputedly bred. The Huns had their westernmost outposts in present-day Hungary, but their political organization was weak, and their troops often enlisted in the service of foreign armies. They had been on particularly good terms with Stilicho, who made a habit of hiring Huns in his personal guard.

Another long-time friend of the Huns was the famous general, Flavius Aëtius, whom historians are accustomed to cite as the last Roman, and who in due course became their conqueror. He was the commander-in-chief of the West, and its most powerful man in the final years of Honorius' reign; when the Western Emperor was succeeded on his death by Galla Placidia's little son, Valentinian, Aëtius placed himself in the service of this sorely tried woman. After returning from the Visigoths, she was reluctantly remarried to a Roman general by the name of Constantius, and had managed to give birth to two children before he died.

Aëtius remained in power for twenty years, and the foundation of his sovereignty lay precisely in his good personal relations with the Huns. On several occasions, he visited their court and headquarters in Pannonia, where he was received with all the possible tokens of friendship. Thus the relationship of the Western Empire with the Huns remained cordial, while the Eastern Empire was caught in unending hostilities and quarrels, which she tried her best to avoid with ever-increasing tributes. Aëtius' dear friend, the Hun king Rugilas, was succeeded by his two nephews, Attila and Bleda, but the former soon murdered the latter, beginning the great era of the Huns.

Attila was not only a military genius, but a brilliant organizer, who soon amassed for himself all the resources of the Huns, thereby controlling both

Scythia and Germania, i.e. the entire region from the Rhine to Central Asia with all its tribes and peoples. He was well aware of his supremacy, for the language he uses in his diplomatic relations was arrogant to the extreme. At first, he nevertheless seemed generous towards Aëtius, who persuaded him to place at his disposal the army with which the Roman general would invade and crush the kingdom which the Burgundii had not long ago established in central Gaul. This event is elaborated in the Nibelung saga, which Richard Wagner has made famous.

The peaceful relations of the Romans with Attila were undermined when the Emperor's ambitious sister, Honoria, attempted an alliance with the king of the Huns without her brother's knowledge. Attila took her offer as a marriage proposal and demanded half of the Western Empire as a dowry. When he was refused, he crossed the Rhine with an army of half a million Huns and allies, flooding over northeastern Gaul. Fortunately, the Visigothic king, Theodoric, saw the danger in time and united his forces with those of Aëtius. This joint army of Germans and Romans met Attila at Champagne, forcing him to withdraw at the famous battle on the fields of Catalaunum near present-day Châlons-sur-Marne, where even more blood would be spilled in modern times.

In the war against the Huns, the Visigoths ended up taking the heaviest blows and Theodoric himself fell. Of the Germanic tribes that fought on the side of Theodoric and the Romans, the 6th-century Gothic historian Jordanes names the Visigoths, the Gepidæ, the Heruli, and the Franks. The unbaptized king of the last mentioned was called Merovech—he was the progenitor of the extraordinary House of the Merovings. Attila retreated to his base in Pannonia, but by the following spring, his horsemen were back in the saddle and headed south. Upon learning of his approach, the people of the northern Italian town of Aquileia took refuge on the inaccessible islands in the coastal lagoons of the Adriatic, where they founded the town of Venice.

At the wish of Valentinian III, the Consul Avienus, accompanied by the Prefect Tigetius and Pope Leo the Great, travelled in 452 to meet the King of the Huns at the Mincio River near Mantua, obtaining from him the promise that he would withdraw from Italy and negotiate peace with the Emperor. Hardly had the pagan Huns turned back when the pirate fleet of the Christian Vandals landed at Ostia under the pious Geiseric, who had given his helmsmen orders to release the wheel and let the ships go with the wind, so that the fleet would drift to a location inhabited by people whom God wished to punish. In 455, the Vandals slayed the newly-elected Emperor, Petronius Maximus, after which they thoroughly pirated Rome[101] and shipped a countless number of treasures and prisoners to Carthage, among them Empress Eudoxia and her two daughters.

Attila had once more returned to Pannonia, where he in 453 celebrated his marriage to the beautiful princess Ildico of the defeated House of the Burgundii. In the dead of the night, he staggered from the great wedding feast to the bridal chamber, and his courtiers, who did not want to disturb the newlyweds, waited quietly behind the closed door almost until noon. When lunch time draw near, they finally found the courage to try and awaken the king with noise and rattle, but as breathless silence endured in the bedroom, they grew anxious and broke in. They encountered the bride sitting by the bed, a veil covering her teary eyes, scared to death by the clear and present danger in which she was. Her husband lay lifeless beside her, having suffered a fatal nosebleed in the course of the wedding night. After the Huns had grieved for their king by pulling their hair and cutting themselves with blades, the royal departed was placed in a three-layered coffin of gold, silver, and steel, and buried beside unimaginable treasures and those unfortunate captives who had been forced to dig his grave. Thereafter, the Huns held a feast that was worthy of their greatest king, for Jordanes tells us that the rumours about these revelries soon reached even distant Constantinople.

Just a few years after Attila's death, the Huns vanished from history; not only their kingdom, but their entire tribe disappeared without a trace, once the Ostrogoths, the Gepidæ, and the Heruli had liberated themselves and defeated the sons of Attila in a single decisive battle. The dynasty of Theodosius the Great died in the West in the mid-5th century with Galla Placidia and her son, during whose reign the real power had rested in the hands of Aëtius, and the rapidly changing emperors of the years that followed were without exception new names and not even any relation to one another. They were called Petronius Maximus, Avitus, Majorian, Libius Severus, Anthemius, Olybrius, Glycerius, and Julius Nepos. Most of them were both inducted into office and dismissed from it by Aëtius' successor as the *magister*

---

[101] Apparently, however, the citizens themselves did more damage than the Vandals—whose name became synonymous with wanton destruction—stripping many of the ancient buildings of their marble.

militum of the West, a Swabian called Ricimer. The succession of despotic warriors was carried on by the Pannonian Orestes, one-time secretary to Attila and the father of young Romulus Augustulus. After bestowing the imperial crown upon his son, who thus gained an entry in all the subsequent encyclopædias and history books, he was attacked by a brave Germanic warrior called Odoacer, who not only defeated him, but ruled Italy in his own name for fourteen years.

The watershed between antiquity and the Dark Ages is customarily set at the year 476, on the day that the underage Romulus Augustulus[102], the last Emperor of the West, whose name alone is a sheer joke, was divested of the purple and left for Misenum to spend his remaining days at the fabled villa of Lucullus[103]. This event caused no stir in the generation that had to witness it; by then, the city of Rome had been conquered and pillaged several times by barbarians, and the people were used to the dismissal of emperors.

In the age of the Shadow Emperors, actual power had been wielded by the "Patricians," that is, the Roman generals Stilicho, Constantius, Aëtius, Ricimer, Orestes, and Odoacer. Eventually, even the pretense of an emperor became unnecessary, for when Odoacer ejected Romulus Augustulus from the throne, he did not appoint a successor. By no means did he abolish the Empire, much less the Roman State; on the contrary, he sent the imperial regalia to Zeno, the Byzantine Emperor, humbly requesting that he might be allowed to remain his vassal with the established title of *Patricius*. He did not touch the laws or institutions of Rome, and established his court at Ravenna. Odoacer and his contemporaries conceived not two Roman Empires, but one, the division of which had been arbitrary and temporary.

It is really a matter of taste when we stop talking of "late Classical" and begin using the term "Byzantine"; there was, of course, no "fall of the Roman Empire" until the 15th century. The traditions lived on unbroken in the Empire in the East right through the Middle Ages, the capital still where Constantine had set it. In the Byzantine State, the splendour and glory of the Roman Empire would last for another thousand years; its citizen were known

---

[102] i.e. "Little Augustus"

[103] from which we derive the expression "to live in Lucullan splendour"

as *Romaioi*, its capital as New Rome.[104] Its laws were Roman, as were its government, army, and its officialdom, and initially also its official language. In fine, the whole organization of Byzantium was that of the Roman Imperial Period, with its hierarchy and bureaucracy in their entirety.

Characteristic to the Byzantine culture was a fertile fusion of Hellenism and Christianity. Byzantium was God's Kingdom on Earth, the only thoroughly Christian state in Europe. In its organization, God's law and Roman law worked in harmony. Byzantium was a wealthy, well-regulated, hierarchical society, on the apex of which stood God's vicegerent on Earth, the emperor. Seven hundred emperors ruled there, each of them carrying all the temporal titles that had belonged to Augustus and Nero, and subject to all the elaborate and extravagant ceremonies, which Diocletian and Constantine had prescribed. Never would they neglect to submit their war plans on the altar of God, accompanied by hymns and prayers, and by the Euphrates and the Danube did their legions kneel the night before battle under a forest of burning candles stuck on their spears.

One of the advantages of having Constantinople as the capital was that it stood on an easily fortified peninsula; as it lay closer to the dangerous frontiers of the Empire than Rome had, imperial armies could respond more rapidly to crises. The strategic location of the city enabled its merchants to make a fortune through their control over the trade routes between Europe and Asia, and the shipping lanes connecting the Black Sea and the Mediterranean. A well-conducted economy was a prerequisite to the much admired and envied wealth, which enabled success in the incessant defensive battle against the Persians, the Arabs, and the Turks. During the ensuing decades, when Western Europe sank into the state which the sophisticated Greeks called barbarism, the Byzantine princesses and noblewomen were in demand at the marriage market of the Western rulers.

At Byzantium, which the hordes of migrations never reached, antiquity lasted long and the Middle Ages began early. This long groundlessly undervalued culture has only during the last century gained the respect it deserves. Without its mediation, it is likely that neither Homer nor Sophocles, Plato or Aristotle, would have found their way to us. Though the Byzantine

---

[104] The word "Hellene," on the other hand, became associated with outlawed religious practices and disloyalty to the State, remaining in bad repute for centuries to come.

Church developed its own literature and philosophy, it nonetheless looked favourably upon the intellectual tradition of Classical scholarship. Students read the ancient Greek classics of literature, rhetoric, philosophy, science, medicine, and art. While Western Europe was threatened with complete barbarization, the Imperial University (est. 425) in the metropolis of Constantinople took ceaseless care of producing capable element to offices both spiritual and profane.

Even as the Greek tongue died in the West, Latin died in the East, increasing the chances to foster the maternal language. Both the secular and ecclesiastical authors wrote in a language which no one spoke, an artificial tongue that imitated Plutarch and the Church Fathers. The reasons to preserve this language were more national than spiritual—it was not a question of protecting sacred literature from profanation, but a matter of keeping alive a tradition that was profane to begin with. This fact also had an effect on the subject matter; princes and laymen distinguished themselves as penmen at least as much as the clergy. The social hierarchy was dominated to the last by Church, but by a Church that had allied herself with hereditary patriotism and humanism.[105]

The ascetic view of life was deeply embedded in the Greek character and strengthened by the high development of monastic institutions, which in turn produced a substantial ascetic literature. The monastic institution was the only form of activity common to the whole Eastern Church; the Rule of St. Basil applied to both monks and nuns. The monasteries of the East were situated in near-impassable locations; men and women entered them to escape the world. They were centres of study, meditation, and devotion; the individual acolyte lived a year separated from other people. Isolation from the mundane prevented all active participation in civic functions—in direct contrast to the West, where the monasteries lent support to the trade and industry of their environs and even engaged in politics.

In the 5th and 6th centuries, Western Europe collapsed into a chaos of

---

[105] The Byzantine mystical writers differed from those of the West mainly in their attitude towards ecclesiastical ceremonial, perceiving it not as a substitution of the spiritual life by external pomp, but rather as a profound allegory of this life. The Eastern mystics therefore adhered strictly to the ceremonial rules of the Church, regarding them as a means to the attainment of ethical perfection.

barbarian nations rampaging back and forth. When a monastery was surrounded with walls, it became a refuge for the local people during war and unrest. A constant problem for monasteries was the ambition of bishops and other clergy to subordinate them to the ecclesiastical hierarchy. In the West, the monastic orders were placed under the control of the local bishop, providing the church with labourers. The monasteries were given duties that bound them to social order, and in time, they became an integral part of the Christian society. They were organized strictly according to gender, and as early as the 5th century, many Western nunneries had become sorts of prisons for women, where in particular the adulterous wives were sent. The monastic rules spelled an end to private expressions of Christian piety; acts of charity, such as maintaining a hospice, were considered the duty of every Western monastery. Many of them boasted libraries, schools, and hospitals; many more were model farms.

Still, during the migrations, and the political anarchy and ceaseless wars that followed, in the world of famine and recurrent epidemics, monasteries were the strongholds of peace and culture. In Italy, Cassiodorus endeavoured, during the latter half of the 6th century, to make the monasteries enduring seats of learning in the troubled times which he describes in his *History of the Goths*. Through them all, the Latin language and the Catholic Church survived, preserving for the West a unity that transcended the political divisions. Regardless of the various regional vernaculars, Latin remained the language of religion and learning, such as there was. The long-neglected Greek vanished with the Roman rule, as did also the imperial organization of education, and most of the secular schools. The Church disapproved of the pagan Liberal Arts; they survived because they were bound to: there was no substitute. The Church needed a literate clergy and had to continue providing for is education, which, however, consisted simply of grammar and rhetoric—that much was essential for a religion with scriptures and a Latin liturgy. Only exceptionally did the clerics, to whom Latin was enough, take notice of the local vernaculars, and the dialects derived from Latin had to wait a long time to appear in print.

During this period, Ireland became a prominent seat of learning, furnishing a dramatic contrast to the low level of scholarship in continental Europe. Whereas both Gaul and Britain had first fallen into the hands of the Romans and then of the Germanic tribes, the remote and isolated location of the

"Emerald Isle" helped it remain a Celtic kingdom and retain the Celtic institutions, laws, art, and literature; the myths and legends lived on in its oral tradition, to be much later written down and utilized in the international poetry that tells of Arthur, Tristan, Ossian, and Parsifal. At Clonmacnoise and Glendalough (Gleann dá Loch)—once called Rome of the West—and in many other places, one can see the remains of churches, towers, and magnificently carved crosses as reminders of ancient monastic communities, where students came from all over the West in search of knowledge, which during the Dark Ages that followed the fall of Old Rome, could not be found anywhere else.

There is no question that in the Christianizing of Ireland the monk came before the priest, the monastery prior to the cathedral. The Irish Church was organized as a monastic church, whose power lay in the religious houses of the various clans.[106] Since the Irish and their princes had already during the age of the Druids gotten used to an extremely theocratical form of government, they soon transferred unto the Christian monks the boundless respect they had had for their pagan priests, and as the saints' legends prove, the equally boundless faith in their magical abilities. Eventually, outside religious and political pressures, the Irish monks adopted a practice of wandering, which ultimately became their trademark and the most remarkable and long-lasting feature of Celtic Christianity.

In the beginning of the 6th century, a band of adventurers led by the northern Irish chieftain Fergus mac Erc arrived in Scotland, at the shore of the Kintyre Peninsula, which already had a struggling Christian colony amidst the heathen Picts (Lat. *Picti*, "painted ones"). The name of *Scotia*, having originally meant Ireland, was transplanted by these settlers on their new land. Fergus soon emerged as the king of all these Gælic immigrants and gradually spread his power. His descendants attained, through wars and the matrimonial alliances they forged with the Pictish royal families, supremacy over the whole country and formed the United Kingdom of Scotland. From Fergus descend all the Scottish kings, and through the Stuarts, the current royal family of Great Britain. Simultaneously with this political invasion, an era of missionary work led by the St. Columba (521-597) of the clan O'Neill began first in Pictland, then among the Saxons of northern England, and nearly all of these regions

---

[106] In this, the Church paralleled Gælic secular society, whose basic unit was the autonomous *túath*.

have the Irish to can thank for their conversion.

Circa 400 to 1000 CE, the Irish missionaries also did a momentous job on the Continent, though their peculiar nature caused great controversy in the countries they visited. But greater was the fertilizing effect of their poetry, music, illuminated manuscripts, and scholarship that gave birth to the great monastic libraries of Europe. The Greek language saw an early renaissance in Ireland, and many modern scholars believe that both the end rhyme and polyphonic music had their origin there. In any case, the basis for hymnody—which subsequently became the most remarkable artistic monument of the Middle Ages—was cast in Ireland. The fame of her monasteries and missionary schools rose to such heights that she was dubbed "The Isle of the Saints."

The conversion of the Germans to Christianity was historically very significant, not due to any significant change in their way of life or in their world of ideas, but because it was effected mainly by Arian missionaries. Virtually all the Germanic tribes were Arian, a fact which greatly hindered the assimilation process between *Romania* and *Barbaricum*.

In the last decade of the 5th century, the Ostrogoths, under commission from the Byzantine Emperor Zeno, and led by their ruthless, powerful king Theodoric, attacked Italy. After defeating the forces of Odoacer in the Battle of Verona and treacherously murdering him, it took Theodoric only three years to subdue the rest of the peninsula, and in 493, he became king of Italy, reigning for the next 33 years. He had for his prime minister a prolific penman, the aforementioned Cassiodorus, whose correspondences form our principal source for the events.

Theodoric the Great was, at the same time, both the King of the Ostrogoths and a Patrician of Rome. He placed third of Italy under the rule of his tribe, while leaving the Romans with their own laws and officials. He had at his disposal an army of 100,000 Goths and a fleet of a hundred ships, which guarded the coast from the raids of the Vandals. In the year 500, he issued an edict in which he outlined the principles by which he intended to rule: he meant to raise the Goths to the level of the Romans and fuse both peoples into one nation.

In spite of his Arianism, he protected the Catholics, but viewed with disfavour the persecutions that Emperor Justinian directed at his brothers in faith, and whenever he discovered hostile attitude towards Arianism at his own court, he severely punished the guilty. By the time he died at Ravenna in 526, his domain consisted, in addition to Italy and Sicily, of western Illyricum, Pannonia, Noricum, Rhætia, Provence, and Spain.

Circa 580, Gregory of Tours published his *Historia Francorum*, an unforgettable depiction of the untamed manners of the Merovingians, but also of the forces that cleared the barbarian woodlands and gave birth to France. The bishop describes in a pious manner how the great Frankish king Clovis (Chlodwig) expanded his realm through a host of the wickedest misdeeds, which are all meticulously recounted. According to this amazing chronicle, the King does not appear to have performed a single good or humane act, yet in the eyes of St. Gregory, he is still the favourite of Heaven, for the benefit of whom miracles constantly take place. For Clovis had, in the beginning of his career, had himself baptized in the one redeeming faith, which says that the Son is of the same substance as the Father, born and not created. The Burgundii, the Ostrogoths, and the Visigoths—all of whom he successfully fought against—were not the adherents of this doctrine, but heretical Arians.

The Burgundian king Gundobad had killed his brother Chilperic and drowned Chilperic's wife by tying a rock on poor woman's neck. The House of the Burgundii had a tradition of persecuting Christians, but Gundobad's niece Clotilda was a Christian, and what is more, an orthodox Catholic. The presently still pagan Clovis heard of her beauty and wanted to marry her, and though the Frankish king already had a son, Theodoric, by one of his mistresses, he chose Clotilda as his sole consort.

Clotilda tried many times to get his husband to convert to the Christian faith, but Clovis was stubborn. He finally gained a glorious victory over his enemies after he had promised to have himself baptized if Christ would help him. The Lord had kept his part of the bargain, and so would the King: he was baptized with over three thousand of his warriors and his two sister, one of whom died shortly after the ordeal—the Franks were not particularly keen bathers and a sudden immersion into cold water proved quite a shock to them. The other sister had previously been an Arian, and her conversion was perhaps more pleasing to the Church than that of a mere pagan; this Lanthechild was, after all, the proverbial strayed sheep, who was thus brought back to the flock.

The conversion of the Franks may not have marked any change in their gruesome customs, but from the perspective of Western history, the efforts of

Clotilda have considerable importance. It was through her influence that the Franks converted to the Catholic instead of the Arian faith, and later on the king of France became a champion of the papacy—"His Most Christian Majesty."

With the blessing of Divine Providence, Clovis put to death practically every member of his own family. Towards his holy contemporary, Bishop Martin of Tours, the King, on the other hand, showed the greatest respect. Whenever necessary, Saint Martin conjured the saving grace of God upon Clovis; once, for example, a pillar of fire blazed up in his cathedral and propitiously shed light for the King and his men on their nightly march to their next foul deed. "For God was laying his enemies low every day under his hand, and was increasing his kingdom, because he walked with an upright heart before him, and did what was pleasing in his eyes," writes of Clovis Martin's successor, Gregory of Tours; in that same complacent manner and comforting spirit, he later describes all those misdeeds which Clovis' children and grandchildren and other members of the Merovingian house committed. Some of Clovis' surviving family also figure in Wagner's operas, *Die Walküre*, *Siegfried*, and *Die Götterdämmerung*.

Clovis, upon whom the Byzantine Emperor had conferred the title of Roman Consul, died in 511, leaving behind an undivided nation and a state obedient to a single ruler, the mightiest of the ones built on ruins of the Western Empire. The long period following his death is almost constant struggle within the borders of his empire and endless confusion in the relations of Church and State. Upon her husband's death, Clotilda withdrew into a convent, but piety did not prevent her from inciting her three sons to mount a war against Burgundy—her parents were, after all, still unavenged. During that campaign, Clotilda's eldest son, King Chlodomer, had his opponent, along with his wife and children, assassinated by ordering them to be cast into a well near Orléans; for this, he was cursed and later died in battle. Clotilda's second son, King Clothar, married his elder brother's widow, while Clotilda took over the raising of her grandsons.

However, Clotilda's grown-up sons, Clothar and Childebert, soon grew jealous of their mother's devotion to the little ones. Afraid that the Queen would allow their nephews to share in the succession, the uncles assumed their wardship by deceit, murdering two of them. The keepers of the third cut the child's long hair—a symbol of royalty in the Merovingian house—and had him enter the priesthood. Later on, he became Saint Claudius, with no other merits than having escaped alive from the clutches of his family. In those times, that kind of achievement was proof aplenty of divine protection.

As an epilogue, Clotilda's son, King Childebert, and her stepson's son, King Theudebert, went to war against their brother, King Clothar. Clotilda summoned through her prayers a terrible storm, which dispersed the troops of Childebert and Theudebert, but kept clear of Clothar, thus ending the conflict before it had even begun. In 554, Queen Clotilda died, eulogized to high heaven. She was buried in Paris and her surviving sons mourned greatly for her. She became, of course, Saint Clotilda.

CHAPTER 14

The state of Italy was wretched, as war, pestilence, famine, and all kinds of other misfortunes had greatly depopulated the country. After the murder (535) of Theodoric the Great's daughter, Amalasuntha, who as regent for her son lay under Byzantine protection, Justinian traitorously reconquered Italy. Rome was garrisoned by the Byzantine general Belisarius, and besieged in vain by the Goths, who only regained the city after his recall. Belisarius was succeeded as the military commander of Byzantium by the eunuch Narses, who with the help of a fresh army, composed primarily of Germans, defeated the Goths near Taginæ. After a few feeble attempts at resistance, the Ostrogothic kingdom fell in 555.

Narses celebrated his triumph in Rome by parading weapons and valuables, trophies that he had collected from the Goths, the Swabians, and the Franks, whilst his troops sung praises to the Emperor. Justinian soon died, however, and was succeeded by his nephew, Justin, who recalled Narses and made Longinus his Exarch, or viceroy, in Italy. Like his barbarian predecessors, the Exarch placed his court at Ravenna, but unlike them, he overturned the local government: the Senate and the Consuls, together with other magistrates, were set aside, while Rome and all other important cities were placed under a *dux* or duke.[107] This division of Italy greatly facilitated her ruin, and hardly had the Ostrogothic saga ended, when the last of the migrating Germanic tribes penetrated into the country and gave the name of Lombardy to that part of Italy which was previously known as Cisalpine Gaul.[108]

Responsibility for this change of name rests with the Lombards, known in the annals as the most ferocious and bloodthirsty of all the Germanic conquerors. Around the fall of the Ostrogoths, they had established themselves in present-day Austria, and passed the time by fighting the other

---

[107] The Byzantine duchy of Rome included Latium and parts of Tuscany.

[108] Similarly, the area around Ravenna became in the Lombard mind *Romania*, and is thus known as "Romagna" to this day.

tribes. The first to be driven out were the Heruli, part of whom returned to their original homeland in modern Sweden, settled themselves next to the Götar, and came to be called Svear. Then the Lombards turned against the Gepidæ, who were living in what is now Serbia.

The king of the Gepidæ was called Cunimund, and he had a beautiful daughter by the name of Rosamund, with whom the Lombard king Alboin was madly in love. For political reasons, Alboin was forced to wed a Frankish princess, Clotosinda, but to his great delight, she soon died and he could seriously consider marrying Rosamund. After her father rejected him as a suitor, the Lombards went to war and thoroughly crushed the Gepidæ. Alboin personally killed King Cunimund and had a goblet made out of his gilded skull. Rosamund he, of course, took for himself as part of the spoils, and made her his wife without asking for her hand.

Emboldened by the victory over the Gepidæ, Alboin subsequently marched with his entire tribe to the Po Valley, and soon the Lombards made themselves masters of a region which the Byzantines, busy fending off the Persians, were unable to defend. After crossing the Julian Alps in 568, Alboin pillaged Venice and Milan, and the towns along the Æmilian Way, but only after 572 did he march a victor into Theodoric's palace in Pavia.

Alboin celebrated his conquest by holding a great banquet at Verona. To solemnize the feast, he ordered Cunimund's skull to be brought to the table, and together with his generals, drank a toast of victory. He then refilled the cup and passed it to Queen Rosamund, so that she too could make merry with her father, as the King himself put it. Rosamund obediently partook of the drink, but set to work on her revenge.

Few of Rosamund's handmaidens had as their lover an officer who served in Alboin's staff, and she snuck into a secret midnight rendez-vous with him instead of her maid servant. At the right moment, she naturally revealed her real identity to the startled paramour, and in fear that the King would learn what had taken place, the officer agreed to put him to death. So the next day, the amorous officer murdered his king, who was unable to draw his sword because the Queen had tied it to its scabbard as a precaution.

Following Alboin's death and the eighteen-month reign of Cleph, no new king was elected and Lombardy fell under the disunited rule of some thirty dukes—the duchies of Spoleto and Benevento in central and southern Italy were set up independently. In 584, the nobles jointly elected Cleph's son,

Authari, as their king to fortify themselves against the hostility of the Byzantines, the Franks, and the papacy.

If any pope, St. Gregory the Dialogist deserves to be called "Great." He was largely responsible for the creation of the Latin Church, which served to counteract the subordination of the Roman popes to the Byzantine emperors, by establishing a common religious policy for Western Europe through the marriage of the papacy with Benedictine monasticism.[109] His reign, around the year 600, was certainly among the most critical: continuous wars, famine, and pestilence spread such abysmal despair that many expected imminent apocalypse; and the nearer the world is to its destruction, the more important the saving of souls becomes.

Gregory was born into a wealthy senatorial family in 540. His father, Gordian, owned sizeable estates in Sicily and a huge mansion on the Cælian Hill in Rome; his grandfather was Pope St. Felix III, and he is supposed to have been related to Pope St. Agapetus I as well. Very little is know about his mother Silvia, who is nonetheless honoured as a saint. Besides Gregory's mother, two of his aunts were canonized—Gordian's two sister, Tarsilla and Æmilians.

Gregory of Tours informs us that in grammar, logic, and rhetoric—stuff of the politician—he was so talented as to be reckoned second to none in all Rome. Had he been born in Ravenna, it is likely that he would have pursued a career in the civil service, but in Rome there were few other opportunities for an ambitious young man than the Church. At the age of just thirty-three, Gregory received the title of Prefect from Emperor Justin II, but soon abandoned the highest civil dignity in the city to become a monk. He gave up his Sicilian estates to found six monasteries there under the Rule of St. Benedict, and his home on the Cælian Hill was converted into another under the patronage of St. Andrew.[110]

The talents and wealth of Abbot Gregory made him dear and near to the Church, and in 578, Pope Benedict I ordained him as one of the seven deacons

---

[109] Before St. Benedict of Nursia, each Western monastery had practically its own rule.

[110] Many other secular buildings were forcibly converted into churches once Gregory became pope.

of Rome, the number of which Gregory would later increase to twenty-four. It was a period of acute crisis: the Lombards were advancing rapidly towards the city, and the famine that resulted from their siege of Rome the following year claimed Benedict as one of its victims. The new pontiff, Pelagius II, dispatched a special envoy to ask for supplies and troops from the Emperor, with Gregory as the *apocrisiarius*, or representative of the Pope to the Patriarch of Constantinople.

But although Gregory's sojourn at the Imperial City lasted for six years, so far as obtaining help for Rome was concerned, the visit was an abject failure. Much attention was, however, drawn to Gregory by his prolonged and bitter controversy with Patriarch Eutychius, concerning the doctrine of Resurrection. The good Patriarch maintained that the risen bodies of the elect would be "impalpable, more light than air," to which view Gregory objected the palpability of Christ's risen body. Finally, Emperor Tiberius himself intervened, deciding in the favour of Gregory, and ordering Eutychius' writings on the subject to be destroyed.

After Gregory was recalled to Rome, he returned to his private monastery with a great increase of reputation. The year 589 saw widespread disaster throughout the Empire: in Italy, there was unprecedented flooding; the overflow of the Tiber destroyed numerous farms and buildings, among them the granaries of the Church with the entire store of grain. Pestilence followed the floods, and Rome was turned into a city of the dead: the streets were deserted, except for the wagons that carried the innumerable corpses for burial in common pits outside the city walls. The next year, Pope Pelagius himself was carried off by the plague.

Without hesitation, the clergy, the nobility, and the people of Rome unanimously elected Gregory for the succession. He, however, not only refused to heed the prayers of his fellow-citizens, but went as far as to write to Emperor Maurice, begging him not to confirm the election. Gregory could thus in good conscience later complain about the countless number of bishops who were "in no way divinely called, but inflamed by their own desire." Though his letter to the Emperor was intercepted by the Prefect Germanus, only after six months of waiting did the imperial confirmation of his election arrive, allowing Gregory to finally be consecrated as pope.

Besides their spiritual jurisdiction, the popes exercised, by this time, a considerable amount of temporal power. The papal estates had reached enviable dimensions, different estimates placing their total area at 1,300 to 1,800 square miles—tilled by a corresponding numbers of slaves. Gregory, no stranger to estate management, made sure the law exempting clerics from lay tribunals was enforced to the letter; the estates increased steadily in value, and the revenues were paid in with unparalleled regularity. By convincing the wealthy landholders and slave-owners that their heirs would never live to enjoy their property, he secured it for the papacy.[111]

Since there was no *magister militum* in Rome any more, even the control of military matters fell to Gregory. His consecration in 590 preceded only by a few days the death of the Lombard king Authari, whose Queen, the famous Theodelinda, had chosen as his successor and as her new husband Agilulf, Duke of Turin, and now ruled as his consort and as mother to Prince Adaloald. It was she who built the Cathedral of Monza, where the Kings of Italy were for a long time crowned with the Iron Crown that supposedly hid a nail from the True Cross in its golden rim.

In addition to being a Catholic, Queen Theodelinda was also a close personal friend to Pope Gregory, who now conceived the idea of himself negotiating a peace treaty with the Lombards. However, the Emperor was still hoping to regain the conquered lands and ignored the papal peace. The breach of the treaty naturally infuriated the Lombards, and after the Exarch of Ravenna retook Perugia, King Agilulf marched on Rome. In his *Epistles*, Gregory refers to himself as "the paymaster of the Lombards," and it was probably a large payment from the papal treasury that finally convinced them to lift the seige.

In spiritual matters, Gregory claimed for himself as pope, a primacy not of honour, but of supreme authority[112]; he impressed upon men's minds to an unprecedented degree the claim that the Bishop of Rome was the sole, supreme, and final authority in the Universal Church. This position made it, of course, impossible for him to allow the use of the title Ecumenical Bishop

---

[111] The Eternal City was still suffering from a dreadful pestilence, in the midst of which Gregory, at the head of a penitential procession, saw the figure of St. Michael hovering over Hadrian's Mausoleum, indicating that the plague had subsided—thus was the greatest funerary monument of antiquity transformed into the castle of Sant' Angelo.

[112] The term "primate" itself derives from the phrase *primus inter pares*, "first among equals."

officially given by the Emperor to the Patriarch of Constantinople in 588, two years prior to Gregory's elevation as pope. A long controversy followed his protest, and the question remained at issue when he died.

But while he lived, Gregory did everything in his power to maintain, strengthen, and extend what he regarded as the just prerogatives of papacy. He used his legal powers, as both first bishop and leading official of Byzantine Italy, to bring the Italian episcopate more and more under papal patronage. During his pontificate, close relations were established between the Church of Rome and those of Spain, Gaul, Africa, and Illyricum, and with the help of Theodelinda, Gregory got even the Arian Bavarians to adopt the Catholic faith. He saw it as a duty of the secular rulers to protect the Church and to preserve the "peace of the faith," and thus he often requested the aid of the secular arm, not merely to suppress heresy and idolatry, but even to enforce discipline among monks and clergy.

Although Gregory was the first monk to become pope, he contributed in no way to monastic ideals or practice. His position only modified St. Benedict's work by aligning it more closely with the organization of the Church and with the papacy in particular. The missionary work of the Irish, begun by St. Columba on the Isle of Iona, spread with St. Columbanus (543-615) and many other saintly monks to the Continent so effectively that Gregory was forced take vigorous measures to stop it. You see, the Irish monks, who had established their monasteries throughout France, southern Germany, Switzerland, and northern Italy, denied the authority of Rome over lands that had never been subject to the Empire.

Unable to come up with a fresh heresy to pin on the Irish, the charges the Roman clergy produced against them centred on form[113], such as tonsure style: instead of using the circular tonsure of the Romans, the Irish were accustomed to shave the whole head in front of a line drawn from ear to ear. This, though no evidence exists to suggest that it was the practice of the Druids, was nicknamed *tonsura magorum*—to this day, the *Magoi* of Matthew 2 are *druidhean* in the Scottish Gælic Bible. The Romans also reviled it as the "tonsure of Simon Magus," in contradistinction to their tonsure of St. Peter,

---

[113] In fact, thanks to its autonomy and geographic position, Celtic Christianity had remained remarkably uncorrupted by either Hellenistic philosophy or Roman jurisprudence.

and gradually, all the Columbanian monasteries gave way to the Benedictine Order.

With the Saxon conquest of Britain, the eastern and central parts of the island had relapsed into paganism; England needed to be Christianized a second time. The missionary work of St. Columba spread down the west coast, where the remaining Britons had been pushed by the Saxon conquerors. Eventually, news of Columba's labours reached Pope Gregory, who decided to take action. Augustine, the prior of the St. Andrew's Monastery in Rome, was appointed with forty other monks to convert the Anglo-Saxons to Catholic Christianity and establish the authority of the Roman See in Britain. The only problem was where to start: observing the fact that King Æthelbert of Kent already had a Catholic wife, a daughter of the Merovingian king Clothar, and some familiarity with the faith through her chaplain, a Frankish bishop called Liudhard, Gregory chose Kent for his destination.

In 597, the very same year that St. Columba died, Augustine and his Benedictine monks arrived in Kent. Æthelbert was quickly converted to Catholicism, gave the Roman monks a mansion in the royal capital of Canterbury, and the liberty to preach the Gospel to his court and his people. In due course, they were able to rebuild ruined churches in and around Canterbury, including the one that became the cathedral—Christ Church. Nevertheless, outside the Kentish kingdom, Augustine's progress was slow; the Welsh rejected his claim of supremacy over all Christians by virtue of his Roman commission, and his monks were expelled from London, where Augustine had hoped to put the Metropolitan See.

Gregory made Augustine the first Archbishop of Canterbury in 601, giving him authority over all of the churches in England, including the York and Celtic ones. To his chagrin, Augustine encountered an independent and resilient Church that refused to acknowledge his novel pretensions. The native Britons regarded him as not only an ally but the pawn of their hated conquerors, the Saxons. In order to erase the discord, a meeting was arranged somewhere in the Severn Valley, where St. Patrick was born. It dissolved after the Celtic bishops and abbots refused to accept any of Augustine's proposals. Why should they, who had protected the faith when deserted by the Romans, trust a newly-converted Saxon king when all the Saxons ever wanted to do was to destroy them? A second and third conference were held, but with no better results; the island was split into two by Roman and Celtic versions of the same religion.

There were a number of further confrontations between the two Churches during the centuries when both were active in Britain, but the most famous is the Synod of Whitby (664), at which King Oswald of Northumbria was asked to choose between them. Though Oswald chose Rome, his decision meant very little in practical terms since Celtic Christianity had spread over a number of kingdoms other than his. The result of Whitby was the introduction of many Roman liturgical and ecclesiastical usages into southern England and the Midlands, but these generally did not penetrate into Wales, Scotland, or Ireland. Throughout the first millennium, the British Church remained a peculiarly monastic Church that maintained its own liturgy and uses, acknowledging Christ alone as its head. The Celtic traditions never completely died out, nor did the Bishop of Rome gain real control over the Church until the 13th century.

St. Gregory the Great was not a man of learning, not a philosopher, hardly even a theologian; he was a trained Roman lawyer and administrator, a leader who regarded himself as "superior in place and rank" to the Exarch, establishing a political influence that would dominate the peninsula for centuries. Gregory's final years, however, were fraught with every kind of suffering, and he himself expected a speedy end to the world. As his continued bodily pains increased and intensified, his mind became filled with so gruesome premonitions that his "sole consolation was the hope that death would come quickly." On the 12th of March, 604, his body was finally laid to rest in front of the sacristy of St. Peter's Basilica.

Man has always demonstrated a twofold approach towards death: on the other hand, the luminous figure of St. Peter awaits him at the Pearly Gates of Heaven, on the other, the gloomy phantom of the Grim Reaper haunts him. Similarly, his funeral ceremonies have reflected both views—some have placed gifts in the graves of their loved ones, so that their lives beyond would be made easier, others have driven stakes through the hearts of the corpses and rolled rocks on the mouths of the tombs in order to prevent haunting.

There was a widespread ancient custom which met both requirements: burning of the dead. The flames were thought to facilitate the release of the soul from the body and its ascension to Heaven; besides, an incinerated corpse could not haunt the Earth. Christians, however, revived the archaic practice of inhumation long superseded by cremation, for the latter went against their belief in resurrection. Because of the prevailing notion, heretics and "witches" were burned at the stake in Catholic countries well into the Modern Era, as fire was believed to consume both the body and the soul—the Roman Church would not permit cremation until 1964.

The All Saints' Day was adopted into the Church calendar in the 7th century, at which time it was made the day commemorating the Christian saints and martyrs in contradistinction to the pagan all dead's day; by this time, there were also so many saints that there were not enough days in the year to accommodate them all. Originally held on the 13th of May, the All Saints' Day was moved to the 1st of November as early as the 8th century in order to avert Christians from celebrating the pagan day of the dead.

From time immemorial, the All Hallow's Eve—or Hallowe'en—was more important than Hallowmas, the traditional cerebration focusing on the 31st of October, beginning at sundown. The Celts called it *Samhain*, literally the "end of warm season," which therefore marked the final harvest of the growing season. Not only was it celebrated as the end of summer, but also, more importantly, as the death of the old year and the birth of the new one; the Celtic New Year begins with the onset of the dark phase of the year, just as the new day begins at sundown. Not that the holiday was Celtic only; an astonishing number of ancient and unconnected cultures, including the ancient Egyptians and the pre-Spanish Mexicans, observed this same day as a festival of the dead.

The Celts believed that the dead could, for this one night, return to the land of the living, and celebrate the New Year with their family, tribe, or clan. In other parts of Northern Europe, the holiday was also celebrated by entertaining the dead, feasting and by the burning of fires, which were supposed to help the Sun survive through the dark season. In a tradition very similar to Yuletide wassailing, roving bands would carry a large bowl from house to house, hoping their neighbours would fill it with drink; in fact, the custom known as "carolling," now connected exclusively with midwinter, was once practised on all major holidays.

(During the 7th century, readable melodies were consciously nursed by the Church: a certain type of music was permissible, certain others prohibited. For example, melismatic singing was early on declared forbidden; in other words, one syllable had to be proportional to a single note, and no melodic embellishment was allowed. By the 9th century, everything had to be fitted into diatonic modes to be officially acceptable.)

In the south, people celebrated the New Year at the Spring Equinox, asserting it to be the first day of the first sign of the Zodiac, Aries; it is, at any rate, a time of new beginning, as attested by a mere glance at nature. There are two holidays in the Christian calendar that get mixed up with the Equinox. The first occurs on the fixed date of the 25th of March in the old liturgical calender, and is called the Annunciation of the Blessed Virgin Mary. On this day, the angel announced to Mary that she was pregnant—announcing it was necessary because, being a virgin, Mary had no way of knowing it. And even if the conception was supernatural, it would take the natural nine months for Mary to carry her pregnancy to term, wherefore it was necessary for her to conceive the Child Jesus nine months before his birth on the Winter Solstice.

The other Christian holiday which gets confused with the Spring Equinox is Easter. In Greek and Latin, this holiday is called *Pascha*, from the Hebrew *Pesach*, "Passover." The most important feast of the Jewish calendar, the Passover was celebrated on the first full moon after the Equinox, with the butchering and eating of the Paschal Lamb. It was largely based on the every spring custom of ancient nomadic shepherds to slaughter a sacrificial lamb, the flesh and blood of which the members of the tribe then consumed in their ritual communion, renewing at the same time their covenant of reciprocal aid and support. The feast of *matzoh*, or unleavened bread, was in turn a traditional Canaan agricultural harvest festival adopted by the Israelites to mark the start of the start of the barley harvest—barley was the first crop to ripen. Because the two events occurred at about the same time each year, they soon became associated with each other.

What is more, they also became associated with the semi-mythical Exodus from Egypt[114]. (There is no evidence in the records of Egypt or of the neighbouring peoples, or from archæological research, that the tribe of Israelites was ever in the country.) According to the biblical legend, it took the death of a perfect first-born male lamb and the shedding of its blood to save the Hebrews. As they crossed the Red Sea, they passed over from death unto life and were baptized into life by God. Only the Chosen Ones could pass through; the Egyptians who tried to follow perished. The great joy awaiting

---

[114] written down during the Babylonian Captivity

those who passed was the Promised Land.

At the beginning, there was little difference between the Jewish and the Christian celebration of the holiday. The 2nd-century Easter homily composed by St. Melito of Sardis was a take-off on the Exodus, except that it presented the Jews in a negative light. The Council of Nicæa, however, decided to separate the Christian Easter from the Jewish Passover altogether. Its decrees stated that "it is unbecoming beyond measure that on this holiest of festivals we should follow the customs of the Jews. Henceforth let us have nothing in common with this odious people." From then on, secular and canon law even prohibited Jews from appearing in public at Eastertide. The Paschal Lamb, however, was not replaced by the human image of the Crucified as the universal symbol of Christ until the Quinisext Council in 692[115]; the *Agnus Dei*[116] chant is still sung or recited in the Catholic Mass during the breaking of the bread, which part of the ceremony continues to be called "the Sacrifice of the Lamb."

All the trappings of the modern Easter, and its associated days, are pagan in origin. As any nature-lover will affirm, Easter is the natural season to celebrate the victory of life over death, the season during which the whole face of nature testifies to a fresh outburst of vital energy. Viewed of old as the time when the world was annually created anew in the resurrection of a deity, it transformed within the Christian Church into a feast of the Resurrection of Christ and got associated with his Passion. After his death on the cross on Good Friday, he is told to have descended into Hell for the three days and three nights that his body lay entombed; but on Easter Sunday, his body and his soul rejoined, he rose from the dead, and ascended up into Heaven. However, most of the pagan religions also speak of a deity descending into the underworld for a period of three days.

The supposed deathday of Jesus and the Saturday that followed were commemorated with rigorous fasting. The austerity of the Christian holy day did not mix well with the pagan fertility feast that was celebrated concurrently with it. Ironically, Easter seems to have been named after the Saxon lunar

---

[115] And, until the late 13th century, it was the resurrected Christ who was depicted on the Cross even in the West, wearing a long robe and not suffering.

[116] i.e. "Lamb of God"

goddess, Eostre, from whom derives also the name for the female hormone, œstrogen. This fact is confirmed by the Venerable Bede[117] (672-735), the same British theologian and historian who coined the phrase *Anno Domini* to mark the passing of the years from the birth of Christ. The Germanic goddesses of fertility were known variously as Eostra, Eostur, Eastra, Eastur, Austron, Ausos, Ostare, Ostara, and Ostern. In many ancient cultures around the Mediterranean, fertility goddesses were known by similar names, such as Ishtar and Astarte, and most of these cultures also had a major seasonal day of religious celebration at or following the Spring Equinox.

The chief symbols of the Germanic goddesses were the hare and the egg, images which have always been difficult for the Christians to explain; both, of course, represent fertility. When the goddess of fertility dies, everything dies, and the other deities beg for her to be restored to life. After she emerges from the realm of the dead with her lover, the earth comes alive again. The annual enactment of these events bore a more-than-passing resemblance to the Christian Easter festivities, the main difference being that the pagan version ended with a public act of sexual intercourse. The Christian Church dreaded this feast to the extent of decreeing that its Easter should never be celebrated during a full moon. Thus, the Christian Easter would be the first Sunday following the first full moon after the Spring Equinox, unless it fell on the full moon itself, in which case it was to be postponed to the next Sunday instead.

Aside from all those other holidays, this movable Easter was also considered the New Year's Day in many quarters of Europe. In the Byzantine Empire, which played a much more important role both politically and culturally than we are accustomed to believe, the New Year's Day fell on the 1st of September, and the popes observed this calendar for quite a long time. The use of the Christian Era with the Julian Calendar did not begin until the 8th century "A.D." and then only among scholars—everyday use came centuries later.

---

[117] *De Temporum Ratione*, i. 5

CHAPTER 15

There had been no break in European intercourse with the Orient since Syrian immigrants had introduced the religious and cultural ideas of the East into the major cities of Gaul and Italy during the early Christian period. The Western Christians journeyed in large numbers to Syria, Egypt, and Palestine, either to follow the ascetic life among the monks of Mount Sinai or the Thebaid, or to visit the holy places. They frequented the tombs of the martyrs in hope of obtaining, through their powerful intercession, every kind of spiritual, but even more often temporal blessing: the cure of their ailments, the preservation of their vigour, the fruitfulness of their wives, and the happiness of their children.

On the miraculous discovery of the Tomb of Christ by Saint Helena three centuries after Jesus' death, and the subsequent erection, by command of the first Christian Emperor, of the magnificent Church of the Resurrection—or the Church of the Holy Sepulchre as it is now called—over the sacred monument, the tide of pilgrimage turned towards Jerusalem, and continued to gather strength as Christianity spread throughout Europe. The pilgrimages promoted piety, superstition, indolence, levity, and immorality, and aroused moral indignation among the more serious and spiritual-minded people.

Even if the Arab invasion made the journey to the Holy Land more difficult, the pilgrimages only intensified, directed by clerics and escorted by armed troops. Islam, the youngest of the great world religions, came into being during a critical period of the Arabian Peninsula in the beginning of the 7th century. The Arab tribes worshipped many genies and deities, most common of which were connected with the celestial bodies, though the highest position was gradually given to Allah (definite article *al* + the word *ilah*, god, that is to say: "the God"), the Lord of the Creation. This nomadic religion was in crisis during the 6th and 7h centuries, for the influence of foreign faiths such as Judaism and Christianity had grown in strength.

Several centuries before the birth of Mohammed in 570 CE, the Jews had built important settlements in Arabia, and had gradually acquired a considerable influence on the Gentile population. At one time, there even existed in Yemen an Arab-Jewish kingdom, which was eventually brought to an end by the Christian king of Abyssinia[118]. But even though they had lost their royal domain, the Arabian Jews remained numerous and powerful. And though there was only a small Jewish population in Mecca, contact with the Jews of his native city was probably one of the means by which the Prophet of Islam became familiar with Judaism, its beliefs, and its Patriarchs. As a youth, he also travelled with the trading caravans to Syria, where he came under the influence of Christian teachings.

According to the Islamic tradition, the Angel Gabriel appeared before Mohammed one night in Ramadân about the year 610, and urged him to "recite." Mohammed (Arab. "to praise") believed himself to be a messenger of God, sent to confirm the scriptures of his predecessors, that is, the New and the Old Testament. His sermons initially concentrated on proclamation concerning the oneness of God, the conversion of polytheists, and the Last Judgement. He accused the Jews of perverting the Old Testament scriptures and the Christians of worshipping Jesus as the son of God, though he had expressly commanded them to worship none but God.

As the Meccan resistance to Mohammed's preaching grew, he moved, in 622, to Yathrib, the chief centre of the Arabian Jews, which was thenceforward known as *Madînat an-nabî*, the City of the Messenger, or in short, Medina. This flight, or *Hegira,* is the starting-point of the Islamic chronology. To win the Jews to his cause, Mohammed, already recognized as a prophet and a political leader, made various concessions to their religion. Over the next eight years, he accumulated so great a political power that in 630, all the tribes of the Arabian Peninsula acknowledged him as their suzerain; he re-entered Mecca in triumph and smashed the idols at the Kaaba. After he had reached a treaty even with the Christian ruler of Aqaba[119], the whole of Arabia was under his control.

The rise of the new religion gave a strong focus for the Arab tribes and enabled them to consolidate their identity; when Mohammed died in 632,

---

[118] Now Ethiophia. The Non-Chalcedonian Abyssinians remained under the jurisdiction of the Coptic Orthodox Church of Egypt until 1959, when they were granted their own Patriarch. Today, the Ethiophian Orthodox Church is the largest of all Oriental Orthodox Churches.

[119] in modern Jordan, near the biblical Elath

there were over 40,000 Muslims, and all of Arabia was politically united. A tidal wave of newly-converted Arabs swept with incredible speed the less devout peoples from its way. While the message of the Koran[120] (Arab. *al-Qur'ân*, "The Recital") may seem rather scanty to the outsider, it is also simple, intelligible to all, and applicable to the conditions of ordinary people, partly explaining the rapid spread of the religion. The Koran offered a firm belief in a few simple theses, a certain hope of paradise for the faithful, and love that barely goes beyond a reasonable amount of charity.

In the early 7th century, the great powers of Rome and Persia began to fall apart, exhausted by prolonged conflict with each other. Between 603 and 617, the Persians occupied Syria, Palestine, and Egypt, and by the time Emperor Heraclius had recaptured the lost provinces in 628, the world was ready to witness the birth of a new superpower. The Arab forces swept both the Romans and the Persians, establishing an Islamic empire that would last for over a thousand years.

Since the Koran demanded kindness from the faithful towards the "People of the Book," by which appellation were meant not only the Jews and the Christians, but all people with recognized scriptures, it was possible for an Islamic ruler to be kind towards non-Mohammedan misbelievers without acquiring a reputation for laxity.[121] On the surrender of the Holy City to the Arabs in 638, the Jews were immediately allowed back into Jerusalem. The privileges and the security of the Christian population were ensured via a guarantee given under the hand and seal of Caliph Omar to Patriarch Sophronius: "From Omar ibn al-Khattab to the inhabitants of Ælia. They shall be protected and secured both in their lives and fortunes, and their churches shall never be pulled down nor made use of by any but themselves."

---

[120] It contains the notes of the proclamations that were delivered to the Prophet in the form of visions. Their collection was completed during the caliphate of Omar, the Prophet's second successor, and an authorized version was established in 646, during the caliphate of Othman, his successor.

[121] However, this tolerance did not, and does not extend to non-theistic or polytheistic religions (such as Buddhism and Hinduism, respectively) or, indeed, any religion founded after the death of Mohammed, the "Last Prophet of God."

The site of the great Jewish temple[122] on Mount Moriah has always been regarded with special veneration by the Muslims. In the year of the first publication of the Koran, Mohammed had directed his followers to make their prayers facing towards it, and on the conquest of Palestine by Omar, it was the Caliph's first care to rebuild "the Temple of the Lord." The Arab geographers called it *Beit Allah*, "the House of God," or *Beit al-Maqdis*, a literal translation of its ancient Hebrew name, *Beth ha-Miqdash*, "the Holy House." From it, Jerusalem derives her Arabic name, *al-Quds*, "the Sacred." Instead of the customary high-sounding titles of sovereignty and dominion, the governor of the city assumed the simple title of *Hami*, or protector.

Only with the campaigns of Islam was the Christian Middle East delivered from the tyranny of the Byzantines, who tried by force to assimilate them into the Roman State Church. When the Muslims marched into Syria, they were welcomed by the Non-Chalcedonian population, which saw them as liberators who freed them from the yoke of Byzantium. Through their co-operation with the Arabs, the Syrians were able to retain not only their churches and monasteries, along with the Apostolic See of Antioch, but their ecclesiastical dogma and liturgy as well.

After the surrender of Cyrus, the Byzantine-appointed Patriarch of Alexandria, who also served as the civil ruler of Egypt, the city was peacefully captured by General Amr ibn al-'As in 641. The Arab civilization was of the land, not of the water, and Caliph Omar had bitter memories about thousands of his men drowning in Persia when a bridge collapsed on the Euphrates. "Let no water intervene between me and thee," he told Amr, "and camp not in any place which I cannot reach riding on my mount."[123] So even though the Arabs admired the glamour and wealth of Alexandria, they moved east of the Nile, where they established another city, al-Fustat, the nucleus of modern Cairo. The old capital, however, remained the chief maritime city of the Levant until the 14th century.

Mohammed, whose Egyptian wife was the only one to bear him a son, had said: "when you conquer Egypt, treat its inhabitants well. For there lies upon

---

[122] of which only a portion of an outer wall erected by Herod the Great remains

[123] Ya'qubi: *Kitâb al-Buldân* (c. 891 CE)

you the responsibility because of blood-tie or relationship of marriage."[124] The Coptic Church continued to flourish, and for the four centuries that followed the Arab conquest, Egypt remained essentially Christian. The Copts replaced the Greek-speakers as civil servants and administrators, since unlike the Arab rulers, they spoke the language of the general population. They also became such an important source of tax revenue that some Arab governors of Egypt actually discouraged conversion to Islam for financial reasons.

Also in Jewish history, the triumph of Islam marks the beginning of a new, happier period. In return for the valuable assistance which the Babylonian Jews had offered in his campaigns against Persia, Caliph Omar granted them various privileges, not the least the recognition of their Exilarch, Bostanai, in 642. Under Mohammed's fourth successor, Ali (r. 656-661), the Talmudic academies of Sura and Pumbeditha flourished once again, and Jews throughout the Muslim world were convinced that there survived in the land of Abraham a Prince of the Captivity who had regained the sceptre of David.[125]

Meanwhile, their fellow-Jews were less fortunate in Christian Spain, where most of the 7th-century rulers enacted severe laws against Judaism. Towards the end of the century, King Egica prohibited them from owning land or houses, from travelling to or trading with North Africa, and even from transacting business with Christians. After the Seventeenth Council of Toledo (694) accused the Jews of plotting with the Moors to overthrow the Visigothic rule, Egica sentenced all the Jews of his kingdom into perpetual slavery and ordered all Jewish children over the age of seven to be separated from their families and raised as Christians.

Thus, when the Caliph of Damascus crossed from Africa into Andalusia in 711, defeating and slaying Roderic, the last Visigothic king of Spain, the Jews hailed the Muslims as saviours and welcomed them with open arms. Whereas the Gothic rulers had been harsh and bigoted, their Moorish successors encouraged a culture which in its creativity and tolerance had seen no equal since the golden age of Hellenistic Alexandria.

By the year 730, Mohammed's followers ruled the entire southern

---

[124] *Sahih Muslim*, Hadith No. 6174

[125] Every nation subjected to the Arab conquerors during the 7th century came with a Hellenistic stamp—the Jews were no exception. Unlike the other peoples, however, they also carried their own developed culture, and in a sense, remained a nation even through the feudal Middle Ages.

Mediterranean world, from Spain and Morocco all the way to the Indus River. They had thus acquired the better part of the former Roman colonies and vast regions besides. In an empire which would take five months for a caravan to cross, and whose scope encompassed many of the principal countries of the ancient Græco-Roman literature, there now reigned a new language and a new literature with its own ideals and its own masters. The Koran had displaced both the Bible and Homer for the over 150 million people who honoured the words of the Prophet. Since every syllable in the Koran was held to be divinely inspired, translations were basically not accepted. The subjugated peoples therefore needed to learn the Arabic language, a fact that caused many difficulties in interpretation, but also created a singular unity within Islam. It was an empire of spectacular strength and grace, while Christendom lapsed into the Dark Ages.

Though the eastern half of the Roman Empire carried on occasionally quite viable, the glory of Byzantium did not illuminate the fields of scientific or philosophical study; her intellectual activities were focussed on the Christian Church and the Christian theology. In the 8th century, small buildings and forts began to arise amidst her ravaged cities; by that time, Constantinople was the only city in the area that had not been conquered—Byzantium had passed from an empire of cities to an empire of castles.

The course of life for Roman citizens had changed completely; even patterns of eating and drinking were altered. The corn in Constantinople had come largely from Egypt, which was now occupied by Arab forces. For the first time in centuries, the free bread dole would cease. Worse than that, the wheat that came from the north actually tasted different. With the loss of Syria to the Arabs, practically all the olive oil trade dried up. The dwellings had to now be lit with wax candles, which were quite expensive to make.

In the face of the Islamic menace, the greatest general of the Empire, Leo the Isaurian, took over the Byzantine government in 717 with scarcely any opposition. Emperor Leo III was, as one Byzantine historian puts it, "of English mentality." He tolerated neither ceremonies nor rituals; he hated the superstition of the Church and planned on restoring the Christian worship to its most ancient and simple form.

The Græco-Roman tradition of having painted panels of deities placed in homes with candles lit in front of them had inspired the development of icons

(Gr. *eikon*, "image"). First used privately, icons with Christian motifs had gradually entered the church. An enormous number of refugees—soldiers, craftsmen, and landowners—had gathered under the shelter of Constantinople's walls, and the churches had been filled with images that came from thousands of far-away shrines. In 726, Leo published the "Iconoclastic edict," forbidding the worship of icons, and followed it with the general destruction of effigies representing Jesus and the saints; they were replaced by symbols, such as the cross.

The Emperor's original motive may have been theological, but the movement soon turned into a political attack on the Church, and particularly its monasteries, the growing power of which was furthered by their possession of holy pictures. Asia Minor and the military forces, mostly Asiatic, were firmly on his side, but in Europe, especially in Greece and Italy, both neglected and obscure provinces, the people held on to their comforting superstition. Numerous riots and revolts broke out in Constantinople; the violent religious debate over devotional religious images devastated much of the Empire for over a hundred years and changed Byzantium for ever.

The Greek resistance was crushed, but Liutprand, perhaps the greatest king of the Lombards, reigning from 712 to 744, exploited the revolt of Italy's southern regions by making conquests in the exarchate of Ravenna and the duchy of Rome. Fearing the growth of the Arian kingdom, the popes aligned themselves against the Lombard king, allying with the Venetians, who by now were organized under their doge, but also with the dukes of Spoleto and Benevento, whom Liutprand soon forced into submission.

The popes then turned to the *Major Domus* of the Franks and the progenitor of the Carolingians, Charles Martel, who had won immortal fame by decimating a Saracen raiding party at the Battle of Poitiers (732); since this skirmish marked the northernmost penetration of the Muslims into France, it took on a symbolic importance, even if Charles did not actually stem an invasion, but only defeated a small army. The Arabs also assaulted Byzantine Asia Minor every now and then, until Leo III personally gained a decisive victory over them at Akroinon, on the western edge of the Anatolian plateau, in 739. The next year, the Emperor died.

Because of their uninterest in the details of government, the later Merovingian kings were dubbed the *rois fainéants*, "idle kings." Gradually, the Mayor of the Palace, whose original duties were mostly domestic, had emerged as the most important figure at the Frankish court. It was the Mayors who ruled the Franks in all essential respects, while the Merovingians became only figureheads. By the early 8th century, the office had become hereditary to the House of Carolus, Charles Martel being the first Mayor of significance; his many military victories helped establish him, rather than the king, as the leading power in the realm.

Charles was succeeded as Mayor of the Palace by his son, Pepin the Short. As the reigning king was an incompetent drunkard, Pepin sent a letter to Pope St. Zachary (741-752) asking for his support in deposing the Catholic prince. When the Pope gave his approval, the last Merovingian, Childeric III, was shut up in a monastery, and in 751, Pepin had himself crowned the King of the Franks on the model of the Anglo-Saxon rulers. He united all of Gaul, large sections of which had become independent during Merovingian era, under his rule.

The reign of the Lombards ended after Liutprand's successor, Aistulf, threatened Rome and demanded a tribute from the Pope. Since Byzantium was unable to send any troops, Pope Stephen III (752-757) called in the aid of the Carolingians, thereby opening a fateful new chapter in Western history. King Pepin twice invaded Italy, in 754 and 756, crushing Aistulf and depriving him of the lands which he had only just conquered from the imperial Exarch, including Ravenna and the Pentapolis[126]. Although the Emperor rightfully demanded these for himself, Pepin donated them to the Pope, laying the foundation for the temporal sovereignty of the papacy, now freed from subservience to Constantinople.

Pepin died in 768, and his elder son, Charles, became the sole ruler of the Frankish kingdom following the younger brother Carloman's death in 771. Charles proved a most capable king, earning the title of *Le Magne*, "the Great," which was appended to his name. In the year 774, Pope Adrian (772-795) conferred upon Charlemagne his father's dignity of *Patricius Romanus*, implying the protection of the Roman Church in all its rights and privileges, but above all in the temporal authority which it had acquired in the formerly Byzantine duchy of Rome and the exarchate of Ravenna. As an ally of the Pope, Charles defeated both the last king of the Lombards, Desiderius, and his son, Adalgisus, at Pavia and Verona respectively, was crowned with the Iron

---

[126] i.e. the five cities of Rimini, Ancona, Fano, Pesaro, and Sinigaglia

Crown of Lombardy at their capital, and still the same year, annexed their lands to his own.

The next twenty-five years of his life were consumed in an astonishing series of rapid marches back and forth across a continent riddled with forests, marshes, and mountains—prompting Napoleon to later study his tactics. During his reign, Charles launched more than four dozen military expeditions, riding at the head of no less than half of them. It was undoubtedly his ability to organize that formed the key to his amazing conquests: even though he led his armies over vast reaches of land with incredible speed, his every move was carefully planned in advance. Before each campaign, Charles would let the counts, dukes, and bishops throughout his realm know how many men they should bring, and what kind of arms and supplies they should carry.

On the fall of the Lombard kingdom, Italy can be seen as being composed of five separate parts: the domains of the Franks and the republic of Venice in the north, the Lombard duchy of Benevento and the cities still held by the Byzantine Empire in the south, and the Papal States in the middle. Charles visited Italy five times in all, strengthening his position in the country more and more each time. On his second visit, he suppressed the revolt of the Lombard dukes, abolished their titles and jurisdiction, installing in their place counts and margraves, who were bound to him by fealty and obliged to military service in compensation for the land they owned. On the third excursion in 780, Charles had his son, Pepin, anointed King of Italy by the Pope; on the fourth, he won the duke of Benevento from his alliance with Constantinople and turned him into his vassal.

However, it was one of his minor, early campaigns that has become the most famous: in 778, Charles led his army into Spain to fight the Saracens, and on its return, a mountain people called the Basques ambushed and wiped out the rear guard, killing Count Roland, one of Charles' twelve legendary Paladins. Charles nevertheless had in his possession all the land as far west as the Ebro, while at the same time, he was already expanding his conquests to eastern Germany. In 786, he crushed the last Arian Lombards of southern Italy, having defeated the pagan Saxons the year before and forced them to embrace Christianity, even if he had to quell sporadic revolts until the end of the century. During these years, he deposed the rebellious duke of Bavaria, fought successfully against the Avars and the Slavs, and forced all the tribes living between the Saale and the Elbe to recognize him as their suzerain. He met with equal success in northern Germany, where he established the firm stronghold of Hamburg by the North Sea.

Charlemagne was one of the principal forces in the civilization of barbarian Europe. He was himself devoted to literature, speaking Latin, Greek, and Frankish (i.e. German), and even tried in his later days to learn how to write, albeit with little success. Instead, he got others to write for him, gathering in his court at Aachen an "Academy," which would oversee the development of schools throughout the West.

Charles sought to re-establish general education because, in his own words, "the study of letters is well-nigh extinguished through the neglect of our ancestors." Under the Merovingians, there was established at the palace a school—called *Scola Palatina* by the 8th-century chroniclers—for the training of the young Frankish nobles in the art of war and the etiquette of the court, but the little education there existed of the literary kind was provided only at the monastic and cathedral schools. The nobility and the people did not generally know how to read or to write, and thus literature was represented for the greater part by lost oral tradition. Charles founded a library at Aachen and had ancient folk songs and hero tales, *antiqua carmina*, collected, for the possession of which modern scholars would give much. After his death, he became himself a centre of a complex cycle of legends rivalled only by the tales surrounding King Arthur.

Unlike most of his peers, Charles believed that the government should be for the benefit of the governed. In general, the nobility, that part of society whose task was to make war and to breed new warriors, considered the peasants, their serfs, as little better than animals. After all, they lived and died like animals in boundless poverty, they knew nothing and did not understand anything. The only thing they were good for was labour—on which everyone else subsisted. As soon as his victories over the Lombards, Saxons, and Moors permitted, Charles initiated a reform of the Palace School, slowly transforming it from a school of military tactics and court manners into a place of learning.

Charles demonstrated as great a wisdom in pacifying, stabilizing, and organizing his new lands as he had strength and courage in conquering them. As a tireless reformer, he strove to improve the lot of his subjects in every possible way: he set up money standards to stimulate trade, and helped increase the supply of food by introducing better farming methods; but, above all, he worked to spread education and Christianity in every class of people—"Let every monastery and every abbey have its school, in which boys may be taught the Psalms, the system of musical notation, singing, arithmetic and grammar." By boys, Charles meant not only the candidates for the monastery and the wards committed to the care of the monks, but also the sons of the village and countryside around the abbey, for whom he had separate schools erected as attachments to the monastic buildings.

It was after the arrival of Alcuin of York at Aachen in 782 that the Carolingian educational reform really took off. This reknown British scholar represented the learning of the School of York, which united in its tradition the currents of educational reform inaugurated in southeastern England and that other current which, starting from the schools of Ireland, spread over the entire northern part of the country. He lived at Charles' court for the next twenty years, propagating the spread of Augustinian theology, laying the foundation for the present-day Vulgate through his text-critical emendations, and leaving his mark on every educational pursuit for a long time to come.

In the Carolingian Renaissance, Christianity and Germanism were allied with the heritage of antiquity, paving the way for the development of the Middle Ages. Charles' aspiration was to turn Aachen into a "Christian Athens"; yet it was almost exclusively the Romans—Vergil and Ovid, Suetonius and Sallust, Martial and Terence, Cicero and Cæsar—who were read at his court. Learning Latin was made compulsory for the sons of the nobility, and at one time, Charles even considered making Latin the vernacular of the people. Scholars not only collected and copied ancient Roman manuscripts that might have otherwise been lost forever, but also developed a new style of handwriting, known as the Carolingian minuscule, which later became the model for printing.

According to Einhard the Monk, Charles' biographer and a scholar at his court, the King "loved the strangers" and "had the Irish in special esteem." Before Alcuin received his invitation, two Irish monks had arrived in Gaul, and having somewhat boastfully made known their desire to impart wisdom, were honourably received by the King of the Franks, one of them even being placed at the head of the Palace School. And after Alcuin had left the court, Clement the Irishman succeeded him as the school master, and had pupils sent to him even from the famous Abbey of Fulda. The grammarian Cruindmelus, the poet Dungal, and Bishop Donatus of Fiesole were also among the many Irish teachers on the Continent who enjoyed the favour of Charles.

When the monastery which St. Benedict had founded at Monte Cassino, in a pagan holy place, was destroyed by the Lombards in 581, the monks had fled to Rome, carrying with them, among other priceless treasures, a copy of the rule "which our holy Father had composed." This manuscript of the Benedictine Rule was presented by Pope Zachary to Monte Cassino in the middle of the 8th century, shortly after the restoration of the abbey which would become regarded as the symbolic centre of Western monasticism. It was discovered by Charles when he visited Monte Cassino towards the end of the century, and he asked that a careful transcript be made for him, as an exemplar to be disseminated throughout the monasteries of his kingdom. In border regions, the Carolingian monasteries served as pioneer institutions in bringing forests and marshlands—the homes of the ancient deities—under cultivation and Christian control.

The expansion of Christianity required not only a trained clergy, but a standardized rite, which was provided by Pope Adrian in the form of the Gregorian Sacramentary, or liturgical use of Rome. Ordered by Charles to be used alone throughout the Frankish kingdom, the Roman Rite spread rapidly all over the West, displacing the old Gallican Liturgy. Musical instruments were considered too tainted with paganism to be used in churches, so in order to revive sacred music, the King had monks sent from Rome to train his Frankish singers. Though the latter adopted the chants and some melodies of the Roman Church, they also significantly modified them. For example, the "eight modes" (Gr. *oktoechos*) schema of Byzantine music was introduced, while singing styles changed. The result was the first music in Western history to leave any clear indication of its style or sound. The schools of church song that Charles founded at Metz, Soissons, and St. Gall spread this Carolingian or "Gregorian" Chant throughout Western Europe. (The earliest authority on St. Gregory the Great's connection with this monophonic, alternating, rule-dominated church song was a late 9th-century deacon, Johannes Hymonides.)

In 794, Charles convoked a synod in Frankfurt to discuss the heresy of Adoptionism and icons. He wished to repudiate the decisions of the Second Ecumenical Council of Nicæa (787), partly because he considered the issues surrounding icons theologically irrelevant, but mostly because he hoped to establish the Frankish Church as the equal of the Church of Byzantium. Three hundred bishops from every part of the West gathered at the synod, making it rival any of the General Councils. To suppress Adoptionism, the participants drew on the arguments of the Third Council of Toledo (589), which had officially voted to insert the phrase *filioque* into the Nicene Creed to defeat Arianism. The promulgation of this new clause may have defeated Adoptionism, but it also contributed greatly to the schism between Rome and Constantinople in 1054.

Some Latin monks from Jerusalem had visited the court of Charles, and when they returned to Jerusalem with the new version of the Creed, the Easterners objected strongly to the novel and patently unbiblical clause. After the Frankish bishops upheld the amendment in a synod held at Aachen in 809, Pope St. Leo III (795-816) intervened, forbidding any interpolations or alterations in the Nicene Creed. He ordered it to be engraved, without the Filioque clause, on two silver plates on the wall of St. Peter's Basilica, in both Latin and Greek. The pope thus avoided a direct confrontation with the East, even though the clause continued to gain ground in the West, and ultimately formed the chief dogmatic dispute between the Eastern Orthodox and the Roman Catholic Churches.

On the 30th of November, the year 800, the day on which Charles arrived in Rome to protect Leo III from his enemies, ambassadors from Harun ar-Rashid (r. 786-809)—best known to the Western world as the Caliph whose court is described in the *Arabian Nights*—delivered the keys of the Holy Sepulchre to the King of the Franks; this was an acknowledgment of the Frankish protectorate over the Christians of Jerusalem, "a recognition that the holiest place in Christendom was under the protection of the great monarch of the West." Churches and monasteries were built there at Charles' expense, along with a hospital for pilgrims after the Muslim example.[127] These were still flourishing at the time of the pilgrimage of Bernard the Monk seventy years later, and alms were sent regularly from the West to the Holy Land.[128]

The turn of the century saw a great event which marked the end of an era and the beginning of a new one. On Christmas Day, while Charles knelt in

---

[127] In particular, the pivotal idea of separate wards for different diseases was a Muslim invention.

[128] The Frankish protectorate of the Holy City was not overthrown until 1027, and then replaced by that of the Byzantine emperors.

prayer at St. Peter's in Rome, Pope Leo removed a golden crown from the altar and placed it on the bowed head of the King—"To Carolus Augustus crowned by God, mighty and pacific emperor, be life and victory." Einhard reports that the coronation surprised and angered the king, who was, on his own right, the undisputed ruler of Western Europe, and who regarded the pope as one of his subjects.[129]

"It was then that he received the titles of Emperor and Augustus," writes Einhard, "to which he at first had such an aversion that he declared that he would not have set foot in the Church the day that they were conferred, although it was a great feast-day, if he could have foreseen the design of the Pope. He bore very patiently with the jealousy which the Roman emperors showed upon his assuming these titles, for they took this step very ill. . ." A widower, Charles had been in the middle of negotiating a marriage with Empress Irene, which would have brought him the imperial dignity without offending the Byzantines, spawning one of the great what-ifs of history.

Constantinople regarded the pope's act as one of schism, for its patriarch had had the exclusive right to crown the emperors from 457 onwards. Emperor Nicephorus, Irene's successor, resumed diplomatic relations with Charles, but would not recognize his imperial character. Finally, in 812, after the death of Nicephorus, the Byzantine embassy at Aachen recognized Charles as *Basileus* of the West in return for the cessation of pressure on western borders. Throughout the Middle Ages, however, the Byzantine emperor would not recognize as his equal anyone but the Caliph of Baghdad, an heir to the great kings of Persia.

---

[129] The view that the division of the Roman Empire was only temporary still prevailed, and Charles knew full well that many centuries before, the right of conferring these titles had passed from Old to New Rome.

CHAPTER 16

The victory of northern barbarians was now officially complete: a Germanic prince, who could not inscribe his name, sat on the throne of the Cæsars. Charles is described by Einhard as being quite tall and powerfully built with a thick neck and deep chest; he had the long, flowing red hair and bright blue eyes of his tribe, and was possessed of both strength and stamina. He was typical of the Franks also in his love for the hunt and the feast, though Einhard insists that his Emperor drank in moderation: a mere three cups of wine with a meal.

By establishing a central government over the West, Charles restored much of the unity of the old Western Empire and paved the way for the development of modern Europe. His coronation as Emperor marks the emergence of a new heritor of Rome and a rival to the Byzantines, one which would come to be called the Holy Roman Empire. It also signals the final union of the Roman and the Germanic, of the Mediterranean and the Northern civilizations. The line of demarcation was now between East and West, the lands west of the Elbe and the Adriatic being regarded by others more and more as a single society. This new society was clearly distinct from both Byzantium and Islam—it was truly a culture of its own.

The early mediæval notions of ancestry and family were thrown into tumult when the laws and customs of Romans and barbarians collided. The Germanic family was an extensive kin community, the duties and responsibilities of which were strictly regulated by law and custom; Roman law, on the other hand, recognized the individual with personal liberty and responsibility. From the 5th century on, Germanic rulers began to reduce the customary tribal laws to writing, but the Germanic peoples had no single law that applied to all the tribes, and both the Roman population and the Christian clergy under Germanic rule continued to live under Roman law. The reformed Frankish law imposed by Charlemagne applied throughout his empire and replaced not only the inefficient and fragmented tribal laws, but the Roman civil law as well.

The spirit of Charles' legislation was essentially religious: he employed as a basis and norm the Roman ecclesiastical canons which he had received from the pope in the shape of the *Collectio Dionysia-Hadriana*. He made the paying of tithes obligatory, and laid the basis for the enormous power and vast lands of the ecclesiastical princes, whom he naïvely hoped would act as a check on the arrogance and violence of the lay princes. To reform the lax and oppressive local barons, he expanded the mandate of inspectors, called *missi dominici*, who were always sent out in teams of two: a nobleman and a clergyman. They rode to all parts of Charles' realm as his personal representatives, inspecting government, administering justice, and reawakening his subjects to their civic and religious duties.

Twice a year, Charles summoned the chief men of his Empire to discuss its affairs. In all issues, he was the final arbiter, even in ecclesiastical matters, for the Church was still very much subject to the State. He convoked the synods and confirmed their decisions, disposed of all ecclesiastical benefices, and in all matters of importance, presided over the ecclesiastical tribunals. Already in antiquity, the Christian Church had embarked on a thankless mission to legislate people's morals. Under both Roman and Germanic law, marriage was a civil contract, regulating the rights and financial relations of the spouses. To the Church, however, marriage and family were not contracts, but moral issues: Christianity saw marriage as part of the Christian life, as a sacred bond between the man and the woman, which ideally precluded sexuality altogether—the regulation of property and rights was of no interest to the Church.

The most important morality to the Christian Church was sexual morality. The issues surrounding it consumed a disproportionate amount of the time and energy of the celibate clergy. Their attempt to apply their own moral rules to matter of finances and inheritance, bred incessant disorder in mediæval society. The implementation of regulations that were utterly incomprehensible, unnatural, and impracticable, into a thoroughly reluctant community taxed the Church for centuries. It gave cause to unending quarrel and even actual warfare between secular rulers and the Church. But the rulers changed, generations were buried, and the opposition grew weary. The Church was unremitting, the Church was eternal; and in the end, she got her way.

The immediate result was, however, an unprecedented chaos and confusion. Over the centuries, even the most basic issues could not be solved. When was a marriage valid? Would divorce be permissible, and under what circumstances? Who could get married and to whom? Should one person be allowed only one spouse, or could there be many?

In the early Church, marriages were concluded secularly, the converts from Judaism observing the Judaic custom, the converts from the Hellenistic circles the Roman one. The evolution of the Christian form of marriage was slow, as it was of no interest to early Christianity, which saw celibacy as the ideal and thought the second coming of Christ imminent. In Alexandria, nuptial benediction had become an accepted custom by the late 4th century, originating from the custom of inviting a priest to the family gathering to "bring together" the bridal couple. Wedding liturgy was introduced around the same time also to the Armenian Church, within which it became compulsory, for the first marriage, in the 5th century. In the Byzantine Church, the weddings were private occasions for a long time, and the bridal couple was married at home in a family gathering. From the 8th century on, however, church wedding was made compulsory.

Many of the Christian wedding customs are of ancient origin, distorted through time. The bridal veil, for example, originally an orange one, was first introduced by the ancient Greeks to protect the bride from the evil eye of jealous rivals. The throwing of rice and candy or confections is, in turn, based on an ancient Hellenic fertility rite, in which the married couple was showered with sweets for good fortune. The same ritual was also performed on every new slave who came to the house. The use of a wedding-ring, again, has its origin in ancient Egypt, and though adopted early by the Hebrews and later also by the Romans, it was not common among Christians until the 9th century. The ring was pressed down the left ring-finger of the bride because, according to an ancient superstition, a vein proceeds from it to the heart. Since the ring is a circular loop and made of gold, the most stable metal known, it was thought to guarantee a perfect and a life-long union for its bearer.

From the point of view of Christianity, marriage was indissoluble. Jesus had said: ". . .from the beginning of the creation God made them male and female. For this cause shall a man leave his father and mother, and cleave to his wife; and they twain shall be one flesh. . . What therefore God hath joined together, let not man put asunder." (Mark 10:6-9, Matt. 19:4-6) In the old Roman

Empire, divorce was easy, and either spouse could file for it. If the cause for separation was not adultery or other misconduct, the husband had to pay indemnity to the abandoned wife. It was this common, customary divorce practice that the Church set about to change.

Not all the learned churchmen were in agreement, however, and in the beginning, further confusion was caused by the fact that the ecclesiastical decrees were not always known or remembered. A strict divorce legislation was advocated precisely by Charlemagne, whose own family life was no paragon of Christian morality. Charles' first wife, Himiltrude, bore him a son, but political reasons demanded that he marry the Lombard princess Desiderata, daughter of King Desiderius. The pope, who hated and feared the Lombards, criticized his monarch as he already had a beautiful Frankish wife: "I cannot permit you to abandon her in order to take a new wife, or that you incestuously involve yourself with a foreign race." *Exogamy*, or mixing with a foreign people or tribe, was generally abhorrent to ancient societies, especially to the Hebrews. Strangely enough, the pope calls incestuous a union which was as far removed from such as possible.

Christianity had inherited its ban on incest from Judaism, and over time, its preoccupation with this sin progressed to a veritable mania, as it had to fight for centuries on behalf of the ban. Among the Germanic peoples, only marriages between parents and their children, and those of siblings, were considered incestuous. Nor were marriages within the family at all unusual in the Classical world; in Greece, an uncle could marry his niece, and as late as the 6th century CE, Emperor Justinian approved marriages between first cousins. The purpose of *endogamy* was to prevent the fragmentation of property.

The Catholic Church issued one regulation after another on who could marry whom, and each time, the circle of forbidden degrees spread like ripples in water. Marriage to one's own blood relations, even to cousins six times removed was, of course, forbidden; but this was not enough for the Church. In marriage, the man and the wife became one flesh, which meant that neither could marry the relatives of the other, even after either had passed away. Due to the unity of flesh, spouses of relatives were also counted as blood relatives, but so were the adopted children of the families of both spouses. The parents-in-law were in the black list, as were the godparents of the children. The fact that not only nuns, but the informal wives of the priests were also within the forbidden degrees just demonstrates the general confusion surrounding the issue.[130]

From the endless injunctions, prohibitions, reprimands, and penalties one can deduce that the regulations were not observed too zealously, if in fact they were even known about. Married couples were obedient when it suited their own purposes: the Church had to forbid mothers from being godparents to their own children, in order that they could not later divorce their husbands on the ground of a forbidden degree. By the turn of the millennium, incest was so abhorred by the Church that virtually anyone could get his or her marriage annulled on account of it; the royal houses of Europe had certainly intermarried thick and fast enough to have no trouble showing incest had taken place within seven generations.

Roman law did not prohibit men from having concubines, and in certain cases, it expressly sanctioned the custom: since the provincial governors were not allowed to bring their wives to their new domiciles, they were permitted to live with a concubine instead. The laws of the Germanic tribes, on the other hand, recognized both concubines and polygamy, especially in reigning families. In his 6th-century *Historia Francorum*, St. Gregory of Tours mentions a Frankish king who had four or five queens—in addition to his concubines.

The Church, however, advocated monogamy as part of the aspiration to the Christian ideal of equality, even if this equality applied only to men: each man was, in theory, allowed only one woman. In practice, there were more women in the disposal of a count than of a serf, who might have had trouble procuring even the one. The question of consent was an issue that took centuries to solve, although the bride's consent was not required anywhere in Europe: her father or guardian had the right to marry her off according to his own discretion; nor was her presence required at the betrothal, and frequently, she would not even meet the bridegroom until the wedding.

Charlemagne always had several concubines, and Queen Himiltrude fades to obscurity, as does also the Lombard Princess Desiderata, whom he abandoned two years after their wedding. The reason for this was apparently the beautiful Hildegarde of Swabia, but his marriage to her came with a price: Charles' own cousin and the most prominent of the Frankish bishops, St.

---

[130] Clerical marriage was not officially banned in the West until the First Lateran Council (1123), while none of the Eastern Churches ever prohibited their lower clergy from marrying.

Adalard of Corbie, would rather leave the luxury and comfort of the court than serve a woman whom he considered an adulteress. Perhaps it was this incident that compelled Charles to hold on to his subsequent queens until they died. Not that he had much luck with them: his union with Hildegarde lasted twelve years; his forth marriage to the imperious and hated Fastrada, daughter of an Austrasian court, eleven; and his fifth and final marriage to Liutgarde, six. Even though the voice of the Church had not affected his decisions in regard to his first two wives, Charles never abandoned Fastrada, and when Liutgarde died, he chose to live with his four surviving concubines instead of ever remarrying again.

Among the peasantry, the divorce controversies between the Church and the nobility were scarcely known about and even less understood. A peasant girl would marry very young to a man considerably older than herself, and serve him until she widowed. The marriage dissolved if one party simply travelled off far enough—something that was rare, however. The husband could also chase his wife away if she committed adultery, but the wife was powerless in regard to his misconduct. The women's former relationships, however, had no bearing on the marriages of the poor, and the Church's views regarding the sanctity of maidenhood, the extent of the incestuous grades, and the implicit perpetuity of wedlock, forced their way into the peasant community only very slowly. The peasants lived in accord with their own traditions like they always had, and like they would still continue to live for centuries to come.

The gap between politics and Christian ethics is apparent in the way Charlemagne treated his daughters. He allowed none of them to marry, for he did not care to have sons-in-law to further complicate the already quite intricate politics of his Empire. The daughters lived in their father's palaces, entered into casual relationships with whom ever they wished, and gave birth to high-born bastards. After Charles' death, moralists attacked the poor women and banished them to the provinces.

The Frankish Emperor died of pleuritis, in his seventy-second year, after forty-seven years of reign. He was buried with great splendour in his capital of Aachen, at the enormous palace chapel which he had built, and from which the city derives its French name, Aix-la-Chapelle. In keeping with the Frankish custom, he had divided his realm between his sons, and named none of them Emperor. According to the will which Charles had drawn in 806, most of what subsequently became France was to go to Louis the Pious; Francia proper, Friesland, Saxony, Hesse, and Franconia were to be the inheritance of Charles the Young; while Pepin would receive Bavaria and southern Swabia, together with Lombardy and its Italian dependancies, including Rome. But Pepin and Charles predeceased their father, and in 813, Louis, son of the Swabian Hildegarde, ascended the imperial throne.

Aptly named the Pious, Louis demonstrated weakness already at his coronation, as one Frankish historian testifies in 816: "He fell thrice on his face before the pope. The emperor no longer affirmed the nomination of the pope. The pope crowned the emperor. The balance had been upset." The heirs of Charlemagne competed for the control of his Empire, and needed the blessing of the papacy just as much as the Church of Rome needed the imperial armies and funds. If now and then a particularly capable emperor would assert imperial unity and authority, for the most of its history, the Empire was, as Voltaire famously gibed, "neither Holy, nor Roman, nor an Empire." While the emperors were supposedly its supreme secular, and the popes its supreme spiritual authorities, both tended to interfere in the domain of the other.

For six hundred years, the popes used a 3,000 word document known as *Donatio Constantini*, the "Donation of Constantine," to support their demands of supremacy over all Christendom. First cited in the 9th century, it claimed Constantine the Great had in 315 donated half of his Empire—which he did not acquire in its entirety until 324—as a reward for his conversion to Christianity (though he did not have himself baptized until he was laying on his death-bed in 337) and for his subsequent recovery from fits of leprosy. The see of Rome was also given spiritual supremacy over that of Constantinople before the latter city had even become the capital, or had even been rechristened after the Emperor. Nevertheless, the document became a mighty weapon in the quarrel between the Western and the Eastern Church, its authenticity not being questioned by the former until the 15th century.

Louis the Pious had four sons, and tried to divide his Empire among them while he lived, but the only result was endless war among the brothers and even against Louis himself. After he died in 840, three of the surviving brothers carried on the battle, which resulted in nothing but bloodshed, until concluding the famous Treaty of Verdun in 843. By this settlement, Louis II was given a Germanic kingdom coinciding approximately with present-day Germany, while Charles the Bald acquired Carolingia, or the land of the Salian

Franks, which would develop into modern France. The eldest brother, Lothair, retained his imperial crown, which he had received in Rome as early as 823, and was allotted the area consisting of the Kingdom of Italy and the broad stretch of land from the North Sea to the Mediterranean, called Lotharingia or Lothringen (or, in French, Lorraine). Thus were created Germany and France, and the rich and desirable lands in between, which both kingdoms coveted, and in turns possessed.

Although political and military disintegration began almost immediately after Charlemagne's death, the Carolingian Renaissance continued for a time within the domain of culture. Many continental Europeans contributed to the furthering of this current, but it is hardly an accident that it was an Irishman, long accused of heresy, who deserves most of the credit for the reforms. His name was John Scotus Erigena, and he was the head of the Palace School during the reign of Charles the Bald. He not only translated into Latin the works of the ingenious writer known by the pseudonym of Dionysius the Areopagite, but paved the way for mediæval Scholasticism with his own thoughts and definitions. His cognomens—*Erigena* (or *Eriugena*) and *Scotus*—allude, the former clearly and the latter in that it can signify both a Caledonian and an Hibernian, to the fact that he came from the *Insula Sacra*.[131]

The Irish teachers naturally flocked to the places that were already known to them by missionary work of their countrymen of earlier generations. Contemporaneously to John, Dunchad taught at Reims, Elias at Laon, Israel at Auxerre, and Sedulius at Liège. Every monastic and cathedral school at which the Irishmen appeared soon showed the beneficial effect of their influence. They augmented the curriculum already en vogue in the Carolingian schools with the study of Greek, and wherever they taught philosophy or theology, they drew largely from the writings of the Neoplatonists and of the Greek Fathers.

While the dawn of the 10th century brought other occupations for the royal mind, the monastic and cathedral schools carried on wherever war and pillage was incapable of undermining their existence. In one way or another, the educational influence of the Carolingian Renaissance continued all the way to the advent of university education in the 13th century.

---

[131] Incidentally, he was the only layman in the long line of mediæval Christian philosophers.

The missionary work of the Catholic Church was organized jointly by the pope and the emperor. The Viking raids—which became the scourge of Western Europe, and in which the fury of the invaders found its primary outlet in smiting down the clerics and ransacking the holy places—were in point of fact the echos of the blows which Charlemagne had delivered upon the paganism of the North. The hundred years from 850 to 950 were filled not only with the worst of the Viking invasions, but Muslim and pirate raids in the South, and Magyar incursions from the East. Against these combined pressures the Carolingians could hardly stand: by 900, the Empire had disintegrated into countless duchies, counties, bishoprics, abbacies, and other semi-independent fiefdoms, while the very title of Emperor disappeared for a time.

The Viking raids on the British Isles also began back in Charlemagne's day, and continued without an interruption. Coastal monasteries were favourite targets on account of the riches they contained. To this end, the Vikings hit Lindisfarne in 793, and Iona in 795, 802, and 806—they had to give the monks enough time to rebuild their holy houses and replace their valuables before invading again. On the last occasion, the entire community was put to the sword, the abbot alone escaping with a beautifully illuminated Book of the Gospels to Ireland, where he founded a new monastery at Kells.

The Vikings resembled the earlier Saxon invaders in a number of ways; both were pagan, both were pirates and raiders, and both spoke a Germanic language. Celts, the ancient inhabitants of Britain, had been pushed to Scotland, Wales, and Cornwall. However, the only place that retained a truly Celtic lifestyle was Ireland, which the Viking plunderers did not manage to take over in any meaningful way, even though they founded the first Irish cities, including Dublin.

In Scotland and Wales, the native Celts emulated the Germanic invaders both in social structure and dress. The word "Welsh" itself is derived from the Saxon word *wealhas*, meaning "foreigner" or "slave," and was applied to all indigenous Britons. The "Celtic" folk lived mainly in harsh lands with scanty resources, and were therefore generally a poor people, many of whose belongings were considered rustic or even archaic by the neighbouring Saxons and Vikings.

At that time, the Anglo-Saxon schools of England, the product of the combination of Irish and Roman learning, were more important and better developed than those anywhere on the Continent. While incapable of defending themselves against the havoc brought on by the Northmen, the Britons rebuilt their fallen schools and monasteries and made new copies of the manuscripts they had managed to save from the bonfires. The invasions of the 9th and 10th centuries did, however, destroy the double monasteries of Britain. This once prevalent system had never been viewed with approval by the Catholic Church, and when the religious houses were restored, it was for one gender only. The dual communities appear to have died out also in other countries around the same time.

After plundering the wealthy monasteries of the British Isles, the Vikings wandered up the Seine, Loire, and Rhône deep into the Frankish inland, ransacking the churches, rummaging the altars and the shrines, and guzzling down the communion wines. Originally a part of Charlemagne's Empire, the area around Rouen was fairly wealthy, with several monasteries and small towns. Lying as it does on the northern coast of France, it was an easy and popular target for the Vikings in the 9th century. By the 10th, they had ravaged it to such an extent that little plunder was left along the rivers, their major avenue of attack. Thus, the region was no longer much of a prize in 911, when Rolf the Viking, a Dane with great many men at his command, came to Charles the Simple, King of the West Franks, with a proposal. Through the Treaty of St-Clair-sur-Epte, Rolf, his men, and their descendants, were granted "the land from the River Epte to the Sea, and the town of Rouen"—effectively the land they already controlled—in exchange for which they would recognize Charles as their king, defend the coast against other Vikings, and accept Christianity.

The pillagers had turned into settlers, establishing their capital at Rouen. Rolf took the baptismal name of Robert, and styled himself as the *Comte de Rouen*, "the Count of Rouen." By 924, the French were forced to grant the Danes the districts of Bayeux, Exmes, and Sées, augmented with the Cotenin and the Avranchin in 933. Within two generations, "Robert" and his followers had adopted not only the religion, but the language, laws, customs, political organization and military strategy of the Franks. He married the daughter of a Frankish count; their son, William Longsword, who married the daughter of another Frankish count, felt obligated to send his son to Bayeux to learn Norse, since it was no longer spoken in their capital. They had become French in all but name, for most people still referred to them as *Nordmanni* or "Northmen"—and the land which was given to them took their name:

Normandy.

The world built on the ruins of the Roman Empire was to greatly exceed it in both size and importance. At first, however, the state of affairs was so unmanageable that a complete and utter disaster seemed more probable. All ties had been broken in highest levels of politics, government, and economy, the only thing that stood fast amidst the chaos being Christianity. The pagan Vikings, the heathen Slavs, and the godless horsemen from the steppes seemed to be able to destroy those loose communities which eventually became viable by organizing themselves into the feudal system. The invaders were unable to form any kind of an alliance, while Western Europe could hope a unifying factor of the papacy, whose ultimate goal was the merging of all mankind into the City of God chalked out by St. Augustine. Through these centuries, the Catholic Church remained the only Western institution which really worked and held together.

The men who had been educated by the Church had the sole right to the intellectual culture. During the Dark Ages, the mere ability to write was proof that the person in question was a cleric. A hand-copied Bible was such an expensive a purchase that not all the parishes could afford one. Prayer books and catechisms often replaced the Word of God for even the learned. In thousands of rural parishes and even in the urban ones, the priest acted as a link to the outside world, the world of new thoughts, wars, taxes, and intrigue. The pulpit gave the mediæval Church a mighty advantage, through which she attained a near monopoly over the shaping of public opinion; the Church alone was capable of effective propaganda—the only other medium through which thoughts could spread among the great masses was the spoken word.

Most people were labourers who seldom left the economically self-sufficient rural villages where they lived—city culture had disappeared from Europe almost completely. At the turn of the millennium, the entire Continent had a population of less than forty million people. The cities of Western Europe were small and far apart; none of them had more than 50,000 residents. They were nothing but local market centres, and even those cities in which life most resembled our image of urban existence were, by and large, administrative centres of the Church, the sees of bishops and archbishops, or centres of population that had grown around the great monasteries. Trade was scarce and limited mainly to luxury items and the raw materials which the feudal warlords needed for forging their swords and armours. The wild forests that the Romans had cut down for timber had grown back, and even the roads they had built were abandoned; travel was done only on foot or horseback, and dangerous even over short distances. Society got divided sharply into two groups: feudal lords on the one hand, peasants and craftsmen on the other. There were so few cities in Western Europe, and they were so small, that the middle classes could not gain the significance they have today; they hardly existed at all.

The art of farming regressed from the highest standard of the Roman Empire, although that level had never prevailed throughout it. The technical standard of craftsmanship was undoubtedly also lowered, since the relationship between master and apprentice had been disrupted. The warlords fought between themselves, usually causing substantial damage in the process to the tillages and other property of the ordinary people. The almost incomprehensible greed of the people was dictated by the ruthlessness of the times: man could only trust in what was firmly in his grasp. The was no such thing as social security; you would die of poverty if you could not provide for yourself. When currency gave way to bartering, large farms became the pillars of trade and industry, leaving the destitute with no other option than to seek the protection of the powerful landowners. This relative feeling of security had to be paid for either by working at the farms or by taking part in the battles which the landlords fought against bandits and one another.

The European feudal system was based on both Roman and Germanic customs. The rich Romans had had their clients, and the Germanic chieftains their armed retainers. The feudal nobility was a class of great landowners and mercenaries, which for centuries formed the one and only military and security force. Landownership was based on a system of fiefs (in Latin, *feudum*) and estates, within the limits of which the people were organized into a hierarchy which culminated in the king or the emperor and trampled the rights of free landowners.

Actually, only men of nobility could be vassals to a feudal lord. The vassal's responsibility was to perform certain services for his lord, and the lord's responsibility in turn was to protect his vassal, an invaluable service indeed. The chain of command was often vague, giving the members of the nobility considerable freedom of initiative and action. Inconveniences were caused by the fact that a duke could get into his possession a parcel of land that was linked with feudal ties to some other duke, to the king directly, or perhaps to a person lower in rank to the duke himself. Because of the ill-defined feudal ties, a vassal could end up having to fight his own liege.[132]

A 10th-century Frankish count could neither read nor write. In his youth, he had learned to handle a horse (the Latin, French, and German words for knight, *eques*, *chevalier*, and *Ritter* respectively, all have as their roots in words for horseman) and a sword, but could—and often would—leave to the bailiffs and clerks the task governing those people whom the ruling class usually relies on to sustain its power. Our modern words "clergy" and "clerk" are both derived from the same Latin word, *clerici*, "clerics." Throughout the Middle Ages, all clerks were clergy, and the term "clerical" still preserves both senses.

In the early Middle Ages, there were so many fewer women than men, that unmarried women scarcely even existed. When they did, they usually worked in the households of their brothers, while the few spinsters of noble families entered convents. There were two reasons for which a woman would be allowed to, or forced to, live in a nunnery: spiritual yearning or some handicap or illness that prevented her from marrying. Not every man could find a wife in a society which had 130 to 150 men per 100 women. Nor could every man marry, since all could not provide for a family. This applied especially to the bottom layer of the peasantry, the descendants of the Roman slaves. Not that everyone even wanted to enter into matrimony: the monastic institution spread while the far-off heathen lands in the East and the North swallowed up martyrs as fast as the monastic schools could produce them.

Not all the cloisters were the halls of piety and learning, however; there were ones which the occupants looked upon as no more than boarding houses. Many powerful families founded their own, private monasteries to act as the heralds of their power and wealth. What is more, a monastery also doubled as a bank during an age when there were no banks: one could stash one's wealth there, and if one donated land to it, that land would remain perpetually at one's disposal, since landed property of religious establishments was non-transferrable. A monastery could also act as a hostelry for visiting relations, as a nursing home for aged family members, and as a prison for unwanted relatives. When supplied with a prominent relic like a piece of the True

---

[132] whence the modern term "feud"

Cross, a shred from the sacred girdle of the Virgin Mary, or the head of John the Baptist, it became the object of holy pilgrimage to distant travellers.

Convents were nevertheless the only place where a woman could acquire an education. The daughters of the noble families were often sent to one for a few years to receive a training appropriate to their high status before being wedded across Europe. Each of them arrived at their respective courts thoroughly familiar with the Latin thoughts of the Church Fathers. They were thrown from the peace of a convent to the blood-soaked reality of the sword, beside an illiterate husband, forced to sit at the same table as his concubines, and to give birth to noble children like a high-born brood mare. Some took the reins into their own hands, and lived their lives unconcerned with the men's world, founding new convents and sending their daughters there.

In general, the role of the women was to take care of everything left behind when the men went away to wage war or to clear the land. And when the husband died on his excursion, the widow was left to protect his small children and property. This was especially true in France and Italy, where the laws were lenient towards noblewomen, who were allowed to allocate land, the wage of the day, to their knights. Such a woman, a countess or a duchess, was *de facto* ruler of vast domains during those turbulent times. In the unending matrimonial troubles that affected the future of kingdoms, the women turned to the papacy, and almost invariably, the pope stood by their cause. Women were the supporters of and the major financial contributors to the Church in many a primitive court occupied with brandishing the sword.

A hundred years after the death of Charlemagne, the state of Germany called for a saviour, and a saviour appeared. During this period, Germany was an immense region, stretching from the lower Elbe all the way to the Rhine, though without including the Low Countries beyond the Ems. When Henry the Fowler, with whom the modern world is acquainted through Wagner's *Lohengrin*, was elected king by the German nobles in 919, he refused to be crowned by the bishops in order to maintain his independence of the Church. He made a truce with the Magyars for nine years, during which time he paid them annual tribute, but also built citadels and fortified cities which could repel the Magyar cavalry, while training his Germans, who until then had only fought on foot, in art of mounted combat. When the Hungarians still demanded their tribute after the nine years had passed, they were sent a dog's carcass by the King, who advised them, if they wanted more, to take it by the sword. The decisive victory over the Magyars came in two battles fought in 933, near Gotha and Ried respectively, spelling an end to their westward advancement.

Aside from repelling the Magyars, the reign of Henry I also marked an epoch in the birth of cities and city life, a development which he encouraged in every way, and which introduced self-governing centres of power to counterbalance the clergy and the nobility. Henry even enacted a law prescribing that the German diets, or national assemblies, were to be held in the cities from now on, and not on open hillsides or mounds after the old Germanic tradition.

But the cities were still small and muddy, and the people had squeezed themselves into narrow candle and torch lit corners. When the darkness fell, it was difficult to continue work and dangerous to walk on the streets. If one did not get robbed, one might slip and fall on either human or animal excrement. The offal was thrown into the alleys, dog carcasses were dumped there, as was the blood the barber-surgeon let out of a patient's vein. Combined with rain water, all this mingled into a sticky and smelly ooze.

Meanwhile, Córdoba in Islamic Spain had paved roads, street lights, and municipal engineering; street cleaners took care of sanitation. It was a city of half a million, not only Muslims, but also Christians and Jews.[133] The city had hundreds of public baths, public schools and libraries. People there washed themselves, went to school, and studied. At a period when even kings could not read or write, the Caliph had a private library of 600,000 books, the largest in the Middle Ages. At a period when ninety-nine percent of the Western people where wholly illiterate, "there was not a village within the limits of the [Moorish] empire where the blessing of education could not be enjoyed by the children of the most indigent peasant"—Samuel Scott in *The History of the Moorish Empire in Europe*. The same times as scholars were burned at the stake in Christian Europe, in Moorish Europe, they were the highest paid men in the whole realm.

Arabs had lived in cities for generations, and their ideal habitat was anything but wild: their parks and gardens were filled with geometrical and Arabesque-

---

[133] Córdoba played a pivotal role in the mediæval history of the Jews, eventually eclipsing in scholarship and culture even the Talmudic academies of Babylonia.

like settings. They liked the sight of man's handiwork, artificial streams and ponds, lakes and fountains. Arab nurserymen brought to Andalusia the sugar-cane, the date palm, the peach tree, and the rice. The local stock of horses was bred into noble steeds. The textile factories poured out silk and linen. Paper, made from rags and hemp, was known in Baghdad by 794, and contributed the explosive spread of Arabic culture by providing an inexpensive, yet high-quality means of transmitting and recording ideas.

Conversely, one of the world's first historians of science, Saïd al-Andalusi, observed that the people of Northern Europe could not well be expected to contribute to civilization since the growth of their brains was stunted by the cold climate in which they lived. Muslims in general were stunned by the coarse manners of the Europeans and their incessant fighting. The Christian castles reeked of mould and mildew; the European stench is the one recurrent point in all mediæval Arabic travel account—the palaces of Baghdad and Córdoba smelled of ambra and aloë, of aromatic oils and perfumes. Wars came and went, sultans led their armies into battle after battle, but these took place outside the city walls, and their outcomes did not greatly affect the lives of ordinary people.

The scholars lived in Córdoba, Cairo, or Baghdad, moving from one great city of Islam to another. The University of Córdoba was one of the best in the world. Book acquisition trips were made around the world from there, and scientists were invited there in a similar manner as much later on in American universities. The warlike and peaceful relations with the Byzantium caused a gradual but steady Hellenization of the Arabs. The exchange of lavish diplomatic gifts coupled with the desire for an opulent court resulted in both of the empires borrowing from each other's cultures, including elements of art and architecture. Islam became an heir to the Roman Empire, not only territorially but also culturally, and this inheritance was in due course passed back to Western Europe.

Classical literature and Greek scientific heritage became known to the Islamic Empire when Arab authorities, particularly Caliph al-Ma'mun (r. 813-833), began the assimilation of Hellenistic learning. The Islamic Caliphs had in their disposal a great number of Greek linguists, among others Nestorian Christians, who were considered heretical in Byzantium. With the aid of the Nestorians, ancient Greek texts were rendered via their native Syriac into Arabic. The writings that the Arabs wanted to understand the most were those which would be useful for governing their vast domains: works on mathematics, geometry, geography, astronomy, physics, medicine, and philosophy. They paid little attention to poetry, history, or rhetoric. Greek literature was very much an enigma even to those Arabs who were best acquainted with it, as made apparent by Ibn Rushd's[134] commentary on Aristotle's *Poetics*; and the Arabic literature was as little understood in the West, as proved by the mediæval Latin translation of that same commentary—thus two worlds meet with neither understanding the other.

Still, without the Arab philosophers there would have never been an Aristotelian Renaissance nor Scholasticism in its highest form. The eagerness to learn, newly awakened in the Arabs, also manifested itself in their swift progress in chemistry, medicine, and mathematics, in which fields they could function as guides to the backward Europeans. To be sure, scientific work was wholly peripheral to the mainstream of Islamic scholarship, valid even in the eyes of the scholars only because it fit well with their vision of Allah and His universe. But unlike Christianity, Mohammedanism was not hostile to the natural sciences, which were allowed to develop normally within Islam, as a means of further glorifying the culture and religion. The Islamic Empire was the most far-reaching civilization in the world, stretching from Portugal to China; Córdoba was the largest city in Europe, rivalled only by Constantinople.

Compared to the incoherent Western Europe, Byzantium was an undivided empire, under the rule of one emperor, having a large and complex official class. Considered as the representative of Christ by the Byzantines, the Emperor at Constantinople was an absolute ruler. The government centred at his palace, while thousands of educated bureaucrats carried out imperial legislation and operations throughout the Empire—an administration unique in its efficiency. At its apogee in the late 10th and early 11th century, the Byzantine Empire stretched from southern Italy to Mesopotamia. In the lands reconquered from the Arabs, Muslims and Muslim converts were fully integrated into Byzantine society; indeed, the principle of autonomous organization of minority communities was enshrined in Byzantine law and had thence been adopted by Islam. Mosques had been permitted within the walls of Constantinople herself since the 8th century, for the use of Mohammedan

---

[134] known in the West as Averroës

visitors and prisoners of war.

This was the other Europe, the eastern, the darker, the more mystical; here shined the icons, worn through by kisses, here burned the incenses. Here the Church would not presume to give strict instructions, but instead left the individual free to aspire on his own and to seek personal mystical experiences. The chief patriarch, that of Constantinople, was devoid of temporal power. His task was to pray for all the Orthodox, perform the divine service, and support the monasteries. The local vernaculars were always employed alongside the generic Greek.

Constantinople was the centre of power, money, and religion, and had magnetism. Sea lanes and caravan routes intersected there. The Russians were so impressed by the grandeur of her cathedral and services that Vladimir the Great (c. 980-1015), previously a fervent pagan, adopted Christianity. The Vikings, too, positively drooled when they spoke of Constantinople, which the Sagas call *Miklagård*, "the Great City." Some of them even stayed there, in the service of the Emperor: the Varangian Guard, composed of seven hundred of them, had fought on Crete; the Imperial Guard also had them in its ranks. The Icelander Bolli Bollason served in the Varangian Guard from 1028 to 1032. When he returned home, he boasted of his apparel, his gear, and his weapons. He was especially proud of his gold-plated gift sword, which he affectionately called *Fótbitr*, "Foot Biter."

Everywhere the Vikings met with success on their fierce raids. They not only roamed along the Volga and the Dnieper, but arrived at the ports of the Mediterranean, where they came in contact with Arab traders, causing products transported from great distances by camels to turn up in the North. Arabian coins were found everywhere around the Baltic. "I have never seen more perfect physical specimens, tall as date palms, blond and ruddy," stated a cultured Baghdad resident Ibn Fadlan admiringly in his travel report from the Volga. But, he was forced to add that: "They are the filthiest of God's creatures."

CHAPTER 17

Only after fiefs had become hereditary around the year 1000 CE, did the feudal system establish itself in Europe. The unique way of life known as chivalry and gradually developed from the feudal class, imposed an extremely strict personal code of conduct on its members. There was always a certain equality within this class, regardless of the great disparity in wealth and power. A knight was always a knight, as subsequently a gentleman would always be a gentleman.

During the earlier centuries, and to a certain degree, all the way to the height of Middle Ages, membership in the knightly class was open to gifted new talent. The external badge of nobility was the title of knight, which a feudal lord could bestow upon a young warrior who had reached maturity, or upon an old dependent whom he found deserving. Knighthood was practically never denied to the high-born, but in addition, it could, for a good reason, be awarded to a low-born. Later on, ascent to the upper classes became difficult, if not impossible.

The office of the Emperor was considered so great and holy that it could not be left to the chance of heredity, and because the motives of the electors were anything but idealistic, occasions for rivalry and civil war were abundant. A knight had plenty of time on his hands, plenty of opportunities to brood insults, wreak vengeance, and maintain a reputation, which he called honour. He could have uncontrolled outbursts of rage, and in his anger, could kill, assault, rape, and break most of the precepts that Christianity never completely ceased to impose on him.

The mediæval knight believed quite firmly in Heaven and even more firmly in Hell. On the one hand, he strived to dedicate himself to God, to his woman, and to his duties, on the other, he was tempted by the natural male urge to fight, gamble, hunt, and copulate. The knight had to struggle increasingly with his conscience as he became more and more aware of this conflict. A knight who had given in to his anger, lust, or greed knew full well that he had sinned, and could embark on disproportionate penances; he could pawn all his earthly possessions in order to join a pilgrimage to the Holy Land, or donate or bequeath enormous sums to the Church.

During these thousand years, the Church had accumulated so enormous endowments from men who had either a clear or guilty conscience, that she had become a significant economic power of her own. The Church not only owned extensive landed property, but collected various "pennies," or stamp taxes, from charters, land sales, and civil cases alike. She placed every parish on the Continent under an obligation to share in both the massive building projects and in the cost of the wars the popes fought. Death was familiar to all, but it was the state of things after death that caused constant anxiety in the common parishioner. The recalcitrant faced the risk of excommunication, which was interpreted as a sentence to eternal damnation.

The small duchy of Normandy on the periphery of the French kingdom was fraught with constant warfare. Viking raids dragged on, of course, but the Normans also fought among themselves, not to mention with their neighbours. The office of duke, like that of the king, was no more powerful than the man behind it, and Normandy was blessed with many strong men. It was not only their thirst for conquest, but the limited available land, that made Normans pursue military goals abroad. In 1016, the Lombards asked a group of scruffy Norman pilgrims at the Holy Shrine of the Archangel Michael at Monte San Angelo on the Gargano Peninsula to fight with them against the occupying forces of the Byzantine Empire, thus unwittingly setting the stage for a Norman kingdom in the south.

However, the first venture of the Normans into southern Italy ended in a quick defeat: the joint Norman-Lombard force was utterly beaten by the Byzantines near Cannæ in 1017—ironically with the help of fellow-Vikings. You see, the forces of Capatan Basil Boioannes, the triumphant Byzantine general, had been augmented with the mighty Varangian Guard, sent to him as a gift from Prince Vladimir of Kiev. Having no money to go home, the remnant of the Norman warriors regrouped under a certain Rainulf, and hired themselves out to various wealthy noblemen in need of a strong military arm. Basil became alarmed by the ever-growing number of Normans arriving in Italy, and in the ancient Roman fashion, started recruiting them into his service in 1021. By splitting up and constantly changing their alliances, the Normans were able to maintain their freedom of action and to ensure that no single interest became too powerful.

In 1025, the Byzantine Emperor, Basil II Bulgaroktonos (Gr. "Bulgar-Slayer"), died after a 49-year reign, in midst of planning new conquests, leaving to his weak brother, Constantine VIII, an all-around expanded Empire, a great and victorious army, and an abundant state treasury. Two years hence, Basil Boioannes was recalled to Constantinople—a colossal mistake from which Byzantium would never recover. With him gone, things began to fall apart, and several small wars broke out, soon engulfing the whole province in conflict. In return for Rainulf and his band of warriors joining him, the Neapolitan duke, Sergius IV, gave him the hand of his sister and the newly-created county of Aversa near Naples, making it the first piece of property owned legally by the Normans in southern Italy.

In 1034, Robert the Devil[135], Duke of Normandy, announced that to atone for his many sins and transgressions, he would make a pilgrimage to the Holy Sepulchre, "barefoot and in fear of God." Such was the magnificence of Duke Robert that when he was passing through Constantinople, her inhabitants mistook him for the King of France. The Duke never reached the Holy City, however, dying somewhere in Asia Minor the next year.

William the Bastard was Robert's son by Arletta, a local tanner's daughter. Although illegitimate, William was nonetheless a direct descendant of Rolf the Viking, and had a good claim to the throne, which he now ascended, at the age of seven. All was well for two years, until the death of William's great uncle, Archbishop Robert of Rouen, who had guarded him with the whole weight of the Church. For the next ten years, his duchy was in a constant state of anarchy, remaining intact only due to the protection of William's feudal overlord, King Henry I of France.

With a steady influx of man-power from Normandy, Rainulf of Aversa continued his phenomenal rise to power in Italy. Under the law of primogeny, the eldest son received the full inheritance of the father, leaving the younger sons to make their own way. Thus, when Tancred de Hauteville's first wife bore him five sons, and his second seven, he informed his offspring that dispersal was their only option. William, Drogo, and Humphrey de Hauteville enlisted in the forces of Rainulf, which in 1038 went to Sicily under the banner of the Byzantine general, George Maniakes, to help the Greeks reconquer the Mediterranean island which had now been under Arab rule for

---

[135] i.e. Robert I

two centuries.

William de Hauteville earned the name *Bras-de-fer*, "Iron-Arm," by slaying the Emir of Syracuse in the battlefield, but two years later, the Normans were still fighting the Saracens in Sicily. The Lombards also continued their efforts to chase the Byzantines from Italy, and gave the Normans the city of Melfi to ensure Norman enthusiasm for the Lombard cause. The Norman-Lombard forces met and defeated the Byzantines three times in 1041, but the next year, Maniakes returned from Constantinople with a new army. He stormed Matera, one of the first Byzantine cities that had declared for the enemy; its inhabitants were struck down, buried alive, hanged, and tortured in many horrible ways.

Just when the Norman-Lombard cause seemed lost, Maniakes fell a victim to Byzantine politics and was recalled to Constantinople. Offended by this interference, he declared himself emperor, and marched with his loyal troops on Constantinople, only to be defeated and killed at Thessalonica. The void left in Italy by his departure was filled immediately by the Hautevilles, notably with William Iron-Arm being invested with Apulia, the heel of the Italian Peninsula, a formerly Byzantine-held territory, inhabited by a Greek-speaking population.[136]

Meanwhile, the rebellion of the Norman barons came to a head in 1047, when the whole of lower Normandy rose against Duke William. With the help of Henry I of France, the twenty-year-old William crushed the revolt at Val-es-Dunes near Caen, and the nobles never challenged the Duke's authority again. King Henry, however, was worried about his vassal's growing power, and set out to crush William before he became too strong to handle. But it was already too late: William successfully resisted not one but two full-scale invasions by his overlord.

In the 10th century, Vikings had hit both Normandy and England quite hard, and the Norman dukes had found a common interest with the rulers of southern Britain in closing the English Channel to Viking fleets. Edward the Confessor, who had lived in exile in Normandy for 25 years before becoming King of England in 1042, found his own earls just as dangerous as he did the Vikings, and turned to his Norman friends for aid against them. To keep the

---

[136] Even today, there are villages in southern Italy where the local population speaks only Greek.

Saxon barons from becoming too strong, the English King gave fiefs to Norman lords. Edward was childless, and his plan was carried to its final conclusion in 1051, when he proclaimed William the Bastard, now twenty-five, as his heir. Two years later, William ignored a papal ban by marrying Matilda, daughter of Count Baldwin the Pious[137] of Flanders and a direct descendant of Alfred the Great, antagonizing both the French King and the German Emperor in the process.

By the 11th century, Rome and the papacy had sunk to their lowest point of degeneracy. Papal elections had fallen under the control of the Roman noble families, each of which would rather have torn Rome apart than allowed another family to gain the upper hand. Indignant at the corruption of the current papacy, the new German Emperor, Henry III, descended into Italy in 1046, deposed three rival claimants to the papal throne, and appointed the first in a series of reformist popes, namely his own cousin, Bishop Bruno of Toul.

Hildebrand, a Cluniac monk, advised Bruno not to accept the papal tiara from the hands of the Emperor, but to wait for canonical election by the people and clergy of Rome. Bruno travelled to Rome as a pilgrim with the monk, and entered the city barefoot to show his deep commitment to the Gospel values. Hildebrand would remain the moving force behind the papacy of not only Bruno but his four successors; the monk's influence and involvement were so pervasive that these pontiffs are known collectively as the Hildebrandian Popes.

Bruno had begun his career in the service of Emperor Conrad II, and although in holy orders, had commanded a cavalry unit in the Italian expedition of 1027. Two years after ascending the papal throne as Leo IX (1049-1054), he put the Church of Rome on a collision course with the Normans, posturing at the head of a conspiracy to remove their presence from southern Italy. William of Apulia's brother and successor, Drogo de Hauteville, was assassinated in 1051 along with most of his chiefs, but Humphrey quickly stepped in to assume his brothers' place.

Roger de Hauteville came to Italy in 1053 to join his half-brother, Robert Guiscard (Ital. *guiscardo*, "weasel"), who had arrived a few years earlier, in

---

[137] i.e. Baldwin V

conquering Calabria from the Byzantines. In the summer of the same year, Pope Leo, feeling the Normans were getting too strong, met them on the field of battle without help from either the German or the Byzantine Emperor. Surveying the immense papal army, however, the Normans realized the odds were against them; they sent a delegation to Leo, pledging loyalty to him and begging his forgiveness—he told them that their only choices were exile or death.

Apart from a unit of Swabian mercenaries, who stood to the last man, the papal forces broke up and fled on first contact. With the papal army destroyed, the inhabitants of Civitella, the papal headquarters, handed Leo over to the Normans, who besought absolution for their crimes, swore fidelity, and were absolved by him. The Pope was none the less held prisoner for another nine months, although treated with the utmost respect, and kept in comfortable quarters at Benevento.

Leo was hoping for a word from Constantinople as to whether the Emperor would send his army to Italy, and maybe rescue him in the process, but eventually, the sick and exhausted Pope agreed to recognize the new Norman nation in the south. After the Byzantine no-show, Leo also issued a papal bull of excommunication against Michael Cærularius, the Patriarch of Constantinople, thus initiating the formal schism between the Eastern and the Western Church.[138] Upon receipt, the Byzantines solemnly burned the bull, and in turn anathematized the offending papal legates, the Pope himself having died some months earlier.

Norman power in southern Italy was further consolidated when the young Prince Pandulf of Capua passed away in 1057, enabling Richard of Aversa to take both the city and the title. The Lombard rule, which had lasted over two centuries, ended that day. The same year, Robert Guiscard succeeded his brother Humphrey as Count of Apulia.

Meanwhile, a great change had taken place in Germany: Henry III had died the year before in the prime of manhood, leaving a son of six years and a widow as regent. The long regency gave an opportunity for the reform party

---

[138] Even if at first, it was only the Patriarch who was excommunicated, not the whole Byzantium: while regular weekly reception of communion was not the practice of either rite at the time, crusaders frequently attended Mass in the Greek churches of the Holy Land more than half a century later.

to secure for the Roman clergy perpetual control of the papal office. Hildebrand and other reformers unleashed themselves upon Christendom, promulgating the Papal Election Decree, which prescribed that popes should be elected exclusively by vote of the cardinals, the chiefs of the Roman clergy. Before, the Roman population had taken part, as had the aristocratic faction within Rome, and, above all, the emperor.

The Roman aristocracy, under the leadership of the counts of Tusculum, took advantage of Hildebrand's absence to reassert their control over the papacy by appointing their first pope in nearly three decades: the Bishop of Velletri, John Mincius, who assumed the ill-omened name of Benedict X. The Roman clergy refused to recognize him, and elected Gerard of Burgundy, Bishop of Florence, in his stead as Nicholas II. After a brief period of impasse, Hildebrand called in Richard of Capua to resolve the schism. The Norman troops besieged Benedict at Galeria, and following the usual Norman scorched earth policy, he was captured, deposed, and imprisoned in Rome. Cardinal Hildebrand was created Archdeacon of the Roman Church, the first dignitary after the pope himself.

The sixth pope in twelve years, Nicholas was destined to reign little longer than the average of his recent predecessors. His reign was, none the less, among the most important, for hardly was he installed before he convened at the Lateran a council which confirmed the law governing papal elections still in force today—namely the one that restricts the vote to the cardinals. Putting it into effect, however, was no easy feat, and to secure the freedom of election from those out of whose hands the new law took it—the Roman aristocracy and the German emperor—Nicholas forged an alliance with the Normans. He persuaded Robert Guiscard and Richard of Capua to become "vassals of St. Peter" for their newly-conquered—and yet-to-be-conquered—territories, and with the help of their armies, he disorganized the Roman nobles.

The council of 1059 was the largest held in Rome down to that time. Though attended by a hundred and thirteen bishops and a multitude of lower clergymen, more than two-thirds of these prelates were Italian, the rest Burgundian and French—Germany was not represented at all. It was no surprise then that a synod of German bishops condemned Nicholas and declared all his ordinances null and void. He died on the 27th of July, 1061, and on 30th of September, the cardinals elected, at some unknown location outside of Rome, Anselm of Baggio, Bishop of Lucca, to succeed him. Anselm was escorted to Rome the following night by Norman soldiers, and consecrated, on the 1st of October, as Alexander II.

Four weeks later, an assembly of German and Lombard bishops met at Basel and chose as pope Bishop Cadalus of Parma, the candidate favoured by the Roman aristocracy. Calling himself Honorius II, he entered Rome with an armed entourage, defeated the troops of Alexander II, and maintained himself in Castel Sant' Angelo for two years. Meanwhile, a palace revolution had taken place in Germany; the new regent, Archbishop St. Anno of Cologne, was a zealous reformer, who summoned a diet to discuss the question at Augsburg. Cardinal St. Peter Damian, Alexander's representative at this diet, declared that it was for the emperor and his bishops to decide which of the rivals was really pope. So, though the diet ended by acknowledging Alexander, the principle that the laity have no right in papal elections had suffered a temporary eclipse.

In his oath of fealty, Robert Guiscard had promised to transfer all the churches in the lands he conquered to the papal jurisdiction. Alexander, returning to Rome in 1063, presented Roger de Hauteville with a papal banner to be carried at the head of his army. As the Pope further granted absolution to any warrior who fought for the Hautevilles in their struggle to deliver Sicily from the Saracens, the Norman conquest of Sicily took on aspects of a crusade.

Henry I of France died in 1060, and the new king, Philip I, was only eight years old. He would rule under the regency of Baldwin the Pious of Flanders, William the Bastard's father-in-law, ending the intermittent war of France with Normandy that had been waged since 1047. During those years, William had gained a great reputation as a warrior, for he had been generally victorious in battle, many of which he had fought against imposing odds.

As a result of the wars, a great amount of land—both conquered territory and confiscations from rebellious vassals—had changed hands. The latter were returned to those loyal to the Duke, transforming the independent baronage into a loyal aristocracy. In 1062, Herbert II of Maine died, and William of Normandy claimed the county on behalf of his son, Robert Curthose. William led the invasion of Maine personally, and by the beginning of 1064, it was completely in his control. He controlled the Norman Church, too, through its central power, the Archbishop of Rouen. The ecclesiastical positions were controlled by the great families, all of which now served the Duke.

Saxon England, on the other hand, was no feudal state, and the English Church was still run from the monastery, not the cathedral. The country was sparsely populated and poor; its peasantry consisted of free farmers and slaves, and there were few cases of land in exchange for service. The king's army was made up of his household, his barons and their retainers, and a general levy of the Saxon peasantry—the rivalrous nobles fought alongside the king only as allies, not as vassals.

And as with most of the successions to the throne in those days, there was more than one claimant to the crown. The leading pretender was a Saxon earl, Harold Godwinson, who started acting as the principal royal counsellor after his sister, Edith, married King Edward. Harold's powerful position, his relationship to the King, and the esteem he enjoyed among his peers made him the logical candidate to the Saxons.

But the Danes also had a claim, and through them, the King of Norway, Harald Hardrada ("Stern Council"), who fancied himself the greatest warrior in Christendom. In his youth, he had served as the commander of the Varangian Guard for many years, leading the Varangians into battle in North Africa, Syria, Palestine, and Sicily. However, his plans to invade Denmark came to naught because his reputation had preceded him, so he had to turn his sights elsewhere. And though the King of Denmark could also have made a claim to the English throne, his major concern was with Hardrada, and therefore, he threw his support behind William.

In 1064, King Edward sent Harold Godwinson to Normandy to confirm publicly William's right of succession. To refuse this command would have been an act of rebellion, and he was not yet ready for open revolt. Whilst crossing the English Channel, Harold was blown off course by a storm, cast ashore in Ponthieu, and there captured by Count Guy, the local lord. Ransoming nobles was a profitable business, so Guy figured he would hang on to the Earl and extract a sizable sum for him. But as Guy's lord, William of Normandy promptly demanded him to release the prisoner into his care.

Rather than arriving at Caen in the full dress of a great baron, Harold made his entrance under guard, not only in William's debt, but like a criminal being escorted to court. Virtually powerless, Harold was made to swear fealty to William, and to futher promise that he would support William's claim to England—vows which he never intended to honour. While taking the oaths, however, Harold had inadvisably placed his hand on a table, the covering of which was removed by William's men once he was done, revealing holy relics underneath. Swearing on relics was another thing altogether, and William took malicious pleasure in having outsmarted his rival.

On the 5th of January, 1066, Edward the Confessor died after a reign of 23 years. The next morning, Harold Godwinson, having ridden all night, arrived at London. He subsequently claimed that Edward had uttered on his deatbed: "Into Harold's hands I commit my Kingdom." On the strength of his word, the royal council, the *Witan* (or *Witanagemot*), composed of Saxon "Wise Men," unanimously elected Harold as king. His coronation took place with an almost indecent haste, the same day that Edward was buried in his newly-completed Westminster Abbey.

At this conjuncture, a "hairy star" (i.e. Halley's Comet) appeared in the sky, a portent which was taken to mean the imminent downfall of a sacrilegious upstart. William immediately prepared to invade England, and due to the dim view of feudal societies towards a broken oath, he found enlisting the support of the other rulers of Christendom to be easy. Prior Lanfranc of the Abbey of Bec, a famed Italian theologian and a trusted servant of William, was entrusted to head a mission to Rome denouncing Harold as a perjurer, and Stigand, the Archbishop of Canterbury who had crowned him, as schismatic. Archdeacon Hildebrand, the political power behind the papacy, knew the Prior from his earlier mission to Rome, during which Lanfranc obtained papal sanction and blessing for the marriage of William and Matilda; it is reasonable to assume that the two powerful churchmen had established a strong and mutually beneficial partnership.

Hildebrand was seeking to create a temporal power base throughout Italy by using the newly-seized territories established by Norman mercenaries, such as Robert Guiscard and Richard of Capua. These new nobles had sworn their oath of fealty to the pope, thus obtaining their political recognition through Rome. By increasing the number of devout Normans eager to conquer new lands and to establish new papal fiefs, the Church could obtain a massive secular base not only in Italy, but beyond the Alps, and indeed, wherever these fiefs should be founded. The only problem was the limited number of Normans capable of conquering such lands; it would further the cause greatly if the Duke of Normandy himself, or better yet, the future King of England, were to lend his support, if not his available men.

With these bounties in mind, Hildebrand used his considerable influence within the College of Cardinals to promote the claims of William the Bastard. Prior Lanfranc presented the arguments in support of his Duke, while the judgement was delivered by the Archdeacon. Not only was Harold of England on trial as a perjurer and a violator of holy relics, but the Chuch and State of England themselves were brought under investigation. It was submitted that the King had failed to pay Rome the levy known as Peter's Pence; that the Church of England had allowed the practice of simony to spread within its body; that the State of England had sunk into a semi-barbarous condition; and that only the appointment of a God-fearing king, who was a dutiful son to the Holy Father, could restore England into the brotherhood of Christendom.

Of course, the fact that England had an extremely devout ecclesiastical body that owned nearly one-fifth of the landed property, or that both simony and withholding Peter's Pence were common in most of the Catholic countries did not come out during the trial. What is more, King Harold was unable to send his own ecclesiastical representative because Archbishop Stigand was not recognized by Rome. The evidence and interests were such that the excommunication of Harold and his supporters was foregone. Papal support to William was issued in the form of a Papal Banner and a papal blessing—copies of the latter were circulated from the Abbey of Bec to all the heads of state who might join the Duke of Normandy in his crusade.

William's claim to the throne and his subsequent invasion received full support from noblemen of not only Normandy, but also of Flanders. The Channel Islands or Îles Normandes, as well as the Counties of Brittany and Maine, were William's personal dependancies, and all three contributed ships and men to the "Great Expedition" of 1066. But although the Duke was ready by August, his fleet was detained at Saint-Valéry by adverse winds, giving Harold time to assemble an army in southern England, his natural power base. He ran into supply problems, however, and his troops were not tied to him by personal oaths of loyalty; in fact, he could not even stop his own exiled brother, Earl Tostig of Northumbria, from raiding the English shores. Thus, on the 8th of September, the King dismissed all but his personal retainers.

Tostig was no threat on his own, but unfortunately, the rogue Earl forged an alliance with the King of Norway, who landed on the Humber River, on the 18th of September, with a huge fleet, probably the largest Viking fleet ever, carrying an army of around 7,000 men. Hardrada would seek the aid of the naturalized Norsemen, which is strange since he was Norwegian and most of the settlers in the Danelaw were Danish. Considering the animosity between Norway and Denmark, his assumption that he would receive wholehearted support on landing seems more than a little arrogant. In some fit of mad overconfidence, the Norwegian King also left a full third of his army to mind the ships, and those who did accopany him left their armour behind.

Nevertheless, only two days later, the Norwegians had already gained a victory over the northern earls and occupied the city of York. Harold Godwinson arrived with his army on the 25th of September, having marched all the way from the south, and met Hardrada at the Stamford Bridge in a day-long battle, which saw heavy losses on both sides. The real slaughter began the following day, when the Norse line broke in a second battle at Fulford. Cut off, unarmoured, and discouraged, the Norsemen lasted only a few moments; Hardrada fell, then Tostig—the rest fled to their ships. So utter was their defeat that of the 240 ships only 24 made the trip back home, concluding the last major Viking invasion of England.

It was only now that William's fleet could set sail, and on the 28th of September, he made landfall on the beach at Pevensey with around 7,000 Norman, Breton, French, and Flemish troops. That he had managed to keep not only his vassals by his side, but even the sailors in hand, for many weeks of frustration, is a testament to his abilities as a leader and an organizer. The landing at Pevensey itself was among the best planned and most complicated manœuvres of its kind in history. In addition to a sizeable army, William had brought with him a prefabricated wooden fortress and a host of craftsmen; upon arriving at the town of Hastings, he immediately erected defensive works around his position, and secured control of the surrounding countryside. He then sent his knights out to ravage the nearby estates which he knew to be the King's personal property—something that was guaranteed to exasperate Harold and to draw him out to face William.

The Battle of Stamford Bridge had greatly reduced the Saxon forces, and Harold needed all the men he could muster. Ignoring the advice of his brothers and his leading councillors, he set out to confront the enemy. Although the King did gather new men on the way, ending up with a similar number to the Normans, most were exhausted by the time they set up camp near Hastings on that fateful day, the 14th of October, 1066. After hearing Mass on the morning of the battle, William reverently suspended from his neck the holy relics on which Harold had sworn. Led by the sound of war trumpets, William's army began slowly to move across the valley towards Harold's position. Archers with bows and arrows were in front, followed by foot soldiers carrying spears and axes, with the knights on horseback close behind them.

The hard-fought battle lasted the entire day, neither side seeming able to gain the upper hand. As the day lingered on, however, the Saxon ranks began to thin. At sunset, the King himself was cut down by a Norman arrow, and finished off by the heavily armoured Norman food soldiers. The bloodshed did not end there, for the Norman cavalry pursued the Saxons well into the night, until, the next day, none were left to stand against the invaders. Before going to battle, William had promised God that if granted victory, he would build an abbey on the battleground with its high altar at the spot where Harold fell. William was a man of his word, and the Battle Abbey still stands at the site of the famous confrontation.

After his triumph at Hastings, William, formerly known as "the Bastard," became known as "the Conqueror." A papal decree followed, setting the penance for having killed in a "public war," a war sanctioned under the terms of the Truce of God. But while William had won a great battle, he had not yet won England. He sent out news of the victory, inviting the Saxon lords to recognize him as their legitimate king—none of them did. Instead, they withdrew to their lands, to guard their own interests. Enraged by such indolence, William ordered his troop to burn and kill in the shires of southern and southeastern England in a systematic, devastating act of attrition. In December, he advanced on London along a circular path across Kent, lighting a ring of fire around the country's principal city. Meanwhile, the Witan had proclaimed the young Edgar Ætheling, last scion of the old Wessex royal line, as the new king.

William needed to take London soon if he wished to enforce his claim before the surviving Saxon nobility would regroup around Edgar and form an organized resistance. Before the Conqueror could find a safe and defensible spot to cross the Thames, however, he had to take a lengthy detour to Wallingford, well west of London. Finally, upon the advice of Archbishop Aldred of York and Earl Morcar of Northumbria, together with his brother Edwin, all the high nobility of London submitted to William. But although they swore an oath of fealty to him, while William promised to be a gracious lord to them, there was still another armed clash that resulted in the massacre of great many Londoners. At the same time, more and more Saxon lords submitted to the Norman Duke, succumbing to the inevitable.[139]

On the 25th of December, 1066, William's victory was complete: he was consecrated King of England in Westminster Abbey by Archbishop Aldred—consciously mirroring the Christmas Day coronations of Clovis and Charlemagne. Those who had fought with William at Hastings were rewarded with lands all over England as fiefs. Problems, however, arose from the promises which the Pope claimed William had made, and which William denied making. The quarrel was primarily over the amount of Peter's Pence owed to Rome, and the right of the Pope to have Norman bishops travel to Rome with a full complement of armed retinues. Bishop Odo of Bayeux was arrested while attempting to obey such a summons, and the claim that the Duke of Normandy had promised to make England a papal fief was denied throughout his life.

King William I established himself as sovereign lord of the Church of England; he continued the Norman practice of appointing bishops and abbots at will, substituting foreign prelates for the English and granting sees as rewards to favoured families. He brought with him even the Norman Church's Romanesque church architecture, hundreds of parish churches being built immediately following the conquest. The old English Church had centered around the monastery; the new Church was supervised from the cathedrals. At Easter, 1070, papal legates presided over the great Council of Winchester, where Stigand was deposed along with several other English bishops, and Lanfranc appointed archbishop.

As the Duke of Normandy, William had nominally been bound by fealty to the King of France, but now that the vassal had conquered a kingdom, he seemed, in the eyes of the world, more prominent than his lord. William well understood that the lesson would not be lost on his own peers, who in turn recognized his suzerainty. Whatever the cost, he had to prevent his vassals

---

[139] King Edgar fled to his sister, St. Margaret of Scotland, who was largely responsible for the Catholization of its native Celtic Church and under the successive rule of whose three sons, the Scottish court gradually became Anglicized, her grandson King Malcolm IV (d. 1165) being the last Scottish monarch to actually have a Scottish name. (All of Margaret's sons had English names—he was named after her husband.)

from following his successful example.

Whenever Norman lords were granted lands in England, it was in exchange for service, and the few Saxon lords who were confirmed in their holdings were brought under the same obligations. Even though England had a much smaller population than France, the English King was able to maintain armies of equal size. As king, William held one-fifth of all land in England, a far greater estate than that held by any king in France. And though half the English fiefs belonged to Norman lords, their holdings were scattered rather than concentrated, which prevented them from ever becoming rivals to royal power. The remaining quarter of the land was held by the Church.

The finishing touch to William's control of England was a military innovation that he had brought with him from the Continent, namely stone castles. The army of Harold Godwinson may have been destroyed at Hastings, but the Saxons resisted the invaders for years, and Norman authority was established only through brute force. Once an area had been secured, castles were raised and garrisoned to keep the locals in check. Eighty-four were built by the end of the century, thoroughly transforming the English landscape.

Due to the strong Norse influence, England had been oriented mainly towards Denmark and Norway; England's destiny was now intertwined with that of France, and the repercussions of this would echo for centuries to come—the Anglo-Norman power had become the principal and most dangerous enemy of the French crown.

In 1073, William could finally return to Normandy, where he spent the better part of the next twelve years, dealing, among other matters, with a rebellion (1078) of his own son, Robert Curthose[140], who had allied himself with King Philip of France. A combined Saxon revolt and a Danish invasion brought William back to England in 1085, and in its wake, he ordered all his nobles to the Salisbury Plain, where they were forced to swear service to the King directly. This arrangement was unique in Europe at the time, as a minor knight usually held a few acres from a baron, who in turn held the land from a count or earl, who again held even larger territories from the king. Still the same year, William ordered into existence his famous "Domesday Book," one of the most far-reaching and thorough-going evaluations of material wealth known in history. This general survey enabled the King to tax England more

---

[140] i.e. Robert II

efficiently than any other monarch had ever been able to tax a kingdom before.

With the Norman Conquest, England became a unified country for the first time since the Romans left six centuries earlier. Language, however, remained a barrier and a divide between the Normans and their Saxon subjects. For the next three hundred years, the rulers of England spoke French, not English. In fact, many of the nobles actually spent all their lives in France, instead of their English estates. Saxon tradition survived at the local level, especially among the peasants, furthering the rift between the conqueror and the conquered—the antagonism between the Normans and the Saxons in the Robin Hood legends mirrors a real one that survived long after William.

CHAPTER 18

In the early 11th century, the enthusiasm of Western Christians for the pilgrimage to the Holy Land continued steadily to increase. Such excursions were believed to be one of the principal acts by which people could shorten their posthumous exposure to the tortures of Purgatory. Not only able-bodied knights and wealthy bishops, but the old and the young, women and children, flocked in crowds to Jerusalem. In the middle of the century, the Arabs were displaced as leaders of Islam by the Seljuk Turks, who came from Central Asia and converted to Islam even as they conquered the Arab world. The Turks disrupted political and social structures in the Middle East, compromised the safety of Western pilgrims, and what is more, even threatened the very existence of the Byzantine Empire.

Up until now, most Muslim rulers of Palestine had been quite tolerant of Christian interest in the holy shrines—with the notable exception of the "Mad Caliph," al-Hakim (996-1020), who had torn down churches and persecuted not only Jews and Christians, but later also his fellow-Muslims. By the second half of the century, pilgrims travelled to the Holy Land mostly in large, armed bands, something which in hindsight seems very much like a crusade rehearsal. In 1070, Jerusalem itself was conquered by the Turks; three thousand of its citizens were summarily massacred, and the hereditary control of the Holy City was entrusted to Emir Ortok, chief of a savage nomad tribe.

The Byzantine Emperor, Romanus IV Diogenes, made a fearless effort to pacify the marauding, quick-moving Turkish cavalry. At first, he had some luck despite the weakening of his army, but in 1071, the Byzantines suffered a crushing defeat against the Seljuk Sultan Alp Arslan at Manzikert in Armenia. The Emperor himself was made captive, and after he had been released in return for ransom, the rival Ducas family put out his eyes. The Empire was thus plunged into civil war just when Turkish tribes were entering its domains unopposed. Over the next ten years, rival factions bid against one another for the services of the Seljuk chiefs, handing many towns over to Turkish garrisons and ensuring the success of the Turkish occupation in the process. Asia Minor was thus overran by Turks, who were a nomadic, not agricultural people; as roads and aqueducts fell into ruin, cultivation ceased and the province declined rapidly into a desert, depriving the Empire of both its main granary and recruiting ground.

With a crisis like that at home, all Byzantine funding to the Norman barons was terminated. In April, 1071, the Byzantine presence in Italy finally came to an end with the fall of Bari, the last major stronghold of the Greeks in Magna Græcia. It had held out for two years and eight months, and received two reinforcement fleets, but with mass starvation in the city and no hope of relief, the inhabitants opened the city gates to Robert Guiscard and his half-brother, Roger. After assembling his fleet and army at Taranto (ancient Tarentum), Robert headed for Sicily in 1072. Roger had gone there shortly after the capture of Bari, and the two met at Messina. With their forces combined, they moved on Palermo—a city of over 300 mosques—which surrendered relatively quickly, on the 10th of January. Its capitulation was made easier by the Norman policy which allowed the Muslim inhabitants to retain their religious beliefs[141] and remain largely self-governing. Though it was Robert, as Duke of Apulia, who appointed Roger as Count of Sicily, it was the latter who ended up in stronger position, for he did not need to spend time and resources keeping rebellious vassals in check.

In twenty more months, all of southern Italy and Sicily, disunited since the Lombard Invasion of 568, was to be theirs, and a new kingdom would begin to emerge in the Mediterranean. The Normans brought this region into the sphere of West European culture vice the culture of the eastern Mediterranean. Richly amalgamating Arab architecture in Christian edifices, they erected a strong Catholic Church where such had not existed in five centuries. Even the language of the region became more Latinized, losing much of its strong Greek ties that dated back to the 8th century BCE. In one form or another, the Norman territorial creation lasted until 1860, when the Spanish Bourbons were toppled in favour of a unified Italy.

On the 22nd of April, 1073, Archdeacon Hildebrand was consecrated pope—the second to be elected by the College of Cardinals exclusively—and assumed the name Gregory VII, in honour of St. Gregory the Great.

---

[141] Even then, many Christians, if mainly in Byzantium, held that Muslims worshipped the same God as they did.

Meanwhile, the Christian population of Jerusalem was fearfully oppressed; the Patriarch of the Holy City was dragged by his hair over the pavement of the Church of the Resurrection, and cast into a dungeon. The pilgrims who made it through the untold perils to the gates of the city, were charged an *aureus*, or piece of gold, as the price of admission to the Holy Sepulchre; those unable to pay the tax were forced to retrace their weary steps to their distant homes in anguish and sorrow. On their return to Europe, they gave exaggerated accounts of the hardships they had faced, and their tall tales grew with the frequent retelling, even after the difficulties had disappeared.

Gregory sent the Patriarch of Venice to meet with the Byzantine usurper, Michael VII Ducas, as the papal envoy; wrote to the princes of Europe, exhorting them to rally the armies of Western Christendom for the defence of the Christian East; and issued a papal encyclical, urging all the faithful to come to the rescue of their Eastern brethren. He even conceived the notion that he himself would lead a great army of Christians to deliver the Holy Places from the infidel—"Fifty thousand men are pledged, if they can have me for their leader and priest, to march against the enemies of God." The so-called Investiture Controversy, however, compelled him to lay aside his plans.

When discussing the *Investiturstreit*, historians tend to deal only with the West and neglect the East, when in fact, the controversy had more to do with the schism between East and West than anything else, for in trying to solve this problem, the papacy became stronger than ever before. A relatively rigid, authoritarian, and static society requires a higher, absolute authority, whose decisions are truly final. In the eastern half of the old Roman Empire, the emperor[142] and later his Russian successor, the czar (from Lat. *cæsar*), were such ultimate authorities, who could dictate their will even to the Church. In the West, no one final authority was ever indisputably accepted, something that would have been necessary for the type of society in which many Western thinkers thought they lived.

The struggle between the popes and the emperors over the status of supreme authority raged all through the Middle Ages. According to mediæval thinking, only God had absolute power, and both parties invoked the same claim: their power had been given to them by God. The pope affirmed his

---

[142] or the empress as the case might be

own power by asserting that spiritual power was higher than the temporal. Ultimately, he proclaimed himself the Vicar of Christ on Earth: how could any Christian not obey the voice of Christ, speaking through the pope? The emperor, on the other hand, invoked God's sovereignty, which He had bestowed upon the government, that is, the emperor, who in turn divided it among his subjects, ecclesiastical and secular princes alike. If the supreme governmental authority was God's, then the supreme secular ruler represented God as the "Sword of Government," emperorship was divive sovereignty, and the emperor should be obeyed like God (cf. Rom. 13:1-4).

Few men have assumed the papacy as well prepared as Hildebrand. During a period covering more than twenty-five years, he had served as secretary, legate, and advisor to six different popes. As Pope Gregory VII, he strongly advocated the reformatory principles emanating from the Abbey of Cluny. He was determined to distinguish priests from the laity by prohibiting under a heavy penalty the marriage of the clergy. In 1074, he sent emissaries throughout the Western Church to see that these rules were enforced, stirring up violent objections among the German bishops and priests. Gregory's decrees were difficult to obey for two reasons: a priest needed a wife to take care of himself and his household, and men struggling with their desires were sent into a hysterical state by the constant sexual temptations. Thus, during the first Christian millennium, priestly celibacy had remained at the level of a mere ideal. When the priests at Vercelli were ordered to leave their wives in 960, their reply was unambiguous: "If our women will not take care of us, we will die of hunger and nakedness." The Church, which abhorred the concubines of its clergy, subsisted partly on their expense.

To secure the necessary influence in the appointment of bishops, and thus break down the opposition of the clergy, Gregory withdrew, at the Lenten Synod of 1075, "from the king the right of disposing of bishoprics in future, and relieved all lay persons of the investiture of churches." Investiture was the public ceremony by which a lord invested a vassal with a fief, usually by handing him a symbolic stone or clod. Just like the fiefdom, the bishopric was an honour, a beneficium granted by the feudal lord. The cleric who received the ring and the staff became the vassal of the prince who conferred them, and at the same time, the lord of other men. By the 11th century, the secular countships had become hereditary, leaving the royal investiture of sees and abbeys as the main check on the tendency of the feudal nobility to nullify the royal power. It was absolutely vital to the stability of the country that the king be assured of both the competence and loyalty of the men to whom the prelacies were invested.

Gregory was in no rush to promulgate the new decree to princes in general, and even his policy in applying it varied considerably. In Norman Sicily, Count Roger was still allowed not only to appoint the bishops at will, but to fix the boundaries of their dioceses; in the English kingdom of William the Conqueror, Gregory never raised the question at all. In Germany, however, where the lands of the prince-bishops encompassed half of the total area, the papal prohibition threatened to remove vast regions from the reach of the country's laws and the authority of its sovereign. Henry IV may have been the King of Germany since he was six years old, but while his mother, Agnes of Poitou, was regent, she had generously given away the duchies of Bavaria, Swabia, and Carinthia to her various feudal counts. So when Henry reached the age to rule, his power was in great jeopardy because his mother had thus imprudently created several strong nobles with their private lands, castles, and armies. It was quite impossible for the young King, who had yet to consolidate his power, to acknowledge the papal decree.

Ignoring Gregory's prohibition, Henry continued to appoint bishops in Germany and Italy. Towards the end of December, 1075, the Pope delivered an ultimatum to the King: if he failed to observe the papal decree, he would not only be "excommunicated until he had given proper satisfaction, but also deprived of his kingdom without hope of recovering it." Henry's answer was to organize all the malcontent ecclesiastics of Germany and Lombardy against Gregory, and with them, there also rose the disgruntled Roman aristocracy; it was not thirty years since Henry's father had removed three popes in as many weeks. In January, 1076, Gregory was deposed by twenty-six bishops at the Diet of Worms, on the ground that his elevation was irregular, and that consequently, he had never even been pope. Henry then addressed a letter "to Hildebrand, at present not pope but false monk":—"I, Henry, king by the grace of God, do say unto thee, together with all our bishops: Descend, descend, to be damned throughout the ages."

Kings and emperors had deposed popes before, but this time the pope would return the favour. In February, at the next Lenten Synod, Gregory addressed St. Peter in a prayer, declaring that "for the honour and security of thy Church, in the name of Almighty God, Father, Son and Holy Spirit, I withdraw, through thy power and authority, from Henry the King, son of Henry the Emperor, who has risen against thy Church with unheard of insolence, the rule over the whole kingdom of the Germans and over Italy. And I absolve all Christians from the bonds of the oath which they have made or shall make to him; and I forbid any one to serve him as king."

The excommunication thus released all of Henry's subjects from their oath of allegiance. Many of them were badly frightened by the supernatural sanctions that were associated with the papal ban; others were all too eager to use any and every weapon that presented itself to regain the powers they had enjoyed during the King's minority. Finally, in October, a diet of the German princes at Tribur obliged Henry to apologize to Gregory, to give a pledge of future obedience and reparation, and to refrain from any actual government as an excommunicate. They further decreed that if the excommunication was not removed within a year and a day, Henry should forfeit his crown. Lastly, it was resolved that Gregory should be invited to Germany to settle the conflict between the king and the princes. Filled with unholy joy, he immediately embarked towards the Alps.

To everyone's great surprise, Henry set out simultaneously to present himself as penitent before the Pope, and thus obtain pardon. In January, 1077, he crossed Mont Cenis and soon arrived at the castle of Canossa, whither Gregory had withdrawn upon learning of the King's approach. Henry had to stand three days at the gates of the castle in the dead of winter, barefoot and in the garb of a penitent, before he received clemency on the appeal of the proprietress, Countess Matilda of Tuscany. When finally admitted to the Pope's presence, Henry presented his apology in tears. His surrender was absolute, and Gregory became *de facto* king of Germany. Through Bismarck, "Canossa" would later become a proverbial term for the humiliation of the State before the Church.

The German enemies of Henry ignored the reconciliation, and proceeded in March to install his brother-in-law, Rudolph of Rheinfelden, as a new king. Henry demanded that the Pope excommunicate his rival or he would set up an antipope. Gregory answered by excommunicating Henry a second time and recognizing Rudolf as the rightful king. However, the second excommunication was widely considered unjustified, and the many who began to realize what the struggle was really about, sided with Henry—the cities in particular stood by him. In June, 1080, the King's bishops deposed Gregory at the Synod of Brixen, and elected as antipope Guibert, the German Archbishop of Ravenna, "otherwise a learned and blameless man" even according to the *Catholic Encyclopedia*.

In October, Rudolph was killed in battle. His duchy was given to Henry's son-in-law, Frederick, a Swabian nobleman, who had built his castle—Waiblingen—in Hohenstaufen, and whose family enjoyed great esteem. Gregory, now virtually defenceless against Henry, made terms with Robert Guiscard, whose attacks on the duchy of Benevento, a papal fief, had resulted in his excommunication six years earlier. After Robert had conquered practically all of Benevento except the city itself, he turned his eyes on the Byzantine Empire. The glory days of the East Rome had come irredeemably to close at the Battle of Manzikert. Not until 1081, when rectifying the state of affairs was already too late, was the throne ascended by a capable young soldier, Alexius Comnenus, founder of the Comneni dynasty. At first, however, Alexius could hardly stand his ground even in Europe, where the Normans ruthlessly pursued him.

Between 1081 and 1084, Henry assaulted Rome four times. Having made an alliance with Alexius in 1083, Henry succeeded in capturing a portion of the city, including the Basilica of St. Peter. He then made use of the generous funds sent by the Byzantine Emperor for an expedition against the Normans to bribe some Romans, who on the 21st of March, 1084, opened to Henry the gates of Rome proper, the part of the city which until then had been held by Gregory. Three days later, a synod convened to confirm the deposition of Gregory and the election of Guibert, who now called himself Clement III. On Easter Sunday, the 31st of March, Clement crowned Henry as emperor in St. Peter's, saluting him as Patrician of the Romans, while the old oaths guaranteeing the emperors' rights in the election of the popes were renewed.

With these solemnities out of the way, Henry laid siege to Castel Sant' Angelo, where Gregory had taken refuge. In the midst of the siege, word reached Rome that Robert Guiscard was marching north with a huge army to defend his lord the Pope. Instead of waiting for his arrival, the Emperor fled. Six days later, on the 27th of May, the Normans turned up, plundering the city so mercilessly that Gregory lost the support of the Romans. When the Normans retired with their booty, Gregory had no choice but to accompany them, first to Monte Cassino, then to Benevento, and finally to Salerno, where he died in 1085, following another ineffectual renewal of excommunication against his opponents.

"Clement III," on the other hand, held the field in Rome for 15 years against Gregory's two successors[143]. Robert Guiscard resumed his eastern wars, moving to Corfù to wait for spring. Before he could launch his forces against Constantinople, however, a typhoid fever epidemic swept his army, and while en route to join his advance party on the Ionian island of Cephalonia, he was himself struck down by the fever, leaving his half-brother Roger as the most powerful Norman lord in southern Italy.

The death of Robert Guiscard (1085) provided Emperor Alexius with sorely needed respite from defending the western front, and after securing the alliance of the Cumans, he succeeded in cleansing the Balkan Peninsula also of the fierce Patzinaks (c. 1091), nomadic people of the Tartar[144] family, who in turn pursued the land. He repulsed the Cumans after they turned against him, and suppressed insurrections in both Crete and Cyprus.

To the east, the Turks were rapidly encroaching upon the Empire, having taken as their headquarters the city of Nicæa, just across the Bosporus from Constantinople. Alexius wrote to his friend Robert[145], Count of Flanders, in 1093, relating stories about atrocities committed by the Turks on Christian pilgrims on their way to—and in—Jerusalem. Robert passed this letter on to Pope Urban II, Gregory's second successor. In March of 1095, Urban presided over an immense assembly at Piacenza, an international congress attended by the loyal supporters of the Gregorian reforms from all over Western Europe.

The two hundred bishops, 4,000 other clerics, and 30,000 laity were addressed by the ambassadors of the Byzantine Emperor. The Seljuk Turks, who had taken Jerusalem, had also destroyed the main Byzantine field army, and the balance of power needed to be restored. Alexius expected the Pope to act like a good Byzantine official and send a few hundred mercenaries, but that is not exactly what he got. Instead of summoning a few barons to go to the aid of the Eastern Emperor, Urban journeyed on in triumphal procession,

---

[143] Perhaps an heir would be a more appropriate term—both were hand-picked by Gregory.

[144] The Tartars derive their name from Tartarus, the lowest region of the Greek underworld, the place where the wicked are punished.

[145] later known as Robert of Jerusalem

surrounded by princes and prelates, from Italy, through Burgundy and southern France, moving about the Rhône Valley for four months, spreading enthusiasm for a crusade. Thousands of knights and nobles encamped on the plain of Chantoin in Auvergne, to the east of Clermont-Ferrand, where Urban convoked his most famous council in November, 1095.

The Council of Clermont met in the Basilica of Notre-Dame-du-Port, and began by renewing the Gregorian decrees against investiture, simony, and clerical marriage. Once more, prelates, monks, and laity came in from all parts: accounts speak of three or four hundred bishops and abbots, but the total number of people drawn to the town by the council may have been as high as 100,000. On Tuesday, the 27th of November, the Pope came forth from the church and addressed the assembled multitudes, relating how Christians in the Holy Land were suffering and dying at the hand of the Turks. He chastised the Christian knights of Europe, who waged perpetual war against one another, and offered them a way to save their souls from eternal torment in the fiery bowels of Hell. All the faithful were exhorted to stop killing one another, travel to the Holy Land, and wage a righteous war against the infidel. A plenary indulgence would be granted to all who should undertake the journey *pro sola devotione*, and anyone who lost his life on this expedition, either in battle or misadventure en route, would be assured a place in Heaven.

The papal appeal inspired extraordinary enthusiasm; cries of *Deus le volt*, "God wills it!"—the same cry which the Normans had used when invading England—began to echo across the city, growing louder and louder with each of Urban's exhortations. Though urged time and again to lead the Crusade personally, the Pope appointed Bishop Adémar of Le Puy-en-Velay, in his stead. After leaving Clermont, Urban travelled from city to city in France, preaching the Crusade, while letters were sent to bishops who had been unable to attend the Council.

It is not clear how many volunteers the Pope expected, possibly he hoped for a few thousand; what he got was a mass migration. Not only did professional soldiers respond to this war of penance, but craftsmen, farmers, and labourers by the thousands sewed a red cross on their shoulder. There sprang up disorganized, undisciplined, penniless hordes in every corner, nearly devoid of any equipment, who enthusiastically undertook "the pious and glorious enterprise" of cleansing the Holy Sepulchre from the abominations of the heathen. Following the likes of Peter the Hermit, a small and dirty man who rode a donkey and lived on a diet of wine and fish, men of all ranks, including monks and priests, flew to arms. A band of Germans followed a goose that they thought was God-inspired.

Surging eastward through the Danube Valley, the loose followers of Peter thieved food and ransacked homes for supplies. They also decided not to bother marching 3,000 miles to kill the enemies of God, when the people responsible for the death of Jesus were already nearby in Europe. As the unofficial army of around 60,000 peasants passed through Europe, great numbers of Jews were challenged "Christ-killers, embrace the cross or die!" The Jewish inhabitants of the German towns of Cologne, Mainz, Worms, Speyer, Trier, Metz, and several smaller villages were slaughtered by crusaders who believed they were carrying out the will of God. In the Rhine Valley alone, 12,000 Jews were murdered. Some Jewish writers refer to this as the "First Holocaust."

In July, 1096, Peter the Hermit and the German knight, Walter the Penniless, finally reached Constantinople with their unruly troops. Despite losing over a quarter of their number on the journey, they were still a sizeable force and a cause of worry for Alexius, who kept the city gates firmly closed. As the rabble that camped outside his city was beginning to loot the surrounding area, Alexius, not wanting them to cause further trouble, made arrangements to have them ferried across the Bosporus—most never saw the Imperial City much to the Emperor's relief. Once in Asia Minor, they felt it was time to start the Crusade in earnest, pillaging, torturing, and massacring indiscriminately. As it turned out, most of their victims were Greek Christians who lived in and around Nicæa. While the regular crusade was being organized in the West, the rabbles that followed Peter the Hermit and Walter the Penniless were either starving in Asia Minor or now slaves in Seljuk cities.

Pope Urban met the crusading princes at Lucca, and bestowed the Papal Banner on Hugh de Vermandois, the younger brother of the King of France. It was apparently this crusading host that enabled Urban, who had been consecrated outside of Rome, to enter the Eternal City, which at this time was still held by the Antipope. With northern and central Italy in the hands of Urban's supporters, the German Emperor was finally forced to leave Italy. Urban was able to celebrate the Christmas festival of 1096 with unusual magnificence; a council convened at the Lateran in 1097, and before the year was out, the Pope could go south again to implore the help of the Normans to regain Castel Sant' Angelo. In 1098, the castle capitulated and Roger de Hauteville was made a "perpetual legate of the Holy See"—around the same time, however, an Arabic coin was minted in Agrigento, presenting Roger as *Imâm* and *Malik* of Sicily.

Archbishop Anselm of Canterbury, who visited Roger during the siege of Capua, was horrified; his biographer reported that the Muslims of Sicily were not only allowed to retain their faith, but St. Anselm was expressly forbidden to convert them to Christianity. Meanwhile, a huge host of Catholic knights, most of them hungry for land, had gathered at Constantinople. Alexius, being already familiar with Peter's troops and well aware of the damage a real army could inflict, wanted some assurance of fidelity from these visiting noblemen. After he had persuaded their leaders to swear fealty and to sign over all conquest of the former Byzantine territories, he furnished them with money, supplies, and transportation to Asia Minor.

The first to arrive was Hugh de Vermandois, from northern France. From southern France came Raymond IV of St-Gilles, Count of Toulouse, who had already fought the Moors in Spain; from Normandy, Duke Robert II, son of William the Conqueror; from Sicily, Marcus Bohemund, Prince of Taranto, son of Robert Guiscard. He was in the company of the two Rogers, his half-brother and his uncle, the Great Count. He had with him over five hundred knights, including five other grandsons and two great-grandsons of Tancred de Hauteville, and a great many foot soldiers. All of Bohemund's men were already accustomed to fighting Byzantines and Saracens, and many could speak both Greek and Arabic.

One after the other, remaining armies turned up, took the oath, and were escorted across the Bosporus to join the rest of the crusading host. Count Stephen of Blois wrote in a letter to his wife, Adèle, daughter of William the Conqueror, "we should be in Jerusalem within five weeks," but it was going to take them slightly longer than that. In fact, it took the crusaders over two years to reach the Holy City.

Their first target was Nicæa, the capital city of the Seljuk Sultan, Kilij Arslan. After what had happened to Peter, the Sultan figured the crusaders would not dare to come through. His army, busy attacking a neighbouring Sultan, could never have arrived in time to reinforce the city. Before the crusaders had the chance to mount an assault, however, Emperor Alexius sent in his messengers under the cover of darkness to strike a deal with the Nicæans—either they could die by the hand of these Western barbarians or they could spare their lives by surrendering to him. Alexius gave the leaders of the crusade a portion of the spoils, but they felt cheated out of a victory. Their plans to hold the family of Arslan for ransom likewise came to naught when Alexius released the valuable prisoners as a courtesy. In the eyes of the crusaders, this made him disloyal to the cause, fuelling their growing dislike of the "prissy" Emperor.

As the main crusading army proceeded towards Antioch, Baldwin de Bouillon broke off alone with a hundred knights and made a detour towards Edessa, the richest and most important Armenian Christian city. Its ruler, Thoros, had captured the city from the Turks only two years earlier, and was in a precarious situation being surrounded by unfriendly emirates. Thoros and the population welcomed Baldwin with open arms; in fact, Thoros went as far as to adopt him as his son and heir. Strangely enough, about four weeks later, a full-scale riot burst out, during which Thoros was torn apart by an enraged mob, making Baldwin the new ruler of Edessa. The crusaders had thus gained their first major foothold in the Holy Land.

Antioch was a city which controlled the route from Asia Minor into Syria, and therefore essential for the crusaders to capture. Though no longer enjoying the opulence that it had in Roman times, it was still a fortress unlike any the crusaders had seen before; a stone edifice with six miles of curtain wall, over 60 feet tall, guarded by 450 towers. After a nine-month siege, Bohemund of Taranto has lost 5,000 of his 7,000 horses to hunger and disease. So many of his men had fallen ill and died so quickly that it has not been possible to bury all the corpses. The way to Antioch was to be through treachery, not through brute force. Bohemund's spies managed to bribe one of the tower guards into letting a small band of knights into the city so they could try to open the city gates. They succeeded and the rest of the crusading army swept into Antioch, massacring everyone in the city, whether Muslim or Christian.

The crusaders then caused the huge Turkish army of Kerbogha—made up of warriors from many separate regions, who generally trusted one another even less than they trusted the fanatical crusaders—to break up and withdraw. Not that the crusaders' own army was a unified whole; there had been a falling out between the Norman and Provençal crusaders, and Hugh de Vermandois had returned to Europe. Bohemund had made himself Prince of Antioch, both in defiance to his oath to the Byzantine Emperor and over the objection of Count Raymond, the papally-appointed leader of the Crusade. When the other Norman nobles moved on with the rest of the crusaders, who had finally decided to march towards their real goal, Jerusalem, Bohemund stayed in his new castle; he founded a line that continued until the fall of the Holy Land, and which would later include kings of Cyprus and of Jerusalem.

As the crusaders marched down the Syrian coast toward the Holy City, they found the towns abandoned and the gates left open for them to enter. The deal they made with the Emir of Tripoli allowed them to pass through his territory without incident, and he even provided them with an escort. They met with no opposition when they reached the Fatimid territories, but as they approached Beirut, they were running dangerously low on supplies. The locals, fearful of crusader destruction, offered them food and free passage to hurry them out of the city. It was the same in Tyre, whose local garrison stayed inside the great fortress while the crusaders passed by. They marched through Haïfa, under Mount Carmel, to Cæsarea. They pushed on to Arsuf, and as they turned inland, the Arab town of Ramallah fled before them. They passed through Emmaus without an incident, and finally, on the 7th of June, 1099, almost three years after setting out, they camped before the gates of Jerusalem.

The crusaders had originally set out to liberate the Holy City from the Turks, but there was one slight snag: it had taken them so long to get there that someone else had beaten them to it. Egyptian forces had expelled the Turkish garrison from Jerusalem the year before, and enjoyed good relations with the local Christian population. The crusaders were not to know this, however, and their attack on Jerusalem began on the 14th of July.

The next day, the crusaders entered the city from all sides, slaying its inhabitants regardless of age, sex, or creed. "They entered the houses of the citizens, seizing whatever they found in them. . . Whoever first entered a house, whether he was rich or poor . . . was to occupy and own the house or palace and whatever he found in it as if it were entirely his own. . . In this way many poor people became wealthy."[146] Emir Iftikhar, governor of Jerusalem,

---

[146] Thus the French cleric and eye-witness Fulcher of Chartres—the sack of Jerusalem barely rated a mention in the Islamic chronicles of the time.

took shelter with his bodyguard in the Tower of David. When Raymond of Toulouse reached the ancient Citadel, he was offered a huge ransom for sparing their lives—they were the only locals to leave the city alive.

The 30,000 Muslims who had fled to the great Aqsa Mosque on Mount Moriah were slaughtered without mercy. After locating about 6,000 Jews holed up in the Great Synagogue, the crusaders set it on fire; those who tried to escape were forced back into the burning sanctuary. The entire population of the Holy City, 70,000 men, women, and children were put to the sword in a genocide that raged for three days. The streets ran ankle-deep in blood of the slain, splashing on the knights as they rode through. Barefoot and weeping, these pious conquerors proceeded to pray at the Holy Sepulchre, before rushing ardently back to the slaughter. When the killing ceased, huge pyramids of bodies were left burning outside the city walls.

Satisfied that they had done their duty to God, most of the crusaders returned home to Europe. Jerusalem was divided under about a hundred knights, who chose as their lord Godfrey de Bouillon, brother of Baldwin of Edessa. Bohemund of Antioch came to Jerusalem to complete his vow, kneeling with Godfrey before the papal legate to whom he now swore fealty; they were thus in a unique positions of owing no allegiance to any overlord apart from the pope. Godfrey took the title of *Advocatus Sancti Sepulchri*, "Protector of the Holy Sepulchre," but his reign was short-lived, as he died a year later, and his brother ascended the throne as a king rather than a protector. After suffering a crushing defeat in 1104, Bohemund went back to Europe, married the daughter of King Philip of France, and secured support for a "crusade" against the Byzantine Emperor. The campaign was unsuccessful, and in 1108, Bohemund was forced to acknowledge Alexius as his suzerain. On Bohemund's death (1111), however, his nephew and successor, Tancred, refused to live up to the treaty and retained Antioch, leaving a legacy of distrust between the Greeks and the Latins.

The capture of Jerusalem by the crusaders was an immense victory for the papacy, which reaped all the credit and profit of that peculiar achievement. Unfortunately, Pope Urban did not live to hear the news; nor could his remains be buried in the Lateran, for Antipope Clement's followers were still in the city. Next year, Clement followed Urban to the grave.

All who went on a crusade had been promised total absolution from all prior, present, and future sins, and Henry IV, anxious to procure the removal of his excommunication, publicly declared his intention of taking the cross and joining the crusaders. This nowise satisfied the new pope, Paschal II, a monk of Cluny and Hildebrand's disciple, who demanded the renunciation of the right of investiture. Young Henry, son of the Emperor, was relieved by Paschal of excommunication and of his oath of allegiance to his father; he organized a revolt and forced the elder Henry to sign his abdication at Ingelheim in 1105. The former Emperor died the next year, still under anathema, and his remains were not graced with Christian burial until the year 1111.

The new monarch, however, had no intention of withdrawing the royal claims in respect of the investitures. The complacency of the German clergy made it evident that their earlier refusal of obedience to the Emperor arose from his excommunication, rather than from any resentment provoked by his interference in the affairs of the Church. In 1111, Henry V marched on Rome with a great army, demanding that the right of investiture be restored and that he be crowned emperor. On Paschal's refusal, Henry seized him and thirteen cardinals, hurrying them away from the city. After two months imprisonment, the Pope acceded to the King's demands, crowning him emperor and granting him unconditional investiture as an imperial privilege, while swearing on oath not to excommunicate him for what had taken place.

The more zealous members of the Gregorian party rebuked the "heretical" pope, compelling Paschal to back down step by step from the position into which he had been driven. Since he did not wish to infringe his oath by withdrawing his promise to Henry directly, he had the Archbishop of Vienne, his legate in France, call a council, declare lay investiture to be heretical, and excommunicate the Emperor, once more furnishing the princes with a pretext for rebellion. Excommunication of the "tyrant of Germany" was repeated by papal legates at Beauvais in 1114, at Reims, Cologne, Goslar, and a second time at Cologne in 1116.

Paschal II died in 1118; his successor, Gelasius II, lived only a year. On the 1st of March, 1119, the cardinals elected as pope Archbishop Guido of Vienne, the same who had excommunicated the Emperor in 1112. It was under him, as Calixtus II, that a nominal reconciliation was reached, against all odds, ten years later. This treaty is known as *Pactum Calixtinum*, or more commonly, the "Concordat of Worms." In it, the Emperor relinquishes his right to appoint bishops and install them with the ecclesiastical symbols, the ring and the staff; the bishops, on the other hand, now have to swear an oath of allegiance over their lands just like the secular princes. The different parts of the Empire were treated differently: in Germany, the investiture was to precede the consecration, while in Lombardy and Burgundy it followed the consecration.

Henry V died at Utrecht after a troubled reign in 1125, and the Frankish imperial dynasty died with him. From Henry IV on, the emperor and the pope were perpetually at war with each other, and every petty prince had to take one side or the other. Consumed by private warfare, the Empire was defenceless against external enemies. As the quarrel between the pope and the emperor spread its tentacles to all sorts of family and territorial relations, the fact that the imperial office was filled through election provided a powerful impetus for rivalry and ambition. Every nobleman with hundred lancers in his command was solicited for help by being granted dignities, privileges, and exemptions from taxes; this state of affairs is one of the principal reasons why Germany entered the Modern Era as a peculiar conglomeration of small principalities, each with their own customs borders, army, and hereditary despotism, each devoid of even the rudiments of political culture.

CHAPTER 19

The pyramid of society rested firmly on two strong hierarchies: the secular, on the head of which stood the king, followed by the dukes, counts, barons, etc. in a descending order; and the ecclesiastical, in which the pope, the cardinals, archbishops, bishops, etc. served a similar function. Both of these social classes were closed in the sense that one was hereditary and the other you could attain only through ordination. From these classes came the proponents of culture, and if such were born without, they could only amount to pale imitations. The creative culture of the Middle Ages was aristocratic and sacerdotal.

It was from within the circle of ecclesiastical music that the most sublime and lasting achievements of mediæval culture emerged. To help remember the pieces, musical signs, *neumes*, were introduced, to which a monk by the name of Guido d'Arezzo (c. 995-1050) added a stave of four lines. The advanced notation also made it possible for polyphony to delevop, and the addition of the latter to the liturgy brought on a tremendous change in music; the Gregorian Chant evolved in the 11th and 12th centuries into the part-singing which in due course came to be known as *Ars Antiqua*. The voices were initially combined *punctus contra punctum*, "note against note," meaning that each note of the original plainchant was doubled by another note, but eventually, the style became more sophisticated, resulting in true polyphonic music with two or more independent melodies. Sacred music was efficiently backed up by the earthly *troubadours* and *trouvères*, *minnesingers* and, in time, the *meistersingers*.

The royal courts and baronial manors became centres of intense literary activity. Even though the representatives of the nobility had been little more than professional soldiers in the darkest ages, with the dawning of the High Middle Ages, their field of interest was already much broader, concentrating on law and government, poetry and romance, on the unique way of life known as chivalry, and at times even on genuine scholarly cultivation of the mind.

France took the point in this activity and maintained her lead through the height of the Middle Ages. Having been one of the darkest regions in the Dark

Ages, France began to evolve into a nation in the modern European sense of the word earlier than any other country. The First Crusade, in which numerous French nobles had taken part, gave their country prestige, while at the same time, the absence of many powerful feudatories gave their king an opportunity to strengthen his position at home. One senses a genuine national spirit already in *Le Chanson de Roland*, the most famous of the *chansons de geste* ("songs of deeds"), the epic poetry that begins the chivalric romances. Its historical basis was the skirmish of 778, where Basques decimated the rear guard of one of Charlemagne's armies; they were now turned into Saracens, as was fairly common in the age of the Crusades. Incidentally, it was precisely this new military, commercial, and cultural involvement in the East, that helped pull Western Europe out of the Dark Ages and back into the annals of world history.

The opulent chivalric culture of France is largely explained by the fact that the material which sustained it was acquired from several different directions. The heritage passed on by the Roman colonists was allied with the warrior's code of the Germanic conquerors, and possibly also with their respectful treatment of women as roughly equal beings. The development of the latter feature into a positive worship of the woman was undoubtedly due to other reasons, and the ever-growing cult of the Virgin Mary can perhaps be seen as fruit of the same tree.

France was in close communication with the British Isles, from whence Celtic poetry poured into the country. Bretons were the descendants of those Britons who in the 5th and 6th centuries had, as a result of the Saxon invasion, emigrated to Armorica, now known as Brittany. They became largely bilingual through intercourse with their continental neighbours, and added French to their native tongue, which remains the last Celtic language spoken today on the mainland of Europe. The Arthurian Cycle, the principal group of poetry in the European Middle Ages, came into being when the poets of Britain and Brittany reworked the old Celtic legends partly into prose narratives, partly into collections of poems. Brittany was abound with *matière de Bretagne*, Celtic legendary material, which formed the basis of the *romans bretons*, Breton popular romances, penned by the French poets in the 12th century. A substantial part of this material was grouped explicitly around King Arthur and his court; even after a lapse of six hundred years, many Bretons still cherished the hope that he would return as a saviour to win back their ancestral home—anyone who dared to publicly dispute this belief in Brittany was in danger of stoning.

The nobility made their greatest literary contribution by creating the vernacular lyric. It came into being at Provence around the year 1100. There had been dance songs and similar improvisations for a couple of centuries already, but it was the Provençal troubadours who turned lyric poetry into an art form. Nearly five hundred of them are known by name: several, like the first, Guillaume de Poitiers, the most famous, Bertrand de Born, and the most talented, Thibaut de Champagne, were gentlemen of eminence; most, however, were of humble birth and made their living by praising noblemen and especially their women, and by reviling their enemies.

Troubadour—*trouvère* in French—means an inventor. The troubadour invention was the *gaya scienza*, the "gay science," the rules of which were held in highest esteem in the ages to come, as was the similarly normative art of love. Like other inventions, both were built on the work of predecessors. The Mohammedan love lyric, vacillating between ambiguous physical and metaphysical passion, must have made a deep impression on the nation which not only was the *primus motor* of the Crusades, but which as a neighbour to Spain had ample opportunity to familiarize itself with Islam. The troubadours bore an uncanny resemblance to Arab singers, both in sentiment and character, but also in the very forms of their minstrelsy. For the first time, people wrote extensively about love; romantic love, adulterous love, courtly love; unachievable, transcendental, insatiable love of the ideal. The troubadour concept of *fin'amors* left an indelible mark on Western culture; it put the woman on an idealized pedestal, adjusting to which can be quite cumbersome in the modern world.

During the 11th and 12th centuries, the region known as the Languedoc, bounded by the foot of the Pyrenees, the upper Garonne River, the Auvergne Mountains, the Rhône, and the Mediterranean, became the most highly civilized province of Christendom. It was a land where something still remained of the tradition of the Moors who had once occupied much of it, an outpost of Muslim culture next to the very heart of Catholic Europe. The Garonne and the Rhône were important routes of communication, and the passage of crusaders on their way to the East gave a tremendous stimulus to trade. Thanks to the Crusades, the West got to know buckwheat, rice, pepper, shallot, melon, sesame, lemon, apricot, playing-cards, and also new fabrics and furniture. The Arabs taught the crusaders chess, introduced them to new arts, dance, metal-workings, and story telling—all of which were incorporated into the crusader culture, as is apparent in clothing, jewelry, and literature.

By the end of the 12th century, the counts of Toulouse, the principal city of Languedoc, were suzerains of practically the entire region. Ruling with great wisdom and tolerance, the counts held a magnificent court that attracted the most talented troubadours and became the artistic and literary centre of mediæval Europe. And even if rival dynastic claims to Aquitaine did bring recurrent warfare with England, the Languedoc itself was scarcely affected. Its pleasant climate and fertile soil provided the means for a life of leisure. Here the Jews were not debarred from public life, and were highly respected as doctors and teachers, earning the region the name of *Judæa Secunda*. Here the Catholic Church no longer held the monopoly on knowledge and was slowly losing its power.

For many centuries, the only people who could read and write were the monks and priests. The first cathedral schools had been founded as early as the 7th century to produce scribes for the Church. In these were taught the basic rudiments of knowledge and before all Latin, which no longer was commonly spoken by any but scholars. The officiating priest at the Mass could easily substitute the words *Hoc est meum corpus*, "This is my body," with *Panis es, et panis manebis*, "Bread it is, and bread it shall remain," and the poor, benighted congregation would be unable tell the difference.

The education of the upper classes, which had been neglected in the Dark Ages, gradually led to the spread of literacy to wide circles of nobility. Nevertheless, the schooling of upper-class children was generally limited to the methods of warfare, hunting, and the management of large estates. Its real heyday came in the 12th century, coincidentally with the great era of Gothic cathedral building and the rise of cities as the prominent centres of culture. There were now increasing number of laymen who were literate—not in Latin, but in their own native vernacular—and the tension between the ruling classes was often reflected in the poetry cherished by the feudal nobility. Though religion itself was never attacked, the poor manners of the clergy incurred frequent and harsh criticism.

Very different was the behaviour of the Cathars (from Gr. *katharos*, "clean" or "pure") who, side by side with the troubadours, spread with incredible rapidity in southern France in the 11th and 12th centuries, preaching apostolic Christianity and simple life according to the Gospel. The great wealth of the monastic orders and the hypocrisy of the bishops had earned the contempt of the aristocracy, who charged them with self-indulgence and disinterest in the poor. Through the neglect of their superiors, the common priests had fallen into discredit because of their poverty and illiteracy. Under these circumstances, the idea of a return to the purity and simplicity of the apostolic age could not fail to attract attention. The strict moral demands of the Cathars made such a profound impression because their words corresponded to their actions.

The closest most laymen ever got to Scripture was when the parish priest would expound the Word of God to them. When the issue of laymen reading the Bible did arise, it was invariably linked to heretical movements. The Latin Vulgate was the product of a Saint, one of the Fathers of the Church. His work was considered divinely inspired, and other translations were not to be trusted.[147] In fact, the leaders of mediæval heresies had usually arrived at their "erroneous" beliefs after reading the Bible for themselves. The Cathars were accused of reading from the Gospels and the Epistles in the vulgar tongue, of citing and interpreting them in their favour and against the condition of the Catholic Church.

The eloquence with which the Cathars presented their beliefs and the selfless care which they showed everyone in need, won the affection of both nobility and common people. They became known by the name of *bons hommes*, "good men," though the women played an equal part as preachers and teachers. By the time the leaders of the Church realized just how widely the movement had spread, it was much too late to stem the tide. The heretics in question comprised a number of different sects, many of which were under the direction of an independent leader, whose followers would assume his name; but they were also frequently stigmatized with the names of much earlier heresies: Arian, Manicæan, and Marcionite.

In many respects, Cathar ritual reflected the early practices of the pre-

---

[147] E.g., to explain how Methuselah lived 14 years after the Deluge (according to St. Jerome), the pious Catholics invented the tradition that Methuselah was snatched up to be with Enoch for the duration of the flood and then set down again. According to the original Hebrew, Methuselah died the year of the Deluge.

Constantine Church. Their services were simple and could be performed anywhere, consisting of Gospels reading, a brief sermon, a blessing, and the Lord's Prayer. They rejected the authority of Rome, and denied the validity of all clerical hierarchies, all official and ordained intercessors between man and God. Under one name or another, the Cathars were denounced and condemned in a whole series of councils, at Toulouse (1119), the Second Lateran (1139), at Reims (1148) and Tours (1163), and in the Third Lateran (1179)—*Extra ecclesiam nulla salus.*

Ecclesiastical learnedness and the aristocratic doctrine of love meet in the person of Peter Abélard (1079-1142). Born into a knightly family in Le Pallet, a small Breton village near Nantes, he renounced his military heritage to study philosophy—then little more than an euphemism for theology—under Roscelin the Nominalist, William of Champeaux, and St. Anselm of Laon, all of whom he eventually debated. His career as a teacher in Paris, from 1108 to 1118, was an extraordinarily illustrious one. He was both a mundane professor and the idol of Paris, eloquent and handsome. Pupils flocked to him from every corner of Europe. He had, as he tells us, the whole world at his feet.

For all that, Abélard's scandalous romance with Héloïse is better known today than any of his writings. In 1117, he managed to obtain a room at the house of her uncle, Canon Fulbert of Notre-Dame, on the pretence that the servants at his own dwelling disturbed his work in addition to being costly. Abélard innocently suggested that by changing lodgings, several birds could be killed with one stone: he would save money and Héloïse could avail herself of his renowned teaching. Since Abélard was willing to sweeten the deal with payment of cash rent, Fulbert, being a greedy man, consented.

Abélard reveals what happened to the studies: "Our speech was more of love than of the books which lay open before us; our kisses far outnumbered our reasoned words." Though Abélard was not a priest or monk, or in any way sworn to celibacy, he was a lecturer at the Cathedral School and would lose his job if he got married. When Héloïse finally got pregnant, Abélard offered to marry her, but she insisted that his work as a great philosopher, destined to reshape the intellectual history of the world, was much too important to be jeopardized.

Unlike today, marriage was not laden with emotional expectations; a peasant had not even heard of romantic love and a knight associated that concept with something altogether different than marriage. In 1118, the pregnant Héloïse was smuggled out of the Canon's house under the cover of night and sent to Abélard's sister at his ancestral home. There Héloïse bore a male child, whom Abélard characteristically named "Astrolabe."

In no wise did Uncle Fulbert act like a gentleman in relation to the incident. He went wild with rage, demanding restitution, and would perhaps have killed Abélard on the spot, had he not feared that his relatives would in turn take their revenge on Héloïse. Abélard promised to marry her on the condition that it would take place in secret—over the objections of Héloïse herself, who would rather have been a lover than a wife. When Fulbert and his servants started spreading rumours about the marriage, Abélard hurried his wife to a nunnery near Paris, further embittering the aged Canon. Together with his relatives, he bribed one of Abélard's servants, and under the cover of night, crept into his bedroom, where Abélard says "they cut off those parts of my body with which I had done that which was the cause of their sorrow."

Humiliated and repentant, Abélard withdrew to a monastery at the Royal Abbey of St. Denis, and assumed the habit of a Benedictine monk: "I must confess that in my misery it was the overwhelming sense of my disgrace rather than any ardour for conversion to the religious life that drove me to seek the seclusion of the monastic cloister." As to Héloïse, she had become a nun, and ended up becoming one of the most literate women of her time. Although she now led a most exemplary and chaste life, she continued to exchange love letters with Abélard. The couple later compiled and published their correspondence, which today stands as a pillar of romantic classics.

While a monk at St. Denis, Abélard got into trouble by establishing that St. Denis of Paris, the patron saint of France, could not possibly be Dionysius the Areopagite; the other monks strongly disagreed with his reasoning, and through their influence, his orthodoxy was impeached, especially on the doctrine of the Trinity, and he was summoned to appear before the Council of Soissons in 1121. Given his reputation as a brilliant debater who could tie anyone in knots, Abélard's opponents were reluctant to challenge him head on. Finally, they succeeded in persuading the presiding papal legate that the mere fact that Abélard had publicly circulated a book on the Holy Trinity without first subjecting it to peer review was reason enough to condemn the work. Besides being ordered to burn his writings, Abélard was sentenced to imprisonment in the Abbey of St. Médard, at the instance of Abbot Adam of St. Denis, whose enmity was implacable.

Abélard fled to a desert place near Troyes, whither pupils soon, however, began to flock. Huts and tents were erected for their reception, and a private chapel was built, and his former success as a teacher renewed. But he soon got into trouble again, for he had dedicated his chapel to the Paraclete, or the "Comforter" (cf. John 14:16, 26), even though there was no precedent for dedicating a chapel to the Holy Spirit. In typical overkill, he replied that while there was nothing wrong with such dedication, when he said "Comforter," he was referring to Christ, the title of Paraclete not being exclusive to the third person of the Trinity, as Jesus expressly calls Him "another Comforter."

The philosophical development which would reach its peak in Scholasticism, acquired powerful stimulus from the Arabs and the Jews, and the gradual reconquest of the multicultural Spain only intensified this exchange of thoughts. Theologians of the day usually proved their points by quoting statements from the Church Fathers, and since the opinions of even the latter differed, the Mohammedans accused Christianity of contradicting itself. Abélard's most famous work, *Sic et Non*, "Yes and No" (1123), was a collection of 158 theological and philosophical writings aimed to resolve these apparent contradictions and to defend Christianity from attacks by other religions. It remains to this day one of the few documents to tie together rationality and Christianity.

Following the death of Abbot Adam, his successor, Suger, absolved Abélard from censure, thereby restoring his status as a monk. In 1125, he accepted a position in Brittany as the abbot of the Monastery of St-Gildas-de-Rhuys, but it turned out that the monks had expected him to be very lax in enforcing the monastic rules, when instead he was quite strict. After they attempted to poison him, he finally packed his bags and left. Meanwhile, the nunnery of Argenteuil, where Héloïse was prioress, had lost its lease, so Abélard had presented his private chapel to her. He now joined his wife and her nuns there, giving them spiritual guidance and composing a monastic rule for them. Some thought this arrangement was suspicious, but he argued that his being a eunuch put him above suspicion.

Around 1136, Abélard returned from seclusion once more and began to teach in Paris again, reviving the renown of the days when "all Europe" had gathered to hear his lectures. In fact, he is considered the founder of the

University of Paris, which grew up around the site of his school. In his teachings, Abélard emphasized the dialectic of Aristotle, maintaining that the system of logic and intellectual reflection could be applied to the truths of faith, pre-dating the Scholastics by a century. His solution of the centuries old philosophical question of universals also anticipates the conceptualism of Thomas Aquinas, while his resolution of the debate between the realists and the nominalists prefigures that of the Saint.

Though Abélard's influence on the philosophers and theologians of the 13th century was very great, his influence on his own generation was minimal, owing to his conflict with the ecclesiastical authorities. He alienated several ecclesiastical councils, bishops, abbots, his own monks, and most notably Bernard of Clairvaux (1090-1153), the most powerful man in the Church in those days.

Born into the highest nobility of Burgundy, St. Bernard was educated at a college of secular canons in the town of Châtillon-sur-Seine. At the age of twenty-three, however, he entered a monastery near Dijon. It was not one of the old established and rich abbeys, but Cîteaux, of a reformed Benedictine sect, recently founded by an Englishman, St. Stephen Harding. The Cistercians pursued self-sufficiency and took a dim view towards mere devout Bible reading within the confines of a monastic cell, labouring in the fields rather than studying in the cloisters. The Order's basic philosophy was crystallized in the water mill: its monasteries were to be built by water, and this water was to run the wheat mill and the tannery, irrigate and wash and aid at the forge shop.

Bernard's example had such a decisive influence on the Cistercian Order that he is sometimes called its "second founder." He convinced thirty young noblemen of Burgundy, among them four of his brothers and one uncle, to leave their knightly status behind and join him at Cîteaux. Others followed, and in such numbers that fours affiliate colonies were established in the three years succeeding Bernard's entry. He himself became abbot of the one at Clairvaux, which in turn became mother to sixty-eight others still in his lifetime. Despite their expressed desire for poverty, the abbeys grew wealthy; in fact, the network of Cistercian monasteries was to form the first supranational economic empire in Europe.

The monks not only planted vines and raised sheep in herds of thousands, but traded in wine and grain all over Europe—the famous red Burgundy wine,

Clos de Vougeot, comes from the founding place of the Cistercian Order. One could even talk of an industrial revolution of sorts; since the Cistercians wasted many hours a day praying, the importance of machines became more pronounced. Through this, the appreciation for handicrafts grew and the wheels of economy began to turn more and more efficiently. The Cistercians were also the first to institute the use of *conversi*, lay brothers who were turned from the service of the world to the service of God. They did only manual labour and lived in the abbey under separate regimen, being excused from many of the normal requirements of the regular monks.

Many of the men who had taken part in the First Crusade had been inflamed by religious zeal, a zeal that faded once the goal was accomplished. The few who had stayed in Palestine were adventurers, mainly from France, with nothing to go back to. Some of them had stayed in the hopes of gaining land that they could not hope to get in Europe; others simply because they had no funds to return. And even if the Holy Land was in Christian hands, pilgrimages were by no means safe. The land route through Constantinople, Nicæa, and Antioch was infested with roving bands of highwaymen. The sea route was just as dangerous, fraught with pirates eager to raid ships and sell the passengers off as slaves. The Kingdom of Jerusalem needed every soldier it could get, but there was no provision for a standing army and few means for conveying supplies to the kingdom. Many of the fighting men were Armenian and Syrian mercenaries, whose loyalty to the ideals of 1095 was doubtful at best. Pilgrims needed to be able to visit the holy places and provide money and supplies to the kingdom.

To redress the situation, one of the most unique and characteristic of mediæval institutions was created—the religious orders of knighthood, called to arms for the defence of the holy places. The oldest of these, the Knights Templar—nine of whom gathered around Hugues de Payens in 1118—served as a model for all the others. The Order's official name, the "Poor Knights of Christ and of the Temple of Solomon," comes from their place of habitation—on the supposed site of King Solomon's Temple on Mount Moriah, where its members took over the former Aqsa Mosque. Their primary function was the protection of pilgrims along the main roads between the coast at Jaffa and the inland city of Jerusalem.

The "Friars of the Hospital of St. John of Jerusalem" originally did duty at the Hospital of St. John, founded by the merchants of Amalfi long before the Crusades began. Commonly known as the Hospitallers, they devoted themselves at first to the purely peaceful function of caring and providing for the poor and pilgrims visiting the Holy Land. Though there is considerable dispute as to the precise date when military functions were assumed "to defend the Holy Sepulchre to the last drop of blood and fight the unfaithful wherever one finds them," it is known that as early as in 1136, the Hospitallers were given the fortified town of Beth Gibelin, a strategic outpost on the southern border of the Kingdom. Not until about 1200, however, under the ninth Master of the Hospital, did their rule make mention of military duties, or draw a distinction between brothers who fought and those who cared for the sick.

After nine years in the Holy Land, Hugues de Payens, leader of the Knights Templar, returned to France to find recruits, accompanied by another founding member, André de Montbard. They had great difficulty getting papal sanction for their military order until a vindication of their aims was written by Montbard's nephew, St. Bernard of Clairvaux. Until his conversion five years earlier, the Saint himself had been destined for a knightly career, and the Templar Order was to be imbued with the ideals and convictions of the knightly class of Burgundy. In the revolutionary document entitled *Liber ad milites Templi: De laude novæ militæ,* "In Praise of the New Knighthood," he outlines the many noble and selfless traits of the Knights Templar, comparing them favourably against the worldly, pompous, and degenerate secular knights of the era.

In 1128, Bernard assisted at the Council of Troyes, convoked by Pope Honorius II and presided over by Cardinal Matthew, Bishop of Albano and papal legate to France. At this council, the Knights Templar were officially recognized as a religious order and Bernard was asked to help create a rule for them. The rule would be that of the Cistercians, of whose white habit the Templars adopted, adding to it a red cross. These warrior-monks, whether knights drawn from the nobility, bailiffs, clerks, or chaplains, pronounced three monastic vows, although it was to the war against the Saracens that they were primarily pledged. A Cistercian thought of cutting down a tree as prayer, given the right circumstances, and the Templars adopted a similar attitude towards the Muslims.

There was not enough room for all the men of noble families back in

Europe, as the eldest son inherited the titles, castles, and lands, while the younger sons had only the Church or military life open to them. They were trained to fight from the age of seven, and that was all they knew. If they made a pilgrimage to the Holy Land, it was at least possible for them to attain some eminence in the endless wars being fought there. The Templars appealed to those of a more religious bent, who thought they could serve their God better by fighting the infidel and giving protection to the faithful.

St. Bernard became the Order's most vocal champion, exhorting men of good family to renounce their sinful lives and take up the sword and cross as Knights Templar. Service in the Order, which combined adherence to strict monastic vows with the constant threat of mutilation or death on the battlefield, was deemed sufficient to atone for any sin or number of sins. Bernard appealed to *sceleratos et impius, raptores et homicidas, adulteros,* "the wicked and the impious, rapists and murderers, adulterers," to save their souls by enlisting as Templars. Thieves, fornicators, and even heretics were welcomed.[148]

As the number of Templars grew, so did gifts of money and other goods. Knights who could not afford horses, armour, or weapons, were given all these upon their entry, along with personal attendants and servants. Like all the other holy orders founded on a vow of poverty, the Templars grew immensely rich; they acquired both in Palestine and in Europe considerable property. Just a year after the Council of Troyes, Hugues de Payens supervised the building of the first Templar shrine outside the Holy Land, in Scotland on the site where the Rosslyn Chapel would later rise—another temple was established at High Holborn in London.

In 1130, Hugues declared one of the nine original knights, Payen de Montdidier, as the Grand Master of France, and returned to Jerusalem with André de Montbard and three hundred newly-initiated members. By the end of the decade, the reputation of the military orders was so great that many knights travelled from Europe with the express purpose of joining either the Templars or the Hospitallers. France and England were soon covered with the houses which served them as recruiting centres. In time, both orders became independent of the authority of both the King and the Patriarch of Jerusalem, their Grand Masters being, like the chief superior of any other religious order,

---

[148] cf. I Cor. 6:9

subject only to the pope himself.

Following the conflict over investiture, the successors of Hildebrand developed the canon law of the Church, which provided the papacy with jurisdiction over the clergy, the rights of inheritance, and the rights of widows and orphans. With the creation of Gratian's *Decretum* in the first half of the 12th century, the papacy systemized and structured the Church, specifying religious duties, protecting parish priests from eviction and guaranteeing them a minimum income, defining and enforcing both ecclesiastical discipline and moral behaviour in general, ensuring the sanctity of wills and testaments, etc. etc.

The designs of the Church stood in the midst of the life of men from cradle to grave. After being born, they were named after the saints who prayed for them. Both the merchants and the craftsmen were organized into guilds which tied them to the religious ceremonies and obligations that were demanded by their trade. Colleagues were linked together on workdays and holidays alike, bound by the dictate of the Church to care for their poor and sick, to support the widows and orphans of the craftsmasters, and to bury their trade's dead during the epidemics, when all others shrank from touching the victims of the plague.

Work was not a means for a labourer to climb the social ladder, nor did anyone work just to "make money" in the modern sense of the term. Earning money in this sense would have been possible only by deceiving someone else and by taking more than one's just share. The fruits of labour, say a pair of shoes made by a professional cobbler, were not dealt with as merchandise is on free market, that is, asked as high a price as the customer is willing to pay. The "just price" consisted of the cost of the raw material, of as much or as little as the labourer needed for maintaining his customary standard of living for the duration of crafting the product, and of a small portion for the retailer, not to be considered as much a trading profit as his salary.

In order to ensure this economic justice, mediæval society gradually developed a highly complex system of regulation. The purpose of the guilds was to guarantee the income of their members during a period when earnings were small. The guild not only determined the prices and the quality of work, but controlled the amount of new labourers and masters, making sure that no outside competition came to the city.

There was no banking institution, so everyone had to look after his own assets personally. People often carried their riches, gold, silver, precious stones, on their person, concealed in their clothing; a larger fortune would be kept in a locked chest in some secure location. Treasures were, however, robbed all the time: the feudal nobility was in turns enriched and impoverished by looting one another. The total amount of wealth remained roughly the same—it just wandered from one possessor to another. Fortune of war had a decisive effect on the estate. Warfare was an imperative: it was the only way to make money.

As a result of the Crusades, international trade picked up and agriculture began to flourish again. The Templar Order, having assumed the duty of protecting Christian pilgrims and merchants travelling through the Holy Land, also undertook to protect the travellers' lands, castles, and other property back home, where Templars from Jerusalem arrived to take charge.[149] Their dwellings enjoyed the privilege of sanctuary, with various papal bulls solemnly decreeing that no person was to lay violent hands either upon the persons or the possessions of those having taken refuge in a Templar house.

One of the key financial activities of the Templars was arranging payments at a distance without physical transfer of funds. In an age when roads were unprotected and plunder was a constant risk, people were disinclined to make pilgrimages if they had to carry valuables with them. This lead the Templars to devise letters of credit: one would deposit a particular sum in one of the European Temples and receive a coupon; one could then travel safely to the Holy Land, most of the Continent, and even Britain—upon reaching one's destination, one would present the coupon and receive cash in whatever currency desired.

In devoting a lot of time and effort to plunder, as they did from the beginning, the Templars behaved like any other knights. In exacting large payments of tribute from Saracen rulers, they again complied with normal feudal practice. But, in one respect, the Templars offended grievously against canon law: this was in lending money and in providing, through their network of preceptories, places of safe deposit. At the pinnacle of their wealth, they are estimated to have had an income of over 350 millions sterling *per annum*. And this money was used to provide what were essentially the first banking services in Europe.

---

[149] And, should the pilgrims fail to return from their journey, their property would naturally pass into the Templars' permanent possession.

In theory, canon law prohibited Christians from engaging in "usury," or collecting interest on loans. The rationale offered by theologians was based on natural law: only living entities can grow—since money is not alive, it must remain a fixed size. The collection of interest on loaned money was unearned income and exploitation of one's neighbour's temporary need. What is today seen as completely acceptable rent, was in the Middle Ages considered mere profiteering. When the Jews of Central and Northern Europe, after centuries of harassment, were in effect deprived of any chance to participate in the various pursuits of landownership, trade, and social life, many sovereigns gave them permission and encouraged them to engage in money-lending. Yet the role of Jewish money-lenders in the evolution and development of West European economic institutions was minor compared to that of the Templars.

The "Poor Knights" lent money—and collected interest—on a massive scale. The strictures of canon law were evaded by the shrewd use of semantics, euphemisms, and circumlocution. The Templars thus not only predated the great Italian merchant houses, but established the machinery and procedures which those houses would later emulate and adopt. They became bankers and creditors, with their Paris Temple becoming the hub of the European financial world. Their rich holdings grew until they were so powerful that they could lend money to reigning monarchs.

Even thought the Templars transformed from an order devoted to poverty into an extremely rich institution, they still asked those who joined to surrender all their worldly goods to the Temple. There was also a rule that no Templar was to be rescued from the hands of the enemy by paying ransom, and many a captured Templar came to his death because of this rule. On the battlefield, the Templars were only permitted to retreat if the odds against them were greater than three to one. Not only were the men who joined the Order expected to die in battle, but most of them did.

When Emperor Henry V of Germany passed away in 1125 without a son to inherit, the imperial succession was open to question for the first time in a century. It should not have been, for Henry had designated his nephew, Frederick of Hohenstaufen, Duke of Swabia, as his successor. The German princes, however, were not about to miss the opportunity now offered to reassert their electoral rights over the claims of family. Pope Honorius II sent his legates to the election, and in combination with the archbishops and bishops of Germany, they secured the choice of Lothair, Duke of Saxony, one of the leaders of the opposition to Henry V.

Lothair's election set in force a great feud, which was to dominate German politics for the rest of the century. On one side were the partisans of Swabia, the family of Hohenstaufen; on the other, adhering not so much to Lothair personally as to the potential gain he represented, the Duke of Bavaria and his family, the Welfs. The Duke, Henry the Proud[150], acquired the duchy of Saxony[151] and became the most powerful German noble through his marriage with Gertrude, the only child of King Lothair II. He fought with him against Frederick of Hohenstaufen and his brother Conrad, who refused to recognize Lothair's election. Conrad was elected antiking in 1127, went to Italy in 1128, and despite excommunication by Pope Honorius, was crowned with the Iron Crown of Lombardy at Milan.

In the south, Duke William II of Apulia had died and his cousin, Roger II of Sicily, son and successor of Roger de Hauteville, laid claim to all of southern Italy. His claim was more than reasonable since William was childless and had himself declared Roger as heir. Though the island that Roger I and his half-brother had conquered was populated largely by Arabs, he had always remained a Norman knight. His son, by contrast, was a man of the Mediterranean, raised in the cosmopolitan, multicultural world of Greek and Muslim tutors and secretaries; he was not only a southerner, but worse yet, he was also an Oriental. Should the young Roger acquire such land and wealth, it would render him more powerful than all of his fellow-Normans put together, and the Pope would have him right on his southern doorstep. Consequently, Honorius forbade him from assuming the position of duke.

By midsummer of 1128, Pope Honorius had raised as large an army as he could, and set out with the intention of crushing the Duke and enforcing papal rule. Roger, however, was a ruler to whom diplomacy, no matter how tortuous, was a more natural weapon than the sword. After a month-long stand off at the Garigliano River, Honorius sent word to Roger announcing his willingness to negotiate. The meeting went well until Roger objected to having his investiture take place on papal land because of the symbolic interpretations that this might warrant. They met again a few days later, this

---

[150] i.e. Henry X

[151] as Henry II

time on the Leproso Bridge outside Benevento, in front of their troops and 20,000 spectators. Here the Pope invested Roger with the triple dukedom of Apulia, Calabria, and Sicily, while Roger in his turn renounced claims to Benevento and Capua. He had now become, at the age of thirty-two, one of the wealthiest and most powerful rulers in Europe.

Following the death of Honorius in 1130, Gregorio Papareschi, a distinguished Roman who had played an important part in the struggle against Henry V, was elected as Innocent II by a minority of cardinals; the majority had elected Pietro Pierleoni as Anacletus II—both were consecrated on the same day. St. Bernard's great fame and influence prompted Innocent to call on him to intervene in the conflict, and he travelled from place to place with the powerful abbot by his side. He was even received in the Saint's humble cell at Clairvaux, but the meanness of the accommodation and the scantiness of the meals left Innocent reluctant to prolong his stay at the monastery. He found a more suitable reception elsewhere, and though banished from Rome, Innocent was, in the words of St. Bernard, "welcomed by the world." Anacletus, in comparison, was supported only by Duke Roger, who got what he wanted for his support when Anacletus crowned him as King of Sicily on Christmas Day of 1130, in the Cathedral of Palermo.

King Lothair led Innocent and Bernard to Rome by armed force in 1132, and received in turn the imperial crown in 1133. But after Lothair's departure, Anacletus regained possession of Rome with the help of King Roger and his Saracenic army. After defeating Conrad and making peace (1135) with him, Lothair returned to Italy and campaigned successfully against Roger (1136), driving him temporarily out of Apulia and Calabria, but died on the journey home (1137). Although Henry the Proud was Lothair's intended successor to the German kingship, the electors were wary to increase his power, and chose Conrad of Hohenstaufen in his stead.

Conrad III deprived Henry of his duchies, giving Saxony to Albert the Bear of Brandenburg and Bavaria to Leopold IV of Austria. Henry retained the loyalty of his subjects, however, and a civil war broke out. In it, or more accurately, at the siege of Weinsberg (1140), figured for the first time the war-cries "Welf" and "Waiblingen," in their Italianized forms "Guelfo" and "Ghibellino." The former came to be the motto of the papal party, the latter that of the imperial party. The feud between the "Guelphs" and the "Ghibellines" would persist in Italy long after the feud between the Welfs and the Hohenstaufen had ended in Germany.

Though Anacletus soon (1138) followed Lothair to the grave, Innocent could not ascend the papal throne forthwith; a certain Victor IV occupied it for several months before retiring from the field through the persuasion of St. Bernard. At last on his throne, and without an antipope to contend with, Innocent decided it was time to settle the score with Roger of Sicily. At the Second Lateran Council, in April of 1139, Innocent pronounced sentence of excommunication against Roger, his sons, and every southern bishop consecrated by Anacletus. The Pope then prepared to carry out the sentence personally and depose the King.

By June, Innocent was on the march, receiving support from Robert II of Capua, a turncoat vassal of Roger. Robert had been confirmed by the Pope in his principality over Roger's claim for his son, Alfonso. Roger met Innocent, but nothing was resolved as the King refused to recognize Robert of Capua, and the Pope Roger's kingship. In the ensuing war, the papal army ended up utterly decimated and the Pope was taken prisoner, though Robert escaped to Roger's great annoyance. Innocent was forced to confront the fact that he had caused the papacy its greatest humiliation since Humphrey de Hauteville and Robert Guiscard had destroyed the army of St. Leo IX at Civitella eighty-six years earlier.

On his release, Innocent was obliged to recognize Roger's kingship and confirm his sons', Alfonso and the young Roger's, claims to the principality of Capua and the duchy of Apulia respectively. With the Pope humbled, all the barons finally fell into line, leaving Roger in total control of the lands that, for the next seven centuries, were to constitute the kingdoms of Naples and Sicily. Roger proceeded to conquer the North African coast from Tunis to Tripoli with the help of his Greek navy, and established a strong central administration, staffed by his Arab subjects. Prosperity returned to the "Jewel of the Mediterranean," and Roger's brilliant court at Palermo became a centre of the arts, letters, and sciences. Half a century later, the blood of his house would be mingled with the blood of the House of Hohenstaufen in the person of the great Frederick II. In their attempt to merge the disparate ethnic groups of the kingdom, the Normans of southern Italy created the first Western state since the ancient Roman Empire to preach religious and racial equality.

CHAPTER 20

Arnold of Brescia was born at the beginning of the 12th century and died around the year 1155. Aspiring to an irreproachable life, he entered a monastery in his native city at a tender age. He was later ordained a priest and appointed provost of his community, finally being placed at the head of the reform movement then stirring Brescia. Arnold had come to the conclusion that the principal causes of the evils afflicting both the city and Church were the wealth of the clergy and the temporal power of the bishop. He proclaimed that like Christ and the Apostles, the Church and the clergy should be devoid of temporal possessions, and subsist on the tithes and the voluntary offerings of the people. He practised what he taught, begging his daily bread from house to house.

At this precise point in history, Brescia, like just about every other Italian town north of the Papal States, was asserting its municipal liberties. The Lombard cities each would form themselves into single republics, in which the authority of the principal landed proprietors, namely the bishops, was superseded by annually elected consuls, who, assisted by a councils of burghers, conducted the government. Arnold's sermons received great popular applause, but also caused bitter disputes between the citizens and the bishop of Brescia. The exhortation to Apostolic Poverty posed a great threat to the Church, which was, after all, the richest institution in Europe. The Bishop of Brescia made a journey to Rome in 1138, as a consequence of which Arnold was charged before the Lateran Council of 1139 with inciting the laity against the clergy. Silence and exile were imposed on him, and he was forbidden to return to Brescia without express permission from the pope.

Arnold may have been a student of Abélard, or the association of the two may have begun when Arnold was banished from his monastery. Either case, in 1140, Arnold found himself in Sens at the side of Abélard, whom St. Bernard had just denounced to the bishops of France. Underestimating the shrewdness of his opponent, Abélard requested a council of bishops, before whom Bernard and he should discuss the matter. Abélard was expecting to debate the points in dispute with Bernard, only to find that the Council of Sens (1141) had already decided to condemn him and would not even let him speak in his own defence. On the eve of the Council, a meeting of bishops had been held, at which Bernard acted as the prosecutor. In that meeting, a number of propositions had been selected from Abélard's writings and condemned; at the Council itself his entire theological work was declared heretical. Arnold fared no better, for both were sentenced to lifelong confinement in separate monasteries in Paris.

Defying the ruling, Abélard undertook a journey to Rome to plead his case there. He collapsed on the way, taking refuge at the Abbey of Cluny, where he stayed under the protection of Peter the Venerable. Abbot Peter was one of the few men who could stand up to St. Bernard, having once written to him: "You perform all the difficult religious duties; you fast; you watch; you suffer; but you will not endure the easy ones—you do not love." After persuading Abélard to leave the future of theology to the theologians of the future, the Abbot reconciled him with Bernard, and obtained from Rome a mitigation of his sentence. Abélard died in 1142 at the Cluniac Abbey in St-Marcel-sur-Saône, and was buried at the Paraclete. In the 19th century, he and Héloïse were reburied together in a single tomb in the famous Père Lachaise Cemetery in Paris.

Unlike Abélard, Arnold of Brescia was never reconciled with Bernard, whom he continued to attack as conceited and narrow-minded. From his enforced retirement at Mont-Sainte-Geneviève in Paris, he began a course of public lectures against the immorality and worldliness of the clergy, accusing Bernard of ungodly ambition and envy against scholars. He addressed in particular the greed of the bishops, citing wealth as the real disease infecting the Church. But his attacks did not stop here; the Roman Church had become corrupt through avaricious and simoniacal priests, bishops, and cardinals, and was no longer the true Church. "The pope," he said, "is no longer the real Apostolicus, and, as he does not exemplify in his life the teachings of the Apostles, there is no obligation of reverence and obedience towards him." The unworthy clergy had forfeited the right to administer the sacraments, and the faithful needed no longer confess to them—it was sufficient that they confessed to one another.

At Bernard's urging, King Louis VII expelled "the incorrigible schismatic, the sower of discord, the disturber of peace, the destroyer of unity" from

France. He fled to Zürich, where he was kindly received by Cardinal Guido, the papal legate to Bohemia and his former fellow-student in Paris. But Bernard pursued him even there, denouncing him to the Bishop of Constance. In this manner, Arnold was driven by persecution from one country to another.

Pope Innocent II died in 1143, and his two successors, Celestine II and Lucius II, reigned but a short time. In 1145, St. Bernard saw one of his own disciples, Bernardo di Pisa, Abbot of Tre Fontane, thereafter known as Eugene III, ascend the papal throne. The "Book of Consideration," *De Consideratione*, was written by the former to instruct the latter in his papal duties. The Monk of Clairvaux had become more influential than the pope.

By the middle of the 12th century, the Crusader States of the East had been completely organized, forming a small but unbroken territory between the Euphrates and the Egyptian frontier, eclipsing in wealth and prosperity most of the Western states. A Latin patriarchate of Jerusalem had been set up, with four metropolitan and seven suffragan bishops depending on it. Through rich and frequent donations, the Latin clergy had not only become the greatest of all the landed proprietors, but also received from the crusaders substantial estates in Europe. The patriarch was practically the king's equal, yet the intermittent strife between the two was only one of the many barriers to real unity.

The second and third generations of crusaders had adopted forms of dress, customs, and manners of the native peoples. Their king gave audiences cross-legged on a carpet, dressed up in a burnous and kaffiyeh. Their nobles wore turbans and shoes with upturned points, the silks, damasks, muslins, and cottons so different from the wool and furs of France. Living in villas with courtyards, fountains, and mosaic floors, they lounged on divans, listening to Arab lutes and watching girls dance. They washed with soap in sunken baths, while their women applied cosmetics with the aid of glass mirrors. Unfortunately, those who came fresh from Europe were a different breed; filthy, unrefined, rude, and fanatical. Once they arrived in the area, they would come across someone they identified as a Saracen, and immediately attack him. Much to their chagrin, they often discovered that they had, in fact, assaulted a fellow-Christian in the local garb. Many a delicate political alliance fell apart exactly because of the newcomer enthusiasm to slay the infidel.

At the end of the First Crusade, the Islamic world had been too divided to act against the Latins. However, as soon as it started to recover from the disruptions caused by the Turkish invasions, major Mohammedan leaders began to emerge. Imad ad-Din Zengi and his son and successor, Nur ad-Din, were the most famous chieftains of the age, regarded by the Muslims as champions who could recover the civil and religious authority of the Caliph in the lost city of Jerusalem and all the holy places deeply venerated by them. In 1127, Zengi, the Atabeg of Mosul, succeeded in creating a new unity with only the city of Damascus, "the Queen of Syria," for a rival. The years from 1131 to 1144 were a period of uninterrupted success for him against the Crusader States. Luckily for them, Damascus narrowly held off Zengi, and finding them useful, its Emir concluded an alliance with the Latin rulers.

There was never a single Crusader State, but rather four distinct ones, the Kingdom of Jerusalem, the Principality of Antioch, and the Countships of Tripoli and Edessa, the rulers of which were constantly at odds with one another. Joscelin de Courtenay, Count of Edessa[152], seemed to enjoy the pleasures of the court rather than attending to the business of government. Taking residence in the old family home at Turbessel instead of the countship's capital, he fell out with his neighbour and overlord, Raymond de Poitiers, Prince of Antioch, to the point that "each rejoiced in the distress of the other and exulted over any untoward mischance." The Count of Tripoli, Raymond II, showed little interest in events so far to the east, and King Fulk of Jerusalem had just died, leaving the government in the hands of Queen Melisende as regent for their 13-year-old son, Baldwin III.

When Joscelin appealed to Raymond of Antioch for support, after Zengi had laid siege to Edessa in 1144, Raymond refused. With only few mercenaries defending the city, Zengi's troops faced no real opposition. On Christmas Day, Edessa capitulated—the first of the crusader conquests had become also the first to be lost. The horrified citizens fled to the safety of the Citadel, only to find the gates locked against them by Archbishop Hugo in a bid to save his own skin. In the panic that followed, many were trampled to death, but the Archbishop got what was coming to him when Zengi smashed the gates of the Citadel and slaughtered everyone inside. Although Zengi made sure that all Latin Christians were executed and their women and children sold

---

[152] as Joscelin II

into slavery, he spared the native Armenian, Syrian, and Greek Christians, who still formed the majority of the population.

In trepidation, the Latin clergy rushed delegations to Rome, begging for the Pope's assistance. Eugene III consequently proclaimed the Second Crusade, granting the same indulgences for it as Urban II had granted to the First. The office of preaching he wisely delegated to his teacher, and on the 31st of March, 1146, St. Bernard held his first crusade sermon in a field outside the town of Vézelay. The response was extraordinary to say the least: the Saint was obliged to use portions of his habit to make crosses to satisfy the zeal of the multitude who wished to take part in the expedition; he is even alleged to have become a miracle worker, reputedly healing the lame and the possessed as he rode from place to place on his humble little ass.

The power of his exhortations to take part in the crusade also bordered on the supernatural. People who did not understand a word of his language were powerless against the fire of his eloquence. As though under spell, princes accepted his orders, bishops did his bidding. His words had such an irresistible emotial appeal that many of those who listened to him took the cross even against their better judgement. The 19-year-old Queen Eleanor of Aquitaine enlisted under the cross with her first husband, Louis VII of France; she galloped through the crowds at Vézelay on a white horse, urging them to join the Crusade. But what Bernard himself described as the miracles of miracles took place in the Cathedral of Speyer: here the German King, Conrad III, scorned all counsels of prudence and adopted the standard of the cross, undeterred even by the disapproval of the Pope.[153]

The German crusaders set off in May of 1146, followed shortly by the French in June. The presence of Queen Eleanor, her ladies, and the wagonloads of female servants, was reproved by chroniclers throughout her adventure. Though dressed in armour and carrying lances, the women never fought. The papal bull for the next Crusade expressly forbade women of all sorts to join the expedition; clerics, especially those charged with duties to a parish or diocese, would also be discouraged from going.

When the German crusaders arrived at Constantinople, Emperor Manuel

---

[153] Realizing that the Welfs and the Hohenstaufen would never be able to co-operate in the Holy Land, the Saint persuaded the Pope to authorize the Wendish Crusade of the Saxon nobility against the pagan Slavs living across the Elbe in what is today eastern Germany.

Comnenus, like his grandfather Alexius during the First Crusade, was eager to ferry off their huge, disorderly army before the French came in. The Germans were ambushed at Dorylæum by a large Turkish force led by the son of Kilij Arslan, the Sultan defeated at that very spot by the armies of the First Crusade fifty years earlier—barely a tenth of them made it back to Nicæa, where they met up with the French crusaders.

In February, 1147, King Louis led his army towards the port of Attalia (now Antalya), but the worsening winter conditions and depleting supplies began to take their toll on the French. Unable to continue by land, the French King gave orders to the Byzantine governor at Attalia to round up a fleet. The governor did what he could, but there were far too few vessels to accommodate the entire army. Louis took his own household and as many of the cavalry as he could with him, leaving the foot soldiers and pilgrims to shift for themselves. The governor wanted the crusaders to leave, for their presence brought Turkish raids, and they finally decided to set out for Antioch on foot. Without food, a leader, and the protection of knights, they were an easy prey, and less than half of them ever reached the city.

At Antioch, Queen Eleanor had rekindled an old friendship with Raymond de Poitiers, her uncle and the prince of the city. Only a few years older than Eleanor, he was far more interesting and handsome than her husband, King Louis. So when Raymond decided that the best strategic objective would be to recapture Edessa, thereby protecting the Latin presence in the Holy Land, Eleanor sided with his view. As a deeply pious man, Louis was fixated on reaching Jerusalem, and when its patriarch arrived in Antioch with news that the German King was already there, he demanded that Eleanor follow him to Palestine. The Queen calmly announced that their marriage was not valid in the eyes of God, for they were related to an extent prohibited by the Church, but the King forced her to honour her marriage vows and ride with him.

In the spring of 1148, the royal couple finally arrived in Jerusalem, having passed down the coast without an incident. They met up with Conrad at Palmarea near Acre, where a council was held to decide on the strategy. The alliance that the Latins had concluded with Damascus was the sort of co-operation with the infidel that completely baffled the crusaders who arrived from the West. In their minds, Saracen were Saracen; they were the enemy they had come to fight. Since regaining Edessa was more than they could hope, it was decided that they would instead attack Damascus—the one force that stood between them and the aggressive Nur ad-Din. No longer the imposing force that had left Europe, the crusader army could not even surround the city[154]; its attacks only succeeded in turning the sole Muslim ally of the Crusader States into their enemy and giving Nur ad-Din's career the boost it needed.

Utterly beaten, the crusaders were harassed all the way back to the Latin territory. Louis and Conrad returned home, and their troops with them, to spread, as widely as the area whence they were recruited, the tale of a great disaster. It was commonly suspected in Europe that the word of pope did not equal the will of God after all; St. Bernard became regarded as a false prophet, and the crowds were as ready to stone him as they once had been to cheer him.

Louis' three-year stay in the East had given the French lords back home an opportunity to hold their own. The eventual annulment of his marriage with Eleanor of Aquitaine also proved perilous to the young monarchy, for Eleanor married Henry Plantagenet, Count of Anjou, who soon became King Henry II of England, and Eleanor's lands, consisting of Guyenne, Poitou, and Saintogne, were removed from France's sphere of power. Added to Henry's own holdings, they gave him control over the better part of western France. Louis, by comparison, was left with little more than his title, and a few thousand acres to his name.

Meanwhile, the people of Rome had asserted the rights of the commune and set up a republic after the ancient model. They had attracted to their cause Arnold of Brescia, who became their leader, eloquently pleading for liberty and democracy. Clad in his monastic habit, he preached to the *patres conscripti* on the ruins of the Capitol, advising them to rebuild the ancient monument and to restore the old order of senators and equites. He referred to the popes and cardinals as scribes and Pharisees, and to their Church as an house of merchandise and a den of robbers. According to Arnold, Eugene III was more concerned "with pampering his own body, and filling his own purse than with imitating the zeal of the Apostles whose place he filled." The Pope had been forced to take exile in France, and for the duration of the Second Crusade, democracy prevailed in the Eternal City.

---

[154] Tellingly, it was still the largest crusading host to ever march in the Holy Land.

Though excommunicated in 1148, Arnold continued to head the republican city-state even after Eugene was permitted to re-enter Rome. He was protected by the Roman Senate and idolized by the people to the end. The Pope had summoned the help of Roger II of Sicily, but all the fighting within the city caused the Pontiff to once again flee Rome. While waiting to return, Eugene entered into negotiations with Conrad III to restore the dignity of the German King who had been so sorely humiliated in the Second Crusade. A huge celebration was planned for the autumn of 1152, where Conrad would have been fêted and crowned emperor, had he not died in mid-February of the year.

Prior to his death, Conrad had named his nephew, Frederick Barbarossa (Ital. "Red Beard"), as his successor, in hopes that Frederick's coronation would end the discord between the Guelphs and the Ghibellines. Frederick's mother, Judith, was a Guelph, and he had frequently acted as a mediator between his Ghibelline uncle and his Guelph cousin, Duke Henry the Lion[155] of Saxony.

Invitations for Frederick to come, armed, into Italy were not few: the Lombard nobles wanted him to suppress the communes; there were many in Sicily who wished to see the Normans driven out; and the pope clamoured for the defeat of Arnold and his followers. Above and beyond, Frederick hoped to restore the imperial power, which had all but disappeared in Italy due to the neglect of his predecessors. In the Treaty of Constance (March, 1153) with Eugene III, Frederick agreed to assist the pope against Arnold of Brescia, but not until the autumn of 1154 was the King ready to advance. By the time he arrived in Italy, Eugene was dead, as was his teacher St. Bernard, along with his short-lived successor, Anastasius IV. The man whom Frederick met was Nicholas Breakspear, Pope Adrian IV—the only pontiff ever to place Rome under interdict.

The Eastertide interdict of 1155 forced the exile of Arnold and allowed Adrian to take possession of the Lateran. After holding a diet on the plain of Roncaglia, Frederick received the iron crown of kingship from the Lombards at Pavia. As a condition of Frederick's coronation with the golden crown of empire, the Pope demanded the surrender of Arnold. Having fallen into the hands of the Cardinal-Deacon of St. Nicholas, Arnold was freed by the

---

[155] i.e. Henry XI, son of Henry the Proud

Viscounts of Campagnatico, who "looked on him as a prophet" and gave him refuge in their territory. However, Frederick was keen on the imperial dignity and saw to it that Arnold was handed over to the Curia—the Pope personally ordered him to be hanged. Asked to recant his teachings, Arnold replied that he was ready to die for them and had nothing to repent. His body was burned after the hanging and his ashes thrown into the Tiber, "for fear lest the people might collect them and honour them as the ashes of a martyr."

The Senate, which had governed Rome in Arnold's days, waited on Frederick with a mixture of petitions and instructions, only to see him turn violently against them. On Whit Sunday (the 18th of June, 1155), he was crowned emperor in St. Peter's. Furious at the reception he had given the Senate, the Romans attacked his troops, ending the day in slaughter. The refusal of his troops to remain in Italy forced Frederick to return to Germany without assisting the Pope against William I of Sicily, who had invaded papal territory. Adrian was obliged to make peace (1156) with William, and acknowledge his titles to the kingdom of Sicily, the duchy of Apulia, and the principality of Capua. This may have infuriated Frederick, who regarded Apulia and Capua as parts of the Empire and had designs on Sicily, but it also served to protect the Papal States against further imperial encroachments.

Characteristic to Frederick's reign was his burning desire to make the imperial dignity totally independent from papal confirmation. Frederick was the first to use the designation "Holy Empire," to emphasize the sanctity of the crown. He proclaimed that he had received it "by the election of the princes from God alone," and got the German princes and people to unanimously support this view. And unanimity gave strength to Germany: Frederick bore the crowns of Germany, Burgundy, Lombardy, and the Roman Empire, and made the kingdoms of Denmark, Poland, Bohemia, and Hungary vassals to him. He placated Henry the Lion by restoring the duchy of Bavaria to him, at the same time erecting the margravate of Austria into an independent hereditary duchy as a counterweight to Henry's power. By openly asserting at the Diet of Besançon (1157) that the Empire was a papal fief, the papal legate, Cardinal Orlando Bardinelli, incurred the wrath of the German princes, and would have been put to death on the spot had the Emperor himself not intervened.

After Frederick had left Italy, the Lombard communes began once more to defend their rights, so he came back in 1158, carried Brescia by storm, and besieged and took Milan. Another diet was held at Roncaglia, in which he laid claim, as Emperor and King of Lombardy, to all former imperial rights, including the appointment of an imperial *podestà*, or chief magistrate, in each city. The presence of the German governors led to the revolt (1159) of Milan, Brescia, and some other communes, encouraged by Pope Adrian and the King of Sicily. After a three-year siege, Frederick thoroughly laid waste to the recalcitrant Milan, ploughing the city with black earth. The assault on Crema was carried through behind the cover of live hostages and prisoners of war.

Adrian, forced by imperial intrigues to leave Rome, died on the 1st of September, 1159, before he could pronounce sentence of excommunication against Frederick. Of the twenty-two cardinals assembled to elect a successor, thirteen voted for Cardinal Orlando, who took the name of Alexander III. In opposition to Orlando, the nine imperialist members of the conclave chose one of their number, Cardinal Octavian of St. Cecilia, who assumed the title of Victor IV, and at once took possession of the Vatican. Alexander fled towards the Norman south; he was consecrated at the little town of Nympha, his rival at the Monastery of Farfa—both were quartered in the Campagna, a few miles from each other, and issued contradictory reports with grave charges of wrongdoing at the election.

The Emperor, being appealed to by both parties, summoned a council at Pavia (1160) to investigate and decide the case. The rival popes were invited to appear in person, but while Victor readily accepted the invitation, Alexander protested against the emperor's right to call a council without his permission. He announced that although he honoured him as a defender of the Church above all other princes, God had placed the pope above kings. Frederick consequently refused to recognize the popeship of Alexander, who responded by solemnly excommunicating the Emperor and releasing his subjects from their oaths of allegiance, thereby encouraging revolt in Lombardy and division in Germany.

Alexander's enforced exile (1162-65) in France brought him into direct contact with Henry II of England, founder of the Plantagenet dynasty and the most powerful sovereign in Western Europe. His continental dominions were, after all, vastly larger than those of the French King, embracing Normandy, Anjou, Maine, Touraine, Brittany, and Aquitaine, and stretching from Flanders to the foot of the Pyrenees. Although the Norman kings had always rejected the right of the papal throne to interfere with the internal affairs of their kingdom, William the Conqueror had unwittingly helped the Church of England to free itself from royal supervision by separating the ecclesiastical tribunals from the secular ones.

The episcopal court used the canon law instead of the common law that was used in the shire courts. Its administration of justice was cheaper, more effective, and, above all, more lenient than that of the royal tribunals, and it was in the interest of every litigant and offender to find his way under ecclesiastical jurisdiction. The Church further held that any felony committed by her clergy had to be tried in their own religious courts of justice and not those of the Crown. Oddly enough, the harshest punishment likely inflicted by a bishop was the defrocking of the felonious cleric and the imposition of penances. Anyone with any dealings with the Church could invoke his right to "trial by clergy," be the accused any person ever taught by the Church or the bishop himself. King Henry was determined to increase his control over his realm by eliminating this custom.

As the highest civil dignitary in England, the chancellor was the custodian of virtually all the royal grants and favours, including vacant bishoprics, abbacies, and other ecclesiastical benefices. For seven years, the chancellorship was occupied by one Thomas Becket, who gave the office a prominence and splendour it never seen before. He aided the King in the restoration of peace and order after the civil war, improving the administration of justice, and even acted as regent during Henry's frequent absences on the Continent. When Archbishop Theobald died in 1161, the King saw an opportunity to increase his influence over the Church by naming his loyal advisor to the highest ecclesiastical dignity in the land. Becket was ordained priest on the Saturday after Pentecost, invested a bishop the next day, and that afternoon, the 3rd of June, 1162, consecrated Archbishop of Canterbury in Westminster Abbey.

Henry trusted that Becket would remain sympathetic to the needs of the Crown, and to the concept of equal justice for all. His trust was disastrously misplaced, for as soon as Becket had been installed, he renounced his ties to the Crown, and became a champion of the Church. Exchanging his splendid court attire for a vermin-infested haircloth, he wandered alone in his cloister, praying for the forgiveness of his past sins. With proud humility and ostentatious charity, he washed the feet of thirteen dirty beggars every day, and gave them four pieces of silver each.

In 1163, a certain canon, Philip of Broi, was acquitted of murder in the bishop's court. Public outcry demanded justice, but Philip refused to plead in a civil tribunal. The matter was taken up by the Archbishop, who imposed but a mild sentence, spurring the King to extend the jurisdiction of royal judiciary over the clergy. Becket's refusal to agree to the changes in the law prompted a royal summons to Henry's court at Northampton. After the King demanded to know what Becket had done with the large sums of money that had passed through his hands as chancellor, the Archbishop sailed for the Continent. King Louis of France, an enemy of Henry and admirer of Becket, received him with honour and recommended him to Pope Alexander, who himself was an exile at Sens.

For the six years of Becket's exile, the contest raged back and forth. Although a reconciliation was eventually reached under the direction of the Pope, the damage had already been done. After overhearing their king talk about ridding himself of the meddlesome priest, four knights of the royal household decided to take matters into their own hands and murdered the Archbishop (1170) in the middle of Mass. This unfortunate turn of events transformed Becket into a martyr, "not of Christianity, but of sacerdotalism," as the English historian H. H. Milman put it. Untold miracles were said to occur at his tomb: "The blind see, the deaf hear, the dumb speak, the lame walk, the lepers are cleansed, the devils are cast out, even the dead are raised to life." Hordes of pilgrims transformed Canterbury Cathedral into a shrine, and only two years after Becket's death, he was solemnly canonized by Alexander III—there scarcely exists another example of such an early recognition of sainthood. A year later, as an act of public penance, Henry donned a sackcloth and walked barefoot through the flinty streets of Canterbury, while eighty monks flogged him with branches. The King's atonement was crowned by his spending the night in the crypt of the Cathedral.

The Pope succeeded in obtaining from the penitent monarch every privilege for which Becket had fought and bled, but this exception aside, the reign of Henry marked the triumph of absolute monarchy in England. In 1155, Pope Adrian IV, the only Englishman ever elected to the Roman See, had presented Henry with a bull promising him the lordship of Ireland, which therefore had to made obedient to Rome and subject to the crown of England. Henry was, at the time, busy attempting to restore order to his own holdings in

Normandy and Britain, and hardly had the resources to embark on such a campaign; but fourteen years later, in early May of 1169, the first Norman ships, about 600 in number, landed at Bannow Bay.

Nominally, the Norman mercenaries were acting on behalf of the English King, but Henry suspected that their leader, Richard FitzGilbert de Clare, the legendary "Strongbow," planned to establish an independent kingdom of his own in Ireland. In 1171, Henry decided it was time to visit the island in person, which he did in company of 4,000 heavily-armed troops. Without a drop of blood, Strongbow and the other Norman warriors capitulated and paid homage to Henry of England, as did all Irish kings and chieftains of note apart from the O'Neills of Tyrone. After Henry had received a congratulatory letter from the Pope, confirming him as "Lord of Ireland," he convoked the Council of Cashel (1172) at which the ancient Celtic Church was finally brought under the yoke of Rome.

Hugh de Lacy was appointed justiciar, to rule in Henry's name in Dublin; the rest of the land was divided between Norman barons, who had the general authorization to subdue their new territories and govern them as they saw fit. Everywhere they went in Ireland, the Normans built castles and cities, just as they had in England. Over the next eighty years or so, they expanded in all directions, until they held about three quarters of the island. Within just a few generations, the Normans were as much a part of the Irish landscape as were the Celts. They intermarried with Gælic nobility, founding the renown Norman-Irish feudal families, such as FitzGerald, Butler, Burke, and Costello, who ruled much of Ireland under nominal suzerainty of England down to the late 16th century.[156]

With Ireland pacified, Henry turned his attention back to Britain. In the north, the Scots had seized three counties from Henry's worthless predecessor, Stephen of Blois, and in the south, the Welsh barons had taken the opportunity to enlarge their domains and reclaim the lands taken by the Normans. The Scottish King, William the Lion, supported a rebellion against Henry, but was subsequently captured by the Normans, who took him to

---

[156] When the Norman kings of England finally adopted the English language, the Norman barons of Ireland found themselves pledging loyalty to English-speaking rulers, rather than their French-speaking rivals in Normandy, further complicating the relations between England and Ireland.

Falaise (1174). He was released only after he had agreed to swear fealty to the King of England, and that all his barons would do so as well—Scotland had become a fief of the English crown. Henry then began rebuilding his fortresses in the south, and to burn down castles that lacked the proper license. When the three campaigns he launched against the Welsh were over, the King returned to England with an oath of fealty from the Prince of Wales.[157]

In 1165, there took place at Aachen the famous schismatic council in which Antipope Paschal III (d. 1168), at the request of the Emperor, decreed the canonization of Charlemagne. His feast (the 28th of January), while never ratified by insertion in the Roman Breviary, was continues to be observed in several German dioceses to this day. The same year, Pope Alexander returned to Italy with the help of Norman forces from Sicily, and took possession of Rome. Frederick withdrew temporarily, but returned after King William died in 1166, capturing Rome the following year, and setting Paschal once more on the papal throne. However, just as the Emperor was preparing to attack Alexander's Sicilian allies, his army was decimated by plague.

The city-states of northern Italy revolted once again and established at the Abbey of Pontida the Lombard League, which rebuilt Milan and constructed the fortress city of Alessandria, named after Pope Alexander, who had placed himself at the head of the movement. Previously, the communes of Lombardy had been divided, some favouring the Emperor, and others favouring the Pope, but now Frederick found that even the imperial cities had joined the alliance against him. Forced again to retreat over the Alps (1168), Frederick decided to increase his territorial power in Germany and pacify her incessantly feuding princes. The Normans of the south exploited the situation by consolidating their positions in Naples and Sicily, and in the end, the Lombard League consisted of thirty-six cities.

Frederick undertook his fifth campaign to Italy in 1174. After destroying Susa, he descended through Piedmont, and laid siege (1175) to Alessandria, where he encountered determined resistance. His forces were further weakened by a harsh winter, prompting the Emperor to request the aid of his cousin and strongest ally, Henry the Lion, who had taken part in his earlier

---

[157] In effect the last piece of Roman Britain, the Welsh principality was finally annexed by England in 1284, but as a show of respect, the heir to the British throne is still styled the Prince of Wales.

Italian expeditions. Henry demanded the imperial city of Goslar in exchange for military support, but Frederick refused and was defeated following a terrible slaughter near Legnano, on the 29th of May, 1176. The Emperor's peace offer was amenably received by the Pope, who realized it was advantageous to reconcile before the opponent would gain reinforcements. In the long negotiations that took place in Venice the next year, Frederick finally agreed to recognize Alexander as true pope and was restored to communion.

To crown and seal his triumph, Pope Alexander III convoked and presided over the Third Lateran or Eleventh Ecumenical Council in 1179. The chronicles of this period frequently refer to this council as the First Lateran, the ecumenical nature of the previous Lateran Councils being suspect. It put an end to the schism within the Roman Church by declaring invalid all ordinations of the antipopes. In order to avoid future schism, it was further decreed that nobody was to be regarded as pope unless elected by two-thirds majority of the cardinals.

As a result of Frederick's reconciliation with the papacy, Henry the Lion was ordered to restore the Saxon church the lands that he had seized. His failure to comply immediately caused the Bishop of Halberstadt and the nobility of Saxony to ally against him. In 1180, the Emperor confiscated Henry's two great duchies, leaving him only with Braunschweig (Brunswick) and Lüneburg (Hanover). After Henry's last stronghold, Lübeck, had surrendered to the imperial forces, he was banished (1182) for three years, which he spent in England. The daughter of Henry II bore him a son, from whom descend the House of Brunswick-Lüneburg and thereby also the Hanoverian royal line of England. Henry's Bavarian lands were given to Otto of Wittelsbach, in the possession of whose family they remained ever after.

Frederick's conciliation with the Lombard towns was confirmed by the Peace of Constance (1183), which restored the rights of the communes, while retaining imperial suzerainty over the cities. Northern Italy was now ruled by autonomous republics, which broke again into rival factions. Peace with southern Italy was ensured through the betrothal (1184) of the Emperor's son and successor, Henry, to Constance, heiress presumptive to the throne of Sicily.

Soon after the Third Lateran, Alexander was once more driven into exily by the Roman republic, and died at Cività Castellana in 1181. His remains were carried to Rome for burial, only to have them pelted with curses and stones by the populace. A day after his death, Cardinal Ubaldo Allucingoli was elected pope at Velletri, where he was crowned as Lucius III on the following Sunday, the 6th of September. At the start of November, he came to Rome, but was compelled to leave in the middle of March the next year. He returned again in 1183, but the people of Rome made his life so difficult that he left the city a second time. The Romans captured twenty-six of his partisans at Tusculum, crowned them with paper mitres inscribed with the names of cardinals, mounted them on asses, and blinded all except one, who was forced to lead them in this condition to "Lucius, the wicked simoniac."

After spending a short time in southern Italy, Lucius went to Bologna, where he consecrated the city's cathedral. The remainder of his pontificate lapsed in Verona, where, with the co-operation of the Emperor, he convened a synod (1184) which condemned as heretical the Arnoldists (i.e. the followers of Arnold of Brescia), who continued to defend the teachings of their master. According to the agreement made here by the Pope and the Emperor, the heretics of every community were to be sought out, brought before the bishop's court, excommunicated, and handed over to the civil authorities for suitable punishment. At this synod, Frederick also promised to undertake preparations for a new Crusade to the Holy Land.

CHAPTER 21

The Seljuks ruled a vast empire reaching from the Great Wall of China to the Mediterranean—but they also fought among themselves for dominance over the loose federation of Turkish monarchs. The only surviving representatives of the Fatimid dynasty were children, and two rival viziers vied for supreme power amid conditions of total anarchy. Egypt had become a battleground between the Turks and the Crusaders, with the Fatimids having lost virtually all control, though they sided mostly with the Latins; fertile and prosperous, she was a prize worth fighting for.

Nur ad-Din, now Sultan of Damascus, was painfully aware of the advantages which the Crusader States would derive from control of Egypt, and was determined to secure the land for himself. In the spring of 1164, he sent his best general, the Kurdish Shírkúh, to invade Egypt before any Latin campaign there could succeed. However, the Egyptian Vizier, Shawer, was as anxious to retain his independence of Nur ad-Din as he was to remain free of the clutches of the *Franji*. Taking advantage of the situation, King Amalric of Jerusalem quickly allied himself with Shawer, besieging Shírkúh's army at the frontier fortress of Bilbeis, the ancient Pelusium. After a siege of three months, an agreement was reached whereby both would back down, but the Latin King would be reimbursed for his trouble by the Vizier. Accordingly, Amalric withdrew from Egypt, all the quicker because his own kingdom had been attacked by Nur ad-Din in his absence.

But the land of Egypt would not be so easily delivered from her enemies. Early in 1167, Shírkúh and his army were once more sent into Egypt, while Amalric went again to the assistance of Shawer. The earlier course of events repeated itself when Shírkúh was besieged in Alexandria, except this time Amalric's reward included an annual tribute of 100,000 dinárs from Egypt and the stationing of a Latin garrison at the gates of Cairo. It was a colossal victory that brought the King of Jerusalem great prestige: if the Latins could not actually conquer Egypt, maybe they could reduce it to a vassal state.

In 1168, a fresh crusader army led by Count William of Nevers arrived in the Holy Land, looking for a war, just as the newly-appointed head of the Hospitallers, Gilbert d'Assalit, was arguing for an attack on Egypt in defiance of treaties. Philip of Naplous, the first Templar Grand Master to be born in Palestine, refused to have anything to do with the expedition, or to allow a single brother of his Order to accompany the King in arms. It was apparently then that Gilbert was authorized by his own brethren to borrow money from the Italian merchants, to take hired soldiers into the pay of their Order, and to organize the Hospitallers as a great military society in imitation of the Templars.

The Latin army set out on the 10th of October, taking the Egyptians completely by surprise. The city of Bilbeis was carried by storm, and the defenceless inhabitants were slaughtered to the last man, woman and child, after which the desolated city was delivered up to the Hospitallers. The Latin fleet entered the Nile, captured the city of Tanis, and put its inhabitants to the slaughter as well. These massacres alienated even those factions in Egypt that had been sympathetic to the Latin cause, especially the Coptic Christians who were numerous in these towns.

Shírkúh's intervention brough about the withdrawal of the Latin troops early in 1169, but he had no intention of withdrawing his men this time. After ordering the assassination of Shawer, Shírkúh had himself proclaimed vizier, if only to die himself just two months later. His nephew and second in command, Salâh ad-Dîn Yûsuf ibn Ayyûb—or Saladin (1138-1193) as he is commonly known—was immediately appointed the next vizier. Young and full of will, he would quickly become one of the most famous figures in mediæval history.

Aided by a Byzantine fleet and army, Amalric invaded Egypt once more that year, but was defeated at Damietta. Saladin retained full sway in Cairo, turning it into an Ayyubid power base, where he used his Kurds in leading positions, while the nominal rules of Egypt, the Fatimids, remained isolated in their palaces. He waited until their Caliph died (1171), whereupon he declared the end of the Fatimid rule and professed allegiance to the Abbasid Caliph of Baghdad, who no longer had any real power. Instead of seizing the Fatimids' wealth or occupying their palaces, the young general opened the gates of Cairo and allowed ordinary Egyptian citizens to live within the city walls in areas which had previously been the exclusive domain of the Fatimid dynasty.

Because of his sincerity and consideration, Saladin became popular among the Egyptians, be they Muslim and Christian—he even had a Jewish personal physician[158]. He was initially not as eager as Nur ad-Din to go to war against the Latins, wherefore the relations of the two Muslim leaders became strained. When he later fought Richard Cœur-de-Lion, legend goes that Saladin ordered his troops to carry ice down the mountains to bring relief to the English King when he was sick; and when the King's steed was slain under him, Saladin sent him two new horses through the lines of battle.

It seemed that the empire which Nur ad-Din had created would soon disintegrate into a number of warring rival states, but before King Amalric could take advantage of this situation, he died (1173), leaving the throne of Jerusalem to Baldwin IV, a child of thirteen, called the "Leper King" for the disease that afflicted him for most of his short life. However, it was the death of Nur ad-Din in 1174 that changed the whole situation: while the Sultan's sons and nephews disputed the inheritance, Saladin took possession of Damascus and conquered all of Mesopotamia, except Mosul. He became Sultan of Egypt and Syria, a title which the Caliph of Baghdad solemnly confirmed. In the ensuing years, Saladin would unite the forces of Islam as no one had ever done before—or has done since.

Even as a child, Saladin was a scholar who studied poetry as well as the Koran, and his scholarly ways would continue throughout his life, even when the thoughts of *Jihad* consumed his mind. The evidence of his tireless work to improve the lot of his subjects endured for centuries: he was responsible for new roads, canals, and sikes, and managed to revitalize the economy of Egypt. In Cairo, Saladin built not only mosques and palaces—in fact, he never build a palace for himself—but also colleges, hospitals, and a fortress, the Citadel, which remains one of the landmarks of the Egyptian capital to this day. Less fortunately, he and his successors used stones from the Pyramids to meet the immense need for building material in the growing metropolis.

As Saladin tightened his grip on a large and powerful Islamic empire, the Crusader States displayed signs of increasingly serious internal tension. The differences between the Westerners who had long been settled in the East and their newly-arrived compatriots permeated not only the internal and foreign policies, but the whole atmosphere of the Kingdom of Jerusalem. "Everyone

---

[158] the famous Maimonides, or more properly, Moses ben Maimon

who is a fresh emigrant from the Frankish lands," wrote one contemporary observer, "is ruder in character than those who have become acclimatized and have held long association with the Moslems." War against the infidel was necessary to achieve the goals of the newcomer faction; namely, land, titles, and positions within the Kingdom for themselves. This was not so for the other party, whose forefathers had come to the East mostly with the armies of the First Crusade, and already held the most desirable ports and lands in the region.

In 1180, a treaty for greater peace was concluded between Saladin and the Latins, the terms of which guaranteed free commercial communications between Christian and Muslim territory. Saladin honoured this as he did all treaties—he was a man who kept his word.[159] However, in the summer of 1181, Reynald de Châtillon, a reckless member of the newcomer faction, succumbed to the lure of easy money and raided a rich caravan of pilgrims en route from Damascus to Mecca. Famous for his cruelty in the Holy Land, he also opposed the Byzantine Emperor and tried to blackmail him several times. After kidnapping the Patriarch of Constantinople, Reynald inflicted many cuts on the eminent churchman's head, covered them in honey, then chained him to a roof, where the scorching summer sun caused bees to attack his wounds till insanity set in.

The violation of the truce in the form of plundering pilgrims so enraged Saladin that he vowed to put an end to the Latins. After setting out with a large army in May, 1182, he never returned to Cairo. Meanwhile, Reynald had hatched a mad scheme to raid the pilgrim ships at sea and in their ports, and even possibly Mecca itself. A fleet of five galleys traversed the Red Sea for a whole year, ravaging the coast as far as Aden; the fleet sank pilgrim ships, burned them at harbour, raided the ports, and even attempted to seize Medina. Eventually, all the Latin ships were destroyed by Saladin.

The Leper King died in 1184, leaving no heir; his little nephew, Baldwin, became king. Raymond III of Tripoli remained in power as regent and sought to negotiate a truce with Saladin. Since the Sultan's attention was diverted by the intrigues of the Turkish chieftains in northern Syria, and he was again engaged in war in Mesopotamia, he agreed to a truce of four years. King

---

[159] The Sultan even boasted to the Caliph that the Latins were selling him arms which he could use against other Latins.

Baldwin V was only five years old and sickly—he died at Acre after a reign of only seven months. There was a skirmish for control within the court, and while the regent, Raymond, was absent, the Templar Grand Master, Gerard de Riderfort, surrounded the royal palace with troops, closed the gates of Jerusalem, and delivered the regalia to Patriarch Heraclius. He then conducted Sibylla, the mother of the deceased monarch, and her second husband, Guy de Lusignan, to the Church of the Resurrection, where they were both crowned by the Patriarch of Jerusalem on the 20th of July, 1186.

Guy de Lusignan was a prince of dashing good looks, but of so ill a repute that his own brother, Geoffrey, was heard to exclaim: "Since they have made him a king, surely they would have made me a god!" The Hospitallers would have no part of this unpopular King, and their Grand Master removed his men from the scene of Guy's coronation in disgust. One reason for the unpopularity of King Guy was that in 1184, he had attacked a peaceful Bedouin tribe who had paid a tribute to the Latins for the privilege of grazing their sheep. After massacring as many of the Bedouins as they could, Guy and his men drove away the rest along with their flock. His accession to the throne of Jerusalem left the newcomer faction in control of the Kingdom, and caused an irreparable rift within the Latin ranks. Raymond of Tripoli refused to do homage and was joined in opposition by Bohemund III of Antioch and several other long-standing members of the Latin nobility. The state was torn by dissent at a time when all the energies of the population were required to defend their land from the Muslims.

At this most inopportune moment, the totally irresponsible Reynald de Châtillon decided once again to break the truce with Saladin. During the years of peace, trade had flourished; unable to resist the temptation, Reynold plundered a caravan bound for Mecca, as he had done five years earlier—only this time, the caravan was carrying the Sultan's own sister. In exasperation, Saladin invaded the Kingdom of Jerusalem, and although King Guy gathered all his forces to repel the attack, Saladin's army utterly decimated them on the 4th of July, 1187, in the deciding battle of the era. Nearly 20,000 Latin troops, including over 1,200 heavily-armed mounted knights, were slain by an equal number of Saracen troops at the Horns of Hattin, near modern Zippori, on the shores of Lake Tiberias.

The King, the Grand Master of the Temple, Reynald de Châtillon, and the most powerful men in the realm were captured and taken to Saladin's camp, where a special tent had been erected for this purpose. The common soldiers were sold into slavery; one Saracen had so many slaves that he was willing to trade one for a pair of shoes. As to the Templars, they were herded into a separate group and beheaded one by one; none except their Grand Master, Gerard de Riderfort, was spared.[160] Many ordinary soldiers, choosing death before a life of slavery in the service of infidels, rushed forward claiming to be Templars.

King Guy lay on the ground of the tent, parched with thirst and paralyzed by fear, when he was offered a bowl of water by the Sultan. As the King began quenching his thirst, Prince Reynald grabbed the bowl, also being thirsty, but Saladin immediately knocked it from his hands, for Muslim hospitality dictated that if a man dined or drank with you, his life was safe in your hands. Upset at the Sultan's behaviour, Reynald reviled the name of the Prophet Mohammed, at which point Saladin drew his scimitar and, with one blow, chopped off the blasphemer's arm. Practically before the limb had even hit the floor, a guard entered and decapitated Reynald. Saladin then turned to Guy, saying, "Have no fear. It is not the custom of kings to kill kings," and gave orders that none of the other captives should be killed.

The city of Tiberias surrendered to Saladin the next day. He then proceeded to Acre, which capitulated almost immediately. Nablus surrendered in a few days and Toron a couple of weeks later. Jaffa made the mistake of resisting; the Sultan's brother carried the city by storm and sold its entire population into slavery. Beirut was the next to fall and Jebail fell a few days after that. Ascalon was captured after a few days' siege, and Gaza surrendered after its garrison had received the order of the captive Templar Grand Master to yield without resistance.

By the beginning of autumn, Saladin had captured nearly all the Latin strongholds south of Tripoli. Finally, on the 2nd of October, just three months after the Battle of Hattin, the city of Jerusalem itself capitulated to Saladin without a fight. The Latins were allowed to buy their freedom: ten dinárs for a man, five for a woman, one for a child. After having paid their ten dinárs, Patriarch Heraclius and the Latin priests fled the Holy City in wagons loaded with gold and silver and sacred relics. The Greek and Syrian Christians

---

[160] That Saladin did not show the same mercy to the warrior monks that he always did to everyone else may well stem from the fact that celibacy is generally regarded as unnatural in Islam.

were allowed to stay, as long as they paid the *jizya*, the poll tax levied on non-Muslims in an Islamic state. Almost all of the holy places were promptly turned over to the Byzantine Church; in fact, the Church of the Holy Sepulchre was closed only for three days, and the influx of Western pilgrims soon resumed.

Saladin had accomplished what seemed impossible to the belligerent Middle Eastern principalities of the time—uniting them to oppose the Western incursions into their native lands. His triumphs did not end at the fall of Jerusalem; soon thereafter, with the exception of a handful of castles by the sea, the entire region was once again free of foreign *kafir* occupation.

When the grave news arrived in the West in October, 1187, the chronicles say that Pope Urban III, already an old man, died of grief. Within a few days, the new pope, Gregory VIII, had proclaimed the Third Crusade. Since peace between the rival Italian seaports of Pisa and Genoa—established as commercial centres with the crusades—was a prerequisite to the transportation of troops and supplies, he proceeded to the former city, where he expired after a pontificate of only two months. He was in turn succeeded by Cardinal-Bishop of Palestrina, Paolo Scolari, the first native of Rome to be elevated to the papal throne since the city's rebellion under Arnold of Brescia. This led to the conclusion of a formal treaty, in which both the papal sovereignty and the municipal liberties were ensured; thus, in February, 1188, papacy was finally allowed to re-enter Rome in the person of Clement III.

In an effort to restore harmony among the warring monarchs and princes of Christendom and to redirect their energies to the reconquest of the Holy Sepulchre, the Pope sent his legates to the various courts of Europe. In Italy, Pisa made peace with Genoa, Venice with Hungary, and Sicily with the Byzantine Empire. North of the Alps, King Philip Augustus[161] of France and Henry II of England were reconciled and took the cross. However, when Henry's son, Richard of Poitou, went to war with the Count of Toulouse, both men appealed to their overlords, and the two kingdoms became embroiled again in war. In a fit of anger, Richard then switched allegiances to the French and made war on his own father. On the 6th of July, the old king died and on the 3rd of September, Richard of Poitou became Richard I of

---

[161] i.e. Philip II

England. He had enlisted under the cross even before Henry had, but would not depart for the Holy Land until the summer of 1190—nearly three years after the fall of Jerusalem.

The first monarch to actually depart was Frederick Barbarossa, who set out from Regensburg in May, 1189, taking the traditional land route down the Danube and across the Balkans to Constantinople with what some chronicles have called an army of 100,000 men. Mediæval estimates are invariably exaggerations, but his forces were definitely in the tens of thousands. Their passage was hindered by the fact that the Byzantine Emperor had made a pact with Saladin to impede the progress of his German counterpart, who, the Sultan was told, was marching with a million men. After crossing Hungary, Frederick took the Balkan passes by storm and sought to outflank Isaac Angelus[162] by attacking the Imperial City. Finally, after the sack of Adrianople, in February, 1190, the Byzantine Emperor surrendered and agreed to transport the crusaders across the Hellespont. In the two centuries of crusading, this was the only occasion on which the German and Byzantine emperors ever met face to face.

The German army continued through Asia Minor, which the Latin chronicles of the 12th century had begun to refer to as "Turkey."[163] After the Battle of Iconium on the 18th of May, the army proceeded through the Taurus mountain passes to Armenian Christian Cilicia on the Mediterranean coast. At Saint Symeon, the aged Emperor shunned his advisors and attempted to cross the turbulent Calycadnus on horseback; by the time they had fished him out of the river, Frederick was dead. Having been intensely worried of the Emperor, Saladin deemed the drowning a miracle of Allah.

Without the leadership of the Emperor, his army began to shatter almost immediately, and his son, Duke Frederick V of Swabia, was left to pick up the pieces. Sections of the army returned home on the spot, others made their way by sea to Tripoli and Antioch, but the bulk of the troops took the land route with the pickled remains of the Emperor. The overland passage proved pernicious during the heat of midsummer; the imperial carcass decomposed badly and was consigned to the grave in St. Peter's Church in Antioch rather

---

[162] i.e. Isaac II

[163] Until then, no land which the nomadic Turks had occupied was identified this way.

than its planned place of rest in Jerusalem. The entourage proceeded thence to Acre, and it was before this port city on the Mediterranean that all the crusading troops ultimately assembled.

By July, the French and English crusaders were gathered at Vézelay, the starting-point for Louis VII's crusade almost half a century earlier. They marched together as far as Lyons, where they separated, the French embarking at Genoa, the English at Marseilles; both arrived at Messina in September. During their sojourn there, lasting until March, 1191, their kings got into quarrel over the paternity of the child of Philip's sister, who was betrothed to Richard. It was rumoured that Richard had a steamier relationship with Philip than with his sister, and the fact is that the "Lion-Heart" was more than once required by the Church to pay fines for the "sin of sodomy"—fines that in today's money would amount close to one million U.S. dollars.

The pope's chief vassal, William II of Sicily, had offered to supply a fleet to accompany the crusaders. But King William had died in November, 1189, leaving the succession in dispute. Henry VI, the son and successor of Frederick Barbarossa, claimed the Norman kingdom on the behalf of his wife Constance de Hauteville, the only legitimate survivor of the House of Roger and the heiress presumptive of Sicily. The Sicilian nobles, anxious to prevent German rule in Sicily, proclaimed Tancred of Lecce, an illegitimate scion of the family of Roger, as king; the pope, whose independence was at peril if the Empire and the Two Sicilies were held by the same monarch, granted Tancred the investiture. When Philip and Richard arrived, Tancred had placed Queen Joanna under house arrest, confiscated the treasure her late husband had left to finance the Crusade, and was expecting an invasion by the Germans; in other words, he was not about to turn away potential allies.

A treaty between all three kings was signed on the 8th of October, 1190, and at this same conference, Philip and Richard negotiated the terms regulating the conduct of their Crusade—including a point that any conquests were to be divided evenly between the two. They had now tarried so long that the weather prevented them from sailing, so they wintered at Messina. Philip finally embarked on the 30th of March, 1191, followed by Richard eleven days later. But while Philip was already landing at Acre, Richard was shipwrecked on the coast of Cyprus. With the aid of Guy de Lusignan, Richard conquered the "Island of Venus" from the Byzantines. The acquisition of Cyprus not only created a new crusader state, but more importantly, with this island in Latin hands, the Byzantine Empire could no longer threaten Antioch from the sea.

Meanwhile, the German King advanced into Italy with a great army to enforce the claim of his queen to the crown of the Two Sicilies. Stopping at Rome, Henry was anointed and crowned as emperor, and Constance as empress, on the 15th of April, by Pope Celestine III, who had ascended the papal throne but a day earlier. However, the commune of Rome, which claimed to rule over the Papal States, particularly the duchy of Rome, would not allow the aforementioned solemnities to take place until both the Pope and the King had helped her subdue the neighbouring Tusculum. Consequently, the town was razed to the ground and delivered to the wrath of the Romans. In defiance of the Pope, the Emperor proceeded south towards Sicily, but was defeated and compelled to withdraw, leaving the Empress a prisoner of her nephew, who soon released her upon papal request.

The Third Crusade saw the birth of a new military order, the Teutonic Knights (The Order of the Hospital of the Blessed Virgin Mary of the German House of Jerusalem), which was founded during the siege of Acre as a field hospital to care for the many sick German crusaders, and confirmed by Pope Celestine in 1196; it was never as important in Palestine as either the Templars or the Hospitallers, but played a central role in the conquest of the Baltic Slavs and in the history of Poland, Livonia, and Lithuania. The siege had already gone on for two years when Philip Augustus and Richard Cœur-de-Lion arrived on the scene, bringing about the capitulation of the city. The walls were breached early in July, 1191, and on the 11th of that month, the Muslim garrison agreed to surrender the city and to hand over the 2,000 Latin prisoners that Saladin was holding. There was no way the Sultan could agree to these terms, but as the garrison had made the agreement in his name, he was honour-bound to respect it.

The garrison left Acre the next day and the crusaders moved in immediately. Even as they were occupying the city, feuds erupted between them. The leader of the German contingent, Duke Leopold V of Austria, set up his banner on an equal footing with those of the two kings, for he represented the German Emperor. King Richard took offence at this, tore down the banner from its staff and threw it into a ditch. His quarrel with the French monarch also broke out again, and on the 28th of July, Philip quit Palestine, leaving Richard in sole command of the Crusade.

One of the Lion-Heart's first acts was such that would earn the condemnation of modern historians. He was still holding a great many Muslim prisoners as hostage for the fulfilment of the terms of capitulation. When Saladin failed, for obvious practical reasons, to deliver all the two thousand prisoners stipulated in one installment, the King declared that the Sultan had violated the said terms, and ordered the execution of all his Muslim prisoners. 2,600 Mohammedans—men, women, and children—were put to death outside the city walls in the plain sight of Saladin's troops, who attempted to rescue them. The massacre took all day, and the Muslim soldiers were driven back. While every Latin chronicler of the era recounts these events with great satisfaction, seeing them as just retribution for the losses suffered at Acre, their contemporary Muslim counterparts speak of those who were killed as martyrs of faith.

Richard compensated for the failure of his planned attack on Jerusalem by brilliant but useless exploits that made his name legendary among the Saracens. After a final expedition to defend Jaffa, Richard came up with a splendid idea: he would give his Christian sister[164] in marriage to the Sultan's brother, if Saladin agreed to an armistice. The Third Crusade ended with the Peace of Ramla, by the terms of which the Latins would get to keep all the towns they had recovered along the coast—except for the stronghold of Ascalon, which was to be returned to Saladin, with its fortifications demolished. Jerusalem was to remain in Muslim hands, but Latin pilgrims would be allowed free and safe access to all the holy places.

Before his departure, Richard sold Cyprus, first to the Templars, who had no more success in governing the island than had the English, and then to Guy de Lusignan, who renounced the crown of Jerusalem in favour of Conrad de Montferrat (d. 1192). Acre, built at one of the few natural harbours on the Palestinian coast, was made the new capital of the Latin Kingdom, and all the three military orders established their headquarters there. The Lusignans in turn would, under the magnificent title of Emperor, rule the Island of Cyprus for almost two hundred years. But whereas the Kingdom of Jerusalem had established a reasonable *modus vivendi* with its native population, tension between the Greeks and Latins persisted in Cyprus until the Turkish conquest in 1571.

In failing to regain Jerusalem, the Third Crusade marked the beginning of

---

[164] Joanna of Sicily

four unbroken decades of crusading; but although every prince in Christendom was thereafter obliged at the very least to make known his intention to win back the Holy City, no subsequent Crusade would achieve anything like the military success of the Third Crusade. Much smaller than the original Kingdom and considerably weaker both militarily and economically, the Second Kingdom would last precariously for another century.

Less than six months after Richard had embarked for Europe, Saladin died of a lingering illness in Damascus. On his death, the Sultan had almost no personal possessions, but his name would be honoured throughout the centuries. With Vergil, Homer, Plato, and Julius Cæsar, he was among the few heathen placed by Dante in Limbo, instead of Hell. He had exhibited the noblest qualities of chivalry at a time when these qualities were in short supply among his fellow-Muslims and Christian knights alike—he is one of the precious few personages of the Crusader era to be positively described in both Western and Eastern sources: the Latins admired him for his considerate treatment of prisoners and his encouragement of East-West trade; not only was he loved and esteemed by King Richard, but it was the consensus among the more chivalrous crusaders that: "If Saladin were only a Christian, he would be the greatest prince on Earth."

Richard did not reach his English realm until April, 1194. Although disguised in the habit of a Knight Templar, he was captured and imprisoned in December, 1192, by his worst personal enemy, Leopold of Austria, who avenged in this way the insults offered him before Acre. Overjoyed to have the King a prisoner, the Duke very reluctantly delivered him up to the Emperor in February, 1193. Henry VI faced a rebellion in Germany, incited by the Rhenish archbishops, who opposed his plans to absorb Thuringia into the imperial demesne. In Richard, the Emperor had a powerful bargaining weapon, for the English King was the brother-in-law and ally of the Guelph leader, Henry the Lion. Not long after Richard had paid a huge ransom of 100,000 silver marks, sworn fealty to Henry VI, and been freed, peace was made in Germany.

When Richard finally arrived in England, he brought to heel his brother, Prince John, who had shamelessly usurped power in his absence. This is the famous return of the King that figures prominently in the Robin Hood legends. *Ivanhoe* portrays Cœur-de-Lion as a strong supporter of the native English Saxons—in truth, he despised England. He only visited the country twice as king and only a few times before that. It is unlikely that he spoke a word of English.

After returning from Palestine, Philip Augustus turned once more to his *raison d'être*: lessening the influence of the English kings in France. Through his first marriage, Philip had acquired new territories in northern France—Artois, Valois, and Vermandois. In 1193, he began to look for allies and happened to think that the Danes, as former Vikings, would be well suited to once more raid the coasts of England. To seal this alliance, Philip, a widower, offered to marry a Danish princess. His intended was Ingeborg, daughter of King Waldemar the Great and sister of Canute VI.

Philip and Ingeborg were married at Amiens and she was crowned Queen of France. But, amidst the wedding festivities, Philip had a change of heart—why fawn upon a petty Danish king when one could just as easily manage relations with the ruler of the Holy Roman Empire himself. Thus, on the morning after the wedding night, Philip told Ingeborg their marriage was over, for they were blood relatives—which came as a surprise to everyone—and she was to go back whence she came.

On the 4th of November, 1193, the Synod of Compiègne declared Philip's second marriage null and void, and the King began to prepare a wedding with Henry VI's cousin, Constance. She did not, however, care to share Ingeborg's fate and secretly married a son of Henry the Lion. Philip decided to marry his mistress, the fair Agnes of Meran, and had her crowned queen. Instead of going home, Ingeborg fled to a convent. The Danes were furious, appealed to the pope, and took the side of the English in the war.

While Capetians and Plantagenets were preoccupied with their struggle against each other at home, the Hohenstaufen assumed the direction of Latin politics in the East. The death of Tancred favoured the success of Henry VI's second Sicilian expedition. Palermo fell in November, 1194, and on Christmas Day, Henry deposed Tancred's infant son, William III, and was crowned King of the Two Sicilies, thus uniting all of southern Italy with the German Empire. This did not satisfy Henry, who already had dreams of further expansion in the Mediterranean—the Sicilian crown made him heir to all the old Norman claims to Byzantine territories they had once occupied. In April, 1195, the Byzantine Emperor, Isaac II Angelus, was deposed and blinded by his brother, who ruled as Alexius III. Not long after the coup, Duke Philip of Swabia, brother of Henry VI, married Irene Angela, daughter of the deposed Emperor. Thus, the Hohenstaufen now had a direct interest in the claims of Isaac II against his upstart brother.

Henry took the cross at Bari on the 31st of May, and began promoting a new crusade, to be directed against Constantinople, after which the combined strength of the two Empires could be focussed on reconquering Jerusalem. In September, 1197, the German crusaders under the Archbishop of Mainz landed at Acre, and quickly recovered Jebail and Beirut for the Latin Kingdom, but were detained before the former crusader castle of Toron from November to February the next year. Upon raising the siege, they learned that Henry had died at Messina, where he had assembled the fleet that was supposed to carry him to Constantinople. On the 1st of July, 1198, the Germans signed a truce with the Saracens, but their future influence in the Holy Land was ensured by the Order of the Teutonic Knights, which was now turned into a military order in imitation of the Hospitallers—the idea of taking over the Byzantine Empire and using its vast resources to "liberate" Jerusalem would also be revived again soon enough.

Before passing away, Henry had induced Pope Celestine to acknowledge his only son, the three-year-old Frederick Roger, as King of the Two Sicilies. Celestine himself was carried off by death, in the ninety-second year of his age. The Emperor's widow, Constance, ruled over Sicily for her little son, but could not stand on her own against the Norman baron of the kingdom, who resented the German rule and refused to acknowledge the infant king. She appealed to the brilliant and power-hungry new pope, Innocent III (1198-1216), to confirm Frederick's title to the Sicilian crown. Innocent exploited this opportunity to reassert papal suzerainty over southern Italy, recognizing Frederick as king only after Constance had surrendered the privileges of the so-called Four Chapters, which King William I had extorted from Pope Adrian IV. Constance survived her imperial husband only a year, and left a will appointing Innocent as guardian of the orphan king. The hereditary foe of the Hohenstaufen was thus entrusted with both the intellectual training and the political destiny of the heir to that august house.

Innocent III has, for a good reason, been dubbed by the reknown German historian, Leopold von Ranke, as Henry VI's real successor. He used the opportunity offered him by the vacancy of the imperial throne to restore papal power in Rome and in the States of the Church. The Prefect of Rome, who ruled the city as the emperor's representative, took an oath of allegiance to the papacy, and Innocent invested him with a mantle and a silver cup. Likewise the Senator, who stood for the communal rights and privileges of the Roman republic, bowed before the authority of the Pope and swore to protect the Holy See and guard the banner of St. Peter. But Innocent would soon push his authority vastly beyond the walls of Rome.

Taking advantage of the rising national feeling of the Italians, Innocent began extending his political power over the peninsula. First, he sent two of his legates to Markward von Anweiler, Henry VI's representative in Sicily, to demand the restoration of the Romagna Region and the March of Ancona to the Holy Mother Church. Upon his evasive answer, the Lord of Palermo was excommunicated by the papal legates and driven away by the papal troops. In the same manner, Spoleto, which had been ruled by a line of German dukes for the last six centuries, was wrested from Conrad von Urslingen, as were the districts of Assisi and Sora. The Tuscan League that had been formed (1197) in imitation of the successful alliance of the Lombard cities was ratified by the Pope after it acknowledged him as suzerain; Florence, Lucca, Siena, Prato, and the other cities, while refusing to renounce their municipal freedom, granted important concessions to Innocent—so total an exercise of papal authority over the States of the Church was unknown before that day.

Immediately upon his accession to the papal throne, Innocent had dispatched two of his legates to Germany, with instructions to release Philip of Swabia from the ban which he had incurred under Celestine III, on condition that he would free the imprisoned Queen Sibylla of Sicily and restore the territory which he had taken from the Church as Duke of Tuscany. By the time that the papal legates arrived in Germany, Philip had already been elected king. Upon his promise to fulfill the proposed conditions, the legates freed him from the excommunication, and after his coronation on the 8th of September, 1198, he sent them back to Rome with letters requesting papal ratification of his election—Innocent refused. Back in April, a small but strong anti-Hohenstaufen group led by the Archbishop of Cologne, had elected Otto of Brunswick, the younger son of Henry the Lion, as antiking. He, too, had appealed to the Pope, and it is no great surprise that the Pope's sympathies were with the Guelph rather than with the Hohenstaufen.

Offended at what they considered an unlawful interference on the part of Innocent, the supporters of Philip sent a letter to the Roman pontiff, in which they protested against his interference in the imperial affairs of Germany. Innocent answered that he had no intention of encroaching upon the right of the German princes to elect their king, but insisted that the right to confer the imperial crown belonged to the pope alone. In the inevitable war, Otto had the support of his uncle, King Richard of England, while Philip was supported by King Philip of France. Though victorious almost everywhere at first, Philip's cause was somewhat weakened in 1201, when Innocent openly declared for the antiking and threatened with excommunication all those who refused to acknowledge him.

Meanwhile, Ingeborg of Denmark had sold her wedding dress and jewels to equip her legate to Rome. After hearing her appeals, the Pope threatened Philip of France with interdict if the King would not be reconciled with his lawful wife within a month. When Philip took no heed of the Pope's warning, Innocent made good on his threat and, on the 5th of February, 1200, placed all of France under interdict. Philip's soul may not have been in peril, but his kingdom was: an interdict was a perfect excuse for all the discontent barons to sharpen their swords. He had to give in, and he did, but in his own way; seven years after abandoning Ingeborg, Philip finally acknowledged her as his lawful wife—but that was all he did. For Ingeborg it was from bad to worse, from a convent to imprisonment in a castle, whose guards treated her roughly. Philip continued to live with Agnes, who bore him another bastard. Though his concubine died soon after giving birth, his wife remained imprisoned and banished from the court for twelve more years. It was not until 1213, twenty years after Philip had abandoned Ingeborg, that he did take her back, but only for the reason that he needed the support of the Pope in an expedition he was planning against England.

CHAPTER 22

When Innocent III issued his crusading bull in August, 1198, he directed the call to arms not to kings and emperors, but to counts and barons and even cities. Bishops and archbishops were likewise expected to contribute soldiers, or a corresponding amount of money. The original date set by the Pope for the departure of the Fourth Crusade was March, 1199, but none sallied forth. Philip and Richard signed a truce, but the latter died soon after, and the war between France and England recommenced. The Pope published more encyclicals, crusading sermons were preached everywhere, and an effort was made to raise money, but still little or nothing happened.

The crusading vows were supposed to be taken only by fighting men or those who could otherwise contribute to a military effort. What is more, they were not to be taken without the permission of the crusader's wife, since his long absence would deprive her of what was delicately called "conjugal rights." In desperate need of troops for his Crusade, Pope Innocent changed all this, and in doing so, violated not only a long-standing Church tradition but the plain intentions of canon law. Yet, until November, 1199, no lords of significance had taken the cross or formally committed enough men to the enterprise for it to be called an army.[165]

It would certainly seem that Innocent lost control of this expedition almost from its inception. Without so much as consulting the Pope, the French knights, having elected Thibaut de Champagne as their leader, decided to launch the Fourth Crusade with a new strategy. Their plan was to attack the Saracens from the opposite direction, travelling by ship to Egypt, from where they would march eastward and northward to the Holy Land. Only the Republic of Venice had the resources for building enough ships to carry an army of such size as the crusaders envisioned.

Venice was not only the richest city in the West, but one that had great

---

[165] Meanwhile, the Muslim rebels in Sicily were identified by its regent as the "enemies of all Christendom," and he offered a full crusading indulgence to any who fought against them.

interest in what happened in the eastern Mediterranean. Although a republic, Venice was in no sense democratic, and political power was wholly in the hands of a narrow élite, consisting of merchants and property owners. This group was represented by the Doge, the chief magistrate of the municipality, who was elected for life by a Council of Ten (the *Dieci*) and exercised considerable power at least up until 1172, when his authority was curtailed by the creation of a Supreme Grand Council of 480 members. The city's wealth derived almost entirely from her entrepôt trade, the moving of goods from the eastern Mediterranean to Lombardy and over the Alps to Central Europe. She held sway over much of the Adriatic as well and had outposts along the coast of Greece, on the Ægean Islands, and even in the Holy Land. She even had a important merchant colony in Alexandria, even though it was a Muslim city.

In March, 1201, six representatives of French lords arrived at Venice to commission the construction of a new fleet of warships and transports for the Crusade. Of course, the service would not be free: the Venetians agreed to supply, at a cost of 84,000 marks—twice the annual income of the French king—transportation and nine months of provisions for a crusader army of 4,500 knights and 19,000 squires and footmen. June of 1202 was set as the date for the crusaders to gather at Venice, pay for the fleet, and embark for the attack on Egypt. In exchange for the promise of one-half of any territory captured on the Crusade, the Venetians agreed to provide fifty additional galleys on their own; they were positively salivating at the prospect of gaining half of Alexandria or Damietta, or even Cairo itself.

On the 24th of June, 1202, Venice had a magnificent fleet ready; as one contemporary observer reported, no Christian had ever beheld a richer or finer collection of vessels. Before the crusaders could even board the ships, however, Thibaut de Champagne died. They chose as his successor Boniface, Marquis of Montferrat and cousin of Philip of Swabia, presently in open conflict with the Pope. Had 4,500 knights arrived as promised, or had those who did arrive been able to pay the agreed 84,000 marks, the course of history might well have been very different. However, only about 1,500 knights gathered at Venice with some 50,000 marks between them. There they sat, unable to pay for the passage, unwilling to go home, and all the while running up tabs with the locals which they were equally unable to pay.

The Venetians were businessmen first and foremost, none of them more so than the Doge, Enrico Dandolo. Their republic had long ruled much of the

Dalmatian coast as a means to secure control of the Adriatic and its lucrative shipping lanes. Of late, however, the King of Hungary had been inciting rebellion in the coastal towns of Dalmatia, offering them his protection. Doge Dandolo now proposed a solution that would solve two problems at once: Venice would defer the balance owned for transportation and supplies if, on the way to Egypt, the crusaders would assist the Venetians in recapturing Zara, one of the towns that had defected to Hungary, and which Venice had for fifteen years been trying to recover. The anomaly of crusaders attacking a Christian city may have been disregarded by the vast majority of the troops, but not by Pope Innocent, who excommunicated all involved. As a last-minute surprise, the Doge himself, over 90 years old and legally blind, announced that he had decided to take the cross. On the 8th of November, 1202, he set sail at the head of a fleet of 480 ships—Zara fell within a week.

In the years at the beginning of the 13th century, the Byzantine Empire was rapidly declining. She had fallen from the cultural, political, and moral pre-eminence that she had enjoyed since the German tribes overran the western half of the Roman Empire. The government funds were wasted in revelry and debauchery; the army broke up, the navy rotted at the docks. When the Bulgars rebelled once again, the usurper, Alexius III, was unable to pacify them; when Serbia transferred her allegiance to Hungary, he could do nothing. And through this all, he never ceased raiding the treasury. Isaac II was blind and wasting away in prison at Constantinople, but his son, young Alexius, had only recently escaped and fled to the West. He and his brother-in-law, Philip of Swabia, came up with a devious plan, which they submitted formally to the forces of the Fourth Crusade while these which were wintering at Zara.

The proposal consisted of two major elements: in return for transporting Alexius to Constantinople and installing him as emperor after deposing his usurping uncle, he would use his imperial power to finance the conquest of Egypt, and what is more, he would also have the Greeks return to the Roman communion. The crusaders agreed with just a handful of defections—since they had already been excommunicated for attacking Zara, proceeding to Constantinople could hardly do any more damage. They sent emissaries to Innocent to try and get reconciled to the Church, and were pardoned on condition that they return the loot they had seized. The Venetians, in what was the first of their many clashes with the papacy, ignored the Pope and kept their share of the booty.

After making a stop to capture the Island of Corfù in May, 1203, the mighty crusader fleet was in sight of Constantinople by June, and on the 5th of that month, anchored at Chalcedon, on the Asian shore across the Bosporus from the Byzantine capital. When the Emperor demanded to know what it was that they wanted, the crusaders replied that they intended to drive him out as a traitor. They then appealed directly to the people of the Imperial City, demanding that young Alexius be placed on the throne immediately, but the Greeks flat out refused to accept anyone advocated by the hated Latins. The only way for the crusaders to put their young pretender onto the throne was by force of arms.

The crusader fleet crossed the Bosporus on the 5th of July, landing at Galata, the water front separated from Constantinople by a broad inlet known as the Golden Horn. Their objective was to capture the fortifications protecting one end of the immense iron chain that stretched straight across the Golden Horn guarding the flank of the city against naval attack. Within a day, the chain was lowered and the mission accomplished. The crusader galleys then sailed in to sink the remnants of the Byzantine fleet anchored there.

On the 17th, a general assault was launched on Constantinople. Though the imperial capital was defended only by a handful of unpaid and rebellious mercenaries, the French crusaders, who attacked the city by land from the west, were driven back. The Venetians also, attacking simultaneously by ship along the coast of the Golden Horn, engaged only cautiously at first. Then, suddenly, a lone galley broke forward, pushing firmly and steadily onto the shore; at her prow stood in full gear the decrepit and blind Doge Dandolo, a man for whom the bottom line was everything. The other galleys dared hang back no longer, proceeding to capture more than twenty-five of the defensive towers of the city. Emperor Alexius III fled the city with his daughter at nightfall, stopping only to retrieve five tons of gold and a sack of jewels.

Isaac II was at once brought out from his prison cell and restored to the throne. The Byzantines then declared that since Isaac was the rightful ruler, there was no need for the Latins to fight on behalf of the young prince. The crusaders agreed, on the condition that Alexius IV Angelus be named co-Emperor, which was done on the 1st of August. His earlier promises to compensate the crusaders were renewed, but by the time he was done handing out gifts, there was not enough money left to pay the debt to the Venetians.

The tax he levied on the citizens to raise the funds eroded his own support in the city, while his promise to place the Byzantine Church under papal authority provoked even more anger and resistance. As if this was not enough, the crusaders, encamped across the Golden Horn at Galata, proved rude and rowdy, refused to pay their bill, and were known to pillage the countryside. On one of their occasional forays into Constantinople, they decided to burn down a mosque, but the flames got out of control and burned down an entire section of the city.

A certain bold and unscrupulous Byzantine nobleman, Alexius Murtzouphlos, rode on the popular wave by posturing as the leader of the anti-Latin faction. A member of the Ducas family and a descendant of Alexius Comnenus, he arranged his own coronation as Alexius V on the 5th of February, 1204—after having Alexius IV assassinated and Isaac II put back in prison, where the old man soon died. The new Emperor, however, had neither funds nor arms, and the crusader leaders decided they would again take over the city, and this time place one of their own number on the throne of the Byzantine Empire. This would surely be the solution to all their problems: the prolonged division of Christendom would be mended, the opulent wealth of the Eastern Empire could be put to good use in the reconquest of Jerusalem, and the Holy Land would no longer be betrayed by the faithless Greeks.

However, the first order of business was to agree on the method of dividing the spoils the Latins would reap from their conquest and pillage of the Great City. The other issue was to decide how to select the new ruler. By a treaty concluded in March between the Venetians and the crusader chiefs, the selection of the ruler was placed in the hands of a twelve-man electoral college. Half of its members were to be appointed by the Venetians and their Doge, the other half by the rest of the crusaders. Whoever the new emperor might be, he would receive one-fourth of Constantinople and the Byzantine Empire; the rest of the city and empire would be divided equally between Venice and the other crusaders. With that all-important business settled, the second assault could commence.

On the 12th of April, 1204, Western crusaders took the Byzantine capital by storm. The next day, the ruthless plunder of its palaces and churches began. Thousands were massacred by the Christian soldiers during a horrific mayhem that went on for days, and virtually every precious object that could be lifted was stolen from the richest city in Christendom. The scale of the destruction and murder was so immense that a contemporary historian regretted that the city had not fallen to the infidel instead. The masterpieces of antiquity that had until then graced the Forum and the Hippodrome were utterly destroyed. Latin clerics, eager to acquire famous and priceless relics, took part in the desecration of Greek churches.[166]

Between the looting and the fires that were started during the two seizures of the city, Constantinople was ravaged so thoroughly that she never fully recovered. Literal shiploads of gold, silver, jewels, art, and relics left the city that year; more booty, it is said, was taken from Constantinople than from all the cities in the world since the Creation. Venice received half of everything; among the countless art treasures she acquired were the four graceful bronze horses that now stand above the portal of the St. Mark's Basilica and the more than 3,000 gems and jewels that adorn the incomparable *Pala d'Oro*, the gold altar screen inside the old brick cathedral, now all but buried under Byzantine marble. There was hardly a church in the West that was not enriched with sacred ornaments stripped from those of Constantinople.

On the 9th of May, the electoral college finally assembled to elect an emperor. After Doge Dandolo refused the honour, Baldwin IX, Count of Flanders, was elected and solemnly crowned in the Hagia Sophia. The Latin Empire of the East, thus created, was a feudal state; the emperor was suzerain of all the princes among whom the Greek Peninsula was divided. Hampered by lack of financial resources and dependence on Venetian fleets, it survived for less than six decades and contributed nothing to the defence of the Holy Land. Nor were the Greeks reconciled with the Church of Rome; most of their bishops abandoned their sees and fled to Nicæa, leaving their churches in the hands of Latin prelates. Thomas Morosini, a Venetian priest, was elected patriarch; Greek monasteries were turned into Cistercian abbeys, into chapters of canons, and into commanderies of Templars and Hospitallers. The frictions and misunderstanding between East and West that had begun with the First Crusade were turned into permanent hatred.

---

[166] The relics of Byzantium were not the bones of some local saints, they were relics from the Holy Land, precious objects touched by Jesus and Mary. Kept in the imperial churches and palaces, they had solidified the sacred status of the Emperor, and would henceforward serve to affirm the divine right of the Western European monarchs.

The feudal princes, busy with their separate interests, gave little support to the Latin Empire, which during its 57-year struggle for existence sank to an infamously low level. Venice, however, achieved her goals: she received as spoils cessions of the eastern shore of the Adriatic, the shores of Thessaly, the Cyclades and the Sporades, the Sea of Marmara, and the Black Sea, thereby holding sway over "a quarter and half a quarter of the Roman Empire." The Venetians now commanded a string of ports in a virtually uninterrupted chain from their lagoons to the Western coast of Caucasus, cementing their control of the trade routes from Europe to Asia. And after having purchased the Island of Crete from Boniface of Montferrat, they controlled the approach to the Adriatic.

In Asia Minor, a strong state rose from the ruins of the Empire, with Nicæa as its capital and the gallant Theodore Lascaris (r. 1204-1222) and his son-in-law, John Ducas Vatatzes (r. 1222-1254), at its head. Two others declared independence, a Comnenus in Trebizond (his empire lasting until 1461) and an Angelus in Epirus (until 1246) who wrested Thessalonica back from the Latins. Kaloyan, Czar of the Bulgarians and Vlachs, invaded Thrace and decimated the crusader army before Adrianople in April, 1205. Emperor Baldwin fell during the battle, and instead of leading a crusade into the Holy Land, his brother and successor, Henry of Flanders, had to ask for Western help and was forced to sign treaties with both the Nicæan Emperor and the Sultan of Iconium.

Even as her territory and resources continued to shrink, Byzantium would never again be able to fully calm internal unrest or to assert independence from outside powers. The war that was fought between the various parts of the old empire and the West Europeans and Venetians, who here and there had obtained a footing on its soil, ultimately, together with the invasion of the Turks and Bulgars, destroyed the Romano-Hellenic social structure. Ironically, the immediate result of the Fourth Crusade was peace for the Middle East. The Ayyubids were greatly alarmed by the fall of Constantinople and about the prospect of united Christendom, even if for nothing. The truce between the Kingdom of Jerusalem and the Sultanate of Damascus remained undisturbed for ten years, and another five-year truce was signed in 1212.

From the second half of the 12th century on, the Cathar movement had spread like wildfire, and if we are to believe the *Catholic Encyclopedia*, "not only menaced the Church's existence, but undermined the very foundations of Christian society." These heretics were known by a variety of different names. In 1165, they were condemned by an ecclesiastical council at the Languedoc town of Albi, for which reason—or perhaps because Albi continued as one of their most important centres—they were often called Albigenses.

Besides theological "discordance," the Cathars practised keen social critique, denouncing the excessively materialistic way of life, the amassing of riches, the sanctimonious morals of the clergy, and the wealth of the Church. They declared themselves to be good Christians, who did not swear, or lie, or speak evil of others; who did not kill any man or animal, nor anything that has the breath of life; and who were persecuted by the Roman Church just as Christ and the Apostles were by the Pharisees.

They were decidedly anticlerical, asserting that there was no need for priests, and that the sacraments, orders, and ceremonies of Catholicism were futile, costly, oppressive, and downright wicked. They attacked and rebutted, in turn, all the sacraments of the Roman Church, especially that of the Holy Eucharist, pointing out that had the body of Christ been as great as the Alps, it would long ago have been consumed and extinguished by those who had partaken of it. They insisted that the host was no different from common bread; it came from straw, passed through the tails of horses (flour was cleaned by a sieve made of horse hair), passed through the body and came to a vile end, which could hardly happen if God were in it.

The Cathars rejected infant baptism, because a child was incapable of deciding about it for himself and could in no way confess his faith. Those who joined their ranks were not baptized with water, but in accordance with the Bible, "with Holy Spirit and with fire" (cf. Matt. 3:11, Luke 3:16). They argued that the water of Holy Baptism was just the same as river water, material and corruptible, and therefore could not sanctify the soul, even if the churchmen sell this water out of avarice—just as they sell earth for the burial of the dead, oil to anoint the sick, and the confession of sins to the priests. Seeing that the priests may be sinners, they cannot loose nor bind, and being unclean themselves, cannot make others clean.

The Cathars also rejected the cross as symbol, asserting that it should not be adored or venerated, because no one would adore or venerate the gallows upon which a father, brother, or friend had been hung. Instead, one important Cathar symbol was the dove. It represented then, as it does now, the notion of "peace," but also more accurately, the concept of "Divine Grace," the state of being in God's love.

Determined to bring an end to this scandalous opposition to his authority, Pope Innocent III dispatched several legates to southern France in order to convert all who had strayed from the one true path. A series of public debates was arranged in the chief towns of the Languedoc. Leading heretics were to meet the papal legates and each side was to expound upon its teachings; as remarkable a gesture as it was to let heretics speak on equal terms with the orthodox, Innocent was convinced that the truth of Catholic dogma would win the day. His legates arrived in their magnificent robes with a vast entourage of supporters, demanding near royal hospitality, while the Cathar *parfaits*, or "perfected ones," appeared in their modest simplicity. The local populace loved the *bons hommes* as much as they despised the pompous representatives of Rome, who made little progress.

An unexpected diversion occurred when two zealous Spaniards, Bishop Diego of Osma, and Domingo de Guzmán, the prior of his cathedral chapter, were sent to Languedoc by the Pope after they had begged his leave to evangelize the Tartars of the Volga. The more active of the two, then known as the "Spanish Canon," but soon to become the famous St. Dominic (1170-1221), reproached the papal legates for their pomp and arrogance, while himself outdoing even the parfaits in asceticism. When the mob flung mud at the Saint and threatened to lynch him, he replied: "Oh I would just ask you not put me to death all at once; but gradually limb by limb to make my martyrdom a slow one, so that hardly human in form, blinded and a mass of blood, I should have a really much finer place in heaven." Despite his fervent eloquence, no converts of any importance appeared.

The churches were abandoned; the voice of St. Dominic rang in vain at the public squares. The heresy stood fast, its prestige unshaken—a prestige in large part due to the complicity of the local princes. In 1203, Innocent sent a Cistercian monk, Pierre de Castelnau, to reprimand the Count of Toulouse, Raymond VI of St-Gilles, for harbouring and supporting the heretics. He ruled as great an area as the King of France did, but his authority within his domains was weak, and many of the towns were controlled by councils. Since the Count failed to keep his subjects in line and to resolve the heretic problem, he was excommunicated in 1207 and his vast territories were laid under interdict. However, because his vassals were unconcerned, Raymond could remain indifferent.

Then, almost certainly without the Count's approval, one of his serjeants kindled the spark that ignited the conflagration. In 1208, while crossing the Rhône on his return to Italy, de Castelnau was murdered, and Innocent did not hesitate to blame the heretics. Instead of directing the forces of Christendom against the Saracens, the Pope disbanded them by proclaiming a crusade against the Cathars. Though there had been sporadic persecutions of heretics throughout the previous century, only now did Rome mobilize her forces in earnest. Secular knights found themselves far more willing to take the cross and go on a crusade if the crusade was as close as southern France. Catharism was to be extirpated once and for all.

Thus began the hideously cruel Albigensian Crusade (1209-29), which thoroughly destroyed the independent culture of Provence and Languedoc. The established lyricism of the troubadours dealt with love, but their accidental poetry was political. Some of these political poems, the so-called *sirventés*, "service songs," were local patriotic protests against the Crusade. However, the influence of these widely-travelled minstrels had already spread to central and northern France, where their counterparts were known as the *trouvères*. In Germany, they were imitated by the *minnesingers*, and the tradition was also carried to Spain and Italy.

Being as they were pacifists, it is hard to see how the Cathars could possibly resist the crusaders. The answer is simple: the local nobles did the fighting for them, since they did not wish to submit to the French King. The alliance of Philip Augustus with Innocent III in connection with the Albigensian Crusade facilitated his relations with the Pope, who considered this crusade to be an exceedingly important one. Northern France was at the time in conflict with the south, which being economically more developed was a menace to it. Crusaders were promised the land that they succeeded in taking from the heretics, and northern French barons under Simon de Montfort rushed to participate.

As the feudal system was weaker in southern France, the local nobles were only too ready to suspect one another of trying to gain undue power. Raymond of Toulouse came up with a clever ruse; he did public penance before the Church of St-Gilles, in the presence of the papal legate, and took the cross. He thus secured the safety of his own people, for the crusader army was now precluded from entering his realm. At the same time, his nephew and vassal, Raymond-Roger III de Trencavel, Viscount of Béziers and Carcassonne, decided to defend his own shires.

On the 21st of July, 1209, an army of estimated 200,000 foot soldiers and 20,000 knights from Northern Europe descended the northeastern foothills of the Pyrenees into the Languedoc. In the war that ensued, the whole region was ravaged, crops were destroyed, towns and cities were laid waste, an entire population was put to the sword. When Simon de Montfort asked the papal legate, Arnaud Amaury, Abbot of Cîteaux, how he might distinguish heretics from true believers, the infamous answer was: "Kill them all. God will know his own."[167] The same legate, writing to Innocent III in Rome, announced proudly that "neither age nor sex nor status was spared." In the town of Béziers alone, at least 15,000 men, women, and children were summarily slaughtered—many of them in the sanctuary of the church itself. The survivors fled the town practically naked, "taking nothing but their sins" as one participant in the Crusade reports. They had been chained to one another, their noses had been chopped off, their eyes had been gouged out. A one-eyed man led the procession to forewarn the next village. Town after town was taken, pillaged, and burnt. Hundreds of thousands fell. The rich provinces of Languedoc and Provence were devastated. Nothing was left but smouldering waste.

In order not to lose his land and power, Raymond of Toulouse refused to participate in the fighting; for this he was excommunicated anew by the Council of Avignon. He then made his way to Rome to clear himself of the murder of Pierre de Castelnau, but on his return, found his estates completely overrun by Simon de Montfort. His brother-in-law and suzerain, King Peter II of Aragón, who had won great fame in fighting the Moors in Spain, came to his rescue in 1213. Though not in particular sympathy with the Cathars, he could not afford to see the important southern French fiefs, commanding as they did the passes of the eastern Pyrenees, fall into the hands of enemies such as the King of France. Peter was killed at the Battle of Muret on the 12th of September, forever relegating the House of St-Gilles to minor status. The decisive victory gained by the crusaders at Muret is matched in its importance to France only by the Battle of Bouvines, for its inevitable consequence was the falling of all Languedoc under the control of the French crown in a matter

---

[167] *Neca eos omnes. Deus suos agnoset.*

of a few years, immensely expanding the power of the Capetians.

Innocent was hardly blind to the vices of luxury and pride that plagued not only the nobility, but the Catholic clergy as well, continuously fanning the flames of the numerous anti-sacerdotal sects of the day. As the best remedy, he saw the mendicant (or "begging") orders founded by St. Dominic and St. Francis (1182-1226). Wanting others to try and lead an evangelical life, they themselves gave up their temporal rank and imitated Christ and the Apostles in their poverty and their disdain for the carnal world. They themselves lived among the poor and gathered around them disciples, who would carry the word of God to the indigent and oppressed. Their preaching was in the local vernaculars, and addressed to whomever would stand in the marketplace to listen. There had, of course, been a multitude of such groups before—but the Church had always suppressed them. Sts. Dominic and Francis were different: as devout Catholics, they respected the sacraments, the dogmas, and even the sinful priests.

The preaching of St. Dominic and his first companions in the Languedoc resulted in the pontifical letter of 1205. The same year, Dominic opened at Prouille, in the diocese of Toulouse, a nunnery for converts from Catharism, living under the Rule of St. Augustine, which he had himself followed for twelve years; this was the definitive, if tentative, beginning of his own Order. In a quite novel adaptation of the monastic code, the Dominicans would vow themselves to no particular house, but instead went wherever preaching took them. The special vocation of the Dominican Order was teaching and defending the "truths of faith," and studying was the first necessity of the Preacher's office, to which everything else in life had to be strictly subordinated. In all cases of conflicting monastic duties, the claim of study was to have precedence. The element of manual labour, once universal in Western religious orders, disappeared from this new monasticism. The Dominican Preachers were to travel in pairs and to possess nothing (Mark 6:7-8), but to live on alms. The growth of his Order was so rapid that, in ten years, Dominic journeyed to the Fourth Lateran Council in Rome with the Bishop of Toulouse, to ask papal confirmation for his Rule.

St. Francis of Assisi—Giovanni de Bernardone by birth—was a son of a wealthy Italian merchant and his Provençal wife. He was an experienced tradesman, soldier, and diplomat, and not half as naïve as the pious legends would have us believe. It was his growing awareness of the distress of the poor that led him to abandon the riches of his father, making his conversion as much social as it was religious. Upon setting his heart on the issue of social equality, he assumed the role of a popular leader, and disciples soon began to flock around him. He wanted to be approved by the Pope, but not to follow any approved rule. The legend is that when St. Francis stood before Innocent III in 1209, wearing his coarse serge garment tied about the waist with a cord, and begged the great Pontiff to approve his movement, he was at first rejected. But while the Pope lay sleeping the night after his meeting with Francis, he had a dream of the Lateran shaken and falling, and a poor beggar holding it up with his shoulders. This beggar he recognized; it was Francis of Assisi. Innocent understood that the new Order would be a pillar of the Church, and was to see St. Dominic in a similar vision five years later.

St. Francis wanted his brethren to approach the people without the burden of wealth and the depravity brought about by books. His disciples and followers looked upon him as their ideal, and for a time, the Order he founded adhered quite well to the requirements set forth by him. However, the line between spirit and flesh is hard to draw. The masses tend to either gravitate towards the more materialistic ends of the social revolution or to settle for what they have. The leaders, in their turn, think up of more subtle and nuanced compromises with the world. Consequently, the Franciscan Order split up almost from the first to two opposing parties: the so-called "Spirituals" demanded unconditional poverty, while the "Conventuals," being realists, never fully renounced property. The realist faction prevailed—already within the second generation after St. Francis' death, the Franciscans would hoard up for themselves a great fortune and were enthusiastically participating in the scholarly pursuits of the High Middle Ages.

Innocent was absorbed over head and ears in power politics. To the papal title, "Vicar of Peter," Innocent added for the first time the title "Vicar of Christ"—a phrase he constantly uses. His power in the Church was therefore absolute, his jurisdiction throughout the Church immediate, and explicitly declared as such: "All things on Earth and in Heaven and in Hell are subject unto the Vicar of Christ." He set aside the decisions of bishops and provincial councils; even the most remote monasteries fell under the rule of papal law and administration; no part of the Church could escape his net.

Innocent's crowning achievement was the Fourth Lateran, otherwise known as the Twelfth Ecumenical Council (1215). It became by far the greatest ecclesiastical council of the Middle Ages, dealing as it would with an enormous number of important issues. All the bishops were invited, as were the heads of all the religious orders, temporal princes, representatives of republics, even of the innumerable, tiny city-states. Besides deciding on a new crusade to the Holy Land, it issued a staggering seventy reformatory canons, the first being the famous profession of faith, *Firmiter credimus*, through which "transubstantiation" was made dogma. Being a statement of Catholic belief directed against the Cathars and the other innumerable anti-sacerdotal movements, the *Firmiter* declared that there was but a single Church for all believers, outside of which no one could be saved; within her, Christ Himself was priest and sacrifice, whose body and blood were truly contained in the sacrament under the appearance of bread and wine, their substance being transformed by the power of God. None, save the priests duly ordained by the power of the Church which Christ gave to the Apostles and their successors, could bring this miracle to pass.

The new "firm" creed further declared that baptism, rightly administered by anyone in the Roman form, was as profitable to salvation of children as of adults, and that sins committed after baptism could be atoned by sincere penance. The twenty-first canon of the Council, *Omnis utriusque sexus*, also prescribed that "everyone of both sexes," under pain of being excluded from the Church while alive and denied Christian burial when dead, should, at least once a year, confess his or her sins to the parish priest, and if only at Easter, receive the Holy Eucharist. The canon concluded with a warning to confessors about the spirit in which they should receive confessions, and of the obligations never to reveal what is confessed to them. Offenders against the seal of the confessional were to be put into a severe monastery, there to do penance for the rest of their lives.

The Fourth Lateran also notoriously approved canon laws that extended to the whole Church the practice, then common in many areas, of requiring Jews (and Muslims) to wear a distinctive badge to enable them to be easily distinguished from Christians. It absolutely prohibited Jews to have Christians in their service, or Christians to enter into the service of Jews, even as nurses or midwives. Attendance by Jewish physicians was equally forbidden, and Christians were not allowed even to lodge with Jews or to maintain any social contact whatsoever, thus laying the foundation of the *ghetto*.

All in all, Innocent's labours in purely ecclesiastical matters were of a decidedly subordinate character when compared with his great politico-ecclesiastical achievements. Before his imperial coronation in 1209, Otto of Brunswick solemnly swore obedience to the Pope and pledged himself to hand over all the territories occupied contrary to the will of the Holy See in the previous twenty-five years (i.e. the Patrimony, Ravenna, Spoleto, Ancona) plus the lands left to the Church by Matilda of Tuscany; he also promised to help maintain papal suzerainty over Sicily, conceded the privilege of episcopal elections and the unrestricted right of appeal to the pope, and renounced the *jus spolii*, or the right to the revenues of vacant sees and to the estates of intestate ecclesiastics.

But scarcely had Otto IV been crowned when he forgot his promises and descended upon central Italy, seizing Spoleto, Ancona, and the bequest of Matilda, distributing the rich estates and provinces among his vassals while sequestrating the revenues of the clergy. The new Emperor then marched on southern Italy, the territory of Henry VI's 16-year-old son, Frederick II, who had been raised under the Pope's guardianship in the court at Palermo. For this he was duly excommunicated in 1210, and Innocent called upon Philip Augustus of France for subsidies and troops to aid him against Otto. As a result of the Pope's negotiations with the German princes, the Diet of Nuremberg (1211) declared the excommunicated Emperor deposed, and after pronouncing in favour of Frederick, sent envoys to Sicily to convey him the message.

By the time Otto crossed the Alps to reclaim his power, it was already too late. Frederick's election was repeated at the Diet of Frankfurt (1212), in presence of a representative of Innocent and of Philip Augustus. Thus was established the policy by which France meddled in the affairs of Germany, and for the first time, the French king claimed, like the Roman pontiff, to have a say in imperial elections. Before leaving Italy, Frederick had again acknowledged Sicily as a papal fief. The following year, he was recognized by nearly all the German princes at Eger, where he disavowed all imperial rights to the States of the Church, and was crowned king at Aachen.

In the ensuing conflict, Otto was supported by the nobles of the Lower Rhine and northeast Germany, as well as by his uncle, King John (1199-1216) of England. Within five years of his coronation, John had found himself on the losing side of a war with Philip Augustus. His shabby treatment of his nephew, Arthur of Brittany, drove Anjou into the hands of the French King. In fact, John lost most of the English possessions in France; the Channel Islands were all that remained, even until today, of the English duchy of Normandy. John's failure in battle earned him the cognomen "Softsword." In 1206, he got into a quarrel with Pope Innocent, a quarrel which would give him the further epithet of "Lackland."

Innocent wanted Cardinal Stephen Langton, Rector of the University of Paris, to become the new Archbishop of Canterbury. King John wanted to decide for himself who should become the Archbishop. In 1208, Innocent placed all of England under interdict; John ordered the clergy to disregard the ban. In 1209, Innocent excommunicated him; John used the excommunication as an excuse to confiscate church lands. Finally, in 1212, Innocent declared that John had forfeited his right to rule, freed his subjects from their oath of allegiance to him, and invited Philip Augustus to land in England and execute the sentence of deposition. The English King then decided on a total reversal of policy, accepting the papal candidate for Canterbury and restoring church property.

However, John was not out of the trouble yet; he needed a way that would make the papacy condemn Philip if he still should launch the invasion fleet of 1,500 ships he had assembled. Consequently, on the 15th of May, 1213, at the House of the Templars near Dover, John resigned the kingdom of England and lordship of Ireland "to God, to the Holy Apostles Peter and Paul, to the Holy Roman Church, his mother, and to his lord, Pope Innocent the Third, and his Catholic successors, for the remission of all sins and the sins of all his people, as well the living as the dead." Innocent then returned England and Ireland to Lackland on condition that he would officially acknowledge, for himself, his heirs, and his successors, Rome's feudal authority under bonds of fealty as vassals of the pope as a feudal prince. In addition to the usual Peter's Pence, the kings of England were obligated to pay the bishops of Rome an annual tribute of 1,000 marks.

To fight the French, John had to levy the first income tax, and the reason for his defeat was the refusal of the English barons to accompany him to France. The allied forces of John and Otto IV were defeated by Philip Augustus at the Battle of Bouvines, on the 27th of July, 1214. With his enemies in disarray, Philip was able to retain everything that he had won over the previous fifteen years, a period in which he had quadrupled the size of the royal domain. He was the master of Normandy, Maine, Anjou, and Touraine, and to some extend in commanding position also in Poitou. The might of the House of Anjou was crushed for good. France was acknowledged as one of the leading European powers, for Philip was without controversy the ruler of most of France. Having lost all influence in Germany, Otto died on the 19th of May, 1218, leaving the Pope's ward, Frederick II, the undisputed Emperor.

For all his ability as a politician, Innocent did not see what was happening in England. After the surrender of the kingdom into the hands of the pope, any who opposed John's high-handed civil administration were subject to religious penalties. When the barons started taking action against the King—incidentally led by the new Archbishop—Innocent started excommunicating the opposition and ended, in fact, by suspending Stephen Langton. By 1215, John had offended all the classes of England to the extent that they forgot their reciprocal jealousies and prejudices, and united in that great league of barons, clergy, and people, which compelled him to approve the *Magna Charta*, regarded by the English as the basis of their political and personal freedom and of their constitutional law. The Pope declared the "Great Charter of Liberties" null and void, and expelled the English from his Church.

When Innocent died (1216), he left the papacy in the zenith of its power, having completely overturned the authority of the emperor and humiliated most of the crowned heads of Europe. In Spain, he had compelled King Alfonso IX (1188-1230) of León to break off his marriage with his cousin, Queen Berenguela (1198-1237) of Castile, and given the crown of Aragón to Peter II (r. 1196-1213), who came to Rome to be crowned by the Pope in St. Peter's. In Portugal, he had likewise induced King Sancho I (1185-1211) to place his newly-risen kingdom under the protection of the Holy See, and also annulled the marriage of the heir to the throne with a too-near relation. In Poland, he had threatened Duke Ladislaus III (1202-1206) with excommunication unless he allowed the reforming Archbishop, Henryk of Gniezno, to return to the country and perform the duties of papal legate.

In Bohemia, Innocent had confirmed Duke Premysl Ottokar I (1197-1230) as king. In Bulgaria, he had similarly acknowledged the czarist claims of Kaloyan, after being promised the union of the Bulgarian Church with Rome.

In Hungary, he had acted as arbitrator between the two sons of King Béla III (1172-1196) who were contending for the crown. In Norway also, he had mediated between the two claimaints for the throne after the death of King Sverre (1184-1202), who was earlier excommunicated by him for standing up to the papacy. Innocent cited Jeremiah in his relationship with secular power: "I set thee over the nations and over the kingdoms, to root out, and to pull down, and to destroy, and to throw down" (1:10). It has been said that more blood was spilled by the Roman Church during his pontificate—and under his immediate successors implementing his policies—than in any other age apart from the Catholic Counter-Reformation of the 16th and 17th centuries.

CHAPTER 23

Although a Hohenstaufen like his namesake grandfather, Frederick II had grown up in Sicily, which, even after 150 years of Norman rule, was more Oriental than European, as much Muslim as Christian. His father, Henry VI, had annexed Sicily to the Holy Roman Empire by his marriage with the Norman princess, Constance de Hauteville, from whom Frederick had inherited his warm southern blood. From his youth, when Pope Innocent III was his guardian and took shameless advantage of this position, Frederick had come to know and despise the Church.[168] As he grew a little older, he made friends with the many different peoples of the island—Greeks, Muslims, Jews, and native Sicilians—learning their tongues and acquiring respect for their cultures. Of his 35 years of reign, he spent only six in Germany; the attraction of Italy was too great for him.

The Sicily of Frederick's childhood was stimulated by influences from the entire Mediterranean region; in it met Córdoba, Rome, Byzantium, Jerusalem, and Egypt. He became fluent in six different languages; not only in German, Italian, and French, but also in Latin, Greek, and Arabic—the scientific language of the day. He was a patron of arts and sciences; and a poet, philosopher, and scientist in his own right. His book, *De Arte Venandi cum Avibus*, on falconry as well as on the anatomy and life of birds, was the first modern ornithology and based almost entirely on his own experimental research. But Frederick was also a lawmaker and political reformer: he created a civil service, the candidates for which were trained at the University of Naples—the first chartered university in Europe—founded by him in 1224. He endowed it with his large collection of Arabic writings, accumulated during his various journeys, and was also a liberal patron of the medical school at Salerno, promoted better ideas of medicine, and embodied them in his laws.

He gathered Provençal troubadours and German minnesingers at his Sicilian

---

[168] One of the conditions of his coronation was death penalty for heretics.

court, which Dante justly called the birthplace of Italian poetry. A fundamental contribution to the development of the new Italian language, this vernacular poetry was so refined in form and so subtle in tenor that even a master like Dante had little to add to it. The most fruitful achievement of the Sicilian School of Poetry is probably the invention of the sonnet. Its work was carried on, among others, by Guido Guinicelli in Bologna and by Guido Cavalcanti in Florence. These love poets carried Platonic spiritualism to such a perfection that Dante regards them as creators of their own, sweet, new style, *il dolce stil nuovo*.

Through Frederick's influence, Florence and other growing cities on the Italian mainland begun to promote lay culture and independent thought, while acquiring the veneration of paganism that is again reflected in Dante. During his reign, German literature—i.e. literature that was written in German, not Latin—also produced its first great monument, an epic known as the "Song of the Nibelungs," in which old myths and the history of the Huns and Theodoric fuse to form astonishingly great and powerful poetry. The *Nibelungenlied* was one of the last echoes of pagan mythological literature, and served as an inspiration to Richard Wagner's massive tetralogy of music dramas, known collectively as *Der Ring des Nibelungen*.

The minnesingers frequenting Frederick's court may have included "der Tannhäuser," whose adventurous wandering became a subject of another legend that inspired Wagner; and Wolfram von Eschenbach, who wrote the famous chivalric poem *Parzivâl*, the source for the libretto of Wagner's last great music drama. The symbolism-filled Grail legend held the possibilities of uniting chivalric and spiritual ideals, which were utilized, in a more skilful manner than the French had, by the aforementioned Bavarian knight-errant. His poem derives largely from distant Eastern sources, and many of its protagonists are both Muslims and real characters, not merely the crude caricatures of the *chansons de geste*. Von Eschenbach was the last great Western writer who professed himself unable to read or write, and boasted of this defect becoming a nobleman. His acquaintance with the French language may have been deficient, but a man who invented anagrams and quoted Latin with understanding, even if only few words, was certainly no illiterate. In fact, he is well-foundedly credited with having authored the first *rites de passage* novel in Europe.

Himself an expert trader engaged in far-flung business activities, Frederick encouraged commerce by enlarging the harbours of his kingdom and establishing a fleet of merchant vessels. If somewhat curbed at first, the cities enjoyed a more generous treatment in the later years of his reign, and many were transformed into important centres of trade—his court in Palermo was certainly one of the most brilliant in Europe. His boldness, his wide range of talents, and his vast erudition, extending to all the vocations of his age, made his contemporaries grace him with the honorific of *Stupor Mundi*, "the Marvel of the World."

At his coronation as King of Germany in Aachen, Frederick, still very young and carried away by the occasion, had announced his intention to go on a crusade, and following his victory over Otto of Brunswick, took the cross at the tomb of Charlemagne.[169] However, no crusade was immediately in sight, and, in any case, he needed to bring order to Germany, so there was never any question of embarking on one then and there. As early as the December of 1216, Pope Honorius III granted him the first delay in the fulfilment of his vow. When the Fifth Crusade (1217-21) finally did set out, the Pope reminded Frederick of his vow, but even as he was raising an army, anarchy broke out in Italy. He delayed, hoping to settle matters quickly at home, but the conflict dragged on, and for five years, Frederick was occupied with suppressing disorder in Sicily.

The centre of Muslim power was now Egypt, and as long as she was strong, there was no point in attacking Jerusalem; however, with the region under Latin control, the Muslims would not be able to defend the Holy City for long. The Fifth Crusade got off to a promising start with the capture of Damietta (1219), a key Egyptian seaport. The crusader strategy called for the taking of Cairo, followed by a campaign to secure control of the Sinai, a link between Egypt and the Latin Kingdom, cutting off the remaining Muslim powers from Egypt's wealth and grain. The Egyptian Sultan, Malik al-Kamil, offered to surrender Jerusalem and other holy places in exchange for Damietta, but Honorius, expecting Frederick to arrive any time now, turned down the generous offer. And as he waited, what had been a winter camp set

---

[169] It should be noted that the word "crusade" is a modern invention; Frederick, at the most, took a vow to make a "pilgrimage," itself a modern word deriving from the Latin *pelegrinatio*, "journey."

up in desperation was turned by al-Kamil into a *bona fide* military city.

Though Frederick never came, he sent much of his army, with Louis of Bavaria as the imperial representative. The Duke argued for an immediate offensive, and since he was assumed to be speaking for the Emperor, the crusaders advanced towards Cairo on the 17th of July, 1221. The attack was abortive and the crusaders were trapped in the Nile Valley.[170] The Sultan no longer needed to offer the surrender of Jerusalem, for he now had the entire crusader army, including John of Brienne, Regent of Jerusalem, at his mercy. But as the Latins still held Damietta, which they had recently fortified, and another crusader fleet was on its way, al-Kamil merely asked that they leave his sultanate. The captured seaport would be returned to the Muslims, and the Latins would observe an eight-year truce with Egypt.[171]

Back in Europe, many blamed Frederick, who had promised to go but had not. Meanwhile, the ambitious ruler had secured imperial coronation (1220) from the ever-optimistic Pope by agreeing to issue laws against heretics. And even though the newly-crowned Emperor had sent troops to the East, many felt that he had shirked his Christian duty as the natural leader of a crusade just so he could look after his own, narrow political interests. Once again, Frederick proclaimed his determination to go, making his preparations even as the dispirited crusaders returned from Egypt. The other European monarchs did little to help him, but his empire was so vast that even unaided he might succeed where all others had failed.

The Kingdom of Jerusalem was at present without a king. John of Brienne, who had been acting as a regent, was now in his seventies and needed to find a husband for his 11-year-old daughter Yolande, who was to be queen. In 1222, the old warrior travelled to Europe, where Hermann von Salza, the Grand Master of the Teutonic Knights, suggested that the girl should marry Frederick, a widower and his close personal friend. It was a momentous proposition, for it would unite the Kingdom with the Empire. Hoping to thereby hasten the departure of the crusade, Pope Honorius encouraged the

---

[170] Their earlier success was largely explained by the fact that the Egyptian navy, so formidable under the Arab Fatimids, languished under the Kurdish Auyybids.

[171] The thousands of European merchants who were in Damietta before the Fifth Crusade remained there, but were henceforward treated with suspicion.

marriage, which took place in 1225, as soon as Yolande reached the legal age of 14. In August of that year, Count Henry of Malta, Admiral of Sicily, arrived at Acre with an entourage to take the young princess back to Italy for her wedding. Before she left, she was crowned queen, and on the 9th of November, at the Cathedral of Brindisi, she was wed to Frederick, who then assumed the title of King of Jerusalem.

In 1226, the Lombard League, originally formed against Frederick's grandfather, was revived in Italy. The following year, Frederick annulled the Treaty of Constance and placed the Lombard cities under the ban of the empire. With all the troubles in Italy, Frederick was in no position to continue the eastern expansion of Germany in its original form, which had been halted at Poland's western border, but saw the local crusading enterprise in Prussia and the Baltic countries, both still under the control of the pagan Wends, as an excellent opportunity to extend imperial influence into an entirely new direction. Receiving assistance from King Ottokar of Bohemia, the Teutonic Knights under Hermann von Salza began subduing the Baltic region in 1226. A network of castles was erected along the coast and a large number of German families settled on the conquered lands. The creation of this new, German Prussia was the most striking success of German colonization, one that has influenced the whole political and ethnic structure of East Central Europe until the present.

In 1227, Frederick had not yet, however, left for Palestine. For fifteen years, he had used the papal protection bestowed upon a crusader to help him consolidate his holdings in Europe, dawdling and droning until the death of Honorius. The new pope, Gregory IX, did not like the Emperor and believed him to be delaying out of cowardice or worse. A nephew of Innocent III, Gregory had espoused all the opinions of Hildebrand, who had declared ecclesiastical power to be in the same relation to its secular counterpart as the Sun was to the Moon. Threatened several times with excommunication if he did not fulfill his coronation pledge, Frederick at last prepared to set out. No sooner had he sailed from Brindisi (ancient Brundisium), than malaria broke out among his troops and soon the Emperor himself took ill. His advisors insisted he return to Italy, and after three days at sea, Frederick finally agreed. Immediately upon their docking at Otranto, he sent a letter to the Pope explaining what had happened, but Gregory would not accept even this excuse—he declared the Emperor excommunicated then and there.

Most of his fleet proceeded on without him, but by the time Frederick himself recovered, it was too late in the year to sail. He assembled a second army the following spring, finally setting out on the 28th of June, 1228. The Pope unhesitatingly excommunicated the Emperor a second time, for leaving without having obtained papal absolution for the first sentence—history thus got to witness the unique spectacle of the temporal head of Christendom leading a crusade in fulfilment of a solemn vow to two popes while under the solemn ban of a third.

Frederick arrived at Acre in September, around the same time as the news of his second excommunication. This made him extremely unwelcome among the crusaders in the Holy Land, since any person aiding an excommunicate or any village harbouring one would automatically be excommunicated as well. Many of his own troops turned around and went home at the first opportunity, so when he finally arrived in Palestine, his army was much smaller than he had intended it to be. In the meantime, his wife Yolande had died giving birth to their son and her heir, Conrad. With the Queen of Jerusalem dead, Frederick no longer had a claim to the throne as far as the local barons were concerned.

So extraordinarily commenced an enterprise proceeded even more extraordinarily. There would be no epic struggle, no heroic battles, no dramatic fight to the death with the infidel. Upon landing at Acre, the Emperor sent his delegates, furnished with ample gifts, to al-Kamil, the Sultan of Egypt, in whose possession Jerusalem still was at the time. The Sultan courteously replied, and aware of the Emperor's interest in rarities, presented him with an elephant and other specimens of tropical wild life, plus a troupe of dancing girls.

The Saracens discovered Frederick to be quite an exceptional type of crusader, and their own prince was likewise a highly intelligent and civilized man, who had even been knighted by Richard Cœur-de-Lion back in 1192. While at Acre, Frederick decided to make a daring excursion without his troops into the Jordan, and have a swim in the river. The Templars, having sided with the Pope, sent a word of Frederick's intention to al-Kamil, informing him how he might entrap his enemy and slay him. The Sultan forwarded the letter to Frederick as a token of how much respect he had for such an advice.

A remarkable correspondence soon developed between the two, discussing the great enigmas of philosophy and culture, and resulting in the lasting friendship of these kindred spirits. By February of 1229, the Sultan and the Emperor had come to an agreement through which Jerusalem, Bethlehem, and Nazareth were all handed over to Frederick with reasonable conditions. The Muslims were to retain possession of al-Aqsa Mosque and the Dome of the Rock, and free access to and within Jerusalem. The mutually agreed upon truce of ten years gave al-Kamil the freedom to concentrate on reuniting Syria with Egypt. All prisoners on both sides were set at liberty.

Frederick entered Jerusalem on the 17th of March, 1229. His small entourage of German and Italian troops was with him, but hardly any of the locals. The Templars and the Hospitallers would still have nothing to do with the double-excommunicate, and the Patriarch, too, refused the invite, leaving the city almost empty. The next day was a Sunday, and Frederick went to the Church of the Holy Sepulchre to attend Mass—only to find that there was no priest present. Unabashed, Frederick proceeded to crown himself King of Jerusalem. He then entered the vacant Hospital of St. John, and set up his court there.

Jerusalem had been liberated and the goal of the Crusade achieved without the striking of a single blow. But Frederick had also raised the ire of the local baronage, most of which refused to recognize the legitimacy of his self-coronation. And in the eyes of Pope Gregory, Frederick's success, attained as it was through the strength of a great personality and by unorthodox means, only added to the Emperor's guilt. A papal legate soon arrived in the Holy City, once again declaring the excommunication of the man who had delivered it, and for harbouring the triple-excommunicate, was forced to lay under interdict the very focus of Christianity, the city of Jerusalem itself.

Frederick was excommunicated for not going on a crusade, for going on a crusade, and on coming back from a crusade—be it not in defeat but in triumph. On returning to Europe, in May, 1229, the crusaders found that they needed to repel another crusade, this time incited by Gregory against themselves. The Pope had raised an army, and proceeded to attack the Emperor's positions in Sicily. The imperial troops bearing the cross of Christ were met on their return by the papal army whose banners were inscribed with the keys of St. Peter. Frederick's army was victorious, and he recovered the lost areas, but did not retaliate by attacking the Papal States.

On the 23rd of July, 1230, a treaty was signed at San Germano by which the Emperor was temporarily reconciled with the Pope. In August, Gregory ratified Frederick's treaty with the Sultan of Egypt as part of the Treaty of San Germano, whereupon the newly-absolved King of Jerusalem sent one of his marshals, Ricardo Filangieri, to rule in his place. In preparation for the inevitable conflict with the revived Lombard League, Frederick then turned to strengthening his Sicilian kingdom. He managed to establish peace, prosperity, and order in the south, promulgating (1231) at Melfi a comprehensive body of laws, the *Liber Augustalis*[172], described as the best issued by any Western ruler since the reign of Charlemagne.

To bring order out of chaos, Frederick substituted the uniform legislation of the Sicilian Constitutions for the irregular jurisdiction of episcopal court and baron. Anxious to thwart imperial encroachments on the strictly spiritual province of doctrine, Pope Gregory deemed it necessary to establish a distinct and specifically ecclesiastical tribunal. He appointed special but permanent judges, invested by him with the right and the duty to deal legally with offences against the Faith. Where they sat, there was the Inquisition (Lat. *inquisitio*, an inquiry). The Inquisitor was subject to no law, only to the pope; he was both the judge and the prosecutor. The trials were secret and the accused had to prove their innocence without either benefit of counsel or knowledge of the charges brought against them. What is more, the names of witnesses were also kept secret, leaving the alleged heretics with virtually no rights at all.

It was regarded as providential by the Pope that only recently there had sprang up two new religious orders, the Dominicans and the Franciscans. Since local prelates, as well as rulers, refused to carry out the "search," Gregory entrusted it to the new Dominican friars, soon to be known, in a Latin pun, as *Domini canes*, "the hounds of the Lord."[173] In 1232, they were sent as inquisitors to Germany, Lombardy, and Spain, and the year following, to France. In short, by middle of the 13th century, the Dominican Inquisition was fully active in every country of Central and Western Europe. The "Friars Preachers" became the Church's agents also for the visitation of sees and monasteries, they acted as its fiscal officials, and they preached the

---

[172] a/k/a "Constitutions of Melfi"

[173] whence the appellation "German Shepherd" given to Pope Benedict XVI on his elevation

crusades—against the Saracens in the Holy Land, against the pagans in Livonia and Prussia, and against the Hohenstaufen in Italy and Germany.

Frederick's commitment to the costly wars in Italy, and the Crusade in Jerusalem, had caused him to neglect the welfare of his German subjects. In 1235, he was betrothed to Isabella, the sister of King Henry III of England, and there was a brilliant celebration in Cologne, where the pair met, and another at Worms, where they were married. The same year, an important diet was held at Mainz with all the major princes present. The Diet of Mainz promulgated a body of laws that would have been quite commendable, had it only been implemented. The hand of the Emperor was clearly discernible in its many enactments. They were no longer mere codification of traditional customs and class privileges, but permeated by the spirit of fundamental rights in the interrelationship of people, and reveal every so often that singular modernity and enlightenment of thought that never ceases to amaze one in Frederick.

To gain support for his campaigns in northern Italy, the Emperor had awarded the German princes virtually all power in their own territory. His first son, King Henry VII, who had ruled Germany since 1228, naturally objected to this, entering into an alliance with the Lombard League. He was promptly deposed and imprisoned by his father, who, after seeing his second son, Conrad (age 9), crowned King of the Romans in Vienna, hurried south to subdue Lombardy. He would never again return to Germany. "Italy," he wrote in answer to the Pope's protests, "is my heritage, as all the world well knows."

Frederick, who lived in the Sicilian paradise of art and culture, who owned a *seraglio* of Oriental beauties and a ban-proof bodyguard of Sarasenic troops, who possessed an insatiable intellectual curiosity, who took interest in the natural sciences and philosophy, who openly disdained the papal hegemony and leaned suspiciously towards heresy, became in the eyes of the Church more than a mere strayed and ambitious mortal—he became the Antichrist himself, the personification of the forces of darkness. The papacy may not have had much in the way of its own army, but was able to send for reinforcements from all over Christendom to do battle with the Emperor of Evil. Frederick had Jerusalem, Germany, and Sicily, as well as supporters on the Italian mainland and in other parts of the Continent. In consequence, the rival parties of the pope and the emperor, the Guelphs and the Ghibellines, fought throughout Europe until the death of Frederick, and in Italy, long afterwards.

The imperial arms seemed completely triumphant by 1237, when Frederick crushed the Lombard League at the Battle of Cortenuova. But the accession of Frederick's favourite, if illegitimate son, Enzio, to the throne of Sardinia, through his marriage with Crown Princess Adelasia, gave new cause of offence to the Pope. Though the kingdom of Sardinia was a papal fief, Gregory had not been consulted over the arrangement. He therefore joined the Lombards in 1239, and on Palm Sunday, pronounced the Emperor excommunicated for the fifth time. "Priests are fathers and masters of kings and princes," wrote the Pope, "and to them is given authority over men's bodies as well as over their souls." In return, Frederick issued his own circular against Gregory, demanding that the Church return to the poverty and saintliness of the primitive Christian community, and seized most of the Papal States. In 1241, he prevented the meeting of a general council that was supposed to meet at Easter by arresting the prelates who undertook the journey to Rome in defiance of the imperial ban, and was threatening the Eternal City itself when Gregory died.

While the Empire and the papacy were thus at swords' points, Europe was threatened by a Mongol invasion under Batu Khan, the grandson of the great Genghis Khan. Having crossed the Volga in 1237, Batu now swept across the vast steppes of southern Russia, pillaging so heartlessly that, as one Russian chronicler put it, "No eye remained open to weep for the dead." Pushing forward through Poland into Silesia, the Mongols decimated a German army at Legnica, pouring over the Carpathians into Hungary and chasing King Béla IV from his country; by the end of 1241, they were on the shores of Dalmatia, and nothing seemed able to check their advance. Then, just as all Europe was seized by terror, the storm abated as suddenly as it had arisen. Great Khan Ögödei died in December that year, and being anxious to influence the choice of successor, Batu withdrew his forces back beyond the Urals.

In 1243, Conrad, Frederick's son from his marriage with the heiress of Jerusalem, came of age, at which point the Palestinian barons announced that the regency of his father was at an end. Since King Conrad was an absentee, the barons conferred the regency to the Queen Mother of Cyprus, Alix de Champagne, on the ground that she was Yolande of Brienne's nearest relative—she was 50 years old at the time. The imperialist garrison at Tyre did what it could to resist, but was quickly forced to surrender. Frederick's treaty with the Egyptian Sultan had thereby expired, and on the 11th of July, 1244, the last Ayyubid ruler of Egypt, as-Salih (1240-1249), broke into Jerusalem, utterly sacking the city, his forces swelled by the sudden addition of ten thousand fellow-Mohammedans—Khwarismian Turks, mercenary horsemen from the north, in flight before the new Mongol victories. Aside from a six-month period in 1300, it would be almost seven hundred years before a Christian army was allowed to enter the Holy City again—under Sir Edmund Allenby in 1917.

After the election (1243) of Pope Innocent IV, following a papal vacancy of an unprecedented twenty months, Frederick sought to make peace with the papacy and its allies, offering to evacuate all papal territories and to release all clerical prisoners. Innocent, however, outwitted his opponent by secretly fleeing to France—a move that left him free to convoke, in 1245, the council which the Emperor's forcible measures had prevented from assembling in Rome. Known as the First General Council of Lyons, or the Thirteenth Ecumenical Council, most of its members held a grudge against Frederick for having been arrested and imprisoned by him. It unanimously re-excommunicated and deposed the Emperor, and proclaimed a new crusade against the Saracens and Mongols. Save for St. Louis IX, who had taken the cross already in December of 1244, no one showed any willingness to lead an expedition to the Holy Land.

Among the grounds for charging Frederick with heresy were his treaty with al-Kamil, fraternizing with Saracens, allowing the name of Mohammed to be publicly proclaimed day and night in the Lord's temple, keeping eunuchs over his wives, and giving his daughter in marriage to the Greek Emperor of Nicæa. His foes were given the privileges of crusaders, and those who had taken the cross were allowed to redeem their vows in Sicily. In reply, Frederick addressed a manifesto to the princes of Europe, reminding them of the power-hungry prelates who set themselves up against lawful sovereigns, warning them that his fate could well be theirs. St. Louis' legitimate crusade desperately needed the Emperor's help, and victory awaited Frederick both at home and in the Holy Land at his sudden death, on the 13th of December, 1250.

The Emperor's passing did little to satisfy Innocent IV, whose struggle with Frederick had drawn the attention away from how he abused his papal privileges, promoting nepotism within the Holy See and seeking personal wealth at the expense of the church coffers. The Supreme Pontiff announced his determination to bring about the downfall of the House of the Hohenstaufen, denouncing its surviving members as the "generation of vipers" and the "venomous brood of a dragon of poisonous race." When Conrad IV ascended his father's throne, the Lombard communes ranged themselves on opposing sides in the fight between the papacy and the Hohenstaufen. The showdown was disastrous; Italy was desolated, papal taxation snowballed, and with it the chorus of complaint.

While abuses continued to accelerate, Innocent preached his crusade against Conrad as St. Louis did his against the Saracens, thus undermining the Pope's ability to muster the necessary force to oust the Hohenstaufen. In 1252, Innocent offered the crown of the Two Sicilies to Richard of Cornwall, brother of King Henry III, who turned it down on the grounds that actually seizing control in Sicily was impossible. Henry himself was later enlisted for this task, being promised the Sicilian crown for his son, Edmund of Lancaster, and the commutation of his crusader's vow to a papally-ordained holy war in Italy. However, the King was obliged to assume responsibility for the enormous papal debt, causing a great uproar in England and ensuring that he would never fulfill his promise.

Conrad was excommunicated in 1254, but died of fever before the war could even begin. Frederick's second illegitimate son, Manfred, became regent for his nephew, Conradin of Swabia. Instead of going after Innocent, he restored the kingdom of Sicily to the papacy, retaining only the principality of Taranto in fief from the pope. But when Innocent decided to annex his lands, Manfred rebelled, and just as the papal army had been routed in Foggia, the Pope passed away in his residence at Naples. The cardinals understandably wanted to set distance between themselves and the victorious Prince, but the podestà of Naples locked them up, and informed them that they would stay locked up until they gave the Church a new pastor.

Alexander IV (1254-1261) re-excommunicated Manfred, who had now assumed leadership of the anti-papal forces throughout Italy, and rejected the peace overtures made by him. Yet the Pontiff was wholly unable to advance against Frederick's son, who maintained himself in Sicily down to Alexander's death. It appeared as if Manfred, himself practically an Italian, was about to unite all of Italy into a single anti-papal monarchy. He reconquered Sicily and southern Italy, and in 1258, had himself crowned king at Palermo. The feud between the Guelphs and the Ghibellines escalated. The Ghibellines of Florence, having been banished from their city after Frederick's death, returned (1260) after defeating the Guelphs at the blood-soaked Battle of Montaperti—the "Hill of Death." The Ghibelline della Scala (Scaligeri) family became lords of Verona, while the Guelph della Torres assumed control in Milan.

Urban IV (1261-1264) was a Frenchman, and offered the crown of Sicily to St. Louis, undeniably the most virtuous ruler in the West, but the King nominated in his stead his brother, Charles of Anjou, a man of quite different character. He was not only ready, but eager, to take over Sicily, with a good amount of papal help, of course. Manfred held his own for several years, but on the 26th of February, 1266, Charles defeated him in a decisive battle near Benevento. The Angevin cavalry, aided by traitors among the Swabian troops, utterly destroyed the Hohenstaufen army, causing the German régime to collapse within a few days. Manfred himself had perished on the battlefield, and his wife, Queen Elena, was arrested in Trani and died a prisoner in a Perugian castle six years later. Her children, separated from their mother, were swallowed by the Angevin prisons. But one last "viper" still remained: the young Conradin, grandson of Frederick II.

Although Conradin's title to the imperial crown was contested from the very beginning, when he came down (1267) from Germany with an army to assert his rights, several Italian cities rallied to his support. In fact, he was received by popular enthusiasm even in Rome, but was no match for the military expertise of Charles of Anjou. Defeated on the 23rd of August, 1268, at Tagliacozzo, "Conrad V" fled to the castle of the Frangipani, who sold him to Charles, was charged with high treason, and given a mock trial. His Bolognese lawyer made a strong plea that the youthful prince had come to Italy not as a robber, but to claim his inheritance. Most of the judges were against the death penalty, but Charles knew no mercy, and it was on his orders that Conradin was beheaded, on the 29th of October, at the town square of Naples, the new capital of southern Italy.

The male line of the Hohenstaufen died with Conradin, and from this time on, the emperors ceased to be a major power in Italy. Lombardy remained officially part of the Holy Roman Empire, but in practice, the cities in the richest, most densely populated, and most urbanized part of Europe, became independent states that owed only nominal allegiance to the German emperors north of the Alps. After the Hohenstaufen, Germany entered upon a so-called interregnum, a twenty-year period of anarchy and internal strife. During the dismal times that followed, Frederick II was remembered with nostalgia, and for about a century after his death, the belief persisted that he was still alive. According to a famous legend, Frederick rests with his knights in a deathless sleep in the caves of the Kyffhäuser Mountains in Thuringia, awaiting the ripe time to return and purge the land of quarrel and iniquity. (Not until the 19th century was this legend reinterpreted to refer to Frederick I.)

The extirpation of the Hohenstaufen by the might of the papacy secured the first place in the West for France, and resulted in the passing of the crown of the Two Sicilies to the Angevin dynasty. For centuries, the House of Anjou, with Naples as its capital, was destined to be a disturbing element in the affairs of not only Italy, but all Europe. It represented a new alliance in the history of the papacy, like their ancestors, the Normans, had in the age of Hildebrand. As supporter and ward of the papacy, Charles of Anjou forever transformed the Two Sicilies. He brutally suppressed the Ghibelline nobles, seizing their estates to pay the French mercenaries. He destroyed the last of the Muslim enclaves, the Islamic Republic of Lucera established by Frederick II in Apulia, and generally replaced German lords with French ones.

The Angevin rule, which introduced feudalism to southern Italy at a time when it was weakening everywhere else, proved highly unpopular. The whole region continued to remain largely agrarian, knowing nothing of the rapid urbanization and economic expansion of the north. The population consisted mainly of impoverished peasants, overtaxed by their French masters while eking out their livelihood on mostly poor-quality land, ruled over by barons who were generally a law unto themselves. Urban and prosperous middle classes were imperative for the development of the artistic and intellectual currents associated with the Italian Renaissance, and these were conspicuous by absence in the south. The deep socio-economic gulf between northern and southern Italy, which continued well into the 20th century, can thus be traced back to the 13th.

In the ferocious duel which was dubbed by the great German historian, Gregorovius, as "the grandest spectacle of the ages," the Holy Roman Empire had been humbled to the dust. On the fall of the Hohenstaufen, even the German Kingdom had become like the Empire, a phantom. The Hohenstaufen duchy of Swabia disintegrated as a political unit, as various sections were acquired by families which were to play important roles in the kingdom's future: Zähringen, Hohenzollern, and Habsburg. In all, Germany was split up into over 270 virtually independent states, and after the Interregnum of 1254-1273 was over, the power of the princes was so firmly entrenched, that the continued existence of a strong central government became impossible.

Finally, the electors raised to the throne with Count Rudolph IV of Habsburg the same house which would sit on the throne of Austria-Hungary till the dissolution of the dual monarchy. Beginning with Emperor Rudolph I, various German kings laid claim to the imperial title, and in several instances, their claims were recognized by the papacy. However, inasmuch as the Empire constituted a loose confederation of autonomous states and principalities, imperial authority was nominal. The Holy Roman Emperors, thought still accorded a formal and ceremonial precedence in the courts of Europe, never more had real importance in Western political and religious developments.

CHAPTER 24

The East had shown the crusaders a civilization superior in many ways to that of Western Europe. They came across large cities, magnificent buildings, highly advanced arts and crafts, medical skills, and scientific knowledge. Yet in the Levant, the Latins were far removed from the great cities of Islam[174], there were few intellectuals among them. To the Mohammedans, the knights and barons of the West were not merely infidels, but barbarians. The sophisticated urban culture of Muslim Sicily, on the other hand, instructed its Christian conquerors, who readily adapted to the superior Islamic culture, drawing knowledge from the fields of architecture, agriculture, medicine, chemistry, geography, astronomy, and mathematics. The Sicilian court of Emperor Frederick II was a centre for learned men such as the astronomer and translator Michael Scot, the physician and alchemist Arnold de Villanova, the mathematician Leonardo Fibonacci[175], and St. Thomas Aquinas.

In the early Middle Ages, Plato and Aristotle were only the revered names of two great ancient philosophers. Knowledge of Greek had gradually fallen into disrepair in Western Europe, and the works of the Greek thinkers were not available for centuries. When the remnants of Classical culture eventually reached the West, it was in translations from Arabic. This was possible only in the fringes of Christendom, where many were proficient, in addition to the local vernaculars, in Arabic, Greek, and Latin alike. Toledo in Spain was the initial port of entry into Western Europe of all the classics the Arabs had gathered from Greece, from the Middle East, and from Asia. Another translating centre was Sicily, and many, including Frederick II, greatly favoured this import which strongly promoted the freedom of thought. The Church considered it dubious, at first, and tried to put a stop to it; soon it,

---

[174] Consequently, the Crusades were also more a nuisance than a serious menace to the Islamic world, and indeed, Muslim chroniclers devote relatively little attention to them.

[175] Also known as Leonardo of Pisa. Discovered the Fibonacci sequence (1, 1, 2, 3, 5, 8, 13, 21, 34, 55, 89, 144 . . .).

however, became clear that she had to take on the challenge, and this brought about one of her greatest triumphs.

The Dominicans were the first order instituted by the Church with an academic mission. From 1220 on, the Friars Preachers laid down as a fundamental principle, that no house of their Order could be founded without a doctor. The Dominican houses were grouped into provinces, and in each province, the goal was to provide a school of higher learning. At the apex of the intellectual organization were the *Studia Generalia*, presided over by a Regent of Studies, who lectured on Holy Writ, and whom two Bachelors assisted, one to lecture on the Scriptural Glosses, the other on the *Sentences* of Peter Lombard. By 1248, there were five such *studia*, one in each of the five great university cities of Paris, Bologna, Oxford, Montpellier, and Cologne. Lectureships were later created for the Liberal Arts, moral and natural philosophy, and, with mission work in view, foreign languages. The Dominican friar was a student for life—whoever entered the Order entered a university.

Born amid the Albigensian heresy and founded especially for the defence of the One True Faith, the Dominicans directed their literary efforts towards reaching every class of dissenter from the Holy Mother Church. Their most powerful works were produced precisely in the sphere of apologetics. The *Summa contra Catharos et Valdenses* (c. 1225) of Moneta—whose intense devotion to study caused him to lose his eyesight in the latter days of his life—was the most complete and widely read work of the Middle Ages against the Cathars (and the Waldenses). The inquisitor-brothers finished the job, and by the middle of the 14th century, the Albigensian heresy had been completely wiped out—Guillaume Bélibaste, the last of the Cathar parfaits, was captured and burned at the stake in Villerouge-Termenès in 1321.

The charges brought against these heretics were astonishingly similar to those brought against "witches" in the following centuries. Renouncing earthly pleasures, an integral part of the Cathar doctrine, resulted in many fantastic claims of secret orgies and debauchery. Behind this strange accusation lay a devious logic: grotesque desecration of the body was assumed to be the most effective means to fight carnality. The principal misdeeds the Cathars were charged with were devil worship, conspiracy against Christendom, sexual dissoluteness and perversion, and the eating and sacrificing of babies—the heretics who eschewed procreation were suspected of performing abortions.

All these accusations were later intrinsic in creating the image of the witch.

The Dominican Order had set as one of its goals the conversion of Jews to Catholicism. This goal, backed up by the power of the Inquisition, led to a new wave of persecution. The traditional Catholic view that Jews were condemned to wander, stateless and despised, as witness to the triumph of Christianity, was furthered by the Angelic Doctor, St. Thomas Aquinas (1225-1274), who, in his instruction *De Regimine Judæorum*, expounded that: "Jews, in consequence of their sins, are destined to perpetual slavery." In Germany and Austria, Jews were made easily distinguishable in the latter half of the 13th century by the compulsory wearing of a "horned hat," otherwise known as the *Judenhut*, an article of clothing that Jews had worn freely before the Crusades. Unwelcome in the West, the Jews of the German-speaking areas began their migration to East Central Europe, where the Kings of Poland were eager to introduce a more sophisticated population to develop their backward country and to strengthen its crown.

For the centuries of the growth of Christendom, the philosophical background of the West was Augustinian and hence Neoplatonic.[176] However, between the middle of the 12th and the middle of the 13th century, virtually the entire works of Aristotle were translated from Arabic into Latin. The Franciscans, like Bonaventura (1221-1274), worked to fit this third-hand Aristotelianism through their own interpretations into the traditional Augustinian moulds. The Dominicans, like Albertus Magnus (1206-1280) and his student, Thomas Aquinas, adhered more strictly to Aristotle's own doctrine, which they succeeded in reconciling with the dogmas of the Church. The aristocratic philosophy of these two saints was of immense value to all the subsequent development. Albertus compiled on the model of Aristotle a vast scientific encyclopædia which had a great influence on the last centuries of the Middle Ages, earning him the title of Universal Doctor. Thomas, on the other hand, erected a metaphysical system that has influenced most of the great thinkers and which the Catholic theoriticians still consider the basis of their thought. By and large, Scholasticism placed its emphasis on deductive Aristotelian logic, and sought to erase the contradictions between reason and Christianity.

---

[176] Since this substrate proved an equally enduring aspect of the Protestant tradition, there is more diffence in doctrine between Western and Eastern Christianity than between Catholicism and Protestantism.

Aspiring to create a great synthesis between the Catholic faith and knowledge, St. Thomas built on Aristotle's thoughts to such an extent that this Greek philosopher rose in the High Middle Ages almost to the status of a Church Father. What had made Aristotle so attractive to the Muslim philosophers of 9th-century Baghdad in the first place was that the Byzantines had already subtly transformed the originals in order to make the metaphysical speculation appear like a "natural theology" of sorts. Similarly, the corpus of Aristotelian thought that revitalized Western Christian learning in the 13th century owed as much to Alfarabius[177] and Avempace[178] as it did to Aristotle. Just like the pagan philosophers of the Classical past, many Muslim scholars were eventually detached from their Islamic roots and grafted onto the same non-denominational tree of learning. While Mohammed suffers torture in Dante's Inferno, Avicenna[179] and Averroës are permitted to spend all eternity in Limbo discussing philosophy with the scholars of antiquity.

Thomas of Aquinas set forth five "proofs" of God's existence. Of these, the arguments of the "Unmoved Mover" and the "Uncaused First Cause" were also reflected in the mediæval conception of the world. The first proof, originating from Aristotle, states that everything is moved by something, and thus somewhere there is something which does not move itself, but which moves all the other objects. This is associated with the mediæval misconception about the nature of motion, according to which movement is only possibly through physical contact. It was commonly believed that movement would stop if some mover did not ceaselessly compel, for example, a flying arrow to move. Having thus arrived at the concept of the First Mover, Thomas audaciously declared that his must, perforce, be God. According to his second proof, nothing can be cause to itself, which is why there had to be a First Cause, "to which everyone gives the name of God."

Aristotle's philosophical method, according to which one must start with the obvious facts and proceed from one inevitable conclusion to another, was very well suited to the Scholastic acceptance of revealed truths and to the Scholastic way of thinking in general. However, an even greater impediment to the advancement of science than the deductive reasoning utilized by the

---

[177] i.e. al-Farabi

[178] i.e. Ibn Bajja

[179] i.e. Ibn Sina

mediæval scholars was their great regard for authorities. Looking upon established written word as authority, even against common sense, was rooted in the way a believer accepted the Bible as the Word of God. Such bounteous readiness to accept miracles was not apt to promote the slow and patient observation of nature, where miracles do not occur.

Indeed, people sought to discover the properties of nature mainly by the means of Scripture and their own logical thinking. It was believed that there existed knowledge that could be ascertained purely through intuition. Of course, observations were talked about as well, but the deductions made from them were not considered as reliable. The experiments made by the Greek and Arab authorities were rarely questioned, and their repetition was not deemed necessary. When the authorities appeared to disagree, the Scholastics did not accept one and reject the other, but instead developed a technique to reconcile the apparent contradictions and explain away the disagreement. Observations and experiments were truly not commonplace in mediæval Europe. The questions that occupied the minds of men were of the following kind: Does God have a free will or not? Has He created evil? Did all the Apostles except John have wives? Is it better to sin openly than in secret? Is the Lord one?

Nevertheless, the greatest obstacle to experimental science was formed by the prohibitions that held back the study of the human anatomy. The Church, holding firm to its doctrine of bodily resurrection, could not permit the dissection of a corpse, for some day this corpse would have to appear before its Maker. With the medical science in such disrepute among Christians, much of the leadership in that field was provided by Jewish and Muslim scholars. The eclectic Normans of southern Italy, who patronized Arab scholarship, created the first medical school in the West at Salerno; the Jewry of France was largely responsible for founding the medical school at Montpellier. And, in spite of all, an activity that could only be described as body-snatching flourished, and Emperor Frederick II exhibited true scientific spirit by granting, from time to time, permissions to dissect human bodies; by further using the Classical and Arabic literature of the trade as guidance, an extensive foundation was cast on which later experimental science could build.

The deductive method of reasoning was unwilling to recognize that it was necessary every now and then to verify the validity of the train of thought by comparing the obtained results with what a scientist calls "facts." The movement of the planets was the movement of the vault of heaven because Aristotle had said so, and if this was in conflict with Ptolemy, then so much worse for Ptolemy. Observation was secondary and the human intellect supreme. Thus the most significant scientific accomplishments of the Middle Ages are found precisely in the field of deductive mathematics, where some of the aforementioned handicaps were a much lesser hindrance than in the field of empirical science.

Without the mediæval strides in mathematics, modern science could not exist. The mediæval mathematicians of Europe borrowed their knowledge from the Mohammedans, who unlike the Romans, had found use for mathematics and astronomy. Via Persia, the Arabs gained contact with India, where mathematics had been en vogue for a long time, and from where they acquired a new number system. This system, preserved for posterity as Arabic numerals, contained an element unknown to the Romans, i.e. the zero, and its adoption by Europeans five centuries later was the most important achievement of mediæval mathematicians. In case this does not seem too remarkable, try and divide for example the number MCCLXXXVII with the number XCIX—using only Roman numerals, of course.

Themselves skilled in mathematics, the Arabs preserved what the Greeks had accomplished in geometry, and themselves created a new branch of mathematics, *algebra*. The words *zero* and *cipher* are also of Arabic origin; as are *zenith*, *nadir*, *azimuth*, *algorithm*, *almanac*, and at least a dozen others in mathematics and astronomy; the principal work of Ptolemy is still known by its Arabic title, *Almagest*. Amazingly, this did little to improve the relationship between Christianity and Islam: the Europeans translated only those works which seemed to answer their needs, and purposely ignored theology, jurisprudence, history, geography, and fiction; thus, Algazel[180], for example, was known in mediæval Europe only as a commentator on Greek philosophy, while the Muslims still know him as the "Proof of Islam," whose great achievement was the reconciliation of Sufi mysticism with orthodox Mohammedism.

In the 13th century, trade with the East also introduced the magnifying glass, the magnetic compass, and the gunpowder—all necessary prerequisites to Europe's geographical and scientific achievements. The introduction of

---

[180] i.e. al-Ghazali

paper had a revolutionary effect on the accessibility of ideas, which had previously been limited to a small, vocal minority of ecclesiastics. Arab treatises on science and philosophy, and Arabic version of Greek thinkers, were rendered into Latin and circulated in the burgeoning schools of the West. For five hundred years or more, books translated from the Arabic language were pretty much the only source of learning and teaching in the Western universities. But since translations were almost invariably the work of hired translators rather than of the scholars themselves[181], an Arab professor would have been unable to converse with Europe's foremost experts on Arabic philosophy even if he could have made his way to Paris or Bologna unmolested.

In the 13th century, students began to pour into the cathedral schools of Europe, attracted by the reputation and erudition of famous schoolmasters such as Abélard or Peter Lombard. Often, though not always, their objective was to enter the holy orders, but before doing that, they wanted to familiarize themselves with rhetoric and philosophy under the guidance of the best lecturers of their time. The male offspring of the well-to-do classes therefore shaved their heads, and grasping a hand-copied Latin grammar, rushed every morning to the hallowed halls of learning. There they sat on the floor upon straw, committing the rules of language to memory while getting acquainted with the thoughts of Aristotle and the Church Fathers.

The best schools soon had so many students that the teachers had to move outside the cathedral walls. Lectures were delivered even in the streets, for actual university buildings did not exist before the 14th century. At the same time, teachers formed associations for the purpose of regulating who may practise the profession; these were usually created to counterbalance the influential unions of students, also known as "nations." This was in imitation of the guild system—the Latin word *universitas* itself signifies a guild—which utilized a gradation of three degrees: an apprentice, fellow, and master; one acquired the master's degree by producing a flawless work sample, e.g. in case of the cobbler's fellow, a perfect pair of shoes.

The same three degrees were also instituted in the universities: *matriculation*, or admission, entitled one to study in the faculty of Liberal Arts,

---

[181] In fact, when the original Greek texts became available in the West during the Renaissance, many Latins continued to prefer the translations from Arabic with which they were already familiar.

also called the philosophical faculty, where the *trivium* of grammar, logic, and rhetoric were taught. Successful completion of this programme awarded one the degree of *baccalaureate*, or Bachelor of Arts. From here, one proceeded to the *quadrivium* of arithmetic, geometry, astronomy, and music. Study of these subjects made one eligible for the degree of Master of Arts, which gave one the license to teach, *licentia docendi* in Latin. One was then admitted to the guild of teachers, and could rent a room and advertise for students, who would provide for one's upkeep. Rich benefactors might establish for the poorer scholars *collegia*, where they would receive free meals and lodging.

The boy who entered a university was the age of 14 or 15, and his work description included—in addition to the wearisome attendance of lectures and the evening's study by candlelight—boozing, brawling, and whoring. The sovereigns, however, granted the newly-founded universities great privileges, including the right to pass independent judgement on their students, who therefore needed not to worry about the consequences of their lesser sins.

Many Masters of Arts, in addition to teaching, went on to study in one of the three higher faculties, the division of which remains the same to this day: theology, law, and medicine. In mediæval thinking, theology was truly the "queen of sciences," and for centuries, philosophy was seen only as the "handmaiden of theology." There were two branches of legal study, civil law and canon law, and one might acquire a degree in either, or graduate as a *juris utriusque doctor* (J.U.D.), Doctor of Both Laws. Few actually became doctors, since for example in the University of Paris, a Doctor of Theology was required, in addition to his extensive studies, to be at least 35 years of age. Originally, the words "master" and "doctor" were synonymous.[182]

The principal tool of a student was his books. Their number was rising rapidly during the 13th century, despite the fact that every single word had to be copied by hand. Therefore, they were also priceless treasures, even if they were bound only in simple wooden covers. An assiduous student could build an entire library by borrowing and copying. This was not easy, however, since to copy a Bible, for instance, would take approximately 15 months. Loan periods this long were naturally a constant cause of quarrel. John of Salisbury, for example, refers to the person who borrowed a book of his as "that thief at Canterbury" who "got hold of the *Policraticus* and would not let it go until he

---

[182] The word *doctor* is simply Latin for "teacher."

had made a copy." Copying was not free of charge either: in England, one had to pay a penny to five pence *per pecia*, meaning 16 columns, with 62 rows each, each row having 32 letters (i.e. 31,744 letters in all); to make a comparison, a chicken cost a half-penny and a sheep 17 pence, whereas an anvil would set you back a staggering 20 shillings, that is, 240 pence.

Cultural evolution, the most important aspect of which is Lamarckism, or the passing of assimilated knowledge from one generation to the next, became in the 13th century a systematic, and therefore very effective, means of indoctrination—a master knew he could hand his know-how over to his apprentice. For the first time in Western society, a systematic and progressive educational institute had been formed that was under public supervision. This supervision was not conducted by some government agency, but by the Catholic Church with its numerous educational and administrative organs, run by its exceptionally well organized clergy. The places of high-born men and women in government were gradually taken over by a host of trained and specialized civil servants, who held to their position because of their knowledge and skills, not because of their noble ancestry.

In the early Middle Ages, young ladies had received their education at the household of some or other noblewoman. By the time of the Renaissance, this custom had been abandoned. Boys and girls alike were taught by a highly-educated, humanist tutor. This tutor was male, since women were denied entrance to universities, and thus could not receive higher education.[183]

From the 13th century onwards, the West was afflicted with a phenomenon known as the *Frauenfrage*, or the "Women Question." This simply meant that whereas there had previously been less women than men, there were now more. The advances in agricultural technology had raised the standard of living to a point where the killing of female infants could be discontinued, while the warfare that raged throughout the Middle Ages kept taking its toll on the male population and thousands and thousands of men entered the clergy. The vocation of women was not taken seriously, women were, after all, fickle creatures incapable of standing firm behind any conviction. The Church could not be persuaded in this matter even by the everyday examples of female heretics, who were ready to suffer torture, humiliation, and death for their

---

[183] Oxford would not admit women until 1920; the first British woman to acquire a degree studied in Islamic Turkey.

beliefs. The religious houses of women were considerably fewer than those of men. The great double monasteries of the preceding centuries had been replaced by male monasteries with nunneries as annexes, where the nuns served the monks by copying manuscripts.

Before the 13th century, most of the learned clerics were monastics, but by the time the cathedral schools had grown and been formalized into universities, most were secular clergy or belonged to one of the two new mendicant orders, the Franciscans or the Dominicans. The intellectual energies of the Schoolmen were dissipated in endless and complex debates on such subjects as the gender of angels. No one was permitted to go beyond the limits laid down by dogma, and those who attempted to do so exposed themselves to dire reprisals. Thomas Aquinas and Bonaventura were in their life time recognized and celebrated figures; their contemporary, Roger Bacon, was thrown in prison for fourteen years because of his opinions.

Bacon was born around 1210 in Somerset, the English county most often associated with the Arthurian legends. He studied at Oxford under Robert Grosseteste (1175-1253), the man responsible for turning the University into an important seat of learning. It was established by Jewish teachers who had been driven out of Spain by the Reconquista and had reached England together with William of Normandy.[184] Like Aquinas, Grosseteste attempted to integrate Greek natural philosophy with Catholic dogma, but in direct contradistinction to the Saint, the future Bishop of Lincoln suggested that when faced with an apparent conflict between observation and dogma, one should go with observation.

Bacon's passions included the natural sciences, mathematics, and criticizing his contemporaries. He exhorted men to learn Arabic and Greek as well as Latin; he demanded that Aristotle and the New Testament be read in the original, and not in the worthless translations that were fraught with errors due to carelessness and stupidity, not to mention the doctoring of the text particularly by the Dominicans. Of mathematics he said, that "one who is ignorant of it cannot know the other sciences." According him, "sciences cannot be learned through logical and sophistic argumentation, as is commonly believed, but only through mathematical proofs which lead to truth."

---

[184] The continuous intercourse between the Norman states of England and Sicily had likewise been instrumental in bringing many elements of Muslim learning to Britain.

Through his own observations and from the Arabic and Greek writings he spent most of his money on, Bacon had acquired encyclopædic erudition in the fields of mathematics, mechanics, optics, and chemical sciences, and on these bases, sought to build a system of empirical philosophy. Upon realizing that it was far superior to the verbiage of the contemporary philosophers and theologians, Bacon, a direct and outspoken man, set it against Scholasticism, which at the time was at the height of its authority. He entered the Franciscan Order in 1250, teaching at Oxford until 1257. By that time, he had caused sufficient amount of grudge and suspicion to be stripped of the right to public lecturing and the writing of books.

The later canonized, retrogressive and dogmatical Fransciscan General Bonaventura, placed Bacon, then thirty-three years old and of great repute at Oxford, under supervision, and sent him to a monastery of his body in Paris. He remained there ten years in "close confinement," deprived of all books on science, all instruments, and even pen and parchment. A lawyer and statesman by the name of Guy de Foulques took interest in Bacon's work, but the distinguished cardinal was for years unable to get into communication with him. When this gentleman became the highly-political Pope Clement IV in 1265, he finally ordered the Friar, against the injunction of the Franciscan Order, to write down his controversial thoughts "without delay, and with all possible secrecy." In fifteen months, Bacon produced three works extending to some six hundred folio pages of print—the *Opus Majus*, *Opus Minus*, and *Opus Tertium*—thanks to which he is to this day remembered by historians, though hardly by anyone else.

When Bacon proclaimed his belief in the experimental method, he was a voice crying in the wilderness of the Middle Ages. He proposed educational reforms based on the value of observation and measurement of nature, recommending that the study of languages, mathematics, and experimental science should replace the then-prevalent university curriculum. "Of the three means in which men think they can acquire knowledge of things: authority, reasoning, and experience, only the last is effective and able to bring peace to the intellect." The *Opus Tertium* further enjoins that: ". . .all the noble deductions of science should be tested with experiments. . . Fools busy themselves argumenting theorems from Aristotle's *De Meteoris* or *Optics*, but all in vain. For in this cases cannot be proved by arguments but by experiments only. And this is why I place experimental foundation around these things, what none of the Latins can understand, save for one, namely Master Peter."

Bacon's greatly-admired "Master Peter" was Peter of Maricourt, a/k/a Petrus de Maharncuria, a/k/a Petrus Peregrinus, under which names he also appears. According to Bacon, Peter the Pilgrim was the most skilful mathematician of his time, but neither acclaim nor riches could persuade him to publish the fruit of his work. He came from Picardy and wrote a work on magnets called *Epistola de Magnete*; or, more correctly, it was a long letter addressed to a soldier called Sygerus of Foucaucourt. This appears to have taken place in 1269, when Peter served as a military engineer of sorts in Charles of Anjou's army as the new King of Sicily was laying siege to the Muslim enclave of Lucera in southern Italy.

In his communication, Peter describes how one can discern the north and south poles from a magnet cut in circular shape. He also knew that cutting a magnet in half produces two new magnets, and that the like poles repel while the opposite poles attract each other, but erroneously imagined that the magnet somehow derives its properties from the celestial poles. And that is all we know about Pierre de Maricourt. The man about whom Bacon said "while others struggle with blinking eyes to see the light of the Sun like bats in the dark, he beholds it in all its glory, for he is the master of experiments," did not really fascinate his age.

The Scholastic belief in the omnipotence of intellect bears witness to an inflated hubris. The outlook of the Schoolmen not only belittled the importance of actual knowledge, but glorified idle theological speculation, while disparaging the perseverance of scientists such as Magister Petrus, who showed at least some intellectual integrity. The forgotten Picard can be seen as a symbol for that vehement opposition which knowledge has had to withstand before breaking through the armour of belief and superstition.

And a symbol was Roger Bacon himself, for although his spirit was modern, he was nevertheless born at the wrong time. He wrote of lenses and mirrors, of geography and rainbows, of gunpowder and Greek fire; he investigated the power of steam, and seems to very nearly have reached some of the principal tenets of modern chemistry; he outlines the principles of the telescope, the inventor of which he could after a manner be considered. He asserted that the propagation of light was not a flow like water, but a kind of pulse as in sound—noting also that light travelled much faster than sound, for if someone at a distance were to bang a hammer, the blow would be seen by us before we heard the sound.

The scientific prophecies made by Bacon were just as astonishing as his discoveries, for he foresaw the invention of the submarine, the motor car, and the aeroplane. But even he did not question religion; on the contrary, his skepticism elevated it infinitely above knowledge, thus creating the basis for the idealization of faith, which was subsequently named *fideism*. It should also be remarked that his stated motives for advocating reform of the Julian Calendar were religious: he complained bitterly in the *Opus Majus* that, owing to calendar defects, Christians fasted a week after the true Easter, and ate meat for a week at Lent.

In the *Opus Tertium*, Bacon thunders that the teachers of Paris have four fatal flaws: "Boundless and childlike vanity, unspeakable dishonesty, profound redundancy, and the ability to disregard all that is praiseworthy." Bacon may have been ahead of his age, but he verily did not know how to win friends or influence people. Clement IV died in 1268, and the same year, Bacon was allowed to return to Oxford. In 1272, he published the *Compendium Studii Philosophiæ*, in which he harshly criticized the scholarly methods of his contemporaries. Accusations of unorthodox teaching led to his imprisonment at the behest of the higher authorities in the Franciscan Order; he was only released after reaching the age of eighty. In 1292, he published his last work, the *Compendium Studii Theologiæ*, which directed the sharp end of his pen towards the theological methods of the Schoolmen. By then, however, his name was so obscure that this unpublished and unfinished essay, much like his death later that same year, went unnoticed by all.

In spite of everything, Bacon's revolutionary notion, that theses should be defended with something besides personal opinions and biblical quotations, was left to smoulder. He is not considered the grave-digger of the Middle Ages and the usher of the Modern Era for nothing. By the end of the 14th century, the "Doctor Mirabilis" had been proclaimed the foremost natural philosopher of his day, and in the 15th, his *alma mater* recognized him as "one of those Oxonians who had kept the brightness of Oxford's fame untarnished." However, when the Renaissance finally came, it did not start at Bologna or in any other Italian university, but at the secular courts of the age. The universities produced no Leonardo and encouraged neither philosophical nor scientific innovation.

CHAPTER 25

The Latin stronghold of Saint-Jean d'Acre, from the time of its capture by the Third Crusade to its final conquest by the Saracens, formed for a hundred years the base of the crusading movement in Palestine. With a population of about 40,000, it was easily the largest city in the Latin Kingdom. Acre's strategic location on the highway along the Mediterranean coast, its communications with Damascus to the northeast and the plain of Megiddo to the south, coupled with the awesome military strength of the rocky promontory on which it stood, lent it exceptional political and commercial importance.

Although Zengi, Nur ad-Din, and Saladin had steadily driven the Latins back to the coasts, reversing almost all the gains of the First Crusade, the West had retained naval control of the Mediterranean and its islands. With the fall of Constantinople in 1204, its influence had spread into the Ægean and the Black Sea, whereas the acquisition of Cyprus in 1191 had provided a useful base from which to threaten Egypt and Syria. Through generous distribution of lands and privileges, Guy de Lusignan succeeded in attracting not a few colonists to his island, while his successors established a government modelled on that of the Kingdom of Jerusalem. Commercial activity became a distinctive characteristic of the Cypriot cities, with the small fishing village of Famagusta developing into one of the busiest ports in the Mediterranean.

A curious assortment of soldiers, clerics, and merchants had taken also residence within the walls of Acre. Each of the great military orders had their fortified tower in the city and shared in the defence of its massive fortifications. From their palaces at Acre, the Grand Masters of the Templars, the Hospitallers, and the Teutonic Knights commanded all the members of their orders throughout Christendom. Every mendicant order also had its house and its church. The Venetians, the Genoese, and the Pisans each had their own merchant quarter near the harbour. Capable of sending for supplies from Cyprus and reinforcements from the West, Acre was the last real foothold of the Latins in the Holy Land.

As the power of the Latin princes was falling rapidly, they were selling their estates and returning to Europe. The commercial rivalry between the Italian cities of Venice, Genoa, and Pisa led to bloody struggles in all the towns still occupied by the Latins in Palestine. In the War of St. Sabas (1256-1269), Genoa allied with the Hospitallers, while Venice and Pisa were aided by the Templars. Despite the papal intervention of 1258, the war raged on, further weakening the remnants of the Latin Kingdom. The Venetians drove the Genoese from Acre and treated the city as conquered territory; in a battle where Christian fought Christian, and the Hospitallers were pitted against the Templars, twenty thousand perished.

In retaliation, the Genoese allied themselves with the Nicæan Emperor, Michael VIII Palæologus, whose general, Alexius Strategopulus, now managed to drive the Latins out of Constantinople, thus overthrowing the Latin Emperor, Baldwin II. Escorted by choirs, soldiers, and priests, the Greek Emperor made his triumphal entry into the imperial city on the 15th of August, 1261; the Latin Empire of Constantinople had ceased to exist, having contributed nothing to the cause of the Crusades, nor having effected the reunion of the Churches. In fact, the Latins had succeeded in losing most of what the Comneni dynasty had gained, making the vast expansion of Venetian power in the eastern Mediterranean the only lasting legacy of the Fourth Crusade. The Genoese, on the other hand, were brought extensive privileges by the Greek recapture of Constantinople. Venice was now faced with a struggle to defend its commercial interests against the favoured Genoa, which began its expansion into the Black Sea area. For the rest of the century, and almost whole of the next, the defeat of Genoa was the primary goal of the Venetians.

The new Emperor had perhaps thought Constantinople would be restored to the centre of the cosmos, but the truth was that the crusaders had wrecked and plundered the city, and the Emperor's return to great power politics was all but suicidal. The commercial concessions granted to his Genoese allies reduced the Empire's revenue and made the gifts of land used to pay frontier forces unaffordable, so he was forced to abolish such holdings in Asia, and thus to weaken his defences. A Venetian ship had rescued Baldwin, the ousted Latin Emperor, who returned to Italy and spent the remainder of his life hatching unsuccessful schemes to recover Constantinople. He first convinced the Pope to preach a crusade for the recovery of Constantinople, but in the end, tranferred his claims on the throne to Charles of Anjou. To repel any attacks by the Latins, Michael Palæologus restored the fortifications of Constantinople, and to prevent the crusade, promised the Pope to work for the reunion of the Churches.

Meanwhile, the power in Egypt had been seized by the Mameluks, the Sultan's bodyguard of Kipchak Turks from the Russian steppes, who also made up the officers of his army. The Arabic word *Mamlûk* means "owned," and the founders of the Mameluk Empire were slaves who had been bought from the market in their youth and given religious and military education. Saladin, the great opponent of the Crusader States in the 12th century, was celebrated for his sense of honour, his generosity, and his distaste for bloodshed by his fellow-Muslims and his Christian adversaries alike. His 13th-century successor, Baybars the Arbelester, was his exact opposite. Bought into the Sultan's service at the age of 14, Baybars established the military school as a model of religious fanaticism with a bloodthirst equal to that of the Christian forces themselves. It was he who had had led the Battle of Gaza (1244), seriously reducing the ranks of both the Templars and the Hospitallers, and he who had finished off the Crusade of St. Louis in 1250. Through intrigue and assassinations, he rose from a slave to a sultan, and acquired an empire that stretched from Egypt to Palestine and Syria. The first target of the Mameluks was not, however, the Crusader States, but a more immediate threat to their rule, namely, the Mongol Horde.

The 13th century was the age of Mongol conquests, the last and most frightful of all the nomadic onslaughts on civilization. Having already rolled over a vast swathe of the globe from Korea to Germany, this gigantic tidal wave of destruction seemed about to engulf Islam completely. Descending on the Middle East from China, a vast Tartar army, in composition more Turkish than Mongol, swept across the land laying waste to everything it encountered. Hülegü Khan was bitterly hostile to Islam, but greatly influenced by his Tibetan Buddhist and Nestorian Christian entourage. His powerful mother, Sorghaghtani Beki, his chief wife, Doquz Khatun, and his principal lieutenant, Kitbogha, were all Christian, and a portable tent church travelled with him, allowing Mass to be celebrated daily. Besides the great number of Nestorians, his vast army included contingents from the Christian kingdoms of Armenia and Georgia—Great Khan Möngke is said to have promised the Armenian King that the Mongols would restore Jerusalem to the Christians after they had destroyed the power of the Muslims. In 1258, they laid waste Baghdad, killed the last descendant of Prophet Mohammed, and advanced towards Syria.

Aleppo resisted and was taken by storm, while her non-Christian inhabitants were massacred; Damascus surrendered without a fight, as three Christian leaders—the Mongol commander Kitbogha, King Hethoum the Great of Armenia, and Prince Bohemund VI of Antioch—rode through its streets and forced Muslims to bow to the cross. The Eastern Christians were filled with extravagant hopes and expected the rapid downfall of Islam, but their Western brethren were less sanguine. They noted that the Mongol rulers were still pagan, and that they had a dreadful reputation for cruelty and perfidy, demanding not friendship and alliance, but abject submission. The Mongols were expected to soon be in Jerusalem or Cairo, and unaware that the Mameluks had taken control, Hülegü sent the Sultan of Egypt the usual peremptory summons to surrender or perish. Needless to say, the Mameluks did not take kindly to the demands and killed the Mongol envoy.

Were Egypt, the last important Muslim centre, to fall, the consequences for Islam would be disastrous. However, the progress of the Mongols across the Holy Land was halted early in 1260, when Hülegü received the news that his brother, the Great Khan, had died in China the preceding December. Seeing as his cousin, Berke, Khan of the Golden Horde, had converted to Islam and was horrified by his treatment of the faithful, Hülegü felt it prudent to return to Mongolia with the bulk of his army to sort out the inevitable succession crisis. Appealing for a total mobilization of faithful Muslims against the heathen murderers of the Caliph, the Mameluks under Baybars marched north to engage what was left of Mongol Horde under Kitbogha. The Crusader States, eager to see the two sides massacre each other, let the Mameluks through their territory unmolested.

The Mongols jeered at Baybars and his army of former slaves: "You are but a slave bought at a market. How dare you challenge the Master of the World." But, in September, 1260, the Mameluk cavalry triumphed over the cocksure invader in the Battle of Ain Jalut near Nazareth, where David is said to have defeated Goliath. One of the decisive battles of world history, it saved Cairo from the fate of Baghdad, and Islam itself from impending destruction, guaranteeing Baybars' position as Sultan and the Defender of the Faith. Egypt, thus spared from the devastation of the Mongols, developed into the leading centre of Islam and the home to what remained of Arab culture. The reign of the Mameluks in Egypt lasted over 250 years: the country grew rich from the long-distance trade that flowed through Cairo, where the architectural monuments of the era can be admired even today; the mosques, hospitals, and schools built by the Mameluk Sultans reveal their pious goals and their aspiration to supremacy over all the Muslims.

The same year that Baybars became Sultan, he captured Damascus, and once more, like in the days of Saladin, Damascus and Cairo were united under a single Muslim leader who was determined to drive the Christians from Syria. Cæsarea was the first crusader city to fall, being completely destroyed by the Mameluks in 1265. Next in line was Haïfa, whose fortifications were dismantled and inhabitants massacred. The Sultan then moved on to Arsuf, where the commander of the Hospitaller garrison agreed to surrender if the survivors could go free. Baybars agreed, but unlike Saladin, was not a man of his word, and the entire population of Arsuf was slaughtered as soon as the gates were opened. Next, in 1267, the Sultan laid siege to Acre itself.

Hugh of Antioch, Regent of Cyprus, came to the defence of Acre with a Cypriot army, whose the valiant fighting, combined with the strong fortifications of the city, forced Baybars to temporarily withdraw. The same year saw the death of the child king, last of the Lusignan in the male line, and the regent succeeded to the throne of Cyprus as Hugh III. Surnamed the Great, Hugh had the advantage of ascending the throne as an experienced man of the world. He was not only a great soldier, but also a generous patron of learning and a pious founder of monasteries. It was to him that St. Thomas Aquinas dedicated *De Regimine Principum*, "On the Government of Rulers," which became a handbook on the relationship of Church and State in the High Middle Ages.

Baybars went on the march again in 1268, capturing Jaffa in March; the Templar castle of Beaufort was taken in April, and the Sultan arrived before Antioch in May. Two years earlier, another Mameluk army had routed the Armenians in Cilicia and captured their capital of Sis, effectively eliminating Antioch's only remaining ally. Prince Bohemund was safe in Tripoli, but his constable was captured on the first day of fighting, and Antioch itself fell on the fifth, or the 18th of May, 1268. One of the Mameluk emirs ordered all gates locked, so no one could escape: all the Latins who were not killed were enslaved, and the once great city was reduced to little more than a village—the principality of Bohemund had ceased to exist.

In 1269, Hugh of Cyprus, a Lusignan from his mother's side, claimed the throne of Jerusalem by right of descent, was recognized as the lawful heir by the barons, and crowned at Tyre. The title was nevertheless contested by Mary of Antioch, granddaughter of King Amalric II. After appealing to the Pope, she sold her rights to the crown of Jerusalem to her grandnephew, Charles of Anjou, whose conquest of the Two Sicilies had made him one of the most powerful princes in Christendom. Charles was not the least bit interested in ruling Jerusalem, but the title lent legitimacy to his scheme for a crusade against Constantinople. He tried to take advantage of the vacancy of the papal chair between 1268 and 1271 to this effect, Rome's negotiations with the Byzantine Emperor for religious union having previously thwarted him, but the invasion of Conradin forced Charles to lay his schemes aside for a while.

St. Louis and his three sons had taken the cross in an assembly of nobles at Paris, on the 24th of March, 1267. Charles, brother of the French King, had most of the old Norman Kingdom under his control, but wished to recover Tunisia as well. He wanted it for its grain and its ports, and more important still, to consolidate his hold on the central Mediterranean. Since he was not strong enough to challenge the Emir of Tunis himself, Charles persuaded his reluctant brother to divert his crusade on Africa by promising to help him later in Palestine. However, the plague broke out in the crusader camp at Carthage, and the King of France was among those carried off (1270) by the scourge. His brother negotiated very favourable terms with the Mohammedans, and the crusaders pushed off. Only Prince Edward, afterwards King Edward I of England, was determined to fulfill his vow, and joined Hugh of Jerusalem at Acre in his attempts to repel the attacks of Baybars on his kingdom. For more than a year, Hugh and Edward remained there, making many useless raids on the Saracenic territory and negotiating without avail.

Overlooking the Homs Gap, which runs from Syria's Mediterranean coast to the country's interior, stands Le Crac des Chevaliers, "the Rock of the Knights," an astonishingly strong fortress with its steeply rising bulwarks and walls several yards thick. Controlling as it did the flow of people and goods between Asia Minor and the Levantine coast, Le Crac was an immensely significant site in the Crusades, holding a garrison of over 2,000 men and horses. A frightful barrier on the road of the conquerors from Damascus to Tripoli and Jerusalem, it was never conquered by force.

When the crusaders first arrived at the spot towards the end of the previous century, there stood only a small Kurdish castle. In 1142, it was given by Count Raymond II of Tripoli into the care of the Hospitallers, who—over the ensuing hundred and fifty years—remodelled and developed it into the most remarkable work of military architecture of its time, enabling it to fend off at least a dozen Saracenic attempts of seizure. The fortress had two weak points: the main gate and the exposed southern flank opposite to the flat plain. The Knights secured the latter by erecting an enormous brick fortification and providing it with three gigantic, interconnecting towers. In addition, the south flank was reinforced with up to 80 feet thick ramparts, made out of macadam and brick, under which it would have been almost impossible to burrow. The problem of the main gate was resolved even more brilliantly: the road leading to the gate was built to wind back and forth on a steep incline, so that the attacker would ever and anon be caught in the direct line of fire.

To assault the fortress would have been senseless waste of human life, and besiegement was just as pointless. Like all the crusader castles, Le Crac had ample reserves of food and water. Its full strength garrison of 2,000 knights could fight and survive on its own for at least a year—in which time reinforcements would surely arrive. The capture of Le Crac seemed impossible, and even Saladin had given up his attempt. But in 1271, another Muslim conqueror, the Mameluk Sultan Baybars, stood before its gates, accompanied by an Egyptian army. At the time, the castle's garrison was a dangerously undermanned. A year earlier, the Eighth Crusade had failed and there was no hope of aid from Europe. Only a handful of Hospitallers had stayed behind to lead the mercenaries who formed the actual garrison.

The Sultan commenced the siege with fanatical determination. His troops spent several weeks digging an underground passage, as a consequence of which the southwestern tower of the outermost wall eventually collapsed. The attackers rushed over the debris of the tower, only to be met with the fortifications of the medial circle. Baybars had no intention of abandoning the siege, but since he was not inclined to undertake a lengthy besiegement either, he resorted to guile. According to the Arab historians, he sent a forged letter to the fortress by means of a carrier pigeon. The letter had been drawn up in the name of the Hospitaller Grand Master, then at Tripoli. In it, the garrison was ordered to surrender, seeing that no aid could be dispatched.

The order was obeyed and Le Crac surrendered, even though its strongest fortifications had not yet even been put to the test. Its chapel was immediately converted into a mosque, and in 1272, Hugh was obliged to conclude a treaty with Baybars, which left him only the city of Acre and the right of pilgrimage to Nazareth. He was supported by the Hospitallers, but obstructed by the Templars; the Genoese aided him, while the Venetians thwarted him. Unable to cope with his unruly subjects, he returned to Cyprus after naming (1276) his brother-in-law, Philippe d'Ibelin, as his regent in Jerusalem.

No sooner had Charles of Anjou recovered from the fiasco of the Eighth Crusade than the agreement of Michael Palæologus to the union of the Churches (1274) frustrated once more his plans to invade Constantinople. In 1275, Pope Gregory X (1271-1276) effected a truce between Charles and the Emperor. The King of France, the King of England, and the King of Aragón all made a vow to go to the Holy Land, and the Byzantine Emperor himself promised to take the cross. The death of Gregory, however, brought these efforts to naught, enabling Charles to resume his plotting once again.

Pursuant to the claims which he had purchased from Mary of Antioch, Charles sent a garrison under command of Roger of San Severino to occupy Acre in 1277. By the order of the Grand Master of the Templars, the Sicilian troops were admitted into the citadel, which they then seized, declaring Charles King of Jerusalem. Hugh led an expedition to recover Acre, but owing to the opposition of the Knights Templar, the attempt was abandoned after a four-month siege, and he returned to Cyprus for good. To repay the treachery of the Templars, Hugh tore down their castles at Limassol, Paphos, and Gastria, and confiscated all their property on the island.

Prompted by political motives, the temporary submission of the Greek clergy to Rome aroused the disgust of the Byzantine citizens, but this was hardly the reason why Pope Martin IV (1281-1285) excommunicated Michael Palæologus from the Church into which he was trying to seduce his people. After the death of Pope Nicholas III (1277-1280), Charles of Anjou had intervened in the papal enclave by imprisoning two influential Italian cardinals, without whose opposition the French Martin could be elected to the papacy. With the tenuous union of the Churches annulled, Charles of Anjou could relaunch his plans for a crusade on Constantinople; an alliance having been signed between himself and Venice, a huge expeditionary fleet assembled at Brindisi for the conquest of Byzantium, set for April of 1283—but the fleet never sailed.

The gauntlet which Conradin had tossed onto the scaffold in 1268 was picked up by John of Procida, the organizer of the so-called "Sicilian Vespers." On the vigil of Easter, 1282, a chance insult suffered by certain Sicilian girls at the hand of a French soldier in Messina raised the cry "Death to the Frenchmen!" which led to the massacre of all the French in the city, meaning that 4,000 men, women, and children would die that night. The revolt soon spread all over the island, and in order to subdue his rebellious subjects, Charles was finally forced to abandon his Eastern designs. The inhabitants of Acre expelled his seneschal and called to their aid King Henry II, son and successor of Hugh III. Having been reconciled with the Templars, the King of Cyprus recovered possession of Acre with the help of the two military orders. In 1286, he was crowned King of Jerusalem at Tyre. Michael Palæologus remained master of Constantinople, and the Palæologi ruled the Byzantine Empire for another two hundred years.

Rejected by the French Pope, the Sicilians turned to Peter III of Aragón for support, no doubt because he was connected to the House of Hohenstaufen by marriage. The Pope used all the available spiritual and material resources against him, excommunicating Peter and declaring his Spanish kingdom forfeit. Charles of Anjou died in 1285, the same year as Pope Martin, having realized scarcely any of his ambitions. Although the Aragonese secured control of Sicily, the Angevins retained the former Norman domains on the mainland as the Kingdom of Naples. Since both attempted to conquer the other and reunite the territory, there followed an amazingly complex story of conflict and conspiracy, made the more confusing by the incessant interference of the papacy. The wars between the two continued until 1373, and they were not restored under unified rule until Alfonso V of Aragón, also known as Alfonso the Magnanimous, conquered Naples in 1442.

Despite Baybars' death in 1277, the Mameluk war-machine continued to roll over the Latins in the East. His successor, Kelaoun, finally concluded a ten-year truce with the Latins, but it was broken by an unpardonable outrage on their part: when some European adventurers, freshly arrived at Acre, robbed and hung nineteen Egyptian merchants, the Sultan of Egypt resumed hostilities with the avowed determination to crush the Latin power in the East for good. The Hospitaller fortress of Margat, the sister castle of Le Crac, capitulated after a fierce siege in 1285; the county of Tripoli, the last of the four major Crusader States, surrendered in 1289; the only response from the

West was the arrival in 1290 of a small volunteer force of peasants and vagabonds. On the 5th of April, 1291, al-Ashraf Khalil, son and successor of Kelaoun, appeared before Acre with 160,000 men.

Not wishing to aid their Venetian rivals, the Genoese loaded their ships and left before the fighting began. The 25,000 quarrelsome Latins who were left to defend the city fought with the courage of despair. After the volley from the Mameluk catapults had rained down on the walls and towers for 33 days and nights, the city was carried by storm. The garrison of the Templar fortress held out ten days longer, only to be completely annihilated; the warrior-monks fought to the last man, and the battle finished on the 28th of May, when their last tower collapsed on them and the attacking Egyptians. Tyre, Sidon, and Tortosa were abandoned without a fight. The King, the Patriarch, and the Grand Master of the Hospital made their escape by sea to Cyprus; of the Knights Templar, including their Grand Master, only ten escaped of five hundred knights. The headquarters of both the Templars and the Hospitallers were moved from Acre to Limassol, that of the Teutonic Knights first to Venice, and thence soon to Marienburg. In July, 1291, the last Crusader settlements in Syria capitulated, and the Latin Kingdom of Jerusalem was no more.[185]

---

[185] The Latin Patriarchate of Jerusalem, whose seat had been moved to Acre in 1187, ceased to exist as well, not to be revived until 1889.

CHAPTER 26

For one hundred and ninety-two turbulent years, a feudal kingdom had been imposed on Palestine, and then it vanished as suddenly as it had appeared, leaving no trace save for the ruins of castles, churches, and fortifications, a couple of place-names, and an undying hereditary hatred of Christianity among the local population. Before the Christian invasions and during its golden age, the Islamic World was far superior to the West in tolerance of intellectual pursuits; it permitted Christians and Jews to live their own lives and practise their cultures. But after having received so much savage treatment for two centuries, the Muslims would act much more harshly towards foreigners, and many of the great political, religious, and military struggles of the early 21st century remain a sad inheritance of the murderous folly known as the Crusades.

The earliest West European accounts of encounter with Mohammedan warriors reassure Christendom that its knights had found a worthy foe in the Saracen. The *trouvères* of mediæval France portray the Muslims as "worthy of respect, a good enemy, difficult to conquer, a chance of glory, always numerous and their leaders notable for prowess." The Norman chroniclers of southern Italy go as far as to contrast the treacherous Lombards and the effeminate Byzantines with the proud and manful Arabs. Unlike other conquerors, however, the Crusaders were not interested in maintaining their hegemony over the region in order to collect taxes; rather, their purpose was to establish resident colonies through the displacement of the Muslim population.

While the Byzantine Church had a specific ritual which enabled Muslims to renounce Islam, no such rite was known to the Latins, whose fanaticism was such that they massacred the male inhabitants of entire cities that resisted their conquest. The baptism of Muslim slaves was further declared illegal, for it could impose limits on their masters' rights and lead to manumission. As a result of the violence inflicted upon them, Muslims developed a strong unity that was essential for survival, a unity that has lasted until present time as Arab leaders still refer to the victories of Saladin.

Still, the most dramatic effects of the Crusades were felt in Europe, not in the Middle East. Ancient trade routes reopened along the Mediterranean because of the flurry of activity under way for the Crusades, generating interest in exploration of the Orient. The experiences of the popes and princes in raising money to finance the crusading expeditions led to the development of direct general taxation, which had important long-term consequences for the fiscal structure of Western governments. The Latin Kingdom of Jerusalem was also one of the first attempts made by Europeans at colonization, establishing the machinery that later generations used and improved upon when settling the territories discovered by the 15th- and 16th-century explorers.

Mediterranean cities that had been abandoned for centuries were restored as centres of trade and shipping. Especially in the 14th and 15th centuries, the number and importance of traders, businessmen, and bankers grew, even if their way and view of life broke only slowly from those of the commoners. In the Middle Ages, the vast majority of Western people lived in rural communities. Small towns and the few bigger cities were urban areas surrounded by walls, at the gates of which opened the vast agrarian districts; the town-dwellers were in constant communication with the rural population of surrounding areas, from whom they acquired most of their foodstuff. The craftsmen could live either in the villages or in the cities, but were quite often farmers at the same time.

The feudal system, based as it was on agriculture and natural economy, began to function more and more poorly the more cities there sprung up and the more money got into circulation. As the townsmen learned to read and write, it became harder for the clergy to uphold their authority and collect their bountiful provisions. Commerce was carried on in utter defiance of all the theological doctrines hampering trade, and the Italian cities continued to hold mercantile relations with the Mohammedans even after the Crusades. The sin of usury, like the sin of trading with Muslims, appears to have been settled by the Italian merchants on their death-beds—greatly to the advantage of the splendid cathedrals and ecclesiastical decorations of their cities. Four of the five largest cities in Europe lay in northern Italy: Venice, Milan, Genoa, and Florence, the population of each approaching 100,000. The fifth metropolis was Paris.

With the Holy Land lost and their fighting force decimated, all that remained for the Knights Templar was their function as maritime traders and bankers to kings and princes. Their Paris Temple was also the most important royal treasury, housing the State's funds as well as the Order's, with the knights' treasurer being also the king's. The English crown, again, was chronically in debt to the London Temple. Though mainly concentrated in France and England, the Templars owned extensive properties also in Germany, Austria, and Hungary, in Italy and Sicily, in Castile, León, and Portugal, as well as in Scotland and Ireland.

Florence began to mint gold coins in 1252. This was a sure sign of the increase in prosperity, for gold coins had not been minted in Europe for six hundred years. Because of the consistency and reliability of its gold content, the coinage of Florence, the *florin*, became the standard of trade throughout the Continent. However, the Florentine coin may not be the earliest gold coin created in this period; at about the same time, or perhaps a little earlier, Genoa began issuing its first gold coins—the Venetian *ducat* came into use in 1284. In the next century, the example was followed not only by other Italian cities, but by the sovereign states of the West, bearing witness to a general revival of trade and economy.

During the struggles between the Guelph and Ghibelline factions in Italy, Florence had become a Guelph city. This alliance with the papacy became traditional, securing for the Florentine bankers the banking business of the popes, and for the Florentine merchants special privileges in regions where the popes had particular influence. The growing prosperity of the Florentine merchant class eventually (1283) enabled them to take over the municipal government. The Guelphs and Ghibillines were displaced in the city by the parties of the Whites and the Blacks, both Guelphs, the Blacks only more vehement.

Ever since the Lateran Council of 1059 had restricted the papal election to the cardinals, the pressure was on to have such a College of Cardinals created that would be open to suggestions as to who should be the next pope. By the 14th century, that person was virtually always an ex-cardinal, and that has hardly changed ever since. The cardinals were enormously powerful, had huge wealth and held series of bishoprics and benefices, and were usually exceedingly capable and experienced men, often lawyers by training. There is a common tendency to think that of the mediæval Church as governed by people who were schooled in theology; this was not the case, however, for it was largely run by lawyers.

The age of Hildebrand had inaugurated an age of zealous ecclesiastical litigation, with papal courts, whether presided over by legates or held in Rome itself, acting as the ultimate seat of judgement. The canon law was based on the decisions of popes and those of church councils, both general and local. Since it constituted one of the professional subjects taught in universities, many men ambitious for advancement in the Church took this degree as a stepping-stone. As the powers of the pope increased, the scope of canon law widened, encompassing an ever-growing variety of cases and instances; the papacy became the final arbiter not only for all disputes between ecclesiastical bodies or officials, but also for those between clerics and laity over penalties, rights, and property. It is therefore only natural that from the elevation of Alexander III (1159) on, popes were generally chosen from among canon lawyers rather than monks, like they had been during the first half-century of the Gregorian Reform.

In 1294, the College of Cardinals, after a deadlock of two years and three months, elected as pope a pious 88-year-old hermit, Pietro di Murrone. He had entered the Benedictine Order at the age of 17, his love of solitude leading him to the Abruzzi Mountains and the caves of Mount Morone, whence his surname. Fasting every day except Sunday, he dedicated each day in its entirety and a great part of each night to prayer and labour. His elevation to papacy was welcomed before all by the "Spiritual" wing of the Franciscans, who perceived it as the realization of the then-topical prophecies that the reign of the Holy Spirit ruling through monks was at hand; they proclaimed Celestine V the first true pope since Emperor Constantine had bestowed wealth and worldly power on "the first rich Father."

For a century and a half, all popes of note had been lawyers. Total chaos ensued as the head of the Church knew nothing about administration, the finer points of bureaucracy, or ecclesiastical jurisprudence. Privileges were accorded arbitrarily, and the same title or benefice could be bestowed upon several different candidates. After just five months, the poor old Pope began to doubt the salvation of his soul—the affairs of state took up time that he felt should be devoted to the sacred exercises of piety. Serious canonical questions arose: Can a vicar of Christ resign? He has no superior on Earth, so is anyone even authorized to accept his resignation?

Solution to the dilemma was offered by a Bologna graduate, Cardinal Benedict Gaëtani, who concluded affirmatively. On the 13th of December, 1294, Pope Celestine V announced his resignation, and declared that the cardinals were free to proceed with a new election. Despite the huge procession of monks and priests, who with tears and prayers implored Celestine to continue his rule, Cardinal Gaëtani was proclaimed as Pope Boniface VIII ten days later. He placed his predecessor in custody, fearing that the supporters of the saintly pope would not concede to the arrangements. Confined to the strong castle of Fumone, near Anagni, Celestine finished his highly unusual career three years later, in his ninety-first year.

Boniface was a puzzling, arrogant, and impassioned man; he, too, would go to far. Holding an exalted view of the pope as a kind of clerical monarch, he insisted that every human creature must be subject to the Roman pontiff in order to be saved. Boniface also had a notorious temper: in one well known incident, he kicked a royal nuncio who he was angry with in the head when the man bowed before the papal throne. It was Boniface VIII who proclaimed to the Christian world the first "Papal Jubilee," thereby recognizing pilgimages to Rome instead of Jerusalem, which was no longer accessible to the Latins. In the Jubilee Year of 1300, pardons and indulgences were sold, not given, to the pilgrims at the tombs of the Sts. Peter and Paul. So many came bringing their donations that the Roman officials had to use rakes and shovels to gather up all the money. Dante, who is assumed to have visited Rome during this year in which the goings-on of his *Divine Comedy* are set, indirectly testifies to the enormous crowd of pilgrims by comparing the sinners walking along a bridge of the Eighth Circle of Hell in opposite directions, to the crowds crossing the bridge of Castel Sant' Angelo on their way to and from St. Peter's.

At this period, Philip IV, grandson of St. Louis, occupied the throne of France. On dying, his grandfather had left the country in leading position in Europe—no other state had managed to achieve the unity which his kingdom possessed. Philip, surnamed the Fair, was one of the most prominent mediæval monarchs of France; proud, arrogant, and determined to have his way. He chose skilled and ambitious advisors to serve in his administration, the best known of whom were Pierre Dubois and Guillaume de Nogaret. Together they worked to remove all restrictions on royal authority, a task which involved obstinately combing out special privileges, local customs, and provincial prerogatives. Barons, bishops, and burghers were all obliged to co-operate with the King, be it in connection with the demands of royal justice or with those of the royal treasury.

The outbreak of war (1294) with England added even greater strain on the already crumbling French economy, and Philip resorted to extraordinary measures to raise additional revenue. After the extortionate tax that was levied on the Italian bankers failed to meet his growing expenses, he opted to recall and melt down all coinage, and then remint it with a much lower precious metal content. While he managed to raise around £1,200,000, he seriously devaluated the livre in the process. The French Church owned extensive properties, but instead of going to the King, much of their revenues went to Rome. In a desperate bid to raise more funds, Philip decided to impose a tax on the French clergy, much to to the disgust of Pope Boniface VIII.

In 1296, Boniface issued his infamous bull, *Clericis Laicos*, declaring himself to be the exclusive proprietor of all property held by the clergy, by the monasteries, and by the universities throughout Christendom, and that no secular authority should derive any income from that property without his express consent. Philip's countermove was to issue a royal edict forbidding the export of gold, silver, and coins from his kingdom without royal permission. This, of course, cut off any revenue Rome was earning from France. Enraged, Boniface issued another bull, *Unam Sanctam* (1302), stating that all monarchs were subject to his rulings in matters temporal as well as spiritual. Again, Philip responded bluntly, publicly burning the bull and sending a message to Boniface: "Philip, by the grace of God, King of the French, to Boniface, who giveth himself out for Supreme Pontiff, little or no health. Let thy extreme folly know, that We are not subject to anyone."

Other European sovereigns objected vigorously to the papal claims of supremacy, and should they all imitate the French King's antics, the papacy would go bankrupt. Philip further claimed that Boniface was not even a legitimate pope but had been elected illegally, and his demands could, therefore, be ignored. What is more, he accused Boniface of all sorts of heinous crimes, not limited to heresy and the murder of his predecessor. Infuriated, Boniface prepared a bull by which the French King would be excommunicated. Unwilling to give his not a few domestic enemies the excuse they needed to foment an open rebellion, Philip had the bull intercepted before his excommunication could be publicly announced.

Allegedly acting in the interest of all Christendom, Philip sent his chief advisor, Guillaume de Nogaret, to Italy, accompanied by a small band of armed officers. Upon arrival, they raised a sizeable force of Italians who were opposed to the worldly Pontiff, and together they travelled to Anagni, which was the favourite summer resort of the popes and where Boniface was staying at the time. The town also happened to be his ancestral home, and when word spread that its noble patron had been arrested by his enemies, its entire population came out to stop them. After several days of deadlock, de Nogaret finally agreed to release Boniface, for he knew it was impossible for him to smuggle the Pope out of the town.

Although set at liberty, the aged Pontiff had been subjected to considerable physical abuse, and died of a seizure only a month later, at Rome. His short-lived successor, Benedict XI (1303-1304), at first appeased Philip by removing the sentence of excommunication that Boniface had placed upon him, but their relationship quickly turned sour; after the Pope attempted to reassert the power of the Church over the French monarch, the King, it is believed, arranged to have him poisoned.

For some time now, the College of Cardinals had been increasingly dominated by Frenchmen, and after Benedict's death, the cardinals elected as pope one Bertrand de Got, Archbishop of Bordeaux. Despite his friendship with Philip, he had been loyal to Boniface in his struggle with the King, but also welcomed Benedict's appeasement policy and renewed his friendship with Philip. In 1305, Bertrand was absent visiting his French see, when he received the news of his election. He summoned the cardinals to Lyons, and was there consecrated under the name of Clement V, in the presence of King Philip and his court.

As one might expect, Clement was immediately besieged with grave dilemmas: the new pope discovered that he could not even travel to Rome the year of his coronation; since the current political climate in Italy was adverse to Frenchmen, most of the cardinals, too, stayed in France. King Philip demanded that the body of Boniface VIII be exhumed and burned as that of a heretic, and that Pope Celestine, his alleged victim, be canonized. Many of the cardinals wanted the matter left alone, and Clement got the King to withdraw the charge of heresy by consenting to repudiate all of Boniface's acts directed against Philip. De Nogaret was likewise absolved, with the penance of making a pilgrimage to the Holy Land in the next crusade, and spending the rest of his days there.

But this was, of course, never to be. With the loss of all Latin territory in Palestine, any serious hope of recovering the Holy City had irredeemably expired. The temporal princes of the West were wholly indifferent to everything that did not directly affect their own petty territorial interests. In fact, it was a common practice for late mediæval monarchs to obtain vast sums of money from the clergy by taking the cross, or by promising to take it, and persuading the pope make the churches of their kingdom to pay a tenth of their wealth towards the fictitious crusade; once the money came into the trusteeship of the royal treasurers, it all somehow disappeared, on one pretence or another, into the general stream of crown finances. Not only had Philip IV acquired a great deal of money with this devious method, but so had his contemporary and rival, Edward I of England.

Since the fall of Acre in 1291, there had been no Latin forces at all in the East. The members of the great military orders who returned to the West, apparently unemployed and yet still enjoying their wealth and privileges, seemed only another offensive addition to the growing class of idle clerical hypocrites. Men began to envy and covet the immense possession of the Knights Templar, who remained entrenched in their preceptories, in various countries of Europe, taking an active part in local politics. The Knights intervened in the quarrels of Western princes, even drawing their swords against fellow-Christians, but their principal occupation was finance. Long before the loss of the Holy Land, their European castles had been established as places where princes, merchants, and the wealthy in general could be certain their gold, silver, and jewels were safe. Philip, for one, was in serious debt to them after borrowing large amounts of money to finance his war with Edward. He had also asked to be received into their Order as an honorary member—the kind of distinction previously conferred on Richard Couer-de-Lion—and had been insultingly turned down.

Finally, the privileges conceded to the Order by the popes made even the Church their enemy. The secular clergy viewed their dispensation from the episcopal jurisdiction with jealousy and resentment. Their exemption from tithe was a source of considerable financial loss to the parsons, who further complained that Templars encroached on their territory by offering burials and other holy services at discount prices in cities where they had their oratories. The privilege they enjoyed of celebrating Mass during interdict brought an abundance of offerings and alms to the chaplains of their Order, regarded by the diocesan priests as robberies committed against themselves.

In 1306, Pope Clement V ordered Jacques de Molay and Foulques de Villaret, the Grand Master of the Temple and that of the Hospital respectively, to France to discuss merging the two orders. This idea had been previously brought up by Pope Nicholas II, and it was then as now bitterly opposed by both the Templars and the Hospitallers, who detested each other and had, on several occasions, fought openly. De Villaret could not attend the meeting, as he was far too busy besieging the Island of Rhodes, but de Molay, who had vainly travelled across Europe seeking support for a crusade, immediately set off for France to put forward his reasons for not combining the orders and to discuss the prospect of retaking the Holy Land. He left the Templar Headquarters on Cyprus, where he had been assembling fresh forces for the enterprise, with a fleet of eighteen warships, which soon anchored the Order's naval base at La Rochelle. He was accompanied by sixty of his most distinguished Knights, 150,000 gold florins, and twelve packhorses carrying unminted silver.

This was a year when Philip was particularly desperate for funds. He had levied a hundred percent tax on all Jewish possessions and ordered the confiscation of all their property, finally deporting the entire Jewish community of France. The consequential depreciation of money caused riots in Paris, and the King was forced to seek refuge from the angry mob in the Paris Temple. The two ringleaders of the riot were arrested, and whilst in prison, confessed to having once been Templars. The two men, Squin de Florian and Noffo Dei, upon being brought before the King and his Council, outlined a list of crimes of which they accused their former Order. Whether these men came up with these charges themselves or whether Philip and his advisors constructed them is unsure, but now he had two ex-Templars who were willing to accuse the Order of heresy—the ultimate crime of the Middle Ages and the only one that allowed him to confiscate their property.

The chief officer of the State, Guillaume de Nogaret, devised and implemented the round-up of the Templars. Acting on sealed orders that were not to be opened until the previous midnight, the royal seneschals descended on all the preceptories of the Order across France in the early hours of Friday, the 13th of October, 1307, and on that single day, arrested every Templar in the realm—an impressive accomplishment considering that there were around

15,000 of them in France at the time. Philip's actions were highly illegal, however, for a king had no authority to arrest members of an order responsibly only to the pope. He had hoped the scurrilous accusations made by the two former Templars would ultimately justify his actions, but since Clement was in no way impressed by their horrendous tales, there began a systematic torturing to wring confessions of guilt from the active Templars themselves.

The formula was simple: pardon for those who confessed, death for all who maintained their innocence. Whenever the released Knights, free of royal jurisdiction, appeared before the bishop's court, they immediately retracted their confessions. Recounting the tortures which they had endured, they professed that they would have sworn to anything, and should those horrors be repeated, they would again admit whatever the tormentors invented. But the Templars were now accused of holding heretical beliefs, so the prosecution, initially undertaken by the King's legal officers, was transferred to the Holy Inquisition, which immediately set to work extracting confessions using any means necessary. Guillaume Imbert[186], Grand Inquisitor of France and personal confessor to Philip, was given the task of interrogating the Templar Grand Master.

Clement still protested, condemning the arrests and suspending the Inquisition in France on the 27th of October, 1307. But by then, Philip was already announcing sensational "discoveries," including a written confession from Jacques de Molay himself, so on the 22nd of November, Clement was finally compelled to issue a bull that called for all rulers in Christendom to have the Templars arrested and their lands seized. The Templar chamberlains were nevertheless to be left alone, for they were responsible, among other things, for the tabulation of papal revenues. Not before the 7th of January, 1308, and with great reluctance, did England begin arresting its Templars, and then only in London. There were no more than 135 in Edward's kingdom, of which only six were knights, and few countries was keen to follow his lead. Scotland had newly declared her independence and lay under papal interdict for years, so the bull was never officially recognized and many Scottish Templars escaped persecution.

Clement had fully intended to return to Rome, but the trial of the Templars

---

[186] a/k/a William of Paris

side-tracked his plans. He certainly did not want to be seen as a mere puppet of the French King, and could no more stay in France than he could go to Italy. Finally, in 1309, he found what he considered a makeshift compromise: Avignon. This pleasant little town on the banks of the Rhône belonged not to the King of France, but to the King of Naples, and was practically surrounded by the papal territory of Comtat Venaissin. The year passed and travelling to Italy still seemed impossible; more and more clerks and officials came from Rome to Venaissin, and there was tons to do, so Clement stayed. In fact, he would never leave—he would spend his entire pontificate at Avignon.

The nature of the charges that were brought against the Templars show that their enemies had no serious crimes to pin on the Order. Their very virtues were turned against them, it being alleged that "to conceal the iniquity of their lives, they made much almsgiving, constantly frequented church, comported themselves with edification, frequently partook of the holy sacrament, and manifested always much modesty and gentleness of deportment in the house, as well as in public." Because the Templars, like the members of every military order, were sworn, under pain of expulsion or death, not to divulge any details of their initiation ceremonies to outsiders, it was fairly easy to invent baseless accusations against them.

It was claimed their secret rites involved, among other things, denying Christ, spitting on the cross, kissing the Devil's genitals, and coercing initiates into homosexual acts—charges that became monotonously familiar in the later witch trials. Nearly all the arrested Templars were tortured in one way or another, and their successful extermination set the pattern for the subsequent persecution of witches. They confessed to every sort of nonsense, most of it obviously invented by their judges. It appears that each Templar confessed to one set of crimes when tortured by one judge, and a completely different set when tortured by another. During their trial at Paris, the court refused to take depositions from no fewer than 573 witnesses for the defence.

Outside France, the Templars were everywhere acquitted; from Spain, Portugal, and Cyprus, where they were still fighting the Saracens, came news that they were innocent, while inquiries in the German Empire also proclaimed them guiltless. There were a few condemnations in Sicily and the Papal States, but not many. Some French Templars managed to flee to England, which had never allowed Rome to set up the Inquisition and where torture was illegal. Finally, Clement wrote to King Edward II, demanding that he use torture, or else he and his court would be excommunicated as impeders of holy justice. Edward was also offered a plenary indulgence for all his past sins as a bribe. He eventually agreed, "out of reverence for the Holy See," stipulating, however, that there must be no "mutilations, incurable wounds, or violent effusions of blood," which may be why, for two years, no English Templar confessed.

Even in France, no sooner had the Knights been released from the hands of their torturers than they repudiated their confessions, maintaining the innocence of their Order. Enraged, Philip had the pardoned brethren brought before a provincial council of the French bishops, and sentence of death was pronounced on them by the Archbishop of Sens in the following terms: "By your own confession and repentance, you have merited absolution, and had once more become reconciled to the Church. As you have revoked your confession, the Church no longer regards you as reconciled, but as having fallen back to your first errors. You are, therefore, *relapsed heretics*, and, as such, we condemn you to the fire." So, on the 12th of May, 1310, fifty-four of the Order were burnt in a single execution at Paris, discouraging the rest and destroying any chance of a defence against the accusations.

The Fifteenth Ecumenical Council, or the General Council of Vienne, which was to decide the guilt or innocence of the Order, opened on the 16th of October, 1311. The original convocation had been for 1310, but Clement postponed the opening by a year to give the Templars time to mount some semblance of a defence. However, the second bull of convocation did something more: it made the singular innovation that not every bishop was summoned to the Council, but only a chosen 231—and of these, sixty-six were struck out by King Philip. What is more, the 114 bishops who finally assembled in Vienne found a new conciliar procedure waiting for them: for each of the main issues before the Council, a commission of all ranks was named and charged with finding a resolution; this was then presented to the Pope and cardinals in consistory, and if accepted, announced to the Council as a whole in the form of a papal bull—there would be no general debates in which the whole Council participated.

The commission on the Templar issue reported in December, having decided that the Knights should be heard before the Council, but this potentially embarrassing act was set aside by Clement for the moment. The new year of 1312 brought Philip to Lyons—just twenty miles away—where the French Estates-General were meeting.[187] From Lyons, the King launched threats to revive his campaign against Boniface VIII, and towards the end of March, appeared in person at the Council. He persuaded the Templars commission to revoke their earlier recommendation and to vote for the suppression of the Order. The second public session of the Council began on the 3rd of April with one final procedural novelty: the Pope forbade any member of the Council to speak, under pain of excommunication; the Order of the Temple was then officially dissolved by the reading of his bull, *Vox in Excelso*, without a definite verdict of guilt or innocence ever being pronounced.

Over the next few years, the Order was abolished in all the European countries, though not a single Templar was condemned to death outside of France. Instead of joining the Hospitallers, many of the ex-Knights assumed a secular habit, blending themselves with the laity and mixing in the pleasures of this world. In a bull addressed to the Archbishop of Canterbury, their marriages were condemned as unlawful concubinages, since notwithstanding the dissolution of their Order, the former-Templars remained bound by their vows of perpetual chastity; they were ordered to be separated from the women they had married, and to be placed in different monasteries, where they were to devote themselves to the service of God.

The Knights had adopted the Oriental fashion of long beards, and during the proscription of their fraternity, when the fugitives who had discarded their habits were hunted down like animals, it was dangerous for laymen to wear beards of more than a few weeks' growth. Bearded men were granted certificates to keep them from being molested by the officers of justice as suspected Templars. Cutting their beards would not solve the problem for the real Knights as they also had tonsured heads at a time when Christian laymen grew their hair long. Some of the Castilian brethren were so horrified by the persecutions that they fled to Granada and turned Muslim, whereas the Portuguese Templars were cleared by an inquiry, and simply changed their name to the Knights of Christ, surviving well into the 16th century.

On the 18th of March, 1314, a large public scaffold was erected before the Notre-Dame Cathedral in Paris, and the citizens were invited to hear the

---

[187] The very first Estates-General was summoned by Philip in 1302 to raise money to aid him against Boniface VIII.

Knights Templar convicted by the testimony of its chief officers. The papal legate, turning towards Jacques de Molay and his companions, demanded that they renew, for all the people to hear, the confessions they had previously made of their guilt. The Grand Master raised his chained arm towards heaven, and advancing to the end of the scaffold, declared to the crowd in a loud voice: "I do confess my guilt, which consists of having, to my shame and dishonour, suffered myself, through the pain of torture and the fear of death, to give utterance to falsehoods, imputing scandalous sins and iniquities to an illustrious order, which hath nobly served the cause of Christianity. I distain to seek a wretched and disgraceful existence by engrafting another lie upon the original falsehood." The moment King Philip was informed of this insulting incident, he ordered, without consulting any ecclesiastical authority, the immediate execution of these gallant noblemen.

Legend goes that as the last Grand Master of the Temple was fastened to the stake, he called for his oppressors to be judged by God before the year was out. Sure enough, a month after the execution, Clement was struck by a dysentery and hurried to his grave. His mortal remains were transported to Carpentras, the capital of the Comtat Venaissin and, at the time, the residence of the Roman Curia; they were placed at night in a church which caught fire, and were almost entirely consumed. His family quarrelled over the immense fortune he had left behind; a huge sum of money, having been deposited for safe-keeping in a church at Lucca, was stolen by a band of German and Italian freebooters.

Before the close of the year, Philip IV died of a lingering illness which baffled all the arts of the royal physicians. His last days had been clouded by misfortunes; the French nobles and clergy had allied against him to fight his exactions; the wives of all his three sons had been accused of adultery, and two of them were publicly convicted of that crime. Guillaume de Nogaret, responsible for drawing up the initial accusations against the Templars, was dead; so were the two convicted felons on the strength of whose information the Templars had originally been arrested—hanged for fresh crimes. Between 1314 and 1328, the King's three sons, young, healthy, and vigorous, held the throne successively, and each died without male heirs, erasing the direct line of descent. The widespread superstition which reckons Friday the 13th as a day of misfortune is believed to stem from Philip's initial raids on the 13th of October, 1307.

By the time Clement V died, most of the Curia was at Carpentras, which could have easily become the new papal residence, had not the Bishop of Avignon, Jacques Duèse, been elected pope—there was a period of more than two years before the conclave could agree. Having lived in Avignon for several years already, it was easy for Pope John XXII (1316-1334) to continue his residence in the Bishop's Palace there; thus began in earnest the Avignon exile or the "Babylonian Captivity" of the papacy, a schism which was to produce rival popes and divide the Catholic Church until 1378. A celebrated canon lawyer under Boniface VIII, whom he had supported, John effected a major administrative reorganization. Out of the poor believers' money, he built the magnificent court of Avignon and palaces for the cardinals. The papal household assumed tremendous proportions and became the true centre of power within the Church, even as a royal household was the true centre of power within a kingdom. The papal court numbered three to four hundred people, and included such indispensable offices as the Keeper of the Papal Seals and the Keeper of the Papal Zoo.

The Avignon exile not only centralized the Church government but also established a system of papal finance; as the popes lost their revenues from the Papal States, which they had abandoned to the factions of Italian nobility, new ways to make money became necessary. Bishops and abbots paid the papacy an *annate*, first year's income; the *spolia*, in turn, referred to the collection of revenues until a new official was appointed. The papacy also sold "expectancies," meaning that the hopeful candidate would pay for the right to be considered to a benefice when it became vacant. Since popes could only collect revenues from those whom they had appointed, they continually expanded their powers of appointment, at the expense of secular rulers. The Church was wealthy, powerful, and woven into the Western politics. The left wing of the Franciscan Order renounced wealth and power; Christ had owned nothing, and therefore the Church, too, should relinquish all wealth and power. John XXII condemned the doctrine of Apostolic Poverty—those Franciscans who disagreed were handed over to the Inquisition and burned at the stake.

By ordering the suppression of the Knights Templar, Pope Clement had dealt a crushing blow to the Crusades; instead of distributing the enormous wealth of the Templars to the remaining military orders as postulated in the papal bulls, King Philip had confiscated it. The Teutonic Knights having established themselves as the theocratic rulers of Prussia, there remained in the East only the Hospitallers, who were lucky enough to find an important role in the Mediterranean as the protectors of Christian shipping, without which new responsibility they too would probably have been dissolved, or at least forced to forgo their military function. By 1312, they were firmly established as sovereign rulers of the Island of Rhodes, which would lead them to change their name into the Knights of Rhodes. Their presence in Greece lasted until 1523, when they were defeated by an enormous Turkish force. Seven years later, they were given a new home on the Isle of Malta, where they remained until 1798, surviving to the present day as the Knights of Malta.

CHAPTER 27

The Capetian dynasty, which had ruled France for centuries, finally died out in 1328. King Philip VI, the first ruler of the Valois branch, had been appointed leader of the crusade by the pope and was preparing to embark when the projects of Edward III of England caused him to return to Paris. Edward refused to pay homage for his French lands to Philip on the strength of his own claim to the French throne as a direct descendant of Philip IV through his mother, Isabella of France. The war that broke out thereafter between France and England proved an insurmountable obstacle for any crusade, and the Turks could easily penetrate the once so well guarded West. The conflict would continue, with periodic truces, until 1451, whence its name—the Hundred Years' War.

The hostilities began in earnest in 1346, when Edward invaded Brittany and marched on Paris. The secret weapon of the English was the longbow: in the great Battle of Crécy, Edward's 10,000-strong army utterly routed twice its number of Frenchmen, as English archers obliterated squadrons of heavily-armed French knights; the English lost only 200 men, whereas the casualties of the French were in excess of 10,000. Due to the military superiority of England, France lost most of the battles in the War. French peasants suffered the most economically, as was usual in mediæval times during war, and physically, as their homes fell prey to French and English mercenaries who lived off the land between fighting.

The Hundred Years' War raged amid perhaps the worst century in the annals of Western civilization. The early 1300s saw meagre harvests created by poor weather, and the resulting mass starvation eliminated in some areas as much as 15 percent of the population. During the first half of the century, the agricultural enterprises of Northern Europe reached the limits of their productivity, and the subdivision of their holdings and expansion into marginally productive areas resulted in a reduced standard of living for the peasantry. Pauses in the virtually continuous international warfare were compensated by local conflicts.

Then, mankind was met with the greatest global scourge that it had ever faced: the Black Death—an exceptionally virulent combination of bubonic and pneumonic plagues. It had set out from the Gobi desert and travelled through the trade routes across the entire Eastern World, leaving millions and millions of dead behind, corpses amounting to nations. In Europe, it is thought to have originated as an early form of germ-warfare: in 1347, Mongols reputedly tossed a body claimed by the plague in the Crimea to the side of their Genoese enemies. In two ticks, the Black Death had spread everywhere in the West, killing millions within twenty-four hours of infection. Appearing as it did during a time of economic depression, the pandemic had a profound impact on the social and economic conditions in Western Europe.

The plague ravaged crowded, musty castles and towns more than it did isolated villages. Where the countryside had previously been overworked to support large populations, there now lay an abundance of land for the survivors, the value of whose labour was greatly enhanced. Serfs were no longer bound to one master: if one lord abandoned the land, another would instantly hire them. Confronted with the prospect of their crops rotting in the fields, many lords rented out their lands, and as the serfs turned into tenant farmers, manorialism came to an end. Prices and wages rose sharply, causing governments to impose wage caps, which led to a number of fierce peasant rebellions. As the gap between the rich and the poor widened, the fashions of the nobility became more extravagant to accentuate social status. The whole socio-economic structure of the West underwent a drastic and irrevocable change.

World War I claimed eight and a half million victims, WWII approximately twenty million; the Black Death killed twenty to thirty million people just between 1347 and 1350. The main reason for this awful sacrifice of life was the lack of all hygienic precautions. Christian religious practice of the 14th century was a far cry from the inspired utterance of John Wesley, that "cleanliness is next to godliness."[188] In fact, it was living in filth that was then regarded by men of cloth as an evidence of sanctity. If the devotion of the clergy to the sick was one reason why they lost so many of their number during the pandemics, their lack of cleanliness must also have contributed it. Not only in the rural areas, but in the principal cities of Europe, the simplest

---

[188] *Sermon 88: On Dress*

sanitary precautions were neglected down to a recent period.

The population of Europe fell by a quarter during the 14th century, in some places a lot more. Nor did the plague disappear after those four fateful years; it recurred again and again until the beginning of the 18th century. Down to the 16th and 17th centuries, the filthiness of everyday life in the West was such as we can today scarcely conceive: fermenting organic matter was left to accumulate and became a part of the earthen floors of dwelling-houses, breeding the germs of many diseases. Death became a towering figure in Western thinking; the peaceful death of old, the humble and dignified resignation before the inevitable, turned into blind thirst for life, bitterness towards the death that deprives man of his earthly existence.

People could not believe that such boundless destruction was God's doing, and harboured ill-will towards those who survived the horrors of the plague with the least hardship. Scapegoats were needed. It was noted that a much smaller percentage of Jews than Christians caught the disease; this was without doubt because of the Judaic sanitary and dietary laws, which had originated thousands of years before in the Levant, and been handed down through Jewish lawgivers and statesmen. Rumours, however, circulated in Germany that the Jewish race was protected by the Devil, whom they repaid by poisoning the wells used by Christians. Even then, the final solution was to plunder, torture, murder, and burn the Jews.

12,000 Jews perished in Bavaria; 6,000 at Mainz; 3,000 in the small town of Erfurt; 400 in Worms; in Strasbourg, the Rue Brulée remains as a monument to the 2,000 Jews burned there for causing the plague of 1348. The rumour spread across Europe that God was angry because Christians had been excessively tolerant towards the murderers of His son—God had cursed Christendom as He did Saul when he showed mercy towards God's enemies in the Old Testament. Blame was put on other scapegoats: heretics, witches, and by many a Frenchman, *les goddams anglais*.

As people became profoundly aware of the brevity of life, spirituality focussed on morbid themes. The suffering and death of Christ were emphasized over His triumphant resurrection, and the mellow Madonna became *Mater Dolorosa*, "the Sorrowful Mother," who shed her tears by the cross of her son. The higher powers were propitiated by penitential processions, or by parading the images of the Virgin or of the saints through plague-stricken towns. The flagellants tried to appease the divine wrath and keep the plague from spreading by flogging their naked bodies and screeching the penitential psalms whilst travelling from one town to another.

There was a steady multiplication of witch trials from the middle of the 14th century on. The increase is explained not only by the atmosphere of terror left by the Black Death, or the social insecurity and turmoil, but by a change in judicial custom that transferred the onus of proof from the plaintiff to an officer of the court; before, the wrongful accuser had to suffer a penalty himself. The legal scholars sincerely believed in witchcraft, and due to the threefold seriousness of the crime (murder, sacrilege, treason), the suspected witches and heretics were dealt with more sternly than others by ecclesiastical and secular tribunals alike.

When the papacy and the Dominican Order framed their theory of witchcraft, they created nothing new, for there had always been witches. Persecuting them, on the other hand, was new everywhere except among the Jews. The Mosaic code ordered to destroy the witch (Exodus 22:18, Leviticus 20:27, Deuteronomy 13:5), and this order was obeyed. Roman law made a distinction between a good witch and a bad witch, and imposed the death penalty on the latter. Early Christianity, again, considered the notion of witchcraft as nothing more than a pagan superstition. The clergymen explained to the superstitious populace that witches could not make weather, good or bad, that love potions were nonsense, and that flying on the broomstick was a delusion of weak minds. Nor were the early Christians especially interested in the Devil: demons were everywhere since the gods and spirits[189] of antiquity had merely been given new names, but Satan[190] himself was a distant creature who had no impact on our earthly existence.

Under paganism, the law on torture had been that it should not be carried beyond human endurance; e.g. Cicero would ridicule it as a method of detecting crime, because the hardened criminal with strong nerves might endure it and go free, while an innocent but physically weak man would be compelled to confess.[191] But even as Christianity became predominant throughout Europe, torture was developed to a whole new level of cruelty. There had evolved a doctrine of "excepted cases," these being heresy and

---

[189] Gr. *daimôn*

[190] Heb. "Hinderer"; in Judaism, Yahweh's subordinate. (See the Book of Job.)

[191] *Pro Sulla*, 28

witchcraft in particular. It was held by a deviously simple and logical process of theological reflection that the Devil would provide his worshippers with supernatural strength, wherefore there should be no limit to the use of torture in dealing with heretics and witches.[192] As a result, the accused not only confessed anything and everything that was suggested to them, but admitted to accomplices, who in turn accused others, and so on and so on, until a great number of blameless people were sentenced to the cruelest death ever invented. They would die alone, unpitied, unremembered; even their own kinsmen would shrink from them as tainted and accursed.[193]

The charges of witchcraft were long read as a part of the charges of heresy: a witch could not be burned at the stake for merely being a witch, so she had to be proven a heretic; which was not hard, actually. If a person was in congress with the Devil knowing that this kind of behaviour was sinful, it indeed was a sin, but not heresy. But should someone have congress with the Devil and not regard it as sin, she would think contrary to the doctrine of the Church and would thus be a heretic. Besides, the great teacher of the Church, St. Thomas Aquinas, was totally convinced of the existence of witches. In his imposing work, *Summa contra Gentiles*, Aquinas reflects upon the relationship of magic and nature. Through logical argumentation, he arrives at the inescapable conclusion that its is impossible to work magic using the natural forces or stars. Since so many spells nevertheless seem to work, there must be unnatural forces behind them. When a witch intones for example a pain-relieving spell, she has to address someone as she obviously does not talk to herself. She does not address God or saints, so the only possibility is that she is communicating with demons. From the point of view of Scholasticism, all magic was thus a plot of Satan.

Many regarded the Black Death as God's punishment on the sinful world, the sinful Church, and especially the sinful pope. As the years went by, the absence of the Bishop of Rome from his see became all the more scandalous:

---

[192] As late as the mid-18th century, Beccaria's *Essay on Crimes and Punishment* (1764), one of the first arguments against torture and capital punishment, was placed on the Index of Prohibited Books.

[193] Their earthly possessions naturally went to the Church; in extreme cases, Inquisitors were known to dig up corpses, convict them of heresy, and confiscate their property— property already inherited by the families of the dead heretics.

cities in the Papal States were becoming independent, and the foreign vicars sent from France to rule in the name of the pope were bitterly detested; central Italy, never the most orderly area of Italy, fell into disorder and anarchy as the local aristocracy sought to carve out their own personal fiefdoms in the ensuing chaos; Rome itself was desolate, economically ruined, and constantly in turmoil. The local bigwigs such as the Orsini, Colonna, and Gaëtani families fought it out like rival Mafia clans.

However, it was not all gloom: the 14th century saw the revival of Classical learning, and Francesco Petrarca (1304-1374), born in exile, came to give the first evidence of Italy's spiritual rebirth, becoming a great forerunner of Renaissance poetry. The world around him raised this lonesome man to the apex of fame, and in 1341, Petrarch was crowned *poëta laureatus* at the Capitol of Rome. An opportunity now opened for Cola di Rienzi, a young Roman of humble birth, to remind his fellow-citizens of their illustrious past and to dispossess the great noble families in favour of the ancient Roman institutions. In 1347, the Romans rose to revolt, banished the aristocrats and senators, and made Rienzi the head of the city government, under the title of Tribune. For a time, Petrarch regarded him with hope, for the celebrated poet himself dreamed of restoring the greatness of Rome. But the enemy proved too powerful, and Rienzi was forced to flee to Naples after a reign of seven months. Petrarch returned to his seclusion and died at the age of seventy by the side of his books. Rienzi's plan had ended in dishonour and death, but his statue, with verses from Carducci on its pedestal, stands on the steps of the Capitol, where he was murdered when he tried to return to power in 1354, and a magnificent street preserves his memory to this day.

Rome continued to degenerate, culturally, politically, and economically; every pope proclaimed his intention and desire to return, if some less sincerely than others. Urban V (1362-1370) actually returned to Rome for three years, but found the situation there too perilous for him and was forced to retreat to the relative safety of Avignon. From the time of his election in 1370, Gregory XI received prophetic admonitions to go to Rome, first from St. Bridget of Sweden and then from St. Catherine of Siena. His return was hindered by an empty treasury, depleted from the past building campaigns in Avignon and the costly wars to subdue the Papal States; by the attachment of many cardinals to southern France, their home; and by the fact that the entire Italian Peninsula had plunged into anarchy. Gregory gave up after less than five months in the

Eternal City, but fell ill and died on the eve of his departure in March, 1378.

Once more a republic was set up, and the people of Rome took to the streets, demanding the election of an Italian to the papacy. The cardinals' choice, Bartolomeo Prignano, was indeed Italian, but had also been a leading figure at Avignon, holding a post in the Apostolic Chancery before succeeding to the highest church office in April. Unexpectedly, he turned zealous on his consecration as Pope Urban VI, and embarked on an active reform with the College of Cardinals as the primary target; he would be the last non-cardinal to be elected to the papacy. In August, the French cardinals met at Anagni to nullify the election on the ground that it was forced on them by the Roman mob—notwithstanding the fact that an entire summer had passed before any irregularity was discovered.

The cardinals proceeded to elect Robert of Geneva, son of Count Amadeus III of Geneva and Marie de Boulogne, as Clement VII. There had been antipopes before, but this time the same cardinals had elected two rival popes. With Clement they returned to Avignon, but Gregory XI was the last pope of French nationality. Clement had been Gregory's legate to Italy, and had led the troops who massacred 4,000 anti-papal rebels at Cesena in 1377. In 1379, he made an abortive attempt to take Rome with the French mercenaries who had already captured Castel Sant' Angelo. Meanwhile, Naples had fallen into the hands of the wretched Countess Joanna of Provence, and Clement acquired the town of Avignon for himself by absolving Joanna of the murder of her husband, Prince Andrew of Hungary.[194]

Fresh on the heels of the "Babylonian Captivity," the Great Western Schism (1378-1417) caused even a greater scandal, further diminishing the falling prestige of the papacy. For the next four decades, there were two popes, two Colleges of Cardinals, two separate ecclesiastical governments. They appointed rival bishops and abbots, collected the taxes twice, imposed contradictory penances, and excommunicated one another's supporters. The faithful of Christendom were stunned and horrified, but almost everyone was forced to choose sides. France and her allies—Spain, Scotland, and some of the German princes—supported the Avignon pope, while England, Portugal, Flanders, Bohemia, Hungary, the Emperor, and most of the German princes

---

[194] For the sordid details, see the novella *Jeanne de Naples* by Alexandre Dumas.

supported his Roman rival. Italy was as divided as she had ever been, her cities habitually changing their allegiances. To endorse one side or the other was to support the ecclesiastical appointments from one pope and to reject those from the other; it also entailed making sure that the tithes went to Rome instead of Avignon, or vice versa.

Early on, it was proposed that both popes would voluntarily abdicate, clearing the way for the election of a compromise candidate. Clement refused to abdicate and hoped to be elected pope also in Rome after the aged Urban died. However, on Urban's death in 1389, the Roman cardinals immediately elected Boniface IX, who went on to excommunicate Clement and the cardinals who had elected him. When Clement himself died in 1394, the French cardinals elected Benedict XIII, thus perpetuating the Avignonese papacy; in Rome, Boniface was succeeded by Innocent VII in 1404. Gregory XII was named pope by the Roman cardinals in 1406, on the understanding that he and Benedict in Avignon would agree to resign together and end the Schism. Neither wished to be the first to abdicate, however, so they would both need to abdicate at the same time, but neither could be induced to meet in the same city with the other.

The Schism involved not only the central power, but bishops, abbots, and even common priests, so the controversy over the status of the pope closely parallelled the controversy over secular power: it was debated whether all power should be in the hands of one person or whether it should be used jointly by those who fell under it. Some argued that a general council might represent the Church and choose the pope. This was an extremely delicate issue, for earlier mediæval popes had largely succeeded in asserting that no authority could pass judgement on a pope; by the early 15th century, however, even cardinals were advocating this last course of action. One further problem still remained: the pope alone could summon a general council.

In 1409, cardinals on both sides nevertheless assembled a council at Pisa, with over five hundred prelates attending. The two popes were deposed as "schismatics, obdurate heretics and perjurers,"[195] and a new pope, Alexander V, was elected in their place. However, both Gregory and Benedict had opposed the convocation of the council, and both immediately denounced and

---

[195] *schismaticos . . . notorios hæreticos et . . . perjuriis*

excommunicated Alexander, causing three rivals to the papacy instead of two. Alexander was succeeded the very next year by John XXIII, and the spectacle of three popes, three Colleges of Cardinals, three bodies of Curia, carried on.

The question of authority was worse than ever, and the only person within Christendom with enough prestige to call another council was the Holy Roman Emperor. In 1414, Emperor Sigismund finally responded to the endless pleas and convoked the great Council of Constance. This four-year assembly transformed the free city of Constance completely: its population rose from six thousand to sixty thousand; the number included approximately 1,200 prostitutes, who attended to the needs of three papal courts. Many wished for sincere reform, however, and hoped that the general council would displace the power of papacy—this was known as "conciliarism."

The Council of Constance coincided with another notable event in Western ecclesiastical history. The heresy that sprang from the English Wycliffe (c. 1328-1384) and the Lollards had penetrated into distant Germany, flourishing especially in Bohemia, where John Hus (1369-1415) had gained great popularity as a critic of contemporary theology and the abuses of the clergy. He was the Rector of the University of Prague, which had been founded by Emperor Sigismund's father, Charles IV of Bohemia, and was the first in Central Europe. His sermons calling a return to biblical teaching and a revolt against papal authority, an authority which the recent events had plunged into rather ill repute, had earned him excommunication. But he did not just preach the reform of the Church, he also wanted to free the Czechs of the psychological oppression imposed on them by the Germans. In him was personified both the national protest against German influence and the religious and moral protest against the dogmas and corruption of the Church.

The Czech reformer was lured into the Council with an absolute safe-conduct granted to him by the Emperor. He was proclaimed a heretic and burned at the stake on the 6th of July, 1415, along with his colleague and collaborator, Master Jerome of Prague. This judicial murder drove the entire Bohemian nation into tumult; thus, although King Wenceslaus IV of Bohemia died childless in 1419, and Emperor Sigismund claimed the throne as his brother, he could not get his hands on it until 1434. Rome began preaching a crusade against the Czechs, and the civil war that broke out between the Hussites and the Catholics ravaged not only Bohemia but also the neighbouring Hungary and Germany. The Hussites defeated the many armies sent against them, and once convinced that subduing the Czechs was impossible, Sigismund made a peace with them, agreeing to their principal religious and national demands (1436). As a result, Bohemia would not return to Catholic orthodoxy until two centuries later, after losing the Battle of the White Mountain (1620) to Austria during the Thirty Years' War.

It is quite an irony that the rivalry between popes should be solved only through the authority of their age-old rival, the emperor. John XXIII, having gone to Constance to bully the attendees, left the town in disguise, and agreed to his own deposition in 1415, dying as the Cardinal-Bishop of Tusculum four years later. Gregory XII actually resorted to the fiction of convening the Council, even though it had already met, then abdicated voluntarily, acting as the Cardinal-Bishop of Porto until his death in 1417. Benedict XIII, however, refused to recognize either the Council or his deposition, retiring to a secluded castle in his native Valencia, wherefrom he excommunicated virtually everyone before finally expiring in 1423.

The Council of Constance declared the Holy See vacant, and on the 11th of November, 1417, a Roman, Oddone Colonna was unanimously elected as Pope Martin V. His consecration ended the Schism, though some wretched remnants endured until 1429. Martin was unable to approve the declaration of Constance, that a general council is above the pope, but fearing to provoke another schism, he cunningly approved whatever the Council had done in a conciliar manner; the revolutionary decrees were carried in a manner far from conciliar, and thus implicitly excluded from the papal approval. Since Constance did validly decree that councils should be held every five years, Martin had to use a variety of tactics to prevent any such assemblage; in fact, he was so successful that not a single council met during his 18-year pontificate.

Since reform was associated with conciliarism, the papacy entered the mid-15th century thinking the matter closed; the issue for papacy was not reformation, but the reassertion of power and authority. At first, Martin was unable to even enter Rome, but through artful diplomacy, the city gates opened to him in 1420. Because of its ruined condition and sparse resources, Martin was forced to devote his time to rebuilding the city and restoring order. But the situation remained far from calm when he died—his successor, Eugene IV (1431-1447), was driven into exile by a republican revolution for nine years between 1434 and 1443, and had to reconquer Rome by force.

Eugene did manage to get started on the refurbishment of the city by clearing and paving the piazza in front of the Pantheon, the best preserved of all ancient buildings; the Lateran palace, however, was never again used as the papal residence, the Vatican being chosen in its place.

Even as the popes returned to Rome, the political conditions of Italy became somewhat more stable. The six principal states of the peninsula, having long competed over its mastership, took the shapes in which they appear in the 19th century. During the reign of the "Red Count" Amadeus VII, Savoy acquired Nice, Ventimiglia, and Chivasso. Emperor Sigismund upgraded Savoy into a duchy for Amadeus VIII, who—before being elected the last antipope in history (Felix V, 1439-1449)—annexed to his lands Piedmont, the stem of present-day Italy. The Visconti expanded Milan by annexing Verona and Padua. The duchy was opposed by the republics of Venice and Florence, until both signed a treaty with her at Ferrara (1428). After triumphing over her rival, Genoa, in the Battle of Chioggia, Venice was recognized as the Queen of the Adriatic. Florence had become more democratic after a proletarian rebellion known as the Ciompi Revolt (1378), and she retained her ardent love of freedom intact into the 15th century, while Naples was still torn by civil war. Queen Joanna II bequeathed her rights to René the Good of Anjou, but he was unable to hold off Alfonso the Magnanimous of Aragón and Sicily; both Sicilies were subsequently part of the history of Spain and Austria.

Italy now consisted of half a dozen major states, each of which sought domination of the peninsula: Savoy, which would ultimately gain it; Milan, which came near to gaining it; Venice, which emerged as one of the great powers in Europe; the Papal States, which in the age of the Borgias competed for the same honour; Tuscany, which loved freedom too much to lust after hegemony, until the Medici turned it into a near autocracy; and the Kingdom of the Two Sicilies, whose internal quarrels and incapable government never gave it the chance. Venice and Florence thus remained the only champions of republican freedom, and the former had her hands full keeping to the golden mean between democracy and monarchy.

Meanwhile, France's fortunes in the Hundred Years' War had not been improved by the long reign of "Charles the Mad," beginning in the late 14th century. In 1415, England's young king, Henry V, invaded France, besieging and capturing the port of Harfleur, but retreated towards Calais after his army was reduced by plague. Attacked by the French en route, the English longbowmen once again annihilated the French knights at the famous Battle of Agincourt, with only around 500 casualties to some 7,000 for France. The English took control of all northwestern districts of the land, from the Atlantic to the Loire, including Paris. Most of the eastern region was occupied by the duchy of Burgundy, a rival to the crown of France itself. When the Dauphin, Charles de Valois, met John the Fearless of Bungundy on the bridge of Montereau (1419) to plan an alliance against the English, the heir to the throne accused the Duke of treason because of his previous inaction against the invader. One of Charles' entourage then stabbed and killed Duke John, a treacherous act of murder which only impelled the Burgundians to ally with the English.

Finally, Queen Isabella betrayed France by persuading her mentally ill husband to sign the Treaty of Troyes (1420), which promised that the English King would receive the hand of the French Princess and inherit the throne upon the death of Charles VI. However, on the 31st of August, 1422, Henry V himself succumbed to dysentery, and John of Lancaster, Duke of Bedford, became regent for the nine-month-old Henry VI. After the French King finally died on the 22nd of October, none of his relatives came to his funeral, but the Duke of Bedford did, and no sooner was the royal tomb closed than the Duke proclaimed his infant ward, "by the grace of God, King of England and France." Although the Dauphin made a counter-claim to the French throne, he was a brooding, indecisive man like his father, reluctant to assert any real leadership and jealous of any nobleman who did; also, he had a terrible fear of horses.

At the time, the most splendid court in Western Europe was that of Philip the Good[196] (r. 1419-1467), son of John the Fearless. Through inheritance, conquest, treaty, and purchase, he more than doubled the Burgundian territory; acquiring Flanders, a fief of France; other former fiefs of Lorraine, Hainaut, Limburg, and Namur; the Dutch Holland, Zeeland, and Friesland; along with Brabant, Luxembourg, Liège, Cambrai, and numerous other cities and dependencies. (This has ironically conferred a "Burgundian" identity on the Low Countries, even though they had no previous connection to

---

[196] i.e. Philip III

Burgundy, which was merely a southern adjacent to Lorraine.) All France north of the Loire was soon in the hands of either the Burgundians or the English, apart from a few pitiful holdouts: Tournai, Mont-Saint-Michel, Vaucouleurs in Lorraine, and Orléans. There seemed to be no hope for the French, and the English thought they had won the Hundred Years' War.

An ancient prophecy by King Arthur's wizard, Merlin[197], foretells that: "Out of the oak forest of the Lorraine will come a virgin to save France." In the village of Domrémy (now Domrémy-la-Pucelle), near Vaucouleurs, lived the Celtic family of Arc. They owned a farm and sheep pasture, but were not serfs to the local lord, Robert de Baudricourt. They had five children, two boys and three girls, one of whom was called Jeanette, or in English, Joan. At the age of thirteen, this illiterate shepherdess first heard the voices that would address her for the rest of her short life. She claimed these voices belonged to Sts. Margaret and Catherine, to the Queens of France, and to the Archangel Michael; they convinced her to remain a virgin "as long as it shall please God." In 1428, when Joan was sixteen, the voices told her to leave her little village—and to rescue Orléans.

Joan went to her cousin, Durant Laxart, whom she called her uncle, because he was twice her age, and told him about her plan, reminding him of the Celtic prophecy that "France would be lost by a woman and saved by a virgin." She asked Laxart to take her to Vaucouleurs, where she told Lord Robert of the voices she had not dared to mention to her family. She was given horses and an escort to travel across Philip the Good's territory to aid the Dauphin, whom she wished to see crowned king. Dressed in male attire—from the fear of rape, as she would later explain—Joan, a knight, his squire, and her two brothers, crossed Burgundy. Since they travelled on horseback only by night, they arrived at the Dauphin's castle at Chinon ten days later, on the 4th of March, 1429.

The Dauphin had Joan quizzed by officials and clergymen for almost a month before she was finally granted his audience. Wearing a special-made suit of white enamelled armour, and carrying a banner of white and blue with two angels and the word "Jesus" on it, she proceeded with an ever-growing army from Chinon to Tours, to Blois, and finally to Orléans. Men who would not have followed a seasoned veteran into such a peril readily heeded her call

---

[197] sometimes alternatively ascribed to the Venerable Bede

to "Follow me." She startled many around her by using the flat of the sword to beat a prostitute following her army, one of several streetwalkers driven away, and even forbade swearing among her men—actions that even the most zealous chaplain would not have risked taking. Much to the amazement of officers, soldiers accepted these strictures with little or no complaint.

Joan was called *la Pucelle*, or "the Virgin," by the French; the English called her "the Maid"—on the rare occasions when they spoke courteously of her. The day after her arrival at Orléans, she and the English commander, John Talbot, Earl of Shrewsbury, shouted at each other from the opposite sides of a bridge: the Earl declared her a whore and the French officers pimps, warning them that if the English captured the "cowgirl," she would burn at the stake—the name "Jeanne d'Arc" would not be used until the 16th century.

The French of Orléans were taking heavy casualties and shrank from launching a major attack against their besiegers. If Joan could not save the town, the English would cross the Loire and conquer the rest of France. She rode on as the French cheered, taking the English camp at Saint-Loup by storm. The other garrisons in the area were so startled at the sound and fury of the assault that they declined to intervene. While every Englishman at Saint-Loup was killed, the French lost all of two men—it was a brilliant victory in a long line of losses.[198]

The French then attacked and took the fort of St-Jean-le-Blanc, from where the English retreated to the larger and stronger Bastille des Augustins, near Les Tourelles. From morning to night on the 7th of May, the French assaulted the latter fortress, held by Lord Talbot himself. Joan was wounded by an arrow, but just as Dunois, the Bastard of Orléans, was about to call off the attack, she returned to the battle. Around five hundred English attempted to flee, but the bridge out had been set on fire and collapsed, killing most of the men. Talbot lifted the siege on the following day, allowing the French to re-enter Orléans. All the English troops south of the Loire were either captured or killed, and those north of the river broke camp and withdrew.

While the Dauphin scarcely mentioned Joan in the news of victory he sent to every French town friendly to him, the Duke of Bedford explained in his letter to the King that the English had lost because of Joan, "a fiend with

---

[198] Joan of Arc remains the only person, of either sex, to have held supreme command of the military forces of a nation at the age of 17.

enchantments and sorcery." After her triumph at Orléans, the number of volunteers to gather under the *fleur-de-lys* banners soared. On the 9th of June, the Loire Campaign began, and within a week, the cities of Jargeau, Meung, and Beaugency fell to the French. Finally, on the 18th of that month, the opposing armies met at Patay for a decisive battle. By the time Joan arrived, the English had lost over 2,000 men, the French but one. The English army was decimated, Talbot unhorsed and captured.

The Maid returned to Orléans to urge that the Dauphin be crowned in the Cathedral of Reims, the place where Clovis had been baptized and crowned king of all Franks in 496. The see of an archbishopric since the 8th century, Reims had become the customary scene for French royal coronations after 1137. In 1429, however, the city was held by the Burgundians, who had taken much of the burden of fighting from the English. En route to Reims, the Dauphin and his cavalcade of nobles were halted at Troyes, occupied by a Burgundian garrison of 600. Calling on knights, equerries, archers, common militiamen, and valets alike to help raise a siege, Joan assured the men that they would enter this city "before three days, either by force or by love." At dawn, everything was ready, and at the sight of the imminent assault, the burghers opened the city gates to the French. Reims, too, yielded without a fight, and on the 17th of July, the Dauphin was officially crowned Charles VII of France.

Joan's troops attempted to re-enter Paris in September, but turned back after she was wounded in the leg while looking for a spot to cross the inner ditch. To stall for time to reinforce Paris with a newly-landed force from England, the Burgundians agreed, insincerely of course, to yield in the city to the French. Joan had been shut out of the negotiations, and her military efforts were undermined by the truce agreed to by the King. Though her army was reduced to little more than her own battalion, she resumed fighting early in 1430. The same year, Philip the Good dispatched his vassal, John of Luxembourg, to seize Compiègne in order to create a passage to Paris. Joan, however, moved first, and in the early hours of the 23rd of May, charged the Burgudian forces gathered outside the town. The French within Compiègne pulled up the drawbridge and closed the city gates, holding off out both friend and foe. Managing to drag her from the saddle amidst the short-lived battle, the Burgundians sold Joan to the English for 10,000 gold livres, after months of auctioning her for the highest price.

The English took Joan north, to the Norman port of Rouen, where they turned her over to an ecclesiastical court, which tried her as a heretic and a witch in a proceeding that flagrantly violated the legal procedures of the era. After fourteen months of interrogation, she was accused of unlawfully wearing masculine attire; while in prison, she was offered women's clothes and then raped. The second charge was that she used magic, because she claimed to hear the voices of saints and angels; the indictment stated that these were actually those of demons. Thirdly, she was accused of heresy for believing that she was directly responsible to God rather than to the Holy Mother Church; while St. Thomas Aquinas himself had insisted on the rights of the individual conscience, he had gone on to argue that heresy was a sin because such ignorance must be the result of criminal negligence.

Of the forty-two lawyers at the trial, all but three asked for lenience and an appeal to a higher court that was not under the English thumb. Of the over 600 witnesses who claimed to know the Maid personally, not one would speak a word against her—and each witness had been chosen by the prosecution, Joan being denied a defence counsel. She was condemned to death, but after she confessed her crimes "out of fear of the fire," her sentence was commuted to life imprisonment. However, she resumed male dress on her return to prison and was condemned anew, this time by a secular court.

On the 30th of May, 1431, in the Old Marketplace within the dark walls of Rouen, in the shadows of the Cathedral of Saint-Sauveur, a gruesome spectacle draws the attention of the populace. A 19-year-old peasant girl, "Jehanne, called la Pucelle," is declared "lying, seducing, pernicious, presumptuous, lightly believing, rash, superstitious, a divineress and blasphemer towards God and the Saints, a despiser of God Himself in His Sacraments; a prevaricator of the Divine Law, of sacred doctrine and of ecclesiastical sanctions; seditious, cruel, apostate, schismatic, erring on many points of our Faith," and burned at the stake. To many of the crowd, she was, however, the innocent would-be saviour of France from a century of foreign occupation. The martyrdom that the English thus conferred upon her would haunt them for the rest of their numbered days on French soil. The hundred-year clash of fickle and greedy feudal princes was turned into a war for national liberation; after Burgundy withdrew from English alliance, Charles VII captured Bordeaux (1453) in the southwest, ending the Hundred Years' War. Calais was all that was left for the English of their numerous conquests on the Continent.

The Christian Church has preserved for posterity to adore the names of countless men who died for their faith. The memory of the martyrs of the Reformation is revered. Statues are erected to those who have died in battle. Of the tens of thousands of women swallowed by the stake, one alone is remembered: the Maid of Orléans, a political victim. After being retried posthumously in a formal trial called by the French King in 1456, she was announced innocent by Pope Calixtus III. In 1920, she was formally declared a saint by Benedict XV.

CHAPTER 28

In its earliest form, the institution of chivalry was partly an attempt to convert the primitive and heathenish warriors to Christianity. After the Crusades began, the image of a knight was changed from that of a robber-warrior to a defender of the weak and the humble. From then on, the rituals of chivalry were a part of the rituals of Christianity, and to many, the knight was at his best as a crusader. The failure of the crusaders to save the Holy Land caused a disenchantment of the public in the abilities and motives of knights in general and military orders in particular. The romantic chivalry of the early Renaissance lifted the religious dominance of the knightly heritage, when the tales of Tristan and Isolde, Lancelot and Guinevere, gave a new twist on the duties a knight owed to women and the helpless. The knight-errant, looking for adventure in a personal quest usually connected with worldly, carnal experience, had little in common with the violent sinners who sought to expiate their grave sins by taking the cross.

The development in England of the longbow had long undermined the feudal armies, which were ultimately destroyed by the introduction of gunpowder. With the advent of modern hired armies, the old form of military service owed to one's immediate lord became obsolete, giving sovereigns a monopoly on war-making. To close ranks and to protect social status, the noble élite diverted their military prowess towards quite elaborate and rather tedious "mock battles." The rules of these jousts and tournaments became so complicated and the protective armours so strong, that in the end, no one suffered much bodily harm, although accidents did of course happen. By the latter half of the 15th century, the knightly battles, which perhaps had once justified the existence of a privileged feudal class, had become as harmless as some of today's more extreme sports. Increasingly elaborate suits of armour were forged purely for display, in extravagantly ornamented imitations of earlier models. The knight was ever vigilant of his honour, of himself as an individual, and of the fact that he himself was the ultimate judge of what was suited his dignity and what did not. This concept of honour became the centre of all, turning the knight into a hysterically sensitive individual who shunned the prosaic values of the world. Ironically, the romantic ideals of knightly honour and courtly love, which will forever be associated with the knights of the Middle Ages, were created by the demise of the very institution that shaped them.

Mediæval political speculation took the Roman Church and Empire for granted, as divinely ordained institutions; thinkers differed only as Guelphs and Ghibellines, leaning either to the papal or the imperial supremacy. The centuries-long conflict between the popes and the emperors was brought to a close by the Concordat of Vienna (1448), by which the Germans remained faithful to the papacy, and King Frederick was assured the crown of the Empire. The first of the Habsburgs to receive the imperial crown in the Eternal City, Frederick III held the office longer than any other emperor before or after him. With his coronation in 1452, the Emperor casually combined the celebration of his marriage to Princess Leonora of Portugal. This ceremony, symbolic of the spiritual and political unity of Western civilization, first performed in 800 CE when Charlemagne was crowned the first Emperor of the West since the collapse of Roman power, would never again take place in Rome.

The ailing Byzantine Empire itself was finally extinguished on the 29th of May, 1453, with the dramatic capture of Constantinople. One reason for the fall of the "New Rome" was the irreconcilable discord between the Roman Catholics and the Eastern Orthodox. The former would not render assistance if the latter did not acknowledge the pope as the head of the Universal Church, while the latter would remain ecclesiastically independent even if it meant falling to the Turks. The Greeks had already lived side by side with them for two centuries before the foundation of the Ottoman Empire, fighting together in wars, even intermarrying. But now the mosques of Constantinople were shut, and the Turkish troops who had been sight-seeing in the city were thrown out of the gates—Byzantium was at war.

The location of Constantinople at the intersection of trade routes was vital to the Turks. They also wished to conquer it in order to improve the supply line of their troops. The walls and moats of the city were a thousand years old, and for the last eight centuries, they had been Christendom's only protection against the surrounding threat of Islam. The Ottoman army, numbering 160,000 Muslims, was commanded by the young sultan Mohammed II (1451-

1481). "Either I shall take this city," he declared, "or the city will take me, dead or alive. If you will admit defeat and withdraw in peace, I shall give you the Peloponnese and other provinces for your brothers and we shall be friends. If you persist in denying me peaceful entry into the city, I shall force my way in and I shall slay you and all your nobles; and I shall slaughter all the survivors and allow my troops to plunder at will. The city is all I want, even if it is empty."

After the Sultan's cannons had hammered Constantinople fifty-three days without breaking through the ancient ramparts, a small group of his soldiers swam inside the wall through the sewer holes and hoisted a flag on the crest. Thinking the battle lost, the Greeks started retreating, and at that moment, the conquering forces poured over the mounds. The last Byzantine Emperor, Constantine XI Dragases was killed in the onslaught; his decapitated body was later identified from the purple imperial boots, adorned with the Roman eagles.

The Turkish soldiers were given free reign in the city for three days before the Sultan himself entered through the gates. For three days, the city was pillaged: 60,000 people were taken into slavery and sold or swapped as it pleased their masters; 120,000 manuscripts are said to have disappeared. Mohammed rode on his white horse over heaps of corpses, and headed straight for the famous Church of Hagia Sophia, where the Christians had fled to pray for divine protection. The Ottoman troops took a ruthless revenge on the city that would not surrender: priests were beheaded in the middle of Mass, women were murdered on their knees before the altar, young boys and girls were raped in the shrines and in the chapels. Upon beholding this havoc, Mohammed wept—he ordered to stop the mayhem. The greatest church in the world was turned into a mosque, and became the cornerstone of the new capital of the greatly expanding Ottoman Empire.

Mohammed, henceforth surnamed *Fatih*, "the Conqueror," built his power on charity and tolerance, and began rebuilding Constantinople. He soon brought about a *modus vivendi*, allowing the non-Muslim inhabitants to return to their former course of life. They were allowed to choose their religious leaders, and free to practise their religion under their guidance. In matters of personal status, they were governed by their own religious laws; i.e. issues such as marriage, divorce, child custody, alimony, and inheritance fell under the jurisdiction of their respective religious authorities. Mohammed wanted to make Constantinople the centre of the Islamic Empire and the most magnificent capital in the world. Attached to every mosque was a soup-kitchen from which 10,000 people got their daily bread. The "Sultan of the Romans" invited the citizens of all countries to his city, and in just eighty years, the population of Constantinople increased tenfold; Christians, Muslims, and Jews lived there side by side in amity.

The Eastern Orthodox having lost their secular head in the person of Constantine XI, the Slavonic principalities of the Balkan Peninsula turned their eyes towards the most powerful of the Orthodox rulers, namely, the Grand Duke of Moscow. Ivan "the Great," who succeeded Grand Duke Vasily II to the throne in 1462, was a cruel, born despot, as one Russian historian famously put it. His second marriage in 1472 to Sophia Palæologus, the niece of the last Byzantine Emperor, only added to his pretension. The princess never forgot the fact that imperial blood flowed in her veins, and through her influence, Byzantine splendour brought colour to the dismal Muscovy court. She brought with her Greek and Italian architects to beautify the city, and the two-headed eagle of Byzantium was added to the arms of Moscow. With the original Rome at an incommunicable distance, and the second Rome captured by the infidel, the leaders of the Russian Church proclaimed their capital as the "Third Rome," heir to the spiritual and political authority of both earlier Romes. By the end of the century, the Grand Duke had thrown off the Mongol yoke, which had weighed heavy on his country for the last two and a half centuries, and established autocratic rule in central and northern Russia, modelling his government on the tyranny of his former masters. The Orthodox Church spread to Asiatic Russia, and through Siberia, all the way to Alaska; its only contact with Catholicism was on the East European Plain through the Poles and Lithuanians, both traditional enemies of the Russians.

Pope Calixtus III opened his pontificate in 1455 by vowing "to Almighty God and the Holy Trinity, by wars, maledictions, interdicts, excommunications and in all other ways to punish the Turks" for the capture of Constantinople. He dispatched legates to all the countries of the West to kindle the zeal of princes in a final effort at a crusade. But the princes were slow to heed the call of the supreme pontiff—their countries were fast emerging from the divisions of their feudal past and becoming national monarchies, worse and worse rivals to one another. France and England were at war, and could not allow their forces to be undermined by participation in the papal plans; Germany was averse to joining an expedition which would give Hungary a direct advantage; Genoa did launch a fleet against the Turks, but only to expose herself to attack by Aragón; Portugal, discouraged by the lack of success, withdrew her fleet; Venice, ever guarding her own commercial interests, made a treaty with the Ottoman Empire.

1456 is remembered as the year when the Turks captured Athens and subsequently all Greece, bringing an end to what remained of Classicism in that country. Before collapsing under superior power, the Byzantine Empire had passed the heritage of the Hellenes to the Arabs and that of Christianity to the Slavs. And on its ruin, it lent its best to Western Europe; for the refugees, arriving mainly via Crete to Venice, laid a foundation for the renaissance of both the Greek language and Plato. The energies of Pope Calixtus, however, were directed too much towards the expedition against the Turks to allow him to devote much attention to the literary revival, and his neglect of the humanists made many of them his enemies in this "Heroic Age of Humanism." In 1457, he convoked another assembly of princes to devise measures against the threat of Islam, but it proved even more futile than the first one. Ultimately, the Pope's dispute with King Ferrante[199] of Naples not only prevented him from continuing the work of the crusade, but alienated from the cause the powerful family of Aragón[200].

Despite the unsettled times, the number of universities grew, and the dissemination of Greek culture all over Christendom revitalized the arts and sciences. The art of paper-making, introduced from China by the Arabs, and very slowly and reluctantly borrowed by the Christians from the Muslims, was developed further in the West. By the middle of the 15th century, real paper was made out of rags and flax so cheaply that when printing was invented—or borrowed from the Chinese—printed books soon became, if not cheap, at least less expensive and more numerous than manuscripts had ever been. The ideas of the Renaissance spread and evolved rapidly, thoroughly reshaping people's lives and habits.

Following in the Roman tradition, the Italian Renaissance was practical and not particularly pious. Morals had, in fact, sunk so low that the great humanist scholar, Æneas Sylvius de' Piccolomini, tells us that "scarcely a prince in Italy

---

[199] i.e. Ferdinand I

[200] to whom he owed his cardinalate and thus, indirectly, his papacy

had been born in wedlock"—a statement as applicable to the princes of the Church as those of the State. As a young man, he earned his living through his wide knowledge of the Classics, and his novel, a depiction of love directed at a married woman, was issued in twenty-seven Latin printings in the latter half of the 15th century and translated into various vernaculars. He had served at the court of Frederick III, helping spread humanism to Germany, but when he was elected to the papacy as Pius II (1458-1464), he forgot all his previous concerns. Bending over backwards to persuade the princes of the West to embark on a new crusade, he wore himself out in the vain attempt to revive something that was decidedly of the past.

The Ottomans had brought peace and prosperity to the regions they had conquered: the sense of security was so strong in the empire that the cities did not even require walls to protect them. The immense land area did not, however, satisfy Mohammed the Conqueror—he wanted to rule the seas as well. In 1463, a 16-year war broke out between the Turks and the Venetians, when the Ottomans challenged Venice's domination of the eastern Mediterranean. Pius declared that he himself would lead the "crusade," but when the Pope went to Ancona in June of 1464 to take command of the expedition, he fell ill and died. The Venetians subsequently invaded the Peloponnese and sacked Athens, but the Turkish fleets in turn penetrated deep into the Ægean; in the last years of the 15th century, the Ottoman cavalry many times came so close to Venice that the fires from the villages it destroyed could be seen from the top of the Campanile of St. Mark's. By the end of the century, the eastern Mediterranean was controlled by the Turks in its entirety.[201]

As the feudal system decayed and perished, monetary economy overturned natural economy, and this development favoured trading nations as much as it had encumbered agricultural societies. Mediæval long-distance trade had always centred around the Mediterranean, and the largest commercial cities, stimulated by their rivalry with the even richer Mohammedans, had long been in Italy. Through most of the late Middle Ages, the peninsula had been fought over by the pope and the emperor, both of whom permitted the rise of

---

[201] As a compensation, Venice embarked upon a policy of territorial expansion within Italy itself.

powerful autonomous communes to further their own aims. The Italian landowning nobility had early on become merchant nobles who took up residence in the towns and held the strings through a network of agents in the major trading centres. The phenomenal growth of wealth in the Italian cities finally led to the emergence of a series of city-states, i.e. individual regions ruled centrally from a single city. Neither popes nor kings could command respect in the hard-boiled businessmen who had made a pact with gold and knew its value in power politics.

The number of wealthy families produced by commerce were still of the nobility, wholly lacking the petty bourgeois characteristics that became so peculiar to their great successors north of the Alps. The Italian bankers, merchants, and businessmen were ambitious aristocrats, who loved the splendour of the old princely style, and spent their money on art in order to accentuate their and their city's eminence. While other countries had adopted the Gothic style of architecture, the Italians preferred the purer lines of the ancient temples, whose awe-inspiring remains still rose from the soil of their homeland, as if to rebuke the barbarism of the era. The appearance of towns was transformed as architects, sculptors, and painters laboured ceaselessly to make the surroundings of their masters as magnificent as possible, to convey with inventive allegories the glory and blessing of absolutism. This then revived the Roman penchant for visiting monuments and collecting works of art for purely æsthetic reasons, in contrast to the concentration on shrines and relics that had characterized mediæval Christendom. As the idea spread to Northern Europe, the well-to-do educated people began visiting the Mediterranean centres of Classical civilization in Italy, Greece, Turkey, and the Middle East. Henceforward, the steps of the pilgrims would be traced by merchants, diplomats, singers, poets, artists, and scientists.

The Italian plutocrats surrounded themselves with a court of artists and poets, whose mission was to praise and legitimate their power. This narrow artistic élite, recipient of generous rewards and conscious of its own importance, soon started to proclaim more its own than its patrons' glory. Thus was brought about the notion that poets and artists, in earlier times but humble, anonymous servants of the Church, equal to the many other craftsmen, represented the peak of humanity and deserved the proper treatment. Art became a matter for the connoisseurs; the painter, the sculptor, or the poet no longer created for all humanity as a herald of great salvific truths, but for a small circle that had the "ability" to appreciate the "finesse" and was capable of creating "resonant images"; the master-builders no longer built their chapels and domes to fulfill public yearning, as they had in the Middle Ages, but as contractors to art-loving princes and fame-seeking private individuals.

The city of Florence, though founded in ancient times, was of little importance before the 11th century. The area around it, called Tuscany, would be the centre of Italian culture from the High Middle Ages through the Renaissance; after the unification of Italy in the 19th century, the Tuscan dialect eventually became the official Italian language. No less significant is the fact that Tuscany was where Francesco Datini, the "Merchant of Prato," introduced the promissory note, which proved so useful for banking transactions. Merchants and bankers established a commanding lead in the civic affairs of Florence, and began beautifying the city. The Medici family was the one to amass the most money and power. First gaining prominence in Florence during the early 13th century, by the 15th, the family had became, through its extensive European commerce and banking, one of the most prominent in all Italy. The city, as it stands today, is largely the creation of the Medici.

The legend about the origins of the Medici relates the story of a Carolingian knight called Averado, who happened to be wandering nearby, when he was called upon to save the Florentines by slaying a giant. This giant supposedly dented the hero's shield several times, accounting for the red circles in the Medici coat of arms. In reality, the origins of the Medici were much humbler: the name suggests a connection with medicine, and the earliest members of the family were, indeed, apothecaries and barber-surgeons. Their coming to power involved no violent coups or takeovers, but was as subtle and gradual as the rise of the middle classes throughout Europe. Having started out as ordinary members of the medical guild, the Medici gradually assumed leading positions within every aspect of Florentine life. Thus, although Florence was still nominally a republic, the wealthy merchant-banker, Cosimo de' Medici (1389-1464), became in 1434 the real ruler of the city. This offended the other great families, and the Albizzi drove Cosimo, later known as the *Pater Patriæ*, "Father of the Land," to exile, but after the brief absence, he rose to even greater power. The Medici would dominate the Tuscan city-state, except for the occasional periods of exile, throughout the next three centuries.

The key to supremacy in the Italian city-states was military command. By the 14th century, the citizen army had given way to hired troops; the northern towns still made war on one another, but the wealthy burghers now paid companies of mercenary adventurers, the *condottieri*, to do the fighting. This change was a result of internal class conflict: whichever faction emerged a victor in the struggle for power was disinclined to let its defeated enemies bear arms. The largest city in Italy was Milan, the city of St. Ambrose. It was ruled by the aristocratic Visconti (Ital. "viscounts") family, which had first risen to prominence in 1262, when Ottone Visconti was made archbishop of Milan. In 1395, Emperor Wenceslaus sold Milan as a hereditary fief to Gian Galeazzo Visconti, but the latter had many rivals, and the duchy was divided after his death. His able and crafty son, Filippo Maria, devoted his skills to regaining the lost territories, enjoying a great measure of success largely because he employed the best mercenary captains money could buy, one of whom was Francesco Sforza, who eventually married the Duke's only daughter.

The Sforza (Ital. "force") were of peasant origin, but their founder, Francesco's father, Giacomuzzo Attendolo, had gained fame as a successful condottiere, and as a proof, changed the family name. When the male Visconti line died out with Filippo Maria in 1447, the people of Milan set up the "Ambrosian Republic" and hired Francesco to defend it. Instead, he laid siege to the city and proclaimed himself duke in 1450. He was assisted in this by Florence, a bitter and long-standing enemy of Milan. The Medici also helped the Sforza in the ensuing war against Venice and Naples, and enabled Francesco to hold on to his new duchy. The Italian states were small and numerous, and the only way for them to successfully maintain territorial integrity was to league up with allies they could not fully trust. The dispute between the principalities and the sovereign cities was settled in the Peace of Lodi (1454), which became the basis for the League of all the Italian states that maintained a precarious peace in the country for the next four decades. Italy had been divided into a number of commonwealths, each governed either by an oligarchy or a prince, but the individual enjoyed considerable liberty, and much encouragement was given to art and literature.

The Sforza clan continued to rule the duchy of Milan for much of the next eighty years. Their rule may have been personal and autocratic, but in their keenness to demonstrate the magnificence of their courts, they patronized architects such as Filarete, Alberti, and Bramante, and humanists such as

Filelfo. Francesco was succeeded by his eldest son, Galeazzo Maria, whose wife, Bona of Savoy, acted as regent for their son, Gian Galeazzo, who acceded to the dukedom at the age of eight on his father's assassination. In 1480, however, her brother-in-law, Ludovico il Moro ("the moor," an epithet which had nothing to do with his complexion), deprived Bona of the regency, and became—in fact though not in name—the ruler of Milan. With his wife, Beatrice d'Este, he held one of the most brilliant of Renaissance courts, pouring vast sums of money into the arts and sciences.

In like manner, Cosimo de' Medici was a generous patron of the humanist scholars in Florence, inviting the two most distinguished ones to take a prominent position as chancellors of the city. He established the first public library in Christian Europe at the Monastery of San Marco, which he rebuilt. He also erected or redecorated many other sacred buildings, including the Medici parish church of San Lorenzo, much of which was designed by the greatest architect of the time, Filippo Brunelleschi (1377-1446), the inventor of linear perspective. The founder of modern sculpture, Donatello, born Donato di Betto Bardi (1386-1466), was also among the artists patronized by Cosimo. While Donatello also worked in many other Italian cities, it was in his native Florence that he created the famous bronze *David* (c. 1435), the first nude statue of the Renaissance. Other cities—Venice, Genoa, Mantua, Urbino, Ferrara, etc.—followed the lead; ultimately even Rome had to adopt this revived fashion.

During the next generation, Florentine artists such as Antonio Pollaiuolo (1431-1498) and Andrea del Verrocchio (1435-1488) came to study anatomy in detail. This idea was taken up by the latter's apprentice, Leonardo da Vinci (1452-1519), who became an independent master in 1478. The proportions of the human body were the basis for a broader understanding of existence—Leonardo studied the functions of the bodily organs in order to better comprehend nature. The introduction of printing had made possible the recording of craft traditions that had been handed down orally in previous centuries, thereby reducing the gap between the artisan and scholar classes; the artist-engineer Leonardo drew up fortresses and weapons, and even outlined the mechanics of a parachute. "Science is the captain, and practice the soldier. Those who fall in love with practice without science are like a sailor who enters a ship without a helm or compass."

While Leonardo's studies of flight and other technological issues were far beyond their time, his innovations in painting influenced the course of Italian art for more than a century after his death. As a contrast to the tedious accuracy of earlier artists, Leonardo filled his paintings with light, shadow, and colour, thus producing a much stronger atmosphere and depth in both the external setting and the mental impression. His first large painting, *The Adoration of the Magi*, was ordered for the Florentine monastery of San Donato a Scopeto in 1481, but left unfinished, for the next year, Leonardo entered the service Ludovico Sforza, not only as an architect, but as the principal engineer in his military enterprises. In between designing battle engines for Il Moro's armies, Leonardo laboured on his masterpiece, *The Last Supper*, a fresco in the refectory wall of Bramante's magnificent new building, the convent of Santa Maria delle Grazie in Milan. He also produced many other paintings and drawings, theatre designs, architectural sketches, and scale models for the dome of Milan Cathedral.

The term "renaissance," a French word for rebirth, was first used by the 16th-century artist and art historian Giorgio Vasari only in reference to the revival in Italy of the ancient Roman architecture. Later historians of course employed the term in a much broader sense, marking the fact that it was not just the pagan architecture that was reborn in the late Middle Ages. They were naturally referring to the revival of Greek and Roman literature and ideals, chiefly during the 15th century. Still, the Italian Renaissance was almost purely Latin, and for a long time, it extended to literature alone. What was adopted from the past was not the typical Classical elements, but mostly the sort of material that already anticipated Christianity. The Renaissance was "paganish" only in some of its individual representatives and even with them only in the negative sense that they held a skeptical and partly atheistic attitude towards the Christian articles of faith.

The competition over writing in Classical Latin, and to a small extent in Greek, led mostly to statistical victories, as is usually the case whenever one attempts to breathe new life into something that is gone for good. With the revival of Classical learning, the scholarship of the Renaissance set about to undermine Mediæval Latin literature. Even the traditional prayers, hymns, and homilies of the mediæval Church were rewritten in the new, Classical style favoured by Renaissance popes. The great poets of the time wrote Ciceronian prose and Vergilian eclogues, but nothing new was created, only perfect imitations of the old. In trying to zealously abide by the examples of the Classical Period, the humanists were embarking to erase, not to reform, the living Mediæval Latin, and—aside from the perseverance of Church Latin—they succeeded.

Greek was, on the whole, studied only at the Platonic Academy founded by Cosimo de' Medici. In 1439, his family had managed to move from Ferrara to Florence the ecclesiastical council summoned to unite the Churches of the East and the West.[202] There was, of course, no great reunion[203]; the real importance of the Council lay in the fact that it had brought Gemistus Pletho (c. 1355-1452) and other eminent learned Greeks to Italy, and introduced the study of Plato to Renaissance Florence. The first of the Renaissance Platonists—responsible for the most important early translations and commentaries of not only Plato but also of the Neoplatonists—was Marsilio Ficino (1433-1499). The rediscovery of Classical learning is considered by many scholars to have specifically begun with his translation of the *Corpus Hermeticum*. Yet, Neoplatonism had never really faded from the Western tradition, nor was the Italian Renaissance a revival of Plato. Rather, it forged new philosophies from Plato and the Platonic tradition.

Since one of the ideas of humanism was that religious truth was in part revealed to all, Christian and non-Christian alike, the humanists sought to conciliate non-Christian thinking, particularly that of Plato and his followers, with Christian thought, and to demonstrate, through exhaustive textual scholarship, the essential similarities between non-Christian and Christian philosophies and religion. In his chief original work, the *Theologica Platonica* (1482), Ficino combined Christian theology with Neoplatonic elements. The

---

[202] The reason given was the unhealthy conditions in Ferrara, but the real grounds were the offer of the Florentines to pay for the expenses, and, by getting away from the seaside, to lessen the chances of the Greeks going home before the conclusion of the union.

[203] The Greeks were motivated wholly by a desire to get the assistance of the West against the advance of the Turks, and only small groups of the Orthodox, as of the smaller non-Orthdox churches, i.e. Armenian, Jacobite, and Nestorian, entered the Roman communion. The patriarchs of Alexandria, Antioch, and Jerusalem issued a joint letter in 1443, denouncing the Council of Florence as a synod of robbers and metrophanes, and the Byzantine Patriarch as a heretic and matricide.

greatest synthesizer of all was, however, Ficino's friend and student, the brilliant young nobleman Giovanni Pico della Mirandola (1463-1494). He brought to this project a tremendous mind, an insatiable curiosity, and an intellectual confidence that few if any have matched before or since; while others endeavoured to show that there was no fundamental disagreement between Classical philosophy and Christianity, Pico sought nothing short of reconciling every human philosophy and every human religion with Christianity. As a byproduct, he revived the study of Hebrew, hitherto all but confined to the rabbis, and introduced Renaissance humanists to the Jewish *Qabalah*. Being as it was based on the renewed study of Hebrew and Greek, the humanism of the Renaissance expressly marked a culture that took in account the forces represented by ancient Judæa and Hellas for the better of Christendom. Jerusalem and Athens had once again become the primary influences on the Western civilization and way of life.

One of the most brilliant figures of the age was Lorenzo de' Medici, who for good reason was dubbed *Il Magnifico*, "the Magnificent." He was only 20 years old when he was called to take his father Piero's place at the head of the city government, and while having no formal power, ruled Florence as autocratically as his grandfather Cosimo had. A multifaceted personage, he could be hard-handed when need arose, but saw to the entertainment of his people by organizing festivities and carnivals, and added to their pageantry with his high-spirited poems, in the improvisation of which he was an adept. While his verses are important to the history of Italian literature, Lorenzo was also the *primus motor* of the Platonic Academy, which had a profound effect on the religious and artistic outlook of the era. All this he could easily combine with falconry and recreational hunting, which formed an essential part of his life throughout the years.

In the end, Lorenzo the Magnificent met his master in the Dominican friar Savonarola, leader of the reaction against the Renaissance. This dogmatic eschatologist from Ferrara made a deep impression upon the greatest minds of the time, ending an era in Florentine history. On the famous "bonfire of the vanities" that this great preacher of penitence erected, burned with the other worldly trifles also the works of Classical antiquity and of humanism. His own fall was not due so much to his severity, as to the pacts he inadvertently concluded with the new political forces.

CHAPTER 29

At the daybreak of the Modern Era, Italy was the most highly civilized country in Europe, famous for its arts, its literature, its science, rich in the products of agriculture, industry, and commerce, gilded by the Sun of Renaissance, nourished by study of the Greek literature that had spread to the West after the fall of Byzantium. One might assume that political stability and economic security would be essential for intellectual and cultural experimentation, but that fact is that some of the most revolutionary and far-reaching cultural work was done in a period of great insecurity.

The Italian Peninsula had been divided into numerous principalities and independent cities, and the forms of government in the various city-states were as varied as the states themselves. These separate states had no common social tie, were founded on no common *jus* or right, but were tangled up in a web of clashing interests and capricious diplomatic unions. They fought for territorial expansion, control of trade routes, access to seaports, and possession of natural resources; just like their internal conflicts, the wars and rivalries between the cities were as a rule bitter, prolonged, and ruthless. There was a war of parties and city-states against one and all, and it was ridiculous to even talk about laws. Justice was given to one who had power, and power could only be obtained by being strong enough, cunning enough, and pitiless enough to orchestrate the demise of one's rivals.

The history of Rome was more than ever that of the papacy. Just like all the other heads of a city-state, the popes of this period were mainly interested in beautifying their city, patronizing its arts and letters, and raising their and their family's fortunes. They were the most magnificent in the history of the Church, holding more territories, enjoying more wealth, and claiming almost unlimited power. The Roman pontificate had become a golden goose for the family who controlled the position; there was no longer a struggle to raise a family's status through the papacy—those who received the office were by definition already members of the privileged class.

Rodrigo de Borja was born at the Valencian town of Játiva, on the 1st of

January, 1431. His parents were Jofre de Borja and Isabella Borgia, sister of the future Pope Calixtus III. Borgia was an Italianized version of the name "Borja," and the two branches were originally of the same family. Though claims of Spanish royalty have been associated with the origins of the Borja family, they seem to have been merely of nobility. When his father died, young Rodrigo was adopted to the immediate family of his uncle, and would thenceforward be known to the Italians as Rodrigo Borgia. Because his uncle was the Archbishop of Valencia at the time, Rodrigo would enter the Church at the youngest age possible: six. At the age of twenty-five, he was made a cardinal by the same uncle, now the Pope. A year later, in 1457, he was made Vice-Chancellor of the Church, and despite the blatant nepotism in his nomination to this very important office, he would continue to hold it under the four subsequent popes. Though it was unusual during this "Golden Age of Bastards" to find an ecclesiastic who did not violate his oath of chastity, Rodrigo, at least, appears to have been faithful to one woman most of his life.[204] To Vanozza dei Cattanei (1442-1518) he fathered his children: Juan, Cesare, Lucrezia, and Jofre, to whom he was without question deeply devoted.

Sixtus IV (1471-1484) was the first pope to have Rome and the neighbouring area thoroughly under his control. However, he acquired the necessary funds by simony, which suddenly grew to unforeseen proportions, and would not have obtained the papal dignity without recourse to the same illicit means. What is more, he practised nepotism on a scale hitherto unknown among popes, appointing every relative he had to high ecclesiastical positions. After his death, his nephew, Cardinal Giuliano della Rovere, competed for the papal tiara with Rodrigo Borgia, until Innocent VIII (1484-1492), the richest member of the College of Cardinals, bought the office. Giuliano gratified his ambition by doing much of the governing for that flaccid pontiff, but Rodrigo won the next election and had little use for his rival, who from then on busied himself with intrigue. For thirty-five years, Rodrigo had

---

[204] Taking a concubine has mostly negative connotations to modern people, but it was a practice that had been around in one form or another since Classical Rome. The legal lines between concubinage and marriage were often blurred, and by the mid-13th century, if a man and woman cohabited openly, they were considered lawfully married. Indeed, there was no law against Catholic laymen having concubines until 1563—in the wake of the Protestant Reformation.

managed the affairs of the Papal Chancery with rare ability and diligence, and though Spaniards were never popular in Italy, his elevation to the papacy was hailed by the Romans with much enthusiasm.

Alexander VI, as Rodrigo was now called, found the Papal States in great disorder. The conflicts of the noble factions, led by the Colonna and Orsini families, had reduced the Eternal City to anarchy under the easy-going Innocent VIII. If Sixtus IV had filled the papal treasury through the sale of spiritual favours and dignities, Innocent, for his part, had established an office for the trade of secular favours, in which pardons for murder were sold for money. Thus, at the end of Innocent's pontificate, the city swarming with licensed and unlicensed assassins, and Alexander proceeded to justify the favourable opinion of the Romans by ordering investigations to be made and every culprit discovered to be hanged on the spot. He divided Rome into four districts, and placed over each a magistrate with plenary powers for the keeping of order, quickly changing the face of the city.

Alexander was a munificent patron of the arts and a brilliant political statesman. He rebuilt the Roman University and made generous provision for the support of its professors; he surrounded himself with scholars and granted absolution to Pico della Mirandola, who had been accused of heresy by the Inquisition under Innocent VIII.[205] Alexander deserves to be known as the real founder of the "Leonine City," for only now did the Vatican Field assume a thoroughly urban character. Under Alexander's orders, the Florentine architect Antonio de Sangallo added bastions to the outer walls of Castel Sant' Angelo, turning the ancient mausoleum into a genuine fortress capable of sustaining a siege; by fortifying the Torre di Nona, Alexander secured Rome from naval attacks. He oversaw the construction of the Passetto[206], a long fortified corridor that links Sant' Angelo and the Vatican Palace; he had Pinturicchio adorn the Borgia Apartment with the now famous frescoes, pointing the way to his immortal disciple, Raphael. Bramante executed the fountains in Piazza Santa Maria, in Trastevere, and in St. Peter's Square as an

---

[205] In 1486, Pico had offered to publicly defend his 900 philosophical and theological theses at Rome. As an introduction to the planned debate, he wrote his *Oration on the Dignity of Man*. The disputation was of course never held, but the *Oration* remains a concise statement of some of Pico's principal ideas, and, indeed, "a manifesto of Renaissance humanism."

[206] later sneeringly referred to as the "Popeduct"

under-architect of Alexander. The Basilica of Santa Maria Maggiore likewise owes its beautiful ceiling to Alexander, in the decoration of which he reputedly employed the first gold brought from the New World by Christopher Columbus.

While the idea of the crusade was never given up altogether, it had taken new forms and adapted itself to the new conditions. The Conquistadores, who went forth to discover new lands, saw themselves as the auxiliaries of the crusade. Vasco da Gama was a Knight of Christ, Henry the Navigator a Grand Master of the Order, and Columbus' flagship, the famous Santa Maria, bore the red Templar crosses on her sails. When they sought the means of doubling Africa or reaching Asia by routes from the East, they were thinking of attacking the Mohammedans in the rear and calculating on the alliance of a fabled Christian king, Prester John. Columbus himself explored partly to find a new route to Jerusalem, and partly to obtain wealth that would enable the Catholic Kings of Spain to carry their Reconquista across North Africa and towards the Holy City.

The popes strongly encouraged the explorers and many of these heralds of the Modern Era were Italian; as early as the 13th century, Marco Polo had reached all the way to China and Southeast Asia, and in the 15th, another Venetian, John Cabot, arrived at Newfoundland. It is with the Crusades that we must connect the origin of their geographical explorations. Arabs taught the Crusaders about navigation, having recently learned to apply the magnetic compass of the Chinese to that maritime activity. The Italian navigators were the first to make use of the device in Europe, but the ordinary seamen were afraid of it. For long, the compass was considered an instrument of witchcraft, as those who applied it might still in Columbus' day be accused of dabbling in the Black Art. Yet, the great voyages of discovery could hardly have been possible without it, for it made possible the maintaining of course on the high seas even in adverse weather, when neither the Sun nor the stars could provide help with navigation. Maps and charts could naturally be used for dead-reckoning at sea, but not for fixing the position of a ship out of sight of land.

The truly significant explorations were of course carried out under the command of the Iberians, not least because in his bull *Romanus Pontifex* (1455), Pope Nicholas V had authorized the Portuguese crown to "invade, search out, capture, vanquish, and subdue all Saracens and pagans whatsoever, and other enemies of Christ wheresoever placed." As soon as Columbus returned to

Europe, Alexander VI put a rein on the fierce competition between Spain and Portugal over the newly-discovered lands. His bulls of 1493 fixed a line of demarcation along a circle passing 100 leagues west of the Cape Verde Islands and through the two poles, giving the entire New World to Spain and Africa and India to Portugal. The Treaty of Tordesillas (1494), however, shifted the line to a circle passing 370 leagues west of Cape Verde, thus giving Portugal a claim to Brazil, though it remains controversial whether the Portuguese yet even knew of its existence. At any rate, a little later the Brazil-goer Amerigo Vespucci, working under the Portuguese, lent his name to the new continent.

There had, at different times, been up to five different Iberian Christian kingdoms, all of which were eventually consolidated. In 1469, the two mightiest kingdoms of the peninsula were united when King Ferdinand II of Aragón married Queen Isabella of Castile. The independent Spanish Inquisition was soon instituted to uphold religious and national unity.[207] Portugal, which had started out as a county of León, was the only kingdom to ultimately maintain independence from the rest of Iberia. The Moorish kingdom of Granada fell to the Catholic Kings in 1492, and all its commercial and monetary advantages to Christian Spain. This may have lessened in the eyes of the Spanish royal couple the importance of the Jewish economic contribution, for still in the same year, Ferdinand and Isabella signed an edict expelling all Jews from their kingdoms.

There were no exceptions by age or condition; after a cruel decade of torture in the hands of the Spanish Inquisition, the Jews were now given the choice of being baptized as Christians or be banished from Spain forever. They had to dispose of their possessions and property at whatever price they could to obtain, but were not allowed to take currency, silver, or gold with them, and had to pay all taxes till the end of the year. Some Jews burned down their own houses just to avoid the injustice of selling a fine piece of property for a fraction of its value. Their synagogues were turned into churches, their cemeteries into pasturage. 200,000 of them left Spain penniless. Many migrated to Turkey, Syria, Palestine, Egypt, and North Africa, where they found tolerance among Muslims—Constantinople alone soon boasted 44 synagogues. Of the Christian nations, only Italy welcomed them with

---

[207] Alarmed at the severity of Torquemada, Alexander VI ordered him to share his duties with two other inquisitor-generals—an order which the royal confessor quickly overrode.

humanity.

Alexander VI's tolerant policy towards the Jewish refugees earned the enmity of his native Spain and the censure of his closed-minded contemporaries. It was not until 1965 that the Catholic Church formally abandoned its teaching that Jews were "Christ-killers," and the year before, when Pope Paul VI visited the Holy Land, he refused to accept any vestige of Israeli statehood, clinging to the dogma that Jews were condemned to wander as punishment for rejecting Jesus. Spain was the last Western country to recognize Israel (1986), and only in 1990 were Jews in Spain given the same legal rights as Catholics.

The subsequent expulsion of the Moors in 1502 had much less impact since far more Moors than Jews pretended to accept Christianity and were allowed to remain in Spain. Moreover, boys under fourteen and girls under twelve were not allowed to leave with their parents, and the Catholic nobility were permitted to retain their Moorish slaves—provided that these were kept in fetters. There would not be a single official Islamic mosque in Granada for over five hundred years, the first being opened as late as 2003.

The conquest of Mexico and Peru, the flow of American gold and silver, and her battlefield superiority made Spain the most powerful European state; she became an Atlantic power, revolutionizing the commerce of the West. Maize and orange, tomato and banana, cacao and potato, coffee and tobacco, cochineal and vanilla, ginger and cinnamon were all among the produces acquired by the Europeans from the New World. The massive import of precious metals which had been so scarce in the Middle Ages, furthered the spread of monetary economy, giving merchants, bankers, and tax collectors a more important role in society. Their commercial activities not only produced wealth, but also seriously redistributed wealth. The leading merchant families such as the Medici, the Fuggers, the Welsers, the Imhoff, and the Tuckers grew rich. The noble families, on the other hand, depended on fixed feudal rents and dues, and because they tended to borrow money only for non-productive purposes such as gambling, partying, and waging war, they more than often defaulted on their loans, each time transferring a part of their property to the new mercantile classes.

Who owned what lands was a matter of no little concern to the pope, since he needed people who would support him in times of invasion placed within his reach. Franceschetto Cibo, the son of Innocent VIII, and the son-in-law of Lorenzo the Magnificent, controlled two papal fiefs that had been seized from the Anguillara family. He sold these to Virginio Orsini for 40,000 ducats with the approval of Piero de' Medici, a relative of both Orsini and Cibo. Not only was it a rule that the pope alone could alter the ownership of papal fiefs, but the transfer of these two estates was viewed by the Sforza as disturbing the balance of power in Italy. Ludovico the Moor and his brother, Cardinal Ascanio Sforza, whom Alexander had raised to the vice-chancellorship, pressed the Pope to check the influence of King Ferrante of Naples, a supporter of the Orsini. Therefore, on the 25th of April, 1493, Pope Alexander, along with Milan and Venice, solemnly proclaimed what was known as the League of St. Mark—even though the Venetians only joined for the purpose of opposing Florence.

The League was cemented by the first of Lucrezia's three marriages. The Pope's 13-year-old daughter was joined in matrimony to the much older Giovanni Sforza, Lord of Pesaro and a cousin of Ludovico and Ascanio. This was not Lucrezia's first betrothal, however; in fact, the King of Naples had hoped her to marry into his family. He talked of war, but through the mediation of Spain, came to terms with Alexander, and even promised to help him win the Cibo estates back. As a pledge of reconciliation, Ferrante gave his granddaughter, Donna Sancia, a mere child, in marriage to the Pope's youngest son Jofre, with the Calabrian principality of Squillace as dowry. Feeling betrayed and fearful of Neapolitan invasion, Ludovico urged King Charles VIII of France to seize the crown of Naples on ground of the old Angevin claim.

An envoy of the French King arrived in Rome just a few days after Ferrante's reconciliation with the Pope, demanding the investiture of Naples for his master. He was flatly refused, and when the King of Naples died in January of 1494, Alexander paid no heed to French protests and threats, confirming the succession of Ferrante's son, Alfonso II, and sending his favourite nephew, Cardinal Giovanni Borgia, to crown him. Meanwhile, Giuliano della Rovere, who had resisted the Pope's policy and fled to Avignon, was joined by other disgruntled cardinals in promoting Charles' invasion of Italy as a means towards deposing Alexander.

In September, 1494, the French King crossed the Alps, marking the beginning of the Italian Wars and an end to the period of relative peace in the peninsula. As Alexander was wont to say, Charles needed no other weapon in his march through northern Italy than the chalk with which he marked out the lodgings of his troops. On his way to Florence, the King paid a visit to Ludovico, who laid sick in Pavia, and then proceeded towards Pisa, which threw off Florentine rule at his approach. Before entering Florence, Charles was met by Savonarola, who had prophesied that God would send an avenger to rescue Italy from her godless condition. The King's appearance seemed to confirm the predictions of the Friar, who now enjoyed the immense prestige of a true prophet. The Medici were banished from the city, and as the "Dictator of Florence," the puritanical monk held a brief sway over the minds and bodies of her citizens.

As if things were not bad enough for Rome already, Charles refused to even speak to the cardinal who was sent out to negotiate with him, because the cardinal was related to prominent Neapolitan families. The King continued his advance, and on the 31st of December, he marched through the Porta del Popolo into Rome. The Roman barons deserted the Pope one after the other; the commander of his army defected; Cardinals della Rovere, Sforza, Savelli, and Colonna had ridden into the city with the French troops, and now clamoured for his deposition. A saintlier pope might have made the fatal mistake of surrendering to the conqueror of Italy, but Alexander VI stared into the mouth of the enemy cannon from the crumbling fortifications of Sant' Angelo, whose defences had yet to be finished.

In the end, it was Charles who surrendered. The King had no desire to humiliate the Pope beyond what was necessary for the success of his designs on Naples. He acknowledged Alexander as true pope, and the disgruntled cardinals, with exception of Giuliano, were reconciled to the Pope. Charles further announced that the conquest of Naples was to be followed by that of Constantinople and the East. For this reason, Alexander turned over to him the valuable Ottoman hostage Djem, brother and rival of Sultan Beyazid II, while the Pope's son, Cardinal Cesare Borgia, accompanied the French troops to Naples as his legate.

When Charles entered Naples on the 22nd of February, 1495, the unpopular Alfonso II had already fled to a remote Sicilian monastery. His son and appointed successor, Ferrantino[208], failed to receive any support and

---

[208] i.e. Ferdinand II

retreated to the protection of Spain. The swiftness and efficiency of Charles' march through Italy caused great alarm, both among the other city-states and outside Italy; the League of Venice was formed (1495) at the instigation of Ferdinand of Aragón, consisting of Spain, Sicily, Venice, the Papal States, and the Holy Roman Empire—the official object of the alliance being the crusade. Ludovico, equally terrified by the speed of the French conquests, joined the League a year after it was created, and the alliance was further strengthened by the accession of Henry VII of England, victor of the Wars of the Roses (1455-1485). Cesare was able to make his escape from the French camp, and Charles, too, quit the garrison, having abandoned himself for several months to the pleasures of Naples.

The French King found that he had to fight his way out of Italy, and after distinguished himself against odds at the Battle of Fornuovo (the 6th of July, 1495), finally made it to Paris. From the innumerable Neapolitan brothels his army had contracted a nasty new illness, which the Italians dubbed the "French Disease" and the French of course called the "Neapolitan Disease." Nowadays, it is known as *syphilis*, but to this day, we cannot be sure where it came from. It may have been brought back by the sailors in Columbus' ships, or it may have come from the East with the Mongol conquests. With Charles' troops it, in any case, soon spread all over Europe, becoming in a short time a fashionable disease of the era. Almost all the notables of the age were, according to their contemporaries, syphilitics. The disease was so widely spread that no one hesitated to acknowledge it in public; it was the topic of the high society; even poems were written about it.

The French invasion taught Alexander that if he wished to be the real master of the Papal States, he must break the power of the disloyal and insolent barons, who had abandoned him in his hour of need. In a typical Renaissance fashion, this otherwise laudable task became identified with schemes for the aggrandizement of his family. In 1497, Juan Borgia was accorded dubious honours by being made lord of several papal fiefs confiscated from the Orsini and Farnese families. A stronger remonstrance than that offered by the Archbishop of Siena echoed through Rome a week later when, on the 16th of June, the lifeless body of the Duke of Gandia was fished out of the Tiber. The bereaved old Pope fasted from Thursday to Sunday, declaring that he loved Don Juan more than anything else in the world, and had he seven papacies, he would give them all to restore his son to life. Distraught with grief, Alexander gave much thought to reform, appointing a six-cardinal commission to draw up a plan for the reformation of the Church. But the mood soon passed, and the proposals of the cardinals were set aside as injurious to the papal prerogatives.

From then on, Cesare's wishes were the commands of the papal court. Yet another Borgia was given the honour of crowning the King of Naples: Ferrantino had died childless and was succeeded by his uncle Frederick of Altamura, whose coronation was one of Cesare's last, though probably also one of his first, ecclesiastical acts. Cesare's intention, opposed at first by his father, was to resign the cardinalate and to become a secular prince. By marrying Frederick's daughter, Charlotte of Aragón, he would have become one of the most powerful barons in the kingdom, but the princess' reluctance could not be overcome. During the suit, the Vatican witnessed another nuptial ceremony. Lucrezia's previous marriage with Giovanni Sforza was annulled on the scandalous and evidently untruthful ground that the husband was impotent and the union had never been consummated. Her hand was then given to a man her own age, namely Duke Alfonso of Bisceglie, an illegitimate son of King Alfonso II.

Around this time, Alexander became the patron of Michelangelo (1475-1564), who has variously been dubbed as the Last of the Gothicists, the Perfecter of Classicism, the Originator of the Baroque, and the Father of Expressionism. A painter, a sculptor, an architect, and a poet, he had fled to Rome when his Medici patrons were temporarily expelled from Florence. The Pope had ordered Savonarola to refrain from preaching, but the Friar of San Marco continued to denounce immorality in the Church. After being excommunicated for insubordination, Savonarola declared Alexander a false pope elected by simony. However, the Florentines themselves soon grew tired of the Friar's rigid demands. Hostility towards him mounted, led mainly by the local Franciscans, until in the March of 1498, the Florentine government, threatened with a papal interdict, asked him to quit preaching. There were riots, for which Savonarola and two of his disciples were arrested by the city. Under torture, he confessed to being a false prophet, and all three were hanged by the people of Florence.[209]

The Florentine Republic was re-established after the execution of

---

[209] For good measure, Savonarola's corpse was then burned at the stake.

Savonarola. At the triumph of the opposition, a young clerk by the name of Niccolò Machiavelli (1469-1527) was appointed head of the second chancery. He was secretary of the magistracy, a ten-man council that controlled the diplomatic affairs and military operations of the republic. It was the Florentines who first maintained permanent ambassadors in foreign capitals, and the chancellor's main duties lay precisely in missions to Italian and foreign courts. For the next fourteen years, Machiavelli was entirely occupied with the voluminous correspondence of his office, various diplomatic missions, and organizing a Florentine militia. He became acquainted with many of the European sovereigns and was able to study their political strategies. So, in the course of his official duties, he gradually acquired the principles and ideas which he later conveyed in his amoral but influential works on statecraft that would make his name a synonym for artfulness and deceit.

Up until Machiavelli's day, Western political philosophy had always presupposed an ideal, be it Hellenic or Judæo-Christian. The reports of the early Italian diplomats, however, contain the first attempts to study politics from a scientific point of view, and some of them are still of value even today. Machiavelli's own diplomatic dispatches[210] reveal the acute perception and profound judgement of a political genius. He studied men not according to the traditional preconceptions, but as he found them. In *Il Principe* (1513), Machiavelli depicts the political situation of Italy without regard to the traditional concepts of constitutional law that had been held to dictate the actions of the prince. Machiavelli reduced the naked, unabashed reasons of state to a system, and sought to justify them with such cynical candour that it is sometimes still assumed today that his most famous work is only a scathing satire on the despots of the time—disregarding the fact that it was not intended for the public but written only for the private use of a Medici.

Whether Machiavelli meant to corrupt or to instruct the world, to give rise to tyrants or to bring about their fall, is completely immaterial. As a man of science, he strove to deduce laws from his subject matter by vigorous study. By focusing on its basic principles, Machiavelli founded the science of politics for the modern world. He observed that the practical policies of the contemporary Italian principalities were dictated by ruthless selfishness, which he assumed to be a part of man's essence. Since internal conflicts were a

---

[210] first published in 1767

constant in the human societies, a strong social force was needed to uphold order. When the need arose, the prince had to scheme and deceive to attain his objectives, for "in the actions of men, and especially of princes, from which there is no appeal, the end justifies the means." One may have wonderful moral aims, but without sufficient power and the readiness to wield it, one will accomplish nothing. Machiavelli therefore demanded, with his characteristic and unabashed frankness, that men who cannot do without the luxury of conscience better leave politics alone. His greatest merit was that he laid bare the inner workings of power politics without resorting to empty phrases and hypocritical words to embellish even the most unseemly details.

Charles VIII of France died in April, 1498, preceded to the grave by his only son. The French crown passed to his cousin, the Duke of Orléans, who, as Louis XII, stood in dire need of not one but two papal favours: firstly, he was anxious to be divorced from his deformed and barren wife, Joan of Valois, whom he had been coerced into marrying in his youth; secondly, it was vital that he should be united to his dead cousin's young widow, for Queen Anne carried the dowry of Brittany with her. Alexander promptly issued the required decree annulling the King's marriage and further granted him a dispensation from the impediment of affinity. The prospect of an alliance between France and the Holy See drove several Western powers to the verge of schism, but threats of a council and deposition did little to intimidate the Pope, who by now had the Curia firmly in control.

Louis had inherited the French claims to the duchy of Milan from his grandmother, Valentina Visconti, and unlike his immediate predecessor, fully planned to enforce them. Alexander did not hesitate to take advantage of this second "barbarian" invasion of Italy for the consolidation of his temporal power and the advancement of his family. No longer a cardinal, Cesare began his political career as papal legate to France on the 1st of October, 1498. Designated Duke of Valentinois and Peer of France, he received the hand of Charlotte d'Albret, King Louis' niece and the sister of the King of Navarre, then a young lady of sixteen. The dowry was handsome, the marriage duly solemnized, and—according to a letter addressed by Cesare to his father—consummated eight times during the wedding night. On the 8th of October, 1499, the French King, accompanied by Duke Cesare, made his triumphal entry into Milan, expelling Ludovico from his duchy and bringing captivity to his brother, the cardinal. Ludovico's attempt to recover his lands was defeated at Novara the next year, when he was betrayed by his mercenaries, and imprisoned in France.

The taking of Milan was a signal to start campaigns against the petty tyrants misruling the Papal States. Even though the German emperors had renounced their claims to Spoleto, Ancona, and the Romagna in the 13th century, actual control by the papacy of its territories did not begin until the 16th. The power of France enabled Alexander VI to conquer all the usurped papal territory and quell any rebellion that might arise in future. As Captain-General of the Church, Cesare made good on the papal claims to Imola, Forlì, Rimini, and other cities, many of his victories being celebrated by services in St. Peter's. Between 1499 and 1501, he subdued the cities of the Romagna one by one—the tyrants who were expelled never returned.

In stark contrast to the religious ends associated by pilgrims with the Jubilee, Cesare's entry in 1500 to Rome was beset with the trappings of a military conqueror, for he dragged behind him, in chains of gold, Catherine Sforza, Lady of Imola and Forlì. In July of that year, Lucrezia's second husband, the Duke of Bisceglie, to whom she had borne a son, was attacked and wounded by five masked assassins on the steps of St. Peter's. Convinced that his brother-in-law was behind the attempt on his life, Duke Alfonso attempted to kill Cesare, only to be dispatched by his bodyguard. In the following April, Cesare was invested by his father with the imposing title of Duke of the Romagna, while his widowed sister was made Regent of Nepi and Spoleto.

The High Renaissance period was initiated by Leonardo da Vinci, who in 1500 returned from Milan to Florence, where he two years later entered the service of Cesare Borgia. The Duke aspired to the conquest of Tuscany, and was therefore a threat to the republic. For this reason, Machiavelli was sent on diplomatic missions to him in 1501 and 1502, and had the opportunity to witness his operating methods. Machiavelli developed the strongest admiration for the way Cesare combined audacity with diplomatic prudence, for his skillful use of cruelty and deception, for his firm and effective administration in conquered provinces, and for his method of gradually replacing his mercenaries with the troops drawn from his own duchy—the Italian states had always used foreign soldiers in their wars, and Machiavelli had himself seen just how conceited, undisciplined, and disloyal they could be. Thenceforward, he cherished the image of an ideal statesman, modelled on

Cesare, and known by the name of Valentino.

On the 27th of June, 1501, Alexander deposed his chief vassal, Frederick of Naples, on the basis of an alleged alliance with the Turks to the detriment of Christendom. The Treaty of Granada (1500), secretly approved by the Pope, partitioned the Kingdom of Naples between Spain and France, with Louis XII acquiring the northern part and the title of king. The motive for the reversal of papal policy in respect of foreign interference was quite patent: the Savelli, the Colonna, the Gaëtani, and other barons of the Patrimony had always been aided in their opposition to the popes by the sympathy of the Aragonese dynasty, without which they felt quite impotent. Having been excommunicated as rebels, they offered to surrender the keys of their castles to the Curia, but Alexander insisted that these be handed over to him personally. The Orsini family was short-sighted enough to assist the Pope in despoiling its hereditary foes. The castles were made over, one after the other.

When Alexander left Rome in July to survey his conquests, the day-to-day business of the Holy See was placed in the hands of his 21-year-old daughter. The twice-widowed Lucrezia had been betrothed by his father to another Alfonso, Alfonso d'Este, son and heir of Duke Ercole of Ferrara. This young scion was only a year of Lucrezia's senior, and himself a widower. Both his father and he were initially opposed to the prospect of a matrimonial alliance between the august House of Este and the illegitimate daughter of a Spanish pope, but the old Duke's prejudices were soon removed through the mediation of the French King and the reduction of the tribute due from Ferrara as a papal fief from 400 ducats to 100 florins.

On the 30th of December, 1501, the third marriage of Lucrezia was celebrated in the Vatican by proxy, with Alfonso's brother, Cardinal Ippolito d'Este, standing in for the still unwilling bridegroom. After the ceremony, which took place in St. Peter's, Lucrezia rode in state through the streets of Rome to Santa Maria del Popolo to give thanks to God and the Madonna. The following week was filled with amusements, including a bull fight in which Cesare, in true Spanish fashion and according to the rules of the craft, killed six wild bulls in the enclosed arena of St. Peter's Square. While her brother continued his infamous career of treachery, debauchery, and cruelty, Lucrezia was thenceforward known as a model wife and mother, celebrated for her amiability, her virtue, and her charity.

There is little resemblance between the historical Duchess of Ferrara and the diabolical Lucrezia Borgia of drama and opera. According to contemporary reports, she was very well-bred and made an excellent consort. Respected by the court and admired by the city, she led a quiet, domestic life until her death in 1519. An influential patroness of arts and letters, she bore a child after another to his husband, who himself was more fond of sport, hunting, and armament than of the finer things. Her bad reputation is largely due to the rumours circulated by the political enemies of her family that she was the lover of both her brother and her father; there are no facts to support these stories about Lucrezia's immorality, and none of her husbands made any allegations against her. A common and popular way to malign one's enemy was—and is—to allude to his or her sexual behaviour, even though this has nothing to do with the actual issue of the power struggle itself. Lucrezia was certainly more constant than Alfonso, who sired many bastards; but the age did not expect fidelity from men.

By the end of 1502, Cesare's possessions were rounded out by Piombino, Elba, Camerino, and Urbino. As the Duke's chief architect and engineer, Leonardo da Vinci supervised work on the fortresses of these newly-ceded papal territories in central Italy. At Urbino, he met Niccolò Machiavelli, and the two masterminds of the Renaissance soon became close friends. On the 31st of December, Machiavelli witnessed the bloody murder at the castle of Sinigaglia of Cesare's captains, who had conspired with the Orsini to destroy him. Afterwards, in letters to his friend and prospective patron, Francesco Vettori, as well as in the pages of *Il Principe*, Machiavelli repeats his belief that Cesare's methods of operation were worthy of all commendation and meticulous imitation. The soul of the conspiracy, Cardinal Orsini, was taken prisoner while on a visit to the Pope; his palace was dismantled, and he was imprisoned in Castel Sant' Angelo, where twelve days later he lay a corpse. Other members of the family were seized and their castles confiscated, until nothing was left to the Orsini except the fortress of Bracciano; by April, 1503, they were begging for ar armistice.

The Roman baronage had been thoroughly humiliated: for the first time in history, the pope truly ruled his states. And, thanks to simony, the Curia now contained so many of Alexander's supporters and countrymen that there were no threats from that direction either. Nor was even the moral indignation of Christendom a source of much danger to him; he whole-heartedly enjoyed and laughed at the circulating lampoons that accused him of heinous crimes, taking no actions to guard his reputation. The majority of Christians throughout the West still believed in the virtue of the papal blessing and consecration, and had scarcely any conception of what was taking place in central Italy. Even the conspirator Vitelozzo Vitelli still prayed to be absolved by Alexander, when the Pope's bastard son had him strangled.

Disagreement between the Spanish and the French over division of the Neapolitan spoils had, however, flared into open warfare, and Alexander was still unsure which side he should support when he died, many contemporaries believed, of poison intended for a cardinal. Modern scholarship is nevertheless convinced that the old man died of malaria. Apparently, after dining at a cardinal's villa, the Pope and his son Cesare had braved the treacherous night air of August and paid the penalty by contracting the baneful "Roman Fever." The Duke had sought to win over the cardinals, so that he could secure the election of a successor to his father who would be favourable to him. However, having caught malaria the same time as his father, he was critically ill and could not even make it to the Vatican from another Roman castle to attend the conclave. Giuliano della Rovere once more competed for the papal tiara and once more lost. Alexander was succeeded by a nephew of Pius II who took the name Pius III, but he was a sick, old man, at whose quick passing, Giuliano finally prevailed. With the help of exuberant promises and bribes, he was unanimously elected pope at a conclave that lasted only one day. He proceeded to call himself Julius II, and with his pontificate, the Borgia dynasty came to a swift end.

CHAPTER 30

The Treaty of Granada, which partitioned Naples between Spain and France, expired in a few years, and in 1504, the French claims on Naples were no longer recognized. Louis XII was forced to accept the Treaties of Blois, retaining Milan and Genoa, but pledging Naples and Sicily to Spain. The year before, the papal throne had been ascended by Julius II, who was determined to curb the power of Cesare Borgia, and to bring his conquest under direct papal rule. The encroachments of Venice upon the Romagna provided the occasion for both Cesare's fall and the full restoration of papal authority in the region. Julius demanded the keys of the Romagna towns as an essential measure for the eviction of the Venetians, at which critical point in his career, the Duke failed to show his usual determination and yielded. He withdrew to Ostia, where he was arrested by the Pope for conspiracy, and obliged to give up the rest of his land and possessions. Set at liberty, Cesare accepted the protection of Gonzalo de Córdoba, the first in a long line of Spanish viceroys in Naples, but was soon detained as the result of collusion between Julius and the Spanish rulers, Ferdinand and Isabella. Sent to prison in Spain, he escaped and finally found refuge at the court of his brother-in-law, the King of Navarre. He was killed in action during the 1507 expedition against Castile.

By early 16th century, the centre of the Renaissance had shifted to Rome and to the court of Pope Julius II. Rome was where the money was, where the patronage was, and therefore also where the leading artists and craftsmen were. The countless artists and architects who served at the papal court were the principal creators of Rome as it stands today. St. Peter's Church and the Sistine Chapel in the Vatican are perfect examples of the immense artistic resources of Renaissance Rome. Few of the great edifices of the world have required the contribution of as many architects as the new St. Peter's. Pope Nicholas V began sketching it around 1450, but it took a further 350 years before the building was completed. During this vast stretch of time, a long line of popes and architects had an opportunity to impress their mark upon it.

The basilica which Constantine the Great had erected in the honour of

Apostle Peter was ancient and difficult to keep in repair. Nicholas V had decided to replace it with a new church, in a more Classical idiom, but its construction was not commenced until 1505, when Julius II thought of building a mausoleum and a great memorial for himself near the Basilica. After changing his mind several time, Julius also gave up the idea of erecting a separate tomb and decided that the old Basilica should be renovated in its entirety. The Pope invited Donato Bramante, the outstanding architect of the period, to oversee the work. The first thing he did was to destroy Constantine's structure along with its fixtures. Bramante had the tombs and altars torn apart, throwing out the effigies, mosaics, and icons. This work of destruction, carried out by 2,500 men over several weeks, must have been a cause of great consternation even given the old Basilica's sorry condition.

The great central space of the new St. Peter's Church was made to accommodate the huge tomb of Julius, which the world's greatest living sculptor, Michelangelo, was hired to create. Michelangelo liked to work on a grand scale: he had just finished his marble *David*, which was to become the symbol of Florence, in the town square of his native city; standing seventeen feet tall, the statue made David appear larger than Goliath. His original plan for the Julius Tomb called for forty ten-foot statues of Christian saints, Hebrew prophets, ancient Roman deities, and nude slave-boys. As a consummate perfectionist, he was fully prepared to spend the rest of his life working on the papal tomb, expending great amounts of money with little visible result; he believed that the figures were imprisoned in the blocks of stone, and that the form could be released by removing the excess stone. About two years after hiring Michelangelo, Julius informed him that his design was too elaborate, and in the end, a simplified version was executed by other artists.

The Pope then gave Michelangelo an assignment that he might actually complete. He was commissioned to redecorate the ceiling of the Sistine Chapel, built for and named after Julius' infamous uncle, Pope Sixtus IV. Michelangelo did not want to paint, however, for he was a sculptor, not a painter. What is more, he was broke from having to pay for the supplies and assistants from a paltry advance. Between 1508 and 1512, working high above the floor while lying on his back on specially designed scaffolding, he nevertheless produced some of the finest ever painted images. He created inside the dome a set of surfaces, which he filled with biblical scenes from the creation of the world to the Deluge and drunkenness of Noah, and around these, pictures of Jesus' predecessors, the prophets and the sibyls—the pagan wise women who had reputedly predicted the coming of Christ—and nude adolescent figures. These images, demonstrating his masterful understanding of the human anatomy and motion, changed the course of Western painting.

Of the Renaissance painters, the one who, in his glorified placidity and composure, corresponded most closely to the Classical ideas and standards on art was Raphael (1483-1520). During his brief life, he underwent an exceedingly great number of development stages, and was virtually unparalleled in versatility of style; the pace and quantity of his production is incredible. After a formative sojourn in Florence, where he studied the works of Leonardo and Michelangelo, Rafael moved to Rome. His Madonnas, seventeen of which were painted during his brief Florentine period, are without doubt the most famous of his creations, but the apex of his art was reached in the decoration of four small *stanze*, or rooms, of the Vatican Palace. Julius II had built his private apartments over those of Alexander VI, whom he despised, and in 1508, commissioned Raphael to execute the frescoes for their interiors.

Dubbed the Warrior Pope, Julius was perfectly happy to lead his armies into battle to subdue the rebellious cities of the Church in between pursuing Michelangelo to finish the frescoes in the Sistine Chapel. He made a far-reaching move in securing the aid of the Swiss, who were known as mercenaries throughout most of their early history. Swiss troops were placed at the disposal of foreign powers via treaties between the Swiss diet, the separate cantons, and the power in question, in return for money. They first rose to prominence in 1494, as an integral part of Charles VIII's army during the rapid French invasion of the Italian Peninsula, and during the next five decades, Swiss mercenaries were found on most battlefields in Italy. In 1506, at the suggestion of the Swiss Cardinal Schiner, Julius concluded a treaty with the cantons of Zürich and Lucerne for 6,000 mercenaries for five years. That spring, he donned the papal armour and mounted his horse to personally lead the forces against the rebellious cities of Perugia and Bologna. With astounding speed, *il Papa Terribile* routed the rebels and captured their castles.

Julius' primary objectives were to evict the Venetians from Romagna and the French from Lombardy. Both the presence of Venice in the Papal States and that of France in northern Italy threatened to turn the papacy into a pawn of either the Venetians or the French. The League of Cambrai, formed by Julius in 1508, pitted almost every power in Europe against Venice, in a pact whose explicitly declared intention was to destroy the Venetian Empire as a prelude to conquering the Turks. However, the leagues for the crusade were no longer anything more than political alliances, and it impressed but a few when Emperor Maximilian took the cross at Metz with all the theatrics. This particular agreement decided on the coldblooded division of the Venetian domains: Maximilian was to receive Verona, Padua, and Aquileia; France, Cremona and Brescia; Spain, the Venetian possession in southern Italy; Hungary, Dalmatia; Savoy, Cyprus; and the Holy See, the portions of the Romagna held by Venice.

On the 27th of April, 1509, Julius fulfilled his promise of adding the punishment of the priestly office to the force of arms by placing Venice under interdict. On the 14th of May, her army was defeated by the French at the Battle of Agnadello. Most of the territories she had occupied on the mainland were lost, as was her navy, and she was forced to open the Adriatic to general commerce. The doge further renounced his time-honoured privilege of nominating to bishoprics and benefices and taxing the Venetian clergy without papal consent. The republic seemed to be on the verge of ruin, but the conflicting interests of the League soon enabled it, through subtle diplomacy, to repossess nearly everything it had held at the beginning of the war, for the various populations found their new masters even less pleasant than the old ones. Julius had, however, accomplished his objective of securing papal power in the Romagna, and could reconcile with the Venetians. By turning Venice into his ally, he hoped to restore the duchy of Ferrara under papal authority and drive out the French.

The Holy League which the Pope proceeded in 1510 to form with his former enemy against "the barbarians" failed, however, to produce any wider Italian unity. With the help of a few rebellious cardinals, the French King inspired at Pisa an ecclesiastical council (1511), which was soon moved to Milan. The League could not conquer back Ferrara, but the French captured Bologna. Since the Florentine Republic sided with the schismatic Pisans, the Pope became a warm supporter of the banished Medici. When Julius fell seriously ill in August of 1511, Cardinal Giovanni de' Medici, son of Lorenzo the Magnificent, was already aspiring to succeed him. In October, the Pope, Venice, and Ferdinand of Aragón devised the second Holy League to reclaim

Bologna, and in November, the League was joined by Ferdinand's new son-in-law, Henry VIII (1509-1547) of England.

In 1512, the French army under the 23-year-old Gaston de Foix, Duke of Nemours, fought a fierce battle against the combined papal, Venetian, and Spanish troops, with which the Medici cardinal was sojourning. The French carried the day on the banks of the River Reno near Ravenna, but the victory did nothing to further their cause. The captured cardinal, who would have been taken to France, managed to escape, and Gaston himself was killed while pursuing the enemy. The Swiss conquests in Lombardy, which would later make up the canton of Ticino, greatly increased the power of the Confederation in Milan, enabling the Swiss to install their nominee, Massimiliano Sforza, son of Ludovico, as its duke. As the French retreated beyond the Alps, the schismatic council moved to Lyons, and Julius not only regained Bologna but was also given Parma and Piacenza.

The Florentines, having been more spectators than actors in these great events, were about to feel their full effect. Giovanni de' Medici led a Spanish army into Tuscany, sacking Prato in August. In September, the terrified Florence deposed her duly elected *gonfaloniere*, and opened her gates to the Medici. In February the next year, Julius II died, and in March, the Medici cardinal became Pope Leo X (1513-1521); as head of the family, he was also the real ruler of Florence. He made his cousin Giulio a cardinal and put him in charge of the Florentine government. The army the French King had sent to reconquer Milan was defeated by the Swiss at Novara on the 6th of June, and the French surrendered the castles of Cremona and Brescia, retreating once again beyond the Alps.

Meanwhile, Henry VIII had formed an alliance with Emperor Maximilian and Ferdinand of Aragón to partition France. Ferdinand conquered the Spanish Navarre in July, while Henry and Maximilian laid siege to Terouenne. On the 16th of August, the French were defeated at "the Battle of the Spurs," and in September, their ally, James IV (1488-1513) of Scotland, lost, and was killed in, the Battle of Flodden Field. Before long, both Ferdinand and Maximilian made a truce with Louis, whereas Henry, on the advice of Cardinal Wolsey, entered into a close alliance with the French King, giving him his younger sister in marriage. Exhausted by his 15-year-old English bride, Louis XII died on the 1st of January, 1515, having lost half of Navarre, Terouenne and Tournai, plus all his Italian holdings. Ferdinand's elderly wife, on the other hand, had passed away eleven years earlier, so when the Spanish half of Navarre was annexed to Castile in 1515, all of modern Spain was finally governed by one man.

High hopes were vested in Pope Leo X by theologians who looked for reforms long overdue, politicians who counted on his flexibility, and by scholars and artists of whom he was already a patron. Unfortunately, he only lived up to the hopes of the artists, humanists, and classicists, who saw the papal court as a centre of entertainment. On his election, he exclaimed: *Godiamoci il papato, poichè Dio ce l'ha dato,* "As God has given us the papacy, let us enjoy it!" He set a splendid table, and with banquets, balls, carnivals, and theatrical performances transformed Rome into a city of pleasure. He spent vast sums on beautifying Rome and the rest of his domains with Renaissance art, leaving enormous debts at his death.

From 1514 to 1516, Leonardo da Vinci lived in Rome under Leo's patronage, but the protection which the Pope extended to Raphael is his strongest claim on posterity. During this period, the master genius finished two of the rooms in the Vatican Palace, including his most famous fresco and arguably the greatest painting of the entire Renaissance, the *School of Athens.* Intended to illustrate that central pillar of human civilization, Christianity, and the greatness of the Church, the "School of Athens" symbolizes "philosophy," which perhaps would have been a more suitable title for the work. It depicts the sages of Classical antiquity, gathered around Aristotle and Plato, strolling in a hall with a soaring dome-shaped ceiling, surrounded with individuals and groups in an harmonic ensemble. These festive and rich, yet clear and illustrative renditions have earned Raphael the reputation of being the all-time greatest creator of figure compositions. Because of his many artistic activities, he had time to paint only part of the third room, and provided just the designs for the fourth.

On Bramante's death in 1514, construction defects were discovered in the new St. Peter's Church, and they proved quite expensive to fix. Bramante may have been a brilliant architect, but he was too impatient to be thorough and too undisciplined to properly supervise his workers. Appointed as the new chief architect by Leo X, Raphael made radical changes to Bramante's plans, but when he himself died six years later, he had produced scarcely more than a column or two, for most of his time had elapsed in repairing Bramante's errors. Papal funds were drained to pay for the numerous other churches, palaces, piazzas, and monuments. The huge treasury left by Julius II was empty in two years, and various dubious and reproachable methods were resorted to for raising more money. Leo created new offices and dignities, and put the most exalted clerical positions for sale; indulgences, too, got degraded into mere financial transactions, yet Leo would never recover from his financial embarrassment.

The conflict of France and Spain in Italy had fostered the introduction of the Renaissance in France. French artists began to adopt Renaissance forms, and the Palace of Fontainebleau became the focal point of the movement. Leonardo da Vinci, the most potent force of the Italian High Renaissance, left Rome for the last time in 1516, to enter the service of King Francis I. Settling at the Château de Cloux, near Amboise, the old master was left free to pursue his own scientific investigations until his death. Leonardo's theories and discoveries are contained in his numerous notebooks which, had they only been published, would have revolutionized 16th-century science. The failure of Louis XII's foreign policy nowise discouraged Francis' designs to extend his influence into northern and southern Italy; as a prestigious Renaissance ruler, devoted to arts and sciences, Francis wished to rule also south of the Alps.

After Francis' great victory over the Swiss at the Battle of Marignano (13-14th of September, 1515), Massimiliano Sforza was driven out from Milan, and the French reoccupied the city. With the rule of the Medici threatened in Florence, Leo agreed to a treaty with France, and arranged to meet with Francis in Bologna. The Pope handed over the cities taken from Milan and from the duchy of Ferrara, and despite the objections of the Sorbonne and the Parlement of Paris, the French King signed the Concordat of Bologna (1516), which virtually abolished the Pragmatic Sanction in France. The Roman pontiff was given supremacy over local ecclesiastical councils, and though the nominations of bishoprics and abbacies were transferred to the king, they required papal ratification. What is more, papal annates where reintroduced, greatly increasing the pontifical revenue.

Also known as the "Battle of the Giants," Marignano was the first battle of the gunpowder era to last more than one day. Among the bloodiest armed engagements in the Italian Wars, it delivered the first serious blow to the Swiss who had dominated European battlefields for over a century, establishing the superiority of artillery and cavalry over their reputedly invincible infantry tactics. With their military ambitions thwarted, the Swiss negotiated in 1516 a "perpetual alliance" with France, establishing the contractual basis of their reticence in foreign policy for centuries. At that time, the Confederation renounced, both for itself and for the individual cantons, wars of aggression, and other trappings of neutrality were added as time went by. The cantons, however, continued to rent out their troops, and Swiss mercenaries continued to serve abroad for another three centuries.

In fact, Francis' advancement into Naples was only averted by the appearance in northern Italy of Maximilian's Swiss troops. The Emperor nevertheless withdrew without striking a blow, and in October, acceded the Treaty of Noyon, which Francis had entered into in August with Charles of Ghent. The last mentioned had succeeded Ferdinand to the Spanish throne in January, and in November, concluded a permanent peace with the Swiss. Ferdinand had left his grandson not only a united Spain, but also Naples, Sicily, Sardinia, and an overseas empire. Charles was the the first in the long line of Habsburg kings that would rule Spain for the next two hundred years, during which time the monarchy became absolute. In 1517, he arrived in Spain from the Netherlands, where he had been born and raised and whose ruler he was. Mistrusted as a foreigner, his initial actions only deepened the nation's animosity towards him. The King, who did not even speak the language of his new subjects, was instructed by his Flemish friends and advisors, whom he had brought with him and who exploited the opportunity to make their fortune.

The humanism of the Renaissance produced a talent for organization and critical thinking, and brought supreme self-confidence to the tasks at hand. Nearly everywhere in Western and Central Europe, local writers were encouraged to create histories and descriptions of their lands, modelled after the Italian humanist historiography and filled with patriotic pride. In Germany, a sense of national identity was fostered by humanist historians who sought to play down the importance of the continued political, economic, geographical, and lingual division of the country. The recently founded universities, where many intellectuals and some princes obtained an education in the Liberal Arts, were unifying institutions that worked toward creating a sense of being German. The *Germania* of Tacitus was printed in Germany as early as 1473, starting a fashion for the use of this collective name for the region. The fact that the ancient historian had called the Germans "the indigenous inhabitants" was first used as proof that Germany should be free from all foreign suzerainty by *Der Erzhumanist*, Conradus Celtis (1459-1508).

In order to refill the depleted papal treasury, Leo X entrusted a German friar called Johann Tetzel with a large-scale sale of indulgences. This sordid traffic had been extended by pope after pope ever since they realized that indulgences could be granted just as readily to those who stayed at home and simply paid the Church the price of a Roman journey as to those who actually made the pilgrimage. Since one was liable to be robbed on the way across Europe, or even in St. Peter's, not to mention the loss of time and business, the easier way proved more popular. However, the stream of gold flowing into Italy could not fail to annoy the German princes, nor did the manner in which the money was utilized in Rome mitigate the issue. Martin Luther (1483-1546), a professor at the University of Wittenberg, had witnessed the reproach personally at its hotbed. In 1511, at the height of the Renaissance, he had travelled via upper Italy to Rome; he had not one praise to breathe about the beauty of the works of art: in Florence, he was impressed mostly by the neatly furnished hospitals, and in Rome, he simply complained about the amount of money that flowed from Germany into the decoration of its buildings. When he in exasperation launched his countermeasures, he could rely on the support of his countrymen.

In 1517, Raphael produced what many reckon to be his loftiest contribution to the *maniera* of High Renaissance, the *Sistine Madonna*. The same year, Tetzel's sale of indulgences near Wittenberg prompted Luther to write a paper challenging the wretched business in theory and practice. On the eve of All Saints, he posted these *95 Theses* on the door of the Wittenberg castle church, offering to debate them with any churchman. This was not a declaration of war, mind you, but the accepted and traditional form of disputation in the academic world. Events where university professors—all of them clerics—debated various propositions in a public forum were a form of entertainment in college towns, attended by factions of the public favouring either side. Luther was an Augustinian monk, Tetzel a Dominican friar, so the natural rivalry between the two orders caused supporters to pour in on both sides. The eventual debate turned out to be both spirited and inconclusive, and in the end, the Dominican and the Augustinian party both went home claiming victory.

Luther went on preaching his ideas, which, in passing, were far from modern or original—Wycliffe, Hus, and many others down the line had said much the same thing. When, in 1518, a summary of his ideas reached Rome, the Pope dismissed the whole affair as just another quarrel among monks; for the different monastic orders did in fact bicker frequently and fiercely, and ever so often their arguments bordered on the extreme. This was the year that saw the appointment of Cardinal Wolsey as papal legate; the Lord Chancellor of England brought about the Treaty of London with France, wherewith Francis bought back Tournai and promised that the Dauphin would be wed to Princess Mary. Since Francis had renounced his claims to Naples in the Treaty of Noyon, retaining only Milan, a short period of universal peace embracing all the principal Western states was at last possible. Huge religious processions were held, a truce of five years was proclaimed throughout Christendom, and all the princes of Europe were exhorted by the Pope to unite in a common effort against the Turks—upon the preaching of the crusade in Germany, one of the countless spiteful pamphlets printed declared the real Turks to be in Italy and that this particular species of demon can only be pacified by means of gold.

On the death in 1519 of his paternal grandfather, Maximilian, Charles of Ghent expanded his already enormous domains by inheriting the Habsburg lands in Austria, where his younger brother, Ferdinand, was governor. Charles' election as Holy Roman Emperor over Henry VIII soon revealed England's status as a secondary power. Francis had also tried to get his hands on the imperial crown, and on his failure, France's relations with the Habsburgs became strained. Besides the three, there had been only one other serious candidate: the Elector of Saxony, Frederick the Wise[211]. Charles had prevailed, not because of having more sympathies or because political considerations would have spoken for him, but simply because the great banking house of the Fuggers had guaranteed the vast amounts of money he had promised the electors. Already by then, the real superpower was no longer Spain, France, or England, but the money-lender with his sacks of gold.

Meanwhile, Luther had upped the ante considerably. He now challenged not only the sale of indulgences, but the right of the pope to issue them, the whole theory of the Treasury of Saints, and by the same token, the authority of Rome in several unrelated areas as well. It was precisely this attack on papal

---

[211] i.e. Frederick III

authority that finally drew official attention to Luther. And it was his debates with the papal opponents sent to silence him that gradually drew him more deeply into a defiant position. By 1520, his defiance of Rome was total: he argued that papacy was a man-made office, without Divine authority, and that the entire doctrine of Apostolic Succession was false.

Luther promulgated his ideas not merely from the pulpit, but more importantly, in pamphlets which the printing press made widely available across Germany. His demagogic genius was manifest in coarseness of speech carefully adapted to the environment, carrying both the pros and cons of genuine vulgarity. As a rule, Luther's pamphlets, especially those written in German, reflect praise and glory of the fatherland, and conversely, hatred and contempt towards "foreigners," in this case, Italians: "For Rome is the greatest thief and robber that has ever appeared on earth, or ever will; and all in the holy names of Church and St. Peter. . . poor Germans that we are—we have been deceived! We were born to be masters, and we have been compelled to bow the head beneath the yoke of our tyrants, and to become slaves. . . It is time the glorious Teutonic people should cease to be the puppet of the Roman pontiff."

On the 15th of June, 1520, Luther was excommunicated in the papal bull, *Exsurge Domine*, which condemned him on forty-one counts. A papal counter-manifesto to Luther's theses, it was the last bull addressed to Latin Christendom as an indivisible entity, and the first to be defied by a significant portion of the same. Many had been excommunicated in the past and had simply chosen to ignore it, but this Saxon monk was of different breed. An excommunication arrives like a writ of summons, delivered personally into the hands of the recipient by a papal nuncio. Upon receiving the document, Luther burned it publicly in the streets along with a book of canon law, while leading a riotous procession.

In October, Charles of Ghent departed from Spain to be crowned King of Germany in Aachen, assuming at the same time the title of *Imperator Romanorum Electus*. This meant the further expansion of his domains with the states of Germany, the Swiss Confederation, the remainder of the Netherlands, and northern Italy. As the dispossessed Sforza now turned for help to Charles, the Italian Wars would soon merge into a larger struggle between the Habsburg dynasty and the French monarchs over conflicting territorial claims, a struggle that defines most of modern European history.

Luther's journey in the spring of 1521 from Wittenberg to the imperial diet at Worms, where he had been summoned to defend himself, was nothing short of a triumphal procession. As he travelled, he was asked to deliver sermons at one church after another, for everyone was anxious to hear what he had to say, whether or not they agreed with all his ideas—he was seen as a German persecuted by foreigners. He preached well, winning over the doubters, and by the time he reached Worms, he was quite the national hero; but his reception at the diet itself was completely different.

As the Holy Roman Emperor, Charles V did not see himself as a German head of state, but as a world ruler, a mediæval autocrat of a universal kingdom; the story goes that he spoke German only to his horse. In 1521, Charles needed the alliance of the papacy for his first campaign against France. At Worms, Luther encountered the 21-year-old Emperor attended by two cardinals and a bevy of churchmen. Charles had his own confession of faith, beginning with an exhaustive invocation of his Catholic ancestors, recited to the diet. He professed himself ready to stake his domains, friends, blood, life, and soul on the extinction of heresy.

The Edict of Worms therefore forbids all subversion and places Luther under the ban of the empire, casting him and his followers outside the protection of the feudal law. But Luther was long gone; under an imperial safe-conduct, he had been able to get away from Worms before the safe-conduct was retracted. Imperial officials searched the countryside, finding nothing but rumours. Soon, however, pamphlets attacking the papacy signed by Martin Luther started appearing. Luther was hiding at Wartburg, one of the castles of Frederick the Wise. Although the Elector of Saxony remained a pious Catholic all his life, he still considered Luther as one of his own subjects, protecting him more on political than on religious grounds. The monk of Saxony was thus given the refuge that earlier reformers like John Hus sorely lacked. Moreover, the Emperor's preoccupation with the war effectively kept him from curbing the spread of Lutheran doctrines.

Immediately following the diet, Charles left for Italy to fight the French King over local claims, and was absent until 1530. Luther made use of the time by issuing a cluster of subversive pamphlets and booklets from his hide-out. Inasmuch as the Papist priest has become a barrier between man and God—this is how Luther himself put it in his plead—let us free ourselves of everything that might form a same kind of barrier in the future; and let every man be his own priest. It is blasphemous to even think that the omnipotent and omniscient God would let such a trifling human institution as the Church interfere in the relationship between Him and His creation.

What is more, God has made his plan known in the Bible, which anyone can read without a priestly intermediary. An integral part of the personal relationship with God was formed by the study of Scripture, which presupposed the ability to read. The dissemination of literacy everywhere and to every social class was the cardinal idea of the Protestant Reformation. This idea, and indeed the whole Reformation, was made possible by the printing press.

Since Luther was active just when the printing industry was booming, presses throughout Germany spread his ideas far and wide at a speed impossible for the authorities to control. In addition to writing his own little treatises, he undertook to translate the Bible into German. Luther's translation of the New Testament was published in 1522, followed by his translation of the Old Testament in 1534. When the Word of God was made available in the German language, the priesthood no longer enjoyed the monopoly position that it had held when the Word existed only in a Latin version. The printing press could not only turn out thousands of copies, but much more importantly, made each copy affordable; not only could a German craftsman read the Good Book for himself, he could own that book.

Luther's translation spread in hundreds of thousands of copies and its impact was proportional. In his day, the German commoners did not yet have a standard language, but only innumerable dialects, and it was the extraordinary diffusion and influence of his Bible translation that finally imposed his particular dialect of German on the great masses and was ultimately accepted as the written standard German. Without Luther, today's Germany would, in all probability, be a bilingual country, with one half speaking Low German, and the other half High German.

All the great reformers made it possible for the Bible to be spread in their native language. The dissemination of literacy greatly increased people's confidence in themselves and in their abilities. Protestantism thus had a reinforcing effect on the formation of common language, culture, and custom in the groups which we now identify as nations. Men like Henry VIII and Philip of Hesse were genuine patriots, who truly believed that the degenerate Italians were exploiting both the souls and bodies of their countrymen. By abolishing the Roman canon law, the privileges of the clergy, and the claims of the Catholic Church to be wholly outside secular authority, they paved the way for the new government of civil servants. The new Protestant rulers sought to create Churches that would, in a sense, function as the moral police force of the State.

Initially, however, the spread of Luther's ideas produced only anarchy, dissent, and rebellion, which seemed to confirm the belief of zealous Catholics that religious dissension brought civil war in addition to spiritual peril. Luther had called for German resistance to Rome in nationalistic terms, and his call was soon answered. Among his new fellow-soldiers of freedom were Ulrich von Hutten (1488-1523) and Franz von Sickingen (1481-1523).

Hutten was not only the greatest German poet of the Latin language at the time, but also a fervent patriot and the sharpest polemist in Germany. His parents had tried to make him into a monk, but he had run away from the monastery, and his subsequent contribution to the infamous anti-monastic lampoon, *Epistolæ Obscurorum Vivorum*, was considerable. He wrote biting satires, attacking the pope and speaking in support of Reuchlin, Erasmus, and, in particular, Luther, whose ideology he perceived as a political "free from Rome" movement. Besides his own attacks on the corruption of the Church and its political yoke, Hutten also published, for example, Lorenzo Valla's refutation of the "Donation of Constantine" and Luther's epoch-making *Address to the German Nobility*.

Sickingen, a *Ritter* whose daring deeds form a part of German legendary lore, provided, for his part, a safeguard for persecuted humanists and reformers. In 1522, he led the knights of the Rhineland in a rebellion against the ecclesiastical princes, who opposed not only Lutheran doctrines but knightly privileges. The lower orders of German knights were suffering both socially and economically. The new methods of warfare had diminished their political importance, while the thriving industrial sector undermined the agrarian interests of small landowners. What is more, the lower nobility were threatened to be reduced to serfdom through the revived Roman law adopted by their liege lords.

Himself a knight, Hutten fought side by side with Sickingen against the ecclesiastical princes, but their attempt to unite the German nobility and free cities against the clerical benefice-hunters ultimately failed. After an unsuccessful last raid on the Archbishop-Elector of Trier, Sickingen was deserted by his allies and besieged at one of his castles, dying of his wounds after barely signing his capitulation. Hutten found refuge in Zürich with Ulrich Zwingli (1484-1531), the leader of the Swiss reform movement, but died of syphilis only a year later. Luther had nothing to do with the rising; regarding as he did the secular authority as divinely ordained, he was opposed to any and all revolutionary violence. Yet, these deaths and desertions inflicted an immeasurable loss on Luther, for he had now found himself struggling against new reformers with whom he disagreed.

As chaplain of the Swiss troops, Zwingli had visited Rome three times, something of which his patriotism later made him greatly ashamed. He voluntarily renounced his papal pension in 1519, and proceeded to attack the ruinous mercenary system. As a result, Zürich remained outside the treaty (1521) by which the other Swiss cantons bound themselves to supply France with some 120,000 levies. As a reformer, Zwingli was the most "protestant" of his contemporaries, teaching that the State and the Church were actually one and the same. In 1522, he began measures to establish the Bible as the sole religious authority for the Christian: e.g. he managed to get the Lenten fast outlawed in his home canton, citing the lack of Scriptural warrant for the custom.[212] The Bishop of Constance naturally attempted to suppress this innovation, but lost to the civil government of Zürich, which assumed control of ecclesiastical matters within its jurisdiction.

Whereas Luther had little interest in broader changes within the Church beyond removing Roman spiritual authority, Zwingli wanted to strip Christianity of every feature that was not supported by biblical warrant. The latter accorded the sacraments only a symbolical significance, claiming that the communion was only a memorial ceremony, and that the host only "signified" the body of Christ. This, to the former, was a shocking diminution of the power of the Real Presence in the elements of the eucharist. Yet, Luther could not and would not admit that the Papists were right, so he had to invent his own peculiar "consubstantiation." Thus, as Voltaire maliciously yet accurately put it: the Catholics "eat God but not bread," the Reformed "eat bread but not

---

[212] A period of fasting, apart from Sundays, Lent (from the Anglo-Saxon *lencten*, "spring") begins on Ash Wednesday, the 40th weekday before Easter Sunday, and is borrowed from the 40 days of mourning for Tammuz, the observation of which the Old Testament expressly condemns (Ezekiel 8:13-14).

God," and the Lutherans "eat both."

The Reformation gained more and more currency especially in the cities, whereas the peasants, who probably did not care about the religious aspect of the quarrel, took advantage of the ferment and the discord of the nobility, which afforded an opportunity to successfully oppose exaction and slavery. The short-lived rebellion of the knights was followed by the infinitely more significant Peasants' War (1524-1526) in southern Germany. This revolt was the largest attempt at social revolution that Germany has ever lived through, and it was only the unruliness of the peasants and the jealousy of their leaders that prevented it from achieving its goals. It derived its justification from early Christian thought, and was principally aimed against the rich hierarchy, a lot less against the secular princes, and not at all against the nobility—it was hoped that the emperor himself would assume leadership of the movement.

For centuries, the entire Western Christian order had been a single piece, ordained by God. It was the common belief throughout the Middle Ages that each social class, from popes and emperors down to the vast multitudes of peasants, had its own proper place in the religious, political, and economic hierarchy. This place was determined by God's natural ordering of all people; it was He who decided who would be born a king, and who a beggar. The most dangerous aspect of the Peasants' War was that it did not confine itself to the rural areas, but spread, from the first, to cities, where there had been a long and intense turmoil among the proletariat, added to which there was a great number of poor clerics; in short, it was an exceedingly far-reaching and thorough-going movement of the fourth estate.

The famous "Twelve Articles" from the year 1525 put forth altogether reasonable demands: the peasants should have the right to choose their own pastors; no taxes beyond grain tithes should be imposed; serfdom should be abolished; the freedom to hunt, fish, and collect firewood should be restored. To these were added—as the revolution progressed—some other fairly rational demands: uniformity of coins and measures throughout Germany, abolition of internal customs duties, and reversal of the new arbitrary and biased judicial system in favour of the customary laws. The nobility would be reimbursed the cost of these reorganizations with ecclesiastical properties, whose total subjugation to secular power was one of the keynotes of the programme. However, since the opposition was unwilling to give in to any concessions, a war broke out into which peasants rushed from all quarters.

The uprising received the blessing of Zwingli, among others, but Luther turned out to be extremely hostile towards the peasants. The roots of his thinking were still in the Middle Ages, for he accepted the mediæval class division and considered the use of violence justified when enforcing the will of God. He cited the book of Sirach: "Fodder, stick, and burdens are for the ass," (33:25) and was referring to the peasants. He answered the Twelve Articles by flatly rejecting almost every demand made therein. To the thoroughly reasonable suggestion that the tithes should in the future pay the salaries of the clergy and the rest should be used to subsidize the needy in the parishes, Luther responds: "This article is sheer looting and marauding, for thereby they intend to wrest for themselves the tithes, which belong not to them but to the government, and do with them what they please. If you want to give and do good, then do it from your own property." As if the tithes, a wholly unjust and cruel tax, which often was one third of income and never accrued to the benefit of any charitable purpose, were not the property of the peasants. Serfdom Luther explains to be an institution entirely favourable to God, using the inerrant Bible as a proof: Did not Abraham and other patriarchs have serfs as well? Did Paul not tell each to stick to the vocation into which one has been called?

The peasant rebellion spread rapidly in breath and severity. The cities offered no serious resistance: in a few weeks all the princes in Franconia and along the Rhine knuckled under; a great peasant diet was called at the free city of Heilbronn to discuss a thorough reform of the kingdom; but the peasant forces, splintered and broken down in sieges and looting expeditions, were defeated—mainly with the advantage of cavalry—in all the seven battles which now followed quickly one after another. It is estimated that a total of 100,000 peasants perished, 6,000 of them being killed in the one-day Battle of Frankenhausen alone. By September, 1525, the rebellion had been thoroughly suppressed; its leaders were cruelly tortured and executed.

The most far-reaching result of the Peasants' War was the transfer of real power to the various German princes. The First Diet of Speyer, held in the summer of 1526 under Archduke Ferdinand, in the name of his brother, the Emperor, decreed that the control of the churches in Germany was to be neither a matter of local congregational power nor that of the popes and bishops. Instead, it was the ruling prince in each of the numerous German principalities who would determine the particular Christian character of his territory. As a rule, the South German princes remained loyal to Rome, whereas the North German princes sided with Luther. At all events, from this date on, it was the princes who got to make that determination.

Due to the Reformation, the Catholic Church had lost its hold over the rulers of Central Europe; in Italy, things were still different. The interregnum between the two Medici popes was filled by a Dutch pope, Adrian VI. His pontificate lasted only a year, and although he was elected at the beginning of 1522, he did not arrive in Rome until August. His efforts to reconcile King Francis and Emperor Charles failed, and during the reign of Clement VII (1523-1534), the latter of the two Medici popes, Francis attacked Pavia.

Charles' life-long struggle with France required vast expenditures, the fiscal onus of which rested squarely on Spain. This provoked violent reaction at first, especially in Castile, whose estates resented the Emperor's high-handedness in procuring funds, but a complete rapprochement soon followed between the pacified nation and their sovereign. The Spanish upper classes were starting to embrace and enjoy their monarch's position as the greatest ruler in Europe, and there quickly developed an emotionally tinged understanding between the Emperor and his Spanish subjects. Thenceforward, not only did the material resources of Spain sustain Charles' far-flung campaigns, but his Spanish troops were also the ones to acquit themselves most boldly and successfully in them. During these wars, the Spanish earned a reputation of invincibility, and the capture of King Francis during the Battle of Pavia (1525) and holding him a prisoner in Madrid further massaged their ego.

The royal captive was forced to sign the humiliating Treaty of Madrid (1526), in which he renounced all his Italian claims and ceded Burgundy to Charles. He even agreed to marry the Emperor's oldest sister, Eleanor of Austria, dowager Queen of Portugal, and handed over his sons as hostages. Immediately on his release, however, Francis reneged on the treaty and formed the anti-imperial League of Cognac with Pope Clement VII and Florence. An illegitimate cousin of Leo X, Clement headed the Medici family and controlled Florence through Ippolito de' Medici, Giuliano's illegitimate son, and Alessandro de' Medici, the illegitimate son of the late papal duke of Urbino. As a cardinal, Clement had been known as the mastermind behind Leo's foreign policy; as a pope, he made the fatal mistake of siding with France just as Charles, backed by the funds and troops of Spain, was becoming master of Italy. The league was further acceded to by Francesco II Sforza, who, being accused of plotting against the Emperor, had been deprived (1525) of most of his duchy—and by Henry VIII of England, who had fought on side of Charles against France, but had been denied any part of the spoils after the Emperor's decisive victory at Pavia.

The year 1527 found Charles' heterogeneous army, composed mostly of German Lutheran mercenaries, at the gates of the Eternal City. Hardly led by Charles de Bourbon, it had squabbled its way through the intricate and ever-changing alliances of the Italian city-states. As a pious Catholic, the Emperor wanted to spare the Pope and Rome, and therefore agreed to an armistice. The infuriated soldiers, reckoning this to be an attempt to cheat them of their well-earned loot, stormed the walls of Rome against the orders of their commanding officers. The Duke of Bourbon himself was hit by an arquebus, and died soon after.

Meanwhile, the soldiers had already forced their way into the city, and it was only the quick reaction of the Swiss Guard that saved Pope Clement from being murdered. Numbering about eight hundred at the time, they died almost to a man buying the Pope time to escape and run for shelter. Since this date, the 6th of May, 1527, there has always been about the Roman pontiff a personal guard of Swiss troops; recruited from the Catholic cantons of central Switzerland and still dressed in uniforms of Renaissance design, with puffed sleeves and knickerbockers, striped in the red, blue, and yellow of the Medici family, the Swiss Guard of the Vatican is one of the longest-serving regiments in the West. To commemorate those killed protecting Clement VII, the Vatican holds the 6th of May as the day that all new recruits take their oath to "faithfully, loyally and honourably serve the Supreme Pontiff and his legitimate successors, and also dedicate myself to them with all my strength, sacrificing if necessary also my life to defend them."

During the infamous Sack of Rome, 3,000 Romans made it to safety of Castel Sant' Angelo at the Vatican before the drawbridge was pulled, and the rest of the citizens were left to the mercy of an army of *lanzichelecchi*. An unearthly massacre went on for eight ghastly days, during which house after house was ransacked, their occupants murdered, maimed, and raped, fingers cut off for rings and ears for earrings, churches and monasteries vandalized for their treasures, priests stripped naked and forced to utter blasphemies under pain of death, nuns dragged into brothels or sold to soldiers in the streets, fires lit on the marble floors of the palaces, graffiti scratched on the frescoes, and the ancient manuscripts either scattered at the flames or used as bedding for horses. An estimated 8,000 people were killed on the first day alone. In all, the occupation lasted for nine months, thirty buildings were destroyed, and the population of the city dropped by half.

The Reformation was no longer a distant rumour reverberating from Germany; it had entered the Vatican. Many Romans saw the psychologically compelling Sack as God's punishment on the papacy for its wickedness. The pontiff himself had managed to sneak away from the besieged Sant' Angelo to the safety of Orvieto, disguised in the cloak and hood of a servant. His efforts to loosen the Spanish hold on Italy had only succeeded in tightening it, bringing closer the day when all Italy, except for Venice, would be either under the direct rule of Spain or at least subservient to the Spanish interests. The Serene Republic, having wisely stayed out of the papal dispute with Charles V, remained independent, strong, and prosperous through the century, and long after the rest of Italy had been subjugated by Habsburg power.

CHAPTER 31

With the spread of the Reformation, Renaissance humanists found new uses for their literary and rhetorical skills, exchanging letters and insults, supporting or condemning the proposed reforms. Perhaps the most famous humanist essay defending the Catholic Church is ironically ascribed to Henry VIII, who subsequently fell out with Rome and declared himself "Supreme Head on Earth of the Church of England." In keeping with the fashion of the period, Henry sought to excel in all fields of endeavour, and to distinguish himself as both a scholar and an athlete, as well as a statesman. He therefore composed a vindication of the seven sacraments against Luther's booklet *On the Babylonian Captivity of the Church*, for which the pope rewarded him with the title of *Defensor Fidei (F D)*, "Defender of the Faith," a title which the British monarchs still retain.

Henry did not, however, have a male heir, and therefore, wanted to separate from his Spanish wife, Catherine of Aragón. Though the term "divorce" is most frequently used in this connection, Henry was actually seeking an annulment. His marriage had been a mere political move, one that had defied the moral standards of the era, and had only been made possible by a special dispensation from the pope. When Henry conceived a fresh passion for the fair lady-in-waiting, Anne Boleyn, he began alluding to the illegality of his marriage. Catherine had previously been betrothed to the King's late elder brother, Arthur, and this made her Henry's sister-in-law, at least nominally: vows had been taken, making it a legal ceremony, but the couple had never consummated their relationship. The Catholic Church has always maintained that when the sacrament of holy matrimony is consummated, "the two become one flesh," and in Henry's case, this would have made Catherine his sister—an incestuous marriage would never have been allowed.

According to the King, Heaven did not look favourably upon his marriage, as evidenced by the fact that except one, all his six children had died, and he had no sons. England had never thus far been ruled by a woman, and the lack of an heir threatened the peace and security of the kingdom as much as it did the fate of the House of Tudor. The pope alone had the power to annul the royal marriage, and Henry asked Clement VII to do just that. It had been done many times before for monarchs throughout Christendom; on this critical moment, however, the Pope was in bad terms with the Emperor, who had him cornered in Italy and was the nephew of Catherine of Aragón.

Clement nowise wished to offend the fearsome Charles V, but at the same time, struggled to appease the devout King of England as much as possible. After all, Henry had lent vigorous support to the papacy against the sweep of Lutheranism throughout the Continent. The Pope therefore instructed the King to take Anne Boleyn as his mistress, promising to legitimize their children. He further suggested that Henry's illegitimate son, Henry FitzRoy, Duke of Richmond, should wed Catherine and Henry's daughter Mary, thereby making him an heir to the throne. Clement even proposed bigamy, sending Catherine to a nunnery—which to some theologians was the equivalent of dying to the world—and marrying Anne. Unfortunately, the King wanted undoubted legitimacy for his second marriage and its prospective offspring, so the Pope was finally forced to send his legate, Cardinal Campeggio, to investigate the validity of Henry's marriage—a concession undone by the secret orders received by Campeggio not to render a decision unfavourable to the Queen.[213]

Following the death of Archbishop Warham, the appointment to the see of Canterbury of one Thomas Cranmer, a good friend of Henry's, was duly approved by Clement. However, immediately after his consecration in May, 1533, Cranmer proceeded to declare null and void the King's marriage to Catherine of Aragón, while Henry had Parliament pass an act forbidding all appeals to Rome. This was somewhat fortuitous, for he had secretly married Anne in January of that year, and she was already pregnant. After she gave birth not to a son but to Elizabeth, another daughter, Anne lost Henry's favour and was beheaded on charges of adultery. The King's third wife, Jane

---

[213] After failing to secure the annulment, Lord Chancellor Wosley suddenly found his office as papal legate declared in violation of the ancient Statute of Præmunire (1353), which forbade direct papal jurisdiction. He was not only a cardinal, but bishop, archbishop, and an abbot, yet the affairs of the state had previously kept him from his ecclesiastical duties. He turned to his archdiocese of York, which he had never visited before, and it was only his timely death in 1530 that saved him from getting executed as a traitor.

Seymour, died giving birth to Edward, his sole surviving son. His latter three marriages, one of which was annulled, and another which ended with a beheading, were childless. But, unlike the churchman Clement, Henry never claimed to lead a holy life.

While the King ultimately failed to overcome the resistance of the Pope, he could go around it by proclaiming himself the head of the Church, and that way, sever all ties with Rome. In doing so, he would achieve a lot more than just the right to remarry. One should, however, bear in mind that the kings of England had, beginning with William the Conqueror, contested the right of the popes to meddle in the bilateral relationship of the English Church and State. The struggle between Henry VIII and Clement VII was just the final phase of an intermittent war which had been waged between the papal and the regal power from the days of the Norman Conquest. The kings had always insisted that the Church of England was subject to their power, and a good many edicts had been passed that forbade such actions which would have presupposed acceptance of the higher jurisdiction of papacy.

All through the Middle Ages, there exists voluminous evidence to suggest that the pope was to the English primarily an outsider, whom they had always treated with childlike reluctance. The second Henry was no less eager to emancipate himself from the power of the Roman pontiff, and the desecration of the shrine of Thomas Becket at Canterbury was eighth Henry's way of redressing a quarrel of three and a half centuries' standing. Henry VIII cited the Saint to appear in court to answer to the charges of treason and rebellion; the case was formally argued at Westminster, his guilt was proved, and St. Thomas was condemned (1538) as "a rebel and a traitor to his prince." The gold and jewels from his opulent shire were carried off in two sturdy coffers, and the rest of the treasure in twenty-six carts.

The most curious thing about Henry VIII is perhaps the fact that, although his sovereignty was absolute, he instituted all his far-reaching reforms through Parliament. It seemingly passed many enactments concerning the Church, though, in fact, it only ratified the decrees of the King. Still, there can be little doubt that the opinions of the members of parliament corresponded to the fancies of Henry. Most Englishmen had something to gain from the nullification of papal power, especially as it meant the annulment of the ecclesiastical tributes that came from their own pockets. A great deal of the Church's wealth passed in donations to the new Tudor nobility and gentry, the supporters of the Tudor monarchy. Thus, in England, the religious controversy did not lead to a civil war, but all the more often to persecutions and executions, the purpose of which was the preservation of unity and royal supremacy. The 16th-century Englishman wanted his Church to be a national one—not some subsidiary of a universal organization, the interests of which were often in conflict with those of his king and country.

Even as Henry became the head of the Church of England, the equivalent happened in literally dozens of petty principalities in Germany. A prince would introduce a preacher with Lutheran sympathies, either keeping his Catholic confessor as well and allowing the minister only to deliver sermons, or completely dismissing the priests. The growing temptation to loot Church property soon created a vested interest in encouraging the change of religion. By attacking Catholic doctrine, for example, in the matters of celibacy in holy orders, a prince could open the door for the confiscation of the immense clerical endowments. Many still believe the Protestant Reformation to have essentially been an economic movement, despoiling of the Church by a new band of robber-barons utterly devoid of scruples. The bourgeoisie, who, as a result of the commercial growth, had gained considerable social standing, were fighting by the side of the gentry and the royalty against the feudal nobility and the papacy.

In the free cities, the town council might invite Lutheran preachers in, and if the ministers were favourably received, allow Lutheran congregations to worship openly, usually in private homes. The city might also sponsor public debates between Catholic and Protestant authorities, or even decide to abandon Catholicism altogether; for a minor alteration in the theological garb, the city would be emancipated from episcopal taxes and courts, and could appropriate extensive parcels of ecclesiastical property. On the other hand, the town council had to put the Protestant ministers on the public payroll, for there was no Church fiscal system to fund them, and needed to replace the cathedral schools with publicly funded ones, marking the rise of public education in Europe.

The liberation of the nuns shut up in convents was considered by the reformers as one of their cardinal duties. Not all inmates had entered the monasteries of their own free will as the result of an inner vocation. The nunnery had largely degenerated into a semi-prison of sorts, where excess daughters could be sent by their parents. Many nuns had been brought to the convents almost from arms of their wet-nurses, and had taken their monastic vows so young (at the age of eleven, for example), that they could not fully comprehend the significance. As they grew older and felt the impulses of youth stir up inside, they often bitterly regretted their promise. Such nuns would leave the convents by the thousands, and by rule, marry quickly. Martin Luther's own wife, Katharina von Bora, was a convent child of this precise type.

On the other hand, some nunneries had become refuges for undowered girls, and not all nuns wanted to face the tumults of the world. Other religious houses, both for men and women, accepted only novices of noble birth, and had developed into opulent centres of an aristocratic way of life, far removed from the ascetic founding principle. Again, another reason for the decay of the monastic institution was the constant lack of funds in the poorer houses. The finances of the monasteries, based as they were on landownership, fell into great difficulties when the West entered into a monetary economy at the end of the Middle Ages. The poorer the monastery, the less donations it received. From poverty, many monasteries lapsed into utter destitution, and their overall standard plummetted. With the Reformation, the monks and nuns were chased out and ordered to find jobs or else leave the domain, while the monastic buildings were converted to other uses.

Luther hardly broke his own vow of celibacy out of some deep inner need, but in order to offer a liberating example, and, above all, to spite the Catholics. The former Augustinian wrote to the knights of the Teutonic Order, inviting them also to renounce their vows and take wives. The Bishop of Sambia, who held the high offices of Regent and Grand Chancellor of Prussia, was the first knight to set aside his vows, and in his Christmas Day sermon of 1523, exhorted the others to emulate him. The year after, the Grand Master himself, Margrave Albrecht von Hohenzollern of Brandenburg, decided to discard his vows, marry, and transform East Prussia into a secular principality. Following the Treaty of Cracow (1525), Albrecht formally converted to Lutheranism, swearing fealty to the King of Poland, who invested him as Duke of Prussia with the right of hereditary transmission. After the Livonian Knights similarly established (1561) the secular duchy of Courland, likewise under Polish suzerainty, the Teutonic Order—as a mediæval crusading entity—came to an end.

In the meantime, Emperor Charles' preoccupation with the continuing war against France over control of various cities and principalities in Italy had effectively distracted him from efforts to silence Luther. Then the Turkish threat to the Habsburg lands arose again: in August, 1526, the Turks defeated and killed Louis II of Hungary and Bohemia in the Battle of Mohács, and Ferdinand of Austria assumed the crowns of Sts. Stephen and Wenceslaus both as the brother-in law of the childless king and by virtue of the Treaty of Pressburg (1491) between his own grandfather and Louis' father, Ladislaus II. Henceforward, the Ottomans were the Habsburgs' greatest concern on land, as they had been on the seas ever since Charles' ascension to the Spanish throne.

The devastating Italian Wars were temporarily ended by the Treaty of Cambrai (1529), known as the Ladies' Peace, because its chief negotiators were Charles' aunt[214] and the mother of Francis[215]. As a result, Charles and Ferdinand pressed the renewal of the Edict of Worms and a revocation of the 1526 devolution of the Lutheran question to the princes at the Second Diet of Speyer, convoked in February of 1529. Several princes objected strongly to this proposal: knowing that the Emperor needed men and money, they saw the diet as a golden opportunity to publicly express their demands for religious reform. This was, of course, exactly what Charles did not wish to see happen, and specifically forbade any mention of religion or of Luther at Speyer. Fourteen of the German princes, including Landgrave Philip of Hesse, refused to attend; instead, they addressed a letter of protest to the Emperor, arguing for the continuance of the devolution—it is this action that most historians regard as the origin of the term "Protestant."

The Peace of Barcelona between the Pope and the Emperor, signed in June of 1529, confirmed Charles' position in Italy. *Quid pro quo*, the treaty stipulated a joint military campaign to reinstate the Medici, who had been banished from Florence two year earlier as a result of the Emperor's invasion of Italy. Clement's native city was fortified in October, 1529, and withstood a gruelling ten-month siege. After it finally capitulated on the 12th of August, 1530, its citizens endured a prolonged witch-hunt of retribution. This time, the rule of the Medici became permanent and absolute; even the pretense of a republic was abandoned, for the Medici, having hitherto shunned titles,

---

[214] Margaret of Austria

[215] Louise of Savoy

became Grand Dukes of Tuscany—the Florentine era of republican freedom was irretrievably over.

Still the same year, Clement travelled to Bologna to formally crown Charles as the Holy Roman Emperor, which favour the Emperor returned by issuing a decree extremely hostile to the Reformation at the Great Diet of Augsburg. Charles was the last German Emperor to be crowned by a pope, and after this practice was abandoned, the coronation ceremonies took place (1562-1792) at the free city of Frankfurt, the seat of imperial elections. The Emperors Elect, after being crowned at the Church of St. Bartholomew by the Archbishop-Elector of Mainz, would proceed with great pageantry to a banquet in the town hall—which is still called the *Römer* (Ger. "Roman") because the Emperors Elect were crowned Kings of the Romans.

The Protestants expressed their views in the famous "Confession of Augsburg," the basic confessional statement of the Lutheran Church, which in an amicable fashion pleads for the redressal of certain grievances and advocates the doctrine of justification by faith alone. It did not touch upon the sensitive communion issue, which had come to the foreground of the dispute, nor upon the claim that the Bible is the sole source of Christian doctrine. In spite of all, the diet denounced the Protestants, confirming, in a slightly expanded form, the resolutions embodied in the Edict of Worms. This decision caused the Lutheran princes to close ranks the following year in the Schmalkaldic League, further widening the rift between Catholics and Protestants.

Just when it seemed that war was about to erupt, Charles agreed in the Religious Peace of Nuremberg (1532) to suspend all actions against the Protestants until a general council could meet, in exchange for armed support against the renewed Turkish onslaught. The Ottoman Empire now extended right along the southern Mediterranean to Morocco and posed a serious threat to the Habsburg lands in Hungary. The Turkish soldiers' discipline and their patient endurance of adversity is often contrasted with the disgraceful behaviour of Christian troops. Despite their tolerance of other religious beliefs, the Turks observed the rituals of their own faith with a seriousness that put most Christians to shame. Luther himself modified his initial opinion and urged the German nobility to defend Christendom against Mohammedans.

When Francesco II Sforza, restored as Duke of Milan by the Treaty of Cambrai, died heirless in 1535, the succession to Milan was once more contested by France and Spain. Eager to recoup in Italy, Francis established friendly relations with the Ottoman Sultan, Suleyman the Magnificent, even though the rest of Christendom were less than pleased by this friendship. The French King explained it in the following, only partly apologetic terms: "I cannot deny that I very much want to see the Turk powerful and ready for war, not for his own sake, for he is an infidel and the rest of us are Christians, but to erode the power of the Emperor and involve him in crippling expense." And although the Treaty of Nice (1538) ended the Franco-Spanish conflict in Italy, the Ottomans continued their raids on the Italian coast.

From the time of Francis, the kings of France did not hesitate to enter into treaties with the Turks to maintain the balance of power in Europe against the Habsburgs. The régime of "capitulations," established under Francis I in 1535, renewed under Louis XIV in 1673, and Louis XV in 1740, permitted the French to reside and trade in the Ottoman Empire without being subject to Ottoman taxation or to the jurisdiction of Islamic courts. As the concessions thus granted were originally intended for the French only, the other Westerners who wished to receive them had to first make an agreement with France. In 1583, the capitulations were extended to the English and the Dutch, which is why Northwest Europeans from the 16th century onwards acquired an increasingly large share in the eastern Mediterranean trade formerly dominated by Italy. As for the Holy Land itself, crusading fervour abated with the realization that the Turks were amenable to running a large-scale tourist service for Christian pilgrims. All Western travellers were allowed access to Jerusalem and to the Holy Sepulchre, which was entrusted to the care of the Franciscan friars. The House of Austria alone, as the mistress of Hungary, the only Catholic country directly threatened by the Turks, felt it prudent to maintain some interest in the crusade.

On the 9th of October, 1533, Pope Clement VII, the man who had crowned Charles of Habsburg as the Holy Roman Emperor, embarked for France to consecrate the marriage of his niece, Catherine de' Medici, to Henry of Valois, future King of France. Clement's indecision has often been cited as his gravest failing, for his vacillation between the two great powers frequently spelled danger for both the city and the Church of Rome. As a pope, he regarded Spain as the worse threat, and therefore, a better ally; as the head of the Florentine Medici family, he feared the Spanish armies quartered in Milan, and needed the protection of the neighbouring France.

Although the marriage Francis thought he was negotiating for his son was with Rome and its Church, Catherine's wedding was a thoroughly Medicean and Florentine affair. If her appearance on the French political stage was made under false pretenses, it was this Italian woman—whose bourgeois parents had died in her infancy and who had been shuffled from convent to convent and court to court all through her childhood—who managed to hold France together, to reconcile the aristocracy of the opposing parties, and to maintain the unity and prosperity of the kingdom, despite a string of weak and impotent monarchs.

When Clement died on the 25th of September, 1534, not a soul shed a tear for him. The night following his death, St. Peter's was broken into and the body of His Holiness, pulled up from its temporary resting-place, was dismembered and a sword contemptuously driven through the heart. In November of the same year, the Supremacy Act was promulgated in England and an oath to the king prescribed, denying the pope any jurisdiction in the island kingdom.

One of the first tangible results of the king's assumption of the highest spiritual powers was the supervision by royal decree of the regular episcopal visitations made to the monasteries. These visitations commenced in 1535 and were overseen by Henry's second administrative genius, Sir Thomas Cromwell[216], whose influence upon the 1530s—one of the most crucial decades in English history—was immense. During the summer of 1535, the houses in the west of England were subjected to inspection; in October, the eastern and southeastern counties underwent the same scrutiny; in December, the midlands; in January, the north.

There were two kinds of religious houses in England: the immensely rich bigwig monasteries populated by the nobility, and then the simple, humble, and poor institutions. The great abbeys of England were large landowners and centres of culture. In addition to scholarship, they were devoted to both secular and ecclesiastical politics. The English Parliament that met in February of 1536 had as its chief business the consideration of the act suppressing the smaller monastic houses. In its final shape, this first measure of suppression enacted that all the monasteries having an annual income below £200 standard of good living should be handed over to the king to be dealt with at his

---

[216] He was made the first Earl of Essex, but later lost favour with the King.

"pleasure, to the honour of God and the wealth of the realm."[217]

Henry knew that an attack against the Church was not likely to arouse much anger if it primarily meant an attack on its immense fortune, and by dividing the spoils, he allowed thousands of his countrymen to derive immediate benefit from the closing down of the monasteries. The only serious revolt against his reforms was the so-called "Pilgrimage of Grace," a popular rising that began in the north of England, the most conservative part of the kingdom, and was contained there (1536). The northern counties were placed under martial law and people would get hanged on mere suspicion of disaffection. By a process called "Dissolution by Attainder," an abbey was considered to fall into the king's hands by the constructive treason of its superior; so, as a consequence of the uprising, several of the larger abbeys, with all their lands and revenues, came into Henry's possession.

At the fall of the English monasteries, an income of whopping £200,000 sterling per annum was taken from the Church and transferred to the royal coffers, though Henry never derived anything approaching that sum from the transfer. It is estimated that the capitalized value derived by the Crown from the monastic wealth seized between 1536 and 1547 was diminished to a fifth by, among other things, gratuitous grants and sales of land at nominal value. But once these monastic lands had been reallocated among the English nobility, going back to Rome became a far more complex affair. Even the nobles who had no sympathy for the Reformation now had a vested interest to uphold the acts of their sovereign.

The increased brutality of the real world often creates the sometimes serious, other times not so serious fantasies of an ideal state. The most famous of these is, for good reason, the *Utopia* of St. Thomas More (1478-1535), which gave the name for this whole genre of literature. Even though this ambiguous little book was printed in Latin as early as 1516, it was not reproduced in English until after a reasonable time had passed since the martyrdom of its author. You see, the Saint had refused to take the Oath of Supremacy, which Henry VIII demanded from all his ministers, was tried for treason, and executed on Tower Hill.

The most imaginative Utopia of the period, however, took the form of a

---

[217] The heads of these establishments were to receive pensions, and the religious were to be admitted to the larger, more well-to-do monasteries, or to be licensed to act as secular clergy.

monastery, and was, indeed, invented by a runaway Franciscan friar. François Rabelais (c. 1494-1553) is generally considered the foremost representative of the French Renaissance. Harassed for his humanist studies, Rabelais first fled to the less conservative Benedictine Order, then became a priest, attending most of the French universities. He studied Greek and Latin, and in addition to graduating in philosophy, law, and arts, took the medical degree at Montpellier. His imaginary abbey was called "Thélème," and its rule was as plain as possible: *Faictz ce que vouldras*, "Do what thou wilt."

This ingenious invention was only one of many that appear in the books which Rabelais published between 1532 and 1552 on the lives of *Gargantua and Pantagruel*. This work is among the most bewildering of all world literature; written as it is by an incomparable punster, translating it is impossible, and reading it difficult, if the reader is only familiar with modern French. It might appear as nothing more than a most impious joke—and this is how many have taken it—for never in that extremely scornful, anticlerical, and anti-Scholastic age has the Church and Scholasticism been mocked anywhere near as immodestly as he had done it. Others, however, have perceived behind its undeniably drastic humour a purposeful satire aimed at the remnants of European mediævalism.

Falling a victim of several inconsistent attempts at interpretation is, of course, the fate of all great minds, and among great minds Rabelais, in any case, has to be counted. His books, in their unrivalled outspokenness, attained immense popularity, but for the same reason, were condemned by the Church one after the other, and Rabelais needed the help of the French King to escape the stake. His affection for tasteless puns was so overwhelming that he is told to have subjected to witticism even his own death, putting on a domino, because it is written in the Scriptures: *Beati qui moriuntur in Domino* (Rev. 14:13).

Luther may have launched the revolution, but he lost control of it practically from the start. His profound conservatism and the restriction of his vision of reform to the context of a perpetual, if theologically reformed, agrarian mediæval order, ensured the confinement of his movement to the largely rural, still feudal North Central Europe. After the Peasants' War, the authoritarian and aristocratic tone of Lutheranism was fairly clear; it was emphatically the Prussian Junker's Church of choice.

The position of the rising European urban middle classes seemed to galvanize around the teachings of the French reformer and Zwingli's self-appointed successor, John Calvin (1509-1564). His "Reformed" movement, despite the different names it took on in different countries, was better disciplined than Luther's, making it the most dangerous enemy of Rome. In no time, Calvin's supporters had gained a strong foothold in the towns and cities of France, England, Scotland, and the Netherlands, come close to breaking down the Lutheran opposition in Germany, and established a totalitarian church state in Geneva. Thereby, Calvinism, in point of fact, realized the Utopia of a spiritual commonwealth, the absolutism of the church that has always been the daydream of papacy.

This social system was predicated on two wholly untenable premises: firstly, on the ludicrous belief that all people are by nature alike or that they can be made alike by using a properly moulded and properly applied die; and secondly, on the equally absurd notion that the government is entitled, and even obliged, to take care of absolutely everything.[218] The greatest legislator of Protestantism set up in Geneva a theocracy that surpassed all that had ever been attempted by the Catholic Church in the fields of supervision and inquisition of the conscience. Whereas Lutheranism took joy in what had not been expressly prohibited and embraced it as a good gift from God, Calvinism interpreted the same points negatively: what was not separately ordained was frivolous, and as such, forbidden.

Everything in Geneva was controlled by the clerical police, almost every natural and innocent expression of *joie d'vivre* was suspected, banned, and penalized. All types of amusement and entertainment, playing, dancing, singing, performing, even the reading of fiction, was strictly forbidden. The punishments for cursing, jesting, joking, and using obscene language were severe. It was a grave offence to laugh during sermons, to name children after Catholic saints, to be unable to recite prayers, or to say that the Pope was a good man. Disrespectful reference to Calvin or the clergy was a crime. First offence was punished with a reprimand, second with a fine, further ones with imprisonment or exile. Fornication was punishable by death—as were

---

[218] Calvin makes a splendid example of how easily theocentricism turns into egocentricism: as the dictator of Geneva, he most thoroughly repudiated the principle of private judgement with which the new religion had begun.

adultery, idolatry, and blasphemy.

Calvin, like Luther, found his way to authentic Christianity via that antiquated pillar of orthodoxy, St. Augustine; yet the respective theologies of the two great reformers differed in a number of ways. Calvin recognized no sacraments at all, and placed a greater emphasis on predestination. According to Calvin, God allowed no freedom whatsoever: in being all-everything—knowing, powerful, what have you—He preordained everything and left people no free choice; everything was through Divine Grace, not through some particular ritual. The connection between Calvin's theological tenets and the economic ideas of his followers has long been a subject of debate. Although Calvinist theology well suited the developing commercial classes, it was probably not planned that way. The doctrine that God would reward those destined for eternal life with prosperity while still on Earth produced a diligent, and often fiercely religious, conduct. Today's sole superpower, the United States of America, has been the promised land to both Calvinism and capitalism.

The old-established feudal classes levied taxes on the merchant, disdained and defrauded him, and helped the Church to sustain the mediæval view that prescribed all goods a "just price" and forbade the collection of interest. The new tradesman wanted to buy from the cheapest market and sell on the highest priced one. He wished not to be the patron and guardian of his employee, but to be just his employer. By the 16th century, he had grown into an embryo of a businessman, and naturally took advantage of Protestantism against the Church which sought to maintain the kind of economic conditions that were disadvantageous to him. Protestantism naturally throve in those parts of Europe where the new tradesmen were wealthiest, and withered where they were poorest. Thus, for example, the progressive England and Holland were converted to Protestantism, while the backward Spain and Poland remained Catholic.

Protestant ideology shaped the people who espoused it, making them even more adapted to making money and to form the middle classes familiar to us today. Luther's idea that every man has a God-given vocation, and that it is God's will that one practise this vocation, helped usher in the Protestant work ethic by exalting ordinary occupations as ways of serving God. However, it was Calvin who provided the spirit of capitalism with a theological basis, and it was precisely in the Calvinist countries where the equity now accumulated with which the Industrial Revolution was later financed. Calvinism not only preached the worth of labour, it downright demanded people to work, because the Devil is on the prowl for the idle and since work is a part of man's debt to the Almighty. Until then, work had been considered a punishment, a necessary evil at best; now it was ennobled, even sanctified.

So it is that the Calvinist works hard and reaps his just desserts; he wastes no time or energy pondering the imponderable—whereas Lutherans agonize over faith, the Calvinist simply has it. He is against luxury, ostentation, and the ornamentation of churches; against all that is not absolutely imperative to a virtuous life. His income, which is consequently greater than his expenditure, he reinvests in commercial ventures. This way, the Calvinist becomes a capitalist, a rich man on his way to Heaven. What is more, he takes pleasure in the certainty that the heavily indebted nobleman, who acts high and mighty with him, will not only die poor, but also—because he is not a Calvinist—end up in Hell.

It is curious that the Reformation, which expressly claims to be a return to the pure word of God, in these several points stands in the sharpest contrast to the Scriptures. The Lord impresses upon Adam right at the beginning of the Old Testament that: "Because thou hast hearkened unto the voice of thy wife, and hast eaten of the tree, of which I commanded thee, saying, Thou shalt not eat of it: cursed is the ground for thy sake; in sorrow shalt thou eat of it all the days of thy life; in sweat of thy face shalt thou eat bread. . ." Not a single syllable is uttered about the "sanctity" or "blessedness" of labour; on the contrary, Adam is damned to toil—apparently the most fearsome punishment God could devise for the crimes of the first man. The bliss and joy of idleness is heralded on nearly every line of the New Testament. The idea of hard work and incessant activity is what still persists of Calvin's doctrine in Western society, for he was successful above everything else in making people feel guilty about "doing nothing."

The Reformation Era was a turbulent one, and no two regions went through exactly the same history. The nature of the reforms and whether they succeeded or not depended as much on the regional conditions and local traditions as on the personalities of the men in power. In France, the unique—and uniquely privileged—situation of the French Church in the Catholic hierarchy meant that a widely-supported evangelical movement would ultimately fail. But particularly in England, Scotland, Holland, and

Germany, there was a total identification between the Reformation and the population. Many an historian make the mistake of painting Henry VIII as the first Protestant king—yet he was never a Protestant: though he had ousted Rome from his nation, he still practised the Catholic religion; however, his struggle for the supremacy brought to power Queen Anne Boleyn, Sir Thomas Cromwell, Archbishop Thomas Cranmer, and other bishops who gave the Henrician reform a distinctly Protestant hue.

Educated and naturally inquisitive, the English people were intrigued by the new Protestant teachings, but they also coveted the vast monastic lands which Henry put to auction. This is the paradox of the Henrician reform: it was motivated both by greed and by genuine religious uproar. It is estimated that during Henry's reign, at least half of his subjects were under the age of eighteen, and as time passed, the new generation of nobles were Protestant because it was expedient and intellectually appealing. With each passing year, more Englishmen were born at a further remove from the old days of Roman supremacy. The aging Henry could still remember the Papist ways—but fewer and fewer of his subjects did. At the same time, some countries began to defensively identify patriotism with Catholicism. This was especially true in the case of subjugated nations such as Ireland, where Protestantism would have no chance of appealing to the people by any ethical, religious, or political ideals.

An Irish parliament, convened by fraud, corruption, and terror in 1536, and composed solely of English colonists, acknowledged Henry VIII as Head of Church and State. The Catholic religion, with its ceremonial and teachings, was declared void and "corrupt for ever." In 1538, Pope Paul III revoked the bull of Adrian IV and all the subsequent papal sanctions of the English conquest, recognizing Conn Bacach O'Neill as the rightful ruler of Ireland in place of the newly re-excommunicated King of England. Without so much as apologizing to the Irish chieftains for past actions, the Pope released them from their feudal obedience to the English kings, who he declared no longer entitled to style themselves "Lords of Ireland." Three years later, the Irish forces were defeated and Conn Bacach surrendered; he accepted the title "Earl of Tyrone" while the Irish parliament proclaimed Henry "King of Ireland" rather than feudal lord. One by one, the Irish nobles were forced to surrender their titles. The unpaid English soldiers had to support themselves by rapine and plunder, whilst the introduction of Reformation principles only added new sources of oppression.

Not only on the Continent, but also in England, the Reformation caused one Church to become three. Henry's third wife, Jane Seymour, mirrored the opinions of the old nobility, arguing for the retention of the monasteries, and even trying to persuade the King to restore the stubbornly Catholic Princess Mary to the succession. As an opponent of Luther and a defender of the Faith, King Henry was not about to allow this faith to be erased. He had rid himself of Rome in order to gain wealth and a son, and had done both. He wanted his people to remain Catholic, but under the king rather than the pope. Thus, in 1539, Henry personally pushed through Parliament the "Bloody Statute" of the Six Articles, a "whip with six strings" that imposed severe penalties against most of the standard Protestant beliefs.

According to the third article, "priests, after the order of priesthood received as afore, may not marry by the law of God." Auricular confession was reintroduced and the Catholic eucharist restored. Anyone with a genuine religious conviction was therefore prey to persecution: devout Catholics, who adhered to the pope and regarded Henry's later marriages as adulterous, were liable to get beheaded for treason; faithful Protestants, who abjured the ceremonial institution and deemed clerical marriages lawful, might be hanged for sacrilege; and stern Calvinists, who denied the conversion of the bread, could be burned for heresy. Such a wide net of potential victims not only inspired further awe for the Crown, but also fostered the tendency among 16th-century Englishmen to consult their law books before making a move.[219] Henry's intolerance towards heretical opinions was all in all essential to England's salvation—as subsequent reigns show, conformity well makes up for the lack of unity when the state is threatened from within and without.

Protestantism would greatly increase the feelings of sinfulness, for no man could any longer be certain of his redemption. All the major Protestant denominations unconditionally espoused St. Augustine's doctrine of Original Sin.[220] Even in his most anarchistic moments, Luther would hold fast to the

---

[219] Among the people executed under the Six Articles was Henry's chief minister, Thomas Cromwell. Charges of heresy and treason were brought against him by his bitter enemy, the Duke of Norfolk, in alliance with the Catholic bishops whom the Earl of Essex had forced from power.

[220] Jews and Orthodox Christians maintain that Adam passed on only the consequence of his sin, that is, death.

idea of man's inherent evil. It was God alone who instilled in man the faith which kept him on the straight and narrow. While deeds meant nothing, faith was more an endless task imposed upon the soul than a pillar of certainty. Calvin, for his part, held that only those whom God has specifically elected are saved, and that the individual can do nothing to affect his salvation[221], wherefore no Calvinist could tell for sure if he was one of the elect or one of the eternally damned.

The individual's political affiliation was determined no longer by race, language, or family ties, but by creed alone. All Europe became a gigantic battlefield for the rival religious parties, where tolerance was condemned as indifference and religious freedom as diabolical—a means of letting each go to Hell his own way. The "Wars of Religion" of the later 16th century were notorious for their brutality, which is an inevitable element of any conflict whose parties regard each other as unworthy of mercy. The Calvinists, for example, with their extremely rigid predestinarianism, were downright obligated to deny every heterodox the right to exist.

---

[221] This strict Calvinism was later refuted by Jacobus Arminius (1560-1609), whose more moderate doctrine was subsequently adopted by the Baptists and the Methodists.

CHAPTER 32

"All witchcraft comes from carnal lust, which in women is unsatiable," says the *Malleus Maleficarum*. Sexuality played an essential role in the phenomenon of witchcraft. Almost every 16th-century book on sorcery mentions the *incubus*, a demon who assumes the appearance of a man to lay with a woman. Intercourse with the Devil was a central source of power for the witch, and the better part of the calamities caused was sexual in nature: barrenness, impotence, unnatural desires, irrational amours, and marital quarrels.

The Christian Church, with its celibate clergy, had, during the last thousand years, elevated misogyny to the level of science. The age of the witch-hunts was a sum total of numerous social, cultural, philosophical, and theological factors, not the hysterical frenzy of superstitious peasants. The witch-hunters were not sexually deviant, screaming hysterics; they were the scholars of their time, widely learned men, eminent officials who wielded not inconsiderable power, legally trained individuals who took pride in their logical thinking. Among them were Luther, Zwingli, and Calvin.

Even though the majority of Protestants quit believing in saints, all of them none the less kept believing in the Devil, in witches, and in all the court of Hell. With the Reformation, superstition rather deepened than weakened. Prior to this, only Jews, Turks, and sorcerers were deemed the Devil's disciples; now the entire world became diabolized: to a Protestant, the pope was the Antichrist, and every Papist was the Devil's own, whereas the Catholic saw Hell's minions in Luther and in all his followers. While Luther said of Dr. Eck and many another of his adversaries that they had made a pact with the Devil, the canon of Breslau, in turn, claimed in his biography of Luther, published only three years after the reformer's death, that he was sired by Satan with the adulteress, Margaret Luther.

In the early Middle Ages, persecution of witches was virtually impossible; the great majority of people were peasants, scarcely better than animals in eyes of the nobility and clergy. The wise men and herbal healers of that time were, in practice, allowed to ply their trade without let or hindrance. Though the Church looked askance at their tricks, official dogma did not give occasion to any measures. Non-Christian customs were, on the one hand, regarded as the deceptions of the Devil, but, on the other, the omnipotence of God and the redemption of Christ at the very least, was considered to render ineffective all the plots of Hell. The peasant and his woman had to be made Christians before they could be accused of dissent. Not until the 16th century, during the Reformation and the Counter-Reformation, can we speak of a truly Christian Europe, barring its furthest fringes. At exactly the same time, the witch-hunts burst into their fullest frenzy.

Still, learned and literate men rarely found themselves on trial for their lives; the kings and princes were in habit of keeping court magicians as their advisors, and a vast body of occult literature emanated from the Renaissance. As long as witchcraft was associated with heterodoxy, the privileged and protected male wizards were entirely safe from prosecution; it was not until later, when the witch-hunts had permeated all layers of society, that this once lucrative profession died out. In building up their theories on the essence of evil, the scholars of the ruling class often outdid the actual government officials in ferocity and narrow-mindedness. During the century following the Reformation, Benedict Carpzov of Saxony, who boasted of having read the Bible 53 times, singularly distinguished himself by his skill in demonstrating the reality of witchcraft, and by his cruelty in detecting and punishing it. The doctrines of, among others, this eminent Lutheran legal scholar and theologian were spread by perhaps the most important individual promoting factor of the witch-hunts—the printing press.

It was witchcraft that made women legally competent to stand trial. Before, women had hardly ever seen the inside of a courthouse, because their fathers and husbands were legally accountable for their actions. Over a duration of two hundred years, from 1450 to 1650, women were sentenced to death for witchery more often than for all the other crimes put together. During this, the most intense period of organized witch-hunts, an average of three quarters of the witches executed were women; but the quarter of men should be substantial enough to show that this dreadful phenomenon was not wholly actuated by misogyny. These events reflect not so much mass psychosis and hysteria as a long-term, from contemporary point of view entirely logical and rational, juridical and philosophical development.

In the Middle Ages, folk medicine was almost exclusively in the hands of women. The common people had always administered their own cures; after all, they could not afford the services of a licensed medical doctor. This was their blessing, for the physicians of the courts and of the rich cities usually killed their patients with excessive bloodletting, purgation, and the bizarre mixtures the sick person was forced to swallow. The least harmful and the most often used medical remedies were prayers. These differed from the spells cast by the witches in that they contained the name of Jesus, the Virgin Mary, or one of the saints. The doctors also employed magical talismans; in contradistinction to the amulets used by the witches, these were called holy relics.

Immense revenues flowed into divers monasteries and churches all around Europe from relics noted for their healing power. Every cathedral, every great abbey, and nearly every parish church claimed possesion of a healing relic. The Church maintained that it was impious to seek a natural cure from a physician, when one could receive supernatural help from God. Its attribution of disease to diabolical influence was particularly prejudicial to the development of medical science; Christians were ordered not to seek healing from Jewish or Muslim physicians and the Christian doctors were forbidden, under pain of excommunication, to undertake medical treatment without calling in ecclesiastical advice.

The Reformation brought no sudden change to the sacred theory of medicine. Luther notoriously and consistently ascribed his own ailments to "Devil's spells," declaring that "Satan produces all the maladies which afflict mankind, for he is the prince of death," but that "no malady comes from God." The concurrent witch-hunts, however, managed to smother the women's healing tradition: it was as dangerous to brew camomile tea as it was poison or love potion. Women could not take a medical degree since they were barred from universities, and only a university graduate was allowed to practise the healer's profession.

Philippus Aureolus Theophrastus Bombastus von Hohenheim, one of the most important Renaissance naturalists, adopted the name of Paracelsus ("exceeding Celsus") to publicize his contempt for Celsus and other medical authorities who had been dead more than a thousand years, yet whose tomes were still current at the height of the Renaissance. The healing art as we know it today would be hard to imagine without the historical influence of Paracelsus, an advocate of experimentation in an age when medical knowledge had become bound in paper and was more or less a matter of received doctrine handed down from antiquity.

It was May Day, 1493, when Paracelsus first saw the light of day, in a house which stood near the Devil's Bridge spanning the River Sihl, in Einsiedeln in the forest canton of Schwyz, a Roman Catholic, German-speaking part of Switzerland. Born as the boy was on the Feast of St. Philip, he was named after the Apostle by his father, Wilhelm Bombast de Riett von Hohenheim, an illegitimate scion of the very old and noble Swabian family whose name he proudly bore. The elder von Hohenheim, a man of intelligence and education but of little means, hoped his son to some day follow him in the medical profession, for which reason, the name of Theophrastus was added, in honour of the ancient physician[222]. It has been suggested that *Aureolus* was an endearment occasioned by the boy's blond hair, most of which he, in older age, ironically lost to baldness. (Aureolus was also the ancient term for an alchemist, and it is entirely conceivable that Paracelsus himself adopted this name later on in connection with his alchemical interests.) Paracelsus' mother, a bondswoman of his native town's great Benedictine cloister, had an unfortunate disposition towards depression, which ultimately made her throw herself into the Sihl from the Devil's Bridge, when her son was only nine years old.

It was following the above tragic incident that the Hohenheims moved to Villach, Carinthia, where Wilhelm would teach in the local mining school—a part of the mining operations controlled by the Fugger family—and double as a physician to the miners and smelters. Here Paracelsus began receiving his education from teachers spiritual and secular, scholarly and artisan alike. He studied grammar, logic, and rhetoric at the nearby Abbey of St. Paul, where he took lessons, by his own account, from several of the Benedictines and, apparently, from the Bishop of Lavant himself.

The book learning of the time tended to treat scientific theories as extensions of philosophy, but the environment Paracelsus grew up in assured he would not merely engage in hair-splitting between philosophical doctrines. Craft traditions of the Middle Ages, alchemy of the metal-smelting laboratories in particular, had continued to develop in an independent

---

[222] Theophrastus of Eresus (c. 371-287 BCE), a student of both Plato and Aristotle and the successor of the latter as the head of the Lyceum.

manner, and the foundry-masters of Villach were always ready to show their physician's eager and clever son things that they jealously guarded from grown-ups as mysteries of the craft. His leisure time adventures consisted in going among the foundries with the unearthly incandescence of their furnaces, watching the glimmery crystalline ore transform into shiny white metal; here he learned about the processes involved in mining, the nature of ores, the stratification of the rocks of the earth, and the properties of mineral water.

At about the age of fourteen, Paracelsus left his father in Villach to become an itinerant student, travelling widely throughout Europe. Although he certainly visited a number of universities in various countries, he is known to have engaged in actual studies only at Ferrara, under Johannes Manardus. Whether he went on to take a degree there, or at any other university, is doubtful, for Paracelsus already had too firm a basis of naturalist knowledge to be able to accept the conventional type of medical science based wholly on Aristotle, Galen (c. 130-200), and Avicenna (980-1037). Extremely frustrated with the dogmatism and pomposity of the privileged class of physicians, he resumed his travels in order to familiarize himself with the methods of abortionists and alchemists, gathering an extensive amount of specific knowledge in the field of medicine, practised in those days by both wisemen and quacks, barbers and blacksmiths alike.

Paracelsus picked up practical medical knowledge by working as a military surgeon in the Venetian service, involving the many wars waged between 1517 and 1524, not only in the countries under Venetian influence, but also in the Netherlands, Prussia, Scandinavia, and possibly the Middle East as well. He claimed to have taken the last boat out of Rhodes before it fell to the Turks on the 24th of October, 1522. While staying with the Grand Duke of Moscow, he was captured during an invasion by the Tartars and taken to their capital. Following a string of abortive attempts to establish a practice in southern Germany or Switzerland, Paracelsus finally (1526) settled in the free city of Strasbourg. He did not, however, enroll himself in the physicians' but in the grain merchants' guild, and it was charged that he had illicitly adopted the title of Doctor. Be it as it may, his disdain for the educational methods and attitudes of the universities frequently surfaced, and he habitually attacked everything he found unsatisfactory in these institutions: "It is the giving of health that makes the physician, and their works that make Masters and Doctors, not emperor, not pope, nor faculty, nor privilegia nor any university. . . . from time to time he must consult old women, gypsies, magicians, wayfarers, and all manner of peasant folk and random people."

Paracelsus challenged the established and virtually undisputed, Galenic theory of illness as a result of conflicts among the "four humours." He was a keen-sighted observer, whose medication was based on diagnoses that are still widely in use today. Though he refused to dissect corpses[223], his findings in medicine, surgery, and chemistry, based on his own practice, paved the way for modern medical science, as well as today's alternative medicines. He understood psychosomatic maladies and noted relationships such as the hereditary pattern in congenital syphilis, the association of cretinism with endemic goitre, and of paralysis with head injuries. He was the first person to recognize an industrial disease, devoting his study *On Diseases of Miners* (1567) to the subject.

The study of alchemy may have estranged Paracelsus from his contemporaries, but it was precisely owing to this that he came to understand the physical and psychological causes behind physiological disorders. In his effort to unite medicine and chemistry into a single science, he became an exemplary precursor to modern chemical pharmacology and the founder of iatrochemistry, the forerunner of modern medical chemistry. He declared that the business of the alchemists should be to make medicines, rather than to seek a means of multiplying gold. Until then, the medical problems had been transfixed by the age-old belief that all cure must proceed either from plants or animals—a vitalism which could not accept body chemicals to be like any other chemicals—thereby confining pharmacy to herbal cures. Paracelsus introduced to the treatment of disease mercury, sulphur, salt, iron, led, arsenic, blue vitriol, and several other valuable and still commonly used chemicals[224], including opium tincture or *laudanum*, by which name the narcotic is known to anæsthesiologists even today.

Paracelsus also discovered and named our metal *zink*, and gave us the word *al-Cohol*, which he took over from Arabic for the spirit of wine; yet, it was his experiments with mercury, the most powerful of alchemical metals, that made

---

[223] Surgeons were not regarded as real physicians until the 18th century, so their trade was practised largely by charlatans, the term "barber-surgeon" being a survival of this.

[224] This was so novel that it took until 1584 for chemical remedies to be banned from Catholic universities.

him famous for all time. The cure for syphilis, the most dangerous disease of his day, regarded as incurable, turned out to depend on the use of this chemical element. The only benefit derived from the prevalent use of guaiacum in its treatment was—as Paracelsus put it—to greedy coffers of the Fugger family, holding as they did the import monopoly on the exotic drug. The printing of his *Eight Books on the Origin and Causes of French Disease* was banned based on the opinion of the Dean of the Leipzig Medical Faculty, Heinrich Ströwer, an associate and beneficiary of the Fuggers.

Even though Paracelsus had the qualifications of a physician, his practical abilities were invariably accompanied by what his envious contemporaries called sorcery. In fact, magic was in those days so common a charge against men of science that many of them seemed to believe it themselves. Paracelsus incensed his peers by proclaiming that "magic is a great secret wisdom, just as reason is a great public folly." This did not, however, mean that he would place any reliance on supernatural forces in his work: on the contrary, he rejected the prevailing notion that health and disease were determined by the influence of saints and demons, and was fond of saying that all the healing prayers put together meant no more than the mud on the soles of his shoes; to him, "magic" simply meant the use of natural forces that were not yet fully understood.

While Paracelsus' colourful aphorisms did little to endear him to his rivals, they made him attractive to other independent minds of the Renaissance. At Strasbourg, Paracelsus depended for the protection from his fellow-physicians upon the local humanists and reformers Nicolaus Gerbelius, Caspar Hedio, and Wolfgang Capito. The latter was the most powerful of the three and a life-long friend of Johannes Œcolampadius, the scholar reformer of Basel. This is how Paracelsus, in 1527, came to be called to Basel where the famed printer of humanist classics, Johannes Frobenius, was suffering from a serious leg infection. His limb was about to be amputated, when Paracelsus threw the learned academics out of the room. He saved the leg and effected a cure which won for him the fame long overdue. His patient was the publisher of Erasmus, among others, and the great Dutch humanist expressed his undying gratitude to Paracelsus by writing: "You have brought back Frobenius, who is half my life, from the underworld."

Although scorned by the medical establishment of Basel, Paracelsus was named municipal physician by the town council. What is more, he was permitted to lecture at the University of Basel by its professor of theology, Œcolampadius, even though he had no official appointment with its medical faculty. Possibly neither the town nor the University realized what sort of man they were admitting to their complacent and peaceful circle, but they were not left in ignorance for long. Paracelsus proceeded to heap scorn on the conservative doctors of the medical faculty, attacking their teaching with ridicule and vulgar invective. He poured out his abusive lectures not in the Latin of academic circles, but in the colloquial German of his fellow-citizens, even boasting that he was the first ever to have lectured in the German vernacular.

On the Midsummer Day of 1527, as the students' traditional St. John's bonfire blazed brightly, Paracelsus threw into the flames, before the astonished eyes of his fellow-townsmen, the revered writings of Avicenna. More properly Ibn Sina, he was an Arab follower of Aristotle; a philosopher who took up medicine as a hobby to become the most famous physician of his day. For a total of six hundred years, his works held sway over the educational institutions of Europe. His book, *al-Qanun*, "the Canon," was thus "the basic medical reference for a longer period than any other book on medicine ever written." It was translated in five Latin volumes and had repeated reprints as the instruction in all the Western universities totally depended on it; unlike in Islamic territories, where clinical medicine was taught in hospitals, the text was interpreted literally and dogmatically rather than experimentally in clinics.

Paracelsus found the cost of breaking with accepted medical views and traditions to be considerable. The pressure against him began to escalate when he lost a major protector with Frobenius' death. After Paracelsus insulted a judge following a prejudiced ruling against him, he was forced to leave Basel, bringing to end the single year of triumph in his otherwise disastrous worldly career. He made his exit in haste, even leaving his manuscripts behind. His subsequent existence was fraught with frustration, persecution, and rejection by the medical community as he resumed his wanderings once more, harshly attacking medical orthodoxy wherever he went. Everywhere he had remarkable successes with patients and, despite his lack of formal academic credentials, obtained several decent position, but always ran afoul of the local élite and was soon forced to flee—often leaving behind his manuscripts as he had in Basel.

He wandered through Switzerland, Germany, Austria, and Bohemia, sojourning here and there, gathering and dispersing knowledge; instead of wearing rich robes and jewels as other physicians, he went about in rags, frequently drunk and always ready to quarrel. He could say of himself: "I have pursued the art in danger of my life and have not been ashamed to learn from strollers, hangmen, and barbers."—not that such intercourse as this would have brought any better repute than in our day—"My teachings have been tested more severely than silver in poverty, anxiety, wars, and perils." In the end, he was called to Salzburg to treat its autocrat archbishop, Ernest of Wittelsbach. It was here that, on the 24th of September, 1541, Paracelsus was flung down a very steep cliff by "unknown assailants" and died of his massive injuries. In this picturesque Austrian town his mortal remains still lie and a statue was erected to him in 1752.

Paracelsus wrote much during his travels, but the mass of information he had gathered lacked both order and coherence. Although he knew Latin, he preferred to write in vernacular 16th-century German, which was not a perfect vehicle for the type of writings that he produced. His style is so marked by obscurity, verbosity, and inconsistent grammar and usage, that it is no wonder that so few of his works have been translated into other languages. They contain a curious mixture of sound observation and mystical jargon, and we may assume that much of what he wrote was in code, familiar to others in his field, but eluding the attention of the Inquisition. Still, most of his numerous writings remained unprinted during his lifetime due to the reluctance of publishers to defy the official strictures passed on his works by various local authorities. His reformatory and unorthodox medical views earned him the title of *Lutherus Medicorum*, the "Luther of Physicians," but unlike his fiery contemporary, Paracelsus never openly renounced the pope or the Catholic Church.

The Reformation had caught the Roman Church by surprise; over the Middle Ages, she had become the largest landowner in Europe but, with the Reformation, vast amounts of landed property was transferred from ecclesiastical princes to secular ones—such a great economic change in so short a time the Western civilization had never seen. However, the rapid victories of the reformed soon set off a powerful counter-attack, and it was natural that it should come from Iberia, as if the first and so far undisputed colonial power had foreseen the imminent danger.

On the eve of the Reformation, the once so liberal Spain, where Muslims, Jews, and Christians at one time co-existed peacefully, had been graced with a semi-national inquisition, which, as such, was independent of Rome. To cover in detail what amounts to a genocide of two distinct and large Iberian communities would be a near-impossible task; but the subsequent success of the Spanish Church and nation in suppressing Protestantism led Pope Paul III, the last of the Renaissance popes and the first pope of the Counter-Reformation, to set up a general inquisition for the whole Church. This "Holy Roman and Universal Inquisition" was in 1542 assigned to the Sacred Congregation of the Holy Office[225], one of the several "congregations" that make up the Curia, specially constituted "against heretical depravity throughout the whole Christian Commonwealth." As a means of European cleansing, the Roman Inquisition was most effective in Italy, where it enjoyed the support of the secular authorities; even there, however, this revival of institutional persecution of heretics was much milder than its Spanish forebear, and very few people got executed.

The Catholic Counter-Reformation was characterized by an intensified spiritual commitment to doctrine, which itself grew narrower and narrower just when worldly knowledge was expanding and increasing. The censorship was nowhere more parochial and implacable than it was in Spain; studying in foreign universities was forbidden under penalty of the most dire punishments, so that the poison of more liberal opinions could not penetrate the country. Of the diverse means by which Protestant teaching could be propagated, the role of the book and the sermon is well known; less famous, but equally important, in the creation of the new Churches is the substantial influence of verse and music. Strong measures were demanded, and the best remedy was provided by Iñigo de Loyola (1491-1556) and the Jesuit Order which he founded. It gave the name to the Jesuit style, which offered a new approach that ignored the Classical principles laid down by the artists of the Renaissance, and is roughly the same as the movement we now call the "Baroque."

Iñigo, or "Ignatius," as this Basque nobleman rechristened himself, was at

---

[225] Far from being abolished, the "Holy Office" was replaced in 1965 by the Congregation of the Doctrine of the Faith, long headed by Cardinal Joseph Ratzinger, now Pope Benedict XVI.

least as proficient an organizer as Calvin, and his *Spiritual Exercises* bear witness to both a deeper self-knowledge and to the fact that he could give instruction in action and contemplation alike. He had begun his career as a handsome, amorous courtier, and a celebrated, fearless officer. Whilst he was fighting audaciously at the siege of Pamplona, a large boulder severed both of his legs. An incompetent court physician repositioned his other leg so poorly that it had to be broken all over again. He had been, as one who knew him says, "prone to quarrels and amatory folly," but lame men do not wisely pick quarrels, and maids do not offer smiles to cripples.

After convalescing somewhat, Ignatius embarked on a pilgrimage to the Holy Land; the passage-money that his brother lent him he gave out to the poor, and aboard the ship, he delivered sermons of repentance scoffed at by the rugged seamen. The friars at Jerusalem promptly shipped him back to Venice as an undesirable, but after his return to Spain, he gained a larger and more sympathetic audience for his sermons. In any case, he did not know a word of any other language than Basque or Spanish, and eventually came to the realization that in leading people knowledge is also required. Thus, at the age of thirty-three, he took great pains to learn Latin; he then entered the University of Alcalá, where he slowly acquired an education and half a dozen close followers in the course of ten years. There they formed a pious student society for promoting the glory of God, the only Jesuitical feature of which as yet was the melodramatic secrecy that Ignatius imposed.

Only after years of intrigue and diplomacy did Ignatius secure his papal charter, for the Protestants of Germany and England had just exposed the pervasive corruption of the monastic orders, and those who endorsed reform in Rome wanted the suppression of all orders rather than the establishment of a new one. In 1540, permission was granted by Pope Paul III to found a "Society of Jesus," whose members were to take the usual vows of poverty, chastity, and obedience, and live in communities without being categorized as monks. They were most strictly precluded from all ecclesiastical offices and dignities, enabling them to concentrate their powers fully to the service of the Order. Their main vow was that of obedience, which was treated with the same rigidity and severity as it is in the military.[226] They were ostentatiously

---

[226] At the head of the *Compañia de Jesus* stood the General of the Order, below whom were the Provincial Generals, and below them,

directed to serve the sick and the poor, and quietly to secure rich novices and the support of wealthy women—a feature which left a permanent stigma on the body.

The Jesuits would become the most excellent companions and the most austere ascetics, the most self-sacrificing missionaries and the most skilled advisors, the most qualified physicians and the most proficient assassins. They acquired great significance in all the areas of culture, thus enabling them to extend their influence all over Europe, including in time even the Protestant countries. In nearly every important city they established their schools and colleges, and for a century and a half, were leaders in European education. They suppressed independent research and made a host of important discoveries themselves—even if their efforts to raise the overall intellectual level of the Roman Church were prejudiced by the stubborn opposition of the Catholic hierarchy to freedom of thought. Their ubiquity was literal: no earthly position was too high for them, none too low; it could not be said for certain of anyone, if he was a Jesuit or at least under the influence of the Jesuits. This stealthiness combined with a certain appeal to the melodramatic and picturesque in human nature enabled the Order to count its thousand members before its founder died.

It was a strange new world across which the new type of preachers were sent; nearly half of Western Christendom was lost to the papacy and the rest was being rapidly contaminated—a pan-European Reformation seemed only a matter of time. A serious effort at conciliation was made in 1541 at the Regensburg Colloquy. It is difficult to question the motives of the participants: the Protestants present clearly wanted some compromise by which they could avoid being branded heretics, and Dr. Eck, the only staunch conservative on the Catholic side, was far overshadowed by the great legate, Cardinal Gasparo Contarini. The latter was there to represent the Pope; he was not a theologian, but a Venetian diplomat and a distinguished scholar, whose ancient aristocratic family has included eight doges and several artists. He had important doctrines in common with the Protestants, especially regarding the key issue of faith and justification.

One of the worries that had prompted Paul III to dispatch Contarini was the fear that an all-German solution to the schism might consolidate imperial

---

numerous ranks all the way down to the common soldier.

power at the expense of the papacy. The Pope had also started a war with an Italian ally of the Emperor, and Contarini was in the awkward position of defending the Pope's actions while maintaining peace with the Emperor. What is more, the King of France felt threatened by the possible unification in the Empire and sent envoys to Regensburg in an attempt to derail the proceedings. Even the Catholic princes convened there were divided over how to deal with the Protestants, some favouring outright war, others being anxious to settle. By the end of May, the parties delivered their conclusions before the Emperor, and called the effort a failure. With a Catholic League now ranged against the Lutheran Schmalkaldic League, open war seemed unavoidable.

However, the Emperor had more pressing matters to deal with first. The anti-Turkish naval alliance, which Charles had formed with the Pope and Venice, had been unsuccessful. The bulk of Muslim sea power was in the hands of well-organized pirates, who operated mainly from North African ports, attacking shipping and raiding the Spanish and Italian coasts. The Ottoman forces also came up against the Habsburgs on dry land, and Ferdinand, having lost his Hungarian capital in August of 1541, pleaded his brother for a land campaign against Suleyman. The Ottoman and pirate fleets had been consolidated under the command of "Barbarossa" ("Hayreddin" in Turkish sources), turning the coastal regions of North Africa into tributaries of the Ottoman Empire.[227] Charles again opted for a naval venture, which failed dismally after an abortive attack on Algiers.

When the Emperor invested his son, Philip, with Milan, the French King, who had hoped to regain control of the Italian city-state himself, again allied with Suleyman, renewing warfare in August, 1542. With Catherine of Aragón long dead, Charles allied in 1543 with Henry VIII of England, whose Six Articles had shown him not to be such a great heretic after all. By September, 1544, Francis had been coerced into signing the Treaty of Crépy, which basically reaffirmed the earlier treaty of Cambrai, while the subsequent truce with the Turks more or less confirmed the *status quo*. Finally, the way was open for the Catholic Counter-Reformation, fervently desired by Charles V and strongly encouraged by St. Ignatius of Loyola. The Pope was forced to summon the Council of Trent (1545-1563) in order to counteract the

---

[227] whence the term "Barbary States"

Protestant Reformation and to organize the Catholic response. The choice of Trent, a little north Italian town amidst the Alps, was a compromise; the city was filled with Italian culture, but was geographically close to Protestant Germany.

The Council was called by an ecclesiastical prince who conducted himself like a Renaissance nobleman and was anything but reform-minded. Paul III's papal coronation had been accompanied by tournaments and pageants, marking an end to the austerity imposed by the Sack of Rome in 1527. He had obtained wealth, power, and the cardinalate because his sister was the mistress of Pope Alexander VI, but he was favoured also by the great Medici Pope, Leo X, whose magnificent father's Florentine circle he had belonged to in his youth. On the Via Giulia in Rome, Paul erected the famous Palazzo Farnese, where his sister's four bastard children were born. The Pope had three illegitimate sons himself, and provoked multiple charges of nepotism by using his influence to further the interests of his offspring and their families. Utilizing the military skill of Pier Luigi, a son by his former mistress, and the diplomatic prowess of his grandson, Cardinal Alessandro Farnese, Paul asserted papal control over central Italy, cleverly evading encirclement by both the Spanish and the French. A patron of learning and the arts, Paul reopened the University of Rome, closed for the entire pontificate of his predecessor, and employed Antonio de Sangallo and a host of lesser architects to restore the fortifications of the Eternal City and the Papal States.

Of Michelangelo's numerous patrons, Pope Paul III was perhaps the greatest and most discerning. The cracks in the pillars and arches that Bramante had built for the new St. Peter's were already sprouting weeds when Paul made the 72-year-old master its new chief architect. This overblown basilica was to be Michelangelo's triumph and torment, an endless series of headaches, from construction failures to administrative intrigue. His initial plan for the church was ready the same year, and the building work itself commenced soon after, but Michelangelo deplored that mistakes were made because he, being old and sometimes incapacitated, was unable to visit the work site every day. Nonetheless, the greatest artist of the Renaissance donated his waning vigour, not to mention the last twenty years of his life, to completing this monstrosity. Its most imposing feature, the immense brick dome, was designed by Michelangelo along the lines of Brunelleschi's cupola in Florence, up until then the largest in the world.

Charges of paganism were levelled against Paul's pontificate for its worldly extravagances. He always consulted his court astrologers prior to any important decision, and Copernicus dedicated his astronomical treatise to him. During the Renaissance, the rich and the poor, the learned and the ignorant, the religious and the irreligious, shared a common belief in the influence of the stars—only very recently has anyone found it strange that a great scientific astronomer should also be an authority in astrological matters.

A distinguished ecclesiastic and a humanist intellectual from Poland, Nicolaus Copernicus was born in 1473. He took orders at a young age and served as a canon at a cathedral near Danzig for much of his life. Travelling to Italy in his youth, he studied canon law and medicine at the University of Ferrara. He also advised his government on currency reform, and Pope Leo X asked his help on the reform of the calendar; indeed, *De Revolutionibus Orbium Cœlestium* had started out as a contribution to the project of calendar reform, and the Gregorian Calendar of 1582 was based on computations that made use of Copernicus' work.

Infected with the rekindled spirit of inquiry and independent thinking abroad, Copernicus became convinced that Ptolemy was wrong to place Earth at the centre of the universe. The Renaissance recovery of Greek scientific writings showed that many ancient authorities had argued that at the centre stood the Sun, not the Earth. The fact is that the idea of a heliocentric system is not a new one; the theory had been forwarded as early as 250 BCE by the ancient Greek astronomer, Aristarchus of Sámos, and many of Copernicus' closer predecessors, including the 14th-century French bishop, Nicole Oresme, had said the very same thing.

Already in 1500, when Copernicus was a professor at Rome, he had announced this pivotal notion there, but more in the manner of a scientific paradox, as it had previously been held by the famed cardinal, Nicolaus Cusanus (1401-1464), than as a statement of fact. Though he wrote down his theories in a book, Copernicus carefully put it away without having it published, and they soon disappeared from the public eye. However, to the professor himself, steadily studying the subject, they became more and more a reality. After the Sack of Rome, he returned to his little town by the Baltic to become a canon at Frauenburg Cathedral.

Canon Copernicus locked his manuscript in a cabinet, making a few adjustments here and there, now and then, while continuing the scrupulous performance of his ecclesiastical duties as if nothing remarkable had ever happened. Only in 1543, after incessant pleas from his friends, did Copernicus, near seventy, finally publish his mathematical description of the heavens. Initially, his world system attracted next to no attention—the new science was considered just another novel way of foretelling the future from the stars. What is more, the noted Lutheran theologian, Andreas Osiander, who oversaw the printing of Copernicus' book in Nuremberg, switched its original, later discovered, preface with his own, branding the 400 pages of text, charts, and tables mere unverified hypotheses and handy rules of calculation. Luckily, Copernicus died in May of 1543, never seeing his work finished.

The first edition of *De Revolutionibus* was only in the amount of one thousand copies, and did not even sell out. Perhaps the Copernican system would have remained a mere curiosity known only among the astronomers if the Protestant leaders, who constantly vied with one another over who could surpass Luther in narrow-mindedness, had not hastened to declaim against it. All the Protestant denominations—Lutheran, Calvinist, and Anglican—denounced the Copernican doctrine outright as contrary to Scripture. The Reformation had renewed the literal study of the Scriptures, and transferred all infallibility from the Church and the papacy to the letter of the Holy Writ. The Bible was to be the true and unquestionable authority, for it was the word of God, not of man. What was written therein, was plainly and literally true, without the slightest extenuation or limitation; not only the meaning, but the words themselves, letters, and even the punctuation were held to proceed directly from the Holy Spirit.

"This fool," says Luther, "wishes to reverse the entire science of astronomy; but Sacred Scripture tells us that Joshua commanded the Sun to stand still, and not the Earth." Even Philip Melanchthon, the man of rare intellect and vast erudition who had served as mediator between Luther and the humanists, cites passages in the Psalms and Ecclesiastes which he declares to affirm positively and clearly that the Earth stands fast and the Sun moves around it, adding eight other proofs that "the Earth can be nowhere if not in the centre of the universe." So zealous does this most moderate of the reformers, who for his leading role in creating the German schools is forever known as "Preceptor of Germany," turn, that he proposes severe measures to suppress such ungodly teachings as those of Copernicus.

In December, 1545, after delay and miscarriage, the Council of Trent was at last convened by Paul III. The new directly papal-subordinate order, the Jesuits, prepared and from the background steered the course of the proceedings. The opening session was not very comprehensive; only thirty-one bishops turned up and only one of them was German. But, as the prestige of the Council grew, so did its attendance. Till then, the Roman Church had either been altogether indifferent or purely politically oriented in the religious issues. It was infinitely more important to the Curia that the House of Habsburg did not become too powerful than that some heretical doctrine was allowed to spread. The Protestant heresy had been thought as easy to suppress as all the preceding ones, and a few times the world got to witness the strange spectacle of the pope supporting the Protestant movement against the emperor.

On both sides of the conflict, there were those who still hoped and believed that concord was possible—it was not. Threatened by religious dissenters and attacked by secular princes, the Church, instead of transcending itself, manifested the desperation of a besieged mentality by turning inward and clinging ever tighter to orthodoxy. The essence of the scheme which the Catholic Church adopted to check the Reformation lay, on one hand, in the prevention of even the slightest possibility of lapsing to heresy by formulating religious doctrine with a clarity heretofore unknown, and, on the other, in the accommodation of the more liberal Catholic movements and contemporary demands by reserving the greatest flexibility and modernity within their boundaries. The insurmountable barrier which was thus erected between Catholicism and Protestantism held out for over four hundred years.

The Council of Trent affirmed basically all of Catholic dogma. According to Trent, Catholic doctrine rests not only on Scripture, but also on "tradition," the papal utterances and the decisions of the ecclesiastical councils, that is to say, it is expanding all the time. The Council confirmed such distinctly Catholic doctrines the Church had accrued over the centuries as penance, Purgatory, and, of course, indulgences. The sacrament of penance had come to be regarded as a means of reducing the amount of purgatorial punishment required for the penitent, while the idea of Purgatory itself was responsible for the popularity and importance of indulgences. Those who donated money for a crusade might receive the same rewards promised to those who actually went on one. Indulgences could also be granted for specific purposes, they might not be full indulgences but buy the remission of a set amount of purgatorial punishment, and could even be purchased on behalf of the souls departed.

Above all, the decrees of Trent reserved for the Holy Mother Church the right of interpreting Scripture and opposing unauthorized circulation of the Bible; thus the root of all heresies—lay Christianity—was eliminated. Traditional biblical exegetics had been challenged on two fronts during the 16th century: on one side, reformers like Luther and Calvin persisted that the original, "evangelical" interpretation of the Bible had been lost owing to mediæval corruptions and that only the Protestants understood the true, ancient meaning of the Scriptures; on the other, humanists like Reuchlin and Erasmus had called traditional interpretations into question, revealing that they rested on corrupt texts or anachronistic assumptions on their meaning. In heat of the Counter-Reformation, these two types of critique often became confused: one faction in the Church, while rejecting Protestantism, was concerned with purifying the established usages and explanations in conformity with qualified scholarship; after the Council of Trent, this so-called "Erasmian" party fell into disrepute.

As a rule, Luther held fast to the literal interpretation of Scripture, his argument against Copernicus being a perfect example of his reasoning in this regard. But, when the impetus for biblical study allied with humanist education, the results could be radical: Luther emphatically denied that the Epistle to the Hebrews was written by Paul, and did this in the exercise of a critical judgement on internal evidence. Though he included Hebrews, James, Jude, and Revelation in his list of the New Testament, he considered them of inferior status; his utterance as to James, which he alluded to as the "Epistle of Straw," became especially famous. The Reformed theologians were more conservative than Luther in accepting the canonical books, but in turn, more steadfast in rejecting the Old Testament apocrypha. As a countermeasure, the Council of Trent reaffirmed the canonicity of twenty-seven books of the New Testament and forty-five of the Old Testament. For Catholics, Trent gave the final list of books; no one, not even the pope, can any longer drop or add any book from or into the Bible.

CHAPTER 33

By 1547, when Ferdinand of Austria signed a five-year truce with the Turks, the Ottomans had moved up from Bucharest, Belgrade, and Budapest to within a few days' march of Vienna, and their Sultan was already calling himself the "Supreme Lord of Europe." But, even though he later ostentatiously added to his many titles "Cæsar of All the Lands of Rome," there they were held. If the Ottomans made small territorial gains at the Habsburgs' expense during the following century, their expansion in Europe was effectively over, and the nearly ceaseless war that Austria had from 1529 on waged against the Turks would not end until she had conquered back all of Hungary.[228]

Emperor Charles, no longer fending off either the Turks or the French, was finally free to concentrate on the German princes and the cities of the Schmalkaldic League. Luther did not live to see the outbreak of what was called the Schmalkaldic War. In February, 1546, just before the war between the two religious faction in Germany broke out, the great Protestant leader died. His death did not ease the tensions within the Lutheran party, for although he had had utmost confidence in Melanchthon as his successor, the educator was unsuited for leadership.

The 50,000 foot soldiers and 7,000 cavalrymen raised by the Schmalkaldic League had a joint commander, but were united neither physically nor in spirit. The imperial armies swept the Protestant forces before them, capturing Memmingen, Reutlingen, Esslingen, Biberach, and Frankfurt just in the first year. Two key centres of reform, Augsburg and Strasbourg, fell early in 1547. In April that year, Charles captured Wittenberg after the decisive Battle of

---

[228] The fact that the Mohammedans had set foot on the European continent was subsequently presented as a major event by both Westerners and Turks. In reality, the idea of a Christian Europe was a purely Latin invention—the Byzantine Empire, like the Græco-Roman world of antiquity, had regarded the Ægean not as a frontier, but as a place of passage.

Mühlberg, where Duke John Frederick the Magnanimous, Elector of Saxony, was captured. By the Capitulation of Wittenberg, John Frederick, who represented the Ernestine branch of the House of Wettin, ceded his electoral dignity to Duke Maurice, of the collateral Albertine branch—though there could be as many Dukes of Saxony as heirs, there could only be one Elector of Saxony.

Philip of Hesse surrendered in June, and in 1548, Charles issued the Augsburg Interim, a compromise profession of faith that he then tried to impose on the German Protestants with the help of his Spanish troops. Intended to establish a religious settlement for all Germany, it encompassed the entire Roman Catholic system of doctrine and discipline, but in a temperate and conciliatory form, without an explicit condemnation of the Protestant views.

Francis I of France had died in 1547; with the Protestant princes crushed and his archnemesis gone, Charles V and Catholicism appeared to have won. However, the Emperor's supporters were alienated by the stationing of Spanish troops in Germany, and by Charles' desire to unite the German and Spanish domains permanently—even the Catholic princes did not wish to see this happen; they had every reason to fear a strong emperor who might take away all the rights and privileges they had managed to usurp. Moreover, the prospect of a united Habsburg Empire so alarmed the new Valois ruler, Henry II, that Catholic France entered into a secret alliance with the German Protestants. As stipulated in the Treaty of Chambord (1551), France would receive three strategically located territories on her eastern frontier—the Catholic bishoprics of Metz, Toul, and Verdun—in return for military assistance. So began the French policy of support for foreign Protestants, which would last until the reign of Louis XIV.

To top it all, Duke Maurice, the new Elector of Saxony, previously a supporter of the Emperor, suddenly deserted. The changed political situation compelled Charles to ratify an agreement made at Passau (1552) between his brother Ferdinand and the rebels, reversing the Interim and granting Lutheranism equal rights with Catholicism. The Treaty of Passau did not end the fighting, however; only after his failed siege of Metz (1552-1553) did Charles leave Germany, never to return. The unity of the Empire was further weakened in 1555, after a religious peace was embodied in the recess of the imperial diet that met at Augsburg and thus became part of imperial law and of the imperial constitution. The Peace of Augsburg permitted each free city and state of Germany to exercise choice between Lutheranism and Catholicism, ensuring state control of both Churches, but at the same time, perpetuating and intensifying Germany's political disintegration.

By the terms of the Peace, every German principality would adhere to whichever faith was professed by its ruler, making the new Churches more dependent on the government and developing in them the characteristics of a State Church. The formula *cuius regio, eius religio* meant a shocking infringement of the religious freedom of all the subjects; the principle which Luther had upheld in the youth of his rebellion, the right of private judgement, was completely discarded.

The issue which for a time threatened the whole settlement was the case of ecclesiastical princes who went over to the new religion. The infamous *reservatum ecclesiasticum*, which led to immediate and bitter disputations and remonstrances, provided that all ecclesiastical lands were to remain in possession of whichever Church that held them in 1552. All prelates who became Lutheran after that date were to forfeit their position, their land, and their income. While the Catholics never considered this arrangement as final, the Protestants constantly violated it, secularizing ever more church lands.

The Peace of Augsburg was a treaty between German Catholics and Lutherans only; Calvinists, who were just then growing in strength and number in Germany, received no legal recognition. Following the Peace, the Lutheran territories became increasingly passive; the Calvinist territories, on the other hand, with their theocratic views of government, became that much more militant. The German Protestants had, already in Luther's life-time, divided themselves into "Gnesio-Lutherans," or genuine Lutherans, and Melanchthonians. In Saxony, these Philippists, as they called themselves after Melanchthon's baptismal name, were persecuted as "Crypto-Calvinists," dismissed from their offices to exile or imprisonment. In the Palatinate, on the other hand, the "Heidelberg Catechism" laid a foundation for Calvinism and every pastor who refused accept it, was deported.

Anabaptists and other "radicals"—regarded today as part of the Reformation mainstream—were anathema to all three sides. The various radical sects attracted especially burghers and artisans of the middle classes. In Western Europe, a believer could of course migrate to a country of his particular faith, but in none of these, much or any tolerance prevailed, as even Protestant lands generally and officially accepted only one sect. Within the Holy Roman Empire, both Catholic and Protestant states strove to enforce their own unique brand of religious orthodoxy inside their borders, while imperial law sought to silence the war of words pouring out from all camps.

Straying from official doctrine could prove fateful: society punished the dissidents by flogging and decades of imprisonment; religious fanaticism, intolerance, and cold-heartedness were the defining qualities of the official religion in Protestant as much as in Catholic Europe. Before the New World opened, the only escape route for dissenters was eastwards: in the Far East of the day, infidel Muslims could be more tolerant of Christian heretics than either Catholics or Protestants. In fact, the infallible tolerance which the Ottoman Empire extended to all the other beliefs it absorbed was one of the complicating factors in the reaction of modern Europe to the Turks. Also, as Christian conquerors were imposing ever-increasing presence on overseas lands that did not want them, it became more difficult to deny the Ottomans their right of occupation. Henceforth, the Christian would fight the Mohammedan over commercial interests rather than over religion.

For centuries, Asia had been the source of many valuable commodities for Europe, in part, manufactured goods which the West could not compete in, such as silks and cottons, rugs, china ware, jewelry, and refined steel, and in part, raw or semi-manufactured drugs and foodstuff, such as sugar and spices. Instead of going to the sources of these Oriental goods, the Europeans had thus far, by and large, depended on Arab or Indian traders who moved the produces of China, India, and the fabled Spice Islands of Indonesia over land by caravan, or by boat through the Persian Gulf or the Red Sea, bringing the goods to the eastern Mediterranean markets. Merchants of East and West had up to now met at such thriving Mohammedan centres as Alexandria or Constantinople.

In order to secure trade supremacy, the Portuguese began in the 16th century a ferocious campaign to destroy the Muslim trade. The latter were supported not only by the Egyptians and the Turks, but also by the Venetians, all of whom had a vested interest in maintaining the established routes of trade. The discovery of new ocean routes moved European trade, previously most active in the Mediterranean, first to the Persian Gulf and thence soon to East Asia. In 1552, the Ottoman fleet was completely routed in the Gulf, ending Muslim control over that trade route; the Turks were able to retain control over the Red Sea route, but Christian trade with the East grew while Muslim trade continued to decline. Portugal invaded several Mohammedan cities in eastern Africa in order to remove the commercial control of the Arabs over the Indian Ocean. The Westerners' new Cape of Good Hope route to India was longer but cheaper than the ancient routes through the Levant. The Cape route avoided the cost of all the loadings and unloadings, of all the customs duties (the source of Ottoman taxation income on trade), and of all the tributes exacted by Bedouin marauders on the way.

Disruptive as the change of trade routes was, the appearance of the Levant companies—large joint-stock ventures organized by the French, English, and Dutch to exploit the resources of the Ottoman Empire—was even more so. As Europe grew wealthier, it became more commercial and manufacturing based; the commerce of the Middle East changed into the colonial variety, turning Turkey into a client for European industry, herself only furnishing raw materials and no longer exporting manufactured goods. The Ottoman Empire was fast becoming a mere funnel through which New World bullion from the West was poured on to the Far East. Even if they had been free of the pervasive corruption, the Ottoman merchants would have been unable to compete with the corporations and cartels that were established in the West.

The intrusion of "high-pressure Atlantic economy" into the "low-tension Ottoman economy" set off an uncontrollable chain reaction that disrupted not only the Turkish economy, but pretty much all other branches of the Ottoman society as well. European silver flooded the Ottoman market, causing prices to double within a very short time. Fixed income groups, such as the landholding *Spahis* or cavalrymen, suddenly found themselves impoverished, and would rather abandon their lands than go on long and costly campaigns. Although they tried, the Ottomans could not rapidly convert enough Spahi lands into tax-paying sources of cash. With no money for salaries, more and more young pages of Christian origin were forcibly recruited from the Balkan provinces of the Ottoman Empire to act as foot soldiers or *Janissaries*; according to Islamic law, Muslims cannot enslave other Muslims, and the word "slave" itself presumably has its origin in the fact that many of the slaves in the pre-Atlantic age were Slavs.

The state sought to compensate escalating treasury expenses by debasing and diminishing the coinage, but these panic measures only made the situation worse. Money taxes became the principal source of state revenue, and a heavy burden on the peoples of the Empire, especially its Christian subjects, which at the time were more numerous than its Muslim population. Discontent was widespread, bribery and misappropriation increased among state officials and soldiers, and the Janissary Corps of the capital mutinied more and more frequently. Without the rivalry of the Western nations, the Ottoman Empire would not have lasted the next three and a half centuries.

For European humanists, the rediscovery of lost texts seemed as exciting as the discovery of new lands made by Western explorers; while the rapidly developing West was ridding itself of all forms of mediævalism, the Ottoman Empire clung ever more zealously to the traditional forms of Levantine civilization, becoming self-complacent, inward-looking, and shut from outside influences. Suleyman's policy of helping any Muslim country threatened by European expansion gave the Sultan the right, in the Turkish view, to declare himself Supreme Caliph of Islam. He alone successfully protected Islam from the *kafirs*, and as the sole Protector of Islam, deserved also to be the sole ruler of Islam.

The role demanded that Suleyman also look after the integrity of the faith itself, and root out heterodoxy. His annexation of Mohammedan territory was justified by the assertion that, like in the case of Arabia, the ruling dynasties had abandoned orthodox beliefs and practices. With the conquest of Iraq in 1553, virtually all of the Arab Middle East was placed under Turkish control. The near-total integration of the Arab world into the Ottoman Empire would last for nearly four hundred years. Knowing the Sultanate's distrust of its own subjects in positions of military and administrative responsibility, many talented Westerners went to Constantinople and turned Muslim to enhance their career prospects, while the Ottomans, convinced of their own religious and political superiority, closed their eyes to the world outside.

It was during this period that the term "Europe" became part of common parlance. Though scholars had known throughout the Middle Ages that they lived on a continent referred to by ancient geographers as *Europa* to distinguish it from *Asia* and *Africa*, the term enjoyed no wider currency. The tiny literate minority harangued the great illiterate majority across from the pulpit as Christians forming the part of the world chosen by Divine Providence as the abode of the one true religion, "Christendom." Before spatially accurate maps and the immensely popular travel journals were introduced with the invention of printing and engraving, the European identity was primarily emotional: us, the faithful, versus them, the godless heathen.

However, by now the notion of Christendom as a sacred sheepfold, within which European nations shared at least the uniformity of faith, had suffered many erosions. Christendom, in the sense of a traveller knowing what to expect when he entered a church abroad or passed men of cloth in a foreign street, was becoming at best the "Christendom of Europe"—as one Roman Catholic scholar put it in the latter half of the 16th century.[229] As the Turks gained foothold in the southeast, its centre of gravity was pushed westwards, while its contact with the other "old" continents was increased, and a "new continent" was discovered. As expected, the West would experience a spectacular renaissance of cartography, and it was maps and atlases above all that spread the notion that those who lived in Europe were Europeans.

In 1553, Mary Tudor, "Bloody Mary," an ignorant bigot and a bitter old maid, became the first queen ever to rule England. If she was the daughter of Henry VIII, she was also the daughter of Catherine of Aragón, a Spaniard and devout Catholic, who had been grievously trespassed against. The memory of her mother, whom she revered as a martyr, acted like a lash on Mary's narrow mind; her zeal to lead England back into the fold of the faithful was an obsession that clouded her judgement and made her singularly blind to the genuine good of her country. She not only desired to effect a reconciliation with Rome, but to harness England to the yoke of Rome by tying the island kingdom to Spain, the champion of Roman Catholicism.

With this in mind, Mary made known her intention to marry the son of Charles V. Philip of Spain himself, about ten years younger than his proposed bride and already betrothed to a pretty Portuguese princess, was notably less enthusiastic; knowing that Mary was not especially attractive and advised that the chances of her bearing children were slim, he agreed to the marriage only out of reverence to his father's wishes. Philip had the reputation of being a sullen, stubborn fanatic, and the widespread opposition to the projected alliance resulted in an open rebellion, which, although suppressed, cost Mary

---

[229] The Reformation, essentially a northern movement, further increased the still apparent division of Western Europe into North and South.

most of her popularity.[230] And even though Mary wilfully went ahead with the marriage in July of 1554, the English Parliament flat out refused to crown her Spanish consort.

Reginald Pole, an expatriate member of the former English ruling house of Plantagenet, would now return to England as the chief advisor to Queen Mary, whom he had once been considered a candidate to marry. After his cousin, Henry VIII, had broken with the pope, the fervently Catholic Pole had been banished to Italy, for his claim on the English throne was a good if not better than Henry's. The King was further enraged when Pole was made a cardinal and appointed Papal Legate to England—at one point, he was almost made pope by imperial acclamation. From 1537 to 1539, Pole was actively trying to organize a league against Henry, and when the news reached him that his mother, the Countess of Salisbury, had been executed for treason in 1541, he remarked: "Hitherto I have thought myself most indebted to Divine Providence for having received my birth from one of the most noble and virtuous women in England, but, henceforth, my obligation will be much greater, as I understand I am now the son of a martyr."

On the 30th of November, 1554, in a ceremony attended by Mary, Philip, and both houses of Parliament, Pole absolved the bowed down kingdom from the sin of schism as the papal legate. In December, this same Parliament completely overturned the Henrician and Edwardian policies, making England Catholic again. This was welcomed by the Irish, but Mary did not appear to consider common religion reason enough to treat Ireland decently. On the contrary, Mary's Irish rule was just as merciless as that of her two male predecessors. She sent an English army into the counties west of Dublin and forcibly removed most of the native Irishmen from the region, giving it to English settlers.

The ancient statutes against the Lollards and heresy were re-enacted and implemented with the full force of the law. Between 1553 and 1558, Pole incited Mary to carry out what many British historians have described as the largest number of politically motivated executions in the history of England. Their assertion is questionable, but some three hundred English and Welsh "heretics" were burned at the stake, giving Britain its first Protestant martyrs

---

[230] The leaders of the uprising were executed, and with them, at the instigation of the Spanish ambassador, the unfortunate Lady Jane Grey, who would not renounce her Protestantism.

and earning Mary her famous epithet. The executions were immortalized in John Foxe's *Book of Martyrs* (1563), a copy of which was later kept in every church in the kingdom, and which thus influenced many generations of British Protestants. In addition to these "Marian Martyrs," there was a larger number of prominent Protestants who fled the country to wait for a better time. These about eight hundred "Marian Exiles" naturally took refuge in the leading Protestant centres on the Continent, where they came into contact with doctrines and practices much more radical than their own. When they returned, they would greatly assist in making the Church of England Protestant for good.

The events orchestrated by Cardinal Pole seemed to many Englishmen to verify the belief that a Catholic restoration would threaten not only their lives but also their precious property. Acting under papal instructions, Pole insisted on full restitution of the church lands and chattels seized by Henry VIII—an action which would have erased a large section of the English upper classes. Mary's father had redistributed much of the land he had seized from the Church to his supporters, who were fast reconstituting themselves as a new gentry or nobility of wealth. For many such families, buying up church lands with the wealth earned from manufacture, mining, trade, and banking, was an important step in rise to prominence. This urban, capitalistic gentry ultimately became a supporter of the Reformation from the fear that the restoration of the Church's status would bring with it the loss of their own. By 1554, Parliament had passed a law prescribing all the confiscated lands to remain in the hands of their new owners, which meant that the English monasteries were not reopened and many returning bishops would find themselves impoverished.

Philip had sailed to England in the summer of 1554, accompanied by a large portion of the Spanish court, but in the summer of 1555, he took the boat to the Netherlands. His father was the ruler of most of Europe and the most powerful man of his time. However, Charles seems to have grown weary of the endless struggles and onerous responsibilities of his scattered realms, for after his abortive last campaign against France, he prepared for his abdication, relinquishing over the next few years, his many titles, one after another. In 1555, he renounced his claims on the Netherlands in favour of Philip, and in 1556, Spain and its territories, including the growing New World empire passed to him. Disembarking in Spain at the end of September, 1556, Charles retired from the world at the Monastery of Yuste, which he had long ago selected as his final refuge, and where he died two years later.

The imperial crown and the Austrian hereditary lands were passed, not to Charles' son, but to Charles' younger brother, Ferdinand, who had acted as the Emperor's deputy in German affairs. Thus the House of Habsburg got divided into its two main branches: the Spanish, which was interrupted in 1700, and the Austrian, which ceased in the male line in 1740.[231] Ferdinand I, who officially became emperor in 1558, was raised in Spain, speaking Spanish. His grandfather, Ferdinand II of Aragón, had considered leaving him his Spanish kingdom, but he ended up being given the rule of Austria by his brother, and as Charles became Spanish in his outlook, Ferdinand of Austria became thoroughly German. On the marriage of Ferdinand and his sister, Mary, to Louis and Anne, the children of the King of Hungary and Bohemia, was built that Austrian monarchy which survived to the end of World War I.

If the imperial title had lost much of its bearing, it remained a valuable symbol of sovereignty to the Habsburgs. The German language, which was the language of the Empire, eventually became the official language for not only Austria, but Bohemia and Hungary as well. To further their state ideology, the Habsburgs employed both of the great forces of their time: the Catholic Church and the nobility. In all three countries, they sought to create an noble class that was dependent on them and served as the principal support of the throne. Since the backing of the Church was a prerequisite to this, the Habsburgs became its steadfast advocates. The Counter-Reformation owed a great deal of its success in the German Empire to their faithful support. In 1557, a Venetian diplomat estimated that Germany was nine-tenths Protestant, a figure which even if an exaggeration, reveals just how low Catholicism had sunk. From this seemingly irredeemable recession the Church was to make an unbelievable recovery.

The Habsburg king Philip II had inherited a vast realm stretching from Spain to Italy, the Netherlands, and the New World. His life was dominated by a single obsession: the complete and absolute restoration of the Universal Church and the dissemination of Spanish autocracy over the entire globe. The Iberian Peninsula possessed all the necessities not only for voyages of

---

[231] Since the two branches of the family continued to coordinate their policies, sealing their co-operation by frequent intermarriages, there still remained strong a consistent Habsburg interest in European affairs.

exploration and overseas conquest, but for all that which spelled the denunciation of, not all, but most of the Renaissance ideals. The Inquisition—justified by, of all things, national honour—would come to symbolize the Spain of Philip II. While the Jesuits throughout Europe waged an underground war against the Reformation, Philip fought the same enemy with overt, inhuman violence. The activities of the Spanish Inquisition were so horrifying that the majority of historians have chosen to mention it only in passing and to push on to other matters. In their defence, the fact is that Philip's reign was one of the most artistically fertile in the history of Spain, with Cervantes and de Vega, El Greco and Velázquez, rising to prominence at his time.

Philip returned to England for a brief period between March and July of 1557. He made a laudable effort to win friends in his wife's homeland, creating an English household that duplicated his Spanish one, and bestowing pensions from his own revenues on privy councillors and other important officials. He even encouraged the pardon of the surviving rebels of 1553 and 1554. In vain. On the surface, the Anglo-Spanish alliance seemed mutually advantageous to both countries, if not because of their common hostility to France, then certainly because of the importance to both of the trade between England and the Netherlands, which was part of Philip's empire. However, Philip effortlessly persuaded his adoring wife into making policies that furthered his continental and imperialistic designs at the cost of England's national interests. Spain was to have the exclusive right on all the riches and natural resources of the New World, and in the name of Spanish interest, Mary—unrequitedly in love with Philip all her life—enacted severe restrictions on English trade.

In 1557, Philip managed to coax Mary into joining him in his war against France. The Spanish gained two great victories, but in January, 1558, the French delivered a serious blow by besieging and taking Calais, the one remaining English possession on the Continent. This was an offence to the English even more grievous than all her cruel reactionary actions; had she ruled a few years more, a revolution would have been inevitable. She never bore the son she twice thought she was pregnant with, nor did she win the affection of her husband, who forsook her after the loss of Calais, followed by misunderstandings with the Holy See for which she had sacrificed so much. Disillusionment broke her health and her will, and she died on the 17th of

November, 1558, missed by hardly anyone. Archbishop Pole, who had defied the instructions to return to Rome and face a trial for heresy, died only hours after the Queen.

In April, 1559, a treaty was signed at Câteau-Cambrésis, by the terms of which France was allowed to retain Metz, Toul, Verdun, and Calais. The peace was cemented by Philip's marriage to Elizabeth of Valois, the daughter of Henry II—ending the first phase in the struggle between France and the Habsburgs that had lasted for nearly four decades and been fought largely on Italian soil.

On the eve of the 17th century, Italy was the most densely populated region in Europe, about to enter a period of decline and rupture, after an age of development and growth. The opening of the Atlantic had reoriented Europe; no longer was the Mediterranean what its name implies, "the middle of the world." The flow of silver and gold from the New World shifted the centre of finance from the coastal cities of the Mediterranean to Northern and Central Europe; disruption in the Asian overland routes and the discovery of sea routes to the East around Africa left the northern Italian city-states bypassed as middlemen of the lucrative eastern trade in spices, silks, perfumes, and jewels. Weakened by their loss of commercial revenues, the city-states declined rapidly in power as the hegemony of Spain over Italy was confirmed.

Only Venice and the Papal States maintained full independence; the independence of the other states was in name only. The duchy of Savoy was returned to Emmanuel Philibert, the commander of the Spanish army against the French at Saint-Quentin (1557), but he was forced to accept the presence of Spanish and French garrisons. Under the Treaty of Câteau-Cambrésis, the French King transferred his claims on Milan and Naples to Philip, acquiring Pignerol and Turin in their stead. Saluzzo also fell to the French; all of Tuscany, except Lucca, to Florence, where the Medici had been restored with Spanish help in 1530. The rule of the Medici, once tolerant and wise, became in the 17th and 18th centuries parochial and repressive.

The cold fist of Spain kept watch through governors and viceroys over the three kingdoms of Naples, Sicily, and Sardinia, and over the duchy of Milan, holding them in the state of lethargy for the next century and a half. Under Spain, southern Italy became one of the most backward and exploited areas in all Europe. Famines were chronic, disease, ignorance, and superstition abound; the exorbitant taxes, from which the clergy and nobility were exempt, flowed into the Spanish treasury. Agriculture suffered dearly from the amassment of immense estates by the quarrelling Italian and Spanish aristocracy and the Church—which at all events served only her own interests in Italy, acting just as any of the other competitors for the dwindling wealth of the peninsula.

In an age of sectarian fragmentation, the Roman Church sought to achieve Catholic unity through intellectual repression—the Counter-Reformation was a response of the established powers against the newfound freedom of the Renaissance. The Church could no longer claim monopoly over the thinking of scholars and preachers, the advent of printing having made a wider range of reading available than had ever existed before. Already during his years as a cardinal, Pope Paul IV (1555-1559) had been given responsibility over the Inquisition, and persuaded the reigning pontiff to compile an index of prohibited books, the readers and publishers of which would automatically be excommunicated.[232] When Paul was elected pope, the activity of the Inquisition, originally instituted as an emergency device, heightened to new levels. The Pope is said to have boasted that if his own father were to be discovered a heretic, he would gather the firewood for the pyre himself.

It is not surprising that Lutheran, Calvinistic, Jewish, and Mohammedan texts (the first known Latin translation of Koran had been in 1143) were banned, but aimed as it was at suppressing books which might endanger the faith, corrupt morals, or promote thinking, the Papal Index eventually read like a Who's Who of world literature. Being indexed became a mark of distinction which placed the author in the company of Abélard, Dante, Machiavelli, Descartes, Hobbes, Locke, Gibbon, Kant, Hugo, and so forth. Not that censorship was by any means the exclusive province of the Roman Church—Protestant authorities, no less than their Catholic counterparts, recognized the importance of censorship in maintaining doctrinal uniformity and the communal conformity that would flow from it.

The Romans rejoiced openly when Paul IV died in 1559. An excited mob swarmed the streets and released the victims of the Inquisition from their dungeons. Since Paul had preferred to act as an autocrat, his pontificate had marked a long adjournment in the Council of Trent, which was now

---

[232] As long as books were produced by the labourious process of copying by hand, book burning had provided a sufficient means of censorship.

reconvened. During the final years of the Council, Catholicism was given a new form. Rome was purged from prostitutes, pimps, and thieves. Popes and bishops superimposed fig leafs into the works of art brimming over with nudity their predecessors had commissioned. It was decreed at Trent that art should produce clear, unembellished depictions of the lives of the saints. The purpose of art was to encourage devotion, not to cause admiration for the brilliance of the artist.

The Council was ordered in such a fashion that papal power would not be reduced. The voting in the councils of previous centuries had been by national delegation; at Trent, abbots and theologians were excluded from the vote, which was granted to bishops and heads of orders alone. Needless to say, there were many more Italian than non-Italian prelates present, and the Italians could be counted on to preserve papal supremacy. In the end, the papacy was to suppress all other powers within the Church. Cardinals, having once acted independently, were reduced to obedient officials, and rigid discipline was imposed even on the common priests who remained loyal to Rome. The Tridentine Creed, the first specifically Catholic confession of faith, introduced a vow of obedience to "the Bishop of Rome, successor to St. Peter, Prince of the Apostles, and Vicar of Jesus Christ."

Another significant change ushered in by Trent was liturgical uniformity, which would have been very difficult, if not impossible, before the invention of printing. Seminaries, where Catholic priests were schooled in preaching the true religion among hostile Protestants, were founded, and bishops and other beneficed clergy were henceforth expected to live amidst their congregation as its exemplary and chaste members.[233]

Though the educational influence of Italy was to continue through the 17th century, when its universities and academies were continental centres for teaching and research in the sciences, the country gradually became marginal to the culture, thought, and politics of modern Europe. The Central European Renaissance opened so vast horizons that they no longer fitted under the concept of renaissance. With the advent of voyages of exploration, states such as Spain, Portugal, England, Holland, and France, saw a remarkable expansion in their economic influence; regardless of all the political and religious

---

[233] Even with printing, however, it took until the mid- to late-1600s before the reforms promulgated by the Council began to take root in the parishes.

differences, trade was the dynamo that made the world go round. Traffic in goods was accompanied by what the Elizabethan polymath, John Dee, would call the "intertraffic of the mind"—the new ideas would flow from place to place with ever accelerating pace, penetrating even the farthest corners of Europe.

This so-called Age of Expansion was a crucial factor in the transition of Northern Europe from the agrarian economy of the Middle Ages to the modern commercial and industrial capitalist system. The slow cutting out of the Mediterranean from the great international trade routes, on the other hand, signalled for the Italian economy the beginning of an inward-looking phase. The interest in the utilization of the land grew, leading to development in agriculture and an increase in the rural population. In moving from trade to agriculture, the northern Italians exhumed a more practical aspect of their Classical past: the Venetian aristocrat on his estate in the Veneto regarded himself as the modern equivalent of a Roman nobleman in his country villa. In no case, however, was a city-state going to be a match for the colonial and maritime powers that were fast becoming modern nation-states.

In England, Mary's persecutions and her connections to Spain brought Protestantism a second and lasting victory. The throne was ascended by her step-sister, Elizabeth, the daughter of Henry VIII and Anne Boleyn, who had through Mary's reign been under the guardianship of Parliament in the sense that it would not allow her to be deprived of the right of succession. Since according to the Catholic Church, Elizabeth was a bastard, she was sure to rule as a Protestant. In 1559, she proclaimed the Crown to again reign supreme over the Church and once more severed communion with Rome.

The "Elizabethan Settlement" as it became known, was the first one to bring a solid measure of religious concord after the upheavals of Henry's reign, and still remains the basis for the Church of England as it exists today. The Act of Uniformity (1559) essentially returned the Anglican Church to the Reformation of Henry's later years: it was headed by the monarch, its priests were called ministers, they celebrated the Lord's Supper, not the Mass, in English, rather than Latin. The Edwardian Prayer Book of 1552—the one more advanced in Protestantism—was restored, and every subject was forced to profess, at least outwardly, the new state religion.

The ease with which the Tudors changed the official religion was largely due to the fact that the religious revival which, on the Continent, had given rise both to the Protestant Reformation and to the Catholic Counter-Reformation made little progress in England until the end of the 16th century. Three times within the space of a generation, the population of England had been coerced on pain of death into changing their religion; three times, the "eternal verities" taught by the town parsons were turned upside down. The psychological and intellectual effects of these change-overs were immense and permanent: there was hardly anyone stupid enough to believe the contradictory pronouncements everyone was required to make over this period, and few devout enough to toy with martyrdom or to attempt the overthrow of a dynasty; the memory of the Wars of the Roses, and later the threat of a Spanish invasion, had most Englishmen clinging too closely to their monarchs to enable rebellion, regardless of the justification.

In 1559, however, the threat to England came from France, not from Spain. That year the dauphin ascended the French throne as Francis II, and his spouse was Mary Stuart, the daughter of James V of Scotland and the granddaughter of Henry VIII's sister, Margaret Tudor. Elizabeth's birth being seen as illegitimate by the Catholics, Mary Queen of Scots, though excluded by the will of Henry VIII, laid claim to the English throne as the legitimate heir. Spanish interests, however, demanded that the crowns of England, Scotland, and France not be united in one person, prompting Philip II to initially support Elizabeth, even though she fought the French menace by aiding the Huguenots, or French Protestants, in their struggle against the French crown. The death of Francis II in 1560 was unexpected stroke of luck for Elizabeth. Mary, temporarily overcome with grief, rose to find all her power gone and rivals occupying her place. For the last four decades of the 16th century, France was torn by the Wars of Religion—wars in which religious, political, and dynastic conflicts were intricately mixed—rendering her incapable of external aggression.

In the absence of the Queen, Scotland was ruled by a council, whose leaders were Protestant. While Mary never consented to the summoning of the so-called Reformation Parliament of 1560, which helped to establish the Reformed Church as the official church of the nation, it was nevertheless the single most important parliament in Scottish history. Had the Queen of Scots managed to rid herself of her enemies at home and to overthrow Elizabeth in England, Protestantism would probably have been crushed in the British Isles—an event which would have greatly strengthened the Catholic forces on the Continent. The whole future of Protestantism was thus decided by the course of events in a small, impoverished, and backward country located on the very fringes of Europe.

Elizabeth's long reign, from 1558 to 1603, was a time of internal and external stabilization for England. All threats to this process were either brutally crushed or else swept away via arbitration by a sophisticated queen who had learned both ruthlessness and resilience in the school of hard knocks. On the whole, she was an excellent judge of character, surrounding herself with capable and devoted advisors. She rebuilt the alliance her father had established with the emerging mercantile lords, encouraging an industrial revolution of sorts. England would, during the course of the 16th century, rise from a small mediæval state to a modern European superpower. The increasing power of trade and cities, the expansion of the industrious merchant class that took interest in technological improvements, and the generation of the capital necessary for the realization of these improvements, all contributed to the formation of the kind of social conditions where science could flourish.

During Elizabethan times, London was a city with 300,000 inhabitants, countless commercial enterprises, a dominant stock exchange, a regular trade exhibition, and nearly two dozen resident theatres. Its streets were thoroughly tiled, its water supply was regulated by wooden ducts, its lighting and fire service had undergone considerable improvements. There were numerous well-organized schools, printing-presses, and dispensaries. Elizabeth's accession brought stability to the universities after the menaces and hardships of Mary's Catholic régime, during which many of the academics felt it prudent to lie low.

As a result of the innumerable voyages of exploration, the physical world was greatly expanded, inspiring scholars while laying increasing emphasis on the sciences of navigation and astronomy. Born near London in 1527, Dr. John Dee, a Welsh mathematician, astronomer, philosopher, alchemist, and magician, was a quintessential figure in the beginning of modern science in England, a brilliant example of a Renaissance man, depicted by Shakespeare as Prospero and by Marlowe as Faust.

Educated at the chantry school in Chelmsford, the county seat of Essex, Dee entered the University of Cambridge in 1542—when he was fifteen. He became a Fellow of St. John's College in 1545 and one year hence one of the first Fellows of Trinity College, largest of the Cambridge colleges, founded by Henry VIII. Dee excelled at Cambridge and was named under-reader, a junior faculty member, before taking his degree. After graduation, he sailed to the Continent to continue his studies in Louvain and in Brussels. A young man still in his early twenties, Dee achieved overnight fame in Paris, when he delivered a series of public lectures on the newly-recovered works of the ancient Greek mathematician, Euclid.

A professorship was offered to Dee at the Univerisity of Paris in 1551, and a position as lecturer at Oxford in 1554. He declined both, for he was accustomed to leading a care-free live on the patronage he received from royalty and nobility. In 1552, King Edward VI granted him an annual pension of £100, after Dee presented him with two treatises he had composed. He exchanged the pension for the Rectorship of Upton-upon-Severn in 1553, a benefice to which he succeeded in holding the claim throughout his life, though he never filled the duties of either this or any other ecclesiastical benefice. In his defence, it must be pointed out that science during this period was by and large a hobby, requiring either a rich upper-class patron, a life of penury, or independent wealth.

Most scientists were also "occultists," for science was the unknown. The then prevailing confusion between science and magic was exceptionally well manifested in the person of John Dee, who was always viewed—often with dread—as a "conjurer." He became astrologer to Mary Tudor, but was shortly after imprisoned under suspicion of heresy, being released in 1555. He met the future Queen Elizabeth while she was under house arrest by Queen Mary, and the two detainees developed a lasting friendship. As queen, Elizabeth gave Dee money, and protected him from those who would accuse him of witchcraft. Having cast horoscopes for the Queen already during the reign of Mary, he received the title of Astrologer Royal, selecting, for example, the day for her coronation.

Dee had brought novel and new scientific instruments into England in 1550 when he returned from the Continent, where he had acquainted himself with its foremost mathematicians. An intrinsic part of their work was the designing, description, and use of instruments in the service of geodesy, cartography, gunnery, etc. Instrument-makers were essential for scientific advance, since ever greater accuracy was demanded. Dee stood early in the process, being the first to build navigational instrument to apply Euclidean geometry. About

1553, he developed what he called the paradoxal compass, a circumpolar chart for navigation in polar regions. Among his many inventions was also an instrument for measuring the variation of the magnetic compass.

The explorations of the 16th and 17th centuries had greater consequences than the excursions of the Vikings, because the critically-thinking geographers and meticulous cartographers combined the stories of the navigators into a coherent, scientific picture of the Earth's surface. Indeed, the study of maps reveals how information was amassed and integrated in the early modern period into forms that became regarded as codified knowledge. An eminent figure in Tudor geography, Dee was not only an advisor to one of the most spectacular of all the Elizabethan voyages, Francis Drake's circumnavigation of the world, but also prepared nautical information for the Muscovy Company during its first thirty-odd years.

First major English joint-stock trading company, the "Compagnie of the Merchant Adventurers for the Discoverie of Regions, Dominions, Islands, and Places Unknown" was initially formed (1553) by John Cabot's son, Sebastian Cabot, together with a number of London merchants, to finance a search for the Northeast Passage, a new faster and easier all-water route to India and China. The commander of the expedition, Sir Hugh Willoughby, was lost in mid-voyage and replaced by Richard Chancellor, who became the first to round the North Cape and get through the perilous arctic waters to the White Sea. He then continued overland across Russia to Moscow, where he established relations with Czar Ivan the Terrible. In 1555, the Muscovy Company was granted a monopoly on the newly opened, highly lucrative Anglo-Russian trade. The Northeast Passage, however, would not be navigated by anyone until late 19th century, when the Finnish-born Swede, A. E. Nordenskiöld, finally carried out the feat.

Through such notables as Abraham Ortelius and Gerardus Mercator[234], Dee's vast geographical influence was transmitted to the Netherlands, promoting the renowned Dutch map-making during what has become known as the "golden age of cartography." In the meantime, numerous Dutchmen had

---

[234] Ortelius' *Theatrum Orbis Terrarum* (1570) was the first modern atlas; the word "atlas" itself derives from Mercator's *Atlas sive Cosmographicæ* (1595), whose frontispiece featured the titan Atlas holding a globe on his shoulders. The Mercator map projection, where any loxodrome is represented as a straight line, is commonly used even today.

been forced to seek refuge in England due to the religious persecution practised by Philip II. His imperialistic programme was in short as follows: in France, cramped by Spain in the west, by Franche-Comté (non-royal Burgundy) in the east, and by the Netherlands in the north, and internally inconvenienced by his alignment with the Papist "Holy League," he intended to place on the throne a member of his own family or else a French cadet branch dependent on himself, and thus to transform the only continental power that posed any threat to him into a Spanish protectorate; England he thought he could easily bring under his control through a personal union, such as had once already existed when he was married to Mary Tudor. As he moreover owned the greater portion of Italy, and as a Habsburg branch sat on the throne of the Holy Roman Empire and ruled the Austrian hereditary lands, this would in effect have resulted in all Europe becoming Spanish and returning to Catholicism—for the Turks could hardly have stood their ground against this unified giant power. Yet, reality frustrated on every point these seemingly so easily realizable plans.

The Spanish government sought to establish the Inquisition in all its dominions, but in the Netherlands, the local officials, be they Protestant or Catholic, would not co-operate. Philip, who was tied to the Netherlands neither by blood nor favour, insulted the local nobility by excluding them from all administrative duties, naming Spaniards in place of the formerly native officials, and maintaining a Spanish army in the country to make sure that his orders were followed. At the same time, the statutes against heresy were brought into force with twice the former severity. Eventually, Philip realized he had raised a storm, but though he recalled the Spanish troops in 1561, the heresy-hunts only grew more violent. Protestants were burned and tortured without mercy, and the administrative officials were commanded to aid the inquisitors. But heresy thrived in the crucible, and the nobles and officials refused to provide assistance when these shameful orders were enforced. The wrathful Philip dispatched a Spanish veteran army, commanded by one Fernando Álvarez de Toledo, the infamous Duke of Alba, to crush all resistance in the Netherlands.

When Alba arrived at Brussels in August of 1567, the cause of freedom appeared to be doomed. The Flemish Protestants had been put down and punished even before he and his 9,000 men got there, but Philip was not thus easily placated. Alba, who wielded dictatorial power, would establish a

Council of Troubles, or the "Council of Blood," as the locals for a good reason nicknamed it, with the task of punishing treason. It was considered treason to have signed a petition to tone down the Inquisition; to not have counteracted such petition; to have, though under obligation, heard evangelical sermons; to have stated that the king had no right to deprive the counties of their freedom; and to suspect that the Council was not bound by any laws. It was clearly near impossible not to make oneself guilty of at least one of these crimes.

The gruelingly logical conclusion of these preposterous premises was that, on the 16th of February, 1568, the entire population of the Netherlands was condemned to death—a political act unparalleled in history. After thousands had been hanged, burned, shut in prison, driven to exile, and deprived of their property, a general amnesty was issued, granting clemency to all those who, within a set grace period, repented and asked for mercy—nor is another such amnesty recorded in world history.

Yet the Dutch were not driven to rebellion by any of this, but only after a financial measure by the vicegerent, which nevertheless stood at par with the rest in its stupidity and infamy. Alba, who had promised Philip he would have a six feet deep stream of gold flowing from the Netherlands to Spain, decreed in March of 1569, that a one percent tax was to be collected on all movable and immovable property, one of five percent on every parcel of property sold, and one of ten percent on every chattel sold; the last-mentioned levy in particular would have spelled the complete ruin of Dutch trade. Until then, only a few noblemen and scattered sectarian hordes had offered resistance—now the whole country would revolt from Spain.

With the cry "Sooner Turkish than Popish!" began the great "Revolt of the Netherlands," a world-renowned, triumphant and heroic struggle of a small merchant nation against the then greatest military power in Europe. After the provisional navy, which William of Orange had recruited to harass the Spanish maritime trade, seized the Dutch port of Brill in 1572, the rebels took control of many northern cities, which became the bases of the revolt. These naval forces, the immortal "Sea Beggars," were the germ of Holland's soon-to-be mighty fleet. Meanwhile, Philip's involvement in an expensive joint-campaign with the pope against the Ottomans in the Mediterranean meant that his mercenary army in the Netherlands could not be paid and turned to pillage or refused to fight.

As it turned out, not even Philip's own family would conform to his plans of world domination. Even though the support of the Roman Catholic faith was one of the fixed points of Habsburg policy, Philip's cousin, Emperor Maximilian II (r. 1564-1576) was personally inclined to Protestantism, while his son and successor, Rudolph II (r. 1576-1612) declared himself to be neither Catholic nor Protestant, but Christian. Philip's attempts to negotiate a marriage with Elizabeth of England failed, and when Henry of Navarre became the leader of the French Protestant cause, the Queen assisted him with money, thus helping him to eventually (1589) ascend the French throne. The first and greatest of the Bourbon kings, Henry IV not only granted the Huguenots equal civil rights with the Catholics through the Edict of Nantes (1598), but also adhered to an intensely nationalistic anti-Spanish policy.

The Netherlands could not afford to alienate any potential support for its cause, including royalists, such as the Queen of England and the Catholic French monarchy, which in their opposition to Spain lent occasional support to the Dutch. Thus, the Netherlands turned into a haven not only for other talented, entrepreneurial Calvinists, fleeing persecution elsewhere in Europe, but for all the other religious minorities escaping the Catholic Inquisition as well. After the devastated Antwerp fell (1585) to the Spanish, prosperity exploded in Amsterdam, the population of which increased from 30,000 to 139,000 between 1570 and 1640. A booming centre of trade, the city became an asylum for such refugees as Spanish and Portuguese Jews, who contributed greatly to the astounding economic development of Holland. By the 17th century, also known as Holland's Golden Age, Amsterdam's commercial terrain encompassed the entire globe.

CHAPTER 34

Queen Elizabeth of England was exceptionally tolerant for her times—not a single Catholic was executed for heresy during her reign. She insisted that her will was not to make windows into men's souls, that she cared not what her subjects thought in the matter of religion, so long as they conformed outwardly by attending the services of the State Church. Through the first decade of her reign, Catholics had by and large been left alone. Nevertheless, in 1570, Pope St. Pius V pronounced the Queen excommunicated and deposed, and exhorted his supporters, English and foreign, to dethrone her.

He could have hardly done a greater favour to Elizabeth, for the most popular item of her policy had been the termination of the submissive relationship to Rome and its secular arm, Spain. Apart from the most implacable Catholics, all Englishmen considered the Pope's action an encroachment on their national sovereignty. Some Catholics became recusants, absenting themselves from the services of the Anglican Church. For the rest of England, the papacy now appeared in the guise of a foreign adversary. The recusants were malcontents, but they were few; during Elizabeth's reign, one in four girls born in England were named after the Queen.

1570 is otherwise notable as the year Dee edited the first English translation of Euclid's *Elements*, adding to it his famous preface in justification of the study of mathematics. The *Mathematicall Præface* contains the earliest account of mathematics a practical and useful skill—and mathematical studies were in urgent need of such organized philosophical support and encouragement. For several hundred years, Aristotelianism had been the background philosophy of all educated men; by relegating mathematics to an altogether inadequate place in the universe of knowledge, the established and orthodox Aristotelian science afforded no impetus to an extensive and painstaking study of the subject, for it denied that any results of value could be obtained thereby. Since these antiquated doctrines on top enjoyed the prestigious support of the Catholic Church, a situation had been reached where the natural sciences could nowise advance.

Throughout the High Middle Ages, scientific inquiry was thus dominated by the qualitative, rather than quantitative, natural philosophy of Aristotle, combined with the Averroist doctrine that inquiry into the physical world should never involve speculations of God or any other kind of metaphysics; nature was hostile and inexplicable, forever a surrogate to a higher reality governed by supernatural forces, angels and demons alike. By the dawn of the Modern Era, the impact of the corrected translations of ancient authors and the discovery of manuscripts lost to scholars for a thousand years was leading in two directions: on one hand, the natural philosophers developed an even greater respect for Aristotle and other ancient authorities; on the other, the recovery of the *Corpus Hermeticum* and other more mystical tomes accentuated the relationship of man to the macrocosm, seeking divine truths in the study of nature. The Renaissance Neoplatonists held the physical universe to be fundamentally mathematical, and that a knowledge of these mathematics held the key to the divine essence, paving the way for the rise of natural science.

However, it was not until Newton that the mathematical view of the universe finally took hold and forever changed the face of Western science. In Dee's day, mathematics still suffered the reputation, deeply entrenched in both the learned and the popular mind, of being a branch of necromancy, or at the very least closely related to the forbidden lore in its more shadowy aspects. It was a reputation fostered by the inevitably isolated and individual activities of the mathematician, for only slowly and in the face of daunting obstacles did the study of mathematics penetrate into the curricula of the universities. The process was slow because it entailed the rejection of Aristotle, and emancipation did not come suddenly. Long after Dee's death, when the Savilian and Sedleian Chairs were established (1619) at Oxford, it was recorded that as a result of such open encouragement of the mathematical sciences "not a few of our then foolish Gentry" refused to send their sons to the University "lest they should be smutted with the Black Art."

Dee had become interested in the "occult" early, already in his student years. Numbers, being pure, abstract ideas of quantity, have always been popular in various mystical and philosophical systems. Pythagoras had contended that everything in the universe could be expressed by numbers and thus made easier for man to understand. Aside from symbolic use, they could be employed as an unlimited indexing system, while the smaller numbers naturally display relationships that lead to philosophical speculations. For example, 1 = the monad, 2 = the duad, 3 = the triad; suggesting thesis, antithesis, and synthesis.

But whereas number-mathematics, or arithmetic, led largely from neo-Pythagoreanism and "Christian Qabalah" of Pico della Mirandola and Reuchlin into metaphysical speculations with no real connection with science, the impact of Euclid as a model of mathematical reasoning was immense and lasting. Euclid's masterpiece, *Elements of Geometry*, a comprehensive treatise on geometry, proportions, and the theory of numbers, written about 300 BCE, is the most long-lived of all mathematical works, having been translated and copied more than any other book except the Bible right into modern times. The first English translation in 1570 disseminated the work for the first time in its complete form, and though credited to Sir Henry Billingsley, who went on to become Lord Mayor of London, it is more than probable that Dee was responsible for part or all of it.

It was precisely this revival of vitally important and proportinately difficult works of ancient Greeks science that began the Scientific Revolution of the 16th and 17th centuries. The rediscovery of Euclid led to the geometrical, Neoplatonic mathematics of Kepler, for example, and what often surprises those who actually bother to read Newton is that his *Principia Mathematica* is framed to a large degree in geometric terms. The ancient Greeks were, of course, driven this way by their exceedingly cumbersome system of depicting numbers, and concrete mathematical developments in physics were postponed until the shift of geometry to algebra in Descartes's coordinate geometry and the Leibniz-Newton invention of the differential calculus. Still, the need for mathematics and its development was felt already in the 16th century, during which its study was vindicated and its importance re-established, effecting a total revaluation of the discipline—for the methods suggested by 16th-century mathematicians commenced a rapid invasion into numerous other fields till then considered utterly foreign to mathematics.

Dee was among the first to recognize the usefulness of mathematics in everyday life. In fact, the whole *Mathematicall Præface* is a manifesto for the practical value of mathematics in all aspects of life, including but not limited to music, architecture, navigation, and mechanics. This unique reorientation of mathematics to physical phenomena has remained to this day the standard world view of Western physics. Without it, the fulfilment of the lavish promises contained in the various newly-recovered works of antiquity would undoubtedly have been still longer delayed.

Dee, who spent much time on astronomy, was also an early supporter of the Copernican theory. As the most rational mathematical universe was one where the Earth and planets orbit the Sun, this, for Dee, represented the physical truth. Besides, like Neoplatonists were wont to point out, how could the radiant Sun have been given any other place in the universe than the centre?

In 1572, a *stella nova*, a new star, was detected in the constellation of Cassiopeia. Brighter than all the rest, it could be seen through clouds at night or in the middle of a sunny day, and remained visible for seventeen months. It was generally considered an extremely ill omen, which would be followed, as was commonly reckoned in England, by such dreadful curses as foul weather, pestilence, and Frenchmen. But the appearance of the new star was also an event of considerable philosophical importance: if the star could be proven to be above the Moon, it would call into question the Aristotelian doctrine of the perfect and unchanging heavens, of the solid concentric orbs in which the stars and planets were set.

Progressive thinkers, like the great Danish astronomer, Tycho Brahe (who was incidentally the first person to observe the new star), were prepared to accept it as a new creation; but since according to the orthodox cosmology, the supralunar world was pure, divine, and immutable, theologians rallied to oppose such a heresy. The only comparable precedent in Europe had been Hipparchus' observation of a new star in 134 BCE—sufficiently remote to be discounted as evidence by the dogmatists—and the qualified exception of the star which had appeared at the birth of the Saviour. Some declared that the star of 1572 A.D. had been there since the beginning of time, being in fact the same star which had guided the three wise men, but had merely remained invisible to men until now. Others dismissed it as merely a meteorological phenomenon, which comets were still generally looked upon as being, a way for the Almighty to admonish the sinful world: "And there shall be signs in the sun, and in the moon, and in the stars; and upon the earth distress of nations, with perplexity; the sea and the waves roaring." (Luke 21:25)

And sure enough, the reigning pope, Gregory XIII, had a medal stuck and a great *Te Deum* celebrated to commemorate the greatest bloodbath of early modern history. In the St. Bartholomew's Day Massacre at Paris, on the 24th of August, 1572, French Catholics fell upon assembled Protestant leaders and their followers and slaughtered three thousand of them. The English Embassy became the asylum for all the escaped heterodox Frenchmen, and those Englishmen, like Elizabeth's ambassador[235] to the court of Charles IX, who witnessed it at first hand, became convinced of the existence of a "Catholic League" intended to extirpate Protestantism from Europe. This greatly affected subsequent Elizabethan foreign policy: it would be impossible thereafter to trust a king of France or any other Catholic; from then on, the only allies to be relied on were fellow-Protestants.

In 1573, Dee published the *Parallacticæ Commentationis praxosque Teoremas Trigonometricos*, a book which perhaps more than any other of his works established his reputation among continental scholars. It gave trigonometric theorems that could be applied to determine the parallax of the star of 1572. Two further works, now lost, were written by Dee on the new star that same year, 1573, receiving much credit and praise from his fellow-astronomers at the time and for long after. He had also continued working on the development of scientific instruments, having in 1572 designed a huge *radius astronomicus* for his former pupil, Thomas Digges (d. 1595), the most important name in introducing Copernican cosmology into England, in order that he might observe the new star. Digges' and Tycho Brahe's observations never differed by more than four minutes of arc, but Dee's own were reserved for yet another book, the non-publication of which Tycho greatly deplored.

Because of their conclusion that the star's position was above the Moon, both Dee and Digges were subject to bitter denunciation by the Scottish reformer, John Craig[236], who obstinately insisted, in spite of all evidence to the contrary, that the star must have been situated below the Moon. In 1576, Digges' addition of *A Perfit Description of the Cælestial Orbes* to his republication of his father's *Prognostication Euerlasting*, included for the first time the idea of an infinite, star-filled universe. The appearance of a comet in 1577 was fortunate for the astronomers of advanced views, for by applying such methods for the determination of parallax as Dee had developed, the "blazing star" could be shown to be a truly celestial and not merely a meteorological

---

[235] i.e. Sir Francis Walsingham

[236] the future court chaplain to James VI and author of the "King's Confession" (1581), the basis for the National Covenant of Scotland (1638)

phenomenon (until then even Tycho had accepted the sublunar nature of comets), dealing a serious blow to the unchanging Aristotelian heavens.

Such phenomena, however, were terrifying to most ordinary Europeans, and horror-stricken masses filled the churches especially in Germany. The comet's appearance also provided the occasion for Kepler's famous astrological predictions—later popularly regarded as foretelling the career of Sweden's Gustavus Adolphus—on which Tycho, too, issued copious prognostications. As for Dee, he spent quite some time closeted with his queen to offer counsel and reassurance. Elizabeth promised that she would protect him from slander and malice of the public, and gave him money so that he could pursue his "rare studies and philosophicall exercises," propaganda for a British empire.

The rise of England as a naval power brought on a corresponding growth in the sense of national pride; Elizabethan geographers and cartographers helped develop a view of the English as separate from and superior to the rest of the world. Between 1576 and 1578, Dee was occupied with one of his most ambitious projects, a four-volume work called *Generall and Rare Memorialls Pertayning to the Perfect Arte of Navigation*, dealing more with the history of discoveries than the science of navigation, and amounting to nothing less than a plan for the establishment of a global British suzerainty with Elizabeth as empress. One of the first, if not the first, to use the term "British Empire," Dee was largely responsible for its popularization.

This was long before the union of England and Scotland gave "Britain" its modern meaning; Dee's *Britannia* was the ancient Britain of King Arthur, embracing England, but before all, his ancestral Wales. The emergence of Protestantism had in a peculiar fashion reinforced the existing nationalistic tendencies of British humanist historians. One of the novel features of the British Protestant historiography was the reawakening of scholarly interest in the period before the Norman Conquest. Dee, who maintained close contact with the leading antiquaries of his day, followed the Tudor historian, Polydore Vergil (c. 1470-1555), in seeing Britain's founding in the mythical landing of the Trojan Brutus, the great-grandson of Æneas.

The Tudors, like Dee, had their origins in Wales, and Welsh interest in the Arthurian tradition was great. A descendant of Brutus, Arthur was one of the Christian princes in southwestern Britain who, after the Romans left in the 5th century, fought against the Saxon invaders and their heathen allies, the Angles, Jutes, Frisians, as well as the faithless Picts coming from the north. The first Tudor monarch, Henry VII, had come to the throne with a very flimsy hereditary claim indeed, and his son and successor, Henry VIII, was particularly eager to identify the family line with the renowned Christian hero-king of the past. Queen Elizabeth, who likewise regarded her Welsh ancestry as important, could thus claim descent from the mythical restorer of the ancient empire of Brutus, an empire that had devolved upon her by virtue of the above descent.

The apocalyptic climate of the 1570s was exceptionally virulent in England, for the overcoming of Antichrist, the pope in Rome, was seen as the chief priority in the scheme of things, an eschatological task assigned by many Britons to Queen Elizabeth. In his *Apologie of the Church of England* (1562), one of the foundation texts of the Anglican Church, Bishop Jewell declares "Christian kings and good princes" as the true heirs of the Roman Empire, whose functions had been usurped by "the tyranny of the Bishops of Rome," and the recent Council of Trent. Examples of good princes of the past were Moses, King David, and Emperor Constantine—all leaders with dual secular and spiritual powers. The last mentioned was a particularly agreeable model for the English Protestants; the first Christian Emperor of Rome, proclaimed as such in York, Constantine, "born in Britain, of a British mother," had summoned and presided over the Council of Nicæa, which was attended by British bishops.

While the ideal of a single world-government, or at least of one great power dominating a federation of other states, owed much to tradition, and though earlier thinkers, like Dante, had argued at length that a world empire was required in order to achieve the abolition of war and the enforcement of universal law, the form in which it appeared in the 16th century, like in *The Arte of Navigation*, is novel in being emphatically nationalistic. The well-known frontispiece to its only published volume, that on *The Brytish Monarchie* (1577), bore an image of the "Imperiall Ship" of Christendom, carrying Empress Elizabeth on a divinely sanctioned mission to restore the ancient British Empire through sea power.

"The Petty Navy Royall," Dee suggests, should be a "fully-equipped expeditionary force," consisting of a whopping total of eighty ships, though still smaller by fifty vessels in comparison to the fleet Philip would eventually send against Elizabeth. Dee's profound patriotism and his unshakeable confidence in an imperial future for Britain based on dominion of the seas was a common theme for the age, reflected in the frequent literary identification of Britain as *Insula Deata*, or the "Fortunate Isles." The great Elizabethan pride in the navy was likewise given expression in Dee, for though the Queen only increased the complement of her fleet from twenty-seven to twenty-nine ships, she maintained it at a remarkable level of efficiency subsequently proven by its wondrous defeat of the "invincible" Spanish Armada.

Drake's return in 1580 with news of "New Albion" may have served as inspiration for the slightly utopistic legal and antiquarian investigations of Dee into Elizabeth's "rightful" *Titles to Far Lands*. Long before the English and Spanish fought out in the English Channel, they fought each other across the Atlantic. It was the intention of Philip II to make the New World into Spain's pacified hunting-ground. In 1580, Portugal, along with its possessions in Asia, Africa, and America, fell to him through maternal inheritance and by force of arms. In Protestant countries, as well as in France, arose an extremely unfavourable view to his colonial régime, which not only entailed the establishment of the Inquisition in the Americas, but also reduced the native peoples to slavery. Philip, however, tolerated no rival conquerors, and debarred foreigners from even trading with his colonies. As a result, Protestant sea captains would visit the Spanish Indies as pirates and privateers rather than as peaceful merchants.

Commissioned by Elizabeth to establish her legal claim to the Americas, Dee went back to Owen Madoc, whose story had been handed down by Welsh bards from the late 12th century. According to the legend, this Welshman of royal lineage had embarked for New England in the Middle Ages with ten ships and several hundred men, established the first overseas colony, and intermarried with the natives. His crew had landed circa 1170 at what is today called Mobile Bay, but which in the 16th century was labelled even by the Spanish cartographers as *Tierra de los Gales*, "Land of the Welsh." As reminders of Madoc's travels there remain the ruins of two mediæval Welsh-style castles near Chattanooga in Tennessee. In addition, remarkable similarities exist between the Welsh Cymri and the near-extinct Mandan Indians. Even the boats of the sometimes fair-skinned, blond-haired, blue-eyed Mandans now inhabiting the upper reaches of the Missouri bear resemblance to the Welsh leather coracles, and thus differ from the wooden canoes of the other Indians. For Elizabeth to plant a colony there was only to "restore her Highnesse aunciente right and interest in those Countries, into the which a noble and worthy personage, lyneally descended from the blood royall, borne in Wales, named Madocke" had first sailed.

It was on the evidence of Prince Madoc's earlier discovery of Florida and the territory northwards that Sir Humphrey Gilbert was granted his long-coveted letters patent for the colonization of North America. For his aid, Dee was ceded by Gilbert all land beyond 50 degrees northern latitude, that is, roughly, Canada. It was undoubtedly also from Dee that Sir George Peckham, who consulted him on the legality of the Spanish-Portuguese partition of the new lands, obtained the bulk of the argument for his famous *True Reporte* of 1583, repeated in Humphrey Lloyd and David Powell's *Historie of Cambria* the next year, and by the geographer Richard Hakluyt in his epic work, *The Principall Navigations*, in 1589. In the following century, Thomas Fuller would still in earnest utilize the legend to warrant the prior rights of the English in the Americas, and Robert Alleyn in his *History of Henry VII* (1638) would consider it proven.

When Gilbert was lost in a shipwreck returning from his Newfoundland voyage, Sir Walter Raleigh pursued and was granted his half-brother's interests in North America. Although the Catholic Church believed that the purpose of overseas expansion was to save souls, it was in fact the explorers, traders, and colonial governors who had the deepest impact on the lives of the people whose lands were invaded, divided, and transformed into European dependencies. England was lucky to give birth to such masters of navigation as Drake, Hawkins, Frobisher, and Davis in an age when the fate of the world was decided at sea. The English "sea dogs," or "merchant adventurers," first on their own, but later under the ægis of a royal prerogative, looted the distant coasts of East and West, yet at the same time establishing commercial enterprises and negotiating trade treaties. It was nothing short of piracy, taking place under government mandate, and at the event of war, dubbed seizure and confiscation. Privateering, smuggling, and slave-trade stood—like it has so aptly been remarked—as godparents by the cradle of the English and all modern-day capitalism.

The Reformation had made such a strong headway that Catholicism could clearly regain its spiritual monopoly only through forcible measures. Spain was without dispute the leading Catholic nation and England was thus far the only major power to have espoused Protestantism. The military effort was preceded by a spiritual expedition of conquest, for in 1580, Gregory XIII, bend on the destruction of Elizabeth, dispatched Jesuits to convert the English. The attempt proved vain, its effects being confined to the tightening of the penalties for demonstrating disobedience to the Act of Uniformity, be the transgressors Catholic or Puritan. Over the next few years, recusancy became subject to heavy fines, attendance at Mass was punishable by imprisonment, and conversion to Catholicism was construed as treason. While Philip of Spain took part in the endless Catholic plots to do away with Elizabeth and release the Queen of Scots, he was, however, unwilling to undertake any active measures in favour of the imprisoned Mary Stuart, whose friendliness to France was no secret, so the great excursion was delayed.

The fact that Dee was both the author of propaganda for colonization of the Americas and a brilliant mathematician who applied the science of arithmetic to surveying and navigation, underlines the inevitable connection between the two endeavours. The study of geography furnished some of the principal politicians and investors of early modern England with a belief that the world could be measured, named, and therefore controlled, as well as with examples of the heroic feats of the champions of British expansion who had gone before—an important counter-argument to the Spanish claim to empire through conquest.

That precise charting and effective colonization were related activities Spain had already recognized, and the men who conceived a British empire were in like manner brought to the realization that to rule the world, the world must first be ruled. Some of this cartographic reconnaissance was to be done "in discreet view," the unpublished 16th-century maps often being regarded as state secrets, tools of surveillance that would enable England to triumph over its enemies. While working as a geographer to Queen Elizabeth, Dee came into contact with her secretary of state, Sir Francis Walsingham, who controlled the early days of British secret service, and shared his advocacy of a blue-water foreign policy of combining Protestant alliances with voyages of exploration and colonization.

Renowned for his development of the art of cryptography, Dee was consulted on ciphers and systems of coding. The role of cryptology in history is poorly understood, and easily understated. Code books were fast becoming the best-selling items of the Renaissance: it was imperative to still be able to safeguard all the precious secrets now that more and more people were learning to read. Clear text could, for example, be replaced with strange symbols or scrambled according to mathematical algorithms, rendering it decipherable only through elaborate "keys"—necessities in the schemes of politics, diplomacy, and commerce alike.

While still actively supplying navigational advice and ideological rationale for projects of discovery and recovery, Dee received a commission to prepare a scheme for the reform of the calendar. That such a reform was scientifically desirable no mathematician could doubt: it was thirty years since Elizabeth's private tutor and a leading intellectual figure of the early Tudor period, Sir Roger Ascham (1515-1568), had declared that if nothing were done, December would in time fall in the middle of the summer. The major stumbling-block was that the reform had elsewhere been propagated as a papal bull, thus being theologically suspect.

The Gregorian Calendar was adopted throughout the Roman Catholic world, albeit mostly at a different time than Pope Gregory XIII had envisaged in his bull. It was by rule rejected in Protestant countries as they rejected the authority of Rome, and in lands where Protestants and Catholics were intermixed, a cause of great quarrel. Some of the disputes (the *Kalenderstreit* of Bohemia being particularly notorious) became known to English diplomats, the spy-master Walsingham receiving a copy of the bull and calendar in diplomatic correspondence. When Walsingham passed these on to Dee, and asked him for his opinion on the behalf of the Privy Council, Dee dropped everything to work on the problem. On the 26th of February, 1583, he delivered to the Queen's most trusted minister, Lord Treasurer Burghley, a 62-page illuminated treatise entitled *A playne Discourse and humble Advise for our gratious Queene Elizabeth, her most Excellent Majestie, to peruse and consider as concerning the needful Reformation of the Vulgar Kalendar for the civile yeres and daies accompting or verifying, according to the tyme truely spent.*

The *Playne Discourse* consisted of two parts: a scientific and a polemical. Successive attempts at rectification of the calendar had been made from the earliest times. Roger Bacon, whose reputation Dee ceaselessly sought to vindicate against suspicions of necromancy, had long ago called upon the pope of the day to implement a reform, and on his treatise on the subject Dee here drew heavily. More recently, in 1514, Leo X had invited Copernicus to assist on the projected reform, and the subsequent observations of the great Polish astronomer Dee now also utilized. He compared the figures given for the length of the year by a number of other astronomers from Classical to early modern times, finishing with the Protestant Michael Maestlin (1550-1631), a vocal critic of the Gregorian Reform and Kepler's future professor at Tübingen. The great difficulty has always lied in the incommensurability of the terrestrial day, the lunar month, and the solar year. The Julian Calendar had fixed the year at 365 1/4 days, which was 11 minutes and 8 seconds too long, and deemed the lunar and solar cycles to coincide every 19 years, which was wrong by 1 hr. 28 min. 11 sec.

Now the Gregorian Calendar is not based on keeping the seasons in step; its aim, like that of all Christian calendars, is to regularize the date of Easter. This greatest of Christian feasts and all those lesser ones that depend on it—Ash Wednesday and Lent, for example, and Pentecost—are movable; they occur on different dates from year to year. The date on which the Feast of the Resurrection falls depends on the time of the Spring Equinox, which is ecclesiastically defined as the 21st of March, but which astronomically-speaking shifts on the Gregorian Calendar over the protracted 400-year leap-year cycle by 53 hours, between the 19th and 21st of that month. From a religious perspective, a calendar which keeps the Equinox on one day would have been far more preferable, necessitating a much shorter leap-year cycle. In the "true Christian kalendar" that Dee came up with, the Equinox fell withing a period of 23 hr. 16 min. on the 21st of March using a cycle of 33 years, the traditional lifetime of Jesus.

In his bull, Gregory XIII had ordered ten days to be removed from October of 1582 to restore the calendar to the relation with the movements of heavens that had prevailed at the time of the Council of Nicæa when the Julian Calendar had been adopted by the Christian Church. But Dee would again argue that while the calendar had indeed drifted out of line by ten days since the time of Nicæa, it had more pertinently drifted by eleven days since the time of Christ, thus drawing a close parallel to the Protestant mission of returning Christianity to its roots. The Queen should issue a special calendar for 1583, to be followed in 1584 by "Elizabeth's Perpetuall Kalendar" for the next couple of centuries, complete with an appeal to all other countries to follow England's lead in what was essentially a Protestant counter-reform of the calendar. Since the Gregorian Reform had yet to widely take root, Dee believed the competing English calendar would, by virtue of its inherent truthfulness, eventually oblige even the pope to "embrace the veritie."

To introduce a 33-year calendar, one would have to establish a new prime meridian 77 degrees west of England, that is, on the eastern seaboard of North America. In 1584, the so-called "Lost Colony" was sent to Roanoke Island, quite a bizarre place to start colonization, but an excellent site from which to make astronomical observations to fix the calendrical meridian. Unfortunately, the small expedition of astronomers and surveyors, who went "50 miles into the main" to Virginia in order to mark "God's Longitude," were lost in what is now called the Great Dismal Swamp, lying just under the single meridian drawn on the map White and Harriot left behind. In Dee's mind, to found a New Albion was only to enable the English Protestants to restore control of the calendar, out of the hands of the Bishop of Rome, into those of "Cæsar's Pere our true Empress," Elizabeth.

The Julian Calendar was "Cæsar's false hypothesis," imposed by him through an *annus confusionis* of 446 days; similarly, Gregory had introduced his with the disruptive removal of the days from the 5th of October, 1582, to the 14th of that month. The Elizabethan calendar was to be introduced gradually and subtly in an *annus reformationis*, by deducting the eleven days in batches of two or three from the ends of the months of May to September, in the year 1583, thus not only minimizing the disruption to contracts and covenants, but also avoiding a change in the nominal date of "any feast or holiday moveable or fixed"; and while both Cæsar and Gregory had proceeded by dictate, Elizabeth was to proceed constitutionally.

A distinctively English version of the calendar reform had an undeniable appeal in a period when the identities of both the Anglican Church and the nascent British Empire were starting to take shape, and Dee's proposal was favourably received by Parliament. It was only the adverse opinion of some Anglican bishops that caused a delay of 170 years: they declared the reform might breed a new schism, and offend the Protestant Churches abroad.[237] There would be no serious attempt at calendar reform in Britain until 1699, and no successful one until 1752, Dee's treatise being consulted on both occasions.

Originally among the Protestant countries most favourable to a reform,

---

[237] Even today, the senior clergy of the Anglican Church retain permanent seats in the British Parliament.

England was to be one of the last to accept one; the Protestants of Central Europe adopted the Gregorian Reform in 1700, Russia only after the October Revolution in 1929. Britain, contrary to the common misconception, never adopted the Gregorian Calendar: it uses what is properly called the British Calendar, as defined in Lord Chesterfield's Calendar Act of 1751; that is the system inherited by the United States, with no specific calendar statute of its own, and much of the rest of the world. As for Dee, he continued to use the system of his own invention, double-dating his private letters and noting the "true date" of every important holiday in his diary.

Throughout the latter half of the 16th century, Dee enjoyed international renown for his vast scholarship. His various recent scientific and mathematical works had won widespread recognition, his opinions were widely consulted, and his authority was invoked in diverse fields of speculation and study. He directed the politically powerful men surrounding the Queen to the necessity of using scholarly knowledge for "the good of the Common Weale," and was employed directly in her affairs on various occasions to the extent that Elizabeth vouchsafed him the title of her philosopher.

Far-sighted enough to have proposed a national scheme for the conservation of ancient monuments, Dee had also done what he could to stimulate interest in the rescuing of manuscripts from the dissolved monastic libraries, and to persuade his queen to house them in a national "Library Royall." He had, on his own, salvaged many ancient scientific volumes that had been scattered when Catholic churches and monasteries were ransacked during the early years of the Reformation, and his Thameside family home of Mortlake would eventually boast the largest library of its time in all Europe. With a catalogue of more than 4,000 printed volumes and over 1,000 manuscript codices, many of which were unique original autographia of famous and rare authors, it was a truly magnificent and luxurious collection for one private gentleman of shaky fortune in the 16th century. Only the great national collections of the next century surpassed it, the libraries of Oxford and Cambridge together numbering less than a quarter of Dee's private library.

While even printed books were difficult to obtain, acquiring manuscript copies took much work and skill, time and money. The text itself was more often than not corruptly rendered by an ignorant or incompetent copyist, so a scholar and collector such as Dee would not be content with owning just one version of a work. In his library, Celtic history, Welsh and Irish, including original historic documents, was most copiously represented after mathematics, astronomy, astrology, and alchemy, and from the 16th century on, maps and atlases were an essential component of any fine library. Several of the manuscripts are now to be found in the British Museum; in Cambridge University Library and Oxford's Corpus Christi College; in Trinity College, Dublin; in the Bibliothèque Nationale de France; and in the prestigious Winthrop Collection at the New York Society Library.

For many years, Dee's house at Mortlake was indeed an important centre of science in England, an Elizabethan equivalent of a university research centre. He had built up an extensive personal acquaintance with many contemporary scholars, who used the resources of his library for their studies. He maintained correspondence with continental scholars at the universities of Heidelberg, Strasbourg, Orléans, Cologne, Bologna, Ferrara, Verona, Padua, Urbino, Rome, etc. Nevertheless, it was towards the end of this period that Dee embarked on the activities that gradually absorbed all his attention, and were to obscure in the memory of subsequent generations all his other pursuits.

It would be difficult to overestimate the depth of the supernatural's presence in Elizabethan England, measured by its appearance in such era-defining plays as *The Spanish Tragedy* of Kyd, *Dr. Faustus* of Marlowe, *The Færie Queene* of Spenser, *Macbeth*, *The Tempest*, *A Midsummer Night's Dream*, and *Julius Cæsar* of Shakespeare, and, if in a satirical vein, *The Alchemist* of Jonson. This was an age given over to the astrologer, alchemist, sorcerer, and soothsayer, when ideas which today seem outlandish and superstitious held sway over the minds of men, regardless of social or intellectual status. One of the first modern scientists, Dee was also one of the last serious astrologers, alchemists, magicians, and crystal gazers.

Already in 1582, Dee's interest in the occult had led to his often remembered association with the dubious Edward Kelly (1555-1595), an "Irish" alchemist thirty years his junior. Born Edward Talbot in Worcester, Kelly conformed almost too closely to the popular image of a magician, and would later act as a scryer in Dee's attempts to communicate with the spirit world. He had begun his career as an apothecary's apprentice, showing some aptitude for this calling; and while he had also attended Oxford for a number of years, he never obtained a degree. In Wales, he apparently chanced upon the sole copy of an alchemical treatise, which explained how to formulate the

Red and White Tinctures for the transmutation of base metals into gold, along with two phials containing samples of these magic powders. Kelly allegedly used them to make gifts of gold for his friends and, more to the point, to impress Dee. Yet Dee was not the unsuspecting dupe that some historians make him out to be; in fact, his extant diaries show that he was often quite critical of Kelly. He nevertheless found certain qualities in Kelly that he valued, and together they ventured into crystal gazing and dowsing for buried treasure.

The Queen was parsimonious with money and honours, believing that men should serve her and England without considerations of reward. Dee seemed dissatisfied with the level of support he received from Elizabeth, though she had always been his "most consistent patron." But while she had invited him to court many times and herself visited his house on several occasions, she did not grant him the lucrative positions he was after, such as provostship of Eton, and several others she had promised him at one time or another. The abortive "Queene Elizabeth's Perpetuall Kalendar" was the culmination of decades of more famous work towards a British world empire, marking the apex of Dee's ambitions, the last and best chance to associate his name in calendrical perpetuity with that of the rightful successor of Cæsar and Constantine, and to become "a Christian Aristotle."

Then, in 1583, Albrecht Laski (1536-1603), a Polish prince with royal pretentions, took a detour from his visit to the English court and presented himself at Mortlake. Evidently fascinated with the occult activities of Dee and Kelly, he promised Dee everything he had failed to get from Elizabeth, and the pair quietly and secretly followed him back to the Continent. Kelly's vision of Laski as King of Poland, dispensing wealth and favour to his two trusted assistants, was of course never realized. The prince, it seems, was heavily in debt, having mortgaged his estates in Poland to raise a loan for a large sum of money. The bond was soon to expire, and with King Stephen Báthory and his all-powerful chancellor, Jan Zamoyski, both set against him, Dee did not see how Laski could possibly redeem his property without the help of the Holy Roman Emperor. Thus, in 1584, Dee, Kelly, and Laski set off to Prague.

The events of the trio's visit to Rudolph II's capital won Dee some notoriety, though his figure in that episode was easily overshadowed by that of Kelly, and their activities were neither remarkable nor singular in that melting-pot of the marvellous, teeming as the city was with impostors encouraged by the credulity of the Emperor. During the Renaissance, princes of Europe sought to assemble all human knowledge in their private libraries, and all useful botanicals in their gardens. Besides the choice art treasures, Emperor Rudolph's precious collections included showcases filled with magnetic stones, Indian feathers, mandrake roots, crocodile skins, and rhinoceros horns; three bagpipes, two nails from Noah's Ark, a "stone that grows, a gift of Herr Rosenberg," a "fleece fallen from heaven," and "various kinds of rare sea-fish, among them a night bat."

For Dee, the seeking of angelic counsel was always knowingly functional, intended to guide his various enterprises, the exploration of the New World, for example, and the reconfiguration of the political map of Central Europe, with Rudolph II apparently seen as the grand prize.[238] His advisors were naturally envious of this foreigner, and many whispers against the two Britons were afloat, but as the Spanish ambassador told Dee, the Emperor himself was amenable. Still, Dee failed to get the patronage he desired, and on the 10th of April, 1586, three copies of his angelic manuscripts were burned in Prague by order of a papal nuncio. Sixtus V, who had succeeded Gregory as pope, issued a papal edict, dated the 29th of May, 1586, banishing Dee and Kelly from the Empire within six days.

Being dismissed in a state of near poverty seemed to bother the pair very little, for Dee was already away on a visit to a new patron. Count Wilhelm von Rosenberg, who took them under his protection, was immensely influential with Rudolph, being not only Viceroy of Bohemia, but Burgrave of Prague as well. On the 8th of August, Rosenberg obtained from the Emperor a partial revocation of the decree against them, and for the next two years, they enjoyed his hospitality, being permitted to reside freely in any of His Lordship's towns and castles. Kelly was constantly riding to Prague and back, and making longer journeys to Poland in hopes of getting more money from Laski. His hopes seem to have been realized, for in March, 1587, Dee notes in his diary that Kelly gave him some 500 ducats. The abundance of gold

---

[238] He may have also been hoping to persuade the Emperor and thus all Holy Roman Empire, to desert the corrupt papal calendar for his superior Protestant one. The fact is, Rudolph was becoming increasingly estranged from Catholicism, and on his death-bed refused the last rites of the Roman Church.

undoubtedly gave rise to the idea that they were actually producing it—had Kelly not once claimed to possess a magical powder that would transform pile of lead into heaps of money?

All Dee's influence and friendship with Rosenberg would gradually be undermined by Kelly's continued pretense of making gold, causing coldness and jealousy to eventually fall between the pair. The Count seems to have had implicit faith in Kelly's powers, even inducing the Emperor to knight him as a reward for his alchemical works. Rudolph was to establish Sir Edward at his court in Prague as a councillor of state, but later imprison him when he failed to deliver the quantities of alchemical gold that he had promised. He would die whilst attempting to escape from one of the Emperor's castles.

Man of science and for two decades England's leading mathematician, it is only recently that Dee's reputation has begun to recover from the stigma attached by the Age of Reason to his brief angel raising episode. His conjuring table, which contains the "Enochian Keys,"[239] a series of nineteen magical incantations received during that period of spirit scrying, now rests in the British Museum. Hard as Dee and Kelly worked to produce this mountain of occult material, they seem to have never done anything with it. Indeed, some modern researchers have concluded that the Enochian language in fact concealed counter-espionage codes[240], and it appears that Laski (or de Lacy, as his Anglo-Norman ancestors chose to be called) was actually an English spy, informing Dee on the current events at and political plans of the Polish court. The secret signature later borrowed by Ian Fleming, and used by Dee in his covert letters sent back to the Crown, was "007." The two zeros actually represented Dee's eyes as the "eyes for the Queen" and the number seven, or rather, the bar at the side and top, signified "under cover."

A revolt against Spanish rule had been going on for years in the Netherlands, and the English had been aiding the rebels unofficially. In 1584, William of Orange, the Dutch leader in the fight against Spain, was

---

[239] Named after the apocryphal Book of Enoch (Heb. *Henoch*, "initiated"), which describes a rebellion of the angels and served as an inspiration for Milton's allegorical masterpiece, *Paradise Lost*.

[240] Even the most complex cipher is relatively easy for a skilled mathematician to crack, whereas deciphering codes with their own unique grammar and signifier relations, such as strange languages, is virtually impossible.

assassinated, and the Estates-General turned abroad for help. Henry III of France was not prepared to intervene in the feud and Dee, all the while in constant communication with England, expressed regret that Elizabeth did not accept the proffered crown. Nevertheless, she did send a small army led by her then favourite, Lord Robert Dudley, Earl of Leicester, to aid the Dutch in 1585. Although this expedition proved ineffectual, it was an open declaration of war against Spain.

In 1586, a Catholic conspiracy, the goal of which was to assassinate the Queen, was revealed. Though it was led by Anthony Babington, behind him stood Philip II, and behind Philip the papacy, which was to lose the last bit of respect it had enjoyed in England, having advocated murder as an instrument of politics. After being a party to a number of conspiracies against Elizabeth, Mary Stuart finally implicated herself so deeply in the Babington Plot that she was tried and found guilty by a court, by the Star Chamber, and by Parliament. Her part in the plot was uncovered by Walsingham's expert intelligence department, and it was the cryptanalysis and successful decipherment of secret messages sent between Mary and her co-conspirators in France, that provided the evidence needed for her conviction.

Four years earlier, Kelly had had a prophetic vision of the execution of a beautiful woman having her head cut off by a tall black man. In spite of Elizabeth's reluctance, her Catholic cousin was finally beheaded on the 18th of February, 1587, giving cause to public jubilation. Mary had already appointed Philip II as the heir to her rights, thus passing over her son, James VI of Scotland, on ground of his affiliation with the Reformed Church. In his vision, Kelly had also beheld the sea, covered with many ships, and been warned by the Archangel Uriel that foreign powers were providing ships "against the welfare of England, which shall shortly be put in practice." In 1587, Walsingham's elaborate spy network provided his government with minute details of the impending attack of the armada that Philip had been preparing since 1585. With the pope's aid, Spain had assembled the largest fleet the world had seen; it would sail from Portugal in late May, 1588, on a mission to convert the English back to Catholicism.

Philip's crusade was funded with the riches of the colonies, where the Spanish acted not only like common thieves, but like commonly stupid thieves. The Spanish warrior-nobility, having nothing to do after the Moors had been expelled in 1492, saw a chance for new adventures across the ocean.

The Conquistadores set upon the New World, operating rather like the bandits who dig out the jewels from a priceless mosaic and kill the milk cow, with which they could have nourished themselves for years on end, just to devour its meat. By the mid-16th century, five hundred tons of silver and ten tons of gold flowed annually from America to Spain, flooding the European market and producing a sharp inflation. Prices and wages rose approximately twice as high in Spain as in Northern Europe, heavily penalizing Spanish industry, the products of which became too expensive to compete in the international market.

The only economic principle that the conquerors seemed to know was the primitive plundering of the natives, the wanton destruction of local flora and fauna, the erratic sucking dry of the soil that everywhere betrayed their visits. The obliteration of million of Incas and Aztecs, the extermination of very unique and highly civilized cultures, was not, however, an inevitable result of the thirst for gold and silver. With their temples also got destroyed their literature and science, which the Spanish deemed idolatrous, unmasking the ideals of the Crusades rather than those of the Renaissance. The Iberian Reconquista, the holy war against Muslims by which the peninsula was reclaimed into Christian hands, was repeated throughout Latin America with deplorable results. The Aztec capital, Tenochtitlán, was as big as Rome and London put together—the Spanish conquerors were enraged by the fact that such a great city should have been built by a heathen people not even mentioned in the Bible.

Even if the Spanish would have only had their Portuguese colonies, they would have had quite plenty, for these consisted, along with much else, of the eastern and western coasts of Africa, the Moluccas, and the enormous Brazil. In America, it was the spirit of the Counter-Reformation that induced the Jesuits, appointed by the pope to convert the natives, to work for the Indians, usually in opposition to the secular authorities. Some individual missionaries, like Las Casas, wrote and published widely-read reports describing the atrocities inflicted upon the natives, and after prolonged legal and theological debates, restrictions were placed on the forced labour of Indians. These New Laws immediately led to the importation of African slaves, at least 100,000 of whom had been shipped to Latin America by the mid-16th century with the complicity and blessing of the Catholic Church. From this large-scale human traffic the "Dark Continent" never recovered.

Almost all the slaves in Europe were domestic servants; it was the discovery of the New World that turned African slaves, previously a Muslim monopoly, into a valuable commodity. While the Spanish and Portuguese exploited the domestic slave-trade in sub-Saharan Africa, the shipment of black Africans as labourers and military auxiliaries to the overseas colonies was hardly even noticed in Europe. To cultivate the sugar of the Americas, a new kind of "plantation slave" became necessary. Since sugar planting was a labour-intensive industry, this new type of slave was acquired for purely economical reasons, that is, for being the cheapest conceivable labour. By the 17th century, the cost of slaves was so low in Africa that it was cheaper for the Brazilian and Caribbean planters to work their slaves to death and buy new ones than it was to raise them from birth. The missionaries in Spanish America were wholly uninterested in the transplanted customs and beliefs of the Africans who, as commodity imports, were irrelevant to the task of saving indigenous souls. And even in Africa itself, missionaries scarcely tried to understand the men and women they rushed into baptism and whose idols they destroyed.[241]

With the incorporation of Portugal into the Iberian Union, the country that boasted a long Atlantic coast-line was brought to permanent ruin, its colonies went to waste or fell into decay, and its share in the world trade shrunk sparser and less significant with every passing year. Although its maritime empire had begun to decline even before the 60 years of "Spanish Captivity," this period undoubtedly hastened the process. The Portuguese, dragged into Spain's wars with Holland and England, began to see these two countries attack their holdings in Asia, as well as Brazil. Products from the East had originally entered Europe through Lisbon, but war with Spain and Portugal meant that Dutch merchants had to obtain the spices themselves, leading to the foundation of companies in Zeeland[242] and various towns in Holland[243]. In time, these would unite, and by the time Portugal regained its independence, it had lost its commercial monopoly to the Dutch East India Company (est.

---

[241] The situation was entirely different in East India, where the Europeans came in contact with civilizations more sophisticated than their own.

[242] which would later lend its name to New Zealand, discovered by the Dutch explorer Abel Tasman in 1642

[243] Australia was known to the first Europeans as New Holland.

1602) in the Far East, and to the English East India Company (est. 1600) in India.

Philip of Spain supported the one institution in Portugal that he thought could unite the two countries: the Inquisition. As a result, the Marranos, Spanish and Portuguese Jews who had been baptized under duress in the previous century, were persecuted even more severely. Many of them had been prosperous merchants with clear economic reasons for not wanting to flee; in fact, Spanish propagandists and paranoiacs accused their descendants of monopolizing the trade of Spanish America "from the vilest African Negro to the most precious pearl." The Netherlands was meanwhile fighting a brave war of independence against Spain, and the Marranos, who already had trade links with Amsterdam, felt drawn to a country where the spirit of liberty was strong.

Moving to Holland and openly returning to the synagogue's fold after having been forcibly separate from it for so long, the Marranos were in many regions trailblazers who would form the cores of new Jewish communities. By the end of the 17th century, the Spanish and Portuguese Jews in Amsterdam would own a quarter of the shares of the Dutch East India Company, and be engaged in trade and industry ranging from Japan to the Americas. Indeed, the first book on the workings of a stock market[244] was penned in Spanish by Josef de la Vega, a Dutch Sephardic Jew. The Amsterdam community was not only financially prosperous, but an intellectual focus graced by such figures as the Portuguese-speaking Baruch Spinoza (1632-1677), who abandoned the commercial world to become a leader in the movement towards rationalism. Its descendants also became the first Jews to set foot in New Amsterdam, now known as New York.

The Inquisition was one of the main factors that contributed to the economic and cultural downfall of Spain, the rapidity of which knows no parallel in history aside from disastrous wars. Moriscos, the Christian descendants of the Moors, still widely spread in the south, were driven to despair by the most senseless and intolerable statutes. After a bloodily suppressed rebellion, many of them fled across the sea; which is exactly what Philip had aimed at with his measures, senselessly depriving himself of his most intelligent, skilful, and industrious subjects. It was the Moriscos that the

---

[244] *Confusión de Confusiones* (1688)

region had to thank for the *huertas*, the marvellous irrigation devices that had transformed the arid plains of Iberia into a fertile garden; they were in charge of the rice production, the sugar refining, the cotton industry, the silk and paper manufacture—all trades on which the wealth of Spain was based. Half a million Moriscos quit Spain, carrying their property and arts, the patrimony of a state. The economic burst that the country had experienced in the first half of the 16th century was to end in the complete collapse of its national economy.

This remarkable disintegration of Spain is the key note in its history from 1550 to 1650. A great part of the trade and most of the agriculture had long been in the hands of the Moors, for pride drove the Spaniards, when at all possible, to positions in the court, in the military, or in the Church. Finally the government had to resort to the desperate measure of pledging every farm-hand a hereditary title, but even this proved ineffective since every free man in Spain looked upon work as shameful. Although the nobility and higher clergy comprised less than two percent of the population, they owned about 96 percent of the land and had all the social status and prestige. Because they looked down on careers in commerce as demeaning for a gentleman, this became the national norm; the ambition of a successful merchant was to acquire an estate, buy a title from the impoverished crown, and abandon his trade to become an *hidalgo*. The land grew impoverished and neglected, the richest and most fertile valleys dried up and were deserted, and the once populous cities of Andalusia fell into decay. Scarcely even now has the Spanish agriculture recovered from the blow it received from the driving away of the Moors.

Around 1588, Dee was spreading prophecies from his base in Bohemia about the "imminent fall of a mighty kingdom amid fearsome storms." Whether or not we believe in the legend that he conjured up the tempest which crowned the English victory over the "Invincible Armada," the ability of Spain to wage war abroad was thereby drastically curtailed. While the Spanish plan for world dominion rested on conquest and the resulting mineral wealth, the other maritime nations were less sure of their methods of expansion and the results they desired. At any rate, after this decisive Spanish defeat, England, Holland, and France quickly established overseas colonies of their own, while the once mighty Spain slowly sank to oblivion. The net effect of Spain's American enterprise was to fuel the booming economy of Northwest

Europe, with its clear primacy of trade and commerce over conquest and glory. Up to 90 percent of the manufactured goods imported by Brazil and Spanish America was supplied by Northwest Europeans, as was a large portion of similar goods consumed in the Iberian Peninsula itself. In addition, most of the carrying trade with the Iberian colonies was controlled by the Dutch, and later by the British.

Dee's letter of congratulations to the Queen upon the splendid victory of her navy is now on display in the manuscript galleries of the British Museum. The letter was sent from the home of the *Kalenderstreit*, and is dated not "new style" or "old style" but *stylo vere*. Patriot that Dee was, he rejoiced in the timely arrival of Elizabeth's "Brytish Earthly Paradise," and brought out his Elizabethan calendar to welcome it. In March, 1589, he left for England, "being favourably called home by her Majestie." Although it was unnecessary and even absurd, he insisted on travelling with huge train of coaches and wagons, complete with an armed escort, its journey taking a year and three-quarters, and costing nearly £800. When Dee finally reached England, he found himself generally shunned, his house ransacked, and much of his property either stolen or destroyed. His financial situation was precarious, and although Elizabeth had promised him a gift of £100, he eventually got £50. She finally granted him the wardenship of Christ's College, Manchester (1595-1604), but the reign of James deprived him of that office. And though he died destitute in 1608, Dee's vast geopolitical mosaic would play a revolutionary role for the next three centuries in Western civilization. The real magical child of Dee's occult workings was not the misinterpreted angelic language, but the subsequent entity known as the British Empire.

CHAPTER 35

At exactly the time when astrologers, alchemists, and magicians were laying the foundations for the sciences of astronomy, chemistry, physics, and mathematics, their activities would become suspect first among Protestants, and then among Catholics, who could not afford to seem less devout than the heretics. The suspicion that modern-day Christian fundamentalists have towards natural science has its roots deep in the 16th century. The supposed astronomical stand of the Bible was at that time backed by an eminent scientific authority: the Danish mathematician, Tycho Brahe (1546-1601). He could never accept the notion that Earth, like the other planets, orbits the Sun, and aimed his work at proving right his personal view, which differed from those of both Ptolemy and Copernicus.

With his king's help, Tycho built a magnificent observatory, but had to leave his native country after Frederick II died, and in 1600 ended up an astrologer to Rudolph II, who was beset by many anxieties, not least the astrological significance of the dawning of a new century. At Prague, Tycho complained that he was disturbed by the nightly devotions at the nearby Strahov Monastery, while the monks in turn did not appreciate the close proximity of a heretic, let alone one enjoying the patronage of the Holy Roman Emperor. Rudolph had given the castle of Benatky to his use, and it was there that, on the 2nd of February, 1600, he first met his equally famous associate, Johannes Kepler (1571-1630).

Tycho was 53, Kepler half his age. Kepler had been driven to Prague by the Counter-Reformation, Tycho by his own arrogance—the one historical fact that remains when all else in forgotten is Tycho's fake nose, there to disguise the loss of his real one, in a duel over who was the better mathematician. Kepler had already written his first book on astronomy and worked several years as a professor at the Lutheran Academy in Graz, leaving town after only Jesuit schools were allowed following the outlawing of Protestant religion. This is when Kepler called to mind the great astronomer, who had once before invited him to join his team. It was just a year and a half later that

Tycho died, and on his death-bed, implored Kepler to use his observations to prove the Tychonic system correct.

Apart from the inadequate and irregular pay of Imperial Mathematician, which position Kepler inherited at Tycho's death, the rest of his life was made difficult by the fact that he and his family were persecuted as heretics. They were Protestant, so they had to change domicile several times during his life as the rulers fitfully demanded Protestants either to leave or to convert to Catholicism. Both his wife, Barbara, and their six-year-old son died in Prague, and his employer, Emperor Rudolph, ultimately lost what was left of his sanity and was forced to abdicate. A wandering astrologer, Kepler moved from one German principality to another, at times being even spit on by people in the streets.

The superficial view of Kepler, derived from hundreds of popular histories of modern science, including highly reputable ones, is that of a great modern astronomer, who took Brahe's scrupulous observations, and by the aid of hard mathematical thinking, unimpeded by Ptolemy or Aristotle, unravelled the Laws of Planetary Motion—which is in a curious way true, yet a travesty of the truth. Kepler sought cosmology, the truths pertaining to the true nature of the universe, just as Plato and St. Thomas Aquinas had done, but because Kepler had the training of a natural scientist, the updated observations forced him to throw out the elaborate system named *Mysterium Cosmographicum* that he had developed in his youth, and to start again from scratch. Facts do not as markedly inconvenience philosophers.

At bottom, Kepler was not an astronomer, and certainly not an observer, but a mathematician. Not a mathematician of the modern, Leibniz-Newton kind, mind you, but a Neoplatonic mathematician of the Ficino school. The concept of mathematical harmony was central to Kepler, and in this, he mirrored Neoplatonism even closer than Copernicus, who wished to reverse the roles of the Sun and the Earth in order to save the ideal of uniform circular motion. Copernicus had stated quite openly that he had arrived at his revolutionary insight by studying the occult writings of ancient Egypt, including the works of the god Thoth himself. In like manner, Kepler confessed that in formulating his Laws he was simply "stealing the golden vessels of the Egyptians." Like most of his contemporaries, Kepler took astrology seriously: both he and Tycho compiled heaps of astrological predictions, but Kepler actually existed largely on his astrological practice, for which he in fact gained something of a reputation.

After Tycho died, Kepler spent the remaining twenty-nine years of his life trying to find patterns in Tycho's two decades worth of data; the result of these efforts was the *Astronomia Nova*. Having tread a long, slow road, Kepler saw the light in the orbital parameters of Mars, and believed and knew that the planetary orbits were elliptical. Gone were epicycles and uniform circular motion, gone were regular polyhedra and Platonic harmony, gone was the Tychonic system. Gone were all theological arguments for the shape and form of the heavenly movements, for though Kepler was never especially fond of ellipses, Nature had spoken. Not that Kepler ever abandoned his mathematical-harmonical speculations, which he himself considered his actual life's work; his thinking constantly recalls a neo-Pythagorean world of number-forms and solid mathematical figures, all fitting into a harmony that makes sense of the whole—a view of the world that Ficino and Pico della Mirandola would have fully sympathized with.

This type of "Neoplatonism" has, in fact, remained the guiding principle of theoretical thinking. Today, more than ever before, we believe and hope that the world is governed by numerical harmonies. The theories of modern particle physics are based on symmetries just as the circular path of planets was once seen as the most symmetrical and divine of all motions. The theoretical speculations towards a grand unified theory are predicated on the notion that still more intricate and profound, though broken, harmonies prevail in nature than we have thus far been able to ascertain. So the next time you browse through a *Scientific American*, remember that the fundamental understanding of the universe employed therein has its origins in Renaissance Neoplatonism.

Turning to Italy, we find Galileo Galilei (1564-1642) about to declare that "the book of the universe is written in the language of mathematics." As great a physicist as an astronomer, he gave a mathematical formulation to many physical laws. Galileo was also the founder of dynamics, a wholly new branch of science, which had been foreign to the scholars of the old because they knew only of studies concerning statics. His experiments on the laws of bodies in motion produced results so contradictory to the teachings of Aristotle that strong antagonism arose in and around the University of Pisa, where Galileo worked as a professor from 1589 to 1592. It should, however, be noted that Galileo, just like Tycho and Kepler, was a deeply religious man, and never felt that he was compromising his faith by conducting scientific investigations.

In 1592, Galileo began lecturing on mathematics at the more liberal University of Padua, where he remained for the next 18 years. There, in 1609 (the same year as Kepler's *Astronomia Nova* was first published), he heard reports of a simple magnifying instrument put together the previous year by a Dutch lens-grinder, who had hit upon the idea of putting two lenses at each end of a tube and looking through it. Forthwith, he ground his own lenses, constructed his own tube, and produced the first complete astronomical telescope, with a magnification twice as powerful as the one made in Holland. He then climbed to the top of the Campanile in Venice, and pointed his spy-glass skywards, becoming the first person ever to behold the four moons[245] around Jupiter, four new worlds that clearly did not move on circular orbits around the centre of the universe, be that centre the Earth or the Sun. As the British ambassador to the Doge's court reported to his superiors in England, Galileo ran "a fortune to be either exceedingly famous or exceedingly ridiculous."

Galileo figured that his reputation was now great enough for him to leave the protection of the essentially anticlerical, safe Republic of Venice, and to return to his native Florence as philosopher and mathematician to Cosimo II de' Medici, Grand Duke of Tuscany. Years before, the opponents of Copernicus had declared to him: "If your doctrines were true, Venus would show phases like the Moon." Copernicus had answered: "You are right; I know not what to say; but God is good, and will in time find an answer to this objection." The God-given answer came in 1611 when Galileo, after improving the magnification of his rude telescope from 8 times to 30 times, saw the "Mother of Love" cycling through phases from full to new, just as the Moon did. The only explanation for this was that Venus is in orbit around the Sun, that the Earth is in orbit around the Sun, and that the orbit of Venus lies inside our own.

Galileo was giddy with triumph, knowing full well the significance of his discoveries—a rudimentary optical instrument had revealed the unseen. "I render infinite thanks to God," he cried, "for being so kind as to make me alone the first observer of marvels kept hidden in obscurity for all previous centuries." Everywhere he blazoned them, deriding as a fool anyone who was

---

[245] i.e. the four large moons, Io, Europa, Ganymede, and Callisto—the number of the smaller satellites is 59 and counting.

not immediately convinced of their accuracy. In an incisive letter written in 1613, Galileo ridiculed the supporters of the Ptolemaic theory, while attempting to illustrate that the Copernican system was not only correct but consistent with the Catholic interpretation of the Bible. This is what eventually got him into trouble, for in the second point of the Tridentine Creed, every Catholic accepts "the Holy Scripture according to that sense which our holy mother the Church hath held, and doth hold, to whom it belongeth to judge of the true sense and interpretation of the Scriptures."

Brought to Rome in 1616 to testify about the said letter, Galileo was reprimanded by a pope and a cardinal inquisitor, but cleared of heresy charges. They admonished him to curtail his forays into the supernal realms: the motion of the heavenly bodies, having been touched upon in the Bible, was a matter best left to the Holy Fathers of the Church. A prohibition on teaching the Copernican theory was now, and only now, imposed on every Catholic, and a decree condemning *De Revolutionibus* was issued by the Congregation of the Index on the 5th of March, 1616—more than seventy years after the work was first published.

Prior to this, the cardinals had in fact congratulated and celebrated Galileo, finding nothing offensive in his propositions; among his supreme judges were people who had just a moment ago fully agreed with him. For centuries, popes and ecclesiastics had relied on astronomers to set a date for Easter Sunday years in advance, thus reinforcing the power and unity of the Church. Rome had worked hard to collect astronomical instruments, measurements, tests, and lore; as recently as 1613, a Jesuit professor by the name of Christoph Scheiner (1573-1650) had undertaken the task of building the first telescope with two corvex lenses, as proposed by Kepler in his *Dioptrice* (1611). During the 16th century, the Church had adapted a number of cathedrals across Europe (and a tower at the Vatican itself) so that their darkened vaults could serve as solar observatories, employed for example by the Jesuits to confirm theories about the Earth's revolution which they were now forbidden to teach.

The opposition that had begun to mount thus slowly would suddenly snowball: some arch-conservatives downright refused to even look through a telescope; in order not to make the observations which could overturn a theory that was 1,500 years old. Or, if they did look, they denounced what they saw—such as moving spots upon the Sun indicating its rotation—as illusions from the Devil. The haughty and arrogant behaviour of Galileo, who was too bold even by Kepler's standards, did nothing to further his cause. Some of Galileo's most bitter opponents were the Jesuits, whom he had offended by ignoring their prior studies. Even his great admirer, the famed Jesuit Cardinal St. Robert Bellarmine, would ultimately turn against him.

For seven cautious years, Galileo obeyed the orders of the Vatican, turning his efforts to less dangerous pursuits, such as harnessing the Jovian satellites in the service of navigation, to help mariners determine their longitude at sea. By modifying his telescope, he also developed a compound microscope. In 1623, however, Galileo found reason to return to the heliocentric theory like a salmon to its spawning ground. That year, the intellectual Cardinal Maffeo Barberini ascended the Chair of Peter as Urban VIII. The new pope was a lover of the arts: he, more than any other pontiff, was responsible for the interior decoration of St. Peter's, aided by the foremost representative of the Italian Baroque, Gianlorenzo Bernini; it was Urban who commissioned Gregorio Allegri to write a *Miserere* for nine voices, a masterpiece for long afterwards reserved exclusively for the Vatican, sung by the castrati[246] of the Papal Choir at the Sistine Chapel every year during Holy Week. In his younger days, Urban had himself written poems, and more to the point, a sonnet of compliments to the Florentine astronomer, mentioning the sights revealed by "Galileo's glass."

Galileo was thus induced to visit Rome again, and had six long talks with the newly-elected pope in 1624. He hoped that Urban, who had admired him so long and well, would let the new scientific ideas flow quietly into the Church until they inconspicuously replaced the old—that was, after all, how the pagan ideas of Aristotle and Ptolemy had become Christian doctrine in the first place. Urban quietly hinted that the restriction on Copernican teaching would indeed be relaxed, so the next year, Galileo began to write the *Dialogue concerning the Two Chief World Systems* believing that the Pope was on his side. Early in 1632, this massive conclusion, six years in the writing, to his exhaustive investigations, was published in Florence. To get it licensed by the Church, he had managed to collect no fewer than four imprimaturs.

Back in 1616, Galileo had publicly sworn not to "hold, teach, or defend" the

---

[246] Whereas women were forbidden to perform in churches and theatres throughout the Papal States, surgically-altered male vocalists were admitted to Catholic choirs as early as 1599, and the practice was not abandoned until the 19th century.

Copernican theory, so all he did in his *magnum opus* was to prove the Ptolemaic view impossible. As was customary of the time, he put forth his ideas in a dialogue form, with a moronic character by the name of Simplicio offering the most asinine counter-arguments against the new world system. The purpose was obviously to mock the Aristotelians, but the Dominicans succeeded in convincing the Pope that the above character was actually a caricature of His Holiness. Urban at once ordered the presses stopped and all the copies bought back—the book had been sold out by then.

Galileo was once again summoned before the Holy Roman Inquisition. Many in Rome were hesitant to prosecute him because his violation was questionable, but on the 12th of April, 1633, Galileo was finally conducted to the Dominican church of Santa Maria sopra Minerva, where his trial was conducted by the Commissar-General of the Inquisition. There were ten judges at the trial, all of whom were Dominican cardinals; one of them was Pope Urban's brother, another his nephew. Threatened with torture, Galileo renounced the doctrines of Copernicus, and was made to swear on his knees that he "abjured, cursed, and detested" the theory according to which the Earth goes round the Sun and rotates on its axis.

From this period then stems the contrariety between Catholicism and the new astronomy. As you may recall, Copernicus himself had dedicated his work to the pope, his patron, and the Jesuits, among them the prior mentioned Father Scheiner, had taken an active part in the new studies. Had Galileo been more discreet and had he not, above all, dabbled in biblical exegesis, he would have been allowed to write about anything, including the rotation of the Earth. He would spend the rest of his life confined under strict house arrest in his villa near Florence, forbidden to publish anything.

Of course, nothing was going to stop Galileo from writing the book the trial had interrupted, a book on physics—not in the heavens, but here on Earth. In the opening pages of the *Dialogue*, he had twice said that Italian science was in danger of being overtaken by northern rivals. The Italian academies suffered from the condemnation of Galileo and soon disappeared, putting a full stop to the scientific tradition in the Mediterranean. From then on, the Scientific Revolution moved permanently beyond the Alps. Galileo's book on the *New Sciences* was printed by a Protestant publisher in the Netherlands two years after it was completed. The Pope forbade the erection of a monument to this great man when he died at the ripe old age of seventy-eight, even though the geocentric world view had by then been completely overturned.

This pivotal event of heliocentrism was one of the most important in intellectual history. It effects were far-reaching and consequential: the coming generations of scholars never forgot the lesson of Galileo, that no amount of rhetoric can defeat the power of instruments and precise, systematic observations. By condemning the Copernican system, the Church and its theologians did a disservice to themselves, for soon Western people refused to bow their heads before the ancient authorities any longer. The Church injured itself more than the scholars it persecuted, for it thereby got entangled in the fateful battle against all the forward-moving forces of the next centuries, a battle which it was bound to lose. The spark of curiosity that had began to flicker in the Middle Ages, burst into an open flame when it was fanned by the plain truth of heliocentrism, and once flared up, it could no longer be smothered.

There have been great many attempts in recent years to play down the Catholic persecution of science. An investigation launched by Pope John Paul II into the "Galileo case" in 1979 reported "grave reciprocal misunderstandings" and errors on both sides, all having happened in a "cultural context very different from ours."[247] The 1616 prohibition was consequently reversed, and in 1993, the Polish Pope delivered an apologetic message to the conference commemorating the 450th anniversary of the publication of *De Revolutionibus* at Copernicus' *alma mater*, the University of Ferrara. His fellow-countryman was, according to John Paul II, a man both of science and of faith.

With the rise of natural science, it was becoming painfully obvious that Aristotle's deductive method, considered the basis of reasoning for over two thousand years, could only demonstrate truths which were already implied in the premises. It was imperative that the study of natural science be made respectable by furnishing it, if not with separate metaphysics, at least with a method and aim of its own. In the writings of the great English statesman, Sir Francis Bacon (1561-1626), did the philosophical basis for the Scientific Revolution eventually find its expression.

Bacon began his studies at Trinity College, Cambridge, when he was 12

---

[247] *Conclusions of the Pontifical Academy of Sciences in the Galileo Case* (Oct 31, 1992)

years old; he later described his teachers as "men of sharp and strong wits . . . shut up in the cells of a few authors, chiefly Aristotle, their dictator." His father died when he was only 18, and being the youngest of six sons, this left him virtually penniless. Turning to the law, his brilliant political career got an early start when he was elected to the House of Commons at the age of 23. In 1591, he became confidential advisor to Robert Devereux (1567-1601), Earl of Essex, who soon replaced Raleigh as the Queen's favourite. Bacon would subsequently serve as an advisor to both Elizabeth and King James I. He was knighted by the latter in 1603, and made Lord Chancellor and Baron Verulam in 1618; in 1621, he was also created Viscount St. Albans. Further serving as regent in the King's absence, he was left in almost complete charge of the English government. The whole world looked at him, all light gathered around his person, causing not only his philosophical achievements to appear more luminous, but also his moral indiscretions to seem more blatant than they actually were. The two great scandals he got entangled in were the trial against the Earl of Essex at the end of Elizabeth's reign and the trial against himself at the end of James'.

Essex had become a national hero in 1596, when he had shared command of the expedition that captured Cádiz from Spain. Three years later, he would accept, against Bacon's advice and to the great joy of his rivals, the position of Lord Deputy of Ireland. He was sent with a large army to Ulster, the northeastern quarter of the island, with the task of quelling the rebellion of one Hugh O'Neill. Essentially a provincial figure, this renegade Earl of Tyrone nevertheless wrapped himself in the rhetoric of a broad Irish Catholic nationalism. O'Neill fought, he said, so that "the Church of Ireland be wholly governed by the pope," and "that all principal governments of Ireland, as Connaught, Munster, etc., be governed by Irish noblemen." Yet the Norman-Irish lords, the descendants of the original 12th-century Anglo-Norman conquerors, categorically refused to participate in a revolt whose sole intention was to secure the supremacy of an ambitious Gælic chieftain.

Alarmed by reported intrigues against him at home, Essex arranged a hasty truce with O'Neill and hurried back to London, in direct disobedience of Elizabeth's explicit orders not to abandon his command. On his arrival at her court, he was committed to custody, and after eight months without access to his wife or newly-born child, charged with insubordination and deprived of his offices. Though given his freedom after Bacon had pleaded for him, Essex was henceforth banned from the court and not allowed to approach the Queen. While imprisoned, the Earl had hatched a plan to rid the court of the enemy party and to establish his own about Elizabeth. To these ends, he sought support from his former army in Ireland and even entered into negotiations with the King of Scotland. The Queen's government was perfectly prepared, however, and the attempted coup of the Earl and his followers ended with the siege of Essex House on the 8th of February, 1601.

In his defence, Essex asserted that the insurrection was aimed solely at his greatest competition for the Queen's favour, the man responsible for the introduction of the potato to Ireland and tobacco to England—Sir Walter Raleigh. Bacon again pleaded in private for his former patron, but as a lawyer sworn to defend the Queen and a member of her Learned Council, he would be instrumental in securing for Elizabeth a guilty verdict at the trial. It is doubtful, however, that Bacon ever thought the sentence of death would be carried out: the expected sign of contrition sent by the Earl while confined in the Tower was never delivered. After the execution, Bacon wrote at the behest of the Queen, *Declaration of the Practices and Treasons attempted and committed by Robert late Earl of Essex and his Complices*. So widespread was the involvement of nobles and officers in the Irish army that many of the co-conspirators were treated with remarkable leniency, being either sentenced only to a fine and imprisonment or condemned to death and then pardoned. The involvement of Lord Mountjoy, Sir Charles Blount—the new Irish commander and Lord Deputy of Ireland—was blankly overlooked due to his success against the Gælic rebels in Ulster.

The wars in Ireland and against Spain were expensive, inflation soared, and Elizabeth would be over £400,000 in debt before she died. In order to get more money, she had to go to Parliament, which was already angry about the privileges she had granted her favourites. She gave way graciously, delivering her "Golden Speech," a model for the relationship between monarch and subjects in future years, with obligations on both sides. A few months later came news of victory in the prolonged battle against the Gælic rebels. For a year, Mountjoy had fought a war of attrition, burning homes, destroying cattle and crops, laying waste large areas in the north of Ireland. In September of 1601, the Spanish allies of Tyrone landed at the southern town of Kinsale; by October, Mountjoy had them firmly besieged within the city walls. Early in December, O'Neill marched south to relieve the siege—the battle on the morning of Christmas Eve would last less than three hours: after the Irish dispersed and fled, the Spanish surrendered. O'Neill himself would finally submit to Mountjoy on the 30th of March, 1603, six days after the Queen's death.

Elizabeth was the last of Henry VIII's children and none of them had any children of their own. Her parliaments had broached the question of the succession several times, urging the "Virgin Queen" to marry, but she had always managed to avoid wedlock. The English crown would consequently pass into the hands of the Stuart dynasty that had long ruled in Scotland: after Elizabeth's forty-five year reign, her throne was taken by James, the son of Mary Queen of Scots, and a descendant of Henry Tudor's daughter in the fourth generation. The Welsh were factored into the Jacobean equation by their conciliation to the idea that James was the true heir of that first Tudor, transforming the Elizabethan pretentions of "Britishness" into something more than a mere antiquarian interest.

James was also the first English monarch to have more than one name: his full name was Charles James Stuart; the "Charles" was in honour of Mary Stuart's brother-in-law, Prince Charles of France. Though Mary had been an ardent Catholic, her son had been raised in Protestant circles, and the Irish Supremacy Act of 1603 once more asserted the English king's power over Irish churches. James was willing to let the subjugated Irish chieftains to live on their ancestral lands as English-style nobles, but not as petty kings of the old Gælic social order. Unhappy with their new roles, O'Neill and a boatload of other Gælic chiefs took ship to Spain in 1607. This "Flight of the Earls" gave James the excuse he needed to confiscate the most fertile lands of Ireland and sponsor settlements of English and Scottish Protestants throughout Ulster.[248]

That the Ulster Plantation was perceived as forming part and parcel of the reconstruction of "Great Britain" in the aftermath of the Union of the Crowns is well illustrated in Bacon's *Certain Considerations Touching the Plantation in Ireland* (1609). The planters were to admit no Irish customs, never to intermarry with the Irish, and to permit no Irish on their lands, giving rise to

---

[248] The Latinate neologism "Gælic" also applies to the Scottish form of the language which in pre-Reformation Scotland was known as "Erse," or Irish.

the only ethnic British identity in the world.[249] With the qualified exception of royal weddings, the streets of England, Scotland, and Wales never see the levels of British paraphernalia that appear every summer in the loyalist communities of Northern Ireland.

James was of an unusually timid and distrustful disposition, living in an incessant fear of conspiracies and assassination attempts. He was especially anxious of the power of sorcery, fully believing that the tempests which beset his 15-year-old bride, Anne, on her voyage from Denmark were raised by witches. Himself the author of a treatise on *Dæmonologie* (1597), James ordered all the copies of Reginald Scot's *Discoverie of Witchcraft* (1584), a scholarly exposé of the fraud involved in witch trials, to be burned. A law that subjected witches to death on the first conviction, whether they had done any harm or not, was passed by Parliament in 1604 and disfigured the English statute book for the next 150 years.

James was very proud of his theological erudition, and to the horror of his neighbours, made a constant exhibition of it in pedantic debates. This combination of learning and lack of tact led Henry IV of France to refer to him as "the wisest fool in Christendom." To make matters worse, James was a leading theoretician of the divine right of kings. In Scotland, he had been overshadowed by Parliament, and came to England determined to be a true king. He delivered long speeches to the English Parliament, informing the wealthy merchants of London that policy was the "king's craft" and thus "far above their reach and capacity." Unfortunately, the burgeoning middle classes had the capital needed by the King to wage his wars and conduct the royal business. James was unable to assert England as a great power because war required taxes and taxes required the approval of Parliament. English naval power grew so weak that even ships bringing coal coastwise from Newcastle to London were not protected from pirates. When James had done ruling, it was said that Great Britain was smaller than Britain.

It was in the course of the struggle between King and Parliament that Bacon's own fall also came about. Nineteen years into the reign of James, when Bacon was at the peak of his fame and power, he himself was brought

---

[249] Subsequently thought of as one of the British Isles, Ireland was frequently depicted in mediæval maps as lying closer to Spain than to England.

under charges: he was accused of having accepted bribes while Lord Chancellor, and on the strength of numerous testimonies and his own admission, sentenced unanimously by the House of Lords to the Tower of London, fined £40,000, prohibited from holding public office or sitting on Parliament. Bribery was perfectly common among government officials at that time, and the suit was brought against Bacon not because of exceptionally serious chancellorial misconduct, but because targeting a person of a peculiarly visible status would impact the whole system. This was precisely why the King asked Bacon to submit without protest to the judgement: James promised to reinstate him to his former position at the first available opportunity, as long as he waived all defence, as easy as it would have been considering his great renown, his extraordinary eloquence, and the relaxed opinion of the time towards the type of crime with which he was charged. Bacon's sentence was remitted, he paid no fine, and spent only four days in the Tower. However, instead of taking office or a seat in Parliament again, he put his talents to better use writing books.

Generally considered the founder of English empirical philosophy, Bacon sought to develop a systematic model of scientific thought and practice. He planned, and in part put to writing, a major work known as the *Instauratio Magna* or *Novum Organum* (1620), which became one of the last principal works to be written in Latin within the Western culture. Like the title indicates, it was intended to be no less than a "Great Reformation" of Sciences, and therefore contained a "New Instrument" to replace that of Aristotle. Scholastic, or Aristotelian, logic was concerned with the formal properties and not the factual accuracy of an argument. Its principles were abstracted by Aristotle from the reasoning then current among Greek mathematicians. But mathematics alone cannot provide adequate description of phenomena: e.g. geometry can render an account of an optical phenomenon, but cannot explain why it happens. To Bacon, mathematics was therefore but a sterile manipulation of numbers, and as such, unable to advance our knowledge of the universe.

According to Bacon, true knowledge proceeds solely from observations of nature, not from calculations, authority, belief, reason, accepted opinion, or religious dogma. Mediæval "sciences" were overthrown because human reason now had recourse to instruments that made up for the limitations of human perception. The naked eye is weak and can see neither the very small nor the very distant, but microscopes and telescopes compensated for this deficiency. The mind itself is prone to all kinds of error, miscalculation, and prejudice, but new methods of reasoning would direct it to sure and reliable conclusions. For Bacon, logic should supply the intellect with the instruments necessary for detecting and overcoming the perils that threaten its pursuit of scientific knowledge.

Particularly in the first volume of his *Instauratio Magna*, Bacon traces a systematic study of the way illogical and unempirical factors affect the function of the human mind. Reason needs to interpret nature in the same manner as a good commentator expounds an author by seeking to penetrate as deep as possible into the nature of the work. "False notions," deeply entrenched in our thinking habits, distort our understanding of the "nature of things," thereby erecting a barrier for the formation of correct judgements. Bacon distinguishes four categories of such deceptions or "idols": the first, called the *Idola Specus*, is formed by those delusions that result from the personal character of every private individual. The second group, otherwise the *Idola Theatri*, stems from received traditions, which are blindly given credence to, although they are as fictitious as the fables of the theatre.

The third section of idols, the *Idola Fori*, are "the false appearances imposed upon us by words," that is, they cause the conventional labels of things to be confused with the things themselves. The last division, the greatest and the hardest to conquer, consists of the *Idola Tribus*, the innate delusions of our race, which constantly makes us interpret physical nature as human, causing the original to lose its peculiarity and assume the tone of its translator. To Bacon, the human mind is in fact a mirror of things, but ground in a way that alters the things it mirrors. What he calls "nature" is not the product of our apperception, but something whose true appearance human sensibility can full well recognize, if only it frees itself from idols.

The vernacular tongues were fast replacing Latin as languages of culture, but had not yet achieved the consistency, richness, and precision necessary for philosophical and scientific purposes; in early English use, "grammar" meant only Latin grammar, as Latin was the only language taught grammatically. However, if an author wished to be broadly read and understood, he had to pen his writings in these "vulgar" languages, and Bacon therefore put forth many of his ideas in the King's English. While all of Bacon's works were banned by the Spanish Inquisition, his *Of the Proficience and Advancement of*

Learning, Divine and Humane (1605) also gained the distinction of being listed on the Roman Index.

Filled with attacks on Aristotle and his mediæval disciples, it draws an analogy between the great voyages of discovery and the exploration leading to the advancement of learning. It likens the mediæval sciences to a nun wedded to Christ, shut in a convent, and thus left barren, the works of Aristotle to light tablets ever staying above water due to their inferior weight, and truth to naked, bright day-light that cannot display the masks, disguises, and pageants of the world half as magnificent as the candlelight of falsehood. Bacon fancied himself an inventor of a process that would kindle "a light in nature . . . which would eventually disclose and bring into sight all that is most hidden and secret in the universe." All in all, he gave an imposing call to scientific research, and from his time onward, Britain contributed greatly to this progress.[250]

The main reason for Bacon's pre-eminent influence was the fact that he was the greatest penman of the age, not to mention one of the most consummate English prose writers of all time. Ben Jonson says already of the parliamentary speeches of the young Bacon that "no man ever spoke more neatly, more pressly, more weightily, or suffered less emptiness, less idleness, in what he uttered," that "his hearers could not cough or look aside from him without loss," and that "the fear of every man that heard him was lest he should make an end"; indeed, his method of induction itself has been shown to derive from humanist rhetorical techniques.

One curious idea introduced by his later admirers is that Bacon was the true author of the works that are usually considered the intellectual property of one William Shakespeare. The Bard of Avon never personally published any of his own plays, since he saw no right of existence for them outside the stage. He was presumably born in 1564, married in 1582, appeared in London after unknown events in 1592—already a known and admired theatrical director and actor—returned in 1610 to his native town of Stratford, where he died in 1616. Any closer details about the world's most versatile dramatist have not

---

[250] In his famous essay, Macaulay asserts that since the aim of Bacon's philosophy was to multiply the human enjoyments and to mitigate human sufferings, it was raised above all preceding philosophy, which deemed it inappropriate to serve pleasure and progress, and was content to remain idle.

been brought out by the exceptionally vigorous investigation.

It appears that the ability to produce stylish verses was exceptionally common among the Englishmen of that era. In fact, Bacon complains that during the course of the 16th century, the "affectionate study of eloquence and copie of speech . . . grew speedily to an excess; for men began to hunt more after words than matter; and more after the choiceness of the phrase, and the round and clean composition of the sentence, and the sweet falling of the clauses, and the varying and illustration of their works with tropes and figures, than after the weight of matter, worth of subject, soundness of argument, life of invention, or depth of judgment."

However, as of yet, there practically existed no narrative prose literature in the English language. Its primary source of inspiration would be the King James Bible, first published in 1611—over two centuries after Wycliffe had completed his translation of the Vulgate. This "Authorized Version" was rendered in clear, idiomatic English by a conclave formed of the leading prose writers of the Jacobean period, among them naturally Sir Francis Bacon.[251] Rightfully described as "the purest well of our native English, in its grand simplicity standing out in contrast to the ornate and affected diction of the language of that time," no other book has had a greater or more healthier influence on the English prose style.

Back in the 15th century, the several emigrant Byzantine scholars had brought into Italy thousands of Greek manuscripts of the New Testament, which the new art of printing made widely available in the West. The new biblical scholarship thus brought forth not only pointed out multitudes of errors in the Latin Vulgate, but gave the scholars a sense of personal judgement superior to that of the Church. Some of the errors had crept in over the centuries, but some had obviously been made by St. Jerome himself. As to the Old Testament, the Hebrew text itself was found to be full of errors due to the carelessness, ignorance, and doctrinal zeal of early scribes. In pursuit of a purer version of the Word, some humanists began working on new editions, based on previously unused ancient texts.

However, with the transfer of authority from the Church to the letter of the Scriptures, it was harder to acquire a printing permit for a Bible than it was

---

[251] To Bacon, religion was above reason, but not opposed by it; on the contrary, the office of reason was to meet the objections and refute the arguments that were set against the truths of revelation.

the original text. William Tyndale, who became the first to translate the New Testament directly from the language it was originally written, had to leave England to get his work published (1524); many of his translations were burned at special ceremonies in London and Antwerp, and he was himself later sent to the stake. It has been estimated that about 90 percent of the New Testament in the King James Version is the work of Tyndale—which might explain its status as the "only literary masterpiece ever to have been produced by a committee." The verse division it utilizes was first added by a French printer, Robert Estienne, in his 1551 edition of the Greek New Testament. The focus of religion was no longer the life and passion of Christ, but a description of these: a book. From this first dawn of a literary age leads a straight line to rational religion and rational culture, to "enlightenment."

It was Bacon who lent the ambitions of the age, aspiring as it passionately did to knowledge and power, the fitting catch-phrase: *Scientia potestas est*, "Knowledge is power." The perfect vehicle for his contemplation of the future, so far as the advancement of learning was concerned, is his unfinished romance, *The New Atlantis* (1627). Written late in life and published posthumously, it recounts the story of a secret house of learning, set like More's *Utopia* in an unknown part of the world. It was, in fine, a college instituted for attaining to knowledge of the physical world by organized observation of its regularities, the ultimate aim of such understanding being man's mastery of his environment.

This "College of the Six Days' Works" pursued the "knowledge of causes, and secret motions of things" in high towers set upon high mountains, as well as in deep caves dug under great hills. In all directions new and great discoveries were made, aimed collectively at the construction of a complete "natural history," from which the primary laws of nature would be apparent. According to Dr. William Rawley, Bacon's chaplain and literary executor, he had also intended to construct a "frame of laws" as the machinery of an ideal commonwealth, but had laid it aside in favour of his natural history, which "he preferred many degrees before it"—thus leaving it to subsequent thinkers to apply the scientific method to social and political issues.[252]

The New Atlantis marks the beginning of a long tradition in Western

---

[252] Thomas Hobbes, who went on to write *Leviathan* (1651), the most influential political treatise of the age, served as Bacon's last secretary.

literature where scientists are seen as redeemers. While the Reformation, the scientific advances, and the social upheavals had shattered the foundation upon which the human mind had built, it was still quite inconceivable that science and religion would go their separate ways. Material as they were in paving the way for the Age of Enlightenment, the various internationalist groups forming across Europe in the 17th and 18th centuries have often received only a passing mention or footnote reference in the historical writings on the period. Rather than referring themselves to old mysteries, such mystical societies as the Rosicrucians were on the contrary very much an image of their time, seeking a common ground between faith and science.

The Rosicrucians made their existence first known in the early 1600s, with the publication in Germany of three anonymous documents, directed at "all of the scholars and rulers of Europe." The first and most important was the *Fama Fraternitatis*, published as a prefix to a larger work, called the *Allgemeine und General-Reformation der ganzen weiten Welt* (1614). The second was a twelve-page booklet entitled *Confessio fraternitatis Roseæ Crucis, ad eruditos Europæ*, issued by the same publisher in Kassel the following year. They presented the Rosicrucians not as a secret society, but as a fraternity of men, united by common philosophy and by a freely accepted discipline of anonymity. By working together with those of like mind, they hoped to bring about a Utopian epoch of peace and justice, where all social and political institutions would be purged of the tyranny of the past.

The thinkers of the era were no longer content to view the cosmos and the life it contains as a mystery to be simply accepted: the true natural magician of the Renaissance would be able to understand man, the microcosm, through his study of the macrocosm of nature, since the former was a perfect representation of the latter. This call for observations in nature could be seen as an act of devotion: Christians should study not only the Holy Bible, but also the Book of Nature, the second book of divine revelation. It was believed that the study of science enabled man, created in God's image, to recover the knowledge and mastery of nature that he had possessed before the Fall. The Rosicrucians saw science not as an enemy of religion, but as the highest expression of religion, to know and understand the mysteries of God's universe.

The third and most elaborate Rosicrucian text was issued in another town by a different publisher from the other two. A book of 146 pages in its

German edition, the *Chymical Wedding* (Strasbourg: 1616) is generally considered to be the work of a young Lutheran pastor from Württemberg by the name of Johann Valentin Andreæ (1586-1654).[253] Also known as the *Hermetick Romance*, it is an extended alchemical allegory, most likely based on Andreæ's experience of the symbolic ceremonies of the Order of the Garter, conducted at the ducal court of Württemberg and the University of Tübingen while he was a student there.

Following the tradition of imaginative analogues to individual spiritual transformation that had developed during the Renaissance, the *Chymical Wedding* uses techniques of mediæval allegorical narrative, combined with metaphorical meditation and elements of popular storytelling. Brimming with personified concepts and their emblematic accoutrements, ciphered messages, and paradoxal formulæ, its essential idea is a wedding of the elements, symbolizing the spiritual joining of man with God. Ceaselessly demanding interpretation from the reader while never offering a key to restrict its meaning, we can trace from its achievement the entire allegorical tradition, across such works as Bunyan's *The Pilgrim's Progress*—now considered a forerunner of the modern novel—all the way to Lewis Carroll's *Alice in Wonderland*.

Especially in England, the early Rosicrucian movement became deeply involved with alchemy. The works of such writers as Robert Fludd (1574-1637), the person responsible for introducing Rosicrucianism to Britain and giving it its English name, show how large a part alchemy played in Rosicrucian literature. While nowadays routinely dismissed as an immature precursor to modern chemistry, alchemy never implied solely the making of gold. In fact, most alchemists were theoreticians who studies philosophy rather than chemistry. A London physician, Fludd distinguished his spiritual—and emphatically Christian—form of alchemy from "laboratory" alchemy, which he counted equally with other arts and sciences, describing it only as the "art correcting Nature in the mineral realm."

More important than transmuting base metals into gold was the separation of the pure essence of a substance from its impurities. To the alchemists, the

---

[253] The rationale of seeking to make gold out of the baser metals was for generations predicated on the Christian doctrine of bodily resurrection, Luther himself subscribing to the theory of transmutation by this analogy.

immutable gold represented the divine spark in man—their quest to make gold and to find the "elixir of life" were one and the same endeavour. The *arcanum*, that mysterious substance which they sought, was at the same time supposed to be a universal remedy against all diseases, a master-key that would unlock all the mysteries of nature, a general emancipatory formula that would solve all the riddles of the universe; this is the deeper meaning of the "philosopher's stone." Through observance of extensive and careful rituals, the alchemical initiate would create a stone that could turn lesser minerals into the purest of all metals, just as his heart and mind were rid of base thoughts and left pure. The process of transmutation was intended as a transitory rite of purification, rather than as a means to quick financial gain; the "Great Work" of the true alchemist would thus lead to self-transformation and, ultimately, to regeneration of the whole world.

Fludd was followed in Britain by the famous Welsh alchemist, Thomas Vaughan (1622-1665)—twin brother of the noted metaphysical poet Henry Vaughan—who translated, under the pseudonym of Eugenius Philalethes, a number of "Hermetic" works from the Continent, including the Rosicrucian manifestos. These anonymous documents were copied, translated, and circulated around Europe. Though no one openly admitted to being a member of the Order, Rosicrucian philosophy quickly became popular and fashionable. Between 1614 and 1620, about four hundred pamphlets were published on the subject in various countries.

One morning in March of 1623, the people of Paris woke to find the walls of their city covered with posters carrying the following message: "We, deputies of the principal College of the Brethren of the Rose-Cross, have taken up our abode, visible and invisible, in this city, by the grace of the Most High, towards whom are turned the hearts of the just. We show and teach without books or signs, and speak all sorts of languages in the countries where we dwell, to draw mankind, our fellows, from error and from death." The Parisians were worried because daring to assert that there was an alternative way of salvation to that of the Church made these posters look like Huguenot propaganda. Most Frenchmen had never equated Frenchness with Calvinism, like most North Germans had equated Germanism with Lutheranism. On the contrary, after the prolonged civil wars (1562-1598) had finally ceased, the average Frenchman tended to equate Protestantism with treason.

CHAPTER 36

In the period between the Peace of Augsburg (1555) and the outbreak of the Thirty Years' War (1618-1648) falls the terminal struggle of the European Renaissance. Although the Peace was a great victory for Protestantism, it did not settle the religious conflict in Germany, and hence could be nothing more than a truce. The Protestants were weakened not only by doctrinal divergences between Lutherans and Calvinists, but the failure of a number of Protestant states to join the Protestant Union (1608), allied with England and the Netherlands. As a response, the Catholic League had been formed in 1609, allying with Spain, which meant that if and when war broke out, most of Europe would be involved, and the fear of this disaster kept the peace for another decade. It was a minor local skirmish on the fringes of the Holy Roman Empire that finally set off the Thirty Years' War, the most bitter and costly conflict fought on European soil prior to the 20th century.

Emperor Rudolph had been succeeded by his brother, Matthias; but like Rudolph, Matthias was forced aside before his death, and from 1617 on, Duke Ferdinand of Styria, the grandson of Emperor Ferdinand I, wielded all the real power in Austria and the Empire. A year later, he received the crowns of Bohemia and Hungary, but the Bohemian nobles, aware of the ruthlessness with which he had sought to eradicate Protestantism from Styria, rose against him. They offered the crown of their humble country to Elector Frederick of the Palatinate, the son-in-law of King James of England, and the most prominent member of the Protestant Union. Shortly after accepting the crown, Frederick V was forced to flee, earning the name of the "Winter King." He was also deprived of his Rhenish estates, which were given to the Duke of Bavaria, founder of the Catholic League.

The division of the Protestant party prevented the sending of assistance to the Protestants of Bohemia, and their rebellion was suppressed within two years. In 1619, Ferdinand had ascended the throne of the Holy Roman Empire as Ferdinand II, and Catholicism was now reimposed in Bohemia through cruel oppression. The Jesuits, who recognized the brutal fact that Catholicism had no chance as long as the arts and sciences were allowed to remain in the hands of anti-Catholic forces, came to play a crucial role in this. They took over the University of Prague and developed a powerful network of colleges, confiscated the Protestant printing presses and systematically burned all Czech books and manuscripts, tainted as they were with heresy. The German language was introduced in Bohemian government, education, and judiciary. From then on, until the formation of Czechoslovakia (1918), the history of Bohemia was merely a part of the history of Austria.

Most of Germany was overrun by Catholic armies early on in the Thirty Years' War, and German Protestantism was threatened with extinction. The commander-in-chief of the Catholic League was one Johannes Tserclæs (1559-1632), Count of Tilly, who had already helped Ferdinand suppress the Bohemian rebellion. Dubbed a "monk in the garb of a general," he had consecrated his banner to the Blessed Virgin, but let his mercenaries loot freely, for "after all they are not nuns." However, the War lost its religious character within its first decade, and became more and more politicized as it spread. There were shifting alliances and local peace treaties throughout what was actually a series of wars which directly or indirectly consumed virtually every nation in Europe.

The entry of Gustavus Adolphus, considered the last decisive Scandinavian intervention in European affairs, was not primarily motivated by the aiding of fellow-Lutherans, who, in fact, strongly protested to his invasion. The King was simply practising Swedish power politics, and turned against the imperial party above all because it supported his hereditary enemy in Poland, and its claim to the throne of the Vasa. What is more, he was alarmed by the designs of Albrecht von Wallenstein, whom Ferdinand II had appointed "General of the Baltic and Oceanic Seas" and who did his damndest to be worthy of that title. Following the Second Battle of Leipzig, the Lutheran king of Denmark prevented Sweden from taking advantage of her gains by making war against her. In the Peace of Prague, which falls approximately at the midpoint of the War, the leading Lutheran power, Electoral Saxony, went over to the imperial side. As to Wallenstein, he realized the restoration of the Empire to be impossible as long as it was impeded by the union with papacy, and was preparing to defect with his armies to the Swedish side, before he was dismissed from his office and murdered by order of the Emperor in 1634.

The now commencing last phase was entirely under the sway of France, which entered the War as the ally of Protestant Sweden, as it appeared that the Habsburgs might unite all Germany under their rule. The promoter and organizer of this policy was a Catholic cardinal, Richelieu (1585-1642), and the War spilled over to Italy, when he renewed the French efforts to gain foothold there. Upon Richelieu's death, his life's work was taken over and brought to conclusion by Mazarin (1602-1661), another Roman cardinal. In the end, it was just Emperor Ferdinand and his ever faithful comrade-in-arms, Maximilian of Bavaria, who fought in the name of the Virgin Mother, their belovèd "Generalissima." Both died before the War was over, and eventually everyone had forgotten why it had started, with Catholics fighting in Swedish, and Protestants in imperial armies.

During those thirty years, huge portions of Central European population were wiped out by war, famine, plague, and pillage. There were parts of the Continent where unburied corpses lay so thick that the regions had to be avoided until nature had done its work with the decaying bodies of the dead. The population of Germany was slashed by more than a half and its landscape was utterly destroyed: most of the cities were in ruins, the flourishing unions of towns had dissolved, commerce, industry, and crafts were in a slump. Switzerland, on the other hand, a country whose religions divisions had not prevented it from remaining neutral throughout the War, was an island of affluence when its independence was formally recognized by the Peace of Westphalia in 1648. The treaty did not include France and Spain, which kept fighting each other for another dozen years.

The Westphalian Treaties sealed the political and religious disunion of the Holy Roman Empire, and turned it virtually into an inland state. Hardly any major mouth of water remained German: the Rhine was Dutch, the Weser, the Elbe, and the Oder Swedish, the Weichsel Polish; the Baltic was fought over by the Polish, the Swedish, and the Danish; the North Sea by the French, the English, and the Dutch. In the Vatican, far away from the horrors of war, Innocent X still urged to carry on the battle, sending his legate to contest the peace at Westphalia. In his bull, *Zelo Domus Dei* (1648), the Pope denounced the first treaty to use the term "toleration" in connection with religion as "null, void, invalid, iniquitous, unjust, damnable, reprobate, inane, and devoid of meaning for all time." But he was not given ear to, and the peace endured, laying the foundation for the construction of German political and religious life. The German Calvinists were offered the same rights as were already widely enjoyed by Catholic and Lutherans.

In the place of the mediæval ideal of a united "Christendom" appeared the set of international rules that is still familiar: Europe was to consist of several independent and sovereign states, the leaders of which would emerge by a formula to be derived internally. As a result, the office of the emperor became less and less significant, and his power was confined to the Habsburg hereditary lands in Austria, Hungary, and Bohemia. The emerging global powers of the 17th century—Britain, Holland, and France—were growing in strength by carving out direct and indirect spheres of influence in Germany and Italy, and divvying up the imperial possessions of Spain and Portugal—all regions formerly dominated by the Habsburgs. For the first time, the German states, great and small, claimed political sovereignty in the French sense: they could have their own armies and currencies, and make their own economic legislation; they could establish relations with foreign courts, make war and conclude treaties and enter into alliances, as long as they did not attack the emperor himself.

The absolute monarchism of Catholic princes was to destroy the influence of the papacy in the south as truly as Protestantism had destroyed it in the north. No longer able to use the imperial framework as a broad European vehicle for propagation of the faith, Catholicism began to fragment along national and secular lines. Catholic princes would limit the authority of the Roman Church, challenge papal leadership, and undermine the power of the religious orders, though always only to the degree compatible with orthodoxy. Behind the Catholic clergyman stood, as ever, the confidence-boosting, all-powerful Church, whereas the Protestant minister was sustained only by his obsequious parish. The former was a servant of the still great, universal Church, while the latter was just a lackey of some small, provincial ruler. With this is associated the fact that Protestantism not only produced as rigid intolerance as Catholicism, but that this intolerance was much more stubborn, pedantic, parochial, and sectarian. The varied Protestant sects derided one another in exactly as immoderate and undignified a fashion as they one and all derided "popery."

The Protestant princes were only too glad to be delivered from papal supremacy, and took the new Churches under their fatherly protection, guarding their subjects in all matters of religion in the exact same manner as had previously been done through Rome. They were anxiously concerned to prevent the complete union of the Protestant Churches, and thus religion was irrevocably enclosed within state boundaries. Instead of one vicar of Christ dictating people's relationship to their God, there were several, each less qualified than the next, each having less influence, and as a result, less responsibility. This, combined with the prevailing distaste for the type of religious war where religion soon gets set aside in favour of a temporal power struggle, led the more enlightened circles to set religious fanaticism aside in favour for jaded toleration. The princes still determined which religion their subjects were to profess, but the wandering intelligentsia could move from one to another unrestrainedly or serve them all in turn.

Apart from the largest duchies and electorates, the territorial division of Germany, a legacy of centuries of tumult and strife, cannot be illustrated, or even adequately described, by any map of conventional measures. The Holy Roman Empire of 1648 contained 234 autonomous entities, including 51 self-governing free cities and several independent ecclesiastical states, such as the archbishoprics of Salzburg and Trier, and the bishopric of Münster. Each of these maintained, according to their varying means, regal pomp and decorum by mercilessly taxing the peasant and merchant classes. All commoners, be they burghers or peasants, were despised as scum of the earth, fit only to provide the court with money, soldiers, and servants.

The servility of the Germans before the least of lords was boundless. This was the age that gave birth to the innumerable court offices: that of lord chamberlain, court chaplain, court physician, head stableman, head gamekeeper, and what not; even craftsmen valued, more than any others, the titles of court tailor, court shoemaker, court baker, and head gardener. The increasingly elaborate court ceremonies took their toll from the maestros of word and tune. While these ceremonies were theatrical enough in themselves, actual theatre evolved into the focal point of social life. The modern theatrical terminology—words like *scène*, *rôle*, *stage*, *costume*, and *orchestration*—was conceived in the 17th century. *Scénario* is a fitting term for the theatrical court rule: the ceremonies of the court were not amusements, but the burdensome duty of the élite; as the central social events, they were the primary means of communication before the advent of mass media and general literacy. It was during this époque that the word "political" acquired the additional meaning of sophistication, artfulness, diplomacy, and worldliness that it still retains in popular language today.

Many of the great scholars and thinkers had fled from Germany during the Thirty Years' War, and all the crucial stimuli in the fields of art, luxury, and manners came from abroad. The small princely courts imitated the great courts of south and west, thanks to the numerous diplomatic delegations that actively advised their domestic courts of the policies and culture of foreign countries. The literary language of the nobility was already uniformly French, which still remains the official language of diplomats the world over. And practically everyone was a member of nobility anyway, since it was quite easy to acquire peerage either by purchasing a title or by offering your services to some petty local prince. This *noblesse de robe*, against which the hereditary nobility fought as vehemently as unsuccessfully, finally embraced all the upper ten thousand. After the decisive victory, the characteristic traits of the era became, as is common in cases like this, the object of public contempt. Even today, we are reminded of this in the words "theatrical," "aggrandizement," "sanctimoniousness," and "grandiloquence"—all used in the most defamatory sense.

During the feudal period, society was simply an alliance of families, who swore allegiance to the house of their liege lord. In the beginning of the Modern Era, Western society was transformed from a union of families into a union of subjects—kinsmen became countrymen. As the family relinquished its authority over its members, it also ceased to answer for their actions and well-being. The state took over many of the affairs that had previously been the business of the families, such as public safety and social services. As churches became an arm of the state, welfare and education became government concerns. Through the means of education, subjects would recognize their place in society, and thus be loyal to their ruler out of conviction.

The central political concept of the period was *raison d'état*, good of the country—the duty of the subject was to the sovereign, and to the sovereign alone; he was expected to sacrifice even his life for his king and country. To rebel against your lord was no longer just violating an oath of allegiance, it was high treason, and all the resources of the state would be brought to bear against you. A charge of treason, in its variety of interpretation, could be levelled against anyone from the greatest in the land, such as queen-consorts and the highest nobility, down to humble peasants upset with land changes, and drunken revellers suspected of vandalizing royal proclamations. From then on, national unity played the same role for the new State as the unity of Christianity had played for the Church.

The political and social reconstruction of Europe took the same course in Catholic as in Protestant lands: during periods of unrest, state religion was the guarantor of national unity; in times of peace, it steered towards a Christian way of life, part of which was unconditional obedience to the dictates of the government. The idea of the king as God's deputy became widely accepted, preparing the ground for our modern state-theology, whose dogmatism nowise yields to that of the Church and equally breaks and enslaves the spirit of man. The government now considered its prerogative, nay its duty, to intervene in all aspects of life, to watch and control the private life of the subject like a tyrannical father or husband.

By abolishing the monastic system, the Reformation deprived women of the only chance they had to live their own lives. Protestantism replaced the Catholic ideal of celibacy with the ideal of the Christian home as the proper milieu in which to serve God. In the sex-negative world of the Middle Ages, the purpose of marriage was to procreate and avoid fornication (I Cor. 7). The Protestants added emotions to marriage: those of spiritual partnership, mutual devotion and comfort, intimacy and affection. Reciprocal love, companionship, and the rearing of common children were added to the priorities of the husband's life beside his public activities. However, the ideal was an ideal and seldom reality.

While the husband and wife were expected to love each other, this did not mean that young people would have been allowed to choose their mates. Parents still arranged the marriages, though it was deemed reasonable that the future partners would get to meet each other at least once before the wedding. By love was meant not romantic love or passion, but patient devotion that was presumed to grow with the union. Though it was acceptable for an unmarried woman to be difficult and demanding, the wife's humble submission was an absolute prerequisite to a happy marriage; her sacred duty was not only to love, but also to honour and obey her husband no matter how violent and abusive he might be. The conflict between the absolute rule of the husband and the loving union demanded by religion was unresolvable.

The great family bible was the most important fixture in the house, not only because of its religious function, but because in it were recorded the births and deaths of family members. Grace was said before each meal; home was the second church, where the father of the household held family worship. "Wives, submit yourselves unto your own husbands, as unto the Lord. For the husband is the head of the wife, even as Christ is the head of the church. . . Children, obey your parents in the Lord: for this is right." (Eph. 5:22-23, 6:1) In exactly the same manner, the monarch of the realm was the father of his subjects; obedience towards both the head of family and the head of the state was ordained by God. According to the then prevailing doctrine of "passive obedience," the king had the same authority over his subjects as a father had over his children: he answered only to God, and not to his subjects, who had no right to opposition regardless of how the ruler acted.

The Reformation also eliminated the possibility of getting one's marriage annulled, and Protestant denominations reacted badly to failed marriages. Quarrelsome couples were bullied into reconciliation through various different bed and living arrangements. Receiving a divorce for incompatibility was an immensely difficult and time-consuming process, which humbled and discouraged even the most irreconcilable. Divorce was granted if one party had committed adultery, but not if both had. The guilty party was not allowed to remarry until the innocent party had either died or remarried. Permission to remarry had to be obtained either from the former spouse or the secular ruler.

Bigamy, on the other hand, was easy and common. More and more Western people moved from the country to the cities and no one asked the newcomers if they were married or had children. In England, bigamy was not even a crime in secular courts until the 17th century. Long after the old pagan handfasting had been replaced by the Christian tradition of monogamous marriage, the usual rules of fidelity were invariably relaxed for the annual May Day celebrations. These pagan rites induced pious horror in the Puritans, who sought to suppress the "greenwood marriages" of young men and women, who spent the entire May Eve in the woods and brought back garlands of flowers with which the village was decorated the next morning. "Merrie Olde England" would disappear only with the Puritan Revolution, if then, for that kind of full frontal assault on merry-making and folk culture could ultimately only end in disaster.

Never was there a king more concerned with protecting his poorer subjects than Charles I (1625-1649) of England. He supported the peasant against the landed gentry, the craftsman against the manufacturer, the wage-earner against the employer. Unfortunately, his efforts to set minimum wages enraged the middle classes just as much as his desire to protect peasants from enclosures angered the landowners, estranging Charles from the most powerful classes in his kingdom. So for eleven years, from 1628 to 1639, the headstrong king tried to rule without Parliament, and thus also without the financial support of this powerful section of English merchants, whose ideology was founded on the accumulation of riches.

Charles had for his advisor an extremely capable man, Thomas Wentworth, Lord Deputy of Ireland, who had left Parliament to join the King's service. He pointed out that Charles could manage without Parliament only by economizing, and came up with many extraordinary means by which the Exchequer could be filled without the aid of Parliament: feudal rights of the Crown were revived or extended, titles were sold, tariffs were raised, forced loans were exacted, and monopolies were granted. These measures, most notoriously the extension to the entire kingdom of the "ship money," a tax previously levied only on the seaside towns, naturally stirred up opposition, but Wentworth organized an effective machinery to put down open resistance.

Charles' second chief advisor, Archbishop William Laud, was less successful within his sphere of influence and would ultimately ruin the whole plan. His determination to impose conformity on the Church of England through the Star Chamber turned the court's name into a byword for unfair judicial proceedings. In the early stage of its colonization, the population of New England was made up almost solely of Puritans—people who were discontent with the religious conditions in England and thought the New World would offer them greater freedom of worship. These early colonists therefore celebrated their first divine service together with an especial feeling of thanksgiving.[254] Though this "chosen people" apparently wanted to spread out and live more or less separately, the constant native threat did not permit such a lifestyle. Thus, with an eye to "mutual safety and welfare," the colonies of Massachusetts, Plymouth, Connecticut, and New Haven would combine to form the United Colonies of New England (1643), the first germ of today's

---

[254] "Thanksgiving" is also the literal translation of *eucharistia*, the Greek word for communion.

imposing federal state.

When Archbishop Laud attempted to force his religious establishment on Scotland, Scottish Presbyterians took up arms and invaded England. Charles then turned to Wentworth, who obtained money from the Irish Parliament to raise an 8,000 strong Irish army to fend off the Scots, but the King failed to get similar support from the Short Parliament (1640) and dissolved it in just three weeks. The next English Parliament, known as the Long Parliament (1640-1648), used the crisis to seize control of the government: the new House of Commons impeached and executed Wentworth, newly created Earl of Strafford, on suspicion of intending to use the Irish troops against the King's domestic opponents; the Star Chamber was abolished and the Archbishop burned at the stake. On the 21st of October, 1641, Ireland rose to rebellion, reconquering Ulster practically in one night and driving the British settlers out of the province; to incite their countrymen at home, they spread stories of massacre and Irish cruelty, many of which are still believed in Britain today.

Though the ensuing conflict has long been called the English Civil War, the vast majority of Englishmen were neutral in the struggle. A breakdown of the House of Commons shows that the merchant, the lawyer, and the country gentleman could be found nearly as often on the side of the King as on the Parliamentary camp. The division between Englishmen was along personal and religious, not social lines: those who felt wronged by Charles leaned towards Parliament, while those who had received royal favours tended to support the King; most of the Puritans and other religious radicals belonged to the Parliamentary camp, while most of those who stood by the Crown were either High Church Anglicans or Catholics. The majority of the population never took sides, preferring according to a contemporary account to avoid the hazards of "an unlawful war" in which one "might well be excused for defending neither."

During the first phase (1641-1646) of the War, Parliament allied with the Scottish Presbyterians against Charles and the Royalist forces. The indecisive early engagements were remarkable only for the emergence to military prominence of Oliver Cromwell, an inconspicuous member of the Long Parliament. He strongly championed the Self-Denying Ordinance, by which the weak Parliamentary army of "decayed tapsters" was reorganized (1644-1645) into the New Model Army of "ironsides," middle-class cavalrymen of heterodox religious views. In distinction to the long curls of the aristocratic "cavaliers," they sported a closely cropped haircut that made them look like "roundheads."

Unable to halt the mounting losses of his army, Charles was finally (1647) obliged to surrender himself to the Scots, who sold him for money to Parliament, which tried him for treason. The King managed to escape, however, and gained the Scottish support by promising to establish Presbyterianism in England and Ireland. Once more the Scots invaded England, only to be defeated by Cromwell's troops at the Battle of Preston (1648). Purged from Presbyterians by Colonel Pride, the new Rump Parliament proceeded to terminate the monarchy and abolish the House of Lords. With Charles again in custody, this Parliament voted for his execution in 1649. It was the first time public authority had executed a king, either in England or anywhere else in Europe. This not only showed how far political thought had advanced and how strong the ignoble classes had grown, but also reminded once more just how powerful a political force religion could be.

Often when the resistance to tyranny and the demand for religious freedom are combined, as they were in the Puritan Revolution, the victors set up a new tyranny and intolerance. The Puritans did not seek to end the Established Church; their aim was to capture and control it—and a minority can make the majority conform to its will only by force of arms. Cromwell's oppressive measures to impose Puritanism were vigorously resisted in Wales, and the Welsh supported Charles in the Civil War. Inspired by the legend of Prince Madoc, many Welshmen braved the horrors of the Atlantic passage to flee religious persecution. William Penn planned New Wales, later named Pennsylvania, the Keystone State where the country began. The city of Philadelphia, or "brotherly love," subscribed to a policy of total religious toleration, soon becoming the fastest growing settlement in America. Other Welsh emigrants played as instrumental a role in the founding of the new nation: Robert Morris was the primary financier of the American Revolution; Thomas Jefferson composed the Declaration of Independence and the Virginia Statute for Religious Freedom; Gouverneur Morris wrote the final draft of the U.S. Constitution; and John Marshall became the father of American constitutional law.

Only one time has Great Britain followed an absolute monarch: in Lord Protector Oliver Cromwell. His English Republic (1649-60) would give the British Isles their first unified government—which was mainly due to the fact that he was the only ruler to have a standing army. Before he landed in Dublin, the Irish practically owned Ireland, English power merely clinging by the skin of its teeth to some outer corners of the island. The Irish had for their leader Colonel Owen Roe O'Neill (1590-1649), a scion of the mighty house of Tyrone, who had come to the aid of his native country after serving thirty illustrious years in the Spanish army. From August of 1649 to February of 1650, Cromwell roamed Ireland, leaving behind him a name forever synonymous with ruthless butchery. He relied on massacres and starvation, paying his soldiers and financiers with the vast lands confiscated mostly from the Norman-Irish lords of the Irish midlands, who had joined the rebellion reluctantly and only to defend themselves against Puritan policies. He then turned to Scotland, where he put down a Stuart uprising.

It took Cromwell's successors in Ireland another two years to complete the work that he had left unfinished. The Articles of Kilkenny (1652) finally ended the longest, most appalling, and inhumane war ever visited upon poor, luckless country. Yet her sufferings, great and dreadful as they had been, were far from over. In 1654, some 3,000 of the leading Irish families were banished west of the River Shannon and Cromwell's forces began the "transportation" of Irish Catholics as labourers to the West Indies; by 1656, over 60,000 Irish men and women had been sent as slaves to Barbados and other islands in the Caribbean—many of their descendants later moved to the United States. By 1658, the population of Ireland, estimated at 1.5 million before Cromwell, had been reduced by two-thirds, to 500,000. The Irish calligraphy, illuminations, and portraiture of the Gospel Books that rank among the greatest art treasures of the Western world were ravaged by Puritans during the 17th century. Even greater works of art may have been irretrievably lost to time, plunder, and the wilful destruction of ancient artefacts by the Protestant fanatics.

The Puritan merchants of London and the southeastern coastal cities of England demanded free trade. All industrial monopolies, which had previously covered roughly 700 staple products, were abolished, and all government efforts to supervise the quality, fix prices, control wage rates, maintain employment, or influence worker-employer relations were abandoned. The First Navigation Act (1651) not only gave the mercantile element in the English Parliament virtual monopoly over British foreign trade, but also brought England into a war with the Dutch. By the mid-17th century, the

Netherlands was the foremost commercial and maritime power in Europe, and now her maritime trade was threatened with paralyzation.

The First Anglo-Dutch War (1652-1654) may not have made much sense for a Puritan, but made plenty of sense in the light of the 1,700 ships the British captured. The Dutch were the "carriers" of Europe, boasting a fleet larger than those of Britain and France combined. As Sir Walter Raleigh himself had once reported, the Dutch built "every year near one thousand ships and not a timber tree growing in their own country."[255] Amsterdam was the busiest trading town and the richest city on the Continent. Alongside the entrepôt trade, the city developed a key international money and capital market, and till the 18th century, came to exercise a near monopoly on both the diamond industry and the trade in diamonds. Though the Dutch Republic broke more than even in the naval battles with England, these also laid a firm basis for Britain's future as the world's dominant maritime power; the British Navy became regular military service and was added more warships than the early Stuarts had managed to build during their 40 years of reign.

England's becoming Puritan meant that in some circles there now prevailed a more sympathetic attitude towards Jews, who had been expelled by royal edict in 1290. In fact, the Puritans built so much on the Old Testament that it is difficult to regard them as a Christian sect. They assumed the names of Israelite heroes, prophets, and patriarchs, made use of Hebrew phrases, proverbs, and parables. The first formal petition to readmit the Jews into England was made to the Rump Parliament by two Baptists, Johanna and Ebenezer Cartwright. English millenarians believed that the Second Coming and the Rule of the Saints were close at hand, maybe as close as the Barebones Parliament (1653), a hand-picked selection of the "godly," convened after the Rump was dispersed by Cromwell's troops. The "Fifth Monarchists" (Daniel 2:44) wished to impose the Mosaic code in place of common law and a Sanhedrin of Saints to assume authority of the state (7:18), but their reluctance to terminate the indecisive war against the Dutch forced Cromwell to dissolve the "Nominated Assembly." He would not allow the first Protectorate Parliament (1654-1655) to convene until he had personally made peace with Holland.

---

[255] Oak was imported to the Netherlands mostly from the Black Forest region of Germany.

The Dutch Republic demanded that its Jews be recognized as full citizens abroad and that no restrictions be placed on them when they visited a foreign country. In 1655, Rabbi Menasseh ben Israel (1604-1657) arrived from the Netherlands to address the Lord Protector of England "in behalf of the Jewish nation." Menasseh was more a zealot than a thinker, claiming among other things to have discovered the Ten Lost Tribes of Israel among Native Americans, an idea later revived by the Mormons; the Rabbi argued that the Messiah and the Millennium could not come until the Jews had spread to every corner of the globe, including England, yet it was mainly for commercial reasons that Cromwell was keen to see the Jews return: the Jewish merchants and bankers of Amsterdam were desirable allies in the financial and political war with Spain (1655-1659).

Thus, when the Jews were allowed to resettle in England after an interval of three and a half centuries, Amsterdam became the springboard for their return. However, being only a commoner, Cromwell could not overturn a royal edict; in fact, the edict of expulsion has not been formally revoked to this day. Nevertheless, a large number of Marranos would settle in London from the mid-17th century on, working as merchants. They obviously did business with the Netherlands, but also with Spain and Portugal, and both the East and West Indies. This made them useful to the Lord Protector regarding the plans of the dead king's exiled heir, Charles Lennox, and also of the Spanish and Portuguese in the New World.

In search of greater economical opportunities, a large number of Portuguese Jews had taken part in the Dutch expedition to Brazil. When the Dutch Republic was forced to cede Brazil back to Portugal in 1654, many Brazilian Jews returned to Amsterdam, but several also settled for the first time in North America. They made port in the city of New York, which at that time was still a Dutch colony called New Amsterdam. It was first discovered by Henry Hudson, an English explorer then in the employ of the Dutch East India Company. After voyaging to the river named in his honour, Hudson set sail on an English venture to explore the Northwest Passage to the north of Canada, thought by the early modern navigators to be a fast route to the Far East. By traversing the fabled passage, it was hoped that the Portuguese monopoly over the lucrative spice and silk trades might be broken. Despite the many heroic and often fatal attempts, the passage was not successfully navigated until the early 20th century.

The Sephardic refugees from Brazil were seeking equality in a land of liberty where they could worship freely and have the same rights and responsibilities as the Christian citizens, but the relative Dutch tolerance did not translate from old Amsterdam to New. On the contrary, Governor Peter Stuyvesant wrote to the Amsterdam Chamber of Commerce, complaining that "Spaniards and unbelieving Jews" manipulated the slave-trade and denied black African labour to the good Calvinist burghers of his pious colony. His attempts to deport the unbelievers were, however, overruled by the Dutch West India Company, many investors in which were Amsterdam Jews. The Jews of New Amsterdam, in the meantime, kept putting pressure on Stuyvesant until the Governor finally granted them full rights of citizenship.

When the control of New Netherlands passed peacefully to the British ten years later, many Dutch merchants stayed in New York and the Jewish settlers continued to have full citizenship. Dutch influence over language and culture would remain significant not only in that region but throughout the colonies; the New York *Kehillah* was to provide the other colonial Jewish communities with leadership and resources, in turn looking to London and the West Indies for support and guidance. Home to approximately 2 million Jews, New York City accounts for over one-third of the present Jewish population in the United States, and remains the principal port of entry and place of settlement for new Jewish immigrants, including East European and Middle Eastern Jews.

With the arrogance of one who is convinced that he is carrying out God's will, Cromwell finally decided in favour of a thorough military dictatorship that prefigured European fascism: in March of 1655, Britain was divided into twelve districts, each controlled by a major-general of the army—they were in charge of the local militia, they ran the courts, they appointed the officials. Two years hence, the second Protectorate Parliament offered Cromwell the crown of England, but he declared contemptuously that he wanted to serve the nation "not as a king, but as a constable."

Blue laws suppressing public immorality were strictly enforced: it was of course sinful to drink, play, and make noise, but it was also sinful to dance, to attend the theatre, to write love letters, to wear a stiff collar, and to enjoy good food; on Sundays, everything was a sin. This excessive keeping holy of the Sabbath echoes the spirit of Judaism: the Puritans saw themselves as Yahweh's foot soldiers, whom He had sent to destroy with fire and sword the Sadducees, Canaanites, and Gentiles; their God was the God of Moses, the unmerciful God of vengeance, wrath, and zealous righteousness.

Great as the exertions made by James to extirpate witchcraft were, they fade to insignificance when compared to those made during Cromwell's reign. Under the gloomy tenets of Puritanism, the persecution of witches reached its climax, and for the first time, the trials and executions drew public attention. After the famous Witchfinder General, Matthew Hopkins, had gone through Suffolk testing multitudes of miserable victims with pins and needless, he pronounced it to be infested with witches. Thereupon Parliament appointed a commission, sending two eminent Puritan divines to accompany it, with the result that in this small, rural county alone five dozen people were put to death for witchcraft in just one year. It has been asserted that during the few years of the Commonwealth, more alleged witches perished in England than in the whole period before and after.

An equally bleak chapter was inscribed by witch-hunts also on the early history of New England. The multitudes of nonconformists who had fled from England to America did not learn the lesson of toleration. As soon as they found themselves in a position to persecute, they tried their best to outdo what they had endured. For being absolutely right means that all who disagree are absolutely wrong and must therefore be restrained or eliminated as menaces to society. Among those whom they attacked were the Quakers, who themselves repudiate the use of violence. One of the most subjective and individualistic of Protestant sects, the Society of Friends worships without minister or liturgy, teaching the existence of an "inner light" of divine revelation. Like its predecessor Anabaptism, Quakerism has an honourable record of tolerance, eschewing as it does association with the worldly governments, wherein alone lies the power to persecute.[256]

During the Puritan rule, Christmas celebration was attacked in Britain as paganism for its joyful, often boisterous features. Cromwell's army of gun-toting iconoclasts were ordered to tear down the Christmas decorations, condemned as Popish idolatry. The ban on Christmas also spread to the

---

[256] In pushing for the separation of State and Church, Jefferson and Madison were responding precisely to these inter-Protestant battles for dominance, not to the wars of post-Reformation Europe; unfortunately, when coupled with the republican form of government, this led to the Church gaining in influence what it had lost in power, as observed by de Tocqueville in 1831.

American colonies, where it was to remain in force all the way down to the year 1836, when the narrow-minded descendants of the "Pilgrim Forefathers" would finally overcome their aversion and proclaim the 25th of December a national holiday.

In February, 1658, Cromwell dissolved his fifth and last Parliament, dying in September of the same year. His son, Richard, succeeded him, but the "Tumbledown Dick" was too weak to gain the respect of the army. In the ensuing chaos, General Monk, the Scottish commander, marched on London and recalled the Long Parliament. England welcomed home the murdered king's eldest surviving son in May, 1660, and attempted to bring things back to how they had been before the Puritan Revolution. The Stuart scion was restored to the throne as Charles II, while the body of Oliver Cromwell was exhumed, hung, and beheaded.

The Church of England was restored to its former glory, Christmas, Easter, and Pentecost returned. All Puritan restrictions, be they moral or stylistic, were lifted: people not only rushed to all the pleasures that had previously been strictly prohibited, but also demanded that they be as wild and unruly as possible. The public appetite for high style and a licentiousness that realized the worst Puritan nightmares was generously fed by Restoration comedy; a whole generation of comedy-wrights filled the stage with the most shameless blasphemy and debauchery. Restoration England would not only renounce the Puritan hypocrisy and prudery, but also regard piety and decency as the surest signs of pretense.

CHAPTER 37

Before the Protestant Reformation, the Catholic Church had—even in its periods of decline—provided a universal forum for the otherwise warring princes and statesmen of Western Christendom. Protestantism would completely sever the nominal bond of unity the papacy had constituted for several hundred years, and give birth instead to a dozen greater and hundreds of lesser Churches and denominations, each demanding absolute authority in the matters of religion within their respective jurisdictions. By the mid-17th century, there were 180 independent sects and sub-sects in Europe, all based on the Bible, each more dogmatically intolerant than the next. This multitude of incompatible and contradictory movements, each claiming a monopoly of truth, would inevitably usher in religious skepticism and deism.

With the dissolution of religious orders, the system of initiations with private ceremonies and solemn oaths was adopted by various lay fraternities. At the very period when the Rosicrucians disappeared from the public eye, a movement known as Freemasonry came to fore. While regarded today as a somewhat sinister, secretive gentlemen's club whose continued existence is excused by its donating hefty sums of money to charity every year, Masonry's most fascinating aspect has always been how so many men, from so many different backgrounds, can meet together peaceably without any religious or political quarrel, fondly referring to one another as "brothers." Its ideology, founded on metaphors of the architecture of the universe and the building of the Temple, was, and is, non-confessional; although each candidate was required to confirm his belief in a supreme being—which the brotherhood dubbed the "Grand Architech of the Universe"—it did not expand on the subject, but left religion and its practice to the individual Mason. It furnished an international network of communications that transcended the Roman sphere of influence and threatened to make organized religion redundant.

Though the most recent studies have identified Sir Robert Moray, Secretary of State for Scotland, as the first person recorded to have been made a Freemason (Newcastle, 1641), for long the honour belonged to a fellow-

Royalist, Dr. Elias Ashmole (Warrington, 1646), the famous Rosicrucian apologist and founder of the Ashmolean Museum in Oxford. Ashmole studied law in London from 1633 to 1638, and his principal means of support in the years leading up to the Civil War was soliciting in Chancery. However, while still in his youth, he tells us that he had entered into the condition to which he had always aspired: "That I might be able to live to myself and studies, without being forced to take pains for a livelihood in the world." Evidently Baroness Kinderton, whom the low-born barrister had met through his first wife's family, more or less adopted him, and Baron Kinderton became his patron.

Soon after the outbreak of war, Ashmole retired to his native Staffordshire, where the deposed Charles I had appointed him to collect the excise. In 1645, he was appointed Commissioner of Excise for Worcester, and his official duties brought him frequently to Oxford, which had been selected as the Royalist capital.[257] Although most of its citizens were so anti-Royalist that the King had to disarm them, the University was loyal to the Stuarts, and Ashmole himself became a member of Brasenose College.[258]

Oxford, at the time, was the centre of scientific activity in England. Here first gathered the men who were to form the nucleus of the Royal Society, which for the longest time was synonymous with science in the British public mind. In the first half of the 17th century, there arose a number of groups of men who gathered, usually in private houses, to discuss the latest intelligence in a large number of fields. Much of the business, as well as literary and political discussion, was transacted in these "coffee-houses," forerunners of that most British of institutions, the club. It was the period when the status of natural sciences as a form of social activity became established, as hundreds of active naturalists worked within these societies, maintaining communications with one another through their publications and through a peculiar system of private correspondence.

---

[257] Christ Church provided a good substitute palace, other colleges and halls becoming warehouses for rations and supplies, factories for the manufacture of gunpowder and foundries for cannons. The Royal Mint was brought over from Shrewsbury, and college plate was pillaged for silver and gold to turn into coin. The miracle is that the city emerged virtually unscathed from the siege that subsequently took place, but which was abandoned, without the expected battle.

[258] whence he received his honourary M.D. in 1669

In 1648, the first truly scientific fellowship, the Oxford Philosophical Society, was started in the lodgings of Bishop John Wilkins (1614-1672), then Warden of Wadham College. The brilliant group this man of vision collected round him met weekly to discuss "Philosophicall Experiments." By 1652, it had about thirty members, the most notable being Robert Boyle (1627-1691), who is often considered the founder of modern chemistry; Sir Christopher Wren (1632-1723), who contributed greatly not only to architecture, but also to astronomy and anatomy; and Professor John Wallis (1616-1703), who held the Savilian Chair of Geometry for over half a century. Important in part for his introduction of the use of infinite series as an ordinary part of analysis, Wallis also introduced fractional and negative exponents, and discovered the formula for *pi*, which still bears his name. The meetings at Oxford continued for eleven years, but after Cromwell's death, many of the members returned to London and began meeting at Gresham College.

Ashmole was back in the capital already in 1646. His first wife had died in childbirth, and in 1649, he became the fourth husband to Lady Manwaring, a wealthy widow twenty years his senior. Her estate having established his fortunes, he became something of a patron himself; with the help of her wealth, Ashmole was also able to form an imposing collection of alchemical, astrological, medical, and historical manuscripts. Together with other founding members of the Royal Society, he was among the purchasers of Dee's immense library of mediæval science books. He secured at least five original manuscripts by Dee, and in 1650 edited one of them, *Fasciculus Chemicus*, under the anagrammatic pseudonym of James Hasolle. His groundbreaking *Theatrum Chemicum Britannicum* (1652) was an annotated and linguistically harmonized anthology of all the orthographically heterogeneous works on alchemy by previous English authors. Other alchemical writings followed, influencing both Boyle and Newton.

It must again be emphasized that "occultism" during this age was not invariably distinguishable from what was considered science, or "natural philosophy" as science was still referred to in Ashmole's day. To the 17th-century mind, the worlds of nature, man, and divinity were intrinsically intertwined, and to study one without acknowledging the others would be a distortion of the truth. The view frequently taken by modern writers is that the sole function of alchemy was to provide a starting-point for the more "objective" sciences; yet alchemy was much more than a set of parlour tricks or some vague belief in sympathetic magic—it was, at the time, the state of the art in theoretical sciences, far more advanced in fact than some current science.

As Bacon noted in the *Advancement of Learning*, "the aim of magic is to recall natural philosophy from the vanity of speculations to the importance of experiments." Both alchemy and chemistry place emphasis on carefully conducted practical experiments, and point out that in addition to qualitative observations it is also essential to carry out quantitative measurements. Since the Middle Ages, the alchemists had been using skilfully constructed precision scales, and had recorded a vast amount of experimental data concerning the preparation and properties of different substances. Modern chemistry assimilated all their accumulated knowledge of chemical processes, all their formulas, materials, and techniques dealing with identifiable chemical changes and the physical properties of matter.

It was precisely in the hands of the so-called "Oxford Chemists" that chemical science began to diverge from the art of alchemy: Dr. John Mayow (1640-1679) discovered that air is actually composed of at least two different gases, while Dr. Robert Hooke (1635-1703) came up with the first rational explanation of combustion; it was Boyle who first revived the ancient atomic theory, which perceived an infinite universe of atoms in continual motion through the Void, with matter composed of discrete particles combining in different ways to make up all the diversity we behold. From Boyle onwards, the work of chemists has been predicated on his statement that a chemical element is a pure substance which cannot be broken down into any simpler substances by chemical means. Of course, we now know that nuclear reactions can actually transmute one element into another—modern physics is alchemy that works.

In 1659, Ashmole's collections were considerably enriched when the famous gardener and plant hunter, John Tradescant the Younger (1608-1662), deeded to his fellow-collector his "Closett of Rarities," the initial source of the Ashmolean Museum. The Tradescant collection was almost entirely the creation of the elder Tradescant (d. 1638), and contained not only books and antiquities, but geological and zoological specimens as well—including the stuffed body of the last dodo seen in Europe. The mixture of natural and man-made rarities was typical of the age, but the Tradescants were ahead of their time in opening their private collection to the paying public—a practice continued at the Ashmolean, Britain's first public museum.

After voyaging the high seas with Sir Robert Maxwell, Tradescant the Elder had set up a garden at Lambeth, near London, eventually becoming head gardener to Charles I, a position in which he was succeeded by his son. The discovery of the New World itself had largely been fuelled by a quest for herbs and spices, and during the Tulipomania of 1634, tulips were actually traded at a higher price than gold. The two Tradescants were responsible for what amounts to a monopoly of plant introductions into Britain: they brought over an incredible number of exotic flowers, shrubs, and trees, and many of the best known garden plants will forever be associated with their names. Unfortunately, the exchange of plants in this newly-revived garden culture had a dark side: when the colonists planted gardens on the other side of the Atlantic, some of their most prized botanicals became weeds, choking out the natural vegetation.

The uneasy atmosphere that had prevailed between the Parliamentarians and the academics abated in 1660, when Charles II was restored to the throne. The ghastly tyranny of the Puritans was over, or passed to New England. The kingdom echoed again with the mirth and magic of the Renaissance. Britain took advantage of the situation where continental Latinate culture had collapsed and the use of vernacular languages had fragmented ideas and knowledge along national lines to build its own national scientific culture. The "Royal Society of London for Improving Natural Knowledge" was duly chartered in 1662, with the King not only as its official patron, but also as a Fellow. Moray was elected the Society's first president, Wilkins its first secretary. It was actually founded a couple of years earlier, growing as it did out of the group that had met for some years at Gresham College. For more than a century, it and its offshoots were the only exponents of science in Britain.

It was also the model for the French *Académie Royale des Sciences* (est. 1666), but had three significant advantages: it was free to pursue its diverse interests without interference from either Church or State and it regularly published its *Philosophical Transactions*. These gave it continuity and public standing, not to mention helping spread its findings to the rest of British society. Finally, there was a subscription for membership, largely to pay for its publications, which gave it economic independence of patronage. Once more there had appeared on earth what existed two millennia earlier in Hellenistic Alexandria: an assembly formed by researchers and teachers, laboratories and collections, necessary for the exchange of ideas and knowledge, in short, a favourable social and intellectual environment for the advancement of science.[259]

Bacon's criticism of language had led to an increased interest in linguistics, for it suggested that only a deeper understanding of language and ultimately its reform could protect us from its pitfalls. The Royal Society argued that "philosophical" language should be "stripped of all ornamentation and emotive" expressions. In December, 1664, it appointed a committee from its members on the model of the *Académie Française* (est. 1634) to fix the English language and forever protect it from change or corruption. The English Academy included the historian Sprat, the poets Waller and Dryden, with the diarist Evelyn, but luckily faded after just a few meetings: a language is best developed organically, over time, rather than trusted to an academy that will present its decisions prematurely from a fixed moment in time, with no knowledge of the future requirements from a dynamic, technological and cultural development. English is so vibrant because it grows continually, unlike French, which deliberate national efforts still keep from changing or from absorbing new vocabulary from other languages. As a result of this conservative policy, English has at present some 200,000 words in common use, French only half that number.

It is nowise an exaggeration to say that science gets invented in the Scientific Revolution. The Latin word *scientia* had long been in use, but it only meant "knowledge." In *Novum Organum*, Bacon wrote that knowledge "must begin anew" from its very foundation, new means of evaluating human observations had to be devised in order to organize facts and to explain what exists. Science was magic by new means, mastery of nature through knowledge. Bacon accepted that no one person could know or explain everything and therefore argued for corporate schemes involving both those with the means to sponsor the sciences and those with the ability to be scientists. Only by working jointly over generations could mankind begin to understand all that exists in the

---

[259] The American Philosophical Society, founded in Philadelphia by Benjamin Franklin in 1743, was explicitly modelled on the Royal Society of London. It counted among its members Charles Wilson Peale (1741-1827), the founder of the first public museum in America, and Thomas Jefferson, who remained its president even during his presidency of the United States.

universe. The Royal Society's explicitly Baconian programme for science aimed not only to "improving the useful arts, . . . [but] also to reviving ancient skills and secrets which had been lost and virtues of which would be tested by experiment."

In September, 1666, the Great Fire of London, lasting five days, virtually destroyed the city. It was rebuilt in beauty and grandeur by Sir Christopher Wren, who designed more than fifty churches, notably the rebuilt St. Paul's Cathedral, his masterpiece and one of the finest church designs of the English Baroque. Had he not found his forte in architecture, he would have been better known as the brilliant mathematician and scientist that he in fact was. Savilian Professor of Astronomy from 1661 to 1673, he lived in Oxford at the top of the tower in Wadham College in a room which became known as the "astronomy room." With the equally ubiquitous Robert Hooke, he planned the famous Royal Observatory at Greenwich, the inauguration of which in 1676 is usually considered the starting-point of modern astronomy. Hooke was the first to build a reflecting telescope (1664), which avoids chromatic aberration, the main defect of the early, Galilean telescopes, by using mirrors instead of lenses. However, the mechanism of this colour distortion was not fully understood until Newton proposed his new theory of colour, in which white light consists of different rays with different refrangibilities. Nor was the use of mirrors widely accepted until the following century, finally replacing refracting telescopes in the 20th, when metal mirrors were substituted with crystal ones with silver or aluminium front surface, resulting in completely achromatic images.

Around the Restoration, Ashmole became primarily an antiquary, publishing several exhaustive studies in that field. His loyalty was rewarded by being made Windsor Herald in the restored monarch's first appointment, a post which enabled him to deepen his research into the Order of the Garter, a work he had entered upon five years earlier. He was given the privilege to peruse, collect, and transcribe any documents that he might wish to use in his studies. This eventually led to the publication of his *tour-de-force*, *The Institutions, Laws and Ceremonies of the Most Noble Order of the Garter* (1672), still regarded as the definitive text in the area. Not only an history of the Garter, but an account of all the other chivalric institutions in the West, it was the first literary work to refer favourably to the Templars since their suppression.

In the words of Ashmole, the Knights Templar were "no less famous for martial achievements in the east, than their wealthy possessions in the west. . . Which gave occasion to many sober men to judge, that their wealth was their greatest crime." Within a quarter of a century since their dissolution, a host of new, secular orders began to appear, and continued to appear for centuries afterward. Although at first composed of fighting men, they were not limited to landless knights, provided no military training, were organized around no military hierarchy, had no land or holdings of any kind, and no revenue. Principally honorary establishments by the kings or great nobles, their military accountrements and nomenclature was as metaphorical as those of the Salvation Army; but in their initiations, ceremonies, and secrecy, they would look to the Templars as a model.

When Ashmole was offered the post of Garter King-at-Arms in 1677, he arranged for it to be conferred instead on William Dugdale[260], his father-in-law by his third marriage. By that time, his collection of curiosities had grown in scale and stature to the point where he could donate it to Oxford University as a major scientific resource. Oxford, for its part, was obliged to construct a separate building (1678-1683) in order to house the vast collection, which, according to a contemporary source, consisted of twelve wagonloads. In addition to displaying objects, the Ashmolean Museum was also a centre for scientific research, and remained so for over a century and a half. It contained a library and rooms for undergraduate lectures, and in its basement was the first university chemistry laboratory. In 1706, *The New World of Words* defined the term "Museum"—a novelty in English—as "a Study, or Library; also a College, or Publick Place for the Resort of Learned Men," with a specific entry for "Ashmole's Museum," a "neat Building in the City of Oxford."

In the mid-19th century, the Oxford University decided to establish a new Museum of Natural History, at which point all the scientific specimens were transferred to the new institution. Having lost what had become the most important element of its collection, the Ashmolean was to find a major new role for itself as the Museum of Art and Archæology, one of the most important museums in Britain to this day. Many of the less wholesome exhibits quietly disappeared during the transition to the present Ashmolean building (1848), a handsome neo-Classical structure in whose basement the first *Oxford*

---

[260] a fellow-antiquary, whose works include *History of St. Paul's Cathedral* (1658) and *Baronage of England* (1675-76)

Dictionary was produced. The Old Ashmolean still stands next to the Sheldonian Theatre, and fittingly functions as the Museum of the History of Science. As well as its famous astrolabes, the museum boasts early chemical apparatus, medical instruments, and microscopes, Hooke's drawings of fleas as observed by him under one, a replica of Boyle's air pump, and a contemporary portrait of Halley. The building itself, erected by none other than Sir Christopher Wren, is a beautiful architectural reminder of the Scientific Revolution.

Stuart Britain was both politically and artistically still something of a vassal state of France. The Civil War sent not only the British court, but most leading Englishmen of letters to Paris, with Hobbes, Waller, Evelyn, Davenant, Denham, and Cowley all gathered together in the French capital. Restoration comedy reveals both the influence of Jacobean drama and French farce. Everything pointing at mysticism met with rigid opposition in France of Louis XIV, but rationalist theology was esteemed with all the intellectual pretension of the time. Sir William Davenant, the dramatist and theatre manager, reformed the stage into a great illusionistic Baroque theatre in keeping with the Classical taste of the Sun King, adopting comprehensive use of music, and even reshaping the Shakespearean pieces into dramatic operas, plays with numerous musical scenes. This trend was given the name of French Classicism after its place of birth, or pseudo-Classicism for its alleged inauthenticity.

Due to the recent civil strife, English intellectualism moved to a discussion of linguistic standardization and the authority to maintain it; the common thread between Renaissance and Classicism was the return to ancient ideals, here especially emphasizing the lucidity and simplicity perceived therein. English was still in its formative stages and writers, poets, and correspondents were constantly taking liberties with the language which we would today deem excessive; verbosity, flowery prose, and overt metaphors all had an adverse effect on thinkers, who saw the play of language as a sign of weak thoughts. The Royal Society insisted on the need of a plain and terse style for scientific exposition, meaning that the expression of the metaphysicians was replaced with a parlance that articulates the facts clearly and concisely, as if trying to imitate Bacon, giving greater importance to clarity than to poetic, penetrating analysis—subsequent lexicographers would see the Restoration as the best period for English.

The title of Poet Laureate, adopted from the Græco-Roman custom of crowning with a wreath of laurel, was first accorded to John Dryden (1631-1700), who celebrated the Restoration of the Stuarts with his *Astræa Redux*. Seven years later, he published *Annus Mirabilis*, describing the great English naval victory in the Second Anglo-Dutch War (1664-1667). The "Augustan Age" of English literature is closely reflected in the magnitude and polished elegance of his poems, but even more in their implicit public character. Dryden had a long and varied career, excelling not only in comedy and heroic tragedy, but in verse satire and translation as well—the genres which both his contemporaries and later generations have defined as representative of the period. His essays, many of them prefaces to his plays, constitute the first significant volume of English literary criticism. His successors would address themselves to a wider audience, to ordinary middle-class citizens in addition to scholars and courtiers, but the foundations of the literature of the first half of the 18th century were already laid in the 17th.

Embarrassed by the unsophisticated nonstandardization of English, Dryden took part in the tidying up of Shakespeare's language as practised by the Royal Society, helping establish durable norms for both prose and poetry. However, his comedies and tragedies nowise meet the Classical ideals, and thought the metaphysical echo of his early works soon faded, Baroque continued to live in his output. His close association with Baroque music manifested itself in his cantata for St. Cecilia's Day and even more in his operas. His and Davenant's 1667 adaptation of *The Tempest*, hastily operatized by Shadwell, proved unexpectedly successful thanks more to its music and lavish Frenchified staging and effects than any literary efforts on his part—French Classicism had finally conquered England.

Absolute monarchy or "kingship by the grace of God" was not adopted in England as it had been in France, where the king ruled as God's representative on earth. The subservient clergy provided a theological justification for the divine right at the synod which Louis XIV summoned in Paris, declaring that St. Peter and his successor, the pope, had received power from God only in spiritual, not in secular matters. The claim of the local parlements to a veto over royal decrees was ignored, and the various councils that advised Louis and carried out his instructions were staffed with capable men who were utterly dependent on him for position and income. The attachment of the potentially dangerous *noblesse de l'épée* to prestigious but ceremonial offices in the court left them no time for genuine political activity. The wealthy bourgeoisie was kept satisfied by active governmental promotion of commerce and industry, and by the opportunities to make a fortune from the state expenditures.

However, the bourgeoisie did not always stand behind the monarch. Constitutionalism represented a political theory in which the powers of the government were limited by a constitution. The Popish Plot in 1678 and the attempt to exclude James, Duke of York, Charles' Roman Catholic brother, from the English succession revealed the political parties that were then forming: the Whigs, originally a term of abuse used for Scottish Presbyterians, were the Englishmen who favoured Parliament and hated "popery"—the Tories, a term originally applied to Irish Catholic outlaws, was the derogatory name for those Englishmen, mainly of the country gentry, who still believed in ecclesiastical uniformity, the royal prerogative, and hereditary right to the crown. James VII of Scotland and II of England acceded to the two thrones in 1685. He possessed all the bad qualities of his brother, yet none of his good ones, for he was on the contrary extremely ill-mannered, ignorant, and despotic. Favours were conferred on the Jesuits, payments were offered to eminent individuals if they converted to Catholicism—Dryden himself announced his conversion in *The Hind and the Panther* (1687). The civil, judicial, educational, and military establishments were all filled with Catholic appointees; nonconformists and political adversaries the King treated with barbarous cruelty.

After James had for three years done all he could to embitter even his most loyal and patient subjects, the Whigs and Tories unanimously deposed their monarch. This time, however, there would be no appealing to the masses for support; instead, the English Parliament invited the King's son-in-law, the Dutch Protestant, William III of Orange, to take over the throne, on condition of accepting parliamentary authority. This compromise was known as the "Glorious Revolution" (1688), although it was neither; a victory of Whig principles and Tory pragmatism, it established once and for all the power of the middle classes in England. In Scotland, it took until April of 1689 for the Convention of Estates to agree that James had forfeited the Scottish crown and to recognize William III of England as William II of Scotland—the troubled Stuart dynasty would never again occupy the thrones of either country. James fled to Louis XIV, who treated him not only as an equal sovereign, but even allowed him to retain both the title of King of France and the *fleur-de-lys* in his coat of arms, rights which the Kings of England derived from the day when they were in possession of the greater part of France.

The English cant had no great trouble in reconciling the right to revolution with the obligation to passive obedience. The Glorious Revolution did not entail any democratic reforms, but merely terminated the long struggle between Parliament and monarchy, only consolidating the political hegemony of the ruling class.[261] It overthrew the monarch, but not the monarchy, and the new King was no more popular among the people than his predecessor had been. The monarchy proceeded to reinforce its own political power through the establishment of the Bank of England and the National Debt six years later, providing the financial resources necessary for the exercise of global suzerainty: for making loans and funding enterprises, such as the raising of armies and the staging of revolutions. The ideological father of the Glorious Revolution was John Locke (1632-1704), who had been introduced to William already during his own exile in the Netherlands. He returned to England in early 1689, on the same ship with the new Queen, Mary of York, whom, as the daughter of James, the British incidentally considered their rightful ruler.

In his *Two Treatises of Civil Government* (1690), Locke called for division of state authority between the subjects and the king in the manner suggested by Bacon's "double majesty state" and realized in the Bill of Rights in 1689. Bacon's phenomenological interpretation of law became the basis for the unwritten constitution described by Locke and transliterated into a written constitution by the American Founding Fathers. In direct contravention to the argument of his eminent contemporary, Sir William Temple (1628-1699), that state government arose out of an extension of paternal and patriarchal authority, the Lockean theory of social contract argues that men enter into government to secure those rights which they cannot secure themselves. In his *Letters on Toleration* (1689-1692), Locke further argued that the legislative

---

[261] Sir Christopher Wren was even commissioned to design a new palace that would have exceeded the old in size and grandeur, but it was never built. So until George IV erected the Buckingham Palace in the 19th century, the British monarch was without a principal residence of any scale or majesty.

powers of government reach actions only and not opinions, that religious conscience lies solely between man and his God, and that he owes account to none other for his faith or worship. Indeed, it cannot abide coercion, for religion in its very nature depends on the private, inward persuasions of the mind.

As Britain began to recover from its internal conflicts, science, instead of fighting, became the field in which fame and titles were won. The aim of scientific inquiry as specified by Bacon and the Royal Society was the building of a scientific world view. The revolution that began with Copernicus and led through Tycho Brahe and Kepler to Galileo came to a head in Sir Isaac Newton. Thanks to these men, the beliefs concerning the world were no longer separate and unconnected. They were linked together so that the belief according to which the Earth orbits the Sun got associated with the entirely distinct belief that objects of different weight fall with the same speed.

Newton's theory of celestial mechanics, based on his concept of universal gravitation, explained not only the planetary motions as described by Kepler on basis of Tycho's observations, but also how the Sun and the Moon affect the tides, the complex variations in the Moon's motions, and many other hitherto unexplained astronomical phenomena such as the precession of the equinoxes, first noted by Hipparchus around 120 BCE. Beliefs started to weave together into a web of propositions that were connected to, and could not exist independently of one another. Galileo's dream of a single set of physical laws to govern dynamics on earth and in the heavens was finally realized by Newton. He augmented the earlier discoveries in mechanics and astronomy with several of his own, combining them all in a single system for describing the workings of the universe.

For this purpose, Newton invented a whole new branch of mathematics, the mathematics of instantaneous motion. It is so familiar to us today that we think of time as an inherent element in the description of nature, yet this was not always so. It was Newton who introduced the idea of a tangent, that of acceleration, of slope, and the notion of infinitesimal. His apt name for that flux of time which he made stop like a shutter was "fluxion," but today we clumsily call it the differential calculus, after Leibniz. With it, mathematics finally became a dynamic mode of thought that concentrates on expressing the nature of effects in precise terms and leaves the causes of things to the metaphysician. The publication in 1687 of Newton's *Philosophiæ Naturalis Principia Mathematica*, or "Mathematical Principles of Natural Philosophy," marked the culmination of the Scientific Revolution, the definite break with the old Aristotelian-Ptolemaic world view.

Newton was born into a middle-class Lincolnshire family on Christmas Day, 1642, and to his death in 1727, dominated the intellectual life of England. A scholarly uncle took an interest in his education, sending the young Isaac away to school at Grantham and then on to Cambridge, where he eventually became a Fellow of Trinity College. However, he could not get a promotion in the University because he was a Unitarian, that is, he did not accept the doctrine of the Holy Trinity. Therefore, he could not become a clergyman, wherefore it was impossible for him to become the Master of a College. Thus, in 1696, Newton finally left Cambridge for London, where he was made Warden of the Mint; eventually, he would become Master of the Mint.

Twenty-five years earlier, his mentor, the Cambridge Professor Isaac Barrow, had demonstrated Newton's six-inch telescope before the members of the Royal Society. That day Newton was elected as its Fellow, for the tiny spy-glass showed the moons of Jupiter. Yet it was Edmond Halley (1656-1742) alone, who perceived that all the money in the Mint paled in comparison to the value of Newton's work. The second Astronomer Royal of Great Britain and the last of the brilliant set of Oxford mathematicians and astronomers, Halley paid for the publication of Newton's *magnum opus* out of his own pocket.

Like the great thinkers of the Renaissance, the natural philosophers of the age were still mostly men with a broad vision of science: Newton's another contemporary and life-long rival, Robert Hooke, was not only the greatest experimental physicist before Faraday, but also a chemist, astronomer, biologist, and inventor of scientific instruments. In his post as Curator of Experiments (1662-1688) at the Royal Society, he designed and tested equipment for ideas recommended by Fellows, making him the world's first professional scientist.

Though the microscope had been invented some thirty years before Hooke was even born, for over half a century after its invention, it remained a poor relation to the telescope. Not until Hooke published his own explorations of the minuscule was it made manifest that the microscope revealed a realm of nature as diverse in structure and as vast in scale as the telescopic universe.

Like Newton's *Principia*, Hooke's *Micrographia*, or "Small Drawings" (1665), was one of the formative works of the modern world, the first proper picture book of science. Its sixty Observations were accompanied by fifty-eight skilful engravings of the tiny objects viewed through the lens of his microscope, opening up a hitherto invisible universe to the reading public.

Philosophers had speculated about the vastness of space centuries before the invention of the telescope, but no one had seriously considered the existence of living creatures punier than fleas or inanimate objects more diminutive than specks of dust. The *Micrographia* illustrated how the microscopic analysis of ice crystals could lead to a speculation about atomic structures, how the first recognition of the cellular structure of cork instigated research into the role of air in combustion, and how the anatomical description of a fly evolved into an exploratory essay in aerodynamics and acoustics; not one of the Observations is simple, and each is a detailed starting-point for further scientific inquiry. In its optical chapter, Hooke reported for the first time the phenomenon of interference on a thin film, but it was Newton's *Opticks* (1704) that provided a dominant paradigm for further optical studies throughout the 18th century. On Hooke's death, Newton finally accepted the Presidency of the Royal Society and was knighted by Queen Anne two years later in 1705, thus becoming the first scientist to be elevated to nobility.

Best known for his formulation of the theory of gravity, his laws of planetary motion, and his discovery of the spectrum in white light, Newton was also a passionate mystic and a studious astrologer. During the crucial period of his scientific career, the two decades between his discovery of the law of universal gravitation and the publication of the *Principia*, his overriding passion was alchemy. In the 17th and early 18th centuries, alchemy and astrology were still no different from other sciences, and the scientists of the era preserved to a remarkable degree the outlook of the natural magicians of the Renaissance. The nature of light and colours, the mechanism of eyesight and colour perception, the role of the ethereal medium in the transmission of light, all had serious scientific, philosophical, and religious implications.

Newton was not interested in discovering the calculus so that in the future, pudgy, overindulged, middle-class children could sit in cold white rooms figuring out answers to algebra problems—he was seeking to discern the inner nature of the fundamental principles of the universe. He was convinced that the law of inverse squares was already to be found in Pythagoras, and was much concerned with the recovery of ancient, esoteric understanding of the universe. Bunkered in his solitary live-in laboratory at Trinity College, he spent a lot of time on alchemy, regarding it as important as his other scientific work or the work at the Royal Mint. Here, his friends attested, the fires never went out during six weeks of the spring and six weeks of the autumn; here he pored over occult literature, owning all six heavy quarto volumes of Ashmole, the *Theatrum* being his bible.

Far from being a distraction, Newton's knowledge of alchemy and Hermeticism was in fact the very trigger for his discoveries in the realm of physics. The attractions and repulsions of his speculations were a direct transposition of the occult sympathies and antipathies of Hermetic philosophy. To Newton's great contemporaries, Leibniz and Hooke, the notion that one body could attract another across empty space was mediæval and magical; they subscribed exclusively to mechanical explanations, in which bodies influence one another only by a series of direct pushes and pulls. It is clear, therefore, that without the study of mysticism, Newton never could have made the discoveries that he did; nor did he believe that a science based on occult qualities, such as action at distance by invisible forces, as opposed to observable mechanical interactions, was impossible without a return to the dead end of Aristotelianism. Newton sought the true knowledge of the universe—once known but corrupted through apostasy and idolatry.

Neither Newton nor Leibniz went as far as the people of the next two or three generations who invoked their authority. In the *cause célèbre* between Leibniz and Newton's spokesman, the Rev. Samuel Clarke, the political overtones were such that each party would accuse the other of anti-Christian tendencies. The radical reappraisal of how nature worked that was then taking place was commonly seen as fulfilling Old Testament prophecies—in his long Preface to the *Micrographia*, Hooke expressed the prophetic character of the Scientific Revolution quite succinctly: "And as at first, mankind fell by tasting of the forbidden Tree of Knowledge, so we, their Posterity, may be in part restor'd by the same way, not only by beholding and contemplating, but by tasting too those fruits of Natural Knowledge, that were never yet forbidden."

Locke, like his contemporaries, never renounced religion; in his *Reasonableness of Christianity as Delivered in the Scriptures* (1695), the Philosopher of the Glorious Revolution pleaded in good conscience—as a believing Christian and a loyal Anglican—for the termination of religious strife through the recovery of the truths of primitive Christianity. Outside his scientific activity, Newton was no reformer; he taught himself ancient Greek and various Semitic languages, including Syriac and Aramaic, in order that he could study the original biblical texts.[262] Locke had great respect for Newton as an exegete and submitted his commentaries on the Pauline Epistles to the Father of Physics for review. In his later years, Newton devoted himself almost exclusively to religious questions, authoring meticulous studies on the prophecies of Daniel and the Book of Revelation. Locke, whose theory of knowledge became the basis of Enlightenment ideas, was at least in part merely using new methods to verify ancient wisdom. The search for religious significance lay at the heart of 17th century intellectual culture, and dismissing it would produce as lopsided a picture as if an historian describing the 20th century laughed off the effect of economics.

The repeated references to "Newtonian" mechanics in writings on 18th-century science tend to mislead the reader into thinking that Newton himself subscribed to the mechanistic philosophy of the time, which required no supernatural activity to guide or support the universe. It was precisely the admirable lawfulness of the universe that affirmed Newton's belief in a divine agency. To him, just placing all the planetary orbits into a single plane in such an orderly manner was proof positive that creation was the work of "an intelligent agent, very well skilled in mechanics and geometry." The movement of objects was controlled by the omnipresent laws of mathematics, and Newton stood in great awe of the heavenly engineer who had crafted the universe with such precision. Locke, too, was ready to take for granted the existence of an obliging deity, who, after giving the universe a bit of a nudge, retired into the celestial background for the rest of eternity, allowing men of science to get on with their work; it was the philosophical equivalent of the constitutional monarchy, which incidentally was Locke's political ideal. But these two men, along with the other early members of the Royal Society, were dead before the second half of the 18th century, to be succeeded by

---

[262] From internal evidence, he concluded that the *Pentateuch* must have been made up from several books by several authors, that the Book of Genesis was not written until the reign of Saul, and that the Kings and Chronicles were probably collected by Ezra. We now know that Genesis is the youngest of the five books of the *Torah*, and that none of them predate the Babylonian Captivity.

unbelievers.

Newton has been dubbed the "last of the magicians," the last of those scientists who in their research work combined mathematical precision with metaphysical speculation. As the 17th century passed into the 18th, the investigation of nature and the formation of world view began to be guided by ever narrower research methods. The natural sciences themselves divided into a series of more specialized fields, geology diverging from mineralogy, botany from zoology. The Age of Reason gave up the alchemists' aspiration for a holistic view of the universe. As much as the Hermetic ideal and Rosicrucian internationalism helped usher in the Enlightenment, they were also among its first victims. Classical ideas would influence the philosophy of the day, but mysticism was fast becoming irrelevant; Freemasonry was Rosicrucianism divested of Hermetic teaching.

The novel ideas and controversies of the period were discussed and debated in coffee-houses, salons, reading societies, and of course in those mysterious lodges of the Freemasons. At a time when preachers declaimed against scientists, when street mobs jeered at them, and neither Oxford nor Cambridge would admit science courses, Masonic lodges invited Royal Society members in for lectures and demonstrations. The 18th century witnessed a literary explosion of books, journals, and dissertations, all emphasizing a dispassionate representation of factual information rather than reliance on ancient "wisdom." However, only two countries, England and Holland, provided anything resembling freedom for the new thought of the age and uncensored publication of it. The massive *Dictionnaire* (1695-97) was a reference book through which anyone could familiarize himself with the newest accomplishments of science. Its French author, Pierre Bayle (1647-1706), had taken refuge in the safety of liberal Holland, from where his glad tidings spread to every corner of Europe.

In the Protestant states, where the Enlightenment appeared less scathing in its critique of religion than in other regions, general rationalism was proclaimed not only in æsthetics and philosophy, but also in theology. The Dutch educated deist, John Toland (1670-1722), who in his work, *Christianity not Mysterious* (1696), sought to demonstrate that there was nothing unnatural, nor yet anything irrational in the Gospels, first spoke of the freethinkers, whom Anthony Collins (1676-1729) then discussed in detail in *A Discourse of Freethinking* (1713). Practical morality is independent of dogma, which, on the contrary, has been responsible for so much wickedness throughout the history of the world. Jesus and the Apostles, the prototypes of the freethinkers, never invoked supernatural authority, but rather confined themselves to simple, rational object-lessons. Setting out from Locke's proposition of the identity of the truths of revelation with those of reason, Collins found it an easy step to reject prophecy and miracles as inessential characteristics of religion, amounting to didactic devices at best.

Ideas became the principal elements in the literature of the age, but the doctrine of scientific rationalism moved the focus of philosophy to human motivations; little room was left, except in the increasingly insular Catholic world, for the relation between man and the infinite. Though the great French authors called themselves *philosophes*, this did not mean that they would have wanted to be metaphysical thinkers and creators of subtle philosophical systems; on the contrary, they wanted to be modern conversationalists and popular agitators. Rejecting the guidance of custom and tradition, they urged their countrymen to use reason to discern the natural laws that govern human relations, and to shape new institutions in conformity with them. No longer was the mission of philosophy to reflect the world, or to contemplate another, but to change it; the "philosophers" dedicated all their creative energy to effect a thorough-going change in the way of thinking, to erase all prejudice, and to immerse at the least every civilized person in *l'esprit libertin*.

In the beginning of the Modern Era, rationalism was not yet as evident and potent as Protestantism and humanism, but in the long run, it became more important and more powerful than the two other undoers of the Middle Ages. The attempt to bring all phenomena under the sovereignty of reason became the great theme of Modern Era. Rationalism, when no longer restrained by revelation or respect for ecclesiastical tradition, threw away a much greater part of traditional Christianity than either Protestantism or humanism, and contained none of their obvious paradoxes. Protestantism and humanism tried denial, the latter in claiming that rationalism was identical with art, which for it represented the highest, the former in explaining that rationalism issued from God; one cannot begin to understand the rationalism of Erasmus, Descartes, or Montaigne until one realizes that they were engaged in bitter argument with these very notions. The rationalist was not content with merely dismissing the supernatural from the cosmos, but was fully prepared to put humanity itself within the framework of nature—or the "material universe."

When Roger Bacon had attempted to explore the causes and character of the rainbow in the 13th century, he was accused of black magic and thrown in a dungeon, as his opponents expressly declared, *propter aliquas novitates suspectas*, "on account of certain suspicious novelties."[263] Scientific knowledge, which, since the 16th century, had on all sides been encroaching on theology, now spread widely among the reading public, and natural science became one of the vehicles for the propagation of rationalistic views throughout the Western world. The whole force of the European intellect was concentrated on the study of natural phenomena and the discovery of natural laws. There thus developed a general disposition to attribute a natural cause to every event, soon followed by a conviction of the absurdity of using a supernatural hypothesis to explain phenomena, quickly discrediting the doctrine of witchcraft.

Though the anti-witchcraft laws were still in force, and little or no direct reasoning had been brought to bear on the subject, the witch-hunts effectively ceased by the beginning of the 18th century. Where torture had been abolished, or only made milder, "weather makers" no longer confessed, while the steadily growing number of skeptics laughed at witchcraft as so patently absurd that it would be a waste of time to examine it. The last serious witchcraft panic took place in the town of Salem, in the backwaters of the American colonies; it came to an abrupt end in 1692, when the accused implicated, among others, mayors of nearby cities and the wife of the governor of Massachusetts. The doctrine of witchcraft, though neither scientifically nor philosophically refuted, or even contested in court, would disappear before the Industrial Revolution.

---

[263] *Chronica XXIV Generalium Ordinis Minorum*

CHAPTER 38

The 18th century was undoubtedly one of the great ages of France. The French still speak proudly of *le siècle de Louis XIV*, "the century of Louis XIV," which more precisely fell between 1661 and 1715; by the appellation *Le Grand Siècle*, they refer roughly to the same set of years. This was the period when France was the richest and most powerful nation on the Continent: its culture and politics were examples for the rest of Europe, its taste and styles in architecture, interior decoration, dress, and manners were emulated throughout the Western world, and French became the language of the educated people around the globe.

Nevertheless, in his struggle against all revolutionary tendencies, the Sun King persuaded himself into the revocation of the Edict of Nantes, thus depriving the Protestants of their religious liberties. Though they were expressly told not to leave the country, even the strictest injunctions could not prevent half a million Huguenots from emigrating. This loss meant more to France than just a decrease in population, for the French Calvinists had formed the highest skilled and most industrious segment of the nation: brocade, silk, and velvet industry, the manufacture of fine hats, gloves, and shoes, lace-making, clock-making, glass-cutting, and the tobacco industry had been almost solely in their hands. Their mass exodus not only robbed their mother country of these industries, which she only gradually and not as magnificently could put again in order, but also introduced them to their new homelands, making these more competitive. What is more, they established free press where they could, describing to all the world the selfish and cruel character of the admired government of Louis the Great.

His political programme was no less grandiose than that of Philip II, and was realized to just as small a degree. The last stretch of his reign was consumed by the War of Spanish Succession (1701-14), a thirteen-year conflict in which most of Europe was involved. Louis' most dangerous and consistent enemy was not, however, Spain or even Austria, but William of Orange, who at that time ruled both the Dutch Republic and Great Britain. With William, England also got Holland's war with France; called "Queen Anne's War" in America, after William's sister-in-law and successor, it was the first war to be fought on a world scale. It ended with Newfoundland, Hudson Bay, and the French colony of Acadia, now Nova Scotia, all being ceded to Britain. The Acadians had come from the west of France to fish and farm; those of them who refused to swear allegiance to the English crown were deported, and many moved to the bayou country of Louisiana.

In 1704, the victory of General Churchill at the Battle of Blenheim showed that England was also once again a force to be reckoned with in European affairs. The conquest of Gibraltar the same year by Admiral Rooke turned Britain into a Mediterranean power. Situated in the southernmost extension of Spain, the Rock of Gibraltar spans measly 4 square miles, and has a coast-line of 7.5 miles altogether. Despite its humble dimensions, Gibraltar constitutes the only territorial dispute that still persists today between Spain and Britain. As a lock between the Mediterranean and the Atlantic, its value as a strategic base during the two World Wars was immeasurable; subsequently, however, it has become mainly a financial base. But it also has symbolic value for England, being a relic from the days when she was a true world power.

The Act of Settlement (1701) had decreed that since Anne had no surviving issue, the English throne would pass on her death to the nearest Protestant heir. The marriage of Elector Ernest Augustus of Hanover to Sophia of Bohemia, a granddaughter of James I of England, thus gave his son, Georg Ludwig, a claim to the throne, realized with the "Hanoverian Succession" in 1714. The act, still in force today, requires that the sovereign and his consort must both be Protestants. The Act of Union (1707), which produced the "United Kingdom," in turn ensured that the House of Hanover would succeed in Scotland as well. Even though the two countries were to share a national parliament until 1999, Scotland retained its own system of laws, based on Roman law rather than English common law. The story is that the prime ministership emerged in Great Britain because King George I never learned to speak English and Sir Robert Walpole was one of the few people in Parliament who spoke German.

The Spanish Netherlands became an important pawn in the War of the Spanish Succession, a fateful conflict matched by the ground-breaking peace that redrew the map of Europe. The treaty concluded at Utrecht in 1713 was an ingenious settlement with no clear losers: while France achieved her primary objective, the induction of a Bourbon on the vacant Spanish throne, the two thrones were never to be united; France was given part of Flanders, but the bulk of the Spanish Netherlands became the Austrian Netherlands and the Dutch received a so-called barrier, or buffer zone, on the French border. Gradually overshadowed by the expanding power of Britain on the sea and France on the land, the Dutch Republic ultimately lost its dominant position, with only Amsterdam able to maintain an economic lead.

Partly fought in Italy, the War of Spanish Succession also led to a redistribution of Italian land and ushered in a new period of political stability. The Spanish Habsburgs were no more, but the Austrian branch of the family took over their Italian possessions, replacing Spain as the dominant power in the region. The duchy of Savoy, located between France and the Habsburg possessions in Italy, became the other major force in the area. The kingdoms of Naples and Sardinia, and the duchy of Milan, were given to Austria, while the kingdom of Sicily went to Victor Amadeus II of Savoy, along with the royal title. The lands of the Gonzagas of Mantua, who had sided with France in the War, were divided between Austria and Savoy. In 1720, Victor Amadeus was obliged to cede Sicily to Austria, in exchange for the kingdom of Sardinia. In Florence, which no longer had a central role in the area, the Medici were replaced (1737) by members of the new House of Habsburg-Lorraine, which was Habsburg only in the female line. Austria would continue to exercise dominion over the peninsula throughout most of the second half of the century, but the dukes of Savoy, now styling themselves Kings of Sardinia, would eventually become the kings of a united Italy.

Until the War of the Spanish Succession, none of the innumerable, autonomous German states were kingdoms. Then, in 1701, Elector Frederick III of Brandenburg asked a royal title from Emperor Leopold I as a condition of his entering the War. The state of Brandenburg, with its capital at Berlin, spent four to five times as much per annum on its armed forces as it did on all the other obligations put together. The size of its military establishment at 83,000 men made its army the fourth largest in Europe, even though the state ranked only tenth in territory and thirteenth in population. Instead of assuming a royal crown for a domain that was under imperial jurisdiction, the Elector cleverly chose to use it for Prussia, which lay outside the Empire. However, he really only controlled East Prussia, the isolated German enclave that had been a Polish fief until 1657. His coronation was a challenge to

Poland as West Prussia continued to be a Polish province, and the locution "King in Prussia" was initially used in order to leave things a bit vague.

This subtlety was soon forgotten, for Poland was in no position to enforce suzerainty. The Polish state was entirely without a strong executive and administrative body at a time when all the nations of Europe had embraced the "new monarchy." Frederick Augustus, Elector of Saxony (1694-1733), whom combined Russian and German pressure had in 1697 forced upon the Poles as King Augustus II, was not universally recognized. For long no way inferior to the neighbouring Brandenburg, the economic partnership with the declining Poland greatly diminished the prestige of Electoral Saxony. From the beginning of his reign, King Augustus conspired with Poland's enemies in hopes of establishing absolute rule in the country, but ended up only serving the interests of the Czar of Russia, who needed a "window" on the Baltic.

One of the most notable events of the period was the entry of Russia into the annals of world history. The national states of East Central Europe had fallen under the influence of the great bureaucratic states, Austria and Prussia, and Peter the Great (r. 1682-1725) would now form the third strong government after the German example. He gave his country an army that was trained in the West European manner and equipped it with the best Western weapons. He established in Russia a shipbuilding industry and gave her a navy. The middle part of his career was taken up by the Great Northern War (1700-1721), which was fought in the north and east of Europe at the same time as the War of Spanish Succession was fought in the south and west. It began when, contrary to the interests of Poland, badly in need of peace and internal reforms, King Augustus invaded Livonia. Though there was no direct connection between the two wars, Sweden received ample diplomatic support from France, while England at first supported Russia.

Later on, when the Elector of Hanover ascended the British throne as George I, England became involved in an expensive naval campaign of its own in the Baltic. After gaining some of her greatest military triumphs, Sweden was forced to cede the archbishopric of Bremen to Hanover, while Russia received the Baltic provinces which Ivan the Terrible had tried in vain to conquer, effectively ending the Swedish empire. For East Central Europe, or all the peoples between the German Empire and the new Russian Empire, officially proclaimed after Sweden's final defeat in 1721, the long war, largely fought on their soil, was one more step on the road to perdition, leaving the whole area completely devastated. Far from regaining Riga for herself, Poland was now, over two decades later, in much worse position than at the start of the century. Though still one of the largest countries in Europe, Poland was slowly but surely being turned into a Russian protectorate.

The victory of Russia was also of great concern to the West, which for the first time became aware of the alarming rise of her power. Peter the Great was the instrument to transform Russia and make her people adopt Western customs. When the War was still dragging on, he had already had a castle built at the Gulf of Finland, dedicating it to St. Peter the Apostle, and providing it with garrisons, hospitals, factories, libraries, theatres, and other European innovations. The city that thus rose around St. Petersburg he made his new capital, so it would be closer to Europe. The laws of Russia were reformed on the model of Swedish legislation, while Sweden herself was torn by civil discord and political intrigue. Whereas the Russians had formerly reckoned time from the creation of the world, the Julian Calendar was now introduced. Even the appellation of Czar was discarded, and the Latin title of *Imperator* adopted in its stead.

Before the War, Peter had visited England, Holland, Austria, and Prussia, disguised as a private citizen, to learn more about European life. He had invited many foreign officers and merchants, scholars and artists, to return with him to Russia. There he outlawed the long beards and Oriental costumes, and after dressing his subjects like Europeans, he tried to get them to act in a fashion consistent with their new appearances. The first attempts to implement civilized manners were exceedingly comical: social events where men associated with women—now delivered from their harem-like existence—began with chaos and ended up in drunken revel; the crudeness and obscenity of court banquets was beyond belief. Schools were founded in Moscow for higher education, with British and German professors as instructors, but the great difficulty was that the students had not received even the rudiments of knowledge. The Emperor marched the young nobles to field trips in Europe and forced the masses to attend the newly-founded basic schools. To coerce his subjects into learning, he decreed that noblemen would not be allowed to marry unless they had an education.

It was this level of patrimonialism that made Russia a wholly different state-society from those of the West. Like the prominent Russian statesman Michael Speransky stated as late as the early 19th century, Russia remained a despotism despite all its Western-style institutions. The same was demonstrated by Emperor Nicholas himself to the visiting Marquis de Custine, who remarked: "This empire, vast as it is, is nothing but a prison, whose keys are held by the emperor." Even the Orthodox Church was just a branch of government used to ensure the loyalty of the subjects. When the last Patriarch of Moscow died in 1700, Peter the Great would not appoint a successor to him; instead, the first Russian Emperor established the Holy Synod, that is, a clerical committee directed by a crown appointed president.

Peter confessed his sins and took the communion three times during the last week of his mortal existence. His subjects were sick and tired of his reforming vigour, and the death of the founder of modern Russia came as a relief to them. Yet Russia continued to be a slave-state of sorts, where everyone was forced to serve the state, the nobility directly and the peasantry indirectly, reaching its ultimate perfection in Bolshevism. Lenin himself knew this full well, marking Peter the Great down as his political precursor, and calling him the "first crowned revolutionary." On this basis, Lenin also opposed changing the name of St. Petersburg.

For more than half a century, Europe had stood in the shadow of the Sun King, but on its fringes new powers were rising. France's old archenemy and new superpower, England, had already towards the end of the 17th century began to signify for at least the enlightened Frenchmen a promise of a better tomorrow. Enlightenment, which now evolved into a revolutionary doctrine, went all the way back to Bacon, spreading from Britain to continental Europe in the first half of the 18th century. In France, the combined pressures of Church and State proved at first inimical, and during the reign of Louis XIV, the Enlightened way of thinking could seriously hinder one's advancement. Yet it was to the Island Kingdom that the French thinkers of *L'Age des Lumieres* would look for new ideas.

The book that made Voltaire famous was his *Lettres Philosophiques* (1734), often called the "Letters on the English," because they are devoted to the glorification of all things British. The Lockean tenets had a revolutionary impact on 18th-century France, well illustrated by the fact that the most famous Frenchman dubbed Locke the most sensible man in the world. Voltaire also published the *Éléments de la Philosophie de Newton* (1738), and translated Sir

Isaac directly.[264] He was so enthused by English society that he lauded it as the example to which all European civilization should aspire; English social system, English natural science, even English poetry became a model for the Continent. Baron de Montesquieu, the first great Anglophile, converted the grounds of his family castle into an English garden.

In France, the social controversies were far more impassioned than in England, which can only be taken as a sign of profound social ills. According to Montesquieu, the revival of political liberty was possible only through a constitutional reform that checks the misuse of power. In his seminal historical work, *Considérations sur les Causes de la Grandeur des Romains et de Leur Décadence* (1734), he clearly pointed at democratic England and autocratic France, when he argued that Rome had the Republic to thank for her greatness, and later the Empire for her decline. Following the Western tradition that goes back to the early Middle Ages, Montesquieu regarded the Empire at Constantinople as corrupt and decadent, and could not even bring himself to refer to it with the noble names of "Greek" or "Roman." From the obsolete name of the city, he derived the word "Byzantine" to denote the Empire and its supposed characteristics, namely dishonesty, hypocrisy, and decadence.

The Enlightenment ideal was a world ruled by reason and knowledge, and much of the political, social, and literary activity of the period was characterized by a repudiation of revealed religion. In Protestant England, freethinking was closely connected with deism, but did not break completely with Christianity. It took a more radical form in Catholic France, where the prestige of the Church had suffered as a result of Louis XIV's intolerance. The Church may have held possession of advanced instruction for more than a thousand years, but in the institutions outside the universities, such as the science academies and the publications of individual philosophers, the spirit of the Enlightenment reigned supreme. Defying the pressure from above was the easier the laxer the poorly managed censorship got, and when it effectively evaporated in the mid-18th century, free thought had won the day.

The new ideas were compiled in the *Encyclopédie*, a compendium of human knowledge begun by the French atheist, Denis Diderot, in 1751, and swelling to 35 volumes by 1780, despite the fact that it had to be financed, printed, and

---

[264] Thus promoting the spread of Newtonian physics to the Continent, its acceptance having been hindered by the older Cartesian philosophy and the dispute over priority in the invention of calculus.

distributed in secret. Its editors competed with Voltaire over who could produce the most accessible and informative text, making its publication a major historical and literary event. It contained contributions from many of the other notable philosophers from across Europe, including Montesquieu, Rousseau, Buffon, and Turgot. According to them, traditional learning was fraught with prejudicial and superstitious precepts. "Everything," insisted Diderot, "must be examined, everything must be shaken up, without exception and without circumspection." A proposition like this naturally posed a threat to the religious authority of the Church, and Pope Clement XII ordered all Catholics who owned this great reference work to either hand it over to the clergy for burning or suffer excommunication.

The more educated members of French society came to regard the Church as a means whereby men without scruples swindled the ignorant. The anticlericalism can also be seen in the calls for freedom: religion ought to be, if not outright abolished, at least separated into its own domain in society, thus liberating State from the wardship of Church. For the first time, the individual was demanded statutory freedom from religion; passive freedom of religion, the right to worship, had finally found its active flip-side. Yet even the worship of reason took on religious characteristics: the Enlightenment mirrored the Christian faith, reason becoming its revelation, nature its god; as the *Encyclopédie* became its bible, Freemasonry became its ritual. *The Magic Flute* of Mozart was not only a masterpiece of musical charm, but also a beautifully orchestrated example of Masonic allegory—his seminal opera symbolizes the search of enlightenment and truth. The Masons celebrated the victory of light over darkness, the triumph of reason over ignorance; their lodges gave both moral and financial support to the *philosophes* and Encyclopedists, all of whom were invariably among their number.

Strange as it may seem in an age when the Masonic lodge has been reduced to little more than a cigar lounge for the local bourgeoisie, it was above all in these countless lodges where the intellectual revolution took place. These conclaves, with their metaphorical secrets and lore, were consequently proscribed as the crucibles of "impiety and anarchy" by church dogmatists of the early 18th century. In 1738, Clement XII issued a papal bull excommunicating all Freemasons, pronouncing them enemies of the Roman Church, and forbidding lodge membership for Catholics; it was subsequently asserted that Masonic thought rests on a heresy, the denial of Jesus' divinity, and that the "masterminds" behind Freemasonry were none other than those who engineered the Protestant Reformation—their deistic god is certainly not the god of the Catholic superstition. Eleven more popes, in over 400 additional documents, would condemn Freemasonry in even stronger terms, and the Catholic Church still discourages its members from joining the fraternity.

Not surprisingly, Masonic lodges, in attempting to recruit men of science and intelligence at a period when the pursuit of knowledge required wealth or patronage, soon accumulated men of fortune and power. In 1738, Frederick Lewis, Prince of Wales, was made mason; Crown Prince Frederick of Prussia was "raised" the next year, and on his accession as king in 1740, he became a protector of the "Craft." His father, Frederick William, otherwise known as the "Sergeant King," had had great concerns about him because he appeared to apply himself to philosophy, music, and poetry, rather than to military affairs. Unnecessarily, for by the fifth year of his reign, Frederick II of Prussia was already called "the Great."

All his life, Frederick was driven by one great guiding principle, Plato's call for kings to be philosophers, and philosophers to be kings; the light must govern, the most powerful spirit dominate, the most brilliant mind rule—this alone is the true meaning of "enlightened despotism," the vogue word of the period, which he alone understood in its deeper significance, and which he translated into living reality. The 18th century was, in many respects, a time of transformation, but one thing remained unchanged: war was still seen and practised as "politics by other means," as von Clausewitz would later contend. Frederick the Great was able to turn Prussia into a great power largely because of the army his father had lovingly prepared, but sparingly used.

Frederick deployed, and even exhausted, the Prussian army to seize Silesia from Archduchess Maria Theresa, who had just assumed the succession to Austria, Bohemia, and Hungary. A state formed by two separate coastal areas and a few small strips of land in the west, was not viable in this form; as heir of the house of Brandenburg, Frederick demanded the cession of the four fiefs of Upper Silesia, which should have, by right of succession, been transferred to Prussia already in 1675. Only this addition, increasing the land area by third and the population by half, would give his kingdom the stability and strength of regional foundation, without which a superpower status was unimaginable; scornfully refused by the young Queen, Frederick marched an army of 30,000 into Silesia, commencing the War of the Austrian Succession (1740-1748).

When the Prussians arrived, the prisons of Silesia were filled with Protestants, and the annexation of the province by Frederick was undoubtedly to the good of its people. No person in their right mind could seriously claim that the King of Prussia would have waged the Seven Years' War (1756-1763), in which three great powers were aligned against him, out of anything other than necessity. Only Hanover, whose elector conducted England's European policy more with Germany than Britain in mind, aided Frederick and his forces against the armies of Austria, Saxony, France, Sweden, and Russia. Yet contemporary literature reveals that in every German state, whichever side its prince happened to be in the War, the people looked upon the Prussian King with pride and sympathy. He could have hardly aimed at the complete annihilation of Austria either, for this would have given France an undue advantage; all he wanted was Silesia, on the possession of which the Empress (as Maria Theresa was called after her inconsequential husband, Duke Francis Stephen of Lorraine, had been elected Emperor in 1745) obstinately insisted.

Only the death of Elizabeth of Russia, the last of the Romanovs, and the accession of her nephew, Peter III (r. 1762), a German prince of Holstein-Gottorp and Frederick's ardent admirer, saved him from certain defeat. One of the first and only acts of Peter's short reign was to take Russia out of the Seven Years' War and conclude an alliance with Prussia, thus sacrificing all the advantages she had gained in the conflict that marked her first great venture into purely European affairs. The consequences of this turn of events for West Central Europe are well known, but often underestimated: instead of the Ottoman Empire, which had long ago ceased to be a threat to the West; instead of Sweden, which had been a threat for only a short while; and instead of Poland, which was the last fully independent country in East Central Europe, the West now faced two dynamic hostile powers that had a common interest in destroying the country which separated them from each other.

The Treaty of Hubertusburg (1763) may not have awarded Prussia with any new territory, but it ratified the borders that had existed before the War. Silesia not only strengthened Brandenburg-Prussia, but more importantly, weakened Saxony's physical ties with the Polish-Lithuanian Commonwealth. Augustus III, invaded and humiliated by Frederick the Great at the very beginning of the War, died a few months after the peace, ending the union of Saxony and Poland for good. However, the House of Saxony remained for ever Catholic, having converted merely to facilitate the election of Augustus' father to the throne of Poland. Frederick would live another 23 years, and those years were by no means the least significant of his glorious reign: the bloodless annexation of West Prussia in the First Partition of Poland (1772) with Russia was one of his greatest diplomatic triumphs, for this measure removed the wedge that Casimir IV had driven in the coast between Brandenburg and East Prussia. It was one of the most significant territorial expansions of modern European history, a manifestation of German power beyond the frontiers of the Empire, deep in the East Central European region. All those possessions which, in addition to the tiny bits of western Germany, made up the state of Frederick the Great, now a genuine European superpower, had formerly been either Baltic or Slavic, greatly reducing the non-German, eastern portion of Central Europe.

Called the French and Indian Wars in America, the Seven Years' War marked the end of France as a naval power and global rival to the British. Colonized by the French at the beginning of the 17th century, Canada was ceded to Great Britain in the Treaty of Paris (1763), and remained in its control until the British North America Act of 1867. As Louis XV also ceded Louisiana to his ally, Charles III of Spain, in compensation for Florida, which the Spanish were forced to yield to Britain, France lost all its possessions on the North American continent. Though the French were allowed to return to their posts in East India, they were prohibited from maintaining troops or building forts in Bengal, wherefore India passed in practice to Britain, cementing her colonial and maritime supremacy.

Frederick had managed his wars without incurring any debt, and by the end of them, Prussia had not only doubled its area, but been established as a rival to Austria for domination of the German states. In the last years of that long reign (1740-1786), the "Old Fritz," as Frederick was familiarly known by his now 200,000 strong army, was quite happy to steer clear of conflict and entertain Enlightenment philosophers instead. He made constant tours of inspection throughout his kingdom, seeing to the welfare of the poor in particular, ensuring that justice was served; anyone with a serious cause of complaint could turn to him personally. To all quarters stretched his endless and patient campaign of reform. Not only was the study of nature revived in the re-established Berlin Academy of Sciences, but Frederick aided and defended every institution which might extend education throughout his kingdom. He decreed general compulsory education in 1763, on account of which numerous common schools and seminaries were founded. Youth were not taught by words alone, but given a clear idea of natural things, of moral and physical relations, of history and geography.

Frederick supported George Washington during the Revolutionary War (1776-1783) and was among the first European sovereigns to conclude a commercial treaty (1785) with the United States. He spoke French at court and gathered in his palace of Sans Souci all *les esprits forts* starting from Voltaire, invariably entertained with judicious economy. When not attending to the affairs of the state, the King earned his esteem as a man of science, poet, composer, and flutist. Kant dedicated the *Critique of Pure Reason* (1781) to his Minister of State, Baron von Zedlitz, and in 1784, answered the question "What is Enlightenment?" by equating the "Age of Reason" with the "Century of Frederick." Himself a prolific writer in political, historical, and military subjects, Frederick's complete works, all in French, were published in 30 volumes between 1846 and 1857.

Frederick's example encouraged the literary Germans to publish their opinions and his capital became the asylum of the persecuted. Moses Mendelssohn (1729-1786), dubbed the "Socrates of Berlin" for his brilliant philosophical writings, was born in an age when Jews were no longer massacred or plundered, but none the less oppressed. Freemasonry did not require adherence to any particular faith, and nowhere was anti-Semitism more discredited than in England, the birthplace of Masonry, where Jews were not only joining lodges, but also gaining access to social, political, and public life hitherto denied to them. This was not the case in either France or Germany, where Jews were still denied admission to the order that proclaimed brotherly love because of their religion. Though Masons formed virtually all of the aristocracy as well as the intellectual and military élite in Prussia, Mendelssohn had no trouble finding his way into the vanguard of the high society that gathered around their Grand Master. He taught German society to accept the Jews, and the Jews to accept German society. Subsequent to him, the Jews began to participate in the pursuits of all the nations within which they lived and to which they professed to belong.

Frederick was a tolerant unbeliever, and it was above all his religious enlightenment that made him a true philosopher. One can be a freethinker and—as is the case with most freethinkers—not have any room for understanding the convictions of others; in the words of Laurence Sterne (1713-1768), "Free thinkers are generally those who never think at all." It is the same with conventional toleration: a liberal is tolerant only towards other liberals, while all other people are to him blinded fools, who must be induced to adopt the more reasonable outlook even against their wills. This is also the typical way in which enlightenment was pursued during the age of Frederick; the despots of progress saw it as their duty to coerce the backward humanity into attaining beatitude.

In the Catholic countries, the Church had exercised cultural and political hegemony for a very long time, and the abuses had only become more pointed with its conservatism. The Catholic orders were forced to relinquish their power and the fear of the Jesuits made this society in particular responsible for all the darkness, treachery, and outrage on earth. In Portugal, the Marquês de Pombal accused the Jesuits of taking part in an attempt on the King's life. This tyrant of reason then searched their professed houses, confiscated their property, closed their schools, and finally in 1759 expelled them from the kingdom and its colonies.

The head of the leading Protestant state in Germany, Frederick was much more tolerant towards Catholicism than the Holy Roman Emperor: the same time as the latter abolished monasteries, the former rebuilt burned-down Catholic churches. Frederick practised genuine tolerance, which simply means the recognition of every individual conviction. "Toleration is not the opposite of intoleration," said Thomas Paine, "but is the counterfeit of it. Both are despotisms. The one assumes the right of withholding liberty of conscience, and the other of granting it." Frederick consciously deprived the monarchy of its character as a divine institution, proclaiming a general freedom of religion, "for every man must get to Heaven his own way."[265] He was wholly indifferent to what his subjects thought or believed, as long as they served, paid taxes, and were obedient. To quote Thomas Jefferson, freedom is the most effective remedy against religious dissent and conflict, "the maxim of civil government being reversed in that of religion, where its true from is 'divided we stand, united we fall'."

Five years after their expulsion from Portugal, the Jesuits met the same fate in France and its colonies. The French King wished to salvage the Order and

---

[265] *denn hier muß ein jeder nach seiner Fasson selig werden*

suggested its reformation to Clement XIII, but the Pope uttered his now famous line: *Sint ut sunt, aut non sint,* "Let them be as they are, or not be at all." Soon the example was followed by the other Bourbon states: in 1767, Spain and its dominions, Parma, and the Two Sicilies were all closed to the Jesuits. By 1773, all Pope Clement XIV could do was issue a brief suppressing and abolishing the Society throughout the entire world. Frederick the Great refused to publish the brief, and the Jesuits continued to run their schools and churches in Prussia. When the brief arrived in Poland, it was likewise ordered to be treated as non-existent by Empress Catherine the Great (1762-1796), who proclaimed it her "most important duty to promote national education," wherefore she could not "despoil an Order which devotes itself so zealously to educational work."[266]

In the other countries, the ex-Jesuits became martyrs, proving more dangerous and pernicious than they had previously been powerful and envied, as they were forced to perpetuate their existence under false pretences in disguises of all sorts. They now sought, before all, to infiltrate all kinds of other societies, partly even the kinds with diametrically opposite goals. They could frequently be met within the ranks of freethinkers and Freemasons, manifesting their ability to be all, to become everything, in its most glorious form yet. During the last quarter of the 18th century, there were some seven hundred lodges in France, more than there are today. Their influence with both public opinion and the course of things was great, after all, the "light" of Freemasonry had been attained by nearly every notable in the country.

The origins of the oldest Masonic traditions lay of course in Britain, but the first testimonies are often French, and most of continental Europe and the Americas discovered Freemasonry through French Freemasonry. An amazing number of the Founding Fathers of America were Masons, including every member of the Virginia delegation to the Philadelphia convention, which largely framed the Constitution, itself reflecting the egalitarian ideals of Masonry. Nine of the signatories of the Declaration of Independence, ten signers of the Articles of Confederation, and thirteen of the Constitution, were members of one lodge or other. Washington wore a Masonic apron in the ceremony that took place at the laying of the cornerstone for the U.S. Capitol. The Eye in the Pyramid of the Great Seal of the United States is a

---

[266] *Letter to Pope Pius VI* (c. 1775)

Masonic symbol, though it has also famously but unfoundedly been linked to the Bavarian Illuminati.

The Masonic ideal has always been an old boys' network of enlightened men, whose common interests transcend nationalism and borders. This was especially attractive in 18th-century Germany, divided as it was into a loose string of petty principalities, having virtually no central government. Influential men in society quickly found their way into one of the lodges emerging all over the nation. Of all the societies of the Enlightenment, perhaps none has been so vilified and misunderstood as that known as the Illuminati of Bavaria. Nowhere did the ideas of the Enlightenment meet with such hostility and censure from the clerical and aristocratic establishment than in Catholic Bavaria. According to a contemporary report, there were some 28,000 churches and chapels in this isolated South German electorate, with its capital, Munich, boasting 17 monasteries. Even the Jesuits, though officially banished from Bavaria, were still powerful, tirelessly labouring for the restoration of their order.

The founder of the Illuminati, Adam Weishaupt (1748-1830), was the professor of civil law at the University of Ingolstadt, an institution of learning under the strictest ecclesiastical control. He had himself been a student of the Jesuits, but had acquired a bitter dislike for them. His election in 1773 to the chair of canon law, which until then had been held exclusively by the Jesuits, was a cause of great offence to the Society. In conference with his students, Weishaupt soon conceived the idea of forming an opposing party in the University, organized along similar lines as the Jesuits, but committed to the ideals of the Enlightenment. After so many ages during which the human mind had been held in vassalage by kings and priests, the Illuminati swore to abolish the slavery of despotism, secular and spiritual, so that man might take control of his destiny by discovering the laws of nature and using them in the service of humanity.

Since such ideas and activities were clearly prohibited not only in Bavaria, but throughout most of Europe, the Illuminati did their work in secret, constantly fearing exposure to civil and religious authorities. "As Weishaupt lived under the tyranny of a despot and priests," wrote Jefferson, "he knew that caution was necessary even in spreading information, and the principles of pure morality. This has given an air of mystery to his views. . . If Weishaupt had written here, where no secrecy is necessary in our endeavour to render men wise and virtuous, he would not have thought of any secret machinery for that purpose." But Europe was still governed by dogmatic authority and superstition, embodied in the alliance between priests and kings, Church and State. There were no formal political parties in the 18th century, nor was there yet a formal opposition in parliament; on the contrary, opposition to the royal cabinet was deemed treasonous; universities, controlled by ecclesiastical administrations, were mere handmaidens to the aristocracy.

As originally founded, the Order of the Illuminati was altogether dissimilar to Freemasonry, of which its founders knew little. But since quite a number of distinguished Masons were to become, for a time at least, members of this society, it became an essential part of the history of Freemasonry. Baron Adolph F. F. L. von Knigge (1752-1796), who translated *The Magic Flute* into German and is still remembered as a writer in Germany, was perhaps the most prominent of these men. He appears to have been unsatisfied on the completion of his advancement through the higher Masonic degrees in 1779; he thereupon conceived projects for the improvement of Masonry, travelling extensively, from lodge to lodge, to unite the Masons of Europe. In 1780, he met the Marquis of Costanza, who told him the Illuminati had already forestalled his plans. The next year, Knigge accepted an invitation to visit Bavaria and receive full access to all of Weishaupt's ritual materials, only to find them an incomplete invention of a contemporary German mind. Reverting to his former ambition, he affected a marriage between the advanced degrees of Masonry and those of Illuminism. The lofty goal of promoting enlightened ideas was lost in the mire of secrets and mysteries, dragging Illuminism down without helping Freemasonry much.

Weishaupt's own predilection for organizational detail would also take its toll: as the Illuminati grew in number, eventually reaching the excess of 2,000, the possibility of factionalism, internal strife, and betrayal grew in proportion. Worse still was the growing antagonism between Weishaupt and Knigge. Unlike the anticlericalism of Weishaupt, Knigge's disdain of the clergy did not involve him in contempt for Christianity; on the contrary, he wished to incorporate into the Order the whole pomp of the Church, its consecration, ceremonies, garments, and what not. The two quarrelled over the resulting rituals in 1784, whereupon the latter became disgusted and resigned from the Illuminati, and is said to have retired also from Masonry. Disillusioned by the course of events, four university professors in the lower degrees of the Order disclosed some of its secrets to its enemies. Elector Charles Theodore of Bavaria could remain idle no longer, even though, or maybe because, several of his daily companions, one of his ministers, and members of the first families in the electorate also belonged to it.

A general ordinance was issued, strictly prohibiting all Bavarians from being members of any secret or unauthorized associations. Though this was not specifically directed at the Illuminati, they suspended their meetings, and Weishaupt even approached the Elector, revealing him most of their secrets. To no avail, for in 1785, Charles Theodore published another edict, this time explicitly condemning not only Illuminism but Freemasonry as well; both were thus wiped out from Bavaria and neither ever recovered its former position. The fear of the Jesuits during the Enlightenment was mirrored in the subsequent fears of Illuminist and Freemasonic intrigue: most famously, Abbé Barruel ascribed the whole of the French Revolution to the Duke of Orléans, the Grand Orient of France, and the Illuminati; his work was to set off a wave of hysteria, to inspire a still growing body of similar literature, and to become the bible for all conspiracy theorists. From the paranoid ramblings of this 19th-century Jesuit father derives the clichéd image of Freemasonry as a vast international conspiracy, dedicated to the overthrow of existing institutions and to the establishment of a "new world order."

Weishaupt was discharged from his position at the University of Ingolstadt, and given a pension which he turned down. Banished from Bavaria, he began a pamphlet war at the free city of Regensburg, whose close proximity to the Bavarian territory was a cause of great anxiety to the Elector. However, the efforts made by the latter to check any influence the former might exert to reorganize his secret society were as futile as they were unnecessary. His spirit broken, Weishaupt contented himself with the outpouring of various apologetic fliers, making no effort to restore the Illuminati in his native state. He would soon find a generous patron in Ernest II of Saxe-Gotha, at whose capital he was to remain until the Duke's death in 1804. Weishaupt was then offered professorship at the University of Göttingen[267], where he would publish critical works on Kantian philosophy and die in obscurity quarter of a century later.

---

[267] One of the most illustrious universities in Europe, founded in 1737 by George II of England in his capacity as Elector of Hanover.

CHAPTER 39

The magic word, which the era hoped would solve all the social, moral, and economic problems, was "instruction." Europe was filled with manuals of manners, which were initially directed at adults, but with the newfound zeal for child rearing, were later aimed at the young. Education began to increase rapidly in the 17th and 18th centuries, schools appearing even for some poor children, first in Britain. By the beginning of the 19th century, almost ninety percent of the Scottish and half of the English males of full age were literate; maybe two-thirds of the adult Frenchmen could read and write.

The spread of literacy alone increased people's confidence in themselves and in their abilities. There were many factors in modern Western culture that contributed to the emergence of the individual: the rationalism of the Enlightenment, the individualistic hero of literature, the waning influence of the Church, the pursuit of pleasure—better to rejoice in this life than to wait for the next—and the inventions that allowed man at least a degree of control over the hitherto merciless nature. The modern man saw that he needed not give in to hunger, fear, oppression, or disease; health is one of the principal values of a secularized society.

Since the 17th century, the health of the population has been a subject of political interest and a target of positive measures. The projects of public hygiene and health care became public undertakings that bore upon political order and power structures. They therefore also became the stuff of major political struggles: when physicians in Britain and France began promoting inoculations to prevent smallpox, conservatives on both sides of the Channel were alarmed, and the theologians soon found profound reasons for condemning the new practice. The Christian Church saw grief and suffering as a social necessity, and diseases were regarded as a judgement of God on the sins of the people. The smallpox vaccination, which vanquished one of the worst scourges of Modern Era, was widely denounced as an "encroachment on the prerogatives of Jehovah, whose right it is to wound and smite." By preventing the spread of disease, evil sorcerers and atheists were "flying in the face of Providence" and "bidding defiance to Heaven itself, even to the will of God."

Children used to be baptized at a couple of days old, for they were in constant danger of dying during their first year. The recurrent illnesses and hard work reduced the chance of getting pregnant, and the Catholic Church also placed several restrictions on the frequency of marital intercourse: one had to practise abstinence during Lent and regular fast days, during religious holidays and periods of mourning. An average of two out of the five or six children, to which the mother of the early Modern Era was able to give birth, died before the age of one. The third died before reaching three years, and the fourth likely before fifteen. The death of infants was so common that two living children in one family might well be given the same name as it was expected that one or the other would die before long. Children were not carried off only by hunger and disease, but also by poor care and negligence. When a wife was pregnant or nursing, the Church demanded that she remain celibate so that the fœtus would not be hurt or the milk be spoilt. The children were usually sent to wet-nurses so that the husband would not fall into the sin of fornication, for one's own wife was strictly out of bounds for at least two years per pregnancy.

There was a clear improvement in the standard of health in the European population after the mid-18th century. Infant mortality began to show a slow decrease in Britain and France, and life expectancy at birth was extended in both countries. This beneficial development overlapped with the rapid improvement of medical and health care. Autopsies, while still an abomination unto the Catholic Church, were no longer illegal, but rather common, hastening the transformation of surgery into an experimental science. Reforms were instituted in mental institutions as all forms of insanity were no longer considered demonic possessions. The brutality and cruelty which had prevailed were substituted by kindness and gentleness; the "possessed" were unchained and taken out of their dungeons, given sunny rooms and allowed the freedom of outdoors exercise—while at the same time removed from public display. Though medical science was barely beyond its embryonic stage, it had already robbed theology of its once strongest province, the belief in the supernatural, which had been the greatest stumbling-block in the path of medicine.

The visits by the Grim Reaper at the British and French cradles became less frequent as the method of child care and the general attitude towards children was changed. The little ones were no longer sent to their deaths at the filthy cabins of the wet-nurses, their movements were no longer constricted by swaddling bands, nor were they any longer left alone for hours without supervision. The custom of nursing one's own children spread in the educated middle classes, in the families of doctors, teachers, and merchants, where the ideal image of a bourgeois home was, after all, created. The other social classes were very slow to adopt the custom; even as the shopkeeper's wife began nursing her children, the craftsman's wife, who had formerly taken children in for nursing, sent her own to a nurse upon becoming prosperous.

The doctrine of Original Sin was undoubtedly a result of projecting adult sexuality onto children. The newborn was looked upon as being tainted by the sin that it had inherited from the first parents through its own. Whenever the child followed his own will, the adult construed it as wickedness, disobedience, and wilfulness; in order for the child to be good, the ugly had to be beaten out of him—flogging was an everyday practice in boys' schools. Not until the 18th century was any attention drawn to the actual reason behind the phenomenon, the sadomasochistic homosexuality in which the schoolmasters engaged with the boys. The childhood flagellations left many fond memories for even more men, and the prostitutes of the period were adept at administering the birch.

From the 18th century on, the middle classes of Europe started to modify their attitude towards their children, gradually moving away from the coercive, restrictive approach of patriarchalism. This altered attitude is seen above all in the fact that the child's will was no longer broken with brute force and humiliation. Instead, a kind, permissive, and respectful attitude was introduced, laying the foundation of the modern individual. This change began in Britain, gradually spreading to the Continent, first to France and Scandinavia, then to Central Europe, and finally to Russia. Its significance really cannot be emphasized enough. Already in 1693, Locke had committed to print the thoughts that were in the air, when he rejected the traditional belief in hereditary guilt and the innate wickedness of children. To this eminent English philosopher, the child was, paraphrasing Ovid, like a *tabula rasa*, a "blank slate," which the parents filled with their instruction.

Both the Protestant Reformation and the Enlightenment emanated from the bourgeoisie and carried its ideals. Choosing a mate on basis of finances is now considered contemptible, whereas formerly these were virtually the sole respectable criteria. Leaving one's child in a strange neighbourhood in the care of a stranger and sending him away altogether at the age of seven is considered wholly unnatural today, even though it was a matter of course in the past. The outlook that evolved in the middle classes over the 18th century placed emphasis on feelings, underlining the affection between family members. The modern family was expected to spend a lot of time together as opposed to the traditional family, whose members felt more at home with their peers, giving rise to the now struggling nuclear family.

The three centuries from the Reformation in the beginning of the 16th century to the French Revolution at the end of the 18th were turbulent ones. The discovery of new sea routes gave a powerful boost to the development of Western capitalism. A great amount of trading posts were established in the Americas, on the coasts of Africa, and within the ancient trade zones of Asia during the course of the 16th century. To the Europeans of the 16th and early 17th centuries, the distant lands were an opportunity awaiting exploitation. The first hundred and fifty years of colonialism were a period of conquest, not of scientific exploration. However, the wealth thus generated helped to create a class of people with free time, education, and an interest in science—it also provided the means by which talented but not wealthy individuals would have the opportunity to study nature.

The discovery of America called the universal applicability of European morals, sciences, and religion into question. Here you had an immense landmass, unsuspected by ancient geographers, filled with countless societies covering a great range of sophistication. The Europeans were also introduced to strange new agricultural products, such as potatoes, maize, coffee, and tobacco, each of which changed not only their dietary, but also their cultural practices; nearly half of the crop tonnage of the world is now formed by plants first domesticated by Native Americans. In 1768, Captain James Cook set sail on the *Endeavour* bound for the South Pacific, an event that is said to have ended the era of the great voyages of exploration, and begun the transition to the golden age of scientific expeditions. He was accompanied by the naturalist Joseph Banks, who collected tens of thousands of biological specimens, initiating the exchange of flora and fauna between Europe, the Americas, and the South Seas.

The old narrow-mindedness became impossible; the unfamiliar specimens were a source of both intellectual curiosity and philosophical concern for the

European scientific community. They were not only different from their Old World counterparts, but in many instances, entirely novel. While the alike and near-alike could be associated, the totally dissimilar were more troublesome, upsetting classification systems that had worked fine for thousands of years. Carl von Linné (1707-1778), better known as Carolus Linnæus, revolutionized the science of taxonomy, accounting for some 8,000 species from all parts of the known world. His principal merit lies in the implementation of the so-called "binary nomenclature," i.e. assigning each plant and animal with two Latin identifiers, one for the genus, the other for the species. This set a milestone in the progress of knowledge, and no one knew it better than Linnæus himself, for he was convinced that God Himself had chosen him to arrange all of nature.[268]

Colonialism of the old kind, where the Spanish and Portuguese conquered the New World in order to steal its riches, was nothing but organized pillage. As time went on and permanent colonial settlement began to form, the Europeans also started to transplant their religion and forms of government to the natives. The lessons learned by the English, French, and Dutch during the "first colonial period" were to change the way Britain, France, and Holland would deal with the quite different eastern imperial expansion of the late 18th and early 19th centuries. The colonies and overseas trade increased the gains of Western capitalism, creating fantastic opportunities for profit and loss, and contributing to the advent of industrialism towards the end of 18th century. The mediæval notions of life underwent a thorough-going change; the new era called for new morals. Wars were less profitable than peaceful co-existence; the poor were not in need of alms, but of work; instead of being productive, chivalry and munificence, seclusion and meditation, became counter-productive.

After the mid-18th century, the general prosperity of Europe grew, the population crises ended, and the population rate began to climb. A wealth of new and amazing ideas were formed during this period. The European culture of the 18th century was, like all rich cultures, built on the interplay of opposites. This diversity only expanded towards our own era, for the old-established ideas were constantly augmented by more new ones, while the very old ideas died out in most countries. The evolution of Germany,

---

[268] Son of a minister, he went so far as to term his students as his "apostles."

however, was checked by many factors, not the least the great religious war of the previous century and the fragmentation into petty feudal states that followed. As a result, German literature, unlike the Italian, Spanish, French, and English counterparts, had not yet seen a golden age or even gained any fame outside of home and Scandinavia. The Germans still lived almost exclusively from handicrafts and farming; everything, or at least everything essential, was produced within one's own neighbourhood—the cause and effect was a unique narrowness of view.

The *Sturm und Drang* literary movement, with its obsessive interest in all things mediæval, led to the revival of Romanticism in the late 18th century, affecting artistic, philosophical, and political thinking throughout Europe. The early Romantics of the Jena school started a new trend of thought, the gist of which was a reaction against the French Enlightenment. The *philosophes* believed that the true essence of the universe could be discerned through the use of reason: we may not know what it is yet, but if we continue our study logically and diligently, the dimly visible truth will unveil itself at least to a sufficient degree. The German Romantics blankly dismissed such an optimism; neither the totality nor the absolute, still less the truth, would lend itself to rational analysis, which in any case could not yield results of any interest—these called for poems and myths.

The "Storm and Stress" school got its name from the 1776 play by the author and warrior, F. M. von Klinger, but its members were often called "Goethean," for Johann Wolfgang von Goethe (1749-1832) was considered the true head of the movement. It was formed of the "power geniuses," so named because they felt possessed by a power that fed from their insatiable zest for life, angst of living, passion for action, and longing for death. The basic aims of Romanticism included the exaltation of senses and emotions over reason and logic, a return to nature and to the belief in the basic goodness of people, and the rediscovery of the artist as a supremely individual creator. Their revolt against prescribed rules was the only thing the various Romantic movements had in common; the creative self set itself against the world, the key element being the creative will, which did not acknowledge any pre-existent values. They rebelled against everything and everyone, the superficiality of Classicism, morals, and society.

The modern novel was born only two centuries ago—prior to then the writers had been expected to impress upon the readers the difference between right and wrong. Although he soon distanced himself from the movement, Goethe was generally regarded as the leader of the German youth and made responsible for all its blatant excesses and warped absurdities. Wilhelm Heinse was made infamous by the sexual license displayed in his novel, *Ardinghello* (1787), but ended up a librarian to the Archbishop of Mainz and was later vindicated as a "pioneer" and an "eminent stylist." The advancement of Goethe to a privy councillor is well known, and it is worth mentioning that Klinger himself finally became a lieutenant-general in the service of Russia.

Goethe was born into the upper middle classes and belonged to them his whole life, despite court service and the short artistic-bohemian episode. From 1765 to 1768, he studied law in Leipzig, but nearly all of this time was consumed by social and student life, in addition to art classes. This period gave birth to his remarkable collection of love poems, entitled *Annette* and inspired by a certain Käthchen Schönkopf. Goethe returned home seriously ill, and began dabbling in mysticism during his long convalescence. In the world view of the Romantics, there existed in addition to the ordinary world a realm of spirit, the reflection of which the perceived reality was; nature was a manifestation of the spirit, and every form of being reflected the universe—in the man, nature achieved consciousness of itself, and he became its interpreter. According to the Romantic concept of man, the higher spirituality of the universe could reveal itself under unusual states of mind, such as hypnosis, somnambulism, or delirium. Goethe began studying occult writings, corresponding at length with several acquaintances regarding his growing insights into esoteric knowledge. Being particularly fascinated with the symbolic narratives of the Rosicrucians, he resolved to have a go at this type of open-ended allegorical fantasy. His dramatic take on the old Faust theme proved most fruitful, the result being few of the most powerful scenes of the "Urfaust." But then Goethe got something else to think about.

He travelled to Strasbourg in 1770 to continue his law studies, and after passing the licentiate examination in 1771, joined his father's practice at Frankfurt. During his internship at the Supreme Court of the Empire in Wetzlar, Goethe befriended many intelligent young men and women, who provided the topic for his first great literary success, *Die Leiden des jungen Werthers* (1774). The now world-famous novel met with vehement opposition at first, for the author depicted the events and people as they were, leaving moral judgement to the reader. To the displeasure of the author, it also caused a mild wave of suicides, and still affects minds, albeit in a less grave manner. Romanticism was set in motion by young writers, and it is the young people who have always been the most captivated by it. In "The Sorrows of Young Werther" everyone recognized one's own image, and it became the symbol for and the conclusion to that oscillation between defiance and boredom, which embodied the *Sturm und Drang* period.

Only a year after the first publication of *Werther*, Goethe accepted the invitation of the 18-year-old Duke Charles Augustus (1775-1828) of Saxe-Weimar & Eisenach, and became firmly attached to its miniature court. Small as it was, the 394-square-mile duchy, which resulted from the reunion (1741), was both culturally and politically the most important of the Thuringian principalities. Assisted by Goethe, Charles Augustus made Weimar, the tiny ducal capital of some 6,000 inhabitants, a European centre of literature, art, science, and liberal political thought. He would also help Frederick the Great form (1785) the *Fürstenbund*, a league of princes intended as a check against Austria's ambitions in Germany and Prussia's first attempt to unite the German states under its leadership, not achieved until nearly a century later.

Friedrich von Schiller (1759-1805) was employed at Weimar the same time as Goethe, and the two were forced to be the best of friends for over ten years. Despite the fact that they were complete opposites, they also complemented each other, and together influenced the intellectual life of their people in a most significant manner. Goethe was given practical assignments, which he carried out superbly for more than a decade. During this period, he also joined Amalia Lodge, of which the great Gotthold Ephraim Lessing (1729-1781), whom he deeply admired, was already a member. Goethe deemed Lessing's romantic comedy, *Minna von Barnhelm* (1763), the first literary manifestation of the German national spirit. He was subsequently initiated into all the leading Freemasonic rites of the time, and the literate reader may recall some of his Masonic poems and his allusions to the fraternity in *Wilhelm Meister* (1796). Even by then, however, Masonry seemed already to be suffering from the lack of any interest in its true aims by a significant portion of its membership; Goethe found many of the lodges either silly or subversive, and the members wholly uninterested in scholarship or spiritual discipline.

His nearly two-year-long tour of Italy between 1786 and 1788 was a productive, almost inevitable escape from too much practical work and from too many relationships. In a letter to his mother, Goethe clearly outlines the purpose of this leave: "I count a second birth, a true rebirth from the day I set foot in Rome." The conservative and revolutionary fantasies were over, only Classical antiquity and High Renaissance would do, all else had to go. Even after returning to Weimar, Goethe excused himself from the too onerous administrative and social responsibilities, but was allowed by the obliging Duke to retain a prominent position at the court. He still attended to some of his duties in the coming decades, including the management of the Court Theatre and the University of Jena. Yet he mostly dedicated himself to his literary and scientific pursuits, developing slowly but surely into the *Kunstgreis* mocked by the Young Germans, that is, the "Sage of Weimar" admired by the whole world.

Goethe has to be counted among the great unsung naturalists of the 18th century. Most biologists of that day were still steeped in the Judæo-Christian tradition and believed that there were essential differences between human beings and the rest of creation. Not so Goethe, who during the 1780s discovered in the human *maxilla* a *premaxilla*, which all the other mammals had, but humans in distinction to the "lower beasts" were not thought to possess. In the light of modern knowledge, there is not a single structural element in human anatomy that other primates would not have, although the said *premaxilla* usually fuses with the *supramaxilla* already at the fœtal stage. To Goethe, its existence demonstrated the fundamental affinity between all the many forms of the Natural Kingdom, or at the very least of the Animal Kingdom. His *Metamorphosis of Plants* (1790) advocated exactly the same position, its central thesis being that all the parts of the plant are evolutionary modifications of the type-leaf. His physical studies likewise proceeded from the conviction that one had to seek the "primal phenomenon" unto which the whole complexity of phenomena is of necessity reversible.

Goethe has often been dubbed an "Olympian," an harmonic universal genius, a "favourite of the gods," as he called himself, or even a God-man, which his most devoted admirers saw in him. He wrote expert treatises not only on anatomy, botany, and morphology, but palæontology, geology, and mineralogy as well, ultimately extending his interests to nearly every area of scientific study known in his time. Yet the general public invariably refuses to recognize its leaders' proficiency in more than one field of human endeavour, drawing the conclusion from its own limitation and one-sidedness, though the essence of a genius lay precisely in the fact that he can be creative and pathbreaking in any and every discipline to which he chooses to devote himself. There is hardly anyone in the history of literature who would be able to compete with the versatility of Goethe's genius, and his fate is best illustrated by his own adage that "there is nothing more indispensable and nothing less endurable to humanity than ability."

His Classicistic plays, *Iphigenie* and *Tasso*, received polite but cold reviews, while the eroticism of his *Roman Elegies* was too "pagan" for the growing horde of sentimental romantics. His great novels never appealed to the reading public, and his *Collected Works*, published in eight volumes by Göschen between the years 1787 and 1790, had a grand total of 600 subscribers. The circulation of his separate publications was scarcer still: *Clavigo* sold 17 copies, *Götz* 20, *Iphigenie* 312, *Egmont* 377, even *Werther* only 262. Thanks to *Wilhelm Meister*, *Elective Affinities*, and his autobiography, *Poetry and Truth*, Goethe is today revered by those few who have taken the trouble to dig deep into the heart of his demanding narrative art. The first part of *Faust*, published in its final form in 1808, gained such an immense popularity mostly because of the short Gretchen episode, which the public misconstrued as a love story.

The second part (posth. 1832), finished a few months before Goethe's death, is a cultural panorama that demands a great deal from the active participation of the reader. Although unquestionably an innovative and modern poem, universally recognized as one of the supreme achievements in world literature, it purposely derives much of its thematic and structural material from earlier dramatic works, carrying historical and cultural elements from all the varied sources which Goethe had explored throughout his long and eventful life. Not only are the inexhaustible references to Classical antiquity and to the Hellenic ideals a plot-dependent trope, but the implied parallelism between the dramatic irony of Faust and the typical Greek drama is also what makes this semi-autobiographical work authentic. While its apparent social criticism is often veiled in Classical allusions and planted at metadramatic scenes that call attention to both the ills of society and the evils of man, the dualistic dilemma it clearly outlines between spiritual longing and sensual desires, aspiration and indulgence, has turned Faust into a symbol of Western man and his doomed effort to access the infinite through knowledge. To many, Goethe himself was such a symbol, wholly indistinguishable from his greatest creation.

The "Age of Goethe" was not nearly as enlightened within the wide layers of society as one would assume from the philosophical publications of the period. All the storm and stress, the new ideas and the intellectual brilliance, had relevance only to a minute portion of the European population. Parallel with the great expansion there evolved a great dispersion in Europe: the rapidly expanding mercantile culture produced far more destructive class divisions than had earlier periods; peasants, heavily burdened by taxes, tithes, and feudal obligations, were and remained impoverished, while the income of urban labourers barely kept pace with inflation. The landless population increased with the general growth of population, and a man without land had hardly any other prospects than becoming a labourer. The wages were dismal: a single man could eke out a miserable existence, but in order to provide for a family, the wife or children had to work also. If the husband died or ran away, the only remaining options for a family were either starving to death or applying for parish poor relief—which alternative did not greatly differ from the first one.

Society was unable to solve the increasingly prevalent issue of female majority. The more women there were in the cities, the more difficult it was for them to find a livelihood. Women grew more and more dependent on the head of the family, be he the father, the brother, or the husband. They had no chance to break loose from the family, since a woman could not earn her own living even if she wanted to. Women were regarded as internal to the family, whose provision fell to the husband. Since a man's pay was not adequate to support a family, and since tenth of the population never married, there was a marked increase in the number of unwed women.

A situation where a woman had to take care of herself was considered dishonourable: the women of prosperous, respectable families were always looked after by someone—a lone woman was a failure. The greater part of women still lived in one way or another from agriculture. If a farmer's daughter was lucky, she got to be a maid in some farmhouse. A maid had something a farmer's wife did not necessarily have: meals on the house and a roof over her head. This relative well-being the maid would exchange for the wretched existence of a farmer's wife, after having managed to obtain enough money and linen for a dowry.

Women's chances to subsist on their own labour were greatly diminished after the trade guilds began to degenerate at the dawn of the Modern Era and set up tighter and tighter regulations denying women all professional employment. The female majority and the guilds' anti-women policies produced a great amount of cheap labour, which was forced to sell its goods at any price in order to keep alive. Prostitution mounted as the unemployed women of the cities had to earn their bread by begging and prostituting themselves. However, the connection between prostitution and unemployment remained far from acknowledged as all prostitutes were still considered inherently wicked women.

On the 5th of October, 1789, the palace of Versailles was flooded with a strange crowd. Instead of exquisite minuets and elegant trivialities, the air was filled with cries and gunshots. Instead of rouge silks and powdered wigs, there appeared ragged scarves and modest woollen dresses. Six thousand women had marched twelve miles through rain and mud to ask Louis XVI for bread to give to their children—there had been no bread in Paris for three days. A revolution is ignited when the army no longer functions, and the army ceases to function when the people have nothing left to eat. This, and this alone, is the immediate cause of most, if not all, revolutions.

Many an historian will tell you that the reason for great upheavals is the people's unquenchable thirst for freedom, but of all the untruthful reasons available, this has to be the most untruthful. Most people do not really want freedom, since first of all, they have no concept of it, and secondly, because they would not know what to do with it. Freedom is of value only to two types of people—the so-called privileged classes and the philosophers. The former have labouriously, over generations of practice, acquired the ability to make pleasant and beneficial use of freedom, while the latter invariably have freedom wherever they may find themselves, in every life situation and under any form of government. But the greater part of humanity, whom neither breeding nor philosophy has rendered capable of being free, would be overcome by an unbearable ennui if thousands of restrictive measures did not divert its attention from itself and the emptiness inside.

The Declaration of the Rights of Man[269] is supposed to herald an era of intellectual independence, middle-class self-legislation, and free economic competition. However, the belief in individualism was already prevalent throughout the Western world, deriving theoretical justification and support

---

[269] duly condemned by Pius VI in 1791

from the age-old doctrine of natural rights. Even in the Middle Ages, individuals had their natural rights, certain freedoms or privileges that were held to be an innate part of being human and which could not be denied by society. In 18th-century thinking, rights and reason were intrinsically linked, and by the end of the century, "human rights" had become a stale platitude. The British were inclined to think that they had these inalienable rights without their express formulation, but the French and the Americans in particular deemed it necessary to consolidate them into acts and declarations. The substance of these rights was as varied as the political thinkers who postulated them, but it was above all Locke's views that inspired the writers of the American Constitution. It was he who argued that man's natural and rightful objective in life was temporal happiness, whence the reference to "the pursuit of happiness" in the U.S. Declaration of Independence.

The new economic theory treated happiness the same way as did the new philosophy. Adam Smith (1723-1790), coincidentally in 1776, brought forth the idea of an autonomous economic order governed by the immutable laws of nature. In *An Inquiry into the Nature and Causes of the Wealth of Nations*, the Scottish economist argued that the growing wealth of private individuals would increase collective wealth, while public virtue and prosperity would benefit from private pursuit of happiness. He managed to elevate political economy to the rank of science and succeeded in defining the concept of capital. He saw capitalists as the most important class in society, for by investing their money in production and thus providing work opportunities, they further the economy the most. He called for a complete freedom of trade and traffic, and the abolition of serfdom and trade guilds. While the state ruler and his high officials ought to be freed from the duty of creating commercial enterprises that produce revenue for the nation, the freedom of enterprise should in principle be granted to every individual.

Smith nevertheless represented the moderate wing, and with respect to his temperament, belonged to the first generation of the Enlightenment. He did not believe blindly in totally free economic competition—it was his followers who reduced his doctrines into "crude individualism." His concept of *laissez-faire* economics was popularized by Englishman Jeremy Bentham (1748-1832), whose *Introduction to the Principles of Morals and Legislation* was published in the revolutionary year of 1789; a couple of years later, the author was rewarded with the citizenship of France. Bentham believed that man's instinctive inclination to be happy should provide sufficient motivation to ensure moral behaviour. His optimistic utilitarianism, "the greatest happiness of the greatest number," has become the guiding light of liberals everywhere. Yet it was undoubtedly Benjamin Franklin (1706-1790) who did the most to popularize the new gospel.

When Franklin came to France as the ambassador of his newly-liberated country, he acquainted himself with several of his influential kindred spirits, whom the French Revolution would soon make even more influential. Along with Voltaire and Helvétius, he was also a member of the exclusive Paris lodge of the Nine Sisters, which ceased to be a Masonic body after the Revolution and became *le Société Nationale des Neuf Sœurs*. When he and his compatriots needed to establish a system of government for their country, they recalled closely everything they had learned from the French Enlightenment philosophers, especially "the celebrated Montesquieu."[270] His separation of powers into executive, legislative, and judiciary branches was ultimately realized in the Constitution of the United States.

In France, the ideal shifted in a few years from a limited monarchy to a republic, from humanism to terror. After being forced to abdicate, Louis XVI was condemned for treason and beheaded. Within two years of instituting modern conscription, the French Republic had levied 800,000 soldiers from the provinces, an unheard of number for a European power at that time. The size of these ragged armies made it impossible to provision them in the traditional manner, so they had to live off the land, that is, off the local peasantry.

A far greater threat than the bravely repelled external aggressions was created by the internal mistrust and bickering of the revolutionaries. The public cause of the state had become the private cause of every citizen, now absorbed in a single social unit larger and more complex than any one person could hope to preside over, a microcosm of national interests more varied than any elective body could claim to represent. This led to a reign of terror the kind of which the world had not as yet seen: though rulers have at times been known to terrorize the people, now the people terrorized themselves.

The three watchwords, *Liberté, Égalité, Fraternité*, as luminous as they at first glance seem, are three opposing principles which, if combined, destroy one

---

[270] to use Madison's term

another. Liberty necessarily makes inequality manifest, for if all individuals are allowed to develop at will in conformity with their unique characters, they are no longer equal. Equality is a level which admits no liberty, for if all people are considered identical and therefore given equal rights, duties, and livings, they are no longer free. The pretention of equality sustained by liberty produces interminable strife of people between themselves, rendering fraternity impossible among them.

The Revolution asked everyone if they were in the side of liberty, and should it not receive an unequivocal answer, responded, not with *lettres de cachet* of the *Ancien Régime*, but with the newly invented guillotine. Never before, not under Draco, not under the Czars of Russia, not even under the Spanish Inquisition, had there existed such an illiberty as under the "Friends of Liberty," never before have such completely passive qualities as breeding, reticence, and tolerance been punishable by death. In a similar manner, the Revolution only led to an even more reprehensible form of inequality; the jealous guarding of their own economic liberty did not allow the Third Estate to fraternize with the poor.

By 1795, the joy and jubilation of liberty, equality, and fraternity seemed to be over. As unemployment soared with the flight or ruin of noble and ecclesiastical employers, so did the numbers of those available for immediate political discussion. The financial crisis and the maniacal attempts of people unused to politics to improve their status culminated in a horrible famine winter. After six years of upheavals only one thing had changed: the nation had the same poor as before, but the upper classes were different; whereas under the Old Régime, privileged status was guaranteed by one's ancestry, under the new directorate it was guaranteed by money.

It is often claimed that the great historic significance of the French Revolution was that it brought about the liberation of France and Europe by delivering society from absolutism, from the supremacy of the nobility and the Church. But the Revolution overturned absolutism only temporarily; it first returned as the dictatorship of the Convention and the Commune, then transformed into a personal dictatorship, first of Robespierre and then of Napoleon, following his coup in 1799. Nor did the Revolution crush hereditary kingship, aristocracy, or the clergy: in 1804, Napoleon was crowned "Emperor of the French" with the blessing of the Senate and Pope Pius VII.

Most people are naturally curious about ancient texts and relics; after all, these form the basis of all human culture, philosophy, and religion. Rarely, however, has there been an age that to such an extent and so passionately dressed itself in the bygone way of life. Since "Roman" and "republican" had become thoroughly identified in the consciousness of the period, everywhere stood the graven images of the "heroes of liberty"—Cincinnatus, Demosthenes, Cato, Brutus, Seneca, etc. The Marquis de Lafayette was dubbed "Scipio Americanus," while the Jacobins not only took their name from the Latin form of the name James, but always appealed in the political and economical actions to Rome and Sparta; their characteristic emblem was the "Phrygian cap," an imitation of the scarlet headgear of emancipated slaves in Classical antiquity.

The *Marseillaise* was based on a Roman model, and *R.F.*, the official symbol of the French Republic, was formed after the Roman *SPQR*. The Austrian Netherlands, "liberated" by France, became "Belgium," while Holland was turned into "Batavia," Switzerland into "Helvetia," Genoa into "Liguria," and Naples into "Parthenope." Babeuf changed his first name into Gracchus and named his political journal *Popular Tribune*[271]. The Empire style sponsored by Napoleon accepted only the Classical straight line and rejected every curve. The fact that it was a time of war manifested in the penchant for battle trophies, gauze, and funeral urns. The military headgear took on the shape of a Roman helmet, and tiaras, last popular in Classical antiquity, came back to fashion. Not only the fronts of buildings, but the apartments themselves were stuffed with sphinxes, caryatids, columns, and obelisks. Bookshelves and wardrobes, and even the bedside commodes, were Greek temples with their capitals and architraves; washstands were tripods, chamber-pots urns, urns altars.

The rebuilding of the Louvre, begun by Francis I, was continued in the same Classicistic style. With its extensive Franco-Italian piazzas, the largest palace in Western Europe does not represent a revival of Classical antiquity—ancient Greece and Rome were rather seized as spoils of war. In the *Musée Central de la République*, afterwards the *Musée Napoléon*, were amassed the artefacts looted from all the ancient lands already during the Revolution. Lord Elgin, the British ambassador to the Ottoman Empire, removed 56

---

[271] i.e. *Tribun du Peuple*

sculptures from the Parthenon to London, where the British Museum bought these "Elgin Marbles." The universal interest in archæology was a natural result of the prevailing Classicism. As a scientific study, however, archæology is only about 150 years old: "dilettanti" was the name given to the 18th-century Italian gentlemen who initiated the private collection of art objects from the Classical period. For over a century, relic hunters from the wealthiest families in Europe simply travelled to exotic locations, dug enormous holes, and brought the prettiest artefacts home. Fragile structures and perishable or unimpressive pieces were disregarded for most of the 19th century, as were any earlier prehistoric levels underlying historic sites. Much of even the better-looking objects ended up in unclassified piles in Western museums, far from their countries of origin.

In the 17th and 18th centuries, the chief interests of those travelling to Egypt lay in the pyramids and in the unearthing of lost treasures. Not until 1798, with Napoleon's Egyptian expedition, was the past truly reawakened. After the Battle of the Pyramids was over, Napoleon addressed the 300 draftsmen and scientists, who accompanied his military troops. The mission of these "savants" was to make Egypt known, not only for France, but for all Europe. They needed to familiarize themselves with the lore of the Egyptians, everything had to be surveyed and collected, so that modern Europe could add the ancient knowledge to its own. The record of their work would eventually fill several volumes of *La Description de l'Egypte*.

The more the archæologists of the 19th century excavated, the more surprised they were of what they found. Egyptian religion appears to have been a huge disappointment to the men who had been brought up in the Judæo-Christian tradition and read the Classics in school. They saw that the Egyptian religion did not have the sexual morality of Christianity any more than it had the philosophy of the Græco-Roman tradition. Egyptian sexuality was celebrated in a way that made the early Egyptologists hide things in back rooms, refuse to show certain bits to the public, and look for ways to word the translations so that no one would realize what was really being said. To show his power to rise again after being cut down, Osiris was sometimes depicted with three erect *phalloi*, and most museums of our time continue to have reservations about displaying the divine masturbation of Amoun.

The flow of biological energy, of sexual energy, is still disconcerting to the vast majority of Westerners. The prohibition against self-stimulation is from the Levant, the desert-grown cultures that overwhelmed Egypt and went on to create Judaism, Christianity, and Islam.[272] Far less sophisticated than the Egyptians, these cultures were as unable to deal with sexuality then as now. The same people who dismissed anything they did not understand about the Egyptian religion as "primitive superstition" wore gold crucifixes on chains and believed that a virgin could get pregnant and yet remain one. The arbitrary division between religion and sexuality was foisted upon our culture by the growth of Christianity when it sought to emerge victoriously from the antecedent pagan religions, and despite all that has been done by Freud, Reich, and many others, ours remains a sex-negative culture.

---

[272] In fact, circumcision, both male and female, was instituted primarily to prevent the "sin of Onan."

CHAPTER 40

The 19th century was to witness a social and intellectual boom that has no comparison, an explosion that would sow the seeds of modern industrialism. The real revolution of the turn of the century was not the French, but the Industrial Revolution. Only once before has the lot of ordinary man gone through such a violent change, that is, when Neolithic man was transformed from a hunter and gatherer into a farmer and herder. The starting-point of European industrialization can be placed in those late 18th-century decades which gave birth to both the steam engine and the spinning jenny as well as the first mechanical loom. Steam power freed manufacturing from the restrictions which water power imposed on location and size. Within two generations, the life of the working classes had been completely overturned: before 1760, it was standard to take work to villagers in their own cottages; by 1820, the standard was to bring workers into factories and have them overseen.

The production methods of the old agrarian communities called for a fixed family unit and thus could not sustain divorces. Requiring the distribution of the estate and complicating the matters of inheritance, divorce was an intrusive factor that upset balance and continuity. It affected the very core of the peasant community, the estate. Keeping families together was not in the interest of the urban industrial communities, however, for single people were the best supply of labour. But the increase in divorces was not brought about by industrialization and urbanization alone; as the marrying age fell and the middle age rose, death was simply substituted with divorce.

Throughout the 18th century, the leading thinkers of the time had impressed on their public the importance of mutual affection in successful marriages. The idea of combining marriage and sexuality came from the urban middle classes, who disapproved of the rude and brutal way the peasants treated their wives. The spouses of a bourgeois family had, at least in theory, chosen each other of their own free will, on basis of love. The decisive factors contributing to the birth of the modern nuclear family were the wealth and individualism brought on by market economy. Only among the highest aristocracy was it any longer possible to wed the young ones purely on financial basis, and without them knowing each other before marriage.

While the rationalism of the period had an averse effect on poetry and the sense of tragedy, it encouraged people to explore the everyday reality. This appealed especially to the middle classes, who rejected the old chivalric and pastoral romances in favour of unembellished depictions about their own fates and adventures. The use of the prose form was a given in an age that valued truthfulness and matter-of-factness, regarding the verse form as nothing but an ornate frame. It was a thoroughly literary era: everything was done in writing, discussion, travelling, feuding, and loving; everything was only a matter of literature—state, society, and religion. The world got obsessed by the modern delusion that education is a matter of learning, that books are the great teachers. A veritable reading-frenzy took over all the social classes, the public library came into being, and the pocket book became an essential article of clothing.

The most significant literary event for the rising middle classes was the birth of the periodical. The first regular journal, *The Daily Courant*, was published in London as early as 1702. Nevertheless, only the launch of the "Daily Universal Register," otherwise known as *The Times*, in 1785, marked the advent of the modern newspaper. The most important mechanical invention of that period was the rotary press, which performed the hitherto manual printing independently and several times faster, first in 1814, again naturally in England. Not until the newspaper had thus allied itself with the machine did it gain its universal dominance: words, true and false, fly into the great gaping hole that swallows them, prints them, and duplicates them into thousands of copies, which it then belches out into the bourgeois foyers, peasant cottages, barracks, palaces, cellars, and attics; people no longer have any ideas or opinions of their own, but only what they have gleaned from the media.

The triumph of Fleet Street progressed slowly from west to east, from the British Isles first to France. The sale of single copies instead of the once prevalent, expensive annual subscription turned the newspaper into a public and obtrusive notification and advertisement scheme that united it with the other universal power of the era, namely mercantilism, and introduced the serial novel, ostensibly turning it into literature. Many a famous British novelist, and nearly every French one, begun their career with this journalistic format, and often held on to it for the rest of their lives. Thanks to countless pulp novels, being in love, once likened to a mental disturbance, became a respectable basis for marriage.

In the first half of the 19th century, the number of illegitimate children and pregnant brides grew at an astonishing rate in the lowest classes of Europe.[273] The farmer's daughter, the maid, the seamstress, and the textile worker entered into sexual relationships more readily than before. Instead of chastity and abstinence, Western people valued romance. The search of work sent the young people away from their home village and its traditions. They were unattached and began to look for a companion. The arrival of the nuclear family to the peasant village was signalled by the extinction of the communal gatherings, celebrations, and carnivals. People who had previously associated themselves formally and informally with same-sex peers, now severed their links outside the family; conversely, their relationships with the near kin often improved.

One reason for the greater sexual freedom was the decrease in value of maidenhood. When entering into matrimony, virginity had its exchangeable value; the bride exchanged it for the financial security provided by the groom. But virginity has value only if someone is willing to pay for it. The end of the 18th century saw an explosive increase in farm and factory workers who could barely support themselves, let alone a virgin bride. Virginity was of no use in the farm-hand's shack or in the mill-hand's basement chamber—the health and working capacity of the bride was all that mattered. An illegitimate child was generally the result of either a man of a higher class seducing a lower-class woman or a man and woman of the same class "making love." In the former case, marriage was not even an option, in the latter, promises may have been given, but not kept. Fleeing from responsibility was easy in the new restless society, where the girl could no longer lean on either her parents or relatives, on the Church or the public opinion.

Traditional society was quite successful in regulating sexuality in conformity with its own needs—but different needs call for different measures: labour shortage eased the laws in favour of those whom society needed, and in early 19th century, unwed pregnancy ceased to be a criminal offence. It usually still meant the loss of employment, however, since the employers were of the

---

[273] However, even the Protestant denominations remained totally opposed to contraception until the Church of England took the bold stand in 1930 that birth control might be permissible under certain conditions.

social class which sexual permissiveness did not reach, and which rather tightened its rules. The chastity of its women is a prerequisite to the cohesion of a middle-class nuclear family. The bourgeoisie needed to punish the single mother and her bastard child as an example of the wages of sin for its own young women. Nor did the sexual freedom of the upper-class gentlemen extend to the fathers and husbands of a middle-class family, who had to restrict their sexual liberty, at least on the outside. Here we have the basis for the Victorian way of thinking, for the hypocritical double standard, where a man can do whatever he pleases as long as he does not do it in public.

The 19th century was to be the century of British power and influence. The standard of living was much higher in England than on the Continent, its public health, sports, and hygiene were at a whole other level. The Englishman's attire was the healthiest, the most natural, and the most rational in Europe. The Brits were also the first to dress children differently from adults. The greatest stumbling-block to progress was the mediæval guild system, which retained its status in many countries all the way to the 1860s. Even in England, it was not abolished until 1835, though in practice, it lost its influence by the beginning of the century. Thanks to the break-through of liberalism, Britain became the leading country both in mechanical engineering and industrial development. The Briton had faith in material improvement; virtually throughout the entire Western world, people took for granted that industriousness and inventiveness would produce more and more luxuries. The Utopias of this era are abound with inventions which were quite often also realized in practice.

In the beginning of the century, most houses in London already had water-closets, and as early as 1814, the entire city was given gas lighting. The English streets were in excellent condition and there were many steel bridges and other transport facilities, whereas on the Continent, the roads were intentionally allowed to deteriorate so that the aliens would be forced into a prolonged stay and the citizens would have trouble travelling abroad. There were some two hundred steam engines in France, over five thousand in Britain. Twenty steamers catered for the passenger traffic in English and Scottish waters, while the British mercantile fleet was one-fourth larger than all of the continental ones combined. In an insular kingdom, military power means naval power, and Britain's was unchallenged.

The isolated development of England can be partly traced to the continental blockade which Napoleon decreed in 1806: it forbade the Continent to engage in any trade, traffic, or communication with Britain, and declared every Briton within the French circle of influence a prisoner and all British goods spoils of war. The export trade of England did indeed drop to a half and the value of its government bonds to a third, while the cost of living doubled. But the Continent suffered as great a damage: all over, factories and other large businesses had to be closed, and bankruptcies were rife. The prices of dyes and iron, of cotton, rice, coffee, tobacco, and spices, of all colonial goods in general, went up the roof. The continental blockade made Napoleon the archenemy not only of England, but of all Europe, more than conscription and taxation, more than censorship and police, more than the pillage of countries and the overthrow of governments.

In 1806, Napoleon was at the height of his power; even the States of the Church were annexed by France. The Emperor gave his supporters exalted titles and established new monarchies, often for his relatives, in the territories brought under French control. He made his brother, Joseph Bonaparte[274], King of Naples, but incorporated the rest of Italy into the French Empire—"there is a mistress whose favours I will divide with none."[275] After his victory over the Austrians at Austerlitz, Napoleon formed the Confederation of the Rhine, which counted among its members the newly-created kingdoms of Bavaria, Württemberg, and Saxony, and the grand duchies of Baden, Hesse-Darmstadt, and Berg. Virtually all the German states except Austria and Prussia eventually joined this confederation, disavowing their allegiance to the Holy Roman Empire. Francis II, already styling himself Emperor of Austria, formally dissolved the old Empire on the 6th of August, 1806. Since Napoleon was obviously not going to allow the election of another Habsburg as Holy Roman Emperor, they were one step ahead of him. When Rome was incorporated into the French Empire in 1810, Napoleon declared it "the second city of the empire." A year later, Empress Marie Louise gave birth to Napoleon II, who was proclaimed King of Rome, his father's heir. "Three more years and I will be the master of the universe," announced the new French emperor.

But three years hence, he was already an exile at Elba. In May, 1812, the

---

[274] born Giuseppe Buonaparte

[275] Bear in mind, the Bonapartes were Italians from Corsica.

insatiable conqueror departed from Paris to Dresden, and thence towards Moscow, to bend her to his will. In mid-October, his *Grande Armée* began its long retreat through the snows of Russia. Reduced by nine-tenths, half of the remaining 60,000 troops were killed crossing the Berezina late in November, half of the surviving 30,000 died the following week as the temperature dropped further. By the time the few thousand still alive abandoned their wagons and artillery west of Vilnius, the army had ceased to exist. The Rhenish Confederation collapsed as its members changed sides in the conflict. Napoleon's hold on Italy was similarly weaked in 1813, when Austria invaded northern Italy and a British fleet occupied Genoa. France itself was finally invaded from the east by Austrians, Prussians, and Russians, and from the south by Wellington. In March, 1814, the allies marched on Paris, and Czar Alexander I rode triumphantly through the streets with the King of Prussia by his side. After years of exile in London, Louis XVIII, brother of Louis XVI, was restored to the French throne.

The Enlightenment ended with the American and French Revolutions; after the fall of Napoleon and France, the European governments began to make mutual agreements to check all political and economic reforms. Conservativeness and reactionism were represented by the principles of legitimacy and stability, the twin slogans of the Congress of Vienna, a meeting of the victors[276] convened from September of 1814 to June of 1815. By "legitimacy" they meant restoring the former princes of Europe to their previous positions, by "stability" a balance between the great European powers; the goal was to prevent future revolutions.

The last official link to the Dark Ages had been severed when Napoleon forced the dissolution of the Holy Roman Empire, but the Congress of Vienna saw fit to establish a "German Confederation," another loose association of sovereign states, with exactly the same boundaries as the Empire of 1648. The Confederation would have an appointed, not elected, Federal Diet at Frankfurt, and the Austrian Emperor was to be its *ex officio* President. His Chancellor, Clemens von Metternich, presided over one of the most pervasive police states in history. The ideologue and embodiment of the Congress of Vienna, people said his rule was sustained by a standing army of soldiers, a sitting army of bureaucrats, a kneeling army of priests, and a crawling army of

---

[276] Islamic Turkey was specifically excluded.

informers.

The period of Napoleonic rule had temporarily unified Italy and introduced liberal political principles, but the Congress of Vienna once again divided the country between the Habsburgs in the north, the Bourbons in the Two Sicilies, the Savoy in Sardinia, and the papacy in the centre. The Catholic Church was seen as a bastion of stability in Europe after the long horrors of the French Revolution and the Napoleonic Wars. The new rulers of Italy abolished all liberal institutions, revoked the liberal constitutions, imprisoned and persecuted the liberal elements, while Pope Pius VII re-established the Jesuits as a world order.

The Spaniards had shown indomitable will to independence during the French occupations, incited to resistance by the romance and rhetoric of Quintana's patriotic odes. The name of Prince Ferdinand, imprisoned by Napoleon, became the rallying call of liberal and revolutionary elements throughout the Spanish empire. However, when he was restored to the throne in 1814, he revealed himself a thoroughly reactionary tyrant. One of his first acts as Ferdinand VII was to reintroduce the Spanish Inquisition, abolished by the Cortes just the year before. During his reign, pretty much every Spanish colony in the Americas was lost through the very rebellions that had originally begun as risings in his favour against Napoleon. The spread of national romanticism to Spanish America may have contributed also to the fact that on its liberation it splintered into a plethora of independent states.

In 1815, Napoleon escaped from Elba and returned to power for the so-called "Hundred Days." His final defeat by British and Prussian forces at the Battle of Waterloo in Belgium led to the creation of the short-lived United Kingdom of the Netherlands. Russia, Austria, and Prussia then formed a "Holy Alliance"[277] to oppose all change and revolution, agreeing to base their domestic and foreign policy on Christian principles. Even in liberal England, one Tory ministry followed another, and the chief minister, Lord Castlereagh, an "intellectual eunuch" as Byron called him, smothered every attempt at self-help with emergency legislation—the notorious "gag laws"—until his active paranoia turned passive and drove him to suicide in 1822. The French premier, the Comte de Villèle, similarly curbed civil liberties, suppressed press freedom, and gave the Catholic Church increasing control over

---

[277] a/k/a "White Terror"

education. In 1823, his reactionary government was delegated by the Holy Alliance to crush the liberalism to which Ferdinand VII was finally succumbing. A French army led by a Bourbon prince broke the Spanish constitution and restored the King to absolute power. In the violent repression that followed, liberals were persecuted endlessly, and the justifiability of these persecutions can be deduced from the fact that a woman was executed in Granada for embroidering a banner with the words *justicia, libertad, igualdad*.

When Napoleon conquered Venice at the end of the 18th century, he took half a ton of gold from the Venetian treasury and melted it down to pay his troops. Despite all the losses, it is to this day the only place in the world where one can get a glimmer of the treasure that once filled Byzantium. Modern Greeks call themselves "Hellenes," like the ancient Greeks did; the switch from *Romaioi* back to *'Ellinas*, came from the politics of nationalism in the early 19th century. Except for the brief period (1699-1718) when the Peloponnese was occupied by the Venetians, Greece had been under firm Turkish domination for almost four hundred years. The Greek people were quite heterogeneous, held together in addition to material interests only by religion, and needed West European help to become an independent nation. They were not likely to gain assistance if they were thought of as Byzantines, but if seen as the descendants of Pericles and Plato, the sympathies of every educated Westerner, steeped in the Classical tradition, would be with them.

Throughout Europe, the Greek cause was promoted by eloquent speeches and quotations from Plutarch on the glory days of the past. The Western "Philhellenes," of whose Byron was the most prominent, saw in the Greek War of Independence (1821-1830) also a struggle against slavery. It is true that there were at that time slave markets everywhere in Turkey, like there were in North America, and throughout the war, Greeks were sold on the open market in Constantinople, Smyrna, Alexandria, and other Ottoman cities. However, it was mainly because of the strategic importance of the peninsula that the European powers agreed in 1827 to undertake military intervention, forcing the Sultan to capitulate. Following the peace, Britain, France, and Russia declared Greece an autonomous kingdom under their united protection. Prince Otto of Bavaria, a well-known collector of ancient artefacts and a connoisseur of Greece, was chosen as king. The name *Hellas* may have been revived in order to create a national image that renounced the

"Byzantine" past, but a royal decree (1835) reintroduced "the laws of the Byzantine Emperors," which were to form the cornerstone of the Greek Civil Code.

For twenty years, Napoleon had turned the Continent into an inhumane battleground. The scale of conflict had been completely changed by mass armies, raised at little cost by conscription. The Napoleonic Wars were the most costly and deadly that had thus far visited mankind. But they had also endowed the world with a long-awaited figure of superhuman intellect and the governing skills to match. His fall was perpetrated by subhuman shadows, decrepit puppet kings, insipid petty princes. There is never anything uplifting in the victory of mediocrity over genius, not even when the genius is of the diabolical variety. To cite the French Emperor himself: "Great men are like meteors, which shine and consume themselves to enlighten the earth."

The prophecy uttered by Napoleon in the cabinet of the Hundred Days was fulfilled: "You shall shed bitter tears in remembrance of me." Every word that he had said or left unsaid, was preserved. Busts, drawings, children's books, market stalls, cane handles, and cigarette boxes everywhere bore his image. His mortal remains became sacred relics. People were not afraid to compare Sant Helena with the Calvary, Laetitia with the Sorrowful Mother. Victor Hugo proclaimed Napoleon the "Mohammed of the West," but to most Frenchmen he was simply known as *l'homme*, "the man." Nor was he generally believed to be dead at all: the mountain people of Sicily expected his return and the Arabs, in whose imagination he fused with Alexander the Great, told tales about the reappearance of the Frankish Sultan Iskander.

Before Napoleon, Germany was not a united country: it was made up of 380 entities, mostly independent, ranging from free cities and small ecclesiastical territories to large feudal states such as Prussia. The establishment of the Rhenish Confederation under his control reduced the number of states to a tenth. The thirty-one entities that remained after the Congress of Vienna were an incredible mess: in 1815, the kingdom of Saxony existed alongside the grand duchy of Saxe-Weimar, the duchies of Saxe-Gotha, Saxe-Coburg, Saxe-Meiningen, and Saxe-Hildburghausen—Saxe-Altenburg being the only Saxon division that did not survive. A significant consolidation occurred in 1826, when Duke Ernest of Saxe-Coburg took over Saxe-Gotha, creating the duchy of Saxe-Coburn-Gotha, from which his son

Albert married Queen Victoria of England.[278] (While the name "Windsor" was adopted by the British royal family during World War II, Queen Elizabeth II is still actually a Wettin, descended from Frederick of Saxony.)

The electors of Hanover were also the kings of Great Britain until 1837, when the Salic law, prohibiting female succession, passed over Queen Victoria. Though the British Parliament was always suspicious of the German interests of the Hanoverian kings, Hanover found itself in anti-French alliances just as naturally as England. After the French Revolution and the Napoleonic Wars, when Hanover was generally under French occupation, the electorate emerged as one of the five kingdoms of the German Confederation. Back in 1803, Napoleon had made the landgrave of Hesse-Kassel an elector of the Holy Roman Empire, and since this was an infinitely loftier title than landgrave, the ruler of Hesse-Kassel got it recognized at Vienna—there thus remained one elector of a non-existent emperor until as late as 1866.

Besides the examples offered by Britain and the United States, the primary prerequisite for German nationalism was the fall of the old Empire. Though fragmented Germany could not produce anything comparable to these modern nations, it had its common language. As far as it stretches, also stretches the *Vaterland*, stated Ernst Moritz Arndt, one of the fathers of German nationalism and the coiner of the infamous *Lebensraum*. If nationality is founded on language, literature becomes its most important buttress, and national poets replace the kings and ecclesiastical princes at the top of the hierarchy. A concept of nation of this sort has to build on such Herderian myths as *Volkgeist* or *Stimmen der Völker*, not on practical politics.

By then, most of the German *Klassiker* were dead, and the greatest one alive, Goethe, was not interested in national poetry, but in *Weltliteratur*. While he acknowledged that poetry stemmed from a regional background, he felt that the time of national literatures was past and communication between writers would develop unimpeded by state borders. "If we can find in the world a place, where we can exist peacefully with our possessions, a field to nourish us, a house to shelter us," wrote Goethe in his youth, "have we not then a fatherland? And do not thousands have this in every state? . . . Roman patriotism? Let God keep us from it like from Leviathan! We would not find

---

[278] They were first cousins; in fact, all the surviving royalty of Europe are closely related.

a chair to sit on, a bed to sleep in." And when the Confederation of the Rhine was established, elderly Goethe calls it in his diary "the bickering of a footman and coachman sitting in one seat, that has overwhelmed us with greater passion than the fall of the Roman empire." All ambitions of nationalistic self-sufficiency were clearly alien to him, and when the national enthusiasm rose to its highest pitch, Goethe buried himself in the scientific studies which occupied more and more of his time and interest with every passing year. It was up to the younger generation of German writers to take care of the national revival, which in the cosmopolitan *Weltburger* provoked only irritation.

A few external incentives were all that was needed, and these were provided by the Napoleonic Wars. The French Emperor was not fought only by traditional armies of Austria and Prussia, but citizen volunteers exhibiting the new spirit of German nationalism. The Battle of Leipzig, ending in Napoleon's defeat, was called the "Battle of the Nations." After the War of Liberation, the national slogans were "liberty," "unity," and "Germanism." It was clear, however, that language nationalism would come to a head-on collision with the system of Metternich, and other such efforts to maintain the *status quo* and suppress change. The first German *Burschenschaft* was formed at the University of Jena in 1815, followed three years later by the *Allgemeine Deutsche Burschenschaft*, aimed to generate a united German front at least among the students. In 1819, the Holy Alliance seized the opportunity to enact the notorious Carlsbad Decrees: all student societies were banned, all universities were put under a strict supervision, all books and papers were subjected to censorship. Everyone who had had anything at all to do with the German national movement was met with cruel persecution. A typical episode for this period was the confiscation by the Austrian police of the new edition of Copernicus' treatise, on ground that its title began with the words *De Revolutionibus*, referring of course to the "revolution" of the heavenly bodies.

There was only semi-official journalism in Germany: in all the principal towns, Metternich founded newspapers that contained only government propaganda. At the same time, he managed to obtain the services of many literary talents of the age, partly through detentions and partly through bribes. Outside these compulsory politics, the papers contained only trifling gossip. Censorship arrests, searches and seizures, violations of the privacy of correspondence, covert surveillance through spies and informants were common, not only in every Habsburg country, but also in Prussia, the homeland of Kant and the categorical imperative—where the bureaucracy was even more intransigent than in Austria.

Blaming Napoleon's defeat of the Prussian forces in 1806 on soldiers only thinking about themselves, Baron von Humboldt and his colleagues took the principles set forth by Locke and Rosseau, and created a three-level educational system, the aim of which was "blind obedience and the abolition of independent thinking." Generals von Scharnhorst and von Gneisenau reorganized the Prussian army according to the programme of Baron von Stein, which included West European, in particular Anglo-Saxon type of democratization. Even philosopher Johann Fichte, in his *Address to the German People*, declared that children were to be taken over by the state and told what to think and how to think it. Germany was supposed to become a "land of schools and barracks," and its citizens a "nation of poets and thinkers."

As the French Revolution and all its horrors were blamed on religious skepticism, there were drastic efforts all over Europe during the first quarter of the 19th century to curb its growth and restore the power of Christianity. However, the check of the revolt against the Churches was only a political check, not a spontaneous return to belief. Throughout the Western world and especially in the Catholic countries, the anticlericalism of the Enlightenment lived on, and the skeptical movement became more iconoclastic than ever. But though external religious conformity was no longer enforced by law, leaving a Church was still generally impossible, and freedom of religion was seen as the freedom to practise the particular religion to which one's own society had pledged itself.

When the feudal monarchs of Europe were restored after the fall of Napoleon, the Churches were their strongest allies in every country. Priests and ministers alike insisted that advanced education, not only in literature, but also in science, should be kept under careful sectarian control. Catholic Spain would deny professorship to all men holding the Newtonian theory, Austria and Italy to all those holding objectionable views in regard to the immaculate conception. Following the example of Protestant Britain, the universities of New England would reject professors who had improper opinions regarding the incarnation, infant baptism, the apostolic succession, ordination by elders, or the perseverance of the saints.

In Prussia, Georg Wilhelm Friedrich Hegel (1770-1831) was considered just the right man to oppose revolutionary ideology; few philosophers have had a more pernicious influence on modern philosophy and politics than he has. In 1818, he took over Fichte's chair at the University of Berlin, and remained until his death the professor of philosophy there. Encouraged by his father to become a clergyman, Hegel had initially studied not philosophy, but theology, and in a sense, all his philosophy is essentially theology, exploration of the workings of the "Universal Spirit." Among his first writings were *The Life of Jesus* and *The Positivity of the Christian Religion*, but his circle of interests soon encompassed all conceivable fields of study, from metaphysics to political science, from the interpretation of ancient history to the creation of new.

Thinking and writing similarly about every subject, Hegel did not let his gross ignorance of science get in the way of applying his philosophy to the methods and objects of science. He was the culmination and embodiment of the Kantian school of philosophy, an idealist who claimed to be a rationalist. Following the Greek philosopher Parmenides, he argued that "what is rational is real and what is real is rational." He professed to stand for reason and logic, yet deemed logical contradictions not as evidence of falsity, but as steps in the generation of higher and more comprehensive contradictions—or truth—paving the way for the candid adoption of open hostility towards logic and rationality.

Hegel was a patriotic German, who wished to increase the respect for German traditions at the cost of French ones. He resolved, or rather thought he resolved, the logical difficulties by allowing his Universal Spirit to work through time, attributing human history, with all its revolutions, wars, and scientific discoveries, to an idealistic self-development of an objective intelligence. The philosophical idea of evolution, that the present form of the earth and its inhabitants developed through the ages, was first put forward by Greek philosophers. Among the Romans, Lucretius made much of it, extending the evolutionary process to virtually all things. Hegel, however, rejected the concept of equality, that all societies are the same, just at different levels of evolution. Instead, he developed a classification system that aimed to prove the "natural" sovereignty of German people, and provided an historical rationale for genocide.

Hegel demonstrated with his dialectical method, which his partial disciple Karl Marx would later make even more famous, that monarchy was the highest form of government and that the Prussia of Frederick William III was the greatest of all monarchies. The trouble with Hegel's *Philosophy of Right*

(1820) as an apologetic for the Prussian state is not that the author was corrupted by tenure, but that his entire epistemological system matched exactly the political absolutism upon which he and his sponsoring state readily agreed. Hegel called the state the "march of God through the world" and the "final end." According to him, the state must be worshipped "as the manifestation of the divine on earth." It "has supreme right against the individual, whose supreme duty is to be a member of the state." If the citizen does not recognize the good of the state, and begins to act against the government for example by attempting to bring about universal suffrage, he forfeits his membership in the state. The protesting or rebellious individual can only be justified by success, in which case he can be fitted *ex post facto* into Hegel's dialectic.

The state-worship of the *Philosophy of Right* was not a one-time political requital or temporary enthusiasm. The moral, intellectual, and practical counterpart to Hegelian philosophy came to flourish largely because of the ascendancy of Hegel's patron, the Prussian state. Though long gone, Prussia continues to live in the institutions of social security and police supervision that all Western states have adopted from her. Universal state identification papers, mandatory public education for the purposes of state propaganda, compulsory peacetime recruitment on grounds of national defence and economic stimulation, the disarmament of civilians to prevent resistance to authority, and public pensions to make every citizen dependent on government, all originated in Prussia and constitute "enlightened" features of modern democracies. The older freedoms of voluntary association and private property continue to be dismissed, as they once were by both Hegel and Marx, as "formal" and "insufficient."

At the time of Hegel's death, he was the most prominent philosopher in Germany; his views were widely taught, his students held in high regard. His followers soon divided into two wings, one marching right, the other left—both Fascism and Communism have their philosophical roots in Hegelianism. In his *On Religion: Speeches to Its Cultured Despisers* (1799), the Rev. Dr. Friedrich D. E. Schleiermacher (1768-1834) had advanced the notion that religion is a matter of profound emotions, not of rational arguments. The politically orthodox right-wing Hegelians could continue building on this basis, and at the same time, still remain religious. But opposite conclusions were also possible and equally common: the rebellious left-wing

Hegelians, like Ludwig Feuerbach (1804-1872), considered religious sentiments as products of imagination designed to alleviate life's burdens, as the "opiate of the people," as Marx would soon put it.

The 19th century was characterized by the birth of no major Christian sect, none so successful as the Methodist and Pietistic groups founded at the very height of the Enlightenment. The most significant in number were the two new American groups, Mormons (1830) and the so-called Christian Scientists (1877). But the heterogeneity of religious sects and sub-sects, especially within the circle of Eastern-influenced denominations, was greater than ever. The 1800s were just as colourful and eclectic in the field of religion as they were in the field of architecture.

Knowledge about Oriental religions, brought by missionary work and the translations of sacred texts, taught Westerners that Christianity and religion were not one and the same, that all good was not monopolized by their own belief system. Every culture tends to believe that its own scriptures are received wisdom, that its own chief divinity is a "god above all gods," that its own holy city is the centre of the world, that its own people are the "chosen people." It was the universal belief in the Church that Hebrew was the language spoken by Yahweh and his angels, that it was given by Him to Adam, the first man, transmitted through Noah to the world after the Deluge, and that all other languages were derived from it at the "confusion of Babel."

Until Napoleon took a group of French scholars to the Nile Valley, the ancient Egyptian civilization had been to the Western masses just another nation that lay in darkness and the shadow of death until the light of Christ broke upon the world. The educated knew from Classical literature that Egypt had had a wonderful civilization, that the wisest Greeks and Romans had learned from even earlier Egyptian teachers. The ancient legends ascribed the foundation of several Hellenic cities to men who, like Cecrops and Cadmus, had come from Egypt, or brought Egyptian culture to Greece via Phœnicia or Crete. But Westerners in general knew nothing of these facts—it had been a dogma since the Middle Ages that there was no light or virtue in the world until Judaism gave a dawn and Christianity the full noontide sun.

The West has seen a remarkable revolution of opinion; modern scholars have established that accounts formerly supposed to be special revelations to Jews and Christians are merely repetitions of widespread legends dating from far earlier civilizations, that beliefs formerly thought essential to Judaism and Christianity are based on much more ancient myths, that every fine sentiment in the New Testament has a parallel in the words of Plato or the Stoics. The punctilious 19th-century translations of Indian, Persian, and Chinese scriptures showed the relation of the more Eastern sacred literature to our own, proving once and for all that the ideas of the great world religions were not of sudden revelation or creation, but of slow evolution out of a distant past.

Oriental studies had begun in earnest with the great voyages of discovery, and since the Renaissance and the Reformation, languages had been a favourite study with the divided Western Church. Within the first decade of the founding of the Society of Jesus, St. Francis Xavier had already travelled to India and Japan, and the Jesuits would for long be the main importers of Eastern wisdom to the West. Ethnographic inquiry was in the interest of missionary work: instead of bullying converts into acknowledging beliefs as strange as their own, haltingly using their language augmented by gestures, the languages were learned properly and the native faiths explored. The services of the Jesuit missionaries to the material basis of modern comparative philology were great; as early as 1581, a Jesuit father stationed in India had taken notice of how close the sacred language of the Brahmins was to the European tongues.

However, before the 19th century, languages were studied mainly as a field of theology or philosophy. The real revelation about Sanskrit would come as a by-product of the establishment of direct British rule in India. In 1784, Sir William Jones (1746-1794), a supreme court judge in Calcutta, founded the Royal Asiatic Society of Bengal. Two years later, he suggested that Sanskrit and Persian originated from the same source as Latin and Greek, thus bringing to light for the first time genetic relations between languages. With Jones' realization began the school of comparative historical linguistics, and the small group of scholars who devoted themselves to its study, though almost invariably reverent Christians, were recognized at once as mortal enemies of the sacred theory of language. Not only was the dogma of the multiplication of languages at the Tower of Babel seriously undermined, but the infinitely more important dogma of the divine origin of Hebrew was now in peril, as overwhelming evidence suggested that the various languages of mankind had been produced by natural process of evolution.

Many archæologist began to actively search for the cities and cultures described in the extant ancient writings, such as Homer and the Old Testament, the Vedic and Confucian manuscripts. Schliemann sought Troy of Homer, Botta Nineveh, Gastang and Kenyon Jericho; Woolley dug at Ur of the Chaldees, Evans at Mycenæ. But the most astonishing finds were those made at Babylon by the spade of Koldewey. It appeared that the world had been completely deceived for two thousand years as to the character of the Babylonians. An immense literature and an upright code of laws was found in the ruins of Mesopotamian cities, destroyed before the Hebrews could even write.

The Egyptian discoveries began to unveil pictures of animals with their names in hieroglyphics from a period earlier than that agreed upon by every sacred chronologist as the date of the Creation. During the Christian period, hieroglyphic writing was forbidden, and along with it, much of the subtleties of the language lost. Knowledge lay dormant for centuries, until the Rosetta Stone, discovered by Napoleon's troops in 1799, proved the key to the mystery of hieroglyphics. When the British took possession of Egypt in 1802, they also took possession of the antiquities collection, which is why that famous slab of basalt now rests in the British Museum. The translation and comparison of the Greek inscription with the adjoining hieroglyphic and demotic scripts allowed for the creation of grammar and vocabulary books not only for the hieroglyphics, but also for the demotic language.

At the turn of the century, the Spanish Jesuit, Lorenzo Hervás (1735-1809), enlarged his catalogue of languages to contain specimens of more than three hundred languages and the grammars of more than forty. Protestant Germany, meanwhile, was graced with the work of Johann Christoph Adelung (1732-1806), which contained the Lord's Prayer in nearly five hundred languages and dialects, the comparison of which by such linguists as Jakob Grimm[279], Rasmus Rask, and Karl Brugmann, helped to overturn the tyranny of theological philology. It was a Roman Catholic, namely Friedrich Schlegel (1772-1829), who finally grouped the languages of India, Persia, Greece, Italy, and Germany under the now universally accepted name: Indo-European. Comparative philology revealed beyond a doubt that not only was Hebrew not the most ancient language on earth, but that it was not even the oldest in the

---

[279] Brother of Wilhelm and better known for the *Brothers Grimm Fairy Tales* (1812-15).

Hamito-Semitic group. Though the languages of the Indo-European and Hamito-Semitic families represent only a small fraction of the world linguistic spectrum, they have traditionally received vastly more scholarly attention than the others.

In the late 18th century, when many Sanskrit classics were first translated into European languages, they immediately drew the admiration of intellectual luminaries such as Voltaire and Goethe. Hegel went as far as to declare the German nation's Asian origin as "an incontestable fact." Later, however, the same Hegel dismissed the chronologies of the Puranas as fabrications and disparaged Indian history in general. By the 19th century, there existed a definite Western culture, Western self-awareness. The relatively easy success of the Europeans in subjugating native peoples reinforced their belief in the inherent superiority of their own civilization. The colonized peoples and their cultures came to be seen as inferior, and Hegel's reversal exemplifies this new Eurocentric perspective that has since pervaded the relationship of Western civilization with the rest of the world.

To explain away the common origin of Indo-European languages, 19th-century Western scholars hypothesized an "Aryan" invasion of India. Many of them Christian missionaries unsympathetic to the scriptures of ancient India, they argued that the Vedic culture was that of primitive nomads from Central Asia, who could not have founded the urban Indus Valley culture. The conflict between the powers of light and darkness, a recurrent idea in the Vedic manuscripts, was interpreted to refer to an actual war between light- and dark-skinned peoples. In typical Eurocentric arrogance, it was assumed, without any supporting evidence, that India was invaded and conquered in ancient times by nomadic light-skinned European tribes, who overthrew an earlier, dark-skinned civilization. This rather questionable interpretation of the *Rig-Veda* ignored the sophisticated nature of the culture presented within it, and turned the Vedas into nothing more than primitive poems of uncivilized marauders.

20th-century science provided new methods for archæological research, changing its basis completely. There now exists compelling geological, linguistic, literary, and astronomical evidence for a complete rewrite of the erroneous history books used in schools and universities worldwide. No current archæological data support any European invasion into South Asia, or any Aryan-Dravidian war at any time in the protohistoric period. Instead, a series of cultural changes can be archæologically documented, reflecting indigenous cultural development from prehistoric to historic periods. Rather than a foreign invasion into the area, the early Vedic literature describes a fundamental restructuring of native society. The term *arya* simply means "good," while *dasyu* merely refers to misconduct, both pertaining to quality of behaviour, not race. Genetic evidence points only to a continuity of the same people who traditionally considered themselves "Aryan."

No scholar did more to popularize Indology than the Right Honourable Max Müller (1823-1900), Privy Councillor to Empress Victoria and the author of the standard edition of the *Rig-Veda*. After specializing in Sanskrit at Leipzig, he went to Oxford, where lived the rest of his life—India he never once bothered to visit. He famously asserted that the five layers of the four Vedas and Upanishads were each composed in 200-year periods before Buddha, circa 500 BCE. There are, however, more changes in the Vedic language itself than there are in classical Sanskrit since Panini—also c. 500 BCE—i.e. during a period of 2,500 years. Müller's 200-year figure is obviously far too short, but we should bear in mind that he subscribed to the prevailing Christian belief that the Creation had taken place at 9 a.m. on the 23rd of October, 4004 BCE. This brings us to 2448 BCE for the Deluge, and if another thousand years is allowed for the waters to subside, the soil would be dry enough for the Aryans to begin their invasion around 1400 BCE. Add another two hundred years before they could begin writing the *Rig-Veda*, and we arrive at Müller's date of 1200 BCE.

Only relatively recently have the "standard" textbooks on early Indian history been called to question by postcolonial historians. It is now believed that the *Rig-Veda* was completed as early as 3700 BCE, after which the Indo-European people migrated to Persia, Greece, and further west. The Aryan invasion idea is a perfect example of the adage that history is written by the conquerors: firstly, it provided the British with an excuse for their conquest of India, since they could claim to only be repeating what their Aryan ancestors had done millennia ago; secondly, it divided India into a northern Aryan and southern Dravidian culture, which were declared hostile to each other; thirdly, it made Vedic culture later than, and possibly derived from, Levantine cultures, leaving the Hindu religion only a footnote to the development of religion and civilization in the West; and fourthly, it gave the sciences of India a Hellenic basis, as any Vedic basis was invalidated by the primitive nature of the Vedic culture.

This discredited most of the Hindu tradition and almost all the ancient literature of India: the genealogies of the Puranas with their long list of kings before Krishna and Buddha were stripped of any historical foundation; rather than a civil war in which all the great kings of India participated, the *Mahabharata* became a local skirmish among petty tribal chiefs that was later exaggerated by presumptuous poets. It served the social, political, and economic purposes of imperialism, demonstrating the superiority of Western culture and religion. The Vedic scholars of the West did in the intellectual realm what its armies did in the realm of politics—divided and conquered the non-Westerners.

CHAPTER 41

The Restoration was ultimately nothing but a prologue to a pan-European revolution, not only in politics, but in all the realms of human existence, going deeper, extending further, and lasting longer than the French one. Not a single major war was waged in all Europe between the years 1815 and 1853, and there were only routine colonial wars elsewhere. Many new inventions, and the increase in economic activity necessary for their implementation, accompanied industrialization, reinforcing the positive opinion towards material improvements, faster transportation, bigger cities, better water supply, and richer and more diversified nutrition. Not just a small group of privileged individuals were affected by these improvements, but even the poorest people had hope of eventually partaking in them. Nearly everywhere throughout the Western world, commodities were multiplying and luxury items becoming everyday. No one could fail to notice the clearly growing human capacity to produce goods—be it progress or not.

The emergence of the modern nation-state was intimately connected with the growth of the industrialist and mercantile classes, their desire for political influence, and the consequent development of democratic political theory. The middle classes had long been gaining ground in both Western Europe and North America, but not until the second quarter of the 19th century had industry and commerce obtained such advantage over agriculture that they could demand suffrage. Britain had long been on the cutting edge of the Industrial Revolution, but the Tory landowners were better equipped to guard their interests than the French lords.

The July Revolution of 1830 overthrew King Charles X of France and put on the throne the head of the younger branch of the Bourbon family, Duke Louis Philippe of Orléans, on the precedent of the English Revolution of 1688, which had likewise forced aside the ruling family in favour of the next legitimate branch. The July Monarchy became the first wealth-based bourgeois government: franchise was held by one Frenchman in thirty—the king was nothing more than the first burgher, or rather, the first burgher was the king.

Louis Philippe did not address himself as *Roi de France*, as the Bourbons had done, thereby declaring all of France their property, but as *Roi des Français*, "King of the French," for whom he thereby swore to uphold the constitution.

Britain averted revolution through the Great Reform Bill of 1832, which granted the industrialist middle class the right to participate in parliamentary elections. The next year, slavery was abolished in the Crown Colonies, if less for philanthropical than commercial reasons. There was scarcely an important enterprise in any quarter of the globe that was not to some degree sustained by English capital. To an amazing degree had the British mechanical engineering, railway construction, and steamboat traffic leapt ahead of the Continent. For a long time now, there had also been such wonderful curiosities in England as matchsticks, stearine candles, and steel nibs.

Ever since breaking away from the mother country, the United States had experienced an astonishing economic growth. The traditional images of the American West can be deceptive: the towns may look humble and run-down, but they too are a result of industrialization—it was the machines that won the West. Quite unlike in Europe, railroads preceded the settlement of new regions in America. Rails already ran through its vast uninhabited areas, while stage-coaches still provided the transportation between Munich and Vienna. The physicians of backward Germany resisted the building of the country's first railroad in 1835 on grounds that the amazing speed of trains would surely cause brain damage. The viewing of the quickly changing scenery alone had to be unhealthy, wherefore the doctors demanded that a seven feet fence be erected on both sides of the track.

For the first settlers of America, the prairie, too inhospitable to tame, was a barrier to be crossed, not a land to be settled. They soon found that the promised land was already populated by other cultures, native tribes roaming the plains. The aim of the white people, or their "Manifest Destiny" as they liked to call it, was to expand across the whole continent, by force, if necessary. Millions of colonists crossed the continent on the railroads that the Irish and Chinese labourers built with accelerating pace. The invaders were emboldened by an ever-expanding armament and ammunition industry. Two million cartridges were churned out each day by the Winchester factory alone. The fate of the prairie tribes was directly linked to that of the buffalo: the Indians killed only as many bisons as they needed at a time, and used every part of the buffalo from the horn to the hoof; for the white man, buffalo-hunting was a sport—and yet another way to render the native mode of life difficult. As the colonial settlement spread, the number of the bisons shrunk from 60 million to less than a thousand. It was a stunning demonstration of the power of a society in process of industrialization. The balance of nature was upset, and the prairie tribes were forced to leave their dwellings.

The conquest of enormous fertile regions combined with the vast technological improvements yielded of course extremely beneficial economic results, but only for the proprietary class. In the long run, the spread of Western capitalism would improve the material conditions of life for most of humanity, but only after a great deal of upheaval and destruction. The economic bloom was accomplished through the terrific suffering of the less fortunate: the number of industrial workers began to mount sharply in the 19th century. The most dogmatic practitioners of economic liberalism paid hardly any attention to the concerns of the working classes and did not shrink from using child labour. It was considered a giant step forward when the minimum age of children working in factories was raised to 9 years and the hours were reduced to twelve, not counting overtime. There being no organized strikes during that period, the embitterment of the fourth estate manifested itself in riotous walk-outs and severe unrests, the most frightful of which was that of Birmingham in 1839, when the workers laid waste the whole city, looting the houses and burning down the factories.

Pity, humanism, or even the notion of equality was not self-evident, nor did moral opinion necessarily see any exploitation in society. Dust and gasses may have filled the factories, but mines and workshops had been damp, crowded, and oppressive long before the Industrial Revolution. Neither was pollution from the factories anything new; the mills had always fouled their environment, and factory emissions were just another expression of the wretched indifference that in past centuries had made the plague a yearly visitation. What made the factory different from what had gone before was the domination of men by the pace of the machines: for the first time, the workers were driven by an inhuman clockwork—the same simple and monotonous tasks had to repeated over and over again.

According to a sensational report published in 1842, the life expectancy in a Manchester working-class family was 17 years, twenty years less than in rural Rutlandshire, which was used as a point of comparison. The interest of English poetry in the dark side of factory work, educational system, poor relief, and class entitlement, was initiated by Charles Dickens (1812-1870). The first great urban novelist had had a hard, comfortless life as a boy, working long hours in poverty, yet his accusations were totally devoid of vitriol and purely poetic, giving them the impact they had and preserving their unfading freshness to this day. His sentimental novel, *A Christmas Carol* (1843), popularized the once banned holiday as a family event, making its celebration more common even in still puritanical America. While continuing to write novels, Dickens helped to establish a home for reformed prostitutes and to press for slum clearance, educational reform, sanitary improvements, and the numerous social issues reflected in his fiction.

Besides Dickens, the title of the Apostle of the People was sought by Karl Marx[280] (1818-1883) and Friedrich Engels (1820-1895), who precisely while living in England conceived their politically significant theories about the exploitation of the workers. The social evils they attacked had to do with the break-through of industrialism, but despite the connection of their critique of the capitalist system to this particular point in time, it still inflames passions a century and a half later. In fact, whereas Dickens sold like John Grisham, Marx and Engels did not initially draw much attention at all. Though published simultaneously in German, French, Italian, Flemish, and Danish, the *Communist Manifesto* (1848) was largely disregarded for a couple of decades. Later on, their works were of course read religiously, prompting the famous Polish science fiction author, Stanislaw Lem, to quip that the greatest tragedy of the 20th century was that Communism could not first be tested on mice. In Marx's view, the archetype of the grasping and exploitative capitalism was embodied by the "money-grubbing, avaricious" Jews—this class animus got transformed into race animus when Marxism mutated into National Socialism.

Marx and Engels renounced all previous socialistic theories and claimed to be the first representatives of "scientific socialism." They were particularly influenced by Hegel's dialectical method, which thirty years earlier had already been dubbed "a lasting monument of German stupidity," but in their hands Hegel's idealism turned into realism, and to make matters worse, into materialism. Whereas in Hegel's logic, the thesis-antithesis conflict existed only on a conceptual level, according to the dialectical materialism, it was a concrete conflict existing in the material world. In other words, Marx and

---

[280] born Moses Mordecai Levi in Trier, Prussia

Engels saw history of society as the development of antagonisms between social classes, ending in the collective communistic system as the most highly evolved form of civilization. They opined that social problems could only be solved by vesting workers with property rights in their own jobs, which incidentally is exactly how mediæval feudalism worked. The noble but misguided thought was that workers would be better off with monopoly rents and security, when in fact they would generally be far better off under free market economy, which allowed the growth of wealth and erased the kind of peasant life that most people had under feudalism.

The Revolution of 1848 was unprecedented in geographical reach and number of people involved: the people rose in a united front in almost every European country. King Louis Philippe had to flee to London in February, when the Second Republic was declared, with Napoleon's nephew, Louis Napoleon, as President. From France, the wave of revolution spread to Italy, Germany, Bohemia, Hungary, and Austria, whose mighty prime minister, Metternich, also escaped to England. Within the German Confederation, the revolution took a wholly different form: here monarchy emerged victorious because there was no bourgeoisie that could triumph over it. Far from liberalizing Germany, the Revolution of 1848 led to increased power for Prussia, as a consequence of which liberal institutions, always suppressed, finally perished.

As the rebellion against Austrian domination in Italy turned into an open conflict in March, 1848, more and more Italians treated it as a crusade. Their hopes of a unified, sovereign Italy were dashed when at the end of April, Pope Pius IX refused to join the battle. "As Father of all the Faithful," declared the Pope, "we will take no part in making war on a Catholic nation." This statement provoked a general feeling of betrayal, turning him from the most loved man in Italy into the most hated. After his chief minister was murdered and his summer residence bombed in November, Pius fled Rome disguised as a simple priest. Early the next year, he appealed to the Catholic powers of Austria, Spain, Naples, and France to overturn the Roman Republic, which had been proclaimed in his absence. Despite the military leadership of Giuseppe Garibaldi, the Austrians moved into the north, the Spanish and Neapolitans invaded from the south, and the French troops took Rome, allowing the Pope to finally return in the spring of 1850.

In 1848, there had been April riots even in London, and in July, the patriotic Irishmen rose once again against British domination. Each reconquest of Ireland involved some confiscation of land held by the Catholic Irish and its transfer to successive waves of absentee English landlords, most of whom had little interest in the welfare of their tenants. The infamous Potato Famine together with massive Irish immigration to the Protestant citadel of the northeastern United States made Ireland the only country in Europe whose population actually fell during the 19th century. Unsurprisingly, the Industrial Revolution had almost no influence there, leaving Ireland one of the poorest countries in Europe.

The long reign (1837-1901) of Queen Victoria coincides exactly with the haute bourgeois period. The characteristics of this epoch can therefore be examined almost as a pure culture, for Britain also held the status of the leading superpower of the era. In common parlance, the word "Victorian" has taken on the meaning of pretty much everything that has been eschewed and considered odious in our own era: colonialism and capitalism, bigoted morals and prudishness, complacency and boredom, correctness and conformity.

The technological innovations that became the most striking achievement of modern science were prerequisite for the ascendancy of the middle classes. The change was even more shocking to the people of the time, since the Industrial Revolution took place rather despite those in authority than because of them. The men responsible for the revolution were practical men, simple inventors and craftsmen, who often had little education. In fact, primary education of the time could only dull an inventive mind and the universities, proud of their traditions, took little interest in scientific studies. Until very recently, students in the sciences, not only at Oxford and Cambridge, but also at Harvard and Yale, were treated as intellectually and socially inferior. They were relegated to different buildings and received their degrees on a different occasion with different ceremonies from those appointed for students in the humanities.

Nevertheless, the educated class doing scientific work no longer consisted mostly of gentleman hobbyists. Once science had concrete applications, the old Renaissance man began to make way for engineers and other practical scientists. The weaving industry had become mechanized already during the 18th century, and by the beginning of the 19th, the steam engine was wholly practicable, while iron and coal formed the basis of industrial activity, and consequently, of prosperity. The real revolution took place in the field of transportation: the steamer opened up the Mississippi, the locomotive the American West and Siberia, to international trade and industrial development. Steamboats were not dependent on winds and currents, enabling great migrations across oceans and continents. By the middle of the century, railroads and sea-lanes circled the entire globe, greatly furthering both the exportation of industrial products and the importation of raw materials.

A journey across Europe had once taken weeks—now it took only a few days. The ever-increasing travel necessitated consistent time-keeping throughout the world. The meridian of longitude running through the Royal Greenwich Observatory was designated as prime meridian and Greenwich time[281] became the global mean time. The rest of the world was divided into twenty-four time zones, enabling the compilation of an international timetable for the growing number of tourists. The new transports also changed the nature of war politics by making the supply and maintenance of modern mass armies possible. Heavy industry centralized the power; in the American Civil War (1861-1865), the industrial North crushed the predominantly agrarian South. Industrialization upset the balance of power worldwide as industrial powers assumed world leadership. As we have seen, international and national orientation were equally characteristic of the bourgeois period with its global and conflicting commercial interests.

Britain, the greatest and richest of the competing nation-states, was undoubtedly also the biggest beneficiary of the Industrial Revolution. In 1773, Manchester had a population of 27,000, but by the year 1851, its population exceeded 370,000. By that time, one fifth of Brits already lived in cities with population over 100,000. Not only were people driven to cities by work, but at the same time, the growth of population accelerated rapidly and, all in all, the population of Britain tripled between 1750 and 1850. There were only 22 cities with over 100,000 citizens in all Europe at the beginning of the 19th century. At the end of it, there were 122, filling up with young people from the provinces seeking their fortunes.

Mass production made the increase of wages possible, prosperity increased

---

[281] i.e. GMT. The politically correct modern euphemism is Coordinated Universal Time (UTC).

the demand, and the demand increased the production.[282] During the three-and-a-half centuries prior to the abolition of slavery, some fourteen million slaves were introduced into Latin America, compared with only about half a million brought into the United States.[283] Still in the 19th century, a million new slaves were brought into Brazil alone, and even today, the vast majority of blacks in the Americas speak Portuguese. The about eight million white colonists consciously attracted in the next hundred years exceeded by 15 times the number that had arrived in the preceding 350. These new arrivals would gradually take the reins in the production of coffee, grains, wool, and meat—all destined for the white middle-class markets of Northwest Europe.

The social values of the bourgeoisie would gradually become the values of practically all society. The middle classes valued book learning, and their members might spend as much as fourth of their principal capital on securing a proper education for their children. From their ranks sprang the future natural philosophers: the term "scientist" had not yet been generally accepted; in fact, it was bitterly opposed even in the mid-19th century—only during the last few generations have the natural sciences been accepted into the top echelon of intellectual culture. As a profit-seeking class, the bourgeoisie looked down on art and invested in science. Though the Christian faith played an important part in its moral code, religious fervour had subsided within its ranks. In the latter half of the century, the Industrial Revolution was finally allowed to mature into a scientific revolution.

It was of course the natural scientists who made the most significant contribution to the spread of evolutionism. Charles Darwin (1809-1882) steals, and deserves, most of the credit, but a great body of scientists had for generations before him been formulating the concept of natural evolution. Long before biologists knew that species had evolved, it was clear to philologians that languages had evolved, and the intelligentsia of the 18th century was already familiar with the idea of organic evolution. There was a

---

[282] Also, prior to the Industrial Revolution, tax rates higher than 10 percent were deemed exorbitant. Modern progressive income taxation is largely a Marxist innovation.

[283] The estimates obviously vary a great deal, but the ratio remains about the same. The Middle Passage was far more expensive, which is why the North American slaves were treated better and lived longer, provided that they survived the much longer journey.

conflict over the "antiquity of man" long before Darwin, as men of science dug up prehistoric tools going back tens of thousands of years. In the first quarter of the 19th century, archæologists began to argue against the prevailing theory that the iron tools were for poor people and the bronze ones for the rich, finding the evidence for the three age system—Stone Age, Bronze Age, Iron Age—for use in dating and organizing prehistoric materials. Long before Darwin, geological investigations proved that there was no planet-wide deluge as described in the Bible and that the crust of the Earth had formed gradually over millions of years. There were in rapid succession new discoveries of human skeletons mingled with bones of long extinct animals, placing the origin of man at a period vastly earlier than any which theologians had dared to imagine.

In the *Principles of Geology* (1830), a book that Darwin would later take with him aboard the Beagle, Charles Lyell had discussed the idea of transmutation, the notion that organic forms change and develop over time. It was likely Lyell's discussion that suggested the theory of natural selection to Darwin, but fearing the Church and the critique of his colleagues, he kept his ideas secret for almost twenty years. After learning that another scientist, Alfred Russel Wallace (1823-1913), had come to similar conclusions, Darwin could no longer postpone the publication of his theory. Had Wallace not been such an exceptionally humble individual, "half genius, half madman" as he has been described, we would now be talking about Wallacism, instead of Darwinism. The publication of *The Origin of the Species* in 1859 began one of the greatest conflicts between Christianity and natural science. Like Newton, Darwin incorporated a mass of facts and theories derived from intricate researches into a theory that a normal educated person could assimilate—the first edition sold out in a day.

Darwin's great contribution to science, and his great offence to the Christian Church, was that he first advanced the theory of evolution in a form that drew general attention. The impact of his work echoed in philosophy, economy, and in virtually every still nascent social science. In self-assertion, which had previously been considered the root of all evil, the atonement of which required a supernatural sacrifice, could now be discerned the wise order of nature. Herbert Spencer (1820-1903) applied the biological imperative of the struggle of existence to the development of society in his popular and controversial *Principles of Sociology* (1876). His catch-phrase, "survival of the fittest," implied not only that the fittest would survive, but that he would have to survive. The old doctrine of predestination had taken on a modern form, well suited for the bourgeois period with its free competition and belief in progress—just showing that a favourable social and cultural context is required for acceptance of scientific "truth."

The revival of economy towards the end of the 19th century, coupled with the naïve interpretation of evolution as constant positive development, created a popular evolutionary optimism. Within a community, or political organism as some thinkers were fond of saying, prevailed co-operation, not competition. The competition prevailed for example between Germany and France, but not amongst the Germans or the French. This type of interpretations were frequent in every German daily newspaper during that century, before Darwin's ideas were even fully formed: organic evolution in the form that Darwin and his proponents portrayed it is an exceedingly slow process—the entire historic period from Homer to Keats is in the same proportion to the formation of the fossils of early Cambrian period as five minutes are to a year. Darwinism is rather against than for the childish hopes of the age, for they presupposed a rapid change for the better. In fact, the whole repertoire of Darwin's ideas predicts anything but a future where peace and co-operation prevail and futility and suffering do not exist.

For most of the educated people of the 19th century, natural selection represented merely the clarification and confirmation of the main concept of the Enlightenment, that of the "Great Chain" of human cultural evolution. Over the century, however, it served to reinforce the soon-to-be prevalent notion of national and racial superiority. The colonial powers used quasi-Darwinian doctrines to justify their imperialistic policies: if aggression was natural, then was not war also natural? Were the white troops of the West, with their superior firepower and mobility, not supposed to subjugate the rest of the world?

German nationalism, which at its birth had rested primarily on language, began to look for sustenance from race theories invented largely by H. S. Chamberlain, who posed as a fervent German patriot during World War I despite his English ancestry. Coleridge and Carlyle are other examples of the British enthusiasm for Germany that was a significant strand in 19th-century culture. Many Victorians had ideas of Germany as a sort of alternative England, a romantically rich place of new possibilities, a new country to be constructed. This view was adopted by the Romantics in many other countries as well, both in the Old and the New World, thus making the creation of an original German culture really an international project.

While evolutionary optimism had already an ample basis in the "German wonders" of the period, in theory it was further supported by the active and effective propaganda in favour of scientific truths. Ludwig Büchner, the younger brother of the famous playwright, Georg Büchner, brought about a mass conversion to an oversimplified and populistic materialism. Outlined as early as 1855 in his best-seller, *Kraft und Stoff*, it made Ernst Haeckel world famous when *Natural History of Creation* was published in 1868. Unlike the continental materialists, however, the commonsensical Englishmen wanted to reserve an area for things that could not be known, thereby saving not only their souls, but their social order and poetry as well.

At the beginning of the 19th century, Western science, philosophy, and art all still fit under the same denominator; only half a century later, the paths of science and art had already diverged—the age of the self-taught genius was over. The masters of science would henceforth rise from the bosom of universities, while students of divinity were increasingly driven away to seminaries. Contemporary Protestantism widened, from the other side, the gap between empirical science and theology, between this world and the other, between physics and metaphysics. Religious literature as a separate genre came to an end, while poets and artists turned their backs also to the new technology generated by science.

The rapid industrialization and urbanization that took place in the latter half of the century made hinterlands and backward regions appear exotic and enticing to many Westerners in comparison with the world in which they had suddenly found themselves. Europeans looked back with nostalgia to the mythical golden age, when sinless men lived peaceably together with animals on the fruits of a bountiful nature, without the frets of business life, free from the restrictions of class, laws, and ethics. The big city artists became, in most cases, big city bohemians, who strove to depart as much as possible from the way of life and thought of their employers—it was precisely this period that established the myth about the artist as an asocial superman.

Thanks to all the technical improvements, the tabloids became the cheapest and dearest reading of the public, and due to these same advances, the markets were flooded with factory-made luxury items, the pride of engineers and capitalists. It goes without saying that poets did not feel at home in the bourgeois world, but their displeasure was more æsthetic than political. The refined or, if you like, decadent circles, which they generally found their way into, were not too bad, but otherwise the industrialized nations had become so unsightly that one needed an escape, at the very least in fantasy.

At first glance, Algernon Charles Swinburne (1837-1909), the *enfant terrible* of Victorian poetry, whose work is characterized by political radicalism, blasphemy, androgyny, and sadomasochism, does not seem to have much in common with his contemporaries. Yet this self-proclaimed poet laureate of Italian liberty fits quite comfortably within the context of Victorian literature: an alcoholic son of Admiral Charles Swinburne, he grew up in a conservative High Church family, had a very orthodox upper-class education, attending both Eton and Oxford. The poet who would later become an inspiration and a favourite of the Æsthetes and Decadents displayed the same grave seriousness when dealing with religious and philosophical themes as did Tennyson, Hardy, and Browning. Like them, he had a profound knowledge of Classical and Renaissance literary forms and traditions, as well as of Christianity and biblical exegetics, which he again like them sought to integrate with a devotion to the great Romantics.

With Byron and Shelley, Swinburne was one of the very few poets to come from the aristocracy since the days of Raleigh and Sir Philip Sidney. All of his poetry is marked by the need to free oneself and others from bonds, whether of political oppression, convention, or religion. He was reputedly saved from being expelled for atheism from Oxford by none other than Professor Benjamin Jowett, the great translator of Plato, with the statement that the University should not "sin twice against poetry," the expulsion of Shelley for the very same reason being the first.

Swinburne took a sardonic pleasure in what his biographer, Cecil Y. Lang, has dubbed "Algernonic exaggeration"—when people started to talk disapprovingly about his sexual inclinations, he circulated a story that he had committed pæderasty with a monkey and then eaten the poor creature. Oscar Wilde, wholly capable of inventing his own amusing fables, called Swinburne a "braggart in matters of vice, who had done everything he could to convince his fellow citizens of his homosexuality and bestiality without being in the slightest degree a homosexual or a bestializer."

Swinburne was greatly inspired by ancient Greece and Rome and other bygone times, which could be imagined to be riddled with the thirst of life and longing for death that ate him up inside. Though he renounced Christianity while at Oxford, he never became indifferent to religion, as his *Hymn to Proserpine* and *Hertha* clearly demonstrate. He had a Bible reader's detailed knowledge of the Scriptures and of all the traditional methods of interpretation applied to them, including typology, prophecy, and eschatology. Like Carlyle and Ruskin, he used biblical vocabulary, rhetoric, and iconography partly because that was what his Victorian audience was accustomed to when discussing serious issues, and partly because these suggested that there was common ground even where there was none. Unlike his peers, however, Swinburne blasphemously satirized and savagely attacked both the Christian faith and the Christian establishment, which especially in divided Italy, he perceived as an instrument of oppression.

Masterfully applying the interpretive modes of a religion he despised, Swinburne evoked a vision of a secular redemption where humanity would provide a meaning for existence by fully realizing its powers. He purported to discern the same moral principles in contemporary Italian politics and the Gospel events, comparing Italy's present enslavement with the passion of Christ and her coming freedom with His resurrection. All of her own writers of any note were not only ardent patriots, but usually radicals, liberals, and anticlericals as well. In fact, the powers of culture—religion, tradition, spiritual contemplation—were represented by the Church, while its opponents had on their side the aspirations of civilization: education, progress, material improvements. In *Before a Crucifix*, Swinburne addresses the rood as if it were Christ, and demands if His coming has brought forth anything but a suffering race of men praying to a suffering image of man. The poet then turns to his main target, the Church, and relates to the wooden effigy of Christ how His supposed servants have used His suffering to establish a tyrannical sway over men. Having put it to Him that His priests have enslaved—and crucified—the masses, while enriching themselves, Swinburne ends the poem by urging the people to free themselves from the shackles of religion.

The States of the Church ceased to exist in the course of the unification of Italy under the House of Savoy. After the Austrians left Bologna and the Romagna at the end of the Franco-Austrian War (1859), both united with the kingdom of Sardinia, as did Marche and Umbria following the conquest of the

Two Sicilies (1860). Garibaldi marched on the Patrimony of St. Peter twice between 1860 and 1862, but was twice prevented from taking Rome. By the Franco-Italian Convention of 1864, the French agreed to leave the Eternal City in two years, on condition that the capital of independent Italy be moved to Florence within six months. Florence was indeed the spiritual capital of Italy, but if Rome was not made the capital, Italy was doomed to divide into two. After the withdrawal of the French garrison defending the Pope, Garibaldi succeeded in capturing the papal city of Monte Rotondo a dozen miles east of Rome. The Italian general and his 10,000 volunteers were successfully repelling the papal army of 15,000, when France returned to Italy with a new force of 20,000 and one last time defeated her aspiration for Rome as her capital.

On the 19th of July, 1870, the Franco-Prussian War broke out and the First Vatican Council, having approved the dogma of Papal Infallibility just the day before, was prorogued indefinitely. Napoleon III called the French troops stationed in Rome to come to his aid, and Austria was sounded out, but deemed the time for intervention had passed, leaving Pius IX on his own. King Victor Emmanuel implored the Pope to accept the love and protection of the Italians, rather than cling to a sovereignty that existed only by the support of foreign arms. Negotiations for peaceful surrender having failed, the royal troops entered Rome on the 11th of September and decimated the Swiss Guard. In a plebiscite conducted on the 2nd of October, the Romans voted 153,681 for, and 1,507 against, the new government. On the 30th of June, 1871, Rome was at last inaugurated as the capital of the now fully united kingdom of Italy.

Following the First Vatican Council, a considerable dissent arose among Catholics in parts of Germany, Austria, and Switzerland over its infallibility decree. This stated that the definitions of the pope, when he speaks *ex cathedra* and defines the doctrines concerning faith or morals to be held by all Christians, are irreformable. Some of the dissenters limited themselves to only repudiating the new dogma, but encouraged by a large number of scholars, politicians, and statesmen, others would form independent sects. The "State Catholics," for example, acknowledged the pope's infallibility in the spiritual field, but denied his legitimacy in the secular arena. The "Old Catholics," on the other hand, refused to accept the notion that papal privileges extended any wider than prescribed by the Church Fathers, and sought to adhere to the beliefs and practices of the Church of the post-apostolic era, before the so-called Ecumenical Councils.

In the *Kulturkampf*, the Italian government went much further than that of Germany. It not only decreed a civil marriage, but a civil oath, and not only removed the educational system from the control of the Church, but made religious education voluntary and abolished the theological faculties. Though a number of monasteries were able carry on their work owing to the guarantee of individual liberty, the religious orders and benefices not performing a purely spiritual mission were deprived of their property and legal existence. Pius IX and his successors, however, refused to recognize their loss of temporal power and territorial sovereignty, becoming voluntary "prisoners of the Vatican," the tiny area of about 100 acres around St. Peter's Square. The "Roman Question" remained unsolved until 1929, when the Fascist dictator, Benito Mussolini, achieved what has been described as one of his greatest diplomatic victories. The 60-year-old controversy was settled by his conclusion of the Lateran Treaty, whereby Vatican City became a sovereign state with the pope as its ruler.

Yet even during the early kingdom of Italy, the Roman Church had remained enormously influential while officially in a situation of conflict with the State. Rather than religious liberty, minorities were granted merely "tolerance," an idea that assumes an official religion along with the right of the State to grant or withhold favour to dissenters. Proselytization by non-Catholics was restricted by a rather vague and general notion of "public order," and thus depended largely on the goodwill of the local authorities. Under the Italian legal system, currently based on the post-WWII constitution and a 1984 revision of the concordat with the Holy See, all Italian citizens are obliged to pay a church tax amounting to 0.8 percent of their total income tax bill. While in Germany, for example, tax payers professing to be secular can nowadays refrain from paying the religious tax, in Italy the payment remains statutory.

CHAPTER 42

By the mid-19th century, the Romantic revolt against rationalism had been under way close to a hundred years, stressing the significance of folk tradition in contrast to urban sophistication, spiritual and metaphysical themes to exact science, and exotic lands and events to the ordinary, everyday, mundane. Returning to the old sources revived mysticism: Boehme was studied with newfound enthusiasm and Swedenborg was discovered; profound spirits reverted to Gnosticism and Rosicrucianism, and it was suggested that the East was the source of a "secret wisdom." Buddhism, the most widespread of all religions, would have momentous significance for countless laymen, but the penchant of German Romantics for all things Indian came to a head with Schopenhauer, who aspired to counterbalance "Semitic" Christianity with the ancient wisdom of the Aryans.

To the general public, however, Arthur Schopenhauer (1788-1860) was the avenging angel against the ideology of Hegel, whose pretentiousness and oracular incomprehensibility gained him not only fervent admirers, but bitter opponents as well. The most bitter, or at least the most vocal, was the atheist Schopenhauer, who unlike the devout Hegel, wrote simply and intelligibly. He gained notice in the larger circles only in 1851 with his *Parerga*, though his principal work and one of the great philosophical texts of the 19th century, *The World as Will and Representation*, was published as early as 1818. Its title alone betrays the basic features of his doctrine, elaborated in his subsequent works: his doctrine is subjectivistic like those of other Romantic philosophers, but it sees the inmost essence of the phenomenal world as will, not as reason, emotion, or beauty—according to him, the world is evil because the will is evil.

Schopenhauer was the first Western philosopher to address the suffering which so glaringly surrounds us, the confusion, agony, and evil, things that the other philosophers scarcely seemed to notice and invariably sought to work out into all-embracing harmony and comprehensibility. Reason, omnipotent in the Greek tradition, was finally recognized for the exceedingly imperfect instrument it is; whose methods are entirely empirical, whose terms lack precision, and whose theses cancel each other out. One cannot conceive a more direct antithesis to Hegel's shallow optimism and intellectualism. Schopenhauer neglects no opportunity to mock the "university philosophy" of the "professors of philosophy," the very worst of which was embodied in Hegelianism. Teaching, ostensibly the purpose of academic employment, has become less and less taxing, while the continuous publication of obscure research, comprehensible only to a few cognoscenti, is the key to status and privilege. Schopenhauer's concerns were not just with abstract philosophical problems, but with the existential dilemmas and tragedies of real life.

As the first Western philosopher with access to translations of philosophical material from India, both Vedic and Pali, Schopenhauer was deeply affected by them, to the great interest of many. He had more impact on literature and people in general than on academic philosophy. In fact, he believed that his philosophy was "something quite different from, and indeed dangerous" to that of the academic thinkers, who tried to silence him for fear of being exposed as a coterie of charlatans. Though Schopenhauer had no genuine successors and founded no school, his influence was widespread from the middle of the century onwards, the growing cultural pessimism blazing the trail for a preaching that differed little from ancient, Oriental wisdom, and which only against the background of the vulgar belief in progress could be called pessimistic.

Schopenhauer's most famous disciple was perhaps Richard Wagner (1813-1883), who often acted as if he alone was the philosopher's foremost exponent and apologist. Wagner, too, invited hostility and rejection by the educated, who saw his theatrical and musical innovations as a threat to the traditional cultural ideas and practices. Convinced that Schopenhauer had revealed to him the true meaning of his own early works, the composer felt duty-bound to consciously disseminate Schopenhauerian truths through the medium of his subsequent music dramas. Wagner perceived himself not merely as a creator of epic operas, but also as a writer of profound vision; he openly communicated the great debt owed to his favourite philosopher in his numerous prose works addressing æsthetics, composition, conducting, music history, cultural and political theory, philosophy, and religion—thus Schopenhauer finally became a fashionable philosopher, who was invoked as a counterweight to the more and more vulgar evolutionary optimism.

Though it goes without saying that other values than those in power exist and thrive within society, their official status is usually low, and they are often flouted as antiquated or unenlightened. Wagner's native Saxony suffered the most at the Congress of Vienna, penalized by its old rival, Prussia, for having been an ally of Napoleon. It was forced to cede nearly half of its kingdom, all of Lower Lusatia, part of Upper Lusatia, and all its northern territory, including Wittenberg, to Prussia. Most of the territories were incorporated with several other Prussian districts into the Prussian province of Saxony, with the former ecclesiastical territory, Magdeburg, as its capital. Saxony was thus reduced to parity with Württemberg as one of the smallest of the five kingdoms of Germany, its principal remaining cities being Dresden and Leipzig, Wagner's place of birth.

The value of lost causes is frequently recognized as much more than that of the dispossessed or unfortunate. Even in their failure, they are strangely liberating, a challenge to the notion that justice lay with the conquerors. Art can function as a subversive force against this tyranny, by creating separate worlds where one can ignore the pressure of outside opinion. Wagner became fascinated by literature early on, immersing himself in books and even having a fling at writing his own tragedies. Unlike most other prominent composers, however, he never became proficient on any musical instrument. After having studied music theory at Leipzig under the cantor of the Thomaskirche, Wagner was employed as the chorus master for the Würzburg Theatre. Still in his early twenties, he proceeded in quick succession to new positions in Magdeburg, Königsberg, and Riga as the theatres declared bankruptcy one after the other.

In his youth, Wagner was particularly influenced by the historical novels of Sir Edward Bulwer-Lytton (1803-1873); best known today for beginning his novel *Paul Clifford* (1830) with the line "It was a dark and stormy night," he also coined the phrase "The pen is mightier than the sword." The historical novel itself is a genre that has now and then been derided as mere feminine emotional pornography, but whereas women had dominated both its writing and reading at the beginning of the 19th century, in two decades male writers had reclaimed the genre by turning it into an educational enterprise. After Wagner's first two operas failed to gain any success, he moved via London to Paris, where he hoped to get a production of his third opera, which was based on Lord Lytton's novel, *Rienzi, Last of the Tribunes* (1835). It asserts that the

Roman people rejected his leadership because they were unworthy of him, even as Wagner himself went hungry in France until *Rienzi* was performed successfully (1842) in Dresden. This led to his appointment as both the choirmaster of the Royal Theatre and court conductor *ad vitam*.

In 1843, Wagner finished his first original operatic work, *The Flying Dutchman*, and was given a taste of the difficulties to come, for it failed and was performed only four times. It lacked the popular pageantry and pomposity his previous work, which had been patterned on those of Giacomo Meyerbeer, the leading operatic figure of the day. The public was unenthusiastic about the poetically and musically new and unheard-of psychological drama, the artistic ideas of which diverged sharply from the mainstream of the era. Unwilling to yield an inch of the direction he had chosen, Wagner embarked on new, even more revolutionary projects, giving birth within the next four years to both *Tannhäuser* and *Lohengrin*. Until the political uprising of 1848, he stayed at the Saxon court as a conductor, leaving us with many documents of his theories on conducting and interpretations of the major works that he had conducted. He also began preparing an essay on the *Nibelungenlied* with a view to transforming it into a music drama. As a master of choral works and orchestral music, he also created a new artistic spirit for the Dresden orchestra in his capacity as the chorus master.

Wagner's sound and sensible suggestions to improve the conditions of the orchestra were nevertheless rejected by the director of the opera, while his works failed on the stage one after another. Disillusioned with the theatre and its management, he became involved in the orchestral players union, further widening the rift between him and the management. Bitter at the society that had treated him so badly, he joined the revolutionaries and spoke openly against the state at the meeting of the *Vaterlands-Verein*, attended by nearly 3,000 people. At the same time, however, Wagner extolled the universal mission of German culture—"the rays of German freedom and German gentleness shall warm and transfigure the Cossack and the Frenchman, the Bushman and the Chinese"—and he was to retain this ambivalent attitude towards the *Reich* for the rest of his life. Because of the highly visible role that he played in the Dresden insurrection, Wagner had to flee to Switzerland, the refuge of every politically persecuted or disaffected in Europe. It was more than ten years before he could return to Germany.

While in Zürich, Wagner concentrated on writing essays that outlined his theories on music drama, and his heyday did not dawn until the reign (1862-1890) of Otto von Bismarck, a bourgeois period whose anachronistic longing for romanticism Wagner was able to satisfy better than anyone. With a rare statesmanship, the Prussian Prime Minister made careful use of the advantageous trends during the time he was the true *Führer* of Germany, having first prepared himself for this while serving as a diplomat. He practised a *Realpolitik* well fitting the realist spirit of the era, but had also plenty of the idealism of the Romantics left in him. Although it has often been suggested to the contrary, Bismarck was no militarist, for he deemed war merely an "emetic," and neither was he a monarchist, a reputation he had established during the Revolution of 1848, but a royalist, which is nowise the same thing. Nor was he the stony Roland the people thought he was, but rather a textbook example of a neurotic—an "Iron Chancellor" who has a hissy fit every time he does not get his way is an altogether strange phenomenon.

Wagner returned to political activity in 1864, when he received the invitation of King Ludwig II to settle in Munich. Bavaria is the largest of the modern German states even without the Rhenish Palatinate, which at the time still belonged to it. When the tall and handsome 18-year-old monarch succeeded his father to the throne on the 10th of March, 1864, he gained immediate popularity with the Bavarians. The last of the German feudal princes, Ludwig spent much of the wealth of his kingdom in the pursuit of beauty, with the patronage of the arts, especially architecture, sculpture, painting, literature, and music. At the age of 15, he had seen and heard Wagner's *Lohengrin* and been enchanted by the mythical land created by the composer. As his first act, the new King ordered his cabinet secretary to locate the composer, then in hiding from his numerous creditors. On the 23rd of April, Wagner was uncovered in Stuttgart and given the royal message, which requested his immediate presence at Munich, where all his debts would be paid, and where he would be given everything he needed to continue his composing without interruption. If it was not for Ludwig's generous support, Wagner would probably never have been able to produce *Tristan and Isolde*, complete *The Ring Cycle*, compose *Parsifal*, or carry through the massive Bayreuth project.

Bismarck, in the meantime, initiated the great rise of the Prussian state and army at the cost of Denmark. Thanks to his skill and determination, Denmark faced in 1864 not only her own rebels, but also the armed forces of Prussia and Austria. These quickly occupied the Danish duchies of Schleswig and Holstein, which contained both Danish and German speakers, but their disposal remained at issue for some time. By the Treaty of Gastein (1865), Bismarck purposely imposed a solution that was bound to cause friction with Austria, placing Schleswig under Prussian and Holstein under Austrian rule. This dual administration led, exactly as Bismarck had expected, to enough tension to easily manœuvre Austria into a war with Prussia. It was long past endurance that the backward Austria claimed dominion of the German people, preventing the leading German power, Prussia, from undertaking any viable measures in either domestic or foreign policy. The collapse of the German Confederation had been an historic necessity from the day it was created: the German war of 1866 was not a showdown between the North and the South, but a German *coup d'état*, orchestrated by a single individual. But Bismarck's idea was not understood by his compatriots, and in May, 1866, after there had been an assassination attempt on him (which he survived to the general disappointment), he was the most hated man in all of Germany.

When Austria brought the dispute over the administration of Schleswig-Holstein before the German diet, Bismarck declared that the Gastein Treaty had thereby been nullified. The hostilities began on the 7th of June, when the Prussian Chancellor expelled the Austrians from Holstein, over the objection of his king. The German states, great and small, now had to take one side or the other in a final battle for hegemony: on the 14th of June, the diet voted with a small majority that the German Confederation should proclaim a war on Prussia. All the Catholic states sided with Austria, and some spoke of another Thirty Years' War. Of all the great wars the world has known, it was nevertheless the shortest—the decisive military actions took a week and the length of the interval between the first Austro-Prussian engagement and the final armistice was exactly one month.

The kingdom of Italy allied with Prussia, and though defeated by the Austrians at the battles of Custozza and Lissa, Prussian victory in the war enabled the Italians to seize Venice, completing the unification of their country. However, Bismarck did not want to weaken a potential future ally more than necessary, and demanded no further territory from Austria. Instead, the Prussians annexed the grand duchy of Hesse and the duchy of Nassau, occupied the kingdom of Hanover and deposed George V, who was thrown at the hospitality of his English cousin, Queen Victoria. Up until then, the free city of Frankfurt had held a special status, first as the place of the election and then of the coronation of the Holy Roman Emperors, and finally as the headquarters of the German Confederation, now replaced by the *Norddeutscher Bund*, with Bismarck as Federal Chancellor. The Prussian capital, Berlin, became the seat of the new confederation, from which the South German states were excluded. They were, however, closely bound to it through their membership in the new German Customs Union[284] of 1867, in which also the predominant influence was exercised by Prussia. The same year, Austria was forced to concede autonomy to Hungary, giving birth to the dual monarchy.

Unlike the weak King of Saxony, who had to pay a sizeable indemnity and join the North German Confederation, Ludwig of Bavaria viewed himself as a divinely sanctioned monarch, personally negotiating excellent terms with Prussia. His *leitmotiv* was the swan of Lohengrin: swans could be found in his tapestries, door knobs, and faucets; carved on his furniture, embroidered on his cushions, painted on his china, swimming in his pools. Since the reclusive "Swan King" detested being ogled by the "plebeians," he arranged for special performances of Wagner's operas where he was the only person in the audience. The composer's whimsies where equally regal, and the Bavarian court complained about his meddling in the affairs of the state. Ludwig was finally forced to make a choice between private friendship and public obligations: Wagner was asked to leave Munich, and the next eight years, he was again in Swiss exile, this time living in a house purchased for him by Ludwig, receiving an annual salary from His Majesty.

It was while visiting Leipzig in 1868 that Wagner first met Friedrich Wilhelm Nietzsche (1844-1900), another young enthusiast for his works. Nietzsche was born in Röcken, near Lützen, in Prussian Saxony, on the 15th of October, the same date as Frederick William IV of Prussia, after whom he was baptized. His father was the preacher of the village, "the perfect picture of a country parson," appointed by order of the King. His father's father had also been a pastor, as had his mother's father; indeed, biographers indicate at least twenty clergymen in his family within five generations. When Nietzsche was just under five years old, his father died, followed to the grave by his baby

---

[284] i.e. *Zollverein*

brother only six months later. This left the "little pastor" as the only man in a household consisting of himself, his mother, his younger sister, his maternal grandmother, and two unmarried aunts. There is no question that this veritable matriarchy at such a tender age contributed to the somewhat critical thoughts that Nietzsche later put forward about the fairer sex.

At twelve, Nietzsche earned a full scholarship to Pforta, an élite Lutheran boarding school with only 200 students, the same one that groomed Klopstock, Fichte, Novalis, and Ranke. He immediately excelled academically, showing a lively interest in religious education and the teachings of Christianity. After graduating six year later, he went on to study theology and Classical philology at the University of Bonn. However, at the age of 18, his faith in traditional religion received a fatal blow when he discovered Schopenhauer. He discarded his theological studies and resolved instead to focus on philology at Leipzig. Unfortunately, his years in school had included a great deal of experience with horses, and in 1867, he was conscripted into the Prussian army as an officer in the horse-drawn artillery. He injured himself badly while trying to perform a leaping mount into the saddle and was released from service having not yet completed training.

Nietzsche's outstanding education culminated in a highly unusual appointment to professorship of Classical philology at the University of Basel at the unprecedented age of 24. At that time, he had not yet written his dissertation, let alone taken his doctoral examination, so the University of Leipzig conferred a doctorate on him on the strength of his published writings. Nietzsche was not even a Swiss citizen, so by the same token, Switzerland waived the citizenship requirements for university employment. From the time of his visit to Triebschen the next year, he was a frequent guest at Wagner's villa outside Lucerne. The composer was not only born in the same year as Nietzsche's father, but also had a decided facial resemblance to him, eventually becoming something of a father-substitute for the young professor.

As a boy, Nietzsche had demonstrated such a remarkable talent for music that it was pondered whether he should drop everything else in favour of cultivating his musical gift, and he never entirely gave up composing or playing the piano. While still in his teens, he saw *Tristan and Isolde* three times, growing passionately fond of Wagner's art and its pre-Christian ideal. Like Wagner, the young Nietzsche considered himself a disciple of Schopenhauer, regarding Wagner as the fulfilment of Schopenhauer's ideal of the poet-philosopher, destined to lift the Germans out of barbarity into the sphere of true artistic culture. For a time, Nietzsche acted as Wagner's chief propagandist and commentator, even if the writing of his first book was delayed when Germany and France went to war in 1870.

After her decisive victory over Austria, Prussia had emerged as the pre-eminent power in Central Europe, upsetting the precarious balance of power that had existed since 1815. Until now, Bismarck had held Napoleon III in check by vaguely promising compensation in the Rhineland. When he was asked to fulfill these promises, he arrogantly turned down the idea that an ounce of German land would be transferred to the French. Instead, he pointed out what he saw as the robbery of two traditionally German provinces: in 1697, France had acquired the southern border region of Alsace, and in 1766, assumed control over neighbouring Lorraine. The position was one that rallied even the South German states to the side of Prussia. The immediate occasion for the war was provided by the dispute over the Spanish throne, which the Revolution of 1868 had left vacant. Bismarck urged the candidacy of Prince Leopold, a cousin of King William of Prussia. Napoleon naturally resented this idea and his opposition was egged on by Bismarck until France declared war on Germany.

Wagner had initially opposed Prussia's desire to unify Germany through conquest, believing that Bavaria, as one of the "stem duchies" from the earliest days of the Holy Roman Empire, could become the unifier of Germany. No European monarch was so opposed to war as Ludwig, who detested the greed and bloodshed spawned by it. When his officials came to find him so that the Bavarian King could lead his troops, they were unable to locate him for several days; he was finally found dressed up as Barbarossa, sailing on a lake in a swan-boat with his cousin, who was dressed up as Lohengrin—an orchestra hidden in the bushes was playing Wagner. After his exile from Munich, however, the composer publicly cheered in favour of Prussian conquests, advocating war with the French, whom he had long disdained. As an academic philologian, the young Nietzsche spent his days analyzing Greek and Latin works, wishing he had pursued a more socially valuable career, such as medicine. The Franco-Prussian War provided him an opportunity to obtain leave from the University to serve as a volunteer medical orderly on active duty.

The gist of the Prussian plan was to subdue the French with fierce blows before any European conflicts could arise to neutralize the German victory.

While King Ludwig may have found playing at chivalry and combat as mediæval knights sane and uplifting, fighting wars in the modern manner was barbarous and disgusting to him. At Wissembourg, Froeschwiller, Vionville, Gravelotte, and many other battles, the losses of the victor were often greater than those of the defeated, for the Germans threw battalions of men against the French artillery—the only branch of service in which France was clearly superior. Nietzsche's time as a medic was short, for he contracted dysentery and diphtheria, returning to Basel within a month. Instead of waiting to heal, he pushed headlong into an even more fervent schedule of study. His health had been bad since youth, but from this point onwards he suffered from permanently ill health.

Before long, the Germans had besieged Marshal Bazaine at Metz and driven Emperor Napoleon's army to the pouch of Sedan. A republican government was formed at Paris in September of 1870, and the Germans laid siege to the city, which, being deprived of provisions, capitulated on the 28th of January, 1871. The new German empire of the Kaisers was now brought into being at the expense of the defeated Austria and France, without so much as a nod to the pope or the Catholicism of earlier empires in Francia.

While exploiting the nationalist feelings of German liberals, Bismarck never ceased to view himself in feudal terms as a retainer of the House of Hohenzollern. He represented Prussian particularism and did not want a German nation, pushing instead towards an imperial Germany that brought in thousands of Frenchmen and Poles, Balts and Slavs, and left out millions of Germans. Indeed, to many the "Second Reich" appeared not like a German, but like a Prussian empire.

It adopted, with some minor changes, the constitution Bismarck had prepared for the North German Confederation. A direct male suffrage *Reichstag* was instituted, together with other trappings of liberalism, but the lower house was mainly a deliberative body and the real power remained firmly in the hands of the Kaiser, Chancellor, aristocracy, and military. In order to unite the princes of the realm, Bismarck made the King of Bavaria offer the imperial crown to the King of Prussia in the name of the German princes and free cities. Ludwig resisted for a long time, wanting a rotation of emperorship between the Wittelsbachs and the Hohenzollern, and signed the paper only after realizing that if he did not, the King of Saxony as the next in rank would. He refused to attend the imperial coronation, however, and his early talent for politics notwithstanding, ordered his councillors never to confront him with any political matters again. But even William I was very unhappy about the course of events, being disinclined to accept any title that would efface that of King of Prussia, and publicly evaded Bismarck during the ceremonies.

Much of the admiration for the Germans as a people of culture collapsed after the War. The pursuit of power through military might had long been a Prussian trait, but the German Empire of 1871 contained regions and peoples whose rich traditions were marked more by their economic, intellectual, and cultural achievements. Many Germans had hoped to turn Germany into a liberal society, but in the end, Germany sacrificed liberalism to achieve nationhood. By the Treaty of Paris, roughly a fifth of the ancient duchy of Lorraine, including Briey[285] and Nancy[286], and all of Alsace, except Belfort, were reacquired by Germany. These would form the "imperial land" of Alsace-Lorraine, held in common by all the German states. Rather than submit to Germanization, many Alsatians emigrated to France and the cry for the return of Alsace-Lorraine became a rallying force for French nationalism. Due to the pro-French atmosphere generated by the harsh provisions of the treaty, Germany increasingly perceived herself as being surrounded by enemies. This led to an unprecedented arms race between the European powers, thus setting the stage for the great wars of the 20th century.

Until the annexation of Lorraine, Germany had been poor in iron ore and other industrial raw materials. After the Franco-Prussian War, she entered upon a process of industrialization that was astonishing in its unparalleled rate. She extorted from France a war indemnity of five billion francs, an immense sum by the monetary standards of the time. This led to the "Black Friday," a monumental collapse of the stock market, but the years before and after were rightly called the "founding years." During that time, the nation of poets and thinkers founded such great conglomerates as Krupp and Siemens, whose sphere of operations would span the entire globe. Her economy was, however, lopsided in favour of heavy industry, and burdened with a high-cost agricultural sector and a very limited natural resource base. She could either

---

[285] situated at the edge of immense iron ore fields

[286] located at the centre of a huge iron ore basin

use her heavy industries increasingly for armaments and use war to fulfill her aims and needs, or else she had to find growing export markets at a time when she was hardly alone in that need.

Nietzsche was basically a sensitive moralist, who could not suffer the ugliness, hypocrisy, and stuffiness of the rising Hohenzollern empire. In order to avoid seeing his countrymen, he spent the rest of his life wandering literally as a man without a country: he had given up his Prussian citizenship, but never finished acquiring the Swiss. He greatly admired the ancient Greek civilization and perceived in his two teachers clear resemblances to the greatest of the Hellenes—"between . . . Schopenhauer and Empedocles, Æschylus and Wagner, there is so much relationship, so many things in common, that one is vividly impressed with the very relative nature of all notions of time." In *The Birth of Tragedy* (1872), Nietzsche presented a revolutionary anti-Classicistic, tragic-pessimistic theory on the nature of Greek tragedy and civilization, which has as much to do with psychology as it does with philosophy.

Nietzsche proposed that civilization resulted from a conflict of two human tendencies, the two forms of Greek tragedy: the Apollonian, which stood for the rational desire for order, embodied in the sun-god, Apollo; and the Dionysian, which stood for the irrational desire for ecstasy, embodied in the wine-god, Dionysos. It was Nietzsche's belief in the Dionysian that caused him to initially press Wagner forward as the great reformer and saviour of mankind, the model for his idea of the *Übermensch*. When self-consciousness is destroyed, the whole façade of neurotic character armour collapses, and the self becomes free in a sense indescribable to common sense, itself but a symptom of the psychic defence mechanisms. This Dionysian freedom is not a dream, but a drunkenness; a life complete and immediate, not kept at a distance and seen through a veil. Hence, "the entire symbolism of the body is called into play, not the mere symbolism of the lips, face, and speech, but the whole pantomime of dancing, forcing every member into rhythmic movement." This meant not only returning to the Greek theatre tradition, the ideal of which had been a universal artwork, formed by scenes, text, song, and dance accompanied by the orchestra, but also a sharp renunciation of the classic Italian opera, which emphasized musical aspects alone.

Unlike practically all other opera composers, Wagner created virtually every feature of his works: he not only composed the music, but also wrote the lyrics, designed the sets and costumes, and eventually built his own opera house. His music drama is not just singing and accompaniment, but the steps, gestures, and glances are all carefully governed by the music, and only then does it become a true universal artwork. Wagner claimed that his discovery of Schopenhauer allowed him to "differentiate between intuitions and concepts,"[287] the former being an unmediated, direct grasp of reality, the latter the veil of consciously-held ideas. Once he was able to harmonize the two, he overcame his psychic division, enabling him to see life and art with new eyes. His characters often sing words that express one mental state, while the accompanying music reveals a contradictory state of mind. Wagner thus made known the complexities of the human mind with methods similar to Freud and his contemporaries long before them.

Wagner's librettos were designed to address the philosophical issues that he deemed vital to society, the tension between the physical and the spiritual, between selfishness and redemptive love of another. He considered the German and European culture in the industrial age to be ruled by materialism and greed, with people seeking personal advantage at the cost of empathy, trust, and civic virtue. Wagner perceived himself as a new Æschylus on a holy mission to revitalize German life through his operas, bringing the German people back into contact with the wisdom found in their national myths and poetry. His monumental tetralogy of music dramas based on the Nibelung saga took 26 years to complete and is justly regarded as one of the most ambitious musical projects ever undertaken by a single person. He realized the essential affinity between the Ring Quest and the Grail Quest, that both the Ring and the Grail could bring disaster, albeit by different means. Just as the power of the Grail would wreak vengeance if misused, the power of the Ring had to be withstood or else it would enslave its master. The moral is the same: power is ultimately self-destructive if achieved through selling one's soul.

"In Hellas, the supreme flowering of the state went hand in hand with that of art; so too the resurrection of the German empire should be accompanied by a massive artistic monument to the German intellect." Wagner saw his theatre as the German Delphi, as a place where the renewal myth would be fulfilled. His original intention was to build it in Munich, but when the public opinion there turned against him, he switched his attention to Nuremberg, which would have been especially appropriate for the performance of *The*

---

[287] *Letter to August Röckel* (Aug 23, 1856)

Mastersingers. However, the composer finally chose the small Bavarian town of Bayreuth, partly because back in 1864, he had sold the performing rights of all his forthcoming productions to King Ludwig. It was also suitably situated at a crossroads between Munich and Berlin, Paris and Prague, and Wagner's desire was to have people from all corners of Europe make pilgrimages to the fountain of their spiritual rebirth.

As opposed to the archetypal "village church," standing at the centre of a community, Wagner's *Festspielhaus* towers high above the town, encased by a magic pine forest, a sacred grove. The auditorium, arranged as an amphitheatre, is reminiscent of the raked theatres of antiquity. The three prosceniums create what Wagner referred to as a "mystic gulf" between the audience and the actors. No matter where they sit, the spectators are enclosed in the panorama and forced to surrender to the stage play. The lowering of the orchestra pit under the stage makes the sound rise up in the dark without apparent origin, causing the music to appear like a hallucinatory figment of imagination. Wagner's genius has thus transformed the strikingly simple, factory-like structure into a Dionysian theatre.

Wagner was constantly seeking support and patronage from the state—Germany could become a modern Athens, if only politics and art would go hand in hand. Following his fruitless meeting with Bismarck, he proceeded to assemble from among his friends and admirers throughout Germany and Austria so-called Wagner societies, which were committed to taking care of the expenses arising from the theatre and the performances. Before returning to Switzerland, he visited Leipzig, Frankfurt, Darmstadt, and Heidelberg to enlist members. Through this society activity, Wagnerism finally spread across the German borders to the Baltic and Scandinavian countries. The Mayor of Bayreuth agreed to donate a plot of land on a suitable hill, and on Wagner's 59th birthday, the cornerstone of the *Festspielhaus* was laid at a festive ceremony attended by Nietzsche and 700 other enthusiasts.

By 1874, however, it became apparent that, despite all the efforts, there was not enough funds to complete the project nor any improvement in sight. Wagner's friendship with Ludwig was reaffirmed that year, for the composer received a message saying that the King wished to grant him 200,000 marks and a villa in Bayreuth. Ludwig came to see himself as Wagner's "co-creator," and indeed, Wagner publically hailed him as such[288]. There is no doubt that Ludwig's aid was a major factor in Wagner's success and in his tremendous influence in history, but the extent of the King's financial support is frequently overestimated. The total amount, including all presents, transferred over the 19 years the two men knew each other, stands at 562,914 marks. This should be compared with other figures like the 1.7 million spent on a carriage for the royal wedding that never took place.

Although an overwhelming majority of the visitors to the four-day festival performance of *The Ring Cycle* were friends who had spared no expense to make Wagner's dreams a reality, he was still obsessed with social acceptance and busied himself with the *crème de la crème* of society. The ambivalence in Nietzsche's attitude towards him began to appear in *Richard Wagner in Bayreuth* (1875-6), an essay that heaped praise on the composer while simultaneously describing him as an "Old Minotaur," the seductive destroyer of all who came within his power. Wagner was quite prepared to sacrifice his friends and family for his art, and throughout his life, many of his closest colleagues ended up breaking with him. There is no better example than his relationship with Nietzsche, which had begun with great mutual admiration and ended in equally great hatred and disagreement over German nationalism and anti-Semitism.

In his twilight years, however, Wagner would return to his negative attitude towards the state. The festival had left him in debt once again, and the imperial government refused to grant his theatre the expected subvention as a national institution. Already in his 1870 essay on Beethoven, he had argued that although the German culture is universal by nature, this universality should not mean conquering by force—the German is not a *Welteroberer*[289], but a *Weltbeglücker*[290]. "Even his antagonism towards what he calls the 'Jewish elements' in music and in modern literature springs from the noblest of motives," wrote Hermann Levi, the conductor of the Royal Munich Orchestra, "That he bears no petty animosity, like a Junker or a sanctimonious Protestant, is proven by his behaviour towards me and Joseph Rubinstein, as well as his earlier attachment to Karl Tausig, for whom he had the most tender affection."

---

[288] *Letter to Ludwig II* (11 Aug, 1873)

[289] world conqueror

[290] world beatifier

CHAPTER 43

After the formation of the German Empire, Prussian legislation on the rights of the individual to worship as he pleases was enacted for all of Germany. Unlike in France and Italy, however, in Bismarck's Germany, the conflict between Church and State ended in the victory of the Church. Once liberal freedoms are enjoyed, there are always going to be those whose sense of liberty comes from crying out for a return to old-time traditions. The conflict came to a head when the Curia vainly demanded the Prussian government to expel Old Catholics from teaching positions. Bismarck leaned solely on the liberals, being opposed not only by the conservatives and the centrists, but also the evangelicals and all the national minorities. Government measures such as the "Pulpit Article," aimed against the abuse of the pulpit in political agitation, only incited the clergy into delivering sermons about persecutions of Christian becoming Nero or Diocletian, which Bismarck countered with his famous "Canossa" reference. The death of Pope Pius IX in 1878 finally defused the situation, allowing the old legislation to be restored piece by piece—only state control of education and statutory civil marriage survived.

Rocking the boat with new ideas, finding revolutionary ways of perceiving and doing things, is often deemed blasphemous and evil. Personal creative expression is frequently considered morally suspect, even though the artist, poet, or scholar has no likelihood or intention of harming anyone. All the truly pivotal advances in art, literature, and science incur only the hostility and resistance of the general public. Anything and everything that can potentially transform society is invariably seen as a threat to religious sensibilities. Nietzsche's first book produced such a negative reaction that parents of students protested his presence at the University. He had always been plagued by migraine headaches and poor eyesight, and after his physical condition deteriorated in 1879, he left Basel, receiving a modest pension for the rest of his life. He knew he had come close to death, and perhaps for the first time, found enjoyment in life, renouncing forever the pessimism of Schopenhauer. Increasingly isolated, he saw himself as a heroic wanderer figure, venturing up mountains into new territory.

Much as Wagner's music dramas are not easily pigeonholed, the visionary books Nietzsche wrote during his most productive years defy categorization as philosophy, psychology, sociology, history, poetry, or, indeed, religion. The culmination of both his work and notoriety came with the writing of *Also Spracht Zarathustra* (1882-5). His best-known work took a form that resembles a holy book and was described by him as having been written in a trance state. Like the Bible, it was a narrative, recounting the story of the Persian prophet, Zarathustra, the founder of the Zoroastrian religion. He may be the mythic, order-challenging hero of all Romantics, but the message of the book is not of Romantic nature: "God is dead!"—thus spoke Zarathustra. Other philosophers, including the ultra-conservative Hegel, had used the expression before him, but unlike them, Nietzsche was not presenting the death of God as a philosophical construction or analysis; he was presenting it like the Bible presents the acts of God: as an actual event.

Nietzsche really did intend his book to eventually hold a place like unto that of the Bible in the destiny of mankind: "With that I have given mankind the greatest present that has ever been made to it so far." His analysis of the history of Western civilization led him to the conclusion that Christianity had outdated itself, that science had replaced religion. "The greatest recent event—that 'God is dead,' that the belief in the Christian God has ceased to be believable—is even now beginning to cast its first shadows over Europe." The people themselves have killed God, but as the madman exclaims, "they know not what they do," so have not even realized it. This is particularly true of the clergy, who are rapidly being reduced to mere grave-watchers, presiding over the sepulchres of the once mighty God. The masses have yet to learn the full implication of what they have done: deprived of the Christian God, Western morality has lost its justification.

Christian theologians sought to resolve the obvious discrepancy between the existence of a good and almighty God and the reality of evil by attributing the origin of evil to Adam's rebellion. The human desire for independence from divine authority, the desire to be self-aware and self-governing, was seen by them as the root of all evil. Nietzsche was one of the first philosophers to criticize the morality-obsessed society of the age for its oppressive restraints on individualism, inventiveness, and free expression. He found the death of God good, because the Christian slave-morality would eventually die as well, and humanity would no longer be confined to submissiveness and mediocrity.

Man has long been bound by arbitrary moral codes which tell him how he should or should not behave under this or that circumstance, instead of helping the living individual to function spontaneously. By doing the latter, the organism would fall back instinctively on regulating its own activity through homeostasis, something which has enabled the species to survive over millions of years and evolve into its present incarnation. Once the antiquated values are stripped away, the "will-to-power" will emerge as the natural force behind the development of the individual and society as a whole. Mankind should seek power in themselves and for themselves, not through or because of anyone or anything else.

On the surface, Nietzsche seems to be advocating a barbarous principle of "victory to the strongest," but this is not at all what he is saying and he has been grossly misinterpreted here.[291] Every modern system of psychotherapy is predicated on the basis that each human being has his own essential individuality and that he must regulate his own behaviour in order to remain healthy. As soon as compulsory moral codes are there to repress natural instincts and desires, one sees a conflict-ridden human being, subservient, diseased, and neurotic. Whereas Schopenhauer believed that the fundamental instinct of man was the "will-to-live," Nietzsche believed that even more fundamental than this was his "will-to-power." That is, man instinctively and naturally wants not only to survive, but to be powerful—to further his ability for his own interests. The "will-to-power" is not so much power over others, as it is the power over oneself that is necessary for creativity. Strength is attained through discipline and philosophy, not through the exertion of chaotic force or brute enslavement. In suppressing human creative talent and ability, society stifles human potential.

Nietzsche criticized Christianity for not teaching people to control their basic desires, but to suppress and disregard them altogether. The chronically unsatisfied person suffers from an increased inner excitation that seeks discharge in all kinds of antisocial and violent behaviour unless his energies are blocked and absorbed by moral inhibitions. Conversely, the individual who is satisfied in his sexual and primitive physiological as well as social needs

---

[291] To Nietzsche, the struggle for survival was not the rule, but the exception in human society, and more importantly, it is the strong, not the weak, who always seem to come up short.

requires no artificial moral code for self-control. The Christian slave-morality is thus merely an expression of the resentment born by men who cannot satisfy their own basic needs.

A healthy and positive attitude towards life is manifested in the Overman, who is optimistic of his own free will, without perverted bitterness. Concentrating on real life rather than on the rewards of an afterlife promised by the great religions of salvation, the Overman affirms the fullness of life, including the pain and suffering that come with human existence. We should live as though there was nothing else beyond life: he is "redeemed" who is able to will the "eternal recurrence," who would gladly live every detail of his life over and over again for all eternity—"Dead are all Gods: now we want the Overman to live."

Nietzsche's ideal of redemption arose from his experiences with Wagner, and directly challenged the composer's own vision of mending the fractured human spirit. Wagner claimed that his operas from *Tristan* to *Parsifal* rested on Schopenhauerian philosophical and ethical basis, and for Schopenhauer, supreme wisdom was attained when life was understood as entirely futile, an endless cycle of desire and dissatisfaction. Salvation would be accomplished only by negating the selfish will-to-live in favour of achieving Buddha-like dissolution of the ego. Wagner's intention was to merge all the arts into the higher form of music drama, and in doing so, to supersede dogmatic religion. By making his Bayreuth festival an orgiastic ritual, art could be followed there with a devotion hitherto peculiar only to ancient Greece. He went as far as to boast that, thanks to his neo-pagan, neo-nationalistic achievement, "Church and State will be abolished," having outlived their utility.

However, after the première of *The Ring*, Wagner abandoned his plan to repeat the festival due to lack of funds, and the *Festspielhaus* was kept shut from 1876 to 1882. He was forced to hand over his tetralogy to theatres that in his opinion could not do it justice, and with his health deteriorating, he announced that the festival would die with him. Upon learning of this, King Ludwig made one last financial contribution that not only provided money for another festival, but additional stipends to be awarded annually after the composer's death. While Wagner had termed *The Ring Cycle* a "festival play," his final work, *Parsifal*, over thirty years in the making, was something more, a "sacred festival play," and its performance was forbidden anywhere in the world except at his "festival playhouse." Ludwig allowed Wagner the use of the Munich orchestra and chorus, but insisted that the younger and healthier Levi serve as the conductor. During the last series of performances, Wagner grabbed the baton from Levi in a fit of frustration and finished the final act himself. He died in Venice the next year and was buried in Bayreuth, following a huge public funeral.

Ludwig was often referred to as "Parsifal" by Wagner, and indeed seems to have fancied himself as the Grail King, one in a chain of rulers who knew and drew power from the inner mysteries of Christianity and their pre-Christian origins. Since 1869, he had been rebuilding the ruined citadels near his birthplace of Vorderhohenschwangau in the Bavarian Alps. Located atop a picturesque rock ledge over the Pöllat Gorge with its waterfall, the royal castle Neuschwanstein was intended to represent Monsalvat. Complete with spires, towers, walled courtyard, indoor garden, and an artificial cave, this elaborate reconstruction of a mediæval castle was to be built in the spirit of *Tannhäuser* and *Lohengrin*. A treasure-trove of tapestry and murals, wall-paintings throughout the four floors of the castle depict Wagnerian themes. The "Singers' Hall" on the top floor was designed as a Grail Temple and apparently intended for solemn religious celebrations rather than for the rowdy gatherings of minstrels and jongleurs. It was, however, never used during Ludwig's lifetime; it was first used on the 50th anniversary of Wagner's death.

Few composers have managed to tie up their loose ends as neatly as did Wagner, by creating a work of art that transcended everything he had done previously, fusing the expressive elements of a lifetime into an ultimate, towering legacy. While during his fighting years, he had received empathy only from the few friends who tirelessly fought for him, *Parsifal* seduced, almost from the beginning, not only the susceptible Wagnerians, but the world at large. Wagner and his work are said to have crowned the musical achievements of German Romanticism, and they certainly caused a total re-evaluation of all the operatic art up to that point. They have since become a pervasive part of modern culture, simultaneously celebrated and condemned like the works of no other composer in the history of music. No one saw the flaws and pitfalls of Wagner better than Nietzsche, and yet no one has understood so clearly his unique importance and gift, something that is usually overlooked by both Wagner enthusiasts and their opponents.

Nietzsche had turned against the idol of his youth years before he heard the

Prelude to Parsifal in Monaco, but the apostasy notwithstanding, he was deeply moved: "Putting aside all irrelevant questions (to what end such music can or should serve?), and speaking from a purely æsthetic point of view, has Wagner ever written anything better? . . . We get something comparable to it in Dante, but nowhere else." Nietzsche wrote that it was the discomfiting sensuousness of Wagner's swan song that made it his greatest masterpiece—Wagner is surely the most erotic composer in all of classical music. "In the art of seduction," Nietzsche wrote, "*Parsifal* will always retain its ranks—as the stroke of genius in seduction.—I admire this work; I wish I had written it myself; failing that, I understand it. . . Nowhere will you find a more agreeable way of enervating your spirit, of forgetting your manhood under a rosebush. . . One has to be a cynic in order not to be seduced here; one has to be able to bite in order not to worship here."[292]

Wagner's exploitation of Christian themes, however, Nietzsche found hypocritical, after all, the composer had always idealized the ancient Athenians for their pagan habits, voiced strong anticlerical sentiments, and advocated atheism. Christianity, on the other hand, Wagner had attacked as being against art and free expression, dictating to man and therefore debasing him. Despite Nietzsche's polemic, where he saw the composer "sinking, helpless and broken, before the Christian cross," Wagner never accepted the Christian doctrine. While there are several references to the Saviour in *Parsifal*, there is no explicit reference to Christ. Just like many of his earlier operas, it was concerned with redemption, with a focus on compassion and self-sacrificing love. These are themes that are found in many religions, and appear in a Christian context only because Wagner had a predominantly Christian audience.

Wagner absorbed many elements of Eastern philosophy and they appear also in the libretto of *Parsifal*, in which he used an episode from the *Ramayana*. The Spear of Destiny will not harm the titular hero on account of his karma, and is suspended instead in the air above his head, like the magic weapon was in the 5th-century BCE account of the life of Siddhârtha. The substance of all the Wagnerian myths of redemption is that everything that causes unease, disaffection, or alienation, is an evil that can and should be overcome. Man is constantly being driven into extreme attitudes by the two conflicting

---

[292] *Letter to Peter Gast* (Jan 1887)

tendencies embodied in Amfortas and Klingsor. The former yielded himself to seduction and was thus wounded beyond recovery, while the latter withdraw himself from alike danger and was therefore cast out forever from the Mountain of Salvation. Parsifal is the golden mean, the irrational middle way that allows man to live in harmony with the opposites and to gain deliverance from cosmic tensions. To reconsecrate the temple, the "Holy Fool" has only to thrust the Spear into the Grail, thus exercising the true power of life and redeeming not only Kundry, but himself. By creating a synthesis of East and West, Wagner succeeded in producing a universal drama.

Art as a replacement for religion, which reached its climax in Wagner-worship and Bayreuth pilgrimages, is an important way of looking at Romantic music and Wagner's operas, a topic about which the composer himself wrote at length: "One might say that where religion becomes artificial, it is reserved for art to save the spirit of religion by recognising the figurative value of the mythic symbols which the former would have us believe in their literal sense, and revealing their deep and hidden truth through an ideal representation." By subtly elaborating on the religious metaphor, Wagner was able to offer spiritual insights that could transcend Christianity without being adverse to any denomination.

The heretical Knights of the Grail were the only familiar Christian characters capable of representing the Church not as an institution. In Wagner's *Parsifal*, the holy and great feast of Easter, after having withered and become stereotyped in the hands of priests, is restored its proper power and significance. The old and sick Grail King is healed and the Knights are joyously returned to their worship of the Grail mystery. To Nietzsche, however, Wagner himself is the "Klingsor of Klingsors," who made Bayreuth a shrine where the "Indian Circe" entices the weak-willed to accept his "new Gospel." The virtuous philosopher needs to walk his own unique path "as every free and creative person must," and resist the temptation to gather stupid but adoring disciples who want to enchain themselves to his person and wisdom.

When Nietzsche wrote *Beyond Good and Evil* (1886), he was wrongly assumed to be suggesting that no human action could truly be regarded as evil. He defined evil as an innate human weakness, the inability to resist social stimuli and one's own impulsive desires that ultimately result only in misery for oneself and others—the craving for material gain, money, wealth, land, national identity, and so on across to grander amusements, better social amenities, living space, etc. etc. At the time, the respectable businessman and the incorruptible bureaucrat, the conscientious scholar and the seclusive aristocrat, even the gallant officer and the devout clergyman, were all possessed by a veritable stock-jobbing frenzy. This resulted in overproduction, industrial crisis, mass insolvencies, enormous depreciation, and the collapse of many private fortunes. The Bavarian state was nearly bankrupt due to the King's huge expenditures, and in June, 1886, Ludwig's ministers, along with several members of the royal family, resolved to depose him. They had him examined by Doctor von Gudden, who declared him insane, despite the fact that just a few weeks before another physician had declared him to be perfectly sane.

A host of officials then attempted to arrest the King, arriving at Neuschwanstein in a terrible thunderstorm, only to find themselves arrested by the royal guard and imprisoned. Ludwig's valet finally betrayed him and allowed him to be taken prisoner, but he escaped, drowning in Lake Starnberg under suspicious circumstances. The good doctor was also found in the lake, and according to the official account, he drowned while trying to prevent the King's suicide. The irony is that Ludwig was succeeded by his decidedly insane brother, Otto—his uncle, Prince Luitpold, served as regent until 1912. Ludwig got to live in his dream castle only for 172 days, but it is estimated that at the time of his death, the unfinished building had cost the state over 6 million gold marks. Hundreds of craftsmen had worked for years on its construction, which, since 1869, had provided an entire city with its livelihood. The Western Terrace, the Church Portal, the Knights' House and Baths, were never built; only the work necessary to finish the interior was continued, allowing the castle to be opened to the paying public as early as August, 1886.

The collapse of numerous German companies, the many deductions in wages, and the constant firing of employees, led to demonstrations, strikes, uproars, and anti-capitalist propaganda. Socialist strength created uneasiness and fear among employers, a fear that was shared and exploited by the Junker leaders. Bismarck pushed through a "law against the harmful and dangerous aspirations of Social Democracy,"[293] the implementation of which resulted in

---

[293] *Gezetz gegen die gemeinefährlichen Bestrebungen der Sozialdemokratie*

the suppression of all left-wing associations and newspapers, in countless house searches, arrests, and deportations, coupled with a despicable network of informers, cruel abuses, hateful riots, and socialist martyrdom that won the young party a lot of new friends. The Chancellor himself was far too smart to not know that no ideological movement can ever be suppressed with violence, and tried to woo the workers away from radical or plain reformist doctrines with his social insurance schemes. The first of their kind, they provided against sickness, accidents, disability, and old age, and were promptly denounced as "alms." After Bismarck was finally dismissed by Kaiser Wilhelm II, the political restrictions against socialists were relaxed, and by World War I, the Social Democrats had become the single largest party in Germany and the largest socialist party in the world.

Nietzsche was characterized by his flat refusal to be associated with a particular school of thought, his utter repudiation of the adequacy of any body of beliefs whatsoever, and his dissatisfaction with traditional philosophy as academic, superficial, and remote from life. In such works as the *Genealogy of Morals* (1887) and the *Antichrist* (1895), he sought to expose the predominant ethical and ideological beliefs as prejudice and self-deceit. The essence of his "transvaluation of all values" was the renunciation of both the Christian and the democratic ideals, the close affinity of which he clearly perceived. He considered fundamentally false those virtues that protect the weak from the strong: we are unlikely to become more moral in our behaviour if the only incentive is that staying good will save us from punishment; such coercion only makes people act as though they were highly ethical in public, when they privately harbour deep-rooted and suppressed desire for rebellion, if not revenge—a society that has too many laws unnecessarily restricting human liberty only drives many of its otherwise good members to criminal behaviour.

Today, practically every atrocity committed by a human being is blamed on our estrangement from good old-fashioned religious values. Yet, as Nietzsche so sharply points out to us, there are no such things as "moral facts." All ethical assertions concerning the nature of good and evil are mere value judgements that vary significantly according to time and place. Believing the Christian morality to be quite unnatural, Nietzsche used his knowledge of history as a Classical scholar to investigate the tradition of human morality. He asserted that the aristocrats, who originally dominated society, had defined their own strength, bravery, nobility, and individuality as "good," and the weakness, humility, mediocrity, and conformity of the commoners as "bad." Later, when Christianity rose to power, the slave class embraced democracy and the principle of equality in order to bring the naturally superior class down to its own level. Instead of being a product of affirmation, this second set of values was based on fear and resentment, the distinction between "good" and "evil" emanating from a sense of revenge against the upper classes.

For Nietzsche, there can be no more destructive a feeling than "moral indignation," which allows envy and hatred to be acted out under the guise of virtue. "Is moralizing not immoral?" He asked, passionately believing the Christian ethics to be infinitely more evil than the sinful acts and thoughts against which they were supposed to guard. Man, like all living creatures, adapts and accustoms to the conditions under which he lives and passes on his acquired habits. The descendants of a long line of slaves thus believed slavery to be an essential condition to life, while freedom seemed unthinkable to them. To the slave-moralists, sin was not just extreme acts, such as rape or murder, but any act of nonconformity whatsoever. They would dismiss all forms of human inventiveness as intrinsically evil and contemptible, for "It is not given to men to create, as it is a bad attempt to imitate God."

While one could argue that Western thought has largely abandoned its theologically oriented concept of man, it still remains far from certain that our society has risen "beyond good and evil." We routinely conform at the expense of our personal moral integrity; we all play games with our faces and voices depending on who we are talking to and what we expect from conversing with them. By constantly deceiving one another with such role play, we deprive ourselves of true self-honesty, and for many of us, playing our little roles as stern father, caring mother, obedient worker, or ruthless businessman, can take over life completely. Morality, compulsive imposition of norms, and social inhibition are producing pathological people whose resulting sadomasochistic tendencies can ultimately lead only to the extinction of mankind. Considering himself to be more Darwinian than Darwin himself, Nietzsche saw his Overman as the one and only way to advance the human species.

In spending so much time and energy praying to higher authorities for moral guidance, humanity has long denied itself the freedom to decide for itself what is good and what is evil. Nietzsche called himself the "Antichrist" because he wanted to deliver humanity from all Christian moral impositions.

Moral codes that stipulate a fixed set of rules for every individual to follow equally lower the capacity of each person for their own development in their unique ways. To evolve is, by definition, to become different from what has gone before. All living things have to change and develop, and a fixed code of ethics cannot grow with you. Life says: do not follow after me, but after yourself; only you can judge what action is right for you at any one time—if you become rigid and unbending, you stop growing and begin to die.

Nietzsche's concept of the will-to-power should be understood within the context of his existential idea that the human being strives to "become," rather than simply "to be." The Overman is able to actualize his will-to-power himself and create a "master-morality" that reflects the strength and independence of someone who is liberated from all values, except for those which he himself deems valid. While Nietzsche expressly denied that any such men had yet risen, he lists several individuals who could serve as models, among them Napoleon, Goethe, Shakespeare, Michelangelo, Leonardo da Vinci, and Jesus Nazarene.

"The 'bringer of glad tidings'," says Nietzsche of Jesus, "died as he had lived, as he had taught—not to 'redeem men' but to show how one must live." The life that Christ led was obviously not the life led by the ordinary Christian, nor was his practice that followed by the Church named after him. Slaves often conceive being good as simply not doing anyone any harm personally; however, to change the world in some manner, be it for better or for worse, entails direct involvement in some activity, and whatever one does is inevitably going to offend someone else's notion of what is right or wrong. The Church's lack of courage and will to profess the acts Jesus demanded resulted in the corruption of his teachings: Paul, unable to fulfill even the Jewish life, substituted faith as the path to redemption.

Not only did Paul invent a way for himself and his fellow believers to be redeemed, but this "bringer of ill tidings" also fostered the idea of a place of final judgement in the afterlife, where the unbelievers would be punished. The passion, death, and resurrection of Christ were supposed to give us hope; instead, they gave us only despair. They served as a promise of more pain and suffering to come before the end of times, leaving Christians in panic about whether or not they will gain admittance to Heaven. By sanctioning the ideas of punishment and revenge, Paul betrayed Jesus' basic message of love and forgiveness. In fact, Nietzsche was thoroughly convinced that no Christian ever held true to Jesus' teachings—"In reality, there has been only one Christian, and he died on the Cross."

We retain to this day a romantic idea of self-sacrifice, the sacrifice of the strong for the weak, the kind which is the essence of Pauline Christianity. It goes against all the principles of evolution; the sacrifice is in vain, for the weak are not even saved. The gesture may be magnificent, proof of utmost courage and moral strength—but if everyone acted in this manner the species itself would weaken and die out. Jesus, to Nietzsche, was not a meek and mild son of God, but a rebel and a human teacher with absolutely no divine purpose. When he vandalized the Temple stalls at Jerusalem in protest against the way a holy shrine had been turned into a marketplace, he was committing a criminal felony as an act of civil disobedience. He was a "political criminal," fighting against "caste, privilege, order, and formula. . . He died for his guilt. All evidence is lacking . . . that he died for the guilt of others."

In the past, people have acted immorally and yet still believed; today, self-professed atheists bow down to the Christian code of ethics. Nietzsche saw it as an obligation of the moral philosopher to question religious values; he wanted to be the moralist of the new post-God society, which had to subsist without any divine sanctions. Wishing to effect a "transvaluation of all values," a systemized destruction of systems, he set himself a task that no one could possibly fulfill, finally collapsing under the very weight of the conundrum. Early in 1889, he was walking the streets of Turin, when he encountered a coachman whipping a horse. He ran to the poor animal, put his arms around its neck, and passed out, never to be sane again.

In addition to the various ailments caused by his brief experiences in the military, Nietzsche had long suffered from vision problems, which in turn gave him excruciating migraine headaches and insomnia. Some scholars have suggested that his eventual madness was the result of advancing venereal syphilis, but eleven years is a very long time for anyone to survive the third stage of the disease, let alone someone who was of very poor health throughout his adult life. Among the last near-coherent writings that Nietzsche penned were letters to Wagner's widow, Cosima, in which he addressed her as "Princess Ariadne." He signed these as "Dionysos," others as "The Crucified." In one, he wrote: "When it comes right down to it I'd much rather have been a Basel Professor than God; but I didn't dare to be selfish enough to forgo the creation of the world."

Now widely recognized as one of the most brilliant prose writers of the German language, Nietzsche was notoriously unread in the academic circles during his own lifetime. His work was thought to be unsystematic and not scholarly because it was connected neither in thought or subject, yet working outside of the box was precisely what made Nietzsche one of the most influential philosophers who ever lived. He was adept in the use of contradictions, and often put his provocative ideas forward in the form of masterful aphorisms that have taken a life of their own outside the frame of reference, causing many of his subtler points to be missed. Taken to its extreme, his philosophy borders on the nihilistic, though Nietzsche was nowise a nihilist; taken at face value, it cries out against religion, though Nietzsche did not despise all faiths—he always saw himself as a pagan and an old-fashioned one at that.

Donning the mask of Zarathustra, Nietzsche cautioned his audience to be on guard lest they be deceived or trapped by him. Indeed, he prophecized that his own name would be pronounced "holy" after his death by self-appointed disciples, who would corrupt his teachings, twisting them to justify values and ideals which he himself found repugnant. Most of Nietzsche's final years were spent in his sister Elisabeth's care in Weimar, during which time she became more and more involved in the flourishing anti-Semitic movements of Germany. While he wasted away, she collected and edited some of his discarded notes, which she then published as *Der Wille zur Macht* (1901), a work carefully tailored to suit her own political agenda. As a result of her ruthless control over her brother's literary estate, Nietzsche's altered works became an obsession of Hitler's and a cornerstone of the Nazi Party.

The concept of the Overman has always appealed to both cultivated persons and popular agitators. It has often been misinterpreted as one that postulates a master-slave society and been unjustly identified with totalitarian philosophies. Yet the Nietzschean Overmen do no bother with with the details of government, nor is even the exercise of supreme power over society their main concern; they are the end to which society is a means, living in detached unconcern like Epicurean gods. The Nazis argued that Nietzsche's Overman theory supported their own master race theory, though his only claim was that individuals can be born superior and though he was completely opposed to the collective tendencies that labelled National Socialism; no strong individual, conscious of his will-to-power and identifying with it, would care to live in a society predicated on such conformism. What is more, Nietzsche strongly repudiated both racism and nationalism, asserting that "every great crime against culture for the last four hundred years lies on their conscience." His Overman is "too pure for the filth of the words: revenge, punishment, reward, retribution," viewing competitors for power not as enemies, but as opponents in a great game of human ability that builds our character and teaches us valuable lessons.

As the distortions of Nietzsche's ideas have gradually been exposed, the esteem for him has grown. In fact, his influence so pervades modern culture that many who have never even read his work are indirectly influenced by his thought. The history of 20th-century philosophy, psychology, and theology is wholly unintelligible without him. Since the dawn of time, evil has posed the greatest dilemma for both theologians and philosophers, and Nietzsche overthrew all the previous speculations by asserting that humanity must rise beyong good and evil. Though the idea of the death of God did not begin with Nietzsche, he was the one with whom people consistently associate it, presumably because he had a habit of spelling things out in strong terms. People may accept or reject the idea, but after Nietzsche, no one can ignore it—he called it "philosophizing with a hammer."

Since the time of Nietzsche, dominant currents in Western philosophy, science, and social thought have been engaged in re-examination of man's psychological, physiological, and social being outside religious context. His insistence that the decay of religion requires that individuals take responsibility for their own ethical decisions notably inspired the development of existentialism. His concepts were discussed and elaborated upon by the German philosophers Karl Jaspers (1883-1969) and Martin Heidegger (1889-1976), together with their French colleagues Albert Camus (1913-1960), Jean-Paul Sartre (1905-1980), Michel Foucault (1926-1984), and Jacques Derrida (1930-2004). Both Freud and Jung were profoundly influenced by Nietzsche's work, as was Alfred Adler (1870-1937), founder of the school of individual psychology. It argues that each individual strives for what he termed "superiority," but which today is more commonly known as "self-actualization" or "self-realization." In fact, all branches of humanistic psychology and the entire human potential movement are greatly indebted to Nietzsche's notions of striving and self-creation.

Within prose and poetry, Nietzsche exerted great influence not only on German literature, but French and British literature as well. Especially in his Zarathustra visions and his posthumously published poems, he was the trailblazer for most literary expressionists. The playwright George Bernard Shaw (1856-1950) articulated his own version of the Nietzschean struggle for power in his *Man and Superman*, while the novelist Hermann Hesse (1877-1962) similarly explored the necessity for individuals to transcend traditional ideas and their social training to seek their own way e.g. in *Siddharta*. Rainer Maria Rilke, William Butler Yeats, Thomas Mann, Stefan George, Eugene O'Neill, Knut Hamsun, André Malraux, and André Gide were all influenced by Nietzsche, and each of them found something different in him.

On the surface, the beginning of the 20th century seems little different from the end of the 19th. The bourgeoisie was still dominant, embellished with the fading gilt of monarchy and aristocracy. The pursuit of pleasure and the breaking of family ties became not only lawful, but also recommendable in the name of science and vitality. However, the object of interest during this period was no longer instant gratification, but capital formation. Not until then did capital become an end in itself, an all-consuming beast that devours its own offspring.

The development of science and education, technology and industrialization continued uninterrupted throughout the 20th century. The people of Europe still believed in an unhindered progress towards a growing humanity and prosperity, though the reaction against this optimism also lived on. The average mediæval person of whatever feudal class was no doubt more satisfied with his lot in life than the typical stressed-out citizen of modern society. Most people living in the "deprived" Third World were arguably happier than the average dissatisfied Westerner, and even though Modernist movements one after the other fought Romanticism, it survived. To this day, prominent writers of all genres feel ill at ease in their own environment, are still wont to protest against the complacent middle classes and to fantasize about the more colourful past.

In the Western world of the 19th century, the forms of political and social life still showed considerable variation, from the traditional republic of the United States to the traditional monarchy of Prussia. By the beginning of the 20th century, the political map of Europe had completely changed from what it had been a hundred and fifty years before; yet, in a way, it resembled the much smaller Hellas of the 5th century BCE—the city-states were merely substituted by the nation-states in a much larger scale. During the autocracy of previous centuries, the citizen may have been condemned to a near total insignificance, but his private life was so pleasant, peaceful, and undisturbed that we can hardly comprehend it today. If constitutional monarchy finally gave him political rights, it also made him liable to military service.

There can hardly be a more tangible violation of personal liberty than the requirement to follow for three years the orders of superiors with the authority and disciplinary powers of a prison warden, while performing gruelling hard labour unaccustomed. Yet even constitutional monarchy usually gives way to an even more democratic form of government: the tyrant is eliminated completely and the people rule sovereignly. The inevitable result is that life, which until then had resembled a work camp only during military service, becomes compulsive through and through. The people's government interferes with absolutely everything: a person's every private act is now seen as public business and subjected to the majesty and sanctions of the law.

No form of government can be guilty for more absurdities and atrocities than the democratic one, for it alone has an organic conviction of its infallibility, sanctity, and absolute justification. Absolute monarchy has hundreds of checks, including the ruler's personal liability, his counsellors, the court clique, the Church, and the parallel government which of necessity forms around every monarch. While all self-appointed autocrats are affected by the ever-present fear of dethronement, the democratically elected government is spared from any self-constraint by the circular reasoning that it is legitimate because it represents the will of the people, and that it represents the will of the people because it is legitimate.

SELECT BIBLIOGRAPHY[294]

Abelard, Peter. *Historia Calamitatum: The Story of My Misfortunes*, trans. by Henry Adams Bellows (Saint Paul, 1922)

Aberbach, Alan David. *Ideas of Richard Wagner: An Examination and Analysis of his Major Aesthetic, Political, Economic, Social, and Religious Thoughts* (Lanham, 1984)

Academischen Wagner-Verein zu Berlin. "Deutsche Festspiele in Bayreuth" in *Musikalisches Wochenblatt*, Vol. III (April 26, 1872)

Accius, Lucius. "Atreus" in *Tragicorum Romanorum fragmenta*, ed. by Otto Ribbeck (Leipzig, 1897)

Adams, Henry. *Mont-Saint-Michel and Chartres* (Boston, 1905)

Adas, Michael. *Machines as the Measure of Men: Science, Technology, and Ideologies of Western Dominance* (Ithica, 1989)

Addison, Charles G. *The History of the Knights Templars* (London, 1842)

Adler, Alfred. *Study of Organ Inferiority and its Psychical Compensation*, trans. by Smith Ely Jelliffe (New York, 1917)

Aelian. *Historical Miscellany*, ed. & trans. by Nigel G. Wilson (London, 1997)

Aeschylus. *Eumenides*, trans. by Herbert Weir Smyth (Cambridge, 1926)

Alexiou, Stylianos. *Minoan Civilization* (Heraclion, 1969)

Allegro, John M. *The Sacred Mushroom and the Cross: A Study of the Nature and Origins of Christianity within the Fertility Cults of the Ancient Near East* (Garden City, 1970)

Allen, Don Cameron. *The Star-Crossed Renaissance: The Quarrel about Astrology and its Influence in England* (Durham, 1941)

Allen, Joseph Henry. *Christian History in its Three Great Periods*, 3 vols (Boston, 1883)

Ammianus Marcellinus. *Roman History*, 3 vols, ed. & trans. by J. C. Rolfe (London, 1935-39)

Analecta Franciscana sive Chronica aliaque varia documenta ad Historiam Fratrum Minorum Spectantia, 5 vols, ed. by Bernard of Bessa (Quaracchi, 1885-1910)

Ancient Egyptian Literature: A Book of Readings, 3 vols, ed. by Miriam Lichtheim (Berkeley, 1973-80)

The Ancient Egyptian Pyramid Texts, trans. by R. O. Faulkner (Warminster, 1969)

Ancient Records of Egypt: Historical Documents from the Earliest Times to the Persian Conquest, 5 vols, ed. & trans. by James Henry Breasted (Chicago, 1906-07)

Andreæ, Johann Valentin. *Die Chymische Hochzeit des Christian Rosenkreutz* (Strasbourg, 1616)

The Anglo-Saxon Chronicle, trans. by James Ingram (London, 1823)

---

[294] Of the numerous magazine and journal articles consulted only the ones quoted are cited here.

"Annales Regni Francorum", ed. by Georg Heinrich Pertz, in *Monumenta Germaniæ Historica*, SsrG 6, ed. by Friedrich Kurze (Hanover, 1895)

The Apocrypha and Pseudepigrapha of the Old Testament, 2 vols, ed. by R. H. Charles (Oxford, 1913)

Apollodorus: *Library and Epitome*, 2 vols, ed. & trans. by Sir James George Frazer (London, 1921)

Appian. *The Civil Wars*, trans. by Horace White (New York, 1913)

Après Galilée: Science et foi—nouveau dialogue, ed. by Paul Poupard (Paris, 1994)

Arab Historians of the Crusades, ed. by Francesco Gabrieli, trans. by E. J. Costello (London, 1969)

Aristarchus of Sámos. *On the Sizes and Distances of the Sun and Moon*, ed. & trans. by Sir Thomas Little Heath (Oxford, 1913)

Aristotle. *Theory of Poetry and Fine Art*, 3rd ed., ed. & trans. by Samuel Henry Butcher (London, 1902)

_____. *A Treatise on Government*, trans. by William Ellis (London, 1912)

Armajani, Yahya. *Middle East: Past and Present* (Englewood Cliffs, 1970)

Arndt, Ernst Moritz. *Germanien und Europa* (Altona, 1803)

Arrian. *The Anabasis of Alexander, together with the Indica*, trans. by E. J. Chinnock (London, 1893)

Ashmole, Elias. *The Institutions, Laws and Ceremonies of the Most Noble Order of the Garter* (London, 1672)

_____. "The Life of Elias Ashmole, Esquire by Way of Diary" in *Lives of Those Eminent Antiquaries Elias Ashmole and Mr. William Lilly*, by Elias Ashmole & William Lilly (London, 1774)

_____. *Theatrum Chemicum Britannicum* (London, 1652)

Athenæus of Naucratis. *The Deipnosophists*, trans. by Charles Burton Gulick (London, 1937)

Atiya, Azis S. *A History of Eastern Christianity* (London, 1968)

St. Augustine. "De Civitate Dei", trans. by Marcus Dods, in *Nicene and Post-Nicene Fathers*, Series I, Vol. II, ed. by Philip Schaff (Edinburgh, 1887)

_____. *Confessions*, trans. by William Watts (New York, 1912)

Aurelius, Marcus. *Meditations*, ed. & trans. by C. R. Haines (London, 1916)

Ausubel, Nathan. *The Book of Jewish Knowledge* (New York, 1964)

Babylonian Talmud, Tractate Sanhedrin, trans. by Jacob Shachter & H. Freedman, ed. by Isidore Epstein (London, 1961)

Bacon, Sir Francis. *Certain Considerations Touching the Plantation in Ireland* (1606), British Library Harley MS 6797 fol. 122

_____. "De Hæresibus" in *Meditationes Sacræ* (London, 1597)

_____. "De Interpretatione Naturæ Prooemium" [1620] in *The Works of Francis Bacon*, Vol. III, ed. by James Spedding, Robert Leslie Ellis & Douglas Denon Heath (London, 1859)

_____. *The New Atlantis* (London, 1627)

_____. *Novum Organum* (London, 1620)

_____. *Of the Dignity and Advancement of Science* (London, 1623)

_____. *Of the Proficience and Advancement of Learning, Divine and Humane* (London, 1605)

Bacon, Roger. *Opus Majus*, trans. by Robert Belle Burke (Philadelphia, 1928)

_____. "Opus Tertium" [1268] in *Opera quædam hactenus inedita*, ed. by J. S. Brewer (London, 1859)

Baker, Evan. "Richard Wagner and His Search for the Ideal Theatrical Space" in *Opera in Context: Essays on Historical Staging from Late Renaissance to the Time of Puccini*, ed. by Mark A. Radice (Portland, 1998)

Barber, Malcolm. *The Trial of the Templars* (Cambridge, 1978)

Barberini, Maffeo. *Poemata* (Rome, 1631)

Barraclough, Geoffrey. *The Origins of Modern Germany* (Oxford, 1946)

Barruel, Augustin de. *Memoirs Illustrating the History of Jacobinism* (London, 1798)

Bartholomæus Anglicus. *De Proprietatibus Rerum*, ed. by Robert Steele (London, 1924)

Baugh, Albert C. *A History of the English Language* (London, 1951)

Baxter, Richard. *Reliquiæ Baxterianæ, or, Mr. Richard Baxters narrative of the most memorable passages of his life and times* (London, 1696)

Beck, Hermann. *The Origins of the Authoritarian Welfare State in Prussia: Conservatives, Bureaucracy, and the Social Question, 1815-70* (Ann Arbor, 1995)

Bede, The Venerable. *Opera Historica*, 2 vols, trans. by J. E. King (London, 1930)

Bedoyère, Michael de la. *The Meddlesome Friar: the Story of the Conflict between Savonarola and Alexander VI* (London, 1957)

Belloc, Hilaire. *Characters of the Reformation* (New York, 1936)

Bentham, Jeremy. *A Fragment on Government* (London, 1776)

Bernal, John Desmond. *Science in History*, 4 vols (London, 1954)

St. Bernard of Clairvaux. *The Complete Works of S. Bernard, Abbot of Clairvaux*, 2 vols, ed. & trans. by Samuel J. Eales (London, 1904)

_____. "Liber ad milites Templi: De laude novæ militæ" in *Sancti Bernardi Abbatis primi Clarevallensis opera omnia*, Vol. I, ed. by Jean Mabillon (Paris, 1667)

Beugnot, Arthur Auguste. *Histoire de la Destruction du Paganisme en Occident*, 2 vols (Paris, 1835)

The Bible, King James Version

Bielschowsky, Albert. *Goethe: Sein Leben und seine Werke*, new ed. in 2 vols, rev. by Walther Linden (Munich, 1928)

Billington, James H. *Fire in the Minds of Men: Origins of the Revolutionary Tradition* (New York, 1980)

Biographia Britannica, 7 vols (London, 1747-66)

Boisgelin, Louis de. *Ancient and Modern Malta*, 2 vols (London, 1804-05)

Bolgar, Robert Ralph. *The Classical Heritage and its Beneficiaries* (Cambridge, 1954)

Bonaparte, Napoleon. *The Corsican: A Diary of Napoleon's Life in His Own Words*, ed. by R. M. Johnston (Boston, 1910)

____. *Maxims of Napoleon*, ed. by A. G. de Liancourt, trans. by J. A. Manning (London, 1903)

Bortoft, Henri. *Wholeness of Nature: Goethe's Way toward a Science of Conscious Participation in Nature* (Hudson, 1996)

Boxer, Charles Ralph. *The Dutch in Brazil, 1624-1654* (Oxford, 1957)

Boyer, Carl B. *A History of Mathematics* (New York, 1968)

Brahe, Tycho. *De Nova et Nullius Ævi Memoria Prius Visa Stella* (Copenhagen, 1573)

Brandes, Georg Morris Cohen. *Wolfgang Goethe*, 2 vols, authorized translation from the Danish by Allen W. Porterfield (New York, 1924)

Bray, Gerald Lewis. *Creeds, Councils, and Christ* (Leicester, 1984)

Breccia, Evaristo. *Alexandria ad Aegyptum: A Guide to the Ancient and Modern Town, and to its Graeco-Roman Museum* (Bergamo, 1922)

Brier, Bob. *Ancient Egyptian Magic* (New York, 1980)

Briggs, Lord Asa. *Victorian Cities*, 2nd ed. (Harmondsworth, 1968)

The British Problem, 1534-1707: State Formation in the Atlantic Archipelago, ed. by Brendan Bradshaw & John Morrill (London, 1996)

Bronowski, Jacob. *The Ascent of Man* (Boston, 1973)

Brown, Harold O. J. *Heresies: The Image of Christ in the Mirror of Heresy and Orthodoxy from the Apostles to the Present* (Garden City, 1984)

Brusher, Joseph S. *Popes through the Ages* (Princeton, 1959)

Budge, Sir E. A. Wallis. *Egyptian Magic* (London, 1901)

____. *The Gods of the Egyptians: Studies in Egyptian Mythology*, 2 vols (London, 1904)

____. *Osiris: The Egyptian Religion of Resurrection*, 2 vols (London, 1911)

Bulwer-Lytton, Sir Edward G. D. *Paul Clifford* (London, 1830)

____. *Richelieu; or the Conspiracy* (London, 1839)

Burckhardt, Jacob. *Die Cultur der Renaissance in Italien* (Basel, 1860)

Burke, Peter. *Popular Culture in Early Modern Europe* (London, 1978)

Burkert, Walter. *Ancient Mystery Cults* (Cambridge, Mass., 1987)

____. *Greek Religion: Archaic and Classical*, trans. by John Raffan (Oxford, 1985)

Burkitt, Francis Crawford. *The Religion of the Manichees* (Cambridge, 1925)

Burland, Cottie A. *The Arts of the Alchemists* (London, 1967)

Burman, Edward. *The Templars: Knights of God* (Wellingborough, 1986)

Burnett, Andrew. *Coinage in the Roman World* (London, 1987)

Burns, Thomas S. *Barbarians within the Gates of Rome: A Study of Roman Military Policy and the Barbarians, ca. 375-425 A.D.* (Bloomington, 1994)

Burtt, Edwin Arthur. *The Metaphysical Foundations of Modern Physical Science* (London, 1924)

Byron, Lord George Gordon. *The Intellectual Eunuch Castlereagh* (Venice, 1818)

Cæsar, Julius. *Commentaries on the Gallic and Civil Wars*, trans. by W. A. McDevitte & W. S. Bohn (New York, 1869)

Cæsarius of Heisterbach. *Dialogus Miraculorum* [c. 1230], 2 vols, ed. by Joseph Strange (Cologne, 1851)

Calvin, John. *Institutes of the Christian Religion*, Vol. IV, trans. by Henry Beveridge (Edinburgh, 1846)

Cameron, Kenneth. *English Place-Names* (London, 1961)

Campenhausen, Hans von. *The Formation of the Christian Canon*, trans. by J. A. Baker (Philadelphia, 1972)

Cantù, César. *Storia universale*, Vol. XV (Turin, 1839)

Carlyle, Thomas. *The French Revolution: A History*, 3 vols (London, 1837)

_____. *History of Friedrich the Second, called Frederick the Great*, 6 vols (London, 1858-65)

"Caroli Magni Capitularia" in *Patrologiæ Latina*, Vol. XCVII, ed. by Jacques-Paul Migne (Paris, 1862)

Carradice, Ian & Martin Price. *Coinage in the Greek World* (London, 1988)

Cartwright, Johanna & Ebenezer. *The Petition of the Jews for the Repealing of the Act of Parliament for their Banishment out of England* (London, 1649)

Caspar, Max. *Kepler*, trans. by C. Doris Hellman (London, 1959)

Cassiodorus, Magnus Aurelius. *The Letters of Cassiodorus*, ed. & trans. by Thomas Hodgkin (London, 1886)

The Catholic Encyclopedia, 15 vols, ed. by Charles G. Herbermann et al (New York, 1907-12)

Celtis, Conradus. *Quatuor libri amorum secundum quatuor latera Germanie* (Nuremberg, 1502)

Chadwick, Edwin. *Report on the Sanitary Condition of the Labouring Population of Great Britain* [1842], ed. by M. W. Flinn (Edinburgh, 1965)

Chadwick, Henry. *The Early Church* (Harmondsworth, 1967)

Chadwick, Owen. *The Reformation* (Harmondsworth, 1964)

The Chaldean Oracles of Zoroaster, ed. by W. Wynn Westcott (London, 1895)

Le Chanson de Roland, ed. by Brian Wooledge (London, 1967)

Chapman, Allan. "England's Leonardo: Robert Hooke (1635-1703) and the art of experiment in Restoration England" in *Proceedings of the Royal Institution of Great Britain*, Vol. 67, ed. by Peter Day (Oxford, 1996)

Cicero, Marcus Tullius. *On the Nature of the Gods*, trans. by C. D. Yonge (London, 1907)

———. "Pro Sulla" in *The Orations of Marcus Tullius Cicero*, trans. by C. D. Yonge (London, 1891)

Clausewitz, Karl von. *Vom Krieg* (Berlin, 1832)

Clement of Alexandria. *Recognitions of Clement*, Bk. II, trans. by Thomas Smith, in *Ante-Nicene Fathers*, Vol. VIII, ed. by Alexander Roberts & James Donaldson (Edinburgh, 1867)

———. *The Stromata, or Miscellanies*, Bk. V, trans. by W. Wilson, in *Ante-Nicene Fathers*, Vol. II, ed. by Alexander Roberts & James Donaldson (Edinburgh, 1867)

Clulee, Nicholas H. *John Dee's Natural Philosophy: Between Science and Religion* (London, 1988)

Cobban, Alfred. *The Social Interpretation of the French Revolution* (Cambridge, 1964)

Cochlæus, Johannes. *Commentaria de Actis et Scriptis M. Lutheri* (Mainz, 1549)

Codinus, Georgius. *Excerpta De antiquitatibus Constantinopolitanis*, ed. by B. Medonius (Paris, 1655)

Coil, Henry Wilson. *Coil's Masonic Encyclopedia* (New York, 1961)

Collins, Anthony. *A Discourse of Free-Thinking, Occasion'd by the Rise and Growth of a Sect call'd Free-Thinkers* (London, 1713)

Connolly, Peter. *Living in the Time of Jesus of Nazareth* (Oxford, 1983)

Copleston, Frederick. *A History of Philosophy*, 9 vols (London, 1946-1974)

Cormack, Lesley B. *Charting an Empire: Geography at the English Universities, 1580-1620* (Chicago, 1997)

*Correspondance de Napoléon I*ᵉʳ*, Vol. X, ed. by Henri Plon & J. Dumaine (Paris, 1862)

The Correspondence of Pope Gregory VII, ed. & trans. by Ephraim Emerton (New York, 1932)

Creasy, Sir Edward. *Fifteen Decisive Battles of the World: From Marathon to Waterloo* (London, 1851)

Crombie, A. C. *Robert Grosseteste and the Origins of Experimental Science* (Oxford, 1953)

Cromwell, Oliver. *Letters and Speeches, with Elucidations*, 2nd ed. in 3 vols, ed. by Thomas Carlyle (London, 1846)

Crossan, John Dominic. *The Historical Jesus: The Life of a Mediterranean Peasant* (San Francisco, 1991)

Crusaders as Conquerors: The Chronicle of Morea, trans. by Harold E. Lurier (New York, 1964)

Cumont, Franz. *The Mysteries of Mithra*, trans. by Thomas J. McCormack (London, 1903)

———. *The Oriental Religions in Roman Paganism*, 2nd ed., trans. by Grant Showerman (Chicago, 1911)

Cusanus, Nicolaus. *De Docta Ignorantia*, trans. by Germain Heron (London, 1954)

Custine, Astolphe de. *La Russie en 1839* (Paris, 1843)

St. Cyril of Jerusalem. *Lectures on the Christian Sacraments: the Procatechesis and the Five Mystagogical Catecheses*, ed. & trans. by F. L. Cross (London, 1951)

Dampier, Sir William Cecil. *A History of Science and its Relation with Philosophy and Religion* (Cambridge, 1929)

Daniel, Glyn Edmund. *150 Years of Archaeology* (London, 1975)

Dante Alighieri. *The Divine Comedy*, 3 vols, trans. by John A. Carlyle & P. H. Wicksteed (London, 1900)

_____. *On World Government or De Monarchia*, trans. by Herbert W. Schneider (New York, 1949)

Deacon, Richard. *A History of the British Secret Service* (London, 1969)

_____. *John Dee: Scientist, Geographer, Astrologer, and Secret Agent to Elizabeth I* (London, 1968)

Decrees of the Ecumenical Councils: From Nicaea I to Vatican II, 2 vols, ed. by Norman P. Tanner (London, 1990)

Dee, John. *Brytanici Imperii Limites*, British Library Additional MS 59681

_____. *Generall and Rare Memorialls Pertayning to the Perfect Arte of Navigation* (London, 1577)

_____. "Letter to Elizabeth (Nov 10, 1588 s.v.)", British Library Harley MS 6986 fol. 45

_____. "Mathematicall Præface" in *The Elements of Geometrie of the most aunciente Philosopher Evclide of Megara*, ed. & trans. by Sir Henry Billingsley (London, 1570)

_____. "Note of Advice to Arthur Pet and Charles Jackman" [1580] in *The Principall Navigations, Voiages, Traffiques, and Discoveries of the English Nation*, Vol III, by Richard Hakluyt (London, 1599)

_____. *Playne Discourse* (1583), Ashmolean MS 1789

_____. *The Private Diary of John Dee*, ed. by James Orchard Halliwell (London, 1842)

_____. "Proposals to Mary for the Foundation of a Library Royall" in *Johannis Confratris et Monachi Glastoniensis Chronica sive Historia de Rebus Glastoniensibus*, Vol. II, ed. by Thomas Hearne (Oxford, 1726)

_____. *A True and Faithful Relation of What Passed for Many Yeers Between Dr. John Dee and Some Spirits*, ed. by Meric Casaubon (London, 1659)

Denslow, William R. *10,000 Famous Freemasons*, 4 vols (Trenton, 1957-61)

Desborough, Vincent Robin d'Arba. *The Greek Dark Ages* (London, 1972)

Dictionary of National Biography, 63 vols, ed. by Leslie Stephen & Sidney Lee (London, 1885-1901)

Diderot, Denis. "Encyclopédie" in *Encyclopédie ou Dictionnaire raisonné des sciences, des arts et des métiers*, Vol. V (Paris, 1755)

Digges, Thomas. "A Perfit Description of the Caelestial Orbes According to the Most Aunciene Doctrine of the Pythagoreans lately Revived by Copernicus and by Geometricall Demonstrations approued" in *Prognostication Euerlasting of Ryght Goode Effecte*, by Leonard Digges (London, 1576)

Dio Cassius. *Roman History*, 9 vols, trans. by Earnest Cary, ed. by Herbert Baldwin Forster (London, 1914-1927)

Diodorus Siculus. *Bibliotheca Historica*, 2 vols, trans. by John Skelton, ed. by F. M. Salter & H. L. R. Edwards (London, 1956-57)

Diogenes Laërtius. *The Lives and Opinions of Eminent Philosophers*, trans. by C. D. Yonge (London, 1853)

"Divine Liturgy of James", trans. by William MacDonald, in *The Ante-Nicene Fathers*, Vol. VII, ed. by Alexander Roberts & James Donaldson (Edinburgh, 1872)

"Divine Liturgy of St. John Chrysostom" in *Liturgies Eastern and Western*, Vol. I, ed. by Frank E. Brightman (Oxford, 1896)

Doberer, Kurt Karl. *The Goldmakers: 10,000 Years of Alchemy*, trans. by E. W. Dickes (London, 1948)

Dobbs, Betty J. T. *The Foundations of Newton's Alchemy: The Hunting of the Greene Lyon* (Cambridge, 1975)

Dodds, E. R. "Introduction and Commentary" in *Bacchae*, 2nd ed. (Oxford, 1960)

_____. *The Greeks and the Irrational* (Berkeley, 1951)

Doukas, Michael. *Historia Turco-Byzantina*, trans. by Harry J. Magoulias (Detroit, 1975)

Downey, Glanville. *Late Roman Empire* (New York, 1969)

Downing, F. Gerald. *Christ and the Cynics: Jesus and Other Radical Preachers in First-Century Tradition* (Sheffield, 1988)

Drake, Sir Francis. *The World Encompassed* (London, 1628)

Duby, Georges. *The Three Orders: Feudal Society Imagined*, trans. by Arthur Goldhammer (Chicago, 1980)

Dudo of St. Quentin. "Gesta Normannorum" [c. 1015], ed. by Jules Lair, in *Mémoires de la Société des Antiquaires de Normandie*, Vol. XXIII (Caen, 1865)

Dufour de Pradt, D. G. F. *Histoire de l'Ambassade dans la grande-duché de Varsovie en 1812* (Paris, 1815)

Durant, Will & Ariel. *The Story of Civilization*, 11 vols (New York, 1935-1975)

Eadmer. *The Life of St. Anselm*, ed. & trans. by Richard W. Southern (Oxford, 1962)

The Egyptian Book of the Dead: The Papyrus of Ani in the British Museum, ed. & trans. by Sir E. A. Wallis Budge (London, 1895)

Einhard. *The Life of Charlemagne*, trans. by Samuel Epes Turner (New York, 1880)

Eliade, Mircea. *A History of Religious Ideas*, 3 vols, trans. by Willard R. Trask (Chicago, 1978-85)

_____. *Patterns in Comparative Religion*, trans. by Rosemary Sheed (London, 1958)

Elias, Norbert. *The History of Manners*, trans. by Edmund Jephcott (New York, 1978)

Ellis, Steven G. *Tudor Ireland: Crown, Community and the Conflict of Cultures, 1470-1603* (London, 1985)

Elmacin, George. "Historia saracenica qua res gestæ muslimorum", Lat. trans. by Thomas Erpenius, in *Typographia Erpeniana Linguarum Orientalium* (Leiden, 1625)

Encyclopædia Britannica, 11th ed. in 29 vols (Cambridge, 1910-11)

An Encyclopedia of Archetypal Symbolism, ed. by Beverly Moon (Boston, 1991)

Engels, Friedrich. *The Peasant War in Germany*, trans. by Moissaye J. Olgin (New York, 1926)

Enlightened Absolutism, 1760-1790: A Documentary Sourcebook, ed. by Anthony Lentin (Newcastle, 1985)

St. Ephræm Syrus. *Des heiligen Ephræm des Syrers Hymnen contra Hæreses*, Vol. II, ed. by Edmund Beck (Louvain, 1957)

Epicurus. *Letters, Principal Doctrines, and Vatican Sayings*, trans. by Russel M. Geer (Indianapolis, 1964)

Epiphanius of Samos. *Panarion*, trans. by Frank Williams (Leiden, 1987)

"Epistolæ Stephani III" in *Patrologiæ Latina*, Vol. XCVII, ed. by Jacques-Paul Migne (Paris, 1862)

Erlanger, Rachel. *Lucrezia Borgia: A Biography* (New York, 1978)

Eschenbach, Wolfram von. *Parzival*, trans. by A. T. Hatto (London, 1980)

Euripides. "Bacchæ", trans. by Philip Vellacott, in *The Bacchae and Other Plays* (London, 1954)

European Treaties bearing on the History of the United States and its Dependencies to 1648, ed. by Frances Gardiner Davenport (Washington D.C., 1917)

Eusebius of Cæsarea. *The History of the Church from Christ to Constantine*, trans. by G. A. Williamson (Harmondsworth, 1965)

_____. "The Life of the Blessed Emperor Constantine", trans. by Samuel Bagster, rev. by Ernest Cushing Richardson, in *Nicene and Post-Nicene Fathers*, Series II, Vol. I, ed. by Philip Schaff & Henry Wace (Edinburgh, 1890)

Eutropius. "Breviarium ab urbe condita" in *Monumenta Germaniæ Historica*, AA 2, ed. by Hans Droysen (Berlin, 1879)

Evans, R. J. W. *Rudolf II and his World: A Study in Intellectual History, 1576-1612* (Oxford, 1973)

Evelyn, John. *The Diary of John Evelyn*, 6 vols, ed. by Esmond S. de Beer (Oxford, 1955)

Fahie, John J. *Galileo: His Life and Work* (London, 1903)

Fay, Sidney B. *The Rise of Brandenburg-Prussia to 1786*, rev. by Klaus Epstein (New York, 1964)

Fedden, Robin & John Thompson. *Crusader Castles*, 2nd ed. (London, 1957)

The Federal and State Constitutions Colonial Charters, and Other Organic Laws of the States, Territories, and Colonies Now or Heretofore Forming the United States of America, ed. by Francis Newton Thorpe (Washington D.C., 1909)

Fell-Smith, Charlotte. *John Dee (1527-1608)* (London, 1909)

Fenlon, Dermot. *Heresy and Obedience in Tridentine Italy: Cardinal Pole and the Counter-Reformation* (Cambridge, 1972)

Feuerbach, Ludwig. *Das Wesen des Christentums* (Leipzig, 1841)

Fichte, Johann Gottlieb. *Reden an die deutsche Nation* (Berlin, 1808)

The First Crusade: The Accounts of Eye-Witnesses and Participants, ed. & trans. by August C. Krey (London, 1921)

Flavius Josephus. *Antiquities of the Jews*, trans. by William Whiston (London, 1737)

Fludd, Robert. *Robert Fludd and his Philosophicall Key: Being a Transcription of the Manuscript at Trinity College, Cambridge*, ed. by Allen G. Debus (New York, 1979)

Forbes, Robert James. *A History of Science and Technology*, 2 vols (Harmondsworth, 1963)

Formula Book of English Official Historical Documents, 2 vols, ed. by Hubert Hall (New York, 1908)

Forster, E. M. *Alexandria: A History and A Guide*, 2nd ed. (Alexandria, 1938)

Foucault, Michel. *The History of Sexuality*, 3 vols, trans. by Robert Hurley (New York, 1978-86)

———. *Power/Knowledge: Selected Interviews and Other Writings, 1972-1977*, ed. by Colin Gordon (New York, 1980)

Frawley, David. *The Myth of the Aryan Invasion of India* (New Delhi, 1995)

Frazer, Sir James George. *The Golden Bough*, 3rd ed. in 12 vols (London, 1911-15)

Frederick II of Hohenstaufen. *The Art of Falconry*, ed. & trans. by Casey A. Wood & F. Marjorie Fyfe (Stanford, 1943)

Fredriksen, Paula. *From Jesus to Christ: The Origins of the New Testament Images of Jesus* (New Haven, 1988)

Freeman, Edward Augustus. *History of the Norman Conquest of England: Its Causes and its Results*, 6 vols (Oxford, 1867-79)

Freud, Sigmund. *Civilization and its Discontents*, trans. by Joan Riviere (London, 1930)

Fulcher of Chartres. *A History of the Expedition to Jerusalem, 1095-1127*, trans. by Frances Rita Ryan & H. S. Fink (Knoxville, 1969)

Fuller, Thomas. *The History of the Worthies of England*, ed. by P. Austin Nutall (London, 1840)

Fulop-Miller, Rene. *The Power and Secret of the Jesuits*, trans. by F. S. Flint & D. F. Tait (London, 1930)

Galilei, Galileo. *Dialogue concerning the Two Chief World Systems*, trans. by Stillman Drake (Berkeley, 1953)

———. *Il Saggiatore* (Rome, 1623)

Gay, Peter. *The Enlightenment: An Interpretation*, 2 vols (New York, 1966-69)

The Genius of Arab Civilization: Source of Renaissance, ed. by John R. Hayes (New York, 1975)

The Gesta Normannorum Ducum of William of Jumièges, Orderic Vitalis, and Robert of Torigni, 2 vols, ed. & trans. by Elisabeth van Houts (Oxford, 1992-5)

Gibbon, Edward. *The Decline and Fall of the Roman Empire* [1776-1788], 6 vols, rev. by H. H. Milman (New York, 1845)

Gies, Joseph & Frances. *Life in a Medieval City* (New York, 1969)

Gleason, Elisabeth G. *Gasparo Contarini: Venice, Rome, and Reform* (Berkeley, 1993)

Godwin, Joscelyn. *Robert Fludd: Hermetic Philosopher and Surveyor of Two Worlds* (London, 1979)

Goethe, Johann Wolfgang von. *Gedenkausgabe der Werke, Briefe und Gespräche*, 24 vols, ed. by Ernst Beutler (Zürich, 1948-1964)

____. "Rezension von Über die Liebe des Vaterlands" in *Frankfurter Gelehrte Anzeigen* (May 22, 1772)

____. *Tagebücher*, 3 vols, ed. by Gerhart Baumann (Stuttgart, n.d.)

Goodman, Abram Vossen. *American Overture: Jewish Rights in Colonial Times* (Philadelphia, 1947)

Goodman, Martin. *The Ruling Class of Judaea: Origins of the Jewish Revolt Against Rome, A.D. 66-70* (Cambridge, 1987)

Grant, Michael. *The Classical Greeks* (London, 1988)

Greene, John C. *Darwin and the Modern World View* (Baton Rouge, 1961)

Greene, Kevin. *Archaeology: An Introduction; the History, Principles and Methods of Modern Achaeology* (London, 1983)

Gregorovius, Ferdinand. *History of the City of Rome in the Middle Ages*, 8 vols, trans. by Annie G. Hamilton (London, 1894-1900)

____. *Lucretia Borgia: According to Original Documents and Correspondance of her Day*, trans. by John Leslie Garner (New York, 1903)

St. Gregory the Great. "The Book of Pastoral Rule and Selected Epistles", trans. by James Barmby, in *Nicene and Post-Nicene Fathers*, Series II, Vol. XII, ed. by Philip Schaff & Henry Wace (Edinburgh, 1899)

St. Gregory of Tours. *History of the Franks*, trans. by Ernest Brehaut (New York, 1916)

Griffin, Miriam. "Philosophy, Cato, and Roman Suicide" in *Greece & Rome*, Vol. XXXIII, Nos 1-2 (Cambridge, April/October 1986)

Gui, Bernard. "Inquisitor's Manual", trans. by James Harvey Robinson, in *Readings in European History*, Vol. I (Boston, 1905)

Guignebert, Charles. *Jesus*, trans. by S. H. Hooke (London, 1935)

Gunther, R. T. *Early Science in Oxford*, Vol. I in 4 pts (Oxford, 1921-23)

Guthrie, W. K. C. *The Greeks and Their Gods* (London, 1950)

____. *A History of Greek Philosophy*, 6 vols (Cambridge, 1962-81)

Hadas, Moses. *A History of Latin Literature* (New York, 1952)

ibn Hajjâj, Muslim. *Sahih Muslim: Being Traditions of the Sayings and Doings of the Prophet Mohammad as Narrated by His Companions and Compiled under the Title Al-Jami-as-Sahih by Imam Muslim*, 4 vols, trans. by Abdul Hamid Siddiqi (Lahore, 1971-75)

Hale, John. *The Civilization of Europe in the Renaissance* (London, 1993)

Halecki, Oscar. *Borderlands of Western Civilization: A History of East Central Europe* (New York, 1952)

Halley, Henry H. *Halley's Bible Handbook* (Grand Rapids, 1927)

Harnack, Adolf. *History of Dogma*, 7 vols, trans. by Neil Buchanan (London, 1895-1900)

Harrison, Jane. *Ancient Art & Ritual* (London, 1913)

_____. *Prolegomena to the Study of Greek Religion*, 3rd ed. (Cambridge, 1922)

Harrison, J. F. C. *The Common People: A History from the Norman Conquest to the Present* (London, 1984)

Harwood, William. *Mythology's Last Gods: Yahweh and Jesus* (Buffalo, 1992)

Haskins, Charles Homer. *The Renaissance of the Twelfth Century* (Cambridge, Mass., 1927)

_____. *The Rise of Universities* (New York, 1923)

Hayek, Friedrich A. von. *The Road to Serfdom* (London, 1944)

Hayman, Ronald. *Nietzsche: A Critical Life* (Oxford, 1980)

Heath, Michael. "Unholy Alliance: Valois and Ottomans" in *Renaissance Studies*, Vol. III, No. 3 (September 1989)

Hegel, Georg Wilhelm Friedrich. *Hegels theologische Jugendschriften*, ed. by Herman Nohl (Tübingen, 1907)

_____. *Philosophie der Geschichte* (Berlin, 1837)

_____. *Philosophy of Right*, trans. by S. W. Dyde (London, 1896)

Heilbron, John L. *The Sun in the Church: Cathedrals as Solar Observatories* (Cambridge, Mass., 1999)

Helgerson, Richard. *Forms of Nationhood: The Elizabethan Writing of England* (Chicago, 1992)

Henderson, William J. *Richard Wagner, His Life and His Dramas* (London, 1901)

Hendin, David. *Guide to Biblical Coins* (New York, 1987)

Heraclitus. "Fragments" in *Early Greek Philosophy*, ed. by John Burnet (London, 1892)

Herford, Charles H. *The Age of Wordsworth*, 3rd ed. (London, 1899)

Herodotus. "Euterpe", trans. by G. C. Macaulay, in *The History of Herodotus*, Vol. I (London, 1890)

_____. *The Persian Wars*, 4 vols, trans. by A. D. Godley (London, 1920)

Hesiod. "Theogony", trans. by Hugh G. Evelyn-White, in *Hesiod, the Homeric Hymns, and Homerica* (London, 1914)

_____. "Works and Days", trans. by Hugh G. Evelyn-White, in *Hesiod, the Homeric Hymns, and Homerica* (London, 1914)

Hetoum. *A Lytell Cronycle* [c. 1307], trans. by Richard Pynson, ed. by Glenn Burger (Toronto, 1988)

Hibbert, Christopher. *The House of Medici: Its Rise and Fall* (New York, 1975)

Hill, Christopher. *The Intellectual Origins of the English Revolution* (Oxford, 1965)

Hippolytus. "The Refutation of All Heresies", trans. by J. H. MacMahon, in *The Ante-Nicene Fathers*, Vol. V, ed. by Alexander Roberts & James Donaldson (Edinburgh, 1868)

Historia Augusta, ed. & trans. by David Magie (London, 1922)

Historical Collections of Private Passages of State, 8 vols, ed. by John Rushworth (London, 1659-1701)

The Historie of Cambria, Now called Wales, ed. & trans. by Humphrey Lloyd & David Powell (London, 1584)

The History of Cartography, 6 vols, ed. by J. Brian Harley & David Woodward (London, 1987)

The History of the University of Oxford, 8 vols, ed. by T. H. Aston (Oxford, 1984-2000)

Hitti, Philip K. *History of Syria, Including Lebanon and Palestine* (London, 1951)

———. *History of the Arabs: From the Earliest Times to the Present*, 5th rev. ed. (London, 1951)

Hobsbawm, Eric J. *The Age of Revolution, 1789-1848* (London, 1962)

Hodgkin, Thomas. *Charles the Great* (London, 1897)

———. *Italy and Her Invaders* (Oxford, 1892)

Hodgson, Marshall G. S. *The Venture of Islam: Conscience and History in a World Civilization*, 3 vols (Chicago, 1974)

Hollingdale, R. J. *Nietzsche: The Man and his Philosophy* (Baton Rouge, 1965)

Holmyard, E. J. *Alchemy* (Harmondsworth, 1957)

Homer. *Odyssey*, ed. by Karl Friedrich Ameis, rev. by Carl Hentze (Leipzig, 1895)

The Homeric Hymns, trans. by Andrew Lang (London, 1899)

Hooke, Robert. *Micrographia: or some Physiological Descriptions of Minute Bodies made by Magnifying Glasses with Observations and Inquiries thereupon* (London, 1665)

Horace. "Ars Poëtica" in *Horace*, ed. by Richard Bentley (Cambridge, 1711)

Howarth, David. *1066: The Year of the Conquest* (London, 1977)

Howarth, Stephen. *The Knights Templar* (London, 1982)

Hughes, Glyn Tegai. *Romantic German Literature* (London, 1979)

Hughes, Philip. *The Church in Crisis: A History of the Twenty Great Councils* (London, 1961)

———. *A History of the Church*, 3 vols (London, 1936-48)

Hugo, Victor. *Les Orientales*, 2 vols, ed. by Elisabeth Barineau (Paris, 1952-54)

Hume, David. *The History of England, from the Invasion of Julius Cæsar to the Revolution in 1688*, rev. ed. in 8 vols (London, 1773)

Huxley, Aldous. *Grey Eminence: A Study in Religion and Politics* (London, 1941)

Iamblichus. *Life of Pythagoras, or, Pythagoric Life*, trans. by Thomas Taylor (London, 1818)

St. Ignatius of Loyola. *Spiritual Exercises*, trans. by Joseph Rickaby (London, 1915)

Inalcik, Halil. *Ottoman Empire: The Classical Age, 1300-1600*, trans. by Norman Itzkowitz & Colin Imber (London, 1973)

St. Irenæus of Lyons. "Against the Heresies", trans. by F. R. M. Hitchcock, in *The Ante-Nicene Fathers*, Vol. I, ed. by Alexander Roberts & James Donaldson (Edinburgh, 1867)

Irish Historical Documents 1172-1922, ed. by Edmund Curtis & R. B. McDowell (London, 1943)

Isocrates. "Against the Sophists", trans. by George Norlin, in *Isocrates*, Vol. II (London, 1929)

———. "Panegyricus", trans. by George Norlin, in *Isocrates*, Vol. I (London, 1928)

Israel, Jonathan. *The Dutch Republic: Its Rise, Greatness, and Fall, 1477-1806* (Oxford, 1995)

James, Edward. *The Origins of France: From Clovis to the Capetians, 500-1000* (London, 1982)

James, William. *The Varieties of Religious Experience: A Study in Human Nature* (New York, 1902)

Jardine, Lisa. *Francis Bacon: Discovery and the Art of Discourse* (London, 1974)

Jeanne d'Arc, Maid of Orleans: Deliver of France, ed. by T. Douglas Murray (London, 1903)

Jefferson, Thomas. "Letter to Dr. Jacob De la Motta (Sep 1, 1820)" in *The Occident and American Jewish Advocate*, Vol. I, No. 10, ed. by Isaac Leeser (January 1844)

———. "Letter to Bishop Madison (Jan 31, 1800)" in *The Writings of Thomas Jefferson*, Vol. VII, ed. by Paul Leicester Ford (New York, 1896)

Jewell, John. *Apologie of the Church of England* (London, 1562)

The Jews in Their Land, ed. by David Ben-Gurion (London, 1966)

John of Salisbury. "Epistolæ" in *Patrologiæ Latina*, Vol. CXCIX, ed. by Jacques-Paul Migne (Paris, 1855)

———. "Vita Sancti Thomæ Cantuariensis Archiepiscopi et Martyris" in *Materials for the History of Thomas à Becket, Archbishop of Canterbury*, Vol. II, ed. by James Craigie Robertson (London, 1875)

Johns, Jeremy. *Arabic Administration in Norman Sicily: The Royal Diwan* (New York, 2002)

———. "Christianity and Islam" in *The Oxford Illustrated History of Christianity*, ed. by John McManners (Oxford, 1990)

Johnson, Francis Rarick. *Astronomical Thought in Renaissance England: A Study of the English Scientific Writings from 1500 to 1645* (Baltimore, 1937)

Johnson, Paul. *The Birth of the Modern: World Society, 1815-1830* (London, 1991)

Jones, Alonzo T. *The Two Republics of Rome and the United States of America* (Battle Creek, 1891)

Jones, Gwyn. *A History of the Vikings* (Oxford, 1968)

Jonson, Ben. *Timber, or Discoveries Made upon Men and Matter* (London, 1640)

Jordanes. *The Origin and Deeds of the Goths*, trans. by Charles Christopher Mierow (Princeton, 1915)

Jouin, Ernest. *Papacy and Freemasonry* (Hawthorne, 1930)

Jung, Carl Gustav. *Memories, Dreams, Reflections*, ed. by Aniela Jaffé (New York, 1961)

_____. *Nietzsche's Zarathustra: Notes of the Seminar Given in 1934-1939*, 2 vols, ed. by James L. Jarrett (Princeton, 1988)

St. Justin Martyr. "Dialogue with Trypho", trans. by Alexander Roberts & James Donaldson, in *The Ante-Nicene Fathers*, Vol. I (Edinburgh, 1867)

Justinianus, Flavius Anicius. *Justinian's Institutes*, ed. & trans. by Peter Birks & Grant McLeod (London, 1987)

Justinus, Marcus Junianus. *Epitome of the Philippic History of Pompeius Trogus*, trans. by John Selby Watson (London, 1853)

Kahn, David. *The Codebreakers: The Story of Secret Writing* (London, 1966)

Kant, Immanuel. *Critik der reinen Vernunft* (Riga, 1781)

_____. "Beantwortung der Frage: Was ist Aufklärung?" in *Berlinische Monatschrift* (December 1784)

Kaufmann, Walter. *Nietzsche: Philosopher, Psychologist, Antichrist* (Princeton, 1950)

Kearney, Hugh. *Strafford in Ireland, 1633-1641: A Study in Absolutism* (Manchester, 1959)

Kelly, Amy. *Eleanor of Aquitaine and the Four Kings* (Cambridge, Mass., 1950)

Kepler, Johannes. "Introduction to Book 5" in *The Harmony of the World*, trans. by E. J. Aiton, A. M. Duncan, and J. V. Field (New York, 1997)

Keynes, John Maynard. "Newton the Man: Lecture to the Royal Society (Dec 25, 1942)" in *The Royal Society Newton Tercentenary Celebrations* (Cambridge, 1947)

Kimball, Roger. *Tenured Radicals: How Politics Has Corrupted Our Higher Education* (New York, 1990)

King, Bolton. *A History of Italian Unity: Being a Political History of Italy from 1814 to 1871*, 2 vols (London, 1899)

King, Charles William. *The Gnostics and Their Remains, Ancient and Mediaeval*, 2nd ed. (London, 1887)

Kline, Morris. *Mathematics and the Search for Knowledge* (Oxford, 1985)

Knox, John. *Marcion and the New Testament: An Essay in the Early History of the Canon* (Chicago, 1942)

Koester, Helmut. *Ancient Christian Gospels: Their History and Development* (Philadelphia, 1990)

Koestler, Arthur. *The Sleepwalkers: A History of Man's Changing Vision of the Universe* (London, 1959)

The Koran, 5th ed., trans. by N. J. Dawood (Harmondsworth, 1990)

Kramer, Heinrich & James Sprenger. *Malleus Maleficarum*, trans. by Montague Summers (London, 1928)

Kritovoulos, Michael. *History of Mehmed the Conqueror*, trans. by C. T. Riggs (Princeton, 1954)

Kuhn, Thomas S. *The Copernican Revolution: Planetary Astronomy in the Development of Western Thought* (Oxford, 1957)

Kümmel, Werner Georg. *Introduction to the New Testament*, 17th rev. ed., trans. by Howard Clark Kee (London, 1975)

Lacroix, Paul. "Préface du bibliophile Jacob" in *Rabelais*, ed. by Charles Labiche (Paris, 1840)

Lactantius. "Of the Manner in Which the Persecutors Died", trans. by William Fletcher, in *The Ante-Nicene Fathers*, Vol. VII, ed. by Alexander Roberts & James Donaldson (Edinburgh, 1867)

Lamy, Lucie. *Egyptian Mysteries: New Light on Ancient Knowledge* (London, 1981)

Lane-Poole, Stanley. *The Story of the Moors in Spain* (New York, 1886)

Lang, Cecil Y. "Introduction" in *The Swinburne Letters, New Writings of Swinburne*, 6 vols (New Haven, 1959-62)

Larner, John. *Italy in the Age of Dante and Petrarch, 1216-1380* (London, 1980)

Las Casas, Bartolomé de. *Tears of the Indians*, trans. by John Phillips (London, 1656)

Laslett, Peter. *Family Life and Illicit Love in Earlier Generations: Essays in Historical Sociology* (Cambridge, 1977)

Laven, Peter. *Renaissance Italy, 1464-1534* (London, 1966)

"Laxdæla Saga" [c. 1245], ed. by Einar Ólafur Sveinsson, in *Íslenzk Fornrit*, Vol. V (Reykjavik, 1934)

Lees-Milne, James. *Saint Peter's: The Story of Saint Peter's Basilica in Rome* (London, 1967)

Legge, Francis. *Forerunners and Rivals of Christianity from 330 BC to 330 AD*, 2 vols (Cambridge, 1915)

Lehmann, Winfred P. *Historial Linguistics: An Introductions*, 3rd ed. (London, 1992)

Leonardo da Vinci. *The Notebooks of Leonardo Da Vinci*, 2 vols, ed. by Jean Paul Richter, trans. by R. C. Bell & E. J. Poynter (London, 1883)

L'Epinois, Henri de. *La question de Galilée: Les faits et leurs conséquences* (Paris, 1878)

Lewis, C. S. *The Allegory of Love: A Study in Medieval Tradition* (Oxford, 1936)

Libanius. *Selected Orations*, 2 vols, ed. by E. H. Warmington (London, 1969)

Liberati, Anna Maria & Fabio Bourbon. *Splendours of the Roman World* (London, 1996)

The Life and Letters of Sir Henry Wotton, 2 vols, ed. by Logan Pearsall Smith (Oxford, 1907)

Lightfoot, Joseph Barber. *On a Fresh Revision of the English New Testament* (London, 1872)

Lindberg, Carter. *The European Reformations* (Oxford, 1996)

Lipman, Samuel. *Music after Modernism* (New York, 1979)

Livy. *History of Rome* [c. 9 CE], 14 vols, ed. & trans. by B. O. Foster et al (London, 1919-59)

Locke, John. *An Essay concerning Human Understanding* (London, 1690)

_____. "Four Letters concerning Toleration" in *The Works of John Locke*, Vol. III (London, 1714)

_____. *The Reasonableness of Christianity as Delivered in the Scriptures* (London, 1695)

_____. *Some Thoughts concerning Education* (London, 1693)

_____. *Two Treatises of Civil Government* (London, 1690)

Lombard, Maurice. *The Golden Age of Islam*, trans. by Joan Spencer (Amsterdam, 1975)

Loomis, Roger Sherman. *The Grail: From Celtic Myth to Christian Symbol* (Cardiff, 1963)

Lucretius. *On the Nature of Things*, trans. by Martin Ferguson Smith (London, 1969)

Luther, Martin. *First Principles of the Reformation, or The Ninety-Five Theses and the Three Primary Works of Dr. Martin Luther*, ed. & trans. by Henry Wace & C. A. Buchheim (London, 1883)

_____. *The Table Talk of Martin Luther*, ed. & trans. by William Hazlitt (London, 1846)

_____. "Vorrede zum Neuen Testament" in *Das Neue Testament Deutzsch* (Wittenberg, 1522)

_____. "Wider die räuberischen und mörderischen Rotten der Bauern" [1525] in *D. Martin Luthers Werke, Kritische Gesamtausgabe*, Vol. 18, ed. by J. F. K. Knaake & G. Kawerau (Weimar, 1883 sqq.)

Lyell, Charles. *The Antiquity of Man*, ed. by Robert Heron Rastall (London, 1914)

Maalouf, Amin. *The Crusades through Arab Eyes*, trans. by Jon Rothschild (London, 1984)

Macaulay, Thomas Babington. "Lord Bacon" in *Critical and Historical Essays contributed to the Edinburgh Review*, Vol. II (London, 1867)

MacCulloch, Diarmaid. *Thomas Cranmer: A Life* (New Haven, 1996)

Machiavelli, Niccolò. *Between Friends: Discourses of Power and Desire in the Machiavelli-Vettori Letters of 1513-1515*, ed. by John M. Najemy (Princeton, 1993)

_____. *History of Florence, and of the Affairs of Italy, from the Earliest Times to the Death of Lorenzo the Magnificent*, publ. by H. G. Bohn (London, 1847)

_____. *The Prince*, trans. by Luigi Ricci (Oxford, 1903)

MacKay, Charles. *Extraordinary Popular Delusions and the Madness of Crowds*, 3 vols (London, 1841)

Mackey, Albert G. *An Encyclopedia of Freemasonry and its Kindred Sciences*, 2 vols, rev. by Edward L. Hawkins (Chicago, 1921)

MacManus, Seumas. *The Story of the Irish Race: A Popular History of Ireland* (New York, 1921)

MacMullen, Ramsay. *Christianity and Paganism in the Fourth to Eighth Centuries* (New Haven, 1997)

MacNulty, W. Kirk. *Freemasonry: A Journey through Ritual and Symbol* (London, 1991)

Macoy, Robert. *General History, Cyclopedia and Dictionary of Freemasonry*, rev. by George Oliver (New York, 1869)

Madison, James. "The Federalist No. 47" in *The Independent Journal* (Jan 30, 1788)

Magnusson, Magnus. *B.C.: The Archaeology of the Bible Lands* (London, 1977)

Maitland, Samuel Roffey. *Facts and Documents Illustrative of the History, Doctrine and Rites of the Ancient Albigenses and Waldenses* (London, 1832)

Malek, Jaromir. *In the Shadow of the Pyramids: Egypt during the Old Kingdom* (London, 1986)

Mallett, Michael. *The Borgias: The Rise and Fall of a Renaissance Dynasty* (London, 1969)

Manuale Sacerdotum, ed. by P. Josephus Schneider (Cologne, 1867)

Martial. *Epigrams*, 2 vols, ed. & trans. by Walter C. A. Ker (London, 1919-20)

Marx, Karl. "Zur Judenfrage" in *Deutsch-Französische Jahrbucher* (February 1844)

———. "Zur Kritik der Hegelschen Rechtsphilosophie" in *Deutsch-Französische Jahrbucher* (February 1844)

Mattingly, Garrett. *Renaissance Diplomacy* (London, 1955)

McCabe, Joseph. *A Candid History of the Jesuits* (London, 1913)

McCarthy, Justin. *The Ottoman Turks: An Introductory History to 1923* (London, 1997)

McCormack, John. *One Million Mercenaries: Swiss Soldiers in the Armies of the World* (London, 1993)

McInerny, Ralph. *A History of Western Philosophy*, 2 vols (Chicago, 1963-70)

McIntosh, Christopher. *The Swan King: Ludwig II of Bavaria* (London, 1982)

McNeill, John Thomas. *Celtic Churches: A History, A.D. 200 to 1200* (Chicago, 1974)

McPhee, John. *La Place de la Concorde Suisse* (New York, 1984)

Mead, G. R. S. *Fragments of a Faith Forgotten* (London, 1900)

Medicine from the Black Death to the French Disease, ed. by Roger French (Aldershot, 1998)

Melanchthon, Philip. *Initia Doctrinæ Physicæ* (Wittenberg, 1549)

St. Melito of Sardis. *On Pascha and Fragments*, trans. by Stuart George Hall (Oxford, 1979)

Menasseh ben Israel. *Accounts of the ten tribes of Israel being in America, originally published by R. Manasseh ben Israel*, ed. by Robert Ingram (Colchester, 1792)

———. *Menesseh Ben Israel's Mission to Oliver Cromwell: Being a Reprint of the Pamphlets Published by Menasseh ben Israel to Promote the Re-Admission of the Jews to England, 1649-1656*, ed. by Lucien Wolf (London, 1901)

Michell, John. *Who Wrote Shakespeare?* (London, 1996)

Millard, Alan. *Discoveries from the Time of Jesus* (Oxford, 1990)

Milman, Henry Hart. *History of Latin Christianity*, 4th ed. in 9 vols (London, 1867)

———. *History of the Jews*, 3 vols (London, 1829-30)

Milne, J. Grafton. *A History of Egypt under Roman Rule*, 3rd ed. (London, 1924)

Mitterauer, Michael & Reinhard Sieder. *The European Family: Patriarchy to Partnership from the Middle Ages to the Present* (Oxford, 1982)

Montesquieu, Baron Charles de Secondat. *Considerations on the Causes of the Greatness of the Romans and their Decline*, trans. by David Lowenthal (New York, 1942)

Morgan, George Allen. *What Nietzsche Means* (Cambridge, Mass., 1941)

Müller, Friedrich Max. *A History of Ancient Sanskrit Literature* (London, 1859)

Mundy, Barbara. *The Mapping of New Spain: Indigenous Cartography and the Maps of the Relaciones Geográficas* (Chicago, 1996) ibn Munqidh, Usamah. *An Arab-Syrian Gentleman and Warrior in the Period of the Crusades: Memoirs of Usamah Ibn-Munqidh*, trans. by Philip K. Hitti (New York, 1929)

Murray, Gilbert. *Five Stages of Greek Religion*, 3rd ed. (Oxford, 1951)

The Nag Hammadi Library, ed. by James M. Robinson (San Francisco, 1977)

Nasr, Seyyed Hossein. *Science and Civilization in Islam* (Cambridge, Mass., 1968)

Neillands, Robin. *The Hundred Years War, 1337-1453* (London, 1990)

Nelson, Thomas. *Italy and the World War* (New York, 1920)

Neugebauer, Otto. *The Exact Sciences in Antiquity* (London, 1951)

Newark, Timothy. *Women Warlords: An Illustrated Military History of Female Warriors* (London, 1989)

Newman, Philip. *A Short History of Cyprus* (London, 1940)

The New Oxford History of Music, 10 vols, ed. by Gerald Abraham et al (London, 1957-74)

Newton, Sir Isaac. "Four Letters to Richard Bentley" in *Theories of the Universe*, ed. by Milton K. Munitz (Glencoe, 1957)

_____. *Philosophiæ Naturalis Principia Mathematica* (London, 1687)

The Nibelungenlied, trans. by A. T. Hatto (London, 1962)

Nicene and Post-Nicene Fathers, Series II, vols X & XIV, ed. by Henry R. Percival (Edinburgh, 1899)

Nicholl, Charles. *The Chemical Theatre* (London, 1980)

Nichols, Mike. *The Witches' Sabbats* (Albany, 2005)

Nietzsche, Friedrich Wilhelm. *Also Spracht Zarathustra, Ein Buch für Alle und Keinen*, 4 vols (Chemnitz & Leipzig, 1883-85)

_____. "The Antichrist", trans. by Walter Kaufmann, in *The Portable Nietzsche* (New York, 1954)

_____. *The Birth of Tragedy and The Case of Wagner*, trans. by Walter Kaufmann (New York, 1967)

_____. *The Gay Science: With a Prelude in Rhymes and an Appendix of Songs*, trans. by Walter Kaufmann (New York, 1974)

_____. *Jenseits von Gut und Böse* (Leipzig, 1886)

_____. "Richard Wagner in Bayreuth", trans. by Anthony M. Ludovici, in *The Complete Works of Friedrich Nietzsche*, Vol. I, ed. by Oscar Levy (Edinburgh, 1909)

_____. *Selected Letters of Friedrich Nietzsche*, trans. by Christopher Middleton (Chicago, 1969)

Nigg, Walter. *Warriors of God: The Great Religious Orders and Their Founders*, ed. & trans. by Mary Ilford (London, 1959)

Norwich, John Julius. *Byzantium*, 3 vols (Harmondsworth, 1988)

_____. *A History of Venice* (London, 1982)

_____. *The Normans in Sicily: The Magnificent Story of the Other Norman Conquest* (Harmondsworth, 1992)

Notestein, Wallace. *A History of Witchcraft in England from 1558 to 1718* (New York, 1911)

Notker the Stammerer. "De Carolo Magno", trans. by Lewis Thorpe, in *Two Lives of Charlemagne* (Harmondsworth, 1969)

O'Donoghue, Bernard. *The Courtly Love Tradition* (Manchester, 1982)

Old Oligarch. *Athênaiôn politeia* [c. 443 BCE], ed. by E. Kalinka (Leipzig, 1913)

Oresme, Nicole. *Le Livre du Ciel et du Monde* [1377], trans. by Albert J. Menut (Madison, 1968)

Origen. "Contra Celsum", trans. by Frederick Crombie, in *The Ante-Nicene Fathers*, Vol. IV, ed. by Alexander Roberts & James Donaldson (Edinburgh, 1867)

Orpen, Goddard Henry. *Ireland under the Normans*, 4 vols (Oxford, 1911-20)

Osborne, Francis. *Advice to a Son* [Oxford, 1658], ed. by Edward Abbott Parry (London, 1896)

Ovenell, R. F. *The Ashmolean Museum, 1683-1894* (Oxford, 1986)

Ovid. *Ars Amatoria*, ed. by Edward J. Kenney (Oxford, 1961)

_____. *The Metamorphoses*, trans. by Rolfe Humphries (Bloomington, 1955)

Özal, Turgut. *Turkey in Europe and Europe in Turkey* (High Wycombe, 1991)

Pachter, Henry Maximilian. *Paracelsus: Magic into Science* (New York, 1951)

Pagden, Anthony. *Lords of All the World: Ideologies of Empire in Spain, Britain, and France, 1492-1830* (New Haven, 1995)

Pagel, Walter. *Paracelsus: An Introduction to Philosophical Medicine in the Era of the Renaissance* (Basel, 1958)

Pagels, Elaine. *The Gnostic Gospels* (New York, 1979)

Paine, Thomas. *The Rights of Man: Being an Answer to Mr. Burke's Attack on the French Revolution* (Baltimore, 1791)

Panegyrici Latini, ed. & trans. by C. E. V. Nixon & Barbara Saylor Rodgers (Berkeley, 1994)

Paracelsus. *Der Werke von Paracelsus*, 10 vols, ed. by Johannes Huser (Basel, 1589-1590)

_____. *Selected Writings*, ed. by Jolande Jacobi, trans. by Norbert Guterman (London, 1951)

Pareti, Luigi. *The Ancient World, 1200 BC to AD 500*, trans. by Guy E. F. & Sylvia Chilver (London, 1965)

Parker, Richard A. *The Calendars of Ancient Egypt* (Chicago, 1950)

Parker, Thomas Maynard. *The English Reformation to 1558* (Oxford, 1950)

Parry, J. H. *Age of Reconnaissance: Discovery, Exploration and Settlement, 1450-1650* (New York, 1963)

Parsons, Edward Alexander. *The Alexandrian Library, Glory of the Hellenic World: Its Rise, Antiquities and Destructions* (London, 1952)

Parsons, John Denham. *The Non-Christian Cross* (London, 1896)

Partner, Peter. *The Murdered Magicians: The Templars and their Myth* (Oxford, 1981)

Pannekoek, Antonie. *A History of Astronomy* (London, 1961)

Pausanias. *Description of Greece*, 6 vols, trans. by Sir James George Frazer (London, 1898)

Peckham, Sir George. *A True Reporte Of the late discoveries and possessions taken in the right of the Crowne of Englande, of the Newfound Landes* (London, 1583)

Pellegrino, Charles R. *Unearthing Atlantis: An Archaeological Odyssey* (New York, 1991)

Pendell, Dale. *Pharmako/Poeia: Plant Powers, Poisons, and Herbcraft* (San Francisco, 1995)

Pernoud, Régine. *Joan of Arc: By Herself and Her Witnesses*, trans. by Edward Hyams (New York, 1966)

Peters, H. F. *Zarathustra's Sister: The Case of Elisabeth and Friedrich Nietzsche* (New York, 1977)

Phillips, Edward. *The New World of Words*, 6th ed., rev. by John Kersey (London, 1706)

Phillips, Thomas. *The History of the Life of Cardinal Pole* (Oxford, 1764)

Philo Judæus. "Against Flaccus", trans. by F. H. Colson, in *Philo*, Vol. IX (London, 1941)

Piccolomini, Æneas Sylvius. *Epistolæ familiares ad diversos* (Nuremberg, 1481)

Pierre des Vaux-de-Cernay. *Historia Albigensis* [c. 1219], 3 vols, ed. by Pascal Guébin & E. Lyon (Paris, 1926-39)

Pike, Albert. "A Historical Inquiry in Regard to the Grand Constitutions of 1786" in *Grand Constitutions of Freemasonry* (New York, 1872)

Plato. *The Dialogues of Plato*, 4 vols, trans. by Benjamin Jowett (Oxford, 1871)

_____. *The Seventh Letter*, trans. by John Harward (London, 1928)

Plotinus. *The Six Enneads*, 6 vols, trans. by Stephen MacKenna & B. S. Page (London, 1952)

Plutarch. *The Lives of the Noble Grecians and Romans*, trans. by John Dryden, rev. by Arthur Hugh Clough (London, 1861)

_____. "On Isis and Osiris", trans. by Frank Cole Babbitt, in *Plutarch's Moralia*, Vol. V (London, 1927)

_____. "Progress in Virtue", trans. by Frank Cole Babbitt, in *Plutarch's Moralia*, Vol. I (London, 1927)

_____. "Sayings of Kings and Commanders", trans. by Frank Cole Babbit, in *Plutarch's Moralia*, Vol. III (London, 1927)

_____. "Stoic Essays", trans. by Harold Cherniss, in *Plutarch's Moralia*, Vol. XIII, Pt. 2 (London, 1976)

Poole, Robert. *Time's Alteration: Calendar Reform in Early Modern England* (London, 1998)

Popper, Sir Karl. *The Open Society and its Enemies*, 2 vols (London, 1945)

Porphyry. "On Abstinence from Animal Food" in *Select Works of Porphyry*, trans. by Thomas Taylor (London, 1823)

Porter, Roy. *The Greatest Benefit to Mankind: A Medical History of Humanity from Antiquity to the Present* (London, 1997)

Porter, Whitworth. *A History of the Knights of Malta, or, The Order of the Hospital of St. John of Jerusalem* (London, 1858)

Potthast, August. *Regesta pontificum Romanorum (1198-1304)*, 2 vols (Berlin, 1874-75)

Power, Eileen. *Mediaeval Women*, ed. by M. M. Postan (Cambridge, 1975)

Pozdneyev, Aleksei Matveevich. *Mongolia and the Mongols*, ed. by J. R. Kreuger, trans. by John Roger Shaw & Dale Plank (Bloomington, 1971)

Prag um 1600: Kunst und Kultur am Hofe Rudolfs II, 2 vols, ed. by Eliska Fucikova (Freren, 1988)

Prescott, William Hickling. *History of the Reign of Philip II, King of Spain*, 3 vols (London, 1855-58)

Printing and the Mind of Man, ed. by John Carter & P. H. Muir (London, 1967)

Procopius: *History of the Wars*, 7 vols, ed. & trans. by H. B. Dewing (London, 1914-1940)

Die Publizistik im Zeitalter Gregors VII, ed. by Carl Mirbt (Leipzig, 1894)

Puritans, the Millennium and the Future of Israel: Puritan Eschatology, 1600 to 1660, ed. by Peter Toon (Cambridge, 1970)

Purver, Margery. *Royal Society: Concept and Creation* (London, 1967)

Quinn, David Beers. *England and the Discovery of America, 1481-1620* (New York, 1974)

Rabelais, François. *Gargantua* (Lyon, 1534)

Rajaram, Navaratna S. *The Politics of History: Aryan Invasion Theory and the Subversion of Scholarship* (New Delhi, 1995)

Randall, J. H. *The School of Padua and the Emergence of Modern Science* (Padua, 1961)

Ranke, Leopold von. *Weltgeschichte*, 9 vols (Leipzig, 1881-88)

Ravignan, Père de. *Clément XIII et Clément XIV* (Paris, 1854)

Read, Conyers. *Mr Secretary Walsingham and the Policy of Queen Elizabeth*, 3 vols (Oxford, 1925)

Readings in Ancient History: Illustrative Extracts from the Sources, 2 vols, ed. by William Stearns Davis (Boston, 1912-13)

The Record of the Royal Society, ed. by Sir Henry Lyons (London, 1940)

Reich, Wilhelm. *Die Massenpsychologie des Faschismus: Zur Sexualökonomie der Politischen Reaktion und zur Proletarischen Sexualpolitik* (Zürich, 1933)

"Relazione di Francia di Marino Giustinian (1535)" in *Le relazioni degli ambasciatori veneti al Senato*, Series I, Vol. I, ed. by Eugenio Albèri (Florence, 1839)

"Relazioni di Marino Giorgi (17 marzo 1517)" in *Le relazioni degli ambasciatori veneti al Senato*, Series II, Vol. III, ed. by Eugenio Albèri (Florence, 1846)

Reveal, James L. *Gentle Conquest: The Botanical Discovery of North America with Illustrations from the Library of Congress* (Washington D.C., 1992)

The Rhetorical Tradition: Readings from Classical Times to the Present, ed. by Patricia Bizzell & Bruce Herzberg (Bedford, 1990)

Robert of Clari. *The Conquest of Constantinople*, trans. by Edgar Holmes McNeal (New York, 1936)

Robinson, John J. *Dungeon, Fire and Sword: The Knights Templar in the Crusades* (New York, 1991)

Robison, John. *Proofs of a Conspiracy* (Edinburgh, 1797)

Rocker, Rudolf. *Die Entscheidung des Abendlandes*, 2 vols (Hamburg, 1949)

Rodgers, William Ledyard. *Greek and Roman Naval Warfare: A Study of Strategy, Tactics, and Ship Design from Salamis (480 BC) to Actium (31 BC)* (Annapolis, 1937)

Roller, Duane W. *The Building Program of Herod the Great* (Berkeley, 1998)

Romer, John. *Testament: The Bible and History* (London, 1988)

Ross, Anne. *Everyday Life of the Pagan Celts* (London, 1970)

Ross, Sydney. *Nineteenth-Century Attitudes: Men of Science* (Dordrecht, 1991)

Rossi, Paolo. *Francis Bacon: From Magic to Science*, trans. by Sacha Rabinovitch (London, 1968)

Rostovtzeff, Michael. *The Social and Economic History of the Roman Empire*, 2 vols (Oxford, 1926)

Rufus, Quintus Curtius. *The History of the Life and Reign of Alexander the Great*, trans. by P. Pratt (London, 1809)

The Rule, Statutes and Customs of the Hospitallers, 1099-1310, ed. & trans. by Edwin J. King (London, 1934)

Runciman, Sir Steven. *The Fall of Constantinople, 1453* (Cambridge, 1965)

_____. *A History of the Crusades*, 3 vols (Cambridge, 1951-54)

Sacrorum conciliorum nova et amplissima collectio, 31 vols, ed. by Joannes Dominicus Mansi (Florence & Venice, 1759-1798)

Saïd al-Andalusi. *Book of the Categories of Nations*, ed. & trans. by S. I. Salem & Alok Kumar (Austin, 1991)

Said, Edward W. *Orientalism: Western Conceptions of the Orient* (London, 1978)

Salmi, Hannu. *Imagined Germany: Richard Wagner's National Utopia* (New York, 1999)

Samuel, V. C. *The Council of Chalcedon Re-examined: A Historical and Theological Survey* (Madras, 1977)

Santillana, Giorgio de. *The Origins of Scientific Thought* (Chicago, 1961)

Saunders, John Joseph. *A History of Medieval Islam* (London, 1965)

Schaff, Philip. *History of the Christian Church*, 5th ed. in 8 vols (Grand Rapids, 1910)

Schleiermacher, Friedrich D. E. *Über die Religion: Reden an die Gebildeten unter ihren Verächtern* (Berlin, 1799)

Schlesinger, Arthur Meier. *A Critical Period in American Religion, 1875-1900* (Philadelphia, 1967)

Schopenhauer, Arthur. *Die Welt als Wille und Vorstellung* (Dresden, 1818; 2nd ed. 1844)

Schroeder, H. J. *Disciplinary Decrees of the General Councils: Text, Translation and Commentary* (St. Louis, 1937)

Schwab, Raymond. *The Oriental Renaissance: Europe's Discovery of India and the East, 1680-1880* (New York, 1984)

The Scientific Enterprise in Early Modern Europe, ed. by Peter Dear (Chicago, 1997)

Scott, Martin. *Medieval Europe, 800-1453* (London, 1964)

Scott, Samuel Parsons. *The History of the Moorish Empire in Europe* (Philadephia, 1904)

Scott, Sir Walter. *Ivanhoe: A Romance* [1819], ed. by Ian Duncan (Oxford, 1996)

Select Historical Documents of the Middle Ages, ed. & trans. by Ernest F. Henderson (London, 1896)

Selections from the Sources of English History, B.C. 55 - A.D. 1832, ed. by Charles W. Colby (London, 1920)

Seligmann, Kurt. *The History of Magic* (New York, 1948)

Seneca. "On Tranquility of Mind" in *Moral Essays*, ed. & trans. by John W. Basore (London, 1932)

Setton, Kenneth M. *The Papacy and the Levant (1204-1571)*, 4 vols (Philadelphia, 1976-1984)

Seward, Desmond. *The Monks of War: The Military Religious Orders* (London, 1972)

Shakespeare, William. "Antony and Cleopatra" [c. 1607] in *First Folio*, ed. by John Heminge & Henry Condell (London, 1623)

_____. "Julius Cæsar" [c. 1599] in *First Folio*, ed. by John Heminge & Henry Condell (London, 1623)

Sherman, William H. *John Dee: The Politics of Reading and Writing in the English Renaissance* (Amherst, 1995)

Shorter, Edward. *The Making of the Modern Family* (New York, 1975)

Significant Figures: A History of Mathematics at Oxford, ed. by John Fauvel, Raymond Flood & Robin Wilson (Oxford, 1999)

Skelton, Geoffrey. *Wagner at Bayreuth: Experiment and Tradition* (London, 1965)

Smart, Ninian. *The Religious Experience of Mankind* (New York, 1969)

Smith, Adam. *An Inquiry into the Nature and Causes of the Wealth of Nations*, 2 vols (London, 1776)

Smith, Goldwin. *A History of England* (New York, 1949)

Smith, Lacey Baldwin. *Henry VIII: The Mask of Royalty* (London, 1971)

Smyser, Hamilton M. "Ibn Fadlan's Account of the Rus with Some Commentary and Some Allusions to Beowulf" in *Franciplegius: Medieval and Linguistic Studies in Honor of Francis Peabody Magoun, Jr.*, ed by Jess B. Bessinger Jr. & Robert P. Creed (New York, 1965)

Socrates Scholasticus. "The Ecclesiastical History" in *Nicene and Post-Nicene Fathers*, Series II, Vol. II, ed. by Philip Schaff & Henry Wace (Edinburgh, 1892)

Sozomenus, Salaminius Hermias. "The Ecclesiastical History" in *Nicene and Post-Nicene Fathers*, Series II, Vol. II, ed. by Philip Schaff & Henry Wace (Edinburgh, 1892)

Spedding, James. "Preface to the New Atlantis" in *The Works of Francis Bacon*, Vol. III, ed. by James Spedding, Robert Leslie Ellis & Douglas Denon Heath (London, 1859)

Spence, Lewis. *Ancient Egyptian Myths and Legends* (London, 1915)

Spencer, Herbert. *Principles of Biology*, Vol. I (London, 1864)

Spicilegium sive collectio veterum aliquot scriptorum qui in Galliæ Bibliothecis delituerant, 2nd ed. in 3 vols, ed. by Luc d'Achéry, rev. by Louis-Francois-Joseph de La Barre (Paris, 1723)

Sprat, Thomas. *History of the Royal Society* (London, 1667)

Statutes of the Realm, 11 vols, ed. by Alexander Luders et al (London, 1810-28)

Stauffer, Vernon. *New England and the Bavarian Illuminati* (New York, 1918)

Stavrianos, Leften Stavros. *Global Rift: The Third World Comes of Age* (New York, 1981)

Stearns, Peter N. *European Society in Upheaval: Social History since 1750*, 2nd ed. (New York, 1975)

Steel, Duncan. *Marking Time: The Epic Quest to Invent the Perfect Calendar* (New York, 1999)

Steiner, Rudolf. *Eleven European Mystics: Mysticism at the Dawn of the Modern Age*, trans. by K. E. Zimmer (Englewood, 1960)

Stoddard, John L. *Rebuilding a Lost Faith* (New York, 1826)

Storr, Anthony. *Human Destructiveness: The Roots of Genocide and Human Cruelty* (Brighton, 1972)

Strachey, Lytton. *Elizabeth and Essex: A Tragic History* (London, 1928)

Streeter, Burnett H. *The Four Gospels: A Study of Origins* (London, 1924)

Studies in Early British History, ed. by Nora Kershaw Chadwick (Cambridge, 1954)

Suetonius. "The Lives of Illustrious Men", trans. by J. C. Rolfe, in *Suetonius*, Vol. II (London, 1914)

_____. "The Lives of the Twelve Caesars", trans. by J. C. Rolfe, in *Suetonius*, 2 vols (London, 1913-14)

Sumption, Jonathan. *The Albigensian Crusade* (London, 1978)

Swinburne, Algernon Charles. *Collected Poetical Works*, 2 vols (London, 1924)

Tacitus, Cornelius. *Annals*, trans. by Alfred John Church & William Jackson Brodribb (New York, 1942)

_____. "Germania" [98 CE] in *Libri qui supersunt*, Vol. II, Pt. 2, ed. by Erich Koestermann (Leipzig, 1926)

Tatian. "Address to the Greeks", trans. by J. E. Ryland, in *The Ante-Nicene Fathers*, Vol. II, ed. by Alexander Roberts & James Donaldson (Edinburgh, 1867)

Taylor, Eva G. R. *Late Tudor and Early Stuart Geography, 1583-1650* (London, 1934)

_____. *The Mathematical Practitioners of Tudor and Stuart England* (Cambridge, 1954)

_____. *Tudor Geography, 1485-1583* (London, 1930)

Taylor, Richard. *Richard Wagner: His Life, Art and Thought* (New York, 1971)

Temple, Sir William. "Essay upon the Original and Nature of Government" [1672] in *Miscellanea*, Vol. I (London, 1680)

Tertullian. "The Five Books Against Marcion", trans. by Peter Holmes, in *The Ante-Nicene Fathers*, Vol. III, ed. by Alexander Roberts & James Donaldson (Edinburgh, 1867)

_____. "On Modesty", trans. by Sydney Thelwall, in *The Ante-Nicene Fathers*, Vol. IV, ed. by Alexander Roberts & James Donaldson (Edinburgh, 1867)

Theodoret. "The Ecclesiastical History" in *Nicene and Post-Nicene Fathers*, Series II, Vol. III, ed. by Philip Schaff & Henry Wace (Edinburgh, 1892)

The Theodosian Code and Novels and the Sirmondian Constitutions, ed. & trans. by Clyde Pharr (Princeton, 1952)

Thesaurus novus anecdotorum, 5 vols, ed. by Edmond Martène & Ursin Durand (Paris, 1717)

St. Thomas Aquinas. *Expositio super librum Boëthii De trinitate* [1252-1259], ed. by Bruno Decker (Leiden, 1955)

_____. "De Regimine Judæorum ad Ducissam Brabantæ" [1271] in *Politaca Opuscula Duo*, ed. by Joseph Mathis (Turin, 1924)

_____. "De Regimine Principum ad Regem Cypri" [1267] in *Politaca Opuscula Duo*, ed. by Joseph Mathis (Turin, 1924)

_____. *Summa contra Gentiles*, 5 vols, trans. by A. C. Pegis, J. F. Anderson, V. J. Bourke & C. J. O'Neil (New York, 1955-57)

_____. *Summa Theologica*, Vol. I, trans. by Fathers of the English Dominican Province (New York, 1920)

Thoren, Victor E. *The Lord of Uraniborg: A Biography of Tycho Brahe* (Cambridge, 1990)

Thorndike, Lynn. *A History of Magic and Experimental Science*, 8 vols (New York, 1923-58)

Thucydides. *History of the Peloponnesian War*, 4 vols, trans. by Charles Forster Smith (London, 1919-23)

Tocqueville, Alexis de. *Democracy in America*, trans. by George Lawrence, ed. by J. P. Mayer & Max Lerner (New York, 1966)

Toland, John. *Christianity not Mysterious* (London, 1696)

Tradescant's Rarities: Essays on the Foundation of the Ashmolean Museum, 1683, ed. by Arthur MacGregor (Oxford, 1983)

Treece, Henry. *The Crusades* (London, 1962)

Trevor-Roper, Hugh Redwald. "The European Witch-Craze of the Sixteenth and Seventeenth Centuries" in *Religion, the Reformation and Social Change, and Other Essays* (London, 1967)

Ullmann, Walter. *The Growth of Papal Government in the Middle Ages: A Study in the Ideological Relation of Clerical to Lay Power* (London, 1955)

Vacandard, Elphège. *The Inquisition: A Critical and Historical Study of the Coercive Power of the Church*, trans. by Bertrand L. Conway (London, 1908)

Valla, Lorenzo. *Discourse on the Forgery of the Alleged Donation of Constantine*, trans. by Christopher B. Coleman (New Haven, 1922)

Van Cleve, Thomas Curtis. *The Emperor Frederick II of Hohenstaufen: Immutator Mundi* (Oxford, 1972)

Vasari, Giorgio. *Vite de' più eccellenti architetti, scultori e pittori* (Florence, 1550)

Vergil. *Georgics*, trans. by L. P. Wilkinson (Harmondsworth, 1982)

Vergil, Polydore. *Anglia Historia* (Basel, 1534)

Vicaire, Marie-Humbert. *Histoire de Saint Dominique*, 2 vols (Paris, 1957)

Victor, Sextus Aurelius. *Epitome de Cæsaribus*, ed. by Franz Pichlmayr (Leipzig, 1911)

Viliers, Alan John. *Men, Ships, and the Sea* (Washington D.C., 1962)

Villehardouin, Geoffrey de. *Memoirs or Chronicle of The Fourth Crusade and The Conquest of Constantinople*, trans. by Sir Frank T. Marzials (London, 1908)

Vitæ Sanctorum Hiberniæ, 2 vols, ed. by Charles Plummer (Oxford, 1910)

Voltaire, François Marie Arouet de. *Essai sur les Mœurs et l'Esprit des Nations*, 7 vols (Geneva, 1756)

_____. *Lettres Philosophiques* (Paris, 1734)

Wagner, Nike. *The Wagners: The Dramas of a Musical Dynasty*, trans. by Ewald Osers & Michael Downes (Princeton, 1998)

Wagner, Richard. "Address to the Vaterlands-Verein (1848)", trans. by William Ashton Ellis, in *Richard Wagner's Prose Works*, Vol. IV (London, 1895)

_____. *The Authentic Librettos of the Wagner Operas* (New York, 1938)

_____. *Beethoven* (Leipzig, 1870)

_____. *My Life*, authorized translation from the German in 2 vols (New York, 1911)

_____. "Religion and Art", trans. by William Ashton Ellis, in *Richard Wagner's Prose Works*, Vol. VII (London, 1898)

_____. *Selected Letters of Richard Wagner*, ed. & trans. by Steward Spencer & Barry Millington (London, 1987)

Waite, Arthur Edward. *A New Encyclopædia of Freemasonry*, 2 vols (London, 1921)

Wallace, Alfred Russel. *Travels on the Amazon and Rio Negro: With an Account of the Native Tribes, and Observations on the Climate, Geology, and Natural History of the Amazon Valley* (London, 1853)

Wallace, William E. *Michelangelo: The Complete Sculpture, Painting, Architecture* (Hong Kong, 1998)

Wandruszka, Adam. *The House of Habsburg: Six Hundred Years of a European Dynasty*, trans. by Cathleen & Hans Epstein (London, 1964)

Watson, Derek. *Richard Wagner* (New York, 1979)

Weber, Max. *The Protestant Ethic and the Spirit of Capitalism*, trans. by Talcott Parsons (New York, 1930)

Webster, Charles. *From Paracelsus to Newton: Magic and the Making of Modern Science* (Cambridge, 1982)

Weil, Simone. *La Pesanteur et la Grâce* (Paris, 1947)

Welbon, Guy Richard. *The Buddhist Nirvana and its Western Interpreters* (Chicago, 1968)

Wesley, John. "Sermons III: 71-114" in *The Bicentennial Edition of the Works of John Wesley*, Vol. III, ed. by Albert C. Outler (Nashville, 1988)

Westfall, Richard S. *Never at Rest: A Biography of Isaac Newton* (Cambridge, 1980)

Wheeler, Ramona Louise. *Walk Like an Egyptian* (New York, 1999)

Which Bible?, ed. by Davis Otis Fuller (Grand Rapids, 1970)

White, Andrew Dickson. *A History of the Warfare of Science with Theology in Christendom*, 2 vols (New York, 1896)

White, James F. *Roman Catholic Worship: Trent to Today* (New York, 1995)

White, John. "Return to Roanoke" [1590] in *The Principall Navigations, Voiages, Traffiques, and Discoveries of the English Nation*, Vol. IV, by Richard Hakluyt (London, 1600)

Wilken, Robert Louis. *The Christians as the Romans Saw Them* (New Haven, 1984)

William of Tyre. *A History of Deeds done Beyond the Sea*, 2 vols, trans. by Emily Babcock & August C. Krey (New York, 1943)

Williams, Gwyn A. *Madoc: The Making of a Myth* (London, 1979)

Wilson, Ian. *Jesus: The Evidence* (San Francisco, 1984)

Wiseman, T. P. *Catullus and his World: A Reappraisal* (Cambridge, 1985)

Women of Spirit: Female Leadership in the Jewish and Christian Traditions, ed. by Rosemary Ruether & Eleanor McLaughlin (New York, 1979)

Wood, Charles T. *The Age of Chivalry: Manners and Morals, 1000-1450* (New York, 1970)

Wortman, Richard S. *Scenarios of Power: Myth and Ceremony in Russian Monarchy*, 2 vols (Princeton, 1995-2000)

Wylie, James A. *The History of Protestantism*, 3 vols (London, 1875-77)

____. *History of the Scottish Nation*, 3 vols (London, 1886)

Yadin, Yigael. *Masada: Herod's Fortress and the Zealots' Last Stand*, trans. by Moshe Pearlman (London, 1966)

Yates, Frances A. *Astraea: The Imperial Theme in the Sixteenth Century* (London, 1975)

____. *The Rosicrucian Enlightenment* (London, 1972)

Zanker, Paul. *The Power of Images in the Age of Augustus*, trans. by Alan Shapiro (Ann Arbor, 1988)

Zenobius. *Paroemiographi Graeci*, ed. by Thomas Gaisford (Oxford, 1836)

Ziegler, Philip. *The Black Death* (London, 1969)

Zosimus. *New History*, publ. by W. Green & T. Chaplin (London, 1814)

INDEX

Aachen, 256-257, 259-260, 266, 342, 375, 381, 489
Abélard, Peter, 316-319, 329-330, 400, 546
Abgar the Great, 176
Abraham the Patriarch, 139, 172, 251, 495
absolute truth, 13, 81, 159, 166, 193, 217, 319, 369, 372, 397, 457, 461, 557, 581, 587, 594, 595a, 617, 633, 635, 344, 659, 684, 728
absolutism, see absolute monarchy
Abydos, 8
Abyssinia, 248
Académie Française, the, 622
Académie Royale des Sciences, the, 621
academies of science, 207, 547, 586, 587a, 618-619, 621-623, 625-626, 629-631, 634, 643, 647
Academus, 74; the Academy of Plato, 74, 76-78, 81
Acadia, 638
Accius, Lucius, 140
acoustics, 631
Acre, 334, 349-350, 353-356, 358, 383-384, 407-408, 411-412, 414-416, 424; the fall of Acre, 416, 424; the siege of Acre, 354, 358
Acropolis, 55-56, 62-65
Actium, the Battle of, 128
Acts of the Apostles, the, 146, 170, 173; the Acts of Thomas, 176
Adalard, St., 266
Adaloald, king of the Lombards, 239
Adam, 512, 514a, 686, 723
Adelung, Johann Christoph, 688
Adémar de Monteil, bishop of Le Puy, 303
Adler, Alfred, 735
Adrian I, pope, 254, 258; Adrian IV, 336-338, 340, 358, 513; Adrian VI, 496
Adrianople, 186-187, 203, 352, 367
Adriatic Sea, the, 224, 261, 362-363, 367, 443, 482
adultery, 177, 229, 264, 266, 313, 322, 430, 500, 511, 514, 516, 607
Ægean Sea, the, 20, 22, 58-61, 70, 407, 455, 534a; the Ægean islands, 19-21, 30, 35, 45, 49, 53, 56, 58-59, 102, 187, 302, 353-355, 362, 364, 367, 407, 425, 432; the Ægean region, 19, 22, 26, 31
Ælia Capitolina, see Jerusalem
Æmilian Way, the, 236-237
Æneas, 9, 133, 561
Æschylus, 45a, 49, 66, 718-719

æsthetics, 41, 78, 201, 456, 634, 703, 708, 727
Æthelbert I, king of Kent, 241
Aëtius, Flavius, 223-226
Africa, the Africans, 1, 13-14, 20, 466-467, 538-539, 545, 563, 575-577, 614, 657; North Africa, 20, 37, 54, 98, 105, 107, 116, 124, 126, 142, 175, 181-182, 184-185, 205, 209, 215-216, 218, 240, 251, 287, 328, 412, 466, 528
afterlife, 4a, 7, 144, 161, 172, 177, 188, 200, 216, 242, 245, 279, 303, 356, 369, 373, 397, 421, 512, 515, 649, 725, 732
Agapes, the, 159, 193
Agapetus I, St., pope, 237
Agilulf, king of the Lombards, 239
Agincourt, the Battle of, 444
Agnadello, the Battle of, 482
Agnes of Meran, 357, 360
Agnes of Poitou, 299
Agorâ of Athens, the, 64
agriculture, 1-2, 5, 10-11, 13-15, 19, 21-22, 28-30, 36, 38-40, 54-56, 63, 71, 75, 100, 110,118, 120, 132, 137, 152, 173,229, 238, 244, 256-257, 272, 287, 296, 303, 324, 392, 394, 402, 418, 433-434, 445, 455, 463, 456, 492, 494-495, 509, 548, 578, 638, 657, 659, 664, 666-667, 672, 674, 692, 696, 698, 717
Agrippa, Marcus Vipsanius, 125, 128, 131; Herod, 141, 149; Herod, II, 147
Ahura-Mazda, 99
Ain Jalut, the Battle of, 410
Aistulf of Friuli, 254
Akroinon, the Battle of, 253
Akrotiri, 21
Alaric I, king of the Visigoths, 212-215
al-Ashraf Khalil, 416
Alaska, 453
Alba, duque de, 553-554
Albert the Bear, 327
Albertus Magnus, St., 396
Albigensians, the, see Cathars; origin of the term, 368; the Albigensian Crusade, 370, 395
Albion, see England
Alboin, 236
Albrecht von Hohenzollern, 503
alchemy, alchemists, 394, 519-521, 550, 570-571, 573, 580, 598-599, 619-620, 631-632, 634
alcohol, origin of the term, 521; alcoholic beverages, 2-3, 38, 40-42, 46-48, 130, 159-

160, 207a, 261, 270, 304, 320, 374, 521
Alcuin, 257
Aldred of York, 291-292
Alemannia, see Swabia
Alessandria, 342
Alexander the Great, 18, 78-79, 82-90, 94-95, 97, 99, 112, 138, 142, 680
Alexander, Tiberius Julius, 148
Alexander of Alexandria, St., 191-192, 198
Alexander II, pope, 286; Alexander III, 338, 340, 342-344, 420; Alexander IV, 390; Alexander V, 440-441; Alexander VI, 463-472, 474-478, 481, 529
Alexander I, czar of Russia, 677
Alexandria, 52, 77, 85, 89, 91-94, 103, 115, 120, 125, 127-128, 131, 136-141, 145, 148, 153, 155-156, 163-165, 178, 191-192, 195, 198, 202, 205, 207, 214, 218-221, 250-251, 263, 345, 362, 461a, 537, 621, 679
Alexandrian Wars, the, 115, 117
Alexius II Comnenus, Byzantine emperor, 301-302, 304-308, 334; Alexius III Angelus, 357, 363-364; Alexius IV Angelus, 363-365; Alexius V Ducas, 365
Alexius Strategopulus, 408
Alfarabius, 397
Alfonso V, king of Aragón, 415, 443
Alfonso di Bisceglie, 472, 475
Alfonso IX, king of León, 377
Alfonso II, king of Naples, 469-470, 472
Alfred the Great, 283
Algazel, 399
algebra, 51, 399, 558, 631
Algiers, 528
algorithms, 399, 566
al-Hakim, caliph of Egypt, 295
Ali, caliph of Islam, 251
Alix de Champagne, 388-389
al-Kamil, 381-382, 384-385, 389
Alkmene, 28
Allah, origin of the name, 247
allegories, 74-76, 138-139, 163, 165, 228a, 456, 573a, 598, 644, 660
Allegri, Gregorio, 585
Allenby, Sir Edmund, 389
All Saints' Day, the, 243, 487
al-Ma'mun, caliph of Baghdad, 276
almanac, 119-120, 132; origin of the term, 399
Alp Arslan, 295
alphabet, 9, 23
Alps, the, 101, 109, 111, 113-114, 183, 235-236, 288,

766

300, 342, 351, 362, 368, 375, 392, 456, 469, 483, 485, 529, 586, 726
Alsace, 715, 717; Alsace-Lorraine, 717
Altar of Victory, the, 207
Amadeus VII, count of Savoy, 443; Amadeus VIII, duke of Savoy, 443
Amalasuntha, 235
Amalric I, king of Jerusalem, 345-347; Amalric II, 412
Amazons, the, 36
Ambrose of Milan, St., 190a, 209, 458
Americas, the, 468, 563-565, 575-577; the origin of the name, 467; Latin America, 468, 563, 575-577, 579, 678, 699; North America, 131, 564, 568, 610, 613, 615-616, 636, 638, 647, 679, 692-693, 698, 699a; the Native Americans, 563, 575, 608, 613, 657-658, 693-694
Ammianus, 201-202
Ammonius Saccas, 178
Amoun, 12-13, 16-18, 84-85, 671; the symbols of Amoun, 13; Amon-Ra, 16
Amphictyon, 25; the Amphictyonic league, 79
Amphipolis, 79
Amr ibn al-'As, 250
Amsterdam, 555, 577, 612-614, 639
Anabaptists, 536, 615
Anacletus II, antipope, 327-328
Anagni, 421, 423, 439
Anastasius IV, pope, 336
Anatolia, see Asia Minor
anatomy, 379, 398, 459, 481, 619, 631, 662
Ancona, 254a, 359, 375, 455, 475
Andalusia, 215, 251, 276, 578; origin of the name, 215
André de Montbard, 321-322
Andreæ, Johann Valentin, 598
Angeli dynasty, the, 358, 367
angels, 145, 239a, 244, 248, 280, 403, 445, 448, 557, 572-573, 579, 686
Angles, the, 215, 562
Anglesey, see Mona
Anglican Church, the, 499, 501-502, 531, 542, 548, 556, 562, 568, 608-609, 616, 633, 674a
Anglo-Dutch Wars, the, 612, 626
animals, 1-3, 10-11, 13, 18, 21, 29, 32, 37-38, 46, 63, 74, 84, 368, 521, 658, 662, 688, 700, 702
Anjou, 335, 338, 376-377; the Angevin dynasty, 335, 338, 376-377, 391-392, 415, 469
annates, papal, 431, 485
Anne of Bohemia, 543
Anne of Brittany, 474

Anne of Denmark, 591
Anne, queen of Great Britain, 631, 638
Anno of Cologne, St., 286
Anno Domini, 246
annulment of marriage, 265, 335, 377, 472, 474, 499-501, 607
Annunciation, the, 244
Anselm of Canterbury, St., 305; St. Anselm of Laon, 316
Anterus, St., pope, 178
anthropomorphism, 25, 37, 42, 68
Antichrist, the, 387, 516, 562, 730-731
anticlericalism, 368, 509, 644, 652, 683, 704, 727
Antigonus I Cyclops, king of Macedon, 90; Antigonus II Gonatas, 90;
Antigonus Mattathias, king of Judæa, 127
Antioch, 91, 93, 141, 145-146, 163, 176, 178, 306-308, 320, 332, 334, 349, 352, 354, 410-412, 414; the see of Antioch, 145, 154-155, 163, 170, 191-192, 195, 198, 206, 219-221, 250, 461a
Antipas, Herod, 136
Antipater, the Macedonian general, 90; the founder of the Herodian dynasty, 115-116, 127
antipopes, the, 178, 300-301, 304, 308, 328, 342-343, 439, 443
Antoninus Pius, 158, 161
Antonius, Lucius, 125
Antony, Marc, 122-128
Anubis, 6
Aphrodite, 35
Apis, 84, 93
Apollo, 30, 33, 36, 39, 42, 44a, 46, 130, 183, 718; the temple of Apollo, 130
Apollinarius of Laodicea, 206;
Apollinarianism, 206, 219
Apologists, the Christian, 159, 164, 175, 183, 191
apostles, the Christian, 143, 145-146, 155, 162, 168, 170, 200, 250, 315, 329-330, 335, 368, 372, 374, 376, 378, 547, 635, 658a;
Apostolic Poverty, 329, 431; Apostolic Succession, 374, 489, 683; the Church of the Holy Apostles, 200
Appian, 124
Appian Way, the, 153
Aqaba, 248
Aqiba, Rabbi, 157-158
Aqsa Mosque, the, 308, 320, 385
aqueducts, 55, 131, 136, 296
Aquileia, 178, 201, 206, 224, 482
Aquitaine, 215, 314, 333, 335, 338
Aquyrion, 200

Arabia, the Arabs, 91, 116, 127, 136, 158, 180, 185, 222, 227, 247-253, 275-278, 281, 295-296, 305, 307, 313-314, 318, 326, 328, 382a, 394, 398, 400, 411, 413, 417, 454, 466, 523, 537-539, 680; Arabic language, 9, 250, 252, 277, 305, 379, 394, 396, 398-400, 403-404, 409, 521; Arabic numerals, 51, 399-400
Arabian Nights, the, 259
Aragón, 371, 377, 414-415, 443, 454, 467, 471-472, 482-483, 499-500, 528, 540, 543
Aramaic language, 173, 633
Arcadia, the Arcadians, 34, 38
Arcadius, Flavius, 212, 219
arcanum, the, 599
archæology, 2, 4a, 20-21, 84, 110, 150, 244, 624, 670, 688-690, 700
Archelaus, Herod, king of Judæa, 136; St. Archelaus, bishop of Caschar, 180
architecture, 16, 41, 62, 64, 135, 147, 276, 292, 296, 394, 411, 413, 453, 456, 459-460, 465-466, 472, 477, 479-480, 484, 529, 558, 617, 619, 623, 625, 637, 686, 711
Archytas of Tarentum, 52, 74
Areopagus, 30, 64
Ares, 40
Argonauts, the, 34
Argos, 33
Aristarchus of Alexandria, 120;
Aristarchus of Sámos, 530
Aristobulus II, king of Judæa, 107
aristocracy, the, see the upper classes
Aristophanes, 32a, 66-67
Aristotle, 34, 44, 57, 69, 77-78, 87, 91-92, 95, 138, 179, 227, 277, 319, 394, 396-397, 399-400, 403-404, 484, 519a, 520, 523, 557, 571, 581-582, 585, 587-588, 592, 594; Aristotelians, Aristotelianism, 52, 78, 94, 159, 277, 396-397, 556, 559, 561, 586, 592, 630, 632
arithmetic, 77, 257, 401, 558, 565
Arius of Alexandria, 191-193, 198-199; Arianism, Arians, 198, 202, 204-206, 218-219, 231-233, 240, 253, 255, 259, 315
Arles, 175, 192
Armada, the Spanish, 563, 574, 578
Armenia, 99, 144, 155, 176, 295, 320, 409-411; the Armenian Church, 189, 222, 263, 306, 337, 352, 461a

Armorica, see Brittany
armour, 60, 63, 272, 290-291, 322, 333, 445, 450, 481
Arnaud Amaury, 371
Arndt, Ernst Moritz, 681
Arnold of Brescia, 329-331, 335-337, 344, 351
Arnold de Villanova, 394
Arsuf, 307, 411
art, artists, 8-9, 14-15, 20-21, 25, 29, 36, 38, 42-44, 53, 61, 64, 71, 78, 88, 92, 96, 130-131, 134, 159, 230-231, 276, 314, 328, 366, 379, 387, 392, 394, 454, 456-460, 462-463, 465, 477, 479-481, 484-485, 487, 525, 527, 529, 544, 547, 572, 578, 585, 605, 611, 624-625, 635, 641, 659-661, 670, 679, 699, 702, 709-711, 715, 718-720, 722, 725, 727-728
Arthur of Britain, 230, 256, 312, 403, 445, 561-562
artisans, see craftsmen
Aryans, the, 689-690, 707; meaning of the term, 690
Ascalon, 350, 355
asceticism, ascetics, 35a, 41, 47, 49, 216a, 228, 247, 369, 503, 527
Ascham, Sir Roger, 566
Ashmole, Elias, 618-621, 623-624, 632
Asia, 14, 20, 57, 59, 83, 98, 138, 142, 163, 176, 181, 186-187, 196-197, 227, 367, 394, 453, 466, 537, 539, 545, 563, 576, 657, 687, 689; Asia Minor, 20, 24, 37, 56-58, 60, 71, 78-79, 83, 90-91, 99, 124, 126, 153, 160, 166, 183, 195, 206, 223, 253, 281, 295-296, 304-306, 352, 367, 412; Central Asia, 23, 84, 224, 295; East Asia, see the Far East
Asius, 26
as-Salih, sultan of Egypt, 389
Assembly, the Athenian, 56, 58, 62, 69-70, 154; the Roman, 105-106, 123, 129
Assisi, 359, 372
Assos, 78
Assyria, 15, 54, 85, 92
Astarte, 246
astrology, 89, 99, 156, 197, 530, 551, 561, 570, 580-581, 619, 631
astronomy, 9-11, 50, 91-92, 119-120, 156, 218, 277, 394, 399, 401, 530-531, 550, 559-560, 567-568, 570, 580-586, 619, 623, 629-630, 689
Ataulf, 215
Athanasius of Alexandria, St., 192, 198, 202
atheism, atheists, 7, 95, 101, 144, 154, 460, 643, 654, 703, 707, 727, 733

Athena, 31, 33-34, 40, 44, 63-64
Athenæus, 34
Athens, the Athenians, 25, 29, 33-34, 36, 40, 42, 44, 46, 47a, 48, 53-67, 69-72, 77-80, 82, 87, 95, 97, 125, 130, 135, 154, 156, 201, 212, 454-455, 462, 484, 727
athletics, 50, 58, 65, 67, 174, 477, 499, 675
Atlantic Ocean, the, 444, 468, 538, 545, 563, 576, 610, 621, 638
Atlantis, 20
Atlas, the Greek god, 32, 552a; atlases, 540, 552a, 570
atomic theory, the, 96, 101, 620, 631
Attalia, 334
Attalus, Priscus, 213
Attica, 20, 28, 36, 55-56, 59, 67, 88
Attila the Hun, 223-226
Attis, 98-99
Augsburg, 534; the Augsburg Confession, 505; Augsburg diets, 286, 505, 535; the Augsburg Interim, 535; the Peace of Augsburg, 536, 600
Augustine of Canterbury, St., 241
Augustine of Hippo, St., 33, 174, 195, 201, 215-218, 257, 271, 396, 551, 514; the Augustinian Order, 372, 487, 503
Augustus II, king of Poland, 640, 646-647; Augustus III, 646
Austerlitz, the Battle of, 676
Australia, 576a
Austria, the Austrians, 130, 189, 235, 327, 354, 356, 393, 396, 419, 442-443, 488, 496, 504, 506, 524, 534, 543, 553, 600-601, 603, 637, 639-641, 645-647, 661, 669, 676-678, 682-683, 696, 704-705, 712-713, 715-716, 720; Austria-Hungary, 393, 713; the House of Austria, see the Habsburg dynasty
Austrian Succession, the War of, 645
Austro-Prussian War, the, 712
Authari, 237, 239
authoritarianism, 76, 78, 162-163, 297-298, 316, 388, 398, 404, 441, 489, 493, 518, 531, 557, 587, 592, 595, 607, 617, 652, 723-724
autocracy, see absolute monarchy
autopsies, 398, 521, 655
Auvergne, 303, 313
Avempace, 397
Aversa, 281, 284
Averroës, 277, 397, 557
Avesta, the, 98

Avicenna, 397, 520, 523
Avignon, 371, 427, 431, 438-440, 469; the Avignon exile, 431, 438-440
Ayyubid dynasty, the, 346, 367, 389
Aztecs, the, 575

Babeuf, François Noël, 669
Babington, Anthony, 574
Babylon, the Babylonians, 14-15, 19, 54, 59, 83-86, 89-91, 93, 99, 122, 142, 162a, 179, 216, 275a, 688; Persian Babylonia, 59, 84, 99, 158, 179, 251
Babylonian Captivity of the Jews, the, 142, 244a, 633a; the Babylonian Captivity of the papacy, see the Avignon exile
Bacchos, see Dionysos; the Bacchæ, 42; the Baccheion of Athens, 47a
Bacon, Sir Francis, 587-596, 620, 622-623, 625, 628-629, 642
Bacon, Roger, 403-406, 566, 636
Baghdad, 276, 278, 397, 410; the caliphate of Baghdad, 260, 346-347
Bahram I, king of Persia, 181
Baldwin I, Latin emperor of Constantinople, 366-367; Baldwin II, 408-409
Baldwin I, count of Edessa, 306, 308
Baldwin V, count of Flanders, 283, 286; Baldwin IX, see Baldwin I of Constantinople
Baldwin III, king of Jerusalem, 332; Baldwin IV, 345-348; Baldwin V, 348-349
Balkans, the, 124, 183-184, 187, 302, 352, 453, 538
Balts, the Baltic, 278, 354, 383, 530, 601-602, 640, 647, 716, 720
ban of the empire, 383, 388, 490; papal ban, see interdict
banishment, see exile
banking, banks, 94, 104, 141, 273, 324-325, 418-419, 422, 456-458, 488, 542, 613, 628; the Bank of Alexandria, 94; the Bank of England, 628
Banks, Joseph, 657
baptism, 99, 170, 172a, 174, 177, 180, 186, 200, 204, 232, 244, 267, 270, 368, 374, 417, 447, 467, 576-577, 655, 683
Baptists, 515a, 612
barbarians, 40-41, 57, 79, 99, 119, 142-143, 151, 157, 188, 201, 203, 213-214, 226-229, 231-232, 235, 256, 261, 306, 394, 456, 474, 482, 715
Barbarossa, 528
Barcelona, the Peace of, 504

768

Bardesanes, 175-176
Barebones Parliament, the, 612
Bari, 296, 358
Bar Kochba, Simon, 157-158
barley, 2, 6, 28, 40, 244
Barnabas, St., 163; the Epistle of Barnabas, 210
Baroque, the, 147, 472, 525, 585, 623, 625-626
Barrow, Isaac, 630
Barruel, Augustin de, 653
barter economy, 272, 418, 455
Basel, 286, 522-523, 714, 716, 722
Basil Boioannes, 280-281
Basil II, Byzantine emperor, 281
Basil the Great, St., 202, 208, 211; the Rule of St. Basil, 211, 228
basilica, origin of the term, 194-195; the Basilica of St. John the Lateran, see the Lateran palace
Basilides the Gnostic, 163-164
Basques, the, 255, 312, 525-526
baths, bathing, 65, 135-136, 157, 199-200, 232, 275, 331, 729
Battle Abbey, 291
Batu Khan, 388
Bavaria, the Bavarians, 240, 255, 267, 299, 326-327, 337, 343, 380, 382, 435, 600, 602, 651-653, 676, 679, 711, 713, 715-716, 720, 726, 729
Baybars, 409-415
Bayeux, 270, 292
Bayle, Pierre, 634
Bayreuth, 720, 726; the Festspielhaus of Bayreuth, 711, 719-721, 725, 728
Bec, 288-289
Becket, St. Thomas, 339-340, 501
Bede, the Venerable, 246, 445a
Bedouins, the, 349, 538
beer, 2-3, 40-41, 48
Beirut, 307, 350, 358
Béla III, king of Hungary, 378; Béla IV, 388
Belgium, 669, 678
Belisarius, 235
Bellarmine, St. Robert, 585
Benedict X, antipope, 285; Benedict XIII, 440-442
Benedict of Nursia, St., 237a, 258; the Rule of St. Benedict, 237, 258; the Benedictines, 237, 240-241, 258, 317, 319, 420, 509, 519
Benedict I, pope, 237-238; Benedict XI, Blessed, 423; Benedict XV, 449; Benedict XVI, 386a, 525a
Benevento, 236, 253, 255, 284, 301, 327; the Battle of Benevento, 391
Bentham, Jeremy, 666-667
Berenguela of Cástile, 377
Berenice, 149

Berke Khan, 410
Berlin, 639, 648, 713, 720; the Berlin Academy of Sciences, 647
Bernard of Clairvaux, St., 319, 321-322, 327-331, 333, 335-336
Bernard the Monk, 259
Bernini, Gianlorenzo, 585
Besançon, the Diet of, 337
Bessus, 85
Bethar, 157-158
Beth Gibelin, 321
Bethlehem, 170, 385
Béziers, 371
Bible, the, 18, 25, 112, 138, 168, 184a, 201, 210, 244, 248a, 252, 259, 271, 315, 319, 368, 398, 401, 406, 441, 480, 491, 493, 495, 505, 517, 531, 533, 538, 575, 580, 584, 595-597, 606-607, 617, 633, 700, 703-704, 723; origin of the term, 210; the interpretation of the Bible, 138, 164, 315, 368, 495, 531, 533, 584, 586, 633, 703-704; translations of the Bible, 214, 222, 240, 491, 595-596; the King James Version, 595-596
bigamy, 265, 500, 607
Bilbeis, 345-346
Billingsley, Sir Henry, 558
Bill of Rights, the, 628
biology, 78, 92, 630, 657, 662, 699-700
Bismarck, Otto von, 300, 711-713, 715-717, 720, 722, 729-730
Black Death, the, 434-437, 444, 602
Black Friday, the, 717
Black Sea, the, 21, 37, 58, 70, 134, 197, 203, 227, 367, 407-408
blasphemy, 46, 350, 448, 491, 497, 511, 616, 703-704, 722
Blenheim, the Battle of, 638
Blois, 305, 341, 445; the Treaties of Blois, 479
Blount, Charles, 8th baron Mountjoy, 589-590
Boehme, Jakob, 707
Bœotia, 60, 82
Bohemia, the Bohemians, 331, 337, 377, 383, 440-442, 504, 524, 543, 566, 572, 578, 600-601, 603, 638, 645, 696
Bohemund I, prince of Antioch, 305-308; Bohemund III, 349; Bohemund VI, 410-412
Boleyn, Anne, 499-500, 513, 548
Bolli Bollason, 278
Bologna, 344, 380, 481-483, 485, 505, 704; the Cathedral of Bologna, 344; the Concordat of Bologna, 485

Bona of Savoy, 459
Bonaventura, St., 396, 403404
Boniface VIII, pope, 421-423, 429, 431; Boniface IX, 440
Boniface of Montferrat, 362, 367
books, 9, 50, 100, 102, 110, 134, 155, 163, 168, 191, 217, 226, 269, 271, 275-276, 373, 400-402, 404, 411, 437a, 454, 516, 523, 526, 526, 569, 577, 595-596, 599, 601, 611, 619-620, 631, 634, 673, 682, 689-699
Bora, Katharina von, 503
Bordeaux, 423, 448
Borgia dynasty, the, 443, 464, 478
Borgia, Cesare, 464, 470-472, 474-479; Jofre, 464, 469; Juan, 464, 471; Lucrezia, 464, 469, 472, 475-477; Rodrigo, see Alexander VI
Bornholm, 213
Bosporus, the, 57, 186-187, 192, 196-197, 200, 302, 304-305, 364
Bostanai ben Chaninai, 251
Boston, 190
botany, 9, 572, 621, 634, 657, 662
Bourbon dynasty, the, 296, 555, 639, 650, 678-679, 692-693
bourgeoisie, the, see the middle classes
Bouvines, the Battle of, 371, 377
Boyle, Robert, 619-620, 625
Brahe, Tycho, 559-561, 580-582, 629
Bramante, Donato, 459-460, 465-466, 480, 484, 529
Brandenburg, 327, 503, 639-640, 645-647; the House of Brandenburg, see the Hohenzollern dynasty
Brazil, 467, 575-576, 579, 613-614, 699
bread, 3-4, 29, 46-47, 131, 244, 252, 368, 374, 493-494, 665; the breaking of bread, 46-47, 159-160, 173, 245
Brennus, 214
Brescia, 329, 337-338, 482-483
bridal veil, the origin of the, 263
bridge building, 14, 57, 153, 156, 675
Bridget of Sweden, St., 438
Brindisi, or Brundisium, 108, 114, 123, 125, 383, 414; the Cathedral of Brindisi, 383, the Treaty of Brundisium, 126
Britain, the Britons, 109, 111-112, 153, 156-157, 187, 209, 214-215, 229, 241-242, 246-257, 269-270, 282, 312, 324, 341, 403a, 499, 541-542, 549-550,

561-563, 565, 568, 571-572, 579; Great Britain, 230, 403a, 541-542, 568-569, 579, 583, 590-592, 594, 598-559, 603, 609-612, 614-615, 618-619, 621, 624-625, 628-630, 637-642, 646-647, 650, 654-656, 658, 666, 670, 673, 675-679, 681, 683, 687-688, 690, 692-693, 697-698
Brittany, the Bretons, 289-290, 312-313, 316, 318, 338, 376, 433, 474
Brixen, the Synod of, 301
Bronze Age, the, 21, 25, 700
Brunelleschi, Filippo, 459, 529
Brunswick, 343, 359, 375
Brussels, 551, 553
Brutus the Trojan, 561-562
Brutus, Lucius Junius, 121; Marcus Junius, 121-124, 669
Büchner, Ludwig, 702
Buddhas, Buddhism, 138, 181, 249a, 409, 707; Siddhârta Gautama Buddha, 690-691, 703, 736
Bulgaria, 57, 130, 367, 377-378
bulls, the slaying of, 44, 98, 476; bull-gods, 38, 84; the buffalo, 693-694
Bulwer-Lytton, Sir Edward G. E., 709
Bunyan, John, 598
Burgundy, the Burgundians, 213, 232-233, 285, 303, 310, 319-321, 337, 444-445, 447-448, 496, 553; the Burgundii, 213, 224-225, 232
Burschenschaften, the, 682
Busento, the river, 215
Byblos, 5
Byron, 6th baron, 678-679, 703
Byzantine Empire, the, 78, 119, 188, 196, 200, 208, 214, 220-223, 225-228, 231, 233, 235-238, 240, 246, 249-250, 252-255, 258-262, 263, 276-278, 280-282, 284, 295-297, 301-302, 304-305, 307-308, 320, 333-334, 346, 348, 351-355, 357-358, 363-367, 379, 389, 397, 407-409, 412, 414-415, 417, 451-454, 463, 467, 534a, 595, 643, 679-680; the Byzantine Church, see the Eastern Orthodox Church
Byzantium, the ancient city, 61, 186-187, 196-197

Cabot, John, 466, 552; Sebastian, 552
Cádiz, 101, 588
Cadmus, 686
Cæcilian, bishop of Carthage, 184-185

Cælian Hill, the, 237
Caen, 282, 287
Cæsar, Julia, the aunt of Julius, 105-107; the daughter of Julius, 108, 112, 134
Cæsar, Julius, 101, 103-129, 131-132, 134-135, 141-142, 161, 208, 257, 356, 568, 570-571
Cæsarea, 136-137, 145, 150, 307, 411
Cæsarion, 116, 125, 127-128
Cæsarius of Arles, St., 192
Cairo, 250, 276, 345-348, 362, 381-382, 410-411
Calabria, 215, 284, 327, 469
Calais, 444, 449, 544-545
calculus, 558, 629-632, 643a
calendar, 10-12, 119-120, 243-246; Athenian calendar, 48, 65; the British Calendar, 569; Celtic calendar, 243; Egyptian calendar, 12; the Gregorian Calendar, 530, 566-567, 569, 572, the Julian Calendar, 120-121, 132, 189, 246, 406, 567-568, 641; Seleucid calendar, 91
calendar reform, 120-121, 132, 406, 530, 566-569, 572, 579
Caligula, 140-141
Calixtus I, St., pope, 177-178; Calixtus II, 309; Calixtus III, 449, 453-454, 464
Calvin, John, 190, 510-511, 515-516, 526, 533; Calvinism, Calvinists, 510-512, 514-515, 531, 536, 546, 555, 599-600, 602-603, 614, 637
Cambrai, 444; the League of Cambrai, 482; the Treaty of Cambrai, 504-505, 528
Campanile of St. Mark, the, 455, 583
Campeggio, Lorenzo, 500
Canaan, the Canaanites, 2, 93, 244, 614
Canada, 564, 613, 647
candles, 227, 252, 275, 401, 693
Cannæ, the Battle of, 280
cannibalism, 2
Canossa, 300, 722
Canterbury, 241, 340, 401; Canterbury Cathedral, 340, 501; the see of Canterbury, 241, 288, 305, 339, 376, 429, 500
Capetian dynasty, the, 357, 372, 433
capitalism, 511-512, 542, 548, 564, 657-658, 666, 694-695, 697, 703, 729
Capitol, the Roman, 121, 335, 438; the U.S. Capitol, 650
capitulations, the, 506
Cappadocia, 90, 223
Capua, 114, 284-285, 288, 305, 327-328, 337
Caracalla, 173, 176

caravans, 13, 94, 135, 248, 252, 278, 348-349, 537
Caribbean Sea, the, 576, 611
Carinthia, 299, 519
Carlsbad Decrees, the, 682
Carlyle, Thomas, 701, 704
Carolingian minuscule, the, 267
Carpentras, 430-431
Carpzov, Benedict, 517
Carrhæ, the Battle of, 112
Carroll, Lewis, 598
Carthage, the Carthaginians, 54, 60-61, 100a, 117, 218, 225, 412
cartography, see map-making
Cartwright, Ebenezer and Johanna, 612
Cathars, the, 314-316, 367-372, 374, 395; origin of the term, 314
Cattanei, Vanozza dei, 464
Cashel, the Council of, 341
Casimir IV, king of Poland, 647
Caspian Sea, the, 86
Cassiodorus, 229, 231
Cassius, Roman general, 121-125
Castelnau, Pierre de, 369-371
Castel Sant' Angelo, 158, 239a, 286, 301, 305, 421, 439, 465, 470, 477, 497-498
Castile, 377, 419, 467, 479, 484, 496
castle-building, 252, 276, 293, 341, 383, 413, 424, 563, 641, 726, 729
Castlereagh, 2nd viscount, 678
catacombs, 154, 159
Câteau-Cambrésis, the Treaty of, 545
cathedral schools, 256, 268, 314, 400, 403, 502; the Cathedral School of Paris, 316
Catherine of Alexandria, St., 445; St. Catherine of Siena, 438
Catherine the Great, empress of Russia, 650
Catholicism, Catholics, 162, 165, 170-171, 177, 189, 194, 209-210, 217-218, 221, 229, 231-233, 237, 239-243, 245, 254, 258-259, 262, 264-267, 269-271, 274, 280, 283-285, 288-289, 296, 298-300, 305, 309, 313-316, 319-322, 323, 329-330, 334-335, 338, 340-341, 343, 353, 358-359, 361, 363, 366, 368-370, 372-379, 386-388, 390, 394-398, 402-403, 408-409, 411, 414, 419-420, 423-424, 428, 431, 437-438, 440-442, 448-449, 451, 453, 455, 460-461, 463-464, 466-468, 472, 475, 481, 484, 487, 489-493, 496-497, 499, 501-503, 505-514, 516-519, 521a, 524-525, 527-529, 532-533,

770

535-537, 540-543, 546-550, 553, 555-556, 560, 564-566, 569, 572a, 574-575, 578, 580-581, 584-588, 590, 600-603, 606, 609, 611, 617, 627, 635, 642-646, 649, 651-652, 655, 678-679, 683, 688, 696-697, 705-706, 712, 716, 722
Catholic League, the, 528, 560, 600-601
Cato, Marcus Porcius, 103, 109, 116-117, 124, 669; Publius Valerius, 101
cattle-breeding, 1, 14, 16, 23, 41, 203, 589
Catullus, Gaius Valerius, 100-104
cavaliers, the, 609-610
Cecil, William, 1st baron of Burghley, 566
Cecrops, 25, 34, 686
celestial mechanics, 629
Celestine II, pope, 331; Celestine III, 354, 358-359; St. Celestine V, 420-421, 423
celibacy, 262-263, 298, 316, 350a, 502-503, 516, 606, 655
Celsus, the 1st-century physician, 518; the 2nd-century philosopher, 161-162, 167, 171
Celtis, Conradus, 486-487
Celts, the, 19, 101-102, 109, 111-112, 152, 213a, 214, 230, 243, 269, 312, 341, 445, 570; the Celtic Church, 230, 240a, 241-242, 292a, 341
censorship, 133, 177, 182, 193, 206-207, 210, 219, 238, 318, 437a, 462, 510, 522, 525, 546, 572, 575-576, 580, 584, 591, 593-594, 596, 601, 634, 643-644, 649, 676, 678, 682
Centaurs, the, 24, 48
Cesena, the massacre of, 439
Chæronea, the Battle of, 82, 84
Chalcedon, 187, 196, 364; the Council of Chalcedon, 221-222; non-Chalcedonian Churches, 222, 248a, 250
Châlons, the Battle of, 224
Chamberlain, Houston Stewart, 701
Chambord, the Treaty of, 535
Chancellor, Richard, 552
Channel Islands, the, 289, 376
chansons de geste, the, 312, 380
Chanukah, 189a
charity, 154, 216, 229, 249, 339, 452, 476, 495, 617; the Roman alimenta, 152-153; alms, 259, 372, 425, 427, 658, 730
Charlemagne, 254-262, 264-270, 274, 292, 312, 342, 381, 386, 451
Charles of Anjou, 391-392,

405, 409, 412, 414-415
Charles Augustus, 661
Charles the Bald, 267-268
Charles IV, king of Bohemia, 441
Charles de Bourbon, 497
Charles I, king of England, 590, 607-610; Charles II, 613, 616, 618, 621, 627
Charles VI, king of France, 443-444; Charles VII, 444-447; Charles VIII, 469-471, 474, 481; Charles IX, 560; Charles X, 692
Charles V, German emperor, 486, 488-490, 496-498, 500, 503-506, 528, 534-535, 540, 542-543
Charles Martel, 253-254; the Carolingians, 254, 257-258, 268-269, 457
Charles the Simple, 270
Charles III, king of Spain, 647
Charles Theodore, elector of Bavaria, 653
Charlotte d'Albret, 474
Charlotte of Aragón, 472
chemistry, 9, 92, 277, 394, 404-405, 521-522, 580, 598, 619-620, 624-625, 630
chess, 314
Childebert I, king of Paris, 233-234
Childeric III, king of the Franks, 254
children, 11, 34, 38-40, 43, 48-49, 100, 122, 154, 170-171, 247, 251, 264-265, 274-275, 295, 314, 350, 368, 374, 452, 502-503, 510, 606-607, 631, 654-657, 674-675, 683, 699; child labour, 664, 694; massacre of children, see infanticide
China, the Chinese, 19, 21, 91, 94, 181, 203, 277, 345, 409-410, 454, 466, 537, 552, 687, 693, 710
Chinon, 445
Chioggia, the Battle of, 443
chivalry, 273-274, 279, 293, 303, 311-312, 316-317, 319-322, 324, 370, 380, 384, 392, 424, 450-451, 457, 492, 494, 503, 573, 588, 623-624, 631, 658, 716, 728; origin of the term, 273; chivalric romances, 84, 133, 312, 380, 450, 673; knightly honour, 279-280, 348, 354, 356, 409, 430, 450-451
Chlodomer, 233
chorus, 43-44, 65, 67, 408, 585, 709-710, 726
Christ, 133, 159-160, 164-165, 167, 169, 172a, 174, 177, 181, 183, 189-190, 193-194, 196, 207-208, 232, 242, 245-247, 263, 277, 298, 318, 320, 329, 368, 372, 374, 385, 427, 429,

431, 435, 466, 493, 517, 567, 594, 596, 607, 686, 704, 727, 732; Christology, 191, 198, 219-221; the Vicar of Christ, 298, 373, 420, 547, 604
Christendom, 181, 252, 259, 267, 285, 287-289, 297, 313, 351, 356, 361a, 365-367, 370, 384, 387, 394-396, 407, 412, 417, 422-423, 426, 435, 439, 441, 451, 454, 456, 462, 476-477, 488-489, 500, 505-506, 527, 539-540, 562, 591, 603, 617
Christianity, Christians, 8, 52, 78, 88, 98-99, 134, 137, 142-146, 148, 152-156, 158-737
Christmas, 189-190, 259-260, 292, 304, 327, 615-616, 695
Church Fathers, the, 68, 166, 174-175, 190, 202, 228, 274, 318, 397, 400, 705
Churchill, John, 1st duke of Malborough, 638
Cibalis, the Battle of, 187
Cicero, 35, 79-80, 101, 109, 114, 117, 121-122, 124, 184, 201, 257, 436, 461
Cilicia, 106, 125, 352, 411
Cinna, Gaius Helvius, 102; Lucius Cornelius, 106
Ciompi Revolt, the, 443
ciphers, 565-566, 573a, 574, 598; origin of the term, 399
circle, perfect, 50, 156, 581-583
circumcision, 143, 157, 671a
Citadel of Cairo, the, 347; the Citadel of Jerusalem, see the Tower of David
Cîteaux, 319, 371; the Cistercians, 319-321, 366, 369
civil service, 121, 127, 227, 237, 251, 277, 379, 402, 492, 640, 677, 683, 729
civil war, 148, 279, 295, 327, 339, 441-443, 492, 502, 599, 691, the American Civil War, 698; the English, 609-610, 618, 625; the First Roman, 105-106, 108, 113; the Second Roman, 113-118, 120; the Third Roman, 122, 124, 131
Civitella, 284, 328
Clarke, Samuel, 632
class division, 7, 49, 54-56, 71, 75-76, 79, 96-97, 123, 136, 147, 159, 227, 257, 272-273, 277, 279, 311, 314, 321, 387, 392, 400, 419, 424, 450, 457-459, 463, 468, 491, 494-496, 510-511, 517, 520, 536, 542-543, 550-551, 591, 604, 608-610, 626-628, 656-657, 660, 664-666, 668, 672-675, 681, 692-697,

771

699, 702-703, 730-731, 736
Classicism, 438, 460-462, 472, 480-481, 484, 525, 624-626, 634, 659, 662-663, 669-670, 718; French Classicism, 625-626
Claudius, Roman emperor, 141, 152; St. Claudius, 233-234
Clausewitz, Karl von, 645
Clearchus of Soli, 34
Cleisthenes, 55-56
Clement of Alexandria, 163-165, 172a
Clement III, antipope, 301-302, 308; Clement VII, 439-440
Clement the Irishman, 257
Clement III, pope, 351, 353; Clement IV, 404, 406; Clement V, 423, 425-428, 430-431; Clement VII, 496-498, 500-501, 504-507; Clement XII, 644; Clement XIII, 650; Clement XIV, 650
Cleopatra, 115-116, 125-128, 132a
clergy, Christian, 154-155, 163, 175, 177, 185, 194-195, 200, 208, 228-230, 234, 238, 240, 258, 261-265, 271, 273, 275, 283, 285, 298, 303-304, 309, 314-316, 323, 329-331, 333, 339-340, 368, 372, 374-377, 388, 402-403, 414, 418, 422, 424-425, 430, 434, 436, 440-441, 445, 482, 485, 490-492, 495, 502, 508a, 509-510, 514, 516, 546-548, 568a, 578, 603, 626, 630, 644, 651-652, 668, 677, 683-684, 704, 713, 722-723, 727-729; origin of the term, 273
Clermont, the Council of, 303
Clodia Metelli, 101-102
Clodius Pulcher, 101, 112, 117
Clonmacnoise, 230
Clothar I, king of the Franks, 233-234, 241
Clotilda, St., 232-234
Clovis, 232-233, 292, 447
Cluny, 283, 298, 309, 330
Codrus, 71
coffee, 468, 657, 676, 699; coffee-houses, 618, 634
Cognac, the League of, 496-497
coinage, coins, currency, 56, 85, 94, 129, 149-150, 157, 189, 278, 305, 422, 494, 538, 618a; gold coins, 191, 297, 419, 425, 447, 573, 729; silver coins, 339, 356
Coleridge, Samuel Taylor, 701
college, origin of the term, 117; the College of Cardinals, 285, 289, 296, 309, 311, 327, 335, 338, 343-344, 390, 419-421, 423, 428, 431, 438-441, 464, 469-470, 472, 478, 482, 547, 584, 586

Collins, Anthony, 635
Cologne, 286, 304, 309, 359, 387
colonialism, colonization, 36-37, 56-58, 71, 82, 117-118, 158, 160, 173, 196, 230, 252, 312, 362, 383, 407, 417-418, 513, 525, 538, 548, 563-565, 568, 574-578, 608, 613-616, 621, 636, 638, 647, 649, 657-658, 676, 678, 689-694, 697, 699, 701
Colonna family, the, 438, 465, 476
Colosseum, the, 151
Columba of Iona, St., 230, 240-241
Columbanus of Bobbio, St., 240
Columbus, Christopher, 466, 471
columns, 47a, 63-64, 669; colonnades, 64-65
comedies, 616, 625-626, 661; Greek comedy, 66-67
comets, 123, 134, 288, 559-561
Commons, the House of, 588, 609
Commune of Paris, the, 668
communion, Christian, 159-160, 172a, 208, 270, 284a, 368, 374, 493-494, 505, 514, 548, 608a, 642; pagan, 46-47, 98, 244
Communism, 685, 695-696
Comneni dynasty, the, 301, 334, 365, 367, 408
compass, the, 459; magnetic compass, 399, 466, 552; paradoxal compass, 552
Compiègne, 357, 447
composition, 43, 102, 176, 648, 708-709, 711, 714, 718, 726-727
conciliarism, 441-442
concordant scale, the, 51
concrete, Roman, 136, 146-147
concubinage, 160, 265-266, 298, 360, 464a
condottieri, the, 458
conducting, 708, 710, 721, 726
conformity, 193, 514, 546, 556, 608, 610, 615, 627, 683, 697, 731, 735
Conon the Mythographer, 45
Conquistadores, the, 466, 575
Conrad II, German emperor, 283; Conrad III, king of Germany, 326-327, 333-336; Conrad IV, 390
Conradin of Swabia, 390-391, 412, 415
conscription, 143, 667, 676, 680, 714, 737
Constance, 331, 441, 493; the Council of Constance, 441-442; the Peace of Constance, 343; the Treaty of Constance, 336, 383
Constans, Flavius Julius, 200-201, 203
Constantia, Flavia Julia, 184,

187, 199
Constantine VIII, Byzantine emperor, 281; Constantine XI, 452-453
Constantine the Great, Roman emperor, 182-193, 195-201, 226-227, 267, 316, 420, 479-480; Constantine II, 200-201
Constantinople, 119, 196-197, 200, 205, 212, 214, 225, 227-228, 238, 252-253, 267, 277-278, 281-282, 284, 302, 304-305, 320, 333, 352, 358, 363-367, 407-409, 412, 414-415, 451-453, 467, 470, 537, 539, 579; the First Council of Constantinople, 206; the see of Constantinople, 198, 200, 206, 208, 219-222, 238, 240, 259-260, 267, 278, 284, 348
Constantius Chlorus, 182; Constantius II, 200-201; Constantius III, 223, 226
constitution, Athenian, 57, 71; French, 693; German, 536, 716; Italian, 386, 678, 706; Roman, 106, 114, 129; Spanish, 679; the U.S. Constitution, 610, 628, 650, 666-667
constitutionalism, constitutional law, 173, 377, 473, 568, 610, 627-628, 643
consubstantiation, 493-494
Consuls, Roman, 102, 105, 107-116, 120, 122-125, 224, 233, 235
Contarini, Gasparo, 527-528
convents, see nunneries
conversi, the, 320
Cook, James, 657
Copernicus, Nicolaus, 530-531, 533, 566-567, 581, 583, 586-587, 629, 682; the Copernican system, 530-531, 559-560, 580, 584-587
Copts, the Coptic Church, 248a, 251, 346; Coptic language, 5, 165, 251
Córdoba, 275-7, 379, 479
Corfu, 302, 364
Corinth, 70, 77, 82-83, 117, 159; the Isthmus of Corinth, 144
corn, 1, 3, 4a, 5, 28, 30, 37-40, 47-49, 115, 136, 153, 215, 238, 252, 320, 381, 412, 494, 699; deities of corn, 28, 30, 37-38
cornucopia, 39
Cornwall, 269, 390
Cortenuova, the Battle of, 388
Cortes of Spain, the, 678
cosmopolitism, 88, 90, 93, 96, 98, 137-138, 143, 159, 326, 682
Cotta, 105-106
cottage industry, 672
cotton, 331, 537, 578, 676

772

Council of Troubles, the, 554
Counter-Reformation, the, 378, 517, 525, 528, 533, 543, 546, 549, 575, 580
Courland, 503
courtly love, 102, 135, 313, 316-317, 370, 380, 451, 455
Cracow, the Treaty of, 503
craftsmen, 19-20, 35, 42a, 56, 63, 71, 75, 175, 253, 272, 290, 303, 320, 323, 394, 418, 456, 459, 479, 491, 519-520, 536, 602, 604, 608, 656, 659, 697, 729
Craig, John, 560
Cranmer, Thomas, 500, 513
Crassus, 107-109, 111-112, 120
creation, the, 263, 366, 481, 641, 734; deities of creation, 12-13, 16-17, 32, 42, 138, 164, 247; myths of creation, 31, 180; the date of creation, 688, 690
creativity, 3, 13, 24, 36, 62, 251, 311, 456-457, 461, 635, 659, 663, 722, 724, 728, 731, 735
Crécy, the Battle of, 433
creeds, Christian, 191, 208, 220; the Antiochene Creed, 191-192; the Athanasian Creed, 192; the Firmiter, 374; the Nicene Creed, 205-206, 259; the Tridentine Creed, 547, 584
cremation, 242-243
Cremona, 482-483
Crépy, the Treaty of, 528
Crete, the Cretans, 19-23, 25, 28, 30, 36, 53, 278, 302, 367, 454, 686; Cretan language, 19, 22, 28
Crispus, Flavius Julius, 187, 199
Critias, 71-72
Crœsus, 56-57
Cromwell, Oliver, 609-616, 619; Richard, 616; Sir Thomas, 507-513, 514a
Croton, 49, 52
crucifixion, 106, 174, 181, 704
crusades, crusaders, 284a, 286, 289, 295, 303, 308-309, 312-314, 321, 324, 331-332, 344-351, 358, 374, 381-385, 387, 389-390, 394, 396, 408-418, 423-425, 431-433, 441, 450, 453-455, 466, 471, 482, 488, 503, 506, 532, 574-575, 696; crusading vows, 305, 308, 361, 381, 384, 389-390, 412, 414, 453; the First Crusade, 303-308, 312, 320, 332, 348, 367, 407; the Second, 333-336; the Third, 351-356, 407; the Fourth, 361-367, 408; the Fifth, 381-382; the Sixth, 384-385, 387; the Seventh, 389, 409; the Eighth, 412-414
cryptology, 565-6, 573a, 574

Ctesiphon, 180, 220
Cumans, the, 302
Cunimund, 236
Curia Romana, the, 337, 430-431, 441, 474, 476, 477, 525, 532, 722
Cusanus, Nicolaus, 530
Custine, Astolphe de, 642
customs regulations, 310, 494, 538, 713
Custozza, the Battle of, 712
Cybelê, 26, 99-100
Cyclops, the, 32
Cynegius, Maternus, 206
Cynicism, Cynics, 87-88, 94, 169
Cyprus, the Cypriots, 30, 70, 96, 155, 302, 307, 353-355, 388, 407, 411-412, 414-416, 425, 427, 482
Cyrene, 155
Cyril of Alexandria, St., 218-220; St. Cyril of Jerusalem, 172, 210
Cyrus, patriarch of Alexandria, 250
Cyrus the Great, king of Persia, 54, 56-57, 61, 142
Czars, the, 297, 367, 377-378, 552, 640-641, 668, 677; origin of the term, 297
Czechs, the, see the Bohemians; Czechoslovakia, 601

Dædalus, 20
Dalmatia, 363, 388, 482
Damascus, 251, 332, 334-335, 345, 347-348, 356, 367, 407, 410-412
Damasus I, St., pope, 209
Damietta, 346, 362, 381-382
dance, 38, 44, 65, 67, 313-314, 331, 384, 510, 614, 718
Dandolo, Enrico, 363-366
Danelaw, the, 290
Daniel, the Book of, 142, 149, 612, 633
Dante Alighieri, 356, 380, 397, 421, 546, 562, 727
Danube, the river, 151, 203, 227; the Danube Valley, 19, 184, 203, 304, 352
Dardanelles, the, see the Hellespont
Darius the Great, 57-59, 61; Darius III, 84-85
Darwin, Charles, 699-701, 731
Datini, Francesco di Marco, 457
Davenant, Sir William, 625-626
David, king of Israel, 171-172, 179, 251, 410, 562; the Renaissance statues of David, 459, 480; the Tower of David, 308
Davis, John, 564
dead, cult of the, 26-27, 30, 55, 123, 161; deities of the dead, 7-8, 27, festivals of the dead, 243; realm of the dead, 4, 8, 27, 245-246; the Egyptian Book of the Dead, 7, 9
death, 4, 6-8, 26, 42, 46, 66, 96, 98, 116-117, 123-124,

128a, 144, 149, 161, 167-169, 242-246, 280, 322, 325, 337, 369, 392, 402, 430, 435, 437, 449, 509, 512, 514a, 518, 599, 607, 655-656, 659, 664, 672, 686, 704, 722-723, 732-733, 735; death sentence, 15, 54, 70, 72, 82-3, 90, 125-127, 146, 158, 180-182, 184-7, 199, 201, 206-207, 213, 218, 243, 275, 332, 337, 355, 379a, 391, 395, 402, 426, 428-431, 435-437, 441, 446, 448, 465, 472, 495, 500a, 502, 508, 510-511, 514, 517, 525, 541-542, 553-554, 556, 574, 589, 591, 596, 609-610, 615, 668, 679
Declaration of Independence, the, 610, 650, 666
Declaration of the Rights of Man, the, 665-666
deduction, 50, 78, 396-399, 404, 587
Dee, John, 548, 550-552, 556-574, 578-579, 619
Defensor Fidei, origin of the title, 409
deicide, 304, 435
Deir el-Bahri, 17
deism, 617, 634, 643, 645
Delian League, the, 62, 69-71
della Rovere, Giuliano, see Julius II
Delphi, 42, 79, 197; the oracle of Delphi, 33, 49, 197
deluge, 9, 315a, 481, 686, 690, 700
Demeter, 29-33, 37-39, 48, 50
Demetrius of Phaleron, 93
democracy, 55-56, 58-59, 62, 69-72, 77, 79, 87a, 90, 335, 362, 443, 628, 643, 685, 692, 730-731, 737
demons, demonology, 63, 174, 340, 436-437, 448, 488, 516, 522, 557, 591, 655
Demophilus of Constantinople, 205
Demosthenes, 79, 669
Denis of Paris, St., 317
Denmark, the Danes, 270, 287, 290, 293, 337, 357, 360, 559, 580, 591, 601-602, 695, 711-712
Descartes, René, 546, 558, 635, 643a
Desiderata of Lombardy, 264-265
Desiderius, king of the Lombards, 254, 264
despotism, 14-15, 49, 55-58, 59-60, 62, 71-72, 75, 77, 121, 124, 127, 310, 453, 473, 475, 597, 606, 610, 627, 641, 649, 651, 737
Devereux, Robert, 2nd earl of Essex, 588-589
Devil, the, 395, 427, 435-437, 512, 516-518, 585
Diadochi, the, 90

773

Dickens, Charles, 695
Dictator, Roman, 106, 114, 116
Diderot, Denis, 643-644
diets, federal, 677, 712;
  German, 275, 286, 299-300, 336, 375; imperial, 337-338, 375, 387, 490, 495, 504-505, 535-536
Digges, Thomas, 560
Dio Cassius, 158
diocesis, origin of the term, 194
Diocletian, 178, 181-182, 184a, 185-186, 195, 227, 722
Diodorus Siculus, 45
Dion, 76-77
Dionysius the Areopagite, St., 317; Pseudo-Dionysius, 268
Dionysius the Elder, tyrant of Syracuse, 76; Dionysius the Younger, 76-77
Dionysos, 37-48, 55, 63a, 65-67, 160, 172a, 190, 207, 718, 720, 733; the festivals of Dionysos, 55, 65-66; the Theatre of Dionysos, 55, 65-66
Dioscurus of Alexandria, 220-221
diplomacy, diplomats, 224, 260, 276, 326, 373, 442, 456, 463, 473, 475, 482, 526-527, 529, 543, 566, 604-605, 640, 647, 706, 711
dismemberment, 38, 42, 44-46, 178, 207, 369, 507
dithyramb, the, 66-67
divine right of kings, 17, 299, 366a, 422, 493, 562, 591, 626, 649, 713
divine services, Christian, 154, 165-166, 174-175, 184, 195, 252-253, 278, 316, 424, 475, 502, 556, 607-608, 615, 644, 728; pagan, 4, 27, 30, 35, 38-39, 42, 44, 46-48, 55, 66, 84, 100, 138, 140, 143-144, 165, 174-175, 183, 190, 201-203, 247
divorce, 106-108, 126-127, 173, 203-206, 452, 499, 607, 672
Doge of Venice, the, 253, 362-366, 482, 527, 583
dogma, Christian, 49, 160-164, 171, 180, 191-2, 198, 205-206, 216-217, 220, 232, 238, 250, 259, 317, 369, 372, 374, 386, 396, 398, 403, 418, 431, 436-437, 441, 448, 468, 489-490, 492, 502, 505, 511-512, 514-515, 517, 525, 527, 532, 535, 537, 542, 546, 559, 585, 592, 595, 598a, 600, 617, 630, 635-636, 644, 656, 686-687, 701, 705, 725
Domesday Book, the, 293-294
Dominic of Guzman, St., 369, 372-373; the Dominicans, 372, 386-387, 395-396, 403, 436, 462, 487, 586

Domitian, 151-153
Domrémy, 445
Donatello, 459
Donation of Constantine, the, 267, 492
Donatus, bishop of Carthage, 185; Donatism, Donatists, 185, 191, 217-218
Donatus, St., bishop of Fiesole, 258
Donna Sancia of Aragón, 469
Dorian migration, the, 22-23
Dorylæum, the Battle of, 334
Draco, 54, 668
Drake, Sir Francis, 552, 563-564
dramas, 119, 134, 380, 477, 594, 625, 660, 663, 708, 710, 728; Greek drama, 43-44, 62, 65-67, 663
Dresden, 677, 709-710; the Dresden Theatre, 710
Druids, the, 110, 171, 230, 240
Dryden, John, 622, 627-628
dualism, 75, 89, 180, 663
Dublin, 269, 341, 541, 611
Dubois, Pierre, 421
Ducas dynasty, the, 295, 365, 367
Dudley, Robert, 1st earl of Leicester, 574
Dugdale, Sir William, 624
duke, origin of the term, 235
Dunois, Jean, 446
Dying-God, the, 8, 28, 46, 98, 123, 167, 169, 245, 732
dynamics, 582, 629

eagles, 123, 196, 452-453
Earth, the planet, 1-2, 10-12, 16, 51, 75, 156, 530-531, 552, 559, 580-581, 583-584, 586, 629, 684, 700; Chthonian divinities, 6, 26-33, 39, 46-47, 246; the terrestrial day, 10, 12, 567
East, the, see Asia; the Roman East, 99, 108-109, 112, 114, 118-119, 124-127, 137, 155, 164-165, 182, 186-187, 189, 191-192, 195, 203-204, 206, 208, 210-212, 219-220, 223, 226, 228
Easter, 168-169, 244-246, 292, 374, 388, 406, 415, 567, 616, 728; Easter Sunday, 245, 301, 493a, 567, 584
East Indies, the, 576a, 647; the Dutch East India Company, 577, 613; the English East India Company, 577
Ebro, the river, 255
Ecclesiastes of Solomon, the, 169, 531
Eck, Johann Maier von, 516, 527
economics, 15-17, 20-21, 36, 49, 53-55, 58, 62, 93-94, 119, 127-130, 150, 176, 188, 196, 227, 271-272, 280, 319-320, 323, 325, 347, 370, 392, 418-419,

422, 433-434, 438, 455, 463, 467-468, 486, 492, 494, 502-503, 511, 524, 538, 547-548, 555, 575-579, 603, 608, 613, 633, 639-640, 654, 655-669, 672, 677, 685, 691-696, 700-701, 717-718
ecstasy, religious, 42, 44, 718
ecumenical councils, 192, 205-206, 219, 258, 343, 374, 389, 428, 706
Edessa, 155, 175-176, 220, 306, 308, 332, 334
Edgar Ætheling, 291, 292a
Edmund of Lancaster, 390
Edom, see Idumæa
education, 49, 65, 72, 74-78, 80-82, 95-96, 102, 131, 145, 152a, 159, 161, 163, 172-175, 179, 201-202, 207, 229, 231, 256-258, 268-271, 273-275, 277, 314, 319, 379, 395, 398, 400, 402-404, 409, 411, 456, 486, 502, 513, 519-520, 523, 526-527, 531, 533, 547, 550, 556-557, 580, 601, 605, 627, 630, 637, 641, 644, 647-650, 654, 656-657, 670, 673, 678-679, 683, 685, 694-695, 697, 699, 704, 706, 708, 714, 722, 736
Edward the Confessor, 282-283, 287-288
Edward I, king of England, 412, 424; Edward II, 426-428; Edward III, 433; Edward VI, 501, 541, 548, 551
egalitarianism, 69, 96-98, 265, 279, 339, 650, 668, 694, 731
Egica, king of Spain, 251
Egypt, 1-2, 25, 32, 37, 47, 59, 70, 77, 83-86, 89-94, 109, 114-116, 125, 127-128, 136-137, 140, 142, 148, 153, 156, 160, 165-166, 175-176, 180, 186, 189, 191-192, 195, 198, 206, 211, 219, 222, 243-244, 247, 248a, 249-252, 263, 307, 331, 345-347, 361-363, 379, 381-382, 384-386, 389, 407, 409-411, 413, 415-416, 467, 537, 581, 670-671, 686, 688; Upper Egypt, 8; the Old Kingdom, 5, 8-9, 15-16; the Middle Kingdom, 7, 9, 16; the New Kingdom, 16-17
Einhard, 257, 260-261
Ekklesia, see the Athenian Assembly
Elba, 477, 676, 678
Elbe, the river, 255, 261, 274, 333a, 602
Eleanor of Aquitaine, 333-335
Eleanor of Austria, 496
Eleazar ben Yair, 150
electoral princes, the, 279, 325-327, 393, 488, 535, 604,

774

681; imperial elections, 310, 326, 337, 359, 375, 488, 505, 676
Eleusis, the Eleusians, 29-30, 33, 36, 48, 212; the Eleusian mysteries, 29, 47-49; the Eleusinion, at Athens, 48, 56
Elgin, 7th earl of, 670
elixir of life, the, 599
Elizabeth I, queen of England, 500, 548-551, 555-556, 560-569, 571, 573-574, 579, 588-590; Elizabeth II, 681
Elizabeth, empress of Russia, 646
Elizabeth of Valois, 545
Elkesai, the Elkesaites, 180
Emmanuel Philibert, 545
Empedocles, 49, 718
emperor, origin of the term, 129
empiricism, 68, 75, 399, 404, 592-593, 702
encyclopedists, the, 643-644
endogamy, 264
End Times, the, see eschatology
Engels, Friedrich, 695-696
engineering, engineers, 136, 405, 459-460, 477, 675, 693, 697, 703
England, the English, 110, 189, 230, 241-242, 252, 257, 269, 282-283, 287-294, 299, 303, 314, 319, 322, 335, 338-343, 347, 351-353, 355-357, 360-361, 376-377, 387, 390, 402-403, 412, 414, 419, 422, 424, 426-428, 433, 439, 441, 444-450, 453, 471, 483, 488, 497, 499-502, 506-508, 510-514, 526, 528, 538, 540-542, 544, 547-553, 555-556, 558-571, 573-574, 576-579, 583, 587-596, 598, 600, 602, 607-616, 618-628, 630, 634, 637-638, 640-643, 646, 648, 653a, 654, 656, 658-659, 666, 673, 675-676, 678, 681, 692-697, 701-702, 712; English language, 155, 269, 292a, 294, 341a, 357, 558, 561, 593-596, 598, 619, 622, 624, 626; the Church of England, see the Anglican Church
English Channel, the, 282, 287, 289, 376, 563, 654
English Republic, the, 610
enlightened despotism, 76, 90, 562, 645
Enlightenment, the, 573, 596-597, 633-634, 642-644, 647-649, 651, 653-654, 656, 659, 666-667, 677, 683, 686, 701
Enneads, the, 179
Enoch, 315a, 573
entertainment, 95-96, 125, 131, 140, 144, 178, 395, 462,

476, 484, 510, 729
Enzio of Sardinia, 388
Eostre, 245-246
Ephesus, 151, 175; the First Council of Ephesus, 219-220; the Second Council of Ephesus, 220-221
Ephræm Syrus, St., 176
epics, epic literature, 23, 43, 103, 133, 312, 380
Epicurus of Sámos, 95-96, 98, 101; Epicureanism, Epicureans, 95-98, 101, 734
Epirus, 128, 367
episcopacy, the, 154-155, 174-175, 177, 194-195, 208, 218, 229, 292, 298-299, 310, 329-330, 373, 421-422, 431, 439-440, 495, 542, 547, 568; origin of the term, 194; the ecumenical episcopacy, 221, 239-240; the episcopal symbols, 194
episcopal courts, 195, 339, 386, 424, 502
Epte, the river, 270
Erasmus, Desiderius, 492, 522, 533, 635
Ernest II, duke of Saxe-Gotha, 653, 680
eschatology, 4, 142, 159, 169-171, 210, 237, 239, 242, 462, 562, 633, 704, 732
Eschenbach, Wolfram von, 380
espionage, 566, 573-574, 682
Esquiline Hill, the, 131
Essex, 550
Estates-General of France, the, 429; the Estates-General of the Netherlands, 574
Este dynasty, the, 476; Alfonso d'Este, 476-477; Beatrice, 459; Ercole, 476; Ippolito, 476
Estienne, Robert, 596
eternal recurrence, the, 725
ethics, 50-52, 74-76, 78, 81, 87, 94, 96, 97a, 98, 164, 173, 217, 228a, 262, 266, 315, 323, 330, 368, 395, 472-474, 492, 499, 513, 588, 616, 635, 648, 651, 657-661, 666-667, 670, 685, 694, 697, 699, 702, 704-705, 718, 722-725, 730-733, 735; the Protestant work ethic, 511
Ethiopia, see Abyssinia
etiquette, 15, 45, 90, 161, 212, 256, 276, 314, 605, 637, 641, 654
Eton College, 571, 703
Etruscans, the, 54, 125, 207
eucharist, see communion
Euclid of Alexandria, 551-552, 556, 558
Eudoxia, Licinia, 225
Eugene III, Blessed, pope, 331, 333, 335-336; Eugene IV, 442-443
Eumenes of Cardia, 90
Eumolpus, 48
Euphrates, the river, 85, 91,

99, 109, 155, 176, 227, 250, 331
Euripides, 41, 66-67, 78
Eurocentrism, 689
Europe, 19-20, 31, 43, 57, 59, 79-80, 93, 101, 112, 129, 138, 181, 196, 201, 218, 227, 231, 246-247, 253, 256, 260, 265, 272, 274-279, 293, 297, 301, 303-304, 307-308, 312, 316, 319-320, 322, 324-325, 327, 329, 331, 335, 351, 356, 367, 377, 379-383, 385, 388-389, 392-393, 398-400, 408, 413, 415, 418-419, 421-422, 424-425, 429, 434-436, 443, 457, 459, 463, 466-468, 471, 473, 482, 485, 487-489, 496, 502, 506, 509-511, 515, 517-518, 520, 523-525, 527, 534, 537-540, 542, 543a, 544-545, 547-548, 550, 553-555, 559-561, 564, 569, 572, 575-576, 584, 597, 599-601, 603, 606, 610, 612, 614, 617, 620, 634, 636-644, 646-648, 651-652, 653a, 654-659, 661, 664, 667-668, 670, 672, 674-679, 681a, 683, 687-690, 692-693, 696-698, 702, 710, 715, 717, 719-720, 723, 736-737; continental Europe, 19, 79, 211, 229, 231, 240, 258, 268, 270, 280, 293, 312, 324, 338-339, 340, 387, 419, 449, 500, 514, 542, 544, 547, 549-551, 553, 560, 570-571, 599, 602, 612, 621, 637, 642-643, 650, 656, 675-676, 680, 693, 702; Central Europe, 153, 325, 362, 383, 386, 396, 441, 486, 496, 509, 545, 547, 569, 572, 602, 640, 646-647, 656, 715; Eastern Europe, 278, 383, 396, 453, 614, 640, 646-647; Northern Europe, 243, 258, 261, 269, 273, 276, 278, 325, 371, 433, 456, 506, 509, 540a, 545, 548, 575, 579, 603, 640, 699; Southern Europe, 40, 153, 244, 280, 284, 342, 386, 392, 396a, 603, 640, 696; Western Europe, 3, 16, 43, 65, 72a, 78, 97, 99, 118, 178, 227-230, 237, 256, 258-261, 269, 271-272, 276-277, 296, 301, 312-314, 325, 338, 361, 366-367, 386, 391-392, 394, 396, 398, 400, 402, 417, 419, 424, 431, 434-435, 444, 453-455, 461-463, 468, 478, 486, 497, 503, 506, 523-524, 536-540, 579, 592, 595, 611, 623-

624, 636-637, 640-641, 643, 646, 666, 669, 679, 683, 686-687, 690-692, 699, 701
Eurydice, 46, 134
Eusebius, bishop of Cæsarea, 165a, 183, 184a, 190-193, 199; bishop of Nicomedia, 192
Eutyches, Eutychianism, 220-221
Eutychius of Constantinople, 238
Evangelical League, the, see the Protestant Union
Evans, Sir Arthur, 20, 688
Evelyn, John, 622, 625
evil, 8-9, 75, 97, 154, 162, 215, 302a, 322, 368, 387, 398, 498, 512, 515, 517, 635, 654, 656, 663, 665, 700, 707, 722-723, 727-731, 735; evil spirits, see demons
evil eye, the, 263
evolution, natural, 101, 662, 699-701, 724, 732-733; socio-cultural, 4, 13, 33, 89, 91, 93, 100, 118, 208, 218, 263, 311-312, 325, 402, 436, 454, 604, 642, 657, 659, 664, 684, 687, 696, 699, 701, 732
excommunication, 185, 191, 219-221, 280, 284, 289, 299-302, 309, 326, 328, 336, 338, 344, 359-360, 363, 369, 371, 375-378, 383-385, 387-390, 414-415, 422-423, 428-429, 439-442, 453, 472, 476, 489, 513, 518, 546, 556, 644
executions, see death sentence
Exilarch of Babylon, the, 179, 251
exile, as punishment, 9, 36, 52, 55, 58, 70-71, 82, 109, 114-115, 125, 134, 147, 154, 178, 185-186, 193, 198, 202, 221, 266, 282, 284, 289, 327, 329, 335-336, 338, 340, 343, 360, 391, 438, 442, 457, 467, 470, 482, 504, 510, 536, 541, 554, 572, 611, 613, 628, 653, 676-677, 713, 715
existentialism, 708, 732, 735
Exodus, the Book of, 244-245, 436
exogamy, 264
experimentation, experiments, 76, 78, 379, 398, 404-405, 518, 521, 523, 582, 619-621, 623, 630, 655
expressionism, 472, 736
Ezekiel, the Book of, 149-150, 493a

Fabian, St., pope, 178
factories, see mass production
falconry, 379, 462
Fall of Man, the, 512, 597, 723
Famagusta, 407
famine, 29, 153, 158, 229, 235,
237-238, 545, 602, 668; the Potato Famine, 697
Far East, the, 434, 466, 537-538, 545, 563, 576-577, 613, 647, 657, 686-687, 689, 707-708, 727-728
farming, see agriculture
Farnese family, the, 471, 529; the Palazzo Farnese, 529
Fascism, 614, 685, 706
fasting, 28, 95, 245, 330, 406, 420, 471, 493, 655
Fastrada of Franconia, 266
Fatimid dynasty, the, 307, 345-346, 382a
Faust, 51, 550, 570, 660, 663
Fausta, Flavia Maximiana, 199
Felix III, St., pope, 237
Felix V, antipope, 443
Ferdinand the Catholic, king of Aragón, 466-467, 471, 479, 482-4, 486, 543
Ferdinand I, German emperor, 488, 495, 504, 528, 534-535, 543, 600; Ferdinand II, 600-602
Ferdinand VII, king of Spain, 678-679
Fergus mac Erc, 230
Ferrante of Aragón, king of Naples, 454, 469
Ferrantino of Naples, 470-472
Ferrara, 443, 459, 461-462, 476-477, 482, 485
Fertile Crescent, the, 54, 59
fertility, 26-27, 30, 39, 48, 246; deities of fertility, 2, 38, 246 ; fertility rituals, 28, 245-246, 263
feudalism, 22, 251a, 271-273, 279, 281, 287-288, 298-299, 314, 324, 341, 366-367, 370, 376, 392, 417-418, 448, 450, 453, 455, 468, 490, 502, 509, 511, 513, 605, 608, 659, 664, 680, 683, 696, 711, 716, 736; origin of the term, 272
Feuerbach, Ludwig Andreas, 686
Fibonacci, Leonardo, 394
Fichte, Johann Gottlieb, 683-684, 714
Ficino, Marsilio, 461-462, 581-582
fideism, 406
Fifth Monarchists, the, 612
Filioque clause, the, 259
First Cause, 397
FitzRoy, Henry, 500
flagellants, flagellation, 44, 435-436, 656
flamen Dialis, the, see the priest of Jupiter
Flanders, the Flemings, 283, 286, 289-290, 366-367, 440, 444, 486, 553, 639, 695
Flavian of Constantinople, St., 220
Fleming, Ian, 573
Flight of the Earls, the, 590
Flodden Field, the Battle of, 483
Florence, the Florentines, 91,
285, 359, 380, 391, 418-419, 443, 457-462, 465, 469-470, 472-473, 475, 480-483, 485, 487, 496, 504-507, 529, 545, 583, 585-586, 639, 705; the Council of Florence, 461; the Duomo of Florence, 539
Florida, 564, 647
Fludd, Robert, 598-599
flute, 43-44, 45a, 56, 644, 648, 652
fœderati, the, 203, 212
Foggia, the Battle of, 390
Foix, Gaston de, 483
Fontainebleau, 485
Forlì, 475
fornication, 177, 322, 510, 606, 655
Fornuovo, the Battle of, 471
Forum of Constantinople, the, 197, 366; the Forum of Rome, 112, 122, 126, 147
fountains, 276, 331, 465
Four Chapters, the, 358
fourth estate, the, see the lower classes
France, the French, 37, 101, 110, 118, 213, 232-233, 240, 253, 267-268, 270, 274, 280-283, 285-286, 290, 292-294, 303-304, 307a, 308-309, 311-312, 317, 320-322, 329-331, 333-335, 338, 340, 351, 353-354, 357, 360-362, 364, 369-372, 375-377, 380, 386, 389, 391-392, 398, 412, 414-415, 417, 419, 421-423, 425-430, 433, 435, 438-440, 443-449, 453, 457-459, 469-471, 474-476, 478-479, 481-483, 485-486, 488-490, 493, 496-497, 504-507, 509-510, 512, 528-530, 534-535, 538, 542, 544-545, 547, 549, 553, 555, 559-560, 563, 565, 570, 574, 578, 590-591, 596, 599. 601-603, 612, 621, 625-626, 628, 634-635, 637-640, 642-643, 644, 646-650, 653-659, 666-670, 672-673, 675-684, 686, 692-693, 696, 701, 705, 710, 715-717, 722, 735-736; French language, 102, 118, 135, 213, 266, 268, 273, 313, 341a, 379-380, 446, 460, 605, 622, 637, 648, 695; northern France, 305, 357, 370; southern France, 303, 305, 315, 369-371
Francis of Assisi, St., 372-373; the Franciscans, 373, 386, 396, 403-404, 406, 420, 431, 472, 506, 509; the Conventuals, 373; the Spirituals, 373, 420, 431
Francis I, king of France, 485-486, 488, 496, 504-507,

776

528, 535, 669; Francis II, 549
Francis I, German emperor, 646; Francis II, 676
Franconia, 267, 495
Franco-Prussian War, the, 705, 715-716, 717
Frankenhausen, the Battle of, 495
Frankfurt, 258, 375, 505, 534, 660, 677, 713, 720
Franklin, Benjamin, 622a, 667
Franks, the, 186, 213, 224, 232-233, 235-237, 241, 253-239, 261, 264-268, 270, 273, 310, 447; the Frankish Church, 241, 258-259, 265-266
Frauenfrage, the, 402-403
Frederick V, king of Bohemia, 600
Frederick II, king of Denmark, 580
Frederick I, German emperor, 336-338, 342-344, 352, 392; Frederick II, 328, 375, 377, 379-392, 394, 398; Frederick III, 451, 455
Frederick the Great, 645-650, 661
Frederick IV, king of Naples, 476
Frederick I, king of Prussia, 639; Frederick II, see Frederick the Great
Frederick the Wise, elector of Saxony, 488, 490
Frederick II, duke of Swabia, 325-326; Frederick V, 352
Frederick Lewis, prince of Wales, 645
Frederick William I, king of Prussia, 645 ; Frederick William III, 677, 684; Frederick William IV, 713
freedom, 15, 39, 76, 88, 217, 278, 377, 511, 665-666, 668, 702-704, 718, 722, 728, 731; freedom of association, 685; freedom of enterprise, 666, 696; freedom of expression, 723, 727; freedom of speech, 72; freedom of the press, 634, 637, 643-644; 678; freedom of thought, 394, 441, 527, 634, 643, 649; freedom of religion, 89, 93, 141-142, 181, 183-184, 205, 355, 385, 452, 515, 536, 608, 610, 614, 644, 649, 683
Freemasonry, 617, 634, 644-645, 648, 650-653, 661, 667
freethinkers, 634-635, 643, 648-650
free will, 216-217, 398, 725
Freud, Sigmund, 671, 719, 735
Friars Minor, the, see the Franciscans
Friars Preachers, the, see the Dominicans
Friesland, the Frisians, 267, 444, 562

Frobenius, Johannes, 522-523
Frobisher, Sir Martin, 564
Fugger family, the, 468, 488, 519, 522
Fulda, 257
Fulford, the Battle of, 290
Fulk of Anjou, king of Jerusalem, 332
Fuller, Thomas, 564
Fulvia, 125-126
funerary rites, 6-7, 123, 242; Christian burial, 154, 242-243, 309, 368, 374, 424
Fürstenbund, the, 661

Ga, Gaia, Gê, 26, 28, 31-32
Gabriel the Archangel, St., 248
Gaëtani family, the, 421, 438, 476
Galata, 364-365
Galba, 148
Galen of Pergamum, 520-521
Galerius, 182-183, 186
Galilee, the Galileans, 116, 136, 147, 170
Galilei, Galileo, 582-587, 623, 629
Galla Placidia, 215, 223, 225
Gallic Wars, the, 110-114
Gallipoli Peninsula, the, see Thracian Chersonese
Gama, Vasco da, 466
Gamaliel the Elder, 141
Ganymede, 27, 245a
gardening, gardens, 92, 150, 276, 572, 578, 604, 620-621, 643, 726; the Garden of Epicurus, 97
Garibaldi, Giuseppe, 696, 705
Garonne, the river, 215, 313
Garter, the Order of the, 598, 623-624
Gastein, the Treaty of, 712
Gaugamela, the Battle of, 85
Gaul, 109-114, 118, 125, 171, 182-183, 186, 195, 209, 213, 224, 229, 240, 247, 254, 257; Cisalpine Gaul, 101, 109, 111, 113-114, 235; Gallia Narbonensis, 124; Transalpine Gaul, 109
Gaza, 84, 350; the Battle of Gaza, 409
Geiseric, 218, 224
Gelasius II, pope, 309
Gemistus Pletho, Georgius, 461
generation, deities of, 2, 6, 38
Genesis, the Book of, 2, 633a
Geneva, 439, 510
genius, 108, 223, 268, 473, 484, 489, 507, 509, 659, 662-663, 680, 700, 702, 720, 727; the Genius of the Emperor, 140, 143-144
Genoa, the Genoese, 351, 353, 407-408, 414, 416, 418-419, 434, 443, 454, 459, 479, 669, 677
geocentrism, 156, 530-531, 580, 587
geodesy, see surveying
geography, 37, 156, 250, 277, 394, 399, 405, 539, 552,

561, 564-565, 648, 657; geographical exploration, 9, 37, 418, 466-467, 537, 539-540, 543-545, 547-548, 550-552, 558, 561-566, 572, 576, 585, 594, 613, 621, 657, 687
geology, 620, 634, 662, 689, 700
geometry, 9-10, 50-51, 77, 92, 276-277, 399, 401, 552, 558, 592, 619, 633
George the Arian, 202
George I, king of Great Britain, 638, 640; George II, 653;
George IV, 628a
George V, king of Hanover, 712
George Maniakes, 281-282
Georgia, 99, 409
Gepidæ, the, 224-225, 236
Gerard de Riderfort, 349-350
German Confederation, the, 677, 681, 696, 712-713; the North German Confederation, 713, 716
Germania, the Roman province, 148, 224
Germany, the Germans, 110, 190, 255, 267-268, 274-275, 283-286, 298-301, 304, 309-310, 325-328, 333-334, 336-338, 342, 352-354, 356-360, 370, 375-377, 379-381, 383, 385-388, 391-393, 396, 409, 419, 427, 430, 435, 439-442, 451, 454-455, 475, 486-498, 502, 504-505, 510, 513, 524, 526-529, 531-532, 534-536, 543, 561, 581, 597-598, 600-605, 612a, 639-641, 646-649, 651-652, 659-662, 676, 680-685, 688-689, 693, 695-696, 701-702, 705-707, 709-713, 715-717, 719-722, 726, 729-730, 734-736; German language, 169, 214a, 256, 269, 273, 379-380, 396, 489-491, 519, 523-524, 543, 601, 638, 652, 695, 712, 734; the German tribes, 109, 110a, 111-112, 114, 204, 212-214, 224, 226, 229, 231, 235, 246, 257, 261-262, 264-265, 267, 269, 272, 312, 363; northern Germany, 256, 496, 599, 712-713; southern Germany, 130, 213, 240, 494, 496, 520, 651, 712-713, 715
ghetto, the origin of the, 374-375
Ghibellines, the, 327-328, 336, 388, 391-392, 419, 451
Gibbon, Edward, 213-214, 546
Gibraltar, 109, 218, 638
Gilbert d'Assalit, 346
Gilbert, Sir Humphrey, 564
gladiators, 112, 131, 207
Glendalough, 230

777

Gnosticism, Gnostics, 137, 160-166, 169, 174-177, 179-180, 189, 707; origin of the term, 162
God, the Judæo-Christian, 138-139, 143, 147, 153, 164, 167, 170, 180, 191, 194, 206, 208, 211, 216-217, 219, 225, 227, 233, 244, 247-248, 239a, 250, 260, 263, 271, 279, 281, 291, 296a, 297-299, 303-304, 308, 316, 320, 322, 334-335, 337-338, 368, 371, 374, 376, 397-398, 422, 429-430, 435, 437, 445, 448, 453, 470, 476, 484, 491, 493-495, 508, 510-512, 514-515, 517-518, 526, 531, 557, 583, 598, 604, 606-607, 614-615, 626, 629, 635, 654-655, 658, 681, 685, 723, 731, 733, 735
Godfrey de Bouillon, 308
godparenthood, 264-265
Goethe, Johann Wolfgang von, 659-664, 681-682, 689, 732
Golden Horn, the, 196, 364-365
Golden Speech, the, 589
gold-making, 521, 571, 573, 598-599
Gonzalo de Córdoba, 479
good shepherd, 28, 137
Gordian III, Roman emperor, 178
Goslar, 309, 343
Gospels, the, 165-175, 189, 209, 269, 283, 315-316, 611, 634, 704; the Diatessaron of Tatian, 167-168; the Gospel of John, 167-168, 172, 181, 318; the Gospel of Luke, 167-171, 368, 559; the Gospel of Marcion, 167; the Gospel of Mark, 168-171, 363, 372; the Gospel of Mary, 174; the Gospel of Matthew, 168-171, 194, 221, 240, 363, 368; the Gospel of Thomas, 169; the Q Gospel, 169
Goths, the, 203, 205, 213-215, 224, 229, 231, 235, 251; the Ostrogoths, 203, 225, 231-232, 235; the Visigoths, 203, 212, 215, 223-224, 232, 251
Gothicism, 314, 456, 472
Götterdämmerung, 4, 233
grain, see corn; the grain dole, 117, 130
grammar, 92, 229, 237, 257, 400-401, 519, 524, 573a, 593, 688
Granada, 429, 467-468, 679; the Treaty of Granada, 476, 479
Grand Siècle, Le, 637
grand unified theory, 582
Granicus, the Battle of, 83
Gratian, Roman emperor, 204-206, 208, 212; Italian legal scholar, 323
Gravelotte, the Battle of, 716
Great Fire of London, the, 623; the Great Fire of Rome, 146-147
Great Mother Goddess, the, 25-32, 34-35, 48, 99, 197
Great Northern War, the, 640
Great Reform Bill, the, 693
Great Wall of China, the, 203, 345
Greenwich Observatory, the, 623, 698; Greenwich Mean Time, 698
Gregorian Chant, the, 258, 311
Gregorovius, Ferdinand, 392
Gregory of Nazianzus, St., 202, 205-206, 209-210; St. Gregory of Tours, 232-233, 237, 265
Gregory the Great, St., pope, 237-242, 258; St. Gregory VII, see Hildebrand; Gregory VIII, 351, 353; Gregory IX, 383-388; Blessed Gregory X, 414; Gregory XI, 438-439; Gregory XII, 440-442; Gregory XIII, 559, 565-568, 572
Greece, the Greeks, 5, 8, 12, 14-16, 18-32, 35-38, 40-45, 47-54, 56-73, 75-76, 78-85, 87-92, 94-103, 105, 114-115, 118-120, 122, 126, 131, 136-139, 141-143, 145, 147, 155-156, 158-161, 163-164, 167, 169-172, 175, 178-180, 183, 192, 195-199, 201-202, 208, 210-212, 220, 227-228, 253, 263-264, 268, 276, 281-282, 296, 302a, 326, 328, 362, 366, 379, 394, 397-400, 403-404, 432, 453-454, 456, 460-463, 530, 551, 558, 592, 643, 669, 679-680, 684, 686, 690, 704, 707, 718-719, 725, 737; the Greek city-states, 5, 8, 48, 53, 56-64, 66a, 69-71, 74, 76, 78-80, 82, 88, 95, 97, 100, 105, 117, 119, 156; the Greek islands, see the Ægean islands
Greek language, 19, 22-23, 687-688; ancient Greek, 5, 8, 29, 37-38, 41, 43-44, 62, 69, 80-81, 228, 276-277, 400a, 403-404, 454, 460-463, 509, 530, 551, 558, 595-596, 633, 679, 688, 715; Hellenistic Greek, 88-89, 93, 100, 103, 118-119, 122, 129, 143-143, 150, 154-155, 160-161, 165-166, 170, 172a, 175, 179, 183, 194, 198, 202, 208-210, 228-229, 231, 244; mediæval Greek, 251, 256, 259, 278, 282, 305, 379, 394

Greek War of Independence, the, 679
Gresham College, 619, 621
Grimm, Jakob, 688
Guelphs, the, 327-328, 336, 356, 359, 388, 391, 419, 451; the Blacks and the Whites, 419
Guido d'Arezzo, 311
guild system, the, 323, 400-401, 457, 520, 665-666, 675
Guillaume Bélibaste, 395
Guillaume Imbert, 426
Guillaume de Poitiers, 313
guillotine, 668
guitar, 43-44
Gundobad, 232
gunpowder, 399, 405, 450, 485, 618a
Gustavus Adolphus, 561, 601
Guy de Lusignan, 349, 353, 355, 407
Guy of Ponthieu, 287
Guyenne, see Aquitaine
gymnasion, or gymnasium, 65, 78
gymnastics, see athletics

Habsburg dynasty, the, 393, 451, 486, 488-489, 498, 504-506, 528, 532, 534-535, 543, 545, 553, 555, 603; the Austrian Habsburgs, 488, 543, 553, 602-603, 639, 676, 678, 682; the Spanish Habsburgs, 486, 543, 553, 639
Hades, see the underworld
Hadrian, 155-158; Hadrian's Mausoleum, see Castel Sant' Angelo; Hadrian's Wall, 156-157
Haeckel, Ernst, 702
Hagia Sophia, the, 205, 366, 452
Haifa, 307, 411
Hakluyt, Richard, 564
Halley, Edmond, 625, 630; Halley's Comet, 288
Hallowe'en, 243
Ham, see Khem; Hamito-Semitic languages, 3-4, 689
Hamburg, 256
handfasting, 607
Hanover, 343, 638, 640, 646, 653a, 681, 712; the Hanoverian dynasty, 343, 638, 640, 646, 681
Harald Hardrada, 287, 289-290
Harold Godwinson, 287-291, 293
Harriot, Thomas, 568
Harrison, Jane, 23
Harun ar-Rashid, caliph of Baghdad, 259
harvest, 1-2, 6, 14, 29, 47-48, 243-244, 433
Hasmoneans, the, see the Maccabees
Hastings, the Battle of, 290-293
Hathor, 5
Hatra, 155
Hattin, the Battle of the, 349-350
Hauteville, Constance de, 343,

778

353-354, 358, 379; Drogo, 281, 283; Humphrey, 281, 283-284, 328; Tancred, 281, 305; Roger, 283, 286, 296, 299, 302, 305, 326, 353; William, 281-283
health care, 654-655, 675
Heaven, the heavens, 3-4, 6, 11, 16, 31, 47, 50, 75, 123, 144, 147, 161-162, 171-172, 177, 180, 183-184, 188, 194, 197, 200, 216, 242, 245, 279, 303, 369, 373, 399, 512, 531, 559, 561, 567, 572, 582, 629, 649, 655, 732; deities of the sky, 48-49
Hebe, 27-28
Hebrews, the, 13, 89, 93, 116-117, 138-139, 143, 159, 201, 209-210, 244, 263-264, 480, 533, 688; Hebrew language, 9, 13, 23, 93, 116, 143, 157, 160, 170, 173, 209, 244, 250, 462, 612, 686-689; the Hebrew scriptures, 93, 144, 159, 163-167, 169-170, 173, 201, 209-210, 248-249, 315a, 595, 633a
Hecatæus of Miletus, 37
hedonism, 96
Hegel, G. W. F., 683-686, 689, 695, 707-708, 723
Hegira, 248
Heidelberg, 570, 720; the Heidelberg Catechism, 536
Heinse, Wilhelm, 660
Hekate, 30
Helena, St., mother of Constantine, 182, 199, 247
Helena of Tyre, 145
heliocentrism, 530, 559, 585, 580-581, 583, 586-587, 629
Heliogabalus, 140
Heliopolis, 16
Hell, 245, 279, 303, 356, 373, 421, 512, 515-517
Hellas, the Hellenes, see Greece, the Greeks
Hellenic League, the, 82-83
Hellenistic culture, 87-89, 92, 98-99, 115, 121, 129, 137, 142-143, 155, 159, 160a, 163, 172, 202, 227, 240, 251a, 263, 276
Hellenistic poets, the, 94-95, 103
Hellespont, the, 59-60, 83, 187, 196, 252
Héloïse of Argenteuil, 316-318, 330
Helvetia, the Helvetii, 109, 669
Henry II, king of Cyprus, 415
Henry II, king of England, 335, 338-343, 351-352; Henry III, 387, 390; Henry V, 444; Henry VI, 444; Henry VII, 471, 562, 564, 590; Henry VIII, 483, 488, 491, 497, 499-502, 507-508, 513-514, 528, 540-542, 548-549, 551, 562, 590

Henry I, king of France, 281-282, 386; Henry II, 506, 535, 545; Henry III, 574; Henry IV, 555, 591
Henry I, king of Germany, 274-275; Henry III, 283-284, 299; Henry IV, 284, 299-301, 309; Henry V, 309-310, 325-327; Henry VI, 343, 353-354, 356-359, 375, 379; Henry VII, 387
Henry the Lion, duke of Saxony, 336-337, 342-343, 356-357, 359; Henry the Proud, 326-327, 336a
Henry the Navigator, prince of Portugal, 466
Henry Tudor, see Henry VII of England
Hephaistos, 35
Hera, 31-34; temple of Hera, 34
Heracleon of Sicily, 164
Heraclitus, 49, 68, 74
Heraclius, Byzantine emperor, 249; patriarch of Jerusalem, 349-350
Herakles, 27-28, 31, 34, 48, 98, 119, 171, 190
herbalism, herbs, 3, 516, 521, 621
Herder, Johann Gottfried von, 681
heresy, heretics, 35a, 145, 160, 162, 165-168, 174, 176-177, 181, 186, 198, 205-206, 216-222, 232, 240, 243, 258, 268, 276, 309, 315, 322, 330, 344, 368-371, 379a, 382, 386-387, 389, 395, 402, 422-423, 425-426, 428, 435-437, 440-441, 448, 461a, 465, 490, 514, 525, 527-528, 532-533, 537, 541, 545-546, 551, 553, 556, 559, 580-581, 584, 601, 644, 728
Hermes, 12, 29-31, 35, 38; Hermeticism, 461, 557, 598-599, 632, 634
Hermopolis, 12
Herod the Great, 116, 127, 136, 141, 149, 250a
Herodotus, 18, 25, 40a, 56, 60, 68
heroes, hero-worship, 23-24, 26-28, 31, 67, 74, 123, 133, 144, 256, 457, 652, 612, 626, 654, 669, 722-723, 727
Heruli, the, 224-225, 236
Hervás, Lorenzo, 688
Hesiod, 25, 32, 68, 92, 132
Hesse, 267, 491, 504, 535, 712; Hesse-Darmstadt, 676; Hesse-Kassel, 681; Hesse-Nassau, 712
Hesse, Hermann, 736
Hestia, 32-33
Hethoum the Great, 410
hexameter, 43, 101
hierarchy, ecclesiastical, 154-155, 166, 194, 211, 229,

311, 316, 512, 527; secular hierarchy, see class division
hieroglyphics, 3, 5, 9, 12, 688
hieros gamos, see the sacred marriage
Hildebrand of Tuscany, 208, 283, 285, 288-289, 296-303, 309, 323, 383, 392, 420
Hildegarde of Swabia, 265-267
Himera, the Battle of, 61
Himiltrude, 264-265
Hinduism, Hindus, 98, 138, 249a, 690-691
Hipparchus, 156, 559, 629
Hippias, 58
Hippo, 195, 215, 218; the Council of Hippo, 210
Hippocrates, 50-51, 68, 92
Hippodrome of Constantinople, the, 197, 366
Hippolytus, the Christian saint, 175-178; the tragic hero, 178
history, historians, 62, 68, 79, 89, 102, 110, 119, 146, 148, 155, 158, 168, 170, 183, 188, 191, 199, 206, 214, 223-224, 226, 229, 232, 246, 252, 265, 267, 275-277, 297, 340, 355, 358, 366, 380, 392, 399, 404, 413, 453, 460, 486, 504, 513, 541, 544, 561, 564, 570-571, 581, 597, 619, 622-623, 624a, 625, 633, 643, 648, 665, 684, 689-691, 708, 723, 730
Hitler, Adolf, 734
Hobbes, Thomas, 546, 596a, 625
Hohenstaufen dynasty, the, 301, 325-328, 333a, 357-359, 379, 387, 390-393, 415
Hohenzollern dynasty, the, 393, 503, 716, 718
Holland, see the Netherlands; the Dutch county of Holland, 444, 576
Holstein, see Scheswig-Holstein; Holstein-Gottorp, 646
Holy Alliance, the, 678-679, 682
Holy Grail, the, 380, 719, 726, 728
Holy Land, the, see Palestine
Holy League, the, 482-483
Holy Roman Empire, origin of the term, 337
Holy See, see the papacy
Holy Sepulchre, the, 8, 247, 259, 281, 297, 303, 308, 321, 351, 385, 506
Holy Spirit, the, 145, 149, 165, 168, 170, 193, 206-207, 318, 368, 420, 531, 684
Holy Synod of Russia, the, 642
Homer, 19-20, 23-27, 33-36, 39, 42, 49, 55, 68, 92, 119, 113-114, 171, 201, 210, 227, 252, 356, 688, 701
Homoousians and Homoiousians, the, 191, 198

779

Homs Gap, the, 412
Honoria, Justa Grata, 224
Honorius II, antipope, 286
Honorius II, pope, 321, 326-327; Honorius III, 381-383
Honorius, Roman emperor, 212-215, 223
Hooke, Robert, 620, 623, 625, 630-632
Hopkins, Matthew, 615
Horace, 119, 131-132, 134
Hormizd I, king of Persia, 181
Horus the Elder, 6; Horus the Younger, 2, 6, 8, 16
horses, horsemen, 23-24, 65, 106, 111, 121, 178, 203, 223-224, 271-273, 276, 291, 306, 322, 333, 347, 352 366, 368, 389, 412, 425, 498, 714, 733
hospitals, 229, 259, 321, 354, 411, 487, 523, 641
Hospital of St. John, the, 321, 385; the Hospitallers, 321-322, 346-347, 349, 354, 358, 366, 385, 407-409, 411, 413-416, 425, 429, 432
hotel system, the, 94
Hubertusburg, the Treaty of, 646
Hudson, Henry, 613; Hudson Bay, 638
huertas, the, 578
Hugh the Great, 411-412, 414-415
Hugh de Vermandois, 304-307
Hugo, Victor, 546, 680
hugra phusis, the, 6, 38
Huguenets, the, 549, 555, 599, 637; the Huguenot Wars, see the Wars of Religion
Hugues de Payens, 320-322
Hülegü Khan, 409-410
humanism, humanists, 80, 98, 161, 228, 454-456, 459, 461-462, 465a, 484, 486-487, 492, 499, 509, 522, 530-531, 533, 539, 561, 594-595, 635, 667; the humanities, see the Liberal Arts
humankind, the, 1-5, 7, 9-11, 13, 15, 18, 22, 26-29, 33, 38-40, 47, 49, 61, 63a, 69, 72-73, 81, 87-88, 96-97, 143-144, 154a, 159, 164, 167, 172, 180, 213, 216-217, 219-220, 242, 271, 421, 434, 456-457, 462, 473-474, 511-512, 518, 592-593, 597, 599, 606, 619, 622-623, 632, 635-635, 649, 651, 654, 660, 662-663, 665-666, 672, 680, 686, 692, 694, 699-701, 704, 718-719, 723-725, 727-732, 735
Humboldt, Wilhelm von, 638
Hundred Days, the, 678, 680
Hundred Years' War, the, 433, 443-449
Hungary, the Hungarians, 131, 151, 223, 269, 274-275, 337, 351-352, 363, 378, 388, 393, 419, 439-442, 454, 482, 504-506, 528, 534, 543, 600, 603, 645, 696, 713
Huns, the, 203, 223-225, 380
hunting, 1, 28, 261, 279, 314, 462, 477, 494, 672, 693-694
Hus, John, 441-442, 488, 490; the Hussites, 441-442
Hutten, Urlich von, 492-493
hygiene, see sanitation
Hyginus, St., pope, 163
hymnody, hymns, 176, 178, 208-209, 227, 231, 460; the Hymn of the Pearl, 176
Hypatia of Alexandria, 218
Hyrcanus II, high priest of Judæa, 107

Iacchos, title of Dionysos, 48
Iamblichus of Chalcis, 179
Iason, 31, 34
Iberian Peninsula, the, 466-467, 524-525, 543-544, 575-576, 578-579
Iberian Union, the, 576
Ibn Fadlan, 278
Ibn Rushd, see Averroës
Ibn Sina, see Avicenna
Iceland, 278
Iconium, the Battle of, 352; the Sultan of Iconium, 367
iconostasis, the, 208
icons, 252-253, 258, 278, 480; the Iconoclastic edict, 253
Ideas, Plato's doctrine of, 74-77, 81, 178, 557
Ides, the, 120; the Ides of March, 121
idolatry, 141, 188, 206, 240, 248, 511, 575-576, 615
Idumæa, 116, 127, 148
Ignatius of Antioch, St., 154-155, 172a; St. Ignatius of Loyola, 525-526, 528
Ildico, 225
Iliad, the, 23-24, 55, 119
illegitimate children, 182, 266, 281, 353, 360, 390, 446, 454-455, 464, 472, 476-478, 496, 500, 519, 529, 548-549, 674-675
illuminated manuscripts, 231, 269, 611
Illuminati of Bavaria, the, 651-653
Illyricum, the Illyrians, 79, 109, 186-187, 193, 195, 212, 232, 240
immortality, 7, 42, 47, 111, 123, 128a, 162, 202, 392
Imola, 475
Imperator, 129-130; as title of Russian rulers, 641
imperialism, 53, 69, 90, 113, 544, 553, 562-563, 658, 691, 701, 716
incarnations of deities, 16, 46, 84, 98, 145, 191, 198, 683
Incas, the, 575
incest, 2, 5-6, 32, 92, 115-116, 264-266, 499
incubus, the, 516
Index Librorum Prohibitorum, the, 437a, 546, 584, 594
India, the Indians, 19, 84, 86, 91-92, 94, 98, 138, 178, 220, 399, 467, 537-538, 552, 576a, 647, 687-691, 707-708
Indian Ocean, the, 85, 538
individualism, 24, 63a, 162, 228, 450-451, 457, 598, 615, 617, 644, 649, 654, 656, 659, 666, 668, 672, 723-725, 730-732, 734-736
Indo-European languages, 688-689
indulgences, 333, 361a, 421, 428, 485, 487-488, 532-533
Indus, the river, 86, 252, 689
industrialism, industrialization, see the Industrial Revolution
Infant God, the, 38-40, 48-49, 189
infanticide, 154, 186, 233, 308, 346, 355, 371, 402, 415; infant mortality, 655; infants, see children
Ingeborg of Denmark, 357, 360
Innocent I, St., pope, 210; Innocent II, 327-331; Innocent III, 358-364, 369-379, 383; Innocent IV, 389-390; Innocent VII, 440; Innocent VIII, 464-465, 469; Innocent X, 602
inoculation, 654
Inquisition, the, 386, 395-396, 426-427, 431, 465, 524; the Spanish Inquisition, 467, 525, 544, 553-554, 563, 577, 593, 668, 678; the Universal Inquisition, 525, 546, 555, 584, 586
instruments, agricultural, 10, 38-39, 700; musical, 44, 51, 258, 709; scientific, 404, 466, 551-552, 560, 583-584, 587, 592, 625, 630
interdicts, papal, 336, 360, 369-370, 376, 385, 424-426, 453, 472, 482
interregnum, the German, 392-393
intoxicants, see alcohol
inventing, inventors, 3, 9-10, 14, 43, 51, 68, 80, 92, 154-155, 163, 259a, 313, 380, 405-406, 454, 459, 493, 552, 558, 594, 622, 629-631, 643a, 654, 668, 673, 675, 692, 697, 723, 731
inverse square law, the, 632
investiture, 282, 297-299, 303, 309-310, 323, 326-327, 353, 358-359, 469, 475, 503, 528
Iona, 240, 269
Ionia, the Ionians, 49, 52, 57-58, 60, 70, 302; Ionian philosophy, 49, 52, 75
Ipsus, the Battle of, 91
Ireland, the Irish, 101, 112, 189,

216, 229-231, 240, 257, 268-269, 340-341, 376, 419, 513, 541, 570, 588-591, 608-611, 627, 693, 697; the Irish Church, 216, 230-231, 240, 242, 257, 341; Northern Ireland, see Ulster
Irenæus of Lyons, St., 165-166, 168, 176
Irene Angela, 358
Irene the Athenian, Byzantine empress, 260
Iron Age, 23, 700
ironsides, the, 609
irrigation, 13-14, 319, 578
Isaac Angelus, 352, 357-358, 363-365
Isabella the Catholic, queen of Castile, 466-467, 479
Isabella of France, queen of England, 433
Isabella of Bavaria, queen of France, 444
Isabella Plantagenet, German empress, 387
Isaiah, the Book of, 13, 201
Ishtar, 246
Isis, 2-6, 26, 98; the symbols of Isis, 5
Islam, see Muslims
Isocrates of Athens, 79-82
Israel, the Israelites, 93, 107, 139, 143, 149, 157, 170, 244-245, 612; the state of Israel, 150, 468; the ten lost tribes of Israel, 613
Issus, the Battle of, 84, 88
Italian Wars, the, 469-471, 474, 481-486, 489-490, 496-498, 500, 504-506, 528, 545
Italy, the Italians, 80, 97-98, 108, 113-114, 118, 124-128, 152-153, 166, 175, 182, 195, 197, 209, 213-215, 224, 226, 229, 231-232, 235, 238-240, 247, 253-255, 267-268, 274, 282-285, 288, 299-300, 303-304, 325-326, 328-329, 336-337, 342-343, 346, 351, 354, 359, 370, 372, 379-381, 383, 385, 387-388, 390-392, 406, 408, 414, 418-419, 422-423, 427, 430-431, 438-440, 443, 453-457, 460-466, 469-471, 473-475, 481-491, 496-498, 504-507, 525, 528-530, 541, 543, 545-548, 553, 582, 585-586, 595, 602-603, 639, 659, 661, 669-670, 676-678, 683, 688, 696, 703-706, 712, 718, 722; Italian language, 102, 118, 283, 327, 336, 379-380, 457-458, 464, 688, 695; the Italian city-states, 329, 342-343, 408, 418-419, 456, 458-459, 471, 497, 528, 545; central Italy, 54, 236, 304, 375, 438, 477-478, 529, northern Italy,

101, 224, 240, 304, 343, 387, 392, 418, 470, 481, 485, 487, 489, 545, 548, 677; southern Italy, 37, 49, 51-52, 100, 118, 125, 236, 253, 255, 277, 280-284, 296, 302, 326-328, 343-344, 357-358, 375, 391-392, 398, 405, 417, 482, 485, 545; the unification of Italy, 296, 457, 639, 704-705, 712
Ivan the Great, 453
Ivan the Terrible, 552, 640

Jacobins, the, 669
Jaffa, 320-321, 350, 355, 411
James I, king of England and Ireland, 560a, 574, 579, 588, 590-592, 595-596, 600, 615, 638; James II, 627-628
James of Jerusalem, St., 171
James IV, king of Scotland, 483; James V, 549; James VI, see James I of England; James VII, see James II of England
Jamnia, 141, 148-149
Janissaries, the, 538-539
Janus, 149
Jebail, 350, 358
Jefferson, Thomas, 610, 615a, 622a, 649, 651
Jeremiah, the Book of, 378
Jerome, St., 209, 315a, 595
Jerome of Prague, 441
Jerusalem, 84, 89, 93, 107, 116, 127, 136-138, 147-150, 157-158, 179, 198, 247, 249-250, 259, 281, 295, 297, 302, 305, 307-308, 321-322, 324, 332, 334, 349-356, 358, 365, 379, 381-382, 384-385, 387, 389, 409-410, 413, 421, 424, 462, 466, 506, 526; the Latin kingdom of Jerusalem, 302a, 320, 323, 332, 345, 347, 349, 355, 358, 365, 367, 381-386, 388, 407-408, 412, 414-416, 418; the Temple of Jerusalem, 93, 107, 138, 141, 148-149, 168, 202, 733; the see of Jerusalem, 170-171, 172a, 192, 210, 249, 297, 323, 331, 334, 349-350, 385, 416, 461a
Jesuits, the, 525-527, 532, 544, 565, 575, 580, 584, 600-601, 627, 649-651, 653, 678, 687-688
Jesus, 142, 159-160, 164-166, 168-174, 180-181, 191, 194, 198, 206, 211, 244-245, 247-248, 253, 263, 304, 318, 366a, 445, 468, 481, 518, 526, 547, 567, 635, 684, 732-733; the birth date of Jesus, 189; the birthplace of Jesus, 170; the divinity of Jesus, 171-172, 191, 198, 248, 644; the genealogy of

Jesus, 171-172
jewels, jewelry, 314, 360, 364, 366, 424, 501, 524, 537, 545
Jewish War, the First, 147-150, 168; the Second, 157-158
Jews, Judaism, 88-89, 91, 97, 116-117, 123, 137-143, 145, 148-151, 155, 157-162, 164-165, 167, 169-175, 179-181, 189a, 190, 193a, 194, 201-203, 217, 219, 244-245, 247-251, 263-264, 275, 295, 304, 308, 314, 318, 325, 347, 374-375, 379, 396, 398, 403, 417, 425, 435-436, 453, 462, 467-468, 514a, 516, 518, 525, 546, 577, 612-614, 648, 671, 686-687, 695, 721, 732; Alexandrian, 89, 91-93, 115-116, 136-138, 141, 148, 155, 163-164, 218; Ashkenazi, 304, 325, 396, 435, 614, 648; Babylonian, 91, 93, 179-180, 202, 251, 275a; Hellenistic, 88-89, 93, 137, 142, 175; Palestinian, 89, 93, 107, 115, 127, 137, 147-150, 155, 157-158; Mizrahi, 158, 247-249, 295, 308; Sephardic, 251, 275, 379, 398, 403, 467-468, 525, 555, 577, 613-614
jizya, the, 350-351
Joan of Arc, St., 445-449; St. Joan of Valois, 474
Joanna I, queen of Naples, 439; Joanna II, 443
Joanna of Sicily, 353, 355
John XXIII, antipope, 441-442
John the Baptist, St., 145, 180, 274; St. John the Evangelist, 146, 151; St. John Chrysostom, 208, 210
John of Lancaster, duke of Bedford, 444, 446-447
John of Brienne, 382
John the Fearless, 444
John Lackland, 356, 376-377
John XXII, pope, 431
John of Procida, 415
John of Salisbury, 401-402
John Scotus Erigena, 268
John Frederick I, elector of Saxony, 534-535
John Paul II, pope, 587
Jones, Sir William, 687
Jonson, Ben, 570, 594
Jordanes, 224-225
Joscelin II, count of Edessa, 332
Joseph, St., father of Jesus, 171
Joseph Bonaparte, 676
Josephus, Flavius, 88-89, 147-148, 150
jousting, jousts, 450, 529
Jovian, Roman emperor, 203
Jowett, Benjamin, 703
jubilees, papal, 421, 475
Judæa, 89, 91, 107, 115-116, 127, 136-137, 141-142, 147-150, 155, 157, 462

781

Judah the Patriarch, 173
Judith of Bavaria, 336
Julian the Apostate, 154a, 201-203
Julius II, pope, 464, 469-70, 478-483, 485; the Julius Tomb, 480
Jupiter, the Roman deity, 191; Jupiter-Ammon, 12, 85; Jupiter Capitolinus, 140, 148, 151, 158; Jupiter-Julius, 123; the priest of Jupiter, 105-106
Jupiter, the planet, 583; the moons of Jupiter, 630
Justin Martyr, St., 159-161, 167
Justin II, Byzantine emperor, 235, 237
Justinian I, Byzantine emperor, 78, 231, 235, 264
just price, the, 323, 511

Kaaba, the, 248
Kaiserreich, the, 715-719, 722, 730
Kaloyan, 367, 377-378
Kant, Immanuel, 546, 648, 653, 683-684
Karnak, 16-18
Kelaoun, 415-416
Kells, 269
Kelly, Sir Edward, 570-574
Kent, 111, 241, 291
Kepler, Johannes, 558, 561, 567, 580-585, 629
Kerameikos, the, 64
Kerbogha, atabeg of Mosul, 306
Khem, 2
Kilij Arslan, 305-306, 334
Kilkenny, the Articles of, 611
Kingdom of God, the, 142, 147, 161-162, 171, 177, 227
Kinsale, the siege of, 589-590
Kitbogha, 409-410
Klinger, Friedrich Maximilian von, 659-660
Klingsor, 728
Knigge, Adolph F. F. L. von, 652
Knossos, 20-22
Koinê, the, see Hellenistic Greek
Koldewey, Robert Johann, 688
Koran, the, 249-250, 252, 347, 546
Kore, 29-33, 40, 48-49
Kronos, 31-32
Kurds, the, 345-346, 382a, 413
Kyd, Thomas, 570
Kyffhäuser Mountains, the, 392

Labienus, 125
laboratories, 92, 519, 598, 622, 624, 632
Lactantius Firmianus, 183
Lacy, Hugh de, 341
Ladislaud II, king of Hungary and Bohemia, 504
Ladislaus III, high-duke of Poland, 377
Laetitia Bonaparte, 680
Lafayette, marquis de, 669
Lamarckism, 402

landownership, landowners, 15, 17, 22, 54-55, 69, 71, 75, 132, 147, 203, 239, 253-255, 262, 272-273, 279-283, 285-286, 288-293, 298-299, 305, 310, 322, 324-325, 328-329, 331, 335, 337, 340-343, 348, 357, 359, 362, 367, 375-376, 383, 390, 407-408, 422, 424, 426, 433-434, 443-445, 458, 463, 468-469, 471, 474-476, 482-483, 489, 492, 503, 507-508, 513, 524, 535-536, 538, 542, 576, 590, 604, 608, 611, 639, 692-693, 697, 706
Lanfranc, 288-289, 292
Langton, Stephen, 376-377
Languedoc, 313-314, 368-372
Laon, 268, 316
lapis lazuli, 18
Las Casas, Bartolomé de, 575
Laski, Albrecht, 571-573
last supper, 98, 121, 159, 460
Last Judgement, the, 162, 200, 248, 732
Lateran palace, the, 190, 308, 336, 373, 443; the Lateran Council of 1059, 285, 419; the Lateran Council of 1097, 304; the First Lateran Council, 265, 343, the Second Lateran, 316, 329; the Third Lateran, 316, 328, 343; the Fourth Lateran, 372, 374-375; the Lateran Treaty, 706
Latin language, 2a, 78, 80, 92, 100-102, 110, 118-119, 122, 147a, 152, 154-155, 175, 183, 208-209, 213a, 228-229, 244, 256-257, 259, 268, 272-274, 277, 314-315, 379-380, 381a, 386, 394, 396, 400-401, 403, 455, 460-461, 491-492, 508-509, 523-524, 526, 546, 548, 590a, 592-593, 595, 621-622, 641, 658, 669, 687, 715; Church Latin, 209, 461; Classical Latin, 131, 134, 460-461; Vulgar Latin, 118, 209
Latium, 100, 235a
Laud, William, 608-609
laurel crown, 66, 438, 626
law, lawyers, law-makers, 13-15, 20, 23-24, 29-30, 49, 54-55, 57, 64-65, 70, 87-90, 96-97, 100, 105-107, 109-110, 112-118, 124, 129, 136, 140-141, 144, 146, 151, 154, 157-158, 173, 175, 182-187, 190-191, 193, 195, 202-203, 205-207, 212, 217-218, 226-227, 230-232, 239, 240, 242, 249, 251, 253, 255, 257, 261-265, 270, 274-275, 277, 281, 285, 293, 296, 298-299, 305, 311, 339-340, 344, 358-360, 375, 377, 379, 382-383, 386-388, 391-392, 396, 401, 404, 417, 419-422, 426-427, 430, 435-436, 448, 452, 463, 464a, 467-468, 473, 479, 490, 492-495, 500-502, 504-511, 514, 516-518, 525, 535-538, 541-542, 544, 554-556, 562-565, 568, 574-575, 580, 588-592, 595, 603, 605, 609-610, 612-614, 616, 618, 626-629, 636, 637-638, 641, 643, 648, 650-653, 655, 660, 664-668, 674-675, 677-683, 685-688, 693, 702, 706, 716, 722, 724-725, 729-733, 736-737; agrarian law, 13-14, 29; Athenian law, 34, 54-55, 59, 64-65, 69-71, 72a, 97; canon law, 177, 195, 206, 210, 220, 222, 237, 240, 243-244, 245-246, 259, 264-265, 280, 285, 289, 291, 298-299, 303, 323-325, 329-330, 334, 339, 343-344, 361, 374, 378, 386, 398, 401, 403, 420, 420, 422, 424, 426, 431, 437, 440, 442, 448, 489, 492, 499, 517-518, 525, 530, 533, 546-547, 584, 585a, 586-587, 644, 651, 705; common law, 339, 612, 638; Germanic law, 261-262, 265; Roman law, 97-98, 106, 118, 226-227, 231, 261-262, 265, 436, 638; Jewish law, 89, 93, 97, 137, 149, 157, 173, 179, 435
leap day, leap year, leap month, 12, 120, 567
Lebensraum, 681, 729
Le Crac, 412-415
legends, ancient, 2, 4, 18-20, 24, 26-27, 29, 31-37, 39, 41, 45a, 46, 52, 66, 68, 71, 77, 89, 95, 98, 115, 133-134, 167, 180, 199, 201, 380, 561-562, 659, 686-687, 719; Celtic, 230, 312; Christian, 145-146, 153, 161, 178, 182, 196, 202, 213, 230, 373, 380; mediæval (secular), 255-256, 294, 347, 356, 380, 392, 403, 430, 457, 492, 563-564, 610
Legnano, the Battle of, 343
Legnica, the Battle of, 388
Leibniz, Gottfried W. von, 558, 581, 629, 632
Leipzig, 709, 713, 720; the Battle of Leipzig, 682; the Second Battle of Leipzig, 601
Lenin, Vladimir Ilyich, 642
lenses, 405, 583-584, 623
Lent, 406, 493, 567, 655; the Lenten Synods, 298-300
Leo III, Byzantine emperor, 252-253

782

Leo the Great, St., pope, 220-222, 224; St. Leo III, 259-260; St. Leo IX, 283-284, 328; Leo X, 482-485, 487-488, 496, 529-530, 566
León, 377, 419, 467
Leonardo da Vinci, 406, 459-460, 475, 477, 481, 484-485, 732
Leonine City, the, 465
Leopold IV, duke of Austria, 327; Leopold V, 354, 356
Leopold I, German emperor, 639
Leopold of Hohenzollern-Sigmaringen, 715
Leper King, the, see Baldwin IV
Lepidus (d. 77 BCE), 107; (d. 13 BCE), 122-124, 126, 130
Lesbos, the Lesbians, 45, 78, 102
Lessing, Gotthold Ephraim, 661
Levant, the, see the Middle East; the Levant companies, 538; the Levantine religions, 435, 671, 690
Levi, Hermann, 721, 726
Liber Augustalis, the, 386
Liberal Arts, the, 118, 229, 395, 400-402, 486, 509, 697
liberalism, 88, 525, 634, 649, 661, 667, 675, 678-679, 696, 704, 716-717, 722
liberty, see freedom
Libethra, 45
libraries, 91, 141, 210, 216, 229, 231, 256, 275, 459, 569-570, 572, 619, 624, 641, 660, 673; the Library of Alexandria, 91-93, 115, 137; the Cæsareum library, 156, 219; the Great Library, 93; the Serapeion library, 93, 207; the Library of San Marco, 459
Licinius, Valerius Licinianus, the Elder, 183-184, 186-187; the Younger, 187, 199
Liège, 268, 444
lighting, outdoor, 11, 275, 550, 675
Limassol, 414, 416
Limbo, 356, 397
Lindisfarne, 269
linguistics, 2, 19, 24, 102, 134, 201, 276, 619, 622, 625, 687-689, 699, 714-715
Linnæus, Carolus, 658
Lissa, the Battle of, 712
literacy, 9, 13, 50, 229, 256, 271, 273-275, 314-315, 317, 380, 418, 445, 491, 517, 539, 566, 604, 634, 636, 654, 673, 688
Lithuania, 354, 453, 646
liturgy, 165, 172a, 195, 208-209, 222, 229, 242, 250, 258, 263, 311, 547, 615
Liudhard of Canterbury, St., 241
Liutgarde of Alemannia, 266
Liutprand, king of the Lombards, 253-254

Livia Drusilla, 126
Livius Andronicus, 100
Livonia, 354, 387, 503, 640
Livy, 115, 120-121
Locke, John, 546, 628-629, 632-635, 642, 656, 666, 683
Lodi, the Peace of, 458
logic, 52a, 73, 78, 87, 89, 143, 237, 319, 395-396, 398, 401, 403, 437, 516-517, 519, 554, 592-593, 659, 684, 695
logoi sophon, 169
Logos, the, 73, 96, 139, 164, 172a, 191, 219
Lohengrin, 274, 710-711, 713, 715, 729
Loire, the river, 270, 444-447
Lollards, the, 441, 541
Lombardy, the Lombards, 235-239, 253-256, 258, 264-265, 267, 280, 282, 284, 286, 296, 299, 310, 329, 336-338, 342-343, 359, 362, 383, 386-388, 390-392, 417, 481, 483; the Iron Crown of Lombardy, 255, 326; the Lombard League, 342, 359, 383, 386-388
London, 99, 241, 288, 291-292, 322, 419, 426, 550, 552, 558, 575, 588, 591, 594-596, 598, 611, 613-614, 616, 618-619, 621, 623, 630, 670, 673, 675, 677, 696, 709; the Treaty of London, 488
longbow, the, 433, 444, 450
Long Parliament, the, 609, 616
Lords, the House of, 592, 610
Lorraine, 268, 444-445, 639, 646, 715, 717; origin of the name, 268
Lothair, emperor of the West, 268; Lothair II, German emperor, 326-328
Louis I, duke of Bavaria, 382
Louis VII, king of France, 330, 333-335, 340, 353; St. Louis IX, 389-391, 409, 412, 421; Louis XII, 474, 476, 479, 482-483, 485; Louis XIV, 506, 535, 625-626, 628, 637, 642-643; Louis XV, 647; Louis XVI, 665, 667, 677; Louis XVII, 677
Louis II, king of Hungary and Bohemia, 504, 543
Louis the Pious, emperor of the West, 267; Louis II, 267
Louis Napoleon, see Napoleon III
Louis Philippe, king of France, 692-693, 696
Louisiana, 638, 647
Louvre, 669
lower classes, the, 17, 36, 54-56, 71, 75, 79, 94, 105, 108-109, 117, 123, 126, 130, 136, 152, 154, 157, 159, 214, 217-218, 249, 253, 256-257, 265-266, 269, 271-273, 275-276, 280, 287, 294, 304, 314-315,

317, 321, 323, 372-373, 377, 392, 416, 418, 433-434, 443, 448, 453, 458, 491, 494-495, 516-518, 521, 526-527, 530, 604-605, 607-608, 611, 627, 641-642, 647, 654, 656, 658, 664-668, 672-673, 674, 692, 694-696, 698, 730-731
Lucca, 111, 285, 304, 359, 430, 545
Lucera, 392, 405
Lucerne, 481, 714
Lucius II, pope, 331; Lucius III, 344
Lucretius, 100-101, 684
Lucullus, the villa of, 226
Ludwig II, king of Bavaria, 711, 713, 715-716, 720-721, 725-726, 729
Luitpold von Wittelsbach, 729
Lusatia, 709
Lusignan dynasty, the, 349, 355, 407, 411-412
Luther, Martin, 190, 487-493, 495-496, 499, 503-505, 509, 511, 514, 516, 518, 524, 533-534, 536, 598a; Lutheranism, Lutherans, 490-493, 497, 500, 502-505, 509-512, 517, 528, 531, 533-536, 546, 580, 598-601, 603, 714
Luxembourg, 444, 447
Luxor, 17
luxury items, 13, 41, 94, 272, 512, 625, 675, 692, 703
Lyceum, or Lykeion, 78, 91, 512a
Lydia, Lydians, 42, 56
Lyell, Charles, 700
Lyons, 161, 165, 176, 353, 423, 428-429, 483; the First Council of Lyons, 389
lyre, 43, 45-46
Lysander, 71
Lysimachus, 90
Lytton, 1st baron, see Bulwer-Lytton

Maccabees, the, 127; the Books of the Maccabees, 189
Macedon, the Macedonians, 42, 45, 60, 78-79, 82-83, 88-90, 92, 114, 116, 121, 124, 187
Macedonius of Constantinople, 205; Macedonianism, Macedonians, 205-206
Machiavelli, Niccolò, 473-477, 546
Macrina the Younger, St., 211
Madison, James, 615a, 667a
Madoc, Owen, 563-564, 610
Madrid, the Treaty of, 496
Mæcenas, 131, 133-134
Mænads, the, 42-43, 46
Maestlin, Michael, 567
Magdeburg, 709
Magi, the, 99, 144, 194, 207, 240, 460
magic, magicians, 3, 6, 10-11,

13, 15, 28, 33, 46, 51, 68, 84, 133, 142, 145-146, 179, 230, 437, 447-448, 466, 516-518, 521-522, 550-551, 557, 566, 570-571, 573, 579-580, 591, 597, 620, 622, 631-632, 634, 636, 644, 652, 654; magical spells, potions, etc., 6, 68, 437, 518, 571, 573, 727
Magna Charta, the, 377
Magna Græcia, 51, 70, 118, 296
Magna Mater, see the Great Mother Goddess
magnetism, 278, 399, 405, 466, 552, 572
Magyars, the, see Hungarians
Mahabharata, the, 691
Maine, 286, 289, 338, 377
Mainz, 304, 358, 387, 435, 505, 660
maize, 468, 657
Majorinus, bishop of Carthage, 185
malaria, 383, 478
Malta, 383, 432
Mameluks, the, 409-416; origin of the name, 409
Man, the Isle of, 112
Manchester, 579, 694, 698
Mandæism, Mandæans, 180
Mandans, the, 563-564
Manfred of Sicily, 390-391
Mani, 179-181; Manichæism, Manichæans, 180-181, 216-217, 315
Manifest Destiny, the, 693
manners, see etiquette
Mantua, 224, 459, 639
Manuel Comnenus, 333-334, 348
Manzikert, the Battle of, 295, 301
maps, map-making, 466, 539-540, 551-553, 561, 563, 565, 568, 570, 591a, 604
Marathon, the Battle of, 58-59
marble, 64, 135, 197, 225a, 366, 480, 498, 670
Marcellus the Centurion, St., 181-182
Marche, the, see Ancona
Marcian, 221
Marcion, Marcionites, 166-168, 170, 174, 175a, 315
Marcus Aurelius, 161
Marcus the Conjuror, 165
Mardia, the Battle of, 187
Marduk, 99
Mareotis, Lake, 85
Margaret of Antioch, St., 445; St. Margaret of Scotland, 292a
Margat Castle, 415
Maria Theresa, 645-646
Marie Louise, 676
Marienburg, 416
Marignano, the Battle of, 485
maritime trade, 18-23, 36-37, 54, 57-58, 70, 91, 94, 136-137, 227, 278, 250, 362-363, 367, 380-381, 382a, 407, 418-419, 432, 451,

455-456, 463, 468, 506, 528, 537-538, 544-545, 548, 552, 554-555, 563-564, 575-577, 578-579, 591, 611-614, 647, 657-658, 676
Marius, 105-106
Mark the Evangelist, St., 221; St. Mark's Basilica, 366; the League of St. Mark, 469; the Monastery of San Marco, 459
market economy, 20, 323, 511, 672, 696
Marlowe, Christopher, 550, 570
Marmara, the Sea of, 197, 367
Marranos, the, 577, 613
marriage, 5, 25, 28, 34-35, 39, 45, 47, 92, 115-116, 173, 201, 227, 262-266, 273-274, 316-317, 429, 452, 455, 449-500, 503, 590-591, 606-607, 641, 664, 672-674, 706, 721-722; clerical marriage, 177, 265a, 298, 303, 514; matrimonial alliances, 71, 105-106, 107-108, 112-113, 126, 149, 184, 221, 223-225, 232, 236, 260, 264-266, 270, 283, 287-288, 308, 326, 334-335, 341, 355, 357-358, 377, 379, 382-383, 388-389, 415, 451, 453, 458, 467, 469, 472, 474, 476, 483, 488, 499-500, 506-507, 540-541, 543, 545, 553, 555, 590, 638, 681
Mars, the Roman god, 109; the planet, 582; the Martian Field, 122, 214
Marseillaise, the, 669
Marseilles, 56, 114, 175, 353
Marshall, John, 610
Martial, 152, 257
Martin IV, pope, 414-415; Martin V, 442
Martin of Tours, St., 233
martyrdom, martyrs, 144, 150, 154, 159, 161, 175, 178, 182, 191, 207, 243, 247, 273, 337, 340, 355, 369, 448-449, 508, 540-542, 549, 650, 730
Marx, Karl, 684-686, 695-696, 699a
Mary, St., mother of Jesus, 171, 189a, 219, 244, 274, 312, 354, 366a, 518; Santa Maria, 466; Santa Maria delle Grazie, 460; Santa Maria Maggiore, 466; Santa Maria sopra Minerva, 586; Santa Maria del Fiore, see the Duomo of Florence; Santa Maria del Popolo, 476; Piazza Santa Maria, 465
Mary of Antioch, 412, 414
Mary I, queen of England, 488, 500, 514, 540-542, 544, 549, 551, 553; Mary II, 628
Mary of Habsburg, 543

Mary Magdalene, 174
Mary Stuart, 549, 565, 574, 590
Mary Tudor, see Mary I
Mass, the, 195, 208, 245, 284a, 290, 314, 340, 385, 409, 424, 452, 548, 565
Massachusetts, 608, 636
Massilia, see Marseilles
mass production, 276, 320, 618a, 641, 654, 672, 674-676, 692-694, 697-698, 703
masturbation, 671
Matera, 282
Mater Dolorosa, title of St. Mary, 435, 680
materialism, 95-96, 201, 368, 373, 695, 702, 719
mathematics, 9-10, 49-51, 77, 92, 120, 156, 218, 277, 394, 399, 403-405, 531, 550-551, 556-559, 565-566, 569-570, 573, 580-583, 592, 623, 629-630, 633-634
Matilda of Flanders, 283, 288
Matilda of Tuscany, 300, 375
matriarchy, 25, 31-33, 39, 49
Matthew of Albano, Blessed, 321
Matthew the Apostle, St., 174
Matthias, German emperor, 600
Maurice, Byzantine emperor, 238
Maurice, elector of Saxony, 535
Maxentius, 182-184
Maximian, 182
Maximilian the Great, duke of Bavaria, 602
Maximilian I, German emperor, 482-483, 486, 488; Maximilian II, 555
Maximin Daia, 182-183, 186
Maximinus Thrax, 178
Maximus, Magnus Clemens, 206; Petronius Anicius, 225
Maxwell, Sir Robert, 621
May Day, 519, 607
Mayow, John, 620
Mazarin, Jules, 602
mead, 40
Mecca, 248, 348-349
mechanics, 10, 404, 459, 558, 629
mechanistic philosophy, 632-633
Medici dynasty, the, 443, 457-459, 468, 470, 472-473, 482-483, 485, 496-497, 504-505, 529, 545, 639; the origin of the name, 457
Medici, Alessandro de', 496; Catherine, 506-507; Cosimo I, 457, 459, 461-462; Cosimo II, 583; Giovanni, see Leo X; Giuliano, 496; Giulio, see Clement VII; Ippolito, 496; Lorenzo, 462, 469, 482
medicine, physicians, 3, 9, 62, 68, 92, 118, 228, 275, 277, 314, 347, 374, 379, 394, 398, 401, 430, 457, 509, 517-524, 526-527, 530, 598, 604, 619, 625, 654-656, 693, 715, 729

784

Medina, 248, 348
Mediterranean Sea, the, 21, 37, 85, 142, 176, 227, 268, 278, 313, 345, 407, 418, 432, 455, 537, 545, 548, 638; the eastern Mediterranean, 20, 22, 30, 54, 62, 142, 296, 362, 408, 455, 506, 537; the Mediterranean region, 3, 13, 23, 36, 61, 138, 142, 246, 252, 261, 281, 296, 326, 328, 352-353, 357, 379, 407, 412, 418, 456, 505, 545, 548, 554, 586
Melanchthon, Philip, 531, 534, 536; the Melanchthonians, 536
Meletius of Antioch, St., 206
Melfi, 282, 386; the Constitutions of Melfi, see Liber Augustalis
Melito of Sardis, St., 245
Memphis, 17-18, 89
Menasseh ben Israel, 613
Mendelssohn, Moses, 648
mendicant orders, the, 372, 403, 407
Menes, 18
mental institutions, 655
Mercator, Gerardus, 552
mercenaries, 56, 83, 272, 284, 288, 302, 320, 332, 341, 364, 389, 392, 413, 433, 439, 458, 475, 481, 486, 493, 497, 554, 601
merchants and traders, 13, 18, 20-21, 23, 36-37, 54, 56-58, 67, 70, 76, 91, 94, 99, 136-137, 150, 175, 227-228, 252, 256, 272, 278, 313, 320-321, 323-325, 346, 349, 356, 362, 367, 372-373, 380-381, 382a, 399, 407, 411, 415, 418-419, 424, 434, 451, 455-457, 463, 468, 506, 511, 520, 537-538, 542, 544-545, 548, 550, 552, 554-555, 563-564, 576-579, 591, 604, 608-609, 611-614, 621, 641, 656-658, 664, 666, 673, 675-676, 692, 698
Merlin the Wizard, 445
Merovech, 224; the Merovingians, 224, 232-233, 241, 253-254, 256
Mesopotamia, 85, 115, 176, 179, 186, 202, 220, 277, 347-348, 688
Messenia, the Messenians, 36
Messiah, the, 142, 145, 148, 150, 157, 159-160, 171-172, 613
Messina, 296, 353, 358, 415
metallurgy, 91, 314, 519-520
metaphysics, 74, 81, 95, 313, 396-397, 557-558, 587, 625-626, 630, 634-635, 684, 702, 707
Methodism, 515a, 686
Metternich, Clemens von, 677, 682, 696
Metz, 258, 304, 482, 535, 545,

716
Mexico, 243, 468
Meyerbeer, Giacomo, 710
Micah, the Book of, 170
Michael the Archangel, St., 239, 280, 445
Michael Cærularius, 284
Michael Palæologus, 408-409, 412, 414-415
Michelangelo Buonarroti, 472, 480-481, 529, 732
microscopes, 585, 593, 625, 630-631
Middle Ages, the, 22, 51, 53, 78, 80, 102, 133-135, 153, 156, 158, 179, 209, 216, 226-227, 231, 251a, 257, 260-262, 268, 271-457, 460-461, 468, 490, 494-495, 501, 503, 509, 511, 516-519, 524, 533, 539, 548, 550, 557, 563, 587, 591a, 592, 594, 598, 603, 606, 619-620, 632, 635, 643, 658-659, 666, 675, 686, 696, 716, 726, 736
middle classes, the, 159, 272, 392, 456-458, 502, 507, 510-511, 536, 591, 604, 608-609, 614, 626-627, 630-631, 644, 656-657, 660, 665, 672-673, 675, 692-693, 696-699, 701, 703, 711, 736
Middle East, the, 1, 18, 115, 250, 520, 394, 412, 435, 538-539, 671, 690
Midsummer Day, the, 523
Milan, 184, 186, 190a, 196, 205, 214, 236, 326, 338, 342, 391, 418, 443, 458-460, 469, 474-475, 479, 482-483, 485, 488, 505-506, 528, 545, 639; Milan Cathedral, 460; the Edict of Milan, 184, 211
Miletus, 37, 57-58
military orders, the, 320-325, 346-347, 349-356, 354, 358, 366, 376, 382-385, 407-409, 411, 413-416, 419, 424-432, 450, 466, 503, 598, 623-624, 728
millenarianism, 612-613
Milman, Henry Hart, 340
Milo, 112, 117
Miltiades, 58-59
Milvian Bridge, the, 183
mines, miners, mining, 79, 178, 181, 184, 519-521, 542, 694
minnesingers, 135, 311, 370, 379-380
Minos, 20; Minoans, see the Cretans
Minotaur, the, 20, 721
Mint, the Royal, 618a, 630, 632
Minucius Felix, Marcus, 175
miracles, 3, 142, 145, 160, 183, 189a, 191, 232, 247, 333, 340, 352, 374, 398, 635
mirrors, 331, 405, 623
Misenum, 126, 226; the Treaty of Misenum, 126

Mishnah, the, 173
missi dominici, the, 262
missionary work, 42, 99, 142-143, 148, 158, 162a, 170, 176, 180-181, 185, 191, 202, 217, 230-233, 240-241, 248-249, 268-269, 305, 369, 372, 395-396, 450, 511, 527, 565, 574-576, 581, 627, 686-687, 689, 706
Mississippi, the river, 698
Mithradates, 99; Mithridates IV of Pontus, 105-106
Mithradatic Wars, the, 105-106
Mithras, Mithra, Mitra, 98-99, 144, 171, 188-190, 194, 207; Mithraism, 98-100, 144, 190, 194, 207
mitre, origin of the, 194
Mohács, the Battle of, 504
Mohammed, 247-248, 249a, 250-251, 350, 389, 397, 410; Mohammedans, see Muslims
Mohammed the Conqueror, 451-452, 455
Molay, Jacques de, 425-426, 430
Moluccas, the, 537, 575
Mona, the Isle of, 110
monarchianism, 177
monarchy, 7, 14-18, 25, 75-76, 79, 90, 129, 230, 248, 253-254, 260, 265, 298-300, 338, 366a, 376, 388, 443, 453, 496, 501, 549, 562, 589, 607, 609-610, 627-628, 639, 645, 651-652, 649, 668, 676, 679-681, 683-684, 696, 704-705, 711, 736; absolute monarchy, 55, 57, 77, 90, 277, 297, 340, 421-422, 443, 453, 456, 458, 462, 486, 490, 501, 504, 543, 591, 603, 610, 626-627, 640, 643, 668, 679, 685, 713, 737; constitutional monarchy, 627, 633, 667, 692-693, 679, 716, 737
monasticism, monks, 179, 198, 208, 211-212, 216, 218-220, 228-231, 237-238, 240-242, 247, 250, 253-254, 257-259, 269-270, 272-274, 278, 283, 287-289, 291-292, 298, 303-304, 309, 311, 314-315, 317-321, 327, 329-331, 335, 339-340, 366, 369, 371-374, 386, 403-404, 411, 420-422, 429, 431, 439-440, 459-460, 470, 485, 487-488, 492, 497, 502-503, 507-509, 518-519, 526, 543, 547, 580, 601, 651, 706; origin of the term, 211; double monasteries, 211, 220, 270, 403; monastic schools, 256-258, 268-270, 273; monastic vows, 321-322, 429, 503, 526; the

785

dissolution of monasteries, 502-503, 507-508, 513-514, 542, 569, 606, 649, 706
Moneta of Cremona, 395
Möngke Khan, 409
Mongols, the, 388-389, 409-410, 434, 453, 471
Monk, George, 616
monogamy, 34, 263, 265, 607
monophonic music, 44, 258
monophysitism, 222
monotheism, 47, 68, 96-97, 138-139, 161, 164, 179, 248
Monsalvat, 726, 728
Montaperti, the Battle of, 391
Mont Cenis, 183, 300
Monte Cassino, 258, 301
Monte San Angelo, 280
Montesquieu, baron de, 643-644, 667
Montfort, Simon de, 370-371
Monza, the Cathedral of, 239
Moon, the, 10-12, 156, 383, 559-660, 583, 629; full moon, 10, 244, 246; lunar divinities, 10-11, 245-246; the lunar month, 12, 567
Moors, the, 251, 256, 275, 305, 313, 371, 459, 467-468, 574-575, 577-578
Moray, Sir Robert, 617, 621
More, St. Thomas, 508
Moriah, Mt., 107, 202, 250, 308, 320
Mormonism, 613, 686
Morocco, 252, 505
morphology, 662
Morris, Gouverneur, 610; Robert, 610
Mortlake, 569-571
Moscow, the Muscovites, 453, 520, 552, 641, 677; the see of Moscow, 453, 642; the Muscovy Company, 552
Moses, 139, 184a, 562, 614; the Five Books of Moses, see the Pentateuch; the Mosaic code, 144, 436, 612
mosques, 277, 296, 308, 320, 347, 365, 385, 411, 414, 451-453, 468
Mosul, 332, 347
Mozart, Wolfgang Amadeus, 644
Mühlberg, the Battle of, 534-535
Mühleck, Barbara, 581
multiplication table, the, 51
mummification, mummies, 6, 8, 37
Munda, the Battle of, 117
Munich, 651, 693, 711, 713, 715, 719-721, 726
Muret, the Battle of, 371-372
Muses, the, 30, 43-45, 92; the Museum of Alexandria, 91-93, 115, 137, 156, 178, 207, 218
museums, 618, 620-621, 622a, 624-625, 670; the Ashmolean, 618, 620-621, 624-625; the British Museum, 570, 573,

579, 670, 688; the Musée Napoléon, 670
music, 42-46, 50-51, 65, 80, 134, 151, 231, 257-258, 311, 380, 401, 525, 558, 625-626, 644-645, 708-711, 714, 718-721, 723, 725-728; vocal music, 43-45, 65-67, 80, 102, 176, 231, 243-244, 256-258, 311, 313, 370, 456, 510, 585, 625-626, 709-710, 718-719, 726
Muslims, 78, 88, 156, 185, 247-253, 255, 259, 261, 269, 275-278, 282, 286, 295-296, 305-306, 307a, 308, 312-313, 318, 321-322, 324, 326-327, 331-332, 334-335, 347-351, 354-356, 358, 361, 362, 370, 374, 379-382, 384-385, 387, 389-390, 392, 394, 397-399, 402a, 403a, 405, 407, 409-413, 417-418, 427, 429, 451-455, 466-468, 505-506, 518, 523, 525, 528, 534a, 537-539, 575-576, 671, 677a
Mussolini, Benito, 706
Myazd, the, 98
Mycale, the Battle of, 60-61
Mycenæ, the Mycenæans, 22-23, 29, 688
mystery religions, 8, 28-29, 39, 45, 47-49, 67, 84, 98, 159-160, 172
mysticism, 137, 159, 178, 228a, 278, 399, 557, 631-632, 634, 660, 707
myths, mythology, see ancient legends

Nag Hammadi, 176
Nantes, the Edict of, 555, 637
Naples, 281, 328, 342, 390-392, 415, 427, 438-439, 443, 454, 458, 469-472, 476, 478-479, 486, 488, 545, 639, 669, 676, 696
Napoleon Bonaparte, 255, 668-670, 676-683, 686, 688, 696, 732
Napoleon III, emperor of the French, 696, 705, 715-716
Napoleon II, king of Rome, 676
Napoleonic Wars, the, 676-683
Narses, Byzantine general, 235
National Convention, the French, 668
nationalism, 49, 53, 63a, 103, 150, 213a, 222, 228, 251a, 312, 359, 441-442, 448, 453, 467, 486, 490-492, 502, 513, 525, 544, 555-556, 561-562, 588, 601, 603, 606, 621-622, 661, 678-679, 681-682, 685, 695, 698, 701, 716-717, 721, 725, 729, 734-735; nation-states, 97, 453, 548, 692, 698, 737
National Socialism, 695, 734-735

Nativity of Christ, the, 189
natural economy, see barter economy
natural philosophy, see science
natural selection, 700-701
nature, 3, 6, 10, 28, 33, 39, 47, 96, 244-245, 398, 437, 522, 557, 593, 597-599, 619, 622, 629, 631-632, 634, 636, 644, 654, 658-660, 669-702; nature deities, 37-38, 40; the laws of nature, 10, 50, 398, 404, 437, 459, 557, 581-582, 592-594, 596-597, 599, 622, 629, 631-632, 633, 635-636, 651, 666; the order of nature, 15, 96, 98, 123, 494, 700; the Natural Kingdom, 3, 38, 662
naval warfare, 16, 20-21, 54, 58-62, 69-71, 82-84, 106, 111, 115, 125, 128, 131, 187, 224-225, 231, 278, 282, 289-290, 296, 328, 334, 341, 346, 348, 351, 353, 358, 361-364, 366-367, 376, 382, 384, 407, 412, 414, 425, 454-455, 463, 465, 482, 528, 537-538, 554, 563, 574, 579, 612, 626, 638, 640, 647, 675, 677; British navy, 562-563, 579, 591, 612, 675, 677; Dutch navy, 554, 612
Navarre, 474, 479, 483-484, 555
navigation, 466, 550, 552, 558, 561, 564-566, 585, 613
Navigation Acts, the, 611
Nazareth, 170, 385, 410, 414
Nazism, see National Socialism
necromancy, 145, 557, 566
Nectarius of Constantinople, St., 206
Neoplatonism, 78, 178-179, 216-218, 268, 396, 461, 557-559, 581-582
Neoteric poets, the, 103
Nephthys, 6
Nepos, Cornelius, 102; Julius, 225
nepotism, 390, 464, 483, 529
Nero, 144-148, 227, 722; the Golden House of Nero, 147, 150
Nerva, 152-153
Nestorius of Antioch, 219-221; Nestorianism, Nestorians, 219-221, 276-277, 409, 461a
Netherlands, the, 130, 444, 486, 489, 496, 506, 510-513, 520, 522, 538, 542-544, 547-548, 552-555, 576-579, 583, 586, 600, 602-603, 611-614, 626-628, 634, 637-639, 641, 658, 669; the Austrian Netherlands, 639, 669; the Spanish Netherlands, 638-639
Netjer, 4, 12-13, 16
Neuf Sœurs, le Société Nationale des, 667

786

neuroses, 711, 718, 724
Neuschwanstein, 726, 729
New England, 608, 615, 621, 683
Newfoundland, 466, 564, 638
new gentry, the, 542
New Jerusalem, 162, 172, 184a
New Laws, the, 575
New Model Army, the, 609-610
newspapers, 80, 673, 682, 701, 730
New Testament, the, 165-168, 173, 175, 209-210, 403, 491, 512, 533, 595-596, 687; origin of the term, 175; canon of the NT, 165-166, 173, 209-210, 533; translations of the NT, 209, 403, 491, 596
Newton, Sir Isaac, 557-558, 581, 619, 623, 629-634, 642, 643a, 683, 700
New Year's Day, the, 243-244, 246
New York, 577, 613-614
New Zealand, 576a
Nibelung saga, the, 224, 380, 710, 719
Nicæa, 192, 302, 304-306, 320, 334, 366-367; the Council of Nicæa, 193, 195, 198, 245, 562, 567; the Second Council of Nicæa, 258-259; the Empire of Nicæa, 367, 389, 408
Nice, 443; the Treaty of Nice, 506
Nicephorus I, Byzantine emperor, 260
Nicetas of Remesiana, St., 208-209
Nicholas, St., 192
Nicholas II, pope, 285, 425; Nicholas III, 414; Nicholas V, 466, 479-480
Nicholas I, Russian emperor, 642
Nicomedia, 182, 186-187, 192, 196, 200
Nicopolis, 136
Nietzsche, Elisabeth, 714, 734
Nietzsche, Friedrich Wilhelm, 72a, 713-716, 718, 720-728, 730-736
Nike, 42, 63, 207a
Nile, the river, 1-2, 4a, 5-6, 8-9, 13, 17, 85, 87, 90, 250, 346; the flooding of the Nile, 1-2, 12-14
Nile delta, the, 5, 8, 17, 89; the Battle of the Delta, 116
Nile Valley, the, 2, 8, 13-14, 19, 382, 686
Nineveh, 85, 688
Niš, 196
Nisibis, 155, 176, 220
Noah, 2, 481, 572, 686
nobility, the, see the upper classes
noblesse de robe, the, 605; the noblesse de l'épée, 605, 627
Nogaret, Guillaume de, 421, 423-425, 430

nomads, 2, 11, 14, 23, 203, 244, 247, 295-296, 302, 352a, 409, 689
Nominated Assembly, the, see the Barebones Parliament
Nordenskiöld, Adolf Erik, 552
Normandy, the Normans, 270-271, 280-294, 296, 299, 301-303, 305-307, 326-328, 336-338, 341-342, 353, 357-358, 376-377, 379, 392, 398, 403, 412, 415, 417, 448, 501, 561, 573, 588, 611; the Normans of England, 282-283, 287-294, 299, 338-339, 376, 403a, 573; the Normans of Ireland, 341, 588, 611; the Normans of southern Italy, 280-288, 296, 299, 301-302, 305-307, 326-328, 336-338, 342, 353, 357-358, 379, 392, 398, 403a, 412, 415, 417
Norman Conquest of England, the, 289-294, 303, 403, 501, 561; the Norman Conquest of Ireland, 341, 588; the Norman Conquest of southern Italy, 280-288, 296
North America Act, the, 647
Northeast Passage, the, 552; the Northwest Passage, 613
North Sea, the, 256, 268, 602
Northumbria, 242, 289, 291
Norway, the Norwegians, 287, 289-290, 293, 378
Notre-Dame Cathedral, 316, 429
Novara, 475, 483
Nova Scotia, see Acadia
novels, 380, 455, 598, 659-660, 663, 673-674, 695, 709, 736
Noyon, the Treaty of, 486, 488
Nubia, 2, 18
nuclear family, 657, 672, 674-675
numbers, numerology, 10, 30, 50-51, 120, 171, 179, 399, 557-558, 573, 582, 592
nuns, 211, 228, 264, 317-318, 403, 498, 502-503, 594, 601; nunneries, 229, 233, 273-274, 317-318, 357, 360, 372, 403, 460, 500, 502-503, 507, 594
Nur ad-Din, 332, 335, 345, 347, 407
Nuremberg, 375, 531, 719; the Peace of Nuremberg, 505
nymphs, 26, 31

oaths, 13, 50-51, 68, 90, 151, 284, 288-289, 301, 305, 308-309, 375, 464, 507-508, 586, 617, 693, 706; oaths of allegiance, 58, 150, 182, 300, 308-310, 338, 346, 359, 376, 392, 497, 605, 638, 676; oaths of fealty, 255, 286-288, 291-293, 305, 307-308, 342,

356, 376, 503
obelisks, 17, 140, 197, 669
observatories, 92, 580, 584, 623, 698
occultism, 466, 517, 551, 557, 570-571, 573, 579, 581, 619, 632, 660
Octavia, 126-127
Octavian, 123-129; as Augustus, 129-137, 152-153, 156a, 199, 227; the Cæsareum of Alexandria, 156, 219
Odeion, or Odeon, 65
Odenathus, Septimius, 179
Odo of Bayeux, 292
Odoacer, 226, 231
Odyssey, the, 20a, 24, 55, 100
Œcolampadius, Johannes, 552-553
Œdipus, 119
Old Catholics, the, 705-706, 722
Old Oligarch, the, 95
Old Testament, the, 93, 165, 167, 171, 201, 209, 248, 435, 491, 493a, 512, 533, 595, 612, 632, 688; origin of the term, 175
oligarchy, 54, 69, 71, 458
olives, olive oil, 37, 40-41, 48, 64, 252
Olympia, 34, 53, 64; the Olympic games, 58-59, 82, 207
Olympus, Olympian deities, 25, 27-29, 31-37, 42, 53, 63, 95, 98, 662
Omar, caliph of Islam, 249-251
omophagia, 46, 160
O'Neill, the clan, 230, 341, 513, 588, 590, 611; Conn Bacach O'Neill, 513; Hugh, 588-590; Owen Roe, 611
Onnophiris, title of Osiris, 5
opera, 233, 477, 625-626, 644, 708-710, 713, 718-719, 725-728
optics, 404, 583, 592, 631
Optimates, the, 105, 109, 112-113, 121
optimism, 701-702, 708, 736
oral tradition, 24, 163, 165-166, 168-169, 173, 230, 256, 294, 518, 561, 707
Oresme, Nicole, 530
Orestes, prefect of Alexandria, 218; Roman general, 226
orgiastic religion, 42, 44-46, 725
Origen of Alexandria, 162-164, 172a, 176, 178
Orléans, 233, 445-447, 449, 474, 570, 635, 692
Orpheus, 45-46, 63a, 134, 171; Orphism, Orpheans, 39, 42, 47-50, 63, 95, 172
Orsini family, the, 438, 465, 469, 471, 476-477
Ortelius, Abraham, 552
Orthodox Church, the Eastern, 162, 171, 172a, 192, 209, 221-222, 227-228, 252-253, 258-260, 263, 265a, 267, 276, 278, 284, 296a, 304,

333, 350-351, 363, 365-366, 414, 417, 451, 453, 461a, 514a; the Oriental, 222, 248a, 250, 461a; the Russian, 453, 642
orthodoxy, religious, 67, 95, 149, 160, 162, 165, 167-168, 174-177, 180, 185, 198, 204-205, 211, 217-221, 317, 369, 399, 406, 442, 511, 532, 537, 539, 603
Osiander, Andreas, 531
Osiris, 2, 4-9, 38, 93, 98, 670; the symbols of Osiris, 8; Osiris gardens, 6
Ostia, 213, 224, 479
Oswald of Northumbria, St., 242
Otho, 148
Otto IV, German emperor, 359-360, 375-377, 381
Otto, king of the Hellenes, 679
Overman, the, 718, 725, 731-732, 734-735
Ovid, 134-135, 257, 656
Oxford, 618, 624

Pachomius of the Thebaid, St., 211
Padua, 443, 482
paganism, pagans, 78, 136-139, 143, 145, 154, 158-161, 163-164, 167, 170-172, 181, 183-184, 188-191, 197, 201-203, 206-207, 215-219, 224, 229-231, 241, 243, 245-245, 255, 258, 269, 271, 273, 278, 304, 333a, 356, 380, 383, 387, 397, 410, 436, 450, 460, 466, 481, 530, 540, 562, 575, 585, 607, 615, 663, 671, 725, 727, 734; origin of the term, 217
Paine, Thomas, 649
painting, 2, 17, 21, 42, 64, 252-253, 456, 460, 472, 480-481, 484, 611, 625, 711, 726
Paladins, the, 255
Palæologi dynasty, the, 415, 453
palæontology, 662
Palatine Hill, the, 118, 130
Palermo, 296, 328, 357, 359, 375, 381, 391; the Cathedral of Palermo, 327
Palestine, 83-84, 88-89, 91, 93, 107, 115-116, 127, 136-137, 141-142, 145, 147-150, 155, 157, 166, 172-173, 192, 247, 249-250, 259, 280, 284a, 287, 295, 297, 302-303, 306-308, 320-322, 324, 332, 333a, 334-335, 344-350, 352-358, 361-362, 365, 366-367, 374, 381-389, 407-410, 412, 414, 417, 419, 423-425, 450, 467-468, 506, 526
Palladium, the, 197
Palmyra, 179
Pamplona, the siege of, 526

Pan, 38, 113-114
Panathenaia, 55, 65
Pandora, 32
panegyrics, 82, 117, 119, 183
Pangæus, Mt., 46
Panhellenism, 28, 36, 64, 70, 79, 82, 88
Pannonia, the Pannonians, 187, 203, 223-226, 232
Pantheon of Rome, the, 443
papacy, 163, 165, 175, 177-178, 192, 208-210, 220-222, 224, 233, 237-241, 246, 253-255, 258-260, 262, 264, 267, 269, 271, 274, 280, 283-286, 288-289, 291-292, 296-305, 307-311, 317, 321, 323-324, 326-331, 333, 335-344, 351, 353-354, 357-365, 369-379, 381-393, 404, 408-409, 412, 414-415, 418-431, 433, 436-443, 449, 451, 453-456, 460, 463-472, 474-485, 487-490, 492-502, 504-507, 510, 513-514, 516, 520, 524-533, 541-542, 544-547, 554, 556, 559, 562, 566-568, 572, 574-575, 584-588, 572, 585, 601-603, 617, 626-627, 644-645, 650, 676, 669, 678, 696, 704-706, 716, 722; origin of the term, 208; papal banner, the, 286, 289, 304, 359, 385; papal bulls, 284, 324, 333, 340, 361, 422, 426, 428-429, 431, 466-467, 489, 513, 566-567, 602, 644; papal blessing, 267, 288-289, 478, 575, 669; papal elections, 163, 177, 238, 283, 285-286, 296, 301, 309, 327, 338, 340, 343-344, 389, 414, 419-423, 431, 438-440, 442-443, 455, 464, 472, 478, 484, 496, 546; papal encyclicals, 297, 361; papal fiefs, 285, 288, 292, 301, 337, 358, 375, 388, 390, 469, 471, 476; Papal Infallibility, 705; papal legates, 192, 221, 284, 292, 297-298, 305, 308-309, 317, 321, 326, 331, 337, 351, 359, 369-371, 377, 385, 388, 420, 430, 439, 453, 470, 474, 488, 500, 527, 541, 602
Papal States, the, 238-239, 255, 329, 337, 354, 358-359, 375, 385, 388-389, 427, 431, 438, 443, 465, 471, 475, 477, 479, 481-482, 529, 545, 585a, 676, 704-705
paper, 276, 400, 454, 578; papyrus, 9, 17-18, 91, 115, 210; parchment, 210, 404
Paracelsus, 518-524
Paraclete, the, 181, 318; the Convent of the Paraclete, 318, 330
Paris, 206, 234, 316-317, 319, 325, 330-331, 404, 412, 418-419, 425-429, 433, 444, 447, 471, 559, 599, 625-626, 665, 667, 677, 709, 716, 720; the siege of Paris (1870-71), 716-717; the Treaty of Paris (1763), 647
parlements, the French, 626; the Parlement of Paris, 485
parliaments, British, 568a, 638, 681, 693; English, 500-501, 507, 514, 541-542, 548, 568, 574, 589-592, 594, 608-612, 614-616, 621, 627-628; Irish, 513, 609; Scottish, 549, 591, 638
Parma, 286, 483, 650
Parmenides, 73-74, 684
Parnassus, Mt., 48, 201
Parsifal, 230, 380, 711, 725-728
parthenogenesis, see virgin birth
Parthenon, the, 63-64, 130, 670
Paschal III, antipope, 342
Paschal II, pope, 309
Paschal Lamb, the, 244-245
Passau, the Treaty of, 535
Passetto, the, 465
passion, see suffering; divine passion, 8, 167, 169, 245, 435, 596, 704, 732
passive obedience, 607, 628
Passover, 244-245
Patay, the Battle of, 447
patriarchs, the Hebrew, 248, 495, 612,
patriarchy, 25, 31-35, 39, 49, 180, 628, 656
patricians, the, 105-106, 121; the Patrician of Rome, 226, 231, 301
Patrick of Ireland, St., 241
Patrimony of St. Peter, the, 375, 476, 705
patronage, 93, 131, 151, 379, 398, 411, 456, 458-459, 463, 465, 472, 477, 479, 484, 529, 551, 571-572, 580, 586, 589, 618-619, 621, 645, 653, 685, 711, 720
Paul, St., 141-143, 145-146, 162a, 163, 165-167, 170, 376, 421, 495, 533, 732-733; the Pauline Christians, 146, 166-167; the Pauline Epistles, 159, 166-167, 169-171, 172a, 173-175, 209, 315, 495, 533, 633; St. Paul's Cathedral, 623, 624a
Paul III, pope, 513, 525-530, 532; Paul IV, 546-547; Paul VI, 468
Pavia, 213, 236, 254, 336, 338, 470; the Battle of Pavia, 496-497
Pax Augusta, 130; Pax Romana, 157
peasantry, 36, 54-56, 71, 75, 152, 217, 256, 265-266, 272-273, 275, 287, 294,

788

304, 317, 392, 416, 433-434, 445, 448, 458, 494-495, 516-517, 521, 604-605, 607-608, 642, 664, 666-667, 672-674, 696; peasant rebellions, 434, 494-495
Peasants' War, the, 494-495, 509
Peckham, Sir George, 564
Pedius, Quintus, 123-124
Pelagius, 216
Pelagius II, pope, 238
Pelasgians, Pelasgos, 19, 26, 28
Pella, 78
Peloponnese, the, 126, 452, 455, 679
Peloponnesian War, the, 71
penance, 177, 239a, 279-280, 291, 300, 303, 339, 340, 345-346, 370, 374, 423, 439, 532
Penn, William, 610
Pennsylvania, 610
pentagram, 51
Pentapolis, the, 254
Pentateuch, the, 93, 633a
Pentecost, the, 170, 567, 616
Pentheus, 41-42, 44
Pepin the Short, king of the Franks, 254
Pepin I, king of Italy, 255, 267
Perdiccas, 90
perfumes, scents, incense, 91, 136, 207a, 276, 278, 545
Pericles, 61-65, 70-71, 130-131, 679
periodicity, 6, 10-11
Peripatetic school, the, 78; Peripatetics, see Aristotelians
perjury, 288-289, 440, 464, 536
Persepolis, 54, 86
Perseus, 31
Persia, the Persians, 18, 23, 54, 56-63, 65, 70-71, 82-86, 89-92, 94, 98-99, 112, 120-122, 125-127, 138, 155, 158, 166, 171, 175, 178-181, 199-200, 202, 220, 227, 236, 249-251, 260, 399, 687-688, 690, 723; the Seleucids, 91; the Parthians (Arsacids), 112, 116, 120-122, 125-127, 155, 175, 179; the Sassanids (neo-Persians), 179-180, 222
Persian Gulf, the, 86, 153, 537
Persian Wars, the, 57-61, 63, 65-66, 70, 83
Peru, 14-15, 468
Perugia, 125, 239, 391, 481
pessimism, 708, 722
pestilence, see plague
Peter the Apostle, St., 145-146, 155, 163, 170, 174, 177, 221, 240, 242, 285, 299, 376, 385, 421, 480, 489, 547, 626; the Petrine Christians, 146, 166; the Petrine Epistles, 162, 168, 172; St. Peter's Church, in Antioch, 352; in Rome, 140, 190, 214, 242, 259-260,

301, 337, 377, 421, 475-476, 479-480, 484, 487, 507, 529, 585; St. Peter's Square, 465, 476, 706; Peter's Pence, 289, 292, 376; the Banner of St. Peter, see the papal banner; the Vicar of Peter, 373
Peter II, king of Aragón, 371, 377; Peter III, 415
Peter Damian, St., 286
Peter the Hermit, Blessed, 304-305
Peter Lombard, 395, 400
Peter of Maricourt, 405
Peter the Great, Russian emperor, 640-642; Peter III, 646
Peter the Venerable, Blessed, 330
Petrarch, 438
Petronius, Publius, 141
Pevensey, 290
Pforta, 714
Phædra, 199
phallos, phallicism, 5, 38, 47, 670
Pharaoh, 2, 5-7, 14-18, 22, 84, 128a, 184a
Pharisees, the, 116, 142, 147, 173, 339, 368
Pharos, the lighthouse of, 85
Pharsalus, the Battle of, 114, 116, 121
Pherecydes, 49, 171
Phidias, 64
Philadelphia, 610, 622a, 650
Philip the Apostle, St., 519
Philip I, king of France, 286, 293, 308; Philip II, 351, 353-354, 357, 360-362, 369-371, 375-377; Philip IV, 421-431; Philip VI, 433
Philip the Good, 444-445, 447
Philip of Hesse, 491, 504, 535
Philip of Macedon, 78-79, 82-83, 90
Philip II of Spain, 528, 540-545, 549, 553-555, 563, 565, 574, 577-578, 637
Philip of Swabia, 358-360, 362-363
Philippi, the Battle of, 124, 131
Philius, 27
Philo, 89, 138-139, 166
philology, see linguistics
philosophical dialogue, the, 72-74, 585-586
philosophy, philosophers, 49-50, 52, 62-63, 72-77, 80-81, 87-89, 94-98, 101, 106, 118, 137-139, 143, 145, 151, 156, 159-164, 169, 178-180, 191-192, 201, 207, 218, 228, 240a, 268, 277, 316, 318-319, 379, 385, 387, 394, 396, 397, 399-401, 404, 406, 461-462, 465a, 473, 484, 509, 516-517, 519, 523, 550, 556-559, 569, 581, 583, 587-588, 592-593, 594a, 597-599, 631-636, 643-645,

647-648, 653, 656, 658-659, 664-667, 669-670, 683-685, 687, 700, 702-703, 707-708, 714-715, 718-719, 723-725, 727-728, 730, 734-735; origin of the term, 50
philosopher's stone, the, 599
philosophes, the, 635, 644, 659
Phocæa, 56
Phœnicia, the Phœnicians, 19, 23, 37, 54, 83-84, 96, 145, 686; Phœnician language, 9, 23
Phrygia, the Phrygians, 16a, 90, 99, 669
physics, 78, 92, 101, 277, 558, 580, 582, 586, 620, 630, 632-633, 643a, 662, 702; particle physics, 582, 620; the laws of physics, 581-582, 629, 631
Piacenza, 302, 483
Pico della Mirandola, Giovanni, 462, 465, 558, 582
Picts, the, 230-231, 562
Piedmont, 342, 443
pilgrimages, pilgrims, 48, 247, 259, 274, 280-281, 283, 295, 297, 302, 320-322, 324, 334, 340, 348, 351, 355, 381a, 405, 414, 421, 423, 456, 475, 487, 506, 526, 720, 728
Pilgrimage of Grace, the, 508
Pindar, 43, 49
piracy, pirates, 23, 106, 218, 224-225, 269, 320, 528, 563-564, 591
Pisa, the Pisans, 105, 331, 351, 394a, 407-408, 440-441, 470; the Council of Pisa, 482
Pisistratus, 55
Pius II, pope, 455, 478; Pius III, 478; Pius V, 556; Pius VII, 650a, 669, 678; Blessed Pius IX, 696, 705-706, 722
plagiarism, origin of the term, 152
plague, 235, 237-238, 239a, 323, 342, 412, 434-436, 444, 559, 602, 694, 722
planetary motion, 156, 399, 581-582, 584, 629, 631
Plantagenet dynasty, the, 335, 338, 357, 541
plants, 1-3, 6, 8, 10-11, 37-38, 40, 48, 53, 521, 575, 620-621, 657-658, 662
Platæa, the Battle of, 60
Plato, 20, 49, 68, 71-78, 80-82, 87, 92, 138, 179, 216, 227, 356, 394, 454, 461, 484, 519a, 581, 645, 679, 657, 703; Platonism, Platonists, 73-75, 77-78, 81, 87, 89, 94, 138, 159, 161, 163-164, 178, 216, 380, 454, 461, 582
Platonic Academy of Florence, the, 461-462
plebeians, Roman, 105, 108, 121, 136

Pliny the Younger, 154
Plotinus of Alexandria, 49, 78, 178-179
plough, the, 10, 24, 28-29, 39
Plutarch of Chæronea, 5-6, 38, 77, 111, 116, 125, 228, 679
Pluto, 29-30, 32-33, 48, 49
Pnyx, the, 56
Po River, the, 118; the Po Valley, 101-102, 236
poetry, poets, 9, 23-26, 36, 41, 43, 45, 49, 55, 66, 68, 73, 78, 80, 94-96, 100-104, 131-134, 151, 196, 230-231, 258, 277, 311-314, 347, 370, 379-380, 438, 456, 460-462, 471-472, 492, 585, 599, 622, 625-626, 643, 645, 648, 659-661, 663, 673, 681, 683, 689, 691, 694-695, 702-704, 710, 714, 717, 719, 722-723, 736; the poet laureate, 438, 626
Poitiers, the Battle of, 253
Poitou, 299, 335, 351, 377
Poland, the Poles, 337, 354, 377, 383, 388, 396, 453, 503, 511, 530, 567, 571-573, 587, 601-602, 639-641, 646-647, 650, 659, 716; the Partitions of Poland, 647
Pole, Reginald, 541-542, 545
poleis, see the Greek city-states
political parties, 51, 54, 69-70, 105-109, 109, 112-113, 121, 129, 327-328, 463, 627, 652, 730, 734
political science, 57, 62, 69, 71-72, 74-75, 78, 80-82, 87-88, 90, 97, 105, 108, 133, 143, 237, 246, 248, 270, 310, 326, 363, 375, 377, 379, 383, 393, 417, 431, 438, 451, 453, 456, 463, 465, 473-474, 492, 494, 513, 515, 532, 539, 547-549, 554, 572, 579, 596-597, 603-606, 610, 627-628, 633, 637, 642-643, 645, 648, 654, 659, 661, 666, 668-669, 678, 684-686, 691-692, 695, 698, 701, 703, 708, 711, 717, 720, 736-737
Polo, Marco, 466
polygamy, 34, 263, 265, 607
Polygnotus of Thasos, 64
polyphonic music, 44, 231, 311
polytheism, 248, 249a
Pombal, marquês de, 649
Pompeius, Gnæus, 107-114, 115a, 116, 121, 125; Sextus, 125-126
Pontian, St., pope, 178
Pontifex Maximus, the, 107, 110a, 119-120, 126, 130, 132, 188, 190, 208
Pontus, 105-106, 195
Popish Plot, the, 627
Populares, the, 105-106
Porcia Catones, 124

Porphyry of Tyre, 179
Portugal, the Portuguese, 277, 377, 419, 427, 429, 439, 451, 454, 466-467, 496, 537-538, 540, 547, 555, 563-564, 574-577, 603, 613, 649, 658; Portuguese language, 118, 577, 699
Portus Itius, 111
Poseidon, 31-35, 37
potatoes, 468, 589, 657, 697
Prætorian Guard, the, 130, 152, 184, 188; the Prætorian Prefects, 130
Prætors, the, 107, 121
Pragmatic Sanction, the, 485
Prague, 571-573, 580-581, 720; the Peace of Prague, 601
prairies, the, 693-694
Prato, 359, 457, 483
praying, prayers, 7, 15, 33, 43, 50, 68, 211, 227, 234, 250, 260, 278, 299, 308, 320-323, 339, 420, 452, 460, 510, 518, 522, 704, 731; the Lord's Prayer, 316, 688; prayer books, 271, 548
predestination, 216, 511, 515, 701
Prefect of Rome, the, 205, 213, 218, 224, 237-238, 358-359
Premysl Ottokar I, king of Bohemia, 377
Presbyterians, 609-610, 627
Pressburg, the Treaty of, 504
Prester John, 466
Preston, the Battle of, 610
Pride, Thomas, 610
priesthood, Egyptian, 6, 7a, 12, 17-19, 37, 84, 92; Greek, 46-49, 66; Jewish, 93, 107, 137, 147, 149, 157-158; Persian, 99, 181, 194; Roman, 105-106, 208
prince, origin of the term, 129
printing, 80, 257, 454-455, 459, 488-489, 491, 517, 539, 546-547, 550, 552-524, 531, 569, 586, 595-596, 601, 643, 673
Prisca, wife of Diocletian, 181, 186
Priscillian of Ávila, 206
privacy, 229, 263, 606, 617-618, 682, 737
privateering, 563-564
Proclus of Athens, 78, 179
proletariat, the, see the lower classes
Propertius, 119
prophets, prophecies, 45, 121, 133, 142, 147-148, 163, 165, 168, 170, 174, 180-181, 248, 249a, 335, 337, 406, 420, 438, 445, 470, 472, 574, 578, 632, 635, 680, 704, 734; Hebrew, 149, 157, 159, 170, 201, 480-481, 612, 632-633; pagan, 33, 46, 184a, 723
prose literature, 201, 217, 312, 461, 594-595, 625-626, 673, 708, 734, 736

prostitution, prostitutes, 42a, 145, 188, 401, 441, 446, 547, 656, 665, 695
protagonist, origin of the term, 67
Protectorate Parliaments, the, 612, 614
Protestantism, 396a, 491-493, 502, 505, 510-511, 513-514, 516, 525-529, 531-537, 541-543, 546-550, 553-555, 560-563, 565-569, 572a, 580-581, 586, 590, 599-604, 606-607, 611, 615, 617, 627, 634-635, 637-638, 643, 646, 649, 674a, 683, 688, 697, 702, 721; origin of the term, 504; the Protestant Reformation, 449, 464a, 490-494, 496, 498-499, 502-503, 505, 508-514, 516-518, 522, 524-525, 527, 529, 531-534, 536, 540a, 542, 544, 549, 560, 564, 569, 590a, 597, 606-607, 615a, 617, 645, 656-657, 687
Protestant Union, the, 600
Provence, the Provençals, 232, 306, 313, 370-372, 379, 439; Provençal language, 118
provinces, Roman, 101, 106-107, 109, 111-113, 116-118, 121, 123-125, 127-128, 130, 132, 135-136, 147, 152-153, 155, 162a, 182, 184-185, 187, 192, 200, 212-213, 215, 218, 249, 253, 281, 296; provincial governors, 107, 109, 111-114, 116, 118, 121, 136-137, 141, 148, 155, 157, 218, 265, 334
Prudentius, Aurelius Clemens, 178, 209
Prussia, the Prussians, 383, 387, 432, 503, 509, 520, 639-641, 645-648, 650, 661, 676-678, 680, 682-685, 695a, 696, 705, 709, 711-718, 722, 736; East Prussia, 503, 639, 647; West Prussia, 640, 647
Psalms of David, the, 531; the Psalms of Solomon, 107
psychology, 78, 521, 710, 718, 723, 735
Ptolemæus the Valentinian, 164
Ptolemies, the, 90-93, 136-137; Ptolemy I Soter, 90, 92-93; Ptolemy II Philadelphus, 92-93; Ptolemy XI Auletes, 115; Ptolemy XII Neos Dionysus, 115-116
Ptolemy, the ancient astronomer, 156, 399, 530, 580-581, 585; the Ptolemaic theory, 156, 530, 580, 584, 586, 630
Publicans, the, 109
Pulcheria, St., 221
Pulpit Article, the, 722
Punic Wars, the, 100

790

Puranas, the, 689, 691
Purgatory, 295, 532-533
Puritanism, Puritans, 190, 565, 607-612, 614-616, 621
pyramids of Giza, the, 15, 347, 670; the Battle of the Pyramids, 670
Pyrenees, the, 215, 313, 338, 371
Pythagoras, 31, 49-52, 73, 557, 632; Pythagoreanism, Pythagoreans, 49-52, 68, 74, 77, 159, 558, 582; the Pythagorean Theorem, 51

Qabalah, 462, 558
quadrivium, the, 401
Quakers, the, 615
Quinisext Council, the, 245
Quintana, Manuel José, 678

Ra, 6, 16
Rabelais, François, 509
rabbis, 142, 148-149, 157-158, 160, 172-173, 194, 462, 613; Rabbinical Judaism, 158, 166, 173, 251, 275a
racism, 435, 515, 690, 695, 701, 734-735
railroads, 153, 693, 698
Rainulf of Aversa, 280-281
raison d'état, 605
Raleigh, Sir Walter, 564, 588-589, 612, 703
Ramadān, 248
Ramayana, the, 727
Ramesses III, 22
Ramla, the Peace of, 355
Ranke, Leopold von, 358, 714
Raphael, 465, 481, 484, 487
rationalism, 95-96, 396, 522, 559, 573, 592-593, 595a, 596, 634-635, 643-644, 648-649, 659, 666, 675, 684-685, 707, 718
Ravenna, 213-215, 226, 232, 235, 237, 253-254, 301, 375; the Battle of Ravenna, 483; the Exarch of Ravenna, 235, 239, 242, 254
Rawley, William, 596
Raymond I, prince of Antioch, 332, 334
Raymond IV, count of Toulouse, 305, 307-308; Raymond VI, 369-371
Raymond II, count of Tripoli, 332, 413; Raymond III, 348-349
Raymond-Roger de Trencavel, 371
Reason, the Age of, see Enlightenment
rebellion, 36, 52, 57-60, 89, 93, 105, 111, 113, 118, 125, 141, 147, 149, 155, 157, 253, 255, 282, 286-287, 293, 296, 309, 338, 341-342, 351, 356, 361a, 363-364, 390, 415, 422, 434, 438-439, 443, 475-476, 481, 492, 494-495, 501, 508, 535, 540, 541a, 544, 549, 554, 573, 577, 588-589, 600-601, 605, 609, 611, 678, 685, 696, 711
rebirth, 6, 163, 189, 460
Reconquista, the Iberian, 318, 403, 466, 575
recusancy, recusants, 556, 565
redemption, see salvation
Red Sea, the, 85, 184a, 244, 348, 537-538
Reformed Church, the, 493, 510, 533, 549, 574
Regensburg, 352, 653; the Regensburg Colloquy, 527-528
regicide, 122
Reims, 268, 309, 316, 447; the Cathedral of Reims, 447
reincarnation, 49, 162, 178
relics, 39, 274, 288-289, 291, 350, 366, 456, 518, 669-670, 680
Religion, the Wars of, 515, 549, 599
renaissance, origin of the term, 460; the Carolingian Renaissance, 257, 268; the European Renaissance, 485-486, 499, 509, 517-518, 522, 530, 547, 550, 557, 566, 572, 575, 582, 597-598, 600, 621, 625, 630-631, 687; the Italian Renaissance, 80, 91, 392, 400a, 402, 406, 438, 450, 454, 457, 459-463, 465a, 471, 475, 477, 479, 481, 484-485, 487, 497, 525, 529, 544, 546, 662, 703
republicanism, 122, 152, 329, 335-336, 343, 359, 439, 442-443, 610, 615a, 643, 667, 669, 696, 716, 736
reservatum ecclesiasticum, the, 536
Restoration of the Stuarts, the, 616, 623, 625-626
resurrection, 6-8, 38, 46, 47a, 116, 149, 161-162, 168-169, 174, 238, 243, 245, 398, 435, 598a, 704, 732; the Feast of the Resurrection, see Easter Sunday
Reuchlin, Johann, 492, 533, 558
Revelation of St. John, the, 210, 509, 533, 633
revolutions, 14, 105, 442, 493-494, 637, 642, 665, 677-678, 682-684, 693; the Agricultural Revolution, 1-2, 672; the American Revolution, 610, 648, 677; the French Revolution, 653, 657, 667-668, 670, 672, 678, 681, 683, 692; the Glorious Revolution, 627-628, 633, 692; the Industrial Revolution, 512, 636, 672, 677, 692, 694, 697-699; the July Revolution, 692; the October Revolution, 569, the Puritan Revolution, 607, 610, 616; the 1848 Revolution, 696, 710-711; the 1868 Revolution, 715; the Scientific Revolution, 558, 586-588, 622, 625, 629-630, 632
Reynald de Châtillon, 348-350
Rhætia, 118, 232
Rhea, 32
rhetoric, rhetoricians, 62, 73, 79-81, 106, 109, 163, 201, 205, 228-229, 237, 277, 400-401, 499, 519, 587-588, 594, 678, 704
Rhine, the river, 224, 274, 602; the Lower Rhine, 111, 375-376; the Rhine Valley, 99, 148, 151, 186, 204, 224, 304, 495; the Confederation of the Rhine, 676, 680, 682
Rhineland, the, 492, 715
Rhodes, 85, 106, 425, 432, 520
Rhône, the river, 270, 313, 370; the Rhône Valley, 303, 427
rice, 263, 276, 313, 578, 676
Richard of Aversa, prince of Capua, 284-285, 288
Richard Cœur-de-Lion, 347, 353-356, 360-361, 384, 424
Richard of Cornwall, 390
Richelieu, duc de, 602
Ricimer, Flavius, 226
Rienzi, 438, 709-710
rights, civil, 69, 89, 91, 116, 118, 173, 377, 468, 535, 555, 602, 614, 628; communal rights, 335, 337, 343, 359; human rights, 94, 387, 665-666; natural rights, 666; the right of individual conscience, 448, 536, 649, 722
Rimini, 254a, 475
roads, 14, 20, 94, 275, 320, 324, 347, 413, 675; Roman roads, 135, 153, 156, 272, 296
Roanoke Island, 568
Robert II, prince of Capua, 328
Robert II, count of Flanders, 302
Robert Grosseteste, 403
Robert Guiscard, 283-286, 288, 296, 301-302, 305, 328
Robert I, duke of Normandy, 281; Robert II, 286, 293, 305
Robert de Evereaux, archbishop of Rouen, 281
Robert de Baudricourt, captain of Vaucouleurs, 445
Robespierre, Maximilien F. M. I. de, 668
Robin Hood, 294, 356
Roderic, king of Spain, 251
Roger I, count of Sicily, see Roger de Hauteville; Roger II, king of Sicily, 326-328, 336
Roland of Brittany, 255, 312
Rolf the Viking, 270, 281
Romagna, the, 235a, 359, 475, 479, 481-482, 704
Roman army, the, 99, 106-109,

791

112-114, 116a, 122, 124-126, 128, 144, 147-150, 158, 181-183, 186-189, 191, 194, 200, 203, 206, 212-214, 224, 227, 235
Roman Empire, the, 8, 16, 29, 48-49, 53, 88, 97-100, 118, 125-227, 252, 260a, 261, 263-264, 271-272, 276, 297, 328, 337, 363, 367, 453, 464a, 534, 562
Roman Question, the, 706
Roman Republic, the ancient, 97, 103-124, 128-131, 152, 643, 669, 704; the mediæval, 335, 343, 359, 439
Romance languages, 102, 118
Romanticism, 659-661, 663, 678, 701-703, 707, 711, 723, 726, 728, 736
romantic love, 313, 317, 606, 672, 674
Romanus Diogenes, 295
Rome, the city, 91, 97, 100-101, 105-110, 112-119, 121-124, 126, 128-131, 134-135, 140-142, 145-148, 150, 152, 163, 175-179, 183-184, 189-190, 194, 196-199, 201, 205, 207a, 208-209, 212-214, 220-221, 225-227, 230-231, 235, 237-239, 241, 253-254, 258-260, 267-268, 283, 285-286, 288, 292, 301-302, 304, 309, 327, 329-330, 333, 335-338, 342-344, 351, 354, 358-360, 371-372, 377, 388-389, 391, 420-421, 423, 426-427, 437-440, 442-443, 451, 453, 459, 463-465, 469-472, 475-476, 479, 481, 484-485, 487-488, 493, 496-498, 506, 526, 529-530, 545, 547, 562, 575, 584-586, 662, 676, 696, 704-705; the Romans, 28, 52, 96, 98-103, 108-110, 112, 114, 117-120, 123, 127-131, 135, 137, 141, 143, 147, 149, 151, 154, 157, 159, 175, 190a, 196-197, 201, 213-215, 224-225, 227, 229, 231, 238, 241, 261, 263, 272, 283, 285, 294, 301, 335-337, 344, 351, 354, 391, 399, 438-439, 465, 497-498, 546, 562, 684, 686, 705; Roman citizenship, 97-98, 114, 116-118, 136, 142, 144, 154, 170, 196, 226, 252
Romulus Augustulus, 226
Roncaglia, the diets of, 336, 338
Rooke, Sir George, 638
Rosamund, 236
Roscelin, 316
Rosenberg, Wilhelm von, 572-573
Roses, the Wars of the, 471, 549
Rosetta Stone, the, 688

Rosicrucians, the, 597-599, 617-618, 634, 660, 707
Rosslyn Chapel, 322
rotary press, the, 673
Rouen, 270, 281, 286, 448
roundheads, the, 609-610
Rousseau, Jean Jacques, 644
Royal Society of London, the, 618-619, 621-623, 625-626, 629-631, 634
Rubicon, the river, 113-114
Rudolph I, German emperor, 393; Rudolph II, 555, 571-573, 580-581, 600
Rudolph of Rheinfelden, 300-301
Rugilas, 223
Rump Parliament, the, 610, 612
Russia, the Russians, 278, 297, 388, 409, 453, 552, 569, 640-642, 646-647, 656, 660, 668, 677-679

Saale, the river, 255
Sabazios, 40-41, 46
Sabbath, the Jewish, 141, 166, 173, 190; the Christian Sabbath, 190, 614
Sabines, the, 151
sacraments, the, 47, 98-99, 160, 200, 258, 330, 368, 372, 374, 427, 448, 493, 499, 511, 532
sacred marriage, the, 34, 49
sacrifice, 15, 29-30, 32, 47, 63, 110a, 144, 202, 207, 245, 374, 700, 733; animal sacrifice, 28-29, 32a, 44, 46, 58, 63, 98, 244; human sacrifice, 110, 154, 395
sacrilege, 46, 65, 288-289, 436, 514
Sadducees, the, 137, 142, 614
sadomasochism, 656, 703, 731
Saint-Loup, 446
Saint-Quentin, the Battle of, 545
saints, Catholic, 146, 168, 176, 204-205, 207, 230, 233-234, 237, 240, 243, 247, 253, 315, 317, 319, 321, 323, 327, 333, 340, 366a, 369, 372, 389, 396, 403, 435, 437, 445, 448-449, 480, 488, 501, 508, 510, 516, 518, 522, 547, 612, 683
Saladin, 346-352, 354-356, 407, 409, 411, 413, 418
Salamis, the Battle of, 59-60
Salem witch-craze, the, 636
Salerno, 301; the Medical School of Salerno, 379, 398
Salisbury, 293, 401, 541
Sallust, 103, 257
Salome Alexandra, Queen of Judæa, 107
salvation, 7, 47, 49, 95, 145, 159-161, 169, 179-180, 192a, 218-219, 232, 303, 322, 374, 420-421, 514-515, 517, 564, 599, 649, 704, 725, 727-728, 732-

733; soteriology, saviours, 7, 28, 68, 90, 98, 132, 160, 164, 171-172, 181, 184, 597, 718, 727-728; the Mountain of Salvation, see Monsalvat
Salza, Hermann von, 382-383
Salzburg, 524, 604
Samaria, the Samaritans, 89, 93, 136, 145, 150
Sámos, 49, 56
Samothrace, 30
Sancho I, king of Portugal, 377
Sangallo, Antonio de, 465, 529
San Germano, the Treaty of, 385-386
Sanhedrin, the, 93, 136-137, 141, 149, 194, 612
sanitation, 275, 434-435, 654, 675, 695
Sanskrit, 9, 687, 689-690
Sans Souci, 648
Sant Helena, 680
Sappho, 43, 45, 102
Saracens, the, see the Muslims
Sardinia, 100a, 111, 118, 124-126, 178, 388, 486, 545, 639, 678, 704
Satan, see the Devil
satires, 473, 492, 509, 570, 626; Greek satire, 66
Satyrs, 44
Saul of Tarsus, see St. Paul
Savelli family, the, 470, 476
Savonarola, Girolamo, 462, 470, 472-473
Savoy, 443, 459, 482, 504a, 545, 639, 678, 704
Saxa Rubra, the Battle of, 183
Saxony, the Saxons, 215, 245, 255-256, 267, 269, 326-327, 333a, 336, 343, 488-490, 517, 535-536, 646, 676, 680-681, 709-710, 713, 716; the English Saxons, 230, 241, 254, 269, 283, 287-288, 290-294, 312, 357, 493a, 562; Electoral Saxony, 488, 490, 535, 601, 640; Prussian Saxony, 709, 713
Scandinavia, 520, 601, 656, 659, 720
Scheiner, Christoph, 584, 586
Schiller, Friedrich von, 661
Schiner, Matthäus, 481
schisms, 178, 185, 191, 220, 260, 285, 288, 330, 342-343, 448, 474, 482-483, 527, 541, 568; the Great Eastern Schism, 208, 259, 284, 297; the Great Western Schism, 431, 439-440, 442
Schlegel, K. W. Friedrich von, 688
Schleiermacher, F. D. E., 685
Schleswig-Holstein, 712
Schmalkaldic League, the, 505, 528, 534; the Schmalkaldic War, 534-535
scholars, 78, 80, 91-93, 118, 137, 158, 218, 228-229, 231, 246, 257, 275-277, 311, 314, 330, 347, 373,

792

397-398, 400-401, 406, 436, 454, 459-461, 465, 484, 499, 507, 516-517, 519, 522, 527, 533, 539-540, 546, 550, 557, 560-561, 569-570, 582, 587, 591, 595, 597, 605, 626, 630, 641, 661, 686-687, 689-691, 705, 722, 729-730
Scholasticism, the Schoolmen, 268, 277, 318-319, 396-398, 403-406, 437, 509, 592
Schönkopf, Anna Katharina, 660
Schopenhauer, Arthur, 707-708, 714-715, 718-719, 722, 724-725
Schwyz, 519
science, scientists, 9-11, 49-53, 62, 68, 75, 77-78, 80-81, 91-92, 96, 119, 156, 218, 228, 252, 276-277, 328, 379, 387, 394-401, 403-406, 454, 456, 459, 463, 473, 485, 518-522, 530-531, 547, 550-552, 556-558, 560-561, 565-566, 569-570, 573, 575, 580-582, 585-587, 592-594, 596-598, 601, 618-625, 629-636, 643, 645, 647-648, 655, 657-658, 661-662, 666, 670, 682-684, 689-690, 695, 697, 699-702, 707, 722-723, 735-736; the terms, 699
Scipio, 113, 116, 669
Scot, Michael, 394; Reginald, 591
Scotland, the Scots, 153, 230, 240, 242, 268-269, 292a, 322, 341-342, 419, 426, 439, 483, 510, 512-513, 549, 560-561, 565, 574, 589-591, 609-611, 616-617, 627, 637-638, 654, 666, 675; origin of the name, 230
sculpture, 42, 62-64, 197, 456, 459, 472, 480, 670, 711
Scythia, the Scythians, 23, 57, 61, 213, 224
seasons, the, 10-12, 14, 17, 30, 120, 189, 243, 245-246, 567
Second Coming of Christ, the, 263, 612
Sedan, the Battle of, 716
Seine, the river, 270, 319
Seleucia, 155
Seleucus Nicator, 90-91
Self-Denying Ordinance, the, 609
self-discipline, 41, 50, 96, 155, 724
Semele, 43, 46, 48
seminaries, 547, 648, 702
Semitic languages, see Hamito-Semitic languages
Senate, the Roman, 105, 107-114, 117, 122-124, 128-130, 132, 144, 152, 155-156, 158, 184, 197, 207,

235, 237, 335-337, 359, 438
Seneca the Elder, 115; Seneca the Younger, 669
Sens, the Council of, 329-330
separation of powers, the, 667
Septuagint, the, 93, 209
Serapis, 93, 207
Serbia, 196, 236, 363
serfdom, serfs, 36, 256, 265, 434, 445, 492, 494-495, 666
Sertorius, 107
Set, 5-6, 8
Settlement, the Act of, 638
Seven Years' War, the, 646-647
Severus, Alexander, 178; Flavius Valerius, 182, 186; Julius, 157; Libius, 225; Septimius, 156a, 197
sexuality, 35a, 135, 180, 246, 262, 298, 477, 516, 606, 656, 670-672, 674-675, 703, 724
Seymour, Jane, 500-501, 514
Sforza dynasty, the, 458, 469, 489, 505; origin of the name, 458
Sforza, Ascanio, 469-470; Catherine, 475; Francesco, 458-459; Francesco II, 497, 505; Giovanni, 469, 472; Ludovico, 459-460, 469-471, 474-475, 483; Massimiliano, 483, 485
Shadwell, Thomas, 626
Shakespeare, William, 122, 126, 134, 550, 570, 594-595, 625-626, 732
Shapur I, king of Persia, 180-181; Shapur II, 199-200
Shaw, George Bernard, 736
Shawer, 345-346
Sheldonian Theatre, the, 625
Shelley, Percy Bysshe, 703
Shepherd of Hermas, the, 210
ship money, 608
Shirkûh, 345-346
Short Parliament, the, 609
Siberia, 453, 698
Sibylla of Acerra, Queen of Sicily, 359
Sibylla of Jerusalem, 349
sibyls, the, 481
Sicarii, the, 149
Sicilian Vespers, the, 415
Sicily, the Sicilians, 37, 60, 70, 74, 76-77, 100, 107, 124-126, 232, 237, 281-282, 286-287, 296, 299, 305, 326-328, 336-338, 342-343, 351, 353-354, 355a, 357-359, 361a, 375, 379-381, 383, 385-387, 389-392, 394, 403a, 405, 412, 414-415, 419, 427, 443, 470-471, 479, 486, 545, 639, 650, 678, 680, 705; the Two Sicilies, 354, 357-358, 390, 392, 412, 443, 650, 678, 705
Sickingen, Franz von, 492-493
Siena, 359, 438, 471

Sigismund, German emperor, 441-443
Silesia, 388, 645-646
silk, 91, 193, 213, 276, 331, 537, 545, 578, 613, 637, 665; the Silk Road, 176
Silva, Lucius Flavius, 149
Silvia of Rome, St., 237
Simon Magus, 145-146, 240; Simon Peter, see St. Peter
simony, 289, 303, 330, 344, 464, 472, 477; origin of the term, 146
sin, 97, 159, 177, 208, 216, 264, 279, 281, 309, 322, 339, 353, 368, 371-372, 374, 376, 396, 398, 401, 418, 421, 428, 430, 437, 448, 450, 514, 559, 614, 654-655, 671a, 675, 703, 731; the confession of sins, 330, 368, 374, 514, 642; the remission of sins, 99, 177, 184, 281, 300, 308-309, 322, 339, 363, 374, 376, 421, 428, 450, 541; the doctrine of Original Sin, 216, 514, 656
Sinai, Mt., 139, 210, 247; the Sinai Peninsula, 381
Sinigaglia, 254a, 477
Sinuhe, 9
Sirach, the Book of, 169, 495
Sirius, see Sothis
sirventés, the, 370
Siwa, 84
Six Articles, the Act of, 514, 528
Sixtus IV, pope, 464-465, 480; the Sistine Chapel, 479-481, 585; Sixtus V, 572
skepticism, 161, 217, 406, 460, 617, 636, 683
slaves, slavery, 21, 25, 27, 54, 56, 69, 75, 94, 96, 99, 125, 148-149, 152, 158-159, 214-215, 239, 251, 263, 269, 273, 287, 304, 320, 333, 350, 396, 409-411, 417, 452, 468, 480, 494, 538, 563-564, 575-576, 611, 614, 642, 669, 679, 693, 699, 723-725, 731-732, 734; origin of the term, 538; abolition of slavery, 693, 699
Slavs, the, 19, 190, 255, 271, 333a, 354, 453-454, 538, 647, 716
smallpox, 654
Smith, Adam, 666
Smyrna, 56, 679
Social Darwinism, 700-701
Socialism, 695-696, 729-730; Social Democrats, 730; the Anti-Socialist Law, 729-730
sociology, 700, 723
Socrates, 88, 71-74, 77, 80, 87-88, 98, 648
Soissons, the Abbey of, 258; the Council of Soissons, 317-318
Solon, Solonic laws, 27, 54-55, 64, 71

793

Somerset, 403
son of god, 6, 8, 16, 25, 28, 30-31, 39, 46, 49, 129, 133-134, 171, 188, 191, 193, 198, 219, 232, 248, 299, 733
Sophia Palæologus, 453
Sophists, 73, 80-81, 94
Sophocles, 49, 66-67, 227
Sophronius I, patriarch of Jerusalem, 249
sorcery, see magic
Sosigenes of Alexandria, 120
Soter, 28, 90, 93, 98, 160a, 164, 172
Sothis, 11-12
soul, human, 4, 7, 13, 41, 44, 47, 50, 68, 76, 95, 101, 111, 123, 162, 178, 202, 237, 242-243, 245, 303, 322, 360, 368, 388, 420, 490-491, 515, 533, 556, 564, 576, 702, 719
Spahis, the, 538
Spain, the Spanish, 37, 100a, 101, 107, 111, 113-114, 116, 118, 124-125, 152-153, 155, 204, 215, 232, 240, 251-252, 255, 275, 296, 305, 313, 318, 369-371, 377, 386, 394, 403, 415, 427, 439, 443, 464-469, 471, 476, 478-479, 482-486, 488-489, 496-499, 504-506, 511, 525-526, 528-529, 535, 540-549, 553-556, 563-565, 570, 572-579, 588-590, 591a, 593, 600, 602-603, 611, 613-614, 637-640, 647, 650, 658-659, 668, 678-679, 683, 688, 696, 715; Spanish language, 118, 526; unification of Spain, 467, 484; Hispania Terraconensis, 148; Hispania Ulterior, 107
Spanish Succession, the War of, 637-640
Sparta, the Spartans, 36, 53-54, 59-62, 69-71, 82-83, 97, 669
Spear of Destiny, the, 727
Spencer, Herbert, 700-701
Spenser, Edmund, 570
Speransky, Michael, 641-642
Speusippus, 77
Speyer, 304; the Cathedral of Speyer, 333; the First Diet of Speyer, 495; the Second Diet of Speyer, 504
spices, 136, 213, 537, 545, 576, 613, 621, 676; the Spice Islands, see the Moluccas
Spinoza, Baruch, 577
Spoleto, 236, 253, 359, 375, 475
Sprat, Thomas, 622
spring, religious associations of, 6, 28, 34, 38, 48, 55, 66-67, 244, 493a; the Spring Equinox, 244, 246, 567
Spurs, the Battle of the, 483

Stadion, or Stadium, 64-65
Stagira, 78
stake, the, 181, 243, 275, 395, 430-431, 437, 441, 446, 448-449, 472a, 509, 541, 596, 609
Stamford Bridge, the Battle of the, 290
St. Andrew's Monastery in Rome, 237, 241
Star of Bethlehem, the, 559
Star Chamber, the, 574, 608-609
state religion, 49, 99, 176, 202, 250, 536, 548, 556, 606, 615
St. Bartholomew's Day Massacre, the, 559-560
St-Clair-sur-Epte, the Treaty of, 270
steam power, 405, 672, 675, 697; steamboats, 675, 693, 698
Stein, H. F. Karl von, 683
Stephen Báthory, 571
Stephen of Blois, 305, 341
Stephen Harding, St., 319; St. Stephen of Hungary, 504
Stephen I, St., pope, 221; Stephen III, 254
Sterne, Laurence, 649
St. Gall, 258
St-Gilles, 305, 369-371
Stigand, 288-289, 292
Stilicho, Flavius, 212-213, 223, 226
Stoa Poikile, the, 64, 97; Stoics, Stoicism, 28, 88-89, 96-98, 151, 154a, 159, 161, 687
stock market, 550, 577, 717, 729; joint-stock companies, 538, 552
Stone Age, 700; the Neolithic period, 2, 10, 672
St. Petersburg, 641-642
Strasbourg, 435, 520, 522, 534, 598
Stratford-upon-Avon, 594
Strongbow, Richard, 341
St. Sabas, the War of, 408
Stuart dynasty, the, 230, 549, 590, 611-612, 616, 618, 625-628
Sturm und Drang, 659, 661, 664
Stuyvesant, Peter, 614
Styria, 600
Suetonius, 104, 106, 122-123, 145, 149, 151, 257
suffering, 5, 96, 330, 594a, 654, 701, 704, 707, 725, 732
Sufism, 399
sugar, 276, 537, 576, 578
suicide, 72, 116a, 124, 128, 148-150, 212, 661, 678, 729
Suleyman the Magnificent, 506, 528, 539
Sulla, 105-108, 129; the Sullan proscriptions, 108
Sun, the, 8, 10-12, 18, 46, 75-76, 123, 156, 188-189, 243, 348, 383, 405, 466, 530-531, 559, 580-581, 583-584, 586, 629; solar divinities, 6, 16, 46, 98, 183, 188-190, 197, 718; Sunday, 190, 195, 245-246, 420, 493a, 614; sun spots, 584; the solar year, 12, 119, 567
surgery, surgeons, 520-521, 655
Susa, the Italian city, 85-86; the Persian city, 342
supernatural, 4, 26, 191, 244, 300, 333, 437, 518, 522, 557, 570, 633, 635-636, 655, 700
Supremacy Acts, the, 507-508, 590
surveying, 9, 86, 551, 565, 568
survival of the fittest, 701, 724a
Sverre Sigurdsson, 378
Swabia, the Swabians, 213, 226, 235, 265, 267, 284, 299, 301, 325-326, 352, 358-359, 362-363, 390-391, 393, 519; the Suebi and the Alemanni, 109, 213
Sweden, the Swedes, 236, 438, 552, 561, 601-602, 640-641, 646
Swinburne, Algernon Charles, 703-704
Swiss Guard, the, 481, 497, 705
Switzerland, the Swiss, 130, 189, 240, 481, 483, 485-486, 489, 493, 497, 519-520, 524, 602, 669, 705, 710, 713-714, 718, 720; Swiss mercenaries, 481, 486, 493, 497
Symmachus, Quintus Aurelius, 205
synagogues, 140-141, 158, 467; the Great Synagogue of Jerusalem, 308
syphilis, 471, 493, 521-522, 733
Syracuse, 49, 60-61, 77, 282
Syria, the Syrians, 83-84, 90-91, 111-112, 115-116, 121, 124, 127, 136-137, 141, 145, 147-148, 160, 163, 166-167, 173, 176, 180, 186, 189, 192, 195, 206, 220, 222, 247-250, 252, 287, 306-307, 320, 332, 347-348, 385, 407, 409-412, 416, 467; Syriac language, 165, 222, 276, 633; the Syrian Church, 167-168, 189, 191-92, 195, 211, 219-220, 222, 250, 333, 350-351

Tacitus, 146, 148, 214, 486
Tænarum, Cape, 53
Tagliacozzo, the Battle of, 391
Talbot, John, 446-447; Edward, see Edward Kelly
Talmud, the, 116; the Talmudic academies of Babylonia, 251, 275a
Tanakh, the, see the Hebrew scriptures
Tancred of Antioch, 308
Tancred of Lecce, 353, 357

Tannhäuser, 380, 710, 726
Taranto, or Tarentum, 52, 74, 100, 126, 296, 305-306, 390
Tarsus, 186
Tartars, the, 302, 369, 409, 520; origin of the name, 302a
Tatian, 167
taurobolium, the, 99
taxes and tributes, 20, 56, 66a, 69, 85, 93-94, 111-112, 118, 127, 136-137, 143-144, 147-148, 151, 185, 188, 212-213, 217, 223, 251, 254, 262, 271, 274, 280, 289, 292-294, 297, 310, 324, 329, 345, 349, 351, 365, 376, 390, 392, 417-418, 422, 424-425, 439-440, 467, 476, 482, 494-495, 501-502, 506, 511, 538, 546, 554, 591, 604, 608, 649, 664, 676, 699a, 706; tax collectors, 109, 141, 468; direct general taxation, 418; ecclesiastical taxes, 262, 280, 289, 292, 329, 376, 390, 424, 439-440, 494-495, 501-502, 664, 706; income tax, 376, 699a, 706
taxonomy, 658
technology, 10, 402, 460, 550, 622, 694, 697, 702, 736
telescopes, 405, 583-585, 593, 623, 630-631
Temple, Sir William, 628
Temple Mount, see Mt. Moriah
Temple of Solomon, the, 250, 320; the Knights Templar, 320-325, 346, 349-350, 354-356, 366, 376, 384-385, 407-409, 411, 414-416, 419, 424-431, 466, 623-624
temples, Egyptian, 4, 8, 14-18, 20, 84, 93; Greek, 27, 29, 34, 47a, 50, 55, 62-64, 92, 669; Roman, 130, 136, 144, 148-149, 151, 156, 178, 190, 202, 206-207, 218, 456
Tenochtitlán, 575
Terouenne, 483
Tertullian, 174-175, 177
tetrarchy, the Roman, 182
Tetzel, Johann, 487
Teutonic Knights, the, 354, 358, 382-383, 407, 416, 431-432, 503
Thames, the river, 291, 569
Thanksgiving, origin of, 608
Thapsus, the Battle of, 116
theatres, Greek, 65-67, 718-720; the Theatre of Dionysos, see Dionysos
theatres, Roman, 131, 135, 156-157, 174; the Amphitheatre of Alexandria, 207; the Flavian Amphitheatre, see the Colosseum; the Theatre of Marcellus, 131; the Theatre of Pompey, 122
Thebaid, the, 247
Thebes, the Egyptian city, 12, 16; the Greek city, 41-42, 52-53, 59, 82, 97
theocracy, 14-15, 216, 230, 432, 510, 536
Theocritus of Syracuse, 132
Theodelinda, 239-240
Theodore of Mopsuestia, 221
Theodoret of Cyrus, 166a, 220-221
Theodoric the Great, king of the Ostrogoths, 231-232, 235-236
Theodoric I, king of Reims, 380
Theodoric I, king of the Visigoths, 224
Theodosius the Great, St., 204-208, 212, 225; Theodosius II, 219-221
Theodotus the Valentinian, 164-165
theology, Christian, 163, 168, 174-175, 178, 185, 198, 216, 219, 242, 246, 252-253, 257-258, 268, 288, 316, 318-319, 325, 330, 368, 397, 401, 404-406, 418, 420, 437, 441, 461, 465a, 484, 500, 502, 509, 511, 516-517, 523, 527, 531, 533, 547, 559, 566, 575, 582, 587, 591, 625-626, 634, 636, 654-655, 684, 687-688, 700, 702, 706, 714, 723, 731, 735; Jewish, 93, 138; pagan, 7a, 25, 31-32, 42, 46, 89, 179, 202
Theon of Alexandria, 218
Theophilus of Alexandria, St., 207; St. Theophilus of Antioch, 170
Theophrastus of Eresus, 519
Theotokos, the, 219
Thera, 20-21
Theseus, 20, 31, 36, 178
Thespis, 66
Thessalonica, 186-187, 196, 204, 282, 367
Thessaly, the Thessalians, 24, 34, 60, 83, 367
Theudebert I, king of Reims, 234
Thibaut III, count of Champagne, 361-362; Thibaut IV, 313
Thirty Years' War, the, 442, 600-602, 605, 712
Thomas Aquinas, St., 319, 394, 396-397, 403, 411, 437, 448, 581
Thoros of Edessa, 306
Thoth, 6, 7a, 9-13, 581; the symbols of Thoth, 9-10, 13
Thrace, the Thracians, 37, 40-42, 45-46, 48, 58-60, 78-79, 82, 90, 187, 192, 195, 197, 367; Thracian Chersonese, the, 59, 61, 82
Thrasybulus, 71-72
Thucydides, 20, 95
Thuringia, 356, 392, 661
Thyiades, the, 42, 48
thyrsus, 47
Tiber, the river, 106, 131, 158, 183, 196, 214, 238, 337, 471
Tiberius (d. 33 BCE), 126; (42 BCE-37 CE), Roman emperor, 137, 140, 152; Tiberius II, Byzantine emperor, 238
Ticino, 483
Tigris, the river, 85
time zones, 698
Timoleon, 77
Titans, the, 31-33, 47, 49, 552a
tithes, 262, 329, 424, 440, 494-495, 664
Titus, 148-152, 157
tobacco, 468, 589, 637, 657, 676
Toland, John, 634
Toledo, 394, 553; the Third Council of Toledo, 259; the Seventeenth Council of Toledo, 251
tolerance, religious, 98, 140-141, 143, 154, 174, 182, 184, 186, 203, 205, 249a, 251, 295, 314, 417, 435, 452, 467-468, 505, 514-515, 536-537, 556, 602-604, 610, 614-615, 617, 629, 643, 648-649, 706
Tomis, 134
tonsures, 240-241, 429
tools, see instruments
Tordesillas, the Treaty of, 467
Tories, the, 627, 678, 692
Toron, 350, 358
torture, 218, 282, 295, 304, 348, 397, 402, 426-428, 430, 435-437, 467, 472, 495, 553, 586, 636
Tostig Godwinson, 289-290
Toul, the bishopric of, 283, 535, 545
Toulouse, 305, 308, 314, 316, 351, 369-372
Touraine, 338, 377
Tournai, 445, 483, 488
Tours, 232-233, 316, 445
Tower of Babel, the, 686-687; the Tower of David, 308, 332; the Tower of London, 508, 589, 592
trade routes, 13, 16, 176, 227, 278, 306, 313, 367, 418, 434, 451, 463, 466, 537-538, 545, 548, 552, 613, 657
Tradescant, John, 620-621
tragedies, 126, 149, 570, 626; Greek tragedy, 44, 66, 140, 199, 709, 718
Trajan, 153-155
translation, translators, 92-93, 100, 102, 119, 165, 208-209, 214a, 222, 252, 268, 277, 315, 394, 396, 399-400, 403, 455, 461, 491, 523-524, 546, 556-558, 595-596, 599, 626, 643, 652, 670, 686-689, 703, 708
transubstantiation, 374, 493
travel, 34, 37, 43, 53, 135, 153,

795

174, 248, 272, 276, 278, 313, 324, 370, 456, 520, 524, 539, 652, 670, 673, 675-676, 687, 692-693, 698
treason, 15, 144, 207, 217, 364, 391, 436, 444, 500a, 501, 508, 514, 541, 554, 565, 589, 599, 605, 610, 652, 667
Trebizond, 367
Trent, the Council of, 528-529, 532-533, 547, 562
Tribune, Roman, 109, 112-114, 155, 438, 669, 709
Tribur, 300
Triebschen, 714
Trier, 196, 214, 304, 492, 604, 695a
trinities, 30-31, 139; the Holy Trinity, 317-318, 453, 630
Trinity College, Cambridge, 551, 588, 630, 632; Dublin, 570
Tripoli, the Lebanese city, 307, 332, 348-350, 352, 411, 413-415; the Libyan city, 328
Triptolemus, 28-29, 31, 33
Tristan, 230, 450, 711, 714, 725
triumphal arches, 184
triumphal processions, or triumphs, 107-108, 110, 116-117, 127-128, 149, 235
Triumvirate, the First, 108-110, 112; the Second, 123-124, 126
trivium, the, 401
Trojan War, the, 23-24
troubadours, 135, 311, 313-315, 370, 379; trouvères, 311, 313, 370, 417; origin of the term, 313
Troy, 83, 145, 196, 688
Troyes, 318; the Council of Troyes, 321-322; the siege of Troyes, 447; the Treaty of Troyes, 444
True Cross, the, 197, 239, 274
Tserclæs, Johannes, count of Tilly, 601
Tudor dynasty, the, 499-502, 540, 548-549, 552-553, 561-562, 566, 590
tulips, 621
Tunis, 328, 412; Tunisia, 99, 100a, 412
Turin, 183, 213, 239, 545, 733
Turkey, 352, 402a, 467, 538, 677a, 679
Turks, the, 227, 296, 352a, 367, 409, 433, 516; Turkish language, 197, 528; the Khwarismian Turks, 389; the Kipchak Turks, 409; the Ottoman Turks, 355, 432, 451-455, 461a, 470, 476, 482, 488, 504-506, 520, 528, 534, 537-540, 553-554, 646, 670, 679; the Patzinak Turks, 302; the Seljuk Turks, 295-296, 302-

305, 306-307, 332, 334, 345, 348
Tuscany, 235a, 300, 359, 375, 443, 457, 475, 483, 505, 545, 583; the Tuscan League, 359
Tusculum, 285, 344, 354, 442
Twelve Articles of the Upper Swabian Peasants, the, 494-495
Tyndale, William, 596
Typhon, 32
tyranny, see despotism
Tyre, 84-85, 145, 179, 307, 389, 412, 415-416
Tyrone, 341, 513, 588-589, 611

Ulfilas, 214
Ulster, 588-591, 609; the Ulster Plantation, 590-591
underworld, the, 29-30, 32, 48, 68, 245, 302a
Uniformity, the Act of, 548, 565
United Kingdom of Great Britain, the, 638; the United Kingdom of the Netherlands, 678; the United Kingdom of Scotland, 230
United States, the, 276, 511, 569, 610-611, 614, 622a, 628, 648, 650, 666-667, 669, 677, 681, 686, 693, 695, 697-699, 736
universities, 97, 268, 276, 379, 395, 400-404, 406, 420, 422, 454, 486-487, 509, 518, 520-521, 523, 525, 547, 550, 557, 570, 624, 643, 652, 682-683, 689, 697, 702, 708, 714; origin of the term, 400; origin of the degrees, 400-401
University of Alcalá, the, 526; Basel, 522-523, 714-715, 722, 733; Berlin, 684; Bologna, 395, 400, 406, 421, 570; Bonn, 714; Cambridge, 551, 569-570, 588, 630, 634, 697; Cologne, 395, 570; Constantinople, 228; Córdoba, 276; Ferrara, 520, 530, 570, 587; Göttingen, 653; Ingolstadt, 651-653; Jena, 659, 662, 682; Leipzig, 522, 660, 690, 714; Louvain, 551; Montpellier, 395, 398, 509; Naples, 379; Oxford, 395, 402a, 403-404, 406, 551, 557, 569-570, 619-620, 623-625, 630, 634, 690, 697, 703-704; Padua, 570, 583; Paris, 319, 376, 395, 400-401, 406, 551; Pisa, 582; Prague, 441, 601; Rome, 529-530, 570; Strasbourg, 570, 660; Tübingen, 567, 598; Wittenberg, 487
Upanishads, the, 690
upper classes, the, 2-737

Urban I, St., pope, 178; Blessed Urban II, 302-305, 308, 333; Urban III, 351; Urban IV, 391; Blessed Urban V, 438; Urban VI, 439-440; Urban VIII, 585-586
Urbino, 459, 477, 496, 570
Uriel the Archangel, St., 574
usury, 325, 418
utilitarianism, 27, 103, 667
Utopias, 76, 508-510, 596-597, 675
Utrecht, 310; the Treaty of Utrecht, 638

Valencia, 442, 463-464
Valens, Flavius, 187, 203
Valentinian I, Roman emperor, 203-204; Valentinian II, 212; Valentinian III, 223-224
Valentinus of Alexandria, 163-164; Valentinianism, Valentinians, 164-165, 168, 174
Valeria, Galeria, 181, 186
Val-es-Dunes, the Battle of, 282
Valla, Lorenzo, 492
Valois, 357; the Valois dynasty, 433, 444, 474, 506, 535, 545
Vandals, the, 215, 218, 224-225, 231
Varangian Guard, the, 278, 280, 287
Varro, Marcus Terentius, 101, 108
Vasari, Giorgio, 460
Vaterlands-Verein, the, 710
Vatican, the, 140, 210, 338, 465, 472, 476, 479, 497-498, 584-585, 602, 706; the Vatican Palace, 443, 465, 478, 481, 484; the First Vatican Council, 705
Vaucouleurs, 445
Vaughan, Thomas, 599
Vedas, the, 98, 689-690; the Rig-Veda, 689-690
Vega, Joseph de la, 577; Lope de, 544
vegetation, deities of, 6, 8, 37-38
Venaissin, 427, 430
Venice, the Venetians, 224, 236, 253, 255, 297, 343, 351, 361-367, 407-408, 414, 416, 418-419, 443, 454-455, 458-459, 466, 469, 471, 479, 481-483, 498, 520, 526-528, 537, 543, 545, 548, 583, 679, 712, 726
Venus, the Roman goddess, 133, 171, 353; the planet, 583
Vercingetorix, 113
Verdun, the bishopric of, 535, 545; the Treaty of Verdun, 267
Vergil, 39, 49, 101, 131-135, 201, 257, 356, 461
Vergil, Polydore, 561
Verona, 101, 183, 213, 231, 236, 254, 344, 391, 443, 482, 570

796

Vespasian, 147-152, 157
Vespucci, Amerigo, 467
Vesta, 207; the Vestal Virgins, 127, 151
Vézelay, 333, 353
Victor IV, antipope (1138), 328; (1159-1164), 338
Victor I, St., pope, 165, 175
Victor Amadeus II, king of Sardinia, 639; Victor Emmanuel III, king of Italy, 705
Victoria, queen of Great Britain, 681, 690, 697, 712; the Victorians, 65, 675, 697, 701-704
Vienna, 161, 387, 534, 693; the Concordat of Vienna, 451; the Congress of Vienna, 677-678, 680-681, 709
Vienne, 309; the Council of Vienne, 428
Vikings, the, 269-271, 278, 280-282, 289-290, 357, 552
Villaret, Foulques de, 425
Villèle, Joseph de, 678-679
vine, viticulture, 2, 38-41, 320
Virginia, 568, 650; the Virginia Statute for Religious Freedom, 610
virginity, 31, 35a, 127, 191, 445, 590, 671, 674; virgin birth, 31, 49, 171, 189, 219; virgin mother of god, 49, 171, 197, 219
virtues, ancient, 28, 75-76, 82, 103, 124, 134, 730-731; Christian, 216, 391, 427, 512, 541, 724, 730-731
Visconti dynasty, the, 443, 458, 474
Vitellius, 148
Vladimir the Great, 278, 280
Volga, the river, 278, 369, 388
Volkgeist, 681
Voltaire, 267, 493, 642, 644, 648, 667, 689
Vulgate, the, 209, 257, 315, 595

Wadham College, 619, 623
Wagner, Cosima, 733
Wagner, Richard, 224, 233, 274, 380, 708-711, 713-715, 718-721, 723, 725-728, 733; the Wagner societies, 720
Waiblingen, 301, 327
Wales, the Welsh, 241-242, 269, 341-342, 541, 550, 561-564, 570, 590-591, 599, 610, 645
Wallace, Alfred Russel, 700
Wallenstein, Albrecht von, 601
Waller, Edmund, 622, 625
Wallis, John, 619
Walpole, Sir Robert, 638
Walsingham, Sir Francis, 560, 565-566, 574
Walter the Penniless, 304
Washington, George, 648, 650
Waterloo, the Battle of, 678
wedding-ring, the origin of the, 263
Weimar, 661-662, 680, 734; the Weimar Theatre, 662
Weinsberg, the siege of, 327
Weishaupt, Adam, 651-653
Welf dynasty, the, 326-328, 333a
Wellington, 1st duke of, 677
Wenceslaus of Bohemia, St., 504; Wenceslaus IV of Bohemia, German emperor, 441, 458
Wends, the, 333a, 383; the Wendish Crusade, 333a
Wentworth, Thomas, 1st earl of Strafford, 608-609
Wesley, John, 434
Wessex, 291
West, the, see Western Europe; the American West, 693, 698
Westminster Abbey, 288, 292, 339, 501
West Indies, the, 611, 613-614; the Dutch West India Company, 614
Westphalia, the Peace of, 602
wet-nurses, 374, 503, 655-656
Wettin dynasty, the, 535, 681
Wetzlar, 660
wheat, 1-2, 252, 319
Whigs, the, 627
Whitby, the Synod of, 242
White, John, 568
White Mountain, the Battle of the, 442
Wilhelm I, Kaiser, 712, 715-717; Wilhelm II, 730
Wilkins, John, 619, 621
William I, count of Apulia, see William de Hauteville
William II, duke of Apulia, 326
William of Champeaux, 316
William the Conqueror, 281-283, 286-294, 299, 305, 339, 403, 501
William III, king of England, 627-628, 637-638
William the Lion, 341-342
William Longsword, 270
William I, king of Sicily, 337, 358; William II, 353; William III, 357
William II, prince of Orange, 554, 574; William III, see William III of England
William I, king of Prussia, see Kaiser Wilhelm I
will-to-live, the, 724-725; the will-to-power, 724, 732, 735
Winchester, the Council of, 292
Windsor family, the, 681
wine, 2, 38, 40-42, 46-48, 130, 159-160, 207a, 261, 270, 304, 320, 374, 521, 718
winnowing-fan, the, 38-40
Winter Solstice, the, 189, 244
wisdom literature, see logoi sophon
Wisdom of Faith, the, 174; the Wisdom of Solomon; 169
Witan, the, 288, 291
witchcraft, witch-hunts, 35a, 243, 395-396, 427, 435-437, 447-448, 466, 516-518, 522, 551, 570, 591, 615, 636, 654
Wittelsbach dynasty, the, 343, 524, 716
Wittenberg, 487, 490, 534, 709; the Capitulation of Wittenberg, 535
Wolsey, Thomas, 483, 488
women, 4, 21, 25-28, 30-34, 35a, 38-40, 42, 45-46, 49-50, 56, 63, 69, 74, 88, 96, 100, 102, 116, 125, 131, 150, 152, 173-175, 203, 211-212, 218, 227-229, 246, 262-263, 265-266, 273-274, 279, 295, 298, 308, 312-313, 315, 317, 331-333, 346, 350, 355, 371, 402-403, 415, 445, 448-450, 452, 464, 481, 499, 503, 507, 516-518, 521, 527, 541, 574, 576, 585a, 606-607, 611, 639, 641, 660, 664-665, 671a, 674-675, 679, 681, 709; the Women Question, see the Frauenfrage
work, 14, 18, 42a, 75, 181, 229, 256, 271-273, 275, 320, 323, 372, 400, 420, 434, 511-512, 575-576, 578, 611, 614, 655, 658, 664-666, 672, 674, 693-696, 698, 737
World War I, 434, 543, 638, 701, 730; World War II, 434, 638, 681, 706
Worms, 304, 387, 435; the Concordat of Worms, 309-310; the Diet of Worms (1076), 299; (1521), 490; the Edict of Worms, 490, 504-505
Wren, Sir Christopher, 619, 623, 625, 628a
writing, 2, 9, 13, 19-20, 23, 101, 210, 230, 261, 380, 398, 491, 673, 688
Württemberg, 213a, 598, 676, 709
Wycliffe, John, 441, 488, 595

Xavier, St. Francis, 687
Xerxes, 59-60

Yahweh, 39, 138-139, 143, 202, 436a, 614, 686
Yehod, see Aristobulus II
Yemen, 248
Yeshua, 39, 160
Yochanan ben Zacchai, 148-149
Yolande of Brienne, 382-384, 388
Yonatan, see Hyrcanus II
York, 196, 257, 290-291, 500a, 562, 627-628; the Church of York, 241; the School of York, 257
Yule, 190, 243

Zachary, St., pope, 254, 258

797

Zara, 363
Zarathustra, or Zoroaster, 171, 723-724, 736; Zoroasterism, Zoroastrians, 99, 138, 181, 723
Zealots, the, 137, 147-150
Zeeland, 444, 576

Zengi, 332-333, 407
Zeno, the founder of Stoicism, 96-97, the Byzantine emperor, 226, 231
zero, the, 399
Zeus, 12, 20, 28-36, 39, 44, 48-49, 85, 93; altar of Zeus, 58-59; statue of Zeus, 64; temple of Zeus, 34
zither, 43, 151
Zosimus the Historian, 188
Zürich, 331, 481, 493, 710
Zwingli, Ulrich, 493, 495, 510, 516

www.ingramcontent.com/pod-product-compliance
Ingram Content Group UK Ltd.
Pitfield, Milton Keynes, MK11 3LW, UK
UKHW041433180426
11947UKWH00007B/409